STREET ON TORTS

STREET ON TORTS

Thirteenth Edition

JOHN MURPHY

Professor of Common Law, University of Manchester

CHRISTIAN WITTING

Professor, Durham Law School, Durham University

With contributions from

JAMES GOUDKAMP

*Fellow and Tutor, Balliol College, Oxford, and University Lecturer,
University of Oxford*

OXFORD
UNIVERSITY PRESS

OXFORD
UNIVERSITY PRESS

Great Clarendon Street, Oxford OX2 6DP
United Kingdom

Oxford University Press is a department of the University of Oxford.
It furthers the University's objective of excellence in research, scholarship,
and education by publishing worldwide. Oxford is a registered trade mark of
Oxford University Press in the UK and in certain other countries

© Oxford University Press 2012

The moral rights of the authors have been asserted

Tenth edition 1999
Eleventh edition 2003
Twelfth edition 2007

Impression: 1

Contains public sector information licensed under the Open Government Licence v1.0
(http://www.nationalarchives.gov.uk/doc/open-government-licence/open-government-licence.htm)

Crown Copyright material reproduced with the permission of the
Controller, HMSO (under the terms of the Click Use licence)

British Library Cataloguing in Publication Data
Data available

Library of Congress Cataloguing in Publication Data
Data available

ISBN 978-0-19-955444-7

Printed in Great Britain by
Ashford Colour Press Ltd, Gosport, Hampshire

This book is dedicated to our children:
Lauren, Lukas, Nicholas, and Xavier

PREFACE

The first and most obvious point to make in relation to this edition is that editorial responsibility is now shared. Tort law's size and dynamism renders the job of editing a book of this kind a Herculean task when tackled alone. John Murphy was delighted to welcome on board Christian Witting and James Goudkamp. The former shouldered the burden of attending to practically half the text, while the latter brought to the feast not just his particular expertise on tort law defences but also his willingness to manage the companion website that will now accompany this title. Notwithstanding the division of labour, all three of us consider this a joint project.

Important changes have not been confined to editorship. Indeed, since the last edition appeared in 2007, there have been some very significant developments in the law. Undoubtedly, the most notable of these occurred in the context of the economic torts. The decision of the House of Lords in *OBG Ltd v Allan* appeared, at a stroke, to simplify and render coherent a formerly confused and confusing branch of the law. But the ink was barely dry on the speeches in that case when a differently constituted House decided *Total Network v Revenue and Customs Commissioners*, introducing a series of novel and difficult issues that will need to be addressed in future.

In *Bocardo SA v Star Energy UK Onshore Ltd*, the Supreme Court considered the validity of the proposition that the possessor of land is entitled to possession of all that lies below the surface to the centre of the Earth. *Rothwell v Chemical & Insulating Co Ltd* helped to clarify what counts as actionable damage in the law of negligence. Its companion case, *Grieves v FT Everard & Sons Ltd*, dealt a blow to those suffering psychiatric illness as a result of their fear of future disease caused by negligent exposure in the workplace. Controversially, perhaps, in *Sienkiewicz v Greif (UK) Ltd* the Supreme Court extended the *Fairchild* approach to causation to a case involving only one potential tortfeasor, while *Gray v Thames Trains* and *Stone & Rolls Ltd v Moore Stephens* considered the defence of illegality. Finally, *Spiller v Joseph* renamed the fair comment defence to defamation as 'honest comment'. The Government has also proposed reform to various aspects of the law of defamation and has published a Draft Defamation Bill 2011.

In terms of continuity, the chief aims of the book remain the same as for previous editions: namely, to provide a comprehensive, accurate, and accessible account of tort law. In order to accommodate new material while keeping the book from expanding to a size that would make it unmanageable for those studying tort under a semesterised model of teaching, a good deal of painstaking editing and judicious pruning has been necessary. Nothing of great substance has been sacrificed in order to make room for the new material. Rather, it was the footnotes – which have been greatly slimmed down in this edition – that have principally made way for the new law.

In terms of thanks, we owe a debt of gratitude to Jennifer Courage, at Oxford University Press, who responded positively and speedily to our many queries and procured for us a sizeable array of materials that assisted the preparation of this edition. John and Christian are also grateful for the patience and understanding of their families. Getting to grips with a large body of material within the relatively short period permitted for editing a book of this size is no easy matter. It takes its toll in many ways as Anne, Lauren, Lukas, Nicholas, Rita, and Xavier could readily testify.

We have attempted to state the law as it stood and was available to us on 1 June 2011, though it was possible to add some material that post-dates this at proof stage.

JM and CW
27 August 2011

NEW TO THIS EDITION

The thirteenth edition of *Street on Torts* has been thoroughly revised to reflect all important developments in the law and academic literature since publication of the twelfth edition, including:

- Coverage of the following key recent cases: *R v Rimmington and R v Goldstein* (on public nuisance); *OBG Ltd v Allan* and *Total Network v Revenue and Customs Commissioners* (on the economic torts); *Smith v Chief Constable of Sussex and Trent Strategic HA v Jain Police* (on public authority negligence liability); *Ashley v Chief Constable of Sussex Police* (on self-defence); *Douglas v Hello!* (on privacy); *Austin v Commissioner of Police of the Metropolis* (on the interrelationship between the tort of false imprisonment and Article 5 of the European Convention on Human Rights); *Corr v IBC Vehicles Ltd* (on causation and on contributory negligence); *Gray v Thames Trains Ltd* and *Stone & Rolls Ltd v Moore Stephens* (both on the defence of illegality).

- Consideration of the Draft Defamation Bill 2011.

- The chapters on negligence have been rewritten from a more conceptual standpoint, in order to assist students in their understanding of case law.

- A new 'Key Issues' feature has been incorporated into the beginning of each chapter, drawing out the significant details within each topic.

- References to a wide range of authoritative texts at the end of each chapter have been carefully updated to ensure further reading is well directed.

CONTENTS

PART I INTRODUCTION

PART II NEGLIGENT INVASIONS OF INTERESTS IN THE PERSON, PROPERTY INTERESTS, AND ECONOMIC INTERESTS

PART III INTENTIONAL INVASIONS OF INTERESTS IN THE PERSON AND PROPERTY

PART IV   INTERFERENCE WITH ECONOMIC AND INTELLECTUAL PROPERTY INTERESTS

PART V   TORTS INVOLVING STRICT OR STRICTER LIABILITY

TABLE OF CASES

TABLE OF STATUTES

TABLE OF STATUTORY INSTRUMENTS

TABLE OF TREATIES AND CONVENTIONS

TABLE OF EUROPEAN SECONDARY LEGISLATION

TABLE OF NATIONAL LEGISLATION

PART I

INTRODUCTION

1

OVERVIEW OF TORT LAW

KEY ISSUES

(1) The place of tort law

Tort law is a branch of the law of obligations, which also includes contract and the law of unjust enrichment.

(2) Definition

Tort obligations are owed by one person to another and embody norms of conduct that arise outside contract and unjust enrichment. Tort enables the person to whom the obligation is owed to pursue a remedy on his own behalf where breach of a relevant norm infringes his interests to a degree recognised by the law as such an infringement.

(3) Bases of liability

Tort law imposes liability for the breach of norms of conduct by reference to two main factors: the type of interest at stake and the degree of fault present in the 'doer' of harm. Generally speaking, where the interest at stake is an important one (such as bodily integrity or property), the degree of protection offered is less likely to depend upon the presence of (a substantial degree of) fault in the doer. This is another way of saying that liability is likely to be stricter as regards these important interests.

SECTION 1   WHAT IS A TORT?

The very word tort may pose a conundrum for the novice law student. Crime and contract will be terms with which he or she is already familiar, but what does tort mean? What is tort law about? Much ink has been spilt in attempts to define tort with only limited success; at least for the student new to the subject. Winfield's classic definition declared:

> Tortious liability arises from the breach of a duty primarily fixed by law; such duty is towards persons generally and its breach is redressable by an action for unliquidated damages.[1]

---

[1] Winfield, *Province of the Law of Tort* (1931), 92.

A more recent definition, offered by Peter Birks, suggests that a tort is:

> [T]he breach of a legal duty which affects the interests of an individual to a degree which the law regards as sufficient to allow that individual to complain on his or her own account rather than as a representative of society as a whole.[2]

Yet the first of these definitions does little more than point towards one kind of remedy that is available in tort and towards certain distinctions between tort and other branches of the law,[3] while the second may be unhelpfully vague to the newcomer to tort. As we shall see at the end of this chapter, even those distinctions between tort and other branches of law are sometimes blurred.[4] Partly for this reason, a satisfactory definition of tort remains somewhat elusive. Perhaps the best working explanation that can be offered at this stage is this:

> Tort is that branch of the civil law relating to obligations imposed by operation of law on all natural and artificial persons. These obligations, owed by one person to another, embody norms of conduct that arise outside contract and unjust enrichment.[5] Tort enables the person to whom the obligation is owed to pursue a remedy on his own behalf where breach of a relevant norm of conduct infringes his interests to a degree recognised by the law as such an infringement.

No further attempt at defining tort will be made here. But something should be said about the functions and purposes of tort law, and these are matters that can be explained in comparatively simple terms. Tort law defines the obligations imposed on one member of society to his or her fellows and provides a range of remedies for harms caused by breach of those obligations. Tort is often described as centrally concerned with corrective justice – that is, the circumstances in which a wronged party is able to obtain recompense or reparation from a wrongdoer.[6] In consequence, tort law is often judged by its success or otherwise as a compensation system. In simple terms, since most tort actions have as their objective monetary compensation for a loss inflicted on the claimant by the defendant, the question that most often arises is 'who should bear the relevant cost?' Should it lie where it falls on the unfortunate claimant; or is the conduct of the defendant such that the law should shift the loss to him? In the tort of negligence, as well as many other torts later in this book, loss fixing is a core issue.[7]

---

[2] Birks, 'The Concept of a Civil Wrong' in Owen (ed), *Philosophical Foundations of Tort Law* (1995), 51.

[3] For a fuller account of the distinction between tort and other branches of the civil law, see Sappideen and Vines (eds), *Fleming's The Law of Torts* (2011), 3–5 and Cane, *The Anatomy of Tort Law* (1997), 182–96.

[4] See generally Waddams, *Dimensions of Private Law: Categories and Concepts in Anglo-American Legal Reasoning* (2003).

[5] On norms, see Smith (2011) 31 OJLS 1.

[6] M Stone (1996) 11 Can J L & Juris 235, 253. There is now a voluminous literature on tort law and corrective justice, but especially good is Weinrib (1989) 23 Valp ULR 485. See also Wright, 'Right, Justice and Tort Law' in Owen (ed), *Philosophical Foundations of Tort Law* (1995), ch 7. On some of the limitations of corrective justice and other theories, see Hershovitz (2010) 63 Stan LR 67.

[7] *Caltex Oil (Australia) Pty Ltd v The Dredge 'Willemstad'* (1976) 136 CLR 529, at [51].

Tort's 'success' in these areas must therefore be judged, at least in part, by its efficacy as a compensation system.

But compensation is not tort's only concern, and monetary damages are not the only available remedy. Torts are also designed to protect fundamental human interests. Here, 'interests' may be defined as the kinds of claims, wants, or desires that people seek to satisfy in life, and which a civilised society ought to recognise as theirs as of right. Tort therefore serves to determine which of the many human (and related) interests are so fundamental that the law should impose duties upon us all that are designed primarily to protect those interests and, secondarily, to provide a remedy when those interests are wrongfully violated by others.

In the first edition of this work, Street's emphasis on the claimant's interests as opposed to the defendant's wrongdoing was perceived as radical, even bizarre. While we have elected not to follow the hierarchical interest-based structure that characterised previous editions in favour of one that maps more neatly on to the kinds of tort syllabuses that nowadays exist in leading law schools, it is nonetheless worth making clear that there is still a great deal to be said for an interest-based approach[8] (although it has its imperfections and some notable inconsistencies). Certainly, no claim in tort can succeed, however morally reprehensible the defendant's conduct, unless the court first recognises some form of harm suffered by the claimant that involves a violation of an interest sufficient to confer on the claimant a legal right to protection of that interest.[9] It is still useful, therefore, to consider the various rights and interests which tort law protects.

SECTION 2   PROTECTED RIGHTS AND INTERESTS

(A) HUMAN RIGHTS

Tort law has always protected certain 'human rights'. Indeed, tort disputes are by definition about the competing claims of persons to protected interests and we might well denominate the more frequently upheld interests as 'rights'. This is not problematic, so long as the term is not used in a rigid way.[10] The enactment of the Human Rights Act 1998 significantly 'enhanced' this protection (most immediately with respect to

---

[8]   See Cane, *The Anatomy of Tort Law* (1997).

[9]   See, eg, *Rogers v Rajendro Dutt* (1860) 25 JP 3; *Bradford Corpn v Pickles* [1895] AC 587; *Pickering v Liverpool Daily Post and Echo Newspapers plc* [1991] 2 AC 370. For academic explanations of this, see Goldberg and Zipursky (2002) 88 Virg LR 1625; Perry, 'Risk, Harm and Responsibility' in Owen (ed), *Philosophical Foundations of Tort Law* (1995), ch 14; Ripstein, *Equality, Responsibility, and the Law* (1999), 75. See also the analysis of the decision in *Barker v Corus UK Ltd* [2006] UKHL 20 in ch 4.

[10]   As, we would respectfully submit, it is in Stevens, *Torts and Rights* (2007) and Beever, *Rediscovering the Law of Negligence* (2007). See Witting (2008) 71 MLR 621; Hedley, 'Looking Outward or Looking Inward? Obligations Scholarship in the Early 21st Century' in Robertson and Wu (eds), *The Goals of Private Law* (2009), ch 8; and Bagshaw 'Tort Law, Concepts and What Really Matters' in Robertson and Wu (eds), *The Goals of Private Law* (2009), ch 10.

actions of public authorities), in the sense of formalising recognition of rights and
in systemising consideration of their breach by courts. Indeed, the Act's passing
prompted academics and judges almost immediately to rethink the boundaries and
substance of tort law,[11] but the full effects of the Act on tort law are, no doubt, yet to
emerge. To understand the various ways in which the Act is significant for tort law, it
is necessary to say a little about its workings.

Contrary to what is often said, the Human Rights Act did not incorporate the
European Convention on Human Rights into English law. Rather, the Act provides
(1) that, wherever possible, primary and subordinate legislation must be interpreted
in a way that is compatible with 'Convention rights'[12] and (2) that it is unlawful for
any public authority (including a court of law,[13] but excluding the legislature[14]) to
act in a way that is incompatible with a 'Convention right'.[15] 'Convention rights' are
the fundamental rights and freedoms set out in Articles 2 to 12 and Article 14 of the
Convention, as well as Articles 1 to 3 of the First Protocol (concerning rights to property, education, and free elections) and Articles 1 and 2 of the Sixth Protocol (abolish-
ing the death penalty).[16] Section 11 of the Human Rights Act 1998 makes it clear that
'Convention rights' exist in addition to, not in substitution for, rights and freedoms
already endorsed at common law. Reference to several of these Articles and Protocols
will be made from time to time throughout this book.

It may at first glance seem odd that no express provision of the Act appears to require
that the judges develop the common law in a manner consistent with 'Convention
rights'. Two factors explain that apparent omission. First, for some years now, English
judges have, wherever possible, sought to ensure that the common law is consistent
with such rights.[17] Second, and more importantly, section 6 of the Act makes it unlawful, as we have already seen, for any public authority, including a court, to act in a way
that is incompatible with 'Convention rights'. That being so, a judge adjudicating on a
claim in tort must develop the common law compatibly with 'Convention rights' with
a view to ensuring consistency between common law and 'Convention rights'.[18]

---

[11] For comprehensive treatment, see Wright, *Tort Law and Human Rights* (2001). And for a useful introductory account see Buxton (2000) 116 LQR 48.

[12] Human Rights Act 1998, s 3. For an introductory account of the Act, see Ewing (1999) 62 MLR 79.

[13] Human Rights Act 1998, s 6(3)(a).

[14] Human Rights Act 1998, s 6(3)(b).

[15] Human Rights Act 1998, s 6(1). For these purposes, 'acts' include 'failures to act'– eg, failures to fulfil
the several positive obligations that exist under the Convention. See, eg, *Z v UK* (2002) 34 EHRR 97 where
local authorities failed to take all reasonable steps to avoid a real and imminent risk of ill-treatment of children of whom they had actual or imputed knowledge. See also *Anufrijeva v Southwark LBC* [2004] QB 1124
and Murphy [2003] LS 102. Note, however, that under s 6(6) a failure to introduce a proposal for legislation
does not amount to an unlawful act for these purposes.

[16] Human Rights Act 1998, s 1.

[17] See, eg, *Rantzen v Mirror Group Newspapers* [1993] 4 All ER 975; *Olotu v Home Office* [1997] 1 WLR
329; *R v CC of North Wales Police, ex p AB* [1998] 3 WLR 7.

[18] Otherwise the court itself acts unlawfully under the Human Rights Act 1998, s 6. But note that s 6 does
not require the courts to create brand-new rights that mirror those in the Convention.

Apart from these general points, the most crucial element of the Act for a tort law-yer is the provision that 'Convention rights' are directly enforceable against public authorities, thus permitting an individual who considers his rights to have been vio-lated to sue for damages.[19] However, recourse to such damages under the Act may not be the only option available in response to such violations. This is because the self-same rights conferred by the Convention *might* already be protected by tort law. For example, Article 5 provides for a right to liberty and security and protects the citizen against arbitrary detention.[20] But the ancient tort of false imprisonment does likewise. Equally, a person alleging unlawful arrest by the police will not need to claim a breach of Article 5. He, too, can perfectly well sue in false imprisonment; and, indeed, may well prefer to do so.[21] Even so, in determining whether that arrest was lawful, the court will be mindful of the provisions of Article 5 and the jurisprudence of the European Court of Human Rights.[22]

But what if a 'Convention right' is not so well established in domestic law? Privacy is such a case.[23] The claimant might then elect to bring his claim under the Act alleg-ing breach of Article 8 (which requires respect for private and family life). If he elects for a Convention remedy, the claimant can sue under the Act *so long as* the defendant is a public authority. The question of what constitutes a public authority would then, possibly, arise. If I were to discover that the Home Office is bugging my office, suing a government department as a public authority should be straightforward. But, if a tabloid newspaper invades my home life, splashing my private business all over its front page, what then?[24] It is arguable that the newspaper, too, may be classified as a public authority, for section 6(3)(b) classifies as a public authority 'any person certain of whose functions are functions of a public nature'. State schools and universities thus clearly qualify as public bodies, as do charities such as the NSPCC. But the status of other bodies remains unclear for the present.[25]

Next, let us consider the situation where the wrongdoer is an entirely private individual – let us say, a neighbour who invades my privacy by persistently peering through my window and monitoring my private correspondence. Some common-law

[19] Human Rights Act 1998, ss 7–8.

[20] See, eg, *Austin v Comr of Police* [2009] UKHL 5 for discussion.

[21] Generally, tort damages are intended to return the claimant to the position he was in prior to the com-mission of the tort, but in respect of this tort, exemplary damages might be available. Not only would exem-plary damages not be available under the Act, it is by no means clear that C would even be restored to his or her *ex ante* position since under the Act, 'in considering whether to award compensation and, if so, how much, there is a balance to be drawn between the interests of the victim and those of the public': *Anufrijeva v Southwark LBC* [2004] QB 1124, at [56]. The Law Commission has suggested a range of factors that would be relevant in this context: Law Com No 266, [4.44]; see also *McGregor on Damages* (2003), 1549ff.

[22] As is already the case, well illustrated in the judgments of the members of the Court of Appeal in *Olotu v Home Office* [1997] 1 WLR 328.

[23] For the limited extent to which tort law protects privacy, see ch 22.

[24] A particularly pertinent question at the time of going to press, with the *News of the World* scandal having raged for weeks.

[25] But see Sunkin [2004] PL 643 and *Cameron v Network Rail Infrastructure Ltd* [2006] EWHC 1133 (Railtrack was held not to be a public authority for the purposes of maintaining railway safety standards).

remedy may often be found in such circumstances. The 'snooper' who peers through windows and opens mail could be liable for harassment[26] or trespass to goods.[27] But if the facts of the case do not lend themselves to the invocation of an existing common-law action, the position is not entirely clear. This is important because, despite a marked move in the direction of allowing an invasion of privacy to be treated as a full-blown tort (as it is in the USA and New Zealand), English tort law has gone no further than to allow a claimant to sue in respect of the misuse of private personal information.[28] There is full discussion of the protection of privacy in chapter 22 of this book. But for now it suffices to note that the English courts seem generally to be moving towards a convergence of common law and Convention rights in this area. Yet the obligation to develop the common law in a manner consistent with the Convention does not empower the courts to engage in free-and-easy judicial legislation, especially in an area so politically charged as privacy rights.[29] Article 6 (which grants a right to a fair trial) cannot be invoked to chivvy the courts along in this respect, for Article 6 does not carry with it any substantive civil law rights: it merely provides a procedural guarantee.[30]

The judicial view of the impact of the European Convention on Human Rights on the development of the common law is still developing. However, as we shall see in the next chapter, the position of the Supreme Court appears (at the moment) to be that, where there is a Convention right, the need for protection of that right *in tort law* is diminished.[31] This is to say that the existence of an enforceable Convention right reduces the need for an action to be available in tort. (This is similar to the House of Lords' view of the tort in *Wilkinson v Downton*[32] following the passage of the Protection from Harassment Act 1997).[33] If this is the case, it would appear that certain parts of tort law might become 'frozen in time' – a rather ironic outcome. As Steele notes: 'The emerging separation of tort from HRA actions contradicts a generally held view at the time of enactment that tort, being closely akin to the new action, was sure to adapt and expand in order to protect Convention rights more fully'.[34]

Finally, in the context of human rights, we must note that, in relation to primary legislation, the courts' role remains limited by the doctrine of Parliamentary sovereignty. Thus, section 3 of the Act (which requires the judges to interpret domestic statutes consistently with 'Convention rights' so far as it is possible so to do) does

---

[26] See ch 8.

[27] See ch 9.

[28] See *Campbell v MGN* [2004] 2 AC 457; *Douglas v Hello! Ltd (No 6)* [2006] QB 125.

[29] In *Wainwright v Home Office* [2004] 2 AC 406, Lord Hoffmann expressed the view (at [31]–[33]) that that matter was one that would require an Act of Parliament.

[30] See the twin decisions of the European Court of Human Rights in *Z v UK* (2002) 34 EHRR 97 and *TP and KM v UK* (2002) 34 EHRR 42. See also Gearty (2002) 65 MLR 87 and id (2001) 64 MLR 159.

[31] See *Smith v CC of Sussex Police* [2008] UKHL 50 (the assumption being that the views of the House of Lords have been carried over to the Supreme Court).

[32] [1897] 2 QB 57.

[33] See *Wainwright v Home Office* [2004] 2 AC 406.

[34] Steele [2008] CLJ 606, at 606.

not give the courts the power to strike down legislation that contradicts Convention rights. In such cases, there is merely a power for the higher courts to issue a declaration of incompatibility.[35]

(B) OTHER INTERESTS PROTECTED BY TORT LAW[36]

One important issue that must be identified here is that it is not uncommon for the central question in a tort claim to be how the law must reconcile competing interests. A classic example concerns the fact that every citizen can assert both a right to free speech and a right to freedom from the deliberate publication of words injurious to his or her reputation. Thus, protecting A's compelling interest in the latter may involve restricting B's right to the former. Hence, certain defences that justify what would otherwise constitute defamation may be of crucial importance.

We look now at the kinds of interests that tort law protects.

(1) Intentional invasion of personal and proprietary interests

The protection of the person from deliberately inflicted physical harm, restrictions on freedom of movement, and the protection of interests in tangible property – especially the right to non-interference with land and goods – were originally the most important concerns of tort law. The relevant modern torts include interference with goods and trespass in its various forms. It is these torts which provide the foundation of the protection of 'Convention rights' to life (Article 2),[37] freedom from torture or degrading treatment (Article 3), freedom from slavery (Article 4), liberty (Article 5), and peaceful possession of property (First Protocol, Article 1).

(2) Interests in economic relations, business and trade interests[38]

The extensive protection afforded to individuals' interests in freedom from physical harm and in their property is not mirrored by similar protection of interests in economic and business activities. The economic torts presently remain somewhat unclear in their scope.[39] Furthermore, very real difficulties exist in reconciling protection of one individual's economic interests with another's ability to engage in free competition in a market economy. In addition to the classic economic torts of interference

---

[35] Human Rights Act 1998, s 4.
[36] Cane has supplied a simpler list than the one provided here. It covers broadly the same ground, but differs in emphasis. He suggests that tort law protects (i) interests in the person, (ii) property interests, (iii) contractual interests, (iv) non-contractual expectancies, (v) trade values, and (vi) wealth: see Cane, *The Anatomy of Tort Law* (1997), 66–89.
[37] The focus of protection offered under the Convention and under the common law may be different, although their areas of operation overlap. With respect to Article 2, see, eg, *Savage v South Essex Partnership NHS Trust* [2008] UKHL 74, at [91].
[38] For thoroughgoing consideration see Carty, *An Analysis of the Economic Torts* (2nd edn, 2010). See also chs 12–14.
[39] See further ch 14.

with contractual relations, conspiracy, and intimidation, other torts of significance in this context are passing off and deceit.

(3) Interests in intellectual property

Interests in tangible property, land, and goods are, as we shall see, well protected by the common law. By contrast, intellectual property in confidential information, copyright, and patents presents greater problems. Much of the law in this field is statutory; and interests in intellectual property generally overlap with interests in economic relations. But this is not invariably so. For example, the emerging tort based on the misuse of private personal information may soon embrace both a patient's right to confidentiality from his doctor and a multinational company's right to protection of its trade secrets.

(4) Negligent interference with personal, proprietary, and economic interests

If tort law's protection of persons and property were limited only to deliberately inflicted harm, it would be manifestly inadequate in our complex and overcrowded world. Nor would such limited protection reflect the requirements of the Human Rights Act 1998 in so far as it seeks to safeguard and protect life and bodily security.[40] Since the landmark decision in *Donoghue v Stevenson*,[41] however, the courts have developed the tort of negligence to provide further protection to personal safety (including, within limits, mental integrity), property, and economic interests. But for a variety of reasons, including the absence of any requirement that harm be inflicted 'directly' in the tort of negligence, the judges have adopted a cautious approach to protecting economic interests from negligently inflicted harm.

(5) Further protection of personal and proprietary interests

Personal and proprietary interests rank so highly within the hierarchy of protected interests in tort law, and within the hierarchy of 'Convention rights', that further torts have emerged offering protection for those interests against conduct which is not necessarily, or cannot be proved to be, either intentional or negligent. There are, for example, torts of ancient origin – such as nuisance – as well as others of more recent vintage – such as the rule in *Rylands v Fletcher* (developed during the height of the industrial revolution when a new range of threats to private property were born almost overnight)[42] – which protect these interests. The former highlights the (arguably

---

[40] Undoubtedly there would also be a contravention of Article 13 of the European Convention on Human Rights: see *Z v UK* (2002) 2 FLR 549.

[41] [1932] AC 562.

[42] For the significance of the industrial revolution in grounding this rule, see Murphy (2004) 24 OJLS 643.

perverse)[43] degree of importance vested by the common law in the landowner's interest in his property.

The action for breach of statutory duty represents the common law's response to comparatively recent welfarist legislation, usually designed to improve standards of public health and personal safety.[44] But in addition, albeit at the behest of the former European Community, Parliament has also introduced a regime of strict liability for injuries caused by defective products.[45]

(6) Reputation

Tort law has long protected an individual's interest in his reputation via the torts of libel and slander. But these torts are of limited scope and fall a long way short of providing comprehensive protection to an individual's privacy interests, as we shall see in chapter 22. In addition, they are also subject to a wide range of partial and complete defences which further circumscribe their import.[46]

(7) Due process

A right to protection from malicious abuse of the judicial process is recognised in the tort of malicious prosecution and its ancillary tort of abuse of process. Now it seems that a tort to prevent abuse of the administrative process is also in its early infancy; and Article 6 of the European Convention on Human Rights may well contribute significantly to its development.[47]

(8) Miscellaneous interests: 'Convention rights' and European Union law rights

The antiquity and somewhat piecemeal development of torts means that there are a number of residual torts that defy classification. More importantly, however, a question now arises as to whether the principles developed by the common law offer adequate coverage of 'Convention rights'. Does the European Convention on Human Rights recognise interests unknown to the common law? The most obvious example of a possible lacuna in tort law has already been noted: the protection of privacy guaranteed in the Convention by Article 8. However, privacy is also an excellent example of how dangerous it may be to look at any alleged human right in isolation. Article 10 establishes a right to freedom of expression, to hold opinions and disseminate information. The media and others fear that a right to privacy, if developed without proper

---

[43] For the argument that, for the purposes of injunctive relief, property is treated more highly than the interest in bodily integrity, see Murphy (2007) 27 OJLS 506.

[44] See N Foster (2011) 33 Syd LR 67.

[45] See ch 15.

[46] See, eg, the defences available in defamation discussed in ch 21.

[47] It has already been raised on a number of occasions in connection with the striking out of negligence claims: see, eg, *Z v UK* (2002) 34 EHRR 97 and *TP and KM v UK* (2002) 34 EHRR 42. See also Gearty (2002) 65 MLR 87.

safeguards, could undermine that latter right.[48] Unscrupulous individuals whose conduct adversely affects others' interests would seek to use Article 8 to prevent public knowledge of their own activities. But Article 8 would permit the publication and dissemination of such information so long as it could be shown to be necessary within the specific terms mentioned in Article 8(2).[49]

Turning to European Union law rights, it has for some time been recognised by the English courts that directly applicable EU law can create obligations the breach of which entitle affected persons to sue for the harm thereby caused.[50] But as originally understood, these 'Eurotorts'[51] were strictly limited to instances in which the European legislation in question imposed obligations on private individuals. Thus, in one case where the United Kingdom was in breach of its obligations and imposed an unlawful ban on the importing of turkeys from France,[52] it was held that no private law right of action arose and that only public law redress by way of judicial review was available. Since then, however, the European Court of Justice has recognised a much wider principle of state liability that undermines the reasoning in this case.[53] In *Francovich v Italian Republic*,[54] the European Court held that failure by a member state to implement an EU directive designed to create rights on the part of particular individuals would give rise to a claim in damages on the part of those individuals. What was perhaps most significant and remarkable about the decision in *Francovich* was that the EU legislation in question was not directly effective (which meant that, in the absence of an action against the state, there would have been no one against whom an action could have been brought). But it has now been made clear by the European Court that the *Francovich* principle applies equally where the legislation *is* of direct effect,[55] where the breach of EU law entails a legislative act (not merely an omission),[56] in the failure by a national court to observe EU law,[57] and in respect of administrative decisions.[58]

---

[48] See, eg, *Jameel v Wall Street Journal Europe SPRL* [2006] UKHL 44.

[49] See *Campbell v MGN* [2004] 2 AC 457.

[50] *Garden Cottage Foods Ltd v Milk Marketing Board* [1984] AC 130. On the topic covered in this section, see Craig and de Búrca, *EU Law: Text, Cases and Materials* (4th edn, 2008), 328ff.

[51] It has been confirmed that an action for a breach of EU legislation is of the same order as an action for breach of statutory duty and that therefore the action is one in tort: see *R v Sec of State for Transport, ex p Factortame (No 7)* [2001] 1 WLR 942.

[52] *Bourgoin SA v Ministry of Agriculture* [1986] QB 716.

[53] The House of Lords also doubted its correctness in *Kirklees Metropolitan BC v Wickes Building Supplies Ltd* [1993] AC 227.

[54] [1993] 2 CMLR 66. See Craig (1997) 113 LQR 67.

[55] *Brasserie du Pêcheur SA v FR of Germany* (Case C–46/93) [1996] ECR 1–1029.

[56] *R v SS for Transport, ex p Factortame Ltd* (Case C–48/93).

[57] *Köbler v Republik Österreich* (Case C–224/01) [2003] ECR 1–10239, considered in *Cooper v HM Attorney-General* [2010] EWCA Civ 464.

[58] *R v Ministry of Agriculture, Fisheries and Food, ex p Hedley Lomas (Ireland)* (Case C–5/94) [1996] ECR 1–2553.

The conditions that must be satisfied in order to sue according to this 'Eurotort' principle were set out by Lord Slynn in *R v Secretary of State for Transport, ex p Factortame Ltd*. He said:

> Before a member state can be held liable, a national court must find that
> (i) the relevant rule of EU law is one which is intended to confer rights on individuals;
> (ii) the breach must be sufficiently serious;
> (iii) there must be a direct causal link between the breach and the loss complained of.[59]

The similarity between the first requirement and the test adopted in relation to an action for breach of (domestic) statutory duty is immediately striking.[60] Furthermore, it is clear that this requirement can be invoked to restrict the operation of the *Francovich* principle. Thus, in *Three Rivers District Council v Bank of England (No 3)*,[61] the House of Lords held that a failure to comply with a banking directive concerning the regulation of credit institutions was fundamentally concerned with harmonising banking practice, and not with protecting depositors. Therefore the EU legislation in question was not viewed as intended to confer rights on individuals, and the 'Eurotort' action in that case failed at the first stage.

It has since been explained in relation to the second limb that the pivotal phrase 'sufficiently serious' does not necessarily require negligence or fault (although fault may be a material consideration), and that the seriousness of the breach must be judged in the context of the clarity of the EU law breached and, where appropriate, the legislative discretion afforded to the member state.[62]

SECTION 3 THEORETICAL PERSPECTIVES ON TORT LAW

In recent decades there has been much theorising about the proper parameters of tort law;[63] about the bases of tortious liability;[64] and about whether tort law should serve individual or collective goals.[65] In this section, some of these perspectives are considered in order to supply readers with a wider theoretical context in which to set the remaining chapters.

---

[59] [1999] 4 All ER 906, at 916. These conditions derive directly from the decision of the European Court of Justice in *Brasserie du Pêcheur SA v Federal Republic of Germany* (Case C–46/93) [1996] ECR 1–1029, at [74].

[60] See ch 19.

[61] [2000] 2 WLR 1220.

[62] *R v SS for Transport, ex p Factortame Ltd (No 5)* [1999] 4 All ER 960.

[63] See, eg, Weinrib (1989) 23 Valp ULR 485 and id, *The Idea of Private Law* (1995).

[64] See, eg, Coleman, *Risks and Wrongs* (1992). Cf Abel (1982) Maryland LR 695.

[65] See, eg, Weinrib (1989) 23 Valp ULR 485. Cf Schwartz (1997) 75 Tex LR 1801 and Waldron, 'Moments of Carelessness and Massive Loss' in Owen (ed), *Philosophical Foundations of Tort Law* (1995), ch 17.

(A) TORT LAW OR A LAW OF TORTS?

It is sometimes said that it makes more sense to talk in terms of a law of torts than simply tort law, given the various bases of liability that apply to different torts, given the range of interests that these torts protect, and given the peculiar historical genesis of the various nominate torts.[66] There is doubtless something in this, but it is largely an academic point. When considering the vast body of authorities, it is clear that in *practical terms* it counts for little to contend that the infliction of unjustifiable harm is always a tort,[67] or that there is a fixed catalogue of circumstances which alone, and for all time, mark the limit of what are torts.[68] There is no problem peculiar to tort law here. Certain situations have been held to involve torts and will continue to do so in the absence of statutory repeal. Similarly, others have been held not to be tortious, and the courts upon which those decisions are binding will likewise continue to follow them.[69] These fundamental points are also often camouflaged behind the Latin maxims *damnum sine injuria* and *injuria sine damno*, which (not because of their aid to understanding, but because the student may meet them elsewhere) must be shortly explained. *Damnum sine injuria* – harm without (recognised) injury – merely means that one may have suffered harm and yet have no action for damages in tort; in short, that the damage of which he complains is not an interest protected by tort law.[70] *Injuria sine damno* – (recognised) injury without harm – is a shorthand version of the rule that some interests are so important that their violation is an actionable tort without proof of tangible damage. Battery is a classic example of a tort that adopts this principle.

(B) WRONGFULNESS IN TORT LAW

The relationship within tort law between rights and wrongs must very briefly be addressed. It is not enough merely to identify the kinds of interest that tort protects. The kinds of wrongdoing considered sufficient to violate those interests must also be identified.[71] The deliberate invasion of an interest can easily be classified in terms that

---

[66] See Ibbetson, *A Historical Introduction to the Law of Obligations* (1999); Stevens, *Torts and Rights* (2007), 286.

[67] An especially good example is the action for breach of confidential information which may be thought of either (as is common) in terms of a breach of an equitable duty or in terms of a tortious breach of duty (see, eg, *Campbell v MGN Ltd* [2004] 2 AC 457, at [14]).

[68] See further Murphy [1999] Adel LR 115.

[69] This is not to say that the superior courts will not, on occasion, part company with the past: see, eg, *Campbell v MGN* [2004] 2 AC 457 in which Lord Nicholls (at [14]) seemed to want to break free of the shackles of the action in equity for breach of confidentiality in order to give the protection of tort law to the misuse of private information.

[70] For the argument that *damnum sine injuria* should support a claim for injunctive relief, even though it would not ground an action for damages in certain circumstances, see Murphy (2007) 27 OJLS 506. For more general discussion of what amounts to recognised harm see Tettenborn, 'What is a Loss?' in Neyers (ed), *Emerging Issues in Tort Law* (2007), ch 17.

[71] See Cane, *The Anatomy of Tort Law* (1997); Lucy, *Philosophy of Private Law* (2007), ch 6.

demand that the law should intervene to require the defendant to compensate for the harm he has caused the claimant. Certain interests, however, may be so crucial to the claimant, and so vulnerable to accidental harm, that negligence on the part of the defendant suffices to engage his liability in tort. Exceptionally, the relationship of the claimant and the defendant, or the nature of the defendant's conduct, will give rise to *strict* liability. In such instances, the law requires the defendant to bear a greater (but not absolute) responsibility for protecting the claimant's interests.

It is not, however, necessary to dwell here on the importance of motive or malice. It follows from what has already been said that an act, even though it is malicious, will not incur tortious liability unless the interest that it violates is protected by an extant tort.[72] On the other hand, the interest interfered with is occasionally rated so low in the hierarchy of protected interests that only malicious invasions are forbidden. Which these interests are, the reader will discover as he or she progresses through the chapters of this book.

(C) GHOSTS FROM THE PAST: FORMS OF ACTION[73]

Until the passing of the Common Law Procedure Act 1852 and the Judicature Act 1875, a claimant could only sue in tort if he brought his cause of action within a recognised form of action – that is, one for which some particular writ of summons was available. Although the forms of action have now been abolished, many old cases cannot be understood without some knowledge of what they were.[74] Moreover, classifications of torts derive from the various writs grounding suit, so that rules worked out under them have necessarily been the starting point for any growth in tort law which has taken place since. Many seemingly arbitrary divisions today between one tort and another are explained only by reference to the forms of action. Thus, the writ of trespass lay only for direct injuries, while the form of action known as 'action on the case' developed separately for indirect injuries. And it will be seen in due course that, even now, trespass is not committed where the injury is indirect.[75]

A claimant does not have to plead the tort of negligence, trespass or whatever; he merely sets out the relevant facts said to demand redress.[76] Yet torts can overlap so that on any given facts a claimant may succeed by contending at trial that the facts satisfied the requirements of either of two (or more) torts. On the other hand, the claimant may fail where he relies on, say, the rule in *Rylands v Fletcher*, rather than

---

[72] Fierce competition that damages one's business interests and is prompted by malice, for example, will not by itself usually suffice to invoke the protection afforded by the economic torts. There must normally also be some illegal act on the part of D.

[73] See Maitland, *The Forms of Action at Common Law* (1909); Ibbetson, *A Historical Introduction to the Law of Obligations* (1999), ch 3; Gordley, *Foundations of Private Law: Property, Tort, Contract and Unjust Enrichment* (2006), ch 9.

[74] For an accessible account, see Williams and Hepple, *Foundations of the Law of Tort* (1984), ch 2.

[75] See chs 8, 9, and 10.

[76] *Letang v Cooper* [1965] 1 QB 232, 242–3.

private nuisance, if he argues only that the facts proved satisfy all the requirements of *Rylands v Fletcher* (but they in fact do not) and he could have advanced further facts (but did not) which would have satisfied the tort of nuisance. The claimant's error will be one of oral argument, not of pleading, except when he fails to plead an allegation of fact which, although not material in one tort, would have been a prerequisite of the other. Strictly speaking, a judge could find for the claimant merely by holding that, on the facts proved, there was a tort. But, given the splitting up into compartments of tort law, the judge will ordinarily decide that the claimant wins because the defendant has committed some specific tort. The law does not say that intentionally and carelessly inflicted harm will be tortious in certain circumstances. Instead, it defines the limits of each tort and says to the claimant: 'You win if you establish facts which satisfy the definitions of any one of those torts'. With regard to any particular decided case, the tort student is thus concerned to know, not only that the claimant has succeeded on certain facts, but also which tort has been committed. In short, it is important to know both the ingredients of each particular tort and the general principles of tortious liability.[77]

(D) CONFLICT BETWEEN CERTAINTY AND JUSTICE

The conflict between the demands of certainty and justice is a recurrent theme in case law. The claims of certainty are less pressing in the case of tort law than in some other branches of the law – for example, the law of property. The purchaser of land must be assured that the law on the faith of which he acquires a good title is not liable to change; it is less important that the law should settle precisely and for all time, say, the limits of liability of doctors for harm caused to their patients. On the other hand, the development of some torts has been seriously affected by the judicial urge for that certainty which is believed by many to result from making rigid categories. The courts, for example, once thought fit to divide entrants on to land into three rigid categories – invitees, licensees, and trespassers – in order to determine the duty of occupiers to them in respect of their personal safety, with the result that in 1957 the Occupiers' Liability Act was passed in order to clear up the confusion that this method had brought about.[78]

A significant measure of difficulty in this context stems from the fact that there are profoundly competing accounts of what justice entails. Such disagreement over the appropriate conception of justice – corrective, distributive, or even retributive – bedevils the debate about the appropriate balance between justice and certainty.[79] To some extent, then, the fact that common agreement on the justice of any given case is

---

[77] See Cane, 'General and Special Tort Law: Uses and Abuses of Theory' in Neyers (ed), *Emerging Issues in Tort Law* (2007), ch 1.

[78] See ch 7.

[79] See, eg, Coleman 'The Practice of Corrective Justice' in Owen (ed), *Philosophical Foundations of Tort Law* (1995), ch 2.

likely to be elusive perhaps explains why the courts sometimes emphasise certainty,[80] even though the need for certainty within tort law is not of paramount importance.

(E) LOSS DISTRIBUTION, DETERRENCE, AND ECONOMIC ANALYSIS

The traditional approach of tort law has been to ask whether a loss that B has suffered should be shifted to A.[81] If A were at fault, the answer would usually be to shift that loss from innocent victim B to wrongdoer A.[82] There is, however, another view. By spreading the loss from an individual victim to the many that benefit from an activity that has caused it, the loss is more easily and more fairly borne.[83] The employer whose worker is injured can spread the loss through raising the price of his product. The same argument applies where his product injures a consumer. This concept of loss distribution is sometimes, for example, advanced as a justification for the vicarious liability principle which makes an employer answerable for the torts committed by those who work for him.[84] Equally, loss distribution is reinforced by widespread insurance.[85] The vehicle owner can readily insure – and is indeed required by law to do so – against the risk of his negligently inflicting harm on third parties. His premium (and the premium of other drivers) falls short of the amount payable in damages for a typical road accident. Yet, in this way, the aggregate cost of all car accidents is distributed among all properly insured car drivers. Some judges even acknowledge that they are the readier to find negligence, or to make high compensatory awards, when they know that the damages will be paid by an insurance company (and thus, in turn, premium payers).[86]

But, while loss distribution through insurance can better guarantee tort victims that there will be money available to pay them the damages they are awarded in court, it also has the capacity to undermine another of tort law's goals: deterrence. The imposition of tort liability operates not only to transfer the relevant loss from the victim to the tortfeasor, but also (especially where the tort requires intentional wrongdoing or

---

[80] On the other hand, the judiciary in recent years have made explicit their pursuit of justice within tort law, especially in the twin areas of liability for pure economic loss and for psychiatric harm: see, eg, *White v Jones* [1995] 1 All ER 69 and *White v CC of South Yorkshire* [1999] 2 AC 455.

[81] *Caltex Oil (Australia) Pty Ltd v The Dredge 'Willemstad'* (1976) 136 CLR 529, at [51].

[82] Loosely, this account may be termed corrective justice, and it is based on the conception of torts as being based exclusively on bipolar relations: see Weinrib (1989) 23 Valp ULR 485.

[83] This is what is meant by the term 'distributive justice'. For other arguments against simplistic loss shifting see Cane, *Atiyah's Accidents Compensation and the Law* (2006).

[84] For critique of this as a complete justification for vicarious liability, see Neyers (2005) Alberta LR 1; and Murphy, 'Juridical Foundations of Common Law Non-Delegable Duties' in Neyers (ed), *Emerging Issues in Tort Law* (2007), ch 14.

[85] See Cane, *The Anatomy of Tort Law* (1997), ch 9; Stapleton (1995) 58 MLR 520.

[86] See *Murphy v Brentwood DC* [1990] 2 All ER 908, at 923. See also *Nettleship v Weston* [1971] 2 QB 691. But not all insurance is the same. There seem to be good reasons for distinguishing between compulsory motor insurance and other types: *Imbree v McNeilly* [2008] HCA 40, at [99]ff.

malice) to deter tortious conduct from the outset. Put at its simplest, the more a person commits a tort, the more he will have to pay in damages. Accordingly, he will generally endeavour not to commit such torts in the first place.[87] Good examples include the imposition of strict liability for breaches of statutory duty by employers, and on manufacturers of defective products who are encouraged to maintain high standards of safety in their goods in order to avoid liability.

However, the role of deterrence within tort law should not be overestimated, nor is it without other problems. To begin with, there are many instances in which the tortfeasor's conduct is in no sense deliberately harmful or even what might be termed 'calculated negligence'.[88] In such cases, where his conduct is at worst inadvertent, it is difficult to see how the tortfeasor could have been deterred. Second, for the courts to ensure in other areas that 'tort does not pay', recourse to exemplary damages is sometimes thought to be necessary.[89] This is problematic because punishment is not generally taken to be one of tort law's functions; it is, instead, seen as the role of the criminal law. Third, judges are sometimes cautious about invoking principles of deterrence, fearful that it will lead to over-cautious, defensive conduct. This concern is particularly evident in connection with medical litigation, despite the fact that there is scant evidence of defensive medicine.

Finally, we should note in this context that much academic work has been done on the economic analysis of tort law.[90] According to this school of thought, the law is criticised and evaluated according to the criterion of economic efficiency. Thus, in the present context, the crucial issue becomes whether the rule governing a particular tort is cost effective.[91] Perhaps the classic example is the test for negligent conduct propounded by Learned Hand J in *United States v Carroll Towing Co*:[92] 'if the probability be called P; the injury, L; and the burden, B; liability [in negligence] depends on whether B is less than L multiplied by P'. In other words, the test operates by permitting and requiring the defendant to assess the probability and costs of accidents, and then to compare them with the cost of precautions. The defendant is not negligent if his conduct is vindicated according to this test, for the objective is not to eliminate all damage, but rather to deter conduct that results in damage where the cost of preventing the accident is less than the cost (in damages) of the accident occurring. On such criteria, any change from fault-based liability to strict liability would have to depend on proof that the total additional costs to the potential defendants – additional

---

[87] This deterrent effect is not entirely absent in contexts where there is compulsory insurance, since repeated car accidents, for example, will lead to the tortfeasor having to pay higher and higher insurance premiums.

[88] The driver who takes the odd chance with amber traffic lights might appropriately be described thus.

[89] See, eg, *Cassell & Co v Broome* [1972] AC 1027 (D published defamatory material concerning C in the expectation that profits would outweigh an award of compensatory damages). See further Law Commission Report, *Exemplary, Aggravated and Restitutionary Damages*, Law Com No 247 (1997).

[90] For a general introduction to economic analysis see Burrows and Veljanowski, *Readings in the Economics of Law and Regulation* (1984).

[91] Calabresi, *The Cost of Accidents* (1970); Posner, *The Economic Analysis of Law* (6th edn, 2003).

[92] 159 F 2d 169 (2d Cir 1947) at 173.

precautions, insurance, and so on – did not exceed the total cost to individuals of the risk created by the enterprise. Normal concepts of fairness and justice can be relevant only if susceptible to being assigned economic value.[93]

Economic analysis is a useful tool to attain an understanding of the operation of certain torts, in particular negligence, nuisance, and product liability. It offers a measure by which our often confused system of compensation law may be judged and found wanting. However, economic analysis can never be an all-embracing explanation of the objectives of tort law; it fails to account, for example, for broader considerations of justice. As two of the leading lawyer-economists in England have pointed out, '[e]fficiency is, of course, not the only guideline to the right [legal] principles'; thus, efficiency must 'at some points yield before, and at other points compromise with, other guidelines, notably those of justice and fairness'.[94] Not surprisingly, then, English judges are often wary of relying on academic expositions of economic analysis when deciding cases.[95] Quite apart from its limitations, economic analysis has powerful detractors, foremost among whom is Ernest Weinrib.[96]

(F) THE JUDGES AND LAISSEZ-FAIRE

Much of the law relating to economic transactions is only understood if the implied judicial acceptance of laissez-faire is considered. This is merely one facet of the individualism of tort law, especially prominent during the nineteenth century. It is an influence which still persists, although less pervasively, in the face of the modern tendency towards welfarism.[97]

(G) LIMITS ON THE EFFECTIVENESS OF TORT LAW

Though there is much theorising about what should and should not be actionable in tort,[98] tort law remains essentially practical. Judges have little patience with trivial claims. For example, they may deny a remedy by way of trespass to the person for mere touching.[99] They recognise the limits of the wrongs that the law is capable of redressing, however morally reprehensible they may be. For example, avarice, brutal words, and

---

[93] Some lawyer-economists, of course, contend that an economic approach to tort law is a fair one precisely because it can be justified in accordance with objective, economic criteria. But this argument presupposes that the objective economic criteria are themselves fair.

[94] Ogus and Richardson [1977] CLJ 284, 294.

[95] Although they do take economic efficiency into account in determining the limits of liability for negligence on occasion: see, eg, *Stovin v Wise* [1996] AC 923.

[96] See, eg, Weinrib (1989) 23 Valp ULR 485. And for a highly accessible account of the various arguments for (and against), and the proponents of, economic analysis, see Cane (2005) 25 OJLS 203.

[97] See generally Cane, *Tort Law and Economic Interests* (2nd edn, 1996).

[98] And, indeed, what might properly be taken to constitute tort law: see McBride and Bagshaw, *Tort Law* (2005), 30–5 and 727–88.

[99] See *Collins v Wilcock* [1984] 1 WLR 1172. See also *White v Withers LLP* [2009] EWCA 1122, [72] (insusceptibility of courts to actions brought to 'prove a point').

ingratitude cannot form the basis of an action in tort law. Along with this is a judicial dread of a flood of actions. It is often avowedly for this reason that the courts have so far been reluctant to allow claims for negligently inflicted pure economic loss where the range of claimants as a result of one incident might be large.[100] The courts also display a marked caution in the context of awarding damages for non-material harms.

Another problem is that damages in many torts cannot be fixed with mathematical precision. For example, the calculation of damages in, say, the tort of false imprisonment, cannot be conducted in the same way as damages for breach of a contract based on failure to fulfil a sale of goods agreement. For this reason, the courts have rightly been on their guard to restrain 'gold-digging' actions. Nonetheless, it is apparent that they have sometimes been excessively wary; and later courts have had to overrule earlier decisions. The cases on the negligent infliction of psychiatric harm illustrate this point.[101]

SECTION 4 TORT AND OTHER BRANCHES OF COMMON LAW

For some writers, the juridical divisions between torts and other areas of the common law – principally the law of contract and the law of unjust enrichment – have become so blurred that they prefer not to talk of three separate branches of the civil law but, instead, of a general law of obligations.[102] Historically, contract law alone was concerned with the obligation to fulfil undertakings voluntarily made (so long as good consideration had been provided). By contrast, as we have seen, the obligations underlying torts require us to refrain from violating another's non-contractual, legally recognised rights and interests. Finally, with its roots in Roman law, the law of unjust enrichment concerns the obligation to reverse unjust and unjustifiable gains.[103] However, while 'obligations lawyers' recognise that it is broadly possible to distinguish these three areas of law in this way, they nonetheless contend that these divisions are imperfect. They believe that there are too many areas of overlap (in terms of the bases of damages awarded and the sources of the obligations) for this tripartite classification to be worthwhile. For example, the tort law associated with 'assumptions of responsibility' stemming from the decision in *Hedley Byrne & Co v Heller & Partners Ltd*[104] is seen by some to undermine the cardinal principles that only contractual obligations

---

[100] See ch 3. See also Barker, 'Economic Loss and the Duty of Care: A Study in the Exercise of Legal Justification' in Rickett (ed), *Justifying Private Law Remedies* (2008), ch 8 .

[101] As in *White v CC of South Yorkshire Police* [1999] 1 All ER 1. For analysis of the legitimacy of the courts' stance in this context see Murphy (1995) 15 LS 415.

[102] For some of the debate see Cane, *The Anatomy of Tort Law* (1997), 182–96, and Waddams, *Dimensions of Private Law: Categories and Concepts in Anglo-American Legal Reasoning* (2003).

[103] See Giglio (2003) 23 OJLS 455.

[104] [1964] AC 465. See also *White v Jones* [1995] 1 All ER 69; *Henderson v Merrett Syndicates* [1994] 3 All ER 506.

are created by the parties themselves, and that tortious obligations are imposed by rules of law.[105]

Similarly, contract and tort are connected by the fact that they both generally concern awards of damages for harm done (whether broken promises or broken legs).[106] But this is not exclusively the case. For example, contractual remedies may be assessed in the light of benefits acquired by the other party – and herein lies a point of connection with the law of unjust enrichment.[107] At the same time, however, both tort and unjust enrichment can be linked in that their obligations derive from rules of law rather than reciprocal undertakings.[108]

In the light of these juridical connections, the argument in favour of reconceptualising the common law in terms of a law of obligations is not without some force. Certainly, the divisions between tort, contract, and unjust enrichment law are far from perfect.[109] On the other hand, it is submitted that the clearest grasp of the principles, aims, and objectives of tort law – together with an appreciation of its distinctiveness in terms of the range of interests protected – may best be derived from its exposition in isolation from the law of contract and the law of unjust enrichment.

Finally, it should be noted that certain types of conduct may simultaneously constitute both a crime and a tort. Thus it is that the thief who steals your watch commits both the crime of theft and the tort of conversion. This overlap can be explained on the basis that, whereas it is the function of criminal law to protect the interest of the public at large (or the state), it is primarily tort law that protects the interests of individuals (hence sanctioning compensation and injunctions rather than fines or imprisonment).

FURTHER READING

BIRKS, 'The Concept of a Civil Wrong' in Owen (ed), *Philosophical Foundations of Tort Law* (1995), ch 1

CANE, *The Anatomy of Tort Law* (1997)

---

[105] For a particularly trenchant attack on the language of assumed responsibility in this context, see Barker (1993) 109 LQR 461. See also Witting, *Liability for Negligent Misstatements* (2004), 173–7.

[106] Furthermore, while the measure of damages in contract was once distinctively that of 'expectation loss', this has begun to feature also in the law of tort: see *White v Jones* [1995] 1 All ER 69. See also Murphy [1996] CLJ 43.

[107] In contract, if A builds B a fence for which B fails to pay, B is in breach of contract. If the benefit is conferred extra-contractually, however, the action will lie in unjust enrichment (eg, *Greenwood v Bennett* [1973] QB 195: A, believing the car he bought from a thief to be his own, effected several improvements upon it; B, the true owner, to whom the car had to be returned was liable to A in respect of his unjust enrichment in the form of those car improvements).

[108] Occasionally, contractual obligations are imposed by rules of law – eg, the duty to perform a service with reasonable care imposed by the Supply of Goods and Services Act 1982, s 13. But these obligations are imposed only within the pre-existing framework of reciprocal, voluntary obligations.

[109] See Waddams, *Dimensions of Private Law: Categories and Concepts in Anglo-American Legal Reasoning* (2003).

CANE, 'General and Special Tort Law: Uses and Abuses of Theory' in Neyers (ed), *Emerging Issues in Tort Law* (2007), ch 1

GOLDBERG AND ZIPURSKY, 'Unrealized Torts' (2002) 88 *Virginia Law Review* 1625

GORDLEY, *Foundations of Private Law: Property, Tort, Contract and Unjust Enrichment* (2006), chs 9–12

MURPHY, 'Formularism and Tort Law' [1999] *Adelaide Law Review* 115

SCHWARTZ, 'Mixed Theories of Tort Law: Affirming both Deterrence and Corrective Justice' (1997) 75 *Texas Law Review* 1801

STAPLETON, 'Tort, Insurance and Ideology' (1995) 58 *Modern Law Review* 520

STEELE, 'Damages in Tort and under the Human Rights Act: Remedial or Functional Separation?' [2008] *Cambridge Law Journal* 606

WEINRIB, 'Understanding Tort Law' (1989) 23 *Valparaiso University Law Review* 485

WRIGHT, 'Right, Justice and Tort Law' in Owen (ed), *Philosophical Foundations of Tort Law* (1995), ch 7

PART II

NEGLIGENT INVASIONS OF INTERESTS IN THE PERSON, PROPERTY INTERESTS, AND ECONOMIC INTERESTS

2

DUTY OF CARE I: FOUNDATIONAL PRINCIPLES

KEY ISSUES

(1) Negligence elements
The tort of negligence is composed of several elements. The claimant must prove the existence of a duty of care owed to him at the time of the alleged injurious interaction, breach of the duty, and causation of damage.

(2) Duty of care elements
The duty of care comprises three stages: reasonable foreseeability of injury to a class of persons including the claimant, a sufficient relationship of proximity between the claimant and defendant, and inquiry into whether it would be fair, just and reasonable to recognise a duty.

(3) Reasonable foreseeability
This is an objective test of capacity. The court is concerned with whether a reasonable person in the position of the claimant could have reasonably foreseen that carelessness might lead to injury of the kind suffered (whether bodily, psychiatric, property damage, or purely economic) to a class of persons including the claimant.

(4) Proximity
This test is concerned with whether there existed, prior to the defendant's failure to take care, sufficient factual links between the parties so as to establish proximity (in the sense of 'neighbourhood' or 'closeness') such as would support the imposition of a duty of care.

(5) Fair, just, and reasonable limb
Where foreseeability and proximity are found to have existed, the court will have the ability to recognise a duty of care. In determining whether or not to do so, it may assess various mid-level 'policy' issues that argue in favour of and/or against the imposition of a duty of care.

SECTION 1   INTRODUCTION

Far more people suffer damage from the careless acts of others than from intentional wrongdoing. Accordingly, carelessly inflicted harm occupies a central position in tort law, and it has long been recognised that, in certain circumstances, persons guilty of careless conduct should be liable to their victims. Indeed, the liability of those engaged in certain common callings – such as smiths and innkeepers – goes back to the fourteenth century. Furthermore, many actions in nuisance and trespass were once based upon negligent conduct. Gradually, however, a large variety of situations in which negligence was the common element were subsumed under the action on the case. But not until around 1825 was there any discernible emergence of negligence as a separate tort. There existed merely a list of situations where the victims of careless conduct might recover damages. Thereafter, actions on the case for negligence became common, no doubt spurred on at first by the increase in negligently inflicted injuries through the use of new mechanical inventions such as the railways, and later by the abolition of the forms of action.[1] The concrete emergence of negligence as a separate tort with a distinct set of principles became irresistible, and in practical terms it is now the most common (and most important) tort of all. It must be realised, however, that negligently inflicted harm does not always sound in negligence alone; negligent conduct relating to the use of land may well, for example, give rise to nuisance liability.[2]

It is essential to grasp from the start of any consideration of negligence law that it is not the case that anyone who suffers harm as a result of another's carelessness can sue. The tort of negligence requires more than 'heedless or careless conduct'.[3] The injured party must establish that the defendant owed him a duty to take reasonable care to protect him from the kind of harm suffered,[4] that he was in breach of that duty, and that it was the defendant's breach of duty that caused the claimant's injury. Duty, breach, and causation must all be established in every successful claim in negligence.[5] This chapter therefore starts by seeking to identify the fundamental principles underpinning the duty of care. The concept of duty is fundamental, for without it no legal obligation on the part of the defendant to take care with respect to the claimant arises.

SECTION 2   THE EMERGENCE OF A GENERAL TEST

The concept of duty of care in negligence[6] emerged towards the end of the eighteenth century, and is now so firmly rooted that there can be no doubt that actions in

---

[1] The main milestones were *Vaughan v Menlove* (1837) 3 Bing NC 468; *Winterbottom v Wright* (1842) 10 M & W 109; *Heaven v Pender* (1883) 11 QBD 503.

[2] But for criticism see Gearty [1989] CLJ 214.

[3] *Lochgelly Iron and Coal Co v M'Mullan* [1934] AC 1, at 25.

[4] In *Caparo Industries plc v Dickman* [1990] 605, at 627, Lord Bridge said: 'It is never sufficient to ask simply whether A owes B a duty of care. It is always necessary to determine the scope of the duty by reference to the kind of damage from which A must take care to save B harmless'. Accordingly, where X is instrumental in injuring Y in circumstances where no duty was owed to Y to take care not to injure Y *in that way*, X will not be liable for want of duty: *Sam v Atkins* [2005] EWCA Civ 1452.

[5] However, judges by no means always clearly distinguish between the three. In *Roe v Minister of Health* [1954] 2 QB 66, at 85, Lord Denning LJ opined that the three questions were in many cases simply different ways of looking at one and the same thing: 'Is the consequence fairly to be considered within the risk created by the negligence?'

[6] Duties similar to those discussed here under common-law negligence may also arise under statutes or contracts. See, eg, the 'common duty of care' under the Occupiers' Liability Act 1957, s 2(2).

negligence must fail where a duty is not established.[7] There are many strands to this requirement of duty, as we shall see. But to begin with, it is important to stress that there must be one of those general situations which the law recognises as being capable of giving rise to a duty; for in a number of situations it has been held that there can be no such duty.[8] The first attempt to rationalise the situations in which a duty may be imposed was made in *Heaven v Pender* by Brett MR. He said:

> [W]henever one person is by circumstances placed in such a position with regard to another that everyone of ordinary sense who did think would at once recognise that if he did not use ordinary care and skill in his own conduct with regard to those circumstances he would cause danger or injury to the person or property of the other, a duty arises to use ordinary care and skill to avoid such danger.[9]

In 1932 came the famous dictum of Lord Atkin in *Donoghue v Stevenson* in which he enunciated the seminal 'neighbour principle'.

> The rule that you are to love your neighbour becomes in law, you must not injure your neighbour; and the lawyer's question, Who is my neighbour? receives a restricted reply. You must take reasonable care to avoid acts or omissions which you can reasonably foresee would be likely to injure your neighbour. Who, then, in law is my neighbour? The answer seems to be persons who are so closely and directly affected by my act that I ought reasonably to have them in contemplation as being so affected when I am directing my mind to the acts or omissions which are called in question.[10]

This 'neighbour principle' is not the *ratio decidendi* of the case and it is probable that Lord Atkin never intended it to be an exact or comprehensive statement of law.[11] However, the importance of *Donoghue v Stevenson* was twofold. (1) It firmly established a new category of duty, namely that of a manufacturer of goods to the eventual users of those goods (a category that has since developed far beyond the limits of the facts of that case).[12] (2) It finally set at rest any possible doubts about whether the tort of negligence was capable of further expansion.

Although Lord Atkin's neighbour principle was established as a broad guide to the circumstances in which a duty of care may be imposed, it must not be forgotten that the question of duty is one of law, not fact. As such, the question of whether a duty exists is often straightforward, for there are numerous and extensive categories of situation which are already treated by the courts as imposing a duty of care. Examples include

---

[7] *Heaven v Pender* (1883) 11 QBD 503, at 507; *Thomas v Quartermaine* (1887) 18 QBD 685, at 694; *Le Lievre v Gould* [1893] 1 QB 491, at 497; *Grant v Australian Knitting Mills Ltd* [1936] AC 85, at 101; *Hay (or Bourhill) v Young* [1943] AC 92.

[8] See, eg, *Mulcahy v Ministry of Defence* [1996] QB 732.

[9] (1883) 11 QBD 503, at 509.

[10] [1932] AC 562, at 580.

[11] Cf *Haseldine v CA Daw & Son Ltd* [1941] 2 KB 343, at 362.

[12] This was an instance of the courts taking account of the new conditions of mass production and complex marketing of goods (wherein there are many intermediaries between manufacturer and consumer), and imposing on manufacturers certain minimum standards of care in favour of the consumer. The clearest exposition of this function of *Donoghue v Stevenson* is the speech of Lord Devlin in *Hedley Byrne & Co Ltd v Heller & Partners Ltd* [1964] AC 465.

makers or repairers of goods owing a duty to those who use those goods, and those carrying out activities on a highway owing a duty to other highway users. Accordingly, before one falls back on any general test, one must ascertain whether on similar facts the courts have already recognised a duty.

There are, of course, other cases where the law has unequivocally *denied* the existence of a duty. A landowner, for example, may with impunity abstract percolating water from below the surface of his land even though this results in a settlement of a claimant's adjoining buildings. He is not liable because he owes no duty of care in respect of percolating water.[13] Similarly, there is no duty in respect of economic loss caused by damage to the property of an individual other than a person with a current proprietary interest in the damaged property.[14]

SECTION 3   THE RISE AND FALL OF *ANNS*

Were it to be the case that the courts would hold that no duty exists unless an earlier precedent established such a duty, tort law would remain frozen and static for all time. Yet Lord Macmillan stated in *Donoghue v Stevenson* that the 'categories of negligence are never closed'.[15] This means at the very least, as Asquith LJ said in *Candler v Crane Christmas & Co*, 'that in accordance with changing social needs and standards new classes of persons legally bound or entitled to the exercise of care may from time to time emerge'.[16] So, over the several decades beginning with Lord Atkin's formulation of the 'neighbour principle', new duty-situations were readily recognised by the courts. Thus, for example, it was held that an education authority owes a duty to the driver of a vehicle to exercise reasonable supervision over children in its nursery adjoining the highway so as to prevent them from endangering his safety on the road.[17] And an electricity authority that had high-voltage wires near a climbable tree was held liable to the personal representatives of a child who trespassed off a nearby footpath, climbed the tree, and was killed.[18]

What each of the above examples has in common is that the defendant failed his 'neighbour'. He could have foreseen, and should have taken steps to prevent, the injury suffered by the claimant. So was the 'neighbour test' the sole criterion determining whether or not a duty arose? In a series of judgments from 1970 to 1982 the courts came close to accepting as much. First, in *Home Office v Dorset Yacht Co Ltd*, Lord Reid declared:

> The time has come when we can and should say that it [ie, Lord Atkin's neighbour principle] ought to apply unless there is some justification or valid explanation for its exclusion.[19]

---

[13] *Langbrook Properties Ltd v Surrey CC* [1969] 3 All ER 1424; *Thomas v Gulf Oil Refining Ltd* (1979) 123 Sol Jo 787; *Midland Bank v Bargrove Property Services* (1991) 24 Con LR 98.

[14] *Leigh & Sillivan Ltd v Aliakmon Shipping Co Ltd* [1986] AC 785.

[15] [1932] AC 562, at 619.

[16] [1951] 2 KB 164, at 192.

[17] *Carmarthenshire CC v Lewis* [1955] AC 549; *Barnes v Hampshire CC* [1969] 3 All ER 746.

[18] *Buckland v Guildford Gas Light and Coke Co* [1949] 1 KB 410.

[19] [1970] AC 1004, at 1027.

Then in *Anns v Merton LBC*, Lord Wilberforce proposed a two-stage test for duty:

> the position has now been reached that in order to establish that a duty of care arises in a particular situation, it is not necessary to bring the facts of that situation within those of previous situations in which a duty of care has been held to exist. Rather the question has to be approached in two stages. First, one has to ask whether, as between the alleged wrongdoer and the person who suffered damage there is a sufficient relationship of proximity or neighbourhood such that, in the reasonable contemplation of the former, carelessness on his part may be likely to cause damage to the latter, in which case a *prima facie* duty of care arises. Secondly, if the first question is answered affirmatively, it is necessary to consider whether there are any considerations which ought to negative, or to reduce or limit the scope of the duty of the class of person to whom it is owed or the damages to which a breach of it may give rise.[20]

The two-stage test looked deceptively simple. Applied fairly literally, a judge ruling on a novel duty-situation might reason thus: (1) Was the harm to the claimant foreseeable, so bringing him within the 'neighbour principle'? (2) If yes, was there any valid policy reason to deny the existence of a duty to the claimant?[21] In effect, the claimant having established foreseeability raised a presumption of the existence of a duty which the defendant then had to rebut on policy grounds. Lord Wilberforce himself, however, recognised that policy factors had a central role to play in determining the scope of a duty in *McLoughlin v O'Brian*: 'at the margin, the boundaries of a man's responsibilities for acts of negligence have to be fixed as a matter of policy'.[22]

But in the very same case, Lord Scarman, who was fearful that judicial conservatism would lead to unjust rigidity in the common law, came close to declaring foreseeability to be the *sole* test of the existence of a duty. Rejecting any policy-oriented limitations on liability for psychiatric harm, he argued:

> if principle inexorably requires a decision which entails a degree of policy risk, the court's function is to adjudicate according to principle, leaving policy curtailment to the judgment of Parliament.[23]

During the period from 1970 to 1984, the categories of negligence looked infinitely expandable. The boundaries of liability expanded in respect of both psychiatric

---

[20] [1978] AC 728, at 751–2.

[21] For example, to refuse a remedy to C, a criminal, who is injured by the negligence of his drunken companion while driving their getaway car. Injury to C was readily foreseeable but as a matter of policy no duty was recognised as owed by one participant in crime to another: *Ashton v Turner* [1981] QB 137. And a claim by a child for 'wrongful life'– ie, a claim that the doctors acted negligently in not aborting her – was rejected on policy grounds. The consequences of failing to diagnose the rubella in her mother were foreseeable, but the Court of Appeal held (inter alia) that such claims would, if allowed, undermine the sanctity of human life: *McKay v Essex AHA* [1982] QB 1166.

[22] [1983] 1 AC 410, at 421.

[23] *McLoughlin v O'Brian* [1983] 1 AC 410, at 430.

harm[24] and pure economic loss.[25] The tort of negligence even looked set to undermine the very boundaries of contract and tort, and, more particularly, the doctrines of consideration and privity of contract.[26] From 1984 onwards, however, judicial caution resurfaced and the House of Lords led a retreat from *Anns*, bringing the tort of negligence back to a much more category-based approach. Their Lordships' determination to restrict the unchecked expansion of the tort and to prevent the emergence of any presumption that all kinds of harm were the responsibility of someone other than the claimant, was summed up neatly by Lord Hoffmann in *Stovin v Wise*:

> The trend of authorities [since 1984] has been to discourage the assumption that anyone who suffers loss is *prima facie* entitled to compensation from a person (preferably insured or a public authority) whose act or omission can be said to have caused it. The default position is that he is not.[27]

The retreat from *Anns* began in *Governors of the Peabody Donation Fund v Sir Lindsay Parkinson & Co Ltd*.[28] There, the House of Lords denied a remedy to a development company suing a local authority for the financial loss occasioned to that company by an inadequate drainage system, the plans for which they alleged the authority had negligently approved. Lord Keith said of the *Anns* test:

> There has been a tendency in some recent cases to treat these passages as being themselves of a definitive character. This is a temptation to be resisted in determining whether or not a duty of care of a particular scope was incumbent on the defendant. It is material to take into consideration whether it is just and reasonable that it should be so.[29]

In effect Lord Keith demanded that the *claimant* identify policy grounds why a duty should arise and why the defendant should be made responsible for his welfare.

Judicial disapproval of the *Anns* test continued apace thereafter.[30] It became clear beyond doubt that foreseeability of harm alone is not enough to create a duty of care:

> It has been said almost too frequently to require repetition that foreseeability of likely harm is not in itself a sufficient test of liability in negligence. Some further ingredient is invariably needed to establish the requisite proximity of relationship between the [claimant] and defendant, and all the circumstances of the case must be carefully considered and analysed in order to ascertain whether such an ingredient is present.[31]

---

[24] See, eg, *McLoughlin v O'Brian* [1983] 1 AC 410, at 430; *Attia v British Gas plc* [1988] QB 304.

[25] See, eg, *Ross v Caunters* [1980] Ch 297; *Junior Books Ltd v Veitchi Co Ltd* [1983] 1 AC 520 (the high water mark of foreseeability sufficing to impose a duty).

[26] Since then, much of the doctrine of privity has been unpicked by the Contracts (Rights of Third Parties) Act 1999.

[27] [1996] AC 923, at 949.

[28] [1985] AC 210.

[29] [1985] AC 210, at 240.

[30] *Yuen Kun-yeu v A-G of Hong Kong* [1988] AC 175, at 190–4; *Rowling v Takaro Properties Ltd* [1988] AC 473, at 501.

[31] *Hill v CC of West Yorkshire* [1988] 2 All ER 238, at 241.

Foreseeability of harm to the claimant remains a necessary precondition of liability. But there must also be proximity of relationship between the claimant and the defendant; the 'neighbourhood' or closeness and directness of which Lord Atkin originally spoke in *Donoghue v Stevenson*. Although this would appear a rather intuitive concept, the courts have had some difficulty in further defining it, especially in cases involving indirectly caused harms – a matter to which we shall return.

In addition to the foreseeability and proximity requirements, it was subsequently reasserted that the courts would require, also, that there be proper grounds on which to impose on the defendant responsibility for the harm in question; reasons, in other words, why it would be fair to expect the defendant to safeguard the claimant's interests rather than to expect the claimant to look after himself. How difficult a task the claimant faces in this respect will vary depending on the kind of harm he has suffered. The courts are more ready to impose responsibility to safeguard others from physical injury and damage to their property, than from economic losses. Lord Bridge said in *Caparo Industries plc v Dickman*:

> One of the most important distinctions always to be observed lies in the law's essentially different approach to the different kinds of damage which one party may have suffered in consequence of the acts or omissions of another. It is one thing to owe a duty to avoid causing injury to the person or property of others. It is quite another to avoid causing others to suffer purely economic loss.[32]

Where physical harm is caused to a person (or his property) by another's carelessness, establishing that the claimant is proximate and that it is fair that the defendant *ought* to be responsible for the harm thus inflicted is often unproblematic. As Lord Oliver put it in *Caparo*: 'the nexus between the defendant and the injured claimant can rarely give rise to any difficulty [in such cases]'.[33] And in *Murphy v Brentwood District Council*[34] he further implied the presumption of a duty in such cases, stating that '[t]he infliction of physical injury to the person or property of another universally requires to be justified'.

Nonetheless, the House of Lords made it clear in *Marc Rich & Co AG v Bishop Rock Marine Co Ltd*[35] that, even with respect to claims of physical damage, foreseeability alone is insufficient to create a duty of care. Lord Steyn confirmed[36] that, *whatever the nature of the relevant harm*, the court must consider, not only the foreseeability of such harm, but also the relationship between the parties and, in every case, be 'satisfied that in all the circumstances it is fair, just, and reasonable to impose a duty of care'. The facts of the case were as follows:

> Cs' cargo had been loaded on D1's vessel under contracts incorporating the usual terms and conditions of international shipping contracts. Mid-voyage, the ship put into port

---

[32] [1990] 1 All ER 568, at 574.
[33] Ibid at 585.
[34] [1990] 2 All ER 908, at 935.
[35] [1996] AC 211.
[36] Ibid at 235.

with a crack in her hull. A surveyor employed by D3, a classification society responsible for checking the safety of ships at sea, inspected the vessel and certified that after some temporary repairs it should proceed on its voyage. A few days later the ship sank and the cargo worth £6m was lost. Cs recovered some of that sum from D1, but D1's liability was limited by statute. Cs then attempted to recover the balance of the loss from D3. Cs had suffered readily foreseeable physical damage to property as a result of the society's negligent inspection of the ship and the subsequent 'green light' the society's surveyor had given for the ship to carry on with the voyage.

Giving the majority speech in the House of Lords and finding no duty to the cargo owners, Lord Steyn acknowledged that, where one person's carelessness *directly* causes physical damage to another, the law will more readily recognise a duty. The infliction of loss to the claimants in this case was, however, indirect. There was no contract between the claimant and the society and no direct reliance by the claimants on the expertise of the society. Imposing a duty would undermine the framework established by the Hague-Visby Rules (an international maritime Convention).[37] Equally, it was considered relevant that classification societies are independent, non-profit-making bodies that act in the public interest to promote the collective welfare of people and property on the seas. Faced with litigation of this sort, such societies might act defensively, refusing to carry out urgent or problematic inspections with a high risk of liability. Furthermore, limited resources would be diverted from the societies' fundamental work to conduct complex litigation. It would thus be unfair and unjust to impose a duty in respect of the claimants' lost cargo. The societies' responsibility was primarily towards the collective welfare of those at sea, and individual cargo owners should be left to their contractual remedies.

Lord Lloyd dissented. He perceived the facts as little more than a straightforward application of *Donoghue v Stevenson*. The surveyor certifying the ship as fit to sail de facto controlled its fate. Had he refused a certificate, the ship-owners would not have continued the voyage. He argued, therefore, that in instances of physical damage it would require an exceptional case to refuse to impose a duty on the grounds that it would not be fair, just, and reasonable. In other words, Lord Lloyd felt that in a case of physical harm to people or property, once foreseeability of harm is proven there should be a strong presumption of liability. He concluded that: '[o]therwise there is a risk that the law of negligence will disintegrate into a series of isolated decisions without any coherent principles at all, and the retreat from *Anns* will turn into a rout'.[38]

But what Lord Lloyd had to say must be read in the light of *Sutradhar v NERC*,[39] where a unanimous House of Lords insisted that proximity must still be shown in cases where physical injury results from careless certification. Crucial to the non-liability of the NERC (which failed to identify the presence of arsenic in a potential Bangladeshi water supply upon testing the water) was the fact that there was 'nothing

[37] For analogous reasoning, see *Raja v Austin Gray* [2002] EWCA Civ 1965.
[38] [1996] AC 211, at 230.
[39] [2006] UKHL 33.

like the directness and immediacy between the defendant's role in events and the claimant's injuries...the essential touchstones of proximity are missing'.[40] In other words, given that the testing had been commissioned by a third party, the claimant who suffered arsenical poisoning in consequence of drinking the water was unable to establish a sufficiently close relationship between himself and the NERC, and it was not enough that it was foreseeable that someone would suffer such poisoning if the water was certified to be reasonably pure by the NERC.

A crucial question was left unanswered in *Marc Rich*. Had lives been imperilled when the ship sank, would the classification society have owed a duty to the dead sailors? Counsel for the society appeared to concede a duty in relation to personal injury. Lord Steyn's robust speech, suggesting that it is unreasonable to attach legal consequences to the society's carelessness, makes it difficult to judge whether, if the personal injury issue had arisen, a duty of care would have been held to exist.[41]

Notwithstanding the universal support in *Caparo* for the tripartite test based on foreseeability, proximity, and it being fair, just, and reasonable to impose a duty, it was simultaneously asserted in that case that the component limbs of the test are inherently vague. Concepts such as proximity and fairness, for instance, were thought by Lord Bridge to be 'not susceptible of any precise definition as would be necessary to give them utility as practical tests.'[42] And the need to introduce some element of predictability into the development of duty-situations perhaps underscores the comment he made immediately after this acknowledgment.

> Whilst recognising...the importance of the underlying general principles common to the whole field of negligence,...the law has now moved in the direction of attaching greater significance to the more traditional categorisation of distinct and recognisable situations as guides to the existence, the scope and the limits of the varied duties of care which the law imposes. We must now...recognise the wisdom of the words of Brennan J in the High Court of Australia in *Sutherland Shire Council v Heyman*,[43] where he said:
>
>> It is preferable...that the law should develop novel categories of negligence incrementally and by analogy with established categories, rather than by a massive extension of a *prima facie* duty of care restrained only by indefinable 'considerations, which ought to negative, or to reduce or limit the scope of the duty or the class of person to whom it is owed'.[44]

Lord Bridge was not arguing for a return to a pre-*Donoghue v Stevenson* approach. A claimant in an action for negligence will not fail simply because the duty-situation he relies on has never previously been recognised. The House of Lords have not closed the

---

[40] [2006] UKHL 33, at [47]–[48]. See also at [38].

[41] For some intimation that it might, see *Perrett v Collins* [1998] 2 Lloyd's Rep 255.

[42] *Caparo Industries plc v Dickman* [1990] 1 All ER 568, at 574. See also the speech of Lord Oliver (at 585): 'to search for any single formula which will serve as a general test of liability is to pursue a will-o-the-wisp'.

[43] (1985) 60 ALR 1, at 43–4.

[44] [1990] 1 All ER 568, at 574. See also *Murphy v Brentwood DC* [1990] 2 All ER 908, at 915.

categories of negligence.[45] Rather, a claimant seeking recognition of a novel duty of care *will* now have to argue his case in the context of existing authority and to persuade the court that to extend liability into this new situation accords with previous analyses of policy and justice in analogous cases. Moreover, a finding of no duty in analogous cases will tell against the claimant. So, in *X v Bedfordshire County Council*,[46] it was sought to establish that local authorities owe a duty of care in relation to their powers to protect children from abuse and neglect. There was no precedent in relation to a public authority's administration of a social welfare scheme. However, Lord Browne-Wilkinson[47] looked at analogous powers vested in the police to protect society from crime and in the financial regulatory bodies to protect investors from fraud. Finding no duty in either of those contexts, he suggested that establishing a duty in relation to child protection would be very incongruous.

Similar reasoning has also been applied in relation to economic loss arising out of property damage. In *Leigh & Sillivan Ltd v Aliakmon Shipping Co Ltd*,[48] Lord Brandon[49] denied the existence of a duty of care in respect of economic loss to X arising out of damage to Y's property. He noted authorities dating back prior to 1980[50] insisting that a duty of care would be owed only to those with the requisite proprietary or possessory interest in the property concerned.[51] He was adamant that well-established authority had settled the matter,[52] and thus, regardless of how foreseeable consequential loss to others might be, that loss was irrecoverable. There could be no question, he thought, of 'the existence of a duty of care in a factual situation in which the existence of such a duty had been repeatedly held not to exist'.[53]

Judicial refusal to review proposed categories of negligence previously ruled 'out of court' does to some extent fossilise the tort of negligence. But consider some of the reasons justifying such an approach. Principles in tort need to be reasonably predictable otherwise litigation can proliferate fruitlessly; and tort law helps to define those obligations imposed on us by law. Whereas we know what our contractual obligations entail because we chose to enter into them, justice demands that we have some means of knowing what other obligations we must honour. There is also the question of insurance. In many tort cases, the dispute is not really between the claimant and defendant but between their insurers.[54] The decision as to when a person should insure against loss to himself and when he should insure against liability to others depends on an understanding of the circumstances in which a duty of care will arise. If you know it is

---

[45] See, eg, *Spring v Guardian Assurance plc* [1995] 2 AC 296.

[46] [1995] 2 AC 633.

[47] Ibid at 751.

[48] [1986] AC 785.

[49] Ibid at 815.

[50] See *Margarine Union v Cambay Prince Steamship Co Ltd* [1969] 1 QB 219; *The Mineral Transporter* [1986] AC 1.

[51] Cf *Shell UK Ltd v Total UK Ltd* [2010] EWCA Civ 180.

[52] See also *Stephens v Anglian Water Authority* [1987] 1 WLR 1381.

[53] [1986] AC 785, at 815.

[54] See Stapleton (1995) 58 MLR 820.

highly likely that a certain kind of loss will be left to lie where it falls, you, as a prudent person, will insure yourself against that loss. Similarly, if you know that a particular sort of careless conduct will probably give rise to liability towards another person, you will prudently insure against that liability.

A final factor to note in the context of the retreat from *Anns* is the parallel growth in the willingness of the judges to address openly the issue of insurance.[55] The fact that one party might be insured was formerly said to be irrelevant to liability.[56] However, *who*, given the economic and social realities of the parties' relationship, *ought* sensibly to have insured against the relevant loss is now a factor sometimes used to determine whether it is fair, just, and reasonable to impose a duty on the defendant.[57] That said, Lord Lloyd in his dissent in *Marc Rich & Co AG v Bishop Rock Marine Co Ltd*[58] sounded a note of caution. He remarked that judicial statements on insurance are not necessarily based on empirical factual evidence and that too often they may be no more than assumptions about common practice unsupported by conclusive evidence. Indeed, this sentiment is true of most reasoning about consequences to future parties from the imposition of particular legal rules, including the duty of care.[59]

SECTION 4   MODERN APPROACHES TO THE DUTY OF CARE

Although modern judicial conservatism and the adoption by the House of Lords of Brennan J's dictum in *Sutherland Shire Council v Heyman* have not resulted in a finite set of duty categories, they do of course serve to constrain the future growth of the tort. First, by suggesting that new duty-situations ought to develop only incrementally, it is now much harder to establish a new category of negligence that is significantly different from, or wider in scope than, any of its predecessors.[60] Second, as we have already seen, where a duty-situation is not entirely novel, but analogous to a category in which courts in earlier decisions refused to recognise a duty, the door indeed seems closed to imposing a new duty.[61] On the other hand, it must not be overlooked that it is the tripartite *Caparo* test that now provides the primary mechanism according to

---

[55]   An early example can be seen in *Spartan Steel and Alloys Ltd v Martin & Co (Contractors) Ltd* [1973] QB 27, at 38.

[56]   *Capital and Counties plc v Hampshire CC* [1997] 2 All ER 865, at 891.

[57]   See *Murphy v Brentwood DC* [1990] 2 All ER 908, at 923; *Marc Rich & Co AG v Bishop Rock Marine Co Ltd* [1996] AC 211, at 241; *Stovin v Wise* [1996] AC 923, at 954.

[58]   [1996] AC 211, at 228.

[59]   Witting (2005) 25 OJLS 33.

[60]   Note the reliance placed by Lord Steyn in *Marc Rich & Co AG v Bishop Rock Marine Co Ltd* [1996] AC 211 on the absence of precedent for ship-owners suing classification societies.

[61]   But see below for the impact of the human rights dimension on the negligence liability of public authorities in *D v East Berkshire Community NHS Trust* [2005] 2 AC 373. See also Murphy [2003] LS 103.

which new duties of care will be recognised; so the frontiers of negligence are clearly capable of gradual expansion.

(A) THE *CAPARO* TEST

According to their Lordships in *Caparo Industries v Dickman*, a duty of care may now be imposed if three requirements are satisfied: (1) The claimant must be reasonably foreseeable (bearing in mind the kind of harm involved). (2) There must be a relationship of proximity between the claimant and the defendant. (3) It must be fair, just, and reasonable in the circumstances for a duty of care to be imposed on the defendant. Each limb of this test requires closer consideration.

(1) The reasonably foreseeable claimant

The test for reasonable foreseeability is objective in nature; it is concerned with what the reasonable person in the position of the defendant could have reasonably foreseen prior to the injurious interaction between the parties. The threshold of foreseeability is not particularly high, envisaging real possibilities rather than probabilities. But the concept is somewhat malleable in nature. Thus, in *Grieves v FT Everard & Sons*, Lord Hoffmann stated that the 'answers to a test of foreseeability will vary according to, first, the precise description of what should have been foreseen and, secondly, the degree of probability which makes it foreseeable'.[62]

What must be reasonably foreseen is the possibility that if care is not taken, injury may be caused to a certain class of persons. Duty of care being about persons – who owes a duty of care to whom? – the foreseeability inquiry is usually concerned with whether or not injury to *a class* of person including the claimant is foreseeable. However, in some cases, it may suffice for the court to focus upon foreseeability of injury to the claimant – especially where the facts are not likely to recur. Another point to keep in mind is that foreseeability of harm to persons, being about future possible consequences of failures in care, is affected by the kind of injury in question.[63] Thus, while foreseeability of directly caused injury is often quite straightforward, foreseeability of indirectly caused injury may be more difficult to establish. To take an example: it is easily foreseeable that a failure by a driver to take care in driving a vehicle will cause bodily injury to persons in the immediate vicinity, such as pedestrians. But is it reasonably foreseeable that a psychiatric illness might be caused to another driver after a minor prang? Is it reasonably foreseeable that the stricken driver's children may no longer be able to attend private schools and that their future earning power will be diminished? These are questions the answers to which are less intuitive and with respect to which matters of reasonableness – of judgment about what is foreseeable – become more important.

---

[62] [2008] 1 AC 281, at [29].
[63] See also Goldberg and Zipursky, *The Oxford Introductions to US Law: Torts* (2010), 81.

The operation of the reasonable foreseeability requirement is neatly illustrated by *Haley v London Electricity Board*.[64] There, the defendants dug a trench in the street with statutory authority. They took some measures to help ensure the safety of passers-by, but these precautions were only adequate to the needs of passers-by with decent eyesight. The claimant, who was blind and alone, suffered serious injury when he tripped over a long hammer left lying on the ground by the defendants. The House of Lords held that it was incumbent on the defendants to take reasonable care for the safety of all persons using the highway, including the blind and the infirm. Just because blind persons constitute only a small percentage of the population does not make them unforeseeable. As Lord Reid asserted:

> We are all accustomed to meeting blind people walking alone with their white sticks on city pavements…I find it quite impossible to say that it is not reasonably foreseeable that a blind person may pass along a particular pavement on a particular day.[65]

As will become apparent in the chapters on breach and remoteness of damage, foreseeability is a component of a number of elements in negligence. The focus is slightly different at each stage. At the duty stage, foreseeability is important as an objective test of minimal capacity to comprehend risk of injury *to persons* and without it there is no need to go further because no duty of care will be owed.

(2) Proximity[66]

In many instances proximity and reasonable foreseeability may be thought of as informing each other. In the case of road users, for example, the duty of care that is owed is in part founded on the fact that one can readily foresee that careless driving by X may result in adverse consequences for innocent driver Y, who was unfortunate enough to be in X's vicinity. But the thing that makes Y a reasonably foreseeable claimant is the fact that he is on the same stretch of road as X at the time of X's careless driving. In other words, Y's proximity (relational and spatial) is a determinant of his reasonable foreseeability.[67]

However, it is clear that the requirement of proximity is a distinctive limb of the *Caparo* test.[68] The Court of Appeal's decision in *Goodwill v British Pregnancy Advisory Service*[69] illustrates this nicely.

---

[64] [1965] AC 778.

[65] Ibid at 791.

[66] In the US, the 'proximity' inquiry tends to occur when considering causation: see Goldberg and Zipursky, *The Oxford Introductions to US Law: Torts* (2010), 98ff.

[67] It might also be thought that the fact that C was both foreseeable and proximate is what makes it fair, just, and reasonable to impose a duty of care on D. In other words, it could be argued that the three elements are really only 'three facets of the same thing' and 'not to be treated as wholly separate and distinct requirements': see *Marc Rich & Co AG v Bishop Rock Marine Co Ltd* [1996] AC 211, at 235.

[68] This proposition has been denied in Australian cases: eg, *Sullivan v Moody* (2001) 207 CLR 562; *Miller v Miller* [2011] HCA 9, at [59] (the demise in Australian law of proximity 'is now complete'). Instead, the court will examine the ' "relations, juxtapositions, situations or conduct or activities" in question'! ([2011] HCA 9, at [64]).

[69] [1996] 1 WLR 1397. See also *Roe v Minister of Health* [1954] 2 QB 66.

D performed a vasectomy on a man who three years later became C's lover. Knowing that he had had a vasectomy, the couple did not use contraception. But C became pregnant and gave birth to a child. The vasectomy had, as a tiny number of such procedures do, spontaneously reversed. C claimed that D owed her a duty and was negligent in failing to warn her lover of the possibility that he might regain his fertility. Her claim was struck out.

Peter Gibson LJ suggested, *obiter*, that if the claimant's lover had been her husband or partner, and if the doctor had known that the vasectomy was intended to be as much for her benefit as the patient's, a duty might have been owed to the claimant. But without such a connection between the doctor and the woman – who, after all, was merely one of an indeterminate class of women with whom the man in question might have had sexual intercourse during his lifetime – the relationship with the defendant was insufficiently proximate for a duty to be imposed on the doctor in her favour.

As we have seen, the House of Lords in *Caparo* admitted to the 'vagueness' of the three-stage test and of the use of concepts underlying it.[70] How to define what constitutes 'proximity'? This issue has been the subject of significant academic debate. One debate has been about whether or not the proximity limb of duty of care includes both the positive – that is, features of the relationship between claimant and defendant – as well as the normative – that is, elements of policy reasoning. This issue has not been authoritatively resolved and is thus a matter for argument.

In our view, the position should be viewed as this: policy factors have influenced the development of the proximity concept; they 'underpin' (in Cane's terminology)[71] the use of the concept in the three-stage test for duty. The main policy behind the use of the concept is the simple one that parties who are proximate to each other ought usually to be careful because of the capacity to harm that such closeness brings with it. This policy is reflective of the internal logic of the structure of the tort of negligence.[72] But policy factors need not be invoked upon the application of the proximity test itself, even if (as is obvious) what constitutes proximity is undoubtedly a matter of judgment. The proximity test is applied simply according to a judgment of the evidence of the facts surrounding the injurious interaction between the parties. If proximity is present between the parties, then the case will support the recognition of a duty of care; the prerequisite of proximity is fulfilled.

But we still have not answered the question – what *is* proximity? Clearly, proximity, 'neighbourhood', and 'closeness' were intended by Lord Atkin in *Donoghue v Stevenson* to be synonymous concepts. Proximity, we might therefore surmise, is concerned with the factual relationship between the parties. Logically, it is concerned with the existence of that relationship *prior to* the failure in care – it is *because of* the presence of proximity that a duty is recognisable and, where recognised, gives rise to an obligation of care. Our best explanation is that proximity is concerned with the factual relations

---

[70] *Caparo Industries plc v Dickman* [1990] 1 All ER 568, at 574.

[71] Cane (2004) 120 LQR 189, 192. See also MacCormick, *Legal Reasoning and Legal Theory* (1978), 263.

[72] This point has been the hobby horse of one of the editors: Witting (2007) 71 MLR 621; id (2007) 31 MULR 569. But he definitely claims to have drawn inspiration from his co-editor!

between the parties which signified the potential for the defendant to cause harm to the claimant (and persons similarly placed). It is because of the closeness between the parties that pathways to harm are created. These pathways are not restricted to those which signify the potential for physical injury. They include other pathways to recognised forms of harm.

The judges have not, however, explained the concept of proximity in this way – and in some instances have used the concept in ways which are inconsistent with this conception (such as when they mix positive and normative issues). Even if this is so, we hope that our conceptualisation of proximity will assist the student in analysing the cases and thinking through legal problems. But it is important to remember that the mere fact that proximity is present does not automatically entail the recognition of a duty. Indeed, we now look at a class of case where proximity between the parties often is not enough to ground a duty of care.

(a) Omissions

Where, temporally speaking, there is no prior relationship between the parties, an omission to act will not constitute actionable negligence, however readily foreseeable the harm to the claimant[73] and despite the physical proximity between the parties. A passer-by who stands and watches a child drown in a shallow pool is under a negative duty of care not to harm the child. But this will not be the relevant issue in an omissions case. The issue is whether there is a positive duty to act and save the child from drowning and here the law is quite clear that the passer-by is not liable for failing to intervene to save her, even though he could do so at minimal risk to himself. A 'Bad Samaritan', who neglects even to summon aid to the victims of a road accident and prioritises getting to work on time, is not liable for his omission. English law imposes no duty to rescue.[74] Lord Nicholls elegantly summed up the distinction between acts and omissions declaring it to be:

> one matter to require a person to take care if he embarks on a course of conduct which may harm others. It is another matter to require a person, who is doing nothing[,] to take positive action to protect others from harm for which he is not responsible.[75]

The rule against liability for pure omissions was justified by Lord Hoffmann in *Stovin v Wise* according to an array of political, moral, and economic arguments.

> In political terms it is less of an invasion of an individual's freedom for the law to require him to consider the safety of others in his actions than to impose upon him a duty to rescue or protect. A moral version of this point may be called the 'Why pick on me?' argument. A duty to prevent harm to others or to render assistance to a person in danger or

---

[73] *Sutradhar v NERC* [2006] UKHL 33; *Glaister v Appelby-in-Westmorland Town Council* [2009] EWCA Civ 1325.

[74] Such a duty is imposed in a number of civil law systems: see *Smith v Littlewoods Organisation Ltd* [1987] 1 All ER 710, at 729.

[75] *Stovin v Wise* [1996] AC 923, at 930.

distress may apply to a large and indeterminate class of people who happen to be able to do something. Why should one be held liable rather than another? In economic terms, the efficient allocation of resources usually requires an activity should bear its own costs. If it benefits from being able to impose some of its costs on other people (what economists call 'externalities') the market is distorted because the activity appears cheaper than it really is. So liability to pay compensation for loss caused by negligent conduct acts as a deterrent against increasing the cost of the activity to the community and reduces externalities. But there is no similar justification for requiring a person who is not doing anything to spend money on behalf of someone else.[76]

This is the rule in cases of pure omissions – that is, where the defendant's omission directly, and without more, causes loss to the claimant. But this presumes a rather difficult issue: that it is easy to classify any given conduct as nonfeasance (an omission) rather than misfeasance (requiring positive conduct). Is, for example, failing to apply the brakes of a car at a red traffic light an omission to act, or is it simply active, careless driving?[77] It is almost certainly the latter. Yet a failure to repair expeditiously a breached sea wall such that subsequent flooding to a claimant occurred was not culpable misfeasance. The threat posed by the breach in the sea wall had arisen naturally, and the defendants' duty did not stretch to the prevention of future damage for which they were not responsible. Nor were they under a duty to shorten the period in which such damage could occur.[78]

One thing that does seem clear is that, when the defendant's prior act creates a duty to take care, the fact that an omission is the immediate cause of harm will not prevent the defendant from being liable. Thus, if a hospital admits a patient, a duty to provide care then arises. So, too, does a duty to supervise a drunken soldier arise where the company commander organises the evening's drinking and transportation home.[79] And similarly, as *Kent v Griffiths*[80] illustrates, if an ambulance service once accepts an emergency call, a duty to provide an ambulance in good time then arises in favour of the patient. By contrast, however, if a person injures himself in his (criminal) attempt to escape arrest, no duty is owed, even if the attempted escape was foreseeable.[81]

---

[76] [1996] AC 923, at 943–4. Cf Weinrib (1981) 90 Yale LJ 247; Honoré, 'Are Omissions Less Culpable?' in Cane and Stapleton (eds), *Essays for Patrick Atiyah* (1991), 31ff; Simester, 'Why Omissions are Special' (1995) 1 Legal Theory 311; Beever, *Rediscovering the Law of Negligence* (2007), 205–10.

[77] In *Johnson v Rea Ltd* [1962] 1 QB 373, Ds (who were stevedores), without lack of care, dropped soda ash on a surface over which they subsequently invited C to pass. It was held that D had a duty to take care that the surface was safe, and the failure to remove the ash was actionable. But was this an omission or merely negligence in a chain of positive conduct beginning with the unloading of the bags of soda ash? See also *Kane v New Forest DC* [2001] 3 All ER 914.

[78] *East Suffolk Rivers Catchment Board v Kent* [1941] AC 74, at 105.

[79] *Jebson v Ministry of Defence* [2000] 1 WLR 2055. In *Reeves v MPC* [2000] 1 AC 360 it was held that the police may owe a duty to even a sane person placed in their cells where it is foreseeable that the prisoner may attempt suicide. But the risk of suicide must certainly be foreseeable: see *Orange v CC of West Yorkshire* [2002] QB 347.

[80] *Kent v Griffiths* [2001] QB 36. See also *Reeves v MPC* [2001] 1 AC 360.

[81] *Vellino v CC of Greater Manchester* [2002] 1 WLR 218.

In other cases there may be a subsisting relationship from which there flows a positive duty to act. Thus, for example, there may be liability on the part of an education authority in certain circumstances towards a pupil in respect of a negligent omission.[82] Similarly, a general practitioner who has accepted a patient on to his NHS list may be liable if he later negligently omits to treat the patient, refusing to visit her, or turning her away from the surgery. Accepting responsibility for the patient's NHS care imposes a positive duty to act. But if a doctor simply 'happened to witness a road accident' there would be no duty since the doctor, in the absence of a previously cemented relationship with the accident victim 'is not under any legal obligation to [provide assistance]'.[83] For exactly the same reason – that is, the absence of sufficient proximity – a research body that fails to test for, or detect, arsenic in water is not under a duty to warn of its presence to those that subsequently drink the water.[84]

Despite the fact that these exceptions to the general rule about omissions are not easily explained according to any obvious general principle (and certainly not by any tenets of morality), it is submitted that they each do have something in common: the absence of anything other than a fortuitous physical proximity between the claimant and defendant.[85] A mere fortuitous physical proximity is insufficient to create a duty; where even this is absent, it becomes even more obvious that there must be a special reason for recognising a duty. In *Kent v Griffiths*, for example, it was the undertaking to provide assistance upon receipt of the emergency telephone call that constituted the factual link between the claimant and the defendant. For as Stuart-Smith LJ explained in *Capital and Counties plc v Hampshire County Council*:

> As a general rule a sufficient relationship of proximity will exist when someone possessed of a special skill undertakes to apply that skill for the assistance of another person who relies upon such skill and there is direct and substantial reliance by the plaintiff on the defendant's skill.[86]

It is notable that undertakings other than those associated with persons of special skill seem now also to suffice. Consider *Barrett v Ministry of Defence*.[87]

> A sailor drank himself insensible and later asphyxiated on his own vomit after being put in his bunk at a remote base. The Court of Appeal held that the Navy owed no general

---

[82] See *X v Bedfordshire CC* [1995] 2 AC 633, at 735. Another illustration is where D's conduct lulls C into a false state of dependence on D. A railway company which omitted to lock a crossing on the approach of a train was held liable to a person injured because of its previous regular practice (on which C reasonably relied) of locking the crossing at the train's approach: *Mercer v South Eastern and Chatham Rly Co's Managing Committee* [1922] 2 KB 549. (This might be viewed as an early case of assumption of responsibility, on which see ch 3.)

[83] *Capital and Counties plc v Hampshire CC* [1997] QB 1004, at 1060 (*obiter*).

[84] *Sutradhar v NERC* [2006] UKHL 33.

[85] For fuller accounts of this argument, see Murphy [1996] CLJ 43.

[86] *Capital and Counties plc v Hampshire CC* [1997] QB 1004, at 1060. See also *White v Jones* [1995] 2 AC 207.

[87] [1995] 3 All ER 87.

duty to prevent him abusing alcohol. But when colleagues put him in his bunk the Navy had (vicariously) undertaken responsibility for his welfare once he could no longer care for himself.

(b) Failure to control or guard against the acts of third parties[88]

A related problem to the one just considered is that of harm caused to a claimant because of a failure on the part of a defendant to control, or guard against, the acts of one or more third parties. This problem is often dealt with alongside the supposed liability to control dangerous things. But the leading authority for this putative category is *Goldman v Hargrave*,[89] in which nuisance (not negligence) liability was imposed for failure to avert the spread of a fire.[90] And even if liability had been imposed in negligence in that case – something Lord Goff perceived to be a distinct possibility in *Smith v Littlewoods Organisation Ltd*[91] – it could certainly be argued that the basis of the duty was an implied undertaking by one landowner or occupier in favour of his neighbour.[92] As such, the duty would be attributable to the parties pre-existing' relationship and not, per se, to the dangerous nature of the thing causing harm to the claimant. Furthermore, it is notable that the House of Lords have rejected the notion that mere knowledge of a source of danger created by someone else could give rise to a duty to remove that source of danger.[93]

As a general rule, individuals are not subject to any duty to protect their 'neighbours' from others' tortious conduct outside the circumstances in which the principles of vicarious liability operate.[94] And this is so even if the loss or injury in question is readily foreseeable and preventable.[95] Thus, it was said by the Court of Appeal in *Glaister v Appelby-in-Westmorland Town Council*:

> A defendant, D, is not ordinarily liable to a claimant, C, for personal injuries or physical damage caused by the negligence of a third person, T, merely because D could have

---

[88] Note that in the human rights context, certain positive duties are now imposed on certain public bodies: see, eg, *Keenan v UK* (2001) 33 EHRR 913. For the general common law position, see Markesinis (1989) 105 LQR 104.

[89] [1967] 1 AC 645.

[90] In other cases such as *Haynes v Harwood* [1935] 1 KB 146 and *Topp v London Country Bus (South West) Ltd* [1993] 1 WLR 976 the actions of a third party were crucial to the final decision. Indeed, in *Smith v Littlewoods Organisation Ltd* [1987] AC 241, Lord Goff explained the former in terms of a danger liable to be 'sparked off' by a third party.

[91] [1987] AC 241.

[92] See below.

[93] See *Stovin v Wise* [1996] AC 923.

[94] One exception is where D owes his neighbour a non-delegable duty of care in respect of certain operations on D's land: see Murphy, 'The Juridical Foundations of Common Law Non-Delegable Duties' in Neyers (ed), *Emerging Issues in Tort Law* (2007), ch 14.

[95] *Weld-Blundell v Stephens* [1920] AC 956, at 986; *Smith v Leurs* (1945) 70 CLR 256, at 261–2; *Glaister v Appelby-in-Westmorland Town Council* [2009] EWCA Civ 1325, at [45].

foreseen and prevented it. Something more is required to place on D a duty to protect C from the consequences of foreseeable negligence on the part of T.[96]

An omission to warn a next-door neighbour that she has left a door open, or a failure to telephone the police when you see a suspicious person in her garden, results in no liability on your part for the burglary committed by that person. Again, a town council involved in the organisation of an annual horse-fair (along with eight other public bodies) is not liable for a failure to ensure the segregation and tethering of horses so that they do not cause injury to attendees; or in failing to ensure that adequate public liability insurance is in place in the case of accidents.[97] Mere ability to prevent injury does not entail responsibility for it. Indeed, both the third party undertaking the relevant activity and the at-risk claimant are usually in a better position to guard against foreseeable physical risks than is a public body with a degree of regulatory or organisational control over the activity. However, the situation might be different where the defendant with control also had a greatly superior ability to identify the particular risks of harm in question.

Distilling the various speeches in *Smith v Littlewoods* (but especially that of Lord Goff), it would seem that a positive duty to act to prevent third parties causing harm to another might be grounded if two conditions are satisfied.

(1) There must exist either between D and the third party, or between D and C, some special relationship which properly demands of D that he safeguard C from the wrongful conduct of the third party.
(2) The damage done by the third party must be closely related to, and a very probable result of, some failure in care by D.

Whether both these issues go to the existence of a duty, or the first to duty, and the second to remoteness of damage, is a nice point. Oliver LJ put the question thus:

> I think that the question of the existence of duty and that of whether the damage brought about by the act of a third party is too remote are simply two facets of the same problem: for if there be a duty to take reasonable care to prevent damage being caused by a third party then I find it difficult to see how damage caused by that third party consequent on the failure to take such care can be too remote a consequence of the breach of duty. Essentially the answer to both questions is to be found in answering the question: in what circumstances is a defendant to be held responsible at common law for the independent act of a third person whom he knows or ought to know may injure his neighbour?[98]

For convenience, the second condition will be dealt with in this book in chapter 5 on causation and remoteness. In relation to the first condition, however, there appear to be two factual bases that justify the imposition of a duty of care in respect of a failure to control, or guard against, the injurious actions of third parties: either the existence of a

---

[96] *Glaister v Appelby-in-Westmorland Town Council* [2009] EWCA Civ 1325, at [45].
[97] Ibid.
[98] *Perl (P) (Exporters) Ltd v Camden LBC* [1983] 3 All ER 161, at 167.

special relationship between the defendant and the third party, *or* a special relationship between the defendant and the claimant.[99] At first sight, these appear to be alternatives. But in fact – or at least so it is submitted – they are both reducible to, and ought to be viewed as, the proximity requirement central to the operation of the *Caparo* test.

Where the defendant has the right to control the conduct of the third party, a failure of control resulting in the very kind of damage likely to result from lack of control might be actionable by the claimant. Thus, where parents or teachers fail to supervise young children adequately, they may be in breach of a duty not only to the child if she injures herself, but also to any other person injured by intentional or negligent wrong-doing by that child.[100] In *Home Office v Dorset Yacht Co Ltd*,[101] the Home Office's contention that no duty could arise in the case of a wrong committed by a person of full age and capacity who was not the servant of, or acting on behalf of, the defend-ant, failed. The statutory duty to control the detainees in that case was the source of a duty of care to those who were at immediate risk of loss or damage from any neg-ligent failure to exercise carefully that control. The duty placed the borstal officers in a 'special relationship' with the detainees which, coupled with the existence of an identifiable and determinate class of potential victims (the yacht owners) gave rise to the duty owed to the latter.[102] This was because, in the words of Lord Pearson, 'con-trol imports responsibility'.[103] And in this context, the 'responsibility' was that of the officers towards those members of the public whose property would foreseeably be adversely affected by borstal boys attempting an escape.[104] In other words, 'responsi-bility' was synonymous with the required relationship of proximity. Lord Diplock was similarly of the view that the critical factor was the relationship of proximity between the officers and the yacht owners. He said:

> To give rise to a duty on the part of the custodian owed to a member of the public to take reasonable care to prevent a borstal trainee from escaping from his custody before

---

[99] *Glaister v Appelby-in-Westmorland Town Council* [2009] EWCA Civ 1325, [47].

[100] Eg, when lack of supervision allows a child to stray on to a road where a driver is injured swerving to avoid him: *Carmarthenshire CC v Lewis* [1955] AC 549.

[101] [1970] AC 1004.

[102] Note that it was not the statutory duty alone that gave rise to the common-law duty. This is because, as Lord Hoffmann explained in general terms in *Commissioners of Customs and Excise v Barclays Bank plc* [2006] UKHL 28, at [39]: '[a] statute either creates a statutory duty or it does not…But you cannot derive a common law duty of care directly from a statute'. In similar vein see *Gorringe v Calderdale MBC* [2004] 1 WLR 1057.

[103] [1970] AC 1004, at 1055. See also *LaPlante v LaPlante* (1995) 125 DLR (4th) 569 for a case involving a defendant other than a public body having control over the relevant third party.

[104] Proximity was absent where the mother of a serial killer's last victim sought on behalf of her daughter's estate to sue the police for negligence in failing to apprehend the killer earlier: *Hill v CC of West Yorkshire* [1989] AC 53. Unlike the Home Office in *Dorset Yacht*, there was, before his arrest, no right vested in the police to control the killer's conduct; nor was there anything to distinguish Miss Hill from any other mem-ber of the public. For similar reasons, a rape victim who was no more foreseeable than any other woman is not owed a duty of care by those negligently releasing the rapist from custody: *K v Secretary of State for the Home Department* [2002] EWCA Civ 775. Even where proximity is present, the courts are reluctant to recognise a duty of care which would require protection of particular individuals from identifiable persons: *Smith v CC of Sussex Police* [2008] UKHL 50.

completion of the trainee's sentence there should be some special relationship between the custodian and the person to whom the duty is owed which exposes that person to a particular risk of damage in consequence of that escape which is different in its incidence from the general risk of damage from criminal acts of others which he shares with all members of the public.[105]

In the second category of cases – where the defendant has a special relationship with the claimant – the proximity requirement is simply being spelt out. Cases within this category are therefore uncontroversial. However, the fact that they are uncontroversial does not necessarily mean it is always easy to identify cases falling within this category: the threshold test of a 'special relationship' is somewhat vague. Consider *Perl (P) (Exporters) Ltd v Camden LBC*.[106]

> The local authority owned a block of flats the basement flat of which was unoccupied. Cs were tenants of an adjoining flat. The empty flat was left unsecured and there had been several burglaries in the area. Burglars entered the empty flat, knocked a hole through the 18-inch common wall and burgled Cs' property.

The Court of Appeal found that the authority owed the claimants no duty of care in respect of the loss inflicted by the burglary. The relationship of neighbouring property owners was, of itself, not sufficiently 'special' to justify the imposition of a duty of care to guard the claimants against the foreseeable risk of burglary by way of an unsecured property. Similarly, in *Smith v Littlewoods Organisation Ltd*[107] the House of Lords rejected a claim for damage caused by a fire started by vandals in a disused cinema owned by the defendants that spread to the claimants' property.[108]

If, however, there is something more specific about the relationship between the claimant and the defendant, the courts are more likely to treat that relationship as possessing sufficient proximity to impose a duty of care. In *Stansbie v Troman*,[109] for example, a decorator engaged by the claimant left the door of the claimant's house open while he went to get wallpaper. In his absence, a thief entered the house and stole a diamond bracelet and some clothes. The Court of Appeal held that a duty existed in this case, and that the decorator was liable for the claimant's loss.

Two final points ought to be made in this context. First, in relation to the duties of neighbouring property owners, consideration must always also be given to potential duties created by the torts of private nuisance and the rule in *Rylands v Fletcher*. But second, Lord Hoffmann's trenchant support in *Stovin v Wise*[110] for rigorously limiting liability for omissions based on political, moral, and economic arguments, should not be overlooked, even in the context of these torts.

---

[105] [1970] AC 1004, at 1070.
[106] [1984] QB 342.
[107] [1987] 1 All ER 710.
[108] Of crucial importance in both cases was the issue of, if a duty were imposed, how it could be fulfilled. This is a question of breach, as to which see ch 4.
[109] [1948] 2 KB 48.
[110] [1996] AC 923, at 944.

(3) Fair, just, and reasonable

While in *Anns v Merton LBC* the House of Lords made explicit reference to the role of 'policy', it is apparent in the wake of *Caparo* that the same kinds of concerns as are embraced by the term 'policy' are now to be considered under the banner of what is 'fair, just, and reasonable'.

There is a continuing scholarly debate about this limb of the *Caparo* test for duty of care. On the one hand, Allan Beever believes that there is no need for it.[111] He believes that the duty inquiry is fact-based: '[t]he duty of care is concerned to link the parties by tracing the defendant's negligence to the claimant'.[112] On the other hand, Jane Stapleton believes that most choices about the imposition of the duty of care are policy choices.[113] Undoubtedly, the 'truth' lies somewhere in the middle of these claims. This is to say that a finding of both foreseeability and proximity cannot automatically translate into a duty of care. The judicial function has a normative aspect to it; it is concerned with the imposition of norms for the solution, inter alia, of co-ordination problems.[114] The court must apply itself to the question whether or not to impose a duty of care. In this sense, the fair, just, and reasonable inquiry is a logical imperative. This is not to say that the discretion inherent within this inquiry should overwhelm the process of determining the duty of care.[115] The fair, just, and reasonable inquiry should have its main impact upon the *development* of the duty concept – taking it into new areas or withdrawing it from its current area of operation. Policy should not be used to re-make the law on duty in every single case. (Indeed, duty of care questions are rare in practice – despite the attention that they obtain in student texts such as this one!)

In a thought-provoking paper, Andrew Robertson has argued that policy considerations grouped together under the fair, just, and reasonable limb of the *Caparo* test logically fall into two categories – one that relates to 'justice between the parties'[116] and one that relates to wider, systemic concerns which he terms 'justiciability, community welfare and other non-justice considerations'.[117] Robertson argues that clarity

---

[111] Beever, *Rediscovering the Law of Negligence* (2007), 29–30.

[112] Ibid at 129.

[113] Stapleton 'Duty of Care Factors: A Selection from the Judicial Menus' in Cane and Stapleton (eds), *The Law of Obligations: Essays in Honour of John Fleming* (1998), ch 4; Stapleton (2003) 24 Aust Bar Rev 135, at 136. See also Rogers, *Winfield and Jolowicz on Tort* (18th edn, 2010), 181 and 189.

[114] See Witting (2007) 71 MLR 621, 630; Smith (2011) 31 OJLS 215.

[115] There is a debate about whether the term 'discretion' is proper. The Master of the Rolls would argue that the matter is one of judgment – 'Even though one can qualify it as being a "value" judgment or describe it as a balancing exercise, it raises a question of law, to which, as a matter of principle, and however difficult it may be to resolve, there is only one right answer': *Flood v Times Newspapers Ltd* [2010] EWCA Civ 804, at [46] (discussing the role of an appeal court in a case of qualified privilege to defamation). See also ibid at [49] and [107].

[116] Eg, inconsistency with the contractual matrix and unreasonableness of the burden upon the defendant: Robertson (2011) 127 LQR 370, 380.

[117] Ibid at 372. Eg, 'justiciability' and the 'effect on class of potential defendant': ibid at 385–6.

of thought is aided by separating these two kinds of policy. The crucial point concerns the second part of the policy inquiry, which

> is concerned only with issues going beyond the interests of the parties themselves, such as concerns about the adverse effects that recognition of the duty may have on the legal system or on people's behaviour.[118]

One possible objection to Robertson's framework is that it is liable to see a distinction between types of 'policy' argument that is more apparent than real. To the extent that the court's concern is about the likely consequences of the imposition of a duty of care for future parties, the dispute before it will (surely) be a test case and the issue a live one. To the extent that the court seeks to determine negligence cases by reference to the potential impact of a decision upon others of whom the parties are not representative, such as courts themselves, this is very dangerous ground and could rarely justify a decision that would not otherwise be taken by the court.[119]

So much for theory. It is important to appreciate that most of the problematic duty cases that have come *before the appellate courts* in the past 20 years or so have been dominated by two broad kinds of policy issue: (1) whether certain areas of activity (eg, the work of public authorities, or certain professionals) warrant the imposition of a duty of care, and (2) whether the risk of certain kinds of harm (eg, economic loss and psychiatric harm) can rightly be encompassed by the law of negligence. It is in such contexts that arguments about whether it is fair, just, and reasonable to impose a duty of care are most likely to surface. And in relation to certain areas of activity, it is mid-level economic and political arguments that come to the fore. Thus, for example, it is often thought that many actions of public authorities should be non-justiciable, not only because their limited funding is better spent on discharging their statutory functions, but also because they are often involved in the formulation and deployment of matters of public policy with which the courts should not interfere. In relation to certain forms of harm, such as pure economic loss, the concerns tend to centre on ensuring some measure of proportionality between the nature of the defendant's wrongdoing and the extent of his liability. Beyond this guidance, it is difficult to state with any precision what the courts will consider in relation to the question of whether it is fair, just, and reasonable. Much will turn on the facts of each case.[120]

(a) Fair, just, and reasonable: negative usage

In much the same way that policy was invoked under the test formulated in *Anns* to deny the existence of a duty of care, so too are notions of fairness, justice, and reasonableness often used to limit the circumstances in which a duty will be imposed. In *Marc*

---

[118] Robertson (2011) 127 LQR 370, 371.

[119] Although Robertson does not argue for it, this would be even more of a concern if courts, in determining the duty question, tried to predict movements in the future cost and availability of insurance arising from a new rule.

[120] See, eg, *McLoughlin v Grovers* [2001] EWCA Civ 1743 (a very novel case of psychiatric harm).

Rich & Co AG v Bishop Rock Marine Co Ltd,[121] the facts of which case we have already noted, the House of Lords held that no duty was owed by the defendant classification society to a cargo owner whose claim in damages had been limited to an amount fixed according to an international maritime convention. Their Lordships conceded that the requirements of foreseeability and proximity were satisfied in the case, yet held that it was not ultimately fair, just, and reasonable to impose a duty of care. In particular, their Lordships noted that a fine balance of risks was established by the convention in question, and that the recognition of a duty of care in this case would subvert that balance of risks with severe potential consequences for both marine insurance and freight costs. It was also pointed out that the imposition of a duty of care might lead to classification societies refusing to survey high-risk vessels in the future with potentially harmful consequences for public safety at sea.[122]

Other cases decided by the appellate courts also confirm this negative usage of the 'fair, just, and reasonable' limb of the *Caparo* test. For example, in *X v Bedfordshire County Council*[123] the risk of defensive practices to which liability *may give rise*,[124] coupled with the fact that it would be improper for the courts to second-guess local authority decisions, was cited among the reasons for the non-imposition of a duty of care. Equally, in *Elguzouli-Daf v Metropolitan Police Commissioner*[125] it was felt to be inappropriate, for similar reasons, to impose a duty of care on the Crown Prosecution Service in respect of those suspects they decide to prosecute.

(b) Fair, just, and reasonable: positive usage

It was previously noted that, in the immediate wake of *Anns*, policy factors tended to be invoked by the courts in order to justify the *non-imposition* of a duty of care. However, in the post-*Caparo* era, it has become clear that considerations of fairness, justice, and reasonableness can also be employed to ground the *imposition* of a duty of care; either in circumstances in which no such duty has previously existed, or in circumstances where a duty has previously been denied.

In *Stovin v Wise*, Lord Hoffmann recognised this judicial about-turn on the *Anns* approach and summarised what he perceived to be its replacement, thus:

> [s]ubsequent decisions in this House and the Privy Council have preferred to approach the question the other way round...asking whether there are considerations of analogy, policy, fairness and justice for extending [the duty of care] to cover a new situation.[126]

---

[121] [1996] AC 211. See also *White v Jones* [1995] 2 AC 207.

[122] Cf *Perrett v Collins* [1998] 2 Lloyd's Rep 255.

[123] [1995] 2 AC 633.

[124] For doubt about the soundness of this fear, see *Phelps v Hillingdon LBC* [2001] 2 AC 619, at 672. See also *Barrett v Enfield LBC* [2001] 2 AC 550, at 568 and 589; *Gregg v Scott* [2005] 2 AC 176, at [55]–[56], and the criticism of this argument in Markesinis et al, *Tortious Liability of Statutory Bodies: A Comparative and Economic Analysis of Five English Cases* (1999), ch 3.

[125] [1995] QB 335.

[126] [1996] AC 923, at 949.

While it is by no means the case that this positive approach has become the norm, as Lord Hoffmann misleadingly intimated,[127] there is certainly ample evidence of policy considerations being used in this way at the highest judicial level. In *White v Jones*,[128] for example, the facts were as follows:

> D, a solicitor, was instructed by a testator to draw up a new will to replace an earlier one. Due to D's negligence, the new will had not been drafted by the time the testator died. Under the new will, unlike the old one, the testator's daughters would have been named as beneficiaries. The testator's daughters therefore mounted an action in negligence against D alleging that his negligence had cost them their inheritance. By a majority of three to two, the House of Lords held that the daughters were owed a duty of care.

The foreseeability of the daughters' loss was not in question. Equally, in recognising the solicitor's assumption of a responsibility to draft a replacement will, their Lordships were also satisfied that the requirement of a relationship of proximity between the defendant and the claimants existed.[129] But their Lordships ran up (among other things)[130] against the problem that the case involved an omission to act on the part of the solicitor. As we have already seen, the courts are generally loath to impose liability in cases of nonfeasance. However, Lord Goff, in a section of his speech headed 'The Impulse to do Practical Justice', noted four reasons why a duty should be imposed; and each of those reasons was clearly rooted in considerations of fairness and justice. He said:

(1) In the forefront stands the extraordinary fact that, if such a duty is not recognised, the only persons who might have a valid claim (ie, the testator and his estate) have suffered no loss, and the only person who has suffered a loss (ic, the disappointed beneficiary) has no claim...

(2) The injustice of denying such a remedy is reinforced if one considers the importance of legacies in a society which recognises...the right of citizens to leave their assets to whom they please...

(3) There is a sense in which the solicitors' profession cannot complain if such a liability may be imposed upon their members. If one of them has been negligent in such a way as to defeat his client's testamentary intentions, he must regard himself as very lucky indeed if the effect of the law is that he is not liable...

(4) That such a conclusion is required as a matter of justice is reinforced by consideration of the role played by solicitors in society. The point was well made by Cooke J in *Gartside v Sheffield Young and Ellis*:[131]

> To deny an effective remedy in a plain case would seem to imply a refusal to acknowledge the solicitor's professional role in the community. In practice the public relies on solicitors...to prepare effective wills....

---

[127] Both *Marc Rich* [1996] AC 211 and *Elguzouli-Daf* [1995] QB 335 supply ample evidence of policy factors being invoked in the traditional way to negative the imposition of a duty.

[128] [1995] 2 AC 207.

[129] This is questionable: see Murphy [1996] CLJ 43.

[130] See Benson, 'Should *White v Jones* Represent Canadian Law? A Return to First Principles' in Neyers (ed), *Emerging Issues in Tort Law* (2007), ch 6.

[131] [1983] NZLR 37, at 43.

I respectfully agree with Nicholls V-C [in the Court of Appeal] ... that the court will have to fashion 'an effective remedy for the solicitor's breach of his professional duty to his client' in such a way as to repair the injustice to the disappointed beneficiary.[132]

While *White v Jones* constitutes an example of the courts invoking the third *Caparo* limb in order to justify the creation of a *new duty situation*,[133] the decision of the House of Lords in *Arthur JS Hall & Co v Simons* arguably goes one step further by employing it to justify the imposition of a duty of care on advocates who had formerly enjoyed a well-established immunity in respect of their conduct of (at least civil) litigation on a client's behalf. In removing that immunity, Lord Hobhouse declared:

[i]n the civil justice system ... the legitimate interest of the client, the appropriateness of the tort remedy and the absence of clear or sufficient justification all militate against the recognition of an advocate immunity.[134]

A final cautionary note should be entered here. It is this: just because we can identify clear positive and negative usages of policy considerations does not make the task of predicting the outcome of new cases any easier. Indeed, it is perhaps for the reason that the *Caparo* test (especially the third limb) lends itself so well to individual judicial impressions of where lines should be drawn that a great many of the cases concerning the duty of care have been pursued in recent decades at least to the Court of Appeal, with scores even reaching the House of Lords.

(B) INCREMENTALISM

We have already noted that, in *Caparo*, the House of Lords approved Brennan J's dictum in *Sutherland Shire Council v Heyman* suggesting that '[i]t is preferable ... that the law should develop novel categories of negligence incrementally and by analogy with established categories'.[135] But we have yet to explore the nature of this incremental approach and its relationship with the tripartite test that also emerged from the *Caparo* decision.

In *Perrett v Collins*, a case in which a certificate of airworthiness was negligently issued in respect of a light aircraft, with the consequence that a passenger in it was subsequently injured, Hobhouse LJ said:

[t]he over-arching formula [in *Caparo*] does not affect the outcome. Established categories, with or without the assistance of 'common sense and justice', provide the answer. The certainty provided by the previous authorities is not undermined ... It is a truism to say that any case must be decided taking into account the circumstances of the case, but where those circumstances comply with established categories of liability, a defendant should not be allowed to seek to escape from liability by appealing to some vaguer concept of justice

---

[132] [1995] 2 AC 207, at 259–60.
[133] To like effect, see also *Spring v Guardian Assurance plc* [1995] 2 AC 296.
[134] [2002] 1 AC 615, at 749–50.
[135] (1985) 60 ALR 1, at 43–4.

or fairness; the law cannot be re-made for every case. Indeed, the previous authorities have by necessary implication held that it is fair, just and reasonable that the [claimant] should recover in the situations falling within the principles they have applied. Accordingly, if the present case is covered by the decisions in, or the principles recognised by, previous authorities – and it is ... we remain bound to follow them.[136]

It is clear from this passage that his Lordship envisaged that the tripartite test could be ousted in circumstances where an incremental step beyond existing authorities could be taken. Certainly, such an approach seeks to guarantee a measure of consistency in the ever-growing body of case law by adherence to the doctrine of precedent. But it is questionable whether, as it may ostensibly appear, this approach is truly a rival to the three-limbed *Caparo* test. For while it is consonant with the technique of analogical reasoning so central to the common law, it does not tell us how far any given incremental step may take us beyond the decided cases. Ultimately, therefore, the courts will have recourse to concepts such as justice and reasonableness in order to set the limits to what amounts to legitimate incrementalism. In doing so, they are effectively applying the very *Caparo* test to which incrementalism is said to be an alternative. Where the instant case is closely analogous to a previously decided case in which a duty has been imposed, all the court is doing is assuming that the proximity and foreseeability requirements are probably satisfied in the case before it and simply asking whether it is fair, just, and reasonable to extend the duty of care by the marginal amount required in order to cover the particular facts of the case.[137]

(C) ASSUMPTION OF RESPONSIBILITY

In *Hedley Byrne & Co Ltd v Heller & Partners Ltd*,[138] the House of Lords recognised the possibility of negligence liability in respect of negligent misstatements where a defendant 'voluntarily assumes' responsibility for the accuracy of a statement made to a claimant in circumstances where a special relationship exists between the two of them and the claimant places reasonable reliance on the accuracy of the statement. At the heart of the decision was the insistence upon the defendant's 'assumption of responsibility'.

Although originally *Hedley Byrne* was only concerned with the question of whether a duty could be imposed in connection with economic loss caused by negligent misstatements, its 'assumption of responsibility' criterion has since been suggested to form a more general test according to which a duty of care may be ascribed, even

---

[136] [1998] 2 Lloyd's Rep 255, at 263.

[137] For oblique support see, eg, *Islington LBC v UCL Hospital NHS Trust* [2006] PIQR P29 and *White v CC of South Yorkshire* [1999] 2 AC 455, at 511. And for an explicit confirmation that the two tests may be used together (with recourse also to the 'assumption of responsibility' test), see *Commissioners of Customs and Excise v Barclays Bank plc* [2006] UKHL 28.

[138] [1964] AC 465.

beyond the confines of economic loss and negligent misstatements. In *White v Jones*, Lord Browne-Wilkinson said that:

> a duty of care will arise if there is a special relationship between the parties. [And] such special relationships can be held to exist...where the defendant has voluntarily answered a question or tenders skilled advice or services in circumstances where he knows or ought to know that an identified [claimant] will rely on his answers or advice.... [T]he special relationship is created by the defendant voluntarily assuming to act in the matter by involving himself in the [claimant's] affairs or by choosing to speak...[And] although the extent of the duty will vary from category to category, some duty of care arises from the special relationship.[139]

The relationship between the *Caparo* three-stage test for duty and that of 'assumption of responsibility' was the subject of important discussion by the House of Lords in *Commissioners of Customs and Excise v Barclays Bank plc*,[140] the purport of which is that the former encompasses the latter. It was observed in *Barclays* that the 'test' for an assumption of responsibility is objective in nature; it does not depend upon the subjective attitude of the defendant.[141] Rather, in conformity with the approach of Lord Steyn in *Williams v Natural Life Health Food Ltd*, the court will examine the exchanges that 'cross the line' between the parties.[142] This is very similar to the exercise of determining whether or not there is proximity between the parties. *Ipso facto* it makes sense to view 'assumption of responsibility' as a type of proximity,[143] ordinarily of importance in misstatement and negligent provision of service cases. Where an 'assumption of responsibility' is apparent, there is no need to look for any further indication of proximity between the parties.[144] But it is important to acknowledge that both of these are organising concepts, which direct consideration to the more detailed factors that link the parties one to the other.[145] Furthermore, in most cases it is likely to be unnecessary to consider the third stage of the *Caparo* test where the assumption of responsibility test is satisfied; such a finding will itself speak of the fairness of imposing a duty of care.[146]

(D) SCOPE OF DUTY

There may be important limits to the *scope* of the defendant's duty of care. A duty will not always be imposed for the general benefit of the claimant: in some cases it will be imposed in respect of a certain type of activity or a certain type of loss. The easiest

---

[139] [1995] 2 AC 207, at 273.
[140] [2006] UKHL 28.
[141] Ibid at [5], [35], [86].
[142] [1998] 1 WLR 829, at 835.
[143] [2006] UKHL 28, at [5], [35], [73].
[144] Ibid at [4]. By contrast, where there is no assumption of responsibility, the court will apply a more general test of proximity: ibid at [87].
[145] Ibid at [83].
[146] Ibid at [35], [93].

illustration of this is the duty of the occupier. The occupier must take care with respect to the state of the premises; but not with respect to all activities that take place on the premises.[147]

Mitchell v Glasgow City Council[148] is a recent case that illustrates that a landlord (who is an occupier of premises only when they are *not* leased out) owes a duty of restricted scope to his tenant. The duty will include, inter alia, an obligation to let premises which are habitable and safe for occupation.[149] The question was whether the landlord, the defendant council, was required to warn a tenant, the claimant, of the fact that it had arranged a meeting with the claimant's neighbour, who was violent and abusive and whom the defendant was seeking to relocate after numerous nasty disputes between the neighbours. Consistent with *Smith v Littlewoods*, discussed above, it was held that the duty of care which was owed by the defendant to the claimant, as its tenant, did not extend to protecting him from the acts of a third party criminal.[150] It was noted that the defendant had provided no undertaking to warn;[151] and a host of policy reasons were invoked, which need not be rehearsed here.

Another illustration, removed from the occupation and control of land, is *Calvert v William Hill Credit Ltd*,[152] where it was held that the defendant bookmaking agency owed a pathological gambler a limited duty of care to abstain from taking telephone bets from him after he attempted to exclude himself from this activity. The Court of Appeal noted that the defendant 'did not assume a responsibility to prevent him from gambling in other ways – in betting shops or on the internet – nor with other bookmakers'.[153]

Again, the scope of a duty might be limited with respect to kinds of loss. While a defendant may be under a duty to protect the claimant from personal injury, he may not be under a similar duty in respect of pure economic loss.[154] A general practitioner advising her patient on treatment for his heart condition and high blood pressure owes a duty to safeguard that patient's health, but will not be liable for the financial loss caused to the patient if she also gives him an unsuccessful tip for the Grand National and the horse comes in last!

Furthermore, even where a defendant does owe a duty in respect of economic loss under either the original or extended *Hedley Byrne* principles (considered in the next chapter), there may still be a limit to the scope of the defendant's duty where the so-called *SAAMCO* principle applies. This principle, which derives its name from

---

[147] For a case considering the potential liability of an occupier for certain acts of third parties on the premises, see *Everett v Comojo (UK) Ltd* [2011] EWCA Civ 13. Cf *Modbury Triangle Shopping Centre v Anzil* (2000) 205 CLR 254. See ch 7.

[148] [2009] UKHL 11.

[149] Landlord and Tenant Act 1985, ss 8 and 10; Housing Act 2004.

[150] [2009] UKHL 11, at [26]–[28], [41], [62], [77], and [82].

[151] Ibid at [29], [63], and [83].

[152] [2008] EWCA Civ 1427.

[153] Ibid at [47]. The reasoning is criticised in Stigglebout [2010] LS 558, esp. 559–63.

[154] *Desmond v CC of Nottinghamshire Police* [2011] EWCA Civ 2, at [35].

the case in which the principle was introduced – *South Australia Asset Management Corp v York Montague Ltd*[155] – is complicated and multi-faceted, making it far from obvious where exposition of the principle is best located.[156] It need only be noted here that the principle operates to set limits on a defendant's liability for certain forms of loss where other factors (extraneous to both parties) play a part in exacerbating the actual loss suffered. Those interested in a full exposition of the principle should skip forward to chapter 5.

SECTION 5   PUBLIC AUTHORITIES AND THE DUTY OF CARE

(A) BACKGROUND

Public authorities, such as the emergency services and local authorities, require special consideration. This is because the foundational principles governing negligence liability in such cases frequently need to be formulated bearing in mind the statutory and public law dimensions (including the Human Rights Act 1998) that are often present in this arena.[157] These dimensions, as we shall see, impact mainly upon the assessment of whether it is fair, just, and reasonable to impose liability on a public authority.[158] But they may also impinge upon the logically prior question of justiciability.

The starting point is to note that there is no general rule granting public authorities immunity from liability in negligence just because they are public, not private, bodies.[159] A pedestrian knocked down by a council truck can perfectly well sue the local council, and a schoolgirl injured by a dilapidated ceiling collapsing on her in the classroom can sue the education authority. On the other hand, difficulties do tend to arise where the alleged negligence of a public body derives from its exercise of, or failure to exercise, statutory powers that are designed to ensure the provision of some

---

[155]   [1997] AC 191.

[156]   Apart from the possibility of discussing it here, there are three other possibilities. First, since the principle is in practice chiefly concerned with negligence liability for economic loss, it might well have been dealt with in ch 3 (and it should therefore be borne in mind when reading the relevant section of that chapter). Second, since it bears a close relationship with the remoteness of damage principle *in cases of economic loss* it could also be, *and is in fact*, discussed in ch 5. But, third, since the *SAAMCO* principle strictly concerns the quantum of damages to which C is entitled, it might also have appeared in ch 26 (where, once again, it should be borne in mind).

[157]   Sometimes these public law and statutory features are irrelevant (eg, when an action is brought against a public authority qua employer – in respect of, say, an unsafe workplace. The duty in such a case would be the ordinary duty of care owed by any employer to an employee). Sometimes, also, the question of negligence liability is irrelevant (eg, if the statute itself creates a civil law action for breach of statutory duty: see ch 19).

[158]   For the weight that ought to be attached to these concerns (in the light of certain continental experiences) see Markesinis et al, *Tortious Liability of Statutory Bodies: A Comparative and Economic Analysis of Five English Cases* (1999), ch 3.

[159]   *Mersey Docks and Harbour Board Trustees v Gibbs* (1866) LR 1 HL 93; *Allen v Gulf Oil Refining Ltd* [1981] AC 1001; *Desmond v CC of Nottinghamshire Police* [2011] EWCA Civ 3, at [32].

public function or other.[160] The essence of a typical claim is that the claimant has suffered damage because the public body has provided an inadequate service. Many such claims are met with considerable obstacles in establishing a duty of care and a number of factors explain the particular complexities inherent in such cases. These include the following:

(1) Many statutory powers enabling public authorities to provide public services confer on the authority a measure of discretion as to how, or even *whether*, the relevant power should be exercised.

(2) Very often, what the claimant alleges is not that the authority itself negligently created the danger which befell him, but that it failed to protect him from that danger. This then takes us into the familiar, problematic realm of negligent omissions.

(3) The (presumed) effect of frequent litigation on limited public funds and the manner in which statutory functions would be performed in the face of possible negligence actions.

(4) The fact that it would be inapt for the courts to second-guess certain decisions of public bodies made in accordance with the statutory powers of those bodies.

Just as the decision in *Anns v Merton LBC*[161] appeared to trigger a radical expansion of the tort of negligence generally, so, in its specific consideration of the liability of public authorities, did it appear set to extend the liability of public bodies. In the retreat from *Anns*, there was no better example of the courts' hesitancy to expand the frontiers of negligence liability than in relation to public bodies. The decisions of the House of Lords in *X v Bedfordshire County Council*[162] and *Stovin v Wise*[163] sought to place stringent limits on any such actions. And although these limits have since undergone significant refinement – arguably to the point where there is little left of the original *Bedfordshire* decision so far as it allowed for the automatic striking-out of an action against a public body[164] – it may nonetheless remain a considerable task to mount a *successful* negligence action against a public body. Showing a duty of care is, after all, only part of the task: a successful claimant will still need to show a breach of duty (which, it is submitted, future case law will reveal to be far from easy).

(B) JUSTICIABILITY

The point has already been made, but stands reiteration, that in instances in which the public law/statutory dimension is immaterial, the negligence principles governing

---

[160] See, eg, Bailey and Bowman [2000] CLJ 85.

[161] [1978] AC 728.

[162] [1995] 2 AC 633.

[163] [1996] AC 923.

[164] See *Barrett v Enfield LBC* [2001] 2 AC 550; *W v Essex CC* [2001] 2 AC 592; *Phelps v Hillingdon LBC* [2001] 2 AC 619; *B v A-G* [2003] 4 All ER 833; *D v East Berkshire Community NHS Trust* [2005] 2 AC 373.

the liability of public authorities are the same as those applicable in a run-of-the-mill action between two private individuals. But where the statutory powers of a public authority are in issue, the initial question for the courts is whether the alleged negligent act or omission on the part of that public authority is even justiciable.

Ordinarily, public bodies are held to account in respect of their statutory functions by one or more of the following: judicial review, ombudsmen, complaints procedures set out in the enabling legislation,[165] actions based on a breach of the Human Rights Act 1998, and, occasionally, default powers afforded to the relevant secretary of state.[166] In short, public law (in one form or another) ordinarily provides the means of redress in respect of public law wrongs. And allowing private law remedies in such cases might be seen as undermining the public law system.[167] On the other hand, the argument from the corrective justice viewpoint – that damages for negligence ought to be available where a claimant suffers loss or injury – is a powerful one and difficult to resist. That being so, the courts have struggled greatly over recent years to identify clearly the touchstones of justiciability in this context.

As regards the fact that certain decisions are taken by reference to a statutory discretion, Lord Browne-Wilkinson said in *X v Bedfordshire County Council*,[168] a case concerning a local authority, that:

> [i]t is clear both in principle and from the decided cases that the local authority cannot be liable in damages for doing that which Parliament has authorised. Therefore if the decisions complained of fall within the ambit of the statutory discretion they cannot be actionable at common law. However, if the decision complained of is so unreasonable that it falls outside the ambit of the discretion conferred upon the local authority, there is no *a priori* reason for excluding all common law liability.[169]

The fact that a public body has exercised a discretionary power conferred by statute does not necessarily preclude the courts from finding that there has been actionable negligence.

(1) General principles

In *X v Bedfordshire County Council*[170] Lord Browne-Wilkinson sought to rationalise the principles that could be invoked in order to determine the justiciability of public bodies' negligent acts and omissions.[171] The case dealt with two groups of appeals relating to failures in public services. The facts were complex.

> The first group of cases, the 'child care' appeals, comprised two rather different allegations that local authorities had acted negligently in relation to statutory powers to protect children from abuse. (1) Five children of the same parents alleged that Bedfordshire council

---

[165] That is, the legislation that confers upon the public body the relevant powers and duties.

[166] For examples of each of these in relation to local authorities' duties towards children in need, see Murphy [2003] LS 103. Note, too, that an action based on a 'Eurotort' may also be available in this context: see ch 1.

[167] Eg, *Desmond v CC of Nottinghamshire Police* [2011] EWCA Civ 2, at [48]–[49] and [51].

[168] [1995] 2 AC 633.   [169] Ibid at 736.

[170] Ibid.   [171] See Brodie [1998] LS 1.

acted negligently in failing to take them into care after it had received reports of parental abuse and gross neglect. (2) A mother and daughter alleged that their local council, Newham, acted negligently when, on the basis of a mistaken identification of the mother as the child's abuser, the child was removed from its home. Both claimants alleged that their enforced separation had caused them psychiatric harm.

The second group of cases, the 'education' cases, involved three rather different claims that education authorities had acted negligently in the exercise of their powers in relation to the provision of education. (1) In two cases, the actions rested upon the allegation that the children concerned had, because of Ds' negligence, *not* been placed in special schools. (2) In the third case, C alleged that the council had wrongly placed him in a special school, having negligently failed to assess his real needs and potential, and provide appropriate mainstream schooling for him.

Lord Browne-Wilkinson acknowledged the factual diversity of the several claims before him, but nonetheless recognised their common thread: each case raised the fundamental question of the extent to which public authorities charged with statutory duties can be held liable in negligence in relation to the negligent (non-) performance of those duties. Seeking to set out a summary of the relevant principles, his Lordship said:

> Where Parliament has conferred a statutory discretion on a public authority, it is for that authority, not for the courts, to exercise the discretion: nothing which the authority does within the ambit of the discretion can be actionable at common law. If the decision complained of falls outside the statutory discretion, it can (but not necessarily will) give rise to common law liability. However, if the factors relevant to the exercise of the discretion include matters of policy, the court cannot adjudicate on such policy matters and therefore cannot reach the conclusion that the decision was outside the ambit of the statutory discretion. Therefore a common law duty of care in relation to the taking of decisions involving policy matters cannot exist.[172]

In order to understand fully this excerpt – which provides no more than the starting point in understanding public authority negligence liability – it is necessary to unpick and explain each of its key elements.

(1) To begin with, Lord Browne-Wilkinson sought to forge a distinction between (a) *decision-making* cases, where it is contended that the defendant owes a duty of care in respect of the manner in which it exercises a statutory discretion and (b) *implementation* cases, where what is in issue is the manner in which a previously formulated policy is put into practice.[173] Although this distinction between policy formulation and policy implementation has been shown by academics and judges alike to be an imperfect one,[174] the gist of the distinction is

---

[172] Ibid at 738.

[173] A decision to close a school clearly falls into the decision-making category and the day-to-day running of a school falls into the implementation category.

[174] The fallacy of this assumption was most succinctly summed up in an American case where it was said that any act can involve some measure of discretion, even the hammering of a nail (*Johnson v State of*

that, for example, decisions about how to ensure pupil safety would fall into the first category, while the practical measures actually implemented in order to achieve that policy objective would fall into the second.[175] In relation to the implementation of a policy, his Lordship said that the usual *Caparo* test would apply.

(2) Next, wherever a claim relates purely to the exercise of a statutory discretion, his Lordship stated that 'nothing which an authority does within the ambit of that discretion can be actionable at common law'.[176] But if the decision complained of falls outside the statutory discretion, 'it *can* (but not necessarily will) give rise to common law liability'.[177] This, expressed in the language of public lawyers, means that any *intra vires* exercise of statutory discretion cannot give rise to a duty of care for the purposes of negligence law, but that a *Wednesbury* unreasonable decision *may* be justiciable.

(3) Finally, Lord Browne-Wilkinson sought to place even *Wednesbury* unreasonable decision-making beyond the reach of negligence law where the statutory discretion that is alleged to have been abused relates to matters of policy that are unfit for consideration by the courts. In such cases, no action would lie because the courts would simply have no jurisdiction to examine (let alone determine) whether there has been an excess of the discretion afforded.

These three principles must be read subject to the reasoning of the House of Lords in *D v East Berkshire Community NHS Trust*.[178]

> In that case, there were three conjoined appeals. In the first, C was wrongly accused by health professionals of having harmed her own daughter. She sued in negligence on the basis of the resultant anxiety and stress that she suffered. In the second case, a father and daughter brought an action against social workers who removed the daughter into local authority care on the incorrect basis that the father had sexually abused her. In the third case, Cs were a mother and father who were, again, suing on the ground of false accusations that led to a compulsory separation from their daughter. In all three cases, the social services applied to have the negligence actions struck out on grounds of non-justiciability.

The House of Lords rejected the suggestion that a duty might be owed to any of the parents in these cases because of the *perceived* conflict of interests entailed,[179] but conceded

---

California 447 P 2d 352 (1968)). For criticism, see *Stovin v Wise* [1996] AC 923, at 951; Bailey and Bowman [1986] CLJ 430, and, id [2000] CLJ 85.

[175] The fact that the service is provided pursuant to statute is not necessarily incompatible with a normal relationship of proximity between the school and pupils: [1995] 2 AC 633, at 735.

[176] Ibid at 738.

[177] Ibid at 738.

[178] [2005] 2 AC 373.

[179] It was said to be contrary to public policy to hold, in a case where a child was suspected of being abused, that the relevant public authority investigating the case would owe the parents a duty of care in the conduct of its investigation. The thinking was as follows: while the authority would be statutorily bound to

that a duty was arguably owed to the daughter in the second case. Accordingly, their Lordships permitted only the second claim, brought by the daughter, to proceed. It struck out all the remaining actions.

For present purposes, it is also important to note the way in which the Court of Appeal severely circumscribed the principles established in the *Bedfordshire* decision, where it had been held that no duty would be owed in respect of a child wrongfully removed into local authority care. According to the Court of Appeal – and the House of Lords did not disturb this finding – what had materially changed was the enactment of the Human Rights Act 1998. For since its enactment, it had become possible to bring an action directly under that Act in two important circumstances: first, where a child's Article 8 right to respect for privacy and family life would be infringed by taking a child into care where there was no proper basis for so doing, and second, for infringement of the child's Article 3 right to be free from inhuman and degrading treatment where he or she should have been removed into care but was left at home with abusive parents.[180] In short, the Human Rights Act 1998 had already undermined the immunity established in the *Bedfordshire* case, so it was supposed that there was no longer any point in trying to preserve one at common law.[181]

(2) Policy and discretion

In the *Bedfordshire* case, although Lord Browne-Wilkinson gave examples of 'social policy, the allocation of finite public resources [and]...the balance between pursuing desirable social aims as against the risk to the public inherent in so doing',[182] he failed to provide an exact definition of what he meant by a statutory discretion so imbued with considerations of policy as to render it non-justiciable for the purposes of the law of negligence.[183] This lingering uncertainty simply added to that associated with the somewhat difficult policy/implementation dichotomy[184] upon which he also placed great emphasis. So, when should a statutory discretion be regarded as so bound up with policy considerations as to be non-justiciable? This is by no means an easy

---

do what it could to ensure the child's welfare – by, eg, removing the child into care in spite of parental opposition – there would necessarily be a conflict of interests if the authority was liable to be sued in negligence by the parents if it should transpire that the child was not in fact in need of protection. Yet as Lord Bingham observed in his dissenting speech (at [37]), this approach is not wholly convincing since it could well be argued that the prospect of liability towards the parents might galvanise the authority into doing its job with particular care and sensitivity, in which case it would then be performing its statutory functions in the way that we would wish it to perform them in an ideal world.

[180] That these actions would lie was made clear by the twin decisions in *TP and KM v UK* [2001] 2 FLR 549 and *Z v UK* [2001] 2 FLR 612 which arose directly out of two of the appeals in the *Bedfordshire* case.

[181] Arguably, the Human Rights Act had only partially undermined it, since actions under the 1998 Act are subject to a shorter limitation period of just one year: Human Rights Act 1998, s 7(5) and since damages under the Act will not be as generous as those under the law of tort, being assessed on quite separate, narrower bases (on which see ch 1).

[182] [1995] 2 AC 633, at 736.

[183] Any such decisions will, of course, remain open to the public law supervision of the courts by way of judicial review: see *A v Essex CC* [2004] 1 FLR 749, at [33].

[184] For details of the problems associated with this dichotomy, see Bailey and Bowman [1986] CLJ 430.

question to answer, but Lord Slynn provided some guidance in *Phelps v Hillingdon LBC* when he observed:

> The fact that acts which are claimed to be negligent are carried out within a statutory discretion is not in itself a reason why it should be held that no claim in negligence can be brought in respect of them. It is only where what is done has involved the weighing of competing public interests or has been dictated by considerations on which Parliament could not have intended that the courts would substitute their views for the views of ministers or officials that the courts will hold that the issue is not justiciable.[185]

This dictum would appear to explain Lord Browne-Wilkinson's example of competing public interests in the case of decisions concerning the allocation of scarce resources. Take, for example, a local authority that decides to devote certain limited resources to making provision X for children in need rather than provision Y. Its decision so to do (even if negligent) would be non-justiciable because the court is not entitled to substitute its view for that of the public authority on the thorny question of how best to allocate such resources in the furtherance of competing public interests. Applying this approach, it has since been held that the courts are not in a position to second-guess discretionary decisions made by adoption agencies concerning the level of information that is revealed to prospective adopters prior to an adoption.[186] On the one hand, the parents have an interest in knowing a good deal about the child they are proposing to adopt, but on the other, there is the child's interest in keeping certain information confidential (at least so long as the interested parties are merely *prospective* adopters). Parliament has invested adoption agencies with the discretion to decide just how much information to release, and, as the Court of Appeal held, it is not for the courts to second-guess such decisions.

Apart from these illustrations, however, it is difficult to provide hard-and-fast guidance on when a statutory discretion will be regarded as too intricately bound up with matters of policy as to be non-justiciable. The reality seems to be that the negligent exercise of a statutory discretion must always be addressed on a case-by-case basis in order to decide whether policy (or human rights considerations, bearing in mind the *East Berkshire* decision) will render the negligent exercise of that discretion justiciable or not.

(3) The ambit of discretion principle?

While it is easy to state that a decision which falls beyond the discretion conferred upon a public authority is justiciable, it is a good deal more difficult to justify this statement (made, as it was, by Lord Browne-Wilkinson in the *Bedfordshire* case). No matter how appealing the proposition may appear, it nonetheless implies the application of a public law test – that of *Wednesbury* unreasonableness – in the sphere of private law.[187]

---

[185] [2001] 2 AC 619, at 653. To similar effect see *Barrett v Enfield LBC* [2001] 2 AC 550.
[186] *A v Essex CC* [2004] 1 FLR 749.
[187] See *Associated Provincial Picture Houses Ltd v Wednesbury Corp* [1948] 1 KB 223.

As his Lordship said in that case, a decision purportedly taken according to a statutory discretion should be treated as justiciable within the law of negligence if it was 'so unreasonable that no reasonable authority could have made it'.[188] Just why a public law test should be used to determine the existence of a private law cause of action, however, is difficult to comprehend. Yet despite a notable attempt by one Court of Appeal judge in *Carty v Croydon LBC* to relocate the unreasonableness issue to the court's decision on whether there has been a breach of an already established duty of care,[189] it is difficult to square that approach with Lord Browne-Wilkinson's dictum and with the speech of Hale LJ in *A v Essex CC* where she spoke of 'an area of discretion which can only be challenged if it falls outside the realms of reasonableness'.[190] Thus, although the public law principle of *Wednesbury* unreasonableness looks like something of a fish out of water in this context, it nonetheless appears fairly well entrenched as a relevant principle of law in this context.

(C) THE APPLICATION OF *CAPARO*

Once it has been decided that a case is justiciable, it still remains for the claimant to establish that a duty of care was in fact owed to him. This, according to Lord Browne-Wilkinson in the *Bedfordshire* case, should be decided by applying the usual three-stage test established in *Caparo*. And in applying this test, the greatest difficulty that typically arises against public authority defendants comes at the third stage: showing that it would be fair, just, and reasonable to impose a duty of care. In the *Bedfordshire* case, Lord Browne-Wilkinson adverted to a number of factors that might impinge on this question. The first was whether Parliament had created specific remedies within the statute conferring the discretion, for it would be inapt for the courts to superimpose a duty of care on the remedies that had been created by Parliament.[191] (At the same time, the *absence* of a specific statutory remedy will also tell against the existence of a common-law duty of care: '[i]f the statute does not create a private right of action, it would be... unusual if the mere existence of a statutory duty could generate a common law duty of care'.)[192] Second, the fact that the statutory framework in the *Bedfordshire* case required co-operation between many individuals and agencies might mean (1) that it would be unfair to single out any individual or agency for potential liability and (2) that the imposition of a duty of care on the local authority could lead to a disruption in the operation of that partnership. Third, his Lordship was troubled by the fact that no analogous case in relation to a statutory social welfare scheme had been identified where a common-law

---

[188] [1995] 2 AC 633, at 740.

[189] [2005] 1 WLR 2312, at [26] and [32].

[190] [2004] 1 FLR 749, at [48]. But cf the remarks made earlier in her judgment (at [33]) where she seemed fleetingly to pre-echo the approach taken in *Carty*.

[191] [1995] 2 AC 633, at 748–51. The point was endorsed in *Gorringe v Calderdale MBC* [2004] 1 WLR 1057, at [70].

[192] *Gorringe v Calderdale MBC* [2004] 1 WLR 1057, at [23] and [90].

duty had been imposed. This concern, of course, has the capacity – since it was expressed in very general terms – to apply more widely than simply to the facts of the *Bedfordshire* case.

Since the decision in that case, the appellate courts have stressed a number of other factors relevant to the question of whether it would be *fair, just, and reasonable* to impose a duty of care on a public authority. These include the potential for conflict in the exercise of a power between two classes of persons, whose interests are (to a greater or lesser extent) opposed. Thus, in *Jain v Trent Strategic Health Authority*,[193] Lord Scott examined a number of cases where the potential for conflict arose and concluded that there was a general principle underlying them:

> [W]here action is taken by a state authority under statutory powers designed for the ben-
> efit or protection of a particular class of persons, a tortious duty of care will not be held
> to be owed by the state authority to others whose interests may be adversely affected by
> an exercise of a statutory power. The reason is that the imposition of such a duty would or
> might inhibit the exercise of the statutory powers and be potentially adverse to the inter-
> ests of the class of persons the powers were designed to benefit or protect, thereby putting
> at risk the achievement of their statutory purpose.[194]

For this reason, there was no duty to take care imposed upon the defendant authority in making an *ex parte* application to a magistrate under section 30 of the Registered Homes Act 1984 for cancellation of the claimants' registration to operate a nursing home. The effect of the cancellation was the immediate removal of elderly residents from the home and dissipation of the fee income which their residence provided. Although the claimants had their business destroyed as a result of negligence in the exercise of the power, the main object of the power was the protection of elderly care home residents.[195]

Other factors of relevance in determining what is fair, just, and reasonable include the risk that potential liability might lead to defensive practices on the part of the public authority and the wastefulness of a public authority having to devote sizeable amounts of its limited financial resources to defending negligence actions.[196]

The decided cases have also highlighted problems in establishing a sufficient rela-
tionship of *proximity* between public authorities and claimants; especially where the claimants have been children asserting negligence on the part of social services departments or education authorities. To an extent, such problems might have been predicted since not every single child suffering from some form of familial or educational problem is likely to be known personally to the relevant public authorities.

---

[193] [2009] UKHL 4.
[194] Ibid at [28].
[195] Ibid at [20].
[196] *Stovin v Wise* [1996] AC 923; *Gorringe v Calderdale MBC* [2004] 1 WLR 1057; *A v Essex CC* [2004] 1 FLR 749. For a growing judicial scepticism, see *Gregg v Scott* [2005] 2 AC 176 (contrast the speeches of Lord Hoffmann and Lord Nicholls); and for critique, see Markesinis et al, *Tortious Liability of Statutory Bodies: A Comparative and Economic Analysis of Five English Cases* (1999).

It is, therefore, not surprising that the courts have more readily found there to be a sufficient relationship of proximity once the authority has undertaken to provide a particular assessment (in the case of children with educational problems) or welfare service (in the case of children who have been formally admitted to local authority care). In *Barrett v Enfield LBC*, where a child in care complained of a series of negligent acts and omissions on the part of the local authority during his time in local authority care, Lord Hutton made the following point:

> [I]n the present case the [claimant] was not a member of a wide class of society which the defendant was obliged to seek to protect, but was an individual person who had been placed in the care of the defendant by statute, and ... it would not constitute a novel category of negligence to hold that the defendant owed him a common law duty of care.[197]

In a similar vein, recognising the actual connection that existed between the claimant and the defendant, Lord Slynn said in *Phelps v Hillingdon LBC*, where an educational psychologist engaged by the local education authority failed to diagnose the claimant's dyslexia and thence organise special educational provision:

> I see no reason why in this situation [the educational psychologist who failed to diagnose the claimant's dyslexia] did not have a duty of care ... Her relationship with the child and what she was doing created the necessary nexus and duty.[198]

A second difficulty associated with the proximity requirement has arisen in particularly sharp relief where the allegation made is that the public authority has *failed to perform* a statutory function; in other words, where there has been a negligent omission.

Stovin v Wise[199] is illustrative, and the facts were refreshingly simple.

C suffered serious injuries when his motor cycle collided with a car driven by D1 who came out of a junction. The junction was dangerous because a bank on adjoining land obscured road users' views. Accidents had occurred at the junction on at least three earlier occasions. The local council, which was the authority responsible for the highway, was joined as a second defendant. It was alleged that the council owed a common law duty of care to road users. The council was aware of the danger posed by the junction. At a meeting prior to the accident in which C was injured, the council had acknowledged the visibility problems and recommended removal of at least part of the bank so long as the owners of the land, British Rail, agreed. The owners simply did not respond to the council's proposal. They did, however, possess statutory powers to issue a notice compelling British Rail to act to eliminate the danger to the highway.

---

[197] *Barrett v Enfield LBC* [2001] 2 AC 550, at 589. Note that this reasoning was followed by Lord Woolf in *Kent v Griffiths* [2000] 2 WLR 1158, where it was held (at 1170) that the statutory power granted to the ambulance service to answer an emergency call crystallised into a specific duty to respond to a particular 999 call which was owed to C as a particular individual.

[198] [2001] 2 AC 619, at 656.

[199] [1996] AC 923.

One question that arose was whether the council could be liable for its failure to exercise its statutory power to issue a notice to British Rail. Public law demands that councils exercise their power responsibly, but it does not follow that an authority 'necessarily owes a duty of care which may require that the power should actually be exercised'.[200] Thus, while a public authority exercising its statutory powers so as to cause independent or additional damage can sometimes be liable in negligence, it would be rare indeed if the courts were to subvert a discretionary statutory 'power' by imposing a common-law 'duty' that effectively removed that discretion, and forced the authority to act.[201]

Notwithstanding the rejection of a common-law action in that case, it should be observed that *Stovin v Wise* did not completely rule out negligence actions in respect of failures to exercise statutory powers. The minimum preconditions for any such duty were said to be (1) that it would be irrational not to have exercised the power so that there would be a public law duty to act and (2) that there were 'exceptional grounds for holding that the policy of the statute requires compensation to be paid to persons who suffer loss because the power was not exercised'. Since then, Lord Hoffmann has attempted to clarify this rather hazy proposition, explaining that an 'assumption of responsibility' of the extended *Hedley Byrne* variety is what is required to transform a statutory *power* into a common-law *duty*, and that it was just such assumptions of responsibility that underpinned the decisions in *Barrett v Enfield LBC* and *Phelps v Hillingdon LBC*.[202] In such cases, claimants will be required to show evidence of *general reliance* within the community on the provision of the service in question. At the very least, it is difficult to see any clear evidence of *especial reliance* by the children in the *Barrett* and *Phelps* cases. In the context of general reliance, then, it should be established that patterns of behaviour depend on a near-universal and reasonable expectation that the public authority will deliver protection from particular kinds of harm almost as a matter of routine and that the service would be one which was much the same whomever it was provided for. Indeed, Lord Hoffmann suggested that routine building inspections by local authorities might fall within the test as being something upon which there would be universal reliance. By contrast, not all motorists are foolish enough to treat the occasional absence of warning signs along the road as a licence to disregard the obvious risks associated with driving too fast at the crest of a hill. That being so, there will be no liability on the part of a highway authority in respect of a failure to signpost each and every potential hazard on the road.[203]

---

[200] [1996] AC 923, at 950, per Lord Hoffmann. He reiterated this view in *Gorringe v Calderdale MBC* [2004] 1 WLR 1057, at [39]–[40] (and at [73], Lord Scott made the same point).

[201] Cf *Kane v New Forest DC (No 1)* [2001] 3 All ER 914 where the authority had entered into a formal undertaking to improve (but had failed to improve by the time of the accident) visibility where a footpath met the inside of a bend on a main road. It was held that there was a strong possibility of the action succeeding.

[202] *Gorringe v Calderdale MBC* [2004] 1 WLR 1057, at [39]–[40].

[203] Ibid.

An interesting variation upon the theme of failure to exercise a statutory power arose in *Connor v Surrey County Council*,[204] in which the defendant council as employer owed a duty of care to the claimant, an employee head teacher of a primary school. The question was whether the council was negligent for failing to protect the claimant from the machinations of a dysfunctional school governing body. The council had a power under statute to replace the governing board with an interim executive board but did not do so, despite numerous warning signs of disruption in school life and of stress and risks to the claimant's health. As a result of continuous fighting with the governing body, the claimant had to retire early from her post with clinical depression. Although the case was primarily concerned with the question of breach, it demonstrates that the law may require that a pre-existing private law duty of care (here in both contract and tort) be fulfilled by the exercise of a public law power. The proviso is that this can be done 'consistently with the duty-ower's full performance of his public law obligations'.[205] Laws LJ explained:

> The demands of a private law duty of care cannot justify, far less require, action (or inaction) by a public authority which would be unlawful in public law terms. The standard tests of legality, rationality and fairness must be met as they apply to the use of the public law power in the particular case. If the case is one where the action's severity has to be measured against its effectiveness, it must also be proportionate to whatever is the statutory purpose.[206]

(D) VICARIOUS LIABILITY

One further issue that arose in *X v Bedfordshire County Council* concerned the possibility of vicarious liability on the part of public bodies in respect of the acts of their employees.[207] The House of Lords said of such vicarious liability for public service employees generally[208] that the employee would owe a duty of care to the individual member of the public only where (1) the existence of such a duty is 'consistent with the proper performance of his duties to the...authority' and (2) it is appropriate to impose such a duty on the employee. In both *X v Bedfordshire County Council*[209] and *Phelps v Hillingdon LBC*[210] it was recognised that a duty of care was incumbent on the individual professionals for which the council could be vicariously liable.[211] The perceived advantage of pursuing an action on the basis of vicarious liability is, of course,

---

[204] [2010] EWCA Civ 286.

[205] Ibid at [106].

[206] Ibid at [107].

[207] As to the distinction between direct and vicarious liability in this context see *X v Bedfordshire CC* [1995] 2 AC 633, at 739–40.

[208] [1995] 2 AC 633, at 739–40.

[209] Ibid at 763, 766, and 770.

[210] [2000] 3 WLR 776 (negligence of an educational psychologist in failing to diagnose C's dyslexia causing C's future education to suffer could result in the employer-council being held vicariously liable).

[211] See also *Carty v Croydon LBC* [2005] 2 All ER 51.

that it becomes much easier to demonstrate the requisite elements of foreseeability and proximity.

(E) PROPOSED REFORM

In 2008, the Law Commission proposed significant modification of the private law consequences of 'substandard administrative action'.[212] This was on the basis that '[t]he uncertain and unprincipled nature of negligence in relation to public bodies, coupled with the unpredictable expansion of liability over recent years, has led to a situation that serves neither claimants nor public bodies'.[213] Redress in the case of 'truly public' activities would have been restricted to situations where the statutory regime under which the public authority acted was designed to 'confer a benefit on the relevant class of persons' and to failures evidencing 'serious fault'.[214] However, these proposals were dropped after considerable resistance, including resistance by the Government. Law Commission consultees were of the view that the rules of negligence as applied to public authorities are 'appropriate'.[215] Indeed, the law of negligence performs an important role in ensuring proper standards of conduct; it provides a means of accountability for the actions of public officials and assists in improved delivery of their services.[216]

Thus, the law of negligence will continue to play a role as the main means of private law redress for the failure of public bodies. Indeed, in light of developments following the commencement of the Human Rights Act 1998,[217] it is more difficult than in earlier times for a public authority to have a negligence action against it struck out.[218] But this does not mean that public authorities are more likely to be held liable in negligence. Instead, as our survey of the cases has suggested, future decisions will continue to be characterised by three particular difficulties that may present very high hurdles for claimants. These are: (1) showing that in all the circumstances of the case it will be fair, just, and reasonable to impose a duty of care;[219] (2) showing that the claimant

---

[212] Law Commission, *Administrative Redress: Public Bodies and the Citizen* (Law Com Consultation Paper No 187, 2008).

[213] Law Commission, *Administrative Redress: Public Bodies and the Citizen* (Law Com No 322, 2010), at [1.18]. Note that a study of claim rates has found no evidence to support the assertion that claims against local authorities and schools have been rising in recent years, although there is evidence to suggest an increase in claims against the NHS from the 1970s to 2000: Morris (2007) 70 MLR 349, 359–61.

[214] Law Commission, *Administrative Redress: Public Bodies and the Citizen* (Law Com No 322, 2010), at [1.20]–[1.21].

[215] Ibid at [3.7].

[216] See Mullender (2009) 72 MLR 961, esp. 974–5.

[217] Eg, *Osman v UK* (1998) 29 EHRR 245; *TP and KM v United Kingdom* [2001] 2 FLR 549; and *Z v UK* [2001] 2 FLR 612.

[218] But not impossible: see *Brooks v MPC* [2005] 1 WLR 1495.

[219] Thus, there was no departure from the '*Hill* principle' in *Smith v CC of Sussex Police* [2008] UKHL 50.

was in a sufficient relationship of proximity with the public authority;[220] (3) showing that, even if a duty of care existed, the local authority was in breach of that duty of care (given the ongoing resource limitations under which all such authorities continue to operate).

SECTION 6   DUTIES IN TORT AND CONTRACT

There are many circumstances when liability for negligence could arise concurrently in tort and contract. In such cases, the implied duty of care derives from the contract between the parties,[221] the relevant proximity stemming from their contractual nexus.

Concurrent liability was always recognised where the defendant exercised a 'common calling', for example a blacksmith, innkeeper, or common carrier. In such cases, the 'calling' in question imposed a duty to show the degree of skill normally expected of a person exercising that particular 'calling', irrespective of any contract. But in the case of many professionals, such as solicitors and architects, it was traditionally held that, where there was a contract between the parties, the claimant was confined to a remedy in contract alone.[222] A number of Court of Appeal decisions sought to put an end to any such restrictive rule.[223] But subsequent to those decisions, Lord Scarman sought to resurrect the traditional rule and exclude concurrent liability in contract and tort in *Tai Hing Cotton Mill Ltd v Liu Chong Hing Bank Ltd*. He said:

> [t]hough it is possible as a matter of legal semantics to conduct an analysis of the rights and duties inherent in some contractual relationships either as a matter of contract law when the question will be what, if any, terms are to be implied, or as a matter of tort law when the task will be to identify a duty arising from the proximity and character of the relationship between the parties, their Lordships believe it to be correct on principle and necessary for the avoidance of confusion in the law to adhere to the contractual analysis, on principle because it is a relationship in which the parties have, subject to a few exceptions, the right to determine their obligations to each other, and for avoidance of confusion because different consequences do follow according to whether liability arises from contract or tort, eg, in the limitation of action.[224]

A series of conflicting decisions from the Court of Appeal followed *Tai Hing*.[225] At the heart of these cases was an essentially practical question: 'When a person enters

---

[220] See, eg, *Cowan v CC of Avon and Somerset* [2002] HLR 44; *Desmond v CC of Nottinghamshire Police* [2011] EWCA Civ 3.

[221] For an example of a duty of care implied by statute into a contract for services see the Supply of Goods and Services Act 1982, s 13.

[222] *Bagot v Stevens, Scanlan & Co Ltd* [1966] 1 QB 197.

[223] *Esso Petroleum Co Ltd v Mardon* [1976] QB 801; *Midland Bank Trust Co Ltd v Hett, Stubbs & Kemp* [1979] Ch 384; *Batty v Metropolitan Property Realisations Ltd* [1978] QB 554.

[224] [1986] AC 80, at 107.

[225] Cf, eg, *Forsikringsaktieselskapet Vesta v Butcher* [1988] 2 All ER 43 with *Lee v Thompson* (1989) 6 PN 91. See also the disagreement within the Court of Appeal in *Johnstone v Bloomsbury Health Authority* [1992] QB 333.

into a contract, in circumstances where, were there no contract, there would nonetheless be a duty in tort, should he forfeit the potential advantages that suing in tort may have over contract?'[226] The House of Lords in *Henderson v Merrett Syndicates Ltd*[227] finally resolved the issue holding that concurrent liability in contract and tort is generally applicable. Provided that a duty in tort is not contrary to the terms of the contract, a duty in tort arising out of the special relationship between the parties lies concurrently with the obligations imposed by the contract. Lord Goff declared:

> the common law is not antipathetic to concurrent liability, and there is no sound basis for a rule which automatically restricts the [claimant] to either a tortious or contractual remedy. The result may be untidy; but given that the tortious duty is imposed by the general law, and the contractual duty is attributable to the will of the parties, I do not find it objectionable that the [claimant] may be entitled to take advantage of the remedy which is most advantageous to him, subject only to ascertaining whether the tortious duty is so inconsistent with the applicable contract that, in accordance with ordinary principle the parties must be taken to have agreed that the tortious remedy is to be limited or excluded.[228]

A claimant who has either expressly or implicitly agreed to give up any remedy in tort cannot go back on his word. He cannot assert a duty in tort quite contrary to the framework of agreed contractual terms.[229] However, where a contract deals with only part of the relationship between the parties, a duty of care wider than the contractual duty may arise from the circumstances of the case. Such duties may be concurrent but not co-extensive.[230] Thus, if we entrust our portfolio of shares in US companies to a paid financial adviser, our contract will govern his professional liability to us. If that contract excludes a duty in tort, we cannot elect to sue in tort in respect of those dealings between us. If, however, that same defendant also gives us general advice on how to reinvest our US profits elsewhere, no bar exists to a duty of care in respect of those aspects of our relationship not governed by the contract.

It must not be assumed that tort always offers advantages over contract. The disadvantage of a tort action in comparison with contract must also be noted in this context. A surgeon treating an NHS patient can owe him no obligation higher or stricter than that of reasonable care. He does not contract with his patient to 'guarantee' success. In *Thake v Maurice*[231] the claimant paid for a private vasectomy. The operation

---

[226] Such advantages most regularly relate to the rules of limitation of actions. That is, C will normally have longer in which to bring his action if he sues in tort. In contract the limitation period begins to run from the date of the breach of contract. In tort the start may be delayed until the date when C could reasonably have become aware of the breach of the duty. Furthermore, extensions under the Latent Damage Act 1986 apply only to tort actions: *Iron Trades Mutual Insurance Ltd v Buckingham (JK) Ltd* [1990] 1 All ER 808.

[227] [1995] 2 AC 145. See Whittaker [1997] LS 169.

[228] [1995] 2 AC 145, at 193–4.

[229] See *Robinson v PE Jones (Contractors) Ltd* [2011] EWCA Civ 119, where it was held that entry into a NHBC contract for the construction of a house, setting out a staggered-liability regime, was inconsistent with further tortious obligations for purely financial losses.

[230] *Holt v Payne Skillington* [1996] PNLR 179.

[231] [1986] QB 644.

was carefully and competently performed. Some time later, the minute risk of natural reversal of the surgery materialised. The claimant's wife conceived again. In his action for breach of contract the claimant's counsel argued thus: (1) the surgeon never mentioned the possibility of the vasectomy 'failing', therefore, (2) he should be taken to have contracted to render Mr Thake sterile, in which case (3) when he failed to do so, he was in breach of contract. The Court of Appeal ultimately dismissed that claim holding that, in such a contract, a term 'guaranteeing' success could not reasonably be implied.[232] But the argument could never even have been attempted in tort.

Consider also the famous American case of *Hawkins v McGee*.[233] The claimant in that case severely burnt his hand. The defendant, a plastic surgeon, undertook to treat the hand and restore it to perfect condition. After treatment, the hand was in fact much worse than before. The measure of damages awarded in contract was the difference between the hand after treatment and a perfect hand. In tort it would have been the difference between the burnt hand and the hand after surgery. In contract the claimant is awarded damages for his expectation loss; that is, damages for not obtaining the result he contracted for. In tort he is generally[234] only awarded compensation to return him to the position he enjoyed prior to the tort.

The relationship between tort and contract continues to be relevant not only to questions of concurrent liability, but also to cases where a third party seeks to establish that A who owes a duty in contract to B also owes a duty in tort to him.[235] *Donoghue v Stevenson*[236] dismissed the fallacy that privity of contract per se prevents such a duty to the third party ever arising. If there is the necessary proximity between the parties, then a duty in tort may arise independently of any contract between A and B. Nonetheless, the courts will be wary of extending liability in tort to third parties where the defendant's primary duty rests on a contractual obligation to someone else. They will seek to ensure that a duty in tort to the third party does not conflict with the primary contractual duty. The decision of the House of Lords in *White v Jones*[237] (discussed fully in the next chapter) confirms, however, that liability in tort for breach of an obligation owed in contract to another party can arise in appropriate circumstances. Furthermore, in *Williams v Natural Life Health Foods Ltd*[238] the House of Lords acknowledged that tort may play an interstitial role where contract law fails to deliver justice. Privity of contract, then, is not a bar to liability; it is simply a consideration which should not be overlooked.

---

[232] C lost 2–1 in the Court of Appeal. See, however, the judgment at first instance: [1984] 2 All ER 513.

[233] 84 NH 114, 146 A 641 (1929).

[234] For a rare example of expectation losses recovered in tort see *White v Jones* [1995] 2 AC 207.

[235] For a third party statutorily to acquire the benefit of terms included in a contract between two others, three conditions must be satisfied. First, it must be clear that the contract purports to confer a benefit on that third party; second, there must be no contrary agreement in the contract; third, the third party must be expressly identified in the contract: Contracts (Rights of Third Parties) Act 1999: ss 1(1)(b), 1(2), and 1(3).

[236] [1932] AC 562.

[237] [1995] 1 All ER 691.

[238] [1998] 2 All ER 577.

The above discussion has concerned cases where parties are *joined* by contract; but certain parties may be *separated* by contract and the question is what effect does this have upon the operation of the tort of negligence? Where the parties have *structured relations* so that there is no contract between them and so that they deal through an intermediary, this may be an indication of an intention to preclude obligations in tort. Thus, in major projects involving interlocking (especially construction) activities, the conscious structuring of relations may be inconsistent with a duty of care.[239] However, the context will be important. Thus, in *Riyad Bank v Ahli United Bank (UK) plc*,[240] the Court of Appeal held that a Kuwaiti bank owed a duty of care in providing investment advice to a Saudi bank separated by contract in circumstances where the separation was artificially effected for purposes of reputation and marketing of products.

FURTHER READING

BAILEY, 'Public authority liability in negligence: the continued search for coherence' [2006] *Legal Studies* 155

BEEVER, *Rediscovering the Law of Negligence* (2007)

BUXTON, 'How the common law gets made: *Hedley Byrne* and other cautionary tales' (2009) 125 *Law Quarterly Review* 60

FAIRGRIEVE, *State Liability in Tort: A Comparative Law Study* (2003)

HONORÉ, 'Are Omissions Less Culpable?' in Cane and Stapleton (eds), *Essays for Patrick Atiyah* (1991)

PERRY, 'The Role of Duty of Care in a Rights-Based Theory of Negligence Law' in Robertson and Wu (eds), *The Goals of Private Law* (2009), ch 4

ROBERTSON, 'Justice, Community Welfare and the Duty of Care' (2011) 127 *Law Quarterly Review* 370

STAPLETON, 'Duty of Care Factors: A Selection from the Judicial Menus' in Cane and Stapleton (eds), *The Law of Obligations: Essays in Honour of John Fleming* (1998)

WHITTAKER, 'The Application of the "Broad Principle" in *Hedley-Byrne* as between Parties to a Contract' [1997] *Legal Studies* 169

---

[239] *Henderson v Merrett Syndicates Ltd* [1995] 2 AC 145, at 195; *White v Jones* [1995] 2 AC 207, 279.

[240] [2006] EWCA Civ 780.

3

DUTY OF CARE II: RECOGNISED HARM

KEY ISSUES

(1) Hierarchy of protected interests
The law of negligence reflects protective priorities in wider tort law; a duty of care is more readily recognised with respect to physical integrity than with respect to either mental or financial interests.

(2) Impact of European Convention
The extent of protection given to particular interests is apt to change over time and is open to influence by the requirements of the European Convention on Human Rights.

(3) Complex cases
This chapter considers the duty rules that have developed with respect to some complex damage cases. The courts deciding these cases have examined technical factors relating to the causation of damage, but have also been influenced by the desire to keep negligence liability within defensible limits – to prevent the 'floodgates' from opening.

(4) Psychiatric harm
Psychiatric harm cases have been divided into those concerning persons within the area of physical harm or exposure to toxic substances, termed 'primary victims', and those who have suffered illness as a result of witnessing the death, injury, or imperilment of others, termed 'secondary victims'.

(5) Pure economic loss
Pure economic loss cases include those arising by way of defective property and relational economic losses, and through misstatements and poor execution of services. In the latter two categories of case, courts have utilised the concept of 'assumption of responsibility' to determine whether or not to impose duties of care.

SECTION 1 INTRODUCTION

Lord Atkin's famous axiom – '[t]he rule that you are to love your neighbour becomes in law, you must not injure your neighbour' – begs one vital question. What kinds of injury must one take reasonable care to avoid inflicting on one's neighbour? Failing to return his affection may offend him, but no one would suggest that he could sue on this basis. Accordingly, whereas the previous chapter considered the broad framework within which a duty of care will be imposed, this chapter focuses on the kinds of interest that are subjected to such duty.

In the modern era, duties may be imposed to protect against injury to the person (including psychiatric harm), damage to property, and pure economic losses. But such a simple statement provides no hint as to the many intricacies in the law. As we shall see, not always are the distinctions between these categories obvious, nor is each of the various interests afforded the same level of protection. The following points must be borne in mind throughout the chapter.

(1) There are kinds of harm which are currently irremediable in English law even if intentionally and maliciously inflicted: privacy, per se, continues for the present to be an interest not protected in negligence.[1] Furthermore, when the harm of which the claimant complains does not give rise to a tort if committed intentionally, the courts are naturally reluctant to say that such harm gives rise to a cause of action if inflicted carelessly.

(2) The proper functions of tort and contract and the borderline between them may be in issue. Where the substance of the claimant's action is that the defendant failed to provide value for money in terms of services rendered, and where no contract existed between the parties, would imposing a duty of care in such circumstances trespass too greatly on the privity of contract principle (or such of it as remains in the wake of the Contracts (Rights of Third Parties) Act 1999)?[2]

(3) Since the Human Rights Act 1998 came into force, the courts have been forced to rethink some of tort law's foundational principles. The (potential) negligence liability of public authorities has had to be reappraised quite significantly in the light of the decisions of the European Court of Human Rights in *Z v United Kingdom*[3] and *TP and KM v United Kingdom*.[4] And since it became independently possible to hold public authorities liable in respect of breaches of the European Convention on Human Rights,[5] it has been necessary for the courts to show a new-found tolerance in hearing the claims of those seeking to sue public authorities on the basis of common-law negligence.[6]

---

[1] Over the years, via ad hoc applications of several existing torts and the Human Rights Act 1998, many privacy-related interests have received increased protection. But no common-law tort based solely on the invasion of privacy has yet emerged. *Campbell v MGN* [2005] 2 AC 457 seems to create an action for the misuse of private information but *Douglas v Hello! Ltd (No 6)* [2006] QB 125 makes clear that no tort based on an invasion of privacy more generally has yet emerged. See Wacks, 'Why there will never be an English common law privacy tort' in Kenyon and Richardson (eds), *New Dimensions in Privacy Law* (2006), ch 7.

[2] See *White v Jones* [1995] 2 AC 207, at 262–5.

[3] (2002) 34 EHRR 97.

[4] (2002) 34 EHRR 42.

[5] Human Rights Act 1998, s 7.

[6] *D v East Berkshire Community NHS Trust* [2005] 2 AC 373.

(4) Having made the last point, the highest courts in England and Wales have yet properly to determine the appropriate relationship between developments under the Convention and the tort of negligence. One judicial view is that European developments make it unnecessary to expand liability in negligence; if redress is available under the Convention, the domestic law of negligence has no more work to do.[7] This was the view of Lord Brown in *Smith v Chief Constable of Sussex Police*:

> [C]onvention claims have very different objectives from civil law actions. Where civil actions are designed essentially to compensate claimants for their losses, convention claims are intended rather to uphold minimum human rights standards and to vindicate those rights.[8]

The contrary view is that the two areas of law should develop in harmony with each other.[9] There are good arguments each way; but domestic courts will have to be wary of allowing large disparities in protected interests to develop. This is especially so given that negligence is a relatively flexible tort encompassing many forms of damage arising in a wide spectrum of contexts; and given that a failure to provide an adequate domestic remedy to a breach of Convention rights is itself a breach of Article 13 of the Convention.[10]

(5) Claimants are always attempting to test the limits of actionability. In an increasingly complicated world, it is possible to argue that various new interests should be protected. The advent of the Human Rights Act 1998 and protection of European Convention rights has been a catalyst for such arguments. Thus it is that various speculative claims have been made for protection of such things as educational development and even the rather wide interest of 'autonomy'.[11] One issue is whether claims that purport to be about these things are better addressed according to the well-recognised heads of damage in negligence, viz personal injury, property damage, or pure economic loss.[12] With respect to claims for negligent failure to promote the educational development of children, for example, it may be that these are most easily analysed in terms of the diminished earning capacity of the child-cum-adult or expenditure by the relevant parent or guardian to rectify the inadequate provision (both financial losses). The argument against this is that existing categories of damage are too limited and in need of expansion. Thus, it might be argued that the failure of a public authority or school to promote the educational development of the child results

---

[7] *Jain v Trent Strategic HA* [2009] UKHL 4, at [39]; *Smith v CC of South Sussex Police* [2008] UKHL 50, at [136] and [138].

[8] *Smith v CC of South Sussex Police* [2008] UKHL 50, at [138]

[9] Ibid at [58].

[10] *MAK and RK v UK* [2010] ECHR 363, criticised in Greasley (2010) 73 MLR 1026. See also McIvor [2010] CLJ 133, 149–50.

[11] See survey of novel claims in Nolan (2007) 70 MLR 59.

[12] Ibid at 85–6.

in more than just financial loss – in literary, artistic, and social deprivation.[13] True this may be. But it must be accepted also that the law of negligence cannot be seen as the stairway to the Garden of Eden.[14] The aims of this tort are limited and prosaic.[15]

SECTION 2   HARM TO PERSONS

(A) DUTY TO THE UNBORN

Whether a duty of care was owed to a child damaged by another's negligence before its birth remained unresolved at common law until 1992. In *Burton v Islington Health Authority*[16] the Court of Appeal finally held that a duty is owed to the unborn child, but that the duty does not crystallise until the live birth of the child. Prior to that decision, however, Parliament had intervened in the form of the Congenital Disabilities (Civil Liability) Act 1976. There it is provided that a child who is born alive but disabled as a result of an occurrence before its birth may in certain circumstances have a cause of action against the person responsible for that occurrence.[17] Section 4(5) provides that the 1976 Act supersedes the common law in respect of births occurring after its passing. Thus the common-law rule in *Burton, in so far as it is superseded* by the 1976 Act, applies only in relation to children born before 1976.

On the other hand, the Act only applies in respect of children born with a 'disability', and 'disability' is defined in terms of 'any deformity, disease or abnormality including predisposition (whether or not susceptible of immediate prognosis) to physical or mental defect in the future'.[18] It is therefore arguable that any injury which falls short of a disability remains governed by the common law rule established in *Burton.*[19] There are also other limits to the scope of the Act that leave untouched a still wider residual role for the common law. It is therefore necessary to provide some account of the Act.

The duty imposed under the Act relates to any occurrence, whether it is one affecting the reproductive capacity of either parent before conception, or one affecting the mother during pregnancy. The peculiarity of the duty to the child is that it is derivative only. The relevant occurrence must have been capable of giving rise to liability in tort to the affected parent. But it is no answer that the parent suffered no actionable injury

---

[13] There is no injury as such in ignorance: *Donoghue v Copiague Union Free School District* 407 NYS 2d 874, 880 (1978); Nolan (2007) 70 MLR 59, 84–5.

[14] The same can be said for the European Convention of Human Rights: eg, *A v Essex CC* [2010] UKSC 33.

[15] See, eg, *White v CC of South Yorkshire Police* [1999] 2 AC 455, at [98].

[16] [1993] QB 204; and see *De Martell v Merton and Sutton HA* [1992] 3 All ER 820.

[17] Congenital Disabilities (Civil Liability) Act 1976, s 1(1). Note that s 44 of the Human Fertilisation and Embryology Act 1990 extends the 1976 Act to cover negligently inflicted disability in the course of licensed fertility treatment.

[18] Congenital Disabilities (Civil Liability) Act 1976, s 4(1).

[19] See Murphy (1994) 10 PN 94.

so long as 'there was a breach of legal duty which, [had it been] accompanied by injury, would have given rise to...liability'.[20]

Not surprisingly, mothers are made immune from general liability under the Act.[21] How could a mother damaging her baby by smoking or drinking too much be in breach of a duty to herself? Would she be in breach of a duty to the father in damaging his child? Section 2 does expressly provide for the only direct duty owed to her unborn child under the 1976 Act. A woman may be liable for damage to her child inflicted by her negligent driving of a motor vehicle when she knows or ought to know herself to be pregnant. The justification for this exceptional instance of maternal liability is probably that, in such circumstances, her insurers will meet the cost of the child's claim.

One crucial question in the context of pre-natal injuries is the extent to which negligence law recognises 'wrongful life' claims. In *McKay v Essex Area Health Authority*,[22] it was held that English common law recognises no such claims.

C was born before the 1976 Act with terrible disabilities resulting from her mother having contracted rubella during pregnancy. The mother had undergone pregnancy tests when she realised that she had been in contact with the disease and had been negligently told that the tests were negative. She would have opted for an abortion had tests proved positive. Subsequently, the child sued in respect of the harm caused to her by being born disabled. The Court of Appeal held that it was impossible to measure the harm resulting from entry into a life afflicted by disability where the only alternative was no life at all. They were therefore unprepared to impose on doctors a duty of care that was in essence a duty to abort.

In relation to births subsequent to the 1976 Act, Ackner LJ said in *McKay*[23] that the Act gave a cause of action only in respect of occurrences causing disabilities which would otherwise not have afflicted the child. It did not afford a remedy to a child whose birth was caused by the defendant's alleged negligence (even though the child born was afflicted by a disability). His Lordship also emphasised the fact that the Act was equally unsupportive of a claim for 'wrongful life'.[24]

(B) A DUTY TO RESCUERS?

Recognition of a duty in respect of physical and emotional injury to rescuers raises two important questions about the ambit of the duty to avoid harm to persons since the rescuer is only indirectly at risk from the negligent conduct. First, is he a foreseeable claimant? Second, if he is, and given that he 'elects' to undertake the rescue, can he

---

[20] Congenital Disabilities (Civil Liability) Act 1976, s 1(3).
[21] See Congenital Disabilities (Civil Liability) Act 1976, s 1. Fathers are not immune. But what sorts of circumstance could create paternal liability – infecting the mother and baby with AIDS?
[22] [1982] QB 1166.
[23] Ibid at 1187.
[24] See likewise *Harriton v Stephens* (2006) 226 CLR 52; Symmons (1987) 50 MLR 269. Cf Witting (2007) 31 MULR 569.

properly claim that the originator of the danger owes him any obligation in respect of his safety since he has 'chosen' to imperil himself?

In 1935 the Court of Appeal held for the first time that a defendant who owed a duty to another also owed a duty to those who might foreseeably attempt to rescue him from the acute peril in which the defendant's negligence had placed him.[25] Subsequent case law has consistently confirmed the notion that rescuers are foreseeable claimants since it is well understood that '[d]anger invites rescue...[and] [t]he cry of distress is a summons to relief'.[26] Whether the rescuer is a member of the emergency services, whose public duty it is to embark on the rescue mission, or a well-meaning member of the public,[27] the courts will now hold that a duty is owed to him personally.[28] On the other hand, there is no especially favourable duty owed to such persons. It suffices to note here that the usual rules apply[29] and that the controversial question of whether it is generally appropriate to compensate professional servicemen in circumstances where ordinary citizens would recover nothing for psychiatric harm in respect of witnessing a tragic event is considered fully in the following section.

The duty to a rescuer is imposed not only on those who endanger other people or their property so as to invite rescue, but also on anyone endangering himself or his own property so as to make rescue likely. Thus, a householder who negligently set his own roof alight was held liable to the fireman who was later burnt when fighting the blaze.[30]

(C) LIABILITY FOR PSYCHIATRIC HARM

A psychiatric harm is a medically recognised condition of a sustained nature that disturbs the normal functioning of the mind. It might or might not be accompanied by overt physical symptoms.[31] As a broad category, the term 'psychiatric harm' encompasses many more specific illnesses. The relevant case law has, for the most part, concerned physical events (or 'stressors') leading to the onset of post-traumatic stress disorder (PTSD). However, the courts have recognised that this is not the only kind of

---

[25] *Haynes v Harwood* [1935] 1 KB 146.

[26] *Wagner v International Rly Co* 232 NY Rep 176 (1921).

[27] *Baker v T E Hopkins & Son Ltd* [1959] 3 All ER 225; *Chadwick v British Transport Commission* [1967] 2 All ER 945.

[28] In *Videan v British Transport Commission* [1963] 2 QB 650 it was held that a duty was owed to a stationmaster rescuing his small son who had been trespassing on the lines. At that time, no duty was owed to the child trespasser. But the duty owed to the stationmaster was not derived from, or dependent upon, any duty owed to the son. An emergency requiring a rescue was foreseeable, thus creating a direct, personal duty towards the stationmaster.

[29] *White v CC of South Yorkshire Police* [1999] 1 All ER 1.

[30] *Ogwo v Taylor* [1988] AC 431.

[31] See American Psychological Association, *American Diagnostic and Statistical Manual of Mental Disorder* (4th revised edn, 2000), xxxi. See also Handford, *Mullany and Handford's Tort Liability for Psychiatric Damage* (2nd edn, 2006), chs 2–3. The latter work indicates that the term preferred in psychiatry is 'psychiatric disorder': ibid at 30.

compensable psychiatric harm. Thus, in *Vernon v Bosley*, Thorpe LJ stated that while PTSD is a useful classification, it could not 'be adopted in personal injury litigation as the yardstick by which the plaintiff's success or failure is to be measured'.[32] Indeed, more recent times have seen the courts considering arguments for redress in negligence not based upon any external 'event' giving rise to claims for psychiatric illness, including cases in which the claimant has been exposed to some substance (such as asbestos) which causes him to 'fear for the future'.[33]

In terms of what counts as *compensable psychiatric harm* within the law of negligence, consider *Rothwell v Chemical & Insulating Co Ltd*:[34]

> Cs were negligently exposed to asbestos by their employers. They developed pleural plaques, which are 'areas of fibrous thickening of the pleural membrane which surrounds the lungs'.[35] These caused no symptoms. However, because the plaques indicated the presence of asbestos fibres in the lungs, Cs developed anxiety about their conditions, fearing that they would eventually suffer from a life-threatening disease, such as asbestosis or mesothelioma.

The House of Lords affirmed a number of important propositions. First, the claimants had not suffered any form of compensable *physical* harm.[36] Second, the mere *risk* of physical injury arising in the future was not a form of compensable harm.[37] Third, there could be no recovery for mere *grief or anxiety*.[38] These temporary emotional states the law expects persons to endure without compensation. Fourth, the court rejected the claim that it was permissible to *aggregate* the various hurts that the claimants had suffered – the pleural plaques and the anxiety derived from fear for the future – because the sum was greater than its individual parts.[39] Lord Scott put it most bluntly in stating that 'nought plus nought equals nought'.[40]

Consider next the companion case of *Grieves v FT Everard & Sons Ltd*, in which the claimant *had* suffered a psychiatric illness. The concern here was not that the claimant failed to meet the threshold of recognised harm, but about the *manner in which that harm was caused* (its aetiology):

> Again, C was negligently exposed to asbestos dust by his former employers. Following an x-ray examination, he developed clinical depression as a result of his fears that he would eventually develop a life-threatening asbestos-related illness.

---

[32] [1997] 1 All ER 577, at 610. See also ibid at 607.

[33] The full breadth of such claims in considered in Handford, *Mullany and Handford's Tort Liability for Psychiatric Damage* (2nd edn, 2006), ch 27.

[34] [2008] 1 AC 281.

[35] Ibid at [1].

[36] Ibid at [2], [50], [63], and [88].

[37] Ibid at [67], and [88]. See also *Gregg v Scott* [2005] 2 AC 176.

[38] [2008] 1 AC 281, at [2], [66], and [89]. See also, eg, *McLoughlin v O'Brian* [1983] AC 410, at 431; *White v CC of South Yorkshire Police* [1999] 2 AC 455, at 465 and 491; *W v Essex CC* [2001] 2 AC 592, at 600.

[39] [2008] 1 AC 281, at [17] and [73].

[40] Ibid at [73].

Absent some special knowledge about the claimant's durability, it had to be assumed that the claimant was of ordinary mental fortitude.[41] The problem was that it was not reasonably foreseeable to an employer that the claimant would suffer illness in this manner.[42] There was no relevant external event, such as occurs in the more usual psychiatric illness case, with respect to which it had been foreseeable that he might suffer a psychiatric reaction.[43]

Grieves cannot be taken to rule out the possibility that an employer (or other defendant) may be liable in negligence for exposure to asbestos or other substance causing a psychiatric illness because of the claimant's fears of developing a fatal or other disease.[44] However, it does emphasise the importance in such cases of knowledge on the part of the claimant of a susceptibility to psychiatric illness.[45] Unless there was some reason for the defendant to know or have reason to suspect, prior to a failure in care, such vulnerability, claims of this nature will be unavailable.

Much of the case law in this area has concerned allegations of negligence involving some *external event that has occurred* and as a result of which the claimant has suffered a psychiatric illness. In such cases, the claims frequently involve causation of PTSD. As a general proposition, the courts have been very wary of permitting a wide ambit of liability. The reasons for caution are easy to catalogue. They include the risk of fictitious claims and excessive litigation, the problems of proving the causal link between the defendant's negligence and the injury to the claimant, and the difficulties of putting a monetary value on such harm. Gradual, if belated, judicial recognition of the genuine nature of psychiatric harm led to the abandonment of the nineteenth-century attitude that non-physical harm to the person was totally irrecoverable.[46] The courts began to award damages for what was for many years called 'nervous shock'.[47] A claimant who became mentally ill because of the shock to his nervous system caused by an incident that either threatened his own safety,[48] or involved witnessing exceptionally distressing injuries to others,[49] could in certain circumstances[50] recover compensation for psychiatric harm.[51] PTSD can follow from an external incident in a number of ways. First, and most obviously, a claimant who suffers severe physical injury, for

---

[41] [2008] 1 AC 281, at [26] and [99].

[42] Ibid at [57], [75], and [99]–[100].

[43] Ibid at [30].

[44] Cf *Grieves v FT Everard & Sons Ltd* [2008] 1 AC 281, at [2].

[45] See the test laid out in *Hatton v Sutherland* [2002] ICR 613 (applied in *Barber v Somerset CC* [2004] 1 WLR 1089).

[46] For the nineteenth-century view see *Victorian Railways Comrs v Coultas* (1888) 13 App Cas 222. For an analysis of how the law has always 'limped behind medicine' see Sprince [1998] LS 55.

[47] The phrase can be misleading and should be regarded as no more than a customary means of grouping together cases where C becomes mentally ill as a consequence of an assault upon his nervous system: see *Alcock v CC of South Yorkshire* [1991] 4 All ER 907, at 923. See also *McLoughlin v O'Brian* [1982] 2 All ER 298, at 301.

[48] *Dulieu v White & Sons* [1901] 2 KB 669.

[49] *Hambrook v Stokes Bros* [1925] 1 KB 141.

[50] Note the refusal of damages in *Hay (Bourhill) v Young* [1943] AC 92.

[51] The term now preferred to nervous shock: *Attia v British Gas plc* [1987] 3 All ER 455, at 462.

example in a road accident, may well also succumb to mental illness triggered by the terror of the accident and his consequent pain and suffering. Second, a person may be so badly treated following a traumatic event that psychiatric harm ensues.[52] Third, an accident may occur in which the claimant is involved but in which he suffers no bodily injury, only shock and fear that cause psychiatric illness. Fourth, the claimant may not be directly involved in the original accident, and be at no personal risk of physical injury, but nonetheless witness injury to others and suffer psychiatric harm in consequence. (A good example would be a mother who witnesses an horrific injury to her children.)[53] In such cases, the claimant is classified as a *secondary* victim of the defendant's negligence. A series of decisions have set limits, often referred to as 'control mechanisms', on who may claim as a secondary victim of psychiatric harm.[54] These limits will be discussed fully later. But here it suffices to note that they are primarily intended to keep litigation in this area within manageable limits. In essence, and very briefly, to recover damages, a *secondary* victim must generally establish (1) a close tie of love or affection with the primary victim (such a tie being presumed to exist between certain persons such as spouses, or parents and their children) and (2) proximity in time and place to the accident.

Victims of psychiatric illness in the first three categories are *regarded as primary* victims of the defendant's negligence. A person who suffers psychiatric illness as well as physical injury causes us no problems. Such psychiatric harm is part and parcel of his claim for injury. There is ño decided case in which liability has been imposed for a claimant in the second category, which leaves only the third category. Here *Page v Smith*[55] is the leading case.

C was involved in a collision with a car negligently driven by D. He suffered no physical injury. However, almost immediately, he succumbed to a revival in an acute form of the chronic fatigue syndrome (ME) from which he had periodically suffered in the past. He became so ill that he was unable to work. D argued that, as C suffered no physical injury, he was not liable for injury through shock. A normal person with no previous history of psychiatric illness would not be expected to become ill as a result of a minor collision.

The House of Lords found for the claimant. In cases involving 'nervous shock', they said, a clear distinction must be made between primary and secondary victims. In claims by the latter, certain 'control mechanisms' limit the potential liability for psychiatric harm. Shock in a person of normal fortitude must be foreseeable. But Mr Page,

---

[52] See, eg, *Brooks v MPC* [2005] 1 WLR 1495 (although on the facts, there was no duty owed by the police to C, a murder witness). Consider, too, *McLoughlin v Grovers* [2002] QB 1312 where the traumatic occurrence was C's wrongful conviction due to the negligence of his solicitors; it was held that C had an arguable case that he may be entitled to recover in negligence for the psychiatric illness he developed as a consequence of that wrongful conviction.

[53] Eg, *Hambrook v Stokes Bros* [1925] 1 KB 141.

[54] *Bourhill v Young* [1943] AC 92; *McLoughlin v O'Brian* [1983] 1 AC 410. The leading case is now in *Alcock v CC of South Yorkshire Police* [1992] 1 AC 310.

[55] [1996] AC 155, neatly dissected in Bailey and Nolan [2010] CLJ 495.

the claimant, was a primary victim of the defendant's negligence. It was readily fore-seeable that he would be exposed to personal injury, and physical and psychiatric harm were not to be regarded as different kinds of damage. Once *physical* injury to a primary victim is foreseeable, he can recover both for any actual physical harm that he suffers and for any recognised psychiatric illness ensuing from the defendant's breach of duty. Indeed, even if only distress to the claimant is foreseeable, he or she may none-theless sue in respect of any recognised form of psychiatric harm that goes beyond *mere distress* even though that specific illness was not foreseeable.[56] Even so, in the case of primary (just like secondary) victims, damages are available only in relation to a recognised psychiatric illness.[57]

Page v Smith has been subject to criticism,[58] in part because tests for foreseeability in negligence usually encompass a specific form of damage (as discussed in the pre-vious chapter). The test in *Page* conflates two kinds of damage, which are caused (in typical cases) in different ways. Personal injuries usually arise from external impact, whereas psychiatric illness always develops indirectly through a *reaction* to events. The limitations of the *Page* test have become obvious in subsequent cases. It was held in *Grieves v FT Everard & Sons Ltd*, considered already, to be confined to the kind of factual situation that it involved – that is, an external traumatic event. It would not apply in cases of negligent exposure to asbestos, radiation, or contamination of food which had caused no proven physical harm, but which led to anxiety and subsequent psychiatric illness.[59]

The conditions for liability to a *secondary victim* established by the case law up to 1982 generally required that the claimant should be present at the scene of the acci-dent, or very close by, so that he perceived what happened with his unaided senses. But then *McLoughlin v O'Brian*[60] was decided, the facts of which were as follows:

> C's husband and three children were involved in a car accident caused by D's negligence. All four of her family were injured, one so seriously that she died almost immediately. An hour later, a friend told her of the accident at her home two miles away. They went to the hospital where C was told of the death and then saw the three remaining family members before they had been properly cleaned up. Though a woman of reasonable fortitude, C suf-fered severe shock, organic depression, and a change of personality.

---

[56] *Essa v Laing* [2004] ICR 746.
[57] But where the primary victim suffers physically and psychologically, the psychological harm need not be a recognised psychiatric condition. Thus, in *Gregg v Scott* [2005] 2 AC 176, it was held that C could claim for the anxiety caused by a physical condition for which D was answerable in negligence: the anxiety merely falls within the recognised head of 'pain and suffering' that have long been recognised as recoverable in conjunction with physical injuries.
[58] See Jones 'Liability for Psychiatric Damage: Searching for a Path between Pragmatism and Principle' in Neyers (ed), *Emerging Issues in Tort Law* (2007), ch 5; Bailey and Nolan [2010] CLJ 495.
[59] [2007] UKHL 39, at [31]–[34], [53]–[54], [77], [95], and [97]. This ruling has been argued to be arbitrary, adding 'further complexity and uncertainty to the law': Bailey and Nolan [2010] CLJ 495, 524.
[60] [1983] 1 AC 410. For more recent insistence on first-hand experience of traumatic sights, see *Palmer v Tees HA* [1999] Lloyd's Rep Med 351.

The House of Lords insisted that the claimant should demonstrate her proximity in time and space to the traumatic events. But they held also that, in coming upon the 'immediate aftermath' of the accident in which her family had been so grievously injured, she was well within the scope of the duty to avoid nervous shock. Witnessing the aftermath, they said, was equivalent to witnessing the incident itself since nothing in the horror of the sight that met her had changed.

Beyond that, there were distinct differences of approach among their Lordships. But, since the decision was made within the now discredited test for the imposition of a duty laid down by Lord Wilberforce in *Anns v Merton London Borough Council*,[61] these divergent views need not concern us here.[62]

The leading case on liability to secondary victims for psychiatric harm is now *Alcock v Chief Constable of South Yorkshire Police*.[63]

In April 1989, 95 people died and over 400 were injured when South Yorkshire police allowed an excessive number of spectators to crowd into Hillsborough football ground. People were quite literally crushed to death. Cs' actions were for psychiatric illness ensuing from the horror of what had happened to their relatives (or in one case, a fiancé).

In the House of Lords, two issues were pre-eminent: first, could relatives other than parents or spouses bring an action for psychiatric harm? Second, could those who witnessed coverage of the disaster on television recover?

(1) Their Lordships refused to prescribe rigid categories of potential secondary claimants in nervous shock claims. They held that there must generally be a close tie of love and affection between the claimant and the primary victim of the sort normally enjoyed by spouses and by parents and children.[64] Siblings and other more remote relatives, it was held, would generally fall outside such a relationship in the absence of special factors. Consequently, claims by brothers, sisters, and brothers-in-law failed in *Alcock*, while the claim on the part of a fiancé was allowed. However, claims by more distant relatives were not totally debarred. So, for instance, a grandmother who had brought up a grandchild since infancy might qualify upon proof of the required bond of love and affection.

(2) Lord Ackner suggested that, in cases of exceptional horror, where a reasonably strong-nerved individual would suffer shock-induced psychiatric injury, even a bystander unrelated to the victim should be able to recover.[65]

(3) A degree of proximity in time and space between the claimant and the accident is required. The claimant must normally either witness the accident himself or come upon the aftermath within a very short period of time.[66] Identifying a

---

[61] [1978] AC 727, considered in ch 2.
[62] Details can be found in the 10th edition of this work.
[63] [1992] 1 AC 310.
[64] [1991] 4 All ER 907, at 914, 919–20, 930, and 935.
[65] Ibid at 919. See also at 930.
[66] Ibid at 914–15, 920–21, 930–2, and 936. See also *Hunter v British Coal* [1998] 2 All ER 97.

relative several hours after death will not usually suffice. Nor will witnessing the accident via the medium of television generally be sufficient.[67] Parents who watched the Hillsborough disaster unfold on television had their claims rejected. Television pictures cannot normally be equated with actual sight or hearing of the event or its aftermath, especially since the broadcasting code of ethics prohibits graphic coverage of individual suffering.[68] Once again, there might be exceptional cases where simultaneous broadcasts of a disaster that cannot be edited will equate to personal presence at the accident.[69] Indeed, in the Court of Appeal, Nolan LJ gave the example of a balloon carrying children at some live broadcast event suddenly bursting into flames.[70]

(4) The relevant psychiatric illness must be shown to result from the trauma of the event or its immediate aftermath.[71] Psychiatric illness resulting from being informed of a loved one's death, however gruesome the circumstances, is not recoverable in English law.[72] So, if a young child is crushed by falling masonry at school and, within an hour, her mother comes to her deathbed at the hospital, the mother may recover for the trauma of coming upon the immediate aftermath of the accident. But, if the child's father has a heart attack when told over the phone of the girl's fate, his loss remains irrecoverable.[73]

Their Lordships in *Alcock* adopted an avowedly pragmatic approach to psychiatric harm. They rejected a simplistic approach based on fixed categories of who can recover, and in what circumstances. They also refused to extend liability for psychiatric harm indefinitely. Lord Oliver expressly conceded that he could not 'regard the present state of the law as either satisfactory or logically defensible'.[74] He suggested further that Parliamentary intervention may be timely.[75]

A nice point was left open following *Alcock*. Could a primary victim be liable for harm to another person caused by shock where he was the author of his own injury? In *Ogwo v Taylor*,[76] a negligent householder was liable to a fire-fighter injured in a fire caused by his carelessness. But, in *Greatorex v Greatorex*,[77] it was held that a drunk

---

[67] [1991] 4 All ER 907, at 937.

[68] Ibid at 921.

[69] Ibid at 921 and 931.

[70] [1991] 3 All ER 88, at 122.

[71] After *Vernon v Bosley* [1997] 1 All ER 577 it is no longer necessary that it be exclusively shock that triggers C's illness.

[72] [1991] 4 All ER 907, at 914–15. Cf *Tame v NSW* [2002] HCA 35 and *Gifford v Strang Patrick Stevedoring Pty Ltd* [2003] HCA 33. Now that the rule in *Wilkinson v Downton* [1897] 2 QB 57 has been viewed as anomalous (see ch 8), and preferably seen as a case involving negligence, it is a moot point whether in future this rather arbitrary obstacle to recovery for shock-induced psychiatric illness will be upheld in any pertinent future litigation.

[73] As it would be if his illness were precipitated by identifying his daughter at the mortuary next day.

[74] [1991] 4 All ER 907, at 932.

[75] Ibid at 931.

[76] [1988] AC 431.

[77] [2000] 1 WLR 1970.

driver who caused an accident did not owe a duty of care to his father (who happened to be the fireman called to the scene of the accident) in respect of his father's psychiatric harm. To impose such a duty would be, the court said, too much of an imposition on the drunken man's right to conduct himself broadly as he pleased. Our self-determination, the court reasoned, involves the 'right' to injure ourselves without owing others a duty when they witness our injury. Perhaps one distinction between the two cases is that, in *Ogwo*, the claimant suffered physical harm (burns), whereas the fireman in *Greatorex* suffered only psychiatric harm. But as the House of Lords, relying on the formulations contained in the Limitation Acts pointed out in *Page v Smith*,[78] psychiatric harm is merely part of the broader species, 'personal injury'. A second possible distinction is that, in *Ogwo*, the fireman would have satisfied the test of primary victim set out in *White v Chief Constable of South Yorkshire Police*,[79] whereas the claimant in *Greatorex* was in no personal danger (nor in a position to claim reasonably that he thought he was in personal danger). But this, too, is unconvincing, for the primary/secondary victim distinction operates to differentiate between two types of claimant, both of whom are suing for *psychiatric harm*. A third explanation might be that a person rescuing property (as in *Ogwo*) will be owed a duty more readily than a person rescuing fellow human beings (as in *Greatorex*). But such a distinction – if we accept that the law seeks to treat rescuers kindly – runs counter to the usual hierarchy of protected interests in tort law. Perhaps the simplest explanation of the decision in *Greatorex* is the one implicit in the fact that not a single mention of *Ogwo* was made in that case!

Alcock might, at first sight, appear to have settled some firm principles delimiting liability for psychiatric harm. But the decision provoked as many questions as it answered. Let us look, first, at liability to bystanders. Lord Ackner, as we have noted, suggested that a truly horrific disaster might entitle even unrelated bystanders to recover damages for psychiatric illness. Yet consider *McFarlane v EE Caledonia Ltd*.[80]

> C witnessed the destruction of an oil rig from aboard a support vessel involved in attempts to rescue survivors of the explosion which tore apart the rig. He was not himself involved in the rescue effort and was far enough away from the burning rig to be in no personal danger. However, a more horrifying spectacle is difficult to imagine.

The Court of Appeal refused his claim. A rescuer personally at risk in such circumstances would have been entitled to compensation as a participant in the terrifying event. But, crucially, the claimant was neither a rescuer nor otherwise a participant (that is, at no objective risk nor in a position reasonably to believe himself to be at risk).[81] As a bystander only, it was not foreseeable that he would suffer such shock.

---

[78] [1996] AC 155.
[79] [1999] 1 All ER 1.
[80] [1994] 2 All ER 1. For critique, see Murphy [1995] LS 415. See also *Hegarty v EE Caledonia Ltd* [1996] 1 Lloyd's Rep 413.
[81] [1994] 2 All ER 1, at 13.

Stuart-Smith LJ effectively sought to close the door, left ajar in *Alcock*, on liability to bystanders. Practical and policy reasons, he said, militated against such liability: reactions to horrific events were 'entirely subjective'.[82]

White v Chief Constable of South Yorkshire Police[83] further explored the boundaries of *Alcock*.

> Cs were police officers who claimed damages for psychiatric illness resulting from their professional involvement in events at the Hillsborough disaster in which many died or were seriously injured in the crush at the football ground. Five of the six claimants assisted the injured and sought to ensure that, subsequent to the full height of the disaster, no further danger faced those leaving the ground. The sixth claimant was on duty at the mortuary. None of the officers were exposed to any personal risk of physical injury. The Court of Appeal held by 2–1 that a duty of care was owed to the officers actually present at the ground (but not to the one at the mortuary).[84] The decision provoked outrage from the many relatives of those killed and injured at Hillsborough who had been refused compensation in the *Alcock* case. The House of Lords reversed the findings of the Court of Appeal, openly acknowledging the argument that it would be perceived as unacceptable to compensate police officers at the ground in the course of their job and, yet, deny any remedy to brothers and sisters who saw their relatives die horrifically.[85]

By a majority of 4–1, their Lordships ruled that the claimants were not to be classified as primary victims of the defendants' negligence. They observed that an employer's duty to safeguard his employees from personal injury is simply part of the ordinary law of negligence. The claimants' argument (resting upon the assertion that their relationship with the chief constable was akin to a contract of employment) therefore failed: they were in no better position than normal bystanders to sue in respect of psychiatric harm simply by virtue of this relationship. Employers undoubtedly owe a duty where an employee is subjected to such a burdensome workload that stress-related illness is readily foreseeable.[86] But, where it is a form of psychiatric harm (as opposed to mere distress) that results, not from anything directly done to the employee by the employer but, rather, from his traumatic experience of what is done to others, he is to be treated in exactly the same way as any other secondary victim.[87] The Hillsborough police

---

[82] [1994] 2 All ER 1, at 14.
[83] [1999] 1 All ER 1, overturning the decision of the Court of Appeal.
[84] *White v CC of South Yorkshire Police* [1997] 1 All ER 540.
[85] [1999] 1 All ER 1, at 48.
[86] See, eg, *Walker v Northumberland CC* [1995] 1 All ER 737; *Hatton v Sutherland* [2002] 2 All ER 1. (Analogous principles apply in relation to the duty owed by a school to a bullied pupil: *Bradford-Smart v West Sussex CC* [2002] 1 FCR 425.) It may be material to the question of negligence whether, in a job that is known to be stressful, the employer failed to provide counselling services: *Hartman v South Essex Mental Health and Community Care NHS Trust* [2005] ICR 782.
[87] In *Farley v Skinner* [2002] AC 732 it was held that C would have a contractual claim in respect of distress arising out of a breach *where the contract was specifically designed to protect C from distress*. Extrapolating from this, there seems no reason in principle why a tort claim could not be brought in respect of distress if a *tortious duty* to protect C from distress could be found.

officers witnessed the disaster at close quarters, but lacked the requisite close ties of love or affection with the victims in order to be able to sue.

The claimants' alternative argument was that they were owed a duty of care in their capacity as rescuers. Yet here, too, the House of Lords insisted that, *in relation to psychiatric harm*, rescuers must meet the same conditions as any other witnesses of injury to third parties. They must either objectively have exposed themselves to danger or have reasonably believed themselves to have done so.[88] They must also meet the other conditions limiting recovery by secondary victims outlined above.

It appears, then, that *White* has to some extent closed the door on further expansion of liability for psychiatric harm. On the other hand, the courts' repeated insistence upon shock-induced injury now enjoys a lenient enough interpretation so as to embrace a reaction to a protracted event that lasted some 36 hours.[89] Equally, a further important issue that has never much troubled the judiciary in this context is that of the application of the 'egg-shell skull' rule. It may be invoked with respect to psychiatric harm just as it may in relation to physical injury.[90] Thus, if psychiatric harm would have been foreseeable in respect of a reasonably mentally tough individual, the extended degree to which the claimant actually suffers psychiatric harm is irrelevant.[91] And even if psychiatric harm per se is not foreseeable, so long as the physical injury which triggers, or otherwise leads to, psychiatric harm is foreseeable, the claimant may nonetheless recover for the psychiatric illness.[92]

As adumbrated, until the decision in *Vernon v Bosley*,[93] the courts had insisted that a secondary victim of psychiatric harm must show PTSD. In that case, the facts were as follows:

C's two young children were passengers in a car driven by D, their nanny, when it veered off the road and crashed into a river. C did not witness the original accident, but was called to the scene immediately afterwards and watched unsuccessful attempts to salvage the car and rescue his children. These efforts failed and the children drowned. C became mentally ill and his business and marriage both failed. D accepted that C's illness resulted from the tragic deaths of his children, but argued that his illness was caused not by the shock of what he experienced at the riverside, but by pathological grief at his loss in an illness, distinct from PTSD, called pathological grief disorder.

---

[88] See also *Cullin v London Fire and Civil Defence Authority* [1999] PIQR P314.

[89] In *North Glamorgan NHS Trust v Walters* [2003] PIQR P232, the Court of Appeal allowed a claim in respect of a woman who 'reeled under successive blows [to her psyche]' as the condition of her child visibly worsened before her eyes when medics failed to diagnose that the child was suffering from acute hepatitis.

[90] *Brice v Brown* [1984] 1 All ER 997; *Vernon v Bosley* [1997] 1 All ER 577.

[91] *Brice v Brown* [1984] 1 All ER 997.

[92] *Simmons v British Steel Plc* [2004] ICR 565 at [55], per Lord Rodger (with whose speech the remaining members of the House of Lords agreed). For the argument that the egg-shell skull principle is inappropriately applied in the context of psychiatric harm, see Jones, 'Liability for Psychiatric Damage: Walking a Path Between Pragmatism and Principle' in Neyers (ed), *Emerging Issues in Tort Law* (2007), ch 5.

[93] [1997] 1 All ER 577.

The Court of Appeal held that, although damages for ordinary grief and bereavement remain irrecoverable,[94] a secondary victim can recover damages for psychiatric illness where he establishes the general pre-conditions for such a claim (set out above), and that the negligence of the defendant caused or contributed to his mental illness. The claimant in this case was able to do so and could recover compensation regardless of the fact that his illness consisted partly of an *abnormal* grief reaction.[95] On the other hand, the decision in *Vernon v Bosley* does not imply that every person who loses a loved one and becomes ill through grief can sue the negligent individual responsible for the death of the primary victim. For example, the grandmother in Newcastle who is told of the death in a car crash of her grandson in Norwich has no claim in negligence. She cannot establish the requisite conditions limiting any claim by secondary victims.

As Lord Steyn admitted in *White v Chief Constable of South Yorkshire*, 'the law on the recovery of compensation for pure psychiatric harm is a patchwork quilt of distinctions which are difficult to justify'.[96] Even after judicial attempts to clarify the principles governing liability for psychiatric harm and to package claims neatly according to a scheme of primary and secondary victims, loose ends remain. Reflect on the following examples:

(1) A final year student arrives home to witness her hall of residence burning to the ground. In her room are all her revision notes and the only copy of her dissertation. Unsurprisingly, she succumbs to clinical depression. Can she recover damages? If the fire was caused by faulty wiring and the university can be shown to have been negligent in its maintenance of the residence, could she argue that she is a primary victim because her psychiatric illness is consequent on the damage to her property? Might she assert, if a secondary victim, 'a close tie of love and affection to her work'? In *Attia v British Gas plc*,[97] decided before *Alcock*, a woman did win damages after suffering a nervous breakdown caused by witnessing her home burn down.

(2) A second, equally unlucky, student is working in a university laboratory when an explosion rocks the building. He feels the shockwaves and hears the blast, but only minimal damage ensues in the laboratory where he is at the time. Even so, it is immediately clear that the neighbouring laboratory has been completely destroyed and his four closest friends were working there. His fears are justified.[98] All four were killed in the blast. The surviving student succumbs to

---

[94] See also *Alcock v CC of South Yorkshire Police* [1991] 4 All ER 907, at 917.

[95] Note that the courts are prepared to make a discount in the award of damages where C's grief merges with a recognisable psychiatric disorder: see, eg, *Rahman v Arearose Ltd* [2001] QB 351. Furthermore, D will only be liable for that part of C's psychiatric harm that he actually caused: *Hatton v Sutherland* [2002] 2 All ER 1.

[96] [1999] 1 All ER 1, at 38.

[97] [1988] QB 304.

[98] For a case on broadly analogous facts, where C succeeded, see *Dooley v Cammell Laird & Co Ltd* [1951] 1 Lloyd's Rep 271. In *White*, Lord Hoffmann suggested that this case might have to be treated as falling outside the general rules and control mechanisms for secondary victims.

psychiatric illness. If he shows that his illness resulted from reasonable fear to himself, does he recover as a primary victim? If he admits that it was the shock of his friends' fate which triggered his illness, does he fail because of the absence of the requisite 'close tie of love and affection'?

This area of the law is unquestionably very complex. Reform is often called for. Three very different solutions have been advanced. Stapleton advocates the abolition of recovery in tort for pure psychiatric harm.[99] She argues the case for a return to the harsh, but clear rules of the Victorian judges contending that 'no reasonable boundaries for the cause of action [can] be found and this [is] an embarrassment to the law'. Handford contends that no special rules should limit claims for psychiatric illness.[100] Foreseeability of psychiatric injury should be the only condition of recovery of compensation. Finally, the Law Commission recommends a 'middle way'.[101] The condition that secondary victims enjoy a close tie of love or affection with the individual who suffers physical harm would stay. All other 'control mechanisms' would be abolished.[102]

SECTION 3   DAMAGE TO PROPERTY

Recognition of a duty to avoid physical damage to another's property, as much as to his person, raises no unique problem of principle.[103] Should a negligent driver manage by the narrowest of margins to prevent his vehicle actually injuring me, but the vehicle does tear a hole in my new designer suit, I may recover the cost of the suit without problems. Should the careless driver, swerving to avoid me, crash into my colleague's front wall, he may recover the cost of repairing the wall. Whether the damaged property is a chattel or real property, a duty to take reasonable care not to inflict that kind of harm arises.[104] Having said so much, we need to examine two assumptions behind these statements: (1) that the subject matter of the claim is property damage and (2) that the claimant is the right person to sue.

In its core conception, property damage involves some deleterious change in the physical state or structure of property.[105] These changes impair the functional characteristics of the thing in question. Whether the law will regard the physical change

---

[99] Stapleton, 'In Restraint of Tort' in Birks (ed), *Frontiers of Liability* (1994), 83.

[100] *Mullany and Handford's Tort Liability for Psychiatric Damage: The Law of Nervous Shock* (2nd edn, 2006). See also Teff [1998] CLJ 91.

[101] *Liability for Psychiatric Illness*, Law Com No 249 (1998).

[102] For the argument that most of the extant control mechanisms can be rationalised in terms of the general test for the imposition of a duty of care, see Murphy [1995] LS 415.

[103] But note that foreseeability alone is not enough: *Marc Rich & Co AG v Bishop Rock Marine Co Ltd* [1996] AC 211.

[104] [1986] AC 785. See also *The Mineral Transporter* [1986] AC 1; *Tate & Lyle Industries Ltd v Greater London Council* [1983] 2 AC 509. Where, however, the parties are neighbouring property owners, the action may lie in nuisance rather than negligence.

[105] Witting [2002] CLJ 189.

as damage will, at the borderline, depend on 'the evidence and the circumstances'.[106] There are some rather difficult borderline cases. For example, the need to decontaminate a ship after it has been doused in acid, which causes no tangible damage to the ship, has been characterised as physical damage.[107] A similar interpretation has been placed on the ingress of water into a gas supply line such that householders become deprived of a gas supply for several days.[108] In order to be able to recover for property damage, the claimant must suffer more than merely trivial harm.[109]

Property damage is often the result of the operation of some external force, but this need not be so. Cases like *Spartan Steel & Alloys Ltd v Martin & Co (Contractors) Ltd*[110] indicate that the positive acts of the defendant might make it foreseeable that the claimant will react in a certain way causative of damage, perhaps in order to avoid worse consequences occurring. Alternatively, the very failure of the defendant to do something that should have been done might cause damage to property.

The House of Lords in *Leigh & Sillivan Ltd v Aliakmon Shipping Co Ltd* confirmed the rule that a duty in respect of loss or damage to property is owed only to a person having 'legal ownership of, or a possessory title to, the property concerned at the time when the loss or damage occurred'.[111] Should an old house in the process of conversion to flats be destroyed by a fire caused by negligence, only the owner of the house, or a tenant, may recover compensation. The builders, the plumbers, the decorators, all of whom lose out on valuable contracts to convert the property, are left remediless. Contractual rights in relation to property may well be adversely affected by loss or damage to that property, but they are insufficient to give rise to a duty of care.

It has always been clear that physical damage to, or defects in, property which simply render it less than value for money, but *not* dangerous, will be classified as economic loss. So, if one buys a central heating boiler which heats the house inefficiently and at vast expense, the loss one suffers is economic loss alone, readily recoverable in contract, but not normally in tort. Where the defective property is dangerous, however, a line of authority relating to buildings suggests that, if there is an imminent danger of damage to person or other property, the cost of rectifying the defect and avoiding the danger could be categorised as physical damage, although no tangible physical damage has yet materialised.[112] The decision of the House of Lords in *Murphy v Brentwood District Council*[113] rejected that line of authority as being close to heresy. Physical damage means just what it says: actual physical harm to other property. Where no

---

[106] *Hunter v Canary Wharf Ltd* [1997] AC 655, 676.

[107] *The Orjula* [1995] 2 Lloyd's Rep 395.

[108] *Anglian Water Services Ltd v Crawshaw Robbins Ltd* [2001] BLR 173.

[109] Reaffirmed in *Rothwell v Chemical & Insulating Co Ltd* [2008] 1 AC 281, a case concerned with personal injury.

[110] [1973] 1 QB 27.

[111] [1986] 2 All ER 145, at 149. See also *Simaan General Contracting Co v Pilkington Glass Ltd (No 2)* [1988] QB 758.

[112] *Batty v Metropolitan Property Realisations Ltd* [1978] QB 554; *Anns v Merton LBC* [1978] AC 728.

[113] [1991] 1 AC 398.

such damage has materialised, the loss caused by the need to repair defective property, to obviate the danger to person or property, constitutes merely an economic loss.

> C had purchased a house built on an in-filled site over a concrete raft foundation. In 1981 he discovered cracks in the house threatening the whole fabric of the property. Had he done nothing, the house might have collapsed on top of him. He sued the local council for negligently approving the plans for the foundations. The House of Lords held (inter alia) that the council could not be liable unless the builder would have been so liable.[114]

The first question to address was: what was the nature of C's loss? Their Lordships conceded that a builder of premises is subject to the same duty of care in tort as the manufacturers of chattels to 'avoid injury through defects in the premises to the person or property of those whom he should have in contemplation as likely to suffer such injury if care is not taken'.[115] So, to illustrate the points made, if the ceiling had actually collapsed on Mr Murphy, injuring him or destroying his piano, he might have had a claim for personal injuries or property damage against the builder. However, unless and until such actual physical damage occurs, the loss associated with the cost of making the house safe (or any diminution in its value) is purely economic.

One matter must be made clear. Mr Murphy's house at the time of his action was already suffering from serious cracks in the internal walls. Physical damage, you might have thought. Not so; for that damage arose from a defect in the very property in question. There was no question of the defective property causing damage *to* quite separate property. In an earlier decision of the House of Lords, it had been suggested that, where there was a 'complex structure', defects in one part of the structure causing damage to some other part might be regarded as having damaged 'other property'.[116] In *Murphy* this doctrine was questioned, yet not in terms rejected.[117] It has since received further tacit judicial approval.[118] There are, however, limits to this so-called complex structure exception. It can only apply if some distinct and separate item, which is combined with, but distinct from, the product in question, causes damage to the latter. For example, it might apply where C buys a house built by X with a central heating system made and installed by Y, and some months after the purchase an explosion damages the house (but injures no one). In such a circumstance, an action would lie against Y for his negligently manufactured item that has damaged separate property, the house itself.[119]

---

[114] For direct authority on the liability of builders see *Department of the Environment v Thomas Bates & Son Ltd* [1991] 1 AC 499.

[115] [1991] 1 AC 398, at 461. Note that the question of the liability of the council even for physical injury was left open.

[116] In *D & F Estates Ltd v Church Comrs for England* [1988] 2 All ER 992, at 1006–7.

[117] [1990] 2 All ER 908, at 926–8, 932–3, and 942.

[118] *Bacardi-Martini Beverages Ltd v Thomas Hardy Packaging Ltd* [2002] 1 Lloyd's Rep 62.

[119] *Murphy v Brentwood DC* [1990] 2 All ER 908, at 928.

Another limit to the complex structure approach applies where distinct product X is combined with distinct product Y to make product Z – for example, where two products (one a gas, one a liquid) are combined to make a carbonated drink. In such circumstances, it has been held to be inappropriate to speak in terms of the first product damaging the second because there is merely the production of a defective third product (product Z in our example).[120]

Where defective design causes another form of harm to occur – for example, fire damage that would have been avoided if a firewall had been properly designed and constructed – a duty of care *may* be imposed on the architects responsible. But the scope of their duty to a subsequent occupier of the premises is determined by reference to the extent of their original contractual duty. Thus, if they were only contracted to provide the plans for such a wall, but not to supervise its actual construction, no duty would be imposed in respect of the negligent erection of the wall.[121]

Finally in this context, it is worth noting that there can be some strange consequences to applying the *Murphy* doctrine. Assume an impecunious house-owner becomes aware of the worsening condition of her property, but she does nothing about it because she cannot afford to pay for the necessary repairs. Several months later the house collapses injuring her and damaging her priceless furniture. It seems she may then sue to recover compensation for that physical damage.[122] It should be noted that, in a number of cases, Commonwealth jurisdictions have declined to follow the *Murphy* 'doctrine' and preferred to allow claimants in circumstances analogous to Mr Murphy's to succeed.[123]

SECTION 4   UNPLANNED PREGNANCIES AND ECONOMIC LOSSES

Earlier in this chapter, we considered cases in which a duty of care was alleged to be owed to persons when unborn. Another category of case, not far removed from those, concerns the question whether damages are recoverable in respect of the birth of an unplanned baby subsequent to a negligently performed sterilisation. In *Udale v Bloomsbury Area Health Authority*,[124] Jupp J refused the mother compensation towards the upkeep of the child despite the defendant's admission of negligence. Limiting her damages to compensation for the discomfort of her pregnancy, he said that the child's

---

[120] *Bacardi-Martini Beverages Ltd v Thomas Hardy Packaging Ltd* [2002] 1 Lloyd's Rep 62. See further Tettenborn [2000] LMCLQ 338.

[121] *Bellefield Computer Services v E Turner & Sons Ltd* [2002] All ER (D) 272 (Dec).

[122] See *Nitrigin Eireann Teoranta v Inco Alloys Ltd* [1992] 1 All ER 854. Would D be able to plead contributory negligence? See ch 6.

[123] See, eg, *Invercargill CC v Hamlin* [1996] 1 All ER 756; *Bryan v Maloney* (1995) 182 CLR 609. Cf *Woolcock Street Investments Pty Ltd v CDG Pty Ltd* (2004) 216 CLR 515.

[124] [1983] 2 All ER 522.

birth was a 'blessing' and that the financial cost associated with such a 'blessing'[125] was irrecoverable. It offended both society's notion of what is right and the value afforded to human life. Jupp J also thought that the knowledge that his parents had claimed damages in respect of his birth might later distress and damage the child emotionally as he grew to maturity.

A year later, the Court of Appeal in *Emeh v Kensington Area Health Authority*[126] overruled Jupp J on the policy issue. They were unconvinced that the policy objections should prevent recovery of damages. Then, subsequently, in *McFarlane v Tayside Health Board*[127] – another case involving an unplanned child – the House of Lords suggested that damages could be made payable in respect of the pain and suffering associated with an unwanted pregnancy and confinement, but that the costs of bringing up the child were irrecoverable. Largely attempting to side-step the policy issues, their Lordships took the view that child-rearing costs were a form of pure economic loss and thus irrecoverable.[128] Furthermore, it would seem to make no difference if the woman who undergoes a negligently performed sterilisation operation and gives birth is herself disabled: the costs of rearing a healthy child remain irrecoverable.[129] On the other hand, the woman will now be able to recover a fixed sum of £15,000 for the loss of autonomy associated with having the child;[130] and if the child is born with a disability, the *special costs* associated with bringing up that disabled child following a negligently performed sterilisation will be recoverable.[131] Even so, the courts continue to take the view that the birth of *any* child is an unquantifiable benefit at least equivalent to the costs associated with raising a healthy child.[132]

Goodwill v British Pregnancy Advisory Service[133] is also worthy of mention in this context.

C sued the clinic which she alleged had failed to warn her lover of the potential failure rate of vasectomy. Their relationship had begun some time after his surgery. But C nonetheless argued that, had her partner been adequately advised by D, he would have communicated the relevant information to her so that she would then have taken appropriate

---

[125] 'I would have to regard the financial disadvantages as offset by her gratitude for the gift of a boy after four girls': [1983] 2 All ER 522, at 531, per Jupp J.

[126] [1985] QB 1012.

[127] [2000] 2 AC 59.

[128] On the other hand, Lord Steyn ([2000] AC 59, at 82) did recognise the cogency of the policy arguments against the imposition of liability based on the sanctity and value of human life, and Lord Hope (at 97) acknowledged the benefits associated with having a child that (were they calculable) would have to be set off against the costs of bringing up a child (were they recoverable, which they were not).

[129] *Rees v Darlington Memorial Hospital NHS Trust* [2004] 1 AC 309, at [9] and [18].

[130] Ibid at [123]. A subsequent endorsement of compensation for loss of autonomy can be found in the speech of Lord Steyn in *Chester v Afshar* [2005] 1 AC 134, at [18].

[131] *Parkinson v St James and Seacroft University Hospital NHS Trust* [2002] QB 266. This is so regardless of whether it is a matter of pure bad luck that the child comes to be born with a disability, or whether it manifests within a few weeks of birth: *Groom v Selby* (2001) 64 BMLR 47.

[132] *Rees v Darlington Memorial Hospital NHS Trust* [2004] 1 AC 309.

[133] [1996] 2 All ER 161.

contraceptive precautions. She argued that the birth of her child was a consequence of the defendants' negligence.

It was held that the defendants owed no duty of care to the claimant because the claimant was not a person whom they could have been expected to identify as immediately affected by the services they rendered to her lover. The man's future sexual partners were not persons for whose benefit the vasectomy was performed.

Classifying failed sterilisation as economic loss to the parent(s) – whether or not that claim succeeds – has a certain logic to it. The main purpose of compensation will be to meet the costs of raising the child. Yet classifying the loss in this way does not simplify the question of recoverability. The special costs of raising a disabled child, or the special costs of a disabled woman raising *any* child, are equally forms of pure economic loss, yet recoverable according to the Court of Appeal. It is submitted that these decisions were reached only by somewhat clumsy judicial manipulation of 'convenient aspects' of the tripartite *Caparo* test and the extended *Hedley Byrne* assumption of responsibility test. We considered each of these tests in general terms in the previous chapter and will return to their respective applications in the context of pure economic loss in due course. But it is worth setting out in full the compound reasoning of Brooke LJ in *Parkinson v St James and Seacroft University Hospital NHS Trust*.

> I would apply the battery of tests which the House of Lords has taught us to use…My route would be as follows: (i) for the reasons given by Waller LJ in *Emeh v Kensington and Chelsea and Westminster Area Health Authority* the birth of a child with congenital abnormalities was a foreseeable consequence of the surgeon's careless failure to clip a fallopian tube effectively; (ii) there was a very limited group of people who might be affected by this negligence, *viz* Mrs Parkinson and her husband (and, in theory, any other man with whom she had sexual intercourse before she realised that she had not been effectively sterilised); (iii) there is no difficulty in principle in accepting the proposition that the surgeon should be deemed to have assumed responsibility for the foreseeable and disastrous economic consequences of performing his services negligently; (iv) the purpose of the operation was to prevent Mrs Parkinson from conceiving any more children, including children with congenital abnormalities, and the surgeon's duty of care is strictly related to the proper fulfilment of that purpose; (v) parents in Mrs Parkinson's position were entitled to recover damages in these circumstances for 15 years between the decisions in *Emeh's* case and *McFarlane's* case, so that this is not a radical step forward into the unknown; (vi) for the reasons set out in (i) and (ii) above, Lord Bridge of Harwich's tests of foreseeability and proximity are satisfied, and for the reasons given by the Supreme Court of Florida in *Fassoulas v Ramey*[134] an award of compensation which is limited to the special upbringing costs associated with rearing a child with a serious disability would be fair, just and reasonable; (vii) if principles of distributive justice are called in aid, I believe that ordinary people would consider that it would be fair for the law to make an award in such a case, provided that it is limited to the extra expenses associated with the child's disability.[135]

---

[134]   450 So 2d 822 (1984).   [135]   [2002] QB 266, at [50].

SECTION 5   'PURE' ECONOMIC LOSS

We now turn to more orthodox cases of pure economic loss, arising with respect to business-oriented transactions and industrial accidents. Pure economic loss can be defined in the negative as a loss which is not physical damage or injury to intellectual property rights or reputation. It is, furthermore, not merely consequential upon these kinds of injury. The concern is with loss not immediately bound up in one of the primary interests of person, property (including intellectual property), or reputation. In positive terms, pure economic loss involves such things as money expended and opportunities to profit forgone as a result of the defendant's failure to take care. In the hierarchy of protected interests, the law of negligence offers a higher degree of protection to physical interests (and mental integrity) than to purely financial interests.[136]

Classifying the claimant's loss as purely economic does not preclude recovery of that loss altogether. But it does require the claimant to convince the court that the defendant owed him a duty to safeguard him against just that sort of loss. The courts are generally much less willing to find the existence of such a duty than a duty to protect others from physical injury or damage.[137] According to Lord Fraser in *The Mineral Transporter*, 'some limit or control mechanism has to be imposed on the liability of a wrongdoer towards those who have suffered economic damage as a consequence of his negligence'.[138] This restrictive approach to economic loss means that, in practice, economic loss is generally only recoverable when the claimant can establish a 'special relationship' between himself and the defendant,[139] or where the loss is consequential upon physical damage also suffered by the claimant. It is as well to note at the outset that 'special relationships' exist not just where the defendant has made a statement or proffered advice upon which the claimant relies, but also where he has undertaken to perform various forms of service. However, historical development of the law in this area makes it simpler to begin by examining economic loss resulting from inaccurate statements and advice.

(A) STATEMENTS AND 'SPECIAL RELATIONSHIPS'

Two difficulties beset the imposition of any duty to avoid making careless statements. First, there is generally a difference in the potential effects of careless words and careless acts. For while negligent acts will generally have a limited range of impact, negligent words may be widely broadcast without the consent or foresight of the speaker. Second, careless statements are, in general, likely to inflict only economic loss. (But it

---

[136] Reputation is protected through the tort of defamation, as to which see ch 20. Intellectual property rights are protected in torts such as passing off, as to which see ch 13.

[137] See Stapleton (1991) 107 LQR 249; id (1995) 111 LQR 301; Witting [2001] LS 481.

[138] [1985] 2 All ER 935, at 945. See also *White v CC of South Yorkshire Police* [1999] 1 All ER 1, at 31.

[139] *Williams v Natural Life Health Foods Ltd* [1998] 2 All ER 577; *Henderson v Merrett Syndicates Ltd* [1995] 2 AC 145.

should not be overlooked that careless words, whether written or spoken, do have the potential to cause harm to the person.[140] Thus, a doctor whose negligent certification of one claimant as a person of unsound mind leading to his detention in a mental hospital was held liable,[141] while a similar result was reached in a more recent case involving the negligent certification of a light aircraft as suitable to fly.)[142]

The development of the duty to avoid statements causing financial loss is inextricably linked to the troubled history of liability for pure economic loss in general. The original difficulty relating to economic loss resulting from careless statements was this. A person suffering economic loss through relying on a fraudulent statement could sue in the tort of deceit. In *Derry v Peek*,[143] the House of Lords held that to establish deceit the claimant must prove fraud – that is, broadly, that the defendant knew that his statement was untrue, or was reckless as to its untruth. Mere negligence was considered insufficient.[144]

The fallacy in this early case law was exposed by the House of Lords in the landmark decision in *Hedley Byrne & Co Ltd v Heller & Partners Ltd*.[145]

> Cs asked their bankers to inquire into the financial stability of a company with which they were having business dealings. Their bankers made inquiries of Ds, the company's bankers, who carelessly gave favourable references about the company. Reliance on these references caused Cs to lose £17,000. Cs sued Ds for the careless statements. The action failed only because Ds had expressly disclaimed any responsibility.

All five Law Lords re-examined the authorities on liability for careless statements. They rightly limited the rule in *Derry v Peek* to its proper function of defining the limits of the tort of deceit and thus held it to be irrelevant to the issue of whether a duty of care arose in negligence. The absence of a contract was also irrelevant. As Lord Devlin said:

> [a] promise given without consideration to perform a service cannot be enforced as a contract by the promisee, but if the service is in fact performed and done negligently the promisee can recover in an action in tort.[146]

Their Lordships were not however prepared to recognise a duty of care in respect of negligent statements on the basis of the *Donoghue v Stevenson* neighbour principle alone. For liability for statements resulting in economic loss to be imposed, some narrower test than that of foreseeability of the loss had to be satisfied.[147] The House was careful not to formulate rules that might expose a maker of careless statements to liability to a large indeterminate class of claimants. For instance, newspapers were

---

[140] See, eg, *Perrett v Collins* [1998] 2 Lloyd's Rep 255; *Sharp v Avery and Kerwood* [1938] 4 All ER 85; *Bird v Pearce* (1979) 77 LGR 753; *Clayton v Woodman & Son (Builders) Ltd* [1961] 3 All ER 249 (reversed on other grounds [1962] 2 All ER 33).

[141] *De Freville v Dill* (1927) 96 LJKB 1056.   [142] *Perrett v Collins* [1998] 2 Lloyd's Rep 255.

[143] (1889) 14 App Cas 337.   [144] *Candler v Crane, Christmas & Co* [1951] 2 KB 164.

[145] [1964] AC 465.   [146] Ibid at 526.

[147] Ibid at 483 and 537.

not to be accountable to everybody who read their advice columns and suffered loss through relying on their negligent advice.[148] Instead, their Lordships said that the claimant seeking to recover for negligent misstatements must establish that the statement was made within a relationship where the claimant could reasonably rely on the skill and care of the defendant in making the statement. He must show some 'special relationship' with the defendant which properly resulted in the defendant undertaking responsibility for the accuracy of the statements made. These concerns were captured succinctly by Lord Reid:

> [q]uite careful people often express definite opinions on social or informal occasions, even when they see that others are likely to be influenced by them; and they often do that without taking that care which they would take if asked for their opinion professionally, or in a business.[149]

Subsequent case law elucidated to some extent the crepuscular phrase 'special relationship'. In *Mutual Life and Citizens' Assurance Co Ltd v Evatt*,[150] Lord Diplock suggested that liability for misstatements should arise only in the context of certain professional relationships where giving advice was the primary purpose of the relationship. So, solicitors would be responsible for legal advice offered to clients, and stockbrokers for financial guidance, but an insurance company volunteering financial advice to a policyholder should not be liable.

The Court of Appeal, however, largely ignored *Evatt*. In *Chaudhry v Prabhakar*[151] the defendant who considered himself something of an expert on motor cars was held liable to his friend whom he agreed to assist with the purchase of a car when his advice proved to be negligent. Indeed, the trend up until 1989 appeared to be to allow a liberal interpretation of what constituted a special relationship. But two subsequent decisions of the House of Lords – *Caparo Industries plc v Dickman*[152] and *Smith v Bush*[153] – outlined more authoritatively the parameters of liability for economic loss arising from negligent advice.

Although *Caparo* was decided subsequently to *Smith v Bush*, it helps to consider *Caparo* first.

> Ds were auditors who acted for Fidelity plc. They had prepared annual accounts on the strength of which Cs bought shares in Fidelity and then mounted a successful takeover bid. Cs alleged that the accounts were inaccurate and misleading showing a large pre-tax profit when they should have recorded a sizeable loss. Had Cs been aware of this, they would never have bid for Fidelity.

---

[148] [1971] AC 793. A trade association making available certain information about its members' products does not owe a duty of care to those who use that information to contact a member and with whom a contract is subsequently entered into, given that the website itself 'urges independent inquiry': *Patchett v Swimming Pools & Allied Trades Association Ltd* [2009] EWCA Civ 717.

[149] [1964] AC 465, at 487.   [150] [1971] AC 793.

[151] [1988] 3 All ER 718. See also *Esso Petroleum Co Ltd v Mardon* [1976] QB 801.

[152] [1990] 2 AC 605.   [153] [1990] 1 AC 831.

The House of Lords found against the claimants on a preliminary point of law. The auditors owed no duty of care in respect of the accuracy of the accounts either to members of the public who relied on the accounts to invest in the company or to any individual existing shareholder who similarly relied on those accounts to increase his shareholding.[154] Auditors prepare accounts, not to promote the interests of potential investors, but to assist the shareholders collectively to exercise their right of control over the company.[155] Their Lordships held that four conditions must be met for a defendant to be liable for economic loss resulting from negligent advice or information. (1) The defendant must be *fully* aware of the nature of the transaction which the claimant has in contemplation as a result of receipt of the information. (2) He must either communicate that information to the claimant directly, or know that it will be communicated to him (or a restricted class of persons of which the claimant is an identifiable member). (3) He must specifically anticipate that the claimant will *properly* and *reasonably* rely on that information when deciding whether or not to engage in the transaction in question. (4) The purpose for which the claimant does rely on that information must be a purpose connected with interests that it is reasonable to require the defendants to protect.

No duty is owed to all potential investors for such a duty would, in truth, result in unlimited liability. If auditors were liable to *any* investor who relied on the published accounts to deal with the company simply because such conduct is foreseeable, they would equally be liable to anyone else who dealt with the company to his detriment, for example, banks lending the company money, or tradesmen extending credit terms.[156] Caparo sought to argue that the vulnerability of Fidelity to takeover should have alerted the auditors to the likelihood of a company, such as Caparo, mounting a takeover bid, and that they were not just *any* potential investor, but existing shareholders. Their Lordships held that the defendants were under no duty to safeguard the economic interests of corporate predators,[157] and that the statutory duty imposed on them by Parliament was to protect the interests, and existing holdings, of the shareholders in the client company,[158] not to facilitate investment decisions whether by existing shareholders or others.[159]

A positive avalanche of cases on the limits of *Hedley Byrne* liability followed. Just a few examples are given here to illustrate the application of the *Caparo* principles. In one case, it was held that directors of a company who issued a prospectus to invite shareholders to take up a rights issue were not under a duty to those shareholders

---

[154] The Court of Appeal had held that existing shareholders were owed such a duty, distinguishing the shareholder investors from other members of the public: [1989] 1 All ER 798.

[155] [1990] 1 All ER 568, at 580–1 and 600–1.

[156] See *Al Saudi Banque v Clark Pixley* [1990] Ch 313.

[157] Why should auditors be responsible for the success of those actively seeking to destroy their client?

[158] As to whether an existing shareholder might sue if his existing proprietary interest was damaged by negligence on the part of the auditors (ie, sold at an undervalue) see Lord Bridge [1990] 1 All ER 568, at 580–1 (probably yes) and Lord Oliver, at 601 (leaving the question open).

[159] See also *MAN Nutzfahrzeuge AG v Freightliner Ltd* [2007] EWCA Civ 910.

who relied on the prospectus to make further investments.[160] Nor were accountants advising a creditor company on the appointment of a receiver liable to that company's debtors.[161] In both cases, the relationship between the parties lacked the necessary proximity. The defendants had done nothing to make themselves responsible for the financial welfare of the claimants.

But, what if some express representation has been made directly to the claimant, on the basis of which he argues that he then decided to go ahead with a particular trans-action? Much may turn on the facts of the case. In *James McNaughton Paper Group v Hicks Anderson*[162] the defendant accountants became aware that the claimants were considering a takeover of their clients. At a meeting between the two companies, the defendants were asked to confirm the accuracy of draft accounts, and they did this in very general terms. The Court of Appeal found that no duty was owed to the claim-ants. The draft accounts were not prepared for their benefit, and the defendants would reasonably expect a party to a takeover bid to take independent advice and not rely exclusively on draft accounts. However, in another case where it was pleaded that the defendants had prepared profit forecasts expressly in order to induce the claimants to increase their bid for a company at risk of takeover, the Court of Appeal refused to strike out the claim and ordered a full trial on the facts.[163]

Perhaps the key question in this sort of case is whether advice given by the defend-ant has been given in a context in which the assumption that claimants should gener-ally look after their own financial interests can be displaced. Have the defendants in effect induced the claimants to place faith in their judgment? In *Henderson v Merrett Syndicates Ltd*,[164] managing agents at Lloyds, who placed monies entrusted to them by Names at Lloyds in underwriting contracts, owed a duty of care to 'their' Names. The agents undertook responsibility for advising the claimants and finding appropri-ate investments for their money. They effectively 'took over' the claimants' financial affairs.

Williams v Natural Life Health Food Ltd[165] is also instructive. The second defendant set up a company to franchise out health food businesses. The claimants approached the company to obtain a franchise. Having received from the company, Natural Life, a glowing brochure and prospectus which included testimonies to the second defend-ant's experience and success, the claimants went ahead and obtained a franchise. At no stage in the pre-contractual negotiations did they have any contact with the second defendant personally. The enterprise was a disaster and the claimants' shop failed to make money, resulting in severe financial loss to the claimants. The claimants sued both the company, Natural Life, and the second defendant personally. The company

---

[160] *Al-Nakib Investments (Jersey) Ltd v Longcroft* [1990] 3 All ER 321.
[161] *Huxford v Stoy Hayward & Co* (1989) 5 BCC 421.
[162] [1991] 2 QB 113.
[163] *Morgan Crucible v Hill Samuel Bank Ltd* [1991] 1 All ER 148.
[164] [1995] 2 AC 145. As to concurrent liability in tort and contract see ch 2. See also Whittaker [1997] LS 169.
[165] [1998] 2 All ER 577.

went into liquidation so the action proceeded against the second defendant alone. The House of Lords found that there was no special relationship between the second defendant and the claimants because there were no personal dealings between them and neither directly nor indirectly did the second defendant convey to the claimants that he assumed personal responsibility for their affairs. Nor was there evidence that the claimants relied on his personal undertakings to safeguard their economic well-being as franchisers. The dealings were all with the company. Unlike the Lloyds' agents, the second defendant took on no role as an individual in 'managing' the claimants' business interests.

We move now to look at *Smith v Bush*; but we do so noting that in *Caparo*[166] Lord Oliver described *Smith v Bush*[167] as the outer limit of *Hedley Byrne* liability.

> Ds were surveyors acting for the mortgagees. They gave favourable reports on properties to be purchased by C, the mortgagor. An express disclaimer denied any liability to C.[168] Nonetheless the evidence was that 90% of house purchasers do in fact rely on the mortgagees' report[169] and do not engage their own surveyor. C paid the surveyor's fee and Ds were well aware that C (whose identity they knew) would rely on the report and would suffer loss if that report were negligently prepared.

The House of Lords unanimously found that, in such circumstances, a duty of care was owed to the mortgagor. Unlike in *Caparo*, the defendants were well aware of the identity of the claimant, knew that their advice would be transmitted to the claimant, and appreciated exactly how the claimant would act in reliance on that advice. There was no element of uncertainty relating to the transaction consequent on that advice. There was no question of liability other than to one identifiable claimant.[170] There was no conflict between the interests of the surveyors' client and the mortgagors.[171] If the surveyors had done the job properly and produced a proper valuation, they would have discharged their duty to both mortgagee and mortgagor. The claimants who paid their fees were properly entitled to rely on their professional skill and advice.[172]

It is important, of course, to remember that proof of a duty to act carefully in giving advice or information is only the first stage in the claim. Claims may, of course,

---

[166] [1998] 2 All ER 577, at 598.   [167] [1990] 1 AC 831.

[168] The disclaimer was invalid under the Unfair Contract Terms Act 1977.

[169] *Smith v Bush* was a consolidated appeal concerning two separate claimants. In one case the mortgagee showed the actual report to C1. In the other, the report itself was not disclosed to C2.

[170] The likelihood that *a* purchaser may emerge in the future who will suffer loss if a survey is carelessly conducted is insufficient. A particular individual who will almost inevitably place faith in the report and act to his detriment must be within D's contemplation: *The Morning Watch* [1990] 1 Lloyd's Rep 547. Contrast *Smith v Bush* with *Goodwill v British Pregnancy Advisory Service* [1996] 2 All ER 161.

[171] Cf *West Bromwich Albion FC Ltd v El Safty* [2007] PIQR P7.

[172] Lord Griffiths and Lord Jauncey both made references to the reasonableness of purchasers at the lower end of the market relying on the building society survey rather than facing the additional expense of an independent report. Yet the *Smith v Bush* approach was applied to a mid-range property in *Beaumont v Humberts* [1990] 49 EG 46. Cf *Scullion v Bank of Scotland plc* [2011] EWCA Civ 693, where the Court of Appeal rejected a claim that a surveyor providing a valuation for the mortgagee owed a duty of care to the mortgagor of a buy-to-let property.

fail for other reasons. If, for example, it can be shown that the duty extended merely in respect of the provision of information (eg the value of property suggested as security for a loan) upon which the claimant could (but need not) base his financial decisions, the defendant will not be liable for he has not advised upon the wisdom of the financial decision finally taken (because, for instance, the market value of property is susceptible to rapid drops in price).[173] Equally, as with other actions in negligence, want of care may not be proved.[174] Or, alternatively, the claimant may fail to show that his loss resulted from the defendant's carelessness,[175] or, more problematically, that all his loss resulted from the defendant's carelessness.[176] Thus, if the claimant, even though he believed the information, would have acted as he did regardless of the defendant's negligence, his loss is not caused by that negligence.[177]

(B) THE EXTENDED *HEDLEY BYRNE* PRINCIPLE

What, then, is the basis of *Hedley Byrne* liability? Lord Griffiths, in *Smith v Bush*, dismissed as unhelpful the notion that liability rests on an assumption of responsibility by the defendant.[178] Indeed, the defendants in *Smith v Bush* manifested every intention to the contrary, attempting expressly to disclaim liability. A duty, Lord Griffiths argued, can arise, not only where the defendant either expressly or implicitly undertakes responsibility to the claimant for advice or information, but also where the particular relationship between the two is such that it is just that the defendant be subject to such responsibility.[179] Lord Griffiths' criticism of any principle of assumption of responsibility was strongly supported by a number of academic commentators.[180]

However, subsequent decisions of the House of Lords have forcefully endorsed the 'assumption of responsibility' test as the basis of an extended *Hedley Byrne* principle, which embraces negligent performance of services as much as negligent statements

---

[173] *South Australia Asset Management Corp v York Montague Ltd* [1997] AC 191; *Aneco Reinsurance Underwriting Ltd v Johnson & Higgins Ltd* [2002] 1 Lloyd's Rep 157.

[174] *Stafford v Conti Commodity Services Ltd* [1981] 1 All ER 691; *Argy Trading Developments Co Ltd v Lapid Developments Ltd* [1977] 3 All ER 785.

[175] *Banque Financière de la Cité v Westgate Insurance Ltd* [1991] 2 AC 249 (note that their Lordships also found no duty in that case).

[176] The most problematic issues arise where C's financial losses are attributable partly to D's negligent advice and partly to fluctuations in market prices; only those properly attributable to the former are recoverable: *South Australia Asset Management Corp v York Montague Ltd* [1997] AC 191; *Aneco Reinsurance Underwriting Ltd v Johnson & Higgins Ltd* [2002] 1 Lloyd's Rep 157.

[177] *J E B Fasteners Ltd v Marks, Bloom & Co* [1983] 1 All ER 583. See also *Williams v Natural Life Health Foods Ltd* [1998] 2 All ER 577, at 836.

[178] [1998] 2 All ER 577, at 865, confirming the decision of the Court of Appeal in *Ministry of Housing and Local Government v Sharp* [1970] 2 QB 223.

[179] See *Al Saudi Banque v Clark Pixley* [1989] 3 All ER 361, at 367.

[180] See, eg, Barker (1993) 109 LQR 461; Hepple (1997) 50 CLP 69. For a limited defence see Murphy, 'The Juridical Foundations of Common Law Non-Delegable Duties' in Neyers (ed), *Emerging Issues in Tort Law* (2007), ch 14.

and advice;[181] and which – if the courts have not erred in applying the principle – now extends to cases characterised by *both* dependency *and* reliance on the part of the claimant.[182] In *Henderson v Merrett Syndicates Ltd*,[183] for example, Lord Goff rested his finding of liability on the part of the managing agents on their assumption of responsibility towards those who relied on their special expertise in underwriting. In *White v Jones*, Lord Browne-Wilkinson affirmed the centrality within *Hedley Byrne* liability of discovering whether the defendant had assumed responsibility for the advice or task undertaken. Notably, however, he stressed that what is crucial is 'a conscious assumption of responsibility for the *task* rather than a conscious assumption of legal responsibility to the claimant for its careful performance'.[184] (This approach, however, is difficult to square with the notion that an assumption of responsibility is really only a way of characterising the relationship of proximity necessary for the imposition of a duty of care.)[185]

More generally, the three decisions of the House of Lords in *Henderson v Merrett Syndicates Ltd*, *White v Jones*, and *Williams v Natural Life Ltd* have confirmed that *Hedley Byrne* opened the doors to much wider liability in respect of economic loss in tort than had previously been available.[186] In *Hedley Byrne* itself, Lord Devlin stated:

> [c]ases may arise in the future in which a new and wider proposition, quite independent of contract, will be needed. There may, for example, be cases in which a statement is not supplied for the use of any particular individual.[187]

Just such a duty of care came to pass in *So v HSBC Bank plc*,[188] although liability was not established because causation of economic loss could not be proved:

> An employee of the defendant bank signed and stamped a document supplied by and returned to their client, 5th Avenue. The document, which purported to be a letter of instruction relating to the payment of money out of 5th Avenue's bank account for the strict purpose of investment, was obviously capable of misleading third parties. The document was used in order to defraud 5th Avenue's customers, who believed that their payments would be safeguarded by the defendant bank.

---

[181]   *Williams v Natural Life Health Foods Ltd* [1998] 2 All ER 577.

[182]   Even with this description of the extended *Hedley Byrne* principle problems can arise in explaining the decided cases. In some, the courts have had to alight upon tenuous notions of 'an assumption of responsibility' (see, eg, *White v Jones* [1995] 2 AC 207). Equally, there are some rather fictitious instances of reliance to be found in the cases. For some judicial recognition of this, see *Customs and Excise Commissioners v Barclays Bank plc* [2005] 1 WLR 2082 (reversed on other issues [2006] UKHL 28).

[183]   [1995] 2 AC 145, at 182.   [184]   [1995] 2 AC 207, at 274.

[185]   See Murphy [1996] CLJ 43. Note, however, that *White* has been followed in this respect in an analogous case: *Gorham v British Telecommunications plc* [2000] 1 WLR 2129.

[186]   But note that 'extended *Hedley Byrne*' liability is not necessarily confined to economic loss. It has been accepted, for example, that it could in principle be invoked in relation to psychiatric illness caused by being wrongfully convicted due to the negligence of C's solicitors: *McLoughlin v Grovers* [2002] QB 1312.

[187]   [1964] AC 465, at 530.   [188]   [2009] EWCA Civ 296.

The Court of Appeal held that a duty of care was owed to non-clients of the defendant bank on the basis that HSBC had, by providing the document, represented that it 'intended to carry out and had accepted the instructions'.[189]

Seeking to extend yet further the boundaries of a duty to avoid inflicting financial loss on others, a robust approach was taken by Megarry V-C in *Ross v Caunters*.

> D, a solicitor, negligently drew up a will and thereby failed to fulfil his client-testator's instruction to benefit C. C then sued D in negligence.[190]

The claimant could in no sense be said to have relied on the solicitor, yet his action succeeded. The judge held that the law had by 1979 so developed that he should apply the neighbour principle in *Donoghue v Stevenson* in the absence of any policy factors negativing or limiting the scope of such a duty. There was close proximity between the claimant and the defendant. His contemplation of her was 'actual, nominate and direct', so proximity arose out of the duty he undoubtedly owed to the testator. It was in no way 'casual, accidental or unforeseen'. The liability arising from the duty was to one person alone.[191] Accordingly, the spectre of indeterminate liability did not arise.

In *White v Jones*,[192] the House of Lords found for the claimant on facts reminiscent of (but different from) those in *Ross v Caunters*.

> After a family quarrel, the testator (aged 78) disinherited Cs (his two daughters). A few months later, the family was reconciled and, on 17 July, the testator instructed Ds (his solicitors), to draw up a new will including legacies of £9,000 to each daughter. Ds failed to act on those instructions before the testator died some months later. As a result of Ds' negligent delay in acting on the testator's instructions, Cs failed to be awarded their legacies.

The House of Lords held that the claimants could recover. Lord Goff made it clear that their Lordships did not endorse Megarry V-C's simplistic approach basing liability on the neighbour principle alone.[193] The claim by the claimants in *White v Jones*, as in *Ross v Caunters*, posed a number of conceptual difficulties,[194] but principally the following.

(1) D's contractual duty was owed only to his client, the now dead testator. Privity of contract rules excluded the extension of *this* duty to the disappointed beneficiaries.

(2) Cs' actions, being founded on pure economic loss, could succeed only on the basis of some form of application of *Hedley Byrne*; yet there was no obvious assumption of responsibility towards Cs and, still less obviously, any corresponding

---

[189] [2009] EWCA Civ 296, at [40].
[190] [1980] Ch 297. And see *Al-Kandari v JR Brown & Co* [1988] QB 665.
[191] See *Caltex Oil (Australia) Pty Ltd v Dredge Willemstad* (1976) 136 CLR 529 (note the importance in relation to economic loss of there being a single identifiable C rather than a diffuse class of potential Cs).
[192] [1995] 2 AC 207.
[193] Ibid at 268.
[194] Detailed in full in ibid at 260–2.

reliance on their part. For this reason, it was straining logic to suggest that Cs had actually lost anything at all.[195]

(3) If liability were to be imposed, establishing clear and manageable limits to such liability would be near to impossible to achieve.

The majority in the House of Lords thought these difficulties could be surmounted;[196] but the conceptual grounds on which their Lordships did in fact establish liability must be read with some caution.[197] Lord Goff was entirely frank in admitting that he was strongly motivated by an impulse to do practical justice. He pointed out the 'extraordinary fact' that if no duty in tort were owed to the claimants, the only persons who might have a valid claim (the testator and his estate) had suffered no loss, and the only persons who suffered any kind of loss (the disappointed beneficiaries) would have no claim.[198] Lord Browne-Wilkinson warned that his analysis was only what was necessary for the purposes of this case. He made clear that he was 'not purporting to give any comprehensive statement of this aspect of the law'.[199]

So what did *White v Jones* decide? (1) The existence of a contract between the defendants and a third party (the testator) did not by virtue of the rules on privity of contract exclude a duty in tort to the claimant. (2) Such a duty could arise if, quite apart from the contract, the circumstances of the case gave rise to a special relationship between the parties. (3) On the facts of *Hedley Byrne* itself, proof that the claimant relied on the advice given, or statements made, by the defendants, and that the defendants should have foreseen such reliance, was an 'inevitable' condition of liability. However, reliance is *not* a necessary condition for the creation of a special relationship in every case giving rise to a duty to safeguard another from economic loss. (4) A special relationship will arise when the defendant assumes responsibility for providing services knowing and accepting that 'the future economic welfare of the intended beneficiary is dependent on his careful execution of the task'.[200] (5) On the facts of *White v Jones*, there were no reasons of policy why such a duty should not be imposed on the defendants, and indeed very good reasons why it should be so imposed. The actual outcome of the decision in *Ross v Caunters* imposing liability on solicitors for negligently executed wills had worked well and had not given rise to unlimited claims. In such cases there was no conflict of interest[201] between the duty owed to the testator in contract, and the duty owed to the claimants in tort. Fulfilling

---

[195] See Benson, 'Should *White v Jones* Represent Canadian Law?' in Neyers (ed), *Emerging Issues in Tort Law* (2007), ch 6.

[196] Note the powerful dissent of Lord Mustill.

[197] See Murphy [1996] CLJ 43.

[198] [1995] 2 AC 207, at 259–60.

[199] Ibid at 274. But see the application of *White v Jones* in *Gorham v British Telecommunications plc* [2000] 1 WLR 2129.

[200] [1995] 2 AC 207, at 275.

[201] Cf *White v Jones* with *Clarke v Bruce Lance & Co* [1988] 1 All ER 364.

the contractual obligation to the defendant at one and the same time would have discharged the duty of care owed to the claimants.

White v Jones does, therefore, make clear at least three crucial principles. (1) A duty to avoid causing economic loss is confined to special relationships within which the defendant has assumed responsibility for protecting the claimant's economic welfare.[202] (2) Such a relationship will arise only where the claimant is readily identifiable as an individual or a member of a class of persons for whom the defendant undertakes responsibility (in the loosest sense)[203] in the performance of a particular task. (3) 'Extended *Hedley Byrne*' relationships are not confined to negligent misstatements and careless advice. Provision of services, including services provided at the behest of a third party, may create a special relationship in appropriate conditions.[204] Reliance is not an essential ingredient of a special relationship,[205] though in its absence there must be dependency on the part of the claimant (in the sense that the claimant's wellbeing depends upon the care and skill of the defendant).

A willingness to give a liberal, extended interpretation to *Hedley Byrne* liability married to an apparent impetus to do justice to a hard-done-by claimant is once again apparent in *Spring v Guardian Assurance plc*.[206]

C sued his former employers for negligence (among other things). The reference D provided for him when he sought to be appointed as an agent for another insurance company was so unfavourable that the company refused to appoint him. The reference suggested that C was dishonest. The trial judge found that the reference had been carelessly (but not maliciously) prepared and found for C in negligence. In the House of Lords, the majority held that there had been an implied term in the contract of employment that any subsequent reference be supplied with due care. The Law Lords also ruled in C's favour in tort. In supplying a reference – at least in circumstances such as those in the instant case where references were required as a matter of regulation[207] – D assumed the responsibility to prepare the reference with care.

---

[202] Whether all the cases supposedly decided according to this principle actually meet this requirement upon close scrutiny of their particular facts is, however, questionable. See, eg, *Merrett v Babb* [2001] QB 1174.

[203] See Murphy [1996] CLJ 43.

[204] In *West Bromwich Albion FC v El-Safty* [2005] EWHC 2866, it was held that, *if* the three limbs of the *Caparo* test were met, a surgeon whose treatment of a professional player that had been arranged through the club's physiotherapist *would* owe a duty of care to the club in respect of the economic loss it would suffer if the player were to receive negligent treatment ending his career. On the facts, however, the *Caparo* test was not satisfied (affirmed [2006] EWCA Civ 1299). See also *Williams v Natural Life Health Foods Ltd* [1998] 2 All ER 577; *Carr-Glynn v Frearsons* [1998] 4 All ER 225.

[205] C's reliance is often the means by which causation can be established, but it has no normative significance of its own; it tells us nothing about the nature of D's conduct such that it is appropriate for D to be made liable to C.

[206] [1995] 2 AC 296. Note also the growing impetus in negligence law simply to do justice in *Parkinson v St James and Seacroft University Hospital NHS Trust* [2002] QB 266, *Rees v Darlington Memorial Hospital NHS Trust* [2004] 1 AC 309, and *Chester v Afshar* [2005] 1 AC 134.

[207] The regulatory authority (LAUTRO) which governs the conduct of insurance companies required both that the company seeking to appoint C must seek a reference and that Ds must supply such a reference.

That the defendants owed such a duty to the recipient of the reference was established by *Hedley Byrne*. But in the instant case, the duty claimed was one owed to the person about whom it was written, not the person to whom it was sent. It therefore represented an extension of the *Hedley Byrne* principle that could be justified on the basis that an employee relies on his employer to carry out this service with appropriate care. His interests are 'entrusted' to the skill of the referee. His financial prospects are significantly in the hands of that person.

But we must not lose sight of the fact that in *Spring* there was a significant policy issue present that arguably militated against the imposition of liability. Allegations of dishonesty are clearly defamatory. Yet had the claimant sued in defamation, his claim would have been met by a defence of qualified privilege (given the absence of malice). Indeed, the giving of references prepared without malice is a classic example of qualified privilege. It was at least arguable, therefore, that to allow the claimant's action in negligence would be to undermine the principles of defamation law. This, conceivably, might cause employers and others supplying references to be inhibited in what they were prepared to say, and possibly even lead to them being unprepared to supply references at all. Their Lordships nonetheless were dismissive of this line of argument. Lord Woolf acknowledged that public policy required that references be full and frank but countered that public policy also required that references 'should not be based upon careless investigations'. If a negligently written favourable reference could give rise to liability, thought his Lordship, there should be no objection in principle to imposing liability for a negligently written adverse reference. The law should encourage referees to act carefully with proper regard for the interests of both the recipient and the subject of the reference.

A strong desire to offer the claimant redress for a perceived injustice can be seen in the opinions of the Law Lords.[208] Addressing the need to prove malice to succeed in defamation, Lord Woolf declared that:

> [t]he result of this requirement is that an action for defamation is a wholly inadequate remedy for an employee who is caused damage by a reference which due to negligence is inaccurate. This is because it places a wholly disproportionate burden on the employee. Malice is extremely difficult to establish...Without an action for negligence, the employee may, therefore, be left with no practical prospect of redress even though the reference may have permanently prevented him from obtaining employment in his chosen vocation.[209]

Williams v Natural Life Health Foods Ltd[210] confirmed the terms of extended *Hedley Byrne* liability. Lord Steyn made three crucial points. (1) Once it is established that a case falls within the extended *Hedley Byrne* principle – that is, where there is a special relationship between the parties[211] – 'there is no need to embark on any further

---

[208] Cf *Kapfunde v Abbey National plc* [1999] ICR 1.   [209] [1994] 3 All ER 129, at 172.
[210] [1998] 2 All ER 577.   [211] Ibid at 581.

inquiry whether it is fair, just and reasonable to impose liability for economic loss'.[212] (2) He acknowledged, and commended, the 'essential gap-filling role' of the law of tort so that, while contractual privity rules might prevent substantial justice being done in that branch of law, this should not prevent torts from filling that gap. *Spring*, indeed, illustrates that this interstitial role may operate between different torts as well. For, there, negligence was utilised to correct what their Lordships regarded as a deficiency in defamation law. (3) Outside any special relationships blessed by the extended *Hedley Byrne* principle, claimants suffering pure economic loss will not, it seems, recover that loss in tort. Lord Steyn declared:

> The extended *Hedley Byrne* principle is the rationalisation or technique adopted by English law for the recovery of damages in respect of economic loss caused by the negligent performance of services.[213]

(C) OTHER PURE ECONOMIC LOSS CATEGORIES

Outside the extended *Hedley Byrne* principle, it seems that the courts take the view that no duty to protect others from pure economic loss will arise however predictable that loss may be,[214] and however just and reasonable it might appear that the defendant should bear the loss. There is no obvious reason for this stance;[215] yet the judicial sympathy for the claimant abundantly evidenced in *White v Jones* was notably absent in *Murphy v Brentwood District Council*.[216]

First, in *Murphy v Brentwood District Council*, as we have seen, their Lordships classified the loss suffered by the claimant (a subsequent purchaser of a defective dwelling) as pure economic loss. This was notwithstanding the fact that his home, if not repaired, would ultimately have collapsed. Such financial loss is irrecoverable in tort whether the defendant is the builder or the local council approving the original building plans. In the absence of a special relationship of proximity, neither manufacturers of chattels nor builders of property are subject to a duty of care in relation to the quality of their work. To impose any such general duty would introduce into the law of tort transmissible warranties of quality.[217] Such guarantees are provided only by contract. Thus, there was generally perceived to be no need for tort to fulfil an interstitial role.[218] However, the simplicity of this statement is marred somewhat by

---

[212] How this is to be reconciled with the clear emphasis on the endeavour to do practical justice in both *Spring* and *White v Jones* is by no means clear. See also the approach of Brooke LJ in *Parkinson v St James and Seacroft University Hospital NHS Trust* [2002] QB 266, at [17].

[213] *Williams v Natural Life Health Foods Ltd* [1998] 2 All ER 577, at 581.

[214] See, eg, *Simaan General Contracting Co v Pilkington Glass Ltd (No 2)* [1988] 1 All ER 791.

[215] But see McBride and Bagshaw, *Tort Law* (2005), 140–8.

[216] [1991] 1 AC 398. See also *Department of the Environment v Bates* [1991] 1 AC 499; *D & F Estates Ltd v Church Comrs for England* [1988] 2 All ER 992.

[217] *D & F Estates Ltd v Church Comrs for England* [1988] 2 All ER 992, at 1010.

[218] See *Williams v Natural Life Health Foods Ltd* [1998] 2 All ER 577.

a dictum of Lord Bridge suggesting that, even in the absence of a special relationship with the builder:

> if a building stands so close to the boundary of the building owner's land that after discovery of the dangerous defect it remains a potential source of injury to persons or property on neighbouring land or the highway, the building owner ought, in principle, to be entitled to recover in tort ... the cost of obviating the danger ... *to protect himself from potential liability to third parties.*[219]

The Lord Bridge exception, doubted by Lord Oliver,[220] could theoretically drive a coach and horses through the *Murphy* rule. Assume Mr Murphy had children. The cracks in the walls of his house, if left unrepaired with the family remaining in the house, posed a potential source of injury to them. Could Mr Murphy argue he should recover the cost of protecting himself against liability to the children or his visitors? On the one hand, beyond *Hedley Byrne*, the courts strive to provide predictability and restrict claims for economic loss; yet on the other hand they want to retain the ability to meet the really 'hard case'.

A second category of cases where the House of Lords have declared that economic loss is *never* recoverable is more straightforward. A claimant who suffers economic loss consequent on physical damage to another person, or consequent on damage to property in which, at the time damage occurred, he had no proprietary or possessory interest, cannot recover that loss in tort.[221] These are cases of 'relational economic loss'. Loss to the claimant arises because of his dependence upon the continuing integrity of another person or of property owned by another.

In *Weller & Co v Foot and Mouth Disease Research Institute*,[222] the defendants had carelessly allowed cattle to become infected by foot and mouth disease. The claimants were auctioneers, whose business suffered badly when quarantine restrictions prevented them holding auction sales of cattle. Widgery J said that no duty of care was owed to the claimants for their loss of profits. The scope of any duty owed was limited to cattle owners who suffered physical damage to their property when cattle had to be destroyed. The loss occasioned to the auctioneer was readily foreseeable, but so was economic loss to countless other enterprises: the pubs, the cafés, the car parks, the shops which would benefit from the influx into the town of crowds on market day. Policy required that a cut-off point be set. Widgery J set it at those suffering physical harm and, on the facts of *Weller*, it is easy to understand why.

A series of decisions on the damages recoverable when services such as water, gas, or electricity were negligently interrupted confirmed Widgery J's finding that economic loss unrelated to physical damage was irrecoverable. In *British Celanese Ltd v*

---

[219] [1990] 2 All ER 908, at 926 (emphasis added).
[220] Ibid at 936.
[221] For a statutory exception in relation to C's economic loss arising from harm to another, see the Fatal Accidents Act 1976. Note also the Latent Damage Act 1986, s 3.
[222] [1966] 1 QB 569. And see *Cattle v Stockton Waterworks Co* (1875) LR 10 QB 453.

Hunt[223] and *S C M (UK) Ltd v W J Whittall & Son Ltd*,[224] the cutting off of electricity supplies damaged the claimant's machines and materials resulting in a loss of production. The claimants recovered both their additional expenditure in replacing and repairing machinery and their loss of profits on the lost production run. The Court of Appeal in the latter case held that the economic loss (that is, loss of profits) was recoverable, as it was immediately consequent on physical damage to the claimant's property.

In 1973 the Court of Appeal again considered economic loss in *Spartan Steel and Alloys Ltd v Martin & Co (Contractors) Ltd*,[225] the facts of which were as follows:

> The defendants' negligence caused the cable carrying electricity to the claimant's factory to be cut through, interrupting the supply for 14½ hours. To avoid molten metal solidifying in the furnaces, the claimants used oxygen to melt it and pour it out of the furnaces. This reduced the value of the metal and lost the claimants the £400 profit they would have expected to make on that melt. The claimants also lost a further £1,767 on the other four melts which they would normally have completed in the time that the electricity was cut off.

The majority of the Court of Appeal held that they could recover only the loss in value of the metal actually in the furnaces and the loss of profit on that melt. The remaining loss was financial loss unrelated to any physical damage and thus irrecoverable. Edmund-Davies LJ, dissenting, considered that such foreseeable and direct economic loss should be recoverable. For him, the occurrence or non-occurrence of physical damage was a fortuitous event with no relevance in legal principle. In language similar to that later employed by Megarry V-C in *Ross v Caunters*, he argued that if that very kind of economic loss to that claimant was a reasonably foreseeable and direct consequence of want of care, a duty to avoid that kind of loss arose.

Firm endorsement of the majority opinion in *Spartan Steel* was nonetheless supplied by the Court of Appeal in *Muirhead v Industrial Tank Specialties Ltd*.[226]

> C, a fish merchant, devised a plan to buy lobsters in the summer when prices were low and store them to sell at profit on the Christmas market. The lobsters had to be stored in tanks through which seawater was constantly pumped, filtered, and re-circulated. The pumps proved to be defective because the electric motors were not suitable for use in the UK. C sued the manufacturers of the electric motors for (1) the loss of several lobsters that died in the tanks, (2) expenditure on attempts to correct the fault, and (3) loss of profits on the enterprise.

The Court of Appeal affirmed *Spartan Steel*. The claimant could recover only for the loss of his property (dead lobsters) and any loss of profit consequent on those dead lobsters. Only that economic loss directly consequent on physical damage could be

---

[223] [1969] 2 All ER 1252.   [224] [1971] 1 QB 337.
[225] [1973] QB 27 and see *Electrochrome Ltd v Welsh Plastics Ltd* [1968] 2 All ER 205; *The Kapetan Georgis* [1988] 1 Lloyd's Rep 352.
[226] [1985] 3 All ER 705.

recovered in tort. In the absence of any evidence of express reliance on, or close proximity to, the defendants, the defendants owed no duty to protect the claimant against financial loss (whether that loss be wasted expenditure or loss of profit). Manufacturers owe no duty in tort to ensure products are value for money.

In *Leigh & Sillivan Ltd v Aliakmon Shipping Ltd*[227] the claimant had contracted to buy a cargo of steel coils to be shipped from Korea. The cargo was damaged at sea. The contractual and credit arrangements between the claimant and the sellers of the steel coils were such that, although the risk in the cargo had passed to the claimant, it did not own the coils. (Such arrangements, where the party likely to suffer loss is not the owner of a cargo, are not uncommon.) Loss to the claimant was readily foreseeable. Nonetheless, the loss was held to be irrecoverable at common law. Three reasons may explain the refusal to countenance recovery of economic loss in such circumstances:

(1) The indeterminate liability which would otherwise arise requires a fixed cut-off point in the interests of clarity: recall *Weller v Foot & Mouth Institute* where the list of potential claimants – café owners, local shop owners, etc – was virtually endless.

(2) The claimants in *Leigh & Sillivan* suffered damage to their *business* interests. True, the defendants 'caused' that damage, but on what grounds should they have undertaken responsibility for protecting the claimants' business? The risk was as foreseeable to the claimants as it was to the defendants, so they could have protected themselves against that risk via insurance. The defendants had done nothing to indicate their willingness to shoulder the responsibility themselves.[228]

(3) An individual's personality is to some extent constituted by the property he owns. That property thus can be seen as integral to that person's self-definition. Accordingly, damage to his property can be seen as a form of personality damage. It follows, so the argument runs, that such a form of 'consequential' economic loss (as distinct from pure economic loss) 'can be viewed as little more than extra compensation for those who have suffered property damage'.[229] Any loss not thus associated with the claimant's property (and hence his personality) can be viewed as less deserving of compensation in accordance with the general hierarchy of protected interests described in this chapter.

---

[227] [1986] AC 785. Note that in this case as in others, an essential difficulty in imposing a duty in tort derives from the relationship between D's contractual duty to a third party and the purported tortious duty to C. If D (the shippers) had excluded or limited their duty in contract to the sellers, how would that exclusion or limitation affect their duty in tort? See the judgment of Robert Goff LJ in the Court of Appeal: [1985] QB 350, at 399.

[228] But what happens where there is a gap between the time at which D is negligent (C having no proprietary interest at that stage) and the time at which the negligence causes harm (by which time C does have a proprietary interest)? For the suggestion that an interest at the time of harm occurring is enough see *The Starsin* [2001] 1 Lloyd's Rep 437.

[229] Witting [2001] LS 481, 489.

At the beginning of the chapter, we remarked upon the fact that claimants are always seeking to test (through the ingenious argument of their lawyers) the boundaries of actionability in negligence. And so we finish discussion of the relational economic loss cases by noting that the range of potential claimants for pure economic loss was extended by the Court of Appeal in *Shell UK Ltd v Total UK Ltd*[230] in a way that is potentially problematic. The facts were:

> The claimant company, with three other oil companies, was the holder of shares in certain service companies. The service companies held legal title to fuel storage and pipeline facilities that were damaged in a fire caused by the negligence of the defendant. The assets were held 'on trust' for the four oil companies. The oil companies had entered into certain contractual agreements for the use of these facilities but had no possession or immediate right to possession. The claimant argued that it should be entitled to claim as beneficial owner of the damaged property for the economic losses 'consequent' upon the physical damage caused by the fire. These economic losses consisted in increased costs of supply and profits lost from the claimant's reduced ability to supply customers.

The Court of Appeal held that the claimant was indeed the 'beneficial owner' of the damaged property and could, thus, recover its financial losses, at least in circumstances where the legal owner could be joined in the proceedings. The Court explained that 'it would be a triumph of form over substance to deny a remedy to the beneficial owner of that property where the legal owner is a bare trustee for that beneficial owner'.[231] The court effectively set aside the separate legal personality of the service companies and created a new area of liability for financial loss inconsistent with cases we have examined in this section of the book. It can only be hoped that this development is overturned by the Supreme Court.[232]

FURTHER READING

BAILEY AND NOLAN, 'The *Page v Smith* Saga: A Tale of Inauspicious Origins and Unintended Consequences' [2010] *Cambridge Law Journal* 495

HANDFORD, *Mullany and Handford's Tort Liability for Psychiatric Damage* (2nd edn, 2006)

NOLAN, 'New Forms of Damage in Negligence' (2007) 70 *Modern Law Review* 59

STAPLETON, 'Duty of Care and Economic Loss: A Wider Agenda' (1991) 107 *Law Quarterly Review* 249

STAPLETON, 'Duty of Care: Peripheral Parties and Alternative Opportunities for Deterrence' (1995) 111 *Law Quarterly Review* 301

TEFF, *Causing Psychiatric and Emotional Harm: Reshaping the Boundaries of Legal Liability* (2008)

WITTING, *Liability for Negligent Misstatements* (2004)

---

[230] [2010] EWCA Civ 180.

[231] Ibid at [143]. The problem with this is that is completely ignores the very real advantage of limited liability enjoyed by a shareholder in another company.

[232] See Turner [2010] CLJ 445.

4

BREACH OF DUTY

KEY ISSUES

(1) Three steps to breach

In determining whether the defendant was in breach of his duty of care to the claimant, the court will examine (i) the foreseeability of harm to the claimant (or the class to which the claimant belongs) should care not be taken; (ii) the appropriate standard of care owed by the defendant to the claimant, which depends upon a number of factual matters concerning the risk of harm which arose; and the court will (iii) compare the conduct of the defendant with the expected standard of care, to see whether the defendant met the standard or fell below it.

(2) Setting the standard involves considering the circumstances of the case

Ordinarily, in setting the standard of care, the court will be concerned with what the hypothetical reasonable person should have done in the circumstances. This will involve considering factors such as the likelihood of harm, the seriousness of harm, and the social utility of the defendant's activity.

(3) In some cases, the court will consider attributes of the defendant

This will be so where the defendant is a child. Everyone knows of the lesser ability of the child to take care and the law must take this into account. The court might also take into account any physical affliction that overcame the defendant and about which he was not aware at the time of the failure in question.

(4) The claimant might be assisted by the use of the res ipsa loquitur doctrine in concluding that a breach has occurred

Res ipsa loquitur is a mode of reasoning that signifies a likelihood of the defendant having failed to take care in circumstances where the claimant has an accident which ordinarily does not occur without negligence.

SECTION 1 THE STANDARD OF CARE

So far in our consideration of the tort of negligence, only the persons to whom the defendant owes a duty of care and the types of harm to which the duty extends have been considered. We saw, in chapter 2, that the duty of care is concerned with whether or not a legal obligation to take care arises between persons. This chapter is concerned with an examination of what this entails – with what the law requires of the defendant in order to take care and avoid potential liability in negligence. There are a number of components to this exercise:

(1) There is a threshold issue of whether risk of harm to the claimant was reasonably foreseeable by the hypothetical person in the position of the defendant.[1]

(2) If this threshold of reasonable foreseeability is met, the court must then determine the appropriate standard of conduct that was applicable to the interaction between the claimant and the defendant.[2] An objective test is applied.[3] The test is objective in the sense that it is a *generalised* standard, made to suit the hypothetical reasonable person rather than the actual defendant; and it is an *external* standard, in that it focuses upon external acts and omissions (rather than upon any state of mind).[4] The setting of the appropriate standard entails consideration of a number of factors concerned with the nature of the risk that arose in that interaction and the defendant's ability to respond.[5] The result will be a normative statement of what the law expected of the reasonable person faced with a risk of the type that in fact arose. This statement is normative in that it creates a norm – or standard – of conduct.

(3) Lastly there is the question of breach – of whether the defendant fell below the standard of conduct expected by the law.

The question of whether the defendant has breached a duty of care is a mixed one of law and fact;[6] but the standard of care required of the defendant is an exclusively legal construct and based on the standard of a hypothetical reasonable person. If the defendant causes loss or injury to the claimant, but is able to show that he acted in a way that a reasonable person would have acted, no liability will attach.[7]

The logical progression from the duty issue to the breach issue was established in a series of seminal cases. After deciding that the appellants owed a duty to take reasonable care for the safety of children on the premises, Lord Thankerton explained

---

[1] *Overseas Tankship (UK) Ltd v Miller Steamship Co Pty Ltd (Wagon Mound (No 2))* [1967] 1 AC 617. Foreseeability indicates a minimal ability to take steps to avoid harm: Perry 'The Distributive Turn: Mischief, Misfortune and Tort Law' in Bix (ed), *Analyzing Law: New Essays in Legal Theory* (1998), ch 7.

[2] *Orchard v Lee* [2009] EWCA Civ 295, at [7] and [9].

[3] *Glasgow Corpn v Muir* [1943] AC 448.

[4] Goldberg and Zipursky, *The Oxford Introductions to US Law: Torts* (2010), 85–8.

[5] *Morris v West Hartlepool Steam Navigation Co Ltd* [1956] AC 552, at 574; *Baker v Quantum Clothing Group Ltd* [2011] UKSC 17, at [82].

[6] See, eg, *Barber v Somerset CC* [2004] 1 WLR 1089: the appeal to the House of Lords turned on the question of whether the Court of Appeal had been entitled to disturb the trial judge's finding of fact that D had failed to meet the standard of reasonable care.

[7] See, eg, *Al-Sam v Atkins* [2005] EWCA Civ 1452. Note that it is not always easy to specify what is reasonable. Take, as an example, the near-100-page split decision of the Supreme Court concerning whether employers should have supplied protection from noise at work in *Baker v Quantum Clothing Group Ltd* [2011] UKSC 17.

in *Glasgow Corpn v Muir* that a further question had to be settled, namely, 'the test by which...the standard of care is to be judged'.[8] Similarly, in *Bolton v Stone*, Lord Normand commenced his speech as follows:

> My Lords, it is not questioned that the occupier of a cricket ground owes a duty of care to persons on an adjacent highway or on neighbouring property who may be in the way of balls driven out of the ground by the batsman. But it is necessary to consider the measure of the duty owed.[9]

That the threshold issue is one of reasonable foreseeability has been acknowledged in various cases. Thus, it was held in *The Wagon Mound (No 2)* that a person in the position of the defendant must have been able to foresee a 'real' and 'not far-fetched' risk of harm to the claimant or class including the claimant.[10] A failure in care by a motorist might manifest itself in the risk of collision with a vehicle or other object, or in the running down of a person. These risks (normally) are reasonably foreseeable. However, it is not reasonably foreseeable that a failure to drive within the speed limit might give rise to a risk of a piece of space junk falling from the sky and hitting the vehicle, injuring a passenger. There is, therefore, no need to consider taking precautions with respect to the latter risk.

In relation to the 'measure of the duty owed', *Paris v Stepney Borough Council*[11] is instructive. A claim in negligence was brought by a worker, blind in one eye, who had been injured in his one good eye while working without the use of goggles. Lord Oaksey stated that 'the duty of an employer towards his servant is to take *reasonable care* for the servant's safety in all the circumstances of the case'.[12] Taking a lead from this guidance, subsequent cases have now made clear that, as a matter of law, if A owes B a duty of care, A must attain the standard of a 'reasonable person' in order to discharge that duty. In short, the obligation is one to take what amounts to *reasonable care* in the circumstances of the case. Needless to say, if reasonable care was taken by the defendant there is no liability simply on the basis that the defendant, nevertheless, caused harm to the claimant.

In some cases, strong guidance as to the appropriate standard of conduct will be given by statute, custom, or professional standards.[13] The more problematic cases are those 'unbounded' cases in which there are no clear pre-existing norms.[14] The courts might have recourse to a range of factors in determining what reasonableness requires. Some of these factors concern matters extraneous to the defendant – such as whether

---

[8] [1943] AC 448, at 454.   [9] [1951] AC 850, at 860.

[10] *Overseas Tankship (UK) Ltd v Miller Steamship Co Pty Ltd (Wagon Mound (No 2))* [1967] 1 AC 617, at 643. There is no need to take precautions with respect to the proverbial 'one-in-a-million' event: *Craggy v CC of Cleveland Police* [2009] EWCA Civ 1128.

[11] [1951] AC 367.

[12] Ibid at 384 (emphasis added).

[13] Mere failure to conform is not itself determinative of breach: see *Baker v Quantum Clothing Group Ltd* [2011] UKSC 17; *Ryan v Victoria (City)* [1999] 1 SCR 201, at 222 (statute); and *Ward v The Ritz Hotel (London) Ltd* [1992] PIQR 315 (professional standards).

[14] Abraham (2001) 53 Vand LR 1187, 1203.

he acted in an emergency situation created by no fault of his own – while others refer to attributes of the defendant, not as an individual, but as a member of a class, such as his standing as a professional person possessing (or at least professing to possess) certain skills. The factors considered here reflect those commonly referred to by the courts, but they are not presented on the basis that they constitute an absolutely comprehensive list. Indeed, there is no closed list of factors relevant to determining what a reasonable person would do by way of response to a risk.

SECTION 2   FACTORS RELEVANT TO ESTABLISHING THE REQUIRED STANDARD[15]

(A) FACTORS EXTRANEOUS TO THE DEFENDANT

(1) The likelihood of harm

The more likely that a risk of harm will manifest itself, the greater the need for precaution to be taken. Lord Wright in *Northwestern Utilities Ltd v London Guarantee and Accident Co Ltd* said:

> The degree of care which that duty involves must be proportioned to the degree of risk involved if the duty of care should not be fulfilled.[16]

The likelihood of harm occurring is a factual matter to be determined according to the evidence about the harmful interaction that occurred and circumstances surrounding it. *Bolton v Stone*[17] provides a good illustration of the principle:

> Miss Stone was hit by a cricket ball struck from a cricket ground surrounded by a fence 17 feet above the level of the square. The batsman was 80 yards away. The ball was only the 6th in about 30 years to be hit out of the ground. The House of Lords held that there had been no breach of duty by the club in allowing cricket to be played without taking further precautions.

Lord Radcliffe stressed two points: first, the fact that the ball had to clear the fence which itself was a remote possibility and, second, that, having cleared the fence the ball would then have to strike a passer-by (an even more remote possibility). Lord Oaksey said:

> an ordinarily careful man does not take precautions against every foreseeable risk...life would be almost impossible if he were to attempt to take precautions against every risk.[18]

---

[15] See Kidner [1991] LS 1.

[16] [1936] AC 108, at 126 (appd by Lord Normand in *Paris v Stepney BC* [1951] AC 367, at 381). Cf *Palsgraf v Long Island RR Co* 284 NY 339 (1928): 'The risk reasonably to be perceived defines the duty to be obeyed' per Cardozo CJ, and *Glasgow Corpn v Muir* [1943] AC 448, at 456: 'the degree of care required varies directly with the risk involved'.

[17] [1951] AC 850.   [18] Ibid at 863.

In *Bolton v Stone*, the chance of harm occurring was so small that a reasonable person in the position of the cricket club could not be expected to take additional precautions against such a remote possibility. By contrast, where the risk of injury to a road user from a football being kicked from a patch of open land was much greater, the defendant responsible for the land was held to be in breach of a duty of care.[19]

Particular vulnerability on the part of the claimant will be taken to increase the likelihood of harm if the defendant knew, or ought to have known, of that vulnerability. This should not be seen as subjectivising the standard of care: it is just that the standard of care is judged according to the standard of what the reasonable, prudent defendant would do given actual or constructive knowledge of the claimant's vulnerability. Thus, in *Barber v Somerset CC*,[20] for example, it was held by the Court of Appeal that an overworked teacher known to his employers to be suffering from stress was entitled to be treated according to the standard of a reasonable and prudent employer taking positive steps for the safety of his workers in the light of what he knew or ought to have known about their susceptibilities.

(2) The seriousness of harm

Just as the likelihood of harm affects the standard of care demanded, so too does the seriousness of that harm. In *Paris v Stepney Borough Council*[21] the House of Lords held that the gravity of the consequences of an accident befalling an already disabled man had to be taken into account in fixing the level of care required of the defendant.[22] Thus, the risk to the only good eye of the claimant in that case was a material consideration in fixing the standard of care. For a normally sighted individual, there would have been 'merely' the risk of being struck and blinded in one eye. For the claimant, however, the risk of being struck in his one good eye meant a risk of total blindness.

(3) The social utility of the defendant's act

In setting the standard of care, the courts will also take into account any relevant social utility associated with the defendant's conduct. This involves determinations of the general public interest so that matters other than merely those in dispute between the claimant and defendant may be taken into account in assessing the standard of care required of the defendant.

Daborn v Bath Tramways Motor Co Ltd[23] provides a useful illustration of this factor. The relevant issue was whether, during wartime, the driver of a left-hand-drive

---

[19] *Hilder v Associated Portland Cement Manufacturers Ltd* [1961] 1 WLR 1434. See also *Miller v Jackson* [1977] QB 966 (breach of duty where cricket balls were struck out of a ground about eight or nine times every season).

[20] [2004] 1 WLR 1089. See also *Haley v LEB* [1965] AC 778: D's standard of care was set according to the fact that D ought to have foreseen the possibility of blind persons coming into the vicinity of the hole dug by D in the pavement.

[21] [1950] 1 KB 320.

[22] [1951] AC 367. Cf *Withers v Perry Chain Co Ltd* [1961] 3 All ER 676 (the health risk to C had to be balanced against her interest in keeping her job).

[23] [1946] 2 All ER 333.

ambulance had been negligent in turning into a lane on the off-side of the road without giving a signal. Holding that she had not breached the relevant standard, Asquith LJ said:

> In determining whether a party is negligent, the standard of reasonable care is that which is reasonably to be demanded in the circumstances. A relevant circumstance to take into account may be the importance of the end to be served by behaving in this way or that. As has often been pointed out, if all the trains in this country were restricted to a speed of five miles an hour, there would be fewer accidents, but our national life would be intolerably slowed down. The purpose to be served, if sufficiently important, justified the assumption of abnormal risk. The relevance of this applied to the present case is this: during the war which was, at the material time, in progress, it was necessary for many highly important operations to be carried out by means of motor vehicles with left-hand drives, no others being available. So far as this was the case, it was impossible for the drivers of such cars to give the warning signals which could otherwise be properly demanded of them. Meanwhile, it was essential that the ambulance service should be maintained. It seems to me, in those circumstances, it would be demanding too high and an unreasonable standard of care from the drivers of such cars to say to them: 'Either you must give signals which the structure of your vehicle renders impossible or you must not drive at all'.[24]

It has been held that what might be want of care towards an employee in a commercial enterprise will not necessarily be want of care towards a fireman, for 'one must balance the risk against the end to be achieved', and 'the commercial end to make profit is very different from the human end to save life or limb'.[25] Indeed, the courts have demonstrated an increased interest in the importance of community-minded activity, not simply in emergency situations but also in more recreational settings.[26]

By section 1 of the Compensation Act 2006, it is now provided that, where a court is considering a claim in negligence, it shall, in setting the required standard of care, 'have regard to whether a requirement to take those steps [necessary to meet that standard] might (a) prevent a desirable activity from being undertaken at all, to a particular extent or in a particular way, or (b) discourage persons from undertaking functions in connection with a desirable activity'. Since it reflects the existing law, this provision has proved not to have altered the way in which courts approach the question of breach of duty.

---

[24] [1946] 2 All ER 333, at 336. Cf *Quinn v Scott* [1965] 2 All ER 588, at 593, per Glyn Jones J: 'the safety of the public must take precedence over the preservation of the amenities and [I] cannot hold that the [National] Trust's duty to care for the countryside diminishes to any degree the duty not to subject users of this highway to unnecessary danger'.

[25] *Watt v Hertfordshire CC* [1954] 2 All ER 368, at 371. On the other hand, where D can reasonably expect that others will take care for their own safety, and where the cost of eliminating a danger would involve the removal of a social amenity, the social amenity's benefit may well outweigh the obvious risks that exist: see *Tomlinson v Congleton BC* [2004] 1 AC 46 (but note that this is technically a case of whether there was breach of the duty owed under the Occupiers' Liability Act 1984).

[26] Eg, *Cole v Davis-Gilbert* (2007) *Times*, 6 April.

(4) Emergencies

Closely related to the previous factor is that of acts undertaken in an emergency. Frequently, a defendant may act in an emergency, with little time for reflective decision-making, in a manner that falls below the standard of care normally expected of him.[27] It is equally the case that he may act somewhat incautiously in an emergency with a view to assisting another. In either case, the courts will fix the appropriate standard of care mindful of the circumstances. *Watt v Hertfordshire County Council*[28] provides a good illustration.

> The fire service was called upon to save a woman trapped under an over-turned lorry. In order to do so, they needed to use a heavy jack that stood on wheels. They could not transport the jack in the usual vehicle because that vehicle was otherwise engaged. They instead tried to get the jack to the required destination in a surrogate vehicle. While en route, the driver of the vehicle made an emergency stop causing the jack to shoot forwards whereupon it injured C, one of the firemen.

It was held that there was no breach of duty given the short amount of time that the fire service had to act, and in view of the endeavour they were making to save the woman trapped underneath a lorry. On the other hand, it is important to appreciate that an emergency does not exonerate the defendant from displaying any level of care at all; it merely reduces the standard demanded. Thus, if a fire engine goes recklessly through a red light on the way to a fire, there may still be breach.[29]

(5) The relative cost of avoiding the harm

It is relevant to consider how extensive and costly would be the measures necessary to eliminate the risk. In essence there is a balancing of costs: the cost of averting a danger measured against the cost of the danger transpiring.[30] In *Latimer v AEC Ltd*[31] an exceptional storm had caused a factory floor to become flooded. When the water receded, the floor was found to be covered with a slimy mixture of oil and water so that its surface was slippery. The issue was whether the factory owners were in breach of their duty towards a workman who, some hours later, was injured

---

[27] Many of the cases on the standard of care in emergencies deal with contributory negligence: see, eg, *Jones v Boyce* (1816) 1 Stark 493. On primary liability and emergency, see *Parkinson v Liverpool Corpn* [1950] 1 All ER 367; *Ng Chun Pui v Lee Chuen Tat* [1988] RTR 298; *Marshall v Osmond* [1983] QB 1034.

[28] [1954] 2 All ER 368. See also *S (A Child) v Keyse* [2001] All ER (D) 236.

[29] *Ward v London CC* [1938] 2 All ER 341. See also *Craggy v CC of Cleveland Police* [2009] EWCA Civ 1128.

[30] The idea is that if great expense is required to reduce only slightly an existing risk, then it will be acceptable to do nothing. In *US v Carroll Towing Co* 159 F 2d 169 (1947), at 173 Learned Hand J expressed the matter in terms of a formula: 'if the probability be called P; the injury, L; and the burden, B; liability depends upon whether B is less than L multiplied by P; ie, whether B<PL'. See Gilles (2001) 54 Vand LR 813; Witting (2009) Torts LJ 242.

[31] [1952] 2 QB 701, at 711. Cf *Watt v Hertfordshire CC* [1954] 2 All ER 368 (duty of fire authority to firemen in respect of equipment) where the dictum of Asquith LJ, in *Daborn v Bath Tramways Motor Co Ltd* [1946] 2 All ER 333 was also approved.

through slipping on the floor. In holding there to have been no breach, Lord Tucker said:

> The only question was: Has it been proved the floor was so slippery that, remedial steps not being possible, a reasonably prudent employer would have closed down the factory rather than allow his employees to run the risks involved in continuing work?[32]

In *The Wagon Mound (No 2)* the Judicial Committee stated, in similar vein:

> A reasonable man would only neglect...a risk [of small magnitude] if he had some valid reason for doing so, eg, that it would involve considerable expense to eliminate the risk.[33]

These cases are founded on the proposition that risk cannot be eliminated entirely from human behviour.[34] 'Some risk of...injury is the price of activity'.[35] Risks should be reduced where it is practicable to do so, or where otherwise required in the interests of justice. The modest aspiration of tort law is to provide a certain degree of physical safety and to ensure that interactions between persons can be undertaken according to minimal standards of conduct.

The courts will require those who act to do what is reasonable, including the incurring of expense to eliminate risk. In the case of a private individual or enterprise there comes a point where, if the defendant lacks the resources to minimise a significant risk of injury to others, he must cease to engage in the relevant activity. Put otherwise, if the defendant does not possess sufficient resources to undertake an activity with reasonable care, then he should not engage in it at all. Thus, if a sports club cannot afford to replace a wooden spectator stand constituting a fire risk, for example, it should not allow spectators to use that stand.[36] By contrast, where the defendant is a public authority, the position may well be different. This might be because the services provided by the public authority are mandated by statute or are essential, and yet are inadequately resourced. In *Knight v Home Office*[37] the claimant's husband committed suicide while detained in a prison hospital wing. The judge accepted that the standard of care and supervision for suicidal prisoners may well have fallen below that to be expected in an NHS psychiatric facility. Yet he dismissed her claim saying:

> In making the decision as to the standard demanded the court must...bear in mind as one factor that resources available for the public service are limited and that the allocation of resources is a matter for Parliament.[38]

---

[32] [1953] AC 643, at 659.

[33] [1967] 1 AC 617, at 642. See also *Goldman v Hargrave* [1967] 1 AC 645, at 663 and *Baker v Quantum Clothing Group Ltd* [2011] UKSC 17, at [82].

[34] Goldberg (2003) 91 Geo LJ 513, 545.   [35] Keating (2003) 56 Vand LR 573, 701.

[36] See *Latimer v AEC* [1953] AC 643, at 659.   [37] [1990] 3 All ER 237.

[38] Ibid at 243. See the similar reasoning in *Walker v Northumberland CC* [1995] 1 All ER 737: 'The practicability of remedial measures must clearly take into account the resources and facilities at the disposal of the person or body owing the duty of care and the purpose of the activity giving rise to the risk of injury'.

Arguably, cases such as this demonstrate that negligence does not necessarily lie in the final link in a chain of decision-making, where policy is being implemented at the most basic, practical level. In some cases, decisions made at a high political level inevitably entail difficulty in meeting 'service targets', or under-servicing, and thus will result in failures in care. The failures in care that result are systemic in nature. Their 'acceptability' is politically pre-determined and courts might have little authority to redress them.[39] The systemic bias in the National Health Service towards under-treatment might be the best example of this.[40]

Whereas the focus in the English cases is usually upon the cost of *the* untaken precaution that would have prevented harm to *the particular* clamant, the focus has been widened in Australia. The lead was taken by the High Court of Australia in public authority cases,[41] but the matter now finds a place in statute.[42] The effect of the law is that, in all breach cases determined under the statute, the court is required to assess the whole range of risks to which the defendant's activity might foreseeably have given rise, and the whole range of potential responses, including their cost. Although this does seem to focus minds on the practicability of taking precautions, it also creates an evidential burden upon claimants and a complex assessment task for the courts. Inevitably, the effect will be to reduce the chances of claims success in public authority and other cases involving mass production or service provision.

(6) The 'hurly burly' of life

The tort of negligence does not demand perfection.[43] It does not require that those to whom a duty of care is owed should be safeguarded against every conceivable risk. The reasonable person test rests largely upon matters of common sense and the exigencies of everyday life. A good example of the allowance made by the law for the 'hurly burly of life' can be seen in cases relating to parental and quasi-parental duties. In *Carmarthenshire County Council v Lewis*,[44] the defendant council was held liable when a small boy wandered out of his nursery school and on to a nearby road causing an accident in which the claimant's husband died. The council was negligent because premises accommodating small children should be designed to ensure that they cannot wander off, endangering themselves and others. But Lord Reid said that the teacher who had not noticed the boy leave her classroom while she attended to a child with a

---

[39] Witting (2001) 21 OJLS 443.

[40] Klein, Day, and Redmayne, *Managing Scarcity: Priority Setting and Rationing in the National Health Service* (1996), 90. See Law Commission, *Administrative Redress: Public Bodies and the Citizen* (Law Com No 322, May 2010), [3.12]–[3.13]; *Savage v South Essex Partnership NHS Foundation Trust* [2009] AC 681, at [100].

[41] *Vairy v Wyong SC* (2005) 223 CLR 422.   [42] Eg, Civil Liability Act 2002 (NSW), s 5B.

[43] See *Banque Bruxelles Lambert SA v Eagle Star Insurance Co Ltd* [1997] AC 191, where, in considering whether there had been a negligent valuation, the court recognised as reasonable a range of different valuations. See also *Caldwell v Maguire and Fitzgerald* [2002] PIQR P45.

[44] [1955] AC 549.

cut knee was not negligent.[45] The gist of his reasoning was that those in charge of small children cannot have eyes in the back of their heads.

In *Surtees v Kingston-upon-Thames Borough Council*[46] a child was scalded when her mother left her for a moment or two by a wash-basin and she somehow managed to turn on the hot tap and ran scalding water over her foot. The majority of the Court of Appeal held that the mother's apparent oversight was not negligence. Courts should be slow to characterise incidents in family life as negligence 'given the rough and tumble of home life'. Was the Court of Appeal simply acknowledging that a risk-free existence is not feasible, or, in all circumstances, desirable? Beldam LJ dissented. He argued that it would have required only momentary thought to remove the child from the vicinity of the tap.

In *Porter v Barking and Dagenham London Borough Council*[47] a 14-year-old boy, injured when he and a friend were allowed to practise the shot-put unsupervised, failed in his action for negligence against the school authorities. The standard of care in relation to children should not be framed so as to stifle valuable activity or initiative.

(7) General practice of the community

Commonly, a defendant will support his claim to have exercised due care by showing that he conformed to the common practice of those engaged in the activity in question. Such evidence is obviously relevant.[48] Indeed, conforming to the practice of a trade or profession will often (but not always) be conclusive in claims against tradesmen[49] or professionals. So a specialist who failed to diagnose the complaint of the claimant was held not to have been negligent when he used the normal methods of British medical specialists, although the use of an instrument usually employed in the United States might have resulted in a correct diagnosis.[50] By contrast, consider *Cavanagh v Ulster Weaving Co Ltd*.

> C slipped coming down a roof ladder. Despite unchallenged evidence that the 'set-up' was in perfect accord with established practice, the House of Lords restored the jury's verdict that D was negligent.[51]

Commercial enterprises must take steps to keep abreast of scientific developments. Often, this can be done satisfactorily by reference to a code of industry practice which embodies the results of the scientific evidence and collectively agreed responses to risk, but these may not always be determinative.[52] Difficult questions arise about the position of more conscientious enterprises that conduct their own research or investigations

---

[45] Ibid at 564. See also *Kearn-Price v Kent CC* [2003] PIQR P11.
[46] [1991] 2 FLR 559.   [47] (1990) *Times*, 9 April.
[48] See, eg, *Baker v Quantum Clothing Group Ltd* [2011] UKSC 17.
[49] *Gray v Stead* [1999] 2 Lloyd's Rep 559. See also *Baker v Quantum Clothing Group Ltd* [2011] UKSC 17.
[50] *Whiteford v Hunter* (1950) 94 Sol Jo 758. Cf *Vancouver General Hospital v McDaniel* (1934) 152 LT 56; *Wright v Cheshire CC* [1952] 2 All ER 789.
[51] [1960] AC 145.
[52] *Baker v Quantum Clothing Group Ltd* [2011] UKSC 17, at [23], [101], and [126].

into risk – and conclude that the risks are greater than otherwise supposed. The difficulty arises from the fact that the defendant's actual knowledge needs to be taken into
account in setting the relevant standard; but the courts are aware of the disincentive
that arises where the defendant 'ploughing a lone furrow' is held in breach for not taking
precautions that were not to be expected of others in the industry.[53] Where an advance
occurs in knowledge, so that new measures must be taken, the courts accept that there
will often be an unavoidable time-lag between innovation and implementation.[54]

Failure to conform to a standard imposed by a statute, although of course it may
constitute a breach of statutory duty, is not in itself conclusive evidence of negligence.[55]
It may, however, constitute prima facie evidence.[56]

(B) FACTORS PERTAINING TO THE DEFENDANT

Before considering various attributes associated with the defendant that have the
capacity to affect the standard of care demanded, it is useful to consider a fundamental
background principle concerning negligence.

> Negligence is the omission to do something that a reasonable man, guided upon those
> considerations which ordinarily regulate the conduct of human affairs, would do, or
> doing something which a prudent and reasonable man would not do.[57]

It follows from this definition that the standard of care is not the standard of the
defendant himself, but of a person of 'ordinary prudence',[58] a person using 'ordinary
care and skill',[59] a 'hypothetical' person.[60] Lord Macmillan said:

> The standard of foresight of the reasonable man…eliminates the personal equation
> and is independent of the idiosyncrasies of the particular person whose conduct is in
> question.[61]

---

[53] An issue not entirely resolved in *Baker v Quantum Clothing Group Ltd* [2011] UKSC 17.

[54] Ibid at [42] and [105].

[55] In *Powell v Phillips* [1972] 3 All ER 864, it was held that breach of the Highway Code, despite s 37(5)
of the Road Traffic Act 1972, creates no presumption of negligence calling for an explanation. It is just
one relevant circumstance. In *Trotman v British Railways Board* [1975] ICR 95, it was held that breach of
a regulation in the British Railways' Rule Book created a rebuttable inference of negligence. A breach of a
navigational bye-law is particularly cogent evidence of negligence: *Cayzer, Irvine & Co v Cannon Co* (1884)
9 App Cas 873, at 880–1.

[56] *Blamires v Lancashire and Yorkshire Rly Co* (1873) LR 8 Exch 283; *Phillips v Britannia Hygienic Laundry
Co* [1923] 1 KB 539, at 548 (affirmed [1923] 2 KB 832); *Anglo-Newfoundland Development Co Ltd v Pacific Steam
Navigation Co* [1924] AC 406, at 413. See also *Harrison v National Coal Board* [1951] AC 639; *National Coal
Board v England* [1954] AC 403. And compliance with a statutory requirement does not exclude liability in
negligence: *Bux v Slough Metals Ltd* [1974] 1 All ER 262. See also *Budden v BP Oil Ltd* (1980) 124 Sol Jo 376.

[57] *Blyth v Birmingham Waterworks Co* (1856) 11 Exch 781, at 784.

[58] *Vaughan v Menlove* (1837) 3 Bing NC 468, at 475.

[59] *Heaven v Pender* (1883) 11 QBD 503, at 507.

[60] *King v Phillips* [1953] 1 QB 429, at 441.

[61] *Glasgow Corpn v Muir* [1943] AC 448, at 457. Cf the earlier dictum of Holmes J in *The Germanic* 196
US 589 (1904): 'The standard of conduct…is an external standard, and takes no account of the personal
equation of the man concerned'.

In short, it is important to appreciate that the standard of care is objectively set. But even so, it is inaccurate to state that no reference may be made to the attributes of the particular defendant. The definition of the reasonable person is not complete unless the words 'in the circumstances' are appended. And, plainly, these words import the need to take account of the particular defendant. But the overwhelming majority of the cases that explicitly recognise the relevance of who the defendant is, do so in terms that eliminate considerations pertaining to the defendant's idiosyncrasies. Instead, they consider those of his attributes that are characteristic of a class to which the defendant belongs.

(1) Child defendants

In *Mullin v Richards*[62] the Court of Appeal confirmed that, in relation to a child, the test is what degree of care and foresight can reasonably be expected of a child of the defendant's age. In that case, two 15-year-old girls were fooling about during a mathematics lesson, fencing with plastic rulers. One of the rulers snapped and a fragment of plastic entered the claimant's eye ultimately causing her to lose any effective sight in that eye. Adopting the approach of the High Court of Australia in *McHale v Watson*,[63] the Court of Appeal held that the claimant had failed to establish that her school-friend was negligent. A 15-year-old, unlike an adult, might well not foresee the risk of her behaviour, particularly as this kind of tomfoolery had never been banned at school, nor had any similar accident occurred previously. Some degree of irresponsibility may be expected of children playing together.[64] Indeed, the courts appear to look for a clear deviation from the norms of children's behaviour in order to find a breach of the obligation of care.[65]

An unresolved question, in relation to the standard of care demanded of children, is whether the test is entirely objective or whether it will take into account the child's *actual* mental ability, maturity, and experience.[66]

(2) Intelligence and knowledge

The defendant's actions must conform to certain criteria expected of a person of normal intelligence in a given situation. It is no defence that someone acted 'to the best of his own judgment' if his 'best' is below that of the reasonable person.[67] A person whose intellect is lower than average is not thereby excused. And likewise, a woman whose intelligence is superior is not liable for failing to use those above-average qualities,

---

[62] [1998] 1 All ER 920. See also, in relation to contributory negligence, *Yachuk v Oliver Blais Co Ltd* [1949] AC 386; *Gough v Thorne* [1966] 3 All ER 398; *Morales v Eccleston* [1991] RTR 151.

[63] (1964) 111 CLR 384.

[64] *Mullin v Richards* [1998] 1 All ER 920, at 928.

[65] *Orchard v Lee* [2009] EWCA Civ 295, at [12].

[66] Cf *Yachuk v Oliver Blais Co Ltd* [1949] AC 386, at 396 with *McHale v Watson* (1964) 111 CLR 384 where Owen J's yardstick was a 'child of the same age, intelligence and experience'.

[67] *Vaughan v Menlove* (1837) 3 Bing NC 468, at 474.

unless she has professed to have some special skill or expertise, in which case the law demands that she must manifest that skill or expertise to a reasonable degree.[68]

Two branches of knowledge must be considered separately. The first is that of memory and experience. If X had been on a certain highway several times, and a reasonable person who had been there as often would know that it was busy, then X also is expected to know it to be busy, even though his memory is so poor that he does not actually remember it. Similarly, people are deemed to know those things which adults from their experience are expected to know: that some things easily explode, that others burn, that gravity exists, etc.[69] There is one refinement of this rule. Where, in the circumstances, the status of the defendant is relevant, the standard is set according to that status. Thus, in *Caminer v Northern and London Investment Trust* the knowledge required of a landowner with regard to elm trees on his estate, their proneness to disease, lack of wind resistance, and the like, was of a standard between that of an urban observer and a scientific arboriculturist.[70] Taking a similar approach, the Privy Council in *The Wagon Mound (No 2)*[71] said that the ship-owner was liable for a fire caused by discharging oil into Sydney Harbour because the chief engineer should have known that the discharge created a real risk of the oil on the water catching fire. Finally, if someone elects to take on a particular task, although he is not an expert or professional in the field, he will be expected to have the necessary degree of knowledge to complete the task competently.[72]

Second, what knowledge of the facts and circumstances surrounding him must the defendant have? He will not be excused for failing to observe what a reasonable person would have observed. Thus, a dock authority that does not know, but ought to know, that the dock is unsafe may be held negligent.[73] Furthermore, even if a reasonable person could not be expected to know something, he or she may be required to get and follow expert advice. Thus, the landlord of flats must consult a specialist engineer about the safety of his lift if he lacks the relevant expertise himself.[74]

Knowledge – in particular expert knowledge – does not remain static over the years. Scientific and technological advances lead to constant revision of, and improvements in, safety standards.[75] In a negligence action, therefore, the defendant must always be judged in the light of the state of scientific, technological, or other expert knowledge which should have been available to him at the time of the alleged breach. Concrete evidence that a drug damaged a foetus is not conclusive that either the doctor prescribing

---

[68] See *Wooldridge v Sumner* [1963] 2 QB 43.

[69] *Caminer v Northern and London Investment Trust* [1951] AC 88. Cf *Haynes v Harwood* [1935] 1 KB 146, at 153.

[70] [1951] AC 88, at 100. See also *Clarke v Holmes* (1862) 7 H & N 937 (employer required to know more about the dangers of unfenced machinery than workman); *Quinn v Scott* [1965] 2 All ER 588.

[71] [1967] 1 AC 617.

[72] See *Chaudhry v Prabhakar* [1989] 1 WLR 29.

[73] *Mersey Docks and Harbour Board Trustees v Gibbs* (1866) LR 1 HL 93.

[74] *Haseldine v Daw & Son Ltd* [1941] 2 KB 343, at 356.

[75] Eg, *Baker v Quantum Clothing Group Ltd* [2011] UKSC 17.

the drug, or the pharmaceutical company marketing the drug, was negligent.[76] The test in negligence must be: 'At the time when the drug was prescribed or marketed, should the risk of injury to the foetus have been foreseen?'. As Lord Denning put it, when a claimant sought damages in respect of a medical accident which had never occurred before: 'We must not look at the 1947 accident with 1954 spectacles'.[77]

The issue is always one of reasonableness. Less is expected within the realm of the family than in commercial and public service settings. Thus, although a parent hiring a bouncy castle for a children's birthday party might have the ability to obtain technical guidance on the safety of such paraphernalia and form views as to its appropriate use in its light, this is not customarily done and is not expected of the parent by a court.[78]

(3) Skill

It has been seen that a person's conduct must conform to the standard of a person of normal intelligence. When a person holds himself out as being capable of attaining standards of skill in relation to the public generally – for example, by driving a car – he is required to display the skill normally possessed by persons doing that thing.[79] A doctor failing to diagnose a disease cannot excuse himself by showing that he acted to the best of his skill if a reasonable doctor would have diagnosed it.[80] Nor can a young hospital doctor escape liability simply by pleading that he is inexperienced or overworked. He must still attain the level of competence expected from a person holding his 'post' and entrusted with his responsibilities.[81] The same principle presumably applies to newly qualified solicitors.[82] But in such cases, one must be careful to ascertain exactly what skill the defendant did hold himself out to possess.

It is also important to realise that, where a skilled person conforms to practices accepted as proper by *some* responsible members of his profession, he will not be held liable in negligence merely because other members of his trade or profession would take a different view. This principle is most frequently applied in the context of medical

---

[76] The drug thalidomide undoubtedly caused serious deformities in babies whose mothers took the drug in early pregnancy. One of the major obstacles confronting claims for compensation by the damaged children was doubt whether, at the time the drug was first available, as opposed to after the births of several deformed babies, doctors and embryologists appreciated that drugs could cross the placental barrier and injure the foetus.

[77] *Roe v Minister of Health* [1954] 2 QB 66, at 84.

[78] *Perry v Harris (a minor)* [2008] EWCA Civ 907.

[79] It is immaterial if D does not in fact have that skill; if he engages in conduct usually associated with persons having that skill, the standard demanded is that of those who actually do possess that skill: *Adams v Rhymney Valley DC* [2000] Lloyd's Rep PN 777. In *Nettleship v Weston* [1971] 2 QB 691, although the standard of a qualified driver was expected of a learner driver, the point was made that if a uniform standard were not applied, the courts would face insuperable difficulties in assessing the skills and competencies of every individual defendant. See also *Imbree v McNeilly* [2008] HCA 40 (bringing Australian law into line with *Nettleship*).

[80] *Bolam v Friern Hospital Management Committee* [1957] 2 All ER 118.

[81] *Wilsher v Essex Area HA* [1987] QB 730 (reversed on a different point [1988] AC 1074).

[82] *Nettleship v Weston* [1971] 2 QB 691, at 709.

negligence where there are often differences in opinion as to the best way to address any given medical problem. In such circumstances, the courts will not choose between rival schools of professional thought.[83] Nor, in other circumstances where two non-negligent courses of action were possible, will the courts hold a defendant liable for failing to take that course which has been revealed, with the benefit of hindsight, to have been the preferable course.[84]

In one case in which the claimant had her ears pierced by a jeweller and subsequently contracted a disease that might have been avoided had the work been done with normal medical skill, the jeweller was required only to show the skill of a jeweller doing such work, not that of a doctor.[85] A similar approach was taken in *Wells v Cooper*, where a householder fitted a new door handle insecurely. When the claimant pulled on it, he lost his balance and was injured. The defendant householder was only required to show the standard of care of a normal DIY enthusiast, not that of a qualified carpenter.[86] On the other hand, while someone who practises alternative medicine is only liable if he fails to meet the standard applicable to his art, it will nonetheless be relevant to take into account findings within conventional medicine which reveal dangers associated with aspects of his art.[87]

Where someone has not held himself out as having special skill, he is not liable when he shows merely average skill in the circumstances, although he does in fact have special skill.[88] Skill, just like every other aspect of the standard of care, has to be assessed in the light of all the circumstances surrounding the alleged breach of duty, and the degree to which the defendant represents that he holds a particular skill is merely one among several considerations.

Where negligence is alleged in the course of playing a sport, the fact that the object of competitive sport is to win and the fact that spectators attend sporting occasions to see competitors exhibit their skill at the game will be relevant. So, in *Wooldridge v Sumner*[89] Diplock LJ held that, where a show-jumper was concentrating his attention and exerting his skill to complete his round of the show-jumping circuit, this must be taken into account in determining whether a momentary misjudgment constituted negligence.[90] By contrast, in *Condon v Basi*[91] a footballer successfully managed to sue

---

[83]   *Bolam v Friern Hospital Management Committee* [1957] 2 All ER 118.

[84]   *Adams v Rhymney Valley DC* [2000] Lloyd's Rep PN 777. An example given in the case is of a driver who on approaching an amber light notices a car very close behind: should that driver pull up sharply and hope the car behind can avoid a collision, or should the driver risk a collision with another vehicle by proceeding through the junction?

[85]   *Philips v William Whiteley Ltd* [1938] 1 All ER 566.

[86]   [1958] 2 QB 265. If the householder employed a professional carpenter no doubt the latter would be under a contractual duty to him to use the skill of a professional, but what standard would the professional owe to members of the public?

[87]   *Shakoor v Situ* [2001] 1 WLR 410.

[88]   *Wooldridge v Sumner* [1962] 2 All ER 978, at 989.

[89]   [1963] 2 QB 43.

[90]   See, in similar vein, *Caldwell v Maguire and Fitzgerald* [2002] PIQR P45.

[91]   [1985] 2 All ER 453.

in negligence when he suffered a broken leg as a result of a tackle by the defendant which was found by the referee to be serious foul play. The Court of Appeal held that a clear breach of the rules of the game would be a relevant (though not conclusive) consideration in deciding whether there had been actionable negligence. The over-all test – which has since been confirmed by the Court of Appeal[92] – is whether the defendant's disregard for the claimant's safety can be characterised as deliberate or reckless (bearing in mind the level of competency to be expected from players of the defendant's class), in which case the defendant will be held to be in breach.

(4) Disability and infirmity?

It is unclear to what extent the standard of the reasonable person will be adjusted to allow for the incapacities and infirmities of individual adults. In *Daly v Liverpool Corpn*[93] it was held that, in deciding whether a 67-year-old woman was guilty of con-tributory negligence in crossing a road, one had to consider a woman of her age, not a hypothetical pedestrian. But this is only a case on contributory negligence and it is, in any event, by no means easy to square with the objective approach advocated on many occasions since it was decided.

In practice, the matter of the defendant's disability or infirmity will seldom arise in respect of the standard of care demanded for the following reason. If X causes an injury to another because X suffers from some disability or infirmity, he will usually be held negligent, not because of want of care at the time of the accident, but because, being aware of his disability, he allowed himself to be in the situation in the first place. Thus, a motorist with seriously impaired eyesight, who collides with another car because she fails to see it approaching, is not negligent because she is partially sighted, but because, given her defective vision, she was careless enough to drive at the outset.

On the other hand, not all defendants will know of their problem. In *Roberts v Ramsbottom*,[94] for example, the defendant suffered a slight stroke just before getting into his car. He was completely unaware that he had had a stroke although he admitted that he felt somewhat dizzy. A few minutes after starting his journey he was involved in a collision injuring the claimant. It was held that, even though his carelessness resulted from impaired consciousness of which he was, at the time of the collision, unaware, he was nonetheless liable in negligence. Neill J suggested two grounds to support the finding of negligence. He said that the defendant was liable first, because he 'continued to drive when he was unfit to do so and when he should have been aware of his unfitness' and, second, because any disability affecting a defendant's ability to drive could only exempt him from the normal, objective standard of care where the disability placed his actions 'wholly beyond his control'. In *Mansfield v Weetabix Ltd*,[95] however, the Court of Appeal rejected the second of these reasons on the basis that it came close to equating liability in negligence with strict liability.[96] There, a lorry

[92] *Caldwell v Maguire* [2002] PIQR P6; *Blake v Galloway* [2004] 1 WLR 2844.
[93] [1939] 2 All ER 142.   [94] [1980] 1 All ER 7.   [95] [1998] 1 WLR 1263.
[96] But the decision in *Nettleship v Weston* [1971] 2 QB 691 is hard to distinguish from strict liability!

driver was involved in a collision when he partially lost consciousness as a result of a hypoglycaemic state induced by a malignancy of which he was completely unaware. Overruling the trial judge's finding of negligence, the Court of Appeal held that, where a disability or infirmity prevented the defendant from meeting the objective standard of care, and the defendant was not, and could not reasonably have been, aware of his condition, that condition must be taken into account in determining whether or not the defendant was negligent.

It is submitted that *Mansfield* appears inconsistent with the general approach which overlooks the idiosyncrasies of the defendant *unless* it is interpreted as focusing on the standard of care of *all* defendants who suddenly become unconscious, instead of merely *this defendant* who suddenly became unconscious.

(5) Special knowledge concerning the claimant

The defendant's actual knowledge of the claimant's frailties and susceptibilities will affect the required standard of care. Thus, the level of care owed to a woman known to be pregnant,[97] to a workman with one eye,[98] or to employees especially susceptible to stress[99] will take account of these conditions *so long as* the defendant knows of them. If the defendant neither knows, nor ought to know, of these circumstances, however, the standard of care will be unaffected by the claimant's susceptibility. As Lord Sumner explained:

> a measure of care appropriate to the inability or disability of those who are immature or feeble in mind or body is due from others, who know of or ought to anticipate the presence of such persons within the scope and hazard of their own operations.[100]

In *Haley v London Electricity Board*[101] the House of Lords applied Lord Sumner's dictum when they held that a body conducting operations on a city highway should foresee that blind persons would walk along the pavement, and that it owes a duty to take those precautions reasonably necessary to protect them from harm. On the facts, it was held liable although a person with normal vision would not have been injured in consequence of its operations. Similarly, in *Johnstone v Bloomsbury Health Authority*[102] in which the level of care owed by an employer to junior doctors who were required to work excessive hours was in issue, Stuart Smith LJ said:

> [I]t must be remembered that the duty of care is owed to an individual employee and different employees may have a different stamina. If the authority in this case knew or ought

---

[97] *Hay (or Bourhill) v Young* [1943] AC 92, at 109.
[98] *Paris v Stepney BC* [1951] AC 367, at 385 and 386.
[99] *Sutherland v Hatton* [2002] PIQR P241.
[100] *Glasgow Corpn v Taylor* [1922] 1 AC 44, at 67. Of course, there are numerous cases where Ds have not been held in breach of a duty to infants (eg, *Donovan v Union Cartage Co Ltd* [1933] 2 KB 71) or to blind persons (eg, *Pritchard v Post Office* (1950) 114 JP 370).
[101] [1965] AC 778.
[102] [1992] QB 333.

to have known that by requiring him to work the hours they did, they exposed him to risk of injury to his health, then they should not have required him to work in excess of the hours that he safely could have done.

It is no answer to a claim in negligence to respond that you did not appreciate the risk that your conduct would injure the claimant, if the reasonable defendant with your knowledge of the claimant and the circumstances would have perceived that risk. Human frailty must be taken into account and defendants cannot shift their duty to such claimants by arguing that all claimants must always look out for themselves. So, in *Pape v Cumbria County Council*[103] it was found to be insufficient for employers to supply their workers with rubber gloves. They had also to warn them of the risk of dermatitis unless the gloves were worn since the prudent employer would take all reasonable steps to ensure that safety equipment is properly understood and used by employees. By contrast, in *Eastman v South West Thames Regional Health Authority*[104] the defendants were held not liable when the claimant was thrown out of her seat in an ambulance and injured when the driver braked hard. She claimed that the driver had been negligent in not expressly instructing her to wear her seat belt. But a notice in the ambulance carried just that instruction. The claimant was not herself a patient. She was accompanying her mother-in-law to hospital. The court held that the ambulance staff had done all that was reasonably required in the circumstances. Had the claimant been herself a sick and confused elderly person, the outcome might well have been different.

(6) Defendant's ability to foresee acts of third parties

Even where the courts are prepared to find a duty in respect of the acts of third parties, it will often be difficult to decide, when there has been an intervening act of a third party, whether the defendant's act has caused the damage suffered by the claimant. It is important to note that the issue of causation becomes material only after the failure of the defendant to take due care has been proved. Whether the defendant has shown that standard of care will frequently depend on what acts or omissions of another he could reasonably have anticipated. If the claimant is injured because a third party has done something that the defendant could not reasonably foresee he would do, the defendant is not liable.[105] Yet, in *London Passenger Transport Board v Upson*,[106] Lord Uthwatt said:

> It is common experience that many do not [assume a fellow road user will act with reasonable care]. A driver is not, of course, bound to anticipate folly in all its forms, but he is not, in my opinion, entitled to put out of consideration the teachings of experience as to the form those follies commonly take.[107]

---

[103] [1992] 3 All ER 211.   [104] [1991] 2 Med LR 297.
[105] *Donaldson v McNiven* [1952] 2 All ER 691.   [106] [1949] AC 155.
[107] Ibid at 173. Cf *Grant v Sun Shipping Co Ltd* [1948] AC 549, at 567.

Nor can one excuse oneself by relying on another to do an act unless that reliance was reasonable. *Manchester Corpn v Markland*[108] illustrates the point.

> The appellants were the statutory authority for the supply of water to the borough of Eccles. One of the appellants' service pipes in a road in Eccles burst. Three days later, the resulting pool of water froze, and a car skidded on the ice knocking down and killing a man. In a negligence action brought by the dependants of the deceased against the appellants, it was held to be no defence that the appellants chose to rely on Eccles Corporation to notify them of bursts: they should themselves have taken proper precautions.

SECTION 3   THE CONNECTION BETWEEN THE STANDARD AND DUTY OF CARE

Accepting, then, that the standard of care is fixed as a matter of law in the light of the *factual* considerations just outlined, one must ask the further question of whether the standard of care has to be particularised in detail in terms of its obligations. A motorist fails to sound his horn at a crossing and is held liable in negligence to another motorist with whom he collides. The court holds that he should have sounded his horn. Would such a decision thenceforth be authority for the proposition that a motorist has an obligation to sound his horn when approaching an intersection? Although such a suggestion is superficially attractive, we must be cautious of adopting this approach. In 'running down' cases, for example, it will usually be relevant to consider the speed of the vehicles, the degree of visibility, the state of the road, the distance within which the vehicles could have pulled up, etc. Also, how often will the facts of any particular case be exactly replicated in a subsequent case? Are not the circumstances of each case sufficiently different in at least one material respect to make it inapt to formulate a catalogue of obligations based on each individual decision?

 Given this backdrop, it is perhaps unsurprising that, in terms of judicial practice, the higher courts have generally[109] rejected forcefully attempts to particularise obligations in negligence. In *Baker v E Longhurst & Sons Ltd*,[110] for example, Scrutton LJ appeared to lay down a principle that a person driving in the dark must be able to pull up within the limits of his vision. Shortly afterwards, in another road traffic case, Lord Wright said that:

> no one case is exactly like another, and no principle of law can in my opinion be extracted from those cases. It is unfortunate that questions which are questions of fact alone should be confused by importing into them as principles of law a course of reasoning which has no doubt properly been applied in deciding other cases on other sets of facts.[111]

---

[108] [1936] AC 360.
[109] Though, for the contrary approach see, eg, *Caminer v Northern and London Investment Trust Ltd* [1951] AC 88.
[110] [1933] 2 KB 461, at 468.
[111] *Tidy v Battman* [1934] 1 KB 319, at 322. Cf *SS Heranger (Owners) v SS Diamond (Owners)* [1939] AC 94, at 101.

When counsel again relied on the dictum of Scrutton LJ in *Morris v Luton Corpn*, Lord Greene adopted the dictum of Lord Wright 'in the hope that this suggested principle [of Scrutton LJ] may rest peacefully in the grave in future'.[112] Most important of all is the 1959 decision of the House of Lords in *Qualcast (Wolverhampton) Ltd v Haynes*.[113] There, the House of Lords went out of its way to stress that a judge's reasons for finding want of reasonable care are matters of fact, not law, for otherwise 'the precedent system will die from a surfeit of authorities'.[114] That judges now give reasons for conclusions formerly arrived at by juries without reasons must not be allowed to elevate these decisions of fact into propositions of law.

Naturally, in certain common kinds of claim – notably those arising out of road traffic accidents – factual situations do repeat themselves. Judges may properly refer to earlier decisions for guidance as to what constitutes reasonableness in the circumstances. The infinite variability of human conduct, however, makes it undesirable to express such a standard in terms of an inflexible legal duty. *Worsfold v Howe*[115] illustrates the point.

> D, a car driver, edged blind from a side road across stationary tankers and collided with a motorcyclist approaching on the main road past the tankers. Because the Court of Appeal had held in a previous case that a driver so edging out was not negligent, the trial judge felt bound to absolve D from liability.

The Court of Appeal held that the previous decision laid down no legal principle, that such decisions were to be treated as ones of fact, and, in the instant circumstances, held the defendant negligent. In *Foskett v Mistry*,[116] the Court of Appeal reinforced that approach. They ruled that, in 'running down' claims, the question of whether reasonable care had been taken must be judged in the light of all the facts of the particular incident.

SECTION 4   PROFESSIONAL NEGLIGENCE[117]

(A) THE BACKGROUND

There is, in terms of fundamental principle, no distinction between the guidelines ascertaining the standard of care of professionals from those applicable to any other person. Whether the defendant is a plumber or an architect or a consultant surgeon, the primary question is whether in all the circumstances the defendant acted with the skill and competence to be expected from a person undertaking his particular activity

---

[112] [1946] KB 114, at 116. See also *Easson v London and NE Rly Co* [1944] KB 421.
[113] [1959] AC 743.   [114] [1959] 2 All ER 38, at 43–4.
[115] [1980] 1 All ER 1028.   [116] [1984] RTR 1.
[117] For full treatment of this important topic, see Powell, *Jackson and Powell on Professional Negligence* (6th edn, 2010).

and professing his specific skill. But problems do arise in actions against professionals, and include the following:

(1) There may be disputes within the profession as to what constitutes proper practice.

(2) The implications of professional negligence are likely to be more far reaching. When a carpenter makes an error fixing a new door, the householder may suffer personal injury if the door falls off, but the range of potential harm is limited. Should an architect make a design error in his plans for a tower block of flats, however, hundreds of people are at risk, and the financial cost of correcting the error in several blocks of flats may be astronomic.

(3) The potentially high cost of professional negligence has resulted in massive increases in insurance premiums for architects, solicitors, accountants, etc. Many professions are now calling for statutory limits on damages awards made against the relevant professionals even though limited liability partnerships can help.

(4) Particularly acute difficulties affect doctors. Limited funding of the NHS can mean that doctors may often be overworked and hospitals under-resourced, and patients increasingly wish to play a greater part in decision-making these days.

(5) Finally, and rather obviously, a professional defendant will normally be worth suing. The rules of the profession are likely to oblige him to take out professional indemnity cover. On the other hand, professional negligence actions are thus apt to be defended vigorously by the professional backed by his insurers.

Some further guidelines are therefore given here on the current state of the law in England and Wales relating to professional negligence.

(B) DUTY AND BREACH

Very often, the duty of care will arise concurrently in tort and within the contract between the professional and his client. Save where an NHS professional is treating a patient, most professional/client relationships are founded on a contract for services. The client, for example, pays the solicitor or the accountant for her advice. A duty of care will be implied into that contract,[118] but will a duty in tort arise concurrently allowing the client to opt whether to sue in contract or tort? After years of conflicting decisions, the House of Lords in *Henderson v Merrett Syndicates Ltd*[119] ruled in favour of concurrent liability, provided that imposing a duty in tort does not conflict with the contractual terms agreed between the parties.[120] When duties of care do arise

---

[118] See s 13 of the Supply of Goods and Services Act 1982.

[119] [1995] 2 AC 145.

[120] Note, also, *Bellefield Computer Services Ltd v E Turner & Sons Ltd* [2002] EWCA Civ 1823 in which the limit of the contractual duty was relevant to construing the limit of the tortious duty.

concurrently, the question of whether there has been a breach of duty will generally be determined on exactly the same principles, whether the action is framed in tort or contract. However, contract may impose duties beyond those covered by the tortious duty of care.

> In *Thake v Maurice*[121] a surgeon failed to warn a private patient of the risk that a vasectomy may be reversed by a natural process of re-canalisation of the vas. The patient argued that the surgeon contracted to render him sterile and that he was therefore liable for that breach of contract regardless of whether he was negligent when the patient's wife conceived again. The Court of Appeal eventually held, by a majority, that no reasonable man would infer from his contract with a doctor that the doctor guaranteed success.[122]

The case graphically illustrates the separate roles of tort and contract where the claimant seeks to establish a liability independent of classic negligence. The argument pursued by the claimant – that sterility would be guaranteed – could not even have been attempted had he been an NHS patient.

In a number of professional relationships, the core of the professional's duty is to offer advice. Liability in negligence will depend largely on the principles governing liability for negligent misstatements. In *Caparo Industries plc v Dickman*,[123] auditors prepared a report on a company on the basis of which the claimant mounted a successful takeover bid of that company. The claimants alleged that the report negligently suggested pre-tax profits of £1.2 million when in fact there had been losses of £400,000. The House of Lords held that no duty was owed to the claimants. Mere foreseeability of financial loss to a third party was insufficient to create a duty on the part of the professional. For a duty to arise to a third party: (1) the professional must be aware that his advice will be transmitted to the claimant, or to an identifiable class of persons of which the claimant is a member; (2) that advice must be transmitted in order to forward a specific purpose or transaction of the claimants; (3) it must be reasonable in all the circumstances for the claimant to rely on that advice, rather than to seek independent advice of his own, and the professional must be well aware that the claimant will so rely on his advice.[124] But note that no duty will be owed if the professional's contract with his or her client conflicts with the alleged duty owed to a third party.[125]

---

[121] [1986] QB 644. See also *Eyre v Measday* [1986] 1 All ER 488.

[122] But the Court of Appeal unanimously held the surgeon liable in negligence. The failure to warn was held to be negligent, and as a result the wife failed to recognise the symptoms of pregnancy soon enough to be able to opt for an abortion.

[123] [1990] 2 AC 605.

[124] For examples of these criteria being fulfilled, see *Smith v Bush* [1990] 1 AC 831 and *White v Jones* [1995] 2 AC 207.

[125] See, eg, *Clarke v Bruce Lance & Co* [1988] 1 All ER 364.

(C) THE REASONABLE PROFESSIONAL

The standard of care imposed will reflect the level of skill and expertise that the professional holds himself out as having, *or* which it is otherwise reasonable to expect in the circumstances.[126] In the latter case, the defendant must exhibit the degree of skill which a member of the public would expect from a person in his or her position. The law will presume that the professional person will have sufficient time and resources properly to provide the service requested. This includes the time necessary to conduct any research required to reach an informed opinion about a matter.[127] Pressures on him – even pressures for which he is in no way responsible – will not excuse an error on his part. Negligence is not to be equated with moral culpability or general incompetence. In *Wilsher v Essex Area Health Authority*,[128] for example, a premature baby was admitted to a specialist neo-natal unit. An error was made in that the medical staff failed to notice that the baby was receiving too much oxygen and the baby became blind. The Court of Appeal held that the doctors were negligent and, by a majority, that they must be judged by reference to their 'posts' in the unit. It would be irrelevant that they were inexperienced, or doing a job which should have been done by a consultant, or just grossly overworked. The dissenting judge argued that the doctors should be assessed individually. If a particular doctor was too junior for his 'post', then it should be the health authority that was directly liable to the claimant for providing inadequate staffing and resources.[129]

In determining the standard demanded in a particular 'post', expert evidence of proper practice must be called. Where practice is disputed, however, conformity with a responsible body of opinion within the profession will generally suffice.[130] Nonetheless, the court remains the ultimate arbiter of what constitutes reasonable and responsible professional practice. In *Edward Wong Finance Co Ltd v Johnson*,[131] the defendant solicitors followed a uniform practice among the profession in Hong Kong. They paid the purchase price to the vendors in return for the promise to ensure that a property was free of encumbrances. The vendors fraudulently failed to do so, and the claimant thus failed to obtain an unencumbered title to the property. The Privy Council held that, while evidence of the practice of the profession went a long way towards showing that the defendant was not negligent, it was not conclusive. The risk of fraud should have been foreseen and precautions taken to avoid that risk.

Until recently, judges in claims against doctors seemed more than usually unwilling to challenge expert professional opinion. Lord Scarman castigated a trial judge

---

[126] *Chaudhry v Prabhakar* [1989] 1 WLR 29, at 34.

[127] *Independent Broadcasting Authority v EMI Electronics Ltd* (1980) 14 BLR 1.

[128] [1987] QB 730 (reversed on the issue of causation [1988] AC 1074).

[129] On the direct liability of health authorities to patients see Murphy, 'The Juridical Foundations of Common Law Non-Delegable Duties' in Neyers (ed), *Emerging Issues in Tort Law* (2007), ch 14.

[130] *Bolam v Friern Hospital Management Committee* [1957] 2 All ER 118.

[131] [1984] AC 296.

for presuming to prefer one body of distinguished professional opinion to another.[132] However, in *Bolitho v City and Hackney Health Authority*,[133] Lord Browne-Wilkinson stressed that to constitute evidence of proper, non-negligent practice, expert opinion must be shown to be reasonable and responsible: 'the court has to be satisfied that the exponents of the body of opinion relied on can demonstrate that such opinion has a logical basis'.[134] If 'in a rare case' it can be shown that professional opinion cannot withstand logical analysis, then in a claim against a doctor, as much as in a claim against any other professional, a judge is entitled to find that expert opinion is not reasonable or responsible.[135]

Errors of judgment are often the essence of professional negligence. An error is not, of itself, negligence. The issue in all cases is whether the error in question evidenced a failure of professional competence. The virtual immunity offered to doctors for errors of clinical judgment was firmly condemned by the House of Lords in *Whitehouse v Jordan*. As Lord Edmund Davies put it:

> The test [of negligence] is the standard of the ordinary skilled man exercising or professing to have that special skill. If a surgeon fails to measure up to that standard in any respect (clinical judgment or otherwise) he has been negligent.[136]

In assessing that standard, care must be taken to relate what is expected of the professional to the expertise he claims to hold, and not to demand unrealistic standards of skill and knowledge. In *Luxmoore-May v Messenger May-Baverstock*[137] the claimant took a painting to a local auctioneer for valuation and sale. The defendants were held not liable for failing to discover that it was a painting by a well-known artist of the eighteenth century. Similarly, if a general practitioner were to be consulted by a patient complaining of stomach trouble, she would not be expected to have the same level of knowledge as a consultant gastro-enterologist. She must, however, recognise her own limitations and know when the patient needs to be referred to a specialist.

SECTION 5   BREACH OF AN EMPLOYER'S DUTY TO ITS EMPLOYEES

The risk of personal injury suffered either in an accident at work, or by contracting an industrial disease, is particularly acute in certain types of employment. 'Broad' legislative measures have been adopted to prevent such injuries from occurring,[138] focused on the Health and Safety at Work etc Act 1974. These have reduced the importance of

---

[132] *Maynard v West Midlands Regional Health Authority* [1984] 1 WLR 634, at 639.
[133] [1998] AC 232. See also *Hucks v Cole* [1993] 4 Med LR 393.
[134] [1997] 3 WLR 1151, at 1159.
[135] An analysis of when this occurs is provided in Mulheron (2010) 69 CLJ 609.
[136] [1981] 1 WLR 246, at 258.   [137] [1990] 1 All ER 1067.
[138] Information about the legislation is available from the Health and Safety Executive: www.hse.gov.uk. Last accessed 28 September 2011.

the common law, but by no means eliminated it.[139] The general liability of employers under the common law[140] remains liability in negligence alone.[141] The circumstances in which an employer will be held to have been in breach of the duty he owes his employees thus warrants separate consideration.

As will be seen, some of the language deployed to analyse employers' responsibilities is the language of duty. But despite this, at the core of the majority of cases on employers' liability is the issue of the standard of care. The central question discussed here, therefore, is just what kinds of safeguards must employers put in place to discharge their duty in tort for the health and safety of their workers? In answering this question, the courts accept that the concept of 'safety' is relative and not absolute in nature. This is to say that the conception of what is 'safe' will vary according to changes in knowledge and the availability and cost of precautionary measures.[142]

(A) A PERSONAL, NON-DELEGABLE DUTY

The employer's duty is a personal one of a general nature. As will be seen later,[143] there is another form of tortious liability, known as vicarious liability, whereby an employer is held liable not for a breach of his own personal duty, but for the tort of his employee. Until the Law Reform (Personal Injuries) Act 1948, an employer sued by a worker on account of the employer's vicarious liability for the tort of a fellow-worker could successfully raise the defence of common employment. The personal duties of employers have been kept strictly separate from those for which their responsibility is vicarious. It is true that, since that Act abolishes the defence of common employment, this strict marking off of personal duty has become less important in circumstances where the claimant can in any event prove fault by a fellow employee. But it would be misleading to state that the distinction can now be ignored.[144] There will still be many cases where the employer is in breach of his personal duty without any employee being at fault.[145] Furthermore, the distinction remains the basis of judicial thinking on the subject,

---

[139] *Spencer-Franks v Kellogg Brown and Root Ltd* [2008] UKHL 46, at [34].

[140] Breach of the general statutory code on safety provided for by the Health and Safety at Work Act 1974 is not actionable as a breach of statutory duty: s 17(1). But it is reasonable to expect that, in assessing negligence, judges treat conformity with the code as evidence that reasonable care has been taken (and vice versa).

[141] Compensation for industrial injuries is provided for by way of the state scheme relating to industrial injuries. Nonetheless, the higher level of common-law damages ensures that many employees continue to elect for the common-law remedy in negligence. And the Employers' Liability (Compulsory Insurance) Act 1969 requires employers to insure against liability for injury sustained by employees in the course of their employment.

[142] *Baker v Quantum Clothing Group Ltd* [2011] UKSC 17, at [64], [80], [82], [111], [126], and [181]–[182].

[143] Ch 24.

[144] See Murphy, 'The Juridical Foundations of Common Law Non-Delegable Duties' in Neyers (ed), *Emerging Issues in Tort Law* (2007), ch 14.

[145] It may be that there is simply an inadequate system of working (see, eg, *General Cleaning Contractors Ltd v Christmas* [1953] AC 180); or it may be that the individual at fault is not an employee of the employer sued as in *McDermid v Nash Dredging and Reclamation Co Ltd* [1987] 3 WLR 212.

and the development and implications of the cases cannot be understood if this is not grasped.

Employers' responsibilities fall naturally into three divisions: (1) personnel (that is, the provision of competent staff); (2) those concerned with the place of work, machinery, tools, and raw materials (that is, the provision of a safe place of work with proper plant and equipment); (3) the general management or system of work (including supervision).

An important feature of the employer's duty is the fact that it is non-delegable. The true nature of the non-delegable duty has been subject to controversy. There is a lingering argument that it encapsulates an independent head of liability. The courts insist, however, that the non-delegable duty is an aspect of the law of negligence related to the obligation of the employer.[146] Non-delegability places responsibility for taking precautions on the organisation; this reduces the scope for liability gaps especially in cases of failures to act.

In *McDermid v Nash Dredging and Reclamation Co Ltd*[147] C was employed by Ds as a deckhand. He was sent to work on a rig owned by a Dutch company under the control of a Dutch captain employed by that Dutch company. C had no idea that he was not continuing to work on one of Ds' boats under one of Ds' captains. C suffered serious injuries as a result of the Dutch captain's carelessness. Ds denied responsibility on the basis that they were not vicariously liable for the conduct of someone else's employee. The House of Lords held Ds liable on very simple grounds. The evidence showed that C was injured because no safe system of work was in operation. The duty incumbent on his employers to devise and ensure the operation of such a system had not been fulfilled.

The essential characteristic of the employer's non-delegable duty

> is that, if it is not performed, it is no defence for the employer to show that he delegated its performance to a person, whether his servant or not his servant, whom he reasonably believed to be competent to perform it. Despite such delegation the employer is liable for the non-performance of the duty.[148]

Although the duty is personal, and cannot be discharged by entrusting it to a competent delegate, fault must still be proved for negligence liability to be imposed.[149] Thus, Lord Tucker has stressed the importance of not enlarging the employer's duty until it is barely distinguishable from his absolute statutory obligations.[150] On the other

---

[146] The matter received consideration in *Leichhardt MC v Montgomery* (2007) 230 CLR 22.

[147] [1987] AC 906. See also *Kondis v State Transport Authority* (1984) 154 CLR 672.

[148] *McDermid v Nash Dredging and Reclamation Co Ltd* [1987] 3 WLR 212, at 223. See McKendrick (1990) 53 MLR 770.

[149] Cf Stevens, 'Non-Delegable Duties and Vicarious Liability' in Neyers (ed), *Emerging Issues in Tort Law* (2007), ch 13.

[150] *Latimer v AEC Ltd* [1953] AC 643, at 658. See also *Cook v Square D* [1992] ICR 262 (sub nom *Square D v Cook* [1992] IRLR 34). In *Richardson v Stephenson Clarke Ltd* [1969] 3 All ER 705, the employers left it to C, an employee, to choose his equipment. He chose carelessly and was hurt. It was held that the employers

hand, an employer may be liable for a mere omission:[151] actual knowledge of a danger on his part is not insisted on; it suffices if he ought to have known of it.[152] It is a question of fact whether there has been a breach of the duty;[153] precedents relating to industrial practice form guidance as to an employer's breach of duty, but no more than that.[154] Compliance with common practice will constitute strong, but not conclusive, evidence that the employer has discharged his duty. Nevertheless, once a substantial risk of industrial disease, for example, is well known, failure to protect employees against that disease will be actionable even if it is the 'customary practice' of the trade to go on ignoring the risk.[155]

The same defences are available here as in the general law of negligence. But it is worth stressing that the courts are generally reluctant to find that a worker has voluntarily encountered a danger with obvious consequences for the *volenti* defence.[156] On the other hand, where employment necessarily involves particular risks – for example, working as a stuntman – the employer is under no duty to remove these risks, and an employee injured in consequence of undertaking them will not recover in negligence. There is, however, a duty to warn prospective new employees of such risks before they accept the job.[157]

Remembering always that the basic question is whether the employer has failed to take reasonable care for the safety of his employee,[158] and that the tripartite division – based loosely on competent staff, safe places of work, and safe systems of work – is not necessarily an exhaustive list of all possible aspects of an employer's duty towards his employees, it is nonetheless convenient to examine each of those three categories.

(B) THE PROVISION OF COMPETENT STAFF

Prior to 1948, an employee injured by the incompetence of his fellow employee could recover damages in negligence from his employer only by establishing that the employer was himself negligent in employing the fellow employee in the circumstances. Although the negligent engagement of incompetent staff will still today give rise to potential liability, this aspect of an employer's duty towards his employees is no longer of great practical significance: the defence of common employment has ceased

---

had discharged their duty by providing safe equipment and leaving the selection of the equipment to C; C's negligence alone caused the accident.

[151] *Williams v Birmingham Battery and Metal Co* [1899] 2 QB 338; *Barber v Somerset CC* [2004] 1 WLR 1089.

[152] *Baker v James* [1921] 2 KB 674, at 681.

[153] *Latimer v AEC Ltd* [1953] AC 643, at 655. Furthermore, the res ipsa loquitur doctrine applies: *Ballard v North British Rly Co* 1923 SC (HL) 43, at 53.

[154] *King v Smith* [1995] ICR 339.

[155] *Thompson v Smiths Shiprepairers (North Shields) Ltd* [1984] QB 405.

[156] *Smith v Baker & Sons* [1891] AC 325.

[157] See *White v Holbrook Precision Castings* [1985] IRLR 215.

[158] Emphasised again by the House of Lords in *General Cleaning Contractors Ltd v Christmas* [1953] AC 180. Cf *Drummond v British Building Cleaners Ltd* [1954] 3 All ER 507.

to absolve the employer from vicarious liability. Indeed, modern-day cases in this category will now only be relevant where the claimant cannot prove any fault on the part of the other employee and yet can show that his injury results from negligent staffing provision. The most common case will be where the employer appoints an insufficiently qualified or experienced person for a particular task.[159]

(C) ADEQUATE PREMISES AND PLANT

The employer must take reasonable care to provide safe premises[160] and plant for his workers. Both the failure to provide some necessary equipment and the provision of defective appliances will constitute breaches of this duty. So, for example, the failure of ship-owners to provide essential spare ropes for a voyage was actionable negligence.[161] There is probably also a duty not merely to provide the material, but also to maintain it.[162]

(D) A PROPER SYSTEM OF WORKING

The scope of this requirement was considerably increased by the decision of the Court of Appeal in *Speed v Thomas Swift & Co Ltd*.[163]

C was engaged in loading a ship from a barge. Normally, the particular part of this loading operation (requiring the port and starboard winches to be used together), was carried out while the ship's rails were left in position. Only when one winch was being used was it ordinarily necessary to remove a section of the rails in order to prevent their being caught by the hook. The following special circumstances, however, made it dangerous on that occasion to load with two winches without removing the section of the rail. Other sections of the rail had been damaged by accident and had been removed out of necessity; timber was lying against the rails so that it was likely easily to be dislodged; the port winch was not in perfect order. A hook caught in the rail, and the rail and timber fell into the barge injuring C. It was held that he could recover in negligence because D had not, in these particular circumstances, provided a safe system of work.

---

[159] *Black v Fife Coal Co Ltd* [1912] AC 149 (employment of a colliery manager without experience of carbon monoxide in a pit where its presence was a possible danger); esp at 170. In *Hudson v Ridge Manufacturing Co Ltd* [1957] 2 QB 348, knowingly to employ a workman continually indulging in horseplay was held to violate this duty.

[160] 'Whether the servant is working on the premises of the master or on those of a stranger, that duty is still the same; but...its performance and discharge will probably be vastly different in the two cases. The master's own premises are under his control: if they are dangerously in need of repair he can and must rectify the fault at once if he is to escape the censure of negligence. If, however, a master sends his plumber to mend a leak in a respectable private house, no one could hold him negligent for not visiting the house himself to see if the carpet in the hall creates a trap': *Wilson v Tyneside Window Cleaning Co* [1958] 2 QB 110, at 121.

[161] *Vaughan v Roper & Co Ltd* (1947) 80 Ll LR 119.

[162] Dicta in *Wilsons & Clyde Coal Co Ltd v English* [1938] AC 57 and *Toronto Power Co Ltd v Paskwan* [1915] AC 734, at 738.

[163] [1943] KB 557 (approved in *Colfar v Coggins and Griffith (Liverpool) Ltd* [1945] AC 197, where (at 202), however, Viscount Simon LC suggested that the principles laid down there marked the limit of the duty).

Lord Greene MR approved the following description of 'system of work':

> What is system and what falls short of system may be difficult to define…but, broadly stated, the distinction is between the general and the particular, between the practice and method adopted in carrying on the master's business of which the master is presumed to be aware and the insufficiency of which he can guard against, and isolated or day to day acts of the servant of which the master is not presumed to be aware and which he cannot guard against; in short, it is the distinction between what is permanent or continuous on the one hand, and what is merely casual and emerges in the day's work on the other hand.[164]

He added:

> It…may include…the physical lay-out of the job – the setting of the stage, so to speak – the sequence in which the work is to be carried out, the provision in proper cases of warnings and notices, and the issue of special instructions. A system may be adequate for the whole course of the job or it may have to be modified or improved to meet circumstances which arise. Such modifications or improvements appear to me equally to fall under the head of system.[165]

On the other hand, in *Winter v Cardiff RDC*,[166] the House of Lords held that a worker, who was injured because a rope provided by the employer for that purpose had not in fact been used to lash a regulator being carried on a lorry in which he was travelling, could not complain of the system of work. Lord Porter said:

> The difference…is between a case where sufficient and adequate provisions have been made, which will, if carried out, protect the workman unless one of his fellows does not use proper care in carrying out the system, and a case where the system itself makes no such provision.[167]

Does this suggest that, provided a safe system is devised, any failure in operation of the system will not be actionable as a breach of the employer's personal duty? This proposition must be treated with caution after *McDermid v Nash Dredging and Reclamation Co Ltd*. For there Lord Brandon asserted unequivocally that the duty extended to the operation of the system,[168] the crucial factor in that case being perhaps that the relevant carelessness in operating the system was that of the man in control of the operation and not just a fellow employee of the claimant.

The House of Lords has also emphasised that, in considering whether the employers are negligent, regard must be had to their knowledge of physical shortcomings of particular workers, so that it was relevant, in deciding whether the employers had taken reasonable care to protect a worker from flying metal by providing him with goggles, that the employers knew him to be one-eyed.[169]

---

[164] [1943] KB 557, at 562, citing *English v Wilsons and Clyde Coal Co Ltd* 1936 SC 883, at 904.
[165] [1943] KB 557, at 563.   [166] [1950] 1 All ER 819.
[167] Ibid at 822.   [168] [1987] 3 WLR 212, at 223.
[169] *Paris v Stepney BC* [1951] AC 367. On the other hand, in *Charlton v Forrest Printing Ink Co Ltd* [1980] IRLR 331, it was held that an employee attacked by robbers after collecting wages from the bank could not sue his employers on the ground that they neglected his safety by not employing a security firm instead.

Many of the decided cases on employers' liability focus on responsibility for physically dangerous work environments. The risk to the employee is usually of crude injury whether by a mechanical device or via industrial disease. Yet other sorts of risk, for example, also come within the employers' duty. Claims for stress-related illness are rapidly becoming commonplace. In *Johnstone v Bloomsbury Area Health Authority*[170] the Court of Appeal refused to strike out a claim by a junior doctor that the excessive hours which he was required to work had damaged his health. And in *Walker v Northumberland County Council*[171] a social worker recovered damages after his employers failed to reduce his workload on his return from sick leave after suffering a nervous breakdown.[172] The continued stress triggered a second bout of illness. The court held that, given the obvious risk of further mental injury to the claimant, the employer should have taken steps to reduce the level of stress to which the claimant was exposed by his work.

Notwithstanding the foregoing, it must not be forgotten that employers' liability is not unlimited and that an employer does not have to 'insure' his personnel against all work-related risk. In *Reid v Rush & Tompkins Group plc*,[173] for example, an employer was held not liable for failing to provide his employee posted abroad with insurance against risks encountered in that posting.

Consider, too, the rights of workers on premises. If the worker is merely employed by an independent contractor of the occupier, he will of course, have the rights of a visitor against the occupier. He will only have the greater rights of an employee against an employer in respect of the defect on the premises if he shows that the defect was tantamount to a failure on the employer's part to take reasonable care to protect his safety as, for instance, in *General Cleaning Contractors Ltd v Christmas*,[174] where the employee of a firm of window cleaners was held to be entitled to recover from the firm for failure to lay out a safe system on the premises of a customer whose windows he was cleaning. Subject to that, he will normally be limited to the rights of a visitor contained in the Occupiers' Liability Act 1957 or any right of action for breach of statutory duty that there may be. However, even beyond these actions, an employer will be liable for defective equipment negligently provided by a third party in circumstances where, under the Occupiers' Liability Act 1957, an occupier would not be liable for that independent contractor's fault. Furthermore, the employer must insure against this risk.[175]

Particular difficulty may arise where the employee is, at the time of the accident, actually working on a site abroad. In *Cook v Square D*,[176] the claimant suffered injury while working in Saudi Arabia. The Court of Appeal held that the employers did not

---

[170] [1992] QB 333.   [171] [1995] 1 All ER 737.

[172] See also *Sutherland v Hatton* [2002] PIQR P241.   [173] [1989] 3 All ER 228.

[174] [1953] AC 180; *Drummond v British Building Cleaners* [1954] 3 All ER 507; *Smith v Austin Lifts Ltd* [1959] 1 All ER 81.

[175] The Employers' Liability (Compulsory Insurance) Act 1969.

[176] [1992] IRLR 34 (cf the outcome of this decision with *McDermid v Nash Dredging and Reclamation Ltd* [1987] 3 WLR 212).

have a duty to guarantee the safety of premises occupied by third parties. The question must be whether in the light of all the circumstances the employer had done enough to take reasonable steps to protect his staff.

Finally it should be noted that an employer's negligence can incur liability to the employee's family as well as the employee himself. If the employee is exposed to toxic substances at work, or to a transmissible disease,[177] so that unwittingly he endangers his wife who washes his work-clothes, or his family who contract the disease, the employer may owe a duty of care to the family as well. But there must be adequate proof that the level of toxicity, or the risk of infection, did endanger the employee so as to create a real risk to the family.[178]

SECTION 6   ORGANISATIONAL LIABILITY

Related to the issues discussed in the preceding section is that of 'organisational liability'. An organisation, such as a council, health authority, or prison authority, will often owe obligations of care not just to their employees, but to third parties which are 'non-delegable' in nature. This is to emphasise the important expectation that management in an organisation has an obligation to ensure that care is taken with respect to the activities of that organisation that might injure.[179] The non-delegable nature of the obligation means that there is no liability gap where injury occurs, not by way of positive act, but by way of omission – because of a failure to properly organise. The scale of such obligations is growing, in part because of the impact of the Human Rights Act 1998. This requires, for example, prisons and hospitals to have systems of work in place to protect the lives of those involuntarily detained.[180] Reasons for this obligation include the ability of management to organise and oversee, the likelihood of greater resources than those available to individuals, and the advantage of institutional memory. This issue is explored further in chapter 24.

SECTION 7   PROVING NEGLIGENCE

(A) LAW AND FACT

Historically, negligence actions were tried by judge and jury; the judge deciding matters of law and the jury matters of fact. Nowadays, however, they are heard by a judge sitting without a jury: the judge trying issues of both law and fact. It should

---

[177] Consider the potential liability if a health worker becomes infected with hepatitis B and passes on the disease to her husband or any other sexual partner.

[178] *Hewett v Alf Brown's Transport* [1992] ICR 530 (no evidence that the levels of lead waste to which the husband was exposed were sufficient to cause the wife's lead poisoning).

[179] See Chan (2010) 18 Torts LJ 228.

[180] See, eg, *Savage v South Essex Partnership NHS Foundation Trust* [2009] AC 681.

not, therefore, be surprising that many modern judgments do not meticulously separate matters of law from questions of fact. This then evokes the question of where the boundary lies between law and fact.

The following are matters of law:

(1) All questions of duty – was the duty owed to the claimant? What was the scope of the duty? etc.

(2) The standard of care – what was the standard required?

(3) The principles to be applied in determining whether the damage was too remote, and whether there was any evidence of such damage, and whether any recognised heads of damage have not been taken into account.

By contrast, matters of fact include:

(1) Resolving conflicts in the evidence and determining what the circumstances were and what the parties did.

(2) Evaluating the conduct of the parties in the light of the facts found and deciding whether there was a failure to take care, having regard to the standard of care required of the defendant.

(3) Deciding, in the light of the facts found, whether the damage was caused by the defendant, the extent of the damage,[181] and the appropriate level of damages.[182]

When appellate courts largely heard appeals from judges sitting with a jury, they were concerned solely with those matters defined as matters of law. Today the appellate jurisdiction from the judge sitting alone is much broader. '[The court] has ... jurisdiction to review the record of the evidence in order to determine whether the conclusion originally reached upon that evidence should stand; but this jurisdiction has to be exercised with caution.'[183] The court should be 'satisfied that any advantage enjoyed by the trial judge by reason of having seen and heard the witnesses, could not be sufficient to explain or justify the trial judge's conclusion',[184] before it disturbs his findings of fact. On the other hand, where, as often happens, the facts are not in dispute, but the case rests on the inference to be drawn from them, an appellate court is in as good a position as the trial judge to decide the case.[185]

---

[181] These and (2) are matters of inference from (1).

[182] See chs 26 and 27.

[183] *Watt v Thomas* [1947] AC 484, at 486.

[184] Ibid at 488.

[185] *Powell v Streatham Manor Nursing Home* [1935] AC 243, at 267. See also *Benmax v Austin Motor Co Ltd* [1955] AC 370. Appellate courts are these days exercising this power so freely that many decisions now turn solely on matters of inference from facts. *Morris v West Hartlepool Steam Navigation Co Ltd* [1956] AC 552, is a typical example of the House of Lords substituting its own evaluation of the facts for that of the trial judge: nothing else is in issue, yet the case appears in the Law Reports. See also *Whitehouse v Jordan* [1981] 1 All ER 267.

(B) ONUS OF PROOF

Whether what is in issue is the veracity of primary facts alleged or the validity of the inferences to be drawn from those facts, the claimant shoulders the burden of establishing (1) that the defendant was negligent, and (2) that his negligence resulted in the claimant's loss or injury.[186] Should the evidence be evenly balanced so that the accident might have been the result of lack of care or competence, but might just as easily have occurred without carelessness, the claimant fails for he will not have established negligence to the required standard of proof.[187] In *Ashcroft v Mersey Regional Health Authority*,[188] for example, the claimant suffered a partial paralysis in her face when in the course of surgery on her left ear the surgeon cut into a facial nerve. Some expert evidence showed this to be an inherent risk of such surgery even when performed with the greatest skill, while other experts acknowledged that it also sometimes occurred because of a failure in skill. The claimant's action failed.

At least Mrs Ashcroft knew what had happened even though her counsel failed, ultimately, to establish negligence on the defendant's part. In many cases of alleged negligence, the claimant knows only that he has been injured. How he came to be hit on the head by a falling object or a collapsing wall, or why a swab remained in his abdomen after surgery, is a closed book to him. In a number of such cases, however, the claimant may be able to invoke the principle of res ipsa loquitur. In others, section 11 of the Civil Evidence Act 1968 may be of use to him.

(1) Res ipsa loquitur

In *Scott v London and St Katherine's Docks Co*[189] the facts were as follows.

> While near the door of D's warehouse, C was injured by some sugar bags falling on him. The judge directed the jury to find a verdict for D on the ground of lack of evidence of negligence by D, who called no evidence. On appeal a new trial was directed.

The court justified this direction of a new trial in the following terms, which have since become known as the res ipsa loquitur principle.[190]

> There must be reasonable evidence of negligence. But where the thing is shown to be under the management of the defendant or his servants, and the accident is such as in the ordinary course of things does not happen if those who have the management use proper care,

---

[186] Given difficulties of proving breach in certain kinds of negligence case, and given the inadequacy of other private law remedies as well, the Law Commissions have argued for reform of the law regarding misleading consumer practices: see Law Commissions, *Consumer Redress for Misleading and Aggressive Practices: A Joint Consultation Paper* (Law Com Consultation Papers Nos 199 and 149, 2011). See esp ibid at 63–5.

[187] As to why, see Porat and Stein, *Tort Liability Under Uncertainty* (2001), ch 1.

[188] [1983] 2 All ER 245 (affirmed [1985] 2 All ER 96n).

[189] (1865) 3 H & C 596.

[190] Ibid at 601. It is not necessary to plead the doctrine; it is enough to prove facts which make it applicable: *Bennett v Chemical Construction (GB) Ltd* [1971] 3 All ER 822.

it affords reasonable evidence, in the absence of explanation by the defendant, that the
accident arose from want of care.

In the past there has been a tendency to elevate res ipsa loquitur to the status of a
principle of substantive law or at least a doctrine. In the 1970s, however, the Court
of Appeal decisively swung away from that approach. In *Lloyde v West Midlands Gas
Board*, Megaw LJ said:

> I doubt whether it is right to describe *res ipsa loquitur* as a 'doctrine'. I think that it is
> no more than an exotic, although convenient, phrase to describe what is in essence no
> more than a common-sense approach, not limited by technical rules, to the assessment
> of the effect of evidence in certain circumstances. It means that a [claimant] *prima facie*
> establishes negligence where (i) it is not possible for him to prove precisely what was the
> relevant act or omission which set in train the events leading to the accident, but (ii) on the
> evidence as it stands at the relevant time it is more likely than not that the effective cause
> of the accident was *some* act or omission of the defendant or of someone for whom the
> defendant is responsible, which act or omission constitutes a failure to take proper care
> for the [claimant's] safety.[191]

It is still necessary to examine the content of the res ipsa loquitur principle, but always
with that warning in mind. Three separate requirements must be satisfied.

(a) The absence of explanation[192]

This limb merely means that if the court finds on the evidence adduced how and why
the occurrence took place, then there is no room for inference. So, in *Barkway v South
Wales Transport Co Ltd*[193] – where the tyre of a bus burst and the bus mounted the
pavement and fell down an embankment – res ipsa loquitur did not apply because
the court had evidence of the circumstances of the accident and was satisfied that the
system of tyre inspection in the defendants' garage was negligent.

The word 'explanation' must be qualified in this context by the adjective 'exact'.[194]
This is to make it clear that a claimant who is able to present a partial account of
how an accident happened is still not precluded from relying on res ipsa loquitur for
further inferences essential to winning his case. The partial explanation may make it
more obvious that an inference of negligence can be drawn. But of course, as in the

---

[191] [1971] 2 All ER 1240, at 1246. The Court of Appeal in *Turner v Mansfield Corpn* (1975) 119 Sol Jo 629
unanimously affirmed that decision. See also *Ng Chun Pui v Lee Chuen Tat* [1988] RTR 298.

[192] *Barkway v South Wales Transport Co Ltd* [1950] 1 All ER 392, at 394.

[193] [1950] 1 All ER 392. And see *Swan v Salisbury Construction Co Ltd* [1966] 2 All ER 138. In *Richley v
Faull* [1965] 3 All ER 109, D's car hit C's car when D's car was on the wrong side of the road. D proved that
he skidded. Without mentioning res ipsa loquitur, the court reached the solution supported by common
sense that D was liable unless he showed that the skid occurred through no fault on his part. Similarly in
Henderson v Henry E Jenkins & Sons [1970] AC 282, the sudden failure of brakes on a lorry owing to a cor-
roded pipe in the hydraulic braking system was held to impute negligence to the owners.

[194] *Ballard v North British Rly Co* 1923 SC (HL) 43, at 54.

Barkway case, even if res ipsa loquitur is inapplicable because all the material facts are proved, those facts may still be found to constitute negligence.[195]

(b) The harm must be of such a kind that it does not ordinarily happen if proper care is being taken

The courts have applied res ipsa loquitur to things falling from buildings,[196] and to accidents resulting from defective machines, apparatus, or vehicles.[197] It applies also where motor cars mount the pavement,[198] or where aircraft crash on attempting to take off.[199] On the other hand, it was held inapplicable when neighbouring rooms were damaged by fire spreading from a lodger's room in which a fire had been left alight in the grate.[200]

It will be recalled that the classic definition of Erle CJ referred to accidents happening 'in the ordinary course of things'. *Mahon v Osborne*[201] raised the question of whether this means that it must be a matter of common experience, so that the experience of the expert is irrelevant. Goddard LJ held that the principle applied where swabs had been left in the body of a patient after an abdominal operation.[202] But Scott LJ thought that the principle did not apply where the judge could not, as he could with surgical operations, have enough knowledge of the circumstances to draw an inference of negligence.[203] Since then, the Court of Appeal has held it to be prima facie evidence of negligence that a man leaving hospital after a course of radiography treatment on his hand and arm should suffer four stiff fingers and a useless hand.[204] Equally, a court at first instance was influenced by expert evidence in rejecting the application of res ipsa loquitur to a case where a patient sustained a fractured jaw as a result of a dental extraction.[205] Yet where an unexplained accident occurs from a thing under the control of the defendant, and medical or other expert evidence shows that such accidents would not happen if proper care were used, there is strong evidence of negligence.[206]

---

[195] Conversely, D is not liable for an unexplained accident, to which res ipsa loquitur might otherwise apply, if he establishes that he himself was not negligent: *Barkway v South Wales Transport Co Ltd* [1948] 2 All ER 460, at 463.

[196] *Byrne v Boadle* (1863) 2 H & C 722 (flour barrel falling from upper window on to C walking on the street below); *Kearney v London and Brighton Rly Co* (1870) LR 5 QB 411.

[197] *Ballard v North British Rly Co* 1923 SC (HL) 43; *Kealey v Heard* [1983] 1 All ER 973.

[198] *McGowan v Stott* (1930) 143 LT 219n; *Ellor v Selfridge & Co Ltd* (1930) 46 TLR 236; *Laurie v Raglan Building Co Ltd* [1942] 1 KB 152.

[199] *Fosbroke-Hobbes v Airwork Ltd and British-American Air Services Ltd* [1937] 1 All ER 108.

[200] *Sochacki v Sas* [1947] 1 All ER 344.

[201] [1939] 2 KB 14.

[202] Ibid at 50.

[203] Ibid at 23. It is impossible to be certain of the view of MacKinnon LJ, in view of the conflicting reports perhaps the fullest of which is at (1939) 108 LJKB 567.

[204] *Cassidy v Ministry of Health* [1951] 2 KB 343. *Saunders v Leeds Western HA* [1993] 4 Med LR 355.

[205] *Fish v Kapur* [1948] 2 All ER 176. Cf the patient who swallows a throat pack: *Garner v Morrell* (1953) *Times*, 31 October.

[206] *Lillywhite v UCL Hospitals NHS Trust* [2005] EWCA Civ 1466.

(c) The instrumentality causing the accident must be within the exclusive control of the defendant

(i) **The meaning of 'control'**

If the defendant is not in control, res ipsa loquitur does not apply. *Turner v Mansfield Corpn*[207] is illustrative.

> C, a driver of D's dust-cart was injured when its back raised itself up as C drove it under a bridge. It was held that, since C was in control, it was for him to explain the accident. As he was unable to furnish any evidence from which negligence could be inferred, he failed.

McGowan v Stott[208] is an important case also in that it called a halt to previous attempts to insist on complete control of all the circumstances before the rule could apply. Previously, Fletcher Moulton LJ had indicated[209] that the scope of res ipsa loquitur was severely limited in highway accidents because all the essential surrounding circumstances were seldom under the defendant's control. Yet, the court in *McGowan v Stott* refused to follow this approach, declaring the doctrine to be applicable to accidents on the highway where the defendant was in control of the vehicle causing the damage. Two actions brought against railway companies by claimants who had fallen out of trains illustrate the degree of control essential for the doctrine to apply:

> In *Gee v Metropolitan Rly Co*,[210] a few minutes after a local train had started its journey, C leaned against the offside door, which flew open. This was held to be evidence of negligence on the part of the railway company.
> In *Easson v London and North Eastern Rly Co*,[211] C's claim failed, Goddard LJ holding that 'it is impossible to say that the doors of an express corridor train travelling from Edinburgh to London are continuously under the sole control of the railway company'.

(ii) **Where one of two or more persons is in control**

If the instrumentality is in the control of one of several employees of the same employer, and the claimant cannot point to the particular employee who is in control, the rule may still be invoked so as to make the employer vicariously liable. Thus, a hospital authority has been held answerable for negligent treatment where the claimant could not show which of several members of the staff was responsible.[212] Furthermore, if a surgeon is shown to be in general control of an operation, and the patient cannot

---

[207] The case is briefly reported at (1975) 119 Sol Jo 629, but the text here is based on a full Court of Appeal transcript.

[208] (1930) 143 LT 219n. Where the apparatus is in C's house – eg, gas apparatus – the onus is on C to show that it was improbable that persons other than D could have interfered with it. Only then can he invoke res ipsa loquitur: *Lloyde v West Midlands Gas Board* [1971] 2 All ER 1240. In *Ward v Tesco Stores Ltd* [1976] 1 All ER 219, C slipped on yoghurt that had been spilt on the floor of D's supermarket. Even though there was no evidence as to how long the yoghurt had been on the floor it was held to be a case of prima facie negligence.

[209] *Wing v London General Omnibus Co* [1909] 2 KB 652, at 663–4.

[210] (1873) LR 8 QB 161.   [211] [1944] KB 421, at 424.

[212] *Cassidy v Ministry of Health* [1951] 2 KB 343.

establish whether it was the malpractice of the surgeon or one of the theatre staff which inflicted damage on him in the course of that operation, it seems that res ipsa loquitur applies in an action for negligence against the surgeon.[213] If, on the other hand, the surgeon is not in control of all the relevant stages of the treatment, and if the claimant cannot prove that the act complained of took place at a time when the defendant surgeon was in control, res ipsa loquitur cannot be invoked.[214]

Walsh v Holst & Co Ltd[215] extends the principle further. When the defendant's duty is so extensive that he is answerable for the negligence of his independent contractor, and an accident occurs while the independent contractor is performing the work delegated to him, the claimant can invoke res ipsa loquitur against both the defendant and his independent contractor.[216]

A related, though distinct, problem is the position of a claimant who establishes, without invoking the rule of res ipsa loquitur, that the damage to him was caused either by the negligence of A or by the negligence of B. If he is merely able to show that only A or B but not both must have been negligent then he is not entitled to a judgment against both unless the defendants have refused to give evidence, in which case adverse inferences against them may be drawn.[217] It is, however, the duty of the trial court to come to a definite conclusion on the evidence. It must not dismiss the action because of uncertainty as to which party was free from blame.[218] If the inference is that one or other or both have been negligent, the claimant has made out a prima facie case against either A or B, or both.[219] Of course, if the circumstances do not warrant the inference that one or other has been negligent, the claimant fails.[220]

Beyond setting out the above guidance, it is submitted that one cannot define the circumstances where the res ipsa loquitur principle applies. As usual in negligence, some writers list all the circumstances where res ipsa loquitur has been applied as if they were precedents on points of law. But the Court of Appeal has held that such cases do not

---

[213]   *Mahon v Osborne* [1939] 2 KB 14.

[214]   *Morris v Winsbury-White* [1937] 4 All ER 494. Perhaps Somervell LJ disagreed with this statement of law in *Roe v Minister of Health* [1954] 2 QB 66, at 80.

[215]   [1958] 3 All ER 33; *Kealey v Heard* [1983] 1 All ER 973.

[216]   Apparently, the employer conceded that he was liable even though C had not established that the act did not occur within that area of the independent contractor's operations for which the employer is not answerable: viz, acts of collateral negligence.

[217]   *Baker v Market Harborough Industrial Co-operative Society Ltd* [1953] 1 WLR 1472; *Cook v Lewis* [1952] 1 DLR 1 decided that where either X or Y has committed a tort against C and it is the careless act of both of them which prevents C from knowing which caused the harm, both are liable (X and Y were hunters, one or other of whom fired the shot which hit C).

[218]   *Bray v Palmer* [1953] 2 All ER 1449.

[219]   *Roe v Minister of Health* [1954] 2 QB 66; *France v Parkinson* [1954] 1 All ER 739. Where vehicles collide either at crossroads or on the brow of a hill, and both drivers are dead, a passenger has a prima facie case, in the absence of other evidence, against both drivers or either of them: *Davison v Leggett* (1969) 133 JP 552 (head-on collision in the centre lane, negligence by both drivers inferred and more fully reported in *Knight v Fellick* [1977] RTR 316).

[220]   *Knight v Fellick* [1977] RTR 316.

lay down any principles of law; they are merely guides to the kinds of circumstances in which the res ipsa loquitur principle may successfully be invoked.[221]

(d) The effect of res ipsa loquitur[222]

In some cases the inference to be drawn by resorting to the principle is twofold: that the defendant caused the accident, and that he was negligent. In others, the cause is known, and only the inference of negligence arises.[223]

As we have seen, on any given facts it may be just as likely that the event happened without negligence as that it happened in consequence of negligence, in which case there is no hint of negligence. If, however, in such circumstances, res ipsa loquitur applies, its effect is to make it 'relevant to infer negligence'[224] from the fact of the accident. This simply means that there is in law evidence on which the judge may properly find for the claimant.[225] The distinctive function of the rule is to permit an inference of negligence from proof of the injury and the physical instrumentality causing it, even though there is no proof of the facts identifying the human agency responsible. Looked at in this way, its affinity to the ordinary rule of evidence that circumstantial evidence is admissible to prove negligence is clear. As Atkin LJ put it:

> all that one wants to know is whether the facts of the occurrence do as a matter of fact make it more probable that a jury may reasonably infer that the damage was caused by want of care on the part of the defendants than the contrary.[226]

It is clear, then, that the effect of res ipsa loquitur is to afford prima facie evidence of negligence. It does not shift the burden of proof to the defendant[227] in the sense that, in the absence of the defendant rebutting the inference on the balance of probabilities, the courts must find for the claimant. But once res ipsa loquitur has been successfully invoked to raise an inference of negligence against the defendant, if the defendant fails to adduce any countervailing evidence, the judge will be entitled to find for the claimant. Historically, the judge could not have withdrawn the case from the jury. But it may now be that certain facts are so clear that the inference of negligence is sufficiently cogent that the judge must rule in favour of the claimant. On the other hand, this will by no means always be the case. As Du Parcq LJ said:

> The words res ipsa loquitur…are a figure of speech, by which sometimes is meant that certain facts are so inconsistent with any view except that the defendant has been negligent that any jury [or judge] which, on proof of these facts, found that negligence was not

---

[221] Easson v London and North Eastern Rly Co [1944] KB 421, at 423.

[222] For the clearest judicial statement, see the eight rules laid down by Evatt J in Davis v Bunn (1936) 56 CLR 246, at 267–8.

[223] Barkway v South Wales Transport Co Ltd [1950] 1 All ER 392, at 399–400.

[224] Ballard v North British Rly Co 1923 SC (HL) 43, at 54.

[225] Cole v De Trafford (No 2) [1918] 2 KB 523, at 528.

[226] McGowan v Stott (1923), in (1930) 143 LT 219n. Cf Langham v Governors of Wellingborough School and Fryer (1932) 101 LJKB 513, at 518.

[227] On burden of proof generally see Wilsher v Essex Area HA [1988] AC 1074.

proved would be giving a perverse verdict. Sometimes, the proposition does not go as far as that, but is merely that on proof of certain facts an inference of negligence may be drawn by a reasonable jury [or judge].[228]

To sum up, the effect of res ipsa loquitur depends on the cogency of the inference to be drawn, and will vary from case to case. If, for instance, a vehicle mounts the pavement, this *may be* evidence of negligence, but reasonable people may differ about the inference to be drawn from these facts, so that a verdict of no negligence may not be upset. Yet something may fall from the defendant's window in such circumstances that only an inference of negligence can be drawn, in which case a verdict of no negligence should be set aside.

The effect of res ipsa loquitur where the defendant gives evidence must also be considered. Plainly, the effect of the doctrine is to shift the onus to the defendant in the sense that the principle continues to operate unless the defendant calls credible evidence which explains how the accident may have occurred without negligence; and it seems that the operation of the rule is not displaced merely by expert evidence showing theoretically possible ways in which the accident might have happened without the defendant's negligence. But beyond this, the courts describe its effect in two different ways. Sometimes they state that once the defendant has furnished evidence of the cause of the accident consistent with his having exercised due care it becomes a question of whether, upon the whole of the evidence, the defendant was negligent or not; and the defendant will succeed unless the court is satisfied that he was negligent.[229] On other occasions they state that the defendant loses unless he proves that the accident resulted from a specific cause which does not connote negligence on his part but, on the contrary, points to its absence as more probable.[230] There is possibly no inconsistency in these judicial utterances; all may depend on the context of the cases and the cogency of the rebutting evidence in the particular case.[231]

A useful example of how a defendant can rebut an inference of res ipsa loquitur can be seen in *Ng Chun Pui v Lee Chuen Tat*.[232]

> A coach veered across the road colliding with a bus coming in the opposite direction. C called no evidence and the Privy Council held that the facts per se raised an inference of negligence. But Ds testified that an unidentified car cut across their coach causing the driver to brake suddenly and skid across the road. Ds were found to have rebutted any inference of negligence since the driver's reaction to an emergency beyond his control did not constitute any breach of duty.

---

[228] *Easson v London and NE Rly Co* [1944] KB 421, at 425.

[229] Eg, *Ballard v North British Rly Co* 1923 SC (HL) 43, at 54; *The Kite* [1933] P 154; *Colvilles Ltd v Devine* [1969] 2 All ER 53.

[230] Eg, *Moore v R Fox & Sons Ltd* [1956] 1 QB 596.

[231] See, eg, *Lillywhite v University College London Hospitals NHS Trust* [2005] EWCA Civ 1466.

[232] [1988] RTR 298.

(2) Civil Evidence Act 1968, section 11

Whereas res ipsa loquitur can be a seen as a partial exception to the general rule that the claimant must prove the defendant's negligence in that it raises a rebuttable presumption of that negligence, section 11 of the Civil Evidence Act 1968 goes slightly further. It in fact reverses the burden of proof in certain circumstances. Where a defendant has previously been convicted of a criminal offence against the claimant, and the claimant subsequently brings civil proceedings on the basis of the same facts that led to the defendant's conviction, section 11 makes that conviction prima facie evidence of the defendant's civil liability. It then falls to the defendant to demonstrate to the judge (on the balance of probabilities) in civil proceedings that he should not be held liable in damages.[233] This he is entitled to attempt to do,[234] although the court must be mindful of a potential abuse of process whereby the defendant is effectively attempting to re-litigate his criminal conviction.[235] Thus, in *Grealis v Opuni*[236] the fact that the defendant had been in breach of road traffic legislation (by driving at 38mph in a 30mph zone) did not detract from his ability to show that the claimant was contributorily negligent (80% to blame, in fact).

FURTHER READING

BRAZIER AND MIOLA, 'Bye-bye *Bolam*: a medical litigation revolution?' (2000) 8 *Medical Law Review* 85

KIDNER, 'The Variable Standard of Care, Contributory Negligence and *Volenti*' [1991] *Legal Studies* 1

MULHERON, 'Trumping *Bolam*: A Critical Legal Analysis of *Bolitho*'s Gloss' (2010) 69 *Cambridge Law Journal* 609

RAZ, 'Responsibility and the Negligence Standard' (2010) 30 *Oxford Journal of Legal Studies* 1

WITTING, 'The Hand and *Shirt* tests for breach and the Civil Liability Acts' (2009) 17 *Torts Law Journal* 242

---

[233] See *Wauchope v Mordecai* [1970] 1 WLR 317.
[234] *J v Oyston* [1999] 1 WLR 694.
[235] *McCauley v Hope* [1999] PIQR P185.
[236] [2003] 12 LS Gaz R 32.

5

CAUSATION AND
REMOTENESS[1]

KEY ISSUES

(1) Causation in fact

The primary question in the law on causation is whether the defendant can be said to have been a factual cause of the claimant's loss or harm. This question can in most cases be answered by applying what is known as the 'but for' test. According to this test, the defendant can generally be said to have been a factual cause of the claimant's loss or harm if, but for the defendant's breach of a duty owed to the claimant, the claimant would not have suffered in the way that she did. There are, however, quite a number of exceptional types of case in which the application of the basic 'but for' approach will not be practicable. Since the courts cannot shy away from such hard cases, they have been forced to develop a number of alternative tests (sometimes on a seemingly ad hoc basis) in order to resolve them. There is, as a result, no universal test for causation in fact.

(2) Causation in law

There is a second aspect to causation in cases where harm results from a combination of successive events. In such instances, the task for the courts is to identify the legally significant cause: it is reducible to asking whether event X (which occurs subsequent to event Y) can be regarded as a *novus actus interveniens* (or new intervening cause) so as to sever the chain of causation flowing from event X.

(3) Remoteness of damage

The law does not allow recovery for every single form of loss or harm that can, no matter how tenuously, be linked to a prior tort. Limits are placed on the losses for which any given defendant will be held responsible and required to pay compensation. In other words, some forms of loss will be regarded as too remote from the defendant's tort for the defendant to be held liable in respect of those losses. The general test

---

[1] There is a massive literature on causation. Among the best reading is Hart and Honoré, *Causation in the Law* (2nd edn, 1985), Wright (1985) 75 Cal L Rev 1735, and (for treatment of the hardest cases) Porat and Stein, *Tort Liability Under Uncertainty* (2001).

of remoteness in tort law is whether the harm in question was reasonably foreseeable. (In some torts – principally those that involve the intentional infliction of harm – the question of remoteness does not really arise. But one instance in which a test of directness, rather than reasonable foreseeability of harm, is applied is the tort of deceit, and appropriate consideration of the principles at play can be found in chapter 13.)

SECTION 1   INTRODUCTION

Causation is relevant in all torts since problems arise across the board in relation to the twin questions of whether the defendant's wrongful conduct did in fact cause the claimant's loss and whether the defendant ought to be held responsible for the full extent of that loss.

Causation will be dealt with in this chapter in three stages. First, we will consider causation in fact – the matter of how (and to what standard of proof) the claimant must establish that the harm of which he complains resulted from the defendant's negligent conduct. Next, we will consider the question of causation in law: that is, whether a subsequent intervening cause – a *novus actus interveniens* – may be said to sever the chain of causation such that the subsequent cause is treated in law as the only relevant cause of the claimant's loss or injury. Finally, we shall consider the principles governing the related question of remoteness of damage.

A further prefatory point, however, is this. While causation is relevant throughout tort law, it is dealt with here for two reasons. First, very many, though not all, of the more complex causation cases concern negligence. Second, in negligence, unlike those torts actionable per se (at least so far as substantial damages are not sought), causation must be specifically proved before any liability will be imposed. Beyond this, the only other matter that might usefully be mentioned at this stage is that the principles governing remoteness of damage can vary in tort law. The rules discussed here, which pertain to negligence, are the ones most widely applied. Where the rules are different in relation to certain other torts, the relevant principles are explained in the appropriate chapters.

SECTION 2   CAUSATION IN FACT

(A) THE 'BUT FOR' TEST

Establishing cause and effect can be far from easy. Every occurrence is the result of a combination of several different events. Any incident resulting in injury to a claimant is the product not simply of the negligent acts and omissions of the defendant, but also of the conditions in which those events took place. These can include incidents both prior and subsequent to the allegedly tortious conduct of the defendant. Consider the facts of *Wright v Lodge*.[2]

> D2 was driving her car at night along a dual carriageway in the fog. The road was unlit. Her engine failed and the vehicle came to a stop in the near-side lane. A few minutes later, as D2 was trying to restart her vehicle, an articulated lorry being driven at 60 mph by D1 crashed into her car virtually destroying it and seriously injuring a passenger in the back seat. After hitting the car, the lorry careered across the central reservation. The lorry fell on to its side, blocking the road. Four vehicles collided with it. One driver died of his injuries and another was seriously injured.

What or who caused those additional injuries? Had the second defendant not chosen to go out that evening, or had it not been foggy, or had the road been lit, the accident might never have happened. In one sense, then, each of those factors is a cause without which the accident would not have occurred. But the law, of course, looks primarily to the human actors. The unlit road and the fog are merely part of the complex of conditions which produced the accident, but they are not regarded as causes in law. On the other hand, not all human acts constitute the cause in law of an event. No one would suggest that by driving out that night, the driver of the car (or lorry) was responsible for the three claimants' injuries. What must be identified is the operative legal cause or causes (and in this case it was the lorry driver alone who was held liable in respect of the second set of crashes even though his lorry would not have been blocking the carriageway had it not been for the car driver negligently failing to move her car out of the way).

Identifying the operative cause involves considerations of policy as much as it does any strict notion of factual cause and effect.[3] Lord Wright captured the point when he said, '[t]he choice of the real or efficient cause from out of the whole complex of facts must be made by applying common sense standards'. 'Causation is', he continued, 'to be understood as the man in the street, and not as either the scientist or the metaphysician would understand it'.[4] In similar vein, Laws LJ has said that '[t]he law has dug no deeper in the philosophical thickets of causation than to distinguish between a *causa sine qua non* and a *causa causans*'.[5]

It is thus partly as a matter of convenience that the law settles upon a basic 'but for' test of causation whereby the question that the court generally addresses is whether, but for the defendant's tortious act, the harm would have occurred.[6] If the question receives a negative answer, and there is no evidential complication in the case, the court

---

[2] [1993] 4 All ER 299.

[3] In *Gregg v Scott* [2005] 2 AC 176, Lord Hoffmann admitted openly that 'an apparently arbitrary distinction [in the law] obviously rests on grounds of policy'. See also the open use of policy in *Fairchild v Glenhaven Funeral Services Ltd* [2002] 3 All ER 305 and *Barker v Corus UK Ltd* [2005] UKHL 20.

[4] *Yorkshire Dale Steamship Co Ltd v Minister of War Transport* [1942] AC 691, at 706. In similar vein, see *Kuwait Airways Corp v Iraq Airways Co* [2002] 2 AC 883, at [74]. See also Stapleton (1988) 8 OJLS 431.

[5] *Rahman v Arearose Ltd* [2001] QB 351, at [32].

[6] It has famously been suggested that a better explanation of what the courts *in fact* look for is a necessary element in a set of conditions sufficient to bring about the harm (the so-called NESS test): see Hart and

will hold the defendant liable (subject to the harm in question being too remote to permit recovery). Thus, where a man who later died of arsenic poisoning was sent home from a casualty department without treatment after complaining of acute stomach pains, his widow's claim against the hospital failed even though the hospital admitted negligence.[7] Crucially, even if he had been given prompt and competent medical treatment, he would still have died.

(B) EVIDENCE OF CAUSATION

In most cases there is no problem in identifying what has been done (or not done) by the defendant and what in turn this has led to. But sometimes things are less straightforward. In such cases, the standard of proof becomes relevant. That is, it must be shown that it is more likely than not that the wrongful conduct of the defendant caused the claimant's loss or injury.[8]

Where there is some evidence that the defendant's conduct *may* have contributed to the claimant's injury, the burden rests with the claimant. It does not fall to the defendant to rebut the possibility that his conduct *may* have caused the claimant's loss. It thus follows that when the harm in question is a disease, the claimant's task may be a very formidable one. Consider the example of a man claiming that he developed dermatitis because of contact with substances at work caused by his employer's failure to supply proper protective clothing. The medical evidence may well reveal that contact with those substances was merely one possible cause. But it may also indicate that several other possible causes can be identified. In such a case the claimant must show that it was more likely than not that those substances caused the dermatitis;[9] and the question of whether he has produced sufficient evidence to do this is one of law, not fact. Note once again that the exercise is one of identifying the legally operative cause: that of selecting from among a menu of possible causes the 'responsible cause'.

(C) CASES OF EVIDENTIAL UNCERTAINTY

(1) Cases involving the 'loss of a chance'

A number of cases involving 'the loss of a chance' have come before the English courts, and they have served to illustrate the importance of the standard of proof in this context.

> In *Hotson v East Berkshire Area Health Authority*,[10] C fell several feet from a tree injuring his hip. He was rushed to hospital but his injury, thanks to D's negligence, was not

---

Honoré, *Causation in the Law* (1985), xliv). However, it is the language of 'but for', not 'NESS', that is to be found in the English cases.

[7] *Barnett v Chelsea and Kensington Hospital Management Committee* [1969] 1 QB 428.

[8] *Hotson v East Berkshire Area HA* [1987] AC 750.

[9] Cf the exceptional case of mesothelioma: see *Sienkiewicz v Grief* [2011] 2 WLR 523 (discussed below).

[10] [1987] AC 750.

diagnosed until five days later. The hospital admitted negligence and responsibility for the pain C suffered during the five days that treatment was negligently delayed but denied liability for the avascular necrosis that C developed as a result of a failure in the blood supply to his injured hip. The trial judge found (though no one knew for sure) that there was a 75% chance that avascular necrosis would have developed as a result of the injury even if promptly treated, and a 25% chance that it was due to the delay. He held the hospital liable for the loss of the 25% chance that the condition could have been avoided (that is, 25% of the compensation which would have been payable had D been entirely responsible for C's condition). In the House of Lords, it was held fatal to C's case that the accident alone was more than likely the cause of his condition.[11]

According to the House of Lords, if the claimant had been able to show that the delay was the more probable cause of the necrosis, he would have been able to recover in full. But since it was the less likely cause, he could recover nothing.[12] Though a highly contentious decision,[13] it has since been followed by a majority of the House of Lords in *Gregg v Scott*[14] where the claimant sought to claim on the basis of a reduced prospect of surviving cancer based on a doctor's misdiagnosis of his condition and consequent failure to refer him to a specialist for confirmation (or otherwise) of that diagnosis. In fact, the claimant had a malignant lymphoma, but this was not discovered until over one year later. Medical evidence showed that even had there been an immediate referral, the claimant would not, on the balance of probabilities, have secured any greater life expectancy.

Importantly, from a legal perspective, *Hotson* did not involve the loss of a chance (for which loss a claim of proportionate damages could be made). Either the boy's hip was sufficiently damaged at the time of his fall that he would be permanently disabled or it was not. Unfortunately, the evidence available was inadequate to show beyond doubt that it was so damaged. All that could be said, by reference to the available evidence, was that it was more likely than not that, at the time of his fall, the boy's hip was so severely damaged that even prompt treatment could not have prevented his future disability. The decision may appear unpalatable in so far as there was a small chance that immediate treatment may have made a difference. But from the point of view of the law, the fact that it was more probable than not that even prompt treatment would have made no difference, meant that the boy could not be regarded as having lost a chance of being cured. The law treated the onset of avascular necrosis as inevitable.

Perhaps one of the reasons why the House of Lords adopted this approach was because allowing claims generally for lost chances (in the shape of proportionate damages) would radically change the shape of tort law. It would open the way for many more claimants to litigate their cases and might even have serious repercussions

---

[11] [1985] 3 All ER 167, at 240 and 248.
[12] See also *Kay v Ayrshire and Arran Health Board* [1987] 2 All ER 417 (C unable to prove on the balance of probabilities that D who supplied C with an overdose of penicillin had caused C's deafness).
[13] See Stapleton (1988) 104 LQR 389; Lunney [1995] LS 1.
[14] [2005] 2 AC 176.

for insurance companies and the National Health Service given that the deleterious effects of medical mishaps are often uncertain. It would also mean (presumably) a reduction in the damages for those (currently able to recover in full) who are able to show a greater-than-even chance that the defendant's negligence caused them to lose the chance of being cured or the chance of avoiding a particular condition. Weighing up the pros and cons of each approach is by no means easy since a good deal of speculation is required either way. Fully recognising these difficulties, Lord Phillips (in the majority) confined himself to deciding no more than he had to in *Gregg v Scott*. He thus left open the question of whether he would have been prepared to develop the law along the lines of loss of chance in misfeasance cases. That being the case, it may well be that notwithstanding the decisions in *Hotson* and *Gregg*, the Supreme Court may at some future time be required again to again address this difficult issue.[15]

Leaving misfeasance cases to one side, it is certainly true that the loss of a chance is recoverable in circumstances where the claimant's loss is attributable to a negligent omission and the question of causation turns on the hypothetical action of a third party. In *Allied Maples Group Ltd v Simmons and Simmons*[16] the facts were as follows.

> Cs had been advised by Ds (their solicitors) in relation to the purchase of certain businesses from another company. At one stage, the proposed contract included an undertaking by the vendor company that there were no outstanding liabilities in respect of their properties. In the course of negotiations, however, that undertaking got deleted. After purchasing the business, Cs found themselves liable for substantial sums arising from leases previously held by the vendor. The original undertaking would have protected them from such liabilities. Cs therefore argued that Ds were negligent in not advising them that its removal exposed them to liabilities that would not have arisen if the clause had been retained. The issues, therefore, were whether Cs would have tried to insist on its retention had they been properly advised, and whether the vendors would, in turn, have agreed to its retention.

The Court of Appeal held that the claimants had to prove on the balance of probabilities that it was more likely than not that, properly advised, they would have approached the vendors for so showing would establish the loss of a chance to renegotiate the contract. Having done this, they did not need to go on and show that it was also more likely than not that the vendors would have consented to the clause being reinserted. It was enough merely to show a substantial (as opposed to a speculative) chance that they would have agreed.[17] This was enough to make meaningful the claim that the

---

[15] At the very least, *Gregg v Scott* leaves unanswered the question of why the loss of a chance is recoverable in professional negligence cases resulting in economic loss (see, eg, *Allied Maples Group Ltd v Simmons & Simmons* [1995] 1 WLR 1602) but not where the professional negligence is that of a doctor. One might say that it is (in light of the general hierarchy of protected interests in tort law) objectionable to permit claims in respect of the loss of a chance of a financial gain but not the loss of a chance of physical cure. Cf *Gouldsmith v Mid-Staffordshire General Hospitals NHS Trust* [2007] EWCA Civ 397.

[16] [1995] 1 WLR 1602.

[17] A not entirely groundless claim would suffice: *Dixon v Clement Jones Solicitors* [2005] PNLR 6.

claimants had lost a chance to renegotiate the agreement. That said, the probability of the vendors agreeing would need to be determined in order to assess the proper quantum of damages.

Another case in which a claim for a lost chance succeeded was *Spring v Guardian Assurance plc*.[18] There, an employer was found liable for negligently giving a bad reference about the claimant to a new prospective employer. The claimant recovered for his loss of a chance of employment with the new employer. While he could not prove that he would definitely have been given the job, he could at least prove that with a properly written reference he would have had a decent chance of getting it.

These two cases, as well as others in which *Allied Maples* has been applied,[19] can be distinguished from *Hotson*. In that case, it was argued that the boy had lost a 25% chance of recovering had he been treated. But the probability in that case was calculated according to expert evidence grounded on statistical analysis of outcomes in previous cases. Such evidence was of the kind: in 25 out of 100 falls, prompt treatment might save the hip. But this merely means that when the boy came to hospital, he was probably one of the 75 unfortunate ones for whom prompt treatment would make no difference. As such, he could not be heard to argue along the lines that he might 'possibly have avoided the condition' in the same way that, for example, the claimant might 'possibly have got the job' in *Spring*. After the event – that is, after the necrosis had set in – it was simply not possible to say whether he had ever had a chance of recovery (assuming the provision of proper treatment). The uncertainty in *Hotson*, therefore, was of a qualitatively different kind.[20]

In the cases just considered, the courts did not perceive the need to depart from the usual 'but for' test that must be proved on the balance of probabilities. It is true that they possessed a certain amount of evidential uncertainty, but there was enough that was known for sure to stick to the usual rules. In *Allied Maples*, it was certain that the claimant lost the chance to renegotiate the terms of the purchase agreement; in *Spring*, it was certain that the claimant had lost the chance of employment. Furthermore, in both cases there was only one possible cause of the loss of the respective chances: the negligence of the defendant.

By contrast, other cases present far greater problems of evidential uncertainty which go far beyond whether a chance has been lost. In such cases, as we shall see, the courts have rather unsystematically dealt with problems of evidential uncertainty. These largely ad hoc decisions of the English courts seem to create as many problems as they solve, for the 'principles' enunciated are of uncertain scope, and fail to evince a rule capable of universal application that can cope with all the various kinds

---

[18] [1995] 2 AC 296.

[19] See, eg, *Dixon v Clement Jones Solicitors* [2005] PNLR 6 and *Batty v Danaher* [2005] EWHC 2763.

[20] See also *Gregg v Scott* [2005] 2 AC 176, where an earlier diagnosis of C's cancer may or may not have given C better long-term survival prospects.

of evidential uncertainty that have arisen (or may arise in the future).[21] It is submitted that the absence of any such general rule means that future hard cases are likely to be dealt with by a combination of recourse to 'best-fit' analogies and incremental extensions to the various 'principles' that have been deployed in the hard cases to have arisen thus far. With this in mind, let us consider the array of approaches developed in the English courts to date.

(2) Cases involving hypothetical conduct by the claimant

Where it is certain or virtually certain what the claimant would have done had the defendant not acted negligently, there are especial problems for the law of causation. Take, for example, *Cummings (or McWilliams) v Sir William Arrol & Co Ltd*.[22] In that case, an employer failed to comply with a statutory duty to provide a safety harness to an employee who ended up falling from a great height to his death. It was established that even when harnesses had been supplied in the past the employee in question had seldom if ever worn one. That being the case, it was virtually certain that even if the employer had supplied one on the occasion in question, the employee would not have worn it. Accordingly the defendant's negligent non-provision of the harness could not be regarded as the 'but for' cause of the employee's death. (Importantly, the employer's duty was limited merely to providing, but not ensuring or supervising the wearing of the harness.)[23]

Where, by contrast, there is lingering uncertainty about what the claimant would have done had the defendant not acted negligently, matters become much more difficult. The kinds of problem that arise were considered in depth by the House of Lords in *Chester v Afshar*.[24]

> Here, C had a long history of back pain and was advised by D, her surgeon, that she required spinal surgery. What the surgeon failed to tell her was that the operation, which she underwent some three days later, carried with it a risk of neurological damage calculated at 1–2%. In the event, the injury materialised (even though the surgery was not performed negligently) and C brought an action based on the surgeon's negligent failure to disclose the risk of injury.

The difficulty of the case turned on the fact that, had the patient been advised of the risk, she would have sought further medical advice before deciding what to do, and, following that advice, may or may not have had the operation at a later date. Now, if she had merely delayed treatment until after she had received further advice, the

---

[21] Porat and Stein have identified five (sometimes overlapping) kinds of evidential uncertainty: (i) cases of wrongful damage where the wrongdoer is unidentifiable, (ii) cases of wrongful damage where the precise injured party is unidentifiable (eg, cases in which, say, D has emitted radiation affecting many citizens but it is not certain whether C was among their number), (iii) cases of wrongful conduct that may or may not have resulted in damage, (iv) cases of damage wrongfully inflicted by separate wrongdoers, and (v) cases of damage arising from both a wrongful and a non-wrongful cause: *Tort Liability Under Uncertainty* (2001), ch 2.

[22] [1962] 1 All ER 623.

[23] On the relationship between scope of duty and causation, see Stapleton (2003) 119 LQR 388.

[24] [2005] 1 AC 134. For commentary, (2005) 121 LQR 189.

overwhelming probability is that the injury would not have materialised. The operation at that later date would still only have carried a 1–2% chance of the neurological damage occurring. Alternatively, had she ultimately decided not to have the surgery, it would have been impossible to succumb to the neurological damage. So either way, it would have been extremely unlikely that she would have suffered the injury that she ultimately suffered. That being the case, on usual 'but for' principles, the defendant could be held to have caused the claimant's injury. But only by a bare majority did the House of Lords hold that the defendant had caused the claimant's injury; and then on grounds of policy rather than upon conventional 'but for' principles.[25]

What then, was the complicating factor that the House of Lords perceived in the case that caused two members to dissent and the others to reach a policy (as opposed to principled) decision? Put briefly, the perceived complication was that all that the defendant's failure to warn had caused was the patient to undergo the operation on the day that she did. The failure to warn did not, they thought, increase the risk inherent in the surgery: a constant 1–2%.[26] On this analysis, they seemed to be hinting (but not saying explicitly) that the surgery, rather than the failure to warn, was the overwhelming cause of the claimant's injury. However, if one accepted that the failure to warn was legally eclipsed by the subsequent surgery, then this would lead to the conclusion that the duty to warn counted for nothing. As Lord Hope put it, the duty would be 'a hollow one, stripped of all practical force and devoid of all content'.[27] Therefore, he went on, '[the claimant's loss] *can be regarded as having been caused, in the legal sense,* by the breach of that duty'.[28] In order to make the decision more palatable still, their Lordships identified the loss to the claimant as a loss of autonomy (that is, the loss of her right to choose whether to have her operation or delay it until after getting further advice).[29]

---

[25] The majority *did* accept that the 'but for' test was satisfied: [2005] 1 AC 134, at [19], [61], and [94]; but the analysis did not stop there.

[26] See, eg, [2005] 1 AC 134, at [7], [31], and [61]. This assumption is questionable, however, since there may have been something about the patient *or* the surgeon on the particular day that made the risk of injury more likely to occur. All that the 1–2% statistic represents is the fact that either one or two persons out of one hundred undergoing such surgery would succumb to the syndrome that afflicted the claimant. We therefore assert (quite reasonably) in the case of any individual patient, that there is a 1–2% risk of injury. This can be described as 'epistemic probability'. But it does not reflect the actual, subjective probability (which might well vary for any given patient), but which is unknown due to an information deficit (about, for instance, the particular susceptibilities of the claimant, or the relative skills of different surgeons). In short, we simply do not know the precise risk on any given occasion, had we merely alight upon an epistemic risk derived from knowledge of generalities. For further explanation of the difference between epistemic and subjective probability and of their application to causation problems, see Perry, 'Risk, Harm and Responsibility' in Owen (ed), *Philosophical Foundations of Tort Law* (1995).

[27] This too is questionable. If the patient would not have delayed the operation while she sought further advice, but would have declined the operation outright, then the duty to warn would clearly have counted for something. Perhaps this is why Lord Walker did not entirely agree, but preferred to state that the duty would be 'empty in many [but not all] cases': [2005] 1 AC 134, at [101].

[28] Ibid at [87] (emphasis added).

[29] Lord Bingham noted that the rationale of the duty to warn was 'to enable adult patients of sound mind to make for themselves decisions intimately affecting their own lives and bodies', ibid at [5]. See in similar vein the speeches of Lords Hoffmann and Hope at [33] and [56] respectively.

Notably, this approach makes the gist of the action patient autonomy rather than neurological damage; yet it seems that it was for the neurological damage that compensation was awarded. This is by no means explicable in logical terms.[30] In the light of its controversial nature, the Court of Appeal has since been keen to emphasise that the result in *Chester v Afshar* was an extraordinary one reached on policy grounds, and to confine it to its own limited context: that is, cases involving a negligent failure to warn a patient of the dangers associated with a particular medical treatment or procedure.[31] Whether, if the opportunity arises, the Supreme Court will be as keen to confine *Chester v Afshar* in this way remains to be seen. But for the present, it would appear wise to treat the decision as exceptional, and one that does not lay down any general rule capable of universal application.

(3) The material contribution to harm principle

English law allows negligence claims to be brought by a claimant able to show (1) that the defendant was in breach of a duty of care, and (2) that the breach of duty materially contributed to his injury. The fact that the claimant cannot identify precisely the degree to which the defendant's wrongdoing caused his injury is not regarded as a sufficient basis on which to refuse the claimant a remedy. In such cases, according to the Court of Appeal in *Bailey v MOD*, so long as he can 'establish that the contribution of the negligent cause was more than negligible... the claimant will succeed'.[32]

In *Bonnington Castings Ltd v Wardlaw*[33] the facts were as follows:

C, who was D's employee, contracted pneumoconiosis after inhaling silicon dust at work. The dust came from two sources – swing grinders and pneumatic hammers. Only the dust thrown out by the swing grinders was avoidable by use of a proper extraction mechanism. In the absence of such a mechanism, the exposure of C to this dust was regarded as tortious. The dust generated by the hammers was not, however, tortiously produced. The question that arose, then, was whether it was the 'innocent' or the 'tortious' dust that had caused C's condition. There was no evidence at all as to the proportions of 'innocent' and 'tortious' dust that C had inhaled. It was therefore impossible to apply the usual 'but for' test since C could not show on the balance of probabilities that, had a proper extraction mechanism been used, he would not have contracted the disease. The House of Lords nonetheless found for C.

Lord Reid captured the approach taken when he said that 'the source of [the claimant's] disease was the dust from both sources, and the real question is whether the

---

[30] Recognising this, Lord Hoffmann expressly suggested that in respect of the infringement of the patient's right to choose 'there might be a case for a modest solatium': ibid at [34].

[31] See, eg, *White v Paul Davidson & Taylor* [2005] PNLR 15 (*Chester* inapplicable to solicitor's negligent advice); *Beary v Pall Mall Investments* [2005] PNLR 35 (*Chester* inapplicable to negligent advice regarding financial matters).

[32] [2009] 1 WLR 1052, at [46]. See also *Dickins v O2 Plc* [2008] EWCA Civ 1144 (failure to refer an already stressed employee to the works' occupational health department a material contribution to stress-related psychiatric harm).

[33] [1956] AC 613.

dust from the swing grinders materially contributed to the disease'.[34] Importantly, the claimant recovered damages in full despite the fact that the tortious dust only made a contribution to his illness. However, where successive employers expose the claimant to the same harmful agent and the disease the claimant contracts is cumulative (ie, it gets progressively worse with more exposure), each defendant will only be held liable for that proportion of the claimant's disease for which he is responsible (assuming the respective shares can be calculated).[35]

(4) The material contribution to the risk of harm principle

The principle in *Bonnington Castings v Wardlaw* was later extended in *McGhee v National Coal Board*.[36]

> D failed to provide adequate after-work washing facilities so that employees could not remove from their bodies, at the end of the working day, the brick dust to which they were non-tortiously exposed during the working day. The brick dust to which C's skin was exposed caused him to contract dermatitis. But it was unclear whether C would have contracted dermatitis if he had not been exposed to the dust for the prolonged period attributable to D's failure to provide proper washing facilities. C, in other words, could not invoke the usual 'but for' test. The House of Lords nonetheless found for C.

Crucial to the decision in *McGhee* was the tortious quality of the prolonged exposure to the brick dust. The increased danger that the claimant would develop dermatitis could be treated, according to their Lordships, *as though* it had made a material contribution to the claimant's injury. But it will be vital in such cases to show a real increase in the risk of harm: a failure to show any material increase in the danger of harm materialising will yield nothing[37] even though proof of a mere contribution to the risk of harm will enable the claimant to recover damages in full.

Because the claimant in *Bonnington* suffered the onset of pneumoconiosis – a cumulative disease – the House of Lords were at least able to say that the tortious dust had made his illness worse, even if they could not specify the precise extent to which this was the case. Furthermore, there was no doubt that it was silicon dust that had caused the dermatitis. In *McGhee*, by contrast, there was no evidence that the claimant's disease had been caused by occupational exposure to brick dust (whether negligent or not). The experts providing evidence in that case had gone no further than to say that unnecessary exposure to brick dust after work, caused by the non-provision of showering facilities, materially increased *the risk* of the claimant contracting dermatitis. There was, then, even greater evidential uncertainty in *McGhee* than in *Bonnington*.

---

[34] [1956] AC 613, at 621.
[35] *Holtby v Brigham & Cowan (Hull) Ltd* [2000] PIQR Q293. Stuart-Smith LJ (at Q298) was content that there had been no reduction of damages in *Bonnington* simply because this had not been argued. See also *Thaine v London School of Economics* [2010] ICR 1422.
[36] [1972] 3 All ER 1008.
[37] *Wootton v J Docter Ltd* [2009] EWCA Civ 1361.

But the House of Lords, while acknowledging the difference, was prepared to treat the two types of evidential uncertainty *as though* they were the same. Lord Salmon said:

> In the circumstances of the present case, the possibility of a distinction existing between (a) having materially increased the risk of contracting the disease, and (b) having materially contributed to causing the disease may no doubt be a fruitful source of interesting academic discussions between students of philosophy. Such a distinction is, however, far too unreal to be recognised by the common law.[38]

The *McGhee* principle received recent endorsement in *Sienkiewicz v Greif*[39] in which the Supreme Court was required to determine what constitutes a material contribution for these purposes. Karen Sienkiewicz was the daughter of a woman who had died of mesothelioma which she had contracted by virtue of inhaling asbestos fibres during her working life. The fibres that she inhaled came from two sources: her employer's workplace (which was a tortious exposure), and the general atmosphere around where she lived (which was non-tortious). Of the two, the latter was much the more significant. Indeed, the tortious exposure only increased the risk of her contracting mesothelioma by 18%. That being the case, the defendants sought to argue that no liability should be imposed given that, on the balance of probabilities, it was fibres from the non-tortious source that caused her mesothelioma. In essence, there was a claim that the defendants would only be liable if they had more than doubled the risk of the victim contracting the disease. The Supreme Court rejected this argument. They applied the material contribution to risk of harm test holding that a material contribution constituted a more than minimal increase in the risk. Lord Brown put it this way: 'any person who negligently or in breach of duty exposes another more than minimally to the inhalation of asbestos fibres will be liable'.[40] An 18% increase in the risk was clearly more than minimal and the defendants' appeal was dismissed.

(5) The material contribution to the risk of harm among several wrongdoers principle

In *McGhee*, the medical evidence confirmed that the claimant's dermatitis could have begun with a single abrasion, either non-tortiously (while he was working), or tortiously (after work, while he was cycling home with brick dust still on his body). It was conceivable, too, that the disease may have had a non-occupational origin. What at least was clear, however, was that there was only one wrongdoer. But in the case of *Fairchild v Glenhaven Funeral Services Ltd*[41] there were several previous negligent employers as well as other evidential uncertainties.[42]

> C contracted mesothelioma – an invariably fatal form of cancer – by exposure to asbestos during his earlier working life. One complication was the fact that C had worked for several employers, all of whom had negligently exposed him to asbestos. A second

---

[38] [1972] 3 All ER 1008, at 1018.   [39] [2011] 2 WLR 523.
[40] Ibid at [175].   [41] [2002] 3 All ER 305.
[42] For analysis (2002) 10 Torts LJ 276.

complication arose from the fact that medical science does not fully understand the aeti-ology of mesothelioma so that it was impossible to say when he had first contracted the condition (or at least its origins). This meant that the responsible employer could not be identified. Third, because mesothelioma is not a cumulative disease, it was not a case in which the material contribution to harm principle could be applied. Finally, some of C's former employers had ceased to trade, so C was limited in the number of former employ-ers he could attempt to sue.

The House of Lords reasserted the principle espoused in *McGhee* and found for the claimant.[43] But the case, we suggest, can be distinguished from *McGhee*, for if the condition had already been triggered by a period of prior employment, it is entirely feasible that the defendants did not in any meaningful way contribute even to the risk of harm.[44] Further exposure to asbestos would have been more like stabbing a corpse than stabbing the merely wounded.[45] Similarly, if some of the relevant employers had not been in breach of a duty in exposing the claimant to asbestos, and the condi-tion had been triggered while in the employment of one such employer, the defendant would again find himself liable despite the entirely innocent way in which the disease was actually contracted. He would have contributed to neither the harm itself, nor even the risk of the harm.

Somewhat radically, and picking up on the point that was never argued in *McGhee*, the House of Lords later held in *Barker v Corus UK Ltd*[46] that, so long as the claimant had contracted mesothelioma, (1) each defendant could be held liable for exposing the claimant to asbestos dust and (2) each defendant should be held liable *only* for his or her relative contribution to the chance of the claimant contracting mesothe-lioma. In other words, the House of Lords took the view that employers who expose employees to asbestos should be treated as several, not joint, tortfeasors.[47] The effect of the *Barker* decision *in relation to several tortfeasance* was nullified by section 3 of the Compensation Act 2006. That section now makes it clear that the claimant should be entitled to claim in full from a single defendant (whether or not he was the only one exposing the claimant to asbestos in breach of duty).

There was certainly a case for some statutory intervention following *Barker* since it was by no means clear from their Lordships' decision in that case just how the relative

---

[43] Lords Hoffmann, Hutton, and Rodger saw the case as an application of the principle in *McGhee* not-withstanding the additional evidential uncertainty associated with the fact that there were multiple wrong-doers in *Fairchild*: [2002] 3 All ER 305, at [74], [116], and [153].

[44] For the view that each employer can be treated as having, in law, contributed to the risk of harm and that he can be liable for that risk creation (assuming mesothelioma has transpired in the claimant), see *Barker v Corus UK Ltd* [2006] UKHL 20.

[45] Lord Bingham recognised the point given his remark that, '[i]n *McGhee*'s case…unlike the present appeals, the case was not complicated by the existence of additional or alternative wrongdoers' [2002] 3 All ER 305, at [21]. Cf *Barker v Corus UK Ltd* [2006] UKHL 20.

[46] [2006] UKHL 20.

[47] On the distinction between these two categories of tortfeasor, see ch 25.

shares of responsibility between various employers should be computed.[48] However, the unsatisfactory state of the law was hardly resolved by the enactment of the 2006 Act. This is because the statute expressly recognises the right of the defendant[49] to claim a contribution from fellow wrongdoers who also unjustifiably exposed the claimant to asbestos.[50] And in so doing, the Act puts in place a presumptive apportionment between those wrongdoers based on 'the relative lengths of the periods of exposure for which each [tortfeasor] was responsible'.[51] Thus, the statute ends up importing part of what was regrettable about their Lordships' decision in *Barker*, although it is now applied to contribution issues rather than to the extent of an individual wrong-doer's liability. Furthermore, the statutory presumption is of dubious merit since one wrongdoer's share of responsibility will *never* be a simple linear function of the pro-portionate amount of time spent working for him. This is because, even if the intensity of exposure was exactly consistent from one employer to the next (which is highly unlikely), there would still be the problem that a person who had inhaled the fatal fibres while working for X could never have been further jeopardised or harmed by subsequently working for Y and Z.

Perhaps in recognition of the rough and ready nature of this presumption, the Act does go on, in the very same section, to state that the presumption *can* be ousted either (1) where some contrary agreement as to respective responsibility among the vari-ous wrongdoers is reached or (2) the situation is one in which 'the court thinks that another basis for determining contribution is more appropriate in the circumstances of a particular case'.[52] What these two bases for ousting the application of the pre-sumption perhaps have in common is the *suggestion* that a decent amount of available evidence will generally be needed in order to compute an equitable division of respon-sibility for supposed risk.[53] However, if we reflect upon the actual wording of these two exceptions, we might reasonably conclude that the Act is a good deal less helpful than it purports to be. In relation to the first – quite apart from the fact that it does no more than inscribe into the statute the kind of practice that dominates the extra-judicial settlement of tort claims in any event – it is difficult to envisage just when it will be the case that a commercially oriented employer will agree to pay more than he would be

---

[48] Two of their Lordships did suggest, somewhat vaguely, that the respective shares should be determined by reference to the length and intensity of exposure to asbestos dust: [2006] 2 WLR 1027, at [48] and [109].

[49] The Act does not refer to a defendant, per se, but instead uses the term 'responsible person' defined to be someone who has 'negligently or in breach of statutory duty caused or permitted another person ("the victim") to be exposed to asbestos': Compensation Act 2006, s 3(1)(a). That being the case, no liability may attach under the Act to anyone other than a common law or statutory wrongdoer.

[50] Compensation Act 2006, s 3(2). The subsection simultaneously recognises the right to apply the prin-ciple of contributory negligence in order to reduce the extent of a wrongdoer's liability.

[51] Compensation Act 2006, s 4.

[52] Compensation Act 2006, s 4(a), (b).

[53] Indeed, the presumption itself may well have been introduced in recognition of the evidentiary prob-lems that typically surround mesothelioma cases (given that the disease is widely thought to occur by means of a series of medical processes that take decades to unfold).

required to pay by an apportionment based purely on temporal considerations.[54] And in relation to the second exception, it is similarly difficult to predict just when a court will consider that 'another basis for determining contribution is more appropriate',[55] or what that other basis for determining contribution will be. All in all, it might have been more sensible to entitle a court to depart from the presumption in section 3(4) on the basis of the familiar considerations in contribution cases: namely, what it considers to be just and equitable.[56] Without any such constraints, there is a danger that the statute may spawn a fairly unprincipled and ad hoc body of case law.

In summary, then, *Fairchild*, the now-reversed decision in *Barker*, and the 2006 Act (in so far as it deals with liability to contribute) all fail to display or suggest any logically defensible approach to causation in cases of mesothelioma. Certainly, both the cases are characterised by speeches of a rather ad hoc and balance-of-justice nature which, in any event, are intended to be of very limited scope. Taking *Fairchild* first, Lord Nicholls readily admitted that the decision was ultimately rooted in policy rather than established legal principle. He said:

> The unattractive consequence, that one of the [potential wrongdoers] will be held liable for an injury he did not in fact inflict, is outweighed by the even less attractive alternative, that the innocent [claimant] should receive no recompense even though one of the [potential defendants] injured him. It is this balance ('outweighed by') which justifies a relaxation in the standard of causation required. Insistence on the normal standard of causation would work an injustice.[57]

Yet while his Lordship was prepared to concede that, in cases such as *Fairchild*, 'the court is applying a different and less stringent test', he did not explain precisely what that test was. In fact, the only judges to offer any kind of rule-based explanation of the decision were Lords Bingham, Hoffmann, and Rodger. But their three explanations differed significantly from each other. For Lord Bingham, the claimant's case succeeded because it satisfied the following six-part test:

> (1) C was employed at different times and for differing periods by both A and B, and (2) A and B were both subject to a duty to take reasonable care or to take all practicable measures to prevent C inhaling asbestos dust because of the known risk that asbestos dust (if inhaled) might cause a mesothelioma, and (3) both A and B were in breach of that duty to C during the periods of C's employment by each of them with the result that during both periods C inhaled excessive quantities of asbestos dust, and (4) C is found to be suffering from a mesothelioma, and (5) any cause of C's mesothelioma other than the inhalation of asbestos dust at work can be effectively discounted, but (6) C cannot (because of the

---

[54] Perhaps employer X, for whom C worked for five years, may agree to pay, say, 60% of the damages even though C also spent five years working for the actual defendant, Y, if he knows that his workplace was twice as dusty as X's workplace. But even here, why would Y agree to pay 40% of the damages (except perhaps to avoid the hidden costs associated with litigation)?

[55] Compensation Act 2006, s 3(4)(b).

[56] Cf Civil Liability (Contribution) Act 1978, s 2(1). This is equally fluid, but at least imports universality into the law of contribution.

[57] [2002] 3 All ER 305, at [39].

current limits of human science) prove, on the balance of probabilities, that his mesothelioma was the result of his inhaling asbestos dust during his employment by A or during his employment by B or during his employment by A and B taken together.[58]

Lord Rodger offered a far more general test, albeit implicitly, in his somewhat lengthy explanation of the principle applied in *McGhee* (as *he* understood it). He said:

First, the principle is designed to resolve the difficulty that arises where it is inherently impossible for the claimant to prove exactly how his injury was caused…Secondly, part of the underlying rationale of the principle is that the defendant's wrongdoing has materially increased the risk that the claimant will suffer injury. *It is therefore essential not just that the defendant's conduct created a material risk of injury to a class of persons but that it actually created a material risk of injury to the claimant himself.* Thirdly, it follows that the defendant's conduct must have been capable of causing the claimant's injury. Fourthly, the claimant must prove that his injury was caused by the eventuation of the kind of risk created by the defendant's wrongdoing…[That being so] the principle does not apply where the claimant has merely proved that his injury could have been caused by a number of different events, only one of which is the eventuation of the risk created by the defendant's wrongful act. *Wilsher's* case[59] is an example. Fifthly, this will usually mean that the claimant must prove that his injury was caused, if not by exactly the same agency as was involved in the defendant's wrongdoing, at least by an agency that operated in substantially the same way…Sixthly, the principle applies where the other possible source of the claimant's injury is a similar wrongful act or omission of another person, but it can also apply where, as in *McGhee's* case, the other possible source of the injury is a similar, but lawful act or omission of the same defendant.[60]

Different again was Lord Hoffmann's reasoning. In his view, the critical factors justifying the imposition of liability were as follows:

First, [there must be]…a duty specifically intended to protect employees against being unnecessarily exposed to the risk of (among other things) a particular disease. Secondly, the duty is one intended to create a civil right to compensation for injury relevantly connected with its breach. Thirdly, it is established that the greater the exposure to asbestos, the greater the risk of contracting that disease. Fourthly, except in the case in which there has been only one significant exposure to asbestos, medical science cannot prove whose asbestos is more likely than not to have produced the cell mutation which caused the disease. Fifthly, the employee has contracted the disease against which he should have been protected.[61]

There are notable differences between these approaches.[62] On the one hand, Lord Bingham's speech is couched in very narrow terms. It emphasises both the necessity of the claimant having been employed by successive employers both (or all) of whom exposed him to asbestos dust, and the requirement that the relevant form of harm

[58] [2002] 3 All ER 305, at [2].   [59] See below.
[60] [2002] 3 All ER 305, at [170] (emphasis added).
[61] Ibid, at [61].
[62] Curiously, Lord Nicholls agreed with all his brethren: [2002] 3 All ER 305, at [36].

should be mesothelioma. His reasoning, it seems, was designed to resolve the dispute in *Fairchild* but no more: he did not suggest any general principle of law. Lord Hoffmann's approach was almost as narrow, being applicable only to employees exposed to asbestos dust. Thus, elsewhere in his speech, he remarked upon the fact that 'a rule requiring proof of a link between the defendant's asbestos and the claimant's disease would...empty the duty of content'.[63] Only Lord Rodger seemed prepared to propound a relatively broad test. But, if one adopts the usual ex post facto approach to causation in interpreting the italicised sentence in the passage extracted above,[64] it appears that there is a logical flaw in his reasoning. If the defendant must have 'created a material risk of injury to the claimant himself', how can this ever be shown definitively in a case involving anyone other than the first employer in the chain? If we suppose that the claimant's condition was triggered at the first place of employment – which is entirely feasible – how can any subsequent employer have exposed him to, or contributed to, a material risk of mesothelioma? So far as the condition is presently understood, all that would have been necessary for him to have contracted the disease, would have already occurred.

Notwithstanding these differences in approach, the Court of Appeal has on two subsequent occasions made clear that the decision in *Fairchild* is to be applied very narrowly. It cannot, they insist, be applied in any other circumstances than those in which it is scientifically impossible to determine cause and effect.[65] On the other hand, narrowing the scope of the *Fairchild* exception does not answer all the questions to which that case gave rise. And here we must turn again to the *Barker* case, although it has since been nullified by statute *in so far* as it put forward the idea that negligent employers in mesothelioma cases should be treated as several (not joint) tortfeasors.

The best starting point for considering *Barker* is not in fact *Barker* itself, but rather the decision in *Holtby v Brigham & Cowan (Hull) Ltd*,[66] for it was held there that the damages payable should be reduced in circumstances where a defendant was only partly responsible for a claimant's *cumulative* disease.[67] This naturally caused some lawyers to wonder whether liability should also be allocated severally in cases involving an indivisible disease (a matter not pleaded or considered in *Fairchild*). The question, then, following *Fairchild*, was whether a single employer should be held liable for the full amount of a claimant's suffering where multiple previous employers had equally acted in breach of their duties of care towards employees. Certainly, in the immediate

---

[63] [2002] 3 All ER 305, at [62]. This is, of course, untrue. For as Stapleton has pointed out, the employer would still owe a meaningful duty in relation to other conditions, such as asbestosis: see Stapleton (2002) 10 Torts LJ 276, 296.

[64] An ex post facto interpretation would also appear warranted given the past tense in which his dictum is couched: ie, since the language is framed in terms of what D has done, rather than what D may do, it is appropriate to question what may have taken place in fact, rather than what might occur in theory.

[65] *Hull v Sanderson* [2009] PIQR P7, at [52]; *Gregg v Scott* [2002] EWCA Civ 1471, at [100].

[66] [2000] PIQR Q293.

[67] Cf the position in relation to discrete accidents which cumulatively cause a back injury, but do not – *strictu sensu* – cause a cumulative disease: *Environment Agency v Ellis* [2009] PIQR P5.

wake of *Fairchild*, it seemed possible to recover in full from a single employer. Yet if such recovery were possible, it would mean, counterintuitively, that the less the claimant could show in cases of industrial exposure to asbestos (as is the case with mesothelioma where knowledge about the aetiology and triggers of the disease are shrouded in uncertainty), the better off he would be in terms of damages. Thus, if the employee suffered a cumulative disease – such as asbestosis – only a proportion of the damages would be recoverable if several former employers had ceased to exist; whereas if he suffered an indivisible disease – like mesothelioma – he could recover in full. As things turned out, it was just this conundrum that fell to be considered in *Barker*,[68] the second House of Lords mesothelioma case.

There, in a spirited attempt to set the limits to the *Fairchild* exception, a majority of the House of Lords held that full recovery from one among several tortfeasors should not be permitted. Liability, they said, 'must be apportioned to the defendants according to their contributions to the risk [of mesothelioma being contracted]'.[69] But in answering one question, their Lordships raised several others. One of these – namely, the way in which we should calculate contributions to the risk of contracting mesothelioma – we have already encountered. Another, however, lies in characterising risk creation as a recoverable head of damage (although damages for risk creation can only be recovered by those in whom mesothelioma eventuates).[70] For, since the person sued may not have caused the mesothelioma, his liability – effectively for creating a risk – takes English tort law into uncharted territory: territory that may well offer some rewards, but which is nonetheless fraught with dangers where the remedy sought is damages rather than an injunction.[71] Furthermore, there is nothing in the 2006 Act which addresses this problem. Indeed, the contribution provisions of section 3 of the Act leave intact the idea that risk creation alone (albeit only in relation to the risk of mesothelioma) is a wrong that warrants the payment of damages.

(6) The one among several causative agents principle

Given that a decade has now elapsed since the decision in *Fairchild*, it seems safe to say that the case has not given rise to any clear, new, universal principle of law. But what

---

[68] [2006] UKHL 20.

[69] Ibid at [48], per Lord Hoffmann. Lord Scott, Lord Walker, and Baroness Hale all expressly agreed with Lord Hoffmann who also clarified (at [24]) that the *Fairchild* exception was only applicable to cases in which only one agent (or causatively similar/identical agent) caused the disease. Their Lordships unanimously held that it did not matter if not all the exposures were tortious.

[70] *Grieves v FT Everard & Sons* [2008] 1 AC 281.

[71] See the dissenting speech of Lord Rodger in *Barker*: [2006] UKHL 20, at [85]. 'The new analysis which the House is adopting will tend to maximise the inconsistencies in the law by turning the *Fairchild* exception into an enclave where a number of rules apply which have been rejected for use elsewhere in the law of personal injuries. Inside the enclave victims recover damages for suffering the increased risk of developing mesothelioma (or suffering the loss of a chance of not developing mesothelioma) while, just outside, patients cannot recover damages for suffering the increased risk of an unfavourable outcome to medical treatment (or suffering the loss of a chance of a favourable outcome to medical treatment).' For other difficulties and dangers with treating risk as a form of harm see Goldberg and Zipursky (2002) 88 Virg LR 1625.

remains unclear is where the principle in *McGhee* stops, and the rule in *Wilsher v Essex Area Health Authority*[72] begins.

> In *Wilsher*, junior doctors negligently administered excess oxygen to C, a premature infant. C later developed retrolental fibroplasia (RLF) a condition that ultimately left him completely blind. Medical practice required careful monitoring of infants receiving oxygen because of evidence that excess oxygen might cause RLF in premature babies. But there were said to be five other possible causes of RLF in very sick, very premature babies. The trial judge ruled that C, having proved a breach of duty arising from a failure to protect him from the risk of the very sort of damage which in fact materialised, was able to shift the onus of proof to the defendants to prove that some other cause actually resulted in that damage.

The trial judge was severely rebuked by the House of Lords for his endeavour to shift the onus of proof. Nor could their Lordships accept the argument of the majority in the Court of Appeal[73] that the principle in *McGhee* could extend to the facts of *Wilsher*. The claimants had not established that it was more probable than not that an excess of oxygen, rather than any of the other possible causes, had caused the claimant to succumb to RLF. Indeed, although the trial judge largely overlooked it, there was a good deal of conflicting scientific evidence in the case. Their Lordships made it clear that in no circumstances did the burden of proof shift to the defendant and they ordered a retrial on the issue of causation. Lord Bridge warned against the dangers of allowing sympathy for the claimant to overrule the established principles of proof:

> [W]hether we like it or not, the law, which only Parliament can change, requires proof of fault causing damage as the basis of liability in tort. We should do society nothing but disservice if we made the forensic process still more unpredictable and hazardous by distorting the law to accommodate the exigencies of what may seem hard cases.[74]

Wilsher clearly endorses the point made in *Hotson* that causation must be proven only on the balance of probabilities. So, where only two possible causes are in the frame, the court will be entitled to treat the more likely of the two as being the cause of harm *so long as* neither is an improbable cause.[75] However, *Wisher* creates problems, too. For one question that naturally arises in the wake of that decision, but in respect of which there remains no convincing answer, is why a case like *Fairchild* or *Barker* (in which there is a single agent, but several wrongdoers that may have caused the claimant's

---

[72] [1988] AC 1074.   [73] [1987] QB 730.

[74] [1988] AC 1074, at 1092. Note, however, that the court may draw an inference that D's breach of duty did cause C's loss even though C cannot prove the exact causal process so long as damage of the kind that occurred was a probable consequence of such a breach: *Drake v Harbour* [2008] EWCA Civ 25.

[75] *Ide v ATB Sales Ltd* [2009] RTR 8, at [4]. But even if it were not the more likely, it would seem capable of falling within the material contribution to the risk of harm principle: see *Novartis Grimsby Ltd v Cookson* [2007] EWCA Civ 1261, at [72].

harm) should be treated differently from a case like *Wilsher* (in which there is a single wrongdoer, but several agents that may have caused the claimant's harm).[76]

(D) CONCURRENT TORTIOUS CAUSES

Various types of act which may be described as 'concurrent causes' must be looked at separately. If two tortious acts result in damage, and either one would have produced the same damage – as, for example, when two fires are started and merge to burn out a building – then the perpetrator of each act is responsible for the whole damage, because it would be nonsensical to exculpate tortfeasor X (or Y) simply because what tortfeasor Y (or X) did would have resulted in the same harm being suffered. (If the latter approach were adopted, neither party would be held liable, even though both acted in breach of a duty.) So, if two ships negligently collide, injuring a third party[77] – those responsible for the respective negligent acts are each fully liable. Things may be different, however, where a person's negligence combines with a natural force. In such cases, it has been suggested, the fact that the natural force would alone suffice to produce the harm complained of will serve to exculpate the defendant, on the basis that the defendant's negligence would fall short of a material contribution to the harm suffered.[78]

By contrast, if the defendant commits a tort (or an act which will become a tort if non-remote damage ensues) and, before his act spends its force, some later tortious act combines with it to produce a particular result which would not have been produced without the operation of the second act, then the defendant will be liable if, and only if, it is found by applying the rules already stated, that his act caused the damage.[79] In *Hale v Hants and Dorset Motor Services Ltd*, the facts were as follows.[80]

> A corporation negligently allowed tree branches to overhang a highway. C was a passenger in a bus negligently driven by a servant of D (a bus company) in such a way that a branch struck the window of the bus with the result that he was blinded by broken glass.

It was held that the corporation and the bus company were each liable in full to the claimant. Each was negligent in not foreseeing that their negligence would combine with that of the other so as to produce the harm that eventuated.

---

[76] This assumes roughly equal exposures at employers A, B, and C in the multiple wrongdoer scenario, and a roughly equal chance of causing the harm in the multiple agents scenario.

[77] *The Koursk* [1924] P 140. Should D remain liable if the other 'cause' is the non-tortious act of another person, or the act of C himself? Cf *Cummings (or McWilliams) v Sir William Arrol & Co Ltd* [1962] 1 All ER 623.

[78] *Bailey v MOD* [2009] 1 WLR 1052, at [46]. But why not liability for a material contribution to the risk of harm: because there is not sufficient evidentiary uncertainty for that principle to apply?

[79] *Rouse v Squires* [1973] QB 889, at 898, per Cairns LJ: 'If a driver so negligently manages his vehicle as to cause it to obstruct the highway and constitute a danger to other road users, including those who are driving too fast or not keeping a proper lookout, but not those who deliberately or recklessly drive into the obstruction, then the first driver's negligence may be held to have contributed to the causation of an accident of which the immediate cause was the negligent driving of the vehicle which because of the presence of the obstruction collides with it or with some other vehicle or some other person.'

[80] [1947] 2 All ER 628; *Robinson v Post Office* [1974] 2 All ER 737.

Importantly, where an act takes place *almost contemporaneously* with the first negligent act, it seems that the rules on concurrent causes rather than the rules on intervening subsequent causes applies. In *Fitzgerald v Lane*,[81] the claimant was crossing a pelican crossing when he was hit by a car driven by D1. The collision threw him on to the bonnet of the car and back on to the road where he was immediately struck by a car driven by D2. He suffered severe injuries including damage to his neck resulting in partial tetraplegia. Whether it was contact with the car driven by D1 or D2 which caused the injury to the neck could not be established. Both were held jointly liable, and the claimant was held contributorily negligent.

SECTION 3   NEW INTERVENING CAUSES: CAUSATION IN LAW

Sometimes, an event may occur subsequent to the defendant's negligent conduct, which results in further injury to the claimant. For example, the claimant may initially suffer minor injuries at the hands of the defendant, but later die as a result of bungled medical treatment. In such a case, the defendant is not liable for all the ulterior harm. In marking the limits of his liability it will not ordinarily matter whether we use the language of risk or cause. The man run down by the defendant's negligence cannot recover for the extra damage sustained when a tile falls off a roof on to his head while he is on his way to hospital. This is because the defendant's conduct did not create a special risk of harm from that kind of contingency, or because the falling tile was not caused by the defendant's act. It is a mere coincidence. The original negligent driving and the subsequent falling of the tile are independent acts and the conjunction of the two events is an abnormal occurrence not contrived by human agency. In law, we say that the falling tile broke the chain of *legal* causation. It constituted what is called a *novus actus interveniens*: that is, a new intervening act sufficient to relieve the defendant of further liability for the consequences of his tortious conduct.

It is well settled that a *novus actus interveniens* may take one of three forms.

(1)   The intervening event may be an act of nature[82] (or act of God, as it is sometimes described).[83] For example, imagine a child is injured while playing football at school, and, as she is wheeled across the playground to the waiting ambulance she is struck by lightning. The injury inflicted by the lightning is not in any sense a consequence of her sports injury. It is important to note, however, that for an act of nature to constitute a *novus actus interveniens*, it must be something overwhelming and unpredictable and in no sense linked to D's negligence.

---

[81]   [1989] AC 328.
[82]   *Carslogie Steamship Co Ltd v Royal Norwegian Government* [1952] AC 292.
[83]   *Nichols v Marsland* (1876) 2 Ex D 1.

(2) C's own conduct may constitute a *novus actus interveniens*.

(3) The act of a third party may break the chain of causation.[84]

Before considering examples of each type of *novus actus interveniens*, two general points may be made. First, the more foreseeable the intervening cause, the more likely that the court will *not* treat it as breaking the chain of causation. *Reeves v Metropolitan Police Commissioner*[85] illustrates the point.

> C's husband hanged himself in his prison cell. There was no evidence that he had been diagnosed as suffering from any mental disorder but he had been identified as a 'suicide risk'. The Court of Appeal held that his suicide did not constitute a *novus actus interveniens*. The evidence available to Ds of his emotionally disturbed state and suicidal tendencies imposed on them a duty to protect the deceased, effectively from himself. Suicide was a kind of harm which they should have contemplated and guarded against. They failed to do so, and were thus liable when he committed suicide.

Similarly, damage incurred in rescuing a person imperilled by the act of the defendant does not break the chain of causation where such rescue could have been anticipated.[86] Equally, where the injuries negligently inflicted by the defendant on a claimant's husband induced a state of acute anxiety neurosis which persisted for 18 months and caused him ultimately to take his own life, the defendant was held liable to the claimant.[87] In each of these cases, the ulterior harm was within the foreseeable risk.

Second, in respect of intervening causes in the second and third categories, it is generally the case that the smaller the degree to which the conduct in question is a voluntary act of folly, the less likely will be the courts to treat that conduct as a *novus actus*. In *Scott v Shepherd*,[88] for example, it was held to be no defence to the man who first threw a firework into the crowd that the claimant would have suffered no loss had a third party not picked it up and thrown it again after the defendant had thrown it, because the third party, in throwing it, was acting predictably for his self-preservation. In another case, the claimant's ship lost her compass and charts when the defendant's ship negligently collided with it. The claimant's ship consequently ran aground while trying to make for port. The defendant was held liable for this further harm.[89] In both

---

[84] There is an argument that a natural event should not be treated as a *novus actus*. Acts of C and acts of third parties have in common the fact that they tend to involve reactions to (or conduct conditioned by) tortious events. Often they involve acts which are designed in some way to 'deal with' D's initial tortious act. Such acts are therefore intimately related to that initial tortious conduct so that no question of factual causation arises. The only question is one of whether the law is prepared to recognise the fact that D's initial tort was also a cause of the subsequent event. Natural intervening events cannot, of course, be characterised in this way.

[85] [2000] 1 AC 360. Note, however, that a reduction in the damages was made for contributory negligence. Cf *Corr v IBC Vehicles Ltd* [2008] 2 WLR 499.

[86] *Baker v TE Hopkins & Sons Ltd* [1959] 3 All ER 225.

[87] *Pigney v Pointers Transport Services Ltd* [1957] 2 All ER 807. See also *Kirkham v CC of Greater Manchester Police* [1990] 2 QB 283.

[88] (1773) 2 Wm Bl 892.

[89] *The City of Lincoln* (1889) 15 PD 15.

cases, the subsequent events were not sufficiently abnormal responses to the situation created by the defendant's negligence.

With these two general points in mind, let us now consider examples of each type of *novus actus interveniens.*

(A) INTERVENING NATURAL CAUSES

In *Carslogie Steamship Co v Royal Norwegian Government*[90] D negligently caused C's ship to be damaged and require repairs. The ship was out of commission for some time, but she later set sail again for the USA. En route, she suffered storm damage that required further repairs. C argued that the storm repairs would not have been necessary had the ship left for the USA on time and that, since the delay was due to D's initial negligence, D must be held liable in respect of the cost of the further repairs.

It was held that the chain of causation was broken by the storm since the severity of the storm was so unforeseeable that it would be improper to regard it as in any way connected to D's negligence.

In *Jobling v Associated Dairies Ltd*[91] C was partially incapacitated by an accident at work. Later, but before the trial, he suffered the onset of a supervening illness of a kind causing the same type of incapacitation. The House of Lords held that D was only responsible for C's loss of earnings up until the time he succumbed to the illness.

The House of Lords stressed the fact that the object of damages in tort is to place the claimant, so far as money can do it, in the same position he would have been in 'but for' the tort. Claimants are not, they said, supposed to profit. The claimant in *Jobling* would eventually have been unable to work even if the tort had never been committed. Disease, according to the House of Lords, is a vicissitude of life and one in respect of which, on policy grounds, their Lordships were unprepared to make the defendants responsible. Indeed, when awarding damages for loss of future earnings, the courts routinely make allowances for the possibility of some future incapacitation. Where that incapacitation – or even premature death – occurs before the court hears the case, the court is simply able to make an accurate (as opposed to estimated) reduction.[92] And where the claimant commits a criminal offence resulting in his imprisonment, the commission of the offence will be regarded as a vicissitude of life, and the loss of earnings due to imprisonment will be taken into account in just the same way as a supervening illness or disease.[93]

(B) CLAIMANT'S OWN CONDUCT

There is no doubt that the claimant's own conduct can constitute a *novus actus interveniens.* As Lord Bingham has explained: '[i]t is not fair to hold a tortfeasor liable,

[90] [1952] AC 292.   [91] [1982] AC 794.
[92] See, eg, *Whitehead v Searle* [2009] 1 WLR 549.
[93] *Gray v Thames Trains Ltd* [2009] 1 AC 1339.

however gross his breach of duty may be, for damage caused to the claimant not by the tortfeasor's breach of duty but by some independent, supervening cause' and '[t]his is not the less so where the independent, supervening cause is a voluntary, informed decision taken by the victim'.[94]

In *McKew v Holland & Hannens & Cubitts (Scotland) Ltd*[95] D's negligence caused injury to C's leg. C later broke his ankle attempting, while still suffering from the effects of the first injury, to descend a steep staircase unaided. C's imprudent and unreasonable conduct constituted a fresh and separate cause of the second injury. D was only liable for the initial injury.[96]

Compare this with *Wieland v Cyril Lord Carpets Ltd*,[97] where the claimant suffered neck injuries and had to wear a collar in consequence of the defendants' negligence. She later fell downstairs because, as a result of the initial injury and the neck collar, she could not use her bifocal lenses with her usual skill. Her further injury was found to be attributable to the defendants' original negligence. Unlike the rash Mr McKew, Mrs Wieland suffered a further injury triggered by her original disability. There was no unreasonable conduct on her part that could be taken to constitute a *novus actus interveniens* which broke the chain of causation. Similarly, where a defendant's negligence causes X to suffer acute depression, X's subsequent suicide cannot be said to break the chain of causation for the purposes of a fatal accidents claim by X's dependent since X's act – which is influenced by the depression – cannot be characterised as entirely volitional.[98]

Defining unreasonable conduct will not always be easy or uncontentious as *Emeh v Kensington, Chelsea and Westminster AHA*[99] amply illustrates.

C conceived a child after an operation to sterilise her carried out by D. D admitted negligence but denied liability for the cost of the upkeep of the child. That loss to C, he contended, resulted from her 'unreasonable' decision not to seek an abortion, and the judge at first instance agreed with him. The Court of Appeal, however, held that, since by the time C realised she was pregnant she was well into the second trimester of pregnancy, it was not unreasonable for her to refuse the trauma and risk of a late abortion.

Slade LJ made it clear that, save in exceptional circumstances, he would never regard it as unreasonable to refuse an abortion, even early on in pregnancy when the procedure is relatively simple and free of risk.[100] Waller LJ, however, was far less clear about this.[101] The divergence of views simply serves to exemplify the fact that it will frequently be difficult to classify acts or omissions on the part of the claimant as unrea-

---

[94] *Corr v IBC Vehicles Ltd* [2009] 2 WLR 499.
[95] [1969] 3 All ER 1621.
[96] In similar vein, see *Wilson v Coulson* [2002] PIQR P300.
[97] [1969] 3 All ER 1006.
[98] *Corr v IBC Vehicles Ltd* [2008] 2 WLR 499.
[99] [1985] QB 1012.
[100] Ibid at 1053. See also *McFarlane v Tayside Health Board* [1999] 3 WLR 1301.
[101] [1985] QB 1012, at 1048.

sonable where a moral dimension is present.[102] And an additional complication is this: even if the claimant's act may be viewed as immoral or unreasonable, it will not constitute a *novus actus interveniens* where the defendant could foresee such an act and was under a duty to take care to prevent it occurring. Thus, in *Reeves v Metropolitan Police Commissioner*,[103] the fact that a prisoner was a known suicide risk combined with the fact that the defendants were under a duty to take care to prevent his suicide meant that the defendants were causally responsible when he did in fact commit suicide. As Lord Hoffmann explained: 'it would make nonsense of the existence of such a duty if the law were to hold that the occurrence of the very act that ought to have been prevented negatived the causal connection between the breach of duty and the loss'.[104]

There are two final points worth noting. The first is that, in just the same way as we saw in chapter 4 that professional status will cause the standard of care to be raised in relation to professional persons who cause harm to others, so too will higher expectations be placed upon them in respect of the protection of their own interests in this context. (Thus, a former solicitor's failure to take heed of limitation periods of which he was fully aware constituted a *novus actus interveniens* in an action he was attempting to bring against a firm of solicitors acting on his behalf.)[105] The second is that, even where a claimant's own unreasonable act does not sever the chain of causation, it may well lead to a finding of contributory negligence (and pinpointing exactly where contributory negligence stops and a *novus actus interveniens* begins can be hard to do).[106]

(C) ACTS OF THIRD PARTIES

The relevant principles in this category are comparatively flexible and their application is sometimes difficult. The central issue in any case is whether the defendant's negligence was wholly or partly responsible in law for the damage that occurred, even though that damage required the combination of the defendant's negligent act with a subsequent act by a third party. The difficulties in this context stem from the different ways in which the two general principles outlined earlier can be combined.[107] Thus,

---

[102] On the related issue of the duty to minimise damages by accepting medical treatment, see *Selvanayagam v University of the West Indies* [1983] 1 All ER 824.

[103] [2000] 1 AC 360.

[104] Ibid at 367–8. Cf *Grieves v FT Everard & Sons* [2008] 1 AC 281 where C's anxiety about the onset of a long-term asbestos-related disease was foreseeable, but there was no duty to take reasonable care to prevent C suffering such anxiety.

[105] *Kaberry v Freethcartwright (A Firm)* [2002] EWCA Civ 1966.

[106] See *Spencer v Wincanton Holdings Ltd* [2010] PIQR P10, at [45]. However, it is submitted that where C has only contributed to the causation of the damage (as opposed to the accident itself) – eg, where a car passenger fails to wear a seat belt – C's folly can never be a *novus actus inteveniens*. See also *Corr v IBC Vehicles Ltd* [2009] 2 WLR 499.

[107] That the two principles are relevant is clear from Lord Wright's insistence in *The Oropesa* that a third party's act will break the chain of causation if it is '*either* unreasonable *or* extraneous or extrinsic': [1943] P 32, at 39 (emphasis added).

while it can be asserted with some confidence that an unforeseeable and unreasonable premeditated act by a third party will almost certainly sever the chain of causation (and vice versa), it is more difficult to classify unforeseeable reasonable acts, and foreseeable unreasonable acts, as new intervening causes.[108] Furthermore, it may be tricky to determine the reasonableness (or otherwise) of the third party's behaviour.

In *The Oropesa*,[109] a collision at sea was caused by D's negligence. In the ensuing circumstances, the captain of the damaged vessel ordered a lifeboat to be put to sea so that salvage arrangements could be made with D. In traversing the waters between the two ships, the lifeboat capsized and several crew members were lost, including C's son.

While the death of C's son was caused by a combination of the defendant's initial negligence with the captain's subsequent order to board the lifeboat in rough seas, it was nonetheless held that his order was reasonable in the circumstances. But even where (as here) conduct of the third party is in a sense brought about by the initial negligence of the defendant, it is still possible that the subsequent act will constitute a *novus actus*. In *Rahman v Arearose Ltd*[110] the facts were as follows.

C had been assaulted by two youths. The assault left C needing surgery. The surgery that followed was undertaken negligently by D and as a result C was left blind in one eye. Partly in response to the blindness and partly in consequence of the assault, C also suffered a psychiatric response that fell within the definition of PTSD.

It was held that the blindness was exclusively attributable to the negligent surgery even though that surgery had been necessitated by the original torts of the two youths. On the other hand, the careless surgery was only part of the cause of the psychiatric harm and the youths remained partly responsible for that.[111] Similarly, where a patient's GPs failed to refer her to hospital promptly and the hospital, when she was referred a couple of days later, subsequently failed to treat her swiftly such that she suffered permanent damage to her hip, the GPs' negligence was held to remain causatively significant. According to Lord Neuberger MR, 'the negligence of the defendants and the failings of the hospital had a synergistic interaction, in that each tends to make the other worse'.[112]

Issues of remoteness and policy may also complicate matters in this context. In *Lamb v Camden London Borough Council*,[113] for example, the defendants carelessly

---

[108] If, however, the 'unreasonable act' involves deliberate or reckless wrongdoing, that act – even if foreseeable – will sever the chain of causation: *Rouse v Squires* [1973] QB 889, at 898. Certainly, for it not to do so, the subsequent act would have to be more foreseeable (and thus probable) than a mere possibility: *Chubb Fire Ltd v Vicar of Spalding* [2010] EWCA Civ 981.

[109] [1943] P 32.

[110] [2001] QB 351. In similar vein, see *Knightly v Johns* [1982] 1 All ER 851.

[111] [2001] QB 351 at [34]. Cf *Horton v Evans* [2007] PNLR 17 (chain of causation not broken between (i) a pharmacist negligently dispensing tablets that were too strong and (ii) a doctor subsequently following the dosage on the pill bottle provided by the pharmacist).

[112] *Wright (a child) v Cambridge Medical Group* [2011] EWCA Civ 669.

[113] [1981] QB 625.

broke a water main outside the claimant's Hampstead house. The escaping water undermined the foundations and the house subsided so that, until repaired, it was uninhabitable. Squatters moved into the unoccupied house, and by the time they were evicted they had done damage totalling £30,000. The only issue was whether their damage was too remote. Lord Denning MR held that this was to be resolved as a matter of policy. Considering the claimant could readily have insured against the risk and could have taken more steps to guard against squatting, and considering also that the defendants had no right to enter the premises, policy dictated that the damage should be held too remote even though it was foreseeable.[114] Oliver LJ wrestled with the contention that the ratio of Lord Reid's speech in *Home Office v Dorset Yacht Co Ltd*[115] was that the effects of a subsequent act were too remote unless the act in question was likely to happen. He found Lord Reid's statement to be *obiter* and that the subsequent act in the instant case was neither likely, nor even reasonably foreseeable. He added that he did not dissent from the view of Lord Denning that, on grounds of policy, the effect of foreseeable acts could still be regarded as too remote. By contrast, Watkins LJ held that words such as 'possibility' or 'unlikely' did not assist him: even though the acts of squatters were reasonably foreseeable, they were nonetheless too remote.[116] He reached this conclusion by taking 'a robust and sensible approach'. His conclusion was:

> I have the instinctive feeling that squatters' damage is too remote. I could not possibly come to any other conclusions, although on the primary facts I, too, would regard the damage or something like it as reasonably foreseeable in these times.[117]

A final complication arises where the third party's act is said to aggravate a form of harm or loss occasioned by the defendant in circumstances where, but for that initial harm or loss, the subsequent damage would never have occurred. In *Baker v Willoughby*[118] the defendants admitted negligently injuring the claimant in the leg. After that injury, the claimant was forced to take a new job. While working at the new job, but before the action came to trial, burglars shot the claimant in the same leg and it had to be amputated. The House of Lords held that the defendants remained liable for the loss of amenity occasioned by the injury inflicted by them. The fortuitous event of the second tort did not relieve them of liability. Lord Reid explained that a claimant

> is not compensated for the physical injury: he is compensated for the loss which he suffers as a result of the injury. His loss is not in having a stiff leg: it is his inability to lead a full life, his inability to enjoy those amenities which depend on freedom of movement...In this case the second injury did not diminish any of these. So why should it be regarded as having obliterated or superseded them?[119]

---

[114] [1981] QB 625, at 637.   [115] [1970] AC 1004, at 1030.
[116] [1981] QB 625, at 644. See *Rahman v Arearose Ltd* [2001] QB 351.
[117] [1981] QB 625, at 647.   [118] [1970] AC 467.
[119] Ibid at 492.

Though the logic in this reasoning is easy to appreciate, what is less clear is how the *approach* to the occurrence of subsequent harm in this case can be reconciled with the approach taken in *Jobling* (considered earlier). Why the onset of a natural disease should be regarded as having 'obliterated or superseded' the effects of the defendant's negligence in *Jobling*, while the gunshot in *Baker v Willoughby* should be treated as having had no such effect, is difficult to understand. The only explanation hinted at in *Jobling* – the later of the two cases – is that the onset of a natural disease can be regarded as a 'vicissitude of life' severing the chain of causation, whereas a subsequent tortious act is not such a vicissitude. Of the two decisions, *Jobling* seems the preferable one in so far as the claimant would, by 1976, have been incapacitated in any case, and quite irrespective of the defendant's tort. That being the case, it is easy to see why the defendant was not held liable in respect of any incapacitation *after* 1976. Yet although *Baker* looks odd, the Court of Appeal has since stated that subsequent tortious acts are immediately to be disregarded in assessing the damage for which the first tortfeasor will be held responsible.[120] Such an approach seems defensible where, as in one case, the third party's negligence does not contribute materially to the occurrence or severity of an accident.[121] Otherwise, it is hard to justify and reconcile this approach with *Jobling*.

(D) DEFENDANT'S SUPERVENING ACT

It seems well settled that a defendant may not invoke his or her own supervening tortious conduct in order to evidence a break in the chain of causation stemming from the first tortious act.[122] But, in the wake of *Chester v Afshar*, it can legitimately be asked whether, in certain circumstances, a subsequent non-tortious act on the part of the defendant may be considered a *novus actus interveniens*. In *Chester*, it will be recalled, there was unquestionably a breach of duty on the part of the doctor who failed to disclose the risk attending the suggested surgery. But their Lordships stressed the fact that the negligent failure to warn the claimant did not increase the risk associated with the surgery.[123] In so doing, they were all but saying that the non-negligent surgery was unconnected to, and in no way flowed from, the tortious failure to warn; that, on conventional analysis, it might be seen as a supervening proximate cause. Furthermore, given that their Lordships imposed liability *in that particular case* on the basis of *policy reasons*, and given that they fully recognised that on conventional causation principles there would have been no liability, one wonders whether a different result might arise in a case not carrying with it sensitive questions of patient autonomy.

---

[120] *Heil v Rankin* [2001] PIQR Q16.

[121] *Green v Sunset & Vine Productions Ltd* [2010] EWCA Civ 1441.

[122] *Bolitho v City and Hackney HA* [1998] AC 232, at 240, per Lord Browne-Wilkinson: 'A defendant cannot escape liability by saying that the damage would have occurred in any event because he would have committed some other breach of duty thereafter'.

[123] [2005] 1 AC 134, at [22], [81], and [94].

Suppose, for example, there was a case in which the supervening, non-negligent cause was something other than surgery. Suppose further that the initial negligence was something other than negligent medical advice. Might the second, non-negligent act then be taken to constitute a *novus actus interveniens*?

SECTION 4   REMOTENESS OF DAMAGE

Rules which make the wrongdoer liable for all the consequences of his wrongful conduct are exceptional and need to be justified by some special policy. Normally the law limits liability to those consequences which are attributable to that which made the act wrongful.[124] There are however torts – deceit is one example – where imposing liability for all the damage factually related to the relevant wrongdoing is considered justifiable. Such extensive liability is exceptional.[125] In negligence and most other torts, by contrast, certain consequences of the defendant's tortious conduct will be considered too remote from his wrongdoing to impose on him responsibility for those consequences. It is simply considered to be unjust to make the defendant answerable for events thought to be too far removed from his original breach of duty. That being so, we must now consider the content of such rules on remoteness of damage.

(A) *THE WAGON MOUND*

The decision in *The Wagon Mound (No 1)*[126] is the leading authority on the remoteness of damage in negligence.

> Ds carelessly discharged oil from their ship into Sydney Harbour. The oil was carried by wind and tide beneath Cs' wharf, 200 yards away. After being advised that they could safely do so, Cs continued welding operations on their wharf. Later, molten metal from the welding operations, when fanned by the wind, set fire to some cotton waste or rag floating in the oil beneath the wharf. The burning cloth ignited the oil and fire severely damaged the wharf. Ds neither knew nor ought to have known that the oil was capable of being set alight when spread on water.

The Judicial Committee of the Privy Council held that the defendants were not liable in negligence because they could not reasonably have foreseen that the claimants' wharf would be damaged by fire when they carelessly discharged the oil into the harbour. It was, in short, harm of an unforeseeable kind.

---

[124] *Banque Bruxelles Lambert SA v Eagle Star Insurance Co Ltd* [1997] AC 191, at 213.

[125] In respect of wrongful interference with goods, the test for remoteness may, depending on whether D's conduct was intentional or negligent (since both may suffice), be the one relating to the directness of the consequence (as in deceit), or the one (as in negligence) based on the foreseeability of the kind of harm: *Kuwait Airways Corp v Iraq Airways Co* [2002] 2 AC 883.

[126] *Overseas Tankship (UK) Ltd v Morts and Dock & Engineering Co Ltd* [1961] AC 388.

(B) FORESEEABLE TYPE OF HARM

The Wagon Mound established that, if the damage which materialises is damage by fire, then, for the defendant to be liable, he must have been able reasonably to anticipate damage by fire. It was insufficient that he could anticipate damage by fouling the wharf's slipways. An unbroken succession of subsequent cases at all levels – House of Lords,[127] Privy Council,[128] Court of Appeal,[129] and first instance[130] – has followed the principle that the harm suffered must be of a kind, type, or class that was reasonably foreseeable as a result of the defendant's negligence.

Bradford v Robinson Rentals Ltd[131] is a typical illustration of the working of this principle.

> Ds carelessly exposed their employee, C, a van driver, to extreme cold in the course of his duties. In consequence, C suffered frost-bite. The court held that Ds had exposed C to severe cold and fatigue likely to cause a common cold, pneumonia, or chilblains. It held further that since frost-bite was of the same type and kind as these forms of harm, Ds could be held liable.

Where a wife sustained foreseeable psychological damage, the fact that some of it resulted from the effect of her husband's changed behaviour (he was also injured in the accident) did not prevent her from claiming damages: the harm was of a foreseeable type and 'the fact that it arises or is continued by reason of an unusual complex of events does not avail the defendant'.[132]

Notwithstanding the apparent simplicity of the test for the remoteness of damage, there remain areas of uncertainty in defining 'kind of damage', as *Tremain v Pike* illustrates.[133]

> C, a herdsman, while working for Ds, contracted a rare condition called Weil's disease. The disease was caused by coming into contact with rats' urine. Weil's disease, per se, was not foreseeable, even though other diseases associated with rats were foreseeable. Ds were held not liable.

Payne J stated that Weil's disease 'was entirely different in kind from the effect of a rat bite, or food poisoning by the consumption of food or drink contaminated by rats.

---

[127] *Hughes v Lord Advocate* [1963] AC 837; *Donaghey v Boulton and Paul Ltd* [1968] AC 1, at 26; *Banque Financière de la Cité SA v Westgate Insurance Co Ltd* [1991] 2 AC 249.

[128] *The Wagon Mound (No 2)* [1967] 1 AC 617.

[129] *Stewart v West African Terminals Ltd* [1964] 2 Lloyd's Rep 371, at 375; *Doughty v Turner Manufacturing Co Ltd* [1964] 1 QB 518, at 529.

[130] *Wieland v Cyril Lord Carpets Ltd* [1969] 3 All ER 1006, at 1009; *Tremain v Pike* [1969] 3 All ER 1303, at 1308.

[131] [1967] 1 All ER 267.

[132] *Malcolm v Broadhurst* [1970] 3 All ER 508, at 511. See also *Brice v Brown* [1984] 1 All ER 997 (shock foreseeable: thus D liable for C's acute mental illness. No need to foresee exact process leading to the ultimate result); cf *French v CC of Sussex* [2006] EWCA Civ 312.

[133] [1969] 3 All ER 1303.

I do not accept that all illness or infection arising from an infestation of rats should be regarded as of the same kind'.[134]

It is also worth noting the difference between the approaches of the Court of Appeal and House of Lords in *Jolley v Sutton LBC*.[135] There, a 14-year-old boy was injured while playing with a disused boat. In the Court of Appeal, his injury (sustained while crawling underneath the boat which had been propped up) was held to be of an unforeseeable kind: the foreseeable kinds of injury when fooling around with such a boat were those that would occur while climbing upon rotten planking liable to give way. In the House of Lords, however, the foreseeable type of harm was cast much more broadly so as to include any injury occurring in consequence of messing about with a disused boat. As a result, the harm that the Court of Appeal had treated as too unforeseeable became suddenly – because of the broad conception applied – foreseeable. A similar broad conception of the type of harm suffered was used by the House of Lords in *Corr v IBC Vehicles Ltd*, where their Lordships held that the victim's suicide was the same kind of harm as the depression that was negligently inflicted upon him (so as to justify a claim in respect of his death under the Fatal Accidents Act).[136] And, equally, in *Alexis v Newham LBC* it was held that a schoolgirl's prank was all that had to be foreseen when she was allowed unsupervised access to a classroom (rather than the particular act of putting whiteboard cleaning fluid into a teacher's water bottle).[137]

(C) MEANS BY WHICH THE HARM WAS CAUSED

Since *The Wagon Mound*, the courts have frequently reiterated that the defendant may be liable even though he could not envisage that precise set of circumstances which caused harm of the foreseeable kind.

> In *Hughes v Lord Advocate*,[138] C, aged 8, and another boy, aged 10, were playing on an Edinburgh highway. Near the edge of the roadway was a manhole some nine feet deep, over which a shelter tent had been erected. Post Office workmen working on underground cables left the area after dark, placed red paraffin warning lamps there and took the ladder from the manhole and laid it on the ground. The boys came up and started meddling with this equipment and C, while swinging one of the lamps by a rope over the hole, stumbled over the lamp, and knocked it into the hole. An explosion followed. C was thrown into the manhole and was severely burned. The explosion occurred because paraffin from the lamp escaped, vaporised, and was ignited by the flame. D was held liable for the negligence of the workmen.

The defendant was liable because the claimant was injured as a result of the type or kind of accident or occurrence that could reasonably have been foreseen, even though

---

[134] [1969] 3 All ER 1303, at 1308.
[135] [1998] 1 WLR 1546 (CA); [2000] 1 WLR 1082 (HL).
[136] [2008] 2 WLR 499. Whether, on a strict construction of the Act, death must not be too remote is questionable since s 1(1) simply states that death must be 'caused by any wrongful act, neglect or default'.
[137] [2009] ICR 1517.   [138] [1963] AC 837.

the workmen could not have foreseen (1) the exact way in which he would play with the alluring objects that had been left lying around, or (2) the exact way in which, in so doing, he might get hurt. The workmen's conduct created a risk of the relevant kind of harm – personal injury by burning – and this in fact materialised.

If harm of a foreseeable kind occurs, it will normally be no defence that the precise mechanics of the way in which the negligent act results in that harm could not be foreseen.[139] Equally, the fact that an explosion much greater in magnitude than was foreseeable resulted in damage to the claimant will be no defence.[140] In general, it is only when the accident is caused by the intrusion of some new and unforeseen factor that the way in which the damage was caused is relevant. Lord Reid in *Hughes v Lord Advocate* discussed *Glasgow Corporation v Muir*,[141] where the facts were as follows.

> Two picnickers were allowed to carry a tea urn through a passage of D's tea house. For a reason never made explicit, one of the picnickers slipped, and children buying sweets at a counter in the passage were scalded. An action by the children in negligence against D failed.

Lord Reid said of this case that a person carelessly carrying a hot tea urn near children would not be liable if it were upset and caused by an extraneous event, and he gave the example of the ceiling collapsing on to those carrying the urn.

One case is particularly difficult to reconcile with the principles adumbrated here: *Doughty v Turner Manufacturing Co Ltd.*[142]

> Ds placed an asbestos cement cover over a heat treatment bath containing sodium cyanide as a very hot molten liquid. Ds' employees carelessly dislodged this cover so that it slid into the bath. The molten liquid exploded. It erupted from the bath and injured C, a nearby workman. Although it was reasonably foreseeable that damage by splashing would result from dislodging the cover, it was not reasonably foreseeable that an explosion would ensue.

The defendants were held not liable, even though the relevant kind of harm – damage by burning – was foreseeable. They would have been liable for damage by splashing. But since the risk of damage by explosion was not foreseeable, and since this risk differed so substantially from the one that was foreseeable, *Hughes v Lord Advocate* was distinguished. Even so, the distinction drawn between a burn caused by a splash and a burn caused by an explosion is a fine one. This point was noted by the Privy Council in *Attorney-General v Hartwell*, where Lord Nicholls specifically questioned whether the decision in *Doughty* was correct[143] (though of course he was in no position, qua Privy Council judge, to attempt to overturn the decision in that case).

---

[139] *Draper v Hodder* [1972] 2 QB 556; *Wieland v Cyril Lord Carpets Ltd* [1969] 3 All ER 1006.
[140] *Vacwell Engineering Co Ltd v BDH Chemicals Ltd* [1971] 1 QB 88 (on appeal [1971] 1 QB 111).
[141] [1943] AC 448.   [142] [1964] 1 QB 518.   [143] [2004] PIQR P27, at [29].

(D) EXTENT OF THE DAMAGE

Where the very kind of harm that was foreseeable has occurred, it has always been the case that the defendant cannot plead that the claimant was earning more than the average victim, or that goods were exceptionally valuable in order to reduce his liability in damages. This is because damages are not restricted to the average loss of earnings or average value of goods in the circumstances, even supposing that such a sum is calculable. So, if the facts can be proven, the shop assistant who usually earns only £250 per week will recover her full loss if she is knocked down on her way to fulfil a highly lucrative, once-in-a-lifetime television contract.

At one time, it was thought that the claimant's impecuniosity could be relevant in this context. In *Liesbosch (Dredger) v Edison*[144] the claimants' dredger was sunk owing to the negligence of the defendants. It was held that the exorbitant cost of hiring a replacement dredger needed to fulfil an existing contract (and hired because the claimant could not afford to buy a new one), was too remote a loss. Since then, however, the House of Lords has overruled *The Liesbosch*. In *Lagden v O'Connor*, their Lordships decided that losses attributable to a claimant's impecuniosity should be treated no differently from any physical weakness with which the claimant may be afflicted.[145] Thus, the impecunious claimant in that case, whose car the defendant had damaged, and who was only able to obtain a replacement at 30% above the standard rate for car hire, was nonetheless able to recover the full cost of hire.

(E) THE 'EGG-SHELL SKULL' RULE

Before *The Wagon Mound* was decided, it was well established at common law that, in relation to personal injury, the defendant had to 'take the claimant as he found him'. This meant that the victim could claim damages for the entire harm to his person, even though, owing to some special bodily sensitivity, it was greater than would have been suffered by the ordinary individual. Thus, a haemophiliac,[146] or an extreme neurotic,[147] who sustains greater damage than the ordinary person, may recover the full extent of their damage, even though the defendant could not have foreseen such extensive harm. The courts have held that *The Wagon Mound* has not affected this principle, commonly termed the 'egg-shell skull' rule. *Smith v Leech Brain & Co Ltd*[148] is illustrative.

> A negligently inflicted burn on C's lip resulted in him dying of cancer. The tissues in his lip in which the cancer developed were in a premalignant condition at the time when the burn occurred. Ds were held liable for the damage resulting from the death.

---

[144] [1933] AC 449. Cf *The Daressa* [1971] 1 Lloyd's Rep 60.
[145] [2004] 1 AC 1067.
[146] *Bidwell v Briant* (1956) *Times*, 9 May.
[147] *Love v Port of London Authority* [1959] 2 Lloyd's Rep 541; *Malcolm v Broadhurst* [1970] 3 All ER 508; *Brice v Brown* [1984] 1 All ER 997.
[148] [1962] 2 QB 405.

In similar vein, in *Robinson v Post Office*,[149] the defendants carelessly lacerated the claimant's leg. A doctor's subsequent anti-tetanus injection caused encephalitis because the claimant was allergic to the injected serum. The defendants were held liable.[150]

There is no authoritative ruling whether the same principle applies to property damage in tort. In *Parsons v Uttley Ingham*,[151] the defendants negligently failed to install proper ventilation in a device used in the feeding of the claimant's pigs. The ground nuts fed to the pigs went mouldy and the pigs died of a rare disease. Some mild 'food poisoning' might have been foreseen as a consequence of feeding pigs mouldy nuts, but death was a highly unusual consequence. The Court of Appeal held, in effect, that the defendants had to 'take the pigs as they found them', and awarded full compensation for the loss of them. The decision resulted from a claim for breach of contract but the Court of Appeal acted on the interesting, and novel, basis that the rules of remoteness in contract and tort were the same.[152]

Presumably, the defendant takes as he finds them, not only the physical state of the damaged person or property, but also the surrounding external physical circumstances. This is the crux of *Great Lakes Steamship Co v Maple Leaf Milling Co*.[153]

> Ds negligently failed to lighten Cs' ship at the time stipulated. When the water level fell, the ship grounded and was damaged. This damage was more extensive because the ship settled on a large submerged anchor which Ds neither knew nor could have expected to be there. Ds were liable for all the damage to the ship.

The decision is assuredly correct: the damage was of a foreseeable type; it was of a greater extent than foreseeable, not because of internal characteristics of the property, but because of special external circumstances. No doubt the same rule applies to personal injuries. Accordingly, the defendant who negligently causes the claimant to stumble, so that he slides off the edge of a precipice concealed from view, would be liable for those consequences of the risk of stumbling, either before or after *The Wagon Mound*. Once the 'stage is set', the defendant's liability is adjudged accordingly.

(F) SCOPE OF DUTY AND REMOTENESS

In *Caparo Industries v Dickman* Lord Bridge outlined in general terms the important connection between the scope of a duty of care in negligence and the kind of harm for

---

[149] [1974] 2 All ER 737.

[150] See also *Environment Agency v Ellis* [2009] PIQR P5 (C had a degenerative spinal condition prior to the accident for which D was responsible: this was, according to May LJ, at [36], akin to an egg-shell skull).

[151] [1978] QB 791.

[152] This view has since been discredited. In contract, remoteness turns on what was foreseeable to *both the contracting parties*, as opposed to what was foreseeable to the reasonable person: *Jackson v Royal Bank of Scotland* [2005] UKHL 3. But in relation to the foreseeability of illness caused to pigs by mouldy nuts, this later decision is of no import. Such illness would be foreseeable by both contracting parties and the hypothetical reasonable person.

[153] (1924) 41 TLR 21.

which a claimant will be entitled to sue. He said: '[i]t is never sufficient to ask simply whether A owes B a duty of care. It is always necessary to determine the scope of the duty by reference to the kind of damage from which A must take care to save B'.[154] In other words, although the defendant's negligence may be a *causa sine qua non* of a wide range of foreseeable losses, he should only be held liable in relation to those that are specifically within the remit of the duty of care actually owed.[155]

This important interrelation between scope of duty and remoteness has particular significance in cases where a defendant owes a claimant a duty of care either in the performance of a task or in the furnishing of advice. For in such circumstances the duty is specifically owed so as to enable the claimant to avoid a loss or to obtain a benefit. That being so, the claimant will only be able to sue the defendant in respect of those losses which are properly attributable to a breach of that particular duty.[156] This principle is generally referred to as the *SAAMCO* principle and it has its origins in the case of *South Australia Asset Management Corp v York Montague Ltd*[157] (hence the abbreviated name). The way in which the principle works can usefully be illustrated by examining the case itself.

> There were three joined appeals in which Ds had been asked by Cs to supply open market valuations of various properties in relation to which Cs were considering lending money by way of mortgages. In the light of the advice given, Cs lent the money, but in respect of each property, the borrowers defaulted. It further turned out that the properties had been negligently overvalued; while a final complication was the fact that the market for the properties had also fallen since the time of the loans. In one case, C1 had advanced £11 million on a property valued at £15 million, but the true value (at the time of the valuation) was really only £5 million. In the end, the property was sold for only £2.5 million. In a second case, C2 lent £1.75 million on a property valued at £2.5 million. The true value at the time of valuation was £1.8 million, yet after the fall in market value, the property was eventually sold for only £950,000.

It fell to the House of Lords to assess the extent to which the claimants could recover their losses from the negligent defendants. It was held that the valuer's duty of care to a lender was to supply a careful estimate of the market value of the property at the date of valuation. That being the case, the extent of a valuer's liability will be limited to the foreseeable consequences of the information being wrong. These do not include losses associated with the *unforeseeable drop* in market value since a loss of that kind is not a consequence of the valuer's negligence. When applied to the highlighted cases, then, the effects were as follows. In the first case, due to the defendant's negligence,

---

[154] [1990] 2 AC 605, at 627.

[155] Thus, a car driver does not owe a duty of care to protect pedestrians from their own folly when they inappropriately step into the path of an oncoming vehicle: *Al-Sam v Atkins* [2005] EWCA Civ 1452. See also *Calvert v William Hill* [2009] Ch 330. Cf *Bhamra v Dubb* [2010] EWCA Civ 13.

[156] Note that since the duty could be of two kinds – to help C avoid a loss or to help C gain a benefit – the losses in question may, correspondingly, be of two kinds: either (i) losses *simpliciter*, or (ii) losses in the form of C's failure to obtain the benefit that would have been obtained.

[157] [1997] AC 191.

the claimant had £10 million less security than it thought. So as things turned out, the whole of C1's loss (£8.5 million) could be attributed fairly to the defendant. In the second case, by contrast, only part of C2's total loss (£800,000) could be attributed to the defendant, because the claimant had £700,000 less security than it thought. The remaining £100,000 of C2's loss was attributable purely to the unforeseeable drop in market price.

The crucial point in *SAAMCO* was that the claimants had requested from the defendant a valuation *for the specific purpose of avoiding a loss when lending money*. In that circumstance, recoverable losses were confined to those amounts that were attributable to the defendants' overvaluations.

For the sake of completeness, it should be noted that the *SAAMCO* principle can be applied in other kinds of case than merely those involving money lending. Indeed, Lord Hoffmann, in the course of his speech in *SAAMCO*, provided an example of how the principle might apply in a case of personal injury. He gave the following example:

> A mountaineer about to undertake a difficult climb is concerned about the fitness of his knee. He goes to a doctor who negligently makes a superficial examination and pronounces the knee fit. The climber goes on the expedition, which he would not have undertaken if the doctor had told him the true state of his knee. He suffers an injury which is an entirely foreseeable consequence of mountaineering but has nothing to do with his knee.[158]

According to simplistic analysis, it could be argued that the doctor should be held liable because the mountaineer would not have undertaken the expedition in question had he received accurate advice about his knee. But applying the *SAAMCO* principle, we take a more sophisticated approach that restricts the doctor's liability not *generally* by reference to loss or injury that is reasonably foreseeable (the usual remoteness test), but *more specifically* by reference to those losses that are reasonably foreseeable *and* within the scope of the duty owed. As Lord Hoffmann put it:

> The doctor was asked for information on only one of the considerations which might affect the safety of the mountaineer on the expedition. There seems no reason of policy which requires that the negligence of the doctor should require the transfer to him *of all the foreseeable risks of the expedition*.[159]

FURTHER READING

LUNNEY, 'What Price a Chance?' [1995] *Legal Studies* 1

MULLANY, 'Common Sense Causation – An Australian View' (1992) 12 *Oxford Journal of Legal Studies* 431

PORAT AND STEIN, *Tort Liability Under Uncertainty* (2001)

STAPLETON, 'Lords a-Leaping Evidentiary Gaps' (2002) 10 *Torts Law Journal* 276

---

[158] [1997] AC 191, at 213.
[159] Ibid at 213 (emphasis added).

STAPLETON, 'Cause-in-Fact and the Scope of Liability for Consequences' (2003) 119 *Law Quarterly Review* 388

STAPLETON, 'Choosing What We Mean by "Causation" in the Law' (2008) 73 *Missouri Law Review* 433

STAUCH, 'Risk and Remoteness of Damage in Negligence' (2001) 64 *Modern Law Review* 191

WRIGHT, 'Causation in Tort Law' (1985) 75 *California Law Review* 1735

6

DEFENCES TO NEGLIGENCE

KEY ISSUES

(1) Contributory negligence

Contributory negligence is a failure by the claimant to take reasonable care for his own safety that contributes to the damage about which he complains. Contributory negligence results in the apportionment of the claimant's damages. Damages are reduced to such an extent as the court thinks is 'just and equitable' having regard to the parties' respective shares in responsibility for the claimant's loss.

(2) Voluntary assumption of risk

The defence of voluntary assumption of risk, or *volenti non fit injuria*, results in the denial of the claimant's action. It applies when the claimant knew of the risk of injury and freely accepted it. It is unclear whether this defence negates a duty of care or if it is a rule that prevents liability from arising even though all of the elements of the action in negligence are present. The defence has a very limited sphere of application. This is primarily because the courts prefer to avail themselves of the more flexible defence of contributory negligence.

(3) Express exclusion or limitation of liability

Liability may be expressly excluded or reduced by a contract or notice. There are important statutory restrictions on the circumstances in which this defence applies. Legislation provides that liability for personal injury or death resulting from negligence cannot be excluded or limited by a contract or notice in so far as the liability is a 'business liability'. In other cases, liability can only be modified by this defence if the relevant term is 'reasonable'.

(4) Illegality

A claimant who is injured while committing a criminal offence may have his action barred. Where the claimant was engaged jointly with the defendant in a criminal enterprise at the relevant time, liability will be denied if it is impossible or not feasible to ask how the reasonable person in the defendant's position would have acted. Where the parties are not co-offenders, the circumstances in which liability will be denied are unclear but the seriousness of the claimant's offence is a key factor. The illegality defence will usually apply to actions brought in respect of sanctions imposed by the criminal law. The defence may also deny actions in so far as damages are sought in respect of a loss of income if the lost income would have been derived in contravention of the criminal law.

SECTION 1   INTRODUCTION

If the claimant establishes that the defendant committed the tort of negligence, liability will not necessarily arise or arise in full. This is because there are various defences[1] that a defendant who is found guilty of negligence can invoke. This chapter examines four defences to negligence: contributory negligence, voluntary assumption of risk, express exclusion or limitation of liability, and illegality.[2] The plea of voluntary assumption of risk, when accepted, results in the defendant avoiding liability altogether. The defences of express exclusion of liability and illegality, when applicable, generally do too, although they can also merely reduce the extent of the defendant's liability. The doctrine of contributory negligence, unlike the foregoing pleas, only limits the defendant's responsibility for the claimant's damage. It does not eliminate it. Contributory negligence is by far the most important of these defences in practical terms[3] and it has had a substantial impact on the scope of the other defences. For this reason, it will be examined first.

SECTION 2   CONTRIBUTORY NEGLIGENCE[4]

Contributory negligence is a failure by the claimant to take reasonable care for his own safety that contributes to the damage about which he complains. At common law, contributory negligence, however trivial compared with the defendant's negligence, prevented liability from arising. This rule, which was often harsh to claimants,[5] was abolished by section 1(1) of the Law Reform (Contributory Negligence) Act 1945 (the 'Act') and replaced by a system of apportionment of damages for contributory negligence.[6] It is essential to pay close attention to the text of

---

[1] The word 'defence' is used in many different ways by lawyers. This has resulted in considerable confusion. Several meanings of the word are discussed in Goudkamp, 'A Taxonomy of Tort Law Defences' in Degeling, Edelman, and Goudkamp (eds), *Torts in Commercial Law* (2011), ch 19. For the purposes of this chapter, the word 'defence' is used in a loose sense to capture any rule that precludes or reduces a defendant's liability.

[2] These defences are not the only defences to liability arising in the tort of negligence. Many other defences, such as limitation bars (see ch 26, section 3), are available.

[3] Empirical evidence regarding the applicability of the defence of contributory negligence is discussed in Cane, *Atiyah's Accidents, Compensation and the Law* (7th edn, 2006), 59–60.

[4] The leading doctrinal analysis of contributory negligence is Williams, *Joint Torts and Contributory Negligence: A Study of Concurrent Fault in Great Britain, Ireland and the Common-Law Dominions* (1951). For a sophisticated discussion of the philosophical basis of the defence see Simons, 'The Puzzling Doctrine of Contributory Negligence' (1995) 16 Cardozo LR 1693.

[5] It was, however, mollified to some extent by various principles, the most notorious of which was the 'last opportunity rule'. For discussion of this rule see Williams, above n 4 at ch 9. The rule was established in *Davies v Mann* (1842) 10 M & W 546; 152 ER 588 (Exch).

[6] The genesis of this provision is explored in Steele, 'Law Reform (Contributory Negligence) Act 1945: Dynamics of Legal Change' in Steele and Arvind (eds), *Tort Law and the Legislature* (2012) (forthcoming).

this subsection (which is generally referred to as the 'apportionment provision'). It provides:

> Where any person suffers damage[7] as the result partly of his own fault and partly of the fault of any other person or persons, a claim in respect of that damage shall not be defeated by reason of the fault of the person suffering the damage, but the damages recoverable in respect thereof shall be reduced to such extent as the court thinks just and equitable having regard to the claimant's share in the responsibility for the damage.

Section 4 defines 'fault' as 'negligence, breach of statutory duty or other act or omission which gives rise to a liability in tort or would, apart from this Act, give rise to the defence of contributory negligence.' This definition must be read in view of the fact that the word 'fault' refers to fault on the part of the claimant when it is first used in the apportionment provision, and to fault by the defendant on the second occasion that it appears.[8] Accordingly, fault, in relation to the claimant, means 'negligence, breach of statutory duty or other act or omission which...would, apart from this Act, give rise to the defence of contributory negligence.' In so far as the defendant is concerned, 'fault' means 'negligence, breach of statutory duty or other act or omission which gives rise to a liability in tort.'

The onus of pleading[9] contributory negligence and proving[10] that the apportionment provision applies rests on the defendant.

(A) FAULT ON THE PART OF THE CLAIMANT

(1) Definition and examples

As has just been mentioned, the apportionment provision will only be enlivened if the claimant was at 'fault'. The focus of the courts has been on whether the claimant was negligent, although a breach of statutory duty can constitute fault too. A claimant will be negligent for the purposes of the apportionment provision if he failed to take as much care as the reasonable person in his position would have taken for his own safety.[11] Findings of contributory negligence, as with holdings that the defendant

---

[7] 'Damage' is defined in s 4 to include 'loss of life and personal injury'. It extends to economic loss (see, eg, *Calvert v William Hill Credit Ltd* [2008] EWCA Civ 1427; [2009] Ch 330) and to property damage (see, eg, *Sahib Foods Ltd v Paskin Kyriakides Sands* [2003] EWCA Civ 1832).

[8] *Reeves v Commr of Police of the Metropolis* [2000] 1 AC 360 (HL), at 369; *Co-Operative Group (CWS) Ltd v Pritchard* [2011] EWCA Civ 329, at [29]–[30].

[9] *Fookes v Slaytor* [1978] 1 WLR 1293 (CA); [1979] 1 All ER 137.

[10] *Flower v Ebbw Vale Steel, Iron and Coal Co Ltd* [1936] AC 206 (HL), at 216; *Booth v White* [2003] EWCA Civ 1708, at [7]; *Stanton v Collinson* [2009] EWHC 342 (QB), at [140].

[11] There is no need for the defendant to show that the claimant owed him or any other person a duty of care: *Nance v British Columbia Electric Railway Co Ltd* [1951] AC 601 (PC), at 611; *Jones v Livox Quarries Ltd* [1952] 2 QB 608 (CA), at 615; *Sahib Foods Ltd v Paskin Kyriakides Sands* [2003] EWCA Civ 1832, at [62]. This is one important respect in which the doctrine of contributory negligence parts company with the tort of negligence.

was negligent, have no precedential value since they are determinations of fact.[12] Nevertheless, it is worth giving some illustrations of conduct that constitutes contributory negligence. Examples include a motorcycle rider who does not wear a crash helmet[13] or fails to fasten it securely,[14] an employee who has been exposed to asbestos fibres who continues to smoke cigarettes,[15] a passenger in a car who does not wear a seat belt,[16] knows that the car's foot-brake does not work[17] or is aware that its driver is so drunk that his capacity to drive carefully is compromised,[18] a skier who attempts to descend a piste that is too advanced for him,[19] a novice rock climber who attempts to execute a manoeuvre that calls for expertise,[20] and a woman bitten by a dog having put her face in proximity to its jaws.[21]

(2) The standard of care

The principles that are used to ascertain whether a defendant breached a duty of care that he owed to the claimant[22] are, for the most part, applied also to determine whether the claimant is guilty of contributory negligence.[23] For example, both negligence and contributory negligence are objective forms of fault. The fact that the claimant or defendant was incapable of living up to the standard set by the reasonable person is, consequently, no answer in either setting. Similarly, just as the defendant does not have to guard against unforeseeable risks, so too is the claimant entitled to ignore risks of harm that the reasonable person would not have contemplated.[24] Likewise, just as the adequacy of the defendant's conduct must be judged by the standards of the day rather than those prevailing at the time of the trial,[25] so too must the quality of the claimant's behaviour be assessed by reference to how the reasonable person in his position would have conducted himself at the time the injury was sustained.[26] And as is the case when deciding whether the defendant was negligent, in asking whether the claimant failed to take reasonable care for his own safety, the risk of injury and the magnitude of the

---

[12] See above pp 111, 141–1.

[13] *O'Connell v Jackson* [1972] 1 QB 270 (CA).

[14] *Capps v Miller* [1989] 1 WLR 839 (CA); [1989] 2 All ER 333.

[15] *Badger v Ministry of Defence* [2005] EWHC 2941 (QB); [2006] 3 All ER 173.

[16] *Froom v Butcher* [1976] QB 286 (CA). It is worth noting that a failure to wear a seat belt is a criminal offence: Road Traffic Act 1988, s 14; Motor Vehicles (Wearing of Seat Belts) Regulations 1993 (SI 1993/176). The fact that the claimant engaged in criminal conduct at the time of suffering injury may support a finding that he was at fault, but it is not conclusive on this point.

[17] *Gregory v Kelly* [1978] RTR 426 (QBD).

[18] *Owens v Brimmell* [1977] QB 859 (QBD).

[19] *Anderson v Lyotier* [2008] EWHC 2790 (QB).

[20] *Poppleton v Trustees of the Portsmouth Youth Activities Committee* [2007] EWHC 1567 (QB).

[21] *Neeson v Acheson* [2008] NIQB 12 (QBD).

[22] See above ch 4.

[23] Restatement (Third) of Torts: Apportionment of Liability at § 3.

[24] *Jones v Livox Quarries Ltd* [1952] 2 QB 608 (CA), at 615; *Cooper v Carillion Plc* [2003] EWCA Civ 1811 at [16].

[25] See above pp 122–3.

[26] *Smith v Finch* [2009] EWHC 53 (QB), at [43].

potential harm to the claimant is weighed against the cost and inconvenience of taking precautions and the utility of the impugned conduct. Thus, claimants do not have to take the utmost care to avoid getting hurt. A pedestrian, for instance, does not need to keep his eyes glued to the pavement.[27] But where a claimant who has notice of a hazard proceeds without paying proper attention, contributory negligence might be found.[28] Similarly, a passenger in a motor vehicle is not required to interrogate his host before accepting a ride with him as to the precise amount of alcohol that he has consumed.[29] But if the passenger had reason to suspect that the driver is intoxicated, he might be contributorily negligent if he fails to make inquiries in this connection.

(3) Relevance of the claimant's characteristics

The standard of care demanded of child defendants was discussed earlier.[30] It will be recalled that, where it is the defendant's behaviour that is in issue, the fact that the defendant is a child is taken into account in determining the standard of the reasonable person. The defendant's conduct is compared with the benchmark of the reasonable child of the same age. The same rule applies in relation to contributory negligence. Thus, the adequacy of the conduct of infant claimants accused of contributory negligence is judged against the standard of the similarly aged reasonable child[31] rather than against the yardstick of the reasonable adult. As a result, it is ordinarily more difficult for the defendant to establish contributory negligence if the claimant is an infant than where he is an adult. Infants under the age of approximately five are incapable of contributory negligence.[32]

In contrast with the situation that prevails in relation to negligence, where the defendant's characteristics other than his youth are typically excluded from consideration, in the context of contributory negligence the courts are more willing to adjust the standard of care that the claimant is required to achieve on account of his idiosyncrasies. In other words, while the standard that the claimant has to meet remains objective, it is less objective than that which the defendant must attain. Consider the decision in *Condon v Condon*.[33] The claimant passenger in this case, who had been injured in a motor vehicle accident, had failed to wear a seat belt. She did not wear one because she feared that, if she wore one, she would be trapped inside the vehicle if an accident occurred. The court held that this phobia should be attributed to the reasonable person and, accordingly, that the claimant did not fail to take reasonable care for

---

[27] *Piccolo v Larkstock Ltd* [2007] All ER (D) 251.
[28] *Ellis v Bristol City Council* [2007] EWCA Civ 685, at [52]–[53] (claimant employee ignored the risk of slipping in a pool of urine in a home for the elderly despite the existence of signs warning that the floor may be wet).
[29] *Booth v White* [2003] EWCA Civ 1708.
[30] See above p 121.
[31] *Gough v Thorne* [1966] 1 WLR 1387 (CA); [1966] 3 All ER 398; *Morales v Eccleston* [1991] RTR 151 (CA).
[32] *Beasley v Marshall* (1977) 17 SASR 456 (SC), at 459.
[33] [1978] RTR 483 (QBD).

her safety.[34] It is unlikely that a similar allowance would be made for a defendant.[35] Another illustration concerns insanity. Insane defendants are held to the standard of the reasonable sane person.[36] However, in the context of contributory negligence, the claimant's insanity is taken into account in determining how the reasonable person in his position would have acted.[37] The main reason the courts are more lenient towards claimants by taking cognisance of their idiosyncrasies has to do with the differential impact of finding negligence as opposed to contributory negligence. Defendants rarely bear the financial cost of a finding of negligence since they are normally insured. Conversely, claimants usually suffer the monetary consequences of being held contributorily negligent personally.

(4) Emergencies

Claimants who are confronted by an emergency caused by the defendant's negligence are treated leniently. They will not be guilty of contributory negligence simply because they made an error of judgment in the agony of the moment. This principle is nicely illustrated by the decision in *Jones v Boyce*.[38] The claimant in this case, a passenger in a horse-drawn coach, reasonably believed that the coach was about to overturn owing to the negligent driving of the defendant. The claimant therefore jumped off, breaking one of his legs. As things transpired, the coach did not overturn, but the claimant was adjudged not to be contributorily negligent. A more recent decision on point is *Moore v Hotelplan Ltd*.[39] The claimant in this case was riding a snow-mobile while on a holiday that had been organised by the defendant. She was not given proper instructions in the use the snow-mobile by the defendant's representative, who led the claimant's ride. Mistakenly believing that the snow-mobile's brakes had failed, the claimant panicked and accidentally depressed the throttle. Her snow-mobile ran into a car park and collided with a vehicle. The claimant was catastrophically injured as a result. She was found not guilty of contributory negligence. The critical question in cases involving an emergency is whether the claimant behaved reasonably in the light of the dilemma in which the defendant's negligence placed him. Due account

---

[34] See also *Mackay v Borthwick* 1982 SLT 265 (OH) (claimant found to have acted reasonably in not wearing seat belt because using a seat belt would have been painful owing to a hernia from which she suffered).

[35] In *Leahy v Beaumont* (1981) 27 SASR 290 (SC), at 294 White J said: 'Every driver, even a...driver suffering from fear of spiders, bees and moths in the car,...must drive in as good a manner as a driver of skill, experience and care'.

[36] See above pp 120–1, 125–6.

[37] *Mochen v State* 43 AD 2d 484, 488–9 (NY Sup Ct App Div 1974); *Baltimore & PR Co v Cumberland* 176 US 232, 238 (1990); Williams, above n 4 at 357. For further discussion see Restatement (Third) of Torts: Liability for Physical and Emotional Harm at § 11, cmt e. Another example of a case in which the claimant's characteristics were taken into account is *Calvert v William Hill Credit Ltd* [2008] EWCA Civ 1427; [2009] Ch 330, at 352 [70]. In this decision, an allowance was made for the fact that the claimant was a gambler in the grip of an addiction.

[38] (1816) 1 Stark 493; 171 ER 540 (CCP). See also *Baker v TE Hopkins & Son Ltd* [1959] 1 WLR 966 (CA), at 984; [1959] 3 All ER 225, at 244.

[39] [2010] EWHC 276 (QB). See also *Kotula v Edf Energy Networks (Epn) Plc* [2010] EWHC 1968 (QB), especially at [49].

must be taken of the alarm which such a situation would engender in the reasonable person and the fact that the claimant lacked the opportunity for calm reflection as to how he should act.

The 'agony of the moment' principle was extended in *Brandon v Osborne, Garrett & Co*[40] to encompass threats to the safety of the claimant's immediate family. In this case the claimant and her husband were in a shop. Owing to the negligence of contractors working at the premises, a shard of glass fell from the ceiling and imperilled the claimant's husband. The claimant instinctively attempted to pull her husband to a place of safety and strained her leg in the process. Had she not done so, she would not have been injured. She was found to have acted reasonably. Whether the principle extends to instinctive acts performed in an emergency to protect strangers, or interests other than personal safety, is yet to be decided.

(5) Rescuers

Closely related to the principles regarding instinctive reactions in an emergency situation are rules concerning rescuers. Generally speaking, the common law treats rescuers sympathetically.[41] In order to ensure that altruism is not discouraged, the courts are slow to find them guilty of contributory negligence.[42] Only those rescuers who act with reckless disregard for their own safety will be penalised by the apportionment provision. The rule that rescuers must be particularly irresponsible before being found contributorily negligent will often be engaged simultaneously with the agony of the moment principle, which was discussed in the previous section. But these rules do not cover identical terrain. While rescues are often carried out hastily, this is not necessarily the case.

(6) Exercise of right by the claimant

Where the claimant is exercising some right – such as passage along a highway – his deliberately encountering a danger created by the defendant is not necessarily contributory negligence. It will only constitute contributory negligence if, after making due allowance for his right to be there, the claimant showed an unreasonable neglect for his own safety.[43]

(7) Mere inattention by employees

The bare fact that the claimant employee was not paying attention at the time of suffering injury will not constitute contributory negligence, especially when performing

---

[40] [1924] 1 KB 548 (KBD).
[41] See generally Linden, 'Rescuers and Good Samaritans' (1971) 34 MLR 241.
[42] *Baker v TE Hopkins & Son Ltd* [1959] 1 WLR 966 (CA); [1959] 3 All ER 225.
[43] *Clayards v Dethick and Davis* (1848) 12 QB 439 (QB). (In this case the claimant was impeded in taking his horse out of a mews by the only access to the highway because the defendants had dug and negligently fenced a trench at the junction of the mews and highway. In trying to get his horse out, he injured it. The defendant's plea of contributory negligence was rejected.)

repetitive tasks at his place of work.[44] This is because it is the employer's duty to guard against risks of injury resulting from inattention, which is readily foreseeable. As Lord Tucker stated in *Staveley Iron & Chemical Co Ltd v Jones*,[45] not every risky act by an employee 'due to familiarity with the work or some inattention resulting from noise or strain' is contributory negligence.

(8) Expectations that other persons will act reasonably

Claimants are entitled to expect that persons who owe them a duty of care will take reasonable precautions for their safety, although they should not cut things so fine as to leave no room for negligence on the part of others.[46] In *Tremayne v Hill*[47] the claimant pedestrian was struck by a vehicle driven by the defendant. The claimant was crossing the road at a designated crossing area while the defendant was disobeying a red light. The defendant alleged that the claimant was guilty of contributory negligence on the ground that he failed to check for oncoming traffic. This submission was rejected. It was held that the claimant acted reasonably in assuming that drivers would obey traffic signals.[48] This decision sits uncomfortably with *Purdue v Devon Fire and Rescue Services*.[49] In *Purdue*, the claimant was injured when his vehicle entered an intersection and was struck by a fire engine that was proceeding against a red light. The fire engine's lights were illuminated but its driver negligently omitted to sound the siren. It was held that the reasonable driver in the claimant's position would have noticed the fire engine approaching. Hence, the claimant was guilty of contributory negligence.

(9) Intentional conduct on the part of the claimant

Contributory negligence, like negligence, is a type of conduct, not a state of mind. It involves a failure to take as much care as the reasonable person would have taken for his own safety. Accordingly, findings of contributory negligence are not restricted to cases in which the claimant was inattentive to risks. A claimant who deliberately harms himself may be guilty of contributory negligence since the reasonable person does not engage in acts of self-harm. Thus, in *Reeves v Commissioner of Police of the Metropolis*,[50] where a sane prisoner was able to commit suicide owing to negligence on the part of the police, it was held that the act of suicide constituted contributory negligence.

---

[44] *Tafa v Matsim Properties Ltd* [2011] EWHC 1302 (QB), at 166.

[45] [1956] AC 627 (HL), at 648.

[46] *Jones v Livox Quarries Ltd* [1952] 2 QB 608 (CA), at 615 (the claimant's 'reckonings…must take into account the possibility of others being careless').

[47] [1987] RTR 131 (CA).

[48] See also *Grant v Sun Shipping Co Ltd* [1948] AC 549 (HL); *Cooper v Carillion Plc* [2003] EWCA Civ 1811.

[49] [2002] EWCA Civ 1538.

[50] [2000] 1 AC 360 (HL).

(10) Imputed contributory negligence

If a person is vicariously liable for another individual, the contributory negligence of the latter is imputed to the former. For example, just as an employer may be answerable for the negligence of his employee, so too may the contributory negligence of an employee afford one who is sued by the employer with a defence. Suppose that A drives B's car for B and is struck by C's vehicle due to C's negligence. If A was contributorily negligent, his carelessness may count against B in proceedings against C in respect of the damage to his vehicle.[51] However, the contributory negligence of an independent contractor is not imputed to the principal save in those situations in which a principal is vicariously liable for such a contractor.[52] Nor is the contributory negligence of a driver imputed to a passenger,[53] or of a spouse to his or her husband of wife[54] or of a bailee to the bailor.[55] And when a child is accompanied by an adult, the contributory negligence of the adult is not imputed to the child.[56] Consider *Oliver v Birmingham and Midland Motor Omnibus Co Ltd.*[57] In this case the claimant, an infant in the care of his grandfather, was crossing a road when he was injured by the negligent driving of the defendant's bus by its employee. Although his grandfather was also negligent, the infant was entitled to recover in full.

The issue of imputed contributory negligence is also relevant to actions in respect of the death of a person.[58] It is convenient to examine it in relation to its action elsewhere.

(B) THE CLAIMANT'S FAULT CONTRIBUTED TO HIS DAMAGE

The mere fact that the claimant failed to take reasonable care for his own safety is not enough to engage the apportionment provision. His fault must be causally related to the damage about which he complains. As Lord Atkin put it: 'if the [claimant] were negligent but his negligence was not a cause operating to produce the damage there would be no defence. I find it impossible to divorce any theory of contributory negligence from the concept of causation.'[59] This principle was applied in *Lertora v Finzi*.[60] In this

---

[51] *Kenfield Motors Ltd v Hayles and Rees* [1998] CLY 3919 (CC).

[52] Williams, above n 4 at 432.

[53] *Mills v Armstrong (The Bernina)* (1888) LR 13 App Cas 1 (HL) (in this decision the principle was held to apply in the case of ships).

[54] *Mallett v Dunn* [1949] 2 KB 180 (KBD); *Berrill v Road Haulage Executive* [1952] 2 Lloyd's Rep 490 (QBD).

[55] *France v Parkinson* [1954] 1 WLR 581 (CA); [1954] 1 All ER 739.

[56] Although where a disabled child's action rests on the Congenital Disabilities (Civil Liability) Act 1976, his damages will be reduced if it is shown that his parents shared the responsibility for his being born disabled: s 1(7).

[57] [1933] 1 KB 35 (Div Ct). However, if the parent is in breach of his duty to protect the child's safety, the defendant may seek contribution from the negligent parent. Contribution is discussed in ch 25.

[58] See p 724.

[59] *Caswell v Powell Duffryn Associated Collieries Ltd* [1940] AC 152 (HL), at 165.

[60] [1973] RTR 161 (QBD). See also *Condon v Condon* [1978] RTR 483 (QBD); *Toole v Bolton MBC* [2002] EWCA Civ 588; *Stanton v Collinson* [2009] EWHC 342 (QB); *Smith v Finch* [2009] EWHC 53 (QB).

case the defendant motorist failed in his plea of contributory negligence against the driver of another car on the basis that the latter failed to wear a seat belt, as he could not show that his injuries would have been less severe had he used a seat belt.

A case that went the other way was *Jones v Livox Quarries Ltd*.[61] The claimant employee had been riding on the rear of an excavation vehicle contrary to his employer's instructions. While he was in this position, another vehicle struck his vehicle from behind. The claimant was injured as a result. Although the main risks to which the claimant had exposed himself were falling off the vehicle or being trapped in some part of it, the claimant was also vulnerable to being injured in the way that he was. He would not have been injured had he been using the vehicle as instructed. Accordingly, the defence of contributory negligence succeeded. The outcome would have been different if the damage sustained by the claimant had been totally foreign to the risk to which he had negligently exposed himself.[62] Suppose, for example, that the driver of the vehicle on which the claimant was riding negligently caused it to catch on fire with the result that the claimant was burned. As the claimant would have been burned regardless of his carelessness, the plea of contributory negligence would be inapplicable.

Occasionally, a claimant's lack of care may be a necessary condition of the injury about which he complains but nevertheless unrelated to it in the required sense. Consider the case of *St George v Home Office*.[63] The claimant in this litigation was addicted to alcohol and illegal drugs. He had been sentenced to a term of imprisonment for theft. While in custody, he suffered seizures caused by withdrawal symptoms and fell from his bunk, suffering serious injury as a result. The defendant, through its employees, knew that the claimant might experience seizures but negligently allocated him a top bunk. The defendant argued that the claimant was guilty of contributory negligence in becoming addicted to alcohol and drugs. This submission was rejected. The Court of Appeal held that, while the claimant would not have been injured but for this carelessness, his disregard for his own safety 'was too remote in time, place and circumstance and was not sufficiently connected with the negligence of the prison staff'.[64] It was 'no more than part of the history that led to [the claimant's condition] when he was [imprisoned].'[65]

The claimant's fault must be causally related to the loss about which he complains rather than to the accident that caused the loss. This principle is neatly illustrated by *Froom v Butcher*.[66] The claimant in this case was a passenger in a motor vehicle who had been injured by the defendant's negligence. He did not wear a seat belt. He contended that his failure in this regard should be ignored since it did not contribute to

---

[61] [1952] 2 QB 608 (CA).

[62] Singleton LJ took the view that there would be no defence if the claimant carelessly sat upon an unsafe wall, and a driver negligently ran into the wall and injured the claimant (at 612). Similarly, Denning LJ thought that the claimant would succeed if, while riding on the vehicle, he had been hit in the eye by a shot from a gun fired by a negligent sportsman (at 616).

[63] [2008] EWCA Civ 1068; [2009] 1 WLR 1670; [2008] 4 All ER 1039.

[64] [2009] 1 WLR 1670, at 1671 [56]; [2008] 4 All ER 1039, at 1052.

[65] Ibid.   [66] [1976] QB 286 (CA).

the accident. This submission was rejected. Lord Denning MR, speaking for the Court of Appeal, held that the fact that the claimant's carelessness was causally related to his damage was sufficient to trigger the apportionment provision.

(C) THE SCOPE OF THE APPORTIONMENT PROVISION

To which torts other than negligence does the apportionment provision apply? It does not extend to the tort of deceit[67] or other torts based on dishonesty (such as conspiracy or inducing a breach of contract).[68] Nor does it apply to actions in trespass to the person.[69] Section 11 of the Torts (Interference with Goods) Act 1977 excludes contributory negligence as a defence to conversion and trespass to goods. Conversely, in the context of product liability, contributory negligence is a defence under s 6(4) of the Consumer Protection Act 1987. It is unclear whether the defence is available in the setting of negligent misstatement. It cannot apply where the claimant is negligent in relying on the defendant's misstatement.[70] This is because reasonable reliance by the claimant on the misstatement is a definitional element of this action.[71] If, however, the claimant fails to take reasonable care for his own interests in some other respect, the apportionment provision may be triggered. A difficult question is whether the defence of contributory negligence can be invoked in an action for breach of contract.[72] The defence has no place in an action brought only in contract,[73] even if the contractual term breached is framed in terms of exercising reasonable care.[74] However, it may be applicable where the defendant's liability in contract is concurrent with a breach of duty in tort.[75]

(D) APPORTIONMENT OF DAMAGES

(1) General principles

If the claimant is guilty of contributory negligence, it is necessary to consider how his damages should be apportioned. Some reduction must be made.[76] The claimant's

---

[67] *Alliance and Leicester Building Society v Edgestop Ltd* [1993] 1 WLR 1462 (Ch D); [1994] 2 All ER 38; *Nationwide Building Society v Thimbleby & Co* [1999] Lloyd's Rep PN 359 (Ch D).

[68] *Corporacion Nacional del Cobre de Chile v Sogemin Metals Ltd* [1997] 1 WLR 1396 (Ch D); [1997] 2 All ER 917.

[69] *Co-Operative Group (CWS) Ltd v Pritchard* [2011] EWCA Civ 329. See further Goudkamp, 'Contributory Negligence and Trespass to the Person' (2011) 127 LQR 518.

[70] *JEB Fasteners Ltd v Marks Bloom & Co* [1981] 3 All ER 289 (QBD).

[71] See p 99.

[72] See generally Law Commission, *Contributory Negligence as a Defence in Contract*, Report 219 (1993); Spowart Taylor, 'Contributory Negligence – A Defence to Breach of Contract?' (1986) 49 MLR 102.

[73] *AB Marintrans v Comet Shipping Co Ltd (The Shinjitsu Maru No 5)* [1985] 1 WLR 1270 (QBD); [1985] 3 All ER 442; *Barclays Bank Plc v Fairclough Building Ltd* [1995] QB 214 (CA).

[74] *Forsikringsaktieselskapet Vesta v Butcher* [1989] AC 852 (HL).

[75] Ibid. See also *Gran Gelato Ltd v Richcliff (Group) Ltd* [1992] Ch 560 (Ch D), stating that contributory negligence can apply to a claim under s 2(1) of the Misrepresentation Act 1967 where the claim lies concurrently with an action in negligence.

[76] The apportionment provision is couched in mandatory language: 'requires'.

carelessness cannot be disregarded.[77] Nor may a judge evade apportionment by pleading the difficulty of ascertaining the precise degree to which the claimant's carelessness exacerbated his injury.

The apportionment provision directs the courts to reduce the claimant's damages as they think 'just and equitable having regard to the claimant's share in responsibility for the damage'. The way that this provision is applied in practice is as follows. The judge identifies the degree to which each party is responsible for the claimant's loss as a percentage. These percentages add up to 100%. The claimant's damages are then reduced by the percentage allocated to him. For example, if the claimant and defendant are responsible for the claimant's loss in the order of 40% and 60% respectively, the claimant's damages will be cut back by 40%.

In determining the appropriate reduction, two factors must be considered. The first factor is the relative blameworthiness of the parties[78] (evidenced generally by the extent to which they deviated from the standard of the reasonable person). The second is the causal potency[79] of the parties' respective acts in issue. The law on this point was summarised by Lord Reid in *Stapley v Gypsum Mines Ltd*:[80]

> A court must deal broadly with the problem of apportionment and in considering what is just and equitable must have regard to the blameworthiness of each party, but 'the claimant's share in the responsibility for the damage' cannot, I think, be assessed without considering the relative importance of his acts in causing the damage apart from his blameworthiness.

Decisions on apportionment will generally be reached on a common-sense basis.[81] For this reason, and because trial judges have the advantage of observing witnesses, appellate courts are reluctant to disturb findings regarding apportionment. A trial judge's conclusion in this regard will only be interfered with if it is plainly wrong.[82]

(2) Pedestrians and motorists

An important context in which to consider apportionment is actions by pedestrians against motorists. In this setting, the courts have been at pains to point out that both factors relevant to apportionment – blameworthiness and causal potency – support, all other things being equal, assigning the bulk of responsibility for the claimant's

---

[77] Although some cases suggest that damages need not be apportioned where the claimant's contributory negligence is *de minimis*: see, eg, *Boothman v British Northrop* (1972) 13 KIR 112 (CA); *Capps v Miller* [1989] 1 WLR 839 (CA), at 848–9; [1989] 2 All ER 333, at 340. However, where the claimant's fault is very slight, the question arises whether he should have been found contributorily negligent.

[78] *Sahib Foods Ltd, Co-operative Insurance Society Ltd v Paskin Kyriakides Sands (a firm)* [2003] EWHC 142.

[79] *Davies v Swan Motor Co (Swansea) Ltd* [1949] 2 KB 291 (CA), at 326; *Pride Valley Foods Ltd v Hall & Partners (Contract Management) Ltd* [2001] EWCA Civ 1001.

[80] [1953] AC 663 (HL), at 682. See also *Corr v IBC Vehicles Ltd* [2008] UKHL 13; [2008] 1 AC 884, at 913 [44].

[81] *St George v Home Office* [2008] EWCA Civ 1068, at [52]; [2009] 1 WLR 1670, at 1683; [2008] 4 All ER, at 1051.

[82] *Lunt v Khelifa* [2002] EWCA Civ 801, at [19]; *Silverlink Train Services Ltd v Collins-Williamson* [2009] EWCA Civ 850, at [61]; *Robb v Salamis (M&I) Ltd* [2006] UKHL 56; [2007] 2 All ER 97, at 110 [35].

damage to the negligent motorist. This is because of the 'destructive disparity'[83] between a motor vehicle and a pedestrian. As Simon Brown LJ put it, a 'motorist is driving a potentially lethal piece of machinery, whereas [a] pedestrian is basically harmless'.[84] The main situation in which a pedestrian will be found to bear greater responsibility for an accident than a defendant motorist is where he moves suddenly into the defendant's path, especially where the defendant could not see him before he stepped on to the road.[85] Where the pedestrian is intoxicated, the proper approach is to look objectively at how he behaved rather than why he behaved as he did.[86]

(3) Infants

Infant claimants are treated very leniently because of their vulnerability. Even when they are found to be contributorily negligent (recall that the standard of care expected is adjusted where the claimant is a child),[87] apportionment is often made very much in their favour.[88]

(4) Seat belt cases: standard reductions

In seat belt cases, a standard reduction applies. This has been rationalised on the ground that it saves time and expense. The rule was developed by Lord Denning MR (with whom Lawton and Scarman LJJ agreed) in *Froom v Butcher*.[89] In this case, his Lordship suggested the norm of a 25% reduction if wearing the seat belt would have prevented the injury entirely, and a 15% reduction if it would only have reduced the severity of the injury.[90] (If wearing a seat belt would have made no difference to the claimant's injuries, the apportionment provision will be inapplicable.)[91] If the claimant is guilty of contributory negligence not just in failing to wear a seat belt but in some other respect, a greater reduction may be made. Thus, in *Gregory v Kelly*[92] where the claimant did not wear his seat belt and knew also that the car had a faulty foot brake, damages were reduced by 40%. In *Gleeson v Court*,[93] the claimant not only failed to

---

[83] *Eagle v Chambers* [2003] EWCA Civ 1107, at [15].

[84] *Wells v Trinder* [2002] EWCA Civ 1030, at [19]. See also *Henry v Thames Valley Policy* [2010] EWCA Civ 5, at [39].

[85] *Eagle v Chambers* [2003] EWCA Civ 1107, at [16]. For an example where this happened see *Belka v Prosperini* [2011] EWCA Civ 623 (claimant two-thirds to blame).

[86] *Liddell v Middleton* (1996) PIQR P36 (CA), at 40, 43; *Lunt v Khelifa* [2002] EWCA Civ 801, at [16]–[19].

[87] See above p 191.

[88] *Russel v Smith* [2003] EWHC 2060 (QB), at [15]–[16].

[89] [1976] QB 286 (CA). See also *O'Connell v Jackson* [1972] 1 QB 270 (CA) (motorcyclist's damages reduced by 15% for not wearing a crash helmet); *Capps v Miller* [1989] 1 WLR 839 (CA); [1989] 2 All ER 333 (10% where the claimant motorcyclist was wearing a helmet but had not fastened it). Conversely, in *Welsh v Messenger* [2006] CLY 2875 (CC) a passenger on a coach who failed to wear a seat belt and was injured did not have her damages reduced. It was significant in this case that there was no legal requirement to wear a belt on coaches at the time. Nor was wearing a belt on coaches recommended in the Highway Code.

[90] The principles enunciated in *Froom* have survived several challenges: see, eg, *Stanton v Collinson* [2009] EWHC 342 (QB).

[91] See above pp 195–7.   [92] [1978] RTR 426 (QBD).   [93] [2007] EWHC 2397 (QB).

wear a seat belt but also travelled in the boot of a car driven by a driver whom he knew was intoxicated. His damages were reduced by 30%.

(5) 100% contributory negligence?

It is unclear whether damages can be reduced by 100% on account of the claimant's contributory negligence. The issue has been considered on several occasions and the authorities are roughly equally divided.[94] But the better view is clear. A finding of 100% contributory negligence would mean that the claimant is wholly responsible for the damage about which he complains. However, if the claimant's damage is entirely his own fault, the question of contributory negligence cannot arise for consideration. This is because such a claimant will be unable to establish that the defendant's negligence caused his damage. The definitional elements of the action in negligence will be incomplete. For this reason, suggestions that claimants may be found guilty of 100% contributory negligence are incoherent.

(6) Apportionment and exemplary damages

The apportionment provision operates on compensatory damages (which include aggravated damages). What about exemplary damages? The Law Commission suggested that exemplary damages are susceptible to reduction for contributory negligence.[95] This makes little sense. It overlooks the primary rationale of awarding exemplary damages, which is to punish the defendant. Reducing awards of exemplary damages on account of the claimant's fault will undermine the goal of ordering the defendant to pay such damages. Awards of exemplary damages, if apportioned, will not be proportionate to the defendant's culpability.

(7) Multiple tortfeasors

Where two or more defendants cause the claimant indivisible damage (ie where the damage caused by one defendant cannot be separated from the damage caused by the other defendant), the extent of the claimant's contributory negligence is assessed against the totality of the defendants' negligence.[96] Suppose, for example, that C, a pedestrian, is injured by the negligence of D1 and D2, two motorists. C's share of the responsibility for his damage is 30%. D1 and D2 are 40 and 30% responsible respectively. C will be able to recover 70% of his damages from either D1 or D2. Once C has recovered his damages, D1 and D2 will be able to bring proceedings against each other for contribution in an effort to ensure that their liabilities correspond to their

---

[94] Findings of 100% contributory negligence are impermissible according to *Pitts v Hunt* [1991] 1 QB 24 (CA), at 48; *Buyukardicli v Hammerson UK Properties Plc* [2002] EWCA Civ 683, at [7]; *Anderson v Newham College of Further Education* [2002] EWCA Civ 505; [2003] ICR 212. Consider also *Reeves v Commissioner of Police of the Metropolis* [2000] 1 AC 360 (HL), at 372, 387. The converse position is supported by *Imperial Chemical Industries Ltd v Shatwell* [1965] AC 656 (HL), at 672; *McMullen v National Coal Board* [1982] ICR 148 (QBD); *Jayes v IMI (Kynoch) Ltd* [1985] ICR 155 (CA), at 159.

[95] Law Commission, *Aggravated, Restitutionary and Exemplary Damages*, Report 247 (1997), at 81 n 475.

[96] *Fitzgerald v Lane* [1989] AC 328 (HL).

individual responsibility for C's damage. Matters are simpler if the damage is divisible. Suppose that C suffers property damage due to D1's negligence and personal injury because of D2's breach of duty. Assume also that C was contributorily negligent and that his carelessness was causally related to both types of damage. Each defendant's negligence would be compared separately with the claimant's share in the responsibility for the damage in question.

SECTION 3   VOLUNTARY ASSUMPTION OF RISK[97]

(A) THE ELEMENTS OF THE DEFENCE

The defendant will be able to avoid liability in the tort of negligence if he proves that the claimant voluntarily assumed the risk of injury. This plea is often referred to by the maxim *volenti non fit injuria* (no injury is done to one who consents), or '*volenti*' for short. According to Lord Herschell in *Smith v Charles Baker & Sons*, the defence 'is founded on good sense and justice. One who has invited or assented to an act being done towards him cannot, when he suffers from it, complain of it as a wrong'.[98] In order to establish that the claimant was *volens* to the risk of injury, the defendant must prove that the claimant had full knowledge of the risk and voluntarily agreed to incur it. These requirements will be considered shortly. It is convenient, however, to make some general introductory points about the defence. First, in contrast with contributory negligence, the defence of voluntary assumption of risk, when applicable, prevents liability from arising. It does not merely reduce the extent of the defendant's liability. Second, since the enactment of the apportionment provision, the circumstances in which the defence of *volenti* is available have been severely restricted.[99] The courts have usually preferred to award claimants who have been injured through negligence partial damages pursuant to the apportionment provision than to deny liability altogether on the basis of *volenti*.[100] Consequently, nowadays, the defence of voluntary assumption of risk is rarely available. Third, the defence of *volenti*, when exceptionally engaged, can be triggered simultaneously with the apportionment provision, as a person who assumes a risk of injury may be acting unreasonably with respect to his own safety. However, the terrain covered by the *volenti* defence and the apportionment provision is not identical. This is because voluntarily assuming certain risks may not be unreasonable. Fourth, it is unclear exactly how the voluntary assumption of risk defence operates. Some judges have said that, when applicable, it results in a duty of

---

[97] See Jaffey, '*Volenti Non Fit Injuria*' (1985) 44 CLJ 87; Simons, 'Assumption of Risk and Consent in the Law of Torts: A Theory of Full Preference' (1987) 67 BU L Rev 213; Kidner, 'The Variable Standard of Care, Contributory Negligence and *Volenti*' (1991) 11 LS 1; Sugarman, 'Assumption of Risk' (1997) 31 Val ULR 833.

[98] [1891] AC 325 (HL), at 360.

[99] The contraction of the defence is discussed in *ICI Ltd v Shatwell* [1965] AC 656 (HL), at 671–2; *Nettleship v Weston* [1971] 2 QB 691 (CA), at 701.

[100] The preference is made explicit in *Nettleship v Weston* [1971] 2 QB 691 (CA), at 701.

care being waived.[101] On this account, if the claimant is *volens* to the risk of injury, no tort is committed. On other occasions, it has been suggested that, like contributory negligence, it is a rule to which defendants who have committed a tort can appeal.[102] The difference between these views is important. As a matter of principle, the way in which the defence operates ought to affect, for example, the allocation of the onus of pleading and proof in respect of it.

At the outset, it may be helpful to give some illustrations of cases in which the *volenti* defence succeeded. A famous decision is *Morris v Murray*.[103] The claimant in this matter had spent an afternoon drinking heavily with a friend. The claimant then agreed to his friend's proposal that they take a joyride in a light aircraft. At the airport, the claimant helped to prepare the plane and his friend assumed the pilot's seat. Soon after take-off, the plane crashed. The claimant's friend was killed and the claimant was seriously injured. The claimant brought an action in negligence against his friend's estate. The Court of Appeal upheld the estate's plea of *volenti*. Their Lordships said that accepting a flight with an obviously drunken pilot was akin to confronting deliberately some dangerous physical condition brought about by the defendant.

The defence also applied in the recent decision of the Court of Appeal in *Freeman v Higher Park Farm*.[104] This claim arose out of a horse-riding accident. The claimant was an experienced rider who wanted an exciting ride on a lively horse. She attended the defendant's stables and took out one of its horses. She knew that the horse in question had a propensity to buck. When breaking into a canter, the horse bucked and the claimant fell off. She was badly hurt and sued the defendant for damages. The court held that the claimant had voluntarily assumed the risk of injury and that her action in negligence and under the Animals Act 1971[105] therefore failed.

(1) The claimant knew of the risk of injury

The claimant must have been aware of the risk of injury that materialised,[106] for one cannot consent to a risk of injury if one does not know that it exists. The fact that the reasonable person in the claimant's position would have known about the risk is insufficient to satisfy this requirement. Thus, it follows that if, for example, the claimant is too drunk to comprehend a given risk, the defence will not be available if the risk materialises (although he may well be guilty of contributory negligence).[107] Of course, if the reasonable person would have been aware of the risk in issue, that fact may

---

[101] *Thomas v Quartermaine* (1887) LR 18 QBD 685 (CA), at 697–8; *Dann v Hamilton* [1939] 1 KB 509 (KBD), at 512; *Geary v JD Wetherspoon Plc* [2011] EWHC 1506 (QB), at [46].

[102] *Wooldridge v Sumner* [1963] 2 QB 43 (CA), at 69; *Ashton v Turner* [1981] QB 137 (QBD), at 146.

[103] [1991] 2 QB 6 (CA).

[104] [2008] EWCA Civ 1185.

[105] This Act is discussed in ch 18. Section 5(2) of the Act provides for a defence that is essentially equivalent to the common-law defence of voluntary assumption of risk: cf *Cummings v Grainger* [1977] QB 397 (CA), at 408.

[106] *Bennet v Tugwell* [1971] 2 QB 267 (QBD), at 273; *Morris v Murray* [1991] 2 QB 6 (CA), at 18.

[107] This proposition is implicitly supported by *Morris v Murray* [1991] 2 QB 6 (CA), at 16, 27–9, 32.

suggest that the claimant was conscious of it. But this precondition to the defence's application ultimately imposes a subjective test.

A case in which this prerequisite to the defence's application was determinative is *Neeson v Acheson*.[108] This was an action brought by a woman who had been bitten by her neighbour's dog after she placed her face close to its jaws. As she had befriended the animal over the course of several months prior to the incident, she had no reason to expect that it would bite her. The defendant argued that the claimant had voluntarily assumed the risk of injury. This submission was rejected. The judge held that as the claimant did not foresee any risk of injury, the defence was inapplicable.

Another case in which the defence failed for want of full knowledge by the claimant of the risk of injury is *Poppleton v Trustees of the Portsmouth Youth Activities Committee*.[109] The claimant in this case was a novice rock climber. At the relevant time, he was scaling the defendant's artificial climbing wall. Having ascended the wall, the claimant jumped off it and attempted to catch a metal bar running across the ceiling with a view to then dropping safely to the floor. His momentum prevented him from maintaining his grip on the bar and he fell to the ground and broke his neck. The defence of voluntary assumption of risk failed. The court held that the matting on the floor gave the false impression that it was safe to jump from the wall to the ground. The claimant did not, therefore, have comprehensive knowledge of the risk of injury that materialised.

A case that is difficult to reconcile with the requirement of knowledge is *Murray v Harringay Arena Ltd*.[110] This was an action by a six-year-old boy who had been struck in the eye by a hockey puck that had been hit out of an ice rink. The claimant had been taken to the rink by his father. It was held that the claimant was *volens* to the risk of injury. This conclusion is indefensible. The claimant could not have fully appreciated the risk of injury given his age (let alone voluntarily agreed to run it). The case is better explained as one in which there was no negligence on the part of the defendant. Indeed, much can be found in the court's judgment that suggests that the real reason the claimant failed was that the defendant did not breach its duty of care. The court emphasised that the incidence of the escape of pucks from the rink was low and that it would have been unrealistic to expect the defendant to install barriers to protect spectators. These are considerations that go to the negligence calculus.

(2) The claimant voluntarily agreed to incur the risk

It is not enough to enliven the defence of *volenti* that the claimant knew of the risk of injury.[111] He must have also agreed to run the risk. This requirement was explained by Scott LJ in *Bowater v Rowley Regis Corp*.[112] In that case, his Lordship said:

> For the purpose of the rule…a man cannot be said to be truly 'willing' unless he is in a position to choose freely, and freedom of choice predicates, not only full knowledge of the

---

[108] [2008] NIQB 12 (QBD).   [109] [2007] EWHC 1567 (QB).
[110] [1951] 2 KB 529 (CA).   [111] *Nettleship v Weston* [1971] 2 QB 691 (CA), at 701.
[112] [1944] KB 476 (CA), at 479.

circumstances on which the exercise of choice is conditioned, so that he may be able to choose wisely, but the absence from his mind of any feeling of constraint so that nothing shall interfere with the freedom of his will.

Several points should be noticed about this statement. First, it sets the bar very high. If the claimant's decision to expose himself to a risk of injury is influenced by the slightest pressure, the defence will fail. Second, the knowledge requirement is, in a sense, a sub-element of the voluntary agreement requirement. This is because, as Scott LJ observed, an agreement to run a risk without comprehending it is no agreement at all. However, it is convenient for expository purposes to treat the knowledge requirement and the voluntary agreement requirement as distinct. Third, the defendant cannot establish that the claimant consented to the risk of injury merely by pointing to his awareness of it. The rule is *volenti non fit injuria* not *scienti non fit injuria* (no injury is done to one who knows of the risk).

As a result of the voluntary agreement requirement, the *volenti* defence does not lie against rescuers,[113] including professional rescuers whose job requires them to go to a citizen's aid.[114] The decision of a person to assist another imperilled by an emergency is not unencumbered in the sense required to trigger the defence. This is because it is the product of a moral or legal duty to act. The voluntariness requirement also excludes the defence where the claimant engaged in acts of self-harm that the defendant, in breach of a duty owed to the claimant, failed to prevent. The leading decision on point is *Reeves v Commissioner of Police of the Metropolis*.[115] This was a claim by the estate and dependants of a man who committed suicide while in police custody. But for the negligence of the police, the deceased would not have been able to take his own life. As the police were under a duty to prevent the deceased from committing acts of self-harm,[116] it was held that the defendant could not succeed on the *volenti* defence. Their Lordships said that allowing liability to be avoided by way of the defence would effectively empty the duty of its content. The outcome would have been the same had the deceased been a mental patient in the defendant's hospital.

In rare instances, the requirement that the claimant voluntarily assume the risk of injury will be dispensed with and mere knowledge of the risk will bar the claimant. An example of where this will occur is where the claimant is a gratuitous bailee of

---

[113] *Haynes v Harwood* [1935] 1 KB 146 (CA); *Baker v TE Hopkins & Son Ltd* [1959] 3 All ER 225 (CA); cf *Cutler v United Dairies (London) Ltd* [1933] 2 KB 297 (CA). See further Goodhart, 'Rescue and Voluntary Assumption of Risk' (1934) 5 CLJ 192.

[114] *Ogwo v Taylor* [1988] AC 431 (HL) (fireman); *Merrington v Ironbridge Metal Works Ltd* [1952] 2 All ER 1101 (Assizes) (same); *D'Urso v Sanson* [1939] 4 All ER 26 (KBD) (night-watchman extinguishing fire on employer's premises); cf *Sylvester v Chapman Ltd* (1935) 79 Sol Jo 777 (Div Ct) (claimant mauled by leopard at defendant's animal show when he crossed the barrier to extinguish a cigarette smouldering in the straw 'was not rescuing anyone from imminent danger of death, nor even preventing damage to property, since there were people who could easily have done with precautions what he did' (per Lord Wright MR); therefore the defence of *volenti* applied).

[115] [2000] 1 AC 360 (HL).

[116] See *Orange v Chief Constable of West Yorkshire Police* [2001] EWCA Civ 611; [2002] QB 347.

a defective chattel belonging to the defendant and the defendant warns the claimant of its dangerous nature. The defendant can say to the claimant: 'Take it or leave it'. Conversely, reasons of policy sometimes dictate that a claimant will not fail even though he freely encountered a known risk (for example, where the claimant has a right to face the risk, such as when he walks along a highway or exercises a right of access).[117]

(B) SPECIFIC CONTEXTS

(1) Actions by employees against employers

The defence of voluntary assumption of risk used to be especially important in actions by workers alleging negligence by their employers. In the nineteenth-century, it was generally held that the defence would be enlivened if the employee knew of the risk, regardless of whether he had any real choice whether to run it. The House of Lords (no doubt reflecting shifting social and economic attitudes) altered this approach in *Smith v Charles Baker & Sons*.[118] The facts of this landmark case were as follows. The claimant, who was the defendant's employee, was required to drill holes in a rock cutting. He was aware that a crane carrying crates of stones often swung overhead. A stone fell out of a crate and injured him. He brought an action in negligence against the defendant, who pleaded voluntary assumption of risk. The House of Lords held that, notwithstanding the claimant's knowledge of the risk, the evidence justified a finding by the jury that he had not voluntarily assumed it. Hence, the defence was inapplicable. Lord Watson said:[119]

> The question which has most frequently to be considered is not whether [the employee] voluntarily and rashly exposed himself to injury, but whether he agreed that, if injury should befall him, the risk was to be his and not his master's. [Whether continuing to work knowing of the danger will enliven the voluntary assumption of the risk defence] depends...upon the nature of the risk, and the [employee's] connection with it, as well as upon other considerations which must vary according to the circumstances of each case.

A series of employer/employee cases followed *Smith* in which the defence of *volenti* failed for want of consent. *Bowater v Rowley Regis Corp*[120] is typical. The claimant was ordered by his employers to take out a horse known by them to be unsafe. The claimant protested but eventually complied. Later, he was thrown off a cart being drawn by the horse when the horse bolted. The claimant sued his employers in negligence in respect of his injuries. The Court of Appeal rejected the defence of voluntary assumption of risk. Goddard LJ said:[121] 'it can hardly ever be applicable where the act to which the

---

[117] *Clayards v Dethick and Davis* (1848) 12 QB 439; 116 ER 932 (QB).
[118] [1891] AC 325 (HL).   [119] Ibid at 355.
[120] [1944] KB 476 (CA).   [121] Ibid at 480–1.

servant is said to be "*volens*" arises out of his ordinary duty, unless the work for which he is engaged is one in which danger is necessarily involved'.[122]

An important case in which the defence succeeded is *Imperial Chemical Industries Ltd v Shatwell*.[123] In this decision the House of Lords noted that the plea of *volenti* will rarely defeat a claim by an employee against his employer. However, their Lordships held that where the claim rests on vicarious liability for joint and flagrant disobedience of a safety rule by the claimant and a co-employee (where the latter was not the claimant's superior or one whose orders he was bound to obey), the employer could exceptionally succeed on the defence. Thus, the claimant in *Shatwell*, a miner who agreed with a co-worker to detonate an explosive charge in a dangerous manner contrary to safety regulations, was denied recovery in respect of injuries suffered because of the explosion.

(2) Motor vehicle cases

In the past, the defence of *volenti* was often enlivened where the claimant accepted a ride from a driver whom he knew was intoxicated.[124] This situation is now dealt with by statute. Section 149 of the Road Traffic Act 1988, which applies to accidents involving vehicles in respect of which it is compulsory to obtain liability insurance, excludes the defence. Of course, a drunk driver who causes injury to his passenger may be able to reduce his liability on the ground that the claimant was guilty of contributory negligence in accepting a ride from an intoxicated driver.[125]

(3) Dangerous activities

Another context in which the defence of voluntary assumption of risk may be applicable is that of dangerous activities, including sport.[126] As in other settings, before the defence can arise in this context the defendant must show that the claimant consented not only to some risk of harm intrinsic to the activity, but also to the particular risk that culminated in injury to him. *Gillmore v London City Council*[127] illustrates the principle. The claimant was a member of the defendant's physical training class. During an exercise in which the members of the class lunged at each other, the claimant was injured through losing his balance on a floor which was slippery due to the defendant's negligence. Du Parcq LJ held[128] that the claimant had not consented to this specific risk (although, of course, he had consented to the physical contacts which

---

[122] Although even this may not be sufficient. In *Davies v Global Strategies Group (Hong Kong) Ltd* [2009] EWHC 2342 (QB), at [86] the employee was paid 'danger money' to work as a security contractor in Iraq. He was fatally shot by insurgents. The plea of *volenti* was held to be inapplicable in an action by the deceased's dependants against the deceased's employer.

[123] [1965] AC 656 (HL).

[124] See, eg, *Dann v Hamilton* [1939] 1 KB 509 (KBD); *Buckpitt v Oates* [1968] 1 All ER 1145 (Assizes); *Bennett v Tugwell* [1971] 2 QB 267 (QBD); *Ashton v Turner* [1981] QB 137 (QBD).

[125] See, e.g., *Owens v Brimmell* [1977] QB 859 (QBD).

[126] See Yeo, 'Accepted Inherent Risks among Sporting Participants' (2001) 9 Tort L Rev 114.

[127] [1938] 4 All ER 331 (KBD).   [128] Ibid at 336.

might occur in the course of the lunging exercise). Thus, the defence of voluntary assumption of risk failed.[129]

(4) Entrants and occupiers

A statutory defence analogous to that of *volenti non fit injuria* applies in relation to occupiers' liability. This defence is discussed elsewhere.[130]

SECTION 4   EXPRESS EXCLUSION OR LIMITATION OF LIABILITY

The previous section addressed the defence of voluntary assumption of risk. Liability can also be expressly excluded or limited by a contract between the parties or by way of a notice. The relationship between this defence and that of *volenti* is unclear. It is often said that *volenti* is concerned with implicit consent by the claimant to run the risk of injury that caused him damage whereas the defence that is the subject of this section deals with express consent. This understanding is probably not entirely accurate (some cases of *volenti* might be said to involve express acceptance of a risk). But, since it is fairly entrenched, this chapter will not deviate from it.

As a general rule, the parties can reallocate liabilities by a contract or by a notice. This principle is, however, subject to significant exceptions. The most important exception is that created by section 2(1) of the Unfair Contract Terms Act 1977. This subsection provides: 'A person cannot by reference to any contract term...exclude or restrict his liability for death or personal injury resulting from negligence'. Any term that purports to exclude or limit liability in these circumstances is invalid. This subsection only applies to 'business liability'. 'Business liability' is defined as liability arising 'from things done or to be done by a person in the course of a business (whether his own business or another's); or from the occupation of premises used for business purposes of the occupier'.[131]

In the case of loss other than death or personal injury, or in the case of death or personal injury resulting from a tort other than negligence, the 1977 Act provides that an exclusion or limitation of 'business liability' is invalid 'except in so far as the term or notice satisfies the requirement of reasonableness'.[132] The criterion of reasonableness was considered in *Smith v Eric S Bush*.[133] In that case surveyors were instructed by a mortgage provider to inspect and report on a house that the claimant wished

---

[129]   See also *Cleghorn v Oldham* (1927) 43 TLR 465 (KBD). The claimant in this case recovered damages from her golf companion who had injured her with a golf club on the course.

[130]   See p 228.

[131]   Unfair Contract Terms Act 1977, s 1(3).

[132]   Unfair Contract Terms Act 1977, s 2(2). Reasonableness is defined in s 11.

[133]   [1990] 1 AC 831 (HL). See also *Bank of Scotland v Fuller Peiser* 2002 SCLR 255 (OH).

to buy. The surveyors expressly excluded any liability to the claimant. The House of Lords found, first, in the absence of the purported disclaimer, a duty of care was owed to the claimant[134] and, second, in the circumstances, the disclaimer was unreasonable. In the vast majority of cases, house purchasers, as surveyors well know, rely on the report commissioned by the mortgagee (a report for which the purchaser will in fact pay). Lord Griffiths suggested four factors by which to gauge reasonableness:[135] (1) whether the parties were of equal bargaining power; (2) whether it was practicable to expect the claimant to obtain independent advice; (3) the complexity of the task which formed the subject of the disclaimer; (4) the practical consequences of striking down the disclaimer.[136]

To further complicate matters, the 1977 Act must be read in conjunction with the Unfair Terms in Consumer Contracts Regulations 1999[137] which impose additional restrictions on the ability to exclude liability where (i) the tortious duty coexists with a contractual obligation in a consumer contract and (ii) the terms of that contract have not been individually negotiated. Both the Act and the Regulations require further judicial elaboration.

SECTION 5   ILLEGALITY

(A) INTRODUCTION

As a result of the proliferation of criminal offences in recent decades, it is not uncommon for victims of negligence to suffer injury while engaged in an illegal course of conduct. For example, a driver hurt in a motor vehicle accident by the carelessness of another road user may have been driving under the influence of alcohol, without wearing a seat belt, or in excess of the speed limit. Indeed, it has been claimed that most personal injury actions arising out of the use of a motor vehicle involve the commission of an offence by the claimant.[138] The extensive regulation of many of life's ordinary activities by the criminal law thus gives considerable significance to the effect of a claimant's unlawful behaviour on his entitlement to a remedy in tort.

---

[134]   Ibid at 843–5.

[135]   Ibid at 858–9. Had the Unfair Contract Terms Act 1977 been in force at that time, would the disclaimer in *Hedley Byrne & Co Ltd v Heller & Partners Ltd* [1964] AC 465 (HL) (see p 94) have survived judicial scrutiny?

[136]   Presumably, this includes any effect that holding the exclusion clause invalid may have on the cost or availability of the service provided by the defendant.

[137]   SI 1999/2083.

[138]   *Great North Eastern Railway Ltd v Hart* [2003] EWHC 2450 (QB), at [84] per Morland J. Similar comments have been made elsewhere: *Beresford v Royal Insurance Co Ltd* [1937] 2 KB 197 (CA), at 220; *National Coal Board v England* [1954] AC 403 (HL), at 418–19; *Winnik v Dick* 1984 SC 48 (IH), at 54; *Vellino v Chief Constable of Greater Manchester* [2001] EWCA Civ 1249, at [48]; [2002] 1 WLR 218, at 229; [2002] 3 All ER 78, at 88.

In certain situations, tort law grants a negligent defendant a defence[139] if the claimant whom he injured was acting in breach of the criminal law at the relevant time.[140] This defence, which is often referred to by the maxim *ex turpi causa non oritur actio*,[141] assumes different hues depending on the context in which it is raised. There are three different types of case. First, there are cases where the parties were jointly committing a criminal offence when the claimant was injured ('joint illegal enterprise cases'). The second class of case is actions in which the defendant was not implicated in the claimant's illegal conduct ('unilateral illegality cases'). The third type of case is proceedings that are an attempt by the claimant to use tort law to deflect the impact of a sanction imposed on him by the criminal law ('sanction-shifting cases'). The operation of the defence in each of these settings will be examined in due course. The analysis will begin, however, with some general observations.

First, the defence must be pleaded and proved by the defendant. The standard of proof is the balance of probabilities.[142] It is not necessary for the defendant to show beyond reasonable doubt that the claimant committed an offence. Second, the defence is often raised in conjunction with that of contributory negligence. Illegal conduct will usually constitute contributory negligence. But this is not invariably the case. It is possible for a claimant to breach the criminal law yet act reasonably with respect to his own safety. Consider, for example, *Kotula v Edf Energy Networks (Epn) Plc*.[143] The claimant in this case was a bicyclist who was injured by the defendant's negligence. He was illegally riding on the footpath at the relevant time. It was held that in doing so he was taking reasonable care for his own safety (although he may have been acting unreasonably vis-à-vis pedestrians) since it would have been dangerous for him to have used the stretch of road next to the footpath in question because of its narrow carriageway.[144] Third, while the defence is predominantly concerned with illegal conduct, it can also be triggered by grossly immoral behaviour. For a long time, it was doubtful whether this was the case. However, it has recently been confirmed that conduct evincing serious moral turpitude is sufficient.[145] Fourth, if the claimant has

---

[139] The defence of illegality is not confined to the negligence context. It is of general application. It is discussed in relation to intentional torts to the person or to property at pp 345–7.

[140] The defence's arrival in the negligence context was belated. It was not recognised until *Ashton v Turner* [1981] QB 137 (QBD). This important decision is noted in Hervey, 'Caveat Criminalis' (1981) 97 LQR 537; Symmons, 'Ex Turpi Causa in English Tort Law' (1981) 44 MLR 585; Debattista, 'Ex Turpi Causa Returns to the English Law of Torts: Taking Advantage of a Wrong Way Out' (1984) 13 Anglo-Am L Rev 15.

[141] 'No cause of action may be founded upon an immoral or illegal act' (*Revill v Newbery* [1996] QB 567 (CA), at 576 per Neill LJ).

[142] *Hanes v Wawanesa Mutual Insurance Co* [1963] SCR 154 (SCC), at 164; *Lindsay v Poole* 1984 SLT 269 (OH), at 269; *Sloan v Triplett* 1985 SLT 294 (OH), at 296; *Wilson v Price* 1989 SLT 484 (OH), at 486.

[143] [2010] EWHC 1968 (QB).   [144] Ibid at [44].

[145] *Nayyar v Denton Wilde Sapte* [2009] EWHC 3218 (QB) (payment of civil law bribe); *Safeway Stores Ltd v Twigger* [2010] EWHC 11 (Comm); [2010] 3 All ER 577 (anti-competitive behaviour). Suicide is insufficiently turpitudinous: *Kirkham v Chief Constable of the Greater Manchester Police* [1990] 2 QB 283 (CA); *Reeves v Commissioner of Police of the Metropolis* [1999] QB 169 (CA). See further Goudkamp, 'Ex Turpi Causa and Immoral Behaviour in Tort Law' (2011) 127 LQR 26.

a complete defence to criminal liability, the illegality defence is unlikely to apply.[146] Possession of a partial criminal law defence, such as diminished responsibility or loss of control, is probably insufficient to exclude the illegality defence.[147] Fifth, the offending must be contemporaneous. Thus, if the claimant withdraws from a criminal enterprise before suffering damage, the defence will be inapplicable.[148] Sixth, the mere fact that the claimant was engaged in a criminal act at the time of the defendant's tort will not enliven the defence. The claimant's offending must be causally related to his damage. For example, if the claimant's vehicle is struck by another car while he was transporting a person whom he had kidnapped, the defence would be inapplicable in an action brought by the claimant in respect of personal injuries that he suffered. This is because his offending did not materially contribute to his loss. Finally, and perhaps most significantly, not every breach of the criminal law is sufficient to trigger the defence.[149] Only fairly serious offending is sufficient. As Latham CJ said in *Henwood v Municipal Tramways Trust (SA)*:[150]

> there is no general principle of English law that a person who is engaged in some unlawful act is disabled from complaining of injury done to him by other persons, either deliberately or accidentally. He does not become *caput lupinum*.

The courts have stressed the necessity of steering a course between the Charybdis and Scylla that represent the extreme positions of denying all claims affected by illegality and ignoring the claimant's unlawful behaviour.[151] Consequently, the defence has no application to run-of-the-mill personal injury actions that involve no more than trivial infractions of the criminal law.[152]

(B) THREE TYPES OF ILLEGALITY CASE

(1) Joint illegal enterprise cases[153]

Joint illegal enterprise cases are actions in which the defendant injured the claimant while engaged in a criminal enterprise jointly with him. The law applicable to such cases is found in *Pitts v Hunt*.[154] The claimant in this action was hurt while a pillion

---

[146] *Miller v Miller* [2009] WASCA 199; (2009) 54 MVR 367, at 384 [78] (this point was not dealt with on appeal: *Miller v Miller* [2011] HCA 9; (2011) 275 ALR 611; (2011) 85 ALJR 480).

[147] *Gray v Thames Trains Ltd* [2009] UKHL 33; [2009] 1 AC 1339 (noted in Goudkamp, 'The Defence of Illegality: *Gray v Thames Trains Ltd*' (2009) 17 TLJ 205).

[148] *Miller v Miller* [2011] HCA 9, at [106]; (2011) 275 ALR 611, at 639; (2011) 85 ALJR 480.

[149] *Pitts v Hunt* [1991] 1 QB 24 (CA), at 46, 53; *Hewison v Meridian Shipping Services Pte Ltd* [2002] EWCA Civ 1821, at [36]; [2003] ICR 766, at 781.

[150] [1938] HCA 35; (1938) 60 CLR 438, at 446. See also *Revill v Newbery* [1996] QB 567 (CA), at 577, 579.

[151] *Saunders v Edwards* [1987] 1 WLR 1116 (CA), at 1134; [1987] 2 All ER 651, at 665–6.

[152] *Vellino v Chief Constable of Greater Manchester* [2001] EWCA Civ 1249, at [48]; [2002] 1 WLR 218, at 229; [2002] 3 All ER 78, at 88; *Currie v Clamp* 2002 SLT 196 (OH), at 200 [20]–[21].

[153] Weinrib, 'Illegality as a Tort Defence' (1976) 26 UTLJ 28; Goudkamp, 'The Defence of Joint Illegal Enterprise' (2010) 34 MULR 425.

[154] [1991] 1 QB 24 (CA). See also *Ashton v Turner* [1981] QB 137 (QBD).

passenger on a motorcycle. The motorcycle was being driven by his friend, who was 16 years old, unlicensed, uninsured, and intoxicated. When rounding a bend while travelling on the wrong side of the road, the motorcycle collided with an oncoming vehicle. The claimant brought an action against his friend's estate (his friend was killed in the accident). The Court of Appeal[155] held that no duty of care will be recognised between participants to a joint criminal enterprise if the nature of the enterprise is such that it would be impossible or not feasible to ask how much care the reasonable person in the defendant's position would have taken in the circumstances. The court held that this test was satisfied in the instant case. This rule would also prevent recovery by a bank robber injured by his accomplice's negligent handling of an explosive charge[156] and by a thief injured by the careless driving of his getaway driver.[157]

(2) Unilateral illegality cases

Claimants who act unlawfully independently of the defendant at the time of the defendant's tort may also fail due to the illegality defence. A leading case regarding the defence in this context is *Revill v Newbery*.[158] The claimant in this action was attempting to break into a shed owned by the defendant. The defendant was sleeping in the shed at the time in order to protect belongings that he kept inside it. Roused by the claimant's efforts to gain entry, the defendant fired a shotgun through a hole in the door to scare the claimant. The blast struck the claimant. The claimant brought proceedings against the defendant in negligence and under the Occupiers' Liability Act 1984. He succeeded at first instance, although his damages were reduced by two-thirds for contributory negligence. The defendant's appeal to the Court of Appeal was dismissed. Neill LJ, who wrote the principal opinion, held that if the illegality defence applied, it would effectively render the claimant an outlaw and that the legislature, in enacting the Occupiers' Liability Act 1984, implicitly discountenanced such a result.[159]

Another important decision is that in *Vellino v Chief Constable of Greater Manchester*.[160] The claimant in this case had often been arrested by police at his apartment. Although his apartment was situated two floors above street level, the

---

[155] The court was heavily influenced by Australian authority, especially *Jackson v Harrison* [1976] HCA 17; (1978) 138 CLR 438. The High Court of Australia has now taken the jurisprudence regarding the illegality defence in a different direction: *Miller v Miller* [2011] HCA 9; (2011) 275 ALR 611; (2011) 85 ALJR 480.

[156] An example given by Lord Asquith in *National Coal Board v England* [1954] AC 403 (HL), at 429. Consider also the example offered by Lord Mayfield in *Lindsay v Poole* 1984 SLT 269 (OH), at 270: 'An obvious situation [where the defence would apply] would be where two persons embarked on violence towards a third. If one of those two persons struck a blow with a knife and the victim was the other person, his participant, it seems clear that the latter would not have a claim for damages for negligent use of a knife.' Further examples are offered by Scrutton LJ in *Hillen v ICI (Alkali) Ltd* [1934] 1 KB 455 (CA), at 467.

[157] *Ashton v Turner* [1981] QB 137 (QBD).

[158] [1996] QB 567 (CA) (noted in Weir, 'Swag for the Injured Burglar' (1996) 55 CLJ 182).

[159] *Revill v Newbery* [1996] QB 567 (CA), at 577–8. See also at 579 per Evans LJ, 580 per Millett LJ.

[160] [2001] EWCA Civ 1249; [2002] 1 WLR 218; [2002] 3 All ER 78 (noted in Morgan, '*Jus Suum Cuique*' (2002) 118 LQR 527).

claimant would frequently attempt to escape from the police by jumping out of one of the apartment's windows. One evening the police came to the claimant's apartment in response to a complaint about a noisy party. The claimant was arrested. An altercation ensued and the claimant jumped out of a window. On this occasion, he was catastrophically injured by the fall. A majority in the Court of Appeal[161] held that the police did not owe the claimant a duty of care because the seriousness of the claimant's unlawful behaviour meant that the third stage of the *Caparo* test[162] (which asks whether the imposition of a duty of care would be 'fair, just and reasonable')[163] was not satisfied.

It should be noted that the reasons given for the decisions in *Revill* and *Vellino* focused on quite different considerations. In *Revill*, it was important that denying the claimant relief would have sat uncomfortably with the policy behind the Occupiers' Liability Act 1984. In *Vellino*, no such concern arose. The central factor was the seriousness of the claimant's offending, which the Court of Appeal stressed was significant. Unfortunately, therefore, it is difficult to determine what test governs unilateral illegality cases.

The House of Lords recently examined the illegality defence as it applies in the context of unilateral offending in *Stone & Rolls Ltd v Moore Stephens*.[164] The claimant company in this case was owned and controlled by a fraudster. The fraudster used the claimant to commit massive frauds on several banks. When these frauds were discovered, the banks obtained an order for substantial damages against the claimant. The claimant went into liquidation and its liquidators sought an indemnity from its auditor in negligence and in contract in respect of this liability for failing to detect the deception. The auditor relied on the illegality defence. A majority of the House held that the defence applied. Unfortunately, it is difficult to extract general principles applicable to tort law from the decision, for several reasons. First, there were several other significant issues in the case. Second, the reasoning of the majority differed. Third, the proceedings were characterised as essentially brought in contract rather than in tort. However, the majority agreed that, if a claimant needs to rely on his unlawful conduct in pleading his tort action (which was the case on the facts in *Moore Stephens*), he will usually fail on the ground of illegality.[165]

---

[161] Sedley LJ dissented. His Lordship's powerful analysis deserves close reading.

[162] *Vellino v Chief Constable of Greater Manchester* [2001] EWCA Civ 1249, at [8], [28], [62]; [2002] 1 WLR 218 at 222, 226, 233–4; [2002] 3 All ER 78, at 81, 85, 92.

[163] The *Caparo* test is discussed above: see pp 36ff.

[164] [2009] UKHL 39; [2009] 1 AC 1391.

[165] Lord Phillips, Lord Walker, and Lord Brown were in the majority. Lord Walker (at 1480 [128]) and Lord Brown (at 1503 [195]) accepted the reliance principle wholeheartedly. Conversely, Lord Phillips (at 1453 [25]) said that this principle cannot 'automatically be applied as a rule of thumb. It is necessary to give consideration to the policy underlying *ex turpi causa*'. Unfortunately, his Lordship did not identify the relevant policies.

(3) Sanction-shifting cases[166]

Sanction-shifting cases are actions in which the claimant sues the defendant complaining that the defendant's negligence caused him to incur a criminal sanction. Several such cases have been brought. With few exceptions,[167] they have been unsuccessful.[168] The leading decision is that of the House of Lords in *Gray v Thames Trains Ltd*.[169] The claimant in this case was the victim of a train crash that occurred due to the defendants' negligence. His physical injuries were relatively minor but he developed a serious psychiatric illness. Nearly two years after the train accident, the claimant stabbed to death a drunken pedestrian with whom he had an altercation. He was convicted of manslaughter on the ground of diminished responsibility and given a custodial sentence. The claimant then sued the defendant for various losses including several stemming from his conviction such as his loss of freedom, a loss of income while imprisoned, and the damage that his conviction did to his reputation. The House held that these losses were irrecoverable. The House's logic was that to award damages in respect of these losses would mean that tort law would undermine the criminal law (because it would involve restoring that which the criminal law had taken away), and coherence demanded that different branches of the law should not stultify each other. The claimant was, however, entitled to damages in respect of losses that were not associated with the criminal sanction, such as pain and suffering caused by his physical and psychiatric injuries. The non-stultification principle means that, as a general rule, sanction-shifting cases will fail on the ground of illegality. Possibly the only such cases that might succeed are those in which the sentence of the criminal court is solely rehabilitative rather than punitive.

(C) LIMITING REDRESS UNDER SPECIFIC HEADS OF DAMAGES

The illegality defence, when successfully invoked, usually works to completely deny actions. But it can also prevent recovery under specific heads of damages. For example, in *Gray v Thames Trains Ltd*, which was just discussed, recovery was only denied in respect of losses that were caused by the claimant's convictions. The defence can also prevent compensation from being recovered for a loss of earnings where the loss is tainted by unlawful conduct. For example, compensation for a loss of income has been denied where the claimant derived the income concerned by working as an illegal

---

[166] See Goudkamp, 'Can Tort Law Be Used to Deflect the Impact of Criminal Sanctions? The Role of the Illegality Defence' (2006) 14 TLJ 20; Banakas, 'Tort Damages and the Decline of Fault Liability: Plato Overruled, But Full Marks to Aristotle!' (1985) 44 CLJ 195.

[167] See, eg, *Meah v McCreamer* [1985] 1 All ER 367 (QBD).

[168] See, eg, *Clunis v Camden and Islington Health Authority* [1998] QB 978 (CA); *Worrall v British Railways Board* [1999] CLY 1413 (CA); [1999] All ER (D) 455.

[169] [2009] UKHL 33; [2009] 1 AC 1339.

bookmaker,[170] as a crane operator while unlawfully concealing a history of epileptic seizures,[171] without the necessary immigration permit,[172] and in contravention of planning regulations.[173] Damages for a loss of income have also been refused where the claimant had kept earnings secret in order to fraudulently claim social security benefits.[174] Similarly, an action under Lord Campbell's Act was rejected in so far as it relied upon income that the deceased had derived by committing burglaries.[175] No definitive test exists as to when recovery under a specific head of damages will be limited on the ground of illegality. However, the Court of Appeal has indicated that compensation will not be withheld if the loss in question is merely obliquely connected with, or is collateral to, a breach of the criminal law.[176]

(D) REFORM

The illegality defence has been under the scrutiny of the Law Commission for a considerable period of time.[177] In 2010, the Commission published its final report on the defence.[178] It was of the view that the courts should take account of all of the relevant policy considerations in deciding whether the defence applies (these considerations included deterrence, preventing wrongful profiting, and upholding the dignity of the courts). The Commission concluded that recent decisions, especially that in *Gray v Thames Trains Ltd*,[179] were developing the law consistently with its recommendation. Legislative action was not, therefore, required.

FURTHER READING

GOUDKAMP, 'The Defence of Illegality: *Gray v Thames Trains Ltd*' (2009) 17 *Torts Law Journal* 205
GOUDKAMP, 'The Defence of Joint Illegal Enterprise' (2010) 34 *Melbourne University Law Review* 425
LAW COMMISSION, *The Illegality Defence*, Report 320 (2010)

---

[170] *Meadows v Ferguson* [1961] VR 594 (SC).
[171] *Hewison v Meridian Shipping Services Pte Ltd* [2002] EWCA Civ 1821; [2003] ICR 766; cf *Major v Ministry of Defence* [2003] EWCA Civ 1433; (2003) 147 SJLB 1206.
[172] *Lee v McClellan* (1995) 127 FLR 383 (NSWSC).
[173] *McNichols v J R Simplot Co* 262 P 2d 1012 (ID, 1953); contra *Mills v Baitis* [1968] VR 583 (FC).
[174] *Kanu v Kashif* [2002] EWCA Civ 1620. See also *Hunter v Butler* [1996] RTR 396 (CA); cf *Newman v Folkes and Dunlop Tyres Ltd* [2002] PIQR Q2 (QBD).
[175] *Burns v Edman* [1970] 2 QB 541 (QBD).
[176] *Hewison v Meridian Shipping Services Pte Ltd* [2002] EWCA Civ 1821 at [36]–[38], [50]–[51]; [2003] ICR 766 at 781–2, 785–6.
[177] Law Commission, *The Illegality Defence in Tort*, Consultation Paper 160 (2001); Law Commission, *The Illegality Defence: A Consultative Report*, Consultation Paper 189 (2009).
[178] Law Commission, *The Illegality Defence*, Report 320 (2010).
[179] [2009] UKHL 33; [2009] 1 AC 1339.

SIMONS, 'Assumption of Risk and Consent in the Law of Torts: A Theory of Full Preference' (1987) 67 *Boston University Law Review* 213

SIMONS, 'The Puzzling Doctrine of Contributory Negligence' (1995) 16 *Cardozo Law Review* 1693

SUGARMAN, 'Assumption of Risk' (1997) 31 *Valparaiso University Law Review* 833

WEINRIB, 'Illegality as a Tort Defence' (1976) 26 *University of Toronto Law Journal* 28

YEO, 'Accepted Inherent Risks Among Sporting Participants' (2001) 9 *Tort Law Review* 114

7

LIABILITY FOR DEFECTIVE PREMISES AND STRUCTURES

KEY ISSUES

(1) Occupiers' liability

The bulk of this chapter concerns the potential liability of occupiers to those who suffer injury and/or other forms of loss by virtue of the state of the occupier's premises. The means by which an occupier's liability is to be determined is governed almost exclusively by statute. In this respect it is important to appreciate that two statutes exist. The first – the Occupiers' Liability Act 1957 – governs the duty owed by occupiers to visitors. The second, the Occupiers' Liability Act 1984, governs the duty owed by occupiers to non-visitors.

(2) Statutory (not common-law) liability

Because occupiers' liability is governed almost entirely by statute, it is vital to determine liability in accordance with the Acts' pivotal terms – such as 'occupier', 'visitor', 'non-visitor', and 'common duty of care'. Thus, although the Acts impose liability that closely resembles common-law negligence, it is a mistake to assume that the language of the common law can be used interchangeably with the language of the statutes. Rather, it is vital to ascribe to the particular statutory terms that govern liability under the Acts the courts' interpretation of those terms. It is also important to recognise the sometimes subtle differences that exist between liability under the Acts and that under the common law of negligence.

(3) Non-occupiers' liability

The latter part of this chapter considers the residual classes of defendants who may be held liable in tort for losses and injuries arising from the defective state of premises. These non-occupiers include landlords, builders, architects, and engineers; and the rules governing their liability are also to be found in a statute: viz, the Defective Premises Act 1972.

SECTION 1   INTRODUCTION

Liability for defective premises[1] to those who suffer loss or damage on those premises[2] may in general rest with two main types of defendant. The first comprises those persons actually occupying the premises. Here, responsibility is generally for personal injuries such as a broken ankle sustained when a rotten floorboard gives way. Second, someone other than the occupier may be liable for defects in the premises. This latter category of potential defendants is broad in scope and includes landlords, builders, and professionals such as architects and consulting engineers. While in some cases the relevant defect may cause personal injury, in many cases it may only be economic loss that the claimant suffers (such as the discovery that the house one bought from a development company is falling apart after the development company has gone into liquidation). An action against the original builder or architect in such circumstances is designed to recover the financial loss represented by the property's diminished value and/or the cost of repair. In line with the general trend in negligence cases, the liability of non-occupiers for economic loss associated with defective premises is significantly restricted in scope.

SECTION 2   OCCUPIERS' LIABILITY

Occupiers' liability is predominantly defined by statute, but there remains (at least according to case law) a small, residual role for the common law in relation to certain negligently performed activities taking place on the defendant's premises.[3] For this reason, it is necessary to consider the liability of occupiers under three headings: first, the Occupiers' Liability Act 1957 (governing liability to visitors to the defendant's premises); second, the Occupiers' Liability Act 1984 (governing liability to non-visitors); and finally the residual common-law rules (applicable to both visitors and non-visitors injured by particular activities on the defendant's premises).

(A) THE OCCUPIERS' LIABILITY ACT 1957

(1) Who is an occupier?

The first precondition of a defendant's liability under the Occupiers' Liability Act 1957 is that he must be the occupier of the premises on which the claimant's loss occurs. The Occupiers' Liability Act 1957 provides no statutory definition of occupier. Instead, it

---

[1] For the purposes of this chapter, the term 'premises' shall be used for convenience to connote not just any building owned by D, but also any land owned by him, regardless of whether there are any buildings on it.

[2] If C was elsewhere than on the D's premises when he was injured, he must frame his action in negligence, public nuisance, or the rule in *Rylands v Fletcher*.

[3] See, eg, *Ferguson v Welsh* [1987] 3 All ER 777; *Ogwo v Taylor* [1988] AC 431.

states that those who would be treated as occupiers at common law should be treated likewise for the purposes of the Act;[4] and the leading definition of 'occupier' derives from *Wheat v E Lacon & Co Ltd*.[5]

> Ds owned a public house of which Mr R was their manager. Mr R and his wife were allowed by agreement to live in the upper floor, access to which was by a door separate from the licensed premises. Mrs R was allowed to take paying guests on the upper floor. A guest suffered an accident on the staircase leading to the upper floor. It was held that although C was injured in the private area of the premises, Ds (along with Mr and Mrs R) were still liable. They had enough residual control over that part of the premises to be occupiers.

The case thus clarifies that there may be two or more occupiers simultaneously and that exclusive occupation is not required. The test of occupation, then, is whether a person has some degree of control associated with, and arising from, his presence in and use of, or his activity in, the premises. A good example of the scope for multiple occupancy can be seen in *AMF International Ltd v Magnet Bowling Ltd*,[6] where both a contractor and the owner were held to have sufficient control to be joint occupiers of the premises in which the claimant's equipment was damaged by rainwater entering the building via a leaking doorway.[7]

On the question of who may qualify as a sole occupier for the purposes of the Act, it is clear that the following earlier decisions remain sound. A concessionaire without a lease in a fairground is an occupier.[8] So, too, is a local authority that has requisitioned a house[9] (even in respect of those parts of the house in which it allows homeless persons to live),[10] and a contractor converting a ship into a troopship in dry dock.[11] By contrast, a decorator undertaking to do no more than paint a house does not have sufficient control to be regarded as its occupier.[12]

(2) Scope of the act

Prior to the Occupiers' Liability Act 1957, the duty owed by an occupier to entrants upon his land varied according to their common-law status. The highest standard of care was owed to those, such as hotel guests, who were on his land by virtue of contract. A lesser duty was owed to his invitees,[13] and a lower duty still was owed to mere licensees (who were permitted, but not requested, to be there). In relation to

---

[4] Occupiers' Liability Act 1957, s 1(2).
[5] [1966] AC 552.   [6] [1968] 2 All ER 789.
[7] The degree of care that C may expect from each occupier turns on the degree of control held by each: *Wheat v Lacon* [1966] AC 552, at 581 and 601.
[8] *Humphreys v Dreamland (Margate) Ltd* [1930] All ER Rep 327.
[9] *Hawkins v Coulsdon and Purley UDC* [1954] 1 QB 319.
[10] *Greene v Chelsea BC* [1954] 2 QB 127.
[11] *Hartwell v Grayson Rollo and Clover Docks Ltd* [1947] KB 901.
[12] *Page v Read* (1984) 134 NLJ 723.
[13] That is, those who had a mutual business interest with the occupier, such as customers in a shop.

trespassers, the occupier was obliged to do no more than refrain from deliberately or recklessly causing them injury.[14]

A further complexity in the common law lay in the fact that the content of the duty varied according to the manner in which the claimant's injury was sustained. A distinction was drawn between injuries sustained by virtue of something done on the defendant's premises and injuries caused merely by the dangerous state of the premises.[15] The Occupiers' Liability Act 1957 was enacted to give effect to the recommendations contained in the Law Reform Committee's Third Report,[16] which were designed to eliminate the confusion surrounding the common-law rules on liability to entrants. Thus, sections 2 and 3 of the Occupiers' Liability Act 1957 'have effect, in place of the rules of the common law, to regulate the duty which an occupier of premises owes to his visitors in respect of dangers due to the state of the premises or to things done or omitted to be done on them'.[17]

(a) Visitors

The Occupiers' Liability Act 1957 imposes a duty in respect of 'visitors'.[18] And 'visitors' for the purposes of the Act are those persons who were invitees or licensees at common law:[19] that is, anyone to whom an occupier gave any invitation or permission to enter or use his premises. Accordingly, in terms of the level of duty owed, the common-law distinction between invitees and licensees is no longer of any real importance.[20] It does, however, remain important to distinguish between visitors and other types of entrant since the duties of an occupier to those other entrants who fall within the definition 'non-visitors' are governed by the later Occupiers' Liability Act of 1984.[21] This raises the question of whether, in the case of multiple occupiers, a person may be a visitor in relation to Occupier A but a trespasser in relation to Occupier B. Lord Goff answered this question in *Ferguson v Welsh*.

> If it is the case that only one such occupier authorises a third person to come onto the land, then plainly the third person is *vis-à-vis* that occupier, a lawful visitor. But he may not be a lawful visitor *vis-à-vis* the other occupier. Whether he is so or not must, in my opinion, depend on the question whether the occupier who authorised him to enter had authority, actual (express or implied) or ostensible, from the other occupier to allow the third party onto the land...if he had not, then the third party will be, *vis-à-vis* that other occupier, a trespasser.[22]

---

[14] *Robert Addie & Sons (Collieries) Ltd v Dumbreck* [1929] AC 358.
[15] These were termed, respectively, the 'activity duty' and the 'occupancy duty'.
[16] Cmd 9305.
[17] Occupiers' Liability Act 1957, s 1.
[18] In doing so, it envisages not only personal injury suffered by a visitor, but also any property damage he may suffer: Occupiers' Liability Act 1957, s 1(3)(b).
[19] Occupiers' Liability Act 1957, s 1(2).
[20] *Campbell v Northern Ireland Housing Executive* [1996] 1 BNIL 99.
[21] See, eg, *Stone v Taffe* [1974] 3 All ER 1016.
[22] [1987] 3 All ER 777, at 785.

Those entrants covered by the Occupiers' Liability Act 1984 are often called trespass-ers, but the class, 'non-visitors', is not confined only to persons whose presence consti-tutes a trespass. If they are on the premises of the defendant without his permission, then even though they have not gone there voluntarily[23] – for example, if they have been thrown or chased there – they fall within this group, just as much as if they have committed the tort of trespass. Similarly, although he is not a trespasser:

> [a] person entering any premises in exercise of rights conferred by virtue of (a) section 2(1) of the Countryside and Rights of Way Act 2000,[24] or (b) an access agreement or order under the National Parks and Access to the Countryside Act 1949, is not, for the purposes of this Act, a visitor of the occupier of the premises.[25]

It has also been held that the same non-visitor status extends to those using a private right of way.[26] But a more complex situation exists with respect to persons who sustain injury on a public right of way. At one time it was thought that no one using a public right of way could be classed as a visitor for the purposes of the Occupiers' Liability Act 1957.[27] However, the matter was shown to be less straightforward than this in *McGeown v Northern Ireland Housing Executive*.[28]

> C's husband was the tenant of a house on Ds' housing estate. The house was accessed by a path over which the public had acquired a right of way. It was upon this path that C tripped and sustained a broken leg. She argued that Ds were liable to her as a visitor under the Occupiers' Liability Act (Northern Ireland) 1957.[29] The House of Lords held that she was not a visitor and therefore could not sue under the statute.

The complexity in this case stems from the fact that their Lordships confined their deci-sion to persons using a public right of way qua member of the general public (for exam-ple, a hill-walker who neither knows, nor is interested in, who owns the *solum* of the right of way).[30] As Lord Keith put it: '[o]nce a public right of way has been established, there is no question of permission being granted by the owner of the *solum* by [sic] those who choose to use it'.[31] The idea of using a right of way by virtue of 'permission'

---

[23] If D's negligence causes a visitor involuntarily and unpremeditatedly to encroach slightly on land where he has no permission to go, he retains visitor's rights: *Braithwaite v Durham Steel Co Ltd* [1958] 3 All ER 161.

[24] This subsection refers to those exercising a right of access to open land for recreational purposes.

[25] Occupiers' Liability Act 1957, s 1(4).

[26] *Vodden v Gayton* [2001] PIQR P52.

[27] *Greenhalgh v British Railways Board* [1969] 2 QB 286, at 292–3. On the other hand, although no action will lie for nonfeasance according to *McGeown v Northern Ireland Housing Executive* [1995] 1 AC 233, cf *Thomas v British Railways Board* [1976] QB 912 where it was said that an action can be brought in respect of any injury caused by D's misfeasance – eg, digging and leaving uncovered a hole in the right of way into which C later falls.

[28] [1995] 1 AC 233.

[29] This Act is the same, in all material respects, as the English Act of that name and year.

[30] But note that those exercising access rights under the Countryside and Rights of Way Act 2000 are now denied the status 'visitor' under the amended Occupiers' Liability Act 1957, s 1(4)(a).

[31] [1995] 1 AC 233, at 246. Presumably, his Lordship meant to say granted '*to* those who choose to use it'.

is similar to that of using it qua licensee. But what, wondered Lord Browne-Wilkinson, of those who are expressly invited on to the land?

> In the case of an invitee there is no logical inconsistency between the claimant's right to be on the premises in exercise of the right of way and his actual presence there in response to the express or implied invitation of the occupier. It is the invitation which gives rise to the occupier's duty of care to an invitee.[32]

This *obiter* proposition has since been dismissed by the Court of Appeal in *Campbell v Northern Ireland Housing Executive*,[33] where a claimant who was injured on a public right of way, on the way to the shops, was held to be outside the scope of the Occupiers' Liability Act 1957. Despite this rejection of Lord Browne-Wilkinson's distinction, there is much to be said for the logic underscoring his view, even though it would mean giving new life, in the limited context of persons using public rights of way, to the significance of an invitee/licensee dichotomy.[34]

Whether one accepts or rejects Lord Browne-Wilkinson's reasoning, the pre-Act cases on *implied* permissions and invitations to be on the occupier's premises do remain in full force. This is because the Act defines visitors in terms of those who were formerly regarded as invitees and licensees at common law. In *Edwards v Railway Executive*, it was held that permission should not be implied merely because the occupier knew of the claimant's presence or because he failed to take the necessary steps to prevent his entry. Rather, '[t]here must be evidence either of express permission or that the land-owner has so conducted himself that he cannot be heard to say that he did not give it'.[35]

In each case, it is a question of fact whether permission to enter can be implied and the burden of proving it rests with the claimant seeking to rely on it.[36] Although the rules are capable of being applied to adults,[37] they are in practice most pertinent in relation to children who are sometimes able to show an implied permission on the basis of an 'allurement' that would present no temptation to an adult. In *Glasgow Corpn v Taylor*,[38] for example, shiny red berries growing in the open on the defendant's land were held to be an allurement to a child aged seven, to whom the berries looked like cherries or blackcurrants. Similarly, and more recently, the House of Lords held that a rotting boat was a sufficiently alluring plaything to constitute an implied permission.[39] The presence of an allurement in a location that is accessible to children will tend to aid the inference of permission to enter.[40] But the mere fact that the occupier has on his premises a dangerous and alluring object will not, *ipso facto*, make him liable to every child who comes on to his land. For example, the child may be old

---

[32] [1995] 1 AC 233, at 248.   [33] [1996] 1 BNIL 99.
[34] See further Murphy (1997) 61 Conv 362.
[35] [1952] AC 737, at 747.   [36] [1952] AC 737.
[37] See, eg, *Harvey v Plymouth CC* [2010] PIQR P18 (C not on the facts an implied visitor).
[38] [1922] 1 AC 44.
[39] *Jolley v Sutton London BC* [2000] 1 WLR 1082.
[40] *Hardy v Central London Rly Co* [1920] 3 KB 459; *Latham v R Johnson and Nephew Ltd* [1913] 1 KB 398.

enough to read a notice to the effect that the owner did not want him to be present there, in which case the child will be a trespasser, and thus forced to rely on the lower level of protection afforded by the Occupiers' Liability Act 1984. Furthermore, in some circumstances, occupiers are deemed only to permit young children on to their land subject to the condition that they are accompanied by a responsible adult.[41]

Of course, in cases concerning adults, it is clearly inapposite to talk of implied permission based on allurements. But even in such cases, a permission may still be implied. As Lord Porter pointed out in the *Edwards* case:

> an open pathway, as in *Cooke v Midland Great Western Rly of Ireland*,[42] or a knowledge that a track is and has long been constantly used, coupled with a failure to take any steps to indicate that ingress is not permitted, as in *Lowery v Walker*,[43] may well amount to a tacit licence.[44]

Persons entering as of right – such as police with search warrants and a host of other officials statutorily empowered to enter premises – are specifically deemed by the Occupiers' Liability Act 1957 to be present with the occupier's permission,[45] and as such they are afforded the same duty of care as visitors. So, too, potentially, are contractual entrants; for under section 5(1) there is an implied term in the contract whereby, subject to effective contrary provision, the claimant is afforded the very same duty of care.[46]

(b) Against what risks does the Occupiers' Liability Act 1957 afford protection?

The Occupiers' Liability Act 1957 plainly governs the duty of the occupier in relation to structural defects or other dangers due to the state of the premises, or indeed 'things' on the premises such as vicious dogs roaming free in the garden.[47] That this is not the limit of its scope is made clear by the fact that, in addition to dangers arising from the state of the premises, the Act refers also to dangers due to 'things done or omitted to be done on them'. At the very least, then, the Act covers acts and omissions which have created a dangerous condition of a continuing nature which

---

[41] *Latham v R Johnson and Nephew Ltd* [1913] 1 KB 398; *Bates v Stone Parish Council* [1954] 3 All ER 38. In *Phipps v Rochester Corpn* [1955] 1 QB 450, Devlin J criticised this rule on the ground that it was lacking in precision: eg, what degree of incapacity on the part of the child and what qualifications on the part of his companion are called for? But the rule still stands on the authority of the Court of Appeal.

[42] [1909] AC 229 .   [43] [1911] AC 10.

[44] [1952] AC 737, at 744. See also *Robert Addie & Sons (Collieries) Ltd v Dumbreck* [1929] AC 358, at 372–3 and *Darby v National Trust* [2001] PIQR P 372. Cf *Gough v National Coal Board* [1954] 1 QB 191.

[45] Occupiers' Liability Act 1957, s 2(6). Police officers pursuing inquiries without a warrant may take advantage of the generally implied licence to approach a front door via the garden path: *Robson v Hallett* [1967] 2 QB 939. But like other visitors they will cease to have visitor status if they fail to leave immediately the licence is expressly withdrawn: *Snook v Mannion* [1982] RTR 321.

[46] See further below.

[47] *Hill v Lovett* 1992 SLT 994 (OH). At common law, if the danger confronted the visitor while on the premises, although he actually suffered the harm off the premises – eg, by falling off an unfenced cliff into the sea – the rules regulating the duties of occupiers towards visitors applied: *Perkowski v Wellington Corpn* [1959] AC 53. The wording of s 1(1) of the Act is also wide enough to cover this situation.

later causes harm. But a more difficult question is whether the Act also extends to acts (whether of the occupier or others) which themselves directly cause harm to the visitor. Section 1(2) provides that the Act 'shall regulate the nature of the duty imposed by law in consequence of a person's occupation or control of premises'. At common law an occupier had a duty not to permit others to use his premises in such a way that would foreseeably harm other persons on those premises.[48] Regardless of whether such cases previously fell within that branch of the law of negligence imposing special duties on occupiers towards invitees or licensees, it is submitted that the joint effect of subsections (1) and (2) is to bring those situations within the Act – the duty of care arises in consequence of the fact that the defendant is an occupier.[49] On the other hand, activities not directly associated with occupation that caused harm to visitors – such as firing arrows on a farmer's land – were governed by ordinary principles of negligence, and not by the special rules relating to occupiers.[50] It has been stated judicially that the Act does not apply to such activities (regardless of whether the act in question was the occupier's, a contractor's, or a visitor's), since the duty of care is imposed on the actor by virtue of his performing an act foreseeably likely to cause harm to others present on the premises, and not because the actor occupies the land.[51]

Before the Occupiers' Liability Act 1957, it had been held in some cases that a claimant might sometimes have the choice of suing either under the general law of negligence or by virtue of the special duty owed by occupiers.[52] Since the Act seemingly only displaces the common-law rules imposed in consequence of occupation, it follows that if some other duty is imposed by the common law or another statute, the claimant may rely on either the Occupiers' Liability Act 1957 *or* the other cause of action (or both). Thus, a worker injured on his employer's premises may rely on the common duty of care set out in the Act, the duty of the employer to provide a safe system of work, or even some statutory duty of the employer to provide safe access or the like.[53]

---

[48] *Glasgow Corpn v Muir* [1943] AC 448.

[49] All three judges in *Videan v British Transport Commission* [1963] 2 QB 650 were of the same opinion (*obiter*).

[50] See *Ferguson v Welsh* [1987] 3 All ER 777; *Fairchild v Glenhaven Funeral Services Ltd* [2002] 1 WLR 1052.

[51] *Revill v Newbery* [1996] 1 All ER 291. The rationale here is that the restrictive wording of the Occupiers' Liability Act 1957, s 1(2) – 'The rules so enacted shall regulate the nature of the duty imposed by law *in consequence of a person's occupation or control* of premises' – excludes this class of acts. Thus, when premises were set alight by their occupier, this was clearly a negligent act performed otherwise than *in consequence of occupation or control*, and one for which damages under the general law of negligence (rather than the Occupiers' Liability Act 1957) were available: *Ogwo v Taylor* [1988] AC 431.

[52] See, eg, *Slade v Battersea and Putney Group HMC* [1955] 1 All ER 429.

[53] Eg, *Ward v Hertfordshire CC* [1970] 1 All ER 535 (duties of local authority both as education authority and occupier considered when child hurt by playground flint wall, though D held not liable under either head because the wall was not dangerous).

(3) The common duty of care

(a) General principles

The common duty of care is a duty to take such care as in all the circumstances of the case is reasonable to see that the visitor will be reasonably safe in using the premises for the purposes for which he is invited or permitted by the occupier to be there.[54] Thus, a hotelier was not liable in respect of a guest who sustained head injuries from falling out of a window when, in all probability, the guest (who could not recall the incident) had been leaning out too far.[55] There had been no breach of duty because the hotelier had taken reasonable care on the facts, thus illustrating that the duty under the Act is virtually identical to the duty imposed under the common law of negligence.[56] Another example is *Laverton v Kiapasha*,[57] where a takeaway food outlet could not prevent the floor of their premises becoming wet because customers were constantly coming in with wet feet on a rainy evening. There was no liability under the 1957 Act when a customer slipped and injured her ankle since, on the facts, the restaurant had done what was reasonable on a very rainy night to keep the floor as dry as possible. Finally, in one further case, it was held that an occupier cannot reasonably be expected to deal with hazards with absolute immediacy.[58] Had any of these cases been brought under the common law, the respective occupiers would presumably have escaped liability in negligence for precisely the same reason.

Even though the Act stipulates particular considerations that impinge on the standard of care required in relation to child visitors and those who have a particular trade, profession, or skill, the Act still amounts to little more than an echo of well-established common-law principles in these respects. Section 2(3) of the Occupiers' Liability Act 1957 provides:

> The circumstances relevant for the present purpose include the degree of care, and of want of care, which would ordinarily be looked for in such a visitor, so that (for example) in proper cases:
>
> (a) an occupier must be prepared for children to be less careful than adults; and
>
> (b) an occupier may expect that a person, in the exercise of his calling, will appreciate and guard against any special risks ordinarily incident to it, so far as the occupier leaves him free to do so.

Bearing in mind the similarity between the gist of this provision and the ordinary law of negligence, it would seem appropriate to invoke parallel common-law decisions as guides to the way in which this subsection should be applied. In particular, the following common-law principles would appear to be important. First, in deciding whether

---

[54] Occupiers' Liability Act 1957, s 2(2). See also *Baldacchino v West Wittering Estate Plc* [2008] EWHC 3386.

[55] *Lewis v Six Continents plc* [2005] EWCA Civ 1805.

[56] See, eg, *Esdale v Dover DC* [2010] EWCA Civ 409, at [12].

[57] [2002] NPC 145.

[58] *Tedstone v Bourne Leisure Ltd (t/a Thoresby Hall Hotel & Spa)* [2008] EWCA Civ 654.

there was a danger, regard must be had to the limited physical and mental powers of a child visitor: for, what is not a danger to an adult may well be a danger to a child.[59] In determining the standard of care owed to a child who is not accompanied by a guardian, therefore, it will be material to enquire whether, in the circumstances, the occupier could reasonably have expected the presence of the unaccompanied infant.[60] (If the unaccompanied child cannot be expected by the occupier, that child will inevitably be a trespasser. But since the passage of the Occupiers' Liability Act 1984, it is of much less significance that he cannot sue for his injuries qua visitor.)[61] If the child is accompanied by an adult, and the danger would be obvious to the latter, the occupier will have discharged his duty of care.[62]

The significance of section 2(3)(b), in so far as it deals with the care to be shown to visitors possessed of a particular profession, may also be illuminated by decisions at common law. A window cleaner injured through the insecurity of some part of the exterior of the premises which he uses as a foothold or handhold for the purpose of cleaning the outside of the windows can be expected by the occupier to have guarded against this special risk which is ordinarily incidental to the job of a window cleaner.[63] But there is no reason why the occupier should not be liable if the window cleaner is injured through some defect in the staircase when he is going upstairs, in the ordinary way, to reach the windows on an upper floor.[64] Similarly, an occupier can expect a chimney sweep to guard against dangers from flues.[65] But a self-employed plasterer injured when scaffolding collapses beneath him may recover damages from an occupier since the risk was inherent in the defective state of the premises, and was not an expected risk of his employment as a plasterer.[66] In short, the special skills of the entrant are *relevant* to the determination of whether the occupier is in breach of the common duty of care, but they will not automatically absolve the occupier from responsibility (especially where the risk is not one ordinarily encountered by a person possessed of the particular entrant's skills).[67] Nor will the fact that the entrant's employer is under

---

[59] *Cooke v Midland Great Western Rly of Ireland* [1909] AC 229, at 238. Cf *Gough v National Coal Board* [1954] 1 QB 191.

[60] See *Phipps v Rochester Corpn* [1955] 1 QB 450.

[61] The Occupiers' Liability Act 1984 replaced the harsh rules of common law that had traditionally been applied to trespassers. The difference in the child's protection is therefore equal to the discrepancy between the duties imposed by the 1957 and 1984 Acts.

[62] *Phipps v Rochester Corpn* [1955] 1 QB 450. It does not follow, however, that the adult would be liable given that an accident can befall a child at any second: *Bourne Leisure Ltd v Marsden* [2009] EWCA Civ 671, at [17]–[21].

[63] *Christmas v General Cleaning Contractors Ltd* [1953] AC 180.

[64] See *Moon v Garrett* [2007] PIQR P3 (deliveryman injured by virtue of falling into an unguarded trench adjacent to the path).

[65] *Roles v Nathan* [1963] 2 All ER 908. A factory occupier owes a lesser standard of care to a fireman trying to put out a fire than to his employees and has no duty to provide alternative escape facilities: *Bermingham v Sher Bros* 1980 SLT 122.

[66] *Kealey v Heard* [1983] 1 All ER 973.

[67] *Eden v West & Co* [2002] EWCA Civ 991.

a duty to safeguard the visitor exonerate the occupier (though an occupier found liable in such a case can claim a contribution from the visitor's employer).[68]

Another similarity between the duty of care owed under the ordinary law of negligence and the duty owed under the 1957 Act inheres in the fact that no duty is owed under the Act to those who use the premises in excess of their permission to be there. So, someone who was a lawful visitor to the shores of a lake on a hot day became a trespasser once he entered the water in order to swim, when swimming was prohibited.[69] Scrutton LJ neatly encapsulated the principle when he said: '[w]hen you invite a person into your house to use the stairs, you do not invite him to slide down the banisters'.[70] Thus, there is 'no difference between a person who comes upon land without permission and one who, having come with permission, does something which he has not been given permission to do'.[71] This approach, of course, bears a close resemblance to the 'scope of duty' principle in the ordinary law of negligence whereby one asks whether 'the consequence [is] fairly to be considered within the risk created by the negligence'.[72]

A final similarity inheres in the fact that – as was held in *Jolley v Sutton London Borough Council*[73] – the same test for the remoteness of damage applies under the 1957 Act as applies in the ordinary law of negligence.[74] In other words, in order to recover damages, the claimant must be able to show that he suffered loss or injury of a kind that was reasonably foreseeable.

One apparent, if questionable, difference between the two regimes is that the defendant's failure to discharge the common duty of care need not, according to authority, amount to negligent misfeasance. Thus, a football club that can anticipate crowd trouble from visiting supporters, yet fails to make the game all-ticket or ban those visiting supporters, may still be liable in respect of injuries sustained by a policeman when those supporters use loose pieces of concrete as projectiles.[75] But it is difficult to see why the failure of the football club to take preventive steps would not be actionable as common-law negligence. Similar events had occurred at earlier games (making the injury to the policeman foreseeable) and the contractual nexus between the parties would presumably satisfy the proximity requirement.

---

[68] *Lough v Intruder Detection and Surveillance Fire & Security Ltd* [2008] EWCA Civ 1009, at [13].

[69] *Tomlinson v Congleton BC* [2004] 1 AC 46.

[70] *The Carlgarth* [1927] P 93, at 110.

[71] *Tomlinson v Congleton BC* [2004] 1 AC 46, at [13]. Applied in *Maloney v Torfaen CBC* [2005] EWCA Civ 1762.

[72] *Roe v Minister of Health* [1954] 2 QB 66, at 85. See also *South Australia Asset Management Corp v York Montague Ltd* [1997] AC 191.

[73] [1998] 3 All ER 559.

[74] The decision on the facts (but not *ratio*) in this case is highly questionable. The CA categorised the harm – injury caused by an 'alluring', dangerous old boat that fell on to C – as too remote since the injury was caused in an unforeseeable way. This reasoning is difficult to square with the *Wagon Mound* principle that it is the *type* of harm (not the way it occurs) that determines remoteness.

[75] *Cunningham v Reading Football Club* [1992] PIQR P141.

A second difference between the common law and the duty owed under the 1957 Act – and one mentioned briefly in passing – inheres in the fact that, under section 2(6) of the Act, those entering the occupier's premises by virtue of a right conferred by law will also be afforded the common duty of care. Importantly, this subsection *does not* extend the notion of 'visitor' to such persons; it merely broadens the circumstances in which an entrant will be owed the common duty of care by providing that such persons are to be treated as if they were permitted by the occupier to be there for the particular purpose of exercising the specific right conferred by law.[76] By contrast, the common law of negligence does not afford special duties to those exercising rights conferred by law.[77]

(b) Warning

At common law, an occupier discharged his duty to a visitor by a warning sufficient to convey to the visitor full knowledge of the nature and extent of the danger. That rule was changed by section 2(4)(a) of the 1957 Act which now provides that:

> where damage is caused to a visitor by a danger of which he had been warned by the occupier, the warning is not to be treated without more as absolving the occupier from liability, unless in all the circumstances it was enough to enable the visitor to be reasonably safe.

For example, then, the farmer who warns the veterinary surgeon whom he has summoned to the farm at night to attend a sick cow: 'Be careful how you go down the yard or you may fall into a tank', or the railway company which warns of the dangerous roof over what is the sole approach to the ticket office, no longer absolve themselves from liability by such warnings alone. In *Roles v Nathan*[78] Lord Denning provided a helpful example of where the mere provision of a warning would not discharge the duty under the 1957 Act. He suggested that simply warning visitors of the danger of a footbridge over a stream would be insufficient to ensure a visitor's safety if there was only one footbridge and it was essential to use that bridge to enter the defendant's land. But he added that, if there were two bridges and one of them was safe, a warning about the unsafe bridge would then fulfil his duty.[79]

In line with the requirement that the warning must be enough to enable the visitor to be safe, a warning has also been held to be ineffective where it was very small in size and posted in an insufficiently prominent position.[80] On the other hand, if a warning is given, but ignored by the visitor – for example, where a customer fails to observe a shopkeeper's warning not to go to the far end of the shop because of a slippery floor – a court would probably hold that, in all the circumstances, the common duty of care had been discharged. If the defendant does not know of the danger, it is obvious that

---

[76] *Greenhalgh v British Railways Board* [1969] 2 QB 286, at 292–3.
[77] See, eg, *White v CC of South Yorkshire Police* [1999] 1 All ER 1.
[78] [1963] 2 All ER 908.   [79] Ibid at 913.
[80] *D v AMF Bowling* [2002] 12 CL 476.

he cannot rely on section 2(4)(a) of the 1957 Act although he may still have a defence based on exclusion of liability (discussed below).[81]

(c) Assumption of risk

The common duty of care does not impose on an occupier any obligation to a visitor in respect of risks willingly accepted as his by the visitor (where the question of whether a risk is so accepted is to be decided on the same principles as in other cases in which one person owes a duty of care to another).[82] Section 2(5) of the Occupiers' Liability Act 1957 makes clear that an occupier is not in breach of his duty of care where the claimant voluntarily assumed the risk. So, for example, in *Staples v West Dorset District Council*,[83] damages were refused where the claimant slipped and was injured on the defendant council's algae-covered rocks of which he had full knowledge, and in respect of which it was proven that he would have ignored any warning had one been given.[84] Equally, actions will also fail where they are based on mishaps caused either by swimming in deep and murky ornamental ponds that are obviously perilous *for swimmers*, or by diving into shallow water.[85]

(d) Contributory negligence

Section 2(3) of the Occupiers' Liability Act 1957 provides that, in deciding whether the occupier has discharged his common duty of care, the want of care which would ordinarily be looked for in such a visitor is a relevant circumstance. In other words, the claimant cannot by his own carelessness enlarge the duty of care owed to him by the defendant. It is therefore implicit in section 2(3) that the apportionment provisions of the Law Reform (Contributory Negligence) Act 1945 apply to an action for breach of the common duty of care in exactly the same way that they do to any action for negligence *simpliciter*. And a number of cases decided under the Occupiers' Liability Act 1957 have applied these very provisions.[86]

(e) Liability for independent contractors

Section 2(4)(b) of the Occupiers' Liability Act 1957 provides that, where damage is caused to a visitor by virtue of a danger attributable to the faulty execution of any work

---

[81]   *White v Blackmore* [1972] 2 QB 651.

[82]   Occupiers' Liability Act 1957, s 2(5). But where the occupier occupies the premises for business purposes, note the application of the Unfair Contract Terms Act 1977, s 2(3).

[83]   (1995) 93 LGR 536.

[84]   In similar vein, see *Poppleton v Portsmouth Youth Activities Committee* [2009] PIQR P1.

[85]   See, respectively, *Darby v National Trust* [2001] PIQR P372 and *Tomlinson v Congleton BC* [2004] 1 AC 46. Note, however, that it has been held on the highest authority that there is nothing per se dangerous about lakes *for those on land*: *Tomlinson v Congleton BC* [2004] 1 AC 46. But a refinement to this point is required: namely, that for a very young child trespasser, unsteady on his feet and unable to swim, a lake may well constitute a danger. Certainly, in *Donoghue v Folkestone Properties Ltd* [2003] QB 1008 the CA held that s 1 of the 1984 Act permits the court to take account of differences between adults and children who are non-visitors in deciding whether a duty is owed under the 1984 Act.

[86]   Eg, *Bunker v Charles Brand & Son Ltd* [1969] 2 QB 480.

of construction, maintenance, or repair[87] by an independent contractor employed by the occupier, the occupier is not to be treated, without more,[88] as answerable for the danger if, in all the circumstances, he had acted reasonably in entrusting the work to an independent contractor and had taken such steps (if any) as he reasonably ought in order to satisfy himself that the contractor was competent and that the work had been properly done. Notably, the instances of defective construction, maintenance, and repair mentioned in section 2(4)(b) are specifically stated to be no more than examples of the kinds of dangers that can be attributed to independent contractors. Thus, where independent contractors run an amusement facility on the occupier's land, and that facility causes injury to a visitor, the occupier may still be liable if he does not check the contractor's competence in just the same way as he would be liable if he failed to check, say, construction work although only the latter is referred to in section 2(4)(b).[89]

Given that section 2(4)(b) is important both per se and by extension, its terms warrant further analysis. First, in applying this subsection, the courts must consider whether, initially, it was reasonable for the occupier to engage an independent contractor to undertake the construction, maintenance, or repair work. It is not obvious what this entails for it is difficult to envisage a situation in which the court would expect the occupier to have performed construction work himself in preference to engaging an independent contractor.[90] That being the case, we might be tempted to say that it is presumptively reasonable for an occupier to engage a contractor wherever, as in *Haseldine v C A Daw & Son Ltd*,[91] the work to be done requires special skill or equipment not possessed by the occupier. On the other hand, it has been suggested that enquiring as to whether a contractor carries proper insurance is a sensible question that might provide some indication as to his general competence.[92] Also, if he can obtain insurance, this will indicate that the insurance company considers him an insurable risk.[93] Delegation should, at the very least, be reasonable where it is normal

---

[87] This expression covers work incidental to construction and demolition work: see *AMF International Ltd v Magnet Bowling Ltd* [1968] 2 All ER 789 and *Ferguson v Welsh* [1987] 3 All ER 777.

[88] In *Coupland v Eagle Bros Ltd* (1969) 210 *Estates Gazette* 581, C was electrocuted by a live wire which the electrical contractor had not switched off while carrying out electrical work. D knew that the wire was dangerous and had not warned anyone. The 'without more' provision did not absolve him from liability, for he was concurrently careless with the contractor.

[89] *Gwilliam v West Hertfordshire Hospitals NHS Trust* [2002] 3 WLR 1425. Cf *Bottomley v Todmorden Cricket Club* [2003] EWCA Civ 1575.

[90] On the other hand, where the contractor is permitted to run a fairground concession which necessarily carries a risk of injury, the occupier may be required to check whether the contractor is properly insured: *Gwilliam v West Hertfordshire Hospitals NHS Trust* [2002] 3 WLR 1425.

[91] [1941] 2 KB 343.

[92] *Gwilliam v West Hertfordshire Hospitals NHS Trust* [2002] 3 WLR 1425, at [15]; *Naylor v Paling* [2004] EWCA Civ 560, at [19]–[25].

[93] This is markedly different to asking whether he was insured for the purposes of being able to pay any order for damages that may be issued against him. The latter is an illegitimate question associated with the contractor's ability, not to do the work, but to pay damages: see *Glaister v Appleby-in-Westmorland Town Council* [2010] PIQR P6.

commercial practice to engage contractors for such work. A good example might be office cleaning.

Second, the Occupiers' Liability Act 1957 stipulates that the occupier *may* have to check the competence of the contractor. Here, again, it would seem that if the work is of a fairly standard nature the contractor may be trusted.[94] Where, however, the work entrusted to a contractor is of a kind that, after its completion, necessarily involves a risk to future visitors if it has been carelessly executed,[95] the occupier *will* be under a duty to check the competence of the contractor. Third, the occupier will need 'to take such steps as he reasonably ought (if any) in order to satisfy himself that…the work had been properly done'.[96] It is unclear from the statute whether this involves a subjective test or an objective one. If a subjective test were adopted, limited financial resources might provide a sufficient reason for not engaging, say, an architect to assess the quality of the work. If an objective test were used, the only relevant factor would be the degree of risk inherent in the kind of work done.

Since the Occupiers' Liability Act 1957 uses the past tense in relation to work done, it is clear that section 2(4)(b) does not envisage the occupier employing a suitable professional to supervise the ongoing work of an independent contractor. Instead, section 2(4)(b) provides only an example of how the common duty of care might be discharged in such cases. Thus, in some circumstances, it may be expected of the occupier that he will have the contractor's work supervised. In *AMF International Ltd v Magnet Bowling Ltd*,[97] for instance, it was said that if the occupier was going to invite the claimant to bring valuable timber on to the site while construction work was ongoing, then to escape liability he might have to employ a supervising architect to ensure that the contractors had made the premises sufficiently safe for that timber safely to be brought there. On the other hand, it was said in *Ferguson v Welsh*[98] (and reiterated by the Court of Appeal in *Fairchild v Glenhaven Funeral Services Ltd*)[99] that an occupier will not normally be liable to the contractor's employee for injuries sustained because the premises were unsafe by virtue of the dangerous system of work adopted by the independent contractors. But if, according to Lord Keith, the occupier knows or has reason to know that the contractor is using an unsafe system of work, he may be liable for not ensuring that a safe system was employed.[100]

---

[94] *Cook v Broderip* (1968) 206 EG 128.

[95] Eg, the careless repair of a lift clearly poses a risk to subsequent visitors. Here, D is under a duty 'to obtain and follow good technical advice': *Haseldine v Daw & Son Ltd* [1941] 2 KB 343, at 356.

[96] Occupiers' Liability Act 1957, s 2(4)(b).

[97] [1968] 2 All ER 789.   [98] [1987] 3 All ER 777, at 783.

[99] [2002] 1 WLR 1052.

[100] [1987] 3 All ER 777. Note, however, that any such liability would not arise qua occupier but rather qua joint tortfeasor with the contractor: see ibid at 786.

(4) Some special cases falling within the Occupiers' Liability Act 1957

(a) Fixed or movable structures

Section 1(3) of the Occupiers' Liability Act 1957 provides that:

> The rules so enacted in relation to an occupier of premises and his visitors shall also apply, in like manner and to the like extent as the principles applicable at common law to an occupier of premises and his invitees or licensees would apply, to regulate:
>
> (a) the obligations of a person occupying or having control over any fixed or movable structure, including any vessel, vehicle or aircraft.

The term 'movable structures' covers such things as gangways and ladders, as well as vessels, vehicles, and aircraft. The test is probably whether one might go into or upon the structure. It is, however, much more difficult to interpret the expression 'fixed structure', for this term, mentioned in section 1(3), and 'premises', mentioned in section 1(1), must presumably be mutually exclusive under the Act. It is clear that the term 'premises' is not confined simply to land: it also includes permanent buildings erected on the land. Thus, 'fixed structures' must be taken to connote some non-movable chattels constructed on land. No doubt the draftsmen doubted whether docks or erections on part of the land such as garden sheds, or swings in a playground, or even scaffolding or lifts were 'premises' and yet realised that the term 'movable structure' did not cover them either. In the end, all of the aforementioned structures are probably within the Occupiers' Liability Act 1957. Yet it remains important whether a structure falls within section 1(1) or section 1(3) because different approaches may need to be taken under these respective subsections. If Mr X provides a defective ladder for an independent contractor to repair Mr X's premises, the Act does not apply for the benefit of the injured contractor. This is because Mr X has ceased to have enough control of the ladder to be an occupier of it.[101] On the other hand, he may still be liable either as the bailor of goods or as an occupier of premises who intends that the claimant should use his appliances on his land.[102]

(b) Damage to property[103]

Section 1(3) of the Occupiers' Liability Act 1957 also covers:

> (b) the obligations of a person occupying or having control over any premises or structure in respect of damage to property, including the property of persons who are not themselves his visitors.

This subsection will impose a duty on the occupier to prevent damage to goods on the premises arising from the defective physical condition of the premises. The injured visitor would, for example, be able to recover damages for her torn clothes and presumably for damage to her property, even if she is herself uninjured.[104] Where the

---

[101] *Wheeler v Copas* [1981] 3 All ER 405. Cf *Bunker v Charles Brand & Son Ltd* [1969] 2 QB 480.
[102] [1981] 3 All ER 405.   [103] See North (1966) 30 Conv 264.
[104] *AMF International Ltd v Magnet Bowling Ltd* [1968] 2 All ER 789.

entrant is carrying the goods of a third party, it is doubtful whether the Act gives the third party an action.[105] Furthermore, the expression 'damage to property' is not apt to cover loss of property so that the section will not cover the duty of boarding-house keepers to keep safe custody of visitors' goods. Still less will it reverse the common-law decision that a publican owes no duty of care to prevent a customer's motorcycle from being stolen from the yard of the public house.[106] On the other hand, it seems consistent with what was said in the preceding section that, whenever the occupier would have owed a duty at common law to prevent damage to goods on his land due to the state of the premises, the common duty of care will now apply.[107]

(c) Liability in contract

At common law, contracts for the use of premises were deemed to contain various implied terms relating to the safety of the premises.[108] In lieu of those implied terms,[109] section 5 of the Occupiers' Liability Act 1957 provides that:

(1) Where persons enter or use, or bring or send goods to, any premises in exercise of a right conferred by contract with a person occupying or having control of the premises, the duty he owes them in respect of dangers due to the state of the premises or to things done or omitted to be done on them, in so far as the duty depends on a term to be implied in the contract by reason of its conferring that right, shall be the common duty of care.

(2) The foregoing subsection shall apply to fixed and movable structures as it applies to premises.

The effect of this section is as follows. Where a person enters the occupier's premises under a contract between himself and the occupier, the occupier is obliged to extend the common duty of care to that entrant, subject to any effective contrary term in their contract.[110] It is, of course, open to the occupier specifically to increase the level of care by express provision in the contract. And any such protection bargained for in the main contract may extend to certain third parties so long as the terms of the Contracts (Rights of Third Parties) Act 1999 are met.[111] On the other hand, the extent to which he is free to exclude or limit his responsibilities towards contractual entrants is governed by the operation of the rules discussed in the next section.

---

[105] Thus, if the visitor's car is damaged he has a remedy, but the finance company, from whom he has it on a credit agreement, does not.

[106] *Tinsley v Dudley* [1951] 2 KB 18.

[107] Supported by *AMF International Ltd v Magnet Bowling Ltd* [1968] 2 All ER 789.

[108] See especially *Francis v Cockrell* (1870) LR 5 QB 501; *Gilmore v LCC* [1938] 4 All ER 331.

[109] The expression 'the duty…shall be the common duty of care' shows that the duty replaces, and is not merely alternative to, the terms implied at common law.

[110] See, eg, *Maguire v Sefton* [2006] EWCA Civ 316.

[111] Under this legislation, there are three such conditions. First, it must be clear that the contract purports to confer a benefit on a third party (eg, the employee or contractor who has agreed to do work for the occupier); second, there must be no contrary agreement in the contract; third, the third party must be expressly identified in the contract: Contracts (Rights of Third Parties) Act 1999: s 1(1)(b), (2), and (3).

Section 5 of the Occupiers' Liability Act 1957 is not limited in its operation to personal injury caused by the defective state of the occupier's premises; it also covers damage to goods. What is less clear on the face of the Act is whether an action by a contractual entrant must be based solely on contract – on the basis of the term implied into the agreement by virtue of section 5 – or whether he has the alternative of suing in tort. However, the matter was resolved in *Sole v W J Hallt Ltd*.[112] There, a tradesman who had come on to the occupier's premises to perform some plastering work was injured when he fell down an unprotected stairwell. It was held by Swanick J that contractual entrants had the option of suing either in contract (under section 5(1)), or in tort (under section 2(1)).[113]

Another question not resolved by the Act is whether section 5(1) operates where the contract is silent on the issue of the occupier's liability, but it is of a kind that, at common law, traditionally attracted a different implied term. An example would be a passenger on a railway platform who, at common law, was historically protected by a duty owed by the railway company to make the platform reasonably safe.[114] Others present on the platform, such as relatives saying farewell, were afforded the usual duty extended to licensees. But are fare-paying passengers now protected by the traditional common-law implied term which, apart from the statute, would form part of the contract of carriage, or can they invoke only the common duty of care by virtue of section 5(1)? It is submitted that the implied term under the Act applies since the statutory implied term is to be included in the contract *wherever* 'the duty depends upon *a term to be implied in the contract*'.

(5) Exclusion of liability

Section 2(1) of the Occupiers' Liability Act 1957 provides:

> An occupier of premises owes the same duty, the 'common duty of care', to all his visitors, except in so far as he is free to and does extend, restrict, modify or exclude his duty to any visitor or visitors by agreement or otherwise.

The occupier thus has two options if he wishes to modify the common duty of care owed to his visitors. First, where the visitor enters by virtue of a contract – for example, a contractor who enters to carry out work on premises – an express term of the contract may be drafted to govern the situation. Second, in respect of non-contractual entrants, a clear and unequivocal notice,[115] either affixed at the point of entry to the

---

[112] [1973] 1 All ER 1032. *Quaere* the effect of any contributory negligence.

[113] This decision is almost certainly wrong since the Act specifically limits visitors (to whom the Occupiers' Liability Act 1957, s 2(1) refers) to those who were either invitees or licensees at common law. The whole purpose of s 5 is to ensure some protection to contractual entrants where no such protection is mentioned in the contract. It is a decision at first instance and there is no obligation for any future court to follow it.

[114] *Protheroe v Railway Executive* [1951] 1 KB 376.

[115] Note the difference between a notice (excluding or restricting liability) and a warning (alerting entrants to a danger present on the premises).

land,[116] or included in a programme or ticket giving access to the land,[117] will suffice. These two broad options must, however, be read subject to section 3 of the 1957 Act which sets out some important limits on the occupier's freedom to limit or exclude his liability.

Section 3(1) of the Occupiers' Liability Act 1957 provides that the duty of care owed by an occupier to those visitors he is bound to admit on to his premises by virtue of a contract, who are nonetheless 'strangers to the contract',[118] cannot be excluded or restricted.[119] On the other hand, the subsection also provides that any term of the contract which obliges him to increase the level of care shown to such entrants will be effective in determining the standard of care to be shown. Section 3(1) is designed to ensure the protection of employees of the person with whom the occupier has a contract. Thus, if the occupier contracts with Mr A for Mr A's employees to do work on his premises, he may not restrict or exclude any liability to them.

Section 3(2) of the Occupiers' Liability Act 1957 further provides:

> A contract shall not by virtue of this section have the effect, unless it expressly so provides, of making an occupier who has taken all reasonable care answerable to strangers to the contract for dangers due to the faulty execution of any work of construction, maintenance or repair or other like operation by persons other than himself, his servants and persons acting under his direction and control.

On reflection, it is apparent that the burden on the defendant under section 3 appears to be greater than that imposed by the common duty of care because he is unable to delegate to independent contractors any part of his duty to take care.[120] Furthermore, while section 3 places some restrictions on the ability of an occupier to limit or exclude his liability, further restrictions upon his freedom to do so are also imposed under the Unfair Contract Terms Act 1977. This later Act drastically reduces the scope for a person who occupies premises for 'business purposes' to exclude or restrict his liability.[121]

---

[116] *Ashdown v Samuel Williams & Sons Ltd* [1957] 1 QB 409.

[117] *White v Blackmore* [1972] 2 QB 651.

[118] Defined as 'a person not for the time being entitled to the benefit of the contract as a party to it or as the successor by assignment or otherwise of a party to it, and accordingly includes a party to the contract who has ceased to be so entitled': s 3(3).

[119] A similar effect is achieved in relation to contractors who enter premises under a contract with the landlord, where the tenant has agreed with the landlord (extra-contractually) to allow such contractors to enter the premises.

[120] The duty in respect of independent contractors now imposed by s 3(1) and (2) is not exactly the same as the common duty of care imposed by s 2(4)(b). First, s 3(2) limits the liability not only in respect of, as in s 2(4)(b), 'the faulty execution of any work of construction, maintenance or repair' but also in respect of any 'other like operation'. Second, whereas s 2(4)(b) specifies in detail what would be reasonable care by the occupier in relation to the conduct of the independent contractor, s 3(2) states that he shall take 'all reasonable care' without further particularising this standard – it cannot simply be assumed that the two standards are identical.

[121] Note that the Unfair Contract Terms Act 1977 and Occupiers' Liability Act 1957, s 3 will often work in tandem since most, if not all, s 3 cases are likely to involve an occupier for 'business purposes'.

The Unfair Contract Terms Act 1977 renders invalid any contract term or notice purporting to exclude or restrict liability for death or personal injury[122] resulting from breach of the common duty of care under the Occupiers' Liability Act 1957 where the premises are occupied for the business purposes of the occupier.[123] In the case of other loss or damage, any contract term or notice designed to restrict or exclude liability is subject to the requirement of reasonableness.[124] If the exclusion is in the form of a contract term, its reasonableness is to be gauged by reference to 'the circumstances which were, or ought reasonably to have been, known to or in the contemplation of the parties when the contract was made'.[125] If the exclusion of liability is in the form of a notice, then its reasonableness is to be judged in the light of 'all the circumstances obtaining when the liability arose'.[126] Of the two tests, the one relating to notices is the more claimant friendly, for 'all the circumstances' presumably include those both within and beyond the actual or imputed contemplation of the parties. The less claimant-friendly test applied to contract terms can be justified on the basis that the claimant had a chance, at the time of contracting, to bargain against the inclusion of any such term.

Agreement to, or knowledge of, the term or notice will not necessarily be evidence that the visitor has assumed the risk of injury giving rise to the defence of *volenti non fit injuria*.[127] Equally, oral stipulation of any such term or notice, made at the time of the entrant's visit, will similarly fail to render the entrant necessarily *volens*; for under the Unfair Contract Terms Act 1977, any such announcement itself constitutes a notice.[128]

The Unfair Contract Terms Act 1977 clearly leaves an occupier free (via a notice on a front gate) to exclude liability to some of his visitors since its operation is limited to those entering in connection with business purposes;[129] and the Act makes clear that it is the business purposes of the occupier alone which are relevant. In some cases it will be clear that the occupier's business purposes are in issue. Consider, for example, *Ashdown v Samuel Williams & Sons Ltd*.[130]

By a licence granted by D, C crossed D's land. A notice board purported to curtail the liabilities of D to licensees. The Court of Appeal held that because D had taken reasonable steps to bring the conditions of the notice to the attention of C, these conditions (designed to exclude liability for damage sustained in the way in which C's injuries were caused) were effective in excluding D's liability. But if the case had arisen after 1977, D would not have been able to exclude his liability under the Occupiers' Liability Act 1957.

[122] Unfair Contract Terms Act 1977, s 2(1).
[123] Unfair Contract Terms Act 1977, s 1(1)(c).
[124] Unfair Contract Terms Act 1977, s 2(2).
[125] Unfair Contract Terms Act 1977, s 11(1).
[126] Unfair Contract Terms Act 1977, s 11(3).
[127] Unfair Contract Terms Act 1977, s 2(3).
[128] Unfair Contract Terms Act 1977, s 14.
[129] Section 14 of the 1977 Act defines 'business' so as to include 'a profession and the activities of any government department or public or local authority'.
[130] [1957] 1 QB 409.

But what would happen if the facts of *White v Blackmore*[131] were to recur? There, notices at the entrance to the racetrack and in the programme handed to spectators and competitors excluded liability for injuries occurring in jalopy races. The races were being run to raise money for charity. In 1972 the notices sufficed to exclude the organisers' and occupiers' liability. Today, a preliminary question would be whether the track was occupied for business purposes. Similarly, is a Sunday school within the Unfair Contract Terms Act 1977 when a jumble sale is being held there, but not on a Sunday morning? And what of the housewife who does some part-time hairdressing at home, and whose customer is hurt coming downstairs from the bathroom?

The only further attempt at clarification of the definition of 'business purposes' is to be found in section 2 of the Occupiers' Liability Act 1984. That section amends the Unfair Contract Terms Act 1977 to provide:

> but liability of an occupier of premises for breach of an obligation or duty toward a person obtaining access to the premises for recreational or educational purposes, being liability for loss or damage suffered by reason of the dangerous state of premises is not a business liability of the occupier unless granting that person such access for the purposes concerned falls within the business purposes of the occupier.[132]

The purpose of this tortuously worded provision appears to be to allow farmers and owners of countryside areas to exclude liability to day-trippers. The land is occupied for 'business purposes': namely, farming or forestry. But any duty owed to entrants coming to the land to picnic and so on can nonetheless be excluded by agreement or notice.

(B) THE OCCUPIERS' LIABILITY ACT 1984

Liability to trespassers and all other uninvited entrants (such as those using a private right of way)[133] is now governed by section 1 of the Occupiers' Liability Act 1984 which provides that the Act:

> shall have effect in place of the rules of common law[134] to determine –
>
> (a) whether any duty is owed by a person as occupier of premises to persons other than his visitors in respect of any risk of their suffering injury on the premises by reason of any danger due to the state of the premises or to things done or omitted to be done on them;
>
> (b) if so, what that duty is.

Although the Occupiers' Liability Act 1984 avowedly replaces the rules of common law in relation to an occupier's liability towards uninvited entrants, three exceptional instances fall outside the Act because of the terms in which it is drafted. First, section

---

[131] [1972] 2 QB 651.   [132] Unfair Contract Terms Act 1977, s 1(3)(b).
[133] See, eg, *Vodden v Gayton* [2001] PIQR P52.
[134] As to which see *British Railways Board v Herrington* [1972] AC 877.

1(8) expressly confines liability to personal injuries. It therefore follows that the common-law rules in respect of damage to a trespasser's (or other uninvited entrant's) personal property have survived the enactment of the Occupiers' Liability Act 1984. Second, the Act's remit is further limited in that no duty is owed by the occupier of the *solum* of a public right of way to persons using that right of way.[135] (It is arguable, however, that since the Act specifically provides that nothing in its provisions affects any duty otherwise owed to such persons, users of public rights of way are owed the duty of common humanity formulated in *British Railways Board v Herrington*.)[136] Finally, it was held in *Revill v Newbery*[137] that acts of the occupier that are not done in connection with its occupation fall outside the purview of the Act. Put otherwise, liability for acts which do not in themselves affect the safety of the premises is to be determined according to the common law.[138]

A duty to uninvited entrants in respect of any danger due to the state of the premises arises only when three conditions are met.[139]

(1) The occupier must be aware of the danger or have reasonable grounds to believe it exists.

(2) He must have known, or had reasonable grounds to know, that the uninvited entrant either was in, or might come into, the vicinity of the danger. (So, where occupiers had no reason to expect that trespassers were taking shortcuts across their land, no duty arose.[140] And where a trespasser decides to go swimming in a harbour at midnight in mid-winter, the occupier has no reason to suppose that he will be there.)[141]

(3) The risk of injury to an uninvited entrant resulting from that danger was one against which, in all the circumstances of the case, the occupier might reasonably be expected to offer the uninvited entrant some protection.

The test for the existence (as opposed to substance) of the duty of care imposed by the 1984 Act appears, at first sight, to comprise a curious admixture of objective and subjective elements. The first and second limbs seem ostensibly to contain both in referring not only to the *individual occupier's* actual knowledge, but also to that knowledge which he ought reasonably to have. However, it has been held that even the second part of the test contains a subjective element. That is, the occupier either must have actual knowledge of the danger or of the presence of a non-visitor *or* must have actual knowledge of the relevant facts from which a reasonable man would draw the relevant inference (even if he does not himself draw that inference).[142] If he knows neither of

---

[135] Occupiers' Liability Act 1984, s 1(7).

[136] [1972] AC 877. See further Murphy (1997) 61 Conv 362.

[137] [1996] 1 All ER 291.

[138] However, in *Revill v Newbury* it was said that, for the purposes of the common law, the same principles as those contained in the Occupiers' Liability Act 1984 should be applied: [1996] 1 All ER 291, at 298.

[139] Occupiers' Liability Act 1984, s 1(3).

[140] *White v St Albans City and DC* (1990) *Times*, 12 March.

[141] *Donoghue v Folkestone Properties Ltd* [2003] QB 1008.

[142] *Swain v Natui Ram Puri* [1996] PIQR P442.

the danger, nor of the state of affairs, then he will not be liable just because a reasonable occupier would have known of that state of affairs. A landowner who very seldom looks round his grounds, and fails to notice the emergence of a danger, could not be held liable, whereas a landowner who regularly surveys his premises and turns a blind eye to an obvious source of danger would be caught by the subsection.[143] The third limb is mainly objective in nature, emphasising, as it does, all the circumstances of the case. However it is clear that it does not constitute an entirely objective test since it demands only that level of protection which can reasonably be expected of the particular occupier.[144] For these purposes, the personal characteristics of the occupier and the limits on his financial resources may be taken as relevant.

As already noted, section 1(4) of the 1984 Act states that the duty is one 'to take such care as is reasonable in all the circumstances of the case'. Thus, the occupier of an electricity substation is entitled to assume trespassers will not attempt to gain unauthorised entry by scaling both a 13-foot wall and 7-foot spike railings rather than by climbing over a locked metal gate.[145] Relevant circumstances will also include the age and capabilities of the entrant[146] so that greater protection needs to be shown to a child than an adult trespasser where the danger concerned would be more apparent to the latter than the former.[147] Similarly, the entrant's purpose may be relevant, so a burglar can expect far less by way of protection than, say, an 'innocent' child trespasser.[148] On the other hand, where a burglar is injured because of a negligent act on the part of the occupier, the common law will still afford him a remedy. *Revill v Newbery* illustrates this point. There, a burglar whom the defendant negligently shot was able to sue the occupier in negligence even though the case fell outside the Occupiers' Liability Act 1984.[149]

A significant difference between the Occupiers' Liability Act 1984 and the Occupiers' Liability Act 1957 exists in section 1(5) of the later legislation. There it is stipulated that any duty arising under the Occupiers' Liability Act 1984 can:

> in an appropriate case, be discharged by taking such steps as are reasonable in all the circumstances of the case to give warning of the danger concerned or to discourage a person from incurring the risk.

Unlike under the 1957 Act, the warning need not enable the uninvited entrant to be or remain safe on the land. If the occupier of a building site with dangerous concealed

---

[143] In *Swain v Natui Puri* [1996] PIQR P442, the court added the gloss that an occupier cannot be heard to say that he had deliberately shut his eyes to dangers on his land in order to escape liability: knowledge of glaringly obvious dangers will be imputed to him.

[144] This interpretation seems to be borne out by the decision in *Ratcliff v McConnell* [1999] 1 WLR 670, at 680.

[145] *Mann v Northern Electric Distribution Ltd* [2010] EWCA Civ 141.

[146] See *Ratcliff v McConnell* [1999] 1 WLR 670.

[147] Ibid at 683.

[148] See also *Murphy v Culhane* [1977] QB 94, at 98, where Lord Denning MR suggested *obiter* that the defence of *ex turpi causa non oritur actio* might be available in this context.

[149] The court also refused to entertain D's claim that the defence of *ex turpi causa* should apply.

trenches puts up notices[150] around the perimeter of the site saying 'Danger: Concealed Trench', such warnings would be insufficient to discharge the occupier's duty towards his visitors. But since they make specific mention, as the Act demands, of 'the danger concerned', they would almost certainly suffice vis-à-vis an uninvited adult entrant.[151] The fact that a warning notice has been read by an uninvited entrant will not, of itself, render that person *volens*,[152] but the Act does provide for the operation of a very similar defence in this context. It states:

> No duty is owed by virtue of this section to any person in respect of risks willingly accepted as his by that person (the question of whether a risk was so accepted to be decided on the same principles as in other cases in which one person owes a duty of care to another).[153]

In this context it has been held that there need be no warning of obvious dangers, such as those associated with diving head first into the shallow end of a swimming pool with hardly any water in it.[154] Whether a danger is obvious or not may vary according to whether the non-visitor is an adult or a child. But just because a non-visitor is a child does not mean that – even allowing for his lesser appreciation of danger – it will never be appropriate in respect of children to treat a given risk as obvious. Obviousness is a question of fact and degree and it is wrong simply to treat all dangers as non-obvious on the basis of a claimant's immaturity.[155]

As already noted, by virtue of section 1(8) of the 1984 Act, non-visitors are not entitled to sue in respect of property damage occasioned by breach of the section 1 duty. Accordingly, a trespasser who, due to the perilous state of the premises, trips and falls on the occupier's land while snooping there may sue under the Act in respect of his personal injuries but not for the damage caused to his camera.[156]

Finally in this context, we must consider the new provisions that were added to the Occupiers' Liability Act 1984 by the Countryside and Rights of Way Act 2000. As we noted when considering the 1957 Act, those exercising a right of access to open land for recreational purposes under section 2(1) of the 2000 Act are specifically excluded from

---

[150] Note that the Unfair Contract Terms Act 1977 does not apply to the duty created by the 1984 Act and therefore has no impact on the efficacy of such notices so far as they seek to exclude liability.

[151] In relation to an illiterate young child who is allured on to the premises, it is less likely that such a notice would suffice. In any event, he might be classified as a visitor by implied licence.

[152] *Titchener v British Railways Board* [1983] 3 All ER 770.

[153] Occupiers' Liability Act 1984, s 1(6). The difference between this statutory version of *volenti* and its common-law cousin lies in the fact that at common law, C, to be *volens*, must accept both the risk of injury *and* the fact that any resulting loss should be his own. Under the 1984 Act, D can raise the defence in s 1(6) on proof of the former alone. Furthermore, properly understood, *volenti* is to be confined to the assumption of risk in relation to future rather than extant dangers: *Morris v Murray* [1991] 2 QB 6, at 17, 28, and 32.

[154] *Ratcliff v McConnell* [1999] 1 WLR 670. On the other hand, the fact that someone takes such foolhardy action does not negate the existence of a duty to take reasonable steps to prevent such persons from doing those things: *Tomlinson v Congleton BC* [2004] 1 AC 46.

[155] *Keown v Coventry Healthcare NHS Trust* [2006] 1 WLR 953 (11-year-old held *volens* in respect of dangers associated with climbing the exterior of a fire escape).

[156] He may, however, have an action based on the common law which remains untouched by the Act in respect of property damage.

the category, 'visitors'.[157] Instead, they are non-visitors and are owed only a more limited duty under the Occupiers' Liability Act 1984. More specifically, it is now provided that in determining the duty owed to those entering the occupier's land on this basis, regard must be had to 'the fact that the existence of that right ought not to place an undue burden (whether financial or otherwise) on the occupier [and to]...the importance of maintaining the character of the countryside'.[158] Furthermore, the occupier's duty will generally be excluded in the circumstances governed by the new section 1(6A) of the Occupiers' Liability Act 1984;[159] that is, where there is:

(a) a risk resulting from the existence of any natural feature of the landscape, or any river, stream, ditch or pond whether or not a natural feature, or

(b) a risk of [the claimant] suffering injury when passing over, under or through any wall, fence or gate, except by proper use of the gate or of a stile.

It could be argued that these provisions could be interpreted as conferring greater protection on a trespasser than on someone exercising their right to roam since claims by those exercising the right to roam are unquestionably barred where their injury results from a natural feature of the landscape, etc. But, in practice, this may do no more than reflect the law as it stands under the 1984 Act. Take, for example, *Tomlinson v Congleton Borough Council*.[160] In that case, a trespasser was injured in a lake under the control of the defendant council. But it was held that the council did not owe a duty by virtue of section 1 of the 1984 Act as there was no especial danger on the occupier's land, lakes not being inherently dangerous. As Lord Hoffmann put it: '[t]here were no hidden dangers. It was shallow in some places and deep in others, but that is the nature of lakes'.[161]

Suppose the facts were substantially to recur in connection with a lake in the countryside that constituted a natural feature of the land. Any claim based on injury associated with that lake would now fail on the basis of section 1(6A). All that the new provision will have achieved then is the same result via a different route (albeit a more certain route that provides occupiers with some degree of reassurance that they need not be especially careful in respect of those exercising the right to roam). It eliminates the need for the occupier to argue that, taking account of 'all the circumstances of the case' – one of which would presumably be that if the lake happened to be located in an area of natural beauty (which typically attract those exercising the right to roam) – it would have been unreasonable to expect him to undermine or diminish the beauty of the land by erecting artificial fences, warning signs, and the like.[162]

---

[157] Occupiers' Liability Act 1957, s 1(4)(a).
[158] Occupiers' Liability Act 1984, s 1A(a), (b).
[159] Inserted by the Countryside and Rights of Way Act 2000, s 13(2).
[160] [2004] 1 AC 46.   [161] Ibid at [26].
[162] In *Tomlinson v Congleton BC* [2004] 1 AC 46, the House of Lords held that it would have been unreasonable to turn the sandy beaches by the side of the lake that featured in that case into marshland at the cost of the enjoyment of thousands of people who used the beaches for sunbathing. As Lord Hobhouse observed

The only exceptions to the general exclusion of liability under section 1(6A) of the Occupiers' Liability Act 1984 are those set out in section 1(6C). These relate to dangers either intentionally or recklessly created by the occupier. It is submitted that these exceptions are likely to be of little practical significance on the basis that there are likely to be few deliberately or recklessly created perils in the countryside in locations that tend to attract walkers. On the other hand, it is not clear why liability remains excluded in relation to reckless omissions to eliminate dangers that occur otherwise than by the occupier's own creation. If, for example, on a known crumbling cliff-top a favourite viewing point reaches the point of imminent collapse, there is no liability for a failure to address that danger.

(C) COMMON-LAW LIABILITY AND ACTIVITIES ON LAND

Naturally, an occupier who intentionally harms a person whom he has permitted to be on his premises is answerable for so doing under the law of battery considered in chapter 8. But in addition, the occupier may also be under a duty according to the ordinary law of negligence to take reasonable care when conducting certain activities on his land that are foreseeably likely to harm visitors of whose presence he is, or ought to be, aware.[163]

The scope for the residual role of the common law stems from the wording of section 1 of the 1957 Act. It states, first, that the Act 'shall have effect, in place of the rules of common law, to regulate the duty which an occupier of premises owes to visitors in respect of dangers due to the state of the premises *or to things done* or omitted to be done on them'.[164] If it went no further, it would seem that activities – such as driving one's car on the land – would fall within the Act. But it does not stop there: it goes on to provide that the statutory rules shall also 'regulate the nature of the duty imposed by law *in consequence of a person's occupation or control* of premises'.[165] It is arguable, therefore, that activities on the land that are performed otherwise than as a *consequence* of occupation fall beyond the statute. Thus, driving a tractor on a farm may fall within the Act on the basis that tractor driving will be a normal (and, thus, consequential) act performed by the occupier of a modern arable farm. By contrast, riding a bicycle on the farm could well be seen as an act that is anything but naturally ancillary or incidental to farm occupation.

The fact that there is probably a small residual role for the common law in relation to visitors is doubtless a largely academic point, in both the literal and pejorative senses,

---

(at [81]): '[it] should never be the policy of the law to require the protection of the foolhardy or reckless few to deprive, or interfere with, the enjoyment by the remainder of society'.

[163] In *Chettle v Denton* (1951) 95 Sol Jo 802 (D, while shooting game on private land, hit C who was a licensee on the land. D was held liable in negligence in that he would have seen C if he had taken reasonable care).

[164] Occupiers' Liability Act 1957, s 1(1) (emphasis added).

[165] Occupiers' Liability Act 1957, s 1(2) (emphasis added).

since, as we noted at length earlier, there is very little difference between the common duty of care imposed under the Act and the standard of care demanded by the ordinary law of negligence.

So far as the Occupiers' Liability Act 1984 is concerned, however, there are no words equivalent to those located in the 1957 legislation, which might be construed to exclude statutory liability in respect of activities performed on the land. As regards the physical injury of non-visitors, therefore, the pre-existing common law has definitely not survived the passage of the 1984 Act.[166]

(D) LIABILITY TO THOSE OUTSIDE ONE'S PREMISES

The dangers caused by the defective state of premises are not confined to entrants to those premises. Slates falling from roofs, crumbling walls, and dangerous activities carried out on premises are further examples of risks just as likely to endanger passers-by and those on adjoining premises. The circumstances in which the occupier of premises owes a duty to such persons therefore require brief consideration. As will be seen in due course,[167] an action in public nuisance sometimes lies in respect of injuries or loss caused on a highway as a result of harmful conditions on adjoining land. But a claimant may just as well sue for personal injuries in negligence in such cases.[168] Furthermore, occupiers are under a general duty to take reasonable care to prevent dangers on their premises damaging persons or property on adjoining premises.[169] This is so whether the danger arises from the disrepair of the premises, or some man-made or natural hazard such as fire caused by lightning striking a tree.[170] Also, where adjoining properties have mutual rights of support, negligently allowing one property to fall into dereliction so as to damage the adjoining premises is actionable in negligence as well as in private nuisance.[171]

There are two issues of particular difficulty affecting the duties of care owed by the occupiers of adjoining premises. First, where a claimant tenant sues his landlord for damage resulting from the defective state of repair of premises retained by the landlord, the case law is confused. Take first *Cunard v Antifyre Ltd*.[172]

> Some defective roofing and guttering, which formed part of the premises retained by D, a landlord, fell into a part of the premises let by him to C. As a result, C's wife was injured and C's goods were damaged. Damages in negligence were awarded to both C and his wife.

---

[166] See, eg, *Scott v Associated British Ports* 2000 WL 1741511 (youths injured when 'surfing' a ride on a slow-moving goods train).

[167] Ch 16.

[168] Eg, *Hilder v Associated Portland Cement Manufacturers Ltd* [1961] 3 All ER 709.

[169] *Hughes v Percival* (1883) 8 App Cas 443.   [170] *Goldman v Hargrave* [1967] 1 AC 645.

[171] *Bradburn v Lindsay* [1983] 2 All ER 408.   [172] [1933] 1 KB 551.

By contrast, in *Cheater v Cater*[173] the Court of Appeal held that a landlord, who had let a field to a tenant at a time when there was a yew tree on the adjoining premises retained by the landlord, was not liable in negligence when the tenant's horse died through eating leaves from the tree which was then in just the same state as at the date of the lease. Then, in *Shirvell v Hackwood Estates Co Ltd*,[174] the court doubted *Cunard v Antifyre Ltd*, holding that the workman of a tenant could not recover in negligence from the landlord whose tree on adjoining land fell on him. Finally, came *Taylor v Liverpool Corpn*.[175]

> C, the daughter of a tenant of one of D's flats, was injured by the fall of a chimney stack belonging to these flats into the yard adjoining the premises. D had negligently maintained this chimney, which formed part of the building retained by D.

Stable J found for the claimant in negligence, and did so following *Cunard v Antifyre Ltd* while distinguishing *Cheater v Cater* on the ground that the tenant there had impliedly agreed to take the risk in respect of danger existing on the premises at that time. The observations in *Shirvell*'s case were treated as *obiter* on the basis that no negligence had in any event occurred. In any case, the principle in *Cunard v Antifyre Ltd* would appear to be preferable to the one which affords landlords blanket immunity in respect of retained premises in a state of disrepair.[176]

The second area of difficulty in delimiting the duty owed by an occupier to those on adjoining premises relates to damage inflicted on those adjoining premises by third parties. No duty will generally be found to lie where damage is inflicted on a neighbour's property by vandals or burglars[177] even though the wrongdoers' conduct may have been facilitated by a state of disrepair or lax security on the defendant occupier's premises.[178] This approach is in line with the general reluctance on the part of the courts to impose liability on a person who has no special relationship with the relevant third party, for the conduct of that third party.

SECTION 3 LIABILITY OF NON-OCCUPIERS

An occupier of premises may have immediate control over the state of those premises and the capacity to repair defects in them, but in a number of instances – particularly in relation to structural defects – nothing he has done will have caused the relevant defect. Cracks in a house resulting from inadequate foundations will often be the

---

[173] [1918] 1 KB 247 (not cited in *Cunard v Antifyre Ltd*).
[174] [1938] 2 KB 577, at 594–5.
[175] [1939] 3 All ER 329.
[176] It is submitted that the CA thought wrongly in *Shirvell*'s case that the decisions where landlords with no control of defective premises had been held not liable applied in the case before them.
[177] In *P Perl (Exporters) Ltd v Camden London BC* [1984] QB 342 the court did not entirely rule out special circumstances which might give rise to such a duty to adjoining occupiers.
[178] *Smith v Littlewoods Organisation Ltd* [1987] AC 241.

result of the negligence of the builder and they may endanger the occupier as much as any visitor to the property. Parliament passed the Defective Premises Act in 1972 to impose on persons providing dwellings some limited responsibility to subsequent purchasers and their families, and to clarify the responsibilities of landlords. As will be seen, the Act is a far from perfect example of legislation.

(A) THE DEFECTIVE PREMISES ACT 1972

One key feature of the decision in *Murphy v Brentwood District Council*[179] is the repeated insistence of their Lordships that the courts should not seek to impose common-law rules of liability where Parliament, via the Defective Premises Act 1972, had already done so. Since *Murphy*, therefore, the primacy of the 1972 Act cannot be doubted, especially since, under section 6(3) of the 1972 Act, its provisions are made non-derogable.

Section 1 of the Defective Premises Act 1972 imposes on any 'person taking on work for or in connection with the provision of a dwelling' a strict liability to ensure that the work he takes on is 'done in a workmanlike, or, as the case may be professional manner, with proper materials and so that as regards that work the dwelling will be fit for habitation when completed'.[180] Thus, a builder who, reasonably believing that his materials were suitable, used asbestos in roofing materials at a time before the dangers of asbestos were appreciated, would still be in breach of his duty under section 1. The provision covers all those involved in building new homes: from builders and contractors, to architects and developers.[181] However, while fine in theory, section 1 is in practice more or less a dead letter.[182] First, houses built under the National House Building Council scheme, and covered by a National House Building Registration Council Certificate, are exempted from the strict liability regime created by section 1.[183] Second, and much more importantly, the limitation period under the 1972 Act begins to run as soon as the dwelling is completed, which may be a very considerable time prior to a structural defect manifesting itself. (Defects in foundations, for example, usually take a long time to appear.)[184] By contrast, the limitation period in a negligence action begins to run only when the claimant should reasonably have known of

---

[179] [1990] 2 All ER 908.

[180] The section applies to omissions as much as to acts: *Andrews v Schooling* [1991] 3 All ER 723; but it is confined to defects rendering the dwelling (but, importantly, not commercial properties) uninhabitable: *Thompson v Clive Alexander and Partners* (1992) 59 BLR 81.

[181] See the Defective Premises Act 1972, s 1(3) (including local authorities). The fact that all such persons may be liable creates the potential for difficulties in establishing causation. The test to be applied is whether D's breach of the section is a 'significant cause' of the unfitness of the dwelling: *Bayoumi v Protim Services Ltd* [1996] EGCS 187.

[182] See Spencer [1974] CLJ 307 and id [1975] CLJ 48.

[183] Defective Premises Act 1972, s 2.

[184] For an example of the theoretical scope of s 1 made futile by the limitation provisions, see *Rimmer v Liverpool CC* [1985] QB 1.

the relevant damage (subject to a long-stop of 15 years after which any action in respect of property damage is barred completely).[185]

Other provisions of the Defective Premises Act – in particular sections 3 and 4 concerning the survival of a duty of care after disposal of the premises, and landlords' duties of care where there is an obligation to repair – are rather more useful, as we shall see below.

(B) BUILDERS AND CONTRACTORS: PHYSICAL DAMAGE

A builder or contractor actually engaged in construction or repair work on land and premises affixed to that land owes a duty of care[186] to the occupier of the premises, his visitors, and, where their presence is foreseeable, probably to trespassers as well.[187] Any universal exemption from a duty of care in respect of real property did not survive the decision in *AC Billings & Sons Ltd v Riden*[188] where building contractors were employed to make an alteration to the front part of a house. In the course of this work, the contractors failed to take reasonable care to make access to the house safe and Riden, a visitor, was injured when leaving the house in the hours of darkness. The contractors were held liable in negligence.

Subsequent decisions held the original builders of a property liable for personal injury (or physical damage to other property) resulting from the negligent construction or repair of buildings both to subsequent occupiers and to their visitors.[189] Thus, if the defendant contractor negligently erects an unsafe roof which some time later collapses injuring the occupier and her dinner party guests, the victims have a claim against the contractor for those injuries. And if the collapse of the roof also smashes the windows in the adjoining house, the neighbours may also sue the contractor.

The fact that the contractor at the time of the erection of the property was also the landowner no longer affords him immunity from liability in negligence. Most of the content of the maxim *caveat emptor* in relation to the sale of land in this context has now been eroded: '[a] landowner who designs or builds a house or flat is no more immune from personal responsibility for faults of construction than a building contractor, or from personal responsibility than an architect, simply because he has disposed of his house or flat by selling or letting.'[190]

---

[185] Under the Latent Damage Act 1986.

[186] *Miller v South of Scotland Electricity Board* 1958 SC (HL) 20.

[187] The contractor may of course also be the occupier, in which case his liability to trespassers will be governed by the Occupiers' Liability Act 1984. In other circumstances ordinary principles of negligence apply: *Railway Comr v Quinlan* [1964] AC 1054.

[188] [1958] AC 240.

[189] *Sharpe v ET Sweeting & Sons Ltd* [1963] 2 All ER 455.

[190] *Rimmer v Liverpool CC* [1984] 1 All ER 930, at 938.

But this principle covers only negligence in the original construction of the building, not inadequate repairs or maintenance conducted by the original owner and vendor. However, section 3 of the Defective Premises Act provides that where:

> work of construction, repair, maintenance or demolition or any other work is done on or in relation to premises, any duty of care owed because of the doing of the work to persons who might reasonably be expected to be affected by defects in the state of the premises by the doing of the work shall not be abated by the subsequent disposal of the premises by the person who owed the duty.

Thus, a botched job in repairing floorboards will create liability to visitors while the owner remains the occupier; and that liability will survive for the benefit of subsequent occupiers and their visitors when the owner sells or lets the house. But section 3 of the 1972 Act is not comprehensive because it does not cover all possible sources of danger on premises; particularly those caused by omissions. Leaving dangerous refuse on premises and failing to remedy or warn the subsequent occupier about a ruinous defect existing before the vendor came into occupation are probably not covered by the words used in section 3: namely, 'work of construction, repair, maintenance[191] or demolition or any other work'. Thus, the common-law principle that there is no duty not to sell or let a ruinous house probably survives albeit in attenuated form. Only the Supreme Court can finally take up Lord Denning's invitation in *Dutton v Bognor Regis UDC*[192] to overrule the old cases.[193]

It is suggested that today the crucial point is not whether the defendant contractor is or was the landowner but, rather, what kind of damage resulted from his negligence. If actual physical injury to some person, or separate property, is inflicted as a consequence of his incompetence, that injury is likely to be recoverable just as it would be if the 'guilty' cause of the injury were a negligently manufactured chattel.[194]

(C) BUILDERS AND CONTRACTORS: OTHER LOSS

No duty of care will be imposed on a builder or contractor in respect of economic loss occasioned by negligent work of construction or repair, save where some special relationship is found to exist between him and the claimant. Thus, contractors and development companies owe no duty in tort in respect of financial losses occasioned to subsequent occupiers of property with whom they have no contractual relationship. *D & F Estates Ltd v Church Commissioners for England*[195] is illustrative.

> D built a block of flats later occupied by C. Crumbling plasterwork caused by D's negligence forced C to expend considerable sums of money on repairs. The House of Lords found that D was not liable for C's loss. By analogy with liability for chattels, D owed a

---

[191] Could omissions to remove or repair pre-existing defects be caught by the word 'maintenance'?
[192] [1972] 1 QB 373, at 394.   [193] Eg, *Otto v Bolton and Norris* [1936] 1 All ER 960.
[194] See *Murphy v Brentwood DC* [1990] 2 All ER 908, at 917 and 925–6.
[195] [1989] AC 177.

duty to safeguard C against physical damage to person or property caused by negligent construction of the property, but not against loss caused by a defect in the quality of the property itself. Damage to the property itself was a mere defect in quality – the property was simply not value for money.

Recoverable physical damage must be occasioned to separate property.[196] On the other hand, the House of Lords left open the question of 'complex structure' buildings. If a defect in the foundations threatens the structure of a particular flat in a block of flats, or a dwelling house threatens damage to the garden wall, is there damage to separate property?[197]

Some of the questions left open in *D & F Estates* were at least partially answered by the House of Lords in *Murphy v Brentwood District Council*.[198] *Murphy*, strictly speaking, relates to the liability of local authorities, but its applicability to builders and contractors was expressly confirmed in the short judgment in *Department of the Environment v Thomas Bates & Son Ltd*.[199] The facts of *Murphy* were as follows.

> C had purchased from a construction company a semi-detached dwelling constructed on a concrete raft foundation over an in-filled site. Eleven years later, C noticed cracks in the house which proved to be caused by serious defects in the concrete raft. Repairs which were essential to make the house safe and habitable would have cost £45,000. C could not afford that sum and had to sell the house for £35,000 less than he would have received but for the damage caused by the defective foundations. C sued the local council whom he alleged had negligently approved the plans for the foundations.

The House of Lords rejected his claim, classifying the damage he suffered as irrecoverable economic loss. When the claimant argued that the nature of the damage to his home posed an immediate and imminent danger to his and his family's health, the Law Lords unanimously dismissed that contention as irrelevant since the loss was purely economic. Lord Bridge described the distinction between physical damage and financial loss in this way:[200]

> If a builder erects a structure containing a latent defect which renders it dangerous to persons or property, he will be liable in tort for injury to persons or property resulting from that dangerous defect. But, if the defect becomes apparent before any injury or damage has been caused, the loss sustained by the building owner is purely economic.

The effect of *Murphy* would seem to be this. Outside a contractual relationship, negligent construction (and presumably also repair and extension) of a building only results in liability if actual physical damage is caused to a person or property that is not part and parcel of the building. Thus, if defective foundations cause cracks in the walls or threaten damage to any fixture in the building installed by the defendant, the cost of remedying the damage is irrecoverable economic loss. By contrast, if A

---

[196] See *Bellefield Computer Services Ltd v E Turner & Sons Ltd* [2000] BLR 97. Cf *Baxall Securities Ltd v Sheard Walshaw Partnership* [2001] PNLR 257.

[197] See *Murphy v Brentwood DC* [1990] 2 All ER 908, at 1006–7.

[198] [1990] 2 All ER 908.   [199] Ibid.   [200] Ibid at 926.

negligently installs a defective central heating boiler in a building erected by B but which is later bought and occupied by C, and then later still that boiler explodes damaging the building, that loss is recoverable by C against A. A's negligence has caused actual damage to property quite separate from the inherently defective component he installed. Lord Bridge, in *Murphy*, also suggested a new exception to the general refusal of recovery for economic loss. He said that, where the defect in the building requiring repair threatens damage to adjoining land or the highway:

> the building owner ought, in principle, to be entitled to recover in tort from the negligent builder the cost of demolition, so far as that cost is necessarily incurred in order to protect himself from potential liability to third parties.[201]

Consideration of the decision in *Murphy* prompts a number of questions.

(1) Is it just to leave the occupier to bear the loss? Lord Keith maintained that in reality it was not ordinary home-owners who suffered. Disputes such as the one in *Murphy* were essentially quarrels between insurers.[202]

(2) Just how far can Lord Bridge's caveat concerning third party liability be stretched? If one may recover that economic loss occasioned by the need to ensure one's crumbling house does not damage a neighbour's house or crash on to a passer-by on the highway, why is one not able to recover the loss occasioned by the need to ensure that one does not incur similar liability to one's visitors?[203]

(3) Finally, is the following the logical result of *Murphy*? Imagine that X discovers that his house has a latent defect which he has no funds to repair. Three months later the ceiling falls in injuring X and his spouse, and it also smashes the grand piano. Does X then recover for that loss and all its consequences or can he be said to be contributorily negligent for not minimising the loss he suffers, or for not rectifying the defect at his own expense?[204]

Leaving aside economic loss, it has also been held, in *Smith v Drumm*,[205] that builders are liable under section 1 of the Defective Premises Act if their work leaves the premises in a state that is not fit for habitation. In this case, the converted flat was left without either electricity or gas, and on that basis deemed to be unfit for habitation. Had the work simply been rectification work (instead of 'construction, conversion or enlargement', in the words of the Act), no duty under section 1 would have been owed.[206]

---

[201] [1990] 2 All ER 908.

[202] Ibid at 923. No evidence is advanced to support the proposition.

[203] One difference is that I could of course 'obviate' that danger by having no visitors. Another is that I could reasonably warn my visitors; but I could not, for example, practicably warn all passers-by who walk beneath a dangerous overhanging gable.

[204] For a partial answer see *Nitrigin Eireann Teoranta v Inco Alloys Ltd* [1992] 1 All ER 854. See also *Targett v Torfaen BC* [1992] 3 All ER 27: where D lets property, it may in some circumstances be unreasonable to expect a tenant to do repairs that D is obliged to perform.

[205] [1996] EGCS 192.   [206] *Jacobs v Morton & Partners* (1994) 72 BLR 92.

(D) PROFESSIONAL ADVISERS

The strict liability imposed by section 1 of the Defective Premises Act in respect of the construction of buildings is equally incumbent on architects and other professionals involved in the design of the building. Additionally, those professionals owe a duty of care to any person who may be injured on the site in the course of the building work,[207] and to subsequent occupiers of the premises in respect of both their personal safety and damage to property separate from the original property itself. The reasoning in *Murphy* relating to builders applies equally to architects and engineers. Thus, these professionals will not be liable in tort for economic loss arising from the defective nature of the building whether that loss takes the form of the cost of repairs or the diminution in the value of the property.

On subsequent disposal of the premises, surveyors engaged to inspect the property will be liable for any failure to value the property competently or to discover and report on relevant defects in the property. Where the surveyor has been engaged by the building society which is contemplating financing the claimant's house purchase, he will generally be liable, not only to his client (that is, the building society), but also to the purchasers where they have relied on his survey rather than commissioned an independent surveyor.[208] Where, however, a surveyor is expressly commissioned only to value property, he is not under a duty to report on defects generally, or to advise on possible difficulties with resale of the property.[209]

(E) LOCAL AUTHORITIES

Local authorities owe duties to tenants and subsequent purchasers of local authority dwellings as builders and contractors. In *Rimmer v Liverpool City Council*[210] the defendants were held liable to a council tenant injuring himself when he fell against a negligently used, thin, glass panel and the glass shattered.

The decision in *Murphy* removes from local authorities the greatest potential area of liability for defective premises since it is local authorities that are entrusted with the function of inspecting and approving all building work. Negligent exercise of these powers may result in local people purchasing and living in defective, even dangerous, property. *Murphy* makes clear, however, that the local authority will not be liable in tort for any economic loss occasioned by the defects in the property. But would the authority be liable if actual injury was caused to a resident or any of his property that was not an integral part of the premises? The House of Lords suggested that the builder would be so liable. But what if the builder has gone into liquidation? That question was

---

[207] *Baxall Securities Ltd v Sheard Walshaw Partnership* [2001] PNLR 257 (architect liable for sub-standard roof design causing subsequent water damage). But note, also, that the limited scope of an architect's original instructions will define the extent of his or her liability in tort by confining the extent of the duty of care: *Bellefield Computer Services Ltd v E Turner & Sons Ltd (No 2)* [2002] EWCA Civ 1823.

[208] *Smith v Eric S Bush* [1990] 1 AC 831.

[209] *Sutcliffe v Sayer* [1987] 1 EGLR 155. [210] [1985] QB 1.

left open by their Lordships.[211] In the current climate, where restrictions on the duty of care owed by public authorities are being increasingly relaxed, it is very difficult to say. Nonetheless, while it is true that local authorities are granted inspection powers for the purpose of protecting the health and welfare of local people,[212] it is difficult to characterise this as a duty owed to individuals as opposed to the public more generally (because of an absence of proximity). And why, in any event, should the council be liable for what is, at bottom, the negligence of a third party, the builder?

(F) LANDLORDS

Historically, the liability of landlords for defects arising from disrepair on premises let by them was largely limited to contractual liability. A person other than the tenant had no remedy even if the landlord was in breach of a contractual duty to carry out maintenance and repairs.[213] And like vendors, the landlord owed no duty in respect of defects arising before the tenancy was granted. As we have seen, landlords are now liable to tenants, their families, and others injured on the premises just like anyone else in respect of *their* negligent installations or repairs in the premises let by them.[214]

Section 4 of the Defective Premises Act established important duties in respect of landlords under an obligation[215] to carry out repairs or maintenance on the premises, or who are empowered to carry out repairs.[216] A landlord owes to all persons who might reasonably be expected to be affected by defects in the state of the premises a duty to take such care as is reasonable in all the circumstances to see that they are reasonably safe from personal injury or from damage to their property caused by the relevant defects.[217] The landlord is still liable although he did not know of the defect so long as he ought to have known of it.[218] A defect is relevant if it is one in the state of the premises arising from, or continuing because of, an act or omission by the landlord which constitutes or would, if he had had notice of the defect, have constituted, a failure by him to carry out his obligation to the tenant for the maintenance or repair of the premises.[219] The duty is wide: it extends to trespassers and those outside the premises.

---

[211] [1990] 2 All ER 908, at 912 and 917.

[212] See the powerful arguments to this effect in the speech of Lord Wilberforce in *Anns v Merton LBC* [1978] AC 728. Note that *Anns* was only overruled as far as recovery for economic loss was concerned.

[213] But in some circumstances, the Contracts (Rights of Third Parties) Act 1999 may now apply.

[214] *Rimmer v Liverpool CC* [1984] 1 All ER 930; *Boldack v East Lindsey DC* (1998) 31 HLR 41.

[215] This includes statutory obligations.

[216] Defective Premises Act 1972, s 4(4). This extension to the case where the tenant cannot legally insist on a repair, but where the landlord has a power to repair, is important in view of cases like *Mint v Good* [1951] 1 KB 517, deciding that landlords of small houses let on periodic tenancies have such a power.

[217] In the case of children who are injured, however, the landlord is entitled to expect that the parents of the child will take proper precautions to ensure the child's safety: see *B (a child) v Camden LBC* [2001] PIQR P143.

[218] Defective Premises Act 1972, s 4(2).

[219] Defective Premises Act 1972, s 4(3). Failures to remedy such defects are actionable, alternatively, on the basis of common-law negligence: see *Targett v Torfaen BC* [1992] 3 All ER 27.

It also applies where the landlord merely has a right to enter to carry out maintenance or repairs. On the other hand, the duty is not one to make safe premises that are unsafe by virtue of a design defect (rather than a failure to keep those premises in a good state of repair). A defect in design is different from a defect in the performance of a duty to maintain.[220]

The liability of non-occupiers for actual physical damage is now fairly extensive, but by no means comprehensive. If an owner knows of a defect in his premises (not created by him) before he sells or lets, but neither repairs it, nor gives warning of the defect, the 1972 Act imposes no liability on him for harm which results after he has disposed of the premises by sale or lease, and there is no liability at common law.[221] A landlord who fails to repair where he has no obligation or power to do so has no liability under either the Act or the common law.

FURTHER READING

BUCKLEY, 'The Occupiers' Liability Act 1984 – Has *Herrington* Survived?' (1984) 48 *Conveyancer* 413

HOWARTH, 'Negligence after *Murphy* – Time to Re-think' [1991] *Cambridge Law Journal* 58

JONES, 'The Occupiers' Liability Act 1984 – The Wheels of Law Reform Turn Slowly' (1984) 47 *Modern Law Review* 713

LAW COMMISSION REPORT NO 75, *Liability for Damage or Injury to Trespassers and Related Questions of Occupiers' Liability* (Cmnd 6428)

MESHER, 'Occupiers, Trespassers and the Unfair Contract Terms Act 1977' (1979) 43 *Conveyancer* 58

MURPHY, 'Public Rights of Way and Private Law Wrongs' (1997) *Conveyancer* 362

SPENCER, 'The Defective Premises Act 1972: Defective Law and Defective Law Reform' [1974] *Cambridge Law Journal* 307 and [1975] *Cambridge Law Journal* 48

WALLACE, '*Anns* Beyond Repair' (1991) 107 *Law Quarterly Review* 228

---

[220]   *Alker v Collingwood Housing Association* [2007] 1 WLR 2230.
[221]   *Cavalier v Pope* [1906] AC 428; *Bromley v Mercer* [1922] 2 KB 126.

PART III

INTENTIONAL INVASIONS OF INTERESTS IN THE PERSON AND PROPERTY

8

TRESPASS TO THE PERSON AND RELATED TORTS

KEY ISSUES

(1) Wide protection of person and liberty

Tort law is highly protective of the body of the person and of his liberty. This is reflected in the torts discussed in this chapter, which provide redress against various kinds of interference with these interests.[1] Protection is available in battery, assault, and false imprisonment and under the Protection from Harassment Act 1997 following infringement of the protected interest *without* need for proof of harm.[2]

(2) Battery

Battery is any act of the defendant that directly and intentionally (or negligently) causes some physical contact with the claimant's person and without the claimant's consent.

(3) Assault

Assault is any act of the defendant that directly and intentionally (or negligently) causes the claimant reasonably to apprehend the imminent infliction of a battery.

(4) Protection from Harassment Act 1997

Legislation prohibits a course of conduct amounting to harassment of another and the victim of such conduct is granted the ability to sue in tort for either damages or an injunction.

(5) False imprisonment

False imprisonment is an act of the defendant which directly and intentionally (or possibly negligently) causes the claimant's confinement within an area delimited by the defendant.

SECTION 1 INTRODUCTION

The torts of battery, assault, and false imprisonment are among the most ancient and their core features are fairly well settled. While in the last edition of this book the

---

[1] Note, however, that encroachments have been made on the level of protection offered by the common law. See, eg, Criminal Justice Act 2003, s 329, considered in *Adorian v MPC* [2009] EWCA Civ 18, esp. [7] (Parliament could not have intended the wide measure of immunity against suits brought by persons who committed imprisonable offences at the time of the torts in question).

[2] Eg, *Ashley v CC Sussex* [2008] UKHL 25, [60] (discussing trespass to the person).

relative paucity of modern cases concerning these torts was noted, their number is rising again – especially those relating to false imprisonment. Many of the actions are brought against emanations of the state. These cases prove the continuing durability and importance of the core torts to the person. There has also been much recent case law on the modern statutory tort of harassment, a significant number of these concerning the actions of utilities companies and others interested in payment of (alleged) debts.

The judges have shown a willingness to innovate in order to ensure that tort law keeps pace with modern society. Even prior to the enactment of the Human Rights Act 1998, the judiciary sought to test how far the conditions of a particular tort matched the relevant provisions of the European Convention on Human Rights.[3] Articles 2 and 3 respectively guarantee the right to life, and freedom from torture or degrading treatment. Article 5 asserts the right to liberty and security of person and seeks to ensure that the state cannot detain persons without substantial grounds justifying that deprivation of liberty.[4] As we shall see in this chapter, the very same fundamental interests are protected by the existing common law, albeit to a slightly lesser degree and without such clarity of articulation as is found in the Convention.

In time, of course, the protection offered by the Convention and the common law will probably converge now that the Human Rights Act is in force. On the one hand, the courts will have to develop the common law in a manner that is compatible with the Convention rights,[5] while, on the other, claims for battery and false imprisonment against public authorities, such as the police, are frequently litigated in the alternative under the Act.[6]

SECTION 2   BATTERY

There are several key elements in the tort of battery that are evident from the following working definition of the tort:

> Battery is any act of the defendant that directly and intentionally or negligently causes some physical contact with the person of the claimant without the claimant's consent.

(A) DEFENDANT'S STATE OF MIND

Compensation for injuries to the person and to property was first given by the courts from at least the thirteenth century.[7] A suit in trespass could succeed only where the interference was 'direct' and this remains the case today.[8] But if the injury is caused

---

[3] See, eg, *Olotu v Home Office* [1997] 1 All ER 385.   [4] See Art 5(2)–(5) and Art 6.

[5] Human Rights Act 1998, s 6.   [6] Human Rights Act 1998, s 7.

[7] See Maitland, *The Forms of Action at Common Law* (1909).

[8] *Sterman v E W & W J Moore Ltd* [1970] 1 QB 596.

directly, and is attributable to careless conduct on the part of the defendant, must the claimant frame his or her action in negligence, or might battery be an option?

(1) Negligently inflicted battery?

Until the middle of the twentieth century and the decision in *Letang v Cooper*,[9] one would have said with confidence that the torts of battery and negligence were both available in cases of direct injuries sustained as a result of careless conduct. This conclusion would have arisen from the fact that, historically, trespass actions would succeed unless the defendant could show inevitable accident.[10] In other words, mere carelessness on the defendant's part would not allow him to escape liability in trespass.

The largely academic confusion that still surrounds the relationship between negligence and trespass began, however, not in *Letang v Cooper*, but some six years earlier in *Fowler v Lanning*.[11] The latter case concerned a technical point of law about the burden of proof, but in the course of his judgment Diplock J sought to ensure that the claimant could not gain an unfair advantage by relying on trespass rather than negligence on the basis that, according to the former tort, the burden of proof would lie with the defendant to disprove any *negligence* on his part. In so holding, Diplock J aligned trespass to the person with the hitherto anomalous principle applied only in the context of trespass on the highway: namely, that the burden of proof lay on the claimant to show the defendant's negligence.[12]

Although *Fowler v Lanning* did not per se abolish the principle that trespass to the person can be committed negligently, it did leave the claimant with the burden of proving negligence where his injury was caused by negligent conduct. But then came *Letang v Cooper*, the facts of which were as follows.[13]

D negligently drove his car over C's legs while C was sunbathing on the grass car park of a hotel. More than three years later, C sued D. The rules on limitation of actions provided that actions for 'negligence, nuisance or breach of duty' were barred after three years while other tort actions were barred after six years. C relied on trespass in an effort to prevent her action from being time-barred.

The Court of Appeal did not wish to reach the ostensibly absurd conclusion that an action for negligent trespass would lie while an action for negligence *simpliciter* would not. For their part, Lord Denning MR and Danckwerts LJ insisted that there was no overlap between trespass and negligence. They thought that, if an act was intentional, it would result in trespass (not negligence) liability, and that if an act was negligent it would lead to negligence (not trespass) liability.[14] By contrast, Diplock LJ thought that trespass could still be committed negligently, but that in such cases the claimant must prove *both* the negligence alleged *and* that there was resulting harm.[15] In other words,

---

[9] [1965] 1 QB 232.
[10] *Weaver v Ward* (1616) Hob 134. Inevitable accident is discussed at p 327.   [11] [1959] 1 QB 426.
[12] *Holmes v Mather* (1875) LR 10 Ex 261.   [13] [1965] 1 QB 232.
[14] [1965] 1 QB 232, at 240.   [15] Cf intentional trespass which is actionable per se.

the claimant would gain no practical advantage from framing his action in trespass rather than negligence.

In the wake of *Letang v Cooper*, therefore, it would appear that actions for negligent trespass have effectively disappeared: either in juridical terms (for Lord Denning MR and Danckwerts LJ), or in practical terms (for Diplock LJ). But in academic terms we still cannot conclusively assert that trespass has no relevance when negligent conduct is relied on.[16] There may still be particular cases where a claimant perceives there to be an advantage to be gained from framing a claim in trespass rather than in negligence. It is within the divergent principles governing remoteness of damage that this rare advantage may lie. For in negligence law, the defendant is only responsible for injuries or harm of a kind that were reasonably foreseeable,[17] whereas in trespass all the damage actually ensuing from the defendant's unlawful act is generally recoverable.[18]

This minor technical point aside, most modern trespass actions are likely to be based on an intentional act on the part of the defendant. But this merely raises the second, more fundamental question in this context, namely, 'What is meant by an "intentional act" for these purposes?'

(2) Meaning of 'intentional act'

In determining the meaning of 'intentional act' in this context, there are two broad possibilities.

(1) D intended only to act in the way that he did.

(2) D intended *both* to act in the way that he did *and* that the resulting contact with C take place.

In most cases, the distinction is of little consequence. If A aims a punch at B and succeeds in striking B, there is nothing to separate A's act (the thrown punch) from the outcome of that act (for example, B's broken nose). But in some circumstances, A may do a thing without intending a particular outcome. If D aims his rifle at C, then pulls the trigger, there is no doubt that he intended to shoot C. But if D aims his rifle at a partridge on a hunting trip but accidentally shoots C, it is clear that D intended the act (firing the gun) but not necessarily the outcome (C's injury). In such circumstances it may be stretching the tort too far to hold D liable in battery. But if D aimed his gun at a third party, T, then pulled the trigger missing T and shooting C, standing next to T, we might well wish to hold D liable.

In terms of D's mental state in the first example, there is a genuine accident (possibly even without carelessness on D's part). In the second example, D's act was reckless. This may be the basis upon which the English courts might, like the Americans,

---

[16] See Trindade (1982) 2 OJLS 211.   [17] *The Wagon Mound* [1961] AC 388.
[18] *Williams v Humphrey* (1975) *Times*, 20 February. See also *Allan v New Mount Sinai Hospital* (1980) 109 DLR (3d) 634.

borrow the criminal law notion of 'transferred intent' and apply it in tort law.[19] Yet, thus far, there is but limited support for adopting this approach in English law. In addition to a technically non-binding but supportive first instance decision,[20] there is the argument of principle arising from the fact that battery is both a tort and a crime. Thus, as De Grey CJ observed in *Scott v Shepherd*, 'though criminal cases are no rule for civil ones...yet in trespass I think there is an analogy'.[21] In that case there was held to be a battery where D threw a lighted squib into a crowded market place that was tossed from one trader to another before it eventually exploded in the face of C. Nonetheless, the case is inconclusive since the main issue was whether there was sufficient directness to satisfy the requirements of the tort. Further oblique authority can be gleaned from the case of *Haystead v Chief Constable of Derbyshire*.[22] There the defendant punched a woman in the face with the result that she dropped the baby she was holding. He was charged with criminal assault in relation to the baby. Clearly the tortious counterpart of this crime is a battery. The Divisional Court did not even consider the application of the transferred intent doctrine but did say (implying that a battery action may lie) that:

> There is no difference in logic or good sense between the facts of this case and one where the defendant might have used a weapon to fell the child to the floor, save only that this is a case of reckless and not intentional battery.

Here, although the court emphasised the requirement of a sufficiently direct act to ground liability, and although it neglected to address head-on the question of whether the defendant's intention must apply only to his actions, or whether it must also extend to the outcome of those actions, the case does signal a clear unwillingness on the part of the courts to allow defendants in such cases to escape liability.[23]

On balance, then, it seems that there is broad, if still not binding, judicial support for the application of the transferred intent principle in English battery cases. On the other hand, there is a plausible counter-argument that can be made. This is that although certain forms of conduct should be branded morally wrong, and thus deserving of criminal punishment, they may not warrant a remedy in tort to which branch of the law both motive and malice are normally irrelevant in determining liability (if not the amount of damages).[24]

In cases where contact with the claimant is unproblematic, it is well established that the defendant need not have intended the claimant any harm. Battery is actionable per

---

[19] American Restatement, Torts (2d), § 32. See also Prosser (1967) 45 Tex LR 650. In *Livingstone v Ministry of Defence* [1984] NI 356, it was held that where D fired a baton round injuring C it mattered not whether he fired at C or another person – D was liable in battery unless he could prove lawful justification for his act. But that case is not, technically, an authority for the purposes of the law in England and Wales.

[20] *Bici v Ministry of Defence* [2004] EWHC 786, at 71.

[21] (1773) 2 Wm Bl 892, at 899. Cf *Coward v Baddeley* (1859) 4 H & N 478, at 480.

[22] [2000] 3 All ER 890.   [23] In similar vein see *Livingstone v Ministry of Defence* [1984] NI 356.

[24] NB *Haystead* was a criminal (not tort) law case! Cf Gordley, *Foundations of Private Law: Property, Tort, Contract and Unjust Enrichment* (2006), 189ff.

se – that is, without proof of any injury or damage to the claimant. The defendant must merely have understood that his conduct was beyond the bounds of physical contact 'generally acceptable in the ordinary conduct of everyday life'.[25] The Court of Appeal said in *Wilson v Pringle*[26] that the claimant must show that the defendant's touching of the claimant was a 'hostile' touching. Yet the term 'hostility' is not to be equated with ill-will or malevolence. It means merely that the defendant is doing something to which the claimant may object, something that the claimant may regard as an unlawful intrusion on his rights to physical integrity. Thus, the bare allegation that one 13-year-old boy jumped on another in the course of horseplay was insufficient of itself to establish a battery. Further evidence of intent to injure or distress the claimant had to be shown if liability for battery were to be imposed, yet no such evidence was presented (another hearing would have been required to establish that). Had a grown man engaged in similar conduct, the result would almost certainly have been different. Away from the rugby field, mature adults do not generally regard it as acceptable conduct for their peers to leap on them or wrestle them to the ground.

In *F v West Berkshire Health Authority*[27] Lord Goff doubted that the use of the word 'hostile', however defined, was appropriate to describe the necessary state of mind in battery. A surgeon operating on a patient to preserve her life and health may be motivated by his judgment as to her best interests, not hostility towards her. Yet if she is competent to do so, and has refused to consent to a particular course of treatment, the surgeon commits a battery. Lord Goff preferred the following approach. Any deliberate touching of another's body, beyond the bounds of acceptable everyday conduct, is, in the absence of lawful excuse, capable of constituting a battery. Where a person by reason of some permanent or temporary mental incapacity cannot himself consent to medical or other necessary procedures,[28] the requisite lawful excuse may have to be found in the principle of necessity.

(B) NO CONSENT BY THE CLAIMANT

The absence of consent is an element of the cause of action in battery and, consequently, the claimant must prove that he did not acquiesce to the contact with his person. This might at first sight seem rather odd, but any lingering doubt that the onus of proving the absence of consent lies on the claimant was laid to rest in *Freeman v Home Office (No 2)*.[29] There, a prisoner alleged that he had been injected with powerful mood-changing drugs against his will. The judge held that, since the essence of battery

---

[25] *Collins v Wilcock* [1984] 3 All ER 374, at 378.

[26] [1987] QB 237. Cf *Williams v Humphrey* (1975) *Times*, 20 February.

[27] [1989] 2 All ER 545, at 564.

[28] There is a statutory definition of incapacity in the Mental Capacity Act 2005, ss 2 and 3. The gist of this definition is that the defendant is incapacitated when unable to make a decision for himself because of impaired brain function, where the inability to make a decision is to be understood in terms of an inability to understand, retain, or evaluate the information.

[29] [1983] 3 All ER 589, at 594–5; affirmed [1984] QB 524.

is a specific and unpermitted intrusion on the claimant's body, it was for the claimant to establish that he did not agree to the intrusion. This he failed to do.

Part of the rationale for this approach is that the alternative (that is, treating consent as a defence to liability in battery) would potentially have posed severe problems for doctors generally, not just prison medical officers. Any contact with a patient – for example, vaccinations or even examining sore throats with a spatula – would prima facie constitute battery. To escape liability, the doctor would have to justify the intrusion by proving that the patient consented. This might be extremely difficult in cases involving minor procedures where no written consent had been obtained, or if records had been lost, or if the doctor had died.[30]

On the other hand, in the context of actions by suspects against the police, or prisoners against prison authorities, casting the burden of proof on the claimant might vitiate the effectiveness of a battery action as a mechanism for vindicating their civil liberties.[31] In such circumstances, cases would turn on the contest between the word of the prisoner and the word of 'respectable' members of society in a position of responsibility.

That which constitutes a valid consent is often a fundamental issue, especially in cases of trespass in the medical context. There may be a question of exactly what the patient consented to, or indeed whether he was competent to give consent in the first place.[32] Logically, as it is for the claimant to prove absence of consent, it might be expected that we should deal with these issues here. But in practice, once the claimant has raised sufficient evidence to cast doubt on the reality of a purported consent, consent is still treated as a defence.[33] For this reason, it is discussed in greater detail in chapter 11, where general defences to the intentional torts are addressed.[34]

(C) THE CHARACTER OF THE DEFENDANT'S ACT

There can be no battery unless there is a positive act by the defendant. Merely to obstruct the entrance to a room by standing in someone's way is not of itself enough[35] (although there may be an assault if it is clear that if A tries to pass B, B will forcibly

---

[30] As had the prison doctor in *Freeman v Home Office (No 2)* [1984] QB 524.

[31] But see *R (on the application of Wilkinson) v Broadmoor Hospital* [2002] 1 WLR 419.

[32] Where medical treatment is administered to a mental patient without his consent, that treatment may nonetheless be justified so long as it does not amount to inhuman or degrading treatment contrary to Art 3 of the European Convention on Human Rights: *R (on the application of Wilkinson) v Broadmoor Hospital* [2002] 1 WLR 419.

[33] The ingredients of a genuine consent are discussed in ch 11.

[34] See pp 327–33.

[35] *Innes v Wylie* (1844) 1 Car & Kir 257, at 263. A motorist who accidentally drives his car on to a police constable's foot while he is parking commits no battery, but does commit a battery if he then ignores the constable's plea to 'Get off my foot'. See the criminal law case of *Fagan v MPC* [1969] 1 QB 439 (D convicted).

attempt to prevent that happening).[36] Also, no battery is committed if an incident involving contact over which the defendant has no control occurs.[37]

Equally, there can be no battery unless there is contact with the claimant. But is any contact, however slight, enough? Lord Goff has suggested that battery protects a person 'not only against physical injury but against any form of physical molestation'.[38] This formulation provides a guide as to the kind of conduct that the courts will hold tortious, so long as the word 'molestation' is read reasonably broadly. Such a reading explains why spitting in someone's face is battery, while touching another accidentally in a crowd is not. It also explains the view of Holt CJ, 'that the least touching of another in anger is battery' but that 'if two or more meet in a narrow passage, and without any violence or design of harm, the one touches the other gently, it is no battery'.[39] The courts cannot, and should not be expected to, give protection against these unavoidable contacts in everyday life, and thus the second statement just quoted can be classed as an example of a permitted contact.[40] Battery, then, protects a person against all unpermitted contacts which amount to 'molestation', irrespective of whether there is any physical harm.[41] So, taking fingerprints,[42] spitting in another's face (as already noted),[43] and cutting another's hair against his will[44] are all battery.

As with all trespasses to the person, the requirement of directness applies in battery. It is not enough that the act 'causes' the contact. Contact must follow immediately from the act of the defendant;[45] or at least be a continuation of his act.[46] This is to say that there must be no significant acts of volition between D's act and the eventual contact with C's body. It is battery where A strikes B's horse so that the horse bolts throwing B to the ground,[47] or where D punches a third party so that injury results to C.[48] It is also a trespass to the person to overturn a carriage or chair in which the claimant is sitting.[49] Finally, it is battery for a ship to ram another despite the effect of the current.[50]

If battery protected against insult generally, and not merely against bodily infringement, then any intentional contact with anything closely attached to, or associated with, the person of the claimant could conceivably be treated as battery. This very matter was investigated in *Pursell v Horn*,[51] where it was decided that throwing water

---

[36] *Hepburn v CC of Thames Valley Police* [2002] EWCA Civ 1841.
[37] See *Gibbons v Pepper* (1695) 2 Salk 637; *Holmes v Mather* (1875) LR 10 Exch 261.
[38] See *F v West Berkshire HA* [1989] 2 All ER 545, at 563.   [39] *Cole v Turner* (1704) 6 Mod Rep 149.
[40] This explains, too, the dictum in *Tuberville v Savage* (1669) 1 Mod Rep 3 to the effect that striking another on the breast in discourse is not actionable. Cf *Donnelly v Jackman* [1970] 1 All ER 987.
[41] *Ashley v CC Sussex* [2008] UKHL 25, [60].
[42] *Dumbell v Roberts* [1944] 1 All ER 326, at 330; *Callis v Gunn* [1964] 1 QB 495.
[43] *R v Cotesworth* (1704) 6 Mod Rep 172.
[44] *Forde v Skinner* (1830) 4 C & P 239. Cf *Nash v Sheen* (1953) *Times*, 13 March.
[45] *Leame v Bray* (1803) 3 East 593, at 603.   [46] *Scott v Shepherd* (1773) 2 Wm Bl 892, at 899.
[47] *Dodwell v Burford* (1669) 1 Mod Rep 24.
[48] *Haystead v CC of Derbyshire* [2000] 3 All ER 890 (*obiter*).
[49] *Hopper v Reeve* (1817) 7 Taunt 698.   [50] *Covell v Laming* (1808) 1 Camp 497.
[51] (1838) 8 Ad & El 602.

on to the clothes being worn by the claimant was not necessarily battery. But it is probably going too far the other way to suggest that contact with things attached to the claimant can only constitute battery if there is also a transmission of force to the body of the claimant.[52] As suggested, the guide should be whether the action constitutes a molestation – as unnecessary contact with the claimant's underwear would be. The protection from insult or indignity afforded by the tort of battery is limited to insult or indignity arising from the touching.[53]

(D) DAMAGES

As we have already noted, battery, like all suits in trespass, is actionable per se. That being so, damages can be awarded even if the claimant suffers no tangible harm.[54] Furthermore, it seems also that, once the tort is proved, consequential loss in respect of goods, as well as the personal damage sustained, can be recovered.[55] And the courts can also award additional damages on account of insult or injury to feelings in respect of a battery that has caused harm.[56]

SECTION 3   ASSAULT

Though the commission of an assault will often occur just before the commission of a battery, it makes sense to deal with assault second because the tort's definition refers to battery.

An assault is any act of the defendant that directly and intentionally or negligently[57] causes the claimant reasonably to apprehend the imminent infliction of a battery.

The law of assault is substantially similar to the law of battery except that, in assault, a reasonably held apprehension of contact (rather than contact itself) must be established. Usually when there is a battery, there will also be an assault, but not, for instance, when a person is hit from behind. To point a loaded gun at the claimant, to shake a fist under his nose, to aim a blow at him which is intercepted, or to surround him with a display of force,[58] is to assault him. Clearly, if the defendant by his act intends to commit a battery and the claimant apprehends it, it is an assault. Within

---

[52] 'It must imply personal violence': *Pursell v Horn* (1838) 8 Ad & El 602, at 604. In *R v Day* (1845) 1 Cox 207 Parke B held that it was the crime of battery to slit with a knife a victim's clothes.

[53] Thus, an unwanted kiss is actionable: see also Trindade (1982) 2 OJLS 211, at 225.

[54] *Ashley v CC Sussex* [2008] UKHL 25, [60].

[55] *Glover v London and South Western Rly Co* (1867) LR 3 QB 25.

[56] *Loudon v Ryder* [1953] 2 QB 202. There is doubt as to whether such damages are available in cases where the battery does not occasion any physical harm.

[57] By analogy with battery, it would seem to accord with principle to include foreseeable though unintended harm (although actual decisions are lacking).   [58] *Read v Coker* (1853) 13 CB 850.

the tort of assault[59] what must be apprehended, however, is actual physical contact. Photographing a person against his will is not an actionable assault.[60]

The effect of the origins of this tort on the present law is seen when one asks whether to brandish an unloaded pistol is an assault. In 1840 it was still being said that this was not assault because the defendant could not have intended a battery.[61] Tindal CJ had said ten years previously that 'it is not every threat, when there is no actual physical violence, that constitutes an assault, there must, in all cases, be the means of carrying the threat into effect'.[62] These cases have not been overruled, but in criminal law it is firmly established that pointing an unloaded gun at someone is an assault.[63] Reasoning by analogy, it is submitted that a modern-day court would reach the equivalent conclusion in tort. The gist of the tort of assault is an act which would cause a reasonable person to apprehend an imminent battery.[64] The test for what constitutes reasonable apprehension of an imminent battery is objective not subjective, and a reasonable person could not be expected to know that the gun was not loaded. Conversely, if the claimant is paranoid and perceives the defendant's innocuous waving of his hand in the air during conversation as a threat, there is no assault.

Where interventions of the police, or other protective intrusions, ensure that persons cannot carry out threats of violence and abuse, no assault is committed. Thus, where working miners were driven on buses into their collieries with police guards, the threats yelled at them by striking miners were not assaults.[65] The claimants could not reasonably have apprehended that those threats would be carried out there and then and thus fell outside the scope of this tort. It is therefore clear that the tort of assault provides only limited protection from the infliction of mental anxiety.

At one time it was thought that mere words could not constitute an assault.[66] But the House of Lords in *R v Ireland*[67] quashed that fallacy in criminal law. By analogy, words that instil a reasonable fear of an imminent battery should equally amount to a tortious assault for '[the] means by which persons of evil disposition may intentionally or carelessly cause another to fear immediate and unlawful violence vary according to

---

[59] In criminal law it has been held that threatening telephone calls amount to a criminal assault: *R v Ireland* [1998] AC 147.

[60] *Murray v Minister of Defence* [1985] 12 NIJB 12. On the other hand, publishing such photographs might give rise to an action based on the misuse of private personal information. See *Campbell v MGN* [2004] 2 AC 457 and ch 22.

[61] *Blake v Barnard* (1840) 9 C & P 626.

[62] *Stephens v Myers* (1830) 4 C & P 349, at 349–50. In *Osborn v Veitch* (1858) 1 F & F 317 it was held that to point a loaded gun at half-cock at C was an assault but this was because there was 'a present ability of doing the act threatened', the cocking of the gun taking just a split second.

[63] *R v St George* (1840) 9 C & P 483.   [64] *Mbasogo v Logo Ltd (No 1)* [2005] EWHC 2034.

[65] *Thomas v NUM* [1985] 2 All ER 1, at 24.

[66] The case usually relied on is *R v Meade and Belt* (1823) 1 Lew CC 184 at 185, where it was said *obiter*, that 'no words or singing are equivalent to an assault'.   [67] [1998] AC 147.

circumstances'.[68] On the other hand, words accompanying an act may explain away what might otherwise be an assault. Thus, there was no assault in one ancient case where the defendant with his hand on his sword said: '[i]f it were not assize-time, I would not take such language from you'.[69]

SECTION 4 'INTENTIONAL' PHYSICAL HARM OTHER THAN TRESPASS TO THE PERSON?

This somewhat uncertain tort arose from the case of *Wilkinson v Downton*.[70]

> C was told by D, who knew it to be untrue, that her husband had been seriously injured in an accident. Believing this, she suffered nervous shock resulting in serious physical illness, and was held to have a cause of action.

In the case itself, Wright J held the practical joker liable on the basis that he had 'wilfully done an act calculated to cause physical harm to the plaintiff...which in fact caused physical harm to her'.[71] But it was by no means clear that the joker had actually intended the harm caused. For this reason, Wright J explained a little later in his judgment that this intention may sometimes need to be imputed, and duly went on to impute such intention to the defendant. But this seems a rash step given that the defendant intended only a joke. The defendant's act is rather more redolent of negligence even though the joke was intentionally played. And as McPherson J observed in the Australian case of *Carrier v Bonham*.[72]

> Most everyday acts of what we call actionable negligence are in fact wholly or partly a product of intentional conduct. Driving a motor vehicle at high speed through a residential area is an intentional act even if injuring people or property on the way is not a result actually intended. *Wilkinson v Downton* is an example of that kind.[73]

He then went on to note that 'the expression calculated...is one of those weasel words that is capable of meaning either *subjectively contemplated and intended* or, *objectively likely to happen*', before concluding that in *Wilkinson v Downton* those words were 'being used in the latter, not the former sense'.[74] In short, he effectively recast the decision in *Wilkinson v Downton* as a negligence case. And this, it is submitted, is the better way in which *that case* should nowadays be understood given that it was highly improbable that the practical joker had *subjectively intended* anything more

---

[68] [1997] 3 WLR 534, at 550. *R v Ireland* centred on a telephone call, but unless the call is made from a mobile phone just outside C's house, it seems contrary to principle to embrace such a case within the tort of assault for want of the prospect of an imminent battery.

[69] *Tuberville v Savage* (1669) 1 Mod Rep 3.

[70] [1897] 2 QB 57, 66 LJQB 493 (the fuller report). The Court of Appeal later upheld and applied the decision in this case in *Janvier v Sweeney* [1919] 2 KB 316. See Witting (1998) 21 UNSWLJ 55.

[71] [1897] 2 QB 57, at 58.   [72] [2001] QCA 234.   [73] Ibid at [27].

[74] Ibid at [25].

than fleeting or, at most, short-term, distress. What was crucial to Wright J's *particular decision* was the likelihood of harm occurring from the joke (which should be instantly recognised as a central question posed in negligence cases).[75]

There is a historical explanation as to why *Wilkinson v Downton* has traditionally been presented as a kind of intentional tort *sui generis*. The fleeting and insubstantial nature of the 'harm' that was actually intended by the defendant (as opposed to that which actually occurred) would not, at the time, have sufficed to found an action on the case. The Privy Council decision in *Victorian Railways Commissioners v Coultas*[76] then prohibited recovery for nervous shock induced by negligence. It is thus probably partly for this reason that Wright J preferred to impute to the defendant an intention to 'produce some effect *of the kind* that was [actually] produced',[77] even though *that kind of harm* was almost certainly never in the defendant's mind. In the light of the more generous, modern approach to cases of psychiatric harm,[78] it seems high time that we abandoned Wright J's historically rooted legal fiction, and reclassified *Wilkinson v Downton* as a negligence case in which the defendant failed to take appropriate care to avoid causing psychiatric harm to the claimant. Strong support for this reclassification of *the actual decision* in *Wilkinson v Downton* can be taken from the decision of the House of Lords in *Wainwright v Home Office*.[79]

> A mother and her son with learning difficulties were subjected to a strip search before they could enter a prison to visit a second son who was imprisoned there. Although no physical contact was made with the mother, she nonetheless complained of the humiliating and procedurally improper way in which the search was conducted. Her complaint was that the prison staff, in forcing her to undergo the search, had wilfully caused her to do something that infringed her legal right to privacy and exacerbated her existing depression.

In relation to whether liability could be imposed on the basis of the rule in *Wilkinson v Downton*, Lord Hoffmann (with whom the other Law Lords agreed) said:

> [t]he claimants can build nothing on *Wilkinson v Downton*. It does not provide a remedy for distress which does not amount to recognised psychiatric injury and so far as there may be a tort of intention under which such damage is recoverable, the necessary intention was not established. I am also in complete agreement with Buxton LJ [in the Court of Appeal in this case] that *Wilkinson v Downton* has nothing to do with trespass to the person.[80]

Notwithstanding these comments, however, it would be a mistake to discard *Wilkinson v Downton* wholesale.[81] This is because the rule in that case was promulgated in terms wide enough to range well beyond distress falling short of recognised psychiatric harm. There are, quite simply, many intentional (or reckless) acts besides the spoken word that can *indirectly* cause harm and thus defy classification as forms of trespass.

---

[75] See, eg, *Bolton v Stone* [1951] AC 850.   [76] (1888) 13 App Cas 222.
[77] [1897] 2 QB 57, at 59.   [78] See, eg, *Alcock v CC of South Yorkshire* [1992] 1 AC 310.
[79] [2004] 2 AC 406.
[80] Ibid at [47].   [81] Cf McBride and Bagsahw, *Tort Law* (2005), 68–9.

And without the rule in *Wilkinson v Downton*, it is debatable whether there would be a cause of action available in such cases.[82] Thus, putting poison in another's tea or digging a pit into which it is intended that another shall fall are not trespasses, but might comfortably be brought within the *stated* rule in *Wilkinson v Downton*. Furthermore, there are some rather ancient cases declaring that it is a tortious act deliberately to set spring guns or other mechanical devices with the intention of injuring trespassers which might still be explained according to Wright J's principle.[83] And the form of liability embodied in these cases is very similar to that found in the US 'prima facie tort' cases.[84] The only other way of dealing with such cases would be to allow negligence suits based on intentional and reckless conduct. And while this is not per se objectionable,[85] it does run up against the objection that, in *Letang v Cooper*,[86] Lord Denning MR and Danckwerts LJ made a strenuous effort to keep apart negligence and the intentional torts against the person. At the very least, it is to be noted that there has been a marked reluctance to abandon the rule in *Wilkinson v Downton* in the inferior courts.[87]

Even if, notwithstanding what was said in *Wainwright*, we are able to salvage the rule in *Wilkinson v Downton*, it is nonetheless true that it has been a little used tort. For a time, during the mid-1990s, it looked as though the principle would be extended beyond the protection of physical and mental health, to the protection from harassment.[88] Yet dicta in the Court of Appeal decision in *Wong v Parkside Health NHS Trust*[89] halted this expansion of the tort in its tracks. In cases of distress falling short of negligently inflicted psychiatric harm or assault, the preferred route to redress will now ordinarily be the Protection from Harassment Act 1997.[90]

---

[82] Another point is that actions that might fail in negligence because the loss is regarded as too remote, may nonetheless succeed on the basis of the rule in *Wilkinson v Downton* (assuming that the trespass rules on remoteness of damage apply to that tort).

[83] *Deane v Clayton* (1817) 7 Taunt 489; *Bird v Holbrook* (1828) 4 Bing 628. Cf *Townsend v Wathen* (1808) 9 East 277.   [84] See, eg, Vandervelde (1991) 79 Kentucky LJ 519; Witting (1999) 25 Mon ULR 295.

[85] For the suggestion that the tort of negligence logically embraces *intentional* wrongs, see Murphy (2007) 27 OJLS 509.   [86] [1965] 1 QB 232.

[87] See, eg, *C v D* [2006] EWHC 166 and *Bici v Ministry of Defence* [2004] EWHC 786. See also *Wong Kai Wai v Hong Kong Special Administrative Region* (2005) CACV 19/2003.

[88] The decision in *Khorasandjian v Bush* [1993] QB 727 looked for a time as though it might be taking the rule in *Wilkinson v Downton* into new territory: the protection of privacy with no requirement of mental or physical harm. See also *Burris v Azadani* [1995] 1 WLR 1372.   [89] [2001] EWCA Civ 1721.

[90] Three factors may serve to make the remnants of the rule in *Wilkinson v Downton* preferable to an action under the 1997 Act. First, where C's complaint turns on a one-off incident rather than a 'course of conduct', as is required by the Act (see below), C may need to invoke the rule. Second, although there is no specific time-frame under the Act within which the relevant 'course of conduct' must take place, 'the fewer the occasions and the wider they are spread, the less likely it would be that a finding of harassment can reasonably be made [under the Act]': *Lau v DPP* [2000] 1 FLR 799, at [15] (cited with approval in *Pratt v DPP* [2001] EWHC Admin 483, at [9]–[10]; but cf *Jones v Hipgrave* [2005] 2 FLR 174). Third, in cases involving persons who formerly shared an affectionate bond, it seems that pestering conduct that falls short of stalking may prove inadequate for the purposes of invoking the Act: see *R v Hills* [2001] 1 FCR 569, at [31]. But see now Crime and Security Act 2010, s 24.

SECTION 5   PROTECTION FROM HARASSMENT
ACT 1997

This Act creates two criminal offences. The first, created by section 1(1), is the general offence of harassing *one* other person. Under this subsection, conduct amounting to harassment of another person[91] is a criminal offence unless justifiable for the purpose of detecting or preventing crime,[92] or authorised by law, or, in the particular circumstances, the conduct was reasonable.[93] The victim of such harassment, be it actual or apprehended, is granted a right to sue in tort – either for damages or for an injunction[94] – by virtue of section 2 of the Act. But, simple as this sounds, the subsection is not entirely straightforward. For a start, although the Act provides no concrete definition of harassment, it is at least clear that the defendant's conduct can only constitute harassment if he knows or ought to know that his acts amount to harassment.[95] The context will be important. Thus, '[w]hat might not be harassment on the factory floor or in the barrack room might well be harassment in the hospital ward and vice versa'.[96] To take another example, the bringing of legitimate litigation cannot be complained of. But the commencement and dropping of successive lawsuits for the recovery of rental arrears, caused by council ineptitude, provides an arguable case of harassment.[97] The provision appears also to be satisfied where the conduct arises from computer-generated demands for payment erroneously made – as in *Ferguson v British Gas*, where the claimant businesswoman was repeatedly threatened that, unless payment were made, credit-rating agencies would be told that she had not paid her gas bills.[98]

---

[91] A corporate entity cannot claim under the Act (although individual employees targeted by the harassment will be able to do so): *Daiichi Pharmaceuticals UK Ltd v Stop Huntingdon Animal Cruelty* [2004] 1 WLR 1503.

[92] The test for what is necessary in the prevention of crime is to be interpreted objectively and, so far as investigations involve the repeated questioning of certain people, any resulting invasion of their Art 8 right to respect for privacy must satisfy the twin tests of necessity and proportionality: *KD v CC of Hampshire* [2005] EWHC 2550.

[93] In one case, Lord Phillips MR stated, less than transparently, that a newspaper running a campaign against a specific individual would only be acting unreasonably for these purposes if the campaign was 'an abuse of the freedom of press which the pressing social needs of a democratic society require should be curbed': *Thomas v News Group Newspapers Ltd* [2002] EMLR 78, at [50]. No doubt, his Lordship was mindful of the right to freedom of expression afforded to the press under Art 10 of the European Convention on Human Rights.

[94] Protection from Harassment Act 1997, s 3(1). Where an injunction is sought, the civil standard of proof applies: *Jones v Hipgrave* [2005] 2 FLR 174.

[95] For these purposes D ought to know that which a reasonable person in possession of the same information would know: Protection from Harassment Act 1997, s 1(2). The test is a purely objective one: *Banks v Ablex Ltd* [2005] ICR 819, at [20]. That being so, no account is to be taken of any mental deficiency on D's part. Thus, a schizophrenic who sends threatening letters to a local MP is not exempt: *R v Colohan* [2001] 2 FLR 757, at [21].   [96] *Sunderland CC v Conn* [2007] EWCA Civ 1492, at [12].

[97] *Allen v LB of Southwark* [2008] EWCA Civ 1478.

[98] [2009] EWCA Civ 46 (action to strike out). Despite increased use of the Act in consumer cases, the Law Commissions have recommended new legislation to cover aggressive consumer practices: Law

Equally, the precise degree of distress or harm required to invoke the Act remains to be determined. And the courts may choose to be lenient in this respect, preferring not to characterise many forms of undesirable conduct as criminal harassment. Certainly, it has been said that it will be more difficult to rely on pestering that occurs following a relationship breakdown than on stalking.[99] This is borne out by *R v Curtis*, where the Court of Appeal held that there was no sufficient course of conduct in a domestic relationship characterised by 'spontaneous outbursts of ill-temper and bad behaviour, with aggression on both sides...interspersed...with considerable periods of affectionate life'.[100] In any event, because the 1997 Act offence requires there to have been a course of conduct – that is, conduct on at least two occasions[101] – it is clear that one-off incidents of harassing conduct do not fall within the statute.[102]

The second offence contained in the Act was created by an amendment wrought by section 125 of the Organised Crime and Police Act 2005. According to this amendment, there is now also an offence, under section 1(1A), where the defendant pursues a course of conduct that involves harassment of two or more persons, and this harassment is intended to persuade any person *either* not to do something he or she is entitled or obliged to do, *or* to do something that he or she is not obliged to do. In respect of this offence, there is no right to sue for damages, but an injunction may be sought.[103] The test of what the defendant knows or ought to know will be the effect of his conduct applies equally to this offence.[104]

SECTION 6 FALSE IMPRISONMENT

This somewhat inadequately named tort[105] may be defined in the following terms.

An act of the defendant which directly and intentionally (or possibly negligently) causes the confinement of the claimant within an area delimited by the defendant.

Usually when there is a false imprisonment there will also be an assault or battery, but not, for example, where A voluntarily enters a room and B then locks the door

---

Commissions, *Consumer Redress for Misleading and Aggressive Practices: A Joint Consultation Paper* (Law Com Consultation Papers Nos 199 and 149, 2011).

[99] *R v Hills* [2001] 1 FCR 569, at [31]. But note the potential availability of domestic violence protection notices under Crime and Security Act 2010, s 24. [100] [2010] EWCA Crim 123, at [32].

[101] Protection from Harassment Act 1997, s 7(3). Interestingly, this may include a series of newspaper articles, or a series of threatening letters from someone unknown to C, or a series of threatening emails: see, respectively, *Thomas v News Group Newspapers* [2002] EMLR 78, *R v Colohan* [2001] 2 FLR 757, and *Potter v Price* [2004] EWHC 781.

[102] See also Equality Act 2010, s 26, creating offences in relation to, inter alia, harassment 'related to a relevant protected characteristic' and 'unwanted conduct of a sexual nature'.

[103] Protection from Harassment Act 1997, s 3A.

[104] Protection from Harassment Act 1997, s 1(1A).

[105] The term 'false' conveys little to nothing of what this tort concerns.

trapping A inside. The tort protects the interest in freedom from confinement and against the loss of liberty more generally.

There is a substantial overlap between the protection of liberty offered by this tort and the protection to persons available under the European Convention on Human Rights, Article 5(1). According to the European Court of Human Rights in *McKay v United Kingdom*, this provision is 'in the first rank of the fundamental rights that protect the physical security of an individual...Its key purpose is to prevent arbitrary or unjustified deprivations of liberty'.[106] There must be more than a mere restriction of liberty; there must be a deprivation of liberty.[107] As foreshadowed earlier, a remedy may occasionally be available under this provision where the claimant would fail in the common-law tort of false imprisonment.[108]

(A) DEFENDANT'S STATE OF MIND

Normally this tort must be intentional in the sense that the defendant must intend to do an act which is at least substantially certain to effect the confinement. There is no need to show malice. Indeed, even where there is good faith on the part of the defendant, he may still be liable for his intentional confinement of the claimant. Thus, in *R v Governor of Brockhill Prison, ex p Evans (No 2)*[109] a prison governor who calculated the claimant's day of release in accordance with the law as understood at the time of her conviction was held liable when a subsequent change in the law meant that the prisoner should have been released 59 days earlier. On the other hand, since the governor was actually *obliged* to detain the claimant until the law applicable to the calculation of the prisoner's release date was changed – on which date she was duly released – it is difficult to see why the governor could not rely on the defence of necessity, it being required of him that he should detain her until that change in the law occurred.[110] If the law were to have changed before the actual date of release, it would be quite proper that the detainee should be able to sue. This is because an honest mistake – whether negligently made or not – as to the right to continue detention 'does not excuse a trespass to the person':[111] the requisite intention to detain will be present; and that is all that counts in the absence of a recognised justification (such as necessity). But why she could sue on the actual facts of the case is something of a mystery.

---

[106] (2006) 44 EHRR 827, at [30].

[107] *Secretary of State for the Home Department v AP* [2010] UKSC 24, at [2]; *Austin v Commissioner of Police* [2009] UKHL 5, at [16].   [108] Eg, *HL v UK* (2005) 40 EHRR 32, discussed below.

[109] [2001] 2 AC 19. Cf *Olotu v Home Office* [1997] 1 WLR 328.

[110] Their Lordships noted that this involved a hardship to the governor, but felt that it was outweighed by the hardship that would otherwise be done to C were she unable to sue. What perhaps ought to happen, then, is to extend the legislation that currently allows compensation for miscarriages of justice – namely, the Criminal Justice Act 1988, s 133 – to cases like *Evans* (for it currently only applies to cases where an innocent prisoner was wrongly convicted). *Evans* now casts doubt on the decision in *Percy v Hall* [1997] QB 924 where C was held to be unable to sue in respect of arrests made under byelaws that were later declared void for uncertainty.

[111] *Hepburn v CC of Thames Valley Police* [2002] EWCA Civ 1841.

Happily, *R v Governor of Brockhill Prison, ex p Evans (No 2)* has at least been confined to errors on the part of the prison governor by the Court of Appeal's decision in *Quinland v Governor of Swaleside Prison*.[112] In this case, it was judicial error in stating the sentence to be three months longer than it ought to have been that caused the claimant to be detained longer than should have been the case. The Court of Appeal stated that, since the prisoner was unduly detained by virtue of a court order, there would be no remedy apart from the correction of the arithmetical error that had occurred in adding together the various periods of confinement attributable to the various offences of which the claimant had been convicted.

In principle, negligence ought to be enough to engage liability for false imprisonment. Accordingly, if a person locks a door, being negligently unaware of the presence of somebody in the room, this should suffice. On the other hand, a remedy was made available in one case under the auspices of the tort of negligence, but not false imprisonment, when a prisoner was negligently detained for a period that exceeded that authorised by the court.[113] This suggests that the courts might take a dim view of any claim based on 'negligent false imprisonment'.[114]

(B) CHARACTER OF THE DEFENDANT'S ACT

Like other forms of trespass to the person, this tort is actionable per se.[115] However, the courts do insist upon total (as opposed to partial) restraint of the person.[116] Thus, to prevent a man from crossing a bridge except by making a detour around part of the area of the bridge which has been closed off is not false imprisonment. Nor is it false imprisonment if A is able to escape from his confinement by a nominal trespass on the land of a third party.[117] However, there is a breach of Article 5(1) of the Human Rights Convention (the right to liberty) if a mental patient is 'technically' free to leave a mental hospital, but in reality is constantly monitored and subject to immediate compulsory detention should he try to leave.[118]

It is well established that, although confinement must be total, it need not be in a prison as the name of the tort perhaps suggests. One may be confined in a house,[119] in a prison,[120] in a mine,[121] or even in a vehicle.[122] How large the area of confinement can

---

[112] [2003] QB 306.   [113] *Clarke v Crew* [1999] NLJR 899.

[114] A 'dim view' is apparent in the *obiter* comments in *Prison Officers Association v Iqbal* [2009] EWCA 1312, at [71]–[72].

[115] *R (Lumba and Mighty) v Secretary of State for the Home Department* [2011] UKSC 12, at [64], [197], [212], [252], and [343]; *Kambadzi v Secretary of State for the Home Department* [2011] UKSC 23, at [55] and [74]; *Murray v Ministry of Defence* [1988] 1 WLR 692, at 701–2.

[116] Partial restraint was the subject of an action on the case, on proof of damage: *Wright v Wilson* (1699) 1 Ld Raym 739; *Bird v Jones* (1845) 7 QB 742, at 752.

[117] *Wright v Wilson* (1699) 1 Ld Raym 739; the court thought that a special action on the case would lie.

[118] *HL v United Kingdom* (2005) EHRR 32, at [91].   [119] *Warner v Riddiford* (1858) 4 CBNS 180.

[120] *Cobbett v Grey* (1849) 4 Exch 729.

[121] *Herd v Weardale Steel, Coal and Coke Co Ltd* [1915] AC 67.

[122] *Burton v Davies* [1953] QSR 26 (Queensland), driving a car at such a speed as to prevent a passenger from alighting is false imprisonment.

be obviously depends on the circumstances of each particular case. It could be tortious to restrict a man to a large country estate, or perhaps even to restrain him from leaving, say, the Isle of Man. Yet if A prevented B from landing in England from mainland Europe, that act could not be a false imprisonment.[123] The important point is that the boundaries of the area of confinement must be fixed by the defendant. As Coleridge J said in *Bird v Jones*:[124]

> Some confusion seems...to arise from confounding imprisonment of the body with mere loss of freedom...Imprisonment...includes the notion of restraint within some limits defined by a will or power exterior to our own.

Lord Denman, in his dissenting judgment in the same case, said:[125]

> As long as I am prevented from doing what I have a right to do, of what importance is it that I am permitted to do something else?...If I am locked in a room, am I not imprisoned because I might effect my escape through a window, or because I might find an exit dangerous or inconvenient to myself, as by wading through water...?

Although this contention was rejected so far as the adequacy of a partial restraint is concerned, it is suggested that, if someone can only escape at the risk of personal injury, or if it is otherwise unreasonable[126] for him to escape, it constitutes the tort of false imprisonment. On the other hand, the barriers need not be physical. Thus, when a Commissioner in Lunacy wrongfully used his authority to dissuade the claimant from leaving his office, he was liable in false imprisonment.[127] By contrast, where a voluntary mental patient is only restrained in the sense that he would be compulsorily detained under mental health legislation[128] *if he attempted to leave*, there is, according to the present House of Lords authority, no false imprisonment for the purposes of English tort law.[129] This is because the tort turns on actual, not merely potential or conditional, imprisonment.[130] When the case was taken to Strasbourg, however, it was held by the European Court of Human Rights that there was, in these circumstances, an abrogation of Article 5(1) of the Convention.[131] In the light of this later decision, it is likely that the House of Lords will seek to come into line with the Strasbourg ruling at the first opportunity.

Restraint on movement in the street even by a mere threat of force that intimidates a person into compliance without laying hands on him is false

---

[123] But in *Kuchenmeister v Home Office* [1958] 1 QB 496, it was held to be imprisonment for immigration officers to prevent an alien from proceeding from an airport to an aircraft and from embarking on it, even though the Aliens Order 1953 authorised them to prescribe limits within which he must remain.

[124] (1845) 7 QB 742, at 744.   [125] (1845) 7 QB 742, at 754–5.

[126] If A removes B's bathing costume in a swimming pool and B does not leave the pool until she has found someone to lend her another costume, is she falsely imprisoned?

[127] *Harnett v Bond* [1925] AC 669.   [128] The relevant legislation is discussed at pp 332–3.

[129] *R v Bournewood Community and Mental Health NHS Trust, ex p L* [1999] 1 AC 458.

[130] But note the dissent of Lord Steyn in that case ([1999] 1 AC 458, at 495) that it was a 'fairy tale' to suggest that the patient was free to leave.   [131] *HL v UK* (2005) 40 EHRR 32.

imprisonment.[132] A restraint effected by an assertion of authority is enough – so those who seek compensation because they have been wrongfully arrested by policemen claim for false imprisonment, and need not establish that the policeman touched them.[133] The claimant need not risk violence by resisting his arrester even though he is entitled to use reasonable force to resist unlawful restraint.[134]

Once a person is lawfully detained, changes in the conditions of his detention will not render that detention unlawful. In a series of cases, certain prisoners sought to assert that detention in intolerable or unsanitary cells constituted false imprisonment. The House of Lords finally rejected such claims.[135] Once a prisoner is lawfully imprisoned by virtue of the Prison Act 1952, he no longer enjoys any 'residual liberty' vis-à-vis the governor of the prison (and those officers acting in accordance with his instructions), and the governor is entitled to restrain and define his movements.[136] This does not mean, however, that a prisoner subjected to intolerable hardship is remediless. In appropriate circumstances he may have an action for assault and battery, for misfeasance in public office,[137] or, if the conditions of confinement affect his health, under the tort of negligence. It is suggested that similar analysis may be applied to detention by police officers who retain the right to detain (albeit not in the unlawful manner). For, if a remedy in false imprisonment lay, once an arrested person could establish that the conditions of his detention rendered his further detention unlawful, the logical consequence would be that, from that moment on, he could go free, using reasonable force, if necessary, to effect his escape.

Similarly, it has been held that a person held on remand beyond the 112-day limit set by regulations could not sue the prison authorities for false imprisonment.[138] The claimant was lawfully in the custody of the prison governor and only an order of the Crown Court could secure her release. The failure of the Crown Prosecution Service to bring her to trial or arrange her release on bail, and her own surprising failure to apply for bail, did not affect the validity of her detention. The claimant's right was not to be released from prison per se, but to an order of the court releasing her on bail.

---

[132] But can one be imprisoned by telephone, and would a threat of force to a family member suffice?

[133] *Warner v Riddiford* (1858) 4 CBNS 180, especially at 204; *Chinn v Morris* (1826) 2 C & P 361; *Grainger v Hill* (1838) 4 Bing NC 212. What if C is accused of shoplifting, but in order to avoid the embarrassment of a conversation in a crowded store he accompanies the store detective to the office? See *Conn v David Spencer Ltd* [1930] 1 DLR 805.

[134] *R v McKoy* [2002] EWCA Crim 1628.

[135] *R v Deputy Governor of Parkhurst Prison, ex p Hague* [1992] 1 AC 58. But note the *obiter* suggestion in *Toumia v Evans* (1999) *Times*, 1 April that it is arguable that a gaoler who locks a prisoner in his cell in violation of the governor's orders may be liable under this tort.

[136] See *R v Deputy Governor of Parkhurst Prison, ex p Hague* [1992] 1 AC 58, at 164 and 176–8; *Prison Officers Association v Iqbal* [2009] EWCA 1312.

[137] This, however, would require proof of malice: *Three Rivers DC v Bank of England (No 3)* [2000] 2 WLR 1220.

[138] *Olotu v Home Office* [1997] 1 WLR 328 (the Court of Appeal expressly addressed how far their findings were compatible with Art 5 of the Human Rights Convention); *Quinland v Governor of Swaleside Prison* [2002] 3 WLR 807.

Recent cases have held that the Crown is liable in false imprisonment for executive detentions of persons subject to deportation orders, which become unlawful as a result of breaches of public law duties. In *R (Lumba and Mighty) v Secretary of State for the Home Department* a material breach lay in the application of a secret and unlawful policy for detention, rather than the published policy.[139] Liability was held to arise even where the claimants inevitably would have been detained if the published criteria for detention had been applied, because of the risk that they would abscond and commit offences. Lady Hale justified this result by stating that the 'law requires that decisions to detain should be made on rational grounds and in an open and transparent way and not in accordance with arbitrary rules laid down by Government and operated in secret'.[140] In *Kambadzi v Secretary of State for the Home Department* the breach lay in a procedural failure to review the continuing detention of the applicant on the regular basis indicated within published policy guidelines. The system of review was characterised as 'integral to the lawfulness of the detention'.[141] In this case, Lords Brown and Rodger dissented, arguing (cogently, it is suggested) that '[t]heir Lordships in *Christie v Leachinsky* would... be astonished at the suggestion that any failure to give effect to a self-imposed requirement for periodic review of the continuing detention of those awaiting deportation... renders that detention unlawful'.[142]

False imprisonment must result from a direct act of the defendant which deprives the claimant of his liberty.[143] So, it is not false imprisonment to cause a person to be temporarily detained in an asylum by making false statements to the authorities about his behaviour.[144] Again, prison officers do not falsely imprison prisoners who are scheduled for daily release from their cells (but are to remain within the confines of the prison) after the officers have suddenly gone on strike that day.[145]

A false imprisonment will normally result from some positive act;[146] but in *Herd v Weardale Steel, Coal and Coke Co*[147] the question arose as to whether there might be liability in respect of a mere omission.[148]

C, a miner employed by Ds, descended into the mine in pursuance of his contract of employment. During his shift C requested that Ds carry him to the surface in their cage. In refusing this request Ds committed no breach of contract: their contractual obligation

---

[139] [2011] UKSC 12.   [140] Ibid at [205].   [141] [2011] UKSC 23, at [87].

[142] Ibid at [108].

[143] *Prison Officers Association v Iqbal* [2009] EWCA 1312, at [24], [69], and [77]–[78].

[144] But an action on the case lay against a medical practitioner, who negligently certified that C was insane, whereupon she was detained in a mental hospital: *De Freville v Dill* (1927) 96 LJKB 1056. *Quaere*: is it false imprisonment to deflate the tyres of the invalid chair in which a physically disabled person is travelling, or to take away the ladder of a tiler who is on the roof?

[145] *Prison Officers Association v Iqbal* [2009] EWCA 1312; Varuhas [2010] CLJ 438.

[146] Cf *Prison Officers Association v Iqbal* [2009] EWCA 1312, at [21] and [35].

[147] [1913] 3 KB 771; affirmed [1915] AC 67.

[148] Because both are acts of commission, not of omission, consider the example of a student forbidden to leave the lecture room until the end of the lecture, and a conductor who will not allow one who has boarded the wrong bus to alight without paying his fare.

was to transport C to the surface at the end of his shift. The action in false imprisonment also failed.[149]

This case is authority for the proposition that failure to provide a means of egress from premises is not a tort where there is no duty to provide one. Thus, if A falls down B's mine while trespassing on B's land, it is not false imprisonment should B refuse to bring him to the surface in his lift. What the *Herd* case left undecided, however, is whether the failure to carry out a duty – contractual or otherwise – may constitute false imprisonment even though there has been no positive act on the part of the defendant. But the House of Lords in *R v Governor of Brockhill Prison, ex p Evans (No 2)*[150] has now made it clear that the tort is committed where an obligation to release a prisoner who has served his full term is not fulfilled on time. This general approach is fortified by the executive detention case of *Kambadzi v Secretary of State for the Home Department*, already discussed.

Where a direct and intentional confinement can be shown, the burden of proof is upon the defendant to justify that confinement.[151] If this burden cannot be discharged, the defendant is liable no matter how short the period of detention. The length of time imprisoned is a matter for damages.

(C) KNOWLEDGE OF THE CLAIMANT

Surprisingly, perhaps, there is no requirement that the claimant alleging false imprisonment was aware of the relevant restraint on his freedom at the time of his confinement. Prior to 1988 the authorities on this issue were in conflict. In *Herring v Boyle*[152] an action brought on behalf of a schoolboy detained at school by his headmaster during the holidays because his parents had not paid the fees failed. The judge was influenced by the fact that the boy was unaware of his detention. By contrast, in *Meering v Grahame-White Aviation Co*[153] a man persuaded by works police to remain in an office, but unaware that had he tried to leave he would have been prevented from doing so, successfully recovered damages for his imprisonment. The House of Lords in *Murray v Ministry of Defence*[154] endorsed that latter judgment stating that actual knowledge of detention is not a necessary element of false imprisonment. According to Lord Griffiths, proof of a total restraint should suffice. He said:

The law attaches supreme importance to the liberty of the individual and if he suffers a wrongful interference with that liberty it should remain actionable even without proof of special damage.[155]

---

[149] Cf *Robinson v Balmain New Ferry Co Ltd* [1910] AC 295, at 299: 'There is no law requiring the defendants to make the exit from their premises gratuitous to people who come there upon a definite contract which involves their leaving the wharf by another way'.

[150] [2001] 2 AC 19. Cf *Olotu v Home Office* [1997] 1 WLR 328.

[151] *Lumba v Secretary of State for the Home Department* [2011] UKSC 12, at [64].

[152] (1834) 1 Cr M & R 377.   [153] (1919) 122 LT 44.   [154] [1988] 2 All ER 521.

[155] [1988] 1 WLR 692, at 704.

It would also seem to follow from this that, if a 'prisoner' has a reasonable means of escape at his disposal, but does not know of it, there will also be a false imprisonment. The 'prisoner' may, however, need to show that a reasonable person would not have known of the escape route, either.

(D) WHO IS LIABLE FOR A FALSE IMPRISONMENT?

The usual question to be asked when deciding who can be sued for false imprisonment is: who was 'active in promoting and causing' the confinement?[156] It is often necessary to determine who can be sued when a person is detained and charged for an offence where the arrest is unjustified by law.[157] (The separate question of lawful arrest as a defence is examined in chapter 11.)

Giving information to the police, on the basis of which a police officer exercises his own judgment and arrests the claimant, does not impose on the informer responsibility for that arrest, however likely it is that an arrest will ensue from the information proffered. Thus, a store detective was not liable when the claimant was arrested on the basis of information which she gave to police officers, even though her information proved to be erroneous.[158] Even signing the charge sheet at the police station will not necessarily render the private citizen liable for the detention of the claimant.[159] It must be shown that the claimant's detention was truly the act of the defendant rather than of the police officers concerned. So, where a police officer refused to take the claimant into custody unless the defendant charged him and signed the charge sheet, the defendant, not the police officer, was held responsible for that detention.[160]

If the defendant wrongfully delivers the claimant into custody and then the magistrate remands the claimant, the defendant is answerable in false imprisonment for damages only up to the time of the judicial remand. Once a judicial act interposes, liability for false imprisonment ceases.[161] It is important to distinguish false imprisonment from malicious prosecution. The latter is a tort concerned with the abuse of the judicial process, and which, unlike false imprisonment, calls for proof of malice and of absence of reasonable cause.[162] Therefore, if A wrongfully places a complaint against B before a magistrate, who then issues a warrant or tries him forthwith or remands him, A has not committed the tort of false imprisonment,[163] even if the magistrate has no jurisdiction.[164]

---

[156] *Aitken v Bedwell* (1827) Mood & M 68.

[157] See *Pike v Waldrum and P & O Navigation Co* [1952] 1 Lloyd's Rep 431 on the liability of naval authorities and a ship's captain for the arrest of a seaman.

[158] *Davidson v CC of North Wales* [1994] 2 All ER 597. See also *Gosden v Elphick* (1849) 4 Exch 445.

[159] *Sewell v National Telephone Co* [1907] 1 KB 557; *Grinham v Willey* (1859) 4 H & N 496.

[160] *Austin v Dowling* (1870) LR 5 CP 534. See also *Ansell v Thomas* [1974] Crim LR 31 where it was recognised that a person may be liable in false imprisonment either because he himself effected the arrest or – in line with the general principle that he who instigates another to commit a tort is a joint tortfeasor – because he actively promoted the arrest of another.

[161] *Ahmed v Shafique* [2009] EWHC 618, at [78]; *Lock v Ashton* (1848) 12 QB 871.   [162] See ch 23.

[163] *Brown v Chapman* (1848) 6 CB 365.   [164] *West v Smallwood* (1838) 3 M & W 418.

(E) DAMAGES

Like the other intentional torts considered in this chapter, false imprisonment is actionable without proof of damage.[165] In addition to damages for loss of liberty, the court may compensate for injury to feelings and loss of reputation.[166] The effect of the decision of nine justices of the Supreme Court in *R (Lumba and Mighty) v Secretary of State for the Home Department* is that, where false imprisonment has occurred and the claimant was aware of the restraint, damages will be more than nominal in nature. In the view of Lords Rodger and Brown, to hold otherwise would be to 'negate the tort'.[167] However, there is no separate head of 'vindicatory' damages.[168]

In claims for false imprisonment, awards of damages are currently made by juries. The amounts of such awards against the police escalated in recent years with an award of £200,000 in exemplary damages being made in one such action brought by Mr Hsu in *Thompson v Metropolitan Police Commissioner*.[169] There, the police appealed against the award to Mr Hsu, and the Court of Appeal issued guidelines on the criteria which should now determine awards of compensation for false imprisonment and malicious prosecution. Judges directing the jury on the issue of damages must address the following matters.

Save in exceptional cases, damages are to be awarded only to compensate the claimant for the injury suffered, not to punish the defendant. Basic damages to compensate the claimant for loss of liberty would generally start at about £500 for the first hour of detention, but thereafter be calculated on a reducing scale to allow around £3,000 for 24 hours of unlawful imprisonment and a 'progressively reducing scale' for subsequent days. An additional compensatory amount by way of aggravated damages was at one time available in respect of the humiliation, distress, and indignation that are likely to arise upon the commission of an intentional tort against the person. And certainly there is good authority that such an award may be made where the claimant has been humiliated during his or her false imprisonment by the police.[170] But in relation to assault and battery where distress, anger, indignation, and hurt feelings are likely to be present in most cases, it is now thought that the appellation 'aggravated damages' is inappropriate. These forms of injury are, in the context of these torts, merely part and parcel of what a defendant is expected to compensate under the head of general damages. Aggravated damages should thus now only be awarded in a 'wholly exceptional case' of assault and battery.[171]

---

[165] *R (Lumba and Mighty) v Secretary of State for the Home Department* [2011] UKSC 12, at [64], [197], [212], [252], and [343]; *Kambadzi v Secretary of State for the Home Department* [2011] UKSC 23, at [55] and [74]; *Murray v Ministry of Defence* [1988] 1 WLR 692, at 701–2.

[166] *Hook v Cunard Steamship Co Ltd* [1953] 1 All ER 1021.

[167] [2011] UKSC 12, at [344] (paraphrasing). This is subject to the exception noted on the next page.

[168] On this latter point: [2011] UKSC 12, at [101], [170], [195], [236]–[237], and [335].

[169] [1998] QB 498.

[170] See *Wainwright v Home Office* [2002] 3 WLR 405; affirmed [2004] 2 AC 406.

[171] *Richardson v Howie* [2005] PIQR Q3, at [23].

Exemplary damages are always exceptional. They are only granted where the sum of basic and aggravated damages is inadequate to punish the defendant for oppressive and arbitrary behaviour. Juries must note that an award of exemplary damages constitutes a windfall for the claimant and that where damages come out of police funds, the burden of payment falls on the police budget, affecting perhaps the operational efficiency of the police service. The amount of exemplary damages must be no more than is sufficient to mark the jury's disapproval of police behaviour. A particularly disgraceful instance of misbehaviour might merit an award of £25,000; and £50,000 should be regarded as an absolute maximum. The Court of Appeal in *Thompson* reduced the award of £200,000 to £15,000.

Given the facts in both Mr Hsu's case, and the second case with which the police's appeal against his award was joined, it might be asked why, in the light of the gross brutality involved in those cases, the Court of Appeal was so anxious to reduce levels of damages for false imprisonment. Was it solely to protect police funds, and if so, can this be justified in terms of justice?[172] Ironically, it may actually be easier to argue that there should never be exemplary damages by way of vicarious liability in respect of the intentional torts of a police officer (or any other employee), since the employer who would be required to pay will not have been *personally* 'guilty' of outrageous or arbitrary behaviour.[173] As the law currently stands, exemplary damages might be awarded against an employer, but where they are so awarded, there should be no necessary implication that aggravated damages should also be awarded.[174] Another crucial factor might well inhere in the fact that awards for pain and suffering in personal injury claims remain relatively low. A claimant suffering two broken legs, enduring weeks of hospitalisation and some continuing incapacity, might be awarded only about £50,000. Accordingly, how should compensation for loss of liberty and transient humiliation compare to compensation for injury?

In cases of unlawful executive detention in custody where the defendant authority would have had the right to detain if it had applied the proper policy, it has been held by way of exception that damages may be merely nominal.[175] 'The amount of compensation to which a person is entitled must be affected by whether he would have suffered the loss and damage had things been done as they should have been done.'[176]

Quite apart from the common law, it must not be forgotten that an action may lie under the Human Rights Act in respect of a breach of the Article 5 right to liberty. In such cases, the court is required to grant damages that provide 'just satisfaction' to the

---

[172] In relation to the question of whether retributive justice ought to play any part in tort law, see generally Law Com No 247, *Aggravated, Exemplary and Restitutionary Damages* (1997).

[173] For the view that, on this basis, exemplary damages should never be imposed on an employer under the vicarious liability principle, see *Kuddus v CC of Leicestershire* [2002] 2 AC 122, at 128 (*obiter*).

[174] *Isaac v CC of West Midlands* [2001] EWCA Civ 1405.

[175] *Lumba v Secretary of State for the Home Department* [2011] UKSC 12, at [71] and [161].

[176] *Kambadzi v Secretary of State for the Home Department* [2011] UKSC 23, at 74. See also ibid at [89].

claimant.[177] This is a vindicatory award and therefore need not, in principle, be limited to the same compensatory figure that would be awarded under the nominate tort of false imprisonment. For even though there will be some degree of overlap between an action premised on Convention rights and one based on the common law, the two are not coextensive and there is no reason to treat the two causes of action as mutually exclusive.[178] If, however, a claimant does pursue a remedy under the 1998 Act, he or she must demonstrate a causal link between the breach of Article 5 and his detention.[179]

SECTION 7   OTHER FORMS OF COMPENSATION

Many of the torts discussed in this chapter will also be crimes. And any court which has convicted a person of an offence (other than a road traffic offence) may require him to pay compensation to the victim for any personal injury, loss, or damage resulting.[180] The amount of compensation payable is to be determined by the court on the basis of what it considers to be appropriate, having regard to any evidence and to any representations made by or on behalf of the accused or prosecutor.[181] In addition, the Criminal Injuries Compensation Scheme also provides for awards of compensation to victims of crime who have sustained personal injuries.[182] However, detailed discussion of that scheme falls outside the scope of this book.[183]

FURTHER READING

BEEVER, 'Transferred malice in tort law?' (2009) 29 *Legal Studies* 400

CANE, '*Mens Rea* in Tort Law' (2000) 20 *Oxford Journal of Legal Studies* 533

FINNIS, 'Intention in Tort Law' in Owen (ed), *Philosophical Foundations of Tort Law* (1995)

PROSSER, 'Transferred Intent' (1967) 45 *Texas Law Review* 650

TRINDADE, 'Intentional Torts: Some Thoughts on Assault and Battery' (1982) 2 *Oxford Journal of Legal Studies* 211

---

[177]   Human Rights Act 1998, s 8(3). For further details see *R (on the application of KB) v Mental Health Review Tribunal* [2004] QB 936.

[178]   See the Human Rights Act 1998, s 8(3) which specifically requires the court to take into account 'any other relief or remedy granted' and the analogous decision in *Merson v Cartwright* [2005] UKPC 38.

[179]   *R (on the application of Richards) v Secretary of State for the Home Department* [2004] EWHC 93.

[180]   Powers of Criminal Courts (Sentencing) Act 2000, s 130.

[181]   Powers of Criminal Courts (Sentencing) Act 2000, s 130(4).

[182]   See Criminal Injuries Compensation Act 1995.

[183]   For details, see the Criminal Injuries Compensation Authority website at www.cica.gov.uk.

9

WRONGFUL INTERFERENCE WITH GOODS

KEY ISSUES

(1) Wide protection of interests in goods
The common law offers a wide degree of protection not just to the body, but to other physical interests – in this case, interests in goods.

(2) Focus on possession
Protection is offered to those who are owners of goods (especially in negligence and the residual actions on the case), but the main interest protected by the torts of trespass and conversion is that of possession of goods.

(3) Trespass to goods
The action in trespass to goods arises where there has been an intentional or careless direct interference with goods in the claimant's possession at the time of the trespass.

(4) Conversion
The action in conversion arises where the defendant has intentionally dealt with goods in a manner that constitutes a denial of the claimant's rights. The action can be brought by the claimant where the claimant had actual possession or an immediate right to possession of the goods.

(5) Remedies
The remedies available for torts to goods (including relevant actions in negligence) are governed by the Torts (Interference with Goods) Act 1977.

SECTION 1   INTRODUCTION

The law might be expected to protect persons whose title to, or possession of, goods is interfered with, or whose goods are damaged by intentional conduct. Broadly speaking, English law does this, but not in any systematic way; and this is so despite a comprehensive review of these chattel torts by the Law Reform Committee[1] that led to a

---

[1] See the 18th Report of the Law Reform Committee (Conversion and Detinue) (1971) Cmnd 4774.

recommendation that the various torts relating to intentional interferences with goods should be replaced by a single tort of 'wrongful interference with chattels'. In fact, this recommendation was only implemented to a very limited extent in the form of the Torts (Interference with Goods) Act 1977.[2] As such, it is still important to attempt to understand the various chattel torts.

The action for *trespass to goods* affords a remedy where there has been an intentional or careless direct interference with goods in the claimant's possession at the time of the trespass, whether that be by taking the goods from him, or by damaging the goods without removing them. But it is of no help where the relevant interference with the goods was indirect. Nor is a trespass action generally available where the goods were not in the possession of the claimant. Thus if student A lends his book overnight to student B, who gives it or sells it to C, an action in trespass will not lie against C.

The oldest of the chattel torts – the writ of *detinue* – developed to provide a remedy for wrongful detention of goods. A person with a right to immediate possession of goods could, by way of an action in detinue, recover the goods themselves or payment of their value and consequential damages for their detention upon evidence that the defendant had wrongfully refused to surrender the goods on demand. In many instances, the facts that gave rise to a remedy in detinue simultaneously created a cause of action in conversion, the latest of the major chattel torts to evolve. Detinue was abolished by the Torts (Interference with Goods) Act 1977. But the one clear instance of detinue that did not constitute conversion at common law – the loss or destruction of goods in breach of duty by a bailee[3] – was 'transformed' into a *statutory conversion* by section 2(2) of that Act.

The action for *conversion* (originally called trover) developed upon a legal fiction.[4] The original form of the pleadings alleged that the defendant had found the claimant's chattels and had wrongfully converted them to his own use.[5] The allegation of finding could not be contested and the essence of the tort became the wrongful conversion of the goods to the use of the defendant. As seizing goods and carrying them away is quite clearly a wrongful conversion of goods, conversion is also often available concurrently with trespass. But merely moving or damaging goods without converting

---

[2] See Palmer (1978) 41 MLR 629.

[3] When goods are entrusted by one person (the bailor) to another (the bailee) a bailment is created which imposes on the bailee duties towards the bailor in respect of those goods. The nature of the bailment – whether gratuitous or for reward, voluntary or involuntary – will determine the scope of the duty owed by the bailee.

[4] For details of the history of detinue and conversion see Milsom [1954] CLJ 105; Simpson (1959) 75 LQR 364.

[5] The courts wished to encourage the use of conversion but could not do so unless there were some (fictional) reason for which the torts in trespass *de bonis asportatis* and replevin did not apply. 'Loss and finding was convenient…and over time became standard': Green and Randall, *The Tort of Conversion* (2009), 13. The 'need' for an allegation of losing and finding was abolished by the Common Law Procedure Act 1852, s 49.

them to the defendant's own use remains remediable in trespass alone.[6] The action for conversion lies not only where the claimant has actual possession of the relevant goods, but also where he has a right to immediate possession of the goods. Consider again the earlier example of the aggrieved student, A. Should B refuse to return the book to him, he commits conversion. Should B have sold the book to C who also refuses to deliver the book back to A, both B and C may be sued for conversion.

The major chattel torts of trespass and conversion protect interests in possession. But there are also several residual torts derived from the action on the case that protect the rights of owners not in possession in certain cases. Also, where goods are lost or damaged as a result of the defendant's breach of a duty of care, an action may lie in negligence.

The rich history associated with the chattel torts adds to the intrinsic difficulty of the topic of wrongful interference with goods. That difficulty is unavoidable in that, as the essence of trespass or conversion is very often whether the defendant wrongfully and unlawfully dealt with the claimant's goods, the basic question of law in issue may be one of contract or personal property,[7] or even one of mercantile law.[8] For example, if A enters into a hire purchase agreement with B to purchase a car, and before A has completed all the payments on the car he sells it to C, when B seeks to recover the car or its value from C via an action for conversion, the court will have to consider the authority (if any) of A to sell the car to C. That authority will depend on (1) the terms of the contract between A and B; and (2) the relevant personal property rules on title to goods.

The Torts (Interference with Goods) Act 1977 introduces a collective description 'wrongful interference with goods'[9] to cover conversion, trespass to goods, negligence resulting in damage to goods or an interest in goods, and any other tort in so far as it results in damage to goods or an interest in goods. This is done to facilitate common treatment of all chattel torts in respect of remedies and procedure. But the Act neither redefines nor replaces the existing substantive rules on trespass, conversion, or any of the residual chattel torts. The substantive impact of the Act is thus limited. One novel provision, however, does allow bailees to dispose of uncollected goods.[10] But apart from this, the main impact of the 1977 Act is to simplify and rationalise the remedies and procedures relating to chattel torts. This leaves the intricacies of conversion and trespass actions still to be explored.

---

[6] *Bushel v Miller* (1718) 1 Stra 128; *Fouldes v Willoughby* (1841) 8 M & W 540.

[7] See Bell, *Modern Law of Personal Property* (1989).

[8] See *The Future Express* [1993] 2 Lloyd's Rep 542.

[9] Torts (Interference with Goods) Act 1977, s 1.

[10] Without statutory authority to do so bailees (eg, dry-cleaners) disposing of uncollected goods would be liable for conversion for so doing.

SECTION 2   CONVERSION[11]

Conversion involves an intentional[12] dealing with 'goods'[13] that is seriously inconsistent with the possession or right to immediate possession of another person. The tort protects the claimant's interest in the dominion and control of his goods (so long as the interference occurs in England or Wales).[14] It does not protect his interest in their physical condition. This is why the tort is so much concerned with problems of title to personal property, and so often involves complex rules of commercial law.[15]

(A) INTEREST OF THE CLAIMANT

The claimant must have *either* possession *or* the right to immediate possession in order to sue.[16] Equitable rights do not suffice for these purposes,[17] and in any event the law on conversion favours possession at the expense of ownership. Thus, if a landlord has rented out furnished accommodation for a fixed term and a third party commits an act of conversion in respect of some of the furniture, the landlord has no right to sue in conversion; but the tenant may do so.[18]

(1) Bailment

Where goods have been entrusted to another so as to create a bailment, the bailee can sue third parties in conversion.[19] If the bailment is determinable at will, the bailor may

---

[11] A short history can be found in Douglas [2009] CLJ 198. For an excellent, comprehensive treatment, see Green and Randall, *The Tort of Conversion* (2009).

[12] At common law an act of conversion had to be a voluntary act; hence the need to make the wrongful loss or destruction of goods by a bailee in breach of duty a statutory conversion once detinue was abolished.

[13] The term 'goods' is used as a matter of convenience. Technically, conversion is based on property and possession, but it is limited to tangible, movable property. It does not apply to real property (such as land) or intellectual property (such as copyright). It was held by majority in *OBG Ltd v Allan* [2007] UKHL 21 that an invalidly appointed receiver cannot be liable for conversion of contractual rights since conversion cannot be invoked in relation to a *chose in action*. See Green (2008) 71 MLR 114 and discussion in text below.

[14] *Mazur Media Ltd v Mazur Media GmbH* [2005] 1 Lloyd's Rep 41.

[15] As in *The Future Express* [1993] 2 Lloyd's Rep 542. The tort appears to be actionable without proof of special damage: *Hiort v London and NW Rly Co* (1879) 4 Ex D 188. See discussion in text below.

[16] *The Future Express* [1993] 2 Lloyd's Rep 542; *Gordon v Harper* (1796) 7 Term Rep 9. See also Curwen [2004] Conv 308. The Court of Appeal has expressed the view that a contractual right to immediate possession of goods will be a sufficient interest to sue: *Islamic Republic of Iran v Barakat Galleries Ltd* [2008] EWCA Civ 1374, at [30].

[17] *Hounslow LBC v Jenkins* [2004] EWHC 315. 'The reason for equitable interests being an insufficient basis for title to sue in Conversion is very simple: an equitable interest is not a possessory interest per se': Green and Randall, *The Tort of Conversion* (2009), 104.

[18] *Gordon v Harper* (1796) 7 Term Rep 9 and see *Roberts v Wyatt* (1810) 2 Taunt 268; *City Motors (1933) Pty Ltd v Southern Aerial Super Service Pty Ltd* (1961) 106 CLR 477.

[19] The bailment gives him the right to possession of the goods for the period of the bailment. In *The Winkfield* [1902] P 42, the Postmaster-General, as bailee, could recover the full value of mail lost through D's wrongdoing.

also sue because he is then deemed to have an immediate right to possession.[20] A bailment which originally gave to the bailor no immediate right to possess may become a bailment at will. *Manders v Williams*[21] is illustrative.

> C supplied porter in casks to a publican on condition that he was to return the empty casks within six months. It was held that C could sue a sheriff who seized some empty casks (within six months of their being supplied) in connection with a debt owed by the publican. Under the contract, once the casks were empty, the publican became a bailee at will, whereupon C was entitled to immediate possession.

Where a bailor and bailee enjoy concurrent rights to sue in conversion, they cannot both exercise those rights and so effect double recovery against the defendant.[22] The successful claimant who sues first must then account to the other for the proportion of the damages representing his interest in the property. So, where the owner of a car had lent the vehicle to his girlfriend, and the car was damaged while in her possession, his successful claim for damages based on his right to recover the car at will precluded a second action by the girlfriend, albeit she had possession of the car at the time the damage was done.[23]

In very many cases, however, the crucial issue for the bailor who owns the goods is whether he enjoys a right to immediate possession: is the bailment, or has it become, a bailment at will? Or has some wrongful act of the bailee ended the bailment? For if a bailee does a wrongful act which may be deemed to terminate the bailment, the bailor may sue. Sale of the goods by the bailee will ordinarily terminate the bailment and the bailor can then sue either the bailee or the third party.[24] Destruction of the goods[25] or dealing with them in a manner wholly inconsistent with the terms of the bailment,[26] will have the same result. Thus, it will often be a matter of interpreting the contract to decide whether a particular act of the bailee determines the bailment, or, at least, makes it determinable at will. This is especially true in the case of hire-purchase agreements which normally prohibit the hirer from selling or otherwise disposing of the goods,[27] and empower the owner to terminate the agreement if the prohibition is disregarded. If, for example, the agreement dispenses with notice of termination to the

---

[20] As the bailment can be terminated at will, the owner retains the right to demand the goods back instantly: *Nicolls v Bastard* (1835) 2 Cr M & R 659; *Kahler v Midland Bank Ltd* [1950] AC 24, at 56.

[21] (1849) 4 Exch 339.

[22] *Nicolls v Bastard* (1835) 2 Cr M & R 659 (once one has sued, the case is closed).

[23] *O'Sullivan v Williams* [1992] 3 All ER 385.

[24] *Cooper v Willomatt* (1845) 1 CB 672; *Scotland v Solomon* [2002] EWHC 1886. Of course, at the conclusion of the purported act of sale, the bailee's interest is forfeited and the bailor is entitled to immediate possession. But if the sale is one which passes a good title, when can the bailor be said to have an immediate right to possess (ie, a right to sue the bailee in conversion)?

[25] *Bryant v Wardell* (1848) 2 Exch 479, at 482.

[26] *Plasycoed Collieries Co Ltd v Partridge, Jones & Co Ltd* [1912] 2 KB 345, at 351. Presumably, this does not extend to excess of permitted user.

[27] It is standard practice in hire-purchase agreements, by express terms, to make the benefits of the hirer's option to purchase un-assignable: *Helstan Securities Ltd v Hertfordshire CC* [1978] 3 All ER 262.

hirer, the owner can sue a party who purchases from the hirer in unwitting contravention of such a prohibition.[28] Consider *Whiteley Ltd v Hilt*.[29]

> The hire-purchase agreement allowed the hirer to purchase a piano after payment of the
> final instalment. It did not prohibit her from transferring the piano during the hiring
> period. It was held that the owners had no cause of action against the transferee who had
> paid all the instalments that remained owing.

This may be compared with *Belsize Motor Supply Co v Cox*.[30]

> The owners were authorised to determine the agreement if the hirers parted with posses-
> sion of the hired goods. It was held that (i) the owners could recover from a pledgee of the
> hirer only the instalments that were still owing, and (ii) that the agreement continued in
> force despite the transfer of the goods.

In effect, the courts treat hire-purchase agreements as *sui generis*, in that they are
regarded as creating a proprietary interest separate from the contractual interest
under the bailment agreement.[31]

(2) Lien and pledge

In certain cases where goods are entrusted to another to carry out particular services
(for example, repairs or storage), the person in possession of those goods acquires a
lien over the goods. He will thereby ordinarily be entitled to retain the goods until he is
paid for the services.[32] But if title to the goods has passed to some third party (now the
claimant), and the defendant who is holding the goods knows this, the defendant loses
his right to retain the goods and must deliver them up to claimant.[33] The holder of a
lien has a sufficient possessory interest to sue in conversion.[34] But if a lien holder once
wrongfully parts with possession of the goods, he loses his lien, and his act is itself a
conversion which ends the bailment and entitles the owner to sue him.[35]

A pledge (that is, the deposit of goods as security for a debt), however, confers something more than a lien. It confers a power to sell in default of payment on the agreed
date. So, in *Donald v Suckling*[36] it was held that a re-pledge by the pledgee did not end
the pledge and the original pledgor could not sue the second pledgee without tender-
ing the sum owing. Similarly, the assignee of a pledgor cannot sue the pledgee who

---

[28] *North Central Wagon and Finance Co Ltd v Graham* [1950] 2 KB 7 (as explained in *Reliance Car
Facilities Ltd v Roding Motors* [1952] 2 QB 844); *Union Transport Finance Ltd v British Car Auctions Ltd*
[1978] 2 All ER 385.   [29] [1918] 2 KB 808.
[30] [1914] 1 KB 244; *Wickham Holdings Ltd v Brooke House Motors Ltd* [1967] 1 All ER 117.
[31] Cf *Karflex Ltd v Poole* [1933] 2 KB 251, at 263–4; *On Demand Information plc v Michael Gerson
(Finance) plc* [2001] 1 WLR 155, at 171; *VFS Financial Services (UK) Ltd v Euro Auctions (UK) Ltd* [2007]
EWHC 1492.   [32] See Bell, *Modern Law of Personal Property* (1989), ch 6.
[33] *Pendragon plc v Walon Ltd* [2005] EWHC 1082.
[34] In *Lord v Price* (1873) LR 9 Exch 54, the buyer of goods in possession of the seller, who had a lien for
the price, could not sue a third party. Is it desirable to prevent the owner from suing a third party if a carrier
has a lien?   [35] *Mulliner v Florence* (1878) 3 QBD 484.
[36] (1866) LR 1 QB 585.

sells the goods because, until the sum owing is paid, there is no immediate right to possession.[37]

(3) Sale

It is often difficult to discover which of the parties to a contract for the sale of goods has an interest sufficient to support an action in conversion. The crucial question is whether, at the date of the alleged conversion, the buyer has a sufficient right to immediate possession of the goods.[38] In *Empresa Exportadora de Azucar v IANSA*,[39] the claimants had contracted to buy, and had paid for, two cargoes of sugar to be shipped to them in Chile by the defendants from Cuba. On the orders of the Cuban Government, after a military takeover in Chile, the ship discharging the first cargo sailed away with the cargo only partially unloaded and the second ship was diverted back to Cuba part way through its voyage. The buyers were held to have an immediate right to possession of both the partially unloaded cargo and the diverted cargo and succeeded in their action for conversion against the sellers.

Sales on credit terms pose rather more difficulties. In *Bloxam v Sanders*[40] it was held that, where goods were sold on credit, the buyer could ordinarily sue the seller in conversion if he wrongfully sold them to a third party, but that, if the seller exercised his right of stoppage *in transitu* upon the buyer becoming insolvent, the buyer could no longer sue. In the absence of credit terms, the buyer, although he may have property in the goods, has no right to immediate possession until he tenders or pays the price.[41]

(4) Licensee

Sometimes a licensee may be able to sue in conversion. In *Northam v Bowden*[42] the claimant had a licence to prospect certain land for tin, and the defendant, without permission, carted away some of the soil on this land. It was held that 'if the claimant had a right to the gravel and soil for the purpose of getting any mineral that could be found in it, he had such a possession of the whole as entitled him to maintain an action for its conversion against a wrongdoer'.[43] Apart from such cases of *profits à prendre*, licensees of goods are bailees and call for no separate treatment.

(5) Finder[44]

The rule that possession is sufficient to ground a claim in conversion means that, in certain circumstances, someone who finds a chattel can keep it and protect his right to do so against third parties. The rules regarding finding were authoritatively settled

---

[37] *Halliday v Holgate* (1868) LR 3 Exch 299. Cf *Bradley v Copley* (1845) 1 CB 685. The assignee of a bill of sale which authorises the borrower to remain in possession of the goods cannot sue in conversion for a wrongful seizure of the goods by a sheriff, because, until the assignee has demanded payment and been refused, or the borrower has otherwise defaulted in payment, he has no immediate right to possession.

[38] See, eg, *Wood v Bell* (1856) 5 E & B 772.   [39] [1983] 2 Lloyd's Rep 171.

[40] (1825) 4 B & C 941.   [41] Cf *Chinery v Viall* (1860) 5 H & N 288.   [42] (1855) 11 Exch 70.

[43] (1855) 11 Exch 70, at 73.   [44] Hickey, *Property and the Law of Finders* (2010).

in *Parker v British Airways Board* although, as Donaldson LJ pointed out in that case, their application to particular cases is often difficult.

> The finder of a chattel acquires rights over it if the true owner is unknown and the chattel appears to have been abandoned or lost and he takes it into his care and control. He acquires a right to keep it against all but the true owner or one who can assert a prior right to keep the chattel which was subsisting at the time when the finder took the chattel into his care and control.[45]

In the classic case of *Armory v Delamirie*,[46] a chimney sweep's boy who found a jewel was able to sue when the goldsmith's apprentice to whom he had handed the jewel for valuation refused to return it to him. On the other hand, any employee or agent who finds goods in the course of his employment does so on behalf of his employer, who acquires a finder's rights. Anyone with finder's rights has an obligation to take reasonable steps to trace the true owner.[47]

Finally, an occupier of land or a building has rights superior to those of a finder over goods in, under, or attached to that land or building. Thus, a medieval gold brooch buried eight inches under the soil in a public park found by the use of a metal detector,[48] and a prehistoric boat embedded in the soil six feet below the surface,[49] belonged to the respective landowners. Similar rules apply to ships, vehicles, and aircraft. Yet an occupier of premises has rights superior to those of a finder over goods upon or in, but not attached to, the premises only if, before the finding, he has manifested an intention to exercise control over the building and the things which may be upon it or in it.[50]

(6) *Jus tertii* (third party rights)

By virtue of the Torts (Interference with Goods) Act 1977,[51] the defendant in an action for conversion or other wrongful interference is entitled to prove that a third party has a better right than the claimant with respect to all or any part of the interest claimed by the claimant. The aims of this provision are to avoid a multiplicity of actions by allowing interested third parties to apply to be joined in actions, to protect defendants against the risk of being liable to two different claimants in respect of the same interference, and to limit the claimant's damages to his actual loss. The relevant date for ascertaining the interest of the third party is the date of the alleged conversion.[52]

Although the Act abolished the former principle that a possessor of goods could recover for the full amount of their value although he was not the owner, and even

---

[45] [1982] QB 1004, at 1017.   [46] (1722) 1 Stra 505.

[47] Cf Hickey, *Property and the Law of Finders* (2010), 4, summarising the thesis that 'English law can...be shown to encourage a finder to act in favour of the loser, but it does not do so by imposing a specific obligation'.

[48] *Waverley BC v Fletcher* [1996] QB 334. See also *South Staffordshire Water Co v Sharman* [1896] 2 QB 44.   [49] *Elwes v Brigg Gas Co* (1886) 33 Ch D 562.

[50] *Parker v British Airways Board* [1982] QB 1004. In similar vein see *Bridges v Hawkesworth* (1851) 21 LJQB 75 and *Hannah v Peel* [1945] KB 509. Cf *London Corpn v Appelyard* [1963] 2 All ER 834.

[51] Torts (Interference with Goods) Act 1977, s 8(1).

[52] *De Franco v MPC* (1987) *Times*, 8 May.

though he was not personally liable to the owner to that extent, it is unclear whether the Act has this effect where the relevant third party cannot be found or joined in the proceedings.[53] That said, the rules do abolish the principle that a bailee is estopped from denying the bailor's title: when sued by his bailor, he can now have a named third party joined in.

(B) THE SUBJECT MATTER

Any goods can be converted. Although cheques are of value only as *choses in action*, the courts have allowed the full value represented by them to be recovered in conversion, except where the cheque has been altered so as to become a worthless piece of paper.[54] So, where bankers do not handle actual cash, but merely make the appropriate entries by credit or debit balances, the courts treat the conversion as being of the cheque under which the money was transferred, and the value as the sum represented by the cheque.[55] This doctrine, applicable to all negotiable instruments, shows that conversion may occasionally lie in respect of rights in intangible property. But this is not the limit. In *Bavins Jnr and Sims v London and South Western Bank*,[56] the Court of Appeal thought that the full value of a non-negotiable document evidencing a debt could be recovered in an action for conversion. Equally, any intangible right that is represented in the ordinary course of business by a special written instrument, even though not negotiable, seems to be recoverable. Thus, a life insurance policy[57] or a guarantee[58] may also be converted.

In *OBG Ltd v Allan*,[59] the House of Lords was faced with the argument that the tort of conversion should be extended beyond the class of document cases just referred to so as to encompass a chose in action in the form of debts and contractual liabilities.[60] By a majority, the House rejected extension of the tort beyond those cases in which rights are recorded in a document.[61] Lord Hoffmann saw the document cases as consistent with the *historical development* of conversion as protective of tangibles only and (implicitly) saw any further extension as altering the nature of the tort. This was countered by strong arguments from the dissentients Lord Nicholls and Baroness Hale, who saw the *logic* of extending the tort. Lord Nicholls thought that:

> The existence of a document is essentially irrelevant. Intangible rights can be misappropriated even if they are not recorded in a document. In principle an intangible right not

---

[53] See, eg, *The Winkfield* [1902] P 42, for the pre-Act principle. Notwithstanding the literal wording of the Act, it seems that the rule in *The Winkfield* may have survived in such circumstances: see *Costello v CC of Derbyshire Constabulary* [2001] 1 WLR 1437.   [54] *Smith v Lloyd's TSB Group plc* [2001] QB 541.

[55] *Lloyds Bank v Chartered Bank of India, Australia and China* [1929] 1 KB 40, at 55–6.

[56] [1900] 1 QB 270.

[57] *Wills v Wells* (1818) 2 Moore CP 247; *Watson v MacLean* (1858) EB & E 75.

[58] *M'Leod v M'Ghie* (1841) 2 Man & G 326.   [59] [2007] UKHL 21.

[60] These were property because they were 'transferable and therefore had an exchange value': Green (2008) 71 MLR 114, at 118.   [61] [2007] UKHL 21, at [94], [271], and [321].

recorded in writing may merit protection just as much as a right which is recorded in this way.[62]

This is the preferable view. It recognises that a document is ordinarily to be treated as nothing more than evidence of a right; it is not conclusive proof of a right.[63] Relevant rights are, these days, just as likely to be recorded electronically as in 'hard copy' form.[64] Moreover, as Baroness Hale observed, 'it makes no sense that the Defendants should be strictly liable for what is lost on the tangible assets but not for what was lost on the intangibles'.[65]

Advances in medical science pose some further, fascinating problems, in this case concerning property rights in human body products. For example, if a husband about to undergo chemotherapy stores sperm to enable his wife to conceive via artificial insemination at some later date, is the sperm bank liable for conversion if it takes that sperm and uses it, without the donor's consent, to inseminate a patient other than his wife? The authorities that would assist in answering this question are inconsistent. In *Dobson v North Tyneside Health Authority*,[66] the claimants' daughter's brain was removed after she had died in hospital. The brain was initially stored at the second defendant's hospital, but then subsequently disposed of. The claimants sued in conversion alleging that the defendants' failure to keep and preserve the brain deprived them of the opportunity to discover whether the deceased's tumours were benign or malignant. The Court of Appeal dismissed the claim for conversion, reaffirming the principle that generally there is no property right in a corpse, or its parts. Only where some significant process has been undertaken to alter that body, or preserve it for scientific or exhibition purposes, can any title to the body be claimed.[67]

Dobson expressly addressed property in tissues and organs taken from the dead. But *obiter dicta* in the case suggest that a similar approach should be taken in relation to products taken from living human bodies. Indeed, the fact that section 32 of the Human Tissue Act 2004 prohibits commercial dealings in organs for transplant has been argued to be indicative of 'a legislative intent to preclude actions for damages reckoned by their value'.[68]

The question posed above, about the status of stored sperm, came before the Court of Appeal in *Yearworth v North Bristol NHS Trust*.[69] Although the claims for accidental

[62] [2007] UKHL 21, at [230].

[63] There are exceptions to this, eg Statute of Frauds Amendment Act 1828, s 6.

[64] See S Green (2008) 71 MLR 114, 117. See also *Thunder Air Ltd v Hilmarsson* [2008] EWHC 355, at [28]–[29].

[65] [2007] UKHL 21, at [311]. See also Green and Randall, *The Tort of Conversion* (2009), ch 5. Contra Tettenborn 'Intentional Interference with Chattels' in Sappideen and Vines (eds), *Fleming's the Law of Torts* (2011), 68.

[66] [1996] 4 All ER 474.

[67] *AB v Leeds Teaching Hospital* (2004) 77 BMLR 145. So, a museum possessing a valuable Egyptian mummy can assert a claim to that mummy, and, apparently, doctors who deliberately preserved a two-headed foetus could maintain a similar claim: *Doodeward v Spence* (1908) 6 CLR 406. And see now *R v Kelly* [1998] 3 All ER 741.   [68] *Clerk and Lindsell on Torts* (2006), 1024.

[69] [2009] EWCA Civ 37.

destruction of the sperm brought by men who had entered into agreements[70] with the defendant Health Trust for its storage were brought in negligence, the case points towards the availability of an action in conversion. An important issue was whether or not the loss of the sperm constituted damage to the men's property.[71] The court concluded that, although the Human Tissue Act 2004 circumscribed the ability of the men to direct the use of their stored sperm, they had property in it. Steps in the chain of reasoning included the following: First, 'a distinction between the capacity to own body parts or products which have, and which have not, been subject to the exercise of work or skill is not entirely logical'.[72] Second, the men alone generated by their bodies and ejaculated the sperm. Third, the 'sole object of their ejaculation of the sperm was that, in certain events, it might later be used for their benefit'.[73] Fourth, the men retained absolute negative control over the use of the sperm in the sense that they could direct that it not be used in certain ways. Related to this was the fact that 'the Act recognises in the men a fundamental feature of ownership, namely that at any time they can require the destruction of [stored] sperm'.[74] The court concluded that the defendant was liable for losses in tort and also for breach of a bailment agreement. 'The law of bailment provides them with a remedy under which, in principle, they are entitled to compensation for any psychiatric injury (or actionable distress) foreseeably consequent upon the breach'.[75]

Given the reasoning and the result in *Yearworth*, it is not surprising that it has been argued that an action must now lie in conversion for damage to or destruction of sperm[76] – and presumably other bodily parts or products capable of designation as property where brought by their 'originators'.[77] The difficulty, such as it is, would lie in proving possession, or an immediate right to possession of the sperm, stored professionally with a hospital.

(C) TYPE OF ACT

Save for the statutory conversion created by section 2(2) of the Torts (Interference with Goods Act 1977), there can only be a conversion if there is *positive conduct* that interferes with the claimant's goods. *Ashby v Tolhurst*[78] is illustrative.

> A third party had driven away C's car, which he had left in D's car park. At the trial, C gave evidence that the attendant told him that he had 'given' the car to the third party.

---

[70] These were not for consideration; thus no suit could be brought for breach of contract. Claims included damages for psychiatric injury following the accidental destruction of the sperm.

[71] [2009] EWCA Civ 37, at [14]–[15] and [26].

[72] Ibid at [45-d].   [73] Ibid at [45-f].

[74] Ibid at [45-f].   [75] Ibid at [58].

[76] Hawes (2010) 73 MLR 130.

[77] The wider applicability of the principle from this case is foreshadowed in the judgment itself: see [2007] EWCA Civ 37, at [45-f] (example of severed finger). Commentators have presumed that claims may now be made with respect to human tissue in general: Harmon and Laurie [2010] CLJ 476.

[78] [1937] 2 KB 242.

His case in conversion rested upon the assertion that this word 'imports that the attendant took some active step to place this thief in possession of the motor car' but it was found 'impossible to collect that meaning out of the words'. There was therefore no conversion, quite apart from the fact that the conditions on the ticket were also deemed to exclude liability.

If the defendant deals with the goods in a manner which interferes with the claimant's possession or immediate right to possession, his act will constitute conversion, even if he does not 'intend to challenge the property or possession of the true owner'.[79] In other words, liability is strict and it matters not that the defendant commits a conversion by mistake or in good faith.[80] So, vis-à-vis the true owner, it is no defence for an auctioneer, after selling goods on behalf of a client, honestly delivering them to the buyer, and paying the proceeds of sale to his client, to say that he was unaware that his client did not own the goods.[81] On the other hand, if the auctioneer simply redelivers the goods to the apparent owner, there is no conversion since redelivery (as opposed to sale) changes only the position of the goods, not the property in them.[82]

(D) EXAMPLES OF ACTIONS AMOUNTING TO CONVERSION

In some instances, especially those involving a sale of goods, it is eminently clear that the act is sufficiently inconsistent with the rightful possessor's rights to be conversion. In many other instances, however, the courts have a discretion as to whether they will treat the act as sufficiently inconsistent with the possessor's rights to be conversion. This is particularly true in the case of physical damage to the goods and breach of bailment. Regrettably, the courts have not spelt out fully the factors which go to the exercise of their discretion. But the most important are probably the extent and duration of the control or dominion exercised over the goods, the amount of damage to the goods, and the cost and inconvenience to the rightful possessor.[83]

---

[79] *Caxton Publishing Co Ltd v Sutherland Publishing Co* [1939] AC 178, at 202; *Douglas Valley Finance Co Ltd v S Hughes (Hirers) Ltd* [1969] 1 QB 738.

[80] *Fowler v Hollins* (1872) LR 7 QB 616, at 639; affirmed sub nom *Hollins v Fowler* (1875) LR 7 HL 757 (followed in *Union Transport Finance Ltd v British Car Auctions Ltd* [1978] 2 All ER 385, and *R H Willis & Son v British Car Auctions Ltd* [1978] 2 All ER 392). See also *OGB Ltd v Allan* [2007] UKHL 21, at [95] and [311]. The policy reason for this is to ensure that those who deal with goods first ascertain title to them: Green and Randall, *The Tort of Conversion* (2009), 71–3.

[81] *Consolidated Co v Curtis & Son* [1892] 1 QB 495. In *Moorgate Mercantile Co Ltd v Finch and Read* [1962] 1 QB 701, the borrower of a car had it confiscated upon conviction for carrying in it watches not declared to Customs. This was held to be a conversion, for the confiscation was the result of his intentional act of carrying the watches in the car. See also *Chubb Cash Ltd v John Crilley & Son* [1983] 2 All ER 294. Contra Douglas [2009] CLJ 198, at 216.   [82] *Marcq v Christie Manson and Wood Ltd* [2004] QB 286.

[83] As indicated, conversion is a tort of strict liability. This said, intention is sometimes important in characterising the nature of the defendant's act: Green and Randall, *The Tort of Conversion* (2009), 68. However, we do not mention this factor in the body of the text so as to avoid unnecessary confusion.

(1) Taking goods or dispossessing

To take goods out of the possession of another may be to convert them. To steal, or to seize under legal process without justification,[84] is certainly conversion. If, after lopping off the branches of his neighbour's apple tree when they overhang his land, a householder appropriates the fruit, he also commits conversion.[85] Merely to move goods from one place to another, however, is not conversion.[86] Thus, where a porter moved another's goods in order to reach his own, and negligently failed to replace them, he was not liable in conversion for their subsequent loss.[87] It may be conversion, however, if they are moved to an unreasonable place with an intrinsic risk of loss. In *Forsdick v Collins*,[88] for instance, the defendant came into possession of land on which the claimant had a block of Portland stone and the removal of the Portland stone by the defendant 'to a distance' was held to be a conversion. A deprivation of goods that is more than a mere moving (that is, it deprives the claimant of their use for however long), will be conversion,[89] as will forcing the claimant to hand over goods under duress.[90]

(2) Destroying or altering

To destroy goods is to convert them, if the destruction is voluntary.[91] The quantum of harm constituting a destruction for this purpose is clearly a question of degree, but mere damage is not a conversion.[92] A change of identity not amounting to destruction is also enough. For example, to draw out part of a vessel of liquor and fill it up with water is conversion;[93] but perhaps merely to cut a log in two is not.[94] If goods are used for a purpose which eliminates their utility as goods in their original form – for example, making a fur coat from animal skins – this is conversion.[95] But it is not conversion to bottle another's wine in order to preserve it.[96]

(3) Using

To use goods as one's own is ordinarily to convert them. It was thus conversion for a person, to whom carbolic acid drums were delivered by mistake, to deal with them

---

[84] *Tinkler v Poole* (1770) 5 Burr 2657; *Burton v Hughes* (1824) 2 Bing 173; *Chubb Cash Ltd v John Crilley & Son* [1983] 2 All ER 294.   [85] *Mills v Brooker* [1919] 1 KB 555.

[86] *Fouldes v Willoughby* (1841) 8 M & W 540.   [87] *Bushel v Miller* (1718) 1 Stra 128.

[88] (1816) 1 Stark 173. Cf *Sanderson v Marsden and Jones* (1922) 10 Ll L Rep 467.

[89] *Empresa Exportadora de Azucar v IANSA* [1983] 2 Lloyd's Rep 171. But see to the contrary *384238 Ontario Ltd v Canada* (1983) 8 DLR (4th) 676.   [90] *Grainger v Hill* (1838) 4 Bing NC 212.

[91] Purely accidental destruction is not conversion: *Simmons v Lillystone* (1853) 8 Exch 431.

[92] *Fouldes v Willoughby* (1841) 8 M & W 540, at 549.   [93] *Richardson v Atkinson* (1723) 1 Stra 576.

[94] *Simmons v Lillystone* (1853) 8 Exch 431, at 442.

[95] *Jones v de Marchant* (1916) 28 DLR 561 (approved in *Foskett v McKeown* [2001] 1 AC 102). In such cases, the owner of the materials becomes the owner of the product if the material can be wholly or substantially identified in the product: *Glencore International AG v Metro Trading International Inc* [2001] 1 Lloyd's Rep 284.   [96] *Philpott v Kelley* (1835) 3 Ad & El 106.

as his own by pouring the contents into his tank.[97] Equally, a claim 'would not be defeated by the fact that the defendant whom he sues for the misuse of his temporary dominion of the property claims to be an agent for someone else'.[98] However, a mere misuse by a bailee, unaccompanied by any denial of title, is not a conversion, although it may constitute some other tort.[99]

(4) Receipt, disposition, and delivery

Voluntarily[100] to receive goods in consummation of a transaction intended by the parties to give to the recipient some proprietary rights in the goods may be a conversion actionable by the owner.[101] It has been held to be a conversion for a purchaser so to receive goods from someone who has no title.[102] If, however, the defendant receives the goods in good faith for the purposes of storage or transport,[103] he does not commit conversion because there is no assertion of a proprietary interest in the goods. Receipt of goods by way of pledge is conversion if the delivery is conversion.[104]

In relation to disposition and delivery, there is generally no conversion where a person agrees to sell goods to which he has no title, but does not transfer possession of them. This is because bargain and sale are void if the seller has no rights in the goods.[105] On the other hand, a person who without lawful authority disposes of goods with the intention of transferring the title to another, and does deliver the goods, thereby commits a conversion. A sale and a pledge[106] may each constitute such a disposition. In *Syeds v Hay*[107] a sea-captain was liable for delivering goods to another in the wrongful belief that he had a lien on them. In certain circumstances, however, the courts and Parliament have developed exceptions to the *nemo dat* rule (whereby a person who does not have good title may not pass a good title to another). The nature of, and reasons for, these exceptions are not dealt with here, however, for they are properly to be seen as matters of commercial (not tort) law.[108]

---

[97] *Lancashire and Yorkshire Rly Co v MacNicoll* (1918) 88 LJKB 601. It has also been said that '[t]he wearing of a peal is conversion': *Lord Petre v Heneage* (1701) 12 Mod Rep 519, at 520. See also examples in *Mulgrave v Ogden* (1591) Cro Eliz 219.

[98] *Morison v London County and Westminster Bank Ltd* [1914] 3 KB 356, at 386 (*obiter*).

[99] *Lee v Atkinson and Brooks* (1609) Yelv 172; approved in *Donald v Suckling* (1866) LR 1 QB 585, at 615, per Blackburn J, who said that if the act is repugnant to the bailment, it is conversion, but 'where the act, though unauthorised, is not repugnant to the contract as to show a disclaimer' it is not. See also *BMW Financial Services (GB) Ltd v Bhagawani* [2007] EWCA Civ 1230; *Penfolds Wines Pty Ltd v Elliott* (1946) 74 CLR 204. [100] Receipt by an involuntary bailee is not conversion.

[101] Cf *M'Combie v Davies* (1805) 6 East 538, at 540.: [102] *Farrant v Thompson* (1822) 5 B & Ald 826.

[103] *Hollins v Fowler* (1875) LR 7 HL 757, at 767. Cf *Sheridan v New Quay Co* (1858) 4 CBNS 618.

[104] Sale of Goods Act 1979, s 11(2).

[105] *Lancashire Waggon Co v Fitzhugh* (1861) 6 H & N 502; he may, however, be liable for malicious falsehood: see ch 13. [106] *Parker v Godin* (1728) 2 Stra 813.

[107] (1791) 4 Term Rep 260. But if someone entrusts another with a chattel to be used by him, the bailor impliedly authorises the bailee to allow a lien for the cost of necessary repairs to be created over it: *Green v All Motors Ltd* [1917] 1 KB 625; *Tappenden v Artus* [1964] 2 QB 185.

[108] Some illustrative cases were discussed in the 10th edition of this book.

(5) Misdelivery by carrier

A carrier[109] or warehouseman[110] who, by mistake, delivers goods to the wrong person commits a conversion, whether or not his mistake is innocent.[111] But failure to deliver because the goods have been lost or destroyed by accident or carelessness is not conversion.[112] Nor is it conversion for a bailee[113] or pledgee[114] without notice of the claim of the true owner to return goods to the person from whom he received them.

(6) Refusal to surrender on demand

A refusal to surrender goods upon lawful and reasonable demand is a conversion.[115] In particular, this covers the situation where the possession of the defendant was originally lawful. It may be invoked, for example, where the receiving is not itself actionable. The most important case since the abolition of detinue by the Torts (Interference with Goods) Act 1977 is *Howard E Perry & Co Ltd v British Railways Board*.[116]

> The defendants, fearing industrial action by their employees during a national steelworkers strike, refused to surrender to the claimants steel belonging to the claimants that was being held in the defendants' depots. The defendants admitted that the claimants were entitled to immediate possession and it was held that their refusal to allow the claimants to enter the depots and collect the steel was wrongful.

There is a large amount of case law on this topic, but the principles are quite simple. Even if the defendant no longer has possession at the time of the demand and refusal, it is no defence for him to prove that, prior to the accrual of the claimant's title, he wrongfully parted with them.[117] On the other hand, the defendant may postpone surrender until after he has had a reasonable time in which to confirm the title of the claimant,[118] or, if he is an employee, to consult his employer.[119] This reasonableness is a question of fact. Many factors may be relevant – the time of the demand, the expense and inconvenience of immediate compliance, the knowledge on the part of the defendant of the claimant's title, and of his identity, and whether the defendant has adequately conveyed to the claimant the grounds for his temporary refusal. An

---

[109] *Youl v Harbottle* (1791) Peake 68, NP.   [110] *Devereux v Barclay* (1819) 2 B & Ald 702.

[111] If the carrier delivers in accordance with the seller's instructions (or even as a carrier would interpret his instructions according to the usual course of business although he in fact delivered them to a person to whom the seller did not intend delivery to be made) this is not a mis-delivery: *McKean v McIvor* (1870) LR 6 Exch 36. It is conversion by a carrier to deliver goods to another carrier by whom they are misappropriated, unless D carrier is authorised to sub-contract: *Garnham, Harris and Elton Ltd v Alfred W Ellis (Transport) Ltd* [1967] 2 All ER 940.   [112] *Owen v Lewyn* (1672) 1 Vent 223; *The Arpad* [1934] P 189, at 232.

[113] *Hollins v Fowler* (1875) LR 7 HL 757, at 767. Otherwise the bailee would be in an impossible position, for if he retained the goods he could not plead a title paramount of which he was unaware.

[114] *Union Credit Bank Ltd v Mersey Docks and Harbour Board* [1899] 2 QB 205.

[115] *Marcq v Christie Manson and Wood Ltd* [2004] QB 286; *Isaack v Clark* (1615) 2 Bulst 306, at 310.

[116] [1980] 2 All ER 579.   [117] *Bristol and West of England Bank v Midland Rly Co* [1891] 2 QB 653.

[118] *Clayton v Le Roy* [1911] 2 KB 1031. Cf *Gough v CC of West Midlands* [2004] EWCA Civ 206.

[119] *Alexander v Southey* (1821) 5 B & Ald 247.

estoppel may sometimes operate to prevent the defendant from setting up facts which would otherwise have justified a refusal.[120]

If an auctioneer redelivers goods to their apparent owner after he has failed to sell those goods, he cannot be held liable in conversion upon the suit of the rightful possessor so long as his redelivery was made in good faith and without knowledge of the true owner's title.[121]

(7) Goods lost or destroyed

At common law there could be no conversion where there was no voluntary act. Section 2(2) of the Torts (Interference with Goods) Act 1977 therefore provides as follows:

> An action lies in conversion for loss or destruction of goods which a bailee has allowed to happen in breach of his duty to his bailor (that is to say it lies in a case which is not otherwise conversion, but would have been detinue before detinue was abolished).

Bailees are required to take reasonable care of goods in their keeping and are liable for the loss or destruction of such goods unless they can disprove fault;[122] but they are not insurers of the goods. In *Sutcliffe v Chief Constable of West Yorkshire*[123] an arson attack destroyed the claimant's car, which had been lawfully seized by the police and which was being held in a police station yard. The Court of Appeal dismissed the claimant's claim for conversion. The attack was unprecedented, and in respect of the claimant's property the defendant had done all that was reasonable to take care of the vehicle.

Denial of title is not of itself conversion.[124] There may, however, be conversion of goods although the defendant has not physically dealt with them,[125] or been in physical possession of them,[126] if his acts deprive the claimant of his right to possession or amount to a substantial interference with that right.[127] But a mere threat to prevent an owner in possession from removing his goods will not of itself amount to conversion.[128]

Where goods are left on land and occupier B acquires the land on which the goods lie from occupier A, then, if occupier B refuses to allow the rightful possessor to enter

---

[120] *Seton, Laing & Co v Lafone* (1887) 19 QBD 68; *Henderson & Co v Williams* [1895] 1 QB 521.

[121] *Marcq v Christie Manson and Wood Ltd* [2004] QB 286.

[122] A bailee will ordinarily be liable unless he disproves fault: *Houghland v RR Low (Luxury Coaches) Ltd* [1962] 1 QB 694. An involuntary bailee is not liable for failure to return merely because he has lost the goods: *Howard v Harris* (1884) 1 Cab & El 253. However, he is liable if he destroys or damages the goods. If the bailee is unaware that the goods on his premises are not his property (ie, he is an 'unconscious bailee'), he is under a duty to exercise reasonable care to ascertain that they were his own before he destroys them: *AVX Ltd v EGM Solders Ltd* (1982) *Times*, 7 July.   [123] [1996] RTR 86.

[124] Torts (Interference with Goods) Act 1977, s 11(3).

[125] *Van Oppen & Co Ltd v Tredegars Ltd* (1921) 37 TLR 504.

[126] Eg, *Oakley v Lyster* [1931] 1 KB 148.

[127] *Lancashire and Yorkshire Rly Co, London and NW Rly Co and Graeser Ltd v MacNicoll* (1918) 88 LJKB 601; *Oakley v Lyster* [1931] 1 KB 148, at 156; *Club Cruise Entertainment and Travelling Services Europe BV v Department for Transport* [2008] EWHC 2794, at [51].   [128] *England v Cowley* (1873) LR 8 Exch 126.

the land and retrieve them, the refusal is not necessarily conversion.[129] It may become conversion, however, if occupier B himself asserts any right in respect of the goods,[130] or denies the claimant the right to possession for a period which is plainly indefinite.[131] But this needs to be established as a question of fact.

(8) Residual acts amounting to conversion

The foregoing categories of conversion are not exhaustive. There are other acts, not capable of being readily classified, which may yet fall within the definition of conversion.[132] In these residual cases, judicial discretion to treat the act as sufficiently inconsistent with the rightful possessor's rights for a conversion is especially important.

(E) CONVERSION AS BETWEEN CO-OWNERS[133]

Section 10(1)(a) of the Torts (Interference with Goods) Act 1977 provides that co-ownership is no defence to an action founded on conversion where the defendant, without the authority of the other co-owner, destroys the goods, or disposes of them in a way giving a good title to the entire property in the goods, or otherwise does anything equivalent to the destruction of the other interest in the goods. Thus, a partner who paid cheques into a third person's bank account was, by excluding his co-owner's right to enjoy the proceeds, liable for conversion.[134] A co-owner cannot, however, be sued for conversion if he merely makes use of the common property in a reasonable way.[135] Nor was there necessarily a conversion where the co-owner took and kept the goods.[136] The law requires a destruction of the goods or something equivalent to it.[137] The Torts (Interference with Goods) Act 1977 further provides in section 10(1)(b) that it is also no defence to an action founded on conversion where the defendant, without the authority of the other co-owner, purports to dispose of the goods in such a way as would give a good title to the entire property in the goods if he were acting with the authority of all the co-owners of the goods.

---

[129] *Wilde v Waters* (1855) 24 LJCP 193, at 195; *British Economical Lamp Co Ltd v Empire Mile End Lane Ltd* (1913) 29 TLR 386.

[130] *Walker v Clyde* (1861) 10 CBNS 381; *H E Dibble Ltd v Moore* [1970] 2 QB 181.

[131] *Howard E Perry & Co Ltd v British Rlys Board* [1980] 2 All ER 579, at 583; *Bryanston Leasings Ltd v Principality Finance Ltd* [1977] RTR 45.

[132] See the dictum of Bramwell B in *England v Cowley* (1873) LR 8 Exch 126.

[133] Note the Sale of Goods Act 1979, ss 20A and 20B whereby a buyer of a quantity of goods forming part of a larger bulk becomes a proportionate co-owner of those goods.

[134] *Baker v Barclays Bank Ltd* [1955] 2 All ER 571.

[135] As, for instance, by cutting grass and making hay in the common field (*Jacobs v Seward* (1872) LR 5 HL 464) or extracting the oil and the other valuable parts of a dead whale which is owned in common: *Fennings v Lord Grenville* (1808) 1 Taunt 241.

[136] The bailee of common property from one co-owner is not guilty of conversion if he refuses to deliver the property on the demand of another co-owner (*Atwood v Ernest* (1853) 13 CB 881; *Harper v Godsell* (1870) LR 5 QB 422) unless the latter has a special property in the entire chattel (*Nyberg v Handelaar* [1892] 2 QB 202).   [137] *Morgan v Marquis* (1853) 9 Exch 145; *Baker v Barclays Bank Ltd* [1955] 2 All ER 571.

These rules do not affect the law concerning execution or enforcement of judgments, or the law concerning any form of distress.[138]

(F) DAMAGES[139]

As was noted at the start of this chapter, the major impact of the Torts (Interference with Goods) Act 1977 was to rationalise the remedies available to claimants suing in conversion, both in relation to the damages which may be awarded and in making provision for specific return of the goods by way of orders for delivery. Relevant provisions are noted in the exposition of principles that follows. On the other hand, the related issue of remoteness of damage is still governed by the common law, and the test is one of reasonable foreseeability.[140]

The claimant, in conversion, is entitled to be compensated to the extent of the value to him of the goods of which he has been deprived. The prima facie measure of damages is the market value of the goods at the time of conversion.[141] Where goods are of a kind which can be readily bought in the market, the actual market value will be the appropriate measure; otherwise the replacement value in a comparable state,[142] or the original cost minus depreciation will be the standard. It is for the defendant to argue that the appropriate compensatory figure is a lower one.[143]

Consistent with this, the manufacturer of goods who has a contract for their sale is prima facie entitled to the sale value of the goods, including the profit component. It is for the defendant to prove that alleged loss of profits will be recouped by alternative sales.[144] 'It is not for the Claimant to prove a negative, that he has not recouped the

---

[138] Torts (Interference with Goods) Act 1977, s 11(2). The rules apply equally to intentional trespass to goods as they apply to conversion.

[139] See Tettenborn [1993] CLJ 128; id, 'Conversion, Tort and Restitution' in Palmer and McKendrick (eds), *Interests in Goods* (1998).

[140] *Saleslease Ltd v Davis* [1999] 1 WLR 1664; *Kuwait Airways Corpn v Iraqi Airways Co (Nos 4 and 5)* [2001] 3 WLR 1117. At common law, the claimant with a limited interest in the goods could normally recover their full value from a third party. Under s 8 of the Torts (Interference with Goods) Act 1977 and rules of court, however, the claimant now has to identify any other person whom he knows to have an interest in the goods and any such interested party may be joined, whereupon the damages may be apportioned among the interested parties in proportion to their respective interests: Torts (Interference with Goods) Act 1977, s 7(2). Where the other interested party is not traced – as in cases of finding, or a missing bailor – the claimant in possession can recover the full value of the goods, but is liable to account to the true owner. *Wilson v Lombank Ltd* [1963] 1 All ER 740; *O'Sullivan v Williams* [1992] 3 All ER 385.

[141] *Kuwait Airways Corpn v Iraqi Airways Co (Nos 4 and 5)* [2002] 2 AC 883, at [67]; *Zabihi v Janzemini* [2009] EWCA Civ 851, at [43].

[142] *J & E Hall Ltd v Barclay* [1937] 3 All ER 620; *Wilson v Robertsons (London) Ltd* [2006] EWCA Civ 1088, at [43]–[44].

[143] *Sony Computer Entertainment UK Ltd v Cinram Logistics UK Ltd* [2008] EWCA Civ 955, at [37], [45]–[46], and [49].

[144] Ibid.

profit by a substitute sale, but for the Defendant to prove a positive, that the profit has been recouped and thus the loss of profit not suffered after all'.[145]

Where a negotiable instrument or other document ordinarily representing a *chose in action* is converted, the value which the document represents, and not merely its value as a piece of paper, is the basis of the quantum of damages. On the other hand, as indicated above, a purely intangible *chose in action* cannot be converted.[146]

Once a claim for conversion has accrued to the claimant, it is not open to him to delay the issue of his writ and thereby base his action on a subsequent demand and refusal – the duty to mitigate damages operates.[147] Mitigation requires the claimant to do all those things which are reasonable in order to limit his loss. Reasonable costs of mitigation are recoverable by the claimant.[148]

A rule basing damages on the value at the date of conversion can be seen to work to the claimant's benefit in certain circumstances. If the goods decrease in value between the date of the conversion and the date of judgment, the claimant may still recover the value at the date of conversion.[149] However, the general rule is not immutable. In conversion, as in other torts, the normal purpose of an award of damages is to compensate the claimant for the loss he actually sustains.[150] Thus, the market value (even where ascertainable) at the *date of conversion* will not necessarily mark the top limit of damages recoverable in the following instances.

(1) The market value of the goods rises between the date of the cause of action and *trial*.[151] If the act of conversion relied on by the claimant is a sale, and by the time when the claimant knows or ought to know of the sale the value has increased, the claimant can recover that higher value.[152] There is some authority also for the view that, from a broker who has sold his stock, the claimant may recover its increased value within a reasonable time for buying replacement stock;[153] that is, the court estimates the value of the chance of a profit.[154] *Greening v Wilkinson*[155] is illustrative.

> D refused to hand over to C warrants for cotton belonging to C. At the time of the demand and refusal, the warrants were worth 6d per lb, but at the time of the trial they were worth 10½d per lb. The jury awarded damages on the basis of 10½d per lb in accordance with Abbott CJ's ruling that they 'may give the value at the

---

[145] *Sony Computer Entertainment UK Ltd v Cinram Logistics UK Ltd* [2008] EWCA Civ 955, at [49]. It is more doubtful in what circumstances a buyer who does not recover his goods can claim a *loss of resale profit*: *Strand Electric and Engineering Co Ltd v Brisford Entertainments Ltd* [1952] 2 QB 246, at 255.
[146] *OBG Ltd v Allan* [2007] UKHL 21.
[147] *Empresa Exportadora de Azucar v IANSA* [1983] 2 Lloyd's Rep 171; *Uzinterimpex v Standard Bank* [2008] EWCA Civ 819.   [148] Green and Randall, *The Tort of Conversion* (2009), 205.
[149] *Rhodes v Moules* [1895] 1 Ch 236. See also *Solloway v McLaughlin* [1938] AC 247 and *BBMB Finance v Eda Holdings Ltd* [1991] 2 All ER 129.
[150] *Brandeis Goldschmidt & Co v Western Transport Ltd* [1981] QB 864; *IBL Ltd v Coussens* [1991] 2 All ER 133.   [151] *Trafigura Beheer BV v Mediterranean Shipping Co SA* [2007] EWCA Civ 794, at [38]–[41].
[152] *Sachs v Miklos* [1948] 2 KB 23.   [153] *Samuel and Escombe v Rowe* (1892) 8 TLR 488.
[154] *Aitken v Gardiner* (1956) 4 DLR (2d) 119.   [155] (1825) 1 C & P 625.

time of the conversion, or at any subsequent time, at their discretion, because the [claimant] might have had a good opportunity of selling the goods if they had not been detained'.[156]

(2) Whether or not the claimant incurs pecuniary loss (or a potential pecuniary loss) as a direct consequence of the conversion, he may still recover *special damages* in addition to the market value of the goods. Thus, for example, a workman deprived of his tools recovered loss of wages,[157] and the owner of a converted pony could claim the cost of hiring another.[158] In *Strand Electric and Engineering Co Ltd v Brisford Entertainments Ltd*[159] (a detinue case), it was held to be irrelevant that the claimants would not have been able to hire out for the whole period of that wrongful detention those goods that the defendants wrongfully failed to return. This is because the usual 'but for' test of causation does not apply in conversion.[160] Similarly, in *Kuwait Airways Corp v Iraqi Airways Co (Damages)*,[161] it was held that the claimant was not bound to show any actual or probable loss associated with the wrongful retention of aircraft parts. The claimant was entitled to damages representing a reasonable sum by way of hire or rent. On the other hand, there will be a time limit to the period for which he can claim a loss of hire because there will come a time when he will be expected to obtain an alternative chattel to hire out.[162]

(3) Since the effect of a judgment for damages is to transfer the title to the defendant,[163] it follows that the court will not award damages both for loss of use and for the value of the goods where the effect would be doubly to compensate the claimant. The capacity for profitable use is part of the value of the goods. Thus, where the defendant converted manufacturing plant belonging to the claimant, he was liable for the value of the plant when converted but not for loss of use between that date and trial.[164] On the other hand, if the defendant wrongfully detains goods and later sells them, it seems that the claimant can recover, in addition to their value, for the *loss of use* from the date of the unlawful detention until sale,[165] and indeed until the claimant had a reasonable

---

[156] Lord Porter left open the soundness of this judgment in *Caxton Publishing Co Ltd v Sutherland Publishing Co* [1939] AC 178, at 203.   [157] *Bodley v Reynolds* (1846) 8 QB 779.

[158] *Davis v Oswell* (1837) 7 C & P 804.

[159] [1952] 2 QB 246; confirmed in *Inverugie Investments v Hackett* [1995] 3 All ER 841. Where D converted a Rolls Royce on hire from Cs and then put it out of his power to return it, he remained liable for the hiring charges, which came to over £13,000, until it was returned, although its value when converted was only £7,500: *Hillesden Securities Ltd v Ryjak Ltd* [1983] 2 All ER 184.

[160] *Kuwait Airways Corpn v Iraqi Airways Co (Nos 4 and 5)* [2001] 3 WLR 1117.

[161] [2004] EWHC 2603.   [162] *Greer v Alstons Engineering Sales and Services Ltd* [2003] UKPC 46.

[163] *Ellis v John Stenning & Son* [1932] 2 Ch 81.

[164] *Re Simms, ex p Trustee* [1934] Ch 1.

[165] *Strand Electric and Engineering Co Ltd v Brisford Entertainments Ltd* [1952] 2 QB 246, at 255.

opportunity to buy a replacement after learning of that sale,[166] but not for loss of use until trial.

(4) If the general preconditions necessary for an award of *exemplary damages* (discussed in chapter 26 below) are satisfied, such damages may now be claimed in conversion.[167]

Courts will be assiduous not to over-compensate the claimant. Thus, the following further points must be borne in mind:

(1) If the defendant converts the claimant's goods and then *increases their value*, the claimant cannot ordinarily recover that increased value.[168] Thus, where the defendant converted a partially built ship which he then completed at his own expense, the court's view was that the claimant was entitled to recover the market value of the completed ship less the expense incurred by the defendant in completing it.[169] Where the act of conversion relied on takes place after the improvement made to the goods, section 6(1) of the 1977 Act now applies. If the defendant has improved the goods in the mistaken but honest belief that he had a good title to them, an allowance is made for the extent to which (at the time at which the goods fall to be valued in assessing damages) the value of the goods is attributable to the improvement. If, for example, the improver is sued for later selling the goods, the statutory allowance applies.[170] A similar allowance is enjoyed by purported purchasers of goods improved by another, provided again that the purchaser acted in good faith.[171] Subsequent purchasers enjoy the same protection.[172] Thus, an eventual buyer in good faith of a stolen car when sued by the true owner will have the damages reduced to reflect any improvements made to it since the theft. The Act leaves uncertain whether the common law rule that an improver who did not act in good faith was entitled to a deduction still survives, or whether the statutory requirement of good faith must be taken to supersede the common law.

(2) Where the court orders that the defendant pay damages representing the increased value, as at the date of judgment, of goods converted, this will not be accompanied by an *award of interest on the loss of use of money* that would have been obtained by the claimant on an earlier sale of those goods. To award interest in such a case would lead to a 'double benefit'.[173]

---

[166] *Re Simms, ex p Trustee* [1934] Ch 1, at 30.

[167] *Borders (UK) Ltd v MPC* [2005] EWCA Civ 197.

[168] *Caxton Publishing Co Ltd v Sutherland Publishing Co* [1939] AC 178; *Greenwood v Bennett* [1973] QB 195.

[169] *Reid v Fairbanks* (1853) 13 CB 692.   [170] And see *Munro v Willmott* [1949] 1 KB 295.

[171] Torts (Interference with Goods) Act 1977, s 6(2).

[172] Torts (Interference with Goods) Act 1977, s 6(3).

[173] *Trafigura Beheer BV v Mediterranean Shipping Co SA* [2007] EWCA Civ 794, at [42]–[43].

(3) Although detinue was abolished by section 2(1) of the Torts (Interference with Goods) Act 1977, section 3 of that Act preserved the remedies for what would previously have been detinue by making them available in conversion.[174] Where the defendant has possession of the goods at the time that proceedings are begun, he cannot, by disposing of the goods, reduce to its market value his liability for loss caused by detention of a profit-earning chattel. However, where the remedy lies in damages, while the general rule in conversion is that the value of the converted goods is ascertained at the date of conversion, in detinue it was the date of judgment. The approach under the Act was set out in *IBL Ltd v Coussens*.[175] There, the Court of Appeal held that, in cases of temporary deprivation of property (in this case, two cars), where no irreversible act of conversion is committed, evidence must be adduced as to the true loss suffered by the rightful possessor. The measure of damages was not to be fixed arbitrarily at either the date of conversion or the date of judgment.

(4) If the defendant returns the goods before trial, the courts will reduce the damages in conversion by the amount of its value at that time.[176] In short, the court will not enforce a sale on the defendant, and 'subject to the payment of costs and special damages (if there are any) an action for damages for conversion can always be stayed if the defendant offers to hand over the property in dispute'.[177] The value of the goods when returned is *set off* against the damages calculated per the preceding paragraphs. Where goods acquired by the claimant for use in a manufacturing process have been wrongfully detained but later returned, the claimant must show that a loss of profit or other pecuniary loss has resulted from the detention.[178] If he fails to prove that he would have used the goods at any time before their return, he cannot recover the fall in their market value over the period of their detention and may receive only nominal damages.[179] It will, of course, be otherwise where he purchased the goods for resale during the period of detention.[180]

(5) In the case of a conversion of goods the subject of a *hire purchase agreement*, the interest of the owner and rightful possessor in the goods is diminished by the extent to which payments have been made under the agreement. Its interest is in

---

[174] *Hillesden Securities Ltd v Ryjak Ltd* [1983] 2 All ER 184.   [175] [1991] 2 All ER 133.

[176] *Fisher v Prince* (1762) 3 Burr 1363; *Solloway v McLaughlin* [1938] AC 247.

[177] *USA and Republic of France v Dollfus Mieg et Compagnie SA and Bank of England* [1952] AC 582, at 619.

[178] *Brandeis Goldschmidt & Co Ltd v Western Transport Ltd* [1981] QB 864, at 870; *Williams v Peel River Land and Mineral Co Ltd* (1886) 55 LT 689, at 692–3. See also *Williams v Archer* (1847) 5 CB 318; *Barrow v Arnaud* (1846) 8 QB 595.

[179] *Williams v Peel River Land and Mineral Co Ltd* (1886) 55 LT 689, at 692–3; *Bryanston Leasings Ltd v Principality Finance Ltd* [1977] RTR 45; *Brandeis Goldschmidt & Co Ltd v Western Transport Ltd* [1981] QB 864, at 871.

[180] *Brandeis Goldschmidt & Co Ltd v Western Transport Ltd* [1981] QB 864, at 873.

the value of the outstanding payments. Damages will be reduced accordingly.[181] Thus, in *Wickham Holdings Ltd v Brooke House Motors*,[182] the hirer of a car sold the car in breach of his hire-purchase agreement. The finance company that owned the car was held able to recover from the ultimate purchaser of the vehicle only the value of the outstanding hire-purchase instalments due, and not the higher value of the car itself.[183]

(6) Where the *defendant has an interest* in the goods, the claimant's damages in respect of the interference with his interest are limited to the value of that interest.[184] An unpaid seller who sold to a third party was held liable to the original buyer, to whom he had not delivered the goods,[185] who was not in default, for only the value of the goods less the contract price owing to him.

(G) OTHER REMEDIES

The Torts (Interference with Goods) Act 1977 introduced common remedies for all forms of 'wrongful interferences with goods'. Section 3 provides that in proceedings for conversion, or any other chattel tort, against a person in possession or control of the goods, the following relief may be given, as far as is appropriate:[186] (1) an order for delivery and for payment of any consequential damages;[187] (2) an order for delivery of the goods, but giving the defendant the alternative of paying damages by reference to the value of the goods, together in either alternative with payment of any consequential damages;[188] or (3) damages.[189] The first alternative, involving an order for delivery up, is at the discretion of the court.[190] The attitude of the courts is that such an order should not be made with respect to ordinary articles of commerce with no special interest or value to the claimant.[191]

If it is shown to the court's satisfaction that an order for delivery and payment of any consequential damages has not been complied with, the court may revoke the order

---

[181] *Wickham Holdings Ltd v Brooke House Motors Ltd* [1967] 1 WLR 295; *VFS Financial Services (UK) Ltd v Euro Auctions (UK) Ltd* [2007] EWHC 1492, at [103].

[182] [1967] 1 All ER 117.

[183] Cf *Chubb Cash Ltd v John Crilley & Son (a firm)* [1983] 2 All ER 294.

[184] *Johnson v Stear* (1863) 15 CBNS 330; *Belsize Motor Supply Co v Cox* [1914] 1 KB 244.

[185] If an unpaid seller takes goods out of the buyer's possession he is liable in conversion for the full value of the goods without deduction for the unpaid price: *Healing (Sales) Pty Ltd v Inglis Electrix Pty Ltd* (1968) 42 ALJR 280, following *Gillard v Britton* (1841) 8 M & W 575.

[186] Torts (Interference with Goods) Act 1977, s 3(1). See *Secretary of State for Defence v Guardian Newspapers Ltd* [1985] AC 339.

[187] Torts (Interference with Goods) Act 1977, s 3(2)(a). Cf *Howard E Perry & Co Ltd v British Railways Board* [1980] 2 All ER 579.

[188] Torts (Interference with Goods) Act 1977, s 3(2)(b). For principles governing the application of s 3(2)(b) orders see *IBL Ltd v Coussens* [1991] 2 All ER 133. Cf *Howard E Perry & Co Ltd v British Railways Board* [1980] 2 All ER 579.   [189] Torts (Interference with Goods) Act 1977, s 3(2)(c).

[190] But the claimant may elect as between the second and third remedies where the first is not ordered: Torts (Interference with Goods) Act 1977, s 3(3)(b).

[191] *Whiteley Ltd v Hilt* [1918] 2 KB 808, 809; *Tanks and Vessels Industries Ltd v Devon Cider Co Ltd* [2009] EWHC 1360, at [55]–[56].

(or the relevant part of it)[192] and make an order for payment of damages by reference to the value of the goods.[193] Where an order is made for delivery but giving the defendant the alternative of paying damages,[194] the defendant may satisfy the order by returning the goods at any time before execution of judgment, but without prejudice to liability to pay any consequential damages.[195] Where goods are not detained – for example, where they have been destroyed – the normal form of judgment is for damages.

SECTION 3   TRESPASS TO GOODS

This tort protects several interests. First, like conversion (which is more commonly invoked), this tort also protects the claimant's interest in the possession of his goods. Second, trespass protects his interest in the physical condition of the goods and, third, it protects the inviolability of the goods, so that meddling with the goods, such as wrongful wheel clamping, for example, will constitute trespass to goods.[196]

(A) FORMS OF TRESPASS

Trespass takes various forms. Taking goods out of the possession of another,[197] moving them from one place to another,[198] and even bringing one's person into contact with them[199] have been held to be trespasses.

(B) CHARACTER OF THE DEFENDANT'S ACT

There cannot be a trespass if the interference is indirect.[200] Thus, to lock the room in which the claimant has his goods is not a trespass to them.[201] Although he who mixes a drug with the feed of a racehorse commits a trespass to the feed, he does not commit a trespass to the racehorse when it is later given the feed.[202] And it is unclear whether

---

[192] Torts (Interference with Goods) Act 1977, s 3(4)(a).

[193] Torts (Interference with Goods) Act 1977, s 3(4)(b).

[194] That is, under the Torts (Interference with Goods) Act 1977, s 3(2)(b). An order for delivery of the goods under s 3(2)(a) or 3(2)(b) of the Act may impose such conditions as determined by the court, or pursuant to rules of court and, in particular, where damages by reference to the value of the goods would not be the whole of the value of the goods, C may be required to make an allowance to reflect the difference: s 3(2)(b). Where an allowance is to be made under s 6(1) or 6(2) of the Act in respect of an improvement of the goods, and an order is made under s 3(2)(a) or 3(2)(b), the court may assess the allowance to be made in respect of the improvement and by the order require, as a condition for delivery of the goods, that allowance be made by C.   [195] Torts (Interference with Goods) Act 1977, s 3(5).

[196] *Vine v Waltham Forest LBC* [2000] 1 WLR 2383. Cf *Arthur v Anker* [1997] QB 564.

[197] *Brewer v Dew* (1843) 11 M & W 625.

[198] *Kirk v Gregory* (1876) 1 Ex D 55; *Fouldes v Willoughby* (1841) 8 M & W 540, at 544–5.

[199] *Fouldes v Willoughby* (1841) 8 M & W 540, at 549 (*obiter*): 'Scratching the panel of a carriage would be a trespass'.

[200] *Covell v Laming* (1808) 1 Camp 497. Just as in trespass to the person, there will always be difficult questions of where directness ends and indirectness begins. See, eg, *White v Withers LLP* [2009] EWCA 1122.

[201] *Hartley v Moxham* (1842) 3 QB 701.

[202] *Hutchins v Maughan* [1947] VLR 131.

it is trespass to cause the goods of a claimant to come into harmful contact with some other object; for example, to drive sheep over the edge of a cliff into the sea.[203] It is, however, trespass to goods to beat a dog,[204] to shoot racing pigeons,[205] to cut and take away trees,[206] and to wheel-clamp unlawfully.[207] Whether the goods are capable of being stolen is irrelevant.[208]

A dictum of Lord Blanesburgh in *Leitch & Co Ltd v Leydon*[209] is often cited to support the view that trespass to goods is always actionable per se. But technically the matter was left undecided in that case. Some, on the other hand, state that there is clear authority for the proposition that trespass is actionable per se, but only where there is a dispossession of the claimant. Yet in *Kirk v Gregory*,[210] a woman who moved rings belonging to a man who had just died from one room in his house to another was held liable in nominal damages for this. This case has been treated as consistent with this latter view, but an asportation (that is, a moving of the goods) is not necessarily a dispossession.[211] If in gently reversing my car I touch the bumper of another car, the brake of which has not been applied, and, without damaging it, cause it to move a few inches, I have not dispossessed the owner, though I have asported it.

The question arose in *White v Withers LLP* as to the extent to which the law will, in modern times, tolerate actions in trespass to goods which do not involve interferences of a substantial nature.[212]

> D was a law firm which had been provided by C's wife with C's financial and personal papers for the purposes of divorce proceedings. C had not known of or consented to this action. D had the papers photocopied and returned to C only after significant delay.

Sedley LJ appeared doubtful (on an application to strike out) that a technical breach of the so-called 'Hildebrand rules',[213] which governed a spouse's ability lawfully to photocopy such documents without consent, would sound in damages. Furthermore, he stated: 'The claim for a shilling in damages in order to prove a point and obtain an award of costs is history'.[214] But there are good reasons for making all trespasses to goods actionable per se, and this approach is consistent with the bulk of the authorities as well as the general principle in the trespass torts. Otherwise the law would leave remediless the perhaps not oversensitive person who declined to wear her Armani

---

[203] It is not trespass merely because one's animal inflicts direct injury on goods: see *Manton v Brocklebank* [1923] 2 KB 212, esp at 229.

[204] *Wright v Ramscot* (1667) 1 Saund 84.

[205] *Hamps v Darby* [1948] 2 KB 311.

[206] *Heydon v Smith* (1610) 2 Brownl 328.

[207] *Vine v Waltham Forest LBC* [2000] 1 WLR 2383. It is unlawful to clamp without a licence: see the Private Security Industry Act 2001, s 3(2)(j).

[208] [1948] 2 KB 311, at 322.

[209] [1931] AC 90, at 106.

[210] (1876) 1 Ex D 55.   [211] Cf *Burroughes v Bayne* (1860) 5 H & N 296, at 305–6.

[212] [2009] EWCA 1122. The issue in conversion is different, the court having to find a dealing seriously inconsistent with the rights of another.   [213] *Hildebrand v Hildebrand* [1992] 1 FLR 244.

[214] [2009] EWCA 1122, at [72]. See also ibid at [61].

blouse again after her flatmate had 'borrowed' it to wear to a party. Perhaps the correct question, in concert with other trespasses, is whether the relevant touching was beyond what is acceptable in everyday life.[215] Picking up and admiring a friend's Armani blouse (worth £300) may not be so objectionable as wearing it without her permission. That said, a clear rule is usually better than an unclear rule.

(C) DEFENDANT'S STATE OF MIND

The problem of whether there is liability for trespasses which are neither intentional nor negligent has been examined in chapter 8. The same approach is taken in this context so that there is no liability in respect of an act that is neither intentional nor negligent.[216] There is, then, no liability for an accidental trespass to goods.[217] But, if the defendant intended to interfere, his trespass is intentional even though he did not know that his act amounted to a trespass (for example, if he believed the goods to be his own).

(D) THE INTEREST OF THE CLAIMANT

The claimant must be in possession of the goods at the time of the interference. Possession connotes both the power (*factum*) of exercising physical control and the intention (*animus*) to exercise such control on his own behalf. Whether the claimant is the owner is immaterial. So, if A intends to catch a butterfly, which is in his garden, and before he can do so it flies over to the highway where B catches it, A has no possession – there is *animus* but not *factum*. Lord Esher has said that '[t]he [claimant] in an action of trespass must at the time of the trespass have the present possession of the goods, either actual or constructive, or a legal right to the immediate possession'.[218] Thus, a cyclist leaving his cycle outside a shop remains in possession of it but, if a thief rides away on it, the thief then has possession although he obtained it wrongfully.[219] If a lodger holds goods on sale or return from a shopkeeper, and those goods are seized in pursuance of a lawful execution on the landlord's goods, this is trespass to the

---

[215] Cf trespass to the person: *F v West Berkshire HA* [1989] 2 All ER 545.

[216] *National Coal Board v J E Evans & Co (Cardiff) Ltd* [1951] 2 KB 861. Although the *ratio* is probably that the injury was caused by C's conduct (see esp at 875), all three judges gave considered judgments to the effect that there was no liability for accidental trespass to goods.

[217] In *Manton v Brocklebank* [1923] 2 KB 212, at 229, Atkin LJ held that 'whether a horse directly injures goods, or a dog accomplishes an "asportavit" of a golf ball, he does not involve his owner in liability for trespass to goods, at any rate unless the owner has intentionally caused the act complained of'.

[218] *Johnson v Diprose* [1893] 1 QB 512, at 515.

[219] *Costello v CC of Derbyshire Constabulary* [2001] 1 WLR 1437 (confirms that a thief may sue; thus the police who detain a stolen car are liable to C (not actually the thief) when they are unable to identify the real owner).

lodger.[220] Any bailee, even a gratuitous one,[221] can sue in trespass. The Crown could therefore sue in respect of the loss of Post Office mail. [222] Where a landlord demised land to the claimant for 21 years, with liberty to dig a half acre of brick-earth annually, and to dig in excess of that at an agreed price, the claimant could sue a third party who took away brick-earth from the land.[223] A bailor does not have possession and therefore cannot ordinarily sue in trespass for an act done to the goods bailed.[224] If, however, the bailor has an immediate right to possession as in the case of a bailment at will – for example, where a young man had lent his car to his girlfriend while he was on holiday[225] – he may then sue.[226] If A took B's gun and handed it to C, B could not sue the claimant in trespass (unless he showed that the claimant authorised or ratified A's act), because B would have had no possession at the time when the claimant received possession from A.[227] And if X and Y both claim the right to goods which neither has previously possessed, and in a scuffle for them X snatches them from Y's hand, Y has no possession upon which to found a suit in trespass.[228]

Want of possession precluded success in an action brought by the assignees of a bankrupt against a sheriff who seized goods when unaware of a secret act of bankruptcy by the bankrupt.[229] For the same reason a telephone subscriber would have no action if the police tapped his telephone line. But there are three apparent exceptions to the rule that possession is essential.

(1) In *White v Morris*[230] it was held that, where goods were assigned as security for a loan upon trust to permit the assignor to remain in possession until default in repayment, the assignee could sue in trespass while the goods were still in the assignor's possession. It may be assumed, despite lack of authority for such a general proposition, that all trustees may sue for trespass to goods in the hands of the beneficiary on the basis that they share possession with him.[231]

(2) The title of executors or administrators relates back to the death of the deceased, and this entitles them to sue for a trespass between the date of the death and the date of the grant.[232]

---

[220] *Colwill v Reeves* (1811) 2 Camp 575. Cf Lord Ellenborough (at 576, *obiter*): 'If a man puts corn into my bag…because it is impossible to distinguish what was mine from what was his'.

[221] *Rooth v Wilson* (1817) 1 B & Ald 59.

[222] *The Winkfield* [1902] P 42.

[223] *Attersoll v Stevens* (1808) 1 Taunt 183.

[224] *Gordon v Harper* (1796) 7 Term Rep 9; *Ward v Macauley* (1791) 4 Term Rep 489. Cf *United States of America and Republic of France v Dollfus Mieg et Cie SA* [1952] AC 582, at 611.

[225] *O'Sullivan v Williams* [1992] 3 All ER 385.

[226] *Lotan v Cross* (1810) 2 Camp 464; *Penfolds Wines Pty Ltd v Elliott* (1946) 74 CLR 204, at 226–8.

[227] *Wilson v Barker* (1833) 4 B & Ad 614. Cf *Badkin v Powell* (1776) 2 Cowp 476. See also *Wilson v Lombank Ltd* [1963] 1 All ER 740.

[228] *Peachey v Wing* (1826) 5 LJOSKB 55.

[229] *Balme v Hutton* (1833) 9 Bing 471. See also *Taylor v Rowan* (1835) 7 C & P 70. Cf *Wennhak v Morgan* (1888) 20 QBD 635.

[230] (1852) 11 CB 1015.

[231] See *Barker v Furlong* [1891] 2 Ch 172 (conversion).

[232] *Tharpe v Stallwood* (1843) 5 Man & G 760.

(3) The owner of a franchise in wrecks has been deemed to have constructive possession of a wreck so as to enable him to sue in trespass a person who seized a
cask of whisky before he could do so.[233]

'Trespass to goods' is expressly included in the definition of a 'wrongful interference
with goods' within the Torts (Interference with Goods) Act 1977.[234] Thus, by virtue of
the Act's application, the defence of *jus tertii* is no longer available,[235] and the statutory
rules regarding co-ownership apply, as do all forms of relief provided by that Act in
appropriate cases.[236]

(E) DAMAGES

(1) Measure

Where the claimant has been deprived of the goods, he is entitled to their value by way
of damages. This rule applies to suits by bailees against third parties, but when the
assignee under a bill of sale wrongfully seized from the assignor goods comprised in
the bill, the damages awarded to the assignor were limited to the value of his interest in
them.[237] A claimant may recover general damages for loss of use of goods (as distinct
from special damages for loss of profits from the goods) although he would not have
been using them during the period within which he has been deprived of their use.[238]
The provisions of the Torts (Interference with Goods) Act 1977, considered earlier,
apply equally in this context.

(2) Trespass *ab initio*

Where any person having by authority of law[239] entered on land or seized goods, or
arrested a person, subsequently commits a trespass, his original act will in certain
circumstances be deemed itself to be a trespass.[240] The doctrine has little practical relevance today. Its importance is mainly limited to the fact that, presumably, damages
may be assessed on the basis that the entire conduct of the defendant, and not merely
his subsequent wrongful act, is tortious.[241]

---

[233] *Dunwich Corpn v Sterry* (1831) 1 B & Ad 831.
[234] Torts (Interference with Goods) Act 1977, s 1(b).
[235] Torts (Interference with Goods) Act 1977, s 8(1). Section 11(1) excludes contributory negligence as a
defence in proceedings based on intentional trespass.
[236] Torts (Interference with Goods) Act 1977, s 10(1).
[237] *Brierly v Kendall* (1852) 17 QB 937.
[238] *The Mediana* [1900] AC 113, at 117–18.
[239] Authority of law is distinct from permission of another – eg, it covers one who enters an inn, but not
the buyer of a ticket for a seat at a theatre.
[240] The Distress for Rent Act 1737, s 19, abolished this rule in the case of distress for rent.
[241] *Shorland v Govett* (1826) 5 B & C 485.

SECTION 4   RESIDUAL TORTS

There are many circumstances where the violation of interests in goods is not protected by trespass, conversion, or even the tort of negligence. The action analogous
to the old action on the case has generally proved fruitful in filling these gaps. What
follows, therefore, is to be treated as merely illustrative of this wider right of action,
and not as an exhaustive account of the circumstances in which it may be held available in the future. These torts, too, are forms of 'wrongful interference with goods' so
that, where relevant, the provisions of the Torts (Interference with Goods) Act 1977
apply.

Trespass and conversion are especially restrictive in that they are not available to a
claimant who neither possesses nor has an immediate right to possess the goods. Yet
the case of *Mears v London and South Western Rly Co*[242] has firmly established that if
goods are destroyed or damaged, the owner may sue without having possession or an
immediate right to possess. The rule benefits, for example, a bailor, a purchaser where
the vendor has a lien for unpaid purchase money, and a mortgagee. He must prove
damage to his interest; taking the goods from the possessor without affecting title is
insufficient. Presumably, the act complained of must be wrongful in the sense that it
is one which, had the claimant had possession of the chattel (or the immediate right
to it), it would have grounded a suit in trespass, or conversion. So, where the employer
of the claimant, a conductor on a public transport vehicle, endorsed on the claimant's
licence (which was in the employer's possession) the words 'discharged for being 1s 4d
short' he was liable in case for defacing it.[243]

Credit agreements also present interesting problems in this respect. If a car which is
the subject of a credit agreement is seriously damaged, can the owner sue in case? If the
hirer exercises his option to buy, what does the owner lose? And, yet, if (as is likely in
such an event) the hirer does not exercise his option, the owner would be left without
an effective remedy other than in case. It seems, therefore, that, until the hirer opts, the
owner is to be regarded as the reversioner and entitled to sue.

It will be recalled, too, that a bailee disregarding the terms of his bailment may
sometimes be liable in case, though not in conversion, and that to deny the claimant
access to his goods or to interfere with his freedom of using them is also actionable on
the case. Further, to place baited traps on one's land near the highway so as to attract
dogs into the traps, and in consequence of which dogs are so trapped, is a tort in this
category.[244]

---

[242] (1862) 11 CBNS 850.
[243] *Rogers v Macnamara* (1853) 14 CB 27. Cf *Hurrell v Ellis* (1845) 2 CB 295.
[244] *Townsend v Wathen* (1808) 9 East 277.

FURTHER READING

CURWEN, 'The Remedy in Conversion: Confusing Property and Obligation' (2006) 26 *Legal Studies* 570

DOUGLAS, 'The Nature of Conversion' [2009] *Cambridge Law Journal* 198

GREEN AND RANDALL, *The Tort of Conversion* (2009)

HICKEY, *Property and the Law of Finders* (2010)

MILSOM, 'Not Doing is No Trespass' [1954] *Cambridge Law Journal* 105

PALMER, 'The Application of the Torts (Interference with Goods) Act 1977 to Actions in Bailment' (1978) 41 *Modern Law Review* 629

SIMPSON, 'The Introduction of the Action on the Case for Conversion' (1959) 75 *Law Quarterly Review* 364

TETTENBORN, 'Conversion, Tort and Restitution' in Palmer and McKendrick (eds), *Interests in Goods* (1998)

10

TRESPASS TO LAND

KEY ISSUES

(1) Wide protection of possession of land

The law offers a wide degree of protection for those in possession of land – that is, to those with both exclusive occupation of land and the intention to exclude the world at large.

(2) Possession

The possessor of the surface of land is in deemed possession of all the substrata directly below it and of the airspace directly above it in so far as the latter is necessary for the use and enjoyment of the land and any structures upon it.

(3) Elements of trespass

Trespass occurs where the defendant directly and either intentionally or negligently interferes with the claimant's possession of land and is actionable without proof of damage. The action may be defeated by proof of a licence to be on the land or by some other justification.

(4) Remedies

Remedies for trespass include injunctions, actions for the recovery of land, and damages.

SECTION 1   TRESPASS

This tort protects the interest of the claimant in having his land free from the unjustified physical intrusion of another. Because of this emphasis on physical interference with possession,[1] it follows that it is not the function of the tort to protect ownership as such. Nonetheless, the purpose of many lawsuits in trespass is not the recovery of damages but rather the settlement of disputed rights over land, and a judgment may be backed by the sanction of an injunction if the action succeeds. Furthermore, the use of

---

[1] '[A] person does not acquire possession until he obtains exclusive enjoyment; what amounts to exclusive enjoyment of the fee simple depends on the nature of the property...': *Roberts v Swangrove Estates Ltd* [2008] EWCA Civ 98, at [33].

this action in tort as a means of resolving disputes over title has been facilitated by the rule that trespass is actionable per se.[2]

(A) TYPES OF ACT THAT CONSTITUTE TRESPASS

As with all forms of trespass, there must be directness. A claimant landowner who complains that the defendant has erected a spout to drain away water from the eaves of the house of the defendant, as a result of which water has dripped on to the claimant's adjoining land, can sue only in nuisance, not in trespass, because of the indirectness of the invasion.[3] The difficulty with drawing the line between 'direct' and 'indirect' invasions is illustrated by two cases. In *Gregory v Piper*[4] it was held to be trespass where rubbish that was placed near the claimant's land, on drying rolled on to it because of natural forces. By contrast, in *British Waterways Board v Severn Trent Water Ltd*[5] it was made clear that an action may only be brought by the riparian right owner in respect of the direct fouling of a river or other watercourse, but that an action would not lie in respect of the fouling of adjoining land.

Directly causing some foreign matter[6] to enter or come into physical contact with the land of the claimant is a trespass. Thus, placing a ladder against his wall,[7] or driving nails into it,[8] or encouraging a dog to run on to his land,[9] or removing his doors and windows[10] are all trespasses. But in all cases the intrusion on to the claimant's

---

[2] *Bush v Smith* (1953) 162 EG 430. The growing awareness of the scope of the declaratory judgment could lead to a declining use of trespass for this purpose: see *Loudon v Ryder (No 2)* [1953] Ch 423; *Acton Corpn v Morris* [1953] 2 All ER 932. The action for recovery of land is also important in this connection: see section 2(C) below. Where C does not mention trespass to land in his pleadings, he is not restricted to the alternative claim for breach of contract; he may still claim exemplary damages for the trespass: *Drane v Evangelou* [1978] 2 All ER 437.

[3] *Reynolds v Clark* (1725) 2 Ld Raym 1399. Cf *Lemmon v Webb* [1894] 3 Ch 1, at 24: the encroachment of boughs and roots of trees is not trespass, but a nuisance.

[4] (1829) 9 B & C 591.

[5] [2002] Ch 25. This decision is more in line with existing authority such as the decision of Denning LJ in *Southport Corpn v Esso Petroleum Co Ltd* [1954] 2 QB 182, at 195–6 (supported by Lords Radcliffe and Tucker: see [1956] AC 218, at 242 and 244 respectively) where discharge of oil from a ship, which, when carried by tide on to C's foreshore, was held not to constitute a trespass, because it involved consequential, not direct, damage.

[6] Perhaps anything having size or mass, including gases, flames, beams from searchlights and mirrors, but not vibrations.   [7] *Westripp v Baldock* [1938] 2 All ER 779; affirmed [1939] 1 All ER 279.

[8] *Simpson v Weber* (1925) 133 LT 46.

[9] *Beckwith v Shordike* (1767) 4 Burr 2092. But note *League Against Cruel Sports Ltd v Scott* [1986] QB 240 where it was held that the intrusion of D's hounds on to C's land does not necessarily constitute a trespass by D: C must prove that D either intended the hounds to enter C's land, or that D negligently failed to exercise suitable control over the hounds.

[10] *Lavender v Betts* [1942] 2 All ER 72. But this does not apply to D turning off the gas and electricity at the meter in his cellar, for the purpose of evicting the tenant of rooms on an upper floor, because the consequence is indirect: *Perera v Vandiyar* [1953] 1 All ER 1109. This is now a criminal offence under s 1 of the Protection from Eviction Act 1977; but no action for breach of statutory duty lies: *McCall v Abelesz* [1976] QB 585.

land must result from some act or omission on the part of the defendant, or persons for whom he is responsible.

Simply to enter another's land is a trespass.[11] But such an entry may be an assertion of title, in which case an action in trespass will, in effect, determine who has title.[12] To remain on the land after a trespassory entry thereon is in itself also a trespass: a 'continuing trespass', as it is commonly called. Similarly, if A places goods on B's land and is successfully sued by B in trespass for this act, he is also liable to further actions in trespass for the continued presence of the goods on the land if he fails thereafter to remove them.[13] If, on the other hand, he merely commits an act such as digging a hole, or removing goods – that is, if he does not wrongfully allow anything to remain on the land – the fact that the harm thus occasioned continues is not enough to make it a continuing trespass; damages can be recovered only once for such a trespass.[14] In short, there is a continuing trespass only when that which continued after the first action is itself a trespass.

A person who is on land with the permission of the possessor has been held a trespasser if he remains there for an unreasonable time after the termination of that permission.[15] Also:

> [w]hen a householder lives in a dwelling-house to which there is a garden in front and does not lock the gate of the garden, it gives an implied licence to any member of the public who has lawful reason for doing so to proceed from the gate to the front door or back door, and to inquire whether he may be admitted and to conduct his lawful business.[16]

If the licence is withdrawn, he is also not a trespasser during the reasonable time which he takes to leave the premises.[17] There is also the additional reasoning here that trespass is a wrong against possession. Thus, since the termination of the tenancy does

---

[11] A squatter – ie, 'one who, without any colour of right, enters on an unoccupied house or land, intending to stay there as long as he can'– is a trespasser: *McPhail v Persons (Names Unknown)* [1973] Ch 447, at 456. But as to a squatter's ability to dispossess the true paper title owner of his right of possession by acting inconsistently with it for a fixed period of time, without ever himself having any intention of acquiring legal title, see *J A Pye (Oxford) Ltd v Graham* [2003] 1 AC 419; Limitation Act 1980, s 17 (re unregistered land) and Land Registration Act 2002, s 98 (re registered land).

[12] If D has not entered, it will normally be impossible to use an action in trespass as a means of settling a dispute in title.

[13] *Holmes v Wilson* (1839) 10 Ad & El 503. If C seeks an injunction, the court has a discretion to award damages in lieu of such injunction which also take into account the likely future damage. This, in effect, settles the price which D must pay for the right to commit the trespass in the future, and no subsequent action will lie in respect thereof: *Leeds Industrial Co-operative Society v Slack* [1924] AC 851. Nevertheless, the landowner is prima facie entitled to his injunction even where the acts complained of cause no harm: see *Patel v WH Smith (Eziot) Ltd* [1987] 1 WLR 853; *Harrow LBC v Donohue* [1993] NPC 49.

[14] *Clegg v Dearden* (1848) 12 QB 576.

[15] *Minister of Health v Bellotti* [1944] KB 298. Cf conflicting *obiter dicta* in *Winterbourne v Morgan* (1809) 11 East 395, at 402 and 405.

[16] *Robson v Hallett* [1967] 2 QB 939, at 953–4. In *Brunner v Williams* (1975) 73 LGR 266, a weights and measures inspector was held to have no implied licence to enter C's garden to see whether a coal dealer was infringing the Weights and Measures Act 1963; all he may do is go to C's door and ask permission.

[17] *Robson v Hallett* [1967] 2 QB 939, at 953–4.

not coincide exactly with the claimant assuming possession, it follows that a time lag will almost always exist before an action can be brought. But where the claimant has acquired possession and the trespass continues, a lawsuit may be brought. *Konskier v B Goodman Ltd*[18] is illustrative.

> D, a builder had permission from the possessor of a building to leave rubbish there while demolishing part of it. During the currency of this licence, C became tenant of the building and was held entitled to recover in trespass from the builder when the latter did not remove the rubbish after the expiry of the licence.

If a tenant, with the consent of the landlord, stays on at the expiration of his term, so that he thereby becomes a tenant, either from year to year or at will, his remaining there is not an act of trespass so long as the tenancy has not been properly determined.[19] If however, he is a mere tenant at sufferance (thus remaining without the permission of the landlord) the landlord may enter and demand possession and sue in trespass.[20]

Finally, *Watson v Murray & Co* provides an illustration (if not an extension)[21] of the types of acts that may constitute trespass to land.[22]

> Ds, who were sheriff's officers, seized goods in C's shop under writs of execution. It was held that each of the following acts amounted to trespass: locking C's premises so as to exclude her therefrom when they had lotted the goods for the purpose of a sale; opening her premises for a public viewing of the goods; affixing posters on her premises.

(B) WHAT MAY CONSTITUTE THE SUBJECT MATTER OF AN ACTION?

The tort is trespass to land. Obviously, then, merely walking on the surface of the claimant's land is enough to constitute the tort of trespass. Anything attached to the soil, and capable of being separately possessed, may also be the subject matter of trespass such as grass[23] or crops,[24] or a *profit à prendre* (for example, a fishery).[25]

Possession of land may be separated horizontally, as it were, so that, for instance, A may possess the pasturage, B the surface and subsoil, and C the minerals underneath. Each of them may sue if the subject matter of his possession is invaded. Highway authorities, for example, often have the surface of streets vested in them by statute. This being so, it is those authorities (and not the owners of the subjacent or adjoining

---

[18] [1928] 1 KB 421. Presumably, D's successor in title to the chattels would also be liable in trespass for knowingly allowing them to remain on C's land.

[19] *Dougal v McCarthy* [1893] 1 QB 736, at 739–40; *Meye v Electric Transmission Ltd* [1942] Ch 290.

[20] If the deceased tenant's widow remains there after his death she, too, can be sued in trespass: *Thompson v Earthy* [1951] 2 KB 596.

[21] Were all the acts here held to be trespasses sufficiently direct? See *Acton Corpn v Morris* [1953] 2 All ER 932 (not cited in the present case).   [22] [1955] 2 QB 1.

[23] *Richards v Davies* [1921] 1 Ch 90, at 94–5.

[24] *Wellaway v Courtier* [1918] 1 KB 200; *Monsanto v Tilly* [2000] Env LR 313.

[25] Cf *Hill v Tupper* (1863) 2 H & C 121, at 127; *Mason v Clarke* [1955] AC 778. The principle does not, however, extend to an easement: see *Paine & Co v St Neots Gas and Coke Co* [1939] 3 All ER 812.

land)[26] that may sue for surface trespasses, such as breaking up the street,[27] or erecting structures on the highway.[28] Yet a highway is subject to a public right of way.[29] Thus, if a person uses a highway for purposes other than those 'reasonably incident to its user'[30] as a highway (which may include a peaceful demonstration),[31] his act is a trespass. The purpose need not be unlawful in itself.

It may be trespass to tunnel beneath the surface of land, to mine there, to use a cave beneath it, or to drive building foundations through the soil. In the absence of specific provision to the contrary, the owner of the surface is presumed to own that which is underground. This was affirmed by the Supreme Court in *Bocardo SA v Star Energy UK Onshore Ltd*:[32]

> D had been granted a licence under statute to search for, bore for, and get petroleum otherwise vested in the Crown. In order to extract the maximum amount of petroleum from the underground reservoir, D drilled diagonally from an external entry point with pipes that ran under C's land. D's operations took place at a depth of no less than 800 feet under C's land. However, D sought no permission for this and C claimed damages for trespass.

The Supreme Court considered the validity of the proposition that the owner of land is 'entitled to the surface itself and everything below it down to the centre of the earth'.[33] It was held that the proposition represented the law, so far as it was sensible to apply it.[34] This is because 'anything that can be touched or worked must be taken to belong to someone' and there is no better claimant to substrata than the owner of the surface above it.[35] In turn, this means that the person who has lawful possession of the surface also has lawful possession of the earth and minerals below, so far as these have not been alienated to another.[36] It matters not that no use is being made of the substrata by C or his licensees.[37] Trespass was proved on the facts.

However, the proposition operates asymmetrically; it does not entitle the possessor of land to all the airspace above it.[38] Trespass will lie, rather, for invasions of that portion of the airspace which is necessary for the ordinary use and enjoyment of the land

---

[26] In *Hubbard v Pitt* [1976] QB 142 Lord Denning held that where the surface of a pavement was vested in the local highway authority the adjoining owner could not sue for trespass to the pavement.

[27] *Hyde Corpn v Oldham, Ashton and Hyde Electric Tramway Ltd* (1900) 64 JP 596.

[28] *Sewai Jaipur v Arjun Lal* [1937] 4 All ER 5. See also *Tunbridge Wells Corpn v Baird* [1896] AC 434; *Cox v Glue* (1848) 5 CB 533.

[29] *Rangeley v Midland Rly Co* (1868) 3 Ch App 306; *R (on the application of Smith) v Land Registry* [2010] EWCA Civ 200, at [8]–[9] and [16].

[30] *Liddle v Yorkshire (North Riding) CC* [1934] 2 KB 101, at 127; *R (on application of Smith) v Land Registry* [2010] EWCA Civ 200, at [16].

[31] *DPP v Jones* [1999] 2 AC 240, at 256, per Lord Irvine LC: 'the law should not make unlawful what is commonplace and well accepted'.   [32] [2010] UKSC 35.

[33] Eg, *Rowbotham v Wilson* (1860) 8 HL Cas 348, at 360.

[34] Beyond a relatively shallow point in the earth's crust, pressure and heat make any human activity impossible: Sprankling (2008) 55 UCLA LR 979, at 993, fn 84.   [35] [2010] UKSC 35, at [26]–[27].

[36] [2010] UKSC 35, at [27]–[31].   [37] [2010] UKSC 35, at [35].

[38] *Bocardo SA v Star Energy UK Onshore Ltd* [2010] UKSC 35, at [26], affirming *Baron Bernstein of Leigh v Skyviews & General Ltd* [1978] QB 479.

and the structures upon it.[39] Consistently with this, an aircraft does not infringe any of the claimant's rights to airspace by being flown above a reasonable height over his land for the purpose of photographing it.[40]

Apart from the position at common law, the Civil Aviation Act 1982 provides that, with the exception of aircraft belonging to, or exclusively employed in, the service of Her Majesty,[41] no action shall lie in respect of trespass or nuisance by reason only of the flight of an aircraft over any property at a height above the ground, which, having regard to weather and other circumstances of the case, is reasonable.[42] Subject to the same exception, the owner of an aircraft is liable for all material loss or damage to persons or property caused by that aircraft, whether in flight, taking off[43] or landing, or by a person in it or articles falling from it, without proof of negligence or intention or other cause of action.[44]

(C) DEFENDANT'S STATE OF MIND

The leading case on what is required by way of the trespasser's intention is the decision of the House of Lords in *JA Pye (Oxford) Ltd v Graham*.[45]

> Cs had once had an agreement with Ds whereby Ds acquired grazing rights over a portion of Cs' land. Although the agreement came to an end in 1993, Ds continued to use the land exactly as they had done under the agreement for about the next 15 years. Despite Ds' repeated requests, Cs refused to renew the agreement. In 1999, Cs brought possession proceedings against Ds arguing that so long as Ds expressed the hope that the agreement would be renewed, Ds could not have formed the requisite intention to dispossess Cs.

Lord Browne-Wilkinson indicated that possession requires two elements: factual possession *plus* the intention to possess. In relation to the critical second element he approved[46] the dictum of Slade J in *Powell v McFarlane* that there must be an intention 'to exclude the world at large, including the owner with the paper title if he be not himself the possessor, so far as is reasonably practicable and so far as the processes of the law will allow'.[47]

---

[39] *Kelsen v Imperial Tobacco Co of Great Britain and Ireland Ltd* [1957] 2 QB 334; *Anchor Brewhouse Developments v Berkley House Docklands Developments Ltd* (1987) 284 EG 625. The possessor of land has rights to all of the relevant airspace directly above his land. Thus, it is not possible for a person to adversely possess a portion of that airspace: *Stadium Capital Holdings (No 2) Ltd v St Marylebone Property Co plc* [2009] EWHC 2942, at [26] (*obiter*).

[40] That is, the height necessary for ordinary use and enjoyment of land and structures upon it: *Baron Bernstein of Leigh v Skyviews and General Ltd* [1978] QB 479, at 488.

[41] Civil Aviation Act 1982, ss 49(3) and 76(1).

[42] Civil Aviation Act 1982, s 76(1). The section applies to all flights which are at a reasonable height and comply with statutory requirements. But the ordinary liabilities in trespass or nuisance would arise for any other wrongful activity carried on by or from the aircraft, such as deliberate emission of vast quantities of smoke that polluted C's land: *Baron Bernstein of Leigh v Skyviews and General Ltd* [1978] QB 479, at 489.

[43] The ordinary common law applies to accidents caused by the aircraft, while taxiing for take-off: *Blankley v Godley* [1952] 1 All ER 436.   [44] Civil Aviation Act 1982, s 76(2).

[45] [2003] 1 AC 419.   [46] Ibid at [42].   [47] (1979) 38 P & CR 452.

Mistake, as such, is no defence in trespass. It will not avail the defendant that he innocently thought that he was on his own land.[48] On the other hand, there is no liability if the entry was totally involuntary. Thus, for example, a person who is carried on to the land of the claimant by a third party is not liable in trespass.[49] Also, notwithstanding the decision in *Letang v Cooper*,[50] it must be assumed for the time being that a negligent unintentional act of trespass is enough.[51] Thus, if A intentionally throws a stone on to C's land and, as he should have foreseen, it ricochets on to B's land, this is probably trespass to B's land as well as C's.

(D) WHO MAY SUE?

It is generally said that it is possession of the land that entitles a claimant to sue in trespass. Thus, if the claimant has a legal estate and exclusive possession he may sue in trespass. But at the same time, the tenant (not the landlord) can sue if a third party trespasses on the land demised;[52] the owner of an equitable interest with possession can sue;[53] and a statutory possession will also found a trespass action.[54]

The Court of Appeal has held that 'a person may have such a right of exclusive possession of property as will entitle him to bring an action for trespass against the owner of that property but which confers no interest whatever in the land'.[55] Those whose interests fall short of those of a lessee may also be able to sue in trespass if in fact they have exclusive occupation. Thus, whether a lodger can sue in trespass would depend, on the facts, on his having had exclusive occupation – in other words, it would be relevant whether he had an outdoor key and could bar access to the rooms.[56]

---

[48] *Basely v Clarkson* (1681) 3 Lev 37; *Nelson v Nicholson* (2001) *Independent*, 22 January.

[49] *Smith v Stone* (1647) Sty 65. But note that entering the land of others pursuant to threats is no defence for such an entry will be regarded as having been voluntary: *Gilbert v Stone* (1647) Style 72.

[50] [1965] 1 QB 232. For discussion see ch 8.

[51] Certainly in *League Against Cruel Sports Ltd v Scott* [1986] QB 240, Park J expressed the view that liability in trespass could ensue from the negligent failure of D to control hounds properly so that they enter C's land.

[52] *Cooper v Crabtree* (1882) 20 Ch D 589. C with an *interesse termini* could not sue if he never took possession: *Wallis v Hands* [1893] 2 Ch 75.

[53] *Mason v Clarke* [1955] AC 778. Another example is *Loudon v Ryder* [1953] 2 QB 202, where C was entitled to the premises under a declaration of trust merely and yet recovered damages for trespass to the land. A beneficiary under a trust for sale may also sue: *Bull v Bull* [1955] 1 All ER 253, at 255 (*obiter*).

[54] *Cruise v Terrell* [1922] 1 KB 664; *Lewisham BC v Maloney* [1948] 1 KB 50. Whether the landlord of a tenant at will can sue third parties in trespass is undecided: *Attersoll v Stevens* (1808) 1 Taunt 183, cf *Shrewsbury's (Countess) Case* (1600) 5 Co Rep 13b.

[55] *Marcroft Wagons Ltd v Smith* [1951] 2 KB 496, at 501. *Brown v Brash and Ambrose* [1948] 2 KB 247 and *Thompson v Ward* [1953] 2 QB 153 show that a statutory tenant who leaves his premises even for a period of five to ten years with the intention of eventually returning there has the right to sue in trespass. It is sufficient, eg, if he installs someone as licensee yet signals his intention to return by, say, leaving furniture there.

[56] *Lane v Dixon* (1847) 3 CB 776; *Monks v Dykes* (1839) 4 M & W 567; *Helman v Horsham and Worthing Assessment Committee* [1949] 2 KB 335, at 347; *R v St George's Union* (1871) LR 7 QB 90. Similarly, a claimant who could not rely on possession under his lease from the Crown because it was void for non-compliance with a statute was held to have 'actual possession... sufficient to entitle the party possessing it to maintain trespass against persons who have no title at all, and are mere wrongdoers': *Harper v Charlesworth* (1825)

In *National Provincial Bank Ltd v Ainsworth*[57] the House of Lords unanimously held that a deserted wife at that time had only a personal, but no proprietary, interest in the matrimonial home. Nonetheless, Lord Upjohn held that as she had exclusive occupation she could therefore bring proceedings against trespassers. In *Hill v Tupper*[58] the facts were as follows.

> X Co leased to C certain land, which adjoined X Co's canal. C was also given 'the sole and exclusive rights' to rent out pleasure boats for use on the canal. Subsequently, D set up a rival concern, whereupon he was sued in trespass by C. C conceded that X Co could sue D in trespass, but at the same time C argued that he could also sue.

Since the claimant's concession was tantamount to an admission that he did not have exclusive occupation, the court dismissed the action. It did however add that, if a claimant could show that his interest amounted to a new species of property right, he would be able to succeed, subject to the caveat that it was not the policy of the law to allow the courts to create new rights in land. However, in *Manchester Airport plc v Dutton* a licensee who had not yet entered into occupation was entitled to eject trespassers who had set up a protest camp. As Laws LJ explained: 'a licensee not in occupation may claim possession against a trespasser if that is a necessary remedy to vindicate and give effect to such rights of occupation as by contract with his licensor he enjoys'.[59] On the other hand, it was made clear that an action for damages would not have been available on those facts. The action was limited to exercising a superior right in the land in order to gain possession.

It is generally no defence to a trespasser that the claimant's possession of the land is unlawful. The simple fact of possession is normally enough.[60] But as against the true owner, the rule is different. In *Delaney v TP Smith Ltd*[61] the claimant entered property held under a lease that was unenforceable because it did not comply with the requirements of section 40 of the Law of Property Act 1925 relating to a memorandum in writing. That being the case, he was unable to sue his landlord in trespass for ejecting him. Two extracts from earlier cases that were cited are important here:

> A mere trespasser cannot, by the very act of trespass, immediately and without acquiescence, give himself what the law understands by possession against the person whom he

---

4 B & C 574, at 591. The House of Lords in *Street v Mountford* [1985] AC 809 held that where the intention evidenced by the agreement between the parties was to grant exclusive possession for a period of time and at a rent, there will normally be found to be a tenancy in any case.

[57] [1965] AC 1175.   [58] (1863) 2 H & C 121.

[59] [2000] 1 QB 133, at 150. See also *Hounslow LBC v Twickenham Garden Developments Ltd* [1971] Ch 233, at 257. But cf *Street v Mountford* [1985] AC 809 on the distinction between tenancies and occupational licences.

[60] *Graham v Peat* (1801) 1 East 244. In *Mason v Clarke* [1955] AC 778, Viscount Simonds and Lord Oaksey held that the bare possession of a *profit à prendre* was enough to found an action in trespass.

[61] [1946] KB 393.

ejects, and drive him to produce his title, if he can, without delay, reinstate himself in his former possession.[62]

If there are two persons in a field, each asserting that the field is his, and each doing some act in the assertion of the right of possession, and if the question is, which of those two is in actual possession, I answer, the person who has the title is in actual possession, and the other is a trespasser.[63]

If a claimant has a right to immediate possession of the land, he can seek a summary remedy to obtain possession[64] or, if he has already entered upon the land, sue for trespasses committed by third parties between the date of accrual of his right of possession and the actual date of his entry.[65] This is often called trespass by relation.[66] It operates according to the legal fiction whereby, upon his entry on to the land, the party entitled to possession is deemed to have been in possession from the date of his right to such possession accruing.

Although damages in trespass are not available to those without possession whose interests in land are violated, such persons are not entirely without a remedy. A landlord will ordinarily have contractual rights against tenants who damage his interest – for example, by allowing the premises to fall into disrepair – and the law of property will also afford a remedy of a tortious nature to a landlord who establishes that his tenant has damaged the reversionary interest.[67]

If a non-possessory interest in land is violated by a third party, an action derived from the old action on the case may lie. The claimant must prove 'such permanent injury as would be necessarily prejudicial to the reversioner'.[68] Thus, in one case, it was not enough to prove that the defendant's cart-wheels had made an impression on the surface of the land;[69] the impressions lacked permanency.

SECTION 2   REMEDIES

(A) DAMAGES

The claimant is entitled to full reparation for his loss. Generally, the depreciation in selling value will be an adequate measure for destruction of, or damage to, land and

---

[62] *Browne v Dawson* (1840) 12 Ad & El 624, at 629. (In *Portland Managements Ltd v Harte* [1977] QB 306, it was held that if C proves ownership and his intention to resume possession, the onus is on D to prove that he is not a trespasser.)

[63] *Jones v Chapman* (1847) 2 Exch 803, at 821; approved in *Lows v Telford* (1876) 1 App Cas 414, at 426.

[64] Civil Procedure Rules, r 55.21.

[65] *Barnett v Earl of Guildford* (1855) 11 Exch 19.

[66] Suppose that the effect of a proviso for forfeiture in a lease is that the lease subsists until proceedings for forfeiture are brought; this doctrine of trespass by relation would not then allow a lessor, who is entitled by the terms of the lease to forfeit it, to claim damages for the period between the act giving ground for forfeiture and the issue of the writ: *Elliott v Boynton* [1924] 1 Ch 236.

[67] Landlord–tenant relationships of this kind are customarily, and appropriately, dealt with in textbooks on real property, not in those on torts.

[68] *Baxter v Taylor* (1832) 5 B & Ad 72, at 75.

[69] Ibid.

buildings. On occasion, though, the claimant can also recover special damages such as the cost of replacement premises[70] or business profits.[71] Equally, where the cost of reinstatement or repair exceeds the diminution in value of the property, those costs may be awarded as damages provided expenditure on such reinstatement and repair is reasonable.[72] And for these purposes, reasonableness is to be gauged by applying cost–benefit analysis not only to the reinstatement sought, but also to other options that might be available (including halfway-house solutions and the simple payment of damages).[73] Whatever the court's conclusion, the cost of repair will provide important evidence of the claimant's loss, especially where there is no market in which the value of the property may be ascertained, or where the claimant can prove that it was reasonable to have the property restored.[74] All measures of damages – whether based on market value or replacement cost – are subordinate to the general and overriding tort principle of restoring the claimant to the same position he was in before the tort was committed.[75]

The measure of damages for wrongful occupancy of land (*mesne profits*) is generally assessed in terms of the reasonable rental value of the land during the time of the defendant's occupancy.[76] So in *Inverugie Investments Ltd v Hackett*,[77] the claimants were awarded the equivalent of the letting value of the whole of the holiday apartment block wrongfully occupied by the defendant trespassers, even though in practice only about 35–40% of the apartments were actually rented out by the defendants, or could have been by the claimants. The claimants were entitled to compensation for the wrongful use of their property, regardless of whether they had suffered any actual loss from being deprived of the use of that property or whether the defendants had in fact benefited from their wrongdoing. Likewise, in the case of a trespass to the claimant's airspace caused by the erection of an advertising hoarding, it is possible for the claimant to obtain profits made by the defendant in the use of that hoarding representing its letting value.[78] However, the decision in *Davies v Ilieff*[79] provides an important qualification to this approach in that, if the premises concerned are also the claimant's home (rather than merely commercial residential premises), the court should

---

[70] *Dominion Mosaics and Tile Co v Trafalgar Trucking Co* [1990] 2 All ER 246.

[71] *Watson v Murray & Co* [1955] 2 QB 1. Cf *Dunn v Large* (1783) 3 Doug KB 335.

[72] *Heath v Keys* [1984] CLY 3568. Damages based on the cost of repair are only available when C does in fact intend to carry out repairs: *Perry v Sidney Phillips & Son* [1982] 3 All ER 705.

[73] *Bryant v Macklin* [2005] EWCA Civ 762.

[74] For a lucid statement, see *Hutchinson v Davidson* 1945 SC 395.

[75] *Farmer Giles Ltd v Wessex Water Authority* [1990] 18 EG 102. In *Bisney v Swanston* (1972) 225 EG 2299, D put a trailer on C's land so as to interfere with C's business as much as possible. As well as damages for loss of business, £250 aggravated damages were awarded against D for intending to interfere with malice and spite.

[76] *Swordheath Properties Ltd v Tabet* [1979] 1 WLR 285, at 288; *Jones v Merton LBC* [2008] EWCA Civ 660, at [24].

[77] [1995] 1 WLR 713. See also *Whitwham v Westminster Brymbo Coal and Coke Co* [1896] 1 Ch 894; affirmed [1896] 2 Ch 538.

[78] *Stadium Capital Holdings (No 2) Ltd v St Marylebone Property Co plc* [2009] EWHC 2942 (£313,972 for 3½ years).   [79] 2000 WL 33201551.

add to the ordinary letting value a sum in general damages to reflect the insult of the trespass.

Where goods such as coal, minerals, or trees are severed from the land, the measure of damages depends on whether the act is wilful or innocent.[80] If the defendant's severance is innocent, the claimant's damages amount to the value of the goods in their raw state (for example, coal still in a seam) minus the cost of severance and removal.[81] If the act is wilful, however, the claimant's damages will reflect the market value of the goods when they first became a chattel minus only the cost of removal – for example, hauling coal to the surface – but not the cost of severance.[82] Whether in either case the defendant can also deduct an additional sum by way of profit for his work, or whether the claimant is entitled to the value of the severed goods less only the defendant's actual expenses, is not settled.[83] But in the future, it may be that the courts will approach these cases on the basis of the steadily developing law of unjust enrichment rather than the law of trespass (though a sum for the actual trespass will, of course, remain available).

Finally, it is to be noted that aggravated damages are potentially available in the case of a trespass to land, where the interference with possession was high-handed, insulting, or oppressive in nature.[84] And exemplary damages may also (in rare cases) be available, for example in the case of a tenant who is unlawfully evicted by his landlord.[85]

(B) INJUNCTIONS

Injunctions, even of the interim variety, are available in the case of continuing trespasses to restrain the trespasser.[86] And mandatory injunctions can be obtained in order to require a trespasser to restore the land to its former state. In *Nelson v Nicholson*,[87] for example, the facts were these.

> Cs had recently resolved a boundary dispute with their neighbours. In resolving the dispute, it became apparent that Ds had planted a leylandii hedge on Cs' land. They conceded

---

[80] 'Wilful' includes 'fraudulent'; whether it includes 'negligent' is doubtful: *Wood v Morewood* (1841) 3 QB 440; *Re United Merthyr Collieries Co* (1872) LR 15 Eq 46. In *Trotter v Maclean* (1879) 13 Ch D 574, at 587, Fry J said (*obiter*) that the burden of proving wilfulness is on C.

[81] *Jegon v Vivian* (1871) 6 Ch App 742.

[82] *Martin v Porter* (1839) 5 M & W 351; *Morgan v Powell* (1842) 3 QB 278. If C could not himself reach the seam in order to extract the mineral, his damages are based on what a third party would pay him by way of royalty for permission to extract: *Livingstone v Rawyards Coal Co* (1880) 5 App Cas 25.

[83] *Jegon v Vivian* (1871) 6 Ch App 742 and *A-G v Tomline* (1880) 14 Ch D 58 would allow the innocent D his profit. Cf *Re United Merthyr Collieries Co* (1872) LR 15 Eq 46. In *Tai Te Wheta v Scandlyn* [1952] NZLR 30 it was held that even an innocent trespasser could not set off the value of improvements done by him to the land. See also *Lord Cawdor v Lewis* (1835) 1 Y & C Ex 427.

[84] *Stanford International Bank Ltd v Lapp* [2006] UKPC 50, at [39] (*obiter*).

[85] *Drane v Evangelou* [1978] 2 All ER 437. Surprisingly, however, in *Devonshire v Jenkins* (1979) 129 NLJ 849 it was held that exemplary damages were not recoverable if in fact the evicting landlord did not obtain that profit which he sought by his attempted unlawful eviction.

[86] *Patel v WH Smith (Eziot) Ltd* [1987] 1 WLR 853.   [87] (2001) *Independent*, 22 January.

that this constituted a trespass. Cs then sought a mandatory injunction to require Ds to remove the hedge since they could not do so themselves under the terms of a restrictive covenant that prevented them from removing any fence, hedge, tree, or shrubs within 30 feet of the boundary between the two plots of land.

Despite the defendants proposing an undertaking whereby they, the defendants, would keep the hedge trimmed to a height no greater than seven feet, the court granted the injunction sought, making the point that the proposed undertaking would not bind the defendants' successors in title.

Finally, a *quia timet* injunction may be granted to restrain the prospective trespasser; that is, where a trespass is merely threatened. Thus, in one case where the owners of certain incinerators anticipated a trespass by environmental protestors, an injunction was granted to prevent the trespass from occurring. Interestingly, the injunction was granted without the precise identity of the trespassers being ascertained: it was merely aimed at the generic class 'intending trespassers'.[88]

(C) RECOVERY OF LAND

It is an established rule of common law that the person entitled to possession may use reasonably necessary force to remove a trespasser.[89] But in many instances, the rightful occupant may prefer to pursue an action for recovery of land. In order to succeed, the claimant must demonstrate the relative weakness of the defendant's possessory rights. In other words, the claimant need not show that he has perfect title, merely a better title than the defendant. The clearest modern authority on this remedy is *Manchester Airport plc v Dutton*.[90]

Manchester Airport needed to remove certain trees in neighbouring woods and it was granted a licence by the owner to 'enter and occupy the woods' in this connection. Prior to this, however, protestors had occupied the woods. In order to carry out the work, the airport sought an order for possession against the protestors.

Noting that, although Manchester Airport was not the owner of the woods, the Court of Appeal nonetheless granted the order on the basis that the airport had a superior right to occupation than the protestors. What was significant was the fact that the owner had included in the licence a right of occupation. Accordingly, in the ostensibly similar case of *Countryside Residential (North Thames) Ltd v Tugwell*[91] the court refused such an order on the grounds that the licence in question merely conferred permission to carry out work on the land, but not a right to occupy it.

---

[88] *Hampshire Waste Services Ltd v Intending Trespassers upon Chineham Incinerator* [2004] Env LR 9.
[89] *Hemmings v Stoke Poges Golf Club* [1920] 1 KB 720.
[90] [2000] 1 QB 133.
[91] [2000] 34 EG 87.

SECTION 3   DEFENCES

(A) JUSTIFICATION

Occasionally it will be possible to show legal justification for one's presence on another's land. In such circumstances, there is no actionable trespass. Thus, for example, under the Countryside and Rights of Way Act 2000 rights are conferred to enter land to make arrangements for the general public to have access to open countryside. In such circumstances no tort is committed so long as the entrant complies with the specified statutory restrictions within which he must act.[92] Equally, in certain circumstances police officers are permitted to enter land to make an arrest and to search the premises following such an arrest[93] and private individuals have certain similar common-law rights to enter another's land to abate a nuisance or reclaim wrongfully taken personal property.[94]

In fact, there are many forms of justification – whether originating in statute or ancient rules of common law – that are simply too numerous to list here.[95] For present purposes, it suffices to note two general principles: (1) that a recognised legal authority to enter another's land will defeat any prospective trespass action; and (2) that a distinction must be drawn between an absolute right to do an act and a mere power to do an act which the defendant elected to do in a fashion that involved an avoidable trespass.[96]

(B) LICENCE

The defendant may raise the defence of licence where the claimant landowner has granted him a permission, whether express or implied, to enter the land. Such licences do not require that the entrant be granted any proprietary rights in respect of the land; a permission simply to be there suffices. On the other hand, if the entrant exceeds the permission conferred by the licence he becomes a trespasser. Thus, for example, if A is granted permission to enter B's land for the purposes of photographing wildlife, he may not fish in B's lake without becoming a trespasser. Similarly, if the landowner

---

[92] See the Countryside and Rights of Way Act 2000, s 2.

[93] Police and Criminal Evidence Act 1984, ss 17–18.

[94] See also the statutory procedure set out in the Access to Neighbouring Land Act 1992 which permits an applicant to seek an access order from the court in order to enter a neighbour's land to carry out reasonably necessary works for the preservation of his own land.

[95] For full details, see *Clerk and Lindsell* (20th edn, 2010) paras 19–37 et seq.

[96] In *British Waterways Board v Severn Trent Water Ltd* [2002] Ch 25 it was stressed that while a statute authorised certain waterworks, it did not impliedly also confer upon D a right to discharge surplus water into another's watercourse. The court adverted to the crucial difference between mere *convenient* ways of carrying out statutory operations and methods that are *necessary*. A similarly restrictive approach is applied to rights conferred by way of conveyance: see *Martin v Childs* [2002] EWCA Civ 283.

revokes the licence, the entrant may not remain on his land. And this is so regardless of whether the licence was conferred gratuitously or by virtue of a contract.[97]

(C) SEARCH WARRANTS

Under section 8 of the Police and Criminal Evidence Act 1984, magistrates have, in certain circumstances, the power to grant search warrants. The details of this jurisdiction, and the case law associated with the extent of the powers contained in a warrant, are beyond the scope of this book.[98]

FURTHER READING

BIRTS, *Remedies for Trespass* (1990)
HOWELL, '"Subterranean Land Law": Rights Below the Surface of Land' (2002) 53 *Northern Ireland Law Quarterly* 268
POLLOCK AND WRIGHT, *Possession in the Common Law* (1888)
SPRANKLING, 'Owning the Center of the Earth' (2008) 55 *UCLA Law Review* 979

---

[97] Revocation of a contractual licence, it seems, does not require mutually agreed contractual variation. Any complaint about such revocation – effectively a breach of contract – must be pursued under the law of contract: see *Wood v Leadbitter* (1845) 13 M & W 838.

[98] For full details, see *Clerk and Lindsell* (20th edn, 2010) paras 19–61 et seq.

11

DEFENCES TO INTENTIONAL TORTS AGAINST THE PERSON OR PROPERTY

KEY ISSUES

(1) Three types of defence

Tort law provides for a wide range of defences. This is especially so in the case of the intentional torts against the person or property. Defences to these torts can be placed within a threefold system. The first category consists in 'absent element defences'. Defences in this category are denials of one or more of the elements of the tort in which the claimant sues. The second category comprises 'justification defences'. Justifications are pleas that, when accepted, release the defendant from liability on the ground that he acted reasonably in committing a tort. The third category contains public policy defences. These defences are rules that exempt the defendant from responsibility in tort even though he committed a tort for no good reason. They exist in recognition of the fact that unjustified tortfeasors must sometimes be let out of liability to further some important social goal external to those of the law of tort.

(2) Absent element defences

Several rules that are often referred to as 'defences' are in fact merely absent element defences. For example, the plea of consent is an absent element defence to the intentional torts. This is because the absence of consent is an element of these wrongs. The doctrines of inevitable accident, involuntariness, and

physical compulsion are also absent element defences. When they are applicable, these rules merely mean that no tort was committed.

(3) Justification defences

There are many justification defences to the intentional torts. The paradigmatic justification is that of self-defence, which releases persons who use necessary and proportionate force to defend themselves against an aggressor or putative aggressor from liability. An array of other justification defences exist which are variations on the theme of self-defence, including defence of another person, defence of one's property, recapture of land or chattels, and arrest.

(4) Public policy defences

Tort law and its procedural edifice recognise numerous public policy defences. One of the most significant in practice, and the most perplexing, is that of illegality. Broadly speaking, this defence prevents claimants injured by a tort from recovering compensation where they were committing a serious criminal offence at the time of the defendant's tort and their criminal conduct contributed to their damage.

(5) Non-defences

Unlike the criminal law, tort law does not provide for defences of insanity, infancy, duress, or provocation. Nor does it recognise a defence of 'private necessity'.

SECTION 1   INTRODUCTION

This chapter considers the most significant defences available to liability arising in the intentional torts against the person or property. It must not, however, be thought that these defences apply only to these torts. Many of them – for example, consent, statutory authority, and illegality – apply throughout the tort law universe. Nevertheless, the defences under consideration are particularly important in the present context because the key question in proceedings for the intentional torts is often whether the defendant has an answer to liability. For example, most claims in false imprisonment turn on whether the detention of the claimant was justified rather than on whether the definitional elements of this tort are present. The importance of justification defences to false imprisonment is reflected in the European Convention on Human Rights. Article 5 of the Convention protects the rights to liberty and security of the person in just ten words: 'Everyone has the right to liberty and security of person'. By contrast, over a page of text is devoted to articulating the circumstances in which interfering with these rights is justifiable. In short, defences are crucial in defining when liability arises in the intentional torts.

Defences to liability in the intentional torts can be organised within three categories.[1] First, there are denials of one or more of the elements of the tort in which the claimant sues. These defences will be called 'absent element defences'.[2] Justification defences are the second type of defence. They release defendants from liability although they committed a tort on the ground that acting tortiously was reasonable in the circumstances. Finally, there are public policy defences. These are defences that exempt the defendant from liability even though he committed a tort without justification. They exist in recognition of the fact that it is sometimes necessary to release unjustified tortfeasors from liability in order to advance some important social goal that is external to tort law. Justification defences and public policy defences may be referred to collectively as 'affirmative defences' since they exempt the defendant from liability even though he committed a tort.

This classification of defences has important implications. For example, it bears upon the allocation of the onuses of pleading and proof. Absent element defences are merely denials by the defendant that he committed a tort. Accordingly, pursuant to established rules, the claimant carries the burden of negating these defences in his pleadings and in the evidence. In contrast, justifications and public policy defences are affirmative defences. They are therefore for the defendant to plead and prove. Arguably, this classification also affects the permissibility of resisting a defendant. A defendant who has an absent element defence commits no tort. His conduct is lawful (unless, of course, it constitutes a crime or another type of civil wrong). In principle, therefore, others should not generally interfere with his conduct. Doing so is likely to be tortious. The same may hold for justifications. A defendant who is justified

---

[1] Regarding the classification of defences generally see Goudkamp, 'A Taxonomy of Tort Law Defences' in Degeling, Edelman, and Goudkamp (eds), *Torts in Commercial Law* (2011), ch 19.

[2] The terminology is borrowed from Robinson, *Structure and Function in Criminal Law* (1997), at 12.

(for example, is acting in self-defence) acts reasonably. Arguably, therefore, a justified defendant should not be resisted. In contrast, generally speaking, those who can avoid liability only because of the application of a public policy defence may be resisted. This is because their conduct is unreasonable and typically objectionable.

SECTION 2   ABSENT ELEMENT DEFENCES

Recall that absent element defences are contentions by the defendant that one or more of the elements of the tort in which the claimant sues is absent. A selection of absent element defences is discussed here.

(A) INVOLUNTARINESS

No tort is committed by a defendant whose impugned behaviour is involuntary. For example, if the defendant's leg hits the claimant as a result of a muscle spasm, the defendant has not acted tortiously. It is important to be clear about why, precisely, this is the case. Which element, exactly, is negated where the defendant's movements in issue were involuntary? The courts[3] and commentators[4] routinely characterise the plea of involuntariness as a denial of fault. This treatment is to some extent under-standable as a person is not, except in relatively uncommon circumstances, at fault for his involuntary movements.[5] The truth, however, is that there must be some other element that is unsatisfied if the defendant's movements in question were involuntary. This is because involuntariness prevents liability from arising in strict liability torts. It follows that all torts incorporate what may be called an 'act element'. It is this element that is targeted by a plea of involuntariness.

(B) PHYSICAL COMPULSION

Suppose that A grabs hold of B's hand and uses it to hit C. B is not liable to C in battery[6] (although A is of course liable). This is because the act element of battery is not present. It is important to distinguish the plea of physical compulsion from that of duress.[7] Physical compulsion involves a third party using the defendant's body to commit a tort. Duress (which is not a defence) entails the defendant acting tortiously in conse-quence of threats made by a third party.

---

[3] See, eg, *Sik v Lajos* [1962] SASR 146 (SC), at 150; *Smith v Lord* [1962] SASR 88 (SC), at 94–5.

[4] See, eg, Restatement (Third) of Torts: Liability for Physical and Emotional Harm at § 11(b), cmt d.

[5] A defendant will be at fault for his involuntary movements if he could have avoided the movements by taking reasonable care. For instance, a person who experiences an epileptic seizure will be at fault for his seizure if he negligently failed to take his anti-convulsant medication as prescribed by his doctor.

[6] This example is taken from *Ward v Weaver* (1616) Hob 134, at 134; 80 ER 284, at 285 (KB).

[7] Duress is discussed below at pp 347–8.

(C) INEVITABLE ACCIDENT

The law treats an accident as inevitable if it could not have been avoided by taking reasonable care and was not intended by the defendant. Since the intentional torts require proof that the defendant acted intentionally or negligently, the plea of inevitable accident is an absent element defence to these causes of action. It is an assertion by the defendant that he was not at fault.

(D) CONSENT[8]

It is now reasonably clear that, in relation to the intentional torts, the absence of consent is part of the cause of action.[9] Accordingly, consent is an absent element defence to these wrongs. The fact that the issue of consent is internalised within the definitions of the intentional torts rather than treated as an affirmative defence sends an important message: that it is not wrong merely to touch other people or their property. Coming into contact with another person or their property is wrong only when it is non-consensual. This seems to be the correct position for the law to adopt, particularly in relation to sexual batteries. Were a sexual battery constituted simply by proof of sexual intercourse, that would imply that all sexual intercourse is wrong. This would not conform to the prevailing sexual morality in contemporary society. Sexual intercourse is wrong only when it is non-consensual.

(1) Generally

Consent in the context of the intentional torts is the equivalent of the plea of voluntary assumption of risk[10] in relation to the tort of negligence. It may be given expressly. Or it may be inferred from conduct. For example, a boxer's consent to being punched is implicit in his getting into the ring. Likewise, a teenager engaged in horseplay with a friend cannot complain if he is injured by his friend so long as the latter stays within the tacitly agreed rules of that horseplay.[11] Similarly, a footballer consents not only to those tackles permitted by the rules, but also, probably, to those tackles that involve

---

[8] For a philosophical treatment of the concept of consent see Western, *The Logic of Consent: The Diversity and Deceptiveness of Consent as a Defence to Criminal Conduct* (2004).

[9] This is the rule in relation to trespass to the person in England (*Freeman v Home Office (No 2)* [1984] 2 WLR 130; [1983] 3 All ER 589 (QBD); affirmed [1984] QB 524 (CA)), New Zealand (*H v R* [1996] 1 NZLR 299 (HC) at 305) and the United States (*Ford v Ford* 10 NE 474, at 475 (Mass, 1887)). However, in Australia and Canada, at least in relation to certain trespasses to the person, consent is an affirmative defence (*Marion's Case* [1992] HCA 15; (1992) 175 CLR 218, at 310–11; *Non-Marine Underwriters, Lloyd's of London v Scalera* [2000] SCC 24; [2000] 1 SCR 551). There are signs that the English courts are warming to the Australian/Canadian approach: see *Ashley v CC of Sussex Police* [2006] EWCA Civ 1085; [2007] 1 WLR 398, at 410 [31] (the House of Lords did not deal with this issue on appeal: [2008] UKHL 25; [2008] 1 AC 962). On one interpretation, Lord Blanesburgh in *William Leitch & Co Ltd v Leydon* [1931] AC 90 (HL) at 108–9 accepted that the absence of consent is an element of the tort of trespass to goods.

[10] See ch 6, section 3.

[11] *Blake v Galloway* [2004] EWCA Civ 814; [2004] 1 WLR 2844; [2004] 3 All ER 315.

a technical breach of the rules of the game. Where, however, an opponent commits a 'professional foul', the conduct involved is beyond that to which the player agreed when embarking on the game.[12]

Determining what can be inferred from conduct can sometimes be problematic. A modern case in which the scope of a claimant's implied consent was in issue is *Arthur v Anker*.[13] The Court of Appeal in this action held that where a person had unlawfully parked his car on another's land knowing that the latter asserted a right to wheel-clamp trespassing vehicles and charge for their release, he had impliedly consented not only to the otherwise unlawful detention of his car (so that there was no trespass to goods), but also to being required to pay a reasonable fee to ensure the unclamping of the vehicle. *Arthur v Anker* may be contrasted with *Vine v Waltham Forest London Borough Council*[14] where it was held that if the release fee is exorbitant, consent to its payment cannot be implied if the person parking the car does not actually see the sign (even if the sign was both prominently posted and clear in its terms).

Unless the claimant's consent relates to the class of act complained of, it will not prevent liability from arising. For example, the consent of an occupier to a repairman entering her house to fix her boiler would not stop the repairman from being held liable in battery if he has sexual intercourse with the occupier. However, the claimant's consent need not correspond exactly to the defendant's act. Thus, as already noted, in the context of a contact sport, consent generally to the prospect of blows being struck will furnish the defendant with an answer to liability.[15] It need not be shown that the claimant consented to the precise number of blows that were delivered. Of course, determining the generality of the claimant's conduct in a given case can be difficult. Each case will turn on its own facts.

Consent is a state of mind on the part of the claimant. However, the law is yet to determine definitively whether the claimant's mental state is ascertained subjectively or objectively. If a subjective test is adopted, consent will only be present if the claimant in fact agreed to the defendant's contact with his person or property. On an objective test,[16] what was actually running through the claimant's mind at the relevant time is not to the point. What matters is whether the reasonable person would conclude, based on an assessment of the claimant's conduct, that the claimant consented to the contact. A subjective test is more favourable to claimants and promotes rights to personal security. An objective test gives greater weight to the interest in freedom of action. However, it should be noted that the difference between these alternatives is probably not very great in practice. This is because, even if a subjective test is used, the main guide that the court has to the claimant's mental state is his conduct.

---

[12] *Condon v Basi* [1985] 1 WLR 866 (CA); [1985] 2 All ER 453.   [13] [1997] QB 564 (CA).
[14] [2000] 1 WLR 2383 (CA); [2000] 4 All ER 169.
[15] *Blake v Galloway* [2004] EWCA Civ 814; [2004] 1 WLR 2844, at 2851–2 [20]; [2004] 3 All ER 315, at 322–3.
[16] An objective test is supported by *Bennett v Tugwell* [1971] 2 QB 267 (QBD), at 273.

Fraud or deception may vitiate consent. For example, if D impersonates C's partner and C has sexual intercourse with D believing him to be her partner, C's consent to the intercourse will be vitiated.[17] More complex is the situation where one person has sexual intercourse with another and infects the latter with a sexually transmitted disease. In such a scenario, there are two issues at stake: (1) does the second person consent to sexual intercourse? and (2) does that person consent to the risk of being infected with the disease? Consent to sexual intercourse does not mean that there is consent to the risk of infection. Hence, a person who has consensual sexual intercourse with another person without telling the latter that he is carrying a sexually transmitted disease will not be liable in battery in respect of the intercourse but may be liable in battery as a result of any infection that occurs.[18] Also difficult is the case in which the defendant's motive is in question. Suppose that a male police officer 'cuddles' a distressed female victim of crime whom he is questioning. If he puts his arms around her purely in an attempt to ameliorate some of the stress caused by the occasion, and she welcomes such comforting, there will be no battery. But what if he does it for prurient reasons that only transpire later? The criminal law may render the police officer guilty of an offence on the basis that he deceived the complainant as to the nature or purpose of the act.[19] But it is undecided whether a claimant's consent is thus vitiated in tort.[20] On the one hand, tort law typically ignores the defendant's motive.[21] On the other hand, it seems objectionable for the police officer in the scenario to avoid civil responsibility.

Consent that is obtained under duress is no consent at all.[22] For example, a woman who 'agrees' to sexual intercourse with the defendant owing to threats of violence made against her by the defendant does not consent to intercourse.[23] A show of authority may constitute duress. So, for instance, where a police officer, without formally arresting or charging a suspect, asks him with an authoritative air to accompany him to the police station,[24] the claimant may not be treated as having consented. Likewise, if the

---

[17] Sexual Offences Act 2003, s 76(2)(b). This is a criminal law statute. But it undoubtedly reflects the position in tort law.

[18] *R v Dica* [2004] EWCA Crim 1103; [2004] QB 1257. See also *R v EB* [2006] EWCA Crim 2945; [2007] 1 WLR 1567.

[19] Sexual Offences Act 2003, s 76(2)(a).   [20] *KD v CC of Hampshire* [2005] EWHC 2550 (QB).

[21] 'Although the rule may be otherwise with regard to crimes, the law of England does not, according to my apprehension, take into account motive as constituting an element of civil wrong' (*Allen v Flood* [1898] AC 1 (HL), at 92).

[22] Yet in *Latter v Braddell* (1881) 50 LJQB 448 (CA), a servant who complied, crying and under protest, with an order of her mistress that she be medically examined to determine whether she was pregnant, was held to have consented. See also *Centre for Reproductive Medicine v U* [2002] EWCA Civ 565 (pressure applied by a nurse to a patient found to fall short of duress).

[23] Cf Sexual Offences Act 2003, s 75(2)(a).

[24] *Warner v Riddiford* (1858) 4 CBNS 180; 140 ER 1052 (CCP). Submissions in *Freeman v Home Office (No 2)* [1984] 2 WLR 130 (QBD); [1983] 3 All ER 589; affirmed [1984] QB 524 (CA) that the relationship between a prisoner and a prison doctor was such that the former could never freely consent to treatment by the latter failed. But the judge at first instance made it clear that in looking at the reality of a prisoner's consent to medical treatment, the doctor's power to affect the prisoner's situation must be borne in mind.

claimant is so drunk as to be incapable of consenting, any putative consent is treated as invalid.[25]

The overriding interest of the state in maintaining order means that consent is not necessarily an answer to criminal liability. Thus, the consent of a person to the infliction of actual bodily harm is ineffective in the criminal law context unless it is caused for a good reason (such as life-saving surgery).[26] Tort law takes a different approach. As it is concerned with private rather than public interests, consent always prevents liability in tort from arising. It is irrelevant that the act consented to results in the infliction of serious harm for inadequate reasons. It has, for example, been held that a person can consent to the risk of being fatally shot[27] and to being injured in a bar fight.[28]

Difficult issues arise where the defendant mistakenly believed that the claimant consented to contact with his person or property. In the criminal law, a reasonable mistake as to the victim's consent precludes liability for rape.[29] Tort law's position on this issue is unclear. Arguably, however, tort law should adopt a rule that is less favourable to defendants than the criminal law. Unlike the criminal law, which favours the interests of the defendant, in tort law, neither party has a privileged position. If correct, this logic would result in defendants being denied any leeway in consequence of a mistaken belief in consent.[30]

(2) Consent to medical treatment[31]

The law concerning consent to medical treatment is voluminous and intricate. The discussion here gives a highly condensed account of the relevant principles. Interested readers concerned with the fine details are advised to consult a specialist text on medical law. In order to sketch the law on consent to medical treatment, it is necessary to distinguish between four classes of patient: adults with capacity to consent; children; patients suffering from mental incapacity and receiving treatment under the Mental Health Act 1983; patients lacking capacity but falling beyond the scope of the Mental

---

[25] *R v Bree* [2007] EWCA Crim 804; [2008] QB 131.

[26] The leading decision is *R v Brown* [1994] 1 AC 212 (HL). The European Court of Human Rights subsequently ruled that the decision in *Brown* did not violate Art 8 of the European Convention on Human Rights: *Laskey, Jaggard and Brown v United Kingdom* (1997) 24 EHRR 39 (ECtHR).

[27] *Murphy v Culhane* [1977] QB 94 (CA). Consider also *Lane v Holloway* [1968] 1 QB 379 (CA).

[28] *Bain v Altoft* [1967] Qd R 32 (FC), at 41. The Restatement (Second) of Torts § 892C provides that consent bars recovery unless the conduct concerned was criminalised in order to protect the individual consenting to it.

[29] Sexual Offences Act 2003, s 1. The position at common law was different: *Director of Public Prosecutions v Morgan* [1976] AC 182 (HL).

[30] The decision in *Ashley v CC of Sussex Police* [2008] UKHL 25; [2008] 1 AC 962, which is discussed below at pp 334–5, supports this analysis.

[31] See, generally, Mclean, *Autonomy, Informed Consent and Medical Law: A Relational Challenge* (2009); Manson and O'Neill, *Rethinking Informed Consent in Bioethics* (2007); Herring, *Medical Law and Ethics* (3rd edn, 2010) ch 3; Brazier and Cave, *Medicine, Patients and the Law* (4th edn, 2007), ch 6.

Health Act 1983. As we shall see, however, even these categories are not watertight. There is some degree of overlap between them.

(a) Adults with capacity to consent

Any non-consensual physical contact with a competent adult patient is prima facie a battery.[32] This principle reflects the fundamental right to self-determination. As Cardozo J put it in *Schloendorff v Society of New York Hospital*:[33] 'Every human being of adult years and sound mind has a right to determine what shall be done with his own body'. As in other contexts, consent need not be written and may be implied from conduct, such as holding out one's arm to receive an injection. However, where surgery or more serious invasive treatment is contemplated, patients will usually be asked to sign a form agreeing to the procedure.

A patient's consent to medical treatment is ineffective unless he is provided with an adequate explanation of the broad nature of what is to be done to him.[34] But a mere failure to warn the patient of the risks or side-effects of the treatment proposed will not vitiate the patient's consent.[35] At most it will constitute a breach of the doctor's duty to give the patient proper advice and will be actionable as negligence subject to the requirement that the patient suffer damage.[36] Only when the defendant actively misleads the patient will a claim in battery normally be available.[37]

Where it is uncertain whether a patient freely, and with full understanding, rejected life-saving treatment, it is lawful for doctors to err on the side of preserving life.[38] If, however, the patient makes it clear that he does not wish to receive treatment, his wishes must be respected.[39] Thus, if a competent patient requests that his ventilator be disconnected, those providing care must oblige.[40]

(b) Children

Section 8(1) of the Family Law Reform Act 1969 provides that a minor over the age of 16 may provide an effective consent to medical treatment. Accordingly, the consent of such children is placed on a par with that of competent adults. In the case of children under the age of 16, the Act preserves the common-law rule that, provided the individual child is mature enough to make his own decision on the treatment proposed,

---

[32] *In re F (Mental Patient: Serialisation)* [1990] 2 AC 1 (HL).   [33] 105 NE 92, at 93 (NY, 1914).

[34] *Chatterton v Gerson* [1981] QB 432 (QBD), at 443.

[35] The bringing of actions in battery where the essence of the claim is inadequate advice was deplored in *Sidaway v Board of Governors of the Bethlem Royal Hospital and the Maudsley Hospital* [1985] AC 871 (HL), at 883.   [36] See above pp 132–3.

[37] See *Appleton v Garrett* [1996] PIQR P1 (QBD) (dentist withheld essential information from patients). See also the criminal case of *R v Tabassum* [2000] 2 Cr App R 328 (CA) (defendant who performed breast examinations misled victims into believing that he had medical qualifications: liable). Cf *R v Richardson* [1999] QB 444 (CA) (a dentist who provided treatment although she had been suspended from practice not liable for assault despite her patients being unaware of her suspension).

[38] *In re T (Adult: Refusal of Treatment)* [1993] Fam 95 (CA).

[39] See Mental Capacity Act 2005, ss 24–6, which makes provision for advance decisions to refuse treatment to be made.   [40] *Ms B v An NHS Hospital Trust* [2002] EWHC 429 (Fam); [2002] 2 FCR 1.

the child can give an effective consent.[41] Thus, an attempt in *Gillick v West Norfolk and Wisbech Area Health Authority*[42] to ensure that no girl under the age of 16 could lawfully be prescribed the contraceptive pill without parental agreement failed. In this case, the House of Lords held that, if such a girl seeking contraception or an abortion should refuse adamantly to consult her parents, the doctor may lawfully treat her provided that he is satisfied that she has sufficient understanding of what is involved in the treatment and its implications for her.

While a '*Gillick*-competent' child who is not yet 16 can provide effective consent to treatment, the position is otherwise with respect to the *refusal* of treatment, at least in certain situations. In *Re W (A Minor) (Medical Treatment: Court's Jurisdiction)*,[43] the Court of Appeal held that it had jurisdiction to order that medical treatment for anorexia nervosa be provided to a '*Gillick*-competent' child suffering from anorexia nervosa against her wishes. The Court held that account should be taken of the child's wishes, but that it could override them where to do so is in the child's best interests.

In the case of very young children, parental consent to treatment is effective to authorise treatment that is beneficial to the child.[44] No battery is therefore committed when a doctor vaccinates a protesting four-year-old if his parent has given consent. Where the procedure proposed is not clearly and unequivocally beneficial to the child, however, parental consent alone may not be sufficient. In such cases – including, for example, sterilisation – the authorisation of the court must be sought, especially before any such serious and generally irreversible surgery is performed.[45]

(c) Patients lacking capacity and falling within the scope of the Mental Health Act 1983

Where patients are mentally disordered, the terms under which they may be cared for and treated are governed primarily by the Mental Health Act 1983.[46] The details of this statute[47] cannot be given here. It suffices to note that the Act makes provision for treatment according to a complex system that contains many procedural and substantive safeguards.

(d) Patients lacking capacity but falling outside the Mental Health Act 1983

The position in relation to patients who lack capacity but who are not mentally disordered (for example, competent but unconscious patients) and hence fall beyond the scope of the Mental Health Act 1983 is determined by the Mental Capacity Act 2005. Again, a detailed account of this legislation is beyond the ambit of this book. However, it is noted that the Act puts in place a presumption of capacity[48] that is ousted only if

---

[41] Section 8(3).   [42] [1986] AC 112 (HL).   [43] [1993] Fam 64 (CA).

[44] *Gillick v West Norfolk and Wisbech Area Health Authority* [1986] AC 112 (HL), at 166–7.

[45] *Re B (a minor) (Wardship: Sterilisation)* [1988] AC 199 (HL), at 205; *Practice Note (Sterilisation: minors and mental health patients)* [1993] 3 All ER 222.

[46] Section 1(1).

[47] This Act was heavily amended by the Mental Health Act 2007. For analysis, see Bowen, *Blackstone's Guide to the Mental Health Act 2007* (2007).   [48] Mental Capacity Act 2005, s 1(2).

the patient is shown, on the balance of probabilities, to lack capacity (judged according to the patient's ability to understand, retain, and use information relevant to a treatment decision and to communicate his decision).[49] Where the person lacks capacity, he may be treated if the person providing treatment reasonably believes it to be in the patient's best interests, subject to a number of safeguards (concerning matters such as known previous wishes and religious beliefs).[50]

SECTION 3   JUSTIFICATION DEFENCES

Justification defences, recall, are defences that exempt persons from liability who act reasonably in committing a tort. It is important to note that many justification defences are instances of self-help, that is to say, situations where the law permits a defendant to solve his own problems by committing a tort rather than resorting to litigation. Generally speaking, the law takes a dim view of self-help. The circumstances in which it is allowed are narrowly defined. This is because the courts fear that steps taken in self-help will result in violence or the escalation thereof. As Edmund Davies LJ said in *Southwark London Borough Council v Williams*:[51]

> [T]he law regards with the deepest suspicion any remedies of self-help, and permits these remedies to be resorted to only in very special circumstances. The reason for such circumspection is clear – necessity can very easily become simply a mask for anarchy.

(A) SELF-DEFENCE[52]

A battery may be justified on the ground of self-defence. In order to establish this defence the defendant must prove that it was necessary to use force to repel an attack by the claimant or to prevent or terminate a false imprisonment[53] and that the amount of force used was reasonable. The necessity limb of this test means that the defence will be unavailable unless physical force was the only realistic means of avoiding the threat posed by the claimant. Suppose, for example, that a defendant could prevent the claimant from murdering him either by shooting the claimant or by closing and locking a door between him and the claimant. If the defendant opted to shoot the claimant, the defence of self-defence would be excluded. This is because it was unnecessary for the defendant to shoot the claimant in order to save himself.

The criterion of necessity dictates that the threat posed by the claimant must be reasonably imminent. This is because threats that are not proximate can be neutralised

---

[49] Mental Capacity Act 2005, s 3(1).   [50] Mental Capacity Act 2005, ss 4–6.
[51] [1971] Ch 734 (CA), at 745–6. See also *R v Burns* [2010] EWCA Crim 1023, at [11]–[14].
[52] See generally Goudkamp, 'Self-Defence and Illegality Under the Civil Liability Act 2002 (NSW)' (2010) 18 TLJ 61.
[53] This includes an unlawful arrest: *Codd v Cabe* (1875–1876) LR 1 Ex D 352 (CA); *R v McKoy* [2002] EWCA Crim 1628.

other than by using defensive force, such as by seeking help from the authorities. In other words, the defence of self-defence does not create a privilege to commit pre-emptive strikes. Of course, this does not mean that the defendant has to wait until he is actually struck before it is permissible to use defensive force. This would not make sense for, on occasion, if the defendant does not act first, the opportunity for him to save himself may be lost. Thus, the law permits the defendant to strike before the claimant if doing so is necessary.[54] The point is that the defence is unavailable if the threat is so distant that it is speculative. The necessity limb also means that force that comes after a threat has passed will not amount to self-defence. Such force constitutes revenge or retaliation, which is not protected. In summary, defensive force must come neither too soon nor too late.

The reasonableness limb is concerned with whether the amount of force used by the defendant was proportionate to the threat posed by the claimant. What constitutes reasonable force is a question of fact to be determined in the light of the circumstances in each case. It will be relevant to consider, among other things, how the defendant resisted the claimant, whether a weapon was used, and the number of times that the claimant was struck.[55] It is not simply a question of comparing the evil of the response with the evil of the attack. Suppose that A pins B against a wall and repeatedly kisses her against her will. The only means by which B can compel A to desist is by lacerating his hands with a pair of scissors that she is holding. It is not certain that the defence of self-defence will fail simply because the wounding is more severe than the unwanted kisses. Similarly, suppose that C attempts to rape D and that the only way that D can prevent C from raping her is to use lethal force. D would probably be permitted to kill C even though, in doing so, she was causing more harm than that with which she was threatened. It should also be noted that, although self-defence is a type of self-help, the courts are usually generous to the defendant in determining whether the amount of force that he used was proportionate. This is because acts of self-defence are normally carried out under extreme circumstances. As Holmes J famously observed: 'Detached reflection cannot be demanded in the presence of an uplifted knife.'[56]

The defence of self-defence will be available to a defendant who uses force against an innocent person whom he mistook for an aggressor provided that his mistake was reasonable and the requirements of necessity and proportionality are satisfied according to the world as perceived by the defendant. This principle was established

---

[54] *Dale v Wood* (1822) 7 Moore CP 33 (though on the facts the defendant's response was greater than was warranted).

[55] Whether or not the defendant had an opportunity to retreat may not be relevant. In the criminal law context, there is no duty to retreat: *R v Bird* [1985] 1 WLR 816 (CA); [1985] 2 All ER 513. See further Ashworth, *Principles of Criminal Law* (6th edn, 2009), at 120–1.

[56] *Brown v United States* 256 US 335 at 343 (1921). See also *Reed v Wastie* [1972] Crim LR 221 (QBD) per Geoffrey Lane J ('one does not use jewellers' scales to measure reasonable force'); *Cross v Kirkby* (2000) *Times*, 5 April (CA), per Judge LJ ('the law does not require [the defendant] to measure the violence to be deployed with mathematical precision'). See also the Criminal Justice and Immigration Act 2008, s 76(7)(a) ('a person acting for a legitimate purpose may not be able to weigh to a nicety the exact measure of any necessary action').

in *Ashley v Chief Constable of Sussex Police*.[57] This case arose out of a police officer fatally shooting a man whom he mistakenly believed was reaching for a weapon. The deceased's estate and his dependants sued the defendant in several causes of action, including in battery, alleging that he was vicariously liable for the conduct of the officer. The House of Lords, by a majority, ruled that the defence of self-defence is unavailable if the defendant's mistake as to the necessity for defensive force was unreasonable. The House reached this conclusion on the basis that requiring mistakes to be reasonable strikes a fair balance between the interests of both claimants and defendants. Permitting unreasonable mistakes to enliven the defence would be inappropriate, as it would give preferential treatment to defendants. Equally, it would be wrong, the House said, for tort law not to give any leeway for mistakes as to the necessity for defensive force, since this would involve the law affording priority to the interests of claimants. In reaching its decision, the House emphasised differences between criminal law, which extends the defence to unreasonable mistakes,[58] and tort law. The House said that the criminal law and tort law should part company in this connection since the criminal law, with its focus on punishment, must give precedence to the defendant's interests. Tort law, the House stressed, is different. It places the parties on an equal footing.

(B) DEFENCE OF ANOTHER PERSON

The early common law, which saw the exercise of defensive force as a significant threat to the maintenance of law and order, only permitted persons who stood in certain relationships (such as one of employment) with a person confronted by an aggressor to come to that person's aid.[59] Today, the plea of defence of others is probably not limited to specific relationships.[60] Anyone who takes necessary and proportionate defensive measures to save another person from an aggressor should be entitled to it. However, it is conceivable that the relationship between the defendant and the person whom he defended may be relevant to whether the force was proportionate.

(C) PREVENTION OF CRIME

Section 3 of the Criminal Law Act 1967, which applies to both the criminal and civil law, absolves of liability persons who use reasonable force to prevent the commission

---

[57] [2008] UKHL 25; [2008] 1 AC 962, noted in McBride, 'Trespass to the Person: The Effect of Mistakes and Alternative Remedies on Liability' (2008) 67 CLJ 461.

[58] Criminal Justice and Immigration Act 2008, s 76(4).

[59] *Seaman v Cuppledick* (1614) Owen 150; 74 ER 966 (KB); *Tickell v Read* (1773) Lofft 215; 98 ER 617 (KB); *Barfoot v Reynolds* (1733) 2 Str 953; 93 ER 963 (KB); cf *Leward v Basely* (1695) 1 Ld Raym 62; 91 ER 937 (KB).

[60] *Goss v Nicholas* [1960] Tas SR 133 (SC) (stranger).

of any offence recognised by domestic law.[61] This justification defence[62] overlaps significantly with the defences of self-defence and defence of another person. However, unlike the latter defences, the defence in section 3 only applies where the defendant is preventing a 'crime'. Accordingly, in contrast with the common-law defences just mentioned, section 3 probably does not insulate a defendant from liability for restraining a mentally disordered aggressor or a child under the age of 10,[63] since such persons are not criminally responsible for their acts.

(D) DEFENCE OF ONE'S PROPERTY

Where it is necessary to do so, one may use reasonable force to defend property in one's possession against any person threatening to commit or actually committing a trespass to it. But the defendant must have such possession of the property in question as would enable him to sue the claimant in trespass. Thus, the captain of a cricket club who removed the claimant from a field on account of his disruptive behaviour was liable. This was because the captain did not have possession of the field.[64] A lack of possession was also crucial in *Scott v Matthew Brown & Co Ltd*.[65] The defendant in this case was on a plot of land merely as a result of ejecting the claimant, the true owner, by an act of trespass. The claimant re-entered the property and the defendant forcibly removed him. The defendant was held not to have sufficient possession to sue in trespass, and therefore had no defence to liability in battery. If the defendant has a right to possession, but not actual possession, he may have some other defence, such as recapture of land or chattels,[66] but he cannot successfully plead that he was defending his property.

To remain on land after the occupier's consent has been withdrawn is a trespass. Likewise, it is a trespass for a passenger to refuse to alight from a vehicle if its owner rescinds his agreement to the passenger's presence in it. Therefore, the defence of protecting property may be invoked by those who use reasonable force to eject such persons.[67] A threatened intrusion is also sufficient to trigger the defence; so if the claimant has taken the key of the defendant's car and is about to enter it, the defendant is entitled to resist this potential trespass. As with the defence of self-defence, if the defendant reasonably believes that force is necessary to prevent a trespass, he may use force although he is mistaken in thinking it to be necessary.

---

[61] Preventing breaches of international law does not qualify: *R v Jones* [2006] UKHL 16; [2007] 1 AC 136.

[62] See also the broadly analogous defence in s 550A(1) of the Education Act 1996 (teachers may use force against a pupil to prevent the commission of an offence, among other things).

[63] Criminal responsibility begins at the age of 10: Crime and Disorder Act 1998, s 34.

[64] *Holmes v Bagge and Fletcher* (1853) 1 El & Bl 782; 118 ER 629 (QB).

[65] (1884) 51 LT 746; [1881–1885] All ER Rep 1043 (Ch D). See also *Dean v Hogg and Lewis* (1824) 10 Bing 345; 131 ER 937 (CCP) (hirer of steamboat lacked sufficient possession).   [66] See below pp 338–9.

[67] *Green v Bartram* (1830) 4 Car & P 308; 172 ER 717 (KB); *Moriarty v Brooks* (1834) 6 Car & P 684; 172 ER 1419 (Assizes); *R v Burns* [2010] EWCA Crim 1023; [2010] 1 WLR 2694.

Whether force is necessary and reasonable depends on the individual facts of each case. It may be relevant to consider, among other things, whether the defendant requested the claimant to cease the interference with his rights before applying force. The use of force will be unnecessary if the claimant would have ceased his interference with the defendant's property rights following a verbal request from the defendant.[68] However, a defendant is not required to make such a request when to do so would be obviously futile.[69]

As the law does not generally value interests in property as highly as those in bodily security,[70] all other things being equal, the use of force in defence of the former is ordinarily harder to justify than in the case of self-defence.[71] Firing a shotgun at a burglar breaking into a garden shed, but who shows no overt sign of violence towards the owner, was held in *Revill v Newbery*[72] to be unreasonable. May it be, then, that unless the claimant resists his expulsion so as to bring the rules of self-defence into play, the courts will treat force likely to cause death or serious bodily harm as unjustifiable in the defence of property?[73]

The courts have often had to consider the extent to which it is permissible for a defendant to use mechanical devices or barriers to protect his property.[74] The test is, once again, one of reasonableness. Thus, attempting to deter intruders by placing barbed wire or spiked railings on the confines of one's land will ordinarily be reasonable. On the other hand, it is unreasonable to set without notice spring guns or such other devices that are calculated to kill or cause grievous bodily harm.[75] Where dogs (or, theoretically, other animals) are used to protect one's property, the relevant

---

[68] Some old cases suggest that a request must be made before it is permissible to use force: see, eg, *Green v Goddard* (1702) 2 Salk 641; 91 ER 540 (KB).

[69] *Tullay v Reed* (1823) 1 Car & P 6; 171 ER 1078 (Assizes); *Polkinhorn v Wright* (1845) 8 QB 197; 115 ER 849 (QB).

[70] In *Southport Corp v Esso Petroleum Co Ltd* [1953] 3 WLR 773 (QBD), at 779; [1953] 2 All ER 1204, at 1209 Devlin J said that '[t]he safety of human lives belongs to a different scale of values from the safety of property. The two are beyond comparison.' But in relation to injunctive relief, this hierarchy of interests seems to be inverted, with property rights receiving more robust protection: see Murphy, 'Rethinking Injunctions in Tort Law' (2007) 27 OJLS 509.

[71] An interesting examination of the relevant issues at stake here is Posner, 'Killing or Wounding to Protect a Property Interest' (1971) 14 J Law & Econ 201.

[72] [1996] QB 567 (CA). See also *Collins v Renison* (1754) Say 138; 96 ER 830 (KB); *Moriarty v Brooks* (1834) 6 C & P 684; 172 ER 1419 (Assizes).

[73] As to when killing intruding animals is justifiable, see *Hamps v Darby* [1948] 2 KB 311 (CA). See also Animals Act 1971, ss 7 (detention of trespassing livestock) and 9 (destruction of dogs that worry livestock).

[74] See generally Bohlen and Burns, 'The Privilege to Protect Property by Dangerous Barriers and Mechanical Devices' (1926) 35 Yale LJ 525.

[75] *Bird v Holbrook* (1828) 4 Bing 628; 130 ER 911 (CCP). Consider also the Offences Against the Person Act 1861, s 31. In *Attorney General's Reference (No 2 of 1983)* [1984] QB 456 (CA), the defendant had armed himself with petrol bombs to repel rioters who had earlier smashed into his shop. He had been charged with unlawfully being in possession of an explosive device. The Court of Appeal held that the defendant was entitled to acquittal if his object was to protect his family or his property from an imminent attack and he believed that it was both necessary and reasonable to use the petrol bombs to meet the force used by any attackers.

rules concerning the defence of one's property are contained in the Animals Act 1971. Under that Act, a person is not liable:[76]

> for any damage caused by an animal kept on any premises or structure to a person tres-
> passing there, if it is proved either – (a) that the animal was not kept there for the pro-
> tection of persons or property; or (b) (if the animal was kept there for the protection of
> persons or property) that keeping it there for that purpose was not unreasonable.

(E) DEFENCE OF ANOTHER'S PROPERTY

According to Blackstone, it is a defence to use reasonable force to protect the property of other members of one's household.[77] It is unclear, however, if this is the case today. It is difficult to reconcile this proposition with the requirement that only those with sufficient possession of property to enable one to sue for a trespass committed against it may exercise defensive force in respect of it.[78]

(F) RECAPTURE OF LAND OR CHATTELS

A person who enters land in respect of which he has a right of possession and who uses no more force than is reasonably necessary to evict a trespasser will have a defence in an action brought by the trespasser for battery and interference with his chattels.[79] It is unnecessary for such an individual to bring proceedings for possession, although the practicality of obtaining judicial relief will be relevant to whether forcibly re-entering the land was reasonable. This defence is closely related to the defence of property defence. It too is justificatory in nature.[80]

Tort law also recognises a defence of recapture of chattels.[81] Unfortunately, a paucity of modern authority renders it difficult to describe the scope of this answer to liability with precision. Old cases, however, hold that one who has been dispossessed of a chattel may use reasonable force to retake it.[82] It is also permissible for a defendant to enter the claimant's land if doing so is necessary to reclaim a chattel.[83] So, for example, if an apple falls from a tree on the defendant's land and lands on the claimant's property, the defendant is entitled to enter the claimant's land to retrieve it if doing so is reasonable in the circumstances. This justification defence is a variant of that of recapture of land,

---

[76] Section 5(3) (considered in *Cummings v Grainger* [1977] QB 397 (CA)). See further ch 18.

[77] Blackstone, *Commentaries of the Laws of England*, vol 3 (1769), at 3.

[78] This requirement is discussed above at p 336.

[79] *Hemmings v Stoke Poges Golf Club Ltd* [1920] 1 KB 720 (CA); *Manchester Airport Plc v Dutton* [2000] QB 133 (CA).

[80] The defence has been abrogated where the trespasser is a tenant who has held over: Protection from Eviction Act 1977, s 2.

[81] See generally Branston, 'The Forcible Recaption of Chattels' (1912) 28 LQR 262; Hawes, 'Recaption of Chattels: The Use of Force against the Person' (2006) 12 Cant LR 253.

[82] *Blades v Higgs* (1865) 11 HL Cas 621; 11 ER 1474 (HL); *Anthony v Haney and Harding* (1832) 8 Bing 186; 131 ER 372 (CCP).   [83] *Patrick v Colerick* (1838) 3 M & W 483; 150 ER 1235 (Exch).

and the principles that govern its availability are, *mutatis mutandis*, more or less the same. The guiding principle is that the retaking must be reasonable. For example, the defence will not lie where the defendant breaks into the stables of an innocent person in which his horse was placed by a third party. The defence of recapture of chattels is, however, somewhat more generous than that of recapture of land owing to the fact that chattels can be destroyed, concealed, and removed from the jurisdiction.

(G) ABATEMENT

The doctrine of abatement is a defence to liability in trespass to land. It applies where a person takes reasonable steps to ameliorate or terminate a nuisance.[84] This rule's resemblance to the plea of defence of one's property is obvious and, like that defence, it is also a justification. This is because it only extends to objectively warranted steps taken to reduce a nuisance or to bring one to an end. It will be forfeited if, for instance, one uses disproportionate force to eliminate the nuisance,[85] if the more prudent course of action would have been to request the occupier of the land on which the nuisance was situated to terminate it,[86] or if one delayed to such an extent before taking steps to address the nuisance that one could have waited for relief through 'the slow progress of the ordinary forms of justice'.[87]

(H) DISTRESS

If the claimant owes the defendant a debt, the defendant is entitled to distrain chattels belonging to the claimant until the debt is discharged by the claimant. Suppose, for example, that a bus driver negligently loses control of his vehicle and it veers off the road and into the defendant's rose garden. The defendant is entitled to seize the bus until the driver's employer pays for the damage that it caused. This defence is justificatory in nature because it is only available if taking the property is reasonable, the defendant acquired it in a reasonable way, and the defendant took reasonable care of it. Thus, the defence will not lie, for example, if the property taken far exceeds the value of the debt.[88] It should be noted that this defence has little vitality left in it today. It is doubtful whether it is of much relevance in the modern world.

---

[84] Eg, chopping off branches of overhanging trees: *Lemmon v Webb* [1895] AC 1 (HL).

[85] Such as demolishing a house simply because it was used as a brothel: *Ely v Supervisors of Niagara County* 36 NY 297 (1867).

[86] *Lagan Navigation Co v Lambeg Bleaching, Dyeing and Finishing Co Ltd* [1927] AC 226 (HL).

[87] Blackstone, *Commentaries of the Laws of England*, vol 3 (1769), at 6.

[88] As Blackstone said in *Commentaries of the Laws of England*, vol 3 (1769), at 12: 'Distresses must be proportioned to the thing distrained for.... [I]f the landlord distrains two oxen for twelve pence rent; the taking of *both* is an unreasonable distress; but if there were no other distress nearer the value to be found, he might reasonably have distrained *one* of them' (emphasis in original). The defence of distress was abolished in relation to animals by the Animals Act 1971, s 7, and replaced with a substantially equivalent defence of detention of livestock.

(I) PUBLIC NECESSITY[89]

The defence of public necessity exists in order to permit the commission of torts to pre-serve important public interests from danger. It is available if the following circum-stances are met: (1) there is an actual or apparent danger to a public interest;[90] (2) the danger was imminent;[91] (3) the steps taken to protect the public interest from the danger were reasonable;[92] (4) the defendant was not at fault for creating the threat.[93]

The key difference between the defence of public necessity and the defensive force defences is that the latter presuppose that the claimant is a wrongdoer whereas the former contemplates the infliction of harm upon an innocent person. Unsurprisingly, therefore, the defence of public necessity gives greater weight to the interest of the victim of the tort than the defensive force justifications and authorises a lower amount of force as a result. For example, whereas it is permissible to use lethal force in self-defence if one is confronted by a risk of death or serious bodily injury, it is doubtful that such harm can be inflicted pursuant to the defence of public necessity. Indeed, it is questionable whether public necessity allows a person to cause personal injury. Virtually all cases in which it has succeeded involved the destruction of property.

Classic examples of torts that will not be actionable on the ground that they were committed out of public necessity include entering another's land to erect fortifica-tions on it for the defence of the realm[94] or to fight fires,[95] throwing cargo overboard in order to prevent a ship from sinking,[96] and destroying clothing infected with a virulent disease.[97] The defence has also been invoked to justify restraining a crowd of protestors in the interests of public safety[98] and firing a tear gas cylinder into a shop in order to flush out a dangerous psychopath.[99] The defence was of considerable importance in the past in determining when medical treatment could be provided to a

---

[89] A substantial number of the authorities on this defence are discussed in Cohan, 'Private and Public Necessity and the Violation of Property Rights' (2007) 83 ND L Rev 651.

[90] *Cope v Sharpe (No 2)* [1912] 1 KB 496 (CA).

[91] The defence does not, therefore, apply for the benefit of homeless persons who squat in unoccupied premises since they face no immediate peril: *Southwark LBC v Williams* [1971] Ch 734 (CA).

[92] *Cope v Sharpe (No 2)* [1912] 1 KB 496 (CA).

[93] *Rigby v CC of Northamptonshire* [1985] 1 WLR 1242 (QBD); [1985] 2 All ER 985; *Esso Petroleum Ltd v Southport Corp* [1956] AC 218 (HL), at 242.

[94] *The Case of the King's Prerogative in Saltpetre* (1606) 12 Co Rep 12; 77 ER 1294 (KB) (*obiter*).

[95] *Dewey v White* (1827) Mood & M 56; 173 ER 1079 (Assizes) (firemen justified in throwing down the claimant's chimney because of the risk that it would otherwise fall on to highway); cf *Burmah Oil Co (Burma Trading) Ltd v Lord Advocate* [1965] AC 75 (HL (SC)), at 164–5. Fire brigades now have statutory authority to do such things (Fire Services Act 1947, s 30).

[96] *Mouse's Case* (1608) 12 Co Rep 63; 77 ER 1341 (KB). See also the restricted common-law right to devi-ate from a foundrous public highway, at least where the land entered belongs to the person responsible for the highway's foundrous state: *Stacy v Sherrin* (1913) 29 TLR 555 (KBD).

[97] *Seavey v Preble* 64 Me 120 (1874).

[98] *Austin v Commissioner of Police of the Metropolis* [2007] EWCA Civ 989; [2008] QB 660 (the defence was not considered on appeal: [2009] UKHL 5; [2009] 1 AC 564).

[99] *Rigby v CC of Northamptonshire* [1985] 1 WLR 1242 (QBD); [1985] 2 All ER 985.

mentally disordered person.[100] Such cases are now governed by primary legislation.[101] The detailed provisions of this legislation are beyond the scope of this book.

(J) DISCIPLINE

The two main contexts in which torts may be committed to discipline others concern children and unruly passengers on ships and aircraft.

(1) Children[102]

(a) Force used by those with parental responsibility

Those with parental responsibility of a child have the right to chastise the child provided that only reasonable corrective force is used.[103] By legislative fiat, the infliction of 'actual bodily harm' is unreasonable.[104] Parents are also justified in detaining their children to punish them provided that such detention is reasonable in all of the circumstances[105] and so long as it does not breach Article 3 of the European Convention on Human Rights, which prohibits inhuman and degrading treatment.

(b) Force used by schoolteachers and others responsible for children or for their training and education

At one time, schoolteachers, both at boarding and day schools, and in the maintained and the independent sectors, were afforded a broad privilege to use reasonable force to correct children under their tutelage.[106] Nowadays, however, and not least because of the incorporation of the European Convention on Human Rights into domestic law, the ability of persons other than parents to discipline children by using force against them, by detaining them, or by confiscating their property, without incurring liability

---

[100] See, eg, *R v Bournewood Community and Mental Health NHS Trust* [1999] 1 AC 458 (HL).

[101] The most important statutes are the Mental Health Act 1983, the Mental Health (Patients in the Community) Act 1995, and the Mental Capacity Act 2005.

[102] See generally Keating, 'Protecting or Punishing Children: Physical Punishment, Human Rights and English Law Reform' (2006) 26 LS 394; Scutt, 'Sparing Parents Pain or Spoiling the Child by the Rod: Human Rights Arguments against Corporal Punishment' (2009) 28 U Tas L Rev 1.

[103] In *R v H (Assault of Child: Reasonable Chastisement)* [2001] EWCA Crim 1024; [2001] 2 FLR 431 it was held that reasonableness will be judged by reference to (i) the nature and context of the defendant's behaviour, (ii) the duration of the defendant's behaviour, (iii) the physical and mental consequences to the child, (iv) the age and personal characteristics of the child, and (v) the reasons given by the defendant for administering the punishment. These considerations should not be treated as exhaustive.

[104] Under s 58(3) of the Children Act 2004, any battery of a child that causes 'actual bodily harm' cannot be justified under the reasonable chastisement principle. By s 58(4), 'actual bodily harm' bears the same meaning in this context as under s 47 of the Offences Against the Person Act 1861. This Act does not define 'actual bodily harm'. The courts have indicated that these words need no explanation (*DPP v Smith* [1961] AC 290 (HL), at 334). See further David Ormerod, *Smith & Hogan: Criminal Law* (12th edn, 2008), 606–8.

[105] *R v Rahman* (1985) 81 Cr App R 349 (CA).

[106] *Fitzgerald v Northcote* (1865) 4 F & F 656; 176 ER 734 (Assizes) (headmaster, boarding school); *Ryan v Fildes* [1938] 3 All ER 517 (Assizes) (assistant mistress, day school).

in tort is extremely limited.[107] Section 548 of the Education Act 1996, for example, prohibits corporal punishment in both state and independent schools.[108] Similar rules apply to children in community homes[109] or in local authority foster placements.[110] That said, teachers continue to enjoy a residual privilege. The precise scope of this privilege is unclear.

(2) Passengers on vessels

The captain of a ship may use reasonable force against passengers who commit 'some act calculated in the apprehension of a reasonable man to interfere with the safety of the ship or the due prosecution of the voyage',[111] provided that, it seems, he believes that using force is necessary to prevent the act concerned.[112] A captain is not, therefore, justified in detaining a passenger in his cabin for a week because the passenger thumbed his nose to him and did not apologise.[113] A similar power exists in favour of the captain of an aircraft in flight where a person is jeopardising or likely to jeopardise the safety of the flight or persons on board.[114]

(K) ARREST

The powers of arrest conferred on constables and, to a limited extent, on private citizens, are in practice among the most important of the defences discussed in this chapter. The Human Rights Act 1998 requires that the power of arrest meet the principles set out in Article 5 of the European Convention on Human Rights, which guarantees a right to liberty and security.

(1) By a constable with a warrant

A constable is justified in using reasonable force to arrest a person under a warrant. Even if there is a 'defect of jurisdiction' in the magistrate who issued the warrant, a constable is exempt from liability.[115] Thus, a constable is not liable if he obeys even an 'invalid or unlawful warrant'.[116] Obedience to the warrant is always central: thus he is liable if he arrests the wrong person or acts outside his jurisdiction.[117] If he does

---

[107] See generally Education and Inspections Act 2006, Pt 7.

[108] The Act's extension to independent schools, not merely in respect of state-funded pupils, was made clear in *R (on the application of Williamson) v Secretary of State for Education and Employment* [2001] EWHC Admin 960; [2002] 1 FLR 493.   [109] Children's Homes Regulations 1991 (SI 1991/1506), reg 8(2)(a).

[110] Foster Placement (Children) Regulations 1991 (SI 1991/910), Sch 2, para 5.

[111] *Aldworth v Stewart* (1866) 4 F & F 957, at 961; 176 ER 865, at 868 (Assizes).

[112] *Hook v Cunard Steamship Co Ltd* [1953] 1 WLR 682 (Assizes); [1953] 1 All ER 1021.

[113] *Aldworth v Stewart* (1866) 4 F & F 957; 176 ER 865 (Assizes).

[114] Civil Aviation Act 1982, s 94.   [115] Constables Protection Act 1750, s 6.

[116] *McGrath v CC of the Royal Ulster Constabulary* [2001] UKHL 39; [2001] 2 AC 73; *Horsfield v Brown* [1932] 1 KB 355 (KBD), at 369.

[117] As to constables' jurisdiction see the Magistrates' Courts Act 1980, s 125(2).

not have the warrant in his possession, he must produce it on demand as soon as it is practicable to do so.[118]

(2) By a constable without a warrant

The power of arrest without a warrant is governed by section 24 of the Police and Criminal Evidence Act 1984. This section provides that a constable may arrest without a warrant:

(i) anyone who is committing, is about to commit, or has committed an offence; and

(ii) anyone whom he has reasonable grounds for suspecting is committing, is about to commit, or has committed an offence.

Furthermore, a constable must only make an arrest under section 24 if he believes that it is necessary for one or more prescribed reasons. These reasons relate to matters such as ascertaining the name and address of the person in question, preventing the infliction of physical injury (either to the person in question or to some third party), protecting a child, and facilitating the swift investigation of the offence or conduct of the person in question. It is significant that section 24 protects from liability constables who make an arrest as a consequence of a reasonable but mistaken belief that the person arrested was an offender.

(3) Arrest by a private citizen

A person other than a constable may arrest anyone in the act of committing (or reasonably suspected to be committing) an indictable offence.[119] Here, private citizens act at their peril; for if, despite appearances, no offence has actually been committed, they are likely to be liable in false imprisonment.[120] Just as with constables, private citizens may only arrest another where they believe on reasonable grounds that an arrest is necessary according to a list of statutory reasons; but, in addition, it must also appear to the person making the arrest that it is not reasonably practicable for a constable to make that arrest instead.

(4) Breach of the peace

The common law permits both constables and private citizens to arrest without warrant a person committing a breach of the peace or a person who, having committed one, is reasonably believed to be about to renew that breach.[121] Equally, there is a

[118] Access to Justice Act 1999, s 96(4).
[119] Police and Criminal Evidence Act 1984, s 24A(1).
[120] *R v Self* [1992] 1 WLR 657 (CA); [1992] 3 All ER 476 (a store detective arrested a customer whom she saw putting a bar of chocolate in his pocket; the customer was acquitted of theft and the arrest was found to be unlawful).
[121] *Timothy v Simpson* (1835) 1 Cr M & R 757; 149 ER 1285 (Exch); *Bibby v CC of Essex* (2000) 164 JP 297 (CA). Police are not entitled to arrest for obstruction of an officer in the execution of his duty unless the

common-law power to intervene where an imminent breach of the peace is reasonably apprehended.[122] Exceptionally, a person may be detained without a formal arrest in order to prevent or terminate a breach of the peace.[123]

(5) Reasonable grounds for suspicion

The powers of arrest considered above make frequent reference to reasonable grounds for suspicion about the actual or imminent commission of an offence. There is a rich body of case law on the meaning of this phrase. Detailed consideration of the authorities concerned falls beyond the scope of this book.[124] It suffices to note just two things here. First, that reasonable grounds for suspicion are to be judged as a question of fact in each case, and second, that the basic test is one of whether, in all the circumstances, the information available to the person making the arrest, at the time of the arrest, was sufficient to give rise to reasonable grounds for suspicion.

(L) ENTRY, SEARCH, AND SEIZURE

In addition to the power of constables to seek a search warrant from a magistrate, the Police and Criminal Evidence Act 1984 confers on constables powers far greater than those ill-defined powers enjoyed by the police at common law to enter premises, to search persons and property, and to seize evidence.[125] The exercise of these powers will, in an appropriate case, provide a defence to actions for trespass whether to land, person, or goods, and to actions for conversion. Detailed exposition of the relevant powers contained in the 1984 Act is, again, beyond the scope of a general text on torts.[126]

(M) STATUTORY AUTHORITY

Public bodies and officials are invariably empowered or obliged to perform particular acts. If they commit a tort while undertaking the conduct that they are authorised or under a duty to engage in, they may have a defence to liability.[127] Whether or not they enjoy a defence depends upon the construction of the statute that conferred or created the relevant powers or duty. Ultimately, the matter is one of interpretation.[128] Any defence that is found to exist will usually be held only to insulate the defendant

---

disturbance caused, or was likely to cause, a breach of the peace: *Wershof v Commissioner of Police of the Metropolis* [1978] 3 All ER 540 (QBD); (1979) 68 Cr App R 82.

[122] *Foulkes v CC of Merseyside Police* [1998] 2 FLR 798 (CA).

[123] *Albert v Lavin* [1982] AC 546 (HL).

[124] Interested readers should consult *Clerk & Lindsell on Torts* (20th edn, 2010), ch 19.

[125] See also the additional powers of seizure conferred by the Criminal Justice and Police Act 2001, ss 50–1.   [126] For details of the various provisions, see *Clerk & Lindsell on Torts* (20th edn, 2010), ch 15.

[127] *Hammersmith and City Rly Co v Brand* (1869–1870) LR 4 HL 171 (HL).

[128] *Inland Revenue Commissioners v Rossminster Ltd* [1980] AC 952 (HL) is an example of the difficult problems of statutory construction that may arise in this regard.

from liability in respect of torts that could not have been avoided by taking reasonable care.[129] Such defences are justificatory in nature. A statute may also confer immunity. However, the courts are slow to discover immunities owing primarily to the fact that they ignore the extent to which the claimant's rights are infringed.

In determining whether Parliament intended to create a defence, the presence of a provision in the Act for compensating those injured by the activity may be material, and sometimes even decisive. It is also important to look at the nature of the power or duty. Powers to execute some particular work, or to carry on some particular undertaking (such as building a reservoir or a gasworks), 'are, in the absence of clear provision to the contrary in the Act, limited to the doing of the particular things authorised without infringement of the rights of others, except in so far as any such infringement may be a demonstrably necessary consequence of doing what is authorized to be done'.[130] If, however, a public body is required to execute a variety of works at its discretion (many of which are likely to affect private rights), the body will rarely be permitted to infringe those rights, unless respecting the rights concerned would prevent it from doing the very task it was set up to perform.[131]

SECTION 4   PUBLIC POLICY DEFENCES

Public policy defences, to recap, are defences that release the defendant from liability although he committed a tort for no good reason. They exist in order to advance some important goal external to tort law.

(A) ILLEGALITY

The defence of illegality was encountered earlier in the context of the tort of negligence.[132] In relation to that tort, it operates as an absent element defence as it denies the existence of a duty of care. Illegality is also an answer to the intentional torts. In the setting of these torts, it is not an absent element defence (for they do not require a duty of care). Rather, it is a public policy defence since it falls for consideration only once one of these torts is shown to have been committed and is insensitive to the justifiability of the defendant's impugned conduct. Regrettably, the courts have not said clearly when a claim in the intentional torts will fail for illegality. An important decision is *Revill v Newbery*,[133] which was mentioned earlier.[134] Recall that the claimant burglar

---

[129] *Manchester Corp v Farnworth* [1930] AC 171 (HL); *Tate & Lyle Industries Ltd v Greater London Council* [1983] 2 AC 509 (HL); *Geddis v Bann Reservoir Proprietors* (1877–1878) LR 3 App Cas 430 (HL).

[130] *Marriage v East Norfolk River Catchment Board* [1950] 1 KB 284 (CA), at 307; *British Waterways Board v Severn Trent Water Ltd* [2001] EWCA Civ 276; [2002] Ch 25.

[131] *Marriage v East Norfolk River Catchment Board* [1950] 1 KB 284 (CA), at 307–8.

[132] See above ch 6, section 5.

[133] [1996] QB 567 (CA), noted in Weir, 'Swag for the Injured Burglar' (1996) 55 CLJ 182.

[134] See above p 337.

was shot by the defendant occupier while he tried to break into the latter's shed. The occupier's defence of illegality failed. The Court of Appeal held that if the illegality defence applied, it would effectively render the claimant an outlaw and that the legislature, in enacting the Occupiers' Liability Act 1984, which mollified the harsh view that the common law took of the rights of trespassers, implicitly discountenanced such a result.

A different approach was taken in *Cross v Kirkby*.[135] The claimant in this case was a hunting protester. He attacked the defendant, a farmer on whose land he was trespassing for the purpose of disrupting a hunt, with a baseball bat. The defendant wrested the bat from the claimant and used it against him. In resisting an action in battery, the defendant relied on the illegality defence. On this occasion, the Court of Appeal stressed the need to consider whether the claimant's damage was 'closely connected or inextricably bound up' or 'interwoven or linked' with his illegal conduct. In the event, the court held the connection between the claimant's offence and his loss was sufficiently close to enliven the defence. The court attempted to explain the different outcome in *Revill* by asserting that the injury suffered by the claimant in that case was not sufficiently interwoven with his offence. However, it was not made clear why this was so.

A third test was developed in *Lane v Holloway*.[136] The claimant in this matter was an elderly man who provoked the defendant, who was younger and much stronger, by insulting his wife and by striking him on the shoulder (a minor criminal assault). The defendant retaliated with a powerful punch that caused the claimant serious injury. The claimant brought proceedings in battery in respect of this injury. The defence of illegality failed. The Court of Appeal thought that it was significant that the force of the defendant's punch was disproportionate to the gravity of the claimant's offending.

Although no definitive test regarding the defence of illegality emerges from these decisions, they establish two general principles. First, the mere fact that the claimant was acting unlawfully at the time of the defendant's tort will not prevent liability from arising. For example, the defence of illegality will not succeed simply because the claimant was in possession of illegal drugs at the time at which he was beaten by the defendant. Some connection between the illegal act and the damage is essential. Second, trivial offending will not enliven the defence. Only offences entailing moral turpitude[137] will suffice, although exactly how serious the offending must be before the defence will be enlivened is unclear.

It remains to mention the defence created by section 329 of the Criminal Justice Act 2003.[138] This section applies where the claimant sues in trespass to the person and he was convicted of an imprisonable offence in respect of conduct committed at the time of the tort. Where it applies, the defendant will enjoy a defence if the following

---

[135] [2000] All ER (D) 212; (2000) *Times*, 5 April (CA).
[136] [1968] 1 QB 379 (CA).   [137] Sufficiently immoral but lawful acts may also be sufficient: see p 209.
[138] Considered in *Adorian v Commissioner of Police of the Metropolis* [2009] EWCA Civ 18; [2009] 1 WLR 1859; [2009] 4 All ER 227; Spencer, 'Legislate in Haste, Repent at Leisure' (2010) 69 CLJ 19.

conditions are satisfied: (1) his act was not grossly disproportionate; (2) he believed that the claimant was about to commit an offence; and (3) that it was necessary to act to protect himself or his property, to protect the person or property of a third party, or to apprehend the claimant. This section probably adds little to the protection given to defendants by virtue of the defensive force defences and that of illegality.

(B) PRIOR PRIVATE PROSECUTION

Suppose that the claimant brings a private prosecution against the defendant for assault and battery. Irrespective of the outcome of the prosecution, the fact that the prosecution was brought will provide the defendant with a defence to any civil liability that he may have otherwise incurred in respect of the act on which the prosecution was based.[139] The apparent rationale for this defence[140] is that it would be wasteful and unjust to permit the claimant to pursue the defendant in the civil sphere in light of the prior prosecution.

(C) JUDICIAL ACTS

Judicial officers generally enjoy immunity in tort.[141] For example, a judge is not liable in trespass to the person in respect of acts taken against a convicted criminal in the execution of his orders. However, where a judicial order results in an arrest or detention in contravention of the principles embodied in Article 5 of the European Convention on Human Rights, an action for damages may lie under section 9 of the Human Rights Act 1998.

SECTION 5   NON-DEFENCES

In this section, a number of non-defences to liability arising in the intentional torts to the person and to property will briefly be mentioned.

(A) DURESS

It was decided in *Gilbert v Stone*[142] that duress is not an answer to liability in tort. In this case, twelve bandits threatened to kill the defendant if he did not help them to

---

[139] Offences Against the Person Act 1861, ss 44–5.

[140] The Law Commission recommended that this defence be abolished: Law Commission, *Legislating the Criminal Code: Offences Against the Person and General Principles*, Report 218 (1993), at 138 [12.2]. In *Wong v Parkside Health NHS Trust* [2001] EWCA Civ 1721; [2003] 3 All ER 932, at 939 [16] Hale LJ described it as 'anomalous'.

[141] The law in this connection is complex: see Olowofoyeku, *Suing Judges: A Study of Judicial Immunity* (1993), ch 2. Whether judges should enjoy immunity is considered in Murphy, 'Rethinking Tortious Immunity for Judicial Acts' (forthcoming).   [142] (1641) Aleyn 35; 82 ER 902 (KB).

steal the claimant's horse. The defendant yielded to this threat and was sued by the claimant in trespass. It was held that the fact that the defendant's acts were coerced was no defence.[143] The outcome would have been different if the bandits had carried or pushed the defendant on to the claimant's land.[144] This would be a case of physical compulsion rather than duress.

(B) PROVOCATION

The fact that the defendant was provoked into attacking the claimant is not a defence to liability in battery. However, it is a factor that can diminish awards of exemplary damages[145] and possibly compensatory damages.[146]

(C) INSANITY[147]

Unlike the position in the criminal law, insanity is not a defence to liability in tort.[148] Mentally disordered defendants have been held liable in battery,[149] false imprisonment,[150] and trespass to land[151] and goods.[152] It is debatable whether this situation is satisfactory. Arguments advanced in support of the present rule are usually based on deterrence and concerns about defendants faking insanity. These arguments are unconvincing. The insane are unlikely to be deterred by the threat of tort liability (and visiting the insane with liability would not encourage those who care for them to take better care since they already have powerful incentives to act reasonably in the discharge of their responsibilities). Concerns about defendants simulating insanity are unfounded primarily because it is not defendants but their insurers who elect to invoke defences. Defendants simply do not have the opportunity to fake insanity. What arguments are there for admitting insanity as a defence? An analogy might be drawn between involuntariness[153] and insanity. Given that involuntariness is an answer to liability, perhaps insanity should be too. Furthermore, the question arises

---

[143] The courts have had little to say about *Gilbert*. However, it is worth noting that Holmes J singled it out for mention on several occasions. Overall, he remained agnostic on whether it was correctly decided: *Miller v Horton* 26 NE 100, at 102 (Mass, 1891); *Spade v Lynn & BRR* 52 NE 747, at 747 (Mass, 1899); *The Eliza Lines* 199 US 119, at 130–1 (1905).   [144] See above p 326.

[145] *Fontin v Katapodis* [1962] HCA 63; (1962) 108 CLR 177, approved in *Lane v Holloway* [1968] 1 QB 379 (CA); *Hoebergen v Koppens* [1974] 2 NZLR 597 (SC).

[146] Consider *Murphy v Culhane* [1977] QB 94 (CA), at 98; *Cassell & Co Ltd v Broome* [1972] AC 1027 (HL) at 1071; *Wilson v Bobbie* [2006] ABQB 75; (2006) 394 AR 118. See further Nadel, 'Provocation as Basis for Mitigation of Compensatory Damages in Action for Assault and Battery' (1985) 35 ALR 4th 947.

[147] See generally Goudkamp, 'Insanity as a Tort Defence' (2011) OJLS (forthcoming).

[148] *Weaver v Ward* (1616) Hob 134; 80 ER 284 (KB) is generally regarded as the *fons et origo* of this rule.

[149] *Morriss v Marsden* [1952] 1 All ER 925 (QBD); *Beals v Hayward* [1960] NZLR 131 (SC); *Squittieri v de Santis* (1976) 15 OR (2d) 416 (SC); *Delahanty v Hinckley* 799 F Supp 184 (DDC, 1992).

[150] *Krom v Schoonmaker* 3 Barb 647 (NY, 1848).

[151] *Re Meyer's Guardianship* 261 NW 211 (Wis, 1935).   [152] *Morse v Crawford* 17 Vt 499 (1845).

[153] Discussed above at p 326.

whether it is fair to hold the insane liable for their torts. To the extent that liability in tort is a sanction, it seems unjust to impose liability on mentally disordered persons.

(D) INFANCY

The fact that the defendant was an infant at the time of committing a tort is not a defence.[154] As Lord Keynon CJ said in *Jennings v Rundall*, 'if an infant commit an assault, or utter slander, God forbid that he should not be answerable for it in a Court of Justice'.[155] This rule is also controversial. It should be noted that the position that the law takes in relation to infancy should probably mirror that adopted for insanity. This is because infants and the mentally disordered are ultimately in the same position:[156] neither very young infants nor the insane are rational agents. Accordingly, if a defence of insanity is admitted, infants should also be released from liability.

(E) CONTRIBUTORY NEGLIGENCE

This frequently invoked defence is available in relation to certain torts, most notably the tort of negligence.[157] After a long period of uncertainty, it has been settled that it does not apply in proceedings in trespass to the person.[158] Thus, if A goads B into attacking him, A's damages will not be apportioned for his contributory negligence. Nor is contributory negligence a defence in the context of conversion or trespass to goods.[159] It has been argued that apportionment should be unavailable in relation to the intentional torts to the person and to property for several reasons.[160] For instance, it has been suggested that withholding apportionment ensures that tortfeasors are punished more effectively. This argument is weak. This is primarily because the fault elements of the intentional torts are so undemanding that many who commit them do not deserve punishment. It has also been claimed that denying apportionment promotes deterrence. This line of reasoning makes the unrealistic assumption that the average person is aware that apportionment is withheld in the setting of the intentional torts. It also gives no weight to the utility of deterring careless behaviour by claimants. A stronger argument for rejecting contributory negligence as a defence in the domain of the intentional torts concerns the doctrine of provocation, which was discussed above.[161] Arguably, this doctrine permits compensatory damages to be

---

[154] *Ellis v D'Angelo* 253 P 2d 675 (Cal, 1953) (four-year-old capable of being held liable for battery). Consider also the remarks in *Hackshaw v Shaw* [1984] HCA 84; (1984) 155 CLR 614, at 664.

[155] (1799) 8 TR 335, at 337; 101 ER 1419, at 1421–2 (KB).

[156] 'There can be no distinction as to the liability of infants and lunatics' (*Williams v Hays* 143 NY 442, at 451 (1894)).   [157] See ch 6, section 2.

[158] *Co-operative Group (CWS) Ltd v Pritchard* [2011] EWCA Civ 329. See further Goudkamp, 'Contributory Negligence and Trespass to the Person' (2011) 127 LQR 518.

[159] Torts (Interference with Goods) Act 1977, s 11(1).

[160] Williams, *Joint Torts and Contributory Negligence: A Study of Concurrent Fault in Great Britain, Ireland and the Common-Law Dominions* (1951), 198; Dobbs, *The Law of Torts* (2000), 520–1.

[161] See p 348.

reduced in circumstances in which it is thought that contributory negligence should count against the claimant. If this is the case, there may be no need to admit contributory negligence as a defence to the intentional torts.

(F) MISTAKE[162]

In previous chapters it was observed that mistake is not a defence to liability arising in the intentional torts.[163] If the defendant drove his tractor on to the claimant's land, the fact that he mistakenly believed that the land was his own or that the occupier consented to his entry will not prevent the tort of trespass to land from being constituted. This is so even if the mistake was reasonable. Analogous comments can be made about conversion. An auctioneer who sells a stolen chattel is liable in this tort even if he believed that the vendor owned the goods. The reasonableness of his mistake is irrelevant. Likewise, it is a battery to touch another person who does not consent to the touching. It is (probably) no answer to liability that the defendant believed that the claimant was consenting.[164] Although mistake per se is not a defence to the intentional torts, it may be relevant to know in the context of some defences whether the defendant was mistaken as to some fact. For example, as discussed above, a defendant who uses defensive force against a person whom he mistakenly believes is an aggressor may be entitled to the defence of self-defence if his mistake is reasonable.[165]

(G) PRIVATE NECESSITY[166]

The defence of public necessity was discussed earlier.[167] Recall that it applies where the defendant commits a tort to protect a greater public interest from an imminent risk of harm. Private necessity involves the defendant acting tortiously in order to safeguard an interest of his own from a sudden emergency. Unlike public necessity, private necessity is probably not a defence.[168] Discussions of private necessity invariably centre on the famous decision of the Supreme Court of Minnesota in *Vincent v Lake Erie Transportation Co*.[169] The facts of this case were as follows.[170]

---

[162] See Whittier, 'Mistake in the Law of Torts' (1902) 15 Harv L Rev 44; Trindade, 'Intentional Torts: Some Thoughts on Assault and Battery' (1982) 2 OJLS 211.   [163] See chs 8–10.

[164] McBride asserts that the position would be otherwise if the claimant induced the defendant to believe that he was consenting: McBride, 'Trespass to the Person: The Effect of Mistakes and Alternative Remedies on Liability' (2008) 67 CLJ 461, at 462–3.   [165] See above pp 334–5

[166] An exhaustive review of the case law is provided in Cohan, 'Private and Public Necessity and the Violation of Property Rights' (2007) 83 ND L Rev 651.   [167] See above pp 340–1.

[168] Although cf *Cope v Sharpe (No 2)* [1912] 1 KB 496 (CA) (defendant who burned heather on the claimant's land in order to prevent a fire on the claimant's land from spreading to land on which the defendant's master had shooting rights exempted from liability).   [169] 124 NW 221 (Minn, 1910).

[170] *Vincent* has been extensively analysed. For a small selection of the literature see Bohlen, 'Incomplete Privilege to Inflict Intentional Invasions of Interests of Property and Personality' (1926) 39 Harv L Rev 307; Keeton, 'Conditional Fault in the Law of Torts' (1959) 72 Harv L Rev 401, at 410–18; Christie, 'The Defense of Necessity Considered from the Legal and Moral Points of View' (1999) 48 Duke LJ 975; Klimchuk, 'Necessity

The SS *Reynolds*, which was owned by the defendant, was moored at the claimant's dock. A fierce storm spontaneously developed. The captain of the *Reynolds* signalled for a tug-boat to assist her to leave the dock. But no tugboat operator was prepared to help owing to the ferocity of the storm. Accordingly, the captain of the *Reynolds* decided that the ship should remain docked (had the captain cast off, the *Reynolds* would probably have been destroyed). The storm repeatedly threw the *Reynolds* against the dock. The claimant sued the defendant in negligence and trespass in respect of the damage caused to the dock.

The court rejected the claim in negligence on the ground that the captain acted reasonably but found for the claimant in the action in trespass. Although private necessity is not a defence to the intentional torts, it seems that it is a tort to resist a person who acts out of private necessity.[171] It is for this reason that it is sometimes said that private necessity is an 'incomplete privilege'.

FURTHER READING

BRUDNER, 'A Theory of Necessity' (1987) 7 *Oxford Journal of Legal Studies* 339

GILLES, 'Inevitable Accident in Classical English Tort Law' (1994) 43 *Emory Law Journal* 575

GOUDKAMP, 'A Taxonomy of Tort Law Defences' in Degeling, Edelman, and Goudkamp (eds), *Torts in Commercial Law* (2011), ch 19

GOUDKAMP, 'Self-Defence and Illegality Under the Civil Liability Act 2002 (NSW)' (2010) 18 *Torts Law Journal* 61

GOUDKAMP, 'Insanity as a Tort Defence' (2011) *Oxford Journal of Legal Studies* (forthcoming)

HAWES, 'Recaption of Chattels: The Use of Force against the Person' (2006) 12 *Canterbury Law Review* 253

KEATING, 'Protecting or Punishing Children: Physical Punishment, Human Rights and English Law Reform' (2006) 26 *Legal Studies* 394

LAW COMMISSION, *Illegality Defence*, Report 320 (2010)

POSNER, 'Killing or Wounding to Protect a Property Interest' (1971) 14 *Journal of Law and Economics* 201

SUGARMAN, 'The "Necessity" Defense and the Failure of Tort Theory: The Case Against Strict Liability for Damages Caused while Exercising Self-Help in an Emergency' (2005) *Issues in Legal Scholarship* (online journal)

and Restitution' (2001) 7 Legal Theory 59. See also the special issue on *Vincent* in (2005) *Issues in Legal Scholarship* (online journal).

[171] *Ploof v Putnam* 71 A 188 (Vt, 1908).

PART IV

INTERFERENCE WITH ECONOMIC AND INTELLECTUAL PROPERTY INTERESTS

12

BACKGROUND TO THE PROTECTION OF ECONOMIC AND INTELLECTUAL PROPERTY INTERESTS

KEY ISSUES

(1) Abstentionism in the courts

The English courts, unlike their American counterparts, have generally been reluctant to enable tort law to become a tool to ensure fair competition between rival businessmen. On the whole, then, tort law's tendency is to look towards (a) the intentional infliction of economic harm via (b) some or other unlawful means. This means that the economic torts do not inhibit aggressive competition per se, but instead draw the line at excessive competition.

(2) Three broad sources of protection

The protection from excessive competitive practices that tort law provides can be divided into three broad classes. The first concerns the protection granted by the *general* economic torts (of which there are

five). The second comprises the protection afforded by the misrepresentation economic torts (of which there are three). The final class is loosely concerned with the protection of intellectual property (and analogous) rights. So far as this latter category is concerned, the law is largely rooted in statute and is generally these days treated as a specialist area of study (IP Law). There is, however, an analogous action in equity based on breach of confidence that deserves to be mentioned alongside the IP regime. (That said, the breach of confidence action seems now to be giving way to a nascent tort concerning the protection of private, personal information. For this reason full discussion of misuse such information is considered in another part of this book (see chapter 22).)

SECTION 1   GENERAL ECONOMIC INTERESTS

(A) RIGHTS AND ECONOMIC INTERESTS[1]

The law of torts affords every member of society comprehensive protection from deliberately inflicted harm to the rights he has in his physical integrity, his goods, and his land by means of the torts discussed in the previous part of this book. By contrast, the protection afforded by tort law to a claimant's interests in his livelihood, business, and trading interests is significantly less comprehensive. Should my economic prosperity be diminished because I have been physically attacked and can no longer work, my attacker must compensate me for my loss of income. Similarly, if one workman takes the tools of another, he does so at his peril. A misguided belief that the tools were his own will not exculpate him. Yet, if a businessman seduces away from a rival his customers, or if he persuades other traders to discontinue dealing with his rival, that rival *may*, depending on the circumstances, have no remedy in tort for his loss of livelihood.

It was in the landmark decision in *Allen v Flood*[2] that the House of Lords, by a majority, stifled the growth of any general principle of liability in tort for intentional and malicious interference with economic and business interests.[3]

> Flood and Taylor were shipwrights taken on for the day by the Glengall Iron Company to work on the woodwork of a ship. During the day, other employees of the company, who were boilermakers, discovered that Flood and Taylor had previously been employed by another firm working on ironwork. The boilermakers belonged to a union that strongly opposed shipwrights being employed to do ironwork. Allen, an official of the union, sought an interview with an officer of the Glengall Iron Company and told him that unless the respondents were dismissed, all the boilermakers would 'knock off work'. At the end of the day, Flood and Taylor were told that their services would no longer be required. And since they were being engaged on a daily basis only, 'letting them go' in this way involved no breach of contract on the part of the Glengall Iron Company. Flood and Taylor therefore brought an action against Allen for maliciously inducing the company not to employ them on subsequent occasions: that is, for intentionally interfering with their livelihood.

The claimants' case depended largely on establishing a right to the protection of their economic interests. Although Hawkins J, in his advice to the Law Lords, conceived there to be a right 'to pursue freely and without hindrance, interruption or molestation that profession, trade or calling which he has adopted for his livelihood',[4] the majority of their Lordships refused to recognise such a *right*. They recognized only a *freedom* to pursue one's livelihood. They also noted that, because the union members were only engaged on a daily basis, they in turn were no less free to 'knock off' as

---

[1] See generally Carty, *An Analysis of the Economic Torts* (2nd edn, 2010).   [2] [1898] AC 1, at 14.
[3] In *Keeble v Hickeringall* (1706) 11 East 574n Holt CJ enunciated a broad principle to this effect.
[4] [1898] AC 1, at 14.

threatened. Finally, having found nothing intentionally unlawful in what Allen had done, the House of Lords rejected the contention that Allen's motive, to 'punish' the respondents for providing work for Flood and Taylor, transformed an otherwise lawful act (ie, refusing to work the next day) into an actionable tort.

The decision in this case gives rise to a general point, the significance of which ought sensibly to be borne in mind when considering the various economic torts explored in the next chapters. That general point is this: that *Allen v Flood* displays a clear commitment to an abstentionist approach with respect to controlling the intentional infliction of economic harm between business or industrial rivals. Liability, their Lordships suggested, should only be imposed where economic losses were inflicted in ways that involve some or other unlawful means. Specifically, the ones tested (and found to be absent) in that case were: (1) whether any breach of contract had been induced, and (2) whether any unlawful acts (or threats thereof) had been used. In the absence of such unlawful means, losses inflicted by rivals should be considered lawful, and as part and parcel of free competition between economic actors. Notably, in the USA, a more interventionist approach was adopted. So in *Tuttle v Buck*,[5] the claimant recovered where a wealthy defendant set up a rival barber's shop charging much lower prices purely to drive the claimant out of business.

After a lengthy period of time during which the courts got the general economic torts into a dreadful muddle, the orthodoxy and simplicity of *Allen v Flood* was confirmed by the House of Lords in *OBG v Allan*.[6] Alas, as will be explained in the next chapter, almost before the ink was dry on the speeches in that case, a differently constituted House of Lords muddied the waters once again in *Total Network SL v Revenue and Customs Commissioners*.[7] For now, however, it is worth exploring in a little more detail why it is that the courts adopt a relatively hands-off approach to the regulation of aggressive (but not excessive) competition.

(B) FREE COMPETITION, UNFAIR COMPETITION

Why is it that the English courts reject a general right to the protection of economic interests? The clearest explanation is to be found in the following dictum of Atkin LJ in *Ware and de Freville Ltd v Motor Trade Association*.

> [T]he right of the individual to carry on his trade or profession or execute his own activities, whatever they may be, without interruption, so long as he refrains from tort or crime, affords an unsatisfactory basis for determining what is actionable, in as much as the right is conditioned by a precisely similar right in the rest of his fellow men. Such co-existing rights do in a world of competition necessarily impinge upon one another... The true question is, was the power of the [claimant] to carry on his trade etc, interrupted by an act which the law deems wrongful.[8]

---

[5] 107 Min 145 (1909).
[6] [2008] 1 AC 1.   [7] [2008] 1 AC 1174.   [8] [1921] 3 KB 40, at 79.

Historically, English law has favoured free competition. Such a stance is manifestly inconsistent with any assumption that the interest in pursuing a livelihood or a trade is entitled to absolute legal protection.[9] Thus, for the purposes of the general economic torts – of which there are five[10] – interference with another's business is generally only tortious so long as, at some point in the chain of causative events, an independently unlawful act occurs. The one exception to this proposition is the tort of simple conspiracy whose touchstones are malicious purpose and combination.

A second group of economic torts – all of which have at their heart the use of false representations – also seek to censure excessive forms of competition. Thus, the tort of deceit imposes liability for the use of fraudulent representations in reliance on which the claimant suffers damage. At the same time, the tort of passing off prevents the defendant falsely cashing in on the claimant's goodwill by misrepresenting to customers either the provenance or quality of his goods; while the tort of malicious falsehood makes accountable traders who falsely disparage their competitors.

Third, and finally, there is a group of torts concerned with the protection of intellectual property rights. These are for the most part regulated by statutes the details of which fall beyond the compass of a general textbook on tort law. That being so, only the misrepresentation-based torts and the general economic torts will be subjected to detailed analysis in following chapters. The next section of this chapter does, however, provide a brief account of the intellectual property torts; simply in order to complete the picture of liability in respect of interferences with economic interests.

SECTION 2   INTELLECTUAL PROPERTY INTERESTS

The nature of intellectual property and the way in which it is afforded protection under English law is now a well-established, discrete area of study. What follows, therefore, cannot pretend to be more than the very briefest of outlines. Nonetheless, such adumbration is justified in a book of this kind to provide a more complete picture of tort's protection of economic and related interests than would be afforded by an analysis of the economic torts alone.

(A) COPYRIGHT, PATENTS, AND SIMILAR INTERESTS

Intellectual property can be defined broadly as the intangible products of a person's mind and skill. Tangible property, be it land or goods, is protected from intentional interference by trespass and conversion, and from carelessly inflicted harm by the tort of negligence. By contrast, contractual rights are safeguarded to a limited extent

---

[9] Arts 101 and 102 of the Treaty on the Functioning of the EU govern modern competition law.

[10] Viz: (i) inducing breach of contract, (ii) causing loss by unlawful means, (iii) lawful means conspiracy, (iv) unlawful means conspiracy, and (v) intimidation. However, the juridical nature and basis of some of these torts is, as will be seen in the next chapter, highly controversial.

by the general economic torts, while goodwill (built up in the course of a business) is protected by the tort of passing off. But what of a person's interest in the results of his intellectual efforts? To what extent are works of literature or art, or indeed scientific inventions, afforded protection by the law of torts? Statute generally provides the answers. The Copyright, Designs and Patents Act 1988 protects authors, artists, and musicians from those who would 'pirate' their efforts; the Patents Act 1977 safeguards new scientific and technological inventions; the Trade Marks Act 1994 supplements the tort of passing off by enabling traders to register their trade mark, rendering any infringement of that mark actionable; and designs, both registered and unregistered, are protected by the Registered Designs Act 1949 and the Copyright, Designs and Patents Act 1988 respectively.

While the protection afforded by these various statutes is potentially fairly wide ranging, it does not typically apply automatically. The would-be 'intellectual property owner' must generally register his or her claim in order to acquire protection. Thus, for example, the inventor of a product must register a patent in order to protect his intellectual property interest.

While the details of this regulatory web are beyond the scope of this work, it should nonetheless be noted that actions based on infringements of copyright, patents, or trade marks are essentially tort actions. The remedies generally sought include damages, injunctions, and search orders. But given the potential for intellectual property to be the source of huge economic wealth, a number of judges have averred that, in respect of the infringement of patents at least, exemplary damages may be available.[11] And in the wake of the decision in *Kuddus v Chief Constable of Leicestershire*,[12] this view would seem to be palatable enough.

(B) BREACH OF CONFIDENCE

(1) The obligation of confidentiality

The grant of a patent protects research processes only once they have concluded in a novel invention. At that stage, anyone who produces a cheaper, 'copycat' version may infringe the patent. However, where details are leaked to a competitor while the idea is still in the process of refinement and has yet to be expressed in written or other form, there can be no such infringement. How, then, does the law protect such secrets? One partial answer is that, when a competitor seeks to induce an employee to divulge trade secrets, an action for inducing breach of contract may lie.[13] But what of other confidential information, such as lists of clients, special manufacturing processes, and so on? Certainly, the law of equity extends a degree of protection to all victims of breaches of confidential information. The detailed principles need not be reproduced

---

[11] See *Morton-Norwich Products Inc v Intercen Ltd (No 2)* [1981] FSR 337 doubted in *Catnic Components Ltd v Hill & Smith Ltd* [1983] FSR 512.   [12] [2002] 2 AC 122.
[13] *Hivac Ltd v Park Royal Scientific Instruments Ltd* [1946] Ch 169.

here.[14] They are discussed in full in chapter 22, and it suffices to note that an obligation of confidentiality will arise where information is entrusted by X to Y in circumstances where Y is relied upon to keep the confidence.[15]

Although not true of all confidential information,[16] some confidential information may well be valuable as part of a claimant's business and economic interests. Yet even here there may be no need to have recourse to tort law or equity as, sometimes, protection will be available within the law of contract.[17] For example, the duty of fidelity owed by an employee not to disclose his employer's trade secrets derives from his contract of employment. However, an action in contract will not always be available. Consider *Seager v Copydex Ltd.*[18]

> C had told D about a new type of carpet grip. Without conscious plagiarism, D developed this idea which had been divulged in confidence. C was awarded damages to compensate him for the use of his idea by D without paying for it. It was held that, for damages to be available, the information in question must not have been in the public domain; it must not have been public knowledge.

Notwithstanding the availability of damages outside a breach of contract, and in the absence of any harm to tangible or intangible property, the precise nature of the action for breach of confidence remains unclear. Criteria used to determine the measure of damages indicate a judicial perception of the action as one analogous to tort.[19] Equally, the recognition of a *duty* of confidentiality is reminiscent of the law of negligence, while the development of a public interest defence – somewhat akin to qualified privilege in defamation – again suggests a nascent tort.[20] But as will be explained fully in chapter 22, the action for breach of confidence remains, for now, an equitable action (albeit one that, because of the developments it has undergone in the last few decades, has prompted what looks like the emergence of a new tort based on the misuse of private information). Recognising the juridical confusion in this area, the Law Commission proposed clarification some years ago in the form of a statutory tort of breach of confidence,[21] but such a step has yet to be taken.

---

[14] This is mainly because the equitable action looks set to be overtaken by the nascent tort of misuse of private information: see ch 22.

[15] See *Coco v AN Clark (Engineers) Ltd* [1969] RPC 41; *Dunford and Elliott Ltd v Johnston* [1978] FSR 143; *WB v H Bauer Publishing Ltd* [2002] EMLR 145.

[16] See, eg, *Duchess of Argyll v Duke of Argyll* [1967] Ch 302 where C was granted an injunction to prohibit her former husband disclosing certain marital confidences. Equally, the relationship between a doctor and her patients gives rise to an obligation on the doctor to keep her patients' confidences: *X v Y* [1988] 2 All ER 648; *W v Egdell* [1990] Ch 359.

[17] See, eg, *Peter Pan Manufacturing Corpn v Corsets Silhouette Ltd* [1964] 1 WLR 96. The duty may even survive a repudiation of the contract: *Campbell v Frisbee* [2002] EMLR 656.

[18] [1967] 2 All ER 415. See also *WB v H Bauer Publishing Ltd* [2002] EMLR 145.

[19] See *Seager v Copydex Ltd* [1967] 2 All ER 415.

[20] *Initial Services Ltd v Putterill* [1968] 1 QB 396, at 405; *Fraser v Evans* [1969] 1 QB 349, at 362; *Khashoggi v Smith* (1980) 124 Sol Jo 149.   [21] Law Com No 110, *Breach of Confidence* (Cmnd 8388).

(2) Remedies

The most common remedy for a breach of confidence is the injunction. It is clearly preferable to anticipate and prevent the disclosure to the public at large of the relevant information than to wait for such disclosure, then sue for damages. On the other hand, where a breach of confidence has already occurred, damages may of course be awarded. And where the confidential information is of commercial value, an account of profits is also often sought.

FURTHER READING

CARTY, *An Analysis of the Economic Torts* (2nd edn, 2010), chs 1–8

DEAKIN AND RANDALL, 'Rethinking the Economic Torts' (2009) 72 *Modern Law Review* 519

SALES AND STILITZ, 'Intentional Infliction of Harm by Unlawful Means' (1999) 115 *Law Quarterly Review* 411

13

FALSE REPRESENTATIONS

KEY ISSUES

(1) Torts based on false statements protective of economic interests

This chapter considers torts designed to protect the claimant's economic interests from improper actions of others. The unifying feature is a false representation. In most cases, 'the defendant seeks to make a gain which properly belongs to the claimant'.[1]

(2) Deceit

The tort of deceit occurs where the defendant makes a representation knowing of its falsity, or without belief in its truth, or recklessly, careless whether it be true or false, with the intention that the claimant should act in reliance upon it, which causes damage to the claimant in consequence of his reliance upon it.

(3) Passing off

The tort of passing off occurs where the defendant makes, in the course of trade, a false representation that is calculated to deceive the claimant's customers or clients in a way which is really likely to be damaging to the claimant's goodwill. There is no need to prove an intention to harm. The focus is upon the likely effect, objectively considered, of the misrepresentation upon the claimant's goodwill.

(4) Malicious falsehood

The tort of malicious falsehood occurs where the defendant makes a false representation disparaging of the claimant's interest in property, the quality of his goods, or his fitness to offer services, which is maliciously published and really likely to cause, and which does actually cause, damage to the claimant's goodwill.

SECTION 1   DECEIT

Deliberately false representations on which the claimant is induced to, and does, rely to his detriment have been, for more than two centuries, actionable under the tort of deceit.[2] Judicial recognition that fraud never constituted fair competition has a much

---

[1] Carty, *An Analysis of the Economic Torts* (2nd edn, 2010), 3.
[2] *Pasley v Freeman* (1789) 3 Term Rep 51.

longer history;[3] but whether early authorities were founded on contract, equity, or tort is not entirely clear. Whatever their basis, it remains true that the law relating to false representations cannot be understood fully by considering tort alone. A misrepresentation may concurrently create rights of action in tort and contract. A misrepresentation not actionable in tort may give rise to a right to rescind a contract, and misrepresentations unconcerned with contract may create an estoppel. The relationship between common law and equitable remedies for misrepresentation further complicates the picture.

Nonetheless, the development of the separate tort of deceit can be traced fairly precisely to the decision in *Pasley v Freeman*[4] where the defendant falsely misrepresented to the claimant that X was a person to whom the claimant might safely sell goods on credit. The claimant suffered loss by relying on this representation and was held to have an action on the case for deceit. Subsequently, the tort has been defined in terms of several key elements: namely: a false representation made '(1) knowingly, or (2) without belief in its truth, or (3) recklessly, careless whether it be true or false',[5] with the intention that C should act in reliance upon the representation, which causes damage to C in consequence of his reliance upon it.

(A) FALSE REPRESENTATIONS

Usually the representation will consist of written or spoken words. But it may be assumed that any conduct calculated to mislead will suffice[6] – for example, turning back the mileage indicator on the odometer of a car prior to negotiating its sale. Furthermore, '[w]here the defendant has manifestly approved and adopted a representation made by some third person' he may himself be held to commit the tort.[7] And where a statement is simultaneously capable of bearing a true and a false interpretation, and the defendant knows of the false one, there is a false representation for present purposes.[8]

Active concealment of the truth, whereby the claimant is prevented from getting information which he otherwise would have got, is a sufficient misrepresentation although no positive misstatement is made.[9] Equally, although mere non-disclosure is not enough for this tort,[10] a statement which is misleading because it is incomplete

---

[3] There has been a writ of deceit since 1201.   [4] (1789) 3 Term Rep 51.
[5] *Derry v Peek* (1889) 14 App Cas 337, at 374.   [6] Cf *R v Barnard* (1837) 7 C & P 784.
[7] *Bradford Third Equitable Benefit Building Society v Borders* [1941] 2 All ER 205, at 211.
[8] *Smith v Chadwick* (1884) 9 App Cas 187, at 201. If the court construes documents as false, but is not satisfied that D intended to give them that false meaning, he is not liable in deceit: *Gross v Lewis Hillman Ltd* [1970] Ch 445.   [9] Cf *Schneider v Heath* (1813) 3 Camp 506.
[10] There is generally no duty of candour. Even in the exceptional case of insurance contracts, avoidance of the contract (rather than an action in deceit) is the appropriate remedy: *Banque Keyser Ullmann SA v Skandia (UK) Insurance Co Ltd* [1990] 1 QB 665; *HIH Casualty and General Insurance Ltd v Chase Manhattan Bank* [2001] 2 Lloyd's Rep 483.

may be actionable. Thus, Lord Cairns held in *Peek v Gurney*:[11] 'there must...be some active misstatement of fact, or, at all events, such a partial and fragmentary statement of fact, as that the withholding of that which is not stated makes that which is stated absolutely false'.

Where a statement by the defendant was accurate when made but, owing to a change of circumstances of which the defendant has become aware, it ceases to be true, there is an actionable misrepresentation if the defendant, by remaining silent, induces the claimant to act to his detriment on the basis of the original statement. Consider *Incledon v Watson*.[12]

> In an advertisement for the sale of his school, D stated the number of scholars at that time. That statement was not proved to be inaccurate. During the course of negotiations, the number decreased. C, who bought on the faith of the representation, and who was not informed of the reduction in numbers, was held to have an action in deceit for damages.

The case illustrates that what counts is that the statement must be false when the claimant acts upon it.[13] There is support for the view that an action lies if the defendant, though believing the statement to be true when he made it, later learns of its falsity but does not disclose this to the claimant who subsequently relies on the statement.[14] And there are some contracts – for example, contracts of insurance – in which, because only one party can know the material facts, there is a legal duty on that party to disclose all the material information. Breach of this duty renders the contract voidable. Yet, the issue whether such failures to disclose amount to the tort of deceit is undecided.

(B) KNOWLEDGE OF FALSITY

As already noted, in order for the defendant to be liable, he must have made the statement knowingly, or without belief in its truth, or recklessly, careless whether it be true or false. In short, the claimant must prove that the defendant did not honestly believe the statement to be true.[15] Importantly, there is no tort of deceit merely because the claimant does not have reasonable grounds for believing the truth of his statement.[16] The facts of *Derry v Peek* illustrate how onerous the burden of proof is.

> A company was empowered by private Act to run trams by animal power, or, if the consent of the Board of Trade was obtained, by steam power. The directors, believing that the Board of Trade would give this consent as a matter of course (since the Board of Trade raised no objection when the plans were laid before it) issued a prospectus saying that

---

[11] (1873) LR 6 HL 377, at 403. See also *Banque Financière de la Cité v Westgate Insurance Co Ltd* [1990] 2 All ER 947.   [12] (1862) 2 F & F 841. See also *Jones v Dumbrell* [1981] VR 199.

[13] Cf *Briess v Woolley* [1954] AC 333.

[14] *Brownlie v Campbell* (1880) 5 App Cas 925, at 950 (*obiter*); *Templeton Insurance Ltd v Motorcare Warranties Ltd* [2010] EWHC 3113 (Comm), at [168].

[15] Although C need not shoulder a criminal standard of proof, his burden of proving fraud is stricter than that of the ordinary civil standard: see *Hornal v Neuberger Products Ltd* [1957] 1 QB 247.

[16] See, eg, *Niru Battery Manufacturing Co v Milestone Trading Ltd* [2004] QB 985.

the company had the ability to run trams by steam power. Relying on this prospectus, the respondent bought shares in the company. The Board of Trade eventually refused its consent, and later the company was wound up.

The House of Lords held that an action in deceit against the directors failed because no want of honest belief on the part of any director was established by the respondent, and it has since been stated that the absence of any injurious intent – though motive is technically immaterial in deceit – may nonetheless constitute good evidence of an honest belief in the truth of a statement.[17] In the light of this, their Lordships have since insisted upon a special rule for legal counsel: namely, that before counsel could put his signature to an allegation of fraud, he must have received instructions to do so and have evidence before him to make good the allegation.[18] The receipt of instructions is not itself enough; and however negligent a defendant may have been, that is not sufficient to make him liable in deceit.

(C) INTENTION TO DECEIVE

In deceit cases, the claimant must prove that the statement was 'made with the intention that it should be acted upon by the claimant, or by a class of persons which will include the claimant'.[19] Lord Cairns in *Peek v Gurney*[20] might be taken as saying that the claimant must prove that the defendant 'intended'– in the sense that he desired or had the purpose – that the claimant should act on the statement. Intention is, however, best interpreted in the way in which it is normally interpreted in torts: the misrepresentation should be calculated, or its necessary consequence should be to induce the claimant.[21] Thus, a deceit action may be based on an advertisement in a newspaper if the claimant shows that he was one of a class of persons at whom the advertisement was directed.[22]

A misrepresentation need not be communicated to the claimant by the defendant, provided that the defendant intended that it should be communicated to him and that he should rely on it.[23] Furthermore, *Pilmore v Hood*[24] seems to support the imputation of such intention.

A, who was negotiating the sale of a public house to B, made certain false statements to B concerning the takings of the public house. The transaction fell through. To A's

---

[17] *Barings plc v Coopers & Lybrand (No 5)* [2002] PNLR 823. But see now the Financial Services and Markets Act 2000, s 90 and Sch 10 (statutory liability for false prospectuses); HM Treasury, *Extension of Statutory Regime for Issuer Liability* (2008).   [18] *Medcalf v Mardell* [2002] 3 All ER 721.

[19] *Bradford Third Equitable Benefit Building Society v Borders* [1941] 2 All ER 205, at 211.

[20] (1873) LR 6 HL 377.

[21] *Polhill v Walter* (1832) 3 B & Ad 114; *Richardson v Silvester* (1873) LR 9 QB 34 and see support for this view in *Peek v Gurney* (1873) LR 6 HL 377, at 399 and 401.

[22] *Richardson v Silvester* (1873) LR 9 QB 34 (C misled by a false advertisement in the press that a farm was for sale).   [23] *JD Wetherspoon plc v Van De Berg & Co Ltd* [2007] PNLR 28, at [384].

[24] (1838) 5 Bing NC 97. See also *Langridge v Levy* (1837) 2 M & W 519.

knowledge, B passed on to C these false statements. A then sold to C without correcting these statements and was held to be liable in deceit.

The claimant must also have been influenced in the manner intended. If, therefore, company promoters issue a prospectus to the claimant, who buys shares (not by subscribing to this issue, but by purchasing subsequently on the market), and the prospectus was not calculated to influence market dealings, no action will lie.[25] The motive of the defendant is irrelevant. That being so, it was no excuse that the defendant who made a false statement about some company shares genuinely believed that investment in that company would be advantageous to the claimant,[26] or that the defendant did not intend the claimant to suffer any loss in consequence of the misrepresentation.[27] On the other hand, promoters will be liable where they issue false information about a company in order to inflate the market value of shares in that company for their personal gain.[28]

(D) RELIANCE OF THE CLAIMANT

The claimant must prove that the misrepresentation of the defendant both influenced him[29] and caused him to act to his own prejudice as he did.[30] The action lies even if the misrepresentation was only one of several factors impinging on the mind of the claimant.[31] And if the court is satisfied that the false statement was 'actively present to his mind' when the claimant acted, it will not readily hold that he might have acted as he did in any event, even if the false statement had not been made.[32] Relatedly, the courts sometimes say that the misrepresentation must be material. When they do so, they mean that if the claimant acted in a way that a person was likely to act in reliance on the statement of the defendant, this would be prima facie evidence that he did so rely on it.[33] Furthermore, the fact that the claimant acted foolishly is of no moment, because, first, there is no scope for invoking the defence of contributory negligence in

---

[25] *Peek v Gurney* (1873) LR 6 HL 377 had similar facts. Cf *Andrews v Mockford* [1896] 1 QB 372. The Stock Exchange now makes a public advertisement of an issue a condition precedent to the grant of a market quotation, and intention to induce marketing dealings will presumably now be imputed.

[26] *Smith v Chadwick* (1884) 9 App Cas 187, at 201.

[27] *Brown, Jenkinson & Co Ltd v Percy Dalton (London) Ltd* [1957] 2 QB 621.

[28] *Possfund Custodian Trustee Ltd v Diamond* [1996] 2 All ER 774.

[29] *Downs v Chappell* [1996] 3 All ER 344.

[30] *Smith v Chadwick* (1884) 9 App Cas 187; *MacLeay v Tait* [1906] AC 24; *Dadourian Group Int'l Inc v Simms* [2009] 1 Lloyd's Rep PN 601, at [99]–[101]. There must be some conduct of C's in reliance on the representation. Harmful effects produced directly on C (eg, if the false statement causes him to be ill) are not the subject of a claim for this tort, even though C does not recover in the same action for loss suffered through acts performed in reliance: *Wilkinson v Downton* [1897] 2 QB 57.

[31] *Cassa di Risparmio della Republicca di San Marino SpA v Barclays Bank Ltd* [2011] EWHC 484 (Comm), at [468].   [32] *Edgington v Fitzmaurice* (1885) 29 Ch D 459.

[33] *Arnison v Smith* (1889) 41 Ch D 348, at 369.

the tort of deceit,[34] and second, the claimant's act of reliance need not be of the precise kind intended by the defendant.[35]

It is sometimes doubted whether a misrepresentation of an opinion is actionable. An example is the seller who describes his house as highly desirable and commodious and whose sales talk – which is really an expression of opinion – does not incur liability in deceit. Again, a statement by a ratings agency that a complex financial instrument is 'AAA' is said to be an opinion, and not a representation as to default probabilities that could be relied upon by the instrument's purchaser.[36] If both parties have equal access to information about the subject matter, no action is likely to lie. But when the opinion purports to impart information to another who is not on an equal footing,[37] or where the opinion is provided without reasonable grounds such as to evidence dishonesty,[38] an action is possible.

The same general principles govern statements of law.[39] If the representations refer to legal principles, as distinct from the facts on which these principles operate, and the parties are on an equal footing, those representations are only expressions of belief and of the same effect as expressions of opinion between parties on an equal footing. In other cases where the defendant professes legal knowledge beyond that of the claimant, the ordinary rules of liability for deceit apply.

Misrepresentations of intention supply further problems. Certainly, if a defendant promises to do something and fails to carry out his promise, the claimant will ordinarily look to the law of contract for his remedy. If, however, the defendant at the time of his statement lacks either the will or the power to carry out the promise, there is a misrepresentation capable of giving rise to liability for deceit. Thus, it was actionable to state in a company's invitation to the public to subscribe to an issue of debentures that the loan was being arranged in order to improve buildings, when the real purpose was to discharge existing liabilities.[40]

(E) LOSS

There is no cause of action unless the claimant proves that he sustained loss or damage.[41] And while, ordinarily, the damages will be for pecuniary loss (including loss

---

[34] *Standard Chartered Bank v Pakistan National Shipping Corpn (Nos 2 and 4)* [2003] 1 AC 959. On the other hand, a claimant who is aware of the falsity and, perhaps also one who is misled by any patent defect, cannot recover damages. Cf *Horsfall v Thomas* (1862) 1 H & C 90.

[35] *Goose v Wilson Sandford & Co (No 2)* [2001] Lloyd's Rep PN 189.

[36] *Cassa di Risparmio della Republicca di San Marino SpA v Barclays Bank Ltd* [2011] EWHC 484 (Comm), at [265]–[266].

[37] Ibid at [217].

[38] Ibid at [267].   [39] *West London Commercial Bank Ltd v Kitson* (1884) 13 QBD 360.

[40] *Edgington v Fitzmaurice* (1885) 29 Ch D 459.

[41] Damage need not be proved in order to obtain rescission: *Goldrei Foucard & Son v Sinclair and Russian Chamber of Commerce in London* [1918] 1 KB 180, at 192; *Lemprière v Lange* (1879) 12 Ch D 675.

of alternative opportunities to invest money),[42] damages for personal injuries[43] and for loss of property[44] are sometimes also recoverable. Furthermore, the claimant is entitled to recover for all the actual damage directly flowing from the fraud, even if not all of the damage was foreseeable.[45] If, for example, he is induced by fraud to buy business property, he can claim not only the difference between the price paid and the market value, but also for expenses reasonably incurred in trying to run the business fraudulently sold to him,[46] interest on loans entered into to facilitate the purchase of the property,[47] and the loss of the profit which he might reasonably have earned but for the defendant's deceit.[48]

It is technically unclear whether exemplary damages can be awarded in deceit;[49] but in the light of the decision in *Kuddus v Chief Constable of Leicestershire*,[50] such damages certainly ought to be available. By contrast, aggravated damages can definitely be obtained in deceit.[51]

(F) AGENCY

Agency is generally of little relevance in the law of torts, but deceit provides an exception to this rule. As well as being vicariously liable for false statements made by agents who are employees, a principal may also be liable for representations made on his behalf by independent persons acting for him in relation to a particular transaction – for example, an estate agent or broker. A principal who expressly authorises a statement which he and the agent know to be untrue is liable with the agent as a joint tortfeasor.

He is vicariously liable for statements known to be untrue by the agent, and will further be liable where one agent passes on to another information which he knows to be false in order that the second 'innocent' agent may pass it on to the claimant who then acts on it to his detriment.[52] It is unclear whether, if an agent makes a statement

---

[42] *Parabola Investments Ltd v Browallia Cal Ltd* [2010] EWCA Civ 486, at [38].

[43] *Langridge v Levy* (1837) 2 M & W 519; *Graham v Saville* [1945] 2 DLR 489.

[44] *Mullett v Mason* (1866) LR 1 CP 559.

[45] See, eg, *AIC Ltd v ITS Testing Services (UK) Ltd* [2005] EWHC 2122.

[46] *Doyle v Olby (Ironmongers) Ltd* [1969] 2 QB 158; *Banque Bruxelles Lambert SA v Eagle Star Insurance Co Ltd* [1997] AC 191.

[47] *Archer v Brown* [1985] QB 401 (loss resulting from C's impecuniosity did not prevent its recovery).

[48] *East v Maurer* [1991] 2 All ER 733; *Clef Aquitaine Sarl v Laporte Materials (Barrow) Ltd* [2001] QB 488; *Parabola Investments Ltd v Browallia Cal Ltd* [2010] EWCA Civ 486.

[49] *Mafo v Adams* [1970] 1 QB 548; *Archer v Brown* [1985] QB 401; *Metall und Rohstoff AG v ACLI Metals (London) Ltd* [1984] 1 Lloyd's Rep 598. See more generally, Law Com No 247, *Exemplary, Aggravated and Restitutionary Damages* (1997). [50] [2002] 2 AC 122.

[51] *Archer v Brown* [1985] QB 401; *Saunders v Edwards* [1987] 2 All ER 651; *Shaw v Sequence (UK) Ltd* [2004] EWHC 3249.

[52] *London County Freehold and Leasehold Properties Ltd v Berkeley Property and Investment Co Ltd* [1936] 2 All ER 1039 (as explained in *Anglo-Scottish Beet Sugar Corpn Ltd v Spalding UDC* [1937] 2 KB 607).

without knowing it to be untrue, and without authority to make that statement, the principal is liable in deceit if he would have known of the falsity of the statement.[53]

The principal is not liable for merely creating an opportunity to commit deceit.[54] The key question in relation to liability for deceit by agents is generally whether the false representation was made within the scope of the agent's actual or ostensible authority.[55] Was it a representation which the agent was actually authorised to make, or which the principal's conduct of affairs allowed him to appear to be authorised to make?[56] Lord Keith explained the rationale of the rule governing a principal's vicarious liability for deceit thus:

> [T]he question is whether the circumstances under which a servant has made a fraudulent representation which has caused loss to an innocent party contracting with him are such as to make it just for the employer to bear the loss. Such circumstances exist where the employer by words or conduct has induced the injured party to believe that the servant was acting in the lawful course of the employer's business. They do not exist where such belief, although it is present, has been brought about through misguided reliance on the servant himself, when the servant is not authorised to do what he was purporting to do, when what he is purporting to do is not within the class of acts that an employee in his position is usually authorised to do and when the employer has done nothing to represent that he is authorised to do it.[57]

An alternative approach may admit of liability for false representations made opportunistically by the agent in a context that was closely connected to his position as the principal's agent.[58] In either case, the court is entitled to adopt a 'broad approach' to the liability of the principal.[59] Liability arises where the representation as to the agent's authority in respect of the transaction was relied upon by the third party claimant; this involves no question of reasonableness of reliance.[60]

Where the agent is also an employee,[61] the fact that he sets out to deceive his employer as well as the claimant, and intends to benefit himself alone, will not relieve the principal from liability for the agent's deceit.[62]

---

[53] *Armstrong v Strain* [1952] 1 KB 232 (held not to be tortious); but was this decision *per incuriam*? See *Woyka & Co v London and Northern Trading Co* (1922) 10 HL Rep 110.

[54] *Quinn v CC Automotive Group Ltd* [2010] EWCA Civ 1412, at [19].

[55] *Arnagas Ltd v Mondogas SA* [1986] AC 717, at 780–1; *Quinn v CC Automotive Group Ltd* [2010] EWCA Civ 1412, at [19].

[56] *Kooragang Investments Pty Ltd v Richardson & Wrench Ltd* [1982] AC 462; *Petrotrade Inc v Smith* [2000] 1 Lloyd's Rep 486.   [57] *Armagas Ltd v Mundogas SA, The Ocean Frost* [1986] AC 717, at 781.

[58] *Quinn v CC Automotive Group Ltd* [2010] EWCA Civ 1412, at [21], following approach in *Lister v Hesley Hall Ltd* [2002] 1 AC 215.   [59] *Quinn v CC Automotive Group Ltd* [2010] EWCA Civ 1412, at [22].

[60] Ibid at [23].

[61] When the agent is not a servant and the fraud is initially aimed at the principal there will be no vicarious liability to other victims of the fraud: *Kwei Tek Chao v British Traders and Shippers Ltd* [1954] 2 QB 459.   [62] *Lloyd v Grace Smith & Co Ltd* [1912] AC 716.

A principal whose agent has been bribed to induce him to enter into a transaction on the principal's behalf has a claim in tort against the briber for damages.[63] He cannot, however, receive double compensation by pursuing both his equitable remedy to recover the bribe from the agent and his tort action against the briber. He must elect between these two remedies. Where an agent offers a bribe and is acting within the scope of his actual or ostensible authority, the principal will be vicariously liable for that fraud as much as for any other act of deceit.[64]

(G) STATUTE OF FRAUDS AMENDMENT ACT 1828

By section 6 of the Statute of Frauds Amendment Act 1828:

> No action shall be brought whereby to charge any person upon or by reason of any representation or assurance made or given concerning or relating to the character, conduct, credit, ability, trade, or dealings of any other person, to the intent or purpose that such other person may obtain credit, money, or goods...unless such representation or assurance be made in writing signed by the party to be charged therewith.

The section prevents evasion of the Statute of Frauds (which requires guarantees to be in writing) by suing in tort instead of contract, and, in interpreting it, the courts have consistently taken heed of this legislative purpose.[65] The Act does not apply to actions for breach of contract, and in all probability is confined to 'actions upon representations as such'.[66] The signature of a mere agent does not appear to satisfy the requirements of the section.[67] However, signature on behalf of a company by its duly authorised agent is, for the purposes of section 6, the signature of the company.[68] Moreover, a director may be personally liable for signing a document containing a promise by a company to pay for goods to be ordered in the future when that director knows of the company's inability to pay.[69] Even though the defendant has induced the claimant to give credit to secure a pecuniary gain for himself, it seems the Act applies.[70]

(H) MISREPRESENTATION ACT 1967

The Misrepresentation Act 1967, section 2(1) provides:

> Where a person has entered into a contract after a misrepresentation has been made to him by another party thereto and as a result thereof he has suffered loss, then, if the person

---

[63] *Mahesan S/O Thambiah v Malaysian Government Officers' Co-operative Housing Society Ltd* [1979] AC 374.   [64] *Armagas Ltd v Mundogas SA, The Ocean Frost* [1986] AC 717.

[65] *Lyde v Barnard* (1836) 1 M & W 101; *Banbury v Bank of Montreal* [1918] AC 626.

[66] *Banbury v Bank of Montreal* [1918] AC 626.

[67] *Swift v Jewsbury and Goddard* (1874) LR 9 QB 301.

[68] *UBAF Ltd v European American Banking Corpn* [1984] QB 713.

[69] *Contex Drouzhba Ltd v Wiseman* [2007] EWCA Civ 1201, at [16].

[70] So held the House of Lords when interpreting the equivalent provisions of a Scottish statute in *Clydesdale Bank Ltd v Paton* [1896] AC 381.

making the misrepresentation would be liable to damages in respect thereof had the misrepresentation been made fraudulently, that person shall be so liable notwithstanding that the misrepresentation was not made fraudulently, unless he proves that he had reasonable ground to believe and did believe up to the time the contract was made that the facts represented were true.

The important effect of this provision is that, where the misrepresentation by a party induces the claimant to enter into a contract with him, the claimant can recover damages for resulting loss without proving fraud. A claimant may succeed under this Act although he fails in negligence (for want of a duty of care), and the usual burden of proof is reversed: the onus is on the representor to show his belief in the truth of the representation.[71] The Act does not extend the scope of the tort of negligence. Rather, it supplements the tort of deceit,[72] and the rules of deceit, not negligence, govern the measure of damages.[73] On the other hand, contributory negligence is an available defence when liability under the Act is concurrent with liability in common law negligence.[74]

Where the representation falls outside the scope of the Act – for example, where it is made by a person who is not a party to the contract – the victim of negligence will still have to rely on the tort of negligence. The 1967 Act does not impose liability on an agent personally if he makes false representations to induce the making of a contract. His liability, too, remains to be established at common law, in either deceit or negligence.[75]

Prior to the 1967 Act, there were circumstances in which the victim of an innocent misrepresentation could seek rescission of a contract although he could not have sued for deceit. To meet such circumstances, section 2(2) provides the court with a discretion to require the victim of an innocent misrepresentation to accept damages in lieu of rescission. And since rescission can be obtained even though damage is not proven, presumably the court might award damages in lieu of rescission to a person who has not proved damage.

SECTION 2   PASSING OFF[76]

The action for deceit affords a remedy to persons who are the direct target of fraudulent misrepresentation. By contrast, the tort of passing off protects traders against misrepresentations aimed at their customers that are calculated to damage the trader's goodwill. The classic tort of passing off was limited to the use by A of the trade name

---

[71] *Howard Marine and Dredging Co Ltd v A Ogden & Sons (Excavations) Ltd* [1978] QB 574.

[72] The Act does not apply where the representation was made by a third party, including the defendant's agent: *Resolute Maritime Inc v Nippon Kaiji Kyokai* [1983] 2 All ER 1.

[73] *Royscott Trust Ltd v Rogerson* [1991] 2 QB 297.

[74] *Gran Gelato Ltd v Richcliff (Group) Ltd* [1992] Ch 560.

[75] *Resolute Maritime Inc v Nippon Kaiji Kyokai* [1983] 2 All ER 1.

[76] See Carty, *An Analysis of the Economic Torts* (2nd edn, 2010), ch 11.

or trade mark of a rival, B, with a view to inducing B's customers to believe that the goods were produced by B thus cashing in on B's goodwill. But the scope of the tort expanded during the twentieth century so that, in 1979, Lord Parker described the right protected by this tort as the 'property in the business or goodwill likely to be injured by the misrepresentation'.[77]

The extended form of passing off was heralded in *Erven Warnink BV v J Townend & Sons (Hull) Ltd*.[78]

> C manufactured an alcoholic drink known as Advocaat. Its principal ingredients were eggs, spirits, and wine. Ds had for several years manufactured another drink composed of egg and fortified wine known as Egg Flip and up to 1974 marketed it under that name. Because of the vagaries of the excise laws which impose higher duties on spirits than fortified wine, Egg Flip sold at a lower price than Advocaat. In 1974, Ds began selling their product as Keeling's Old English Advocaat and gained a large share of the English Advocaat market.

The House of Lords held that no one was likely to be deceived into believing that the defendants' drink was Dutch Advocaat (that is, that they were buying the claimants' product), and so no cause of action for passing off in its classic form arose. Nevertheless, the name Advocaat was generally understood to denote a distinct species of drink by virtue of which the claimants had built up their goodwill, and the defendants' misrepresentation had induced the public to believe they were buying a form of Advocaat with resulting damage to the claimants' business and goodwill. On these findings, a cause of action arose in tort.

Lord Diplock identified five characteristics necessary to found an action for passing off in its wider form, namely:

(1) a misrepresentation;

(2) made by a trader in the course of trade;

(3) to his prospective customers, or to ultimate consumers of his goods;

(4) calculated to injure the business or goodwill of another trader; and

(5) which causes actual damage to the business or goodwill of the trader by whom the action is brought, or will probably do so.[79]

This broad approach arguably unhinges the tort from its origins, purportedly protecting 'business' (a broad class of interests), rather than goodwill (as originally intended).[80] Thus, analysis of the tort will be undertaken here in accordance with the

---

[77] *A G Spalding & Bros v A W Gamage Ltd* (1915) 84 LJ Ch 449, at 452.

[78] [1979] AC 731. And see *Associated Newspapers plc v Insert Media Ltd* [1991] 3 All ER 535; *Mirage Studios v Counter-Feat Clothing Co Ltd* [1991] FSR 145; *Kimberley-Clark Ltd v Fort Sterling Ltd* [1997] FSR 877.

[79] [1979] 2 All ER 927, at 932. See also the slightly more restrictive definition at ibid at 943. Both are considered in *Anheuser-Busch Inc v Budejovicky Budvar NP* [1984] FSR 413.

[80] Dworkin [1979] EIPR 241; Carty, *An Analysis of the Economic Torts* (2nd edn, 2010), 230.

tripartite framework of the tort that has regained popularity, and which Lord Oliver has described as the 'classic trinity'[81] of misrepresentation, goodwill, and damage.

(A) MISREPRESENTATION

The first requirement in any passing off action is that the defendant must have made a misrepresentation.[82] As Lloyd J has stated, it is insufficient if there has been no misrepresentation, for 'people make assumptions, jump to unjustified conclusions... [and] these are cases of non-actionable confusion'.[83] That said, experience proves that the misrepresentation is likely to be implied rather than express in nature.[84]

(1) Kinds of misrepresentation

Misrepresentations may take many forms, and various titles may be applied to the different kinds.[85] Here, we simply note that they include the following forms.[86]

(a) Marketing a product as that of the claimant

One must not market one's product claiming falsely that it is the claimant's product.[87]

(b) Using the claimant's name

To engage in the same line of business as the claimant and to use a similar name may be passing off.[88] If the defendant carries on business in his own name (or one which he has assumed for some time)[89] then he does not commit this tort unless there are further special circumstances showing dishonesty.[90] This is so because he is entitled knowingly to take advantage of the benefits which may accrue to him from the trade use of his own name.[91] On the other hand, if confusion arises from describing his

---

[81] *Reckitt & Colman Products Ltd v Borden Inc* [1990] RPC 340, at 341. See, more recently, *Phones 4U Ltd v Phone4u.co.uk Internet Ltd* [2006] EWCA Civ 244, at [10].

[82] For emphatic endorsement of the point see *Boehringer Ingleheim KG v Swingward Ltd* [2004] EWCA Civ 129, at [2].   [83] *HFC Bank plc v Midland Bank plc* [2000] FSR 176, at 201.

[84] Carty, *An Analysis of the Economic Torts* (2nd edn, 2010), 236.

[85] See, eg, Carty, *An Analysis of the Economic Torts* (2nd edn, 2010), 237–49.

[86] The list in the text is not necessarily exhaustive. For example, in *Francis Day and Hunter Ltd v Twentieth Century Fox Corpn Ltd* [1939] 4 All ER 192, at 199, Lord Wright thought the tort would be made out where people went to a performance of D's work under the impression that they were going to witness C's work.

[87] *Lord Byron v Johnston* (1816) 2 Mer 29; *C G Vokes Ltd v F J Evans and Marble Arch Motor Supplies Ltd* (1931) 49 RPC 140.

[88] *Tussaud v Tussaud* (1890) 44 Ch D 678; *Boswell-Wilkie Circus (Pty) Ltd v Brian Boswell Circus (Pty) Ltd* [1985] FSR 434.

[89] *Jay's Ltd v Jacobi* [1933] Ch 411.

[90] *Sykes v Sykes* (1824) 3 B & C 541. Cf *Croft v Day* (1843) 7 Beav 84; *Wright, Layman and Umney Ltd v Wright* (1949) 66 RPC 149.

[91] *John Brinsmead Ltd v Brinsmead and Waddington & Sons Ltd* (1913) 29 TLR 237; on appeal (1913) 29 TLR 706; *Burgess v Burgess* (1853) 3 De GM & G 896. There is no similar protection for a nickname: *Biba Group Ltd v Biba Boutique* [1980] RPC 413.

goods by his own name, it is no defence that his use is bona fide.[92] A company does not, however, acquire and incorporate the individual rights of its promoters to carry on business under their names.[93]

(c) Using the claimant's trade name

To use the claimant's trade name – that is, the designation adopted by the claimant to identify goods or services he markets or supplies – may constitute misrepresentation for the purposes of this tort. The following are examples.

> To describe and sell sauce as 'Yorkshire Relish' was to commit a tort against the original manufacturer of sauce under that name.[94]

> At the request of D, C used the name, 'Dr Crock and his Crackpots' when broadcasting with his band on D's programme. When C left this programme, he was entitled to restrain D from putting another band on the programme with the title 'Dr Crock and his Crackpots'.[95]

> Using internet domain names that closely resemble (or incorporate parts of) those used by C.[96]

If the trade name merely describes the goods or their characteristics, then ordinarily the claimant cannot prevent others from using it. For example the terms vacuum cleaner,[97] cellular textiles,[98] and shredded wheat[99] may all be used with impunity. A very heavy burden of proof is cast on the claimant who seeks to establish that a name which is merely descriptive of the product has acquired a technical secondary meaning, so exclusively associated with the claimant's own product, that its use by others is calculated to deceive purchasers. This burden was nonetheless discharged by the makers of 'Camel Hair Belting' in the leading case of *Reddaway v Banham*.[100] The task is a little easier where the descriptive words connect the product with the place of its manufacture. Thus, the manufacturers of 'Glenfield Starch',[101] 'Stone Ales',[102] and 'Chartreuse liqueurs'[103] have all succeeded in passing off actions.

---

[92] *Parker-Knoll Ltd v Knoll International Ltd* [1962] RPC 265; *W H Allen & Co v Brown Watson Ltd* [1965] RPC 191.

[93] *Tussaud v Tussaud* (1890) 44 Ch D 678. Nor has a foreign company a right to set up in England in competitive business with C, a company of the same name: *Sturtevant Engineering Co Ltd v Sturtevant Mill Co of USA Ltd* [1936] 3 All ER 137.   [94] *Powell v Birmingham Vinegar Brewery Co* [1896] 2 Ch 54.

[95] *Hines v Winnick* [1947] Ch 708. Cf *Forbes v Kemsley Newspapers Ltd* [1951] 2 TLR 656.

[96] *Tesco Stores Ltd v Elogicom Ltd* [2006] EWHC 403; *Global Projects Management Ltd v Citigroup Inc* [2005] EWHC 2663.

[97] *British Vacuum Cleaner Co Ltd v New Vacuum Cleaner Co Ltd* [1907] 2 Ch 312.

[98] *Cellular Clothing Co v Maxton and Murray* [1899] AC 326.

[99] *Canadian Shredded Wheat Co Ltd v Kellogg Co of Canada Ltd* [1938] 1 All ER 618.

[100] [1896] AC 199.   [101] *Wotherspoon v Currie* (1872) LR 5 HL 508.

[102] *Montgomery v Thompson* [1891] AC 217.

[103] *Rey v Lecouturier* [1908] 2 Ch 715; affirmed sub nom *Lecouturier v Rey* [1910] AC 262.

The courts are much more willing to protect the use of a 'fancy' name, and one that does not describe the quality of the goods – for example, 'Apollinaris'.[104] It has been suggested, however, that a person originally entitled to protection for a fancy name may lose that right if the name later becomes a mere description of the type of product rather than a word associated with goods of the claimant.[105] Yet no case confirms this,[106] and the attempt failed in *Havana Cigar and Tobacco Factories Ltd v Oddenino*.[107]

> C was the original manufacturer of Corona cigars. D supplied other cigars described as Corona cigars. C successfully sued in passing off, the court rejecting D's argument that the word no longer described a brand of cigar, but only a particular size of cigar.

(d) Using the claimant's trade mark[108]

Historically it was tortious to use the claimant's trade mark – that is, a design, picture, or other arrangement affixed by him to goods which he markets so as to identify them with him.[109] And although the Trade Marks Act 1994 creates separate rights of action in respect of trade mark infringements, section 2(2) of that Act also expressly preserves the common law action of passing off in respect of trade marks. That it does so may prove valuable where the claimant fails to prove registration, or where the registration does not extend to the goods in question, or where it is invalid. For in such cases, the statutory action for infringement of the claimant's trade mark will fail and it will be necessary to have recourse to the common law action.

(e) Imitating the appearance of the claimant's goods

To imitate the appearance of the claimant's goods may be passing off, although it may be difficult to prove that mere imitation sufficiently impacts upon goodwill.[110] The question will be whether the shape and other characteristics of goods have come to denote a particular source in the relevant market.[111] This criterion was satisfied where claimants had, for over 30 years, marketed lemon juice in a distinctive yellow plastic

---

[104] *Apollinaris Co Ltd v Norrish* (1875) 33 LT 242.

[105] Eg, *Ford v Foster* (1872) 7 Ch App 611 (*obiter*).

[106] The cases usually cited here are *Liebig's Extract of Meat Co Ltd v Hanbury* (1867) 17 LT 298 and *Lazenby v White* (1871) 41 LJ Ch 354n. A further case, much more in point is *G H Gledhill & Sons Ltd v British Perforated Toilet Paper Co* (1911) 28 RPC 429. In *Norman Kark Publications v Odhams Press Ltd* [1962] 1 All ER 636, C lost the protection of a trade name in a magazine seven years after its amalgamation with another magazine.

[107] [1924] 1 Ch 179. The same outcome was reached in *Antec International Ltd v South Western Chicks (Warren) Ltd* [1998] 18 LS Gaz R 32.

[108] Cf the related wrong of infringement of a trade mark under the Trade Marks Act 1994. But note that under that Act, there is no need to prove goodwill in a trade mark: *Fisons plc v Norton Healthcare Ltd* [1994] FSR 745.

[109] *Millington v Fox* (1838) 3 My & Cr 338; *Singer Machine Manufacturers v Wilson* (1877) 3 App Cas 376, at 391–2.

[110] The case will be stronger where, eg, a similar name is used for goods. See *Massam v Thorley's Cattle Food Co* (1880) 14 Ch D 748. See also Monaghan (2010) 31 Company Lawyer 184.

[111] *Numatic International Ltd v Qualtex UK Ltd* [2010] EWHC 1237 (Ch), at [39].

squeeze-pack shaped like a natural lemon that the defendants then sought to emu-late.[112] It was also satisfied in the case of a manufacturer, which sought to sell vacuum cleaners that, although not anthropomorphised to the extent of the claimant's prod-ucts, were to feature a bowler hat-shaped lid.[113]

If the appearance complained of is dictated by functional considerations – for exam-ple, the purpose or performance of the goods, or simplicity in handling or processing them – the courts will be reluctant to interfere. An action to prevent the use by the defendant of the normal shape of shaving stick container accordingly failed.[114] Yet the manufacturer of laundry bleach which had a knobbed stick through the middle of the container was able to prevent the defendant from marketing a product similar in appearance, since he satisfied the court that this appearance was more than merely functional. The defendant was at liberty to have a stick in his product, but not one of the same 'get-up' as the claimant's.[115] Protection will not be afforded where the defendant's product is merely similar to that of the claimant in particulars which are common to all types of that product.[116]

(f) Selling goods inferior to claimant's goods, thereby misleading the purchaser

A defendant must not sell goods which are in fact, and which are described as, the goods of the claimant, but which are of a quality inferior to that of the normal new and current product of the claimant, in such a way as to cause prospective purchasers to believe that the goods are the normal, new, and current product of the claimant.

Thus, the manufacturers of Gillette razor blades obtained an injunction restrain-ing the defendant from selling used Gillette blades as 'genuine' ones.[117] On the other hand, a general dealer in a working-class area who advertised in his shop 'All types of electric lamps and fittings at cut prices' was held not liable in passing off to the manu-facturers of Osram lamps for selling old Osram lamps, because it was not established that his acts were calculated to deceive the public into thinking that new lamps were being offered for sale.[118] Judicial reluctance to decide the respective merits of various products[119] led to a denial of a remedy in *Harris v Warren and Phillips*.[120]

> The publishers of a songwriter, who had recently attained fame, were unable to restrain D from passing off as new work the writer's early work (in which D had the copyright, and which, it was contended, was of greatly inferior quality to her latest work). The court held

---

[112] *Reckitt & Colman Products Ltd v Borden Inc* [1990] 1 All ER 873.

[113] *Numatic International Ltd v Qualtex UK Ltd* [2010] EWHC 1237 (Ch).

[114] *J B Williams Co v H Bronnley & Co Ltd* (1909) 26 RPC 765.

[115] *William Edge & Sons Ltd v William Niccolls & Sons Ltd* [1911] AC 693.

[116] *Jamieson & Co v Jamieson* (1898) 14 TLR 160.

[117] *Gillette Safety Razor Co and Gillette Safety Razor Ltd v Franks* (1924) 40 TLR 606. Cf *AG Spalding & Bros v AW Gamage Ltd* (1915) 84 LJ Ch 449; *Wilts United Dairies Ltd v Thomas Robinson Sons & Co Ltd* [1958] RPC 94; *Morris Motors Ltd v Lilley* [1959] 3 All ER 737.

[118] *General Electric Co and British Thomson-Houston Co v Pryce's Stores* (1933) 50 RPC 232.

[119] Cf *White v Mellin* [1895] AC 154.   [120] (1918) 87 LJ Ch 491.

that it could draw no sharp dividing line between the quality of her early and more recent songs.

(g) False advertising

False advertising is largely governed by regulations which provide for complaint to the Director of Fair Trading.[121] However, three cases illustrate when false advertising may also amount to passing off. The first is *Cadbury Schweppes Pty Ltd v Pub Squash Co Pty Ltd*.[122]

C successfully launched a new canned lemon drink with a big media advertising campaign. The following year, D launched a similar drink with a media campaign in which D imitated the slogans and visual images of C's advertising. It was held that such advertising could be passing off, but the action failed: C failed to prove that there had been a confusing misrepresentation.

In *Masson Seeley & Co Ltd v Embosotype Manufacturing Co*,[123] D deliberately created a market for their goods by copying C's catalogue so as to induce the public to believe that goods offered by D were those of C. Customers of C normally ordered goods by reference to certain key words in the catalogue, and D used the same artificial words in their catalogue. Although D's goods were inferior to those sold by C, this was held to be passing off.

In *Associated Newspapers plc v Insert Media Ltd*,[124] D arranged to insert advertising material into C's newspapers without their authority. Readers would assume that the newspaper had sanctioned the inserts, with consequent potential damage to C's reputation and goodwill. D's conduct was found to constitute a misrepresentation amounting to passing off.

On the other hand, if the defendant merely makes inflated claims about his own product, a rival may not sue for passing off even though he thereby suffered loss.[125]

(h) Character merchandising

The developing trade of character merchandising allows great profits to be made from exploiting the popularity of famous television characters, both real and fictional. In particular, children's cartoons have spawned industries of their own. Having seen the Teenage Mutant Ninja Turtles on television, child viewers pestered their parents for Turtle paraphernalia such as Turtle mugs. In recognition of the fact that unlicensed distributors would try to cash in on the craze, an injunction was granted to prevent unauthorised use of the 'Turtle' connection in *Mirage Studios v Counter-Feat Clothing*.[126]

---

[121] Control of Misleading Advertisements Regulations (SI 1988/915) (as amended).
[122] [1981] 1 All ER 213. Cf *United Biscuits (UK) Ltd v Asda Stores Ltd* [1997] RPC 513.
[123] (1924) 41 RPC 160. Cf *Purefoy Engineering Co Ltd v Sykes Boxall & Co Ltd* (1955) 72 RPC 89.
[124] [1991] 3 All ER 535.   [125] *BBC v Talksport Ltd* [2001] FSR 53.
[126] [1991] FSR 145. See also *BBC Worldwide Ltd v Pally Screen Printing Ltd* [1998] FSR 665. But do the public care who makes such goods, and, if not, in what sense have the public been deceived?

(2) Representation must be likely to deceive the claimant's customers

The misrepresentation must be made either to prospective customers of the claim-ant or to ultimate consumers of goods or services supplied by him.[127] It must also be likely to deceive them in a way which is 'really likely to be damaging to the Claimant's goodwill'.[128] Likelihood of deceit is a question of law. The judge must decide on the balance of probabilities whether a substantial number of the members of the public would be misled by the representation.[129] In assessing this, the court will take account of who the likely customers for the product or service are.[130] Thus, although the ordi-nary standard to be applied is that of the unwary member of the public,[131] if the par-ticular trade is exclusively with experts, the test must be whether such an expert is likely to be deceived.[132] To an extent, then, each case must be decided on its own facts, in the light of the particular product or service in question. One case that illustrates this point involved a defendant who put a design of two elephants on yarn tickets of material to be sold in rural districts of India. The fact that his design was different from that of the two elephants pictured on the claimant's yarn tickets did not prevent the House of Lords from finding for the claimant.[133]

Even if the parties have no common field of activity, an action may still lie provided that likely injury to goodwill is established. It is a question of fact and degree.[134] Thus, a moneylender who sets up in trade under the same name as an established bank can be restrained on the ground that it would endanger the bank's reputation if it were thought also to be a moneylender.[135] And *The Times* newspaper obtained an injunc-tion against the defendant who represented it to be his principal or business associate in his cycle dealer business.[136]

However, Granada TV could not prevent Ford from calling a new model 'Granada', for there was neither a connection nor association between the two activities, nor any proved confusion of the public.[137] And the creator of 'The Wombles' could not prevent

---

[127] *Erven Warnink BV v J Townend & Sons (Hull) Ltd* [1979] AC 731, at 742. As regards foreign-based companies, the law is uncertain. According to one account, the foreign-based company must establish that it has customers in England: see *Warnink* [1979] AC 731 and *Athletes Foot Marketing Associates Inc v Cobra Sports Co* [1980] RPC 343. On the other hand, Maxim's, the famous Paris restaurant, succeeded in prevent-ing a Norfolk restaurant from trading under that name despite having no trading base in England: *Maxim's Ltd v Dye* [1978] 2 All ER 55. Note also the perhaps surprising decision in *Burge v Haycock* [2002] RPC 553 where C (a political party) successfully restrained D from dishonestly standing in their name.

[128] *Phones 4U Ltd v Phone4u.co.uk Internet Ltd* [2006] EWCA Civ 244, at [19].

[129] *Neutrogena Corpn v Golden Ltd* [1996] RPC 473; *Arsenal Football Club plc v Reed* [2001] RPC 922.

[130] *Bollinger v Costa Brava Wine Co Ltd* [1961] 1 All ER 561.

[131] *Reckitt & Colman Products Ltd v Borden Inc* [1990] 1 All ER 873, at 888.

[132] *Singer Manufacturing Co v Loog* (1882) 8 App Cas 15.

[133] *Johnston & Co v Orr-Ewing* (1882) 7 App Cas 219. Cf *William Edge & Sons Ltd v William Niccolls & Sons Ltd* [1911] AC 693; *Lee Kar Choo v Lee Lian Choon* [1967] 1 AC 602.

[134] *Phones 4U Ltd v Phone4u.co.uk Internet Ltd* [2006] EWCA Civ 244, at [17].

[135] *Harrods Ltd v R Harrod Ltd* (1923) 40 TLR 195.   [136] *Walter v Ashton* [1902] 2 Ch 282.

[137] *Granada Group Ltd v Ford Motor Co Ltd* [1973] RPC 49.

the marketing of 'Wombles Skips'.[138] But in the light of the developments of a trade in 'character' itself, might these cases be decided differently today? The defendants in the latter case might not be harming the reputation of the originator of the Wombles per se, but what about limiting the profit to be exploited from the character?[139]

Where the misrepresentation relates to a product produced by a group of traders, rather than one single claimant, the group must establish that they constitute a distinctive class of traders who have built up goodwill by the use of a particular name or description of goods. Thus, the French producers of champagne succeeded by establishing they all operated from the Champagne region in France.[140]

(3) Representation in the course of a trade

The representation must be made in the course of a trade. Trade is liberally defined and includes pursuit of a profession[141] and a person's interest in his literary and performance rights.[142] The tort is even available to protect the name of a political party where the party in question can demonstrate that it has valuable property in the form of the goodwill in its name.[143]

(B) GOODWILL

In *A G Spalding & Bros v A W Gamage Ltd*,[144] Lord Parker stated that the tort protected goodwill – that is, 'the attractive force that brings in custom'.[145] The tort of passing off is protective of the trader's goodwill earned through the sale of goods or services.[146] Goodwill is said to be 'local in character and divisible' in the sense that separate goodwill attaches in each market where the business is carried on.[147] A market exists where there are customers among the local general public.[148] Goodwill must exist in the use of the claimant's mark or name immediately before the introduction of the defendant's goods or services to the relevant market.[149] No claim will be available for damage to goodwill where the goodwill is of trivial proportions.[150]

---

[138] *Wombles Ltd v Wombles Skips Ltd* [1977] RPC 99. Cf *Annabel's (Berkeley Square) Ltd v G Schock* [1972] RPC 838 (Annabel's Club and Annabel's Escort Agency).

[139] See *Mirage Studios v Counter-Feat Clothing* [1991] FSR 145.

[140] *J Bollinger v Costa Brava Wine Co* [1960] Ch 262.

[141] *Society of Incorporated Accountants v Vincent* (1954) 71 RPC 325.

[142] See *Lord Byron v Johnston* (1816) 2 Mer 29; *Hines v Winnick* [1947] Ch 708; *Illustrated Newspapers Ltd v Publicity Services (London) Ltd* [1938] Ch 414.   [143] *Burge v Haycock* [2002] RPC 553.

[144] (1915) 84 LJ Ch 449.

[145] Echoing *IRC v Muller & Co's Margarine Ltd* [1901] AC 217, at 223–4. Goodwill is said to be different from reputation, although it is built upon reputation and other factors: Saw [2010] JBL 645, 658–9.

[146] *Star Industrial Co Ltd v Yap Kwee Kor* [1976] FSR 256, at 269.

[147] Ibid at 269.

[148] *Hotel Cipriani SRL v Cipriani (Grosvenor Street) Ltd* [2010] EWCA Civ 110, at [106]. A debate exists about how this should be proved: see Saw [2010] JBL 645.

[149] *Hotel Cipriani SRL v Cipriani (Grosvenor Street) Ltd* [2010] EWCA Civ 110, at [90].

[150] *Knight v Beyond Properties Pty Ltd* [2007] EWHC 1251 (Ch), at [27]; *Sutherland v V2 Music Ltd* [2002] EMLR 568, at [22].

Nearly all the examples so far given constitute passing off in the form of inducing consumers to believe that they are purchasing the claimant's products. But passing off extends beyond such cases. This theme was picked up in *J Bollinger v Costa Brava Wine Co Ltd*.[151]

> D marketed 'Spanish Champagne', a sparkling Spanish wine. C was one of several manu-facturers of champagne in the Champagne region of France. The court found that mem-bers of the public bought D's wine in the mistaken belief that they were buying champagne from the vineyards of Champagne. It was held D had committed the tort of passing off.

Crucially, Danckwerts J held that the description 'champagne' was part of the claim-ants' goodwill and a *right of property*. A group of persons producing goods in a certain locality and naming those goods by reference to that locality were entitled to protec-tion against competitors who sought to cash in on their goodwill and reputation by attaching that name to a product originating from a different locality and with which the competing product has no rational association.[152]

The limitation to goods produced in a certain locality was considered immaterial in *Erven Warnink BV v J Townend & Sons (Hull) Ltd*.[153] The Dutch traders in that case recovered for the loss in their business resulting from the defendants' mislead-ing appropriation of the name Advocaat for their different and cheaper alcoholic egg drink. The crucial issues were:

(1) that there was a 'distinctive class of goods'; and

(2) that those goods were marketed in England by a class of persons whose product was genuinely indicated by the use of the name Advocaat.

This approach continues to be followed, although it has been observed that the more general and descriptive the name of the goods (or services), the more difficult it will be to establish the reputation and goodwill of the claimant in the use of the name.[154] The name must be distinctive of a certain class of goods (or services).[155]

(C) DAMAGE

A passing-off action can be brought even where no damage can be proved.[156] The probability of damage suffices.[157] The crucial test is whether a false representation

---

[151] [1960] Ch 262. Followed in *Vine Products Ltd v Mackenzie & Co Ltd* [1969] RPC 1. See also *Consejo Regulador de las Denominaciones v Matthew Clark & Sons* [1992] FSR 525 and *John Walker & Sons Ltd v Henry Ost & Co Ltd* [1970] 2 All ER 106. But note *Taittinger SA v Allbev Ltd* [1993] FSR 641.

[152] See also *Chocosuisse Union des Fabricants Suisses de Chocolat v Cadbury Ltd* [1998] RPC 117.

[153] [1979] AC 731.

[154] Eg, *Office Cleaning Services v Westminster Window and General Cleaners* [1946] 63 RPC 39; [1944] 2 All ER 269, at 271.

[155] *Diageo North America Inc v Intercontinental Brands Ltd* [2010] EWCA Civ 920, at [24] and [28]; contra *Phones 4U Ltd v Phone4u.co.uk Internet Ltd* [2006] EWCA Civ 244, at [25].

[156] *Draper v Trist* [1939] 3 All ER 513; *Procea Products Ltd v Evans & Sons Ltd* (1951) 68 RPC 210.

[157] *HP Bulmer Ltd and Showerings Ltd v J Bollinger SA* [1978] RPC 79. Note, however, that it might be more accurate to speak of a spectrum of differing requirements for proof of damage: Carty, *An Analysis of the Economic Torts* (2nd edn, 2010), 258.

has in fact been made, fraudulently or otherwise,[158] and whether this will foreseeably result in consumers being misled.[159] Damage subsists in reduced profitability because of, inter alia, diversion of sales and reduced fee-earning opportunities, including that which flows from the misuse of the likeness of a famous person for the purposes of a false endorsement.[160]

Proof of intention to deceive is also not essential (by contrast with the tort of deceit).[161] It is unnecessary (though desirable, where possible) to prove that any members of the public were actually deceived. Thus, where the defendant had done no more than sell to middlemen who were not themselves deceived, the action still lay where it was to be expected that the act of the defendant would be calculated to cause in due course confusion in the minds of the purchasing public.[162]

It is not essential that the person deceived should know the name of the claimant: it is enough 'if a person minded to obtain goods which are identified in his mind with a certain definite commercial source is led by false statements to accept goods coming from a different commercial source'.[163] If the public would not in any sense be confused, there is no tort.[164] But when a cordial was marketed as 'elderflower champagne' it was held that some consumers might link the drink with real champagne, thus damaging the reputation of the genuine article.[165]

(D) DEFENCES[166]

None of the general defences to torts that might apply calls for special attention here. But it is perhaps worth noting that consent is probably the most important in this context.[167]

(E) REMEDIES

(1) Injunction

This remedy is often the most important to the claimant. As always, it is awarded at the discretion of the court, and the actual form of the injunction is often one of the most

---

[158] Indeed, in *Gillette UK Ltd v Edenwest Ltd* [1994] RPC 279 it was held that innocence on the part of D was no defence to an action for damages against him.

[159] *AG Spalding & Bros v AW Gamage Ltd* (1915) 84 LJ Ch 449, at 452. For cases where there was held to be no confusion, see *Grand Hotel Co of Caledonia Springs v Wilson* [1904] AC 103; *Office Cleaning Services Ltd v Westminster Office Cleaning Association* (1944) 61 RPC 133; affirmed (1946) 63 RPC 39.

[160] *Irvine v Talksport Ltd (Damages)* [2003] 2 All ER 881.

[161] *Baume & Co Ltd v A H Moore Ltd* [1958] Ch 907. See explanation in Banfi [2011] CLJ 83, at 93.

[162] *Draper v Trist* [1939] 3 All ER 513.

[163] *Plomien Fuel Economiser Co Ltd v National School of Salesmanship Ltd* (1943) 60 RPC 209, at 214. The same applies even though the drug passed off by imitating get-up was sold on prescription only so that the public had no choice of supplier: *F Hoffman-La Roche & Co AG v DDSA Pharmaceuticals Ltd* [1969] FSR 410.

[164] Examples of failure for this reason include *Cadbury Schweppes Pty Ltd v Pub Squash Co Pty Ltd* [1981] 1 All ER 213 and *Newsweek Inc v BBC* [1979] RPC 441.

[165] *Taittinger SA v Allbev Ltd* [1993] FSR 641.

[166] For full treatment of defences to passing off, see *Clerk and Lindsell on Torts* (20th edn, 2010), [26-21]–[26-22].

[167] *Ex turpi causa* is a defence: *Lee v Haley* (1869) 5 Ch App 155; *Ford v Foster* (1872) 7 Ch App 611, at 630–1.

contested points in this class of litigation.[168] If the defendant's conduct is calculated to divert customers, even though no sale has occurred, then in accordance with general principles, an injunction will lie to prevent the apprehended wrong.[169]

(2) Damages

In the archetypal case, claimants recover damages for the loss of profits sustained in consequence of customers being diverted from them to the defendant. But it is not per se in respect of such loss that they may claim. Rather, all loss must be referable to goodwill, which lies at the heart of the classic trinity. But goodwill has been recognised as capable of being harmed in several ways beyond mere diversion of customers. Loss of business reputation,[170] restriction of the claimant's expansion potential (within limits),[171] and dilution (of the effectiveness of distinctive symbols)[172] are some examples.

The alternative to the common-law inquiry into damages is the equitable remedy of an account of the profits made by the defendant by virtue of the passing off.[173] There are dicta to the effect that an account of profits will not be directed for such period as the defendant's action was innocent.[174] It is uncertain whether more than nominal damages may be awarded when the defendant neither knew nor ought to have known[175] that he was committing the tort of passing off.[176]

(F) UNFAIR TRADING AND PASSING OFF

The House of Lords, in *Erven Warnink BV v J Townend & Sons (Hull) Ltd*, extended the classic tort of passing off to a wider class of misrepresentations resulting in damage to a rival's goodwill. It also paved the way towards the tort becoming a means of controlling unfair competition.[177] Lord Diplock recognised that Parliament has progressively intervened to impose on traders higher standards of commercial candour.[178] He clearly

---

[168] In the absence of a threat to continue the acts complained of, the courts may grant a declaration but not an injunction (though giving liberty to apply for an injunction, eg, if D does continue): *Treasure Cot Co Ltd v Hamley Bros* (1950) 67 RPC 89.

[169] *Reddaway v Bentham Hemp-Spinning Co* [1892] 2 QB 639, at 648.

[170] *AG Spalding and Bros v AW Gamage Ltd* (1918) 35 RPC 101; *Treasure Cot Co Ltd v Hamley Bros* (1950) 67 RPC 89.

[171] *Alfred Dunhill Ltd v Sunoptic SA* [1979] FSR 337; *LRC International v Lilla Edets Sales Co* [1973] RPC 560.   [172] *Taittinger SA v Allbev Ltd* [1993] FSR 641.

[173] In computing this profit, sales by D to middlemen can be considered, although the middlemen were not deceived, and had not passed the goods on to the public: *Lever v Goodwin* (1887) 36 Ch D 1.

[174] *Edelsten v Edelsten* (1863) 1 De GJ & Sm 185, at 199.

[175] This is what 'innocent' means: *Edward Young & Co Ltd v Holt* (1947) 65 RPC 25.

[176] *Draper v Trist* [1939] 3 All ER 513; *Marengo v Daily Sketch and Sunday Graphic Ltd* (1948) 65 RPC 242, at 251.

[177] Cf *Hodgkinson and Corby Ltd v Wards Mobility Ltd* [1995] FSR 169. See also Carty, *An Analysis of the Economic Torts* (2nd edn, 2010), 271ff; and note the protection afforded to a political party to restrain a person standing for election in that party's name in *Burge v Haycock* [2002] RPC 553.

[178] [1979] 2 All ER 927, at 933.

indicated that the steady trend in legislation reflecting the legislative view of what is today acceptable conduct in the marketplace should be matched by the development of the common law. Consequently, earlier decisions that misleading trade practices did not amount, on their facts, to the tort of passing off may now need to be regarded with some caution.[179] However, there may come a point when the extension of passing off becomes a means of protecting a monopoly and of excluding all competition. Lord Bridge in *Reckitt & Colman Products Ltd v Borden Inc* warned of this danger.[180]

SECTION 3   MALICIOUS FALSEHOOD[181]

The tort of malicious falsehood also operates to protect interests in goodwill and economic reputation.[182] Passing off generally prevents competitors from using false representations to cash in on the claimant's goodwill. Malicious falsehood, by contrast, affords a remedy where business reputations are maliciously disparaged even though no aspersion is cast upon the character of an individual sufficient to give rise to a cause of action in defamation. The Court of Appeal set out the parameters of this tort as follows:

> [A]n action will lie for written or oral falsehoods ... where they are maliciously published, where they are calculated in the ordinary course of things to produce, and where they do produce, actual damage.[183]

(A) INTERESTS PROTECTED[184]

Originally, this tort protected persons against unwarranted attacks on their title to land, by virtue of which they might be hampered in the disposal of that land. Hence, it was called 'slander of title'.[185] Later, it was held equally applicable to goods, in which case the tort was usually called 'slander of goods'.[186] By 1874 it was established that disparagements of the quality of property, as well as aspersions on title to it, were tortious.[187] Before the end of the century, *Ratcliffe v Evans*[188] made it clear that the tort could be committed whenever damaging lies about a business were uttered (hence, another name given to this tort – 'trade libel'). Since then, the tort has been referred to by many names;[189] but the term malicious falsehood is preferred here because it is

---

[179] See, eg, *Cambridge University Press v University Tutorial Press* (1928) 45 RPC 335. Cf *Bristol Conservatories Ltd v Conservatories Custom Built Ltd* [1989] RPC 455.

[180] [1990] 1 All ER 873, at 877.

[181] See Carty, *An Analysis of the Economic Torts* (2nd edn, 2010), ch 10.

[182] *CHC Software Care Ltd v Hopkins & Wood* [1993] FSR 241.

[183] *Ratcliffe v Evans* [1892] 2 QB 524, at 527.   [184] See Newark (1944) 60 LQR 366.

[185] Eg, *Gerard v Dickenson* (1590) Cro Eliz 196.

[186] *Malachy v Soper* (1836) 3 Bing NC 371. Cf *Green v Button* (1835) 2 Cr M & R 707.

[187] *Western Counties Manure Co v Lawes Chemical Manure Co* (1874) LR 9 Exch 218.

[188] [1892] 2 QB 524.   [189] See Carty, *An Analysis of the Economic Torts* (2nd edn, 2010), 200–3.

the generic term used in the Defamation Act 1952.[190] The potential ambit and utility of this tort was considerably expanded by two decisions of the Court of Appeal which (1) endorsed its applicability wherever one's economic interests are threatened,[191] and (2) rejected the idea that only truly *commercial* interests are protected. In so saying, the demarcation between malicious falsehood and defamation became partly blurred.[192]

Any type of interest in land, whether vested in possession or not,[193] is protected. Trade marks,[194] patents,[195] trade names,[196] copyright,[197] and company shares[198] may all be the subject of actionable disparagements. The following random illustrations of circumstances treated by the courts as being within the scope of the tort demonstrate its extent:

> an untrue statement by the defendant to a customer that the claimant – a commercial traveller with whom the customer had formerly dealt – was now in the employment of the defendant's firm;[199]

> failure to delete the name of the claimant (a musical accompanist) from the programme of a concert series in which she was no longer to appear (because, as a result of this, others might not offer her engagements);[200] and

> a false statement in the defendant's newspaper that the claimant had ceased to carry on business.[201]

Finally, *Joyce v Motor Surveys Ltd*[202] is a particularly useful example of a successful action in malicious falsehood.

> C became the tenant of one of D's lock-up garages in order to have premises at which he could be registered as a tyre dealer. D subsequently wished to evict C in order to sell the entire property with vacant possession. D therefore told the Post Office not to forward any more mail to him at that address, and told the tyre manufacturers' association that he was no longer trading there. D's conduct was held to constitute malicious falsehood.

The essence of the tort is that the defendant's lies cause economic damage to the claimant, and *Kaye v Robertson*[203] provides a good example of the point. There, an actor was photographed without his genuine consent as he lay in a hospital bed recovering from near-fatal injuries. A newspaper printed a story concerning him as though it had been obtained with his full authority and thereby deprived Mr Kaye of the

---

[190] Defamation Act 1952, s 3.
[191] *Kaye v Robertson* [1991] FSR 62; *Joyce v Sengupta* [1993] 1 All ER 897.
[192] See also Gibbons (1996) 16 OJLS 587.   [193] *Vaughan v Ellis* (1608) Cro Jac 213.
[194] *Greers Ltd v Pearman and Corder Ltd* (1922) 39 RPC 406.
[195] *Wren v Weild* (1869) LR 4 QB 730.
[196] *Royal Baking Powder Co v Wright, Crossley & Co* (1900) 18 RPC 95.
[197] *Dicks v Brooks* (1880) 15 Ch D 22.   [198] *Malachy v Soper* (1836) 3 Bing NC 371.
[199] *Balden v Shorter* [1933] Ch 427. The action failed for a different reason.
[200] *Shapiro v La Morta* (1923) 130 LT 622. The action failed for other reasons.
[201] *Ratcliffe v Evans* [1892] 2 QB 524; *Danish Mercantile Co v Beaumont* (1950) 67 RPC 111.
[202] [1948] Ch 252.   [203] [1991] FSR 62.

opportunity to market his own account. So doing was enough to constitute malicious falsehood because the story would misrepresent the fact that Mr Kaye had given the newspaper an exclusive interview, when the truth was that he was not fully conscious and in fact had no recollection of speaking to the newspaper in question.[204] In *Joyce v Sengupta*[205] the defendant newspaper published an article insinuating that the claimant had abused her position as lady's maid to the Princess Royal in order to steal from her employer personal letters. The claimant argued that the article might well prejudice her future employment prospects and her malicious falsehood claim was allowed to proceed.

(B) DISPARAGEMENT[206]

It is a disparagement if there is some misstatement as to the extent of the claimant's interest in his property, as to the quality of his goods, or as to his fitness to offer services. Thus, a false statement by a newspaper owner that the circulation of his newspaper greatly exceeded that of the claimant's rival newspaper was held to be capable of being tortious.[207]

A threat of proceedings for infringement of a patent[208] or a trade mark[209] may be enough. Section 70 of the Patents Act 1977,[210] section 21 of the Trade Marks Act 1994, section 26 of the Registered Designs Act 1949, and section 253 of the Copyright, Designs and Patents Act 1988 all make it a statutory tort for a person by circulars, advertisements, or otherwise to threaten proceedings for infringement wherever the defendant is unable to prove that the claimant's act constitutes an infringement of the defendant's patent, trade mark, registered design, or design rights.[211] On the other hand, an assertion by way of mere 'puffery' that the defendant's goods are better than the claimant's, is not actionable[212] (unless the defendant's claims are couched in terms of verifiable facts, and those facts can be shown to be untrue, in which case an action will lie).[213] And the courts will not, in such cases, decide the relative merits of competing products.[214] The test is whether a reasonable person would take the claim that denigrates the claimant's goods as one made seriously.[215]

---

[204] It is also worthy of mention that the Court of Appeal was keen to offer protection against the gross invasion of the actor's privacy. [205] [1993] 1 All ER 897.

[206] Most, but not all, cases of malicious falsehood involve disparagement: Carty, *An Analysis of the Economic Torts* (2nd edn, 2010), 203.

[207] *Lyne v Nicholls* (1906) 23 TLR 86. Cf *Evans v Harlow* (1844) 5 QB 624.

[208] *Mentmore Manufacturing Co Ltd v Fomento (Sterling Area) Ltd* (1955) 72 RPC 157.

[209] *Colley v Hart* (1890) 44 Ch D 179, at 183.

[210] See *Johnson Electric Industrial Manufacturing Ltd v Mabuchi-Motor KK* [1986] FSR 280.

[211] For full details of the statutory actions see *Clerk and Lindsell on Torts* (2010), ch 26.

[212] *Young v Macrae* (1862) 3 B & S 264; *Hubbuck & Sons v Wilkinson, Heywood and Clark* [1899] 1 QB 86.

[213] *De Beers Abrasive Products Ltd v International General Electric Co of New York Ltd* [1975] 2 All ER 599; *DSG Retail Ltd v Comet Group plc* [2002] FSR 58. [214] *White v Mellin* [1895] AC 154.

[215] *De Beers Abrasive Products Ltd v International General Electric Co of New York Ltd* [1975] 2 All ER 599; test subsequently applied in *Vodaphone Group plc v Orange Personal Communications Services Ltd* [1997] FSR 34.

Where a statement is capable of being read in a number of ways, at least one of which is not disparaging of the claimant's title, goods, or business, there is no requirement that the court settle upon a 'single meaning' as in the law of libel; the court will consider the impact of the statement in the round.[216]

(C) FALSE STATEMENT

The claimant has the burden of establishing that the disparaging statement was untrue.[217] The statement must be a false one *about the claimant, his property, or his business*; it is not enough that just any false statement resulted in harm to the claimant. Thus, whilst the disparaging statement need not identify the claimant personally, it must at least indirectly refer to him or his interests.[218]

The false statement must be such as is 'calculated' to cause harm[219] in the sense that it is of its nature 'really likely' to cause harm to the claimant's goodwill.

(D) PUBLICATION

Because the essence of the tort is the effect produced by the false statement on persons entering into relations with the claimant, the falsehood must be published to persons other than the claimant.[220] Whether a negligent or accidental publication is sufficient is undecided. However, it is clear that the defendant is liable for a re-publication that is the natural and probable result of his original publication.[221]

(E) MALICE

Since malice is always required to ground liability for this tort, it naturally follows that good faith on the part of the defendant will always be a good defence.[222] But whether the mere absence of good faith should be taken necessarily to imply the presence of malice is unclear due to the different tests for malice that have been put forward from time to time. Malice has been variously defined as 'improper motive',[223] 'intention to injure',[224] and 'want of honest belief in the truth of the statement'.[225] Significantly,

---

[216] *Ajinomoto Sweeteners Europe SAS v Asda Stores Ltd* [2010] EWCA Civ 609.

[217] *Royal Baking Powder Co v Wright, Crossley & Co* (1900) 18 RPC 95, at 99. And see also *Joyce v Sengupta* [1993] 1 All ER 897, at 901. Note that where the statement is 'not obviously untrue', no action will lie: *MacMillan Magazines Ltd v RCN Publishing Co Ltd* [1998] FSR 9.

[218] *Marathon Mutual Ltd v Waters* [2009] EWHC 1931 (QB), at [9-c]; Carty, *An Analysis of the Economic Torts* (2nd edn, 2010), 204.

[219] *Ratcliffe v Evans* [1892] 2 QB 524, at 527; *Kaye v Robertson* [1991] FSR 62, at 67.

[220] Cf *Malachy v Soper* (1836) 3 Bing NC 371.

[221] *Cellactite and British Uralite Ltd v HH Robertson & Co* (1957) *Times*, 23 July.

[222] *Spring v Guardian Assurance plc* [1994] 3 All ER 129; *Kingspan Group plc v Rockwool Ltd* [2011] EWHC 250 (Ch), at [240].   [223] *Balden v Shorter* [1933] Ch 427, at 430.

[224] *Steward v Young* (1870) LR 5 CP 122, at 127.

[225] *Greers Ltd v Pearman and Corder Ltd* (1922) 39 RPC 406, at 417.

the courts have not indicated a preference for any one of these definitions ahead of the others.[226] Thus, while the House of Lords in *White v Mellin*[227] held that either an intention to injure or knowledge of the falsity of the statement would suffice, Lord Coleridge LCJ was of the view in *Halsey v Brotherhood* that mere 'want of *bona fides*' would suffice.[228]

Thus, the claimant may be able to discharge his burden of proving this element of 'malice' in any one of several ways. The defendant is potentially liable if his primary purpose was to damage the claimant's business, even, it seems, although he was also acting for the benefit of his own interests.[229] But malice will be difficult to prove where statements disparaging of the claimant's goods are made against a background of competition for customers and a belief by the defendant in the superiority of its own product, which it attempts to prove, for example, through comparative demonstrations of safety.[230]

(F) DAMAGE

The claimant must prove that the false statement caused him pecuniary loss.[231] A debatable point has been whether the requirement that special damage has to be proved can be discharged by showing general loss of custom without adducing evidence that particular customers have withdrawn their business in consequence of the falsehood.[232] Whether evidence of general loss of business will be sufficient depends on 'the nature and circumstances of the falsehood'.[233] For example, a claimant cannot be expected to identify individuals affected by a statement in a newspaper. Evidence of general business loss will be acceptable in such a case. The same rule has been extended to a circular to customers, where, in the circumstances, the circular was reasonably likely to cause a decline in business.[234] On the other hand, a claimant who complained that

---

[226] Indeed, *British Railway Traffic and Electric Co v CRC Co and LCC* [1922] 2 KB 260 is one of the few cases where the court has held that some particular type of these variants of malice has to be proved. Equally, on only the non-binding authority of a first instance judge, it has been suggested that malice in this context bears the same meaning as in the context of defamation law: *Dorset Flint & Stone Blocks Ltd v Moir* [2004] EWHC 2173.

[227] [1895] AC 154 (the *ratio* is to be found most clearly in the opinion of Lord Herschell LC, at 160). Cf *Shapiro v La Morta* (1923) 130 LT 622, at 628 and *Greers Ltd v Pearman and Corder Ltd* (1922) 39 RPC 406, at 417–18.

[228] (1881) 19 Ch D 386, at 388. Cf *Wren v Weild* (1869) LR 4 QB 730.

[229] The *ratio* of *Joyce v Motor Surveys Ltd* [1948] Ch 252 is supported in *Alcott v Millar's Karri and Jarrah Forests Ltd* (1904) 91 LT 722, at 723. Cf *Mentmore Manufacturing Co Ltd v Fomento (Sterling Area) Ltd* (1955) 72 RPC 157.   [230] See, eg, *Kingspan Group plc v Rockwool Ltd* [2011] EWHC 250 (Ch).

[231] *Ajello v Worsley* [1898] 1 Ch 274; *Shapiro v La Morta* (1923) 130 LT 622; *Allason v Campbell* (1996) *Times*, 8 May. When the damage complained of is physical injury, this tort is presumably not applicable and *Wilkinson v Downton* [1897] 2 QB 57 must be relied on. Cf *Guay v Sun Publishing Co Ltd* [1952] 2 DLR 479; affirmed [1953] 4 DLR 577.

[232] *Malachy v Soper* (1836) Bing NC 371 decided that the tort is not actionable per se.

[233] *Ratcliffe v Evans* [1892] 2 QB 524, at 533.

[234] *E Worsley & Co Ltd v Cooper* [1939] 1 All ER 290. Cf *Lyne v Nicholls* (1906) 23 TLR 86.

the defendants had stated in their newspaper that his house was haunted, but who neither produced witnesses giving evidence that the statement had influenced them to the detriment of the claimant, nor showed that the house had depreciated in value as a result of it, failed.[235] The expenses of bringing litigation in order to remove a cloud hanging over the title caused by the defendant's statement are to be treated as special damage.[236]

The difficulties inherent in proving actual loss caused actions for malicious falsehood to become extremely rare.[237] In consequence, the common-law rules on damage have been modified by the Defamation Act 1952, section 3 of which provides:

> In an action for slander of title, slander of goods or other malicious falsehood, it shall not be necessary to allege or prove special damage – (a) if the words upon which the action is founded are calculated to cause pecuniary damage to the [claimant] and are published in writing or other permanent form;[238] or (b) if the said words are calculated to cause pecuniary damage to the [claimant] in respect of any office, profession, calling, trade or business[239] held or carried on by him at the time of the publication.[240]

For the purpose of this section, 'calculated to cause pecuniary damage' means harm that is objectively likely or probable.[241] And as a result of the section, in the vast majority of cases concerning this tort, it will not be necessary to prove special damage.[242] This is especially important in view of the doubt as to whether an injunction could be obtained before commencement of the Act where damage was merely likely to accrue.[243] The economic damage inflicted on the claimant by the falsehood may be accompanied by considerable mental distress and injury to feelings.[244] The Court of Appeal in *Joyce v Sengupta*[245] suggested that injury to feelings was not per se recoverable. But Sir Michael Kerr suggested that within general damages, an award of aggravated damages might partly reflect the injury to the claimant's feelings and dignity.

(G) DEFENCES

In those circumstances where a defendant in defamation could plead legislative immunity or absolute privilege – for example, in relation to statements in judicial

---

[235] *Barrett v Associated Newspapers Ltd* (1907) 23 TLR 666.

[236] *Elborow v Allen* (1622) Cro Jac 642.

[237] This was the view expressed in *Joyce v Sengupta* [1993] 1 All ER 897.

[238] This includes broadcasting.

[239] These words probably have the same meaning here as in the context of defamation.

[240] Note, too, that in *Joyce v Sengupta* [1993] 1 All ER 897 the court said that the Defamation Act 1952, s 3 is not confined to nominal damages.   [241] *IBM v Web-Sphere Ltd* [2004] EWHC 529.

[242] A claimant who relies on s 3 of the Defamation Act 1952 is not allowed to prove special damage unless he has specifically pleaded it: *Calvet v Tomkies* [1963] 3 All ER 610.

[243] *Dunlop Pneumatic Tyre Co Ltd v Maison Talbot* (1904) 20 TLR 579. Cf *White v Mellin* [1895] AC 154, at 163–4 and 167. Note that *Easycare Inc v Bryan Lawrence & Co* [1995] FSR 597 establishes that the normal rules applicable to the granting of interlocutory injunctions do not apply in cases of malicious falsehood.

[244] In *Fielding v Variety Inc* [1967] 2 QB 841 Lord Denning stated that damages for injured feelings were not recoverable for the tort of malicious falsehood.   [245] [1993] 1 All ER 897.

proceedings – the same defence will be available here. Formerly, it might have been apt to say that the defences of qualified privilege in defamation were similarly applicable, but the requirement of malice in this tort defeats any such claim.

(H) MALICIOUS FALSEHOOD AND DEFAMATION

There are clear similarities between malicious falsehood and the related tort of defamation.[246] It is apparent, for example, that there are occasions when the claimant has a choice between the two. In *Joyce v Sengupta*, where the claimant argued that allegations that she had stolen from the Princess Royal constituted a malicious falsehood threatening her employment prospects, the defendants contended that her proper remedy lay in defamation. By electing to sue in malicious falsehood, the claimant was able to obtain legal aid (which was unavailable in defamation)[247] and the defendant lost the right to trial by jury. The Court of Appeal refused to strike out the claimant's claim.

There is no principle of law that a claimant must pursue the most appropriate remedy. Following *Joyce v Sengupta* she is entitled to elect the action that best suits her. As long as one has an arguable case that defamatory allegations may damage one's financial prospects as well as one's reputation, one may choose whether to sue in defamation or in malicious falsehood. That said, three key differences between malicious falsehood on the one hand, and libel and slander on the other, can be identified.[248] First, while malice is a prerequisite to suing in malicious falsehood, it is not in defamation. Second, X cannot defame Y unless the statement casts aspersions on Y's character, whereas other classes of untruth – such as false statements about Y's business – will suffice in malicious falsehood. This, it has been judicially intimated, may have repercussions in terms of the interrelationship of the tort with Article 10 of the European Convention on Human Rights.[249] Finally, in defamation, the burden of proof lies with the defendant to establish the truth of a defamatory statement, whereas in malicious falsehood it rests with the claimant to show that the defendant's statement was untrue.

FURTHER READING

CARTY, *An Analysis of the Economic Torts* (2010), chs 9–12
NEWARK, 'Malice in Actions on the Case for Words' (1944) 60 *Law Quarterly Review* 366
SAW, 'Goodwill hunting in passing off: time to jettison the strict "hard line" approach in England?'
  [2010] *Journal of Business Law* 645

---

[246] See Gibbons (1996) 16 OJLS 587.

[247] And is nowadays also unavailable in malicious falsehood.

[248] The Court of Appeal has noted differences in the operation of the torts and has indicated its contentment with this: *Ajinomoto Sweeteners Europe SAS v Asda Stores Ltd* [2010] EWCA Civ 609, at [43].

[249] *Charterhouse Clinical Research Unit Ltd v Richmond Pharmacology Ltd* [2003] EWHC 1099, at [14].

14

THE GENERAL
ECONOMIC TORTS

KEY ISSUES

(1) Simplification of the landscape and the identification of the five general economic torts

Prior to 2007, the general economic torts were in a state of complete disarray. There were a large number of principles of liability which, in several cases, were frequently erroneously considered by the courts to be variants of one another. In *OBG v Allan* the House of Lords came close to simplifying significantly the general economic torts into just two varieties. Within a few months of this decision, however, a differently constituted House of Lords, in the *Total Network* case, breathed new life into two largely anomalous causes of action (lawful and unlawful means conspiracy) and in the process of so doing, revitalised the tort of two-party intimidation that had been more or less sidelined in *OBG v Allan*. In the wake of the two cases, we can now identify five general economic torts: the three already mentioned, plus inducing breach of contract and causing loss by unlawful means.

(2) Other causes of action

By analogy with the tort of inducing breach of contract, there is the possibility that it is tortious to induce the breach of other obligations to the detriment of a third party who suffers economic loss as a consequence of that breach. Some judicial support for these satellite causes of action can be identified; but whether they are necessary (bearing in mind other principles and remedies that English law makes available) is debatable.

(3) Lingering controversies

Various matters concerning the economic torts are still somewhat unclear. The nature of the tort of intimidation, and in particular its gist, is a prime example. Also, the interrelation between this tort and the law of contract still needs fully to be explored. Finally, just what will and will not constitute unlawful means for the purposes of the tort revitalised in *Total Network* remains fully to be worked out by the courts.

(4) Trade unions and the economic torts

Trade disputes between unions and employers have, over the years, served to contribute significantly to the development of the economic torts. However, the circumstances in which a trade union or its members can nowadays be held liable for the commission of one of these torts is a matter that needs to be resolved in the light of the various statutory immunities that are afforded in the context of industrial action. A brief sketch of this position is supplied at the end of this chapter.

SECTION 1   INTRODUCTION

This chapter sets out to explain the five general economic torts: viz, inducing breach of contract, causing loss by unlawful means, lawful means conspiracy, unlawful means conspiracy, and intimidation. Although in the wake of the recent decisions in *OBG v Allan*[1] and *Total Network v Revenue and Customs Commissioners*[2] all five torts can be said to stand on House of Lords' authority, it is nonetheless true that the foundations of the third and fourth look less secure under close scrutiny than the others. At the same time, similar close analysis of the tort of intimidation reveals that, while it may sometimes serve to protect economic interests, it is not specifically designed to do this. Notwithstanding such doubts, and in the hope that it promotes a clear exposition of the law as it stands, we endeavour to explain these torts in a way that is consistent with the language and reasoning deployed in those two landmark cases.

SECTION 2   INDUCING BREACH OF AN EXISTING CONTRACT

(A) INTRODUCTION

The modern tort of inducing breach of contract has its origins in the seminal decision in *Lumley v Gye*.[3] There, the facts alleged were as follows.

A famous opera singer was under a contract to sing at C's theatre *and nowhere else*, but she was not C's servant. C claimed that the singer had been induced by D, who knew of this contract,[4] to break it so that she would sing at D's theatre instead.

The court held that, if these facts could be made out, the defendant would have committed a tort in respect of which the claimant would be entitled to a remedy. But as will be seen shortly, the defendant was able to show that he honestly believed that the opera singer was entitled to terminate her contract with the claimant. Nonetheless, the case did establish that a tort will be committed if a defendant knowingly and intentionally induces a third party to break his contract with the claimant with the result that the breach in question causes the claimant to suffer loss. This principle was confirmed a generation later in *Bowen v Hall*[5] where, on similar facts, the Court of Appeal accepted the broad principle enunciated in *Lumley v Gye*. Since that time, a slight qualification has become clear. This is that a defendant who satisfies each of these elements may nonetheless escape liability if she is able to establish that her inducing the breach

---

[1] [2008] 1 AC 1.   [2] [2008] 1 AC 1174.   [3] *Lumley v Gye* (1853) 2 E & B 216.
[4] C failed at the subsequent trial, the jury finding that D did not believe the contract between C and Wagner to be binding: see Waddams (2001) 117 LQR 431.   [5] (1881) 6 QBD 333.

was justified. Six vital aspects therefore require consideration: inducement, breach, knowledge, intention, loss, and justification.

Before considering these six elements, however, it is as well to note that liability for this tort is not primary but secondary: that is, the tortfeasor is a sort of accessory to the primary legal wrong committed by the contract breaker. It is worth bearing this in mind when attempting to distinguish this tort from the other general economic torts. It was, after all, losing sight of just this point that led to so much of the confusion that bedevilled the development of the economic torts during the twentieth century.[6] It is also worth noting that calling it accessory liability *does not* enable us to label the inducer a *joint tortfeasor* for the simple reason that he is an accessory to a breach of contract, not a tort.

(B) ELEMENTS OF THE TORT

(1) Inducement

Prior to *OBG v Allan*, a measure of confusion had crept into the law on what, for the purposes of this tort, could be regarded as inducement. For example, in one strain of cases,[7] it was thought that mere prevention of performance would count. In another – of which *Thomson & Co Ltd v Deakin*[8] is a good example – it was held that mere inconsistent dealings could suffice. Jenkins LJ put it this way: 'if a third party, with knowledge of a contract between the contract breaker and another, had dealings with the contract breaker which the third party knows to be inconsistent with the contract, he has committed an actionable interference'.[9] The tenor of *OBG v Allan*, however, was clearly that orthodoxy should be restored and that the tort should revert to the way in which it had originally been conceived in *Lumley v Gye*. So, for Lord Nicholls, it was 'evident that application of the *Lumley v Gye* tort to a "prevention" case was unfortunate [since] [t]here is a crucial difference between cases where the defendant induces a contracting party not to perform his contractual obligations and cases where the defendant prevents a contracting party from carrying out his contractual obligations'.[10] And while Lord Hoffmann's speech was less clear-cut, he nonetheless identified as the basis of the original decision in *Lumley v Gye* the fact that 'a person...procures another to commit a wrong'.[11] If one adds to this the fact that Arden LJ has since stated that '[t]he tort of inducing a breach of contract is committed when a person, with the requisite knowledge and intention...*procures or persuades* another person to breach his contract with a third party',[12] it seems fairly safe to state

---

[6] For a first-rate critical account of the content and contours of the general economic torts prior to *OBG v Allan*, see Carty, *An Analysis of the Economic Torts* (2nd edn, 2010), chs 2–8.

[7] See, eg, *Torquay Hotel Co Ltd v Cousins* [1969] 2 Ch 106; *Merkur Island Shipping Corpn v Laughton* [1983] 2 AC 570.   [8] [1952] Ch 646.

[9] Ibid at 694.

[10] [2008] 1 AC 1, at [178].

[11] Ibid at [3]. Cf his focus on the causation of breach via 'encouragement, threat, persuasion and so forth' at [36].   [12] *Meretz Investments NV v ACP Ltd* [2008] Ch 244, at [86] (emphasis added).

that the prevention of performance and mere inconsistent dealing ideas have now been consigned to the dustbin of legal history. What this tort now seems to require, then, is direct inducement along the lines of active persuasion or positive encouragement to commit a breach. Mere advice which simply *flags up*, rather than *creates*, a good reason to break a contract, ought not, in our view, to suffice.[13] Nor can there be said to be inducement if it is clear that the contract breaker would have broken the contract in any event.[14]

(2) Breach

Any valid and enforceable contract can found an action for this tort.[15] But if the contract was void or voidable, and therefore unenforceable, any putative procurement of its breach will not of course be actionable.[16] The terms of the contract which are broken need not be the primary terms. So, as the Court of Appeal made clear in *Law Debenture Trust Corpn v Ural Caspian Oil Corporation*,[17] breach of even the secondary contractual duty to pay damages when a primary contractual obligation has been broken can give rise to tortious liability.[18] It would seem to follow from this that, even if the defendant is not responsible for the initial breach of a contract, he will still be liable in tort if he is responsible for procuring the continuing breach of a subsisting contract the obligations of which are ongoing at the time of the inducement.[19] Thus, where the defendant engaged a servant in ignorance of an existing contract of service between the servant and the claimant, he could not escape liability where he continued to employ the servant after learning the facts.[20]

The breach of implied terms will also suffice, as *Hivac Ltd v Park Royal Scientific Instruments Ltd*[21] amply demonstrates.[22] In that case, the claimant had been the only English maker of midget valves for hearing aids. Setting up in competition, the defendant employed some of the claimant's staff in their spare time. It was held that an implied term must be read into the engagement of these staff that the latter should not break their fidelity to the claimant by doing things which would injure the claimant's business. In view of the fact that the claimant had a monopoly on this type of work, and the staff held a monopoly over the relevant skill, an injunction restraining the inducement of breach could be obtained.

---

[13] Cf *Torquay Hotel Co Ltd v Cousins* [1969] 2 Ch 106, at 147.

[14] *Jones Bros (Hunstanton) Ltd v Stevens* [1955] 1 QB 275.

[15] Cf *Thomson & Co Ltd v Deakin* [1952] Ch 646, at 677; *Findlay v Blaylock* 1937 SC 21.

[16] *Proform Sports Management Ltd v Proactive Sports Management* [2007] 1 All ER 542; *Shears v Mendeloff* (1914) 30 TLR 342 (contracts involving minors); *Said v Butt* [1920] 3 KB 497 (mistake); *Joe Lee Ltd v Lord Dalmery* [1927] 1 Ch 300 (gaming).   [17] [1995] Ch 152.

[18] [1994] 3 WLR 1221, at 1235.

[19] *Smithies v National Association of Operative Plasterers* [1909] 1 KB 310.

[20] *Blake v Lanyon* (1795) 6 Term Rep 221; *Fred Wilkins & Bros Ltd v Weaver* [1915] 2 Ch 322. Cf *Read v Friendly Society of Operative Stonemasons* [1902] 2 KB 88, at 95 (on appeal [1902] 2 KB 732). See also *Jones Bros (Hunstanton) Ltd v Stevens* [1955] 1 QB 275.   [21] [1946] Ch 169.

[22] See also *Lonmar Global Risks Ltd v West* [2010] 2878 (QB).

Nor, according to the decision in *Torquay Hotel Co Ltd v Cousins*,[23] need the breach be actionable.

> An injunction was granted against Ds who, in the course of industrial action, were attempting to stop a supplier fulfilling his contract with C. The contract expressly exempted either party from liability for events beyond their control – such as labour disputes – if those events led to a failure to perform. The Court of Appeal interpreted the clause as 'an exception from liability for non-performance rather than an exception from the obligation to perform'.[24] Accordingly, D's conduct still constituted the procurement of a breach, and C still suffered loss (albeit loss that was not actionable under the contract).

The logic of this reasoning seems sound enough even if in other respects (amply exposed by their Lordships in *OBG v Allan*) the decision in the *Torquay Hotel* case was deeply flawed. On the other hand, if a contract is determinable by either party at will, it is not actionable if the defendant induces a party to determine that contract.[25] This is because there has been no breach, but merely a lawful termination of the contract. Similarly, inducing someone to give proper notice in order to terminate a contract lawfully cannot give rise to a tort action.[26] By contrast, however, giving notice of a forthcoming strike is not notice to terminate, but, rather, notice of a forthcoming breach of contract. It thus follows that, where there is a no-strike clause in the contract, inducing a strike will amount to inducing breach of contract.[27] Union officials inducing strike action are thus prima facie open to tort liability. In reality, however, they enjoy certain statutory immunities as a matter of employment law. (These immunities fall beyond the scope this book.)

(3) Knowledge of the contract

That the defendant must have known of the contract between the claimant and the contract breaker was insisted upon in *Lumley v Gye* itself. This insistence was reiterated in *Mainstream Properties v Young*,[28] one of three appeals heard together in *OBG v Allan*.

> D had supplied two of C's employees with funding that enabled them to pursue a personal property development project which had initially been offered to C (a property development company). In pursuing such a project for independent gain, the employees were in breach of their employment contract with C. D knew very well that they worked for C and what C's line of business was. He could not, therefore, deny his awareness of the obvious potential conflict of interest that existed. Nonetheless, because the employees had assured D that there would be no breach of contract if they pursued the project, D was able to

---

[23] [1969] 2 Ch 106.
[24] Ibid at 143.
[25] *McManus v Bowes* [1938] 1 KB 98.
[26] See, eg, *Boxfoldia Ltd v National Graphic Association (1982)* [1988] ICR 752; *Thomson & Co Ltd v Deakin* [1952] Ch 646.   [27] *Rookes v Barnard* [1964] AC 1129.
[28] [2008] 1 AC 1.

escape liability on the footing that he did not subjectively know that there would be a breach of contract.

The defendant was doubtless foolish to believe the employees' lies, but believe them he did. This, Lord Hoffmann said, was enough to exculpate him on the basis that he honestly did not believe that the employees' acts would be in breach of contract and that, therefore, he was procuring a breach of contract. He said:

> It is not enough that you know that you are procuring an act which, as a matter of law or construction of the contract, is a breach. You must actually realise that it will have this effect. Nor does it matter that you ought reasonably to have done so.[29]

In the light of this passage, it might be thought that nothing short of actual knowledge would suffice. However, both Lord Hoffmann and Lord Nicholls were prepared to countenance one exception; and this exception was intended to apply where the defendant deliberately turns a blind eye to facts that would reveal the presence of a breach. In their view, a defendant cannot escape liability if he consciously avoids enquiring into a case simply in order to avoid an inconvenient truth. Thus, as Lord Denning pointed out in *Emerald Construction Co Ltd v Lowthian*[30] – a case where union officials threatened a building contractor with a strike unless he terminated a sub-contract for the supply of labour – the defendants obviously knew that there was a contract (because they wanted it broken). So, '[e]ven if they did not know the actual terms of the contract, but had the means of knowledge – which they deliberately disregarded – that would be enough'.[31] It should, however, be noted that the defendant in *Mainstream Properties* had not turned a blind eye. He had simply been lied to, and he honestly believed those lies to the effect that no breach would occur.

(4) Intention

The need for intention in the tort of inducing breach of contract was asserted forcefully in *OBG v Allan*. For Lord Nicholls, the defendant 'is liable if he intended to persuade the contracting party to breach the contract'.[32] Lord Hoffmann, while equally certain of the need for intention, was less straightforward in the way he expressed things. In his view, intention was to be identified in one of two alternative ways: by reference to whether a breach of contract was intended as an end in itself, or by reference to whether it was sought as a means to an end (such as, say, endeavouring somehow to augment the defendant's own market position).[33] Importantly, both Law Lords stopped short of insisting that the defendant should have intended the breach to result in harm to the claimant. It was enough that a breach – pure and simple – was intended. That being so, there was no absence of the requisite intention in one case in which the defendant union believed that calling a strike of their members would ultimately be to the financial benefit of the mine owner by forcing up the price of coal.[34] On the other

---

[29] Ibid at [39].   [30] [1966] 1 WLR 691.   [31] Ibid at 700–1.   [32] [2008] 1 AC 1, at [192].
[33] Ibid at 43.
[34] *South Wales Miners' Federation v Glamorgan Coal Co Ltd* [1905] AC 239.

hand, nothing in this case should be seen as undermining the additional requirement for this tort that damage actually be suffered.

(5) Harm

It is well settled that the claimant must suffer loss of a more than nominal kind by virtue of the breach of contract in order to be able to invoke this tort.[35] If the breach is of a kind that will, 'in the ordinary course of business' cause damage, then loss may be inferred from the circumstances.[36] If the breach is not of this kind, loss will have to be proved; and this may be no easy matter as is illustrated by *Jones Bros (Hunstanton) Ltd v Stevens.*[37]

> D continued to employ a servant after learning that the servant, in entering into his employment, was breaking his contract with C. It was shown, however, that the servant would not in any event have returned to C's employment. It was held, therefore, that C's action based on this tort failed: no damage had been occasioned.

There appears to be a remoteness test based on reasonable foreseeability of harm with respect to this tort;[38] and – so long as ordinary losses (such as financial loss) can be identified – it seems that aggravated damages may also be recovered in circumstances where the breach was intended to inflict 'humiliation and menace'.[39]

(6) Justification

The point has long been established, and was endorsed in *OBG v Allan*,[40] that, exceptionally, certain circumstances may justify the inducement of a breach of contract. As yet, the courts have not laid down any settled test for this defence; but the dictum of Romer LJ in *Glamorgan Coal Co Ltd v South Wales Miners' Federation* is widely cited.[41]

> [R]egard might be had to the nature of the contract broken; the position of the parties to the contract; the grounds for the breach; the means employed to procure the breach; the relation of the person procuring the breach to the person who breaks the contract; and the object of the person in procuring the breach.

In that case it was held that the defendants were not justified in calling the miners out on strike in order to keep up the price of coal by which the miners' pay was regulated.[42] The breach by a claimant of his contract with the defendant will not justify

---

[35] *Greig v Insole* [1978] 1 WLR 302, at 332.
[36] *Exchange Telegraph Co Ltd v Gregory & Co* [1896] 1 QB 147; *Goldsoll v Goldman* [1914] 2 Ch 603 (on appeal [1915] 1 Ch 292); *Bents Brewery Co Ltd v Hogan* [1945] 2 All ER 570.   [37] [1955] 1 QB 275.
[38] *Boxfoldia Ltd v NGA (1982)* [1988] IRLR 383.   [39] *Pratt v BMA* [1919] 1 KB 244.
[40] [2008] 1 AC 1, at [193]
[41] [1903] 2 KB 545, at 574–5 (approved in *South Wales Miners' Federation v Glamorgan Coal Co Ltd* [1905] AC 239, at 252).
[42] Cf *Temperton v Russell* [1893] 1 QB 715 where trade union officials were not justified in interfering in order to enforce certain conditions of labour in a particular trade; *Read v Friendly Society of Operative Stonemasons of England, Ireland and Wales* [1902] 2 KB 88.

the defendant in inducing a third party to break his contract with the claimant.[43] On the other hand, *Brimelow v Casson* is one of the rare cases in which the defence has succeeded.[44]

> D represented various theatrical unions, and C owned a touring theatrical company. D induced a theatre manager to break his contract with C because C was paying such low wages to his company that some chorus girls were compelled to resort to prostitution. The interest that D had in maintaining professional theatrical standards was held to justify D procuring the breach.

Notwithstanding this decision, it is nonetheless true that the defence of justification is not apt to be widely invoked. Certainly, it has been judicially stated that the role for justification is highly exceptional in relation to procuring a breach of contract.[45] There is a simple reason for this: the interest in maintaining the security of contracts almost always outweighs that of protecting free trade.

(C) ANALOGOUS ACTIONS FOR INDUCING BREACH OF OTHER OBLIGATIONS?

It now seems to be fairly well established that it is tortious deliberately to procure the violation of any enforceable obligation provided a violation of that obligation is itself actionable.[46] So, by analogy with inducing breach of contract, it appears to be tortious to induce a breach of statutory duty (so long as it is a statutory duty breach of which would afford the claimant an action in tort).[47] On the other hand, since all that this really involves is an instance of joint tortfeasance, it can perfectly well be argued that the extension of the *Lumley v Gye* principle to this context was unnecessary.

It has been held in principle that the *Lumley v Gye* tort may be extrapolated to inducing breach of copyright,[48] and it is probably also tortious to induce the breach of an equitable obligation, *except* a breach of trust. So, although a breach of the duty of fidelity owed by a fiduciary is likely to be covered,[49] it is unlikely that mere inducement

---

[43] *Smithies v National Association of Operative Plasterers* [1909] 1 KB 310.

[44] [1924] 1 Ch 302. Yet Simonds J in *Camden Nominees Ltd v Forcey* [1940] Ch 352 treated that decision (at 366) as being based on the separate ground of *ex turpi causa*.

[45] *SOS Kinderdorf International v Bittaye* [1996] 1 WLR 987, at 994.

[46] Cf Bagshaw, 'Inducing Breach of Contract' in Horder (ed), *Oxford Essays in Jurisprudence, 4th Series* (2000) who argues (at 149) that the critical test is 'whether such obligations should be recognized as having a dimension which should be protected against *the rest of the world*'.

[47] *Meade v Haringey LBC* [1979] 2 All ER 1016; *Associated British Ports v Transport and General Workers' Union* [1989] 3 All ER 796 (reversed on other grounds [1989] 3 All ER 822).

[48] *CBS Songs v Amstrad Consumer Electronics plc* [1988] AC 1013 (no liability on the facts where D had only provided X with tape machines that were capable of being used to infringe C's copyright). By contrast, no independent tort lies in respect of inducing breach of tortious obligations; but a separate tort is unnecessary here since such an act would engage the principles of joint tortfeasance.

[49] See, eg, *Boulting v ACTAT* [1963] 2 QB 606, at 627.

of a breach of trust will suffice since it is generally thought that the doctrines of equity provide adequate remedies in that respect.[50]

SECTION 3   CAUSING LOSS BY UNLAWFUL MEANS

(A) INTRODUCTION

This tort was for a time conceived in terms of 'interfering with the trade or business of another person by doing unlawful acts'.[51] These days, however, the ecumenically accepted name for the tort is that of causing loss by unlawful means.[52] Furthermore, despite its patchy history, it is undoubtedly to the House of Lords' milestone decision in *OBG v Allan* that we must turn in order to tease out its essential ingredients. Unfortunately, although this teasing out can be done with a great deal more confidence than was formerly possible, it is an exercise that still reveals a number of lingering ambiguities and uncertainties in the law that will no doubt require consideration by the courts on future occasions. With this sobering thought in mind, we turn first to consider the several elements of the tort that can with certainty be claimed to be vital to its invocation: namely, unlawful means, intention, and harm. Thereafter, we shall examine the lingering uncertainties.

(B) ELEMENTS OF THE TORT

(1) Intention

Just as with inducing breach of contract, intention plays a central role in the operation of the tort of causing loss by unlawful means. However, whereas in the former the defendant must intend to bring about a mere breach of contract (which may or may not result in loss), in this tort 'there must be an intention to cause loss... [meaning] [t]he ends which must have been intended are different'.[53] But apart from the fact that the ends are different, the test is the same. One intends to cause loss by unlawful means if one intends that loss (as opposed to breach of contract) as an end in itself, or as a means to an end (eg, securing a competitive advantage).[54] Whether it makes more sense for the law to adopt a test based on targeted harm is a moot point. Certainly, some writers are of the view that orthodoxy demands a narrow view of intention: one that sees a specific aim of the defendant's act being the infliction of harm on the

---

[50] *Metall und Rohstoff AG v Donaldson Lufkin and Jenrette Inc* [1990] 1 QB 391. Cf *Prudential Assurance Co Ltd v Lorenz* (1971) 11 KIR 78.

[51] *Merkur Island Shipping Corpn v Laughton* [1983] 2 AC 570, at 608.

[52] It is the term used repeatedly in *OBG v Allan* (though not always by Lord Nicholls) and by the Court of Appeal in *Meretz Investments NV v ACP Ltd* [2008] Ch 244.

[53] *OBG v Allan* [2008] 1 AC 1, at [62].   [54] Ibid.

claimant as an end in itself.[55] The test propounded in *OBG v Allan*, by contrast, goes further: it also embraces acts designed to cause harm as a means to some ulterior end (such as self-enrichment). And since Lord Nicholls was content to adopt the same test as Lord Hoffmann as regards intention, it is fairly safe to conclude that, whatever the balance of arguments regarding the need for, or rejection of, a targeted harm test, the law is at least now clear on this matter.

(2) Unlawful means

The question of what constitutes 'unlawful means' in the context of the economic torts has been for some time – and to some extent remains – a controversial issue. However, for the purposes of the present tort, it is now possible to state with some confidence what will be taken to amount to unlawful means. According to Lord Hoffmann's leading speech in *OBG v Allan* (with which Baroness Hale and Lord Brown concurred), unlawful means should generally be taken to constitute 'acts against a third party... [that] are actionable by that third party'.[56] (Examples would include breaches of contract, common law torts,[57] any actionable breach of statutory duty, and (probably) breaches of equitable obligations.)[58] To this general stipulation, his Lordship thought there should be one qualification: namely, 'that they will also be unlawful means if the only reason why they are not actionable is because the third party has suffered no loss'.[59] He then gave as an example the case of *National Phonograph Co Ltd v Edison-Bell Consolidated Phonograph Co Ltd*.[60] In that case the defendant had intentionally caused loss to the claimant by fraudulently inducing a third party to act to the claimant's detriment. Importantly, however, the party who was actually defrauded *did not* suffer any loss. Nonetheless, the fact that the third party had been induced to act in the way that he did was sufficient to constitute unlawful means.

Two general points may be made about this conception of unlawful means. The first is that, because the tort requires an actionable (or potentially actionable) wrong to be committed against an intermediary, the tort of causing loss by unlawful means must *always* involve three parties. This, as will be seen in due course, sets it in contradistinction to the tort of intimidation and unlawful means conspiracy where two-party liability is at play. The second point is that there now seems little to ground either Lord Nicholls' dissenting view that the term unlawful means 'embraces all acts a defendant is not permitted to do whether by the civil or criminal law',[61] or the idea that an agreement made in restraint of trade will suffice. In respect of the latter, it seems we must

---

[55] For details of these writers and the cases upon which they ground their analysis, see Carty, *An Analysis of the Economic Torts* (2nd edn, 2010), 80–2.

[56] [2008] 1 AC 1, at [49].

[57] Intimidation is a prime candidate here since this tort necessarily involves D coercing X into acting in a particular way, including those that harm C: see, eg, *Rookes v Barnard* [1964] AC 1129.

[58] See, eg, *Jarman & Platt Ltd v I Barget Ltd* [1977] FSR 260; *Indata Equipment Supplies Ltd v ACL Ltd* [1998] FSR 248, at 264.   [59] Ibid.

[60] [1908] 1 Ch 335. See also *Lonrho plc v Fayed* [1990] 2 QB 479, at 489.

[61] [2008] 1 AC 1, at [162].

now regard as wrong earlier cases[62] suggesting that such agreements – which are void and therefore legal nullities – would constitute unlawful means.

A further, more particular point also needs to be added; and this is that Lord Hoffmann was not content to control liability for this tort by virtue of a restrictive conception of unlawful means – one which entails only (potentially) actionable civil wrongs. Rather, he additionally insisted that the third party must be one in whom the claimant has an economic interest and that, bearing in mind this interest, the unlawful means must cause loss to the claimant by interfering with the third party's liberty to deal with the claimant. The importance of this rider is that it enabled his Lordship to leave intact two cases involving the infringement of intellectual property rights (which, naturally, would be actionable wrongs in the hands the intellectual property rights holders). The first was *RCA v Pollard*;[63] the second, *Oren v Red Box Toy Factory Ltd*.[64] At the heart of both cases was the fact that the defendant's infringement of a third party's intellectual property right resulted in harm to a claimant who was an exclusive licensee (ie, the only person permitted lawfully to exploit the intellectual property in question). In both cases, the defendant's infringement of the third party's intellectual property right did 'nothing which affected the relations between the owner and the licensee' and therefore fell outside the strictures of Lord Hoffmann's rider in *OBG*.

What might be noted *en passant* is that it would not have been necessary to introduce the rider that he did had the House of Lords made the test for intention for this tort one of targeted harm.[65]

(3) Harm

One thing that has never been in doubt is that the claimant must be able to show that he or she has suffered harm in order to invoke this tort. But quite what form that harm should take was undecided prior to the House of Lords' decision in *OBG v Allan*. According to a good deal of the earlier case law, for example, the tort was conceived in terms of interference with trade or business.[66] Nowadays, however, the preferred name for the tort is simply that of causing loss by unlawful means. It is certainly the name applied by Lord Hoffmann in his leading speech in that case, and the one subsequently adopted by the Court of Appeal in *Meretz Investments NV v ACP Ltd*.[67]

However the simple reference to 'causing loss' is apt to mislead as to the kind of harm that can be said to support liability. This is because Lord Hoffmann's rider on unlawful means makes it clear that the tort protects only economic interests. (Recall his insistence that the third party through whom the claimant is injured must be someone 'in whom the claimant has an economic interest'.) What we are left with, then, in reality,

---

[62] Eg, *Daily Mirror Newspapers Ltd v Gardner* [1968] 2 QB 762; *Associated British Ports v TGWU* [1989] ICR 557.   [63] [1983] Ch 135.
[64] [1999] FSR 785.
[65] For a full account of the argument, see Carty, *An Analysis of the Economic Torts* (2nd edn, 2010), 97.
[66] See the previous edition of this book for examples.   [67] [2008] Ch 244.

is a tort of causing loss to economic interests by unlawful means: a tort with a wider range of application than one that simply protects trade or business, but a tort of insufficient scope to encompass, say, physical injury. That being so, if A intimidates B so that B desists from buying C's house from him, it is probable the tort could be invoked even though C is not a commercial property dealer. Conversely, however, if A intimidates B into punching C, this tort cannot be engaged.[68]

Whether it is appropriate for the tort's remit to be limited by reference to economic interests is an interesting question. Certainly, an argument can be made for using this tort as a platform for the 'development of general principles of liability in respect of harm suffered intentionally'.[69] At the heart of such a development would be two main considerations: namely, (1) the infliction of intentional harm[70] and (2) the requirement that unlawful means be used. These factors do not dictate the limitation of this tort to cases in which economic harm has been caused. Nor is it easy to see why economic interests – which are generally found at the bottom end of the hierarchy of protected interests in tort law – should be singled out for special treatment. Indeed, a cogent argument can be made that this tort could become a 'general principle of liability in respect of harm inflicted intentionally as a counterpart to the generalisation of the reasonable care or reasonable behaviour standard in the non-intentional sphere'.[71]

(4) Justification

A matter not directly considered by the House of Lords in *OBG v Allan* is whether a defence of justification can be raised in relation to this tort. Academic views are divided on the matter. But the present submission is that, so long as the test for unlawful means is that of an actionable (or potentially actionable) civil wrong, there is no conceptual space that the putative defence of justification could occupy. To explain: if the general law says that the unlawful means in a certain case constitute an actionable tort, that carries with it the idea that what the defendant did was not excusable by reference to the general law on tort law defences. That being the case, there is no obvious reason why a more specious defence should be crafted simply to suit this tort. In any event, it is hard to escape the appeal of Webster J's proclamation that 'there can be no justification for a civil wrong'.[72]

---

[68] There is, however, the possibility of being held jointly liable along with the party intimidated on the basis that he *procured* the commission of a battery, for procuring the commission of a tort is a settled basis for the imposition of joint liability: see, eg, *Wah Tat Bank Ltd v Chan* [1975] AC 507.

[69] Sales and Stilitz (1999) 115 LQR 411, at 436.

[70] *Associated British Ports v TGWU* [1989] ICR 557. In this case Stuart-Smith LJ made it clear (at 586) that 'deliberate and intended damage' is required. That view also appears in *Douglas v Hello! Ltd (No 6)* [2006] QB 125 and *Mainstream Properties v Young* [2005] EWCA Civ 861.

[71] Sales and Stilitz (1999) 115 LQR 411, at 430.

[72] *Shearson Lehman Hutton Inc v Maclaine Watson & Co* [1989] 2 Lloyd's Rep 570, at 633.

SECTION 4   LAWFUL MEANS CONSPIRACY

(A) INTRODUCTION

Tortious conspiracy takes two forms. The first form – sometimes formerly called 'simple conspiracy' – is that of lawful means conspiracy. It is thus styled because of the absence of any requirement that the defendant must show the use of unlawful means on the part of the conspirators. The tort is often considered highly anomalous,[73] despite the fact it occupies its place within the common law on the repeated authority of the House of Lords.[74] It is said to be (1) the fact of combination in tandem with (2) the intentional infliction of harm in furtherance of (3) an illegitimate purpose that renders the conspirators' acts tortious.

(B) ELEMENTS OF THE TORT

(1) Combination

The requirement of combination is generally straightforward. The ancient fiction that a husband and wife were one person in the eyes of the common law no longer prevents spouses being liable together for the tort of conspiracy.[75] Directors and their company may conspire together since the company is a separate legal entity.[76] However, to establish such a conspiracy, it is essential to identify the relevant 'mind and will' of the company (normally found in the director who had management or control over the particular act in question).[77] From this, it follows that the relevant alter ego of the company will be located in different people for different purposes (usually discoverable from the company's articles of association).[78]

Combinations with which the tort of conspiracy is concerned may take many forms. Examples include traders combining to ward off the competition of a rival trader;[79] trade union officials combining to compel an employer to dismiss a non-union employee;[80] an employers' federation and a trade union combining to deprive a worker belonging to another union of his job so as to promote collective bargaining in the industry concerned;[81] employees collectively threatening a strike unless the employer dismissed a worker belonging to another union.[82] But these instances by no means constitute an exhaustive list.

---

[73] In *Lonrho Ltd v Shell Petroleum Co Ltd (No 2)* [1982] AC 172 the House of Lords recognised simple conspiracy as a 'highly anomalous cause of action', but one too well established to be discarded.
[74] *Mogul Steamship Co v McGregor* [1892] AC 25; *Quinn v Leathem* [1901] AC 945; *Crofter v Veitch* [1942] AC 435.   [75] *Midland Bank Trust Co Ltd v Green (No 3)* [1982] Ch 529.
[76] *Belmont Finance Corpn Ltd v Williams Furniture Ltd* [1979] Ch 250. And see *Taylor v Smyth* [1991] 1 IR 142 (conspiring with companies under D's control).
[77] *El Ajou v Dollar Land Holdings plc* [1994] 2 All ER 685.
[78] *Meridian Global Funds Management Asia Ltd v Securities Commission* [1995] 3 All ER 918, at 923.
[79] *Mogul Steamship Co v McGregor, Gow & Co* [1892] AC 25.
[80] *Quinn v Leathem* [1901] AC 495.   [81] *Reynolds v Shipping Federation Ltd* [1924] 1 Ch 28.
[82] *White v Riley* [1921] 1 Ch 1.

(2) Preponderantly illegitimate purpose

The second salient ingredient in this tort is that of illegitimate purpose. In order to invoke the tort, the claimant must show that the parties combining against him were preponderantly seeking to secure an illegitimate end. In other words, it is the fact that the conspirators' acts are animated by an injurious motive that is pivotal. In this respect, the tort of lawful means conspiracy contradicts the fundamental proposition in the cornerstone case of *Allen v Flood*[83] that motive alone cannot render illegal that which would otherwise be legal conduct. The contradiction inheres in the fact that, in lawful means conspiracy, defendants are effectively being held liable for doing in combination that which any one of them would be perfectly within their rights to do if acting alone. Nonetheless, as one judge has since explained, the requirement of preponderantly harmful motive is intended to secure the proper 'balance between the defendant's right to exercise his lawful rights and the plaintiff's right not to be injured by an injurious conspiracy'.[84]

Much as it is an easy thing to state that the defendants' acts must be preponderantly calculated to achieve an illegitimate purpose, it can sometimes be rather difficult to establish this. Consider *Crofter Hand Woven Harris Tweed Co Ltd v Veitch*[85] which exemplifies the problem.

> Cs produced tweed cloth on an island in the Outer Hebrides. Only the weaving of their cloth took place on the island; they imported yarn from the mainland. Other firms had their cloth spun as well as woven on the island. Ds were trade union officials of the union to which most of the spinners employed in the island mills belonged. Employers of these men informed Ds that the competition of Cs prevented them from raising wages. Ds (assumed by some of their Lordships to be acting in combination with the mill-owners) instructed dockers at the island's port to refuse to handle yarn imported from the mainland and consigned to Cs. Without breaking their contracts of employment, the dockers (who were members of the same union as Ds) consented. Cs sought to stop this embargo on the ground that it was an actionable conspiracy. They failed. The House of Lords held that the predominant purpose of the combination was the legitimate promotion of Ds' own interests.

So much for the pursuit of self-interest. But what about acts prompted by altruistic concerns: that is, with the interests of others to the fore, such as a group of people against whom the claimant has taken discriminatory action? In *Scala Ballroom (Wolverhampton) Ltd v Ratcliffe*,[86] the defendants sought to justify their acts on just this basis, even though the Court of Appeal went on to find that, properly understood, there was justification for the claimant's imposition of a colour bar at its dance hall. Nonetheless, there were *obiter* intimations in the case that altruism could be taken to constitute a legitimate purpose.

---

[83] [1898] AC 1.   [84] *Crofter v Veitch* [1942] AC 435, at 462.
[85] Ibid.
[86] [1958] 1 WLR 1057.

A further complication in this context may well arise where the defendants are aware that damage to the claimant is an inevitable consequence of their collective action. But being aware of an inevitable consequence cannot be taken to be synonymous with having that consequence as one's predominant purpose. The House of Lords made just this point in *Lonrho Ltd v Shell Petroleum Co Ltd (No 2)*.[87]

> Ds breached sanctions orders against the illegal regime in Rhodesia, substantially increasing their profits at C's expense. Rejecting the claim in conspiracy, the House of Lords found that even if unlawful means were used to further the conspiracy, no liability arose unless Ds acted 'for the purpose not of protecting their own interests but of injuring the interests of [C]'.[88]

Once the bona fides of the defendants is established, it is irrelevant that the damage inflicted to secure the purpose is disproportionately severe.[89] Nor does it matter that, secondarily, the defendants are glad to see the claimant suffer a loss.[90] Furthermore, there is no need for the conspirators to share a common, justificatory, predominant purpose: 'it is sufficient if all the various combining parties have their own legitimate trade or business interests to gain, even though these interests may be of differing kinds'.[91] This dictum tends to limit considerably the practical utility of this tort, since most people have individual (as opposed to collective) interests to pursue.

A final point to note in this context is the fact that it is uncertain whether the burden of proving the predominant purpose of damaging the claimant lies with the claimant or the defendant. In the *Veitch* case, Lords Wright[92] and Porter[93] thought it rested with the claimant; Viscount Maugham held that it lay with the defendant, while the other two Law Lords were silent on the matter. That said, the first view seems preferable since it accords with earlier decisions of the House of Lords and with the expressed intention of the Law Lords in *Lonrho Ltd v Shell Petroleum Co Ltd* to confine the ambit of the tort.[94]

(3) Harm

It is the securing of the defendants' preponderantly illegitimate purpose that forms the gist of this tort. Accordingly, resulting harm on the part of the claimant is an

---

[87] [1982] AC 173.   [88] Ibid at 189.

[89] *Crofter Hand Woven Harris Tweed Co Ltd Veitch* [1942] AC 435, at 447. Cf *Trollope & Sons v London Building Trades Federation* (1895) 72 LT 342.

[90] In *Crofter Hand Woven Harris Tweed Co Ltd v Veitch* [1942] AC 435, Lord Wright said (at 471): 'I cannot see how the pursuit of a legitimate practical object can be vitiated by glee at the adversary's expected discomfiture'. Cf ibid at 444–5 and 450. Yet the court must inquire into the state of knowledge of Ds whenever it is relevant for the ascertainment of their purpose: *Huntley v Thornton* [1957] 1 All ER 234; *Bird v O'Neal* [1960] AC 907.

[91] *Crofter Hand Woven Harris Tweed Co Ltd v Veitch* [1942] AC 435, at 453. Cf the judgment of Evatt J in *McKerman v Fraser* (1931) 46 CLR 343.   [92] [1942] AC 435, at 471.

[93] Ibid at 495.   [94] And see *Sorrell v Smith* [1925] AC 700.

essential requirement, and it has been specifically held that 'a plaintiff in a civil action for conspiracy must prove actual pecuniary loss'.[95]

SECTION 5   UNLAWFUL MEANS CONSPIRACY

(A) INTRODUCTION

The main difference between unlawful and lawful means conspiracy is the obvious one that, in the former, the claimant must show that the defendant used unlawful means to cause harm to the claimant. But another difference is that, in unlawful means conspiracy, the defendant's principal motive is irrelevant. Thus, in *Lonrho v Fayed*,[96] Lord Bridge affirmed that although both forms of civil conspiracy involve intention to harm, in unlawful means conspiracy that intention need not be the defendant's primary design. Indeed, his Lordship explained further that even if the defendants can show that their main purpose was to protect or advance their own interests, this will not avail them of a valid defence. (Indeed, it seems doubtful that any defence of justification can be invoked in relation to this tort.)

In the light of these differences, it is clear that unlawful means conspiracy has little in common with the lawful means tort. What is less clear is the need for the unlawful means version of the tort in the first place. If A and B combine to do something tortious to C, their liability could perfectly well be dealt with according to the rules on joint tortfeasance. However, if the unlawful means by which loss is inflicted on C do not amount to a tort, the joint tortfeasance doctrine has no application. That being the case, the independent vitality of this tort can only be ascertained by reference to what counts as unlawful means. This, and the other chief ingredients of the tort, need therefore to be elucidated.

(B) ELEMENTS OF THE TORT

(1) Combination

Just as with lawful means conspiracy, this tort demands that there be combination between the conspirators. However, whereas conspirators in the lawful means version of the tort need not share the same purpose, the conspirators in unlawful means conspiracy must pursue a 'common design'.[97] A mere association with a primary tortfeasor (or with an extant group of conspirators) will not suffice for these purposes.[98] Thus, in one case[99] in which X sold recording equipment and Y used it to tape copyright material, there was no prospect of X being held liable for the commission of this tort since X only had an interest in selling the recording equipment and was completely

---

[95]   *Lonrho v Fayed (No 5)* [1993] 1 WLR 1489, at 1494.
[96]   [1992] 1 AC 448.   [97]   *Rookes v Barnard* [1964] AC 1129, at 1211.
[98]   *Sandman v Panasonic UK Ltd* [1998] FSR 651.   [99]   *CBS Songs Ltd v Amstrad* [1998] AC 1013.

indifferent to the uses to which it was put after it had been sold. It has further been held that a common design is to be identified in concerted action done in furtherance or pursuit of a common purpose.[100]

(2) Intention

While there is no doubt that the tort of unlawful means conspiracy requires proof of intention, there is no escaping the fact that the meaning of 'intention' in this context is elusive. In the past, there was no settled view.[101] Nor was there a single test of intention to emerge from *Total Network v Revenue and Customs Commissioners*.[102] Lord Walker was alone in adopting the ends/means test propounded in *OBG v Allan* (and discussed above).[103] By contrast, Lords Hope and Mance favoured a test of targeted harm,[104] while Lord Neuberger thought intention could be demonstrated by adverting to the fact that 'injury to the claimant is the direct, inevitable and foreseeable result' of the conspirators' acts.[105] Since then, the Court of Appeal has twice suggested that the appropriate test of intention in relation to unlawful means conspiracy is the same as that employed in the tort of causing loss by unlawful means.[106]

(3) Unlawful means

As noted earlier, the question of whether this tort can be seen as truly juridically independent turns on the question of what constitutes unlawful means. If 'unlawful means' is a mere synonym for some or other tort, then unlawful means conspiracy amounts to no more than an instance of joint tortfeasance. If, however, unlawful means is a term that is to be construed more broadly, the tort does possess free-standing significance. The leading case is *Total Network v Revenue and Customs Commissioners*.

> D had been involved in a complex financial scam known as a carousel fraud. The point of this scam was to cheat the Inland Revenue out of VAT. Importantly, the carousel fraud involved no known tort; but it did amount to the common-law crime of defrauding the Inland Revenue. The Revenue was unable to recover the lost VAT by recourse to any statute, so it turned, instead, to the tort of unlawful means conspiracy. The House of Lords found in its favour, holding that the criminal acts of the conspirators were sufficient unlawful means on which to found this cause of action.

The decision in this case was received as odd among most commentators given the thoroughgoing review of the economic torts that had only a few months earlier been undertaken in *OBG v Allan* in which a differently constituted House of Lords had

---

[100] *Unilever plc v Chefaro* [1994] FSR 135.
[101] Cf the different tests applied in *Ware and De Freville v Motor Traders Association* [1921] 3 KB 40 and *Lonrho v Fayed* [1992] 1 AC 448.   [102] [2008] 1 AC 1174.
[103] Ibid at [100]. The same approach was adopted by the CA in *Meretz Investments NV v ACP Ltd* [2008] Ch 244.   [104] Ibid at [44] and [120] respectively.
[105] Ibid at [224].
[106] *Meretz Investments NV v ACP* [2008] Ch 244, at [146]; *Berryland Books Ltd v BK Books Ltd* [2010] EWCA Civ 1440, at [48].

been at pains to demonstrate that there were only two main economic torts: inducing breach of contract, and causing loss by unlawful means.[107] Nonetheless, the House of Lords in *Total Network* undoubtedly breathed new life into unlawful means conspiracy. In so doing, and in contradistinction to *OBG v Allan*, they alighted upon a conception of 'unlawful means' wide enough to embrace not merely (potentially) actionable civil wrongs, but also criminal acts. The reasoning by which this conclusion was reached was rather involved. However, the nub of the justification for adopting a broader notion of unlawful means in this context was that conspiracy was considered an instance of two-party liability to which, it was said, different considerations apply from those applicable to the three-party tort of causing loss by unlawful means.[108]

Notwithstanding the preparedness of their Lordships to regard criminal offences as 'unlawful means' in *Total Network*, all is not clear in relation to this pivotal concept. This is because the House of Lords was *not willing* to treat *all* crimes as 'unlawful means'. Rather, they were insistent that criminal conduct which was 'wrongful for reasons which have nothing to do with the damage inflicted on the claimant' would not suffice.[109] Thus, although the crime of defrauding the Inland Revenue obviously had as its objective the protection of the claimant, this could not be said of all criminal offences; especially those which may be described as mere regulatory offences and which derive from statutes that have nothing to do with the protection of the interests or well-being of anyone in particular.[110] Unfortunately, their Lordships considered it 'unwise to attempt to lay down any general rule',[111] so whether any given crime will constitute unlawful means may need to be decided on a case by case basis.

(4) Harm

The point has already been made that in the tort of lawful means conspiracy 'a plaintiff in a civil action for conspiracy must prove actual pecuniary loss'. Although this proclamation was made in a case of lawful means conspiracy,[112] it is couched in terms broad enough to encompass also cases of unlawful means conspiracy. Equally, bearing in mind the fact that *Total Network* was plainly dealt with on the basis of unlawful means conspiracy being an economic tort, there is no apparent reason to proceed otherwise than on this basis. Certainly, it has been held that injury to reputation falls beyond the scope of this tort.[113]

A final point that is worthy of note here is that in any case in which a conspirator joins an existing conspiracy, and thus helps add to the injury that has already been visited upon the claimant, that 'new' conspirator will only be liable for participation in

---

[107] Although they stopped short of saying that lawful means conspiracy and two-party intimidation were henceforth defunct, both these torts were plainly regarded as being of questionable standing.

[108] [2008] 1 AC 1174, at [43], [99], [124], and [223].   [109] Ibid at [119].

[110] This is not to say that statutory offences will *never* suffice: see ibid at [45] and [95].

[111] Ibid at [96].   [112] *Lonrho v Fayed (No 5)* [1993] 1 WLR 1489, at 1494.   [113] Ibid at 1509.

inflicting harm that is suffered *after* the time he joined the conspiracy. He cannot be held liable for losses suffered prior to the date on which he joined the conspiracy.[114]

SECTION 6   INTIMIDATION

(A) INTRODUCTION

Intimidation involves the defendant using an unlawful threat successfully to compel another to act (or refrain from acting) in a particular manner that will cause harm.[115] In the leading case of *Rookes v Barnard*,[116] the tort was considered to exist in two forms: a two-party form (where the claimant is the person actually intimidated) and a three-party form (where the claimant is someone at whom the defendant strikes through his intimidating an intermediary into acting to the claimant's detriment). However, since then, the two versions of the tort have been reconsidered, re-conceptualised, and repackaged. In *OBG v Allan*, the House of Lords were clear that the three-party version of the tort was but a mere sub-species of the tort of causing loss by unlawful means. Furthermore, Lord Hoffmann also cast doubt on the continued vitality of the two-party version,[117] though, notably, he stopped short of declaring it completely moribund. That being so, it is submitted that the two-party version of the tort survived the decision in *OBG v Allan*.

One factor that serves to shrink the practical importance of the two-party version of this tort is the Protection from Harassment Act 1997. Under section 3(2) of that Act, damages are available not only for any anxiety caused by harassment of the victim, but also in respect of any financial loss resulting from that harassment. Thus, if harassment is of an intimidatory nature, so long as there has been the requisite course of conduct demanded by that Act, the claimant may well rely on the statute rather than the common law in seeking a remedy.

(B) ELEMENTS OF THE TORT

(1) Unlawful threats

Intimidation is committed whenever an unlawful threat is successfully used deliberately[118] in order to cause another to do something they would not otherwise do, or refrain from doing something that they would otherwise do with the result (in either

---

[114] *Bank of Tokyo-Mitsubishi UFJ Ltd v Baskan Gida Sanayi Ve Pazarlama AS* [2009] EWHC 1276 (Ch).
[115] *News Group Newspapers Ltd v SOGAT '82 (No 2)* [1987] ICR 181.   [116] [1964] AC 1129.
[117] [2008] 1 AC 1, at [61]. He thought two-party intimidation raised 'altogether different issues' from those that had been considered central to his attempt to rationalise the economic torts in *OBG v Allan*. But his reasoning is deeply questionable. For if the two-party version ought not to be seen as a tort (ie, an actionable or potentially actionable wrong), where are the unlawful means for the three-party version he was content to subsume within the unlawful means tort?
[118] *Chet Camp Fisheries Co-operative Ltd v Canada* (1995) 123 DLR (4th) 121, at 127

case) that harm is thereby caused. The requirement that the threat must be coercive in one of these ways is well established.[119]

In terms of the unlawfulness of the conduct threatened, the early authorities on intimidation involved threats of violence.[120] But the modern tort of intimidation is by no means confined to threats of this kind. Indeed it was defined in considerably broader terms than this in *Rookes v Barnard*[121] where the facts were as follows.

C was an employee of the airline BOAC who had resigned from his trade union. Ds were union officials. They threatened BOAC that all union members employed at BOAC would strike unless C was dismissed. BOAC consequently gave C notice and (lawfully) dismissed him. The House of Lords held that the breach of contract threatened by the union members was a sufficiently unlawful form of conduct to substantiate the tort.

Just a few years after the decision in *Rookes v Barnard*, Lord Denning ventured to suggest that any threat of 'violence, or a tort, or a breach of contract'[122] would amount to an unlawful threat for the purposes of this tort: the key being that, in each case, the defendant would be threatening to do something that he was not lawfully entitled to do. Indeed, as Lord Reid put it in *Rookes* itself: 'so long as the defendant only threatens what he has a legal right to do he is on safe ground'.[123]

However, the fact that *Rookes* established that a threat to break a contract would constitute an unlawful threat raised an interesting question about whether the tort was thus set up to usurp the ground occupied by contract law in a case of two-party intimidation. In particular, there may be a tension between the tort of intimidation and the doctrines of anticipatory breach and duress (depending on the nature of the threat). Quite how these potential tensions should be resolved is still relatively unexplored in judicial terms (though, as one might expect, academics have not shied away from offering a view[124]). The best judicial guide that currently exists is probably *Kolmar Group AG v Traxpo Enterprises Pvt Ltd*[125] – a mere first instance decision – in which Christopher Clarke J held in a two-party setting that a threat to break a contract should sound in tort and result in an award of damages for intimidation.

A threat to commit a criminal act of violence will always suffice for the purposes of the tort of intimidation; but a threat to commit a breach of a penal statute is not per se sufficient: the statute must also be intended to create private rights.[126] Following the logic of this, a threat to breach an equitable obligation may also be sufficient.[127]

---

[119] See *Hodges v Webb* [1920] 2 Ch 70; *J T Stratford & Sons Ltd v Lindley* [1965] AC 269.
[120] For a modern example see *Godwin v Uzoigwe* [1993] Fam Law 65.   [121] [1964] AC 1129.
[122] *Morgan v Fry* [1968] 2 QB 710, at 724.
[123] *Rookes v Barnard* [1964] AC 1129, at 1168–9. See also *Hardie and Lane Ltd v Chilton* [1928] 2 KB 306 and *Ware and De Freville Ltd v Motor Trade Association* [1921] 3 KB 40.
[124] See, eg, Bigwood (2001) 117 LQR 376.   [125] [2010] 2 Lloyd's Rep 653.
[126] *Lonrho Ltd v Shell Petroleum Co Ltd (No 2)* [1982] AC 173.   [127] *Dixon v Dixon* [1904] 1 Ch 161.

But what is certainly clear is that words of idle abuse, or words of advice or warning, should not be regarded as threats of the requisite 'or else I will do X' variety.[128]

(2) Intention

It seems beyond doubt that the defendant must intend his threat to cause harm to the claimant. So, for example, in *News Group Newspapers Ltd v SOGAT '82 (No 2)*, Stuart-Smith J insisted that the claimant 'must be a person whom [the defendant] intended to injure'.[129] Since the House of Lords has effectively subsumed cases of three-party intimidation within the tort of causing loss by unlawful means, it must follow that the test for 'intention' in two-party intimidation cases is the same as that used in the unlawful means tort. The reason why this must follow can be explained in stages.

If X threatens Y that unless Y dismisses Z from his workforce, X will take unlawful action against Y, we know that this would, prior to *OBG v Allan*, enable Z to sue X on the basis of three-party intimidation. This is effectively what happened in *Rookes v Barnard*. We may also suppose, however, that employer Y is as dismayed to lose his former star employee Z, as Z is to lose his job. In other words, the self-same threat made by X to Y could just as well form the basis of an action for two-party intimidation. Given this, it would seem entirely indefensible to have a different test of intention depending on which person – Y or Z – was bringing the action. That being so, we may reasonably conclude that the test of whether the defendant intended to injure the claimant is the same in two-party intimidation as it is in the tort of causing loss by unlawful means.

Now, since the test of intention is likely to be regarded as the ends/means test promulgated in *OBG v Allan*, a further potential tension between this tort and the law of contract arises. Suppose A threatens a breach of contract with B intending not just to disappoint B's immediate contractual expectations but also to bring about B's entire financial ruin. Suppose also that the prospect of bringing about B's ruination has only come to A's attention *since the formation of the contract*. In such circumstances, it is entirely possible that the damages available for intimidation would stretch beyond what would be available by reference to the remoteness rules in contract.[130] It is also conceivable that the intentional infliction of harm required by this tort may bring the prospect of exemplary damages into play.[131]

(3) Damage

It has never been entirely clear for what kinds of damage one can sue in the tort of intimidation. The cases abound with statements like Lord Denning's proclamation

---

[128] See *News Group Newspapers Ltd v SOGAT '82 (No 2)* [1987] ICR 181, at 204 (re 'idle abuse'), *Conway v Wade* [1909] AC 506, at 510 (re warnings), and *J T Stratford & Sons Ltd v Lindley* [1965] AC 269 (re advice).
[129] [1987] ICR 181, at 204.
[130] In contract, the remoteness test is set according to things foreseeable by *both parties* at the time of the making of the contract.   [131] *Kuddus v CC of Leicestershire Constabulary* [2001] 2 WLR 1789.

that '[it is] the person damnified by the compliance [with the threat]' that can sue.[132] But unfortunately, such vacuous statements do not really limit or explain the kinds of damage in respect of which this tort can be invoked. All that can be said with confidence is that the types of harm that will be actionable *are not* limited to economic losses. So much is clear from *Godwin v Uzoigwe*,[133] in which case a young woman was intimidated not into suffering financial loss, but into working as a virtual slave in the home of the appellants.

Bearing in mind the lack of clear authority on what constitutes actionable harm for the purposes of this tort, two rather novel suggestions are made here. The first is that intimidation is not *in the strict sense* a specifically economic tort (*Godwin* would be inexplicable if it were). The second is that the gist of the tort is an infringement of the victim's right to free agency/autonomy, and that when economic loss occurs as a consequence, this is the best metric according to which the value of the infringed right can be measured. The cases are certainly littered with references to coercion; and it is one's autonomy, one's right to choose for oneself what one will do or desist from doing, that is infringed when one's will is overborne by intimidation. The mere making of a threat will not amount to intimidation. There must also be compliance and it is the fact of this compliance in conjunction with the consequential harm to which this compliance gives rise that makes intimidation actionable.

Our view is at loggerheads with the understanding of what makes intimidation unlawful proffered by perhaps the leading authority on this area of the law, according to whom what makes intimidation unlawful is the fact that 'threatened unlawful acts are equated with the unlawful acts themselves'.[134] But this latter view can hardly be right given that two-party intimidation is a tort that can be committed by virtue of a threatened breach of contract. If the threat were equated with an actual breach of contract, it would be hard to see why the intimidation in such a case should be regarded as a tortious (not contractual) wrong.

One (arguably) advantageous consequence of refusing to equate the threat with the actual act threatened, and preferring instead to see the infringement of autonomy as the gist of the tort, is the fact that it would enable a case of intimidation to be grounded even if the act threatened were not to be directed at the person threatened. Thus, if A threatened to shoot B's son if B did not comply with A's demand, A might perfectly well be regarded as having been coerced into acting the way that he did without ever being the immediate, prospective victim of the act threatened.

One other consequence of considering two-party intimidation to be a tort that has no necessary connection with the infliction of economic loss is that it casts considerable doubt on the foundations of the decision of the House of Lords in *Total Network*, given that their Lordships sought to make two-party intimidation a significant part of the platform from which they felt able to breathe new life into the (re-conceived)

---

[132] *Morgan v Fry* [1968] 2 QB 710, at 724. [133] [1993] Fam Law 65.
[134] Carty, *An Analysis of the Economic Torts* (2nd edn, 2010), 120.

two-party tort of unlawful means conspiracy. Put otherwise, if two-party intimidation is *not* an economic tort, it can, as a matter of logic, provide but a highly questionable foundation for the distinctly economic tort of unlawful means conspiracy.

SECTION 7   ECONOMIC TORTS AND TRADE UNIONS

It is virtually impossible for a trade union to take effective action in the traditional manner (that is, by striking or threatening a strike) without risking liability arising from one of the economic torts discussed in this chapter. Calling members out on strike may constitute inducing breach of contract. Threatening a strike to preserve a closed shop or to protect a demarcation agreement risks liability for intimidation. Thus, since 1906,[135] the law has witnessed the introduction of statutory immunities afforded to trade unions and their officials for acts done in contemplation or furtherance of a trade dispute. The details of such immunities fall beyond the scope of this book.

FURTHER READING

BAGSHAW, 'Inducing Breach of Contract', in Horder (ed), *Oxford Essays in Jurisprudence, 4th Series* (2000)

CARTY, *An Analysis of the Economic Torts* (2nd edn, 2010)

DEAKIN AND RANDALL, 'Rethinking the Economic Torts' (2009) 72 *Modern Law Review* 519

NEYERS, 'The Economic Torts as Corrective Justice' (2009) 17 *Torts Law Journal* 1

O'SULLIVAN, 'Unlawful Means Conspiracy in the House of Lords' [2008] *Cambridge Law Journal* 459

SALES, 'The Tort of Conspiracy and Civil Secondary Liability' [1990] *Cambridge Law Journal* 491

SALES AND STILITZ, 'Intentional Infliction of Harm by Unlawful Means' (1999) 115 *Law Quarterly Review* 411

WADDAMS, 'Johanna Wagner and the Rival Opera Houses' (1998) 117 *Law Quarterly Review* 431

---

[135] Trade Disputes Act 1906.

PART V

TORTS INVOLVING STRICT OR STRICTER LIABILITY

The common element in the torts discussed in this Part is that a defendant who is not merely being held accountable for the acts of an employee need not have committed the act complained of either intentionally or negligently. They are often referred to as torts of strict liability; yet as the following chapters reveal, the liability threshold in some of these torts is less strict than that in others of them. This being so, it is better to see only some of these torts as involving pure strict liability, while the others impose merely stricter liability than that which characterises the archetypal, fault-based tort of negligence.

15

PRODUCT LIABILITY[1]

KEY ISSUES

(1) Two strands of liability
Liability for a defective product that injures or causes damage to property other than that which is defective arises both in negligence and under the Consumer Protection Act 1987. The former is a fault-based form of liability; the latter is strict liability for defects – that is, liability regardless of fault. Actions are available to the purchasers of goods, to users and to bystanders.

(2) Tort of negligence
Liability for a failure to take care in the manufacture of a product causing personal injury was established in *Donoghue v Stevenson*. It has since been extended to include others involved in the life cycle of products, including assemblers, repairers, testers, and certain

suppliers. In some cases, there may be an obligation to recall unsafe products.

(3) Limitations of negligence
The burden is upon the claimant to prove fault when suing in negligence and this may be a real hurdle, especially in cases of design defects.

(4) Consumer Protection Act 1987
The claimant is likely to find it more advantageous to bring an action for a defective product under the Act because it does not require proof of fault. The Act creates liability in producers and importers of products that are defective in that their safety is not such as consumers generally are entitled to expect and which thereby cause injury or damage to other property. A number of statutory defences to liability are available.

SECTION 1   INTRODUCTION

The complex history of liability for loss or injury caused by defective products illustrates well the gradual development and changing perceptions of the role of tort law and its interrelationship with the law of contract. The classical common-law stance

---

[1] See generally Howells, *Product Liability* (2000); Fairgrieve (ed), *Product Liability in Comparative Perspective* (2005). For developments in the US, see Goldberg and Zipursky, *The Oxford Introductions to US Law: Torts* (2010), ch 10.

towards faulty or useless goods was that of *caveat emptor* (that is, let the buyer beware). The person buying goods was expected either to take steps to ensure that the goods were safe for use and value for money, or to make contractual arrangements which would provide him with a remedy should the goods prove to be defective. If he failed to protect himself, he would bear any resulting loss. In 1893 Parliament gave some protection to purchasers of goods via the first Sale of Goods Act. Then, in 1932, in *Donoghue v Stevenson*,[2] the House of Lords held that the ultimate user of a product might also, in certain circumstances, sue in negligence the manufacturers of a product causing injury to his person or his property. The extent of manufacturers' negligence liability has since been further developed and refined by the courts.

In the meantime, Parliament strengthened the contractual rights of purchasers of goods[3] and services[4] with increasingly interventionist consumer protection laws.[5] And in respect of certain types of goods, the criminal law was used to protect safety standards, and an action for breach of statutory duty[6] was expressly created to allow individuals injured by goods in the specified categories to recover compensation from the manufacturers. Thus, by 1987 little survived of the *caveat emptor* principle. The social and legal climate had changed, but there was a confusing multiplicity of potential remedies available under a range of limited causes of action. Furthermore, the difficulty of proving negligence had become especially problematic in relation to products. Several official bodies[7] therefore advocated that manufacturers should be made strictly liable for defective products.[8] The final victory for proponents of strict liability was won in Europe when on 25 July 1985 the Council of the European Communities issued a Directive[9] requiring all member states to implement a regime of strict liability for defective products. The UK Government responded by enacting the Consumer Protection Act 1987. The Act leaves untouched contractual claims against the retailer, the action in negligence, and, where appropriate, actions for breach of statutory duty. But the Act provides only for claims in relation to personal injury and damage to private property. Damage to business property and economic loss resulting from defective products are outside its remit.

SECTION 2 CONSUMER PROTECTION AND THE CHANGING COMMON LAW

(A) THE LIMITATIONS OF CONTRACT LAW

The primary means invoked to protect consumers against faulty goods has traditionally been the law of contract. The original Sale of Goods Act 1893 has now been replaced by

---

[2] [1932] AC 562.   [3] See the Sale of Goods Act 1979.
[4] See the Supply of Goods and Services Act 1982. Note also the Unfair Contract Terms Act 1977.
[5] Domestic consumer protection legislation has been strengthened further by the European Directive on Unfair Terms in Consumer Contracts 1993.   [6] Consumer Protection Act 1987, s 41.
[7] See *Law Commission Report on Liability for Defective Products* (1977); *Royal Commission on Civil Liability and Compensation for Personal Injury* (1978) (Cmnd 7054–1).
[8] For the reasons and relevant history, see the 10th edition of this book.   [9] 1985/374/EEC.

the Sale of Goods Act 1979 (itself amended by the Sale and Supply of Goods Act 1994). It is that 1979 Act which, among other things, incorporates into every contract of sale terms of satisfactory quality[10] and fitness for purpose.[11] Identical terms are implied by the Supply of Goods and Services Act 1982 into any contract for services in the course of which goods are supplied.[12] Thus, if in the course of private dental treatment a dentist provides her patient with dentures which crumble within the week, it matters not whether any contract of sale for the dentures exists. The patient clearly had a contract for services under which unsuitable dentures were supplied. Terms implied by virtue of the 1979 and 1982 Acts cannot be excluded against the consumer,[13] liability is strict, and it is not limited to protection against injury to the person or property.

There are, however, limitations to the effectiveness of contract as a means of general consumer protection against defective goods. These arise from the rules of privity of contract.[14] A person who is not a party to a contract cannot generally benefit from that contract. So, if one receives as a gift an electric blanket bought by a friend, one has no contractual right to sue the retailer if it proves to be faulty; and where one purchases the faulty blanket oneself, and the retailer goes out of business, one has no contractual claim against the wholesaler.[15] The Contracts (Rights of Third Parties) Act 1999 is unlikely to be of much use in this context, for that Act only confers rights on third parties in respect of whom it is clear that the contract was designed to confer a benefit and who are identified by name, class, or description in the contract.[16]

A number of devices have occasionally been used to evade the consequences of rules of privity. In *Lockett v Charles*,[17] for instance, a wife whose husband bought her a restaurant meal was able to claim for her food poisoning on the basis that her husband had acted as her agent. But the circumstances allowing for an inference of agency are strictly limited. The same is true of the other devices that have been employed to avoid the privity rule.[18] It is thus to tort that a claimant must generally look if she did not purchase the product herself.

(B) THE ACTION FOR NEGLIGENCE

The early development of liability in negligence for defective goods began with *Dixon v Bell*[19] where a master who entrusted a loaded gun to his young servant was found liable

---

[10] Consumer Protection Act 1987, s 14(2).

[11] Consumer Protection Act 1987, s 14(3). Satisfactory quality means 'the standard that a reasonable person would regard as satisfactory taking into account any description of the goods, the price (if relevant) and all the other relevant circumstances'. So, an electric blanket that fails to heat a bed as expected would incur liability as easily as one that causes an electric shock or fire.   [12] Consumer Protection Act 1987, s 4.

[13] Unfair Contract Terms Act 1977, s 6; Supply of Goods and Services Act 1982, s 13.

[14] See Furmston, *Cheshire, Fifoot and Furmston's Law of Contract* (2001), ch 14.

[15] There may, however, be a collateral contract with the manufacturer to the effect that any guarantee given is effective in the hands of the ultimate purchaser. But even if there is no such collateral contract, Art 6 of Directive 1999/44/EC now requires that manufacturers' guarantees should be legally enforceable.

[16] Contracts (Rights of Third Parties) Act 1999, s 1(1)(b) and (3).

[17] *Lockett v A & M Charles Ltd* [1938] 4 All ER 170.

[18] Furmston, *Cheshire, Fifoot and Furmston's Law of Contract* (2001), 502–7.

[19] (1816) 5 M & S 198.

to a third party injured by the servant firing the gun, on the ground that the goods 'were in a state capable of doing mischief'. However, the court in *Langridge v Levy*[20] declined an invitation to deduce from *Dixon v Bell* a general principle of liability for putting into circulation things 'of a dangerous nature'. In *Winterbottom v Wright*,[21] the driver of a coach was seriously injured as a result of a defect in the coach. His action against the defendant (who supplied his employers with coaches and horses) failed because of privity of contract: the claimant could not take advantage of express terms in the contract as to the repair and maintenance of the coach. But what the court in *Winterbottom v Wright* failed to analyse was the possibility of a separate and independent obligation arising within the tort of negligence.

Case law between 1851 and 1932 continued to deny any general duty to take care in the manufacture and distribution of goods although some exceptional cases did hold that a duty existed. Liability was eventually recognised in relation to goods 'dangerous in themselves',[22] in respect of known defects of which no warning was given by the supplier.[23] In addition, occupiers were held liable to their invitees in respect of appliances on their premises which proved to be defective.[24] The boundaries of these instances of liability for defects were unclear, and the need to prove knowledge of the defect in the second category was often fatal to the success of a claim. The decision of the House of Lords in *Donoghue v Stevenson*[25] heralded a new age.

> C drank a bottle of ginger beer, manufactured by D, which a friend bought from a retailer and gave to C. The bottle allegedly contained the decomposed remains of a snail which were not, and could not be, detected (as the bottle was opaque) until most of the bottle had been consumed. C alleged that she was ill as a result, and sued D. The House of Lords had to decide whether the facts disclosed a cause of action. They found for C by a majority of 3 to 2.

Lord Atkin held that:

> a manufacturer of products, which he sells in such form as to show that he intends them to reach the ultimate consumer in the form in which they left him with no reasonable possibility of intermediate examination, and with the knowledge that the absence of reasonable care in the preparation or putting up of the products will result in an injury to the consumer's life or property, owes a duty to the consumer to take that reasonable care.[26]

---

[20] (1837) 2 M & W 519. The court nevertheless found for C on the ground of fraud.

[21] (1842) 10 M & W 109.

[22] See *Longmeid v Holliday* (1851) 6 Exch 761.

[23] *Heaven v Pender* (1883) 11 QBD 503, at 517; *Clarke v Army and Navy Co-operative Society* [1903] 1 KB 155.   [24] *Heaven v Pender* (1883) 11 QBD 503.

[25] [1932] AC 562.

[26] Ibid at 599. This proposition will be called the 'narrow rule' in the case; and the 'neighbour principle', the broad rule.

Others among their Lordships had other reasons for reaching the same result, but since then, negligence liability for defective products has extended its scope and remains important notwithstanding the passage of the Consumer Protection Act 1987. Throughout the remainder of this chapter, therefore, readers ought to bear in mind the following questions:

(1) Are there any persons who may be liable in negligence in respect of defective goods who would not be classified as 'producers' for the purposes of the Consumer Protection Act 1987 (and thus not liable within the terms of the Act)?

(2) Are there any kinds of loss remediable in negligence but not under the Act?

(3) What is the nature of the special limitation rules under the Consumer Protection Act 1987?

(4) How radical a departure from common law negligence is the strict liability regime introduced by the Consumer Protection Act 1987?

With these in mind, let us turn to the modern approach of negligence law.

(1) Range of defendants

Although Lord Atkin imposed liability only on manufacturers, later case law extended liability to, among others, assemblers,[27] repairers,[28] and suppliers of drinking water.[29] Mere suppliers of goods have also been held liable where their function went beyond simple distribution. For example, a car dealer selling vehicles reconditioned by him,[30] and a retail chemist[31] failing to observe the manufacturers' instructions to test the product before labelling it, were both found liable to injured users. Indeed, wherever the circumstances are such that a supplier would normally be expected to check a product, a duty to do so has often been imposed. Second-hand car dealers will be expected to check the steering on used cars.[32] Wholesalers who fail to test a hair dye of dubious provenance will also be held negligent.[33]

A number of categories of persons owing a common-law duty of care will also shoulder responsibility for compensating victims of defective products under the Consumer Protection Act 1987. But this is not so of all those owing a common-law duty of care. For example, suppliers failing to carry out tests may avoid liability under the statute by simply naming the person who supplied the goods to them. Repairers are also beyond the scope of the statute.

---

[27] *Malfroot v Noxal Ltd* (1935) 51 TLR 551.
[28] *Haseldine v C A Daw & Son Ltd* [1941] 2 KB 343.
[29] *Read v Croydon Corpn* [1938] 4 All ER 631; *Barnes v Irwell Valley Water Board* [1939] 1 KB 21.
[30] *Herschtal v Stewart and Ardern Ltd* [1940] 1 KB 155.   [31] *Kubach v Hollands* [1937] 3 All ER 907.
[32] *Andrews v Hopkinson* [1957] 1 QB 229. See also *Fisher v Harrods Ltd* [1966] 1 Lloyd's Rep 500.
[33] *Watson v Buckley, Osborne Garrett & Co Ltd* [1940] 1 All ER 174.

(2) Products

The term 'products' today includes not only food and drink[34] but any product in normal domestic use. Underwear,[35] hair dye,[36] motor cars,[37] computer software,[38] installations in houses,[39] and exterior staircases[40] have all been treated as proper subjects of a duty of care. Pre-*Donoghue v Stevenson* distinctions[41] between products 'dangerous in themselves' and other goods can now be largely disregarded.[42] The distinction remains relevant only in that the greater the potential danger inherent in a product, the more stringent must be the precautions needed to protect the user against injury or loss.[43]

(3) Ultimate 'consumer'

It follows from what has been said about the courts' willingness to expand negligence liability since *Donoghue v Stevenson* that a wide range of claimants may now sue for injuries caused by defective products. Thus, in *Barnett v H and J Packer & Co*,[44] the proprietor of a sweet shop who was injured by a piece of metal protruding from a sweet recovered damages from the sweet's manufacturers. And in *Stennett v Hancock and Peters*[45] a bystander was able to sue after a defendant garage owner negligently reassembled the flange on the wheel of X's lorry so that the flange came off, mounted the pavement, and injured the claimant, a pedestrian. The defendant was held liable for his negligent repair. In neither case was the claimant strictly a 'consumer'.

(4) Sale

There seems no reason why the rule should not apply even where there is no sale of goods distributed in the course of a business, for example, where manufacturers supply free samples.[46] The liability for goods supplied in a domestic or social context is more disputable. Would a housewife who baked a fish pie for a charity fair be liable to the person who bought it, ate it, and succumbed to food poisoning? Would she be liable to her own children who ate a second pie made for their dinner?[47]

---

[34] *Barnes v Irwell Water Board* [1939] 1 KB 21.
[35] *Grant v Australian Knitting Mills Ltd* [1936] AC 85.
[36] *Watson v Buckley, Osborne, Garrett & Co Ltd* [1940] 1 All ER 174.
[37] *Herschtal v Stewart and Ardern Ltd* [1940] 1 KB 155.
[38] *St Albans City and DC v International Computers Ltd* [1996] 4 All ER 481.
[39] *Haseldine v C A Daw & Son Ltd* [1941] 2 KB 343.   [40] *Targett v Torfaen BC* [1992] 3 All ER 27.
[41] See *Dominion Natural Gas Co Ltd v Collins and Perkins* [1909] AC 640.
[42] See *Billings (AC) & Sons Ltd v Riden* [1958] AC 240.
[43] But that must not be construed as a rule distinct from negligence that there is a separate class of dangerous things which D must keep safe at his peril. See *Read v J Lyons & Co Ltd* [1947] AC 156, at 172–3.
[44] [1940] 3 All ER 575. Cf *Mason v Williams and Williams Ltd and Thomas Turton & Sons Ltd* [1955] 1 All ER 808.   [45] [1939] 2 All ER 578.
[46] See *Hawkins v Coulsdon and Purley UDC* [1954] 1 QB 319, at 333.
[47] The narrow rule in *Donoghue v Stevenson* is probably inapplicable to gratuitous transfers. There are cases where liability has been established in respect of dangers known to the transferor: see, eg, *Hodge & Sons v Anglo-American Oil Co* (1922) 12 Ll L Rep 183; *Hurley v Dyke* [1979] RTR 265. Where the defect is not known to the transferor, however, there seems no reason in principle why the *broad rule* should not apply

(5) Intermediate examination

Lord Atkin envisaged that a manufacturer should be liable where:

> he sells in such a form as to show that he intends [his products] … to reach the ultimate consumer in the form in which they left him with no reasonable possibility of intermediate examination.

If the rule is to apply, 'the customer must use the article exactly as it left the maker, that is in all material features, and use it as it was intended to be used'.[48] The effect of intermediate examination seems, therefore, to be this: if someone in the place of the manufacturer would reasonably contemplate that the defect in the goods would remain there at the time of their use by the claimant despite their passing through the hands of intermediaries, he is still liable.[49] The test is not whether intermediate examination is possible.[50] However, where an intermediary does specifically test and certify a product as safe, he may himself incur negligence liability.[51]

This test with respect to defective goods is stricter than it might be for other forms of negligence. *Clay v A J Crump & Sons Ltd*[52] illustrates the point.

> Under the supervision of an architect, D, demolition contractors were demolishing a building, and builders were to construct a new one. On D's advice a wall was left standing on the site. It subsequently collapsed on to C, an employee of the builders. D pleaded that the demolition contractors and their employees had had the opportunity of intermediate examination.

This was held to be a case not of the narrow products rule but of the broad principle, so that the intermediate examination principle did not apply to defeat the claimant's claim against the architect.

(6) Preparation or putting up

There may be liability for a defect in the design of a product,[53] in the container, and, probably also, in the labelling of the package.[54]

(7) Continuing duty of care

What if the product when first put on the market was not manufactured with any lack of care? Imagine that, at that time, on all the reasonably available evidence, the manufacturers could have discovered no defect in their product. Suppose, however, that

---

to gratuitous transfers. What would be the standard of care demanded of the housewife in the example in the text?

[48] *Grant v Australian Knitting Mills Ltd* [1936] AC 85, at 104.

[49] [1936] AC 85 at 105; *Haseldine v C A Daw & Son Ltd* [1941] 2 KB 343, at 376. And see *Nitrigin Eireann Teoranta v Inco Alloys* [1992] 1 All ER 854.

[50] *Dransfield v British Insulated Cables Ltd* [1937] 4 All ER 382, holding the opposite, is best regarded as wrongly decided.   [51] *Perrett v Collins* [1998] 2 Lloyd's Rep 255.

[52] [1964] 1 QB 533.

[53] *Hindustan Steam Shipping Co Ltd v Siemens Bros & Co Ltd* [1955] 1 Lloyd's Rep 167.

[54] *Kubach v Hollands* [1937] 3 All ER 907.

evidence later transpires of risks to person or property posed by a latent defect. Do the manufacturers then owe any duty (1) to attempt to recall the goods, and/or (2) to warn consumers of the danger? It is clear beyond doubt that, even though originally the design of a product may have been made with all due care, once a design defect becomes patent, the manufacturer is liable in negligence if he continues to produce and market the unsafe product.[55] In respect of unsafe products already in circulation, a continuing duty of care is owed to do whatever is reasonable to recall the defective product and warn users of the risk the defect may pose to their health and/or property.[56] As regards the duty to warn, it may be sufficient, according to Canadian authority,[57] if the manufacturer passes the warning on to the intermediary (in that case, a doctor) who supplied the consumer (a patient) with the product rather than warning the consumer directly. So far as the duty to recall goes, it is clear that the recall procedure must also be conducted non-negligently if further liability is to be avoided.[58]

(8) Recoverable loss

The duty of care in respect of defective products remains, in general, limited to a duty to avoid inflicting injury to the ultimate consumer's life or property.[59] But in relation to damage to property, no liability is imposed in respect of damage to the defective product itself. Thus, if pistons in a car's engine fail causing further damage to the engine, there is no liability imposed in respect of the further engine damage.[60] This is pure economic loss and it is not generally recoverable in negligence.[61] It is only where non-integral parts of a car malfunction and cause further damage – such as a CD player that overheats and causes a fire – that an action *may* lie.[62] It would be inapt to conceive of a car without tyres; therefore the tyres are merely parts of an overall defective product. But where an accessory such as a CD player is added, it is possible to talk of product A (the CD player) damaging product B (the car). This example should not be confused, however, with a case in which defective product A is combined with product B to make product C – for example, where two products (a gas and a liquid) are combined to make a carbonated drink. In such a case it is inappropriate to talk of

---

[55] *Wright v Dunlop Rubber Co Ltd* (1972) 13 KIR 255.

[56] *Hobbs (Farms) v Baxenden Chemicals* [1992] 1 Lloyd's Rep 54; *Walton v British Leyland UK Ltd* (1978) *Times*, 13 July; *Rivtow Marine Ltd v Washington Ironworks* (1974) 40 DLR (3rd) 530.

[57] *Hollis v Dow Corning Corpn* (1995) 129 DLR (4th) 609.

[58] *McCain Foods Ltd v Grand Falls Industries Ltd* (1991) 80 DLR (4th) 252.

[59] The property damage must arise from a use to which D might reasonably have expected the property to be put. There was no liability where a waterproofing compound was lost when pails manufactured by D melted in the intense heat of Kuwait: *Aswan Engineering Establishment Co v Lupdine Ltd* [1987] 1 All ER 135.

[60] Analogy drawn from *Hamble Fisheries Ltd v Gardner & Sons Ltd, The Rebecca Elaine* [1999] 2 Lloyd's Rep 1.

[61] *Murphy v Brentwood DC* [1991] 1 AC 398; *Simaan General Contracting Co v Pilkington Glass Ltd (No 2)* [1988] QB 758; *Muirhead v Industrial Tank Specialties Ltd* [1986] QB 507; *Aswan Engineering Establishment Co v Lupdine Ltd* [1987] 1 All ER 135.

[62] For an analogous application of this so-called 'complex structure' approach, see *Jacobs v Moreton & Partner* (1994) 72 BLR 92.

product A damaging product B. Instead, there is merely the production of a defective product, product C, in respect of which the defects are to be treated as irrecoverable, pure economic loss.[63]

(9) Proving negligence

The scope of liability for negligent manufacture, distribution, and repair that has evolved from the rule in *Donoghue v Stevenson* is now very considerable. Yet it is in the formidable task of proving negligence in the narrow sense that claimants confront the greatest difficulty. In the classic application of the narrow rule in *Donoghue v Stevenson* – where the ultimate consumer is suing the manufacturer – it is often verging on impossible to prove absence of reasonable care, at least by direct evidence.[64] The consumer's difficulties may be further compounded by problems of causation; especially, for example, in claims relating to drug-induced injury. Yet the burden of proof remains with the claimant. Lord Macmillan said in *Donoghue v Stevenson* that the burden of proof:

> must always be upon the injured party to establish that the defect which caused the injury was present in the article when it left the hands of the party whom he sues, that the defect was occasioned by the carelessness of that party... There is no presumption of negligence in such a case at present, nor is there any justification for applying the maxim *res ipsa loquitur*.[65]

However, the Privy Council modified this rigid approach in *Grant v Australian Knitting Mills Ltd*.[66] There, the claimant was concerned to prove that the dermatitis he contracted was caused by the presence of invisible excess sulphites in the underwear he purchased and which was made by the defendants. It was explained that the test was whether, on the balance of probabilities, it was a reasonable inference to be drawn from the evidence that the harm was so caused.[67] On the issue of negligence, it was said:

> if excess sulphites were left in the garment, that could only be because someone was at fault. The appellant is not required to lay his finger on the exact person in all the chain[68] who was responsible, or to specify what he did wrong. Negligence is found as a matter of inference from the existence of the defects taken in connection with all the known circumstances.[69]

---

[63] *Bacardi-Martini Beverages Ltd v Thomas Hardy Packaging Ltd* [2002] 1 Lloyd's Rep 62. See also, Tettenborn [2000] LMCLQ 338. [64] See Schwartz (1991) 43 Rutgers LR 1013.

[65] [1932] AC 562, at 622.

[66] [1936] AC 85. [67] Ibid at 96–7.

[68] What if C does not know whether the negligence is that of the manufacturer, the bottler, the wholesaler, the carrier, or the retailer?

[69] [1936] AC 85, at 101. Thus, where there is no evidence of a defect at the time of manufacture, and there exist several alternative explanations of why a malfunction may have occurred, liability will not be imposed on a manufacturer: see *Evans v Triplex Safety Glass Co Ltd* [1936] 1 All ER 283. Cf *Carroll v Fearon* [1998] PIQR P416.

This approach is eminently practical and good law,[70] and it is certainly to be preferred to the *obiter dicta* of Lord Macmillan in so far as the two are in conflict.[71] Where the presence of the defect (in combination with the known circumstances) gives rise to an inference of negligence against the manufacturers, the burden shifts to the defendant to rebut that inference. This may be done either by pinpointing the exact cause giving rise to the defect and establishing that it does not arise from any want of care, or by the manufacturer producing evidence as to his system and establishing that the system was consistent with all due care. In *Daniels and Daniels v R White & Sons Ltd and Tabbard*,[72] the claimant was seriously injured when he drank lemonade containing a large quantity of carbolic acid. The acid presumably came from the washing process used by the defendant manufacturer. The judge accepted evidence of the precautions taken by the defendants to avoid such a contingency and found that the claimants had failed to prove negligence.

The problems faced by the claimant are compounded where the relevant defect is not a construction defect but a design defect.[73] Design defects occur where the basic design of the product proves to be inherently dangerous. Although a construction defect – where something goes wrong that does not normally go wrong – allows the possibility of the court inferring negligence, a similar inference cannot be made with respect to a design defect. In design cases, the claimant must prove (1) that the manufacturer should have been aware of the risk of the defect, and (2) that he could reasonably have avoided the defect. The issue all too often becomes one of whether, at the time the product was put on the market, scientific and technical knowledge available to the manufacturer should have enabled him to identify the danger.

The classic example of the difficulties posed in this connection arise in the medical context where a drug is first marketed without foresight of its possible repercussions, but in the firm belief (based on the best available scientific knowledge), that the drug is safe. In such cases, an action in negligence requires a claimant to prove that according to the state of scientific knowledge at the time of marketing, the manufacturer should recognise the risk.[74]

(10) Proving causation

The next problem faced by the claimant is that of proving causation. Normally, this is done in accordance with the usual 'but for' test.[75] But in relation to certain types of

---

[70] For a lucid and similar explanation of the burden of proof see *Mason v Williams and Williams Ltd and Thomas Turton & Sons Ltd* [1955] 1 All ER 808, at 810.

[71] This was exactly the approach of the House of Lords in *Lockhart v Barr* 1943 SC 1, where the purchaser of aerated water contaminated with phenol recovered from the manufacturer although he could not prove how the phenol came to be in the aerated water.   [72] [1938] 4 All ER 258.

[73] The construction/design dichotomy was rejected as an analytical device in *A v National Blood Authority* [2001] 3 All ER 289. But why? In terms of both conceptual distinctiveness and practical repercussions, the two are readily distinguishable.

[74] While it is very difficult to establish negligence in design defects, it is not absolutely impossible: see *Independent Broadcasting Authority v EMI Electronics and BICC Construction Ltd* (1980) 14 BLR 1.

[75] See ch 5.

product – especially pharmaceutical products – great difficulties can arise.[76] In the case of such products the claimant will frequently already be suffering from some form of illness. Where the claimant's condition deteriorates, or she suffers the onset of a related illness, the question is whether the drug caused the additional illness. Similarly, it is one thing to allege that a drug has caused injurious side-effects, but quite another to prove that it has done so. Thus, in *Loveday v Renton*[77] the action failed because it could not be proved, on the balance of probabilities, that the claimant's brain damage had been caused by the administration of the pertussis vaccine. This was despite the fact that it was known that the pertussis vaccine *could* cause brain damage in children. On the other hand, the courts need not abandon common sense. So in *Best v Wellcome Foundation Ltd*,[78] for example, the Irish Supreme Court held that causation could be inferred from the fact that the first sign of the claimant's brain damage followed closely on the heels of the administration of the pertussis vaccine. There was no other plausible explanation of its cause and it thus satisfied the balance of probabilities threshold.

(C) ACTION FOR BREACH OF STATUTORY DUTY

Before considering the strict liability regime contained in the Consumer Protection Act 1987, a brief mention must be made of the possibility of an action for breach of statutory duty in respect of certain limited categories of goods. The Secretary of State has the power to make safety regulations prescribing detailed rules as to, among other things, the design, manufacture, and packaging of specified classes of goods.[79] Breach of such regulations is a criminal offence.[80] But section 4 of the Consumer Protection Act 1987 also provides that an individual injured by a breach of the regulations will have an action for breach of statutory duty.[81] The regulations cover only a limited class of goods and the action for damages lies only where the defect in the goods derives from breach of the regulations. The action is also subject to the due diligence defence in section 39.

SECTION 3   THE STRICT LIABILITY REGIME

(A) THE CONSUMER PROTECTION ACT 1987

Three prefatory points must be borne in mind when considering the 1987 Act. First, the regime it contains derives from the European Community Directive of 12 July

---

[76] See, eg, Porat and Stein, *Tort Liability Under Uncertainty* (2000).
[77] [1990] 1 Med LR 117.
[78] [1994] 5 Med LR 81.   [79] Consumer Protection Act 1987, s 41.
[80] See General Product Safety Regulations 2005 (SI 2005/1803).
[81] Note that it is only breach of specific safety regulations that gives rise to an action for breach of statutory duty and not infringement of the general safety duty provided for by the Consumer Protection Act 1987, s 10.

1985.[82] And although the Directive allows for some variation in the rules through-out member states, the basic regime throughout the Community is the same. British industry is subjected to the same strict liability rules as its European competitors.[83] Second, industry in the UK – particularly the pharmaceutical industry – persuaded the Government to adopt the controversial 'development risks' defence despite every official report on product liability advising against such a course of action. (The defence, as we shall see, does much to undermine the strictness of liability under the Act.) Third, although it was possible to give direct statutory effect to the Directive, that was not done. Thus, where the interpretation of the 1987 Act is in doubt, it should be construed in the light of the Directive. And should there be any serious conflict between the provisions of the Act and the Directive, the dispute may ultimately have to be decided by the European Court of Justice.[84] That said, there is clear domestic judicial support for the view that the wording of the Directive should prevail in such cases.[85]

(B) WHO CAN SUE UNDER THE ACT?

Wherever a defect in a product wholly or partly causes death or personal injury, the victim or his dependants may sue under the Act.[86] The injured individual need not be a purchaser or even a direct user of the faulty goods. If defective brakes in a new car bought by A suddenly fail causing a road accident in which A, his passenger B, and C, a pedestrian, are seriously injured, all three can sue the car's manufacturer. Where a defective product causes damage to a baby before birth, the baby may later sue in respect of its disabilities.[87] Moreover, although the Act is primarily aimed at protection against personal injuries and death, consumers can also invoke its provisions where a product causes damage to private property (including land) provided the amount to be awarded to compensate for that damage exceeds £275.[88] Damage to the product itself is expressly excluded;[89] and other forms of pure economic loss are also clearly irrecoverable.[90]

---

[82] 1985/374/EEC.

[83] Notably, the European Court of Justice has held that member states may not implement rules more stringent than those contained in the Directive (*European Commission v France* Case C–52/00, 25 April 2002), nor may they retain pre-existing rules that are more stringent than those in the Directive (*Sanchez v Medicina Asturiana SA* Case C–183/00, 25 April 2002).

[84] Interestingly, in *European Commission v UK* Case C–300/95 [1997] All ER (EC) 481, the Commission refused to accept that the UK's adoption of the development risk defence is, despite plausible arguments to the contrary, incompatible with Art 7 of the Directive.

[85] See *A v National Blood Authority* [2001] 3 All ER 289, at 297.

[86] Consumer Protection Act 1987, s 2(1).   [87] Consumer Protection Act 1987, s 6(3).

[88] See the Consumer Protection Act 1987, s 5(4). By s 5(3) property used for business purposes is excluded. See Bell (1992) 20 Anglo-Am LR 371.   [89] Consumer Protection Act 1987, s 5(2).

[90] Economic loss consequent upon physical injury or damage to private property should in principle, however, be recoverable.

(C) ON WHOM IS STRICT LIABILITY IMPOSED?

Liability is not limited to manufacturers alone. Essentially, all those involved in the primary production and marketing of goods are made liable. Repairers and distributors who may owe consumers a duty of care at common law are generally outside the scope of the new strict liability regime.

The Act imposes liability on the following categories of persons.

(1) Liability is imposed on 'producers';[91] and producers are defined as:

   (a) manufacturers;[92]

   (b) in the case of products which are not made, but won or abstracted (for example coal and minerals) the person who won or abstracted the product;[93] and

   (c) in respect of products which are neither made, nor won or abstracted (for example crops), but where essential characteristics of the product are attributable to an industrial or other process, the person carrying out that process.[94]

(2) Liability is imposed on any person who brand names a product or by other means holds himself out as a producer.[95] This does not necessarily mean, however, that if you buy a food processor at Marks & Spencer which bears the brand name 'St Michael', and a part of the machine flies off and injures you, you may sue Marks & Spencer on this basis. Simply placing the 'St Michael' stamp on the processor is probably insufficient, since, in addition, the company must thereby hold itself out as having actually produced the product.

(3) Liability is imposed on any person importing a product into Europe from outside Europe.[96] Had you bought a Japanese food processor you need not concern yourself with the intricacies of suing in Japan; you can proceed against whichever Europe-based person imported it into Europe.

(4) The Directive expressly defines manufacturers of component parts as 'producers' so they, too, are subject to strict liability.[97] The Act achieves the same end by more tortuous means: namely, defining 'product' so as to embrace component parts.[98] The effect is simply illustrated. Should defective brakes in a new car fail causing personal injuries, the injured person may sue both the 'producer' of

---

[91] Consumer Protection Act 1987, s 2(2)(a).

[92] Consumer Protection Act 1987, s 1(2)(a).

[93] Consumer Protection Act 1987, s 1(2)(b).

[94] Consumer Protection Act 1987, s 1(2)(c). The cumbersome definition of this category of producer is explained by reference to the former exemption of primary agricultural produce from the regime instituted by the 1987 Act. This exemption was removed by the Consumer Protection Act 1987 (Product Liability) (Modification) Order 2000 (SI 2000/2771) giving effect to Directive 1999/34/EC.

[95] Consumer Protection Act 1987, s 2(2)(b).

[96] Consumer Protection Act 1987, s 2(2)(c). Note that a person importing a product into the UK from another member state is not made strictly liable under the Act. He may, however, be liable in negligence.

[97] Art 3(1).   [98] See the Consumer Protection Act 1987, s 1(2).

the finished product (that is, the car manufacturer) and the 'producer' of the defective component (the manufacturer of the brakes). Section 1(3), however, provides that a supplier of the finished product shall not be deemed to be liable for defects in all component parts simply because he cannot name the actual manufacturer of each and every component.

(5) Liability is also potentially imposed on distributors. Section 2(3) provides that any supplier of a product will be liable to the injured person *unless* he complies with a request to name, within a reasonable time, the person supplying him with the product. (Recall that a consumer may not know the identity of a manufacturer in a long chain of supply.) Compliance is not present where the supplier merely confirms that it is not the manufacturer without naming the manufacturer.[99]

(6) In *O'Byrne v Sanofi Pasteur MSD Ltd*,[100] the European Court of Justice held upon a reference that pursuant to Articles 3 and 11 of the Directive it was open to a national court to treat a distributor of goods as the producer where the distributor is both a wholly owned subsidiary of the manufacturer and under the control of the manufacturer in that the latter determines when goods are put into circulation. It held that the separate legal status of the two entities was not to 'influence' the court and that 'the fact that the products are invoiced to a subsidiary company and that the latter, like any purchaser, pays the price, is not conclusive'.[101] The Supreme Court later held in *O'Byrne v Aventis Pasteur SA* that the UK distributor of a drug was a correct defendant to proceedings brought by an infant claimant and that there was no need to rely upon the power of substitution available under the Limitation Act 1980 to substitute the French manufacturer for the distributor.[102] The court explained:

> If [the manufacturer] APSA was indeed in a position to decide when the product was to be distributed, then [the distributor] APMSD would be integrated into the manufacturing process and so tightly controlled by APSA that proceedings against APMSD could properly be regarded as proceedings against the parent company, APSA.[103]

---

[99] *O'Byrne v Aventis Pasteur SA* Case C–358/08 (2009) 113 BMLR 1, at [57].

[100] *O'Byrne v Sanofi Pasteur MSD Ltd* Case C–127/04 (2006) 91 BMLR 175.

[101] Ibid at [30]–[31]; affirmed *O'Byrne v Aventis Pasteur SA* Case C–358/08 (2009) 113 BMLR 1. This would allow a national court, where appropriate, to substitute the parent company for the subsidiary in proceedings commenced on time against the subsidiary. For our purposes, the important point is obviously that a suit against the subsidiary is of itself *sufficient* for the purposes of the Directive (and the Consumer Protection Act 1987).

[102] [2010] *O'Byrne v Aventis Pasteur SA* UKSC 23.

[103] [2010] UKSC 23, at [34]. In other words, proceedings against the subsidiary were sufficient for the purposes of the Act. See fn 101 above.

(D) PRODUCTS

'Products' are defined in the Act[104] as 'any goods or electricity' and include component parts, certain substances,[105] and agricultural crops.

In earlier drafts of the Directive, blood and human tissue were expressly excluded from the Directive, but it has since been held that blood and blood products do fall within its compass, even though the Directive and the Act were ultimately silent on the matter.[106] By contrast, the Act does not cover immovable property – that is, land and fixtures on land.[107] But products which become fixtures within immovable property – for example, central heating boilers – are probably within the scope of the Act.[108]

(E) DEFINING 'DEFECT'

Proof that a product resulted in injury is not sufficient to establish liability. The claimant, must show also that *a defect in the product* caused the injury. So long as a defect is proved, there is no need for the claimant to prove the cause of the defect.[109] That is for the defendant to investigate and remedy. Carelessness per se is irrelevant. Thus, if a chef is badly cut when the blade from his new food processor flies off the machine, he will succeed in his claim simply on proof of the obvious: that the processor is unsafe and defective.

Defect is defined in section 3 of the Act in terms that there is a defect in a product if the safety of that product is not such as persons generally are entitled to expect.[110] It is important to note that the standard that a person may be entitled to expect – perfection in some circumstances – may in fact transcend the standard they do *in fact* expect.[111] In assessing what persons generally are entitled to expect, section 3(2) states that all the circumstances are to be taken into account including:

(a) the manner in which, and purposes for which, the product has been marketed, its getup, the use of any mark in relation to the product and any instructions for, or warnings with respect to, doing or refraining from doing anything with or in relation to the product;

(b) what might reasonably be expected to be done with or in relation to the product; and

(c) the time when the product was supplied by its producer to another;

and nothing in this section shall require a defect to be inferred from the fact alone that the safety of a product which is supplied after that time is greater than the safety of the product in question.

---

[104] Consumer Protection Act 1987, s 1(2).

[105] Eg, blood and blood products: see *A v National Blood Authority* [2001] 3 All ER 289.

[106] Ibid.

[107] Liability for defectively constructed buildings remains subject to the general rules of negligence and the Defective Premises Act 1972.

[108] See the Consumer Protection Act 1987, s 45(1) and Art 2 of the Directive.

[109] *Ide v ATB Sales Ltd* [2008] EWCA Civ 424, at [19].   [110] See generally Stoppa [1992] LS 210.

[111] See *A v National Blood Authority* [2001] 3 All ER 289.

It remains for the claimant to prove that, taking into account the criteria outlined in section 3, the product is defective. Hardly any product is entirely safe and free of risk. The test is whether the risk to person and property posed by the product in the context of its common use or uses exceeds what is generally acceptable. Take the example of a sharp knife marketed as a kitchen knife for chopping vegetables and packaged so as to be reasonably child-proof on display. If the knife cuts off the tip of one's finger, one cannot claim that the injury resulted from a defect. A sharp cutting edge is a risk one accepts as the price for a knife which does its job. But if the same knife were marketed as a 'Marvellous Magic Dagger' and a child should cut himself, then the defect would be easier to prove: a risk to children in such a product (clearly aimed at children) would be generally unacceptable. Ultimately, the question is one of whether the manufacturer ought to issue a warning as to dangers one would not expect the product to present. If the danger is both obvious and inherent, and if it is part and parcel of what the consumer would expect, then there is no defect. Thus, hot coffee which inevitably carries the potential to scald is not a defective product.[112]

The test for a defect set out in section 3(2)(a) and (b) might involve the courts in risk–benefit analysis. This can best be illustrated by examples of liability for drugs.[113] Imagine a new and effective antibiotic is introduced. In 99.5% of cases it works well with fewer side-effects than other antibiotics. But 0.5% of consumers develop serious kidney damage caused by the drug. If an identifiable group of persons should or could have been foreseen as susceptible to damage, the failure to warn doctors of the potential allergic reaction may conclude the issue of defect.[114] But in cases where no such reaction is foreseeable, much may turn on the nature of the drug and the condition it is designed to combat. Thus, while a new minor tranquilliser posing a risk of liver damage to however small a group would probably be found defective, an AIDS drug designed to prolong sufferers' lives would probably justify a much higher degree of risk to life and health. Where the consumer of the drug faces a prospect of almost certain and painful death, any product offering a realistic hope of cure or palliation may generally be thought acceptable, even if it is inherently dangerous to some of its users. Existing chemotherapy treatments, for example, fit this analysis.

Section 3(2)(c) of the Act warrants separate consideration. It has two main implications. First, the time when the product was put into circulation is obviously relevant to determine whether the defect was inherent in the product or merely the result of 'fair wear and tear'. Thus, when a child-seat is eight years old and has been used by three different children, can it be expected to be as safe as when new?[115] Second, section 3(2)(c) also provides that safety standards must be judged by the generally acceptable

---

[112] *B v McDonald's Restaurants Ltd* [2002] EWHC 409.

[113] See Newdick (1985) 101 LQR 405. For a more straightforward example, see *Piper v JRI Manufacturing Ltd* [2006] EWCA Civ 1344.

[114] By analogy with *A v National Blood Authority* [2001] 3 All ER 289, and the emphasis placed on strict liability in that case, it is conceivable that even a 0.05% risk would not excuse the manufacturer from liability.

[115] Consider the juridical underpinnings of product liability regimes in Clark (1985) 48 MLR 325.

standards at the time at which the product was put on the market, and not with hindsight, according to standards prevailing when the claim reaches court. Thus, a very old car without rear seat belts ought not to be regarded as defective *purely because* of that absence.

In *Pollard v Tesco Stores Ltd*,[116] the Court of Appeal held that the question of what persons generally are entitled to expect could be determined without reliance upon a published technical standard existing at the time of the accident. The case concerned the ease with which a young child could open a bottle of dishwasher powder. A British Standard established the torque which such a bottle should have required to be opened. Yet this was not decisive, in part for the entirely obvious reason that most members of the public would not have any knowledge of the BS torque measure.[117] The Court set the relevant expectation as being that the bottle should be 'more difficult to open than an ordinary screw top', which it was, and so there was no defect.[118]

In relation to construction and presentation defects, strict liability will probably be easy to establish. Where the manufacturing process breaks down – for example, where snails get into ginger beer bottles – the product will be patently defective. Equally, where instructions on use are inadequate, or warnings as to use fail to make the consumer safe, a defect will also be easy to establish.[119] The need to engage in a rigorous examination of risks and benefits of a product will generally be reserved for design defects[120] where the implications for industry of design defects are potentially much more profound.[121]

The question of what the defendant could (reasonably or otherwise) have done to eliminate or reduce the risks will be irrelevant under the 1987 Act.

(F) GENERAL DEFENCES

Section 4 of the Consumer Protection Act 1987 provides several defences to strict liability. They include the following incidents:

(1) The defect is attributable to compliance with any requirement imposed by legislation (whether domestic or European).[122] On the other hand, the defence is not available where there are no statutory rules on how the product is to be made,

---

[116] [2006] EWCA Civ 393, criticised in Fairgrieve and Howells (2007) 70 MLR 962, at 973.

[117] [2006] EWCA Civ 393, at [16]–[18].   [118] Ibid at [18].

[119] If, however, a warning leaflet is lost, or a consumer chooses not to replace a lost leaflet, the manufacturer cannot be held responsible: *Worsley v Tambrands Ltd* [2000] PIQR P95.

[120] See, eg, *Abouzaid v Mothercare (UK) Ltd* 2000 WL 1918530, where Pill LJ thought the question for the court was one of whether the public could legitimately expect a higher degree of safety from the product than that which was actually present.

[121] Compensating ten victims of a freak construction defect is a less daunting prospect than compensating the thousands who may have suffered injury before a design defect became patent.

[122] Consumer Protection Act 1987, s 4(1)(a). For example drugs which must be licensed under the Medicines Act 1968.

but there are rules requiring licensing of the product by a public body before it can be marketed.

(2) If the defendant proves he never supplied the product to another[123] – for example, if experimental drugs are stolen from a drug company's laboratory and sold by the thieves.

(3) If the defendant did not supply the goods in the course of business.[124] Thus, the defendant is not strictly liable for defects in the food he serves to colleagues at a dinner party.

(4) If the defendant proves that the defect did not exist in the product when it was supplied by the defendant to another.[125] Thus, a chocolate manufacturer would not be liable for chocolates injected with poison on the supermarket shelves by some third party.

(5) Where the defendant makes components, he will not be liable where the defect arose in the finished product and was caused by the faulty design of the finished product or inadequate installation of D's component into the finished product by the manufacturers of that product.[126]

In addition to the defences provided for by section 4 of the Act, section 6(4) provides that the contributory negligence of the consumer is a defence under the Act. Two difficult questions arise, however. The Law Reform (Contributory Negligence) Act 1945 provides that when a finding of contributory negligence is made, apportionment of responsibility between the claimant and defendant (and hence the level of damages) is based on relative fault. But where the defendant is strictly liable, and the claimant has been careless of his own safety, does this mean that the claimant will generally have to bear the lion's share of responsibility, or will the courts at this stage have to revert to considering any evidence of want of care on the part of the defendant?

More problematic still is the matter of defining the circumstances in which a product that is put to improper use is evidence of contributory negligence. Imagine a stepladder is bought for cleaning windows. The 17-year-old son of the purchaser uses it to build an assault course. After a 14-stone friend of his has thundered across it, the wood cracks as the son himself is on the ladder. He falls and breaks a leg. Is he guilty of a degree of contributory negligence, or was the ladder put to a use that it would not generally be expected to withstand (in which case it may not even have been defective)?

(G) THE 'DEVELOPMENT RISKS' DEFENCE[127]

The incorporation of the development risks defence into the Act via section 4(1)(e) is the most controversial part of the legislation. Permitting member states to incorporate

---

[123] Consumer Protection Act 1987, s 4(1)(b).
[124] Consumer Protection Act 1987, s 4(1)(c).
[125] Consumer Protection Act 1987, s 4(1)(d).   [126] Consumer Protection Act 1987, s 4(1)(f).
[127] See generally Newdick [1988] CLJ 455 and id (1992) 20 Anglo-Am LR 309.

such a defence was a compromise by the European Community in order to end the long-drawn-out process of agreeing to implement strict liability at all. Section 4(1)(e) provides that a defendant shall not be liable where he can show:

> that the state of scientific and technical knowledge at the relevant time was not such that a producer of products of the same description as the product in question might be expected to have discovered the defect if it had existed in his products while they were under his control.

The effect of the defence can be explained as follows. Consider a drug-induced injury. A claimant establishes that the product fails to comply with society's legitimate expectations for the safety of that type of product. This means he proves that the risks created by the drug outweigh its potential benefits. The defendant may still escape liability by virtue of the 'development risks' defence if he can prove that the nature of the defect was such that, at the time he marketed the drug,[128] the very best available scientific and technical knowledge[129] would not have revealed the defect.[130] Imagine, for example, that a drug has been developed to alleviate sickness during pregnancy. Imagine further that it leads to unforeseen disabilities in the children born subsequently. In such circumstances, the development risks defence would confer one significant advantage on the parents of the injured babies. In negligence they would have to prove that the defendants should have foreseen the risk. But under the statute, the onus is on the defendants to prove that they could not have anticipated the danger. That being the case, self-interest impels manufacturers to disclose all reports of tests on a product as well as the expert opinion made available to them.

In summary, the Consumer Protection Act 1987 purports to benefit claimants by implementing a regime of strict liability, and despite academic doubts about just how strict liability would prove to be under the Act,[131] the decision of Burton J in *A v National Blood Authority*[132] displays a firm commitment to its strictness. There, the claimants, who had received blood transfusions, were infected with the Hepatitis C virus. The risk of infection had been known, but there was nothing that the defendants could have done to identify which blood products were thus infected. The defendants

---

[128] It will not, once and for always, be enough simply to establish that at the time the design was first put on the market the defect was not discoverable. Once the defect becomes apparent, any further marketing of batches of the drug will engage liability both under the Act and in negligence: see *Wright v Dunlop Rubber Co Ltd* (1972) 13 KIR 255.

[129] The development risks defence in Art 7(e) of the Directive is defined in terms of 'the state of scientific and technical knowledge at the time when he put the product into circulation was not such as to enable the existence of the defect to be discovered'. There is no reference to whether a 'producer of products of the same description might have been expected to have discovered the defect' as in the Consumer Protection Act 1987, s 4(1)(e). But notwithstanding the seemingly more generous test under the Act, relevant case law points to what is unknown to the world of science rather than merely what is unknown to the defendant: see *Richardson v LRC Products Ltd* [2000] Lloyd's Rep Med 280; *A v National Blood Authority* [2001] 3 All ER 289.

[130] It follows that if a risk is known, or ought to be known, in the light of accessible information, the defence is not available: *A v National Blood Authority* [2001] 3 All ER 289.

[131] See, eg, Stapleton (1986) 6 OJLS 392. See also Newdick (1987) 104 LQR 288.

[132] [2001] 3 All ER 289, esp at [69].

were not at fault in causing the claimants' infection. They were nonetheless held liable. Since the overwhelming majority of the blood was free from the virus, it was held that the claimants were entitled to expect a transfusion that was free from the virus (notwithstanding the known, and unavoidable risk). Of course, *A v National Blood Authority* is only a first instance decision, and may well not be the final word on the matter.[133]

(H) CAUSATION

The burden of proof rests with the claimant to show that there was a 'defect' in the product, and that the relevant injury or damage was wholly or partly caused by that defect.[134] This often presents a problem in establishing causation where an improper or unexpected use of the product leads to the claimant's injury: is it the improper use or the defect which caused the injury? Consider the following difficult scenarios.

(1) A new antibiotic is marketed. Information to doctors includes a warning not to prescribe the drug to pregnant women. The drug is only available on prescription. Dr X prescribes the drug for Y. Y feels better the next day. Y discontinues the tablets and gives the remainder to his colleague Z who is ten weeks pregnant. Z takes the tablets and her baby is born seriously damaged.[135]

(2) A trendy student buys a lurid pink dye in a dressmaking shop. She uses it to dye her hair and suffers acute dermatitis as a result.[136]

(3) A wealthy businessman buys domestic heaters and installs them in his swimming pool. One heater explodes, destroying the pool.

One causation issue is, however, somewhat clearer. Intermediate examination of the product will no longer exculpate the manufacturer from liability for defects in the product existing at the time that he put the product into circulation. That some third party may share liability for the injury to the claimant is relevant only to the issue of contribution between the tortfeasors.[137] Equally, certain factual difficulties associated with causation for the consumer seeking to identify and sue the manufacturer

---

[133] For academic discussion of the case, see Howells and Mildred (2002) 65 MLR 95; Hodges (2001) 117 LQR 528.

[134] See the Consumer Protection Act 1987, s 2(1) and Art 4 of the Directive. Causation may be inferred from the facts by a process of eliminating non-causes, so long as the remaining cause is not one which is improbable in nature: *Ide v ATB Sales Ltd* [2008] EWCA Civ 424, distinguishing *Rhesa Shipping Co SA v Edmunds ('The Popi M')* [1985] 1 WLR 948.

[135] Questions of causation can be seen from this example to be inextricably bound up with the definition of a 'defect'. D could argue that the manner in which the product was marketed as a 'prescription only' drug, with appropriate information supplied to GPs, rendered it acceptably safe.

[136] Should dye intended for use on materials be marked 'Not to be used on the hair'?

[137] See Art 8(1) of the Directive. Contribution is not limited to tortfeasors but is available between all persons liable for the same damage: see the Civil Liability (Contribution) Act 1978 discussed in ch 25. Retailers liable to purchasers for breach of the implied conditions of the contract of sale may also seek a contribution from the manufacturers.

will largely be alleviated by the obligation on each supplier to name his supplier or be deemed strictly liable himself.[138] Only where the last party identified is bankrupt will problems arise.

In the US, claims have been litigated where the actual manufacturer of the product – a generic drug – injuring the claimant cannot be traced. The American courts have held that liability should be apportioned between all companies manufacturing the drug in proportion to their share in the market for that drug.[139]

(I) LIMITATION

Actions under Part I of the Consumer Protection Act 1987 are subject to the usual limitation periods with the exception of two special periods of limitation:

(1) The action must be brought within three years of the date on which injury or damage was suffered by the claimant, or, if later, the date on which the claimant becomes aware of the injury or damage.[140] Only in the case of personal injuries does the court have a discretion to override that three-year period.

(2) No action may be brought in any circumstances more than ten years from the date on which the defendant supplied the relevant product to another.[141]

The reason for the provision on which the latter rule is based (Article 11 of the Directive) has been explained by the European Court of Justice as to do, inter alia, with the need for an appropriate balancing between the interests of, on the one hand, injured claimants and, on the other, defendant producers, which are subject to a strict liability regime that represents 'a greater burden than under a traditional system of liability'.[142] The long-stop period is designed to ensure legal certainty, the ability of a producer to insure against liability, and also to ensure continued innovation in industries such as the pharmaceutical industry.[143] Claims such as those brought before the courts in the US by several young women who had developed cervical cancer as a result of a drug (DES) taken by their mothers in pregnancy could not, therefore, have been brought under the 1987 Act. In this country, the young women would have had to fall back on the common law action for negligence.

---

[138] See the Consumer Protection Act 1987, s 2(3).

[139] See *Sindell v Abbott Laboratories* 26 Cal 3d 588 (1980). See also Porat and Stein, *Tort Liability Under Uncertainty* (2001); Newdick (1985) 101 LQR 405.

[140] For example, a person who took a particular drug in 2006 but only became aware of the kidney damage caused by that drug in 2011.

[141] As to time of supply, see discussion of *O'Byrne v Aventis Pasteur SA* [2010] UKSC 23 above.

[142] *O'Byrne v Aventis Pasteur* Case C–358/08 (2009) 113 BMLR 1, at [41]–[42].

[143] Ibid at [41]–[42] and [46].

FURTHER READING

BELL, 'Product Liability Damages in England and Wales' (1992) 20 *Anglo-American Law Review* 371

CLARK, 'The Conceptual Basis of Product Liability' (1985) 48 *Modern Law Review* 325

FAIRGRIEVE (ed), *Product Liability in Comparative Perspective* (2005)

FAIRGRIEVE AND HOWELLS, 'Rethinking product liability: a missing element in the European Commission's third review of the Product Liability Directive' (2007) 70 *Modern Law Review* 962

GOLDBERG AND ZIPURSKY, *The Oxford Introductions to US Law: Torts* (2010), ch 10

NEWDICK, 'Liability for Defective Drugs' (1985) 101 *Law Quarterly Review* 405

NEWDICK, 'The Future of Negligence in Product Liability' (1987) 104 *Law Quarterly Review* 288

NEWDICK, 'The Development Risks Defence of the Consumer Protection Act 1987' [1988] *Cambridge Law Journal* 455

STAPLETON, *Product Liability* (1994)

STOPPA, 'The Concept of Defectiveness in the Consumer Protection Act 1987' [1992] *Legal Studies* 210

TETTENBORN, 'Components and Product Liability' [2000] *Lloyds Maritime and Commercial Law Quarterly* 338

16
NUISANCE

KEY ISSUES

(1) Two torts

There are two torts that fall under the rubric of nuisance law. The first, which turns on the infringement of private rights, is the tort of private nuisance. The second, which enjoys primary significance as a common law crime, and turns on the infringement of public rights, is that of public nuisance.

(2) Private nuisance and protected interests

The tort of private nuisance protects three types of interest: (i) rights in the use of land, (ii) rights in the enjoyment of land, and (iii) rights in land itself so as to protect against physical damage to land.

(3) Private nuisance and strict liability

An especially problematic issue that forever lurks in the background when private nuisance is being examined is whether it constitutes a tort of strict liability. In theory, liability for this tort is strict. That is to say: what counts, ultimately, is the fact that harm of the requisite kind has been suffered.

However, one of the characteristics of the requisite harm – that it be an unreasonable interference with the claimant's rights in or over land tends to confuse. This is because, in deciding whether there has been such an interference, it is material to consider whether or not the defendant engaged in an unreasonable user of his own land. That being the case, the impression can often be created that liability for this tort is governed by a fault-based standard. This appearance can be reinforced by reference to the test for remoteness of damage (ie, whether the harm suffered was of a reasonably foreseeable kind).

(4) Public nuisance

There are two key elements to this tort: viz, showing that (i) there has been infringement of some or other public right, and (ii) the claimant has suffered harm to a markedly greater degree than others of a class of Her Majesty's subjects to which the claimant belongs.

SECTION 1   INTRODUCTORY OBSERVATIONS

(A) SCOPE OF NUISANCE LAW

This chapter deals with two torts: public nuisance and private nuisance. Though both may be actionable under the civil law, the commission of a public nuisance, such as obstructing a public highway, is primarily a criminal offence. We therefore consider public nuisance separately. To begin with, however, and for the greater part of this chapter, we are concerned only with the more prevalent tort of private nuisance.

A private nuisance may be defined as any activity or state of affairs causing a substantial and unreasonable interference with a claimant's land or his use or enjoyment of that land. From this definition we can discern three kinds of interests to which nuisance law affords protection:[1] the protection of land per se; the protection of the use of land; the protection of the enjoyment of land. In each case, the damage must always be referable to the land, and not merely chattels which happen to be on the land.[2] It follows from this that not every interference caused by A to B will amount to an actionable nuisance. Instead, the law calls for reasonable tolerance between neighbours vis-à-vis the respective uses to which each puts his land.[3] Indeed, from time to time, it is almost inevitable that each neighbour will put his land to a use that causes some irritation to the other.[4] It would be absurd for the law to allow an action in nuisance for every minor irritation so caused, for it would unjustifiably circumscribe the freedom to enjoy one's own land. It is for this reason that the law of nuisance insists not simply that there be an interference with the claimant's land in one of the senses adumbrated above, but also that that interference be both *substantial and unreasonable*.[5]

The range of activities that may give rise to an action in nuisance are manifold. They commonly include the emission of noxious fumes, smoke, noise, and heat, or the generation of violent vibrations. But not every instance of smoke or noise emission will sustain a nuisance action: it is impossible to characterise any of the activities just listed as inevitably and incontrovertibly a nuisance. At most, all that can be said about them is that they each have the *potential* to constitute a nuisance. Imagine, for example, that a neighbour's very young child manages momentarily to turn a CD player up to full volume. Naturally, the noise will create a disturbance until the neighbour turns it back

---

[1] Though the enjoyment of land and the use of land may, at one level, be seen as distinct interests, it is important to recognise that they are interrelated: see, eg, *Dodds Properties v Canterbury CC (Kent) Ltd* [1980] 1 All ER 928.

[2] In *Anglian Water Services Ltd v Crawshaw Robbins & Co Ltd* [2001] BLR 273, at [142], Stanley Burnton J opined (in relation to a disrupted gas supply) that 'it is possible to regard the interruption to the supply of gas as an interference with the use of gas appliances rather than with a use of land [since replacement electrical appliances can be obtained]'. But this seems a rather tenuous distinction.

[3] In *Bamford v Turnley* (1862) 3 B & S 66, for example, Bramwell B described nuisance as 'A rule of give and take, live and let live'. As an alternative, in *Hughes v Riley* [2006] 1 P & CR 29, at [29], Chadwick LJ described it as a principle of 'good neighbourliness… [which] involves reciprocity'.

[4] Eg, a 21st-birthday celebration that goes on until late at night.

[5] The *magnitude* and *unreasonableness* of an interference are not mutually exclusive.

down again. In such an instance it would be a very unjust law that characterised such a fleeting disturbance as an actionable nuisance, and it would also be difficult to say that the disturbance caused by a momentary increase in the volume of a CD was either substantial or unreasonable.

While the rigours of the law of nuisance are tempered in this way, it is important to appreciate that there are no precise thresholds beyond which any given disturbance becomes either substantial or unreasonable. The concepts of magnitude and unreasonableness are context dependent;[6] and gauging each depends upon a series of factors explored in depth later in this chapter. One cautionary note that should be entered here, however, is that, unlike the law of negligence, reasonableness in nuisance refers not to the defendant's conduct, as such, but to the outcome of his conduct. We are not strictly concerned with whether the defendant passes the 'reasonable person test' (in the sense of taking reasonable care to avoid causing harm) that is central to the tort of negligence. Rather, we are concerned to assess the reasonableness of the harm occasioned to the claimant.[7] Thus, as Lindley LJ observed in *Rapier v London Tramways Co* – where the nuisance emanated from too many horses crammed into the defendant's stable – 'If I am sued for nuisance, and nuisance is proved, it is no defence to say and to prove that I have taken all reasonable care to prevent it'.[8] On the other hand, it would be wrong to assume that the reasonableness of the defendant's conduct is an irrelevant consideration (especially where what is in question is whether the defendant has adopted or continued a nuisance)[9], for there exists an immutable interrelationship between the unreasonableness of what the defendant does and the unreasonableness of the interference thereby caused to the claimant. Disturbances caused by malice[10] or reckless disregard for one's neighbour – such as persistently playing a musical instrument in the small hours of the morning – as opposed to those caused innocently and unavoidably,[11] are clearly unjustifiable.

As originally conceived, the law of nuisance was not designed to cover personal injuries. It was exclusively concerned with acts or omissions[12] causing violations of interests in or over land.[13] For a time, however, it was thought that personal injuries were actionable in nuisance. Then, in *Hunter v Canary Wharf Ltd*, the House of Lords stated (*obiter*) that such injuries are not recoverable in private nuisance but rather, if at all, in negligence.[14] The fact that the law has fluctuated on this point serves to demonstrate that the boundaries of the law of nuisance are by no means fixed or easy

---

[6] *Sturges v Bridgman* (1879) 11 Ch D 852.   [7] *Walter v Selfe* (1851) 4 De G & Sm 315.

[8] [1893] 2 Ch 588, at 600. See also *Halsey v Esso Petroleum Co Ltd* [1961] 2 All ER 145.

[9] See, eg, *Leakey v National Trust* [1980] QB 485; *Transco plc v Stockport MBC* [2004] 2 AC 1, at [96] (suggesting an overlap between negligence and nuisance law).

[10] Eg, *Hollywood Silver Fox Farm Ltd v Emmett* [1936] 2 KB 468. In *Hunter v Canary Wharf Ltd* [1997] 2 All ER 426, at 465, Lord Cooke expressed the view (*obiter*) that the 'malicious erection of a structure for the purpose of interfering with television reception should be actionable in nuisance'.

[11] Eg, *Moy v Stoop* (1909) 25 TLR 262.

[12] Nuisance can be grounded on either nonfeasance or misfeasance: see *Goldman v Hargrave* [1967] 1 AC 645.   [13] For origins of the tort, see Murphy (2004) 24 OJLS 643.

[14] [1997] 2 All ER 426, at 438 and 442.

to identify.[15] This is in large part because the tort of negligence has, to a considerable extent, eclipsed (or, at least, subsumed) important elements of nuisance law.

(B) NUISANCE AND ENVIRONMENTAL LAW

Nuisance law – whether private or public – plays only a limited role in the protection of the environment.[16] The fact that there has been a steady growth in popular concern for the protection of the environment has resulted in the implementation of a number of statutes imposing a system of regulation that renders the common law very much a secondary means of protection. As Lord Goff put it:

> [S]o much well-informed and carefully structured legislation is now being put in place to effect environmental protection... [that] there is less need for the courts to develop a common law principle to achieve the same end, and indeed it may be undesirable that they should do so.[17]

The point is this. Many of the sorts of conduct that would formerly have sounded in nuisance (and nuisance alone) are now also covered by statutes such as the Clean Air Act 1993 and the Environmental Protection Act 1990.[18] The implementation of such legislation has meant that it is easier and more effective to pursue a grievance via the local environmental health officers (who can prosecute such 'statutory nuisances') than through the courts where the costs of funding, especially in the light of recent restrictions on the availability of legal aid, may be prohibitively high.

A further, related cause of the diminution in the number of nuisance actions has been the effect of planning legislation. Essentially, the requirement that planning permission must be obtained prior to a change in use of existing premises, or the construction of new ones, has meant that some potential nuisances can be avoided prospectively. Thus, where a person is denied the planning permission to turn his house into a small printing works, the obvious potential for disturbance to a neighbour caused by vibrations is avoided in advance. In such cases, nuisance law, which operates retrospectively – that is, in response to an *extant* interference, or state of affairs that threatens interference – is clearly denied any role. It would be wrong, however, to assume that nuisance is a totally redundant tort in the environmental context. On the contrary, it retains the potential to perform at least three useful functions. First, it can operate as an enforcement procedure supplemental to those contained in the relevant statutes (yet where a particular activity has been authorised by planning permission, the courts will naturally be hesitant in finding that it has caused an actionable

---

[15] In *Sedleigh-Denfield v O'Callaghan* [1940] AC 880, at 903, Lord Wright commented that 'The forms which nuisance may take are protean... many reported cases are no more than illustrations of particular matters of fact which have been held to be nuisances'.

[16] See Murphy, 'Noxious Emissions and Common Law Liability – Tort in the Shadow of Regulation' in Lowry and Edmunds (eds), *Environmental Protection and the Common Law* (1999).

[17] *Cambridge Water Co Ltd v Eastern Counties Leather plc* [1994] 2 AC 264, at 305.

[18] For an account of these and other statutory nuisances, see Murphy, *The Law of Nuisance* (2010), ch 8.

nuisance to the claimant).[19] Second, whenever such a case is decided in favour of the claimant, the effect of the judgment may be to establish standards in relation to, say, pollution control, which are additional to those contained in the relevant statute. Third, some statutory nuisances are defined in terms that hinge on the common law concept of nuisance, so the common law elucidates the interpretation of the statute.

(C) NUISANCE AND OTHER TORTS

As Erle CJ once remarked, the law of nuisance is 'immersed in undefined uncertainty'.[20] This uncertainty, Professor Newark forcefully argued, is mainly attributable to the fact that 'the boundaries of the tort of nuisance are blurred'.[21] To begin with, there is a considerable overlap and interrelationship between nuisance and negligence. As Lord Wilberforce remarked in *Goldman v Hargrave*, a nuisance 'may comprise a wide variety of situations, in some of which negligence plays no part, in others of which it is decisive'.[22] Not only does this dictum reveal that the overlap is ill-defined and partial, it also forces us to ask one of the most vexed questions in the whole law of nuisance: namely, whether nuisance liability is strict or fault-based. Consideration of this matter is deferred until later in the chapter. For now, we are concerned only to note that concurrent liability in nuisance and negligence can arise out of a single set of facts. For example, if I were to light a fire next to my neighbour's fence and then leave it unattended, I might be held liable in either negligence or nuisance if the fire were to spread to his fence or shrubs. Indeed, in one case where the action was framed both in negligence and nuisance, the judge, in dismissing the negligence claim, stated that he 'need not discuss the alternative claim based on nuisance... [since the latter] cannot be established unless negligence is proved'.[23] On a practical level, therefore, there is often a choice in terms of the way in which a claimant may frame his action. But on a jurisprudential level, one question that remains is why, when nuisance protects interests in the enjoyment of land, it is necessary to extend the boundaries of negligence to cover similar situations – especially at a time when the judicial trend is to restrain carefully the growth of negligence. Another question is whether nuisance law ought to be reined in and restored to its origins as a strict liability tort protecting only the amenities associated with land ownership.[24]

If the interface between negligence and nuisance leads to some difficult questions about the nature of nuisance liability, these have been compounded by similar questions concerning the interrelationship between nuisance and the rule in *Rylands v*

---

[19] *Gillingham BC v Medway (Chatham) Dock Co Ltd* [1993] QB 343; *Hunter v Canary Wharf Ltd* [1997] 2 All ER 426. An analogous approach may be taken with respect to those granted a waste-management permit: *Barr v Biffa Waste Services Ltd* [2011] EWHC 1003.

[20] *Brand v Hammersmith and City Rly Co* (1867) LR 2 QB 223.   [21] Newark (1949) 65 LQR 480.

[22] [1967] 1 AC 645, at 657.

[23] *Bolton v Stone* [1951] AC 850, at 860. This point was later endorsed by Lord Reid in *The Wagon Mound (No 2)* [1967] 1 AC 617, at 640: 'the similarities between nuisance and [negligence]...far outweigh any differences'.   [24] See Gearty [1989] CLJ 214.

Fletcher[25] (discussed in the next chapter). In juridical terms, the two torts can be distinguished.[26] Yet they share a number of common features which have been taken by the courts and earlier commentators to form the basis for the mistaken idea that the rule in *Rylands v Fletcher* was derived from the law of nuisance.[27]

Trespass to land concerns direct rather than consequential harm and may therefore be distinguished easily from nuisance in both juristic and factual terms. For example, in being actionable per se, trespass does not require the claimant to prove damage.[28] Thus, in *Kelsen v Imperial Tobacco Co (of Great Britain and Ireland) Ltd*, where a sign erected by the defendants projected into the air space above the claimant's shop, it was held that the erection of the sign constituted a trespass but not a nuisance since 'the presence of this sign...caused no inconvenience and no interference with the [claimant's] use of his air'.[29] On the other hand, where damage does occur as a result of a trespass, 'it makes no difference to the result' whether the action is framed in trespass or in nuisance.[30]

The fact that there exists some degree of overlap between nuisance and the other torts mentioned in the preceding paragraphs makes it difficult to classify any of them purely on the basis of the interest protected. If, for example, a neighbour's land is damaged because of an overflow of water, much will depend upon the directness of the invasion (central to trespass);[31] the role of fault (crucial in 'state of affairs' nuisance cases),[32] and whether the invasion was attributable to a foreseeably injurious escape (which lies at the heart of *Rylands v Fletcher* liability).[33]

A final characteristic of the tort of nuisance that should be noted is that the normal remedy sought by the claimant is an injunction rather than damages. His main concern, when subjected to the persistent late-night trumpet playing of his neighbour, for example, is that his neighbour should desist. But, as we shall see, injunctions are granted on a flexible basis reflecting the fact that they form a species of equitable remedy. They may therefore be refused even though an actionable nuisance can be proven. The courts' right to refuse an injunction despite the commission of an actionable nuisance enables them to pursue economic or social objectives.[34] For example, in one case concerning cricket balls being struck from a village green on to the claimants' land, it was stated that:

> it does not seem just that a long-established activity, in itself innocuous, should be brought to an end because someone else chooses to build a house nearby and so turn an innocent pastime into an actionable nuisance.[35]

---

[25] (1866) LR 1 Exch 265.

[26] See *Leakey v National Trust* [1980] QB 485; Nolan (2005) 121 LQR 421; Murphy (2004) 24 OJLS 643.

[27] See, eg, *Cambridge Water Co Ltd v Eastern Counties Leather plc* [1994] 2 AC 264, at 298; and Newark (1949) 65 LQR 480.   [28] *Stoke-on-Trent Council v W & J Wass Ltd* [1988] 3 All ER 394.

[29] [1957] 2 QB 334, at 343. Cf *Smith v Giddy* [1904] 2 KB 448, where it was held to be a nuisance when D allowed his trees to overhang C's land and thus stymie the growth of C's fruit trees.

[30] *Home Brewery Co v William Davies & Co (Loughborough) Ltd* [1987] QB 339, at 354.

[31] *Preston v Mercer* (1656) Hard 60.   [32] *Sedleigh-Denfield v O'Callaghan* [1940] AC 880.

[33] (1868) LR 3 HL 330.

[34] See Ogus and Richardson [1977] CLJ 284.

[35] *Miller v Jackson* [1977] QB 966, at 986. Cf *Kennaway v Thompson* [1981] QB 88.

The extent to which the courts refuse injunctions where nuisance has been established should not, however, be exaggerated. In the vast preponderance of cases where the claimant can prove the commission of a nuisance, he will also succeed in obtaining an injunction. Later in this chapter we shall see that the courts have developed a series of factors to which they will have regard before denying injunctive relief to those who can prove the commission of a nuisance.

SECTION 2   THE BASES OF NUISANCE LIABILITY

According to the definition of nuisance offered earlier, the successful claimant must show a substantial interference either with his land, or with the use or the enjoyment of his land; and he must also demonstrate that the interference was an unreasonable one. As we shall see, the factors taken into account by the courts in assessing both the magnitude and reasonableness of an interference are both manifold and intricately interconnected.

(A) SUBSTANTIAL INTERFERENCE

Before a claimant can succeed in a nuisance action, he must first be able to prove that he has suffered damage, for as we noted when distinguishing nuisance from trespass, nuisance is not a tort which is actionable per se. Since the law of nuisance protects not just against physical damage to land, but also against interferences with the use or enjoyment of it, it is apparent that we require a definition of damage that embraces both tangible and intangible interferences. Thus, in addition to physical harm to land, our concept of damage must also embrace those cases in which the claimant's complaint related to, say, the emission of unpleasant smells, or the generation of loud noise; in short, with things that represented 'sensible discomfort',[36] being interferences with the amenities associated with land ownership.

Although, for the purposes of nuisance, both physical damage and disturbances to the enjoyment of land are actionable, it does not follow that we need not distinguish between the various kinds of interference. Indeed, as we shall see, the case law requires us to treat material harm quite differently from interferences with amenities.

(1) Interference with the use or enjoyment of land

Where interference with the use or enjoyment of land (amenity nuisance) is concerned, the law requires give and take on the part of neighbouring land owners. This principle is neatly encapsulated in the words of Lord Wright in *Sedleigh-Denfield v O'Callaghan* where he said that '[a] balance has to be maintained between the right of the occupier to do what he likes with his own [land], and the right of his neighbour

---

[36] *Hunter v Canary Wharf Ltd* [1997] 2 All ER 426, at 452.

not to be interfered with'.[37] It is implicit in this that, as between neighbours, some measure of interference with the use and enjoyment of each other's land is permissible. In other words, only a *substantial* interference with a claimant's amenities can constitute a nuisance. As Lord Selbourne said in *Gaunt v Fynney*: '[a] nuisance by noise...is emphatically a question of degree...Such things to offend against the law, must be done in a manner which, beyond fair controversy, are to be regarded as excessive'.[38] The same rule, that the nuisance must be substantial, applies equally in respect of other amenities. So, for example, an interference with the right to the free passage of light – acquired by grant or prescription,[39] and sometimes referred to as the right to 'ancient lights'– only amounts to a nuisance where it deprives the claimant of 'sufficient light, according to the ordinary notions of mankind, for the comfortable use and enjoyment of his house'.[40]

One key issue, then, turns on determining when an interference with amenities amounts to a substantial infringement of the claimant's interests. It is certainly the case that the claimant's health need not be shown to have suffered.[41] Indeed, the loss of a single night's sleep has been held to be sufficiently substantial to constitute a nuisance.[42] So, too, has using adjoining premises for the purposes of prostitution (despite the fact that this fails to impinge directly upon the senses of the claimant in the way that, for example, noxious fumes do).[43] The question of whether an interference is sufficiently substantial to amount to an actionable nuisance is one of fact and is to be determined on a case-by-case basis. Not every interference will constitute a nuisance, and an interference that comprises a nuisance in one context may not do so in another.[44] The most commonly cited formulation of the rule by which the interference is to be adjudged substantial is that supplied by Knight Bruce VC in *Walter v Selfe*:[45]

> ought this inconvenience to be considered in fact as more than fanciful, more than one of mere delicacy or fastidiousness, as an inconvenience materially interfering with the ordinary comfort physically of human existence, not merely according to elegant or dainty modes and habits of living, but according to plain and simple notions among the English people?

Over the years, the courts have tended to gauge the seriousness of an interference by reference to two main considerations: the sensitivity of the claimant and the locality in which the alleged nuisance occurs. Neither of these factors is conclusive of whether an

---

[37] [1940] AC 880, at 903; *Delaware Mansions Ltd v Westminster CC* [2002] 1 AC 321.

[38] (1872) 8 Ch App 8, at 11–12.

[39] English common law recognises no automatic right to light, and such a right can only be acquired in connection with a building: *Harris v de Pinna* (1886) 33 Ch D 238.

[40] *Colls v Home and Colonial Stores* [1904] AC 179, at 208.

[41] *Crump v Lambert* (1867) LR 3 Eq 409, at 412.   [42] *Andreae v Selfridge & Co Ltd* [1938] Ch 1.

[43] *Thompson-Schwab v Costaki* [1956] 1 All ER 652. See also *Laws v Florinplace Ltd* [1981] 1 All ER 659 (sex shop established in a residential area).   [44] *Sturges v Bridgman* (1879) 11 Ch D 852.

[45] (1851) 4 De G & Sm 315, at 322.

interference is sufficiently substantial to constitute a nuisance; they are merely *relevant* considerations which ought to be taken into account in all amenity nuisance cases.

(a) The sensitivity of the claimant[46]

If the activity of which the claimant complains only disturbs the use or enjoyment of his land because he carries on there a 'delicate trade', heightening his sensitivity to interference, then the interference complained of will not amount to an actionable nuisance. The disturbance must be such that it would substantially inconvenience a claimant of ordinary sensitivities. In other words, the courts will not allow a claimant to turn an ordinarily innocuous activity into a nuisance. Take for example *Robinson v Kilvert*.[47]

> A landlord who remained in occupation of the cellar let the superjacent floor to C. Because of the landlord's business it was necessary for the cellar to be dry and hot. The heat of the cellar passed through the ceiling to the floor above (which was used by C as a paper warehouse) and caused damage to a stock of brown paper kept there. The court rejected C's application for an injunction to restrain the landlord from keeping his cellar so hot. It was only the fact that he was engaged in an 'exceptionally delicate trade' that caused C to suffer loss.

Similarly, in *Bridlington Relay Ltd v Yorkshire Electricity Board* the defendants' power line was interfering with the claimant's business of providing a radio and television relay service to subscribers. It was said, *obiter*, that because interference with the recreational amenity of television viewing was not a substantial interference, the claimants could not sue for the business interference complained of: 'the claimants could not succeed in a claim for damages for nuisance if... an ordinary receiver of television by means of an aerial mounted on his house could not do so'.[48] It may be important that this case was decided in 1965 when television ownership was rare, rendering viewers unusually sensitive claimants. These days, television viewing is far more common and less easily classified as a hypersensitive activity. Indeed, if the same facts were to arise today, it is possible that the court would hold there to be a nuisance.[49]

Such a possibility was certainly not ruled out in *Hunter v Canary Wharf Ltd* where two members of the House of Lords (Lords Goff and Cooke) suggested that, in certain circumstances, an action for this kind of interference might lie. However, in refusing to award damages to the claimants in that case, Lord Goff stated that while interferences with television reception 'might in appropriate circumstances be protected', it was also the case that 'more is required than the mere presence of a neighbouring

---

[46] Though the hypersensitivity rule is well established, the fact that C must suffer a foreseeable kind of harm may limit its practical import: *Network Rail Infrastructure Ltd v CJ Morris* [2004] Env LR 41, at [35].

[47] (1889) 41 Ch D 88.   [48] [1965] Ch 436, at 446.

[49] As would appear to be the case in Canada: see *Nor-Video Services Ltd v Ontario Hydro* (1978) 84 DLR (3d) 221, at 231.

building to give rise to an actionable private nuisance'.[50] In the wake of *Hunter*, then, it is unclear exactly if and when interferences with television viewing (and, by analogy, other such 'luxury' amenities) might form the basis of a nuisance action. Would there, for example, be an actionable nuisance where the interference is caused by the operation of an existing power station rather than by the construction of a tall building?[51] And bear in mind, too, that the decision in *Hunter* was grounded in part on a long-standing concern to allow landowners the freedom to build on their land (subject, of course, to planning restrictions).[52]

Leaving TV reception to one side, it is well established that '[a] man cannot increase the liabilities of his neighbour by applying his own property to special uses'.[53] On the other hand, he will be compensated in full for all the damage he suffers where a claimant of ordinary sensitivity would also have been able to found a nuisance action in respect of the interference complained of. So, in *McKinnon Industries Ltd v Walker*,[54] damage to the claimant's commercially grown orchids caused by the emission of sulphur dioxide gas from the defendant's factory was held to be actionable since it amounted to a non-remote consequence of what had already been proved to be a nuisance. That said, the fact that the claimant has suffered appreciable financial loss should not be taken, of itself, to amount to a substantial interference[55] (although the infliction of such business losses may be taken into account in deciding whether the interference *as a whole* was substantial).[56]

(b) Location of the claimant's premises

The locality in which the claimant's premises are situated is a second factor which assists the courts in determining whether the interference complained of is sufficiently substantial to amount to a nuisance. The expectations of the claimant, in terms of comfort, peace, and quiet, will naturally vary according to the location of his house or business. The point was succinctly made in *Sturges v Bridgman*,[57] in which case a physician complained about the noise generated by a neighbouring confectioner who was operating a pestle and mortar. There, Thesiger LJ held that the court should take account of the fact that the area consisted largely of medical specialists' consulting rooms since:

> [w]hether anything is a nuisance or not is a question to be determined, not merely by an abstract consideration of the thing itself, but in reference to its circumstances; what would

---

[50] [1997] 2 All ER 426, at 432. Much was made in the case of the fact that D had obtained planning permission to build the tower, but if what is permitted is exceeded – by, say, building too high – a nuisance action may still succeed (or so thought Lord Cooke at 465).

[51] On this, see the view of the Court of Appeal in *Hunter v Canary Wharf Ltd* [1996] 1 All ER 482.

[52] See *A-G (Ex rel Gray's Inn Society) v Doughty* (1752) 2 Ves Sen 453. One answer might be to allow the construction of tall buildings, allow a nuisance action, but restrict the remedy to one of damages: see O'Sullivan [1996] CLJ 184.

[53] *Eastern and South African Telegraph Co Ltd v Cape Town Tramways Companies Ltd* [1902] AC 381, at 393.   [54] [1951] 3 DLR 577.

[55] See *Victoria Park Racing and Recreation Grounds Ltd v Taylor* (1937) 58 CLR 479.

[56] *Thompson-Schwab v Costaki* [1956] 1 All ER 652.

[57] (1879) 11 Ch D 852.

be a nuisance in Belgrave Square would not necessarily be so in Bermondsey; and where a locality is devoted to a particular trade...[the courts] would be justified in finding, and may be trusted to find, that the trade...is not an actionable wrong.[58]

Though locality is relevant in deciding amenity nuisance cases, it is not necessarily a conclusive consideration. Thus, although locality provides a compelling reason for the decision in *Adams v Ursell*[59] – where a fish and chip shop established in a fashionable street was held to be a nuisance – it was not determinative in *Rushmer v Polsue and Alfieri Ltd*,[60] where printing presses were used at night in a printing district. Equally, it should be noted that the character of a locality is susceptible to change over time. Thus, the fact that an area was at one time wholly residential does not mean that the residents will always be entitled to a very high standard of peace and quiet. In *Gillingham Borough Council v Medway (Chatham) Dock Co Ltd*,[61] for example, it was held that planning permission which had been granted to change the use of an old naval dockyard into a commercial port (which turned out to be very noisy at night) should be taken to have effected a change in the character of the neighbourhood. As Buckley J put it: 'where planning permission is given...the question of nuisance will thereafter fall to be decided by reference to a neighbourhood with...[the new] development or use and not as it was previously'.[62]

On the other hand, *obiter dicta* in a decision of the Court of Appeal appear to constrain the effect of Buckley J's judgment to cases in which the interference complained of occurs *after* the character of the neighbourhood has already changed. The Court of Appeal took the view, in *Wheeler v JJ Saunders Ltd*,[63] that the simple grant of planning permission cannot be taken, *ipso facto*, to license what would otherwise be a nuisance. Rather, 'the question whether...planning permission has changed the character of a neighbourhood so as to defeat what would otherwise constitute a claim in nuisance is one of fact and degree'.[64] The court must tread carefully before it concludes that a simple administrative decision (not susceptible to appeal) has effectively extinguished existing private rights, for grants of planning permission will not do this automatically.[65]

(2) Material damage to land

So far we have only been concerned with what amounts to a substantial interference with the use or enjoyment of land (otherwise known as 'amenity nuisance'). In this section we consider cases in which the activity complained of causes actual physical damage to the claimant's land. The kinds of nuisance that concern us here include collapses

---

[58] Ibid at 865.

[59] [1913] 1 Ch 269. See also *Thompson-Schwab v Costaki* [1956] 1 All ER 652 (brothel in high-class street).   [60] [1906] 1 Ch 234 (affirmed [1907] AC 121).

[61] [1993] QB 343.   [62] Ibid at 361.

[63] [1995] 2 All ER 697.   [64] *Watson v Croft Promo Sport Ltd* [2009] EWCA Civ 15, at [24].

[65] The rationale was explained by Lord Goff in *Hunter* when he observed (at 433) that: 'it will usually be open to local people to [complain]...at the stage of the application for planning permission'.

of the defendant's property on to the claimant's land,[66] drenching or flooding,[67] vegetation damage caused by the emission of noxious fumes,[68] the encroachment of roots,[69] and vibration damage.[70] In such instances, the courts will approach the question of substantial interference rather differently from where the claimant complains of amenity nuisance.

To begin with, where physical damage to property is concerned, the character of the district in which the claimant's land lies is *not* a material factor in assessing the gravity of the interference. In *St Helen's Smelting Co v Tipping*[71] – a case in which the claimant's shrubs had been damaged by fumes emitted from the defendants' copper-smelting plant – Lord Westbury held that:

> It is a very desirable thing to mark the difference between an action brought for a nuisance upon the ground that the alleged nuisance produces material injury to the property, and an action...on the ground that the thing alleged...is productive of personal discomfort. With regard to the latter...a nuisance must undoubtedly depend greatly on the circumstances of the place where the thing complained of actually occurs. But where [physical damage is caused]...there unquestionably arises a very different consideration.[72]

One difficulty that arises from the fact that the claimant's location is irrelevant in physical damage cases is that physical damage and interference with amenities can often arise simultaneously, without there being any clear distinction between the two. If, for example, vibrations cause plaster to break off my walls, those same vibrations will probably also adversely affect the comfort and enjoyment of my home. Furthermore, the fact that the defendant engages in such a disturbing enterprise is likely to cause a diminution in the value of my house which is not easy to classify as either an amenity nuisance or an instance of physical damage.[73] Notwithstanding these problems, some attempts have been made by the courts to clarify the meaning of 'material damage'. A dictum of Lord Selbourne suggests that it is enough if science can trace a deleterious physical change in the property.[74] However, in light of the fact that it can be difficult to distinguish between amenity nuisances and those involving physical damage, it is best not to ignore the locality issue in all but the most clear-cut cases.

---

[66]   *Wringe v Cohen* [1940] 1 KB 229. Cf *Sack v Jones* [1925] Ch 235.
[67]   *Sedleigh-Denfield v O'Callaghan* [1940] AC 880; *Hurdman v NE Rly Co* (1878) 3 CPD 168; *Broder v Saillard* (1876) 2 Ch D 692.
[68]   *St Helen's Smelting Co v Tipping* (1865) 11 HL Cas 642; *Manchester Corpn v Farnworth* [1930] AC 171.
[69]   *Masters v Brent LBC* [1978] QB 841.   [70]   *Grosvenor Hotel Co v Hamilton* [1894] 2 QB 836.
[71]   (1865) 11 HL Cas 642.
[72]   Ibid at 650.
[73]   Although the drop in value of the property is a form of economic loss, it seems implicit from *Bone v Seale* [1975] 1 All ER 787 that such loss should be treated as property damage (given that the court treated it separately from the award for the amenity nuisance). Does this mean that diminution in value is to be regarded, in nuisance, as physical damage? If so, it could be argued that *all* amenity cases involve at least some element of physical damage according to this conception (which is the one favoured in *Hunter v Canary Wharf Ltd* [1997] 2 All ER 426). Cf *Mayo v Seaton UDC* (1903) 68 JP 7.
[74]   *Gaunt v Fynney* (1872) 8 Ch App 8, at 11–12.

Just as in the case of amenity nuisance, it is also important to establish in physical damage cases that the nuisance complained of is substantial in nature. Hence, in *Darley Main Colliery Co v Mitchell*[75] it was held that minor subsidence (though identifiable and tangible) which caused the claimant no appreciable harm was not an actionable nuisance.

(3) Interference with servitudes

For the sake of completeness we ought to note (but no more than that) a final category of damage that can, technically, form the basis of a nuisance action. It involves interferences with servitudes such as the right to light and air, and the right to support of land and buildings. The rules in relation to these rights are more suitably the subject matter of a textbook on property law than one on tort.

(B) UNREASONABLENESS

There is perhaps no more confusing matter in the whole of the law of private nuisance than the role played by unreasonableness in the ascription of liability. Conceivably, unreasonableness could relate to one or both of two interrelated issues: the conduct of the defendant and the nature of the interference with the claimant's land. But properly understood, it is the interference, rather than the defendant's conduct, which must be unreasonable.[76] This does not mean, however, that the nature of the defendant's conduct is irrelevant, since the unreasonableness of the defendant's user will impact upon the court's characterisation of the nature of the interference. Imagine, for example, that I regularly fire a gun on my land in order to control vermin posing a threat to my crops. The level of noise made by the gun is precisely the same as if I were firing it out of wantonness. And since the sound level remains constant, so does the degree of disturbance that I cause my neighbour. In only the latter case, however, might a judge declare there to be a nuisance on the basis that the shooting in that instance was completely unwarranted. In the former case, where the shooting was reasonable in order to effect pest control, the judge might easily reach the opposite conclusion.

The difference between the two cases lies in the way in which we characterise the nature of the interference (albeit by reference to the nature of the defendant's conduct). Yet not in every case in which the defendant acts unreasonably will he be liable in nuisance; for the disturbance must still be substantial. So, for example, if I play my CDs late at night and at full volume, I will not be liable in nuisance to my neighbour if she is almost entirely deaf and hears virtually nothing. The interference in such a case will be regarded as *de minimis*. As McNeill J insisted in *Tetley v Chitty*, the claimant must be

---

[75] (1886) 11 App Cas 127.

[76] See, eg, *Sampson v Hodson-Pressinger* [1981] 3 All ER 710 (ordinary use of badly constructed premises caused intolerable noise to neighbours held to be a nuisance). See also *Toff v McDowell* (1993) 25 HLR 650.

able to demonstrate '*a real* interference with *his* use and enjoyment of his premises'.[77] The italicised words make it clear that there needs to be a subjective disturbance. So, it will not matter in such cases that every unreasonable user that gives rise to an interference will *necessarily* give rise to an unreasonable interference. The fact that the interference is not *subjectively substantial* will defeat the claim.

There are several factors that the courts will typically take into account in deciding whether the interference is unreasonable.

(1) The seriousness of the interference

Generally, the more serious an interference with the claimant's interests, the more likely it is that the interference will be regarded by the court as unreasonable. In turn, the seriousness of the interference is influenced by four factors: the duration of the harm, the extent (or degree) of the harm, the character of the harm, and the social value of the use interfered with.

(a) The duration of the harm

The persistence of an interference has a direct bearing on its reasonableness. In general terms, the more persistent an interference, the more likely it is that the courts will deem it to be unreasonable. Self-evidently, it is much less reasonable to expect one's neighbours to tolerate a nauseating smell that is more or less permanent than one that lasts for just a few moments. It follows from this that nuisances normally involve ongoing interferences as opposed to those which are merely transitory or isolated.[78] In some circumstances, however, even isolated or transitory interferences are actionable. For example, if the interference complained of is an isolated event but it causes physical damage, the courts appear willing to tolerate claims in nuisance so long as the damage arose out of a dangerous 'state of affairs'.[79] In *Spicer v Smee* – a case in which defective electrical wiring in the defendant's premises resulted in the claimant's bungalow being destroyed by fire – Atkinson J put the matter thus: '[a] private nuisance arises out of a state of things on one man's property whereby his neighbour's property is exposed to danger'.[80] Similarly, in *Midwood & Co Ltd v Manchester Corpn*,[81] where an accumulation of inflammable gas caused an explosion to occur which set fire to the

---

[77] [1986] 1 All ER 663, at 665. In *Bradford Corpn v Pickles* [1895] AC 587, at 601, Lord Macnaghten stated that no action would lie '[i]f the act . . . gives rise merely to damage without legal injury'. See also *Crown River Cruises Ltd v Kimbolton Fireworks Ltd* [1996] 2 Lloyd's Rep 533.

[78] Thus, in *Cunard v Antifyre Ltd* [1933] 1 KB 551 (where some of D's roofing fell into C's premises) Talbot J stated (at 557) that: 'nuisances, at least in the vast majority of cases, are interferences for a substantial length of time'.

[79] *Midwood & Co Ltd v Manchester Corpn* [1905] 2 KB 597; *Spicer v Smee* [1946] 1 All ER 489. Note, too, that ongoing, but rather short, interferences can perfectly well be nuisances: see, eg, *Crown River Cruises Ltd v Kimbolton Fireworks Ltd* [1996] 2 Lloyd's Rep 533.

[80] [1946] 1 All ER 489, at 493.

[81] [1905] 2 KB 597. See also *Stone v Bolton* [1949] 2 All ER 851; *British Celanese Ltd v A H Hunt (Capacitors) Ltd* [1969] 2 All ER 1252.

claimant's premises, the court again held there to be a nuisance by focusing upon the prevailing state of affairs. Notwithstanding these decisions, it is arguable that these cases would have been better brought in negligence.

Though it is a pre-condition of liability in respect of an isolated event that it arose from a dangerous state of affairs on the defendant's land, it is important to be clear that damages are only awarded for the harm caused. Nothing can be recovered in connection with the menacing state of affairs, per se, for this is merely a prerequisite for, and not the basis of, the defendant's liability. Nuisance law insists that the claimant must demonstrate that he has suffered actual damage.

(b) The extent of the harm

Whether an interference is serious (and hence unreasonable) must be assessed in the light of its impact on the defendant. Whenever I play my piano, I generate a level of noise that may be moderately irksome to my neighbour; but he may easily drown it out by turning on his television or radio. On the other hand, if I were to play my trombone, it would generate much more noise and be likely to remain heard and cause disturbance no matter what normal steps my neighbour might take. The relationship between the degree of interference and its unreasonableness is therefore clear: the louder I play an instrument, or the more odious the smell that my business generates, the more likely it is that the court will find the interference thereby caused to be not only substantial, but also unreasonable.

On the other hand, the gravity of the harm caused must not be gauged on a purely objective basis (for example, by reference only to the loudness of my trumpet playing). There is also an important role for a subjective element in the assessment of whether the interference was unreasonable. Although there is usually a correlation between the magnitude of an interference and its unreasonableness, this is not always the case. Where, for example, I play my trombone late at night generating, say, 20 decibels of noise, this would, nine times out of ten, be considered a very substantial (and hence unreasonable) disturbance to my next-door neighbour. Where, however, my neighbour is practically deaf, she may only faintly hear the trombone. Accordingly, despite the *objective* loudness of my playing, it will not *subjectively* be perceived to be an unreasonable interference. And, as we have already seen, the claimant must show that *she* has suffered a substantial interference, for 'the law does not regard trifling and small inconveniences, but only regards sensible inconveniences which sensibly diminish the comfort... *of the property which is affected*'.[82]

---

[82] *St Helen's Smelting Co v Tipping* (1865) 11 HL Cas 642, at 654 (emphasis added). See also *Sturges v Bridgman* (1879) 11 Ch D 852, at 863: '[where the interference is of] so trifling a character, that, upon the maxim *de minimis non curat lex*, we arrive at the conclusion that the defendant's acts would not have given rise to [liability]'.

(c) The character of the harm

Harm, for the purposes of nuisance law, as we have already seen, may take the form either of physical damage to land or an interference with the use or enjoyment of it. Although all three forms are actionable, physical injury is generally regarded as being inherently of a more serious kind than interferences with a claimant's amenities. Indeed, the distinction drawn in *St Helen's Smelting Co v Tipping* between physical damage and amenity nuisance[83] has been taken by some commentators to support the proposition that physical injury is actionable regardless of whether the defendant's user of his land was objectively reasonable.[84] This proposition probably goes too far,[85] but it does draw attention to the fact that, even in the context of nuisance, the English courts remain chary of protecting trifling personal discomforts falling short of physical injury.[86] The central issue is whether the interference is unreasonable.[87] So, in clear cases of physical injury – which can easily be proven and quantified in terms of damages, and which sit towards the top end of the hierarchy of protected interests in tort law – it is simpler for the courts to find that the interference complained of was unreasonable than in cases of personal discomfort or annoyance.[88] Consequently, physical violations of the claimant's land are tolerated far less readily than disruptions to the peaceful enjoyment of it.

(d) Social value of the use interfered with

The final factor that can affect the seriousness of the harm is the nature of the use to which the claimant puts his land. Where the claimant uses his land in such a way that it can be classified as socially useful, it is more likely that the disruptive interference about which a complaint has been made will be regarded by the court as serious. In *Smith v Giddy*, for example, branches on the defendant's trees which overhung the claimant's land and prevented his commercially cultivated fruit trees from growing properly were held to be a nuisance whereas it was stated *obiter* that, had the claimant not been growing such trees, the mere blockage of light would not have been actionable.[89]

(2) Reasonable user of the defendant's land

Strictly, as we have noted at several points, nuisance liability depends upon there being an unreasonable interference with the claimant's interests rather than there

---

[83] Ibid at 650.

[84] Ogus and Richardson [1977] CLJ 284, at 297.

[85] See *Ellison v Ministry of Defence* (1996) 81 BLR 101.

[86] See the observations of Lord Hoffmann in *Hunter* (noted, at the beginning of this chapter).

[87] See, eg, *Watt v Jamieson* 1954 SC 56, at 58 where Lord President Cooper held that the key question was 'whether what he was exposed to was *plus quam tolerabile*'.

[88] As Lord Selborne put it in *Gaunt v Fynney* (1872) 8 Ch App 8, at 11–12: '[amenity nuisance] is much more difficult to prove than when the injury complained of is the demonstrable effect of a visible or tangible cause'. Note, too, *Ruxley Electronics and Construction Ltd v Forsyth* [1995] 3 All ER 268.

[89] [1904] 2 KB 448.

being unreasonable conduct per se on the part of the defendant. However, there is an immutable and fundamental interrelationship between the reasonableness of the interference and the reasonableness of the user or activity. The fact that one is engaged in an unreasonable user will, *ipso facto*, render any interference thereby caused equally unreasonable: an interference that is caused by an unjustifiable activity cannot itself be justified.[90] The converse, as Lord Goff noted in *Cambridge Water Co Ltd v Eastern Counties Leather plc*, is also true: 'if the user is reasonable the defendant will not be liable for consequent harm to his neighbour's enjoyment of his land'.[91] It thus follows that the question of negligent conduct is a highly relevant consideration, not in itself, but because of its impact on the characterisation of the interference caused. Much may turn on the burden of proof, for, as the Court of Appeal explained in *Marcic v Thames Water Utilities Ltd*:

> Once a claimant has proved that a nuisance has emanated from land in the possession or control of the defendant, the onus shifts to the defendant to show that he has a defence to the claim, whether this be absence of 'negligence' in a statutory authority case or that he took all reasonable steps to prevent the nuisance, [in other cases].[92]

In assessing the reasonableness of the defendant's user the courts resort to a further range of factors. The following comprise the more important of these.

(a) The defendant's motive

In judging what constitutes an unreasonable user, the courts will take into account the main object of the defendant's activity. Thus, for example, in *Harrison v Southwark and Vauxhall Water Co*,[93] the useful nature of the defendants' construction work was part of the reason why the claimant's action was dismissed. Where, however, the defendant's primary aim is to injure his neighbour, there is considerable authority that his malicious motives may render the interference unreasonable. In *Christie v Davey*,[94] for example, the claimants' action lay in respect of noises being made by their defendant neighbours. Central to North J's judgment that the noises were a nuisance was the fact that they were made 'deliberately and maliciously for the purpose of annoying the [claimants]'.[95] Similarly, in *Hollywood Silver Fox Farm Ltd v Emmett*[96] the court held the firing of guns to be actionable where they were fired out of spite, with the object of interfering with the breeding of silver foxes by the claimant. The defendant's malicious purpose was again emphasised. What stands reiteration is that, if nuisance is a strict liability tort, as Lord Goff proclaimed it to be in the *Cambridge Water* case, it is not the unreasonableness of the defendant's conduct, per se, that is of concern. Rather, it is the fact that this has a direct impact on the reasonableness of the

---

[90] Though the unreasonableness of the user will confirm the unreasonableness of the interference, it does not follow that all unreasonable users will result in liability. For example, an unreasonable user that causes minimal interference will not be actionable: the interference must also be substantial.

[91] [1994] 2 AC 264, at 299.

[92] [2002] QB 929, at [85] (reversed on appeal on different points of law: [2004] 2 AC 42).

[93] [1891] 2 Ch 409, at 414.   [94] [1893] 1 Ch 316.   [95] Ibid at 326.   [96] [1936] 2 KB 468.

454   TORTS INVOLVING STRICT OR STRICTER LIABILITY

interference. This is consistent with the definition of nuisance offered at the beginning of this chapter, which does not stipulate unreasonable conduct – for this would blur the distinction between negligence and nuisance liability – but, instead, an unreasonable interference.

An important, and arguably anomalous, case in this context is that of *Bradford Corpn v Pickles*.[97] There, the defendant was exercising his legal right to abstract water percolating beneath his land thereby preventing it from reaching the claimant's adjoining reservoir. In dismissing the claimant's nuisance action, Lord Macnaghten held that:

> it is the act, not the motive for the act, that must be regarded. If the act, apart from motive, gives rise merely to damages without legal injury, the motive, however reprehensible it may be, will not supply that element.[98]

At first sight, this short passage from his Lordship's dictum would appear difficult to square with *Christie v Davey* and the *Hollywood Silver Fox Farm* case. Indeed, a number of commentators have been at pains to reconcile the cases on the basis that *Bradford Corpn v Pickles* is a *sui generis* type of case concerning, as it does, rights in respect of servitudes. But this argument, turning on the claimant's *absolute* right to extract water, is unconvincing, for there is a no less absolute right to use one's land for lawful purposes that have been specifically sanctioned even where a substantial interference is caused to one's neighbour.[99] What the argument fails to recognise is that Lord Macnaghten's focus is not so much on the *reasonableness* of the interference, but rather upon its *gravity*. His concern, it is submitted, is primarily with whether the act complained of has occasioned a substantial interference, since the notions of *factual* and *legal* interference are by no means coextensive. His point, then, is that, in the absence of substantial harm, any action in nuisance based on the malicious conduct of the defendant must fail.[100] This accords with the principle *de minimis non curat lex*, long since deemed to be applicable to nuisance cases.[101] In any event, in *Hunter v Canary Wharf Ltd*, Lord Cooke reasserted the principle that the defendant actuated by malice may incur liability where the same interference, innocently caused, would not lead to this result.[102]

Wanton ill-conduct serves no socially useful function. It necessarily amounts to an unreasonable user, and has the inevitable effect of rendering unreasonable any interference thereby caused to the claimant. Where, however, the defendant's activity does possess some social utility, and it is this social utility that motivates the defendant,

---

[97] [1895] AC 587.   [98] Ibid at 601.

[99] See, eg, *Hunter v Canary Wharf Ltd* [1997] 2 All ER 426, where Lord Goff refused to accept that the lawful construction of a tall building constituted nuisance when its construction caused interference to Cs' television reception.

[100] His dictum is nonetheless misleading in so far as it appears to suggest that D's motive may *always* be disregarded. This is manifestly not the case as the *Christie* and *Silver Fox* cases amply demonstrate.

[101] *Sturges v Bridgman* (1879) 11 Ch D 852.

[102] [1997] 2 All ER 426, at 465ff.

the court will naturally be less inclined to declare any resulting interference to be unreasonable. The country must have power stations, factories, and smelting works. By contrast, the need for motorcycle speedway tracks or racecourses is much less pressing and, consequently, such activities much more readily form the basis of successful nuisance actions.[103]

(b) Location of the defendant's enterprise

Just as the location of the *claimant's* premises is important in determining what constitutes a 'substantial interference' in cases of amenity nuisance, so too is the location of the *defendant's* premises important in assessing the reasonableness of the defendant's conduct. Put simply, we are concerned with the question 'what is it reasonable to do?' and not with the question (relevant when considering the location of the claimant's premises), 'what is it reasonable to put up with?' Thus, in addition to considering the usefulness of the defendant's activity, we must also consider whether it is being carried on in a suitable locality. In this connection, the courts have recognised the national policy of segregating different uses of land and have furthered this policy by taking into account whether the defendant is putting his land to a use which is compatible with the main use to which land in that area is usually put. To take an example, the operation of a chemicals works would not, in every conceivable instance, be considered to be an unreasonable use of land. If it was operated in a residential area, it could be so regarded; but if the factory was located in an industrial area, the activity would probably be considered reasonable.[104]

(c) Fault

The undoubted role that fault can play in determining nuisance liability raises one of the most difficult questions in tort: is nuisance liability strict or fault-based? To answer this question, we must first identify the function served by identifying fault on the part of the defendant and, second, the limits to the role it plays in the ascription of nuisance liability. Much of the confusion that surrounds these issues stems from one famous passage in Lord Reid's Privy Council speech in *The Wagon Mound (No 2)* where he said:

> Nuisance is a term used to cover a wide variety of tortious acts or omissions and in many negligence in the narrow sense is not essential. An occupier may incur liability for the emission of noxious fumes or noise although he has used the utmost care in building and using his premises... [And yet] although negligence may not be necessary, *fault of some kind is almost always necessary* and fault generally involves foreseeability.[105]

---

[103] See, eg, *A-G v Hastings Corpn* (1950) 94 Sol Jo 225.

[104] It was decided in *Ball v Ray* (1873) 8 Ch App 467 that converting part of a house in a residential street into stables caused an unreasonable interference. But a similar degree of interference caused by a piano being played, or crying children, would not be a nuisance: see *Moy v Stoop* (1909) 25 TLR 262.

[105] [1967] 1 AC 617, at 639 (emphasis added).

At first sight, this passage may appear either intractable or inherently self-contradictory. Negligence is the archetypal fault-based tort. How then can it be asserted that while negligence is not required, fault is almost invariably a pre-condition of liability? The answer lies in Lord Reid's qualification that it is only *negligence in the narrow sense* that need not be shown. The first point to note is that 'negligence in the narrow sense' refers to no more than a failure to meet the standard of conduct of the reasonable person. The second point is that, though one undertakes an enterprise with all possible caution, one can seldom guarantee that certain, *foreseeable*, adverse consequences will not arise. I may, for example, drive my car in the winter with all due care but be unable to prevent a collision with another car caused by my skidding on a patch of 'black ice'. In such a case, though it could not be said that my driving was below the standard of the reasonable driver and thus negligent, it might still be said that I was at fault in the rather different sense that I knowingly took the risk of such an occurrence by deciding to drive in the first place. The element of fault in this second sense derives from the foreseeability of an accident even though I drive to an exemplary standard. It is submitted that it is this notion of fault that Lord Reid considered to be crucial to nuisance liability.

The question of whether nuisance involves strict or fault-based liability was revisited by the House of Lords in *Cambridge Water Co Ltd v Eastern Counties Leather plc*.[106] There, Lord Goff, with whom the other four Law Lords agreed, offered a similar interpretation of the role of fault to the one suggested here. He said:

> [T]he fact that the defendant has taken all reasonable care will not of itself exonerate him...But it by no means follows that the defendant should be held liable for damage of a type which he could not reasonably foresee; and the development of the law of negligence in the past 60 years points strongly towards a requirement that such foreseeability be a prerequisite of liability in damages for nuisance, as it is of liability in negligence.[107]

This passage makes it clear that liability in nuisance is strict in the sense that a defendant may be found liable regardless of the care he took in doing what he did to avoid causing harm. But this does not exclude a residual role for fault in the second sense: that is, that liability will only attach to those users of land that involve a foreseeable risk of harm.[108]

(d) The kind of user

A penultimate factor that can influence the court's view of the reasonableness of the defendant's user is the kind of activity in which he is engaged. Here, the concern is simply with the actual use to which the defendant puts his land. If my neighbour disturbs me by operating a noisy printing press in order to produce illegal, proscribed, pornographic literature, his activity can never be justified, for the activity is illegal and

---

[106] [1994] 2 AC 264.   [107] Ibid at 300.
[108] See, eg, *Leakey v National Trust* [1980] QB 485, at 526; *Delaware Mansions Ltd v Westminster CC* [2002] 1 AC 321 (foreseeable root encroachment: D liable).

thus unreasonable. It follows that any substantial disturbance thereby caused can also never be justified. Illegal and extremely dangerous enterprises[109] are, by definition, unreasonable users of land and, apart from the criminal aspects of such activities, any disturbances they cause will, *ipso facto*, be regarded as unreasonable, *regardless* of motive.[110] By contrast, if the defendant is responsible for doing something that is socially useful, it may temper the willingness of the court to find his user to be unreasonable and help persuade the court not to grant injunctive relief even if it finds the activity in question to be a nuisance.[111]

The kinds of activity likely to be deemed unreasonable per se will commonly overlap with those which, for the purposes of liability under the rule in *Rylands v Fletcher*,[112] constitute 'non-natural' users of land. Yet, however clearly related the two notions are, it is nonetheless clear that they are not coextensive. In *Fay v Prentice*,[113] for example, the defendant was found liable in nuisance in respect of water dripping from the eaves of his building although such a user would not be termed non-natural for the purposes of *Rylands v Fletcher* liability. On the other hand, the fact that a given user could be regarded as 'non-natural' for *Rylands* purposes might well be material in deciding whether it was also an 'unreasonable user' for the purposes of nuisance.[114] We return to the question of what constitutes a non-natural user in the next chapter.

(e) Practicability of preventing or avoiding the interference

It will always be material whether the defendant, by taking reasonable, practicable steps to prevent the interference, could still have achieved his purpose without interfering with the claimant's use of his land. If, without excessive expenditure, a factory owner could install equipment that would prevent him causing a disturbance to his neighbours, the courts might treat this as conclusive that the defendant's user was unreasonable. In *Andreae v Selfridge & Co Ltd*, for example, where building operations that were generating noise and dust interfered with the comfortable enjoyment of a neighbour's hotel, it was held that the defendants who had undertaken an ostensibly reasonable user of the land were nonetheless under a duty

> to take proper precautions, and to see that the nuisance is reduced to a minimum. It is no answer for them to say: 'But this would mean that we should have to do the work more slowly than we would like to do it, or it would involve putting us to some extra expense'.[115]

---

[109] Eg, the storing of large quantities of high explosives in a private, terraced house.

[110] In *Cambridge Water Co Ltd v Eastern Counties Leather plc* [1994] 2 AC 264, at 298, Lord Goff identified that unreasonable land use is not necessarily to be equated with negligent land use, though the latter will always be good evidence of the former.

[111] *Dennis v Ministry of Defence* [2003] Env LR 34 (the noise from RAF training aircraft was held to be a nuisance, but damages only were awarded, and continuance of the nuisance permitted).

[112] (1868) LR 3 HL 330.   [113] (1845) 1 CB 828.

[114] But for differences see Murphy (2004) 24 OJLS 643.

[115] [1938] Ch 1, at 9–10. See also the *obiter* endorsement of this approach by the House of Lords in *Southwark LBC v Tanner* [2001] 1 AC 1.

Similarly, in *Leeman v Montagu*[116] a poultry farmer who made no attempt to rearrange his farm was held liable in nuisance in respect of 750 cockerels that crowed between the hours of 2.00 a.m. and 7.00 a.m. On the other hand, in one case involving young children whose crying often caused a disturbance to the claimant, it was held that there was no liability as there was no evidence that the children had been neglected or suffered from a want of care.[117] What was crucial to this finding was the actual ability of the defendant to eradicate or minimise the interference. This principle was endorsed in *Leakey v National Trust* where, despite the defendants ultimately being found liable in respect of an earth-slide from their land, the Court of Appeal expressly declared that '[t]he extent of the defendant's duty [to minimise any interference], and the question of whether he has or has not fulfilled that duty, may ... depend on the defendant's financial resources'.[118] Similarly, in *Holbeck Hall Hotel Ltd v Scarborough Borough Council*,[119] the Court of Appeal stated that in cases involving naturally occurring nuisances – in this case landslips – the defendants' duty would be in part restricted by their ability to avert the nuisance. On the other hand, the Court of Appeal has since held that where the defendant and claimant would both benefit from works done to avoid a nuisance, they should contribute to the cost of those works in proportion to their respective benefit.[120]

SECTION 3   WHO CAN SUE?

Reflecting the fact that nuisance law has traditionally protected interests in land, the conventional approach adopted by the English courts has been to allow only those with a sufficient proprietary interest in the land sue for this tort.[121] In *Malone v Laskey*,[122] a housewife was injured when vibrations generated by the defendant caused an iron bracket designed to support a lavatory cistern to fall off the wall and on to her head. Her claim in nuisance failed because she had no legal or equitable interest in the property. Fletcher Moulton LJ observed: 'a person who is merely present in the house cannot complain of a nuisance'.[123] The point was later endorsed *obiter* by Lord Simmonds in *Read v J Lyons & Co Ltd* when he said: 'he alone has a lawful claim who has suffered an invasion of some proprietary or other interest in land'.[124] And the significance of a

---

[116] [1936] 2 All ER 1677. In similar vein, see *Lambert v Barratt Homes Ltd* [2010] EWCA Civ 681.

[117] *Moy v Stoop* (1909) 25 TLR 262.

[118] [1980] QB 485, at 526. Cf the wholly objective standard that applies in cases of public nuisance: *Wandsworth LBC v Railtrack plc* [2002] QB 756.

[119] [2000] 2 All ER 705. The court emphasised that liability in cases of this type involved nonfeasance and that, therefore, the duty to minimise or avoid an interference to C could be restricted for this reason. Their Lordships even considered, *obiter*, that issuing a warning to C of a known natural danger may suffice in some circumstances.

[120] *Abbahall v Smee* [2003] 1 All ER 465, at [41] (D and C lived beneath a common roof which needed repairs).

[121] *Hunter v Canary Wharf Ltd* [1997] AC 655, at 702.   [122] [1907] 2 KB 141.

[123] Ibid at 153–4.   [124] *Read v J Lyons & Co Ltd* [1946] 2 All ER 471, at 482.

proprietary interest (including, presumably, an equitable interest) was forcefully reaffirmed by a 4:1 majority of the House of Lords in *Hunter v Canary Wharf Ltd*[125] where Lord Goff said:

> an action in private nuisance will only lie at the suit of a person who has a right to the land affected. Ordinarily such a person can only sue if he has the right to exclusive possession of the land, such as a freeholder or tenant in possession, or even a licensee with exclusive possession...But a mere licensee on the land has no right to sue.[126]

Notwithstanding the consistency with which the proprietary interest requirement has been endorsed, there remains some uncertainty in this sphere. To this end, the law as it currently stands is set out under two sub-headings: the first dealing with established claimants, the second dealing with more controversial claimants.

(A) ESTABLISHED CATEGORIES OF CLAIMANT

(1) Those in exclusive possession of the land affected

In the light of what Lord Goff said in *Hunter*, there can be no doubt that freeholders possess *locus standi* to sue in private nuisance. Presumably, too, leaseholders can also be regarded as possessing a sufficient proprietary interest given that their Lordships were prepared to countenance claims by resident tenants enjoying exclusive possession.[127] Put bluntly, their Lordships clearly saw exclusive possession as the main criterion, a matter since confirmed by the Court of Appeal in *Pemberton v Southwark LBC*.[128] So, while a licensee with such possession will be able to sue in nuisance,[129] a claimant with a lesser form of possessory entitlement will not.[130]

One final category of occupier worthy of mention is the successor in title to land afflicted by a continuing nuisance. Such persons are entitled to sue in nuisance even if the interference began prior to their acquisition of the property afflicted.[131] Accordingly, in *Delaware Mansions Ltd v Westminster City Council*,[132] the claimants were freehold owners of certain flats. At the time the damage was first occasioned by the encroachment of the defendant's roots, the claimants were not the freehold owners. But since the defendants had taken no remedial action so as to render the nuisance a continuing one, the flat owners were able to sue in respect of the physical damage caused.

---

[125] [1997] AC 655. The sole dissent was voiced by Lord Cooke.

[126] Ibid at 688.   [127] Ibid at 688 and 724.

[128] [2000] 1 WLR 1672. See also *Foster v Warblington UDC* [1906] 1 KB 648; *Newcastle-Under-Lyme Corpn v Wolstanton Ltd* [1947] Ch 92.

[129] *Newcastle-Under-Lyme Corpn v Wolstanton Ltd* [1947] Ch 92; *Hunter v Canary Wharf Ltd* [1997] AC 655.

[130] *Jan de Nul (UK) v NV Royale Belge* [2000] 2 Lloyd's Rep 700 (C had no exclusive right to possession).

[131] *Masters v Brent LBC* [1978] QB 841, at 848. Where the damage caused by a nuisance remains, but the original nuisance has ceased to operate, only the original owner may sue: *Jeffries v Williams* (1850) 5 Exch 792.

[132] [2002] 1 AC 321.

(2) Reversioners

Another well-settled category of claimants with the right to sue in private nuisance is that of reversioners. But it is not in respect of all nuisances that reversioners are entitled to sue. They may only sue in respect of damage caused to their reversionary interest. Short-term nuisances that are only capable of affecting a tenant currently in occupation will not ground an action by a reversioner. That said, it is certainly going too far to suggest that only a permanent injury to the reversion will suffice. Although Parker J made mention of permanent injuries in *Jones v Llanrwst UDC (No 2)*,[133] he also offered a qualified notion of what amounts to permanent for these purposes. He said:

> I take 'permanent' in this connection to mean such as will continue indefinitely unless something is done to remove it. Thus a building which infringes ancient lights is perma-nent within the rule, for, though it can be removed before the reversion falls into posses-sion, still it will continue until it be removed. On the other hand, a noisy trade and the exercise of an alleged right of way, are not in their nature permanent within the rule, for they cease of themselves, unless there be someone to continue them.[134]

In accordance with this principle, a reversioner may sue where an adjoining land-owner constructs a house, the eaves of which project over his land and discharge rain-water on to it.[135] Similarly, physical damage caused to the reversioner's buildings will afford the reversioner a cause of action.[136] Conversely, no such action will lie where the nuisance complained of comprises merely temporary annoyance caused by the emission of smoke.[137]

(3) Those with easements and *profits à prendre*

As Lord Goff observed in *Hunter v Canary Wharf Ltd*, '[n]uisance is a tort against land, including interests in land such as easements and profits'.[138] In the case of a *profit à prendre*, the claimant can sue without the need to prove that he holds title to the land affected[139] because the person with a *profit à prendre* 'has such possessory rights that he can ... maintain an action on the case for nuisance at common law for such an inter-ference with his right as is proved'.[140] By contrast, easements are always appurtenant to land and the claimant must always be able to show his proprietary or possessory right to the dominant tenement; for, by definition, he can never have title to the servi-ent tenement burdened by the easement.[141] Furthermore, it is also clear that no claim

---

[133] [1911] 1 Ch 393, at 404.
[134] Ibid at 404.   [135] *Tucker v Newman* (1839) 11 Ad & El 40.
[136] *Meux's Brewery Co v City of London Electric Lighting Co* [1895] 1 Ch 287.
[137] *Simpson v Savage* (1856) 1 CBNS 347.   [138] [1997] AC 655, at 702.
[139] *Nicholls v Ely Beet Sugar Factory Ltd (No 1)* [1931] 2 Ch 84, at 88.
[140] *Fitzgerald v Firbank* [1897] 2 Ch 96, at 101–2.
[141] *Paine & Co Ltd v St Neots Gas & Coke Co* [1939] 3 All ER 812, at 823–4.

will lie in respect of a mere trifling interference with an easement, for '[t]he plaintiff cannot complain, unless he can prove an obstruction which injures him'.[142]

(4) Victims of public authority 'nuisances'

Notwithstanding the usual restrictive rules governing *locus standi* in private nuisance, it is clear that those who would otherwise be denied a cause of action – such as the landowner's employees, lodgers, or children – will nonetheless be able to claim a remedy in certain circumstances under the Human Rights Act 1998.[143] This is because the Act effectively imposes a *positive* obligation on all public authorities to ensure that all citizens enjoy equal respect for their private lives.[144] Should they fail to observe this duty, they may be held liable in damages – even to non-landowners – under section 8 of the Act as *Dobson v Thames Water Utilities Ltd*[145] confirms. Such actions are not strictly nuisance actions: they lie for invasion of a privacy right (not a right contingent upon land ownership). That being so, a landowner may seek damages under both heads, and the damages under the Act are not to be deducted from the damages at common law.[146]

The only basis on which the public authority may derogate from this obligation to respect privacy rights is contained in Article 8(2) of the European Convention of Human Rights. There, derogation is only justified if, on balance, it would be in the public interest. But even where the public interest is best served by non-observance of the duty, it is important to note what Buckley J said in *Dennis v Ministry of Defence*:[147] namely, that 'common fairness demands that where the interests of a minority, let alone an individual, are seriously interfered with because of an overriding public interest, the minority should be compensated'.[148] In other words, compensation can still be claimed even if the public authority was not strictly obliged in the circumstances to act in accordance with the claimant's Article 8 right. And while the measure of damages may not equate precisely with the measure of damages available under the common law, there is unlikely to be an appreciable practical difference.[149]

---

[142] *Thorpe v Brumfitt* (1872–73) LR 8 Ch App 650, at 656.

[143] This potential source of redress was recognised by the House of Lords in *Marcic v Thames Water Utilities Ltd* [2004] 2 AC 42 (though on the facts, no action lay because the applicable statutory scheme and tasks of the regulator were found to be compliant with the 1998 Act).

[144] Human Rights Act 1998, s 6; European Convention on Human Rights, Art 8(1).

[145] [2009] 3 All ER 319.

[146] *Dobson v Thames Water Utilities Ltd* [2010] HLR 9, at [44].

[147] [2003] Env LR 34.   [148] Ibid at [63].

[149] Two possible differences are as follows. (1) Actions under the 1998 Act are subject to a shorter limitation period than under the common law (one year: Human Rights Act 1998, s 7(5)). (2) Damages under the Act may not always be as generous as those under the common law as they are assessed on somewhat narrower bases.

(B) MORE DOUBTFUL CASES

(1) Certain claimants relying on the Human Rights Act

For present purposes, *Dobson* and *Dennis* really only establish that those lacking a proprietary interest will nonetheless be able to sue public authorities under section 8 of the Human Rights Act 1998. But in so doing, they raise the question of whether the common law can now sensibly retain its restrictive rules on *locus standi*. There are two arguments against it being able to do so, and both arise from the effect of the Human Rights Act on the development of the common law. The first argument rests upon an analogy with a negligence case, *D v East Berkshire Community NHS Trust*;[150] the second derives from the possible horizontal effect of the Act.

By analogy with the approach of the Court of Appeal in *D v East Berkshire Community NHS Trust* (which was later affirmed by the House of Lords), the Supreme Court may on some future occasion be prepared to change its restrictive approach to *locus standi*. In the *East Berkshire* case, the Court of Appeal held that, although the English courts had traditionally granted public authorities something close to an immunity from suit in negligence, no such immunity could be maintained where an alternative action under the 1998 Act was available since the near-immunity was worthless in the face of an alternative cause of action.[151] (Two members of the House of Lords explicitly confirmed this reasoning on appeal.[152]) Arguably, a similar approach could be adopted in relation to the *locus standi* rule in private nuisance. That is, since there is an effective remedy under the 1998 Act for those suffering public authority interferences with their right to respect for private life, it is now more or less pointless to retain the common law bar on a nuisance action for those lacking a sufficient proprietary interest.[153] For the present, however, the rule in *Hunter* remains intact.

The second argument rests upon the possible horizontal effect of the 1998 Act. That is, since the English courts are public authorities for the purposes of the 1998 Act,[154] it is now unlawful for them to act in a way that is incompatible with a 'Convention right'.[155] Put otherwise, it could be argued that they are now required to develop the common law in a manner that ensures its consistency with the rights embodied in the European Convention on Human Rights.[156] And since Article 8(1) of that Convention affords *all citizens* an equal right to respect for their private lives (regardless of their proprietary rights in land), it becomes possible to contend that the common law of

---

[150]   [2005] 2 AC 373 (affirming the decision of the Court of Appeal: [2004] QB 558).

[151]   [2004] QB 558, at [80]–[87] (composite judgment). Note, however, that a more accurate understanding is that the passage of the Human Rights Act only *partially* undermined the common law position.

[152]   [2005] 2 AC 373, at [30] and [65].

[153]   Such responsibility need not involve the public authority in having, through its employees, directly caused the nuisance. It would suffice if the authority had authorised, continued, or adopted the nuisance (as described below).

[154]   Human Rights Act 1998, s 6(3)(a).

[155]   Human Rights Act 1998, s 6(1). For these purposes, 'acts' include 'failures to act' – eg, failures to fulfil the several positive obligations that exist under the Convention: see, eg, *Z v UK* (2002) 34 EHRR 97.

[156]   For a general discussion of the horizontal effect of the Act, see Hunt [1998] PL 423.

nuisance is presently incompatible with the Convention in so far as only those with a proprietary interest can invoke nuisance law in respect of interferences that disturb their private lives and for which someone *other than* a public authority is responsible. The scope for this argument has chiefly been recognised by academics,[157] but in *McKenna v British Aluminium Ltd*, Neuberger J saw some potential mileage in it.[158] That said, the argument is less than convincing so long as the gist of a nuisance action remains separate from an action based on the right to respect for one's private life.

(2) Spouses in possession of 'home rights'?

If the facts of *Malone v Laskey* were to arise again today, it is by no means certain that the same decision would be reached. This is because section 30 of the Family Law Act 1996 confers upon spouse (or civil partner) X (who has no proprietary interest in the home), certain rights known simply enough as 'home rights' *so long as* his or her spouse (or civil partner) does have a proprietary right to the home. The key question is whether these 'home rights' are sufficient to confer upon spouse (or civil partner) X a sufficient possessory interest to ground a nuisance action. Section 30 of the Family Law Act makes plain that, in these circumstances X has a right not to be evicted by his or her spouse or civil partner (if X is currently in occupation).[159] It also states that X will have a right, so long as the *leave of the court has been given*, to enter and occupy the home.[160] Clearly, the section aims to secure the occupation rights of non-owning spouses and civil partners. But this does not necessarily mean that such rights suffice for the purpose of the *locus standi* rule in nuisance law. The matter was considered in only two of the speeches delivered by their Lordships in *Hunter v Canary Wharf Ltd*, and what they had to say was less than conclusive. So, given that *Hunter* is inconclusive, we can only really speculate on how the matter may be resolved if ever it is litigated. To begin with, it can be argued that the first of the two rights conferred – the right not to be evicted or excluded from the home *by the other spouse or civil partner* – is probably insufficient, because the right is a right as against the other adult occupant. It is, then, properly construed, more in the nature of a personal right than a proprietary right. Also, as regards the second of the two rights – the right to enter and occupy the dwelling house with the leave of the court – it can be argued that there is no automatic right held by the relevant spouse or civil partner (given that the leave of the court must specifically have been obtained). But once such leave has been granted, it could well be seen as possessing a sufficiently proprietary character.

(3) Claimants suffering personal injuries, damage to chattels, or economic loss

It was held in *Hunter v Canary Wharf Ltd*[161] that personal injuries are not, per se, recoverable in an action for private nuisance. Nonetheless, an action will lie where 'the injury to the amenity of the land consists in the fact that persons on it are liable

---

[157] See, eg, Wright, *Tort Law & Human Rights* (2001), ch 8.   [158] [2002] Env LR 34, at [53].
[159] Family Law Act 1996, s 30(2)(a).   [160] Family Law Act 1996, s 30(2)(b).
[161] [1997] 2 All ER 426, at 442.

to suffer inconvenience, annoyance or illness'.[162] The point is one of emphasis. The personal injury, to be recoverable, must be seen in terms of a diminution in the capacity of the land to be enjoyed. That being so, where defective wiring in a neighbouring house causes a fire that spreads to the claimant's house, the claimant should be allowed to recover not only for the damage caused to his house but also for any burns he sustains because it is not only the land, but also the amenity of the land (characterised in terms of the ability to live there free from burns) that has been affected. The matter has resonance at the stage of quantifying damages: 'the reduction in amenity value is the same whether the land is occupied by the family man or the bachelor…the quantum of damages in private nuisance does not depend on the number of those enjoying the land in question'.[163] In other words, there will be no simple multiplication of damages just because more than one person is affected.[164] Yet if the nuisance does affect a whole family, 'the experience of the members of that family is likely to be the best evidence available…upon which the financial assessment of diminution of amenity value must depend'.[165]

So far as damage to chattels is concerned, it is also reasonably well established that, again, private nuisance will afford a remedy. In *Midwood & Co Ltd v Manchester Corpn*,[166] for example, damages were awarded by the Court of Appeal for loss of stock in trade; while in *Halsey v Esso Petroleum Co Ltd*[167] they were awarded for damage to washing on a clothes line. Notwithstanding the fact that in *Hunter* their Lordships staunchly reasserted the principle that nuisance was a tort to *land*, it was also explicitly stated that an action in respect of *consequential* damage to chattels was recoverable.[168]

Finally, let us consider economic loss. In this context, it is clear, as Lord Hoffmann recognised in *Hunter*, that consequential economic loss in the form of the claimant's inability to use the land for the purposes of his business is recoverable.[169] Beyond this, matters are less clear. In two cases[170] decided according to the rule in *Rylands v Fletcher* it has been suggested that, in principle, the recoverability of pure economic loss is possible. Since Lord Goff's view in the *Cambridge Water* case was that the rule in *Rylands v Fletcher* was a tort derived from nuisance, it could be argued that there should be no objection to pure economic loss being recovered in the latter tort, too, *so long as* it arises out of an interference with the amenity of the land.[171]

---

[162] Ibid at 452.
[163] Ibid at 442.
[164] But note that personal injuries are recoverable in the tort of public nuisance (see below).
[165] *Dobson v Thames Water Utilities Ltd* [2010] HLR 9, at [33].   [166] [1905] 2 KB 597.
[167] [1961] 2 All ER 145.   [168] [1997] 2 All ER 426, at 452.   [169] Ibid.
[170] *British Celanese Ltd v A H Hunt (Capacitors) Ltd* [1969] 2 All ER 1252; *Ryeford Homes Ltd v Sevenoaks DC* [1989] 2 EGLR 281.
[171] But cf the (*obiter*) view that the cost of replacement cooking facilities necessitated by a disturbed gas supply is irrecoverable: *Anglian Water Services Ltd v Crawshaw Robbins & Co Ltd* 2002 WL 31523191, at [124].

SECTION 4   WHO CAN BE SUED?

A person is liable in nuisance only if he bears 'some degree of personal responsibility'.[172] Such persons can conveniently be identified under three main heads.

(A) CREATORS

If the actual wrongdoer is invested with the management and control of the premises from which the nuisance emanates, then he is liable irrespective of whether he is an occupier of those premises in the normal sense of the word.[173] Even though the person who created the interference was neither at the time of the proceedings, nor at the time when he created the interference, in occupation or control of the premises from which it emanated, but merely created it with the authority of the occupier of the premises, he may still be liable.[174] Nor will he be excused simply because he lacks the right to enter on to the premises in order to abate it.[175] In accordance with ordinary principles of tortious liability, anyone who authorises another to commit a nuisance is himself also liable. So, for example, a local authority is liable where it authorises the use of its land as a go-kart circuit, where a nuisance is the known and inevitable consequence of go-kart racing taking place there.[176] If, however, land is let by a local authority to persons who may or may not cause a nuisance, no such liability will attach as the eventuality of a nuisance is not inevitable.[177] Nor will a local authority be liable if it lets premises to tenants who, in poorly sound-proofed buildings, cause annoyance to others simply by using their premises in the normal way.[178] It is only the authorisation of conduct that will *definitely* cause a nuisance that enables the courts to treat the landowner as if he had caused the interference himself. Thus, it was held in *Hussain v Lancaster City Council*[179] that since the acts complained of – racial harassment committed by the defendant council's tenants against local shopkeepers – had no direct connection with the tenants' use of the premises they rented from the defendants, nuisance liability could not be imposed on the defendants. The council could only be held liable in respect of uses of the tenants' council houses that they

---

[172] *Sedleigh-Denfield v O'Callaghan* [1940] AC 880, at 897.

[173] *Hall v Beckenham Corpn* [1949] 1 KB 716.   [174] *Southwark LBC v Tanner* [2001] 1 AC 1.

[175] *Thompson v Gibson* (1841) 7 M & W 456. In *Southport Corpn v Esso Petroleum Co Ltd* [1953] 2 All ER 1204, at 1207, Devlin J said *obiter*: 'I can see no reason why...if the defendant as a licensee or trespasser misuses someone else's land, he should not be liable for a nuisance'.

[176] *Tetley v Chitty* [1986] 1 All ER 663.

[177] *Smith v Scott* [1973] Ch 314. Cf *Lippiatt v South Gloucestershire Council* [1999] 4 All ER 149 (travellers on D's land used D's land as a base for forays on to C's land. D knew of these forays and could arguably be deemed to have authorised them. D's strike-out application was therefore refused).

[178] *Southwark LBC v Tanner* [2001] 1 AC 1.

[179] [1999] 4 All ER 125. Cf *Lippiatt v South Gloucestershire Council* [1999] 4 All ER 149.

had authorised and that had caused a nuisance. In this case, there was no such land use by the council tenants.[180]

Where the interference complained of arises from a 'state of affairs' that was created by the defendant,[181] he will again be held liable (even though his initial conduct does not, of itself, amount to a nuisance) *so long as* harm to the claimant is a foreseeable consequence of that initial conduct. Thus, he who plants poplar trees – itself an innocuous act – is liable in nuisance in respect of the indirect harm caused by their roots spreading under neighbouring land.[182] Equally, maintaining defective electric mains gives rise to liability for foreseeable damage that in fact ensues.[183] Where, on the other hand, the defendant creates a state of affairs that will not foreseeably result in a nuisance, the courts will refuse to attach liability.

> In *Ilford UDC v Beal*,[184] D erected a retaining wall along the bank of a river. Because the wall was not constructed in accordance with the best engineering practice it was later completely undermined by the river. This undermining caused the wall to move forward a foot or two where it came to press against, and cause damage to, C's sewer. C neither knew, nor ought to have known, about the presence of the sewer. The damage to the sewer was therefore unforeseeable and D was held not liable in nuisance.

Although the key to liability in such cases is undoubtedly the remoteness of the injurious consequences of the defendant's initial conduct, it is not always easy to distinguish those cases in which the defendant genuinely created the dangerous state of affairs from those in which he merely failed to remedy it. The point can be illustrated by reference to *Goldman v Hargrave*[185] in which the defendant failed to deal adequately with a red gum tree that caught fire after being struck by lightning. One of the Privy Council's findings of fact was that the defendant's method of dealing with the fire gave rise to a foreseeable risk of the embers rekindling and the fire spreading to the claimant's land (as in fact occurred). It is not wholly clear whether the defendant's wrongdoing amounted to misfeasance (in that he dealt inappropriately with a burning tree thereby creating a risk to his neighbour) or nonfeasance (in that he failed to avert an extant risk of fire spreading). Had the tree not been felled in the manner adopted by the defendant, the fire might never have rekindled and spread to the defendant's land. On the other hand, had the tree not been struck by lightning in the first place, a hazardous state of affairs would never have arisen on the defendant's land. Whether

---

[180] But this decision skates rather too close for comfort to supporting the untenable proposition that a nuisance requires an improper use of D's land (on which see *L E Jones (Insurance Brokers) Ltd v Portsmouth CC* [2003] 1 WLR 427).

[181] Cf circumstances in which D only inherits or continues a state of affairs produced by a third party. In such cases, D's liability attaches because of his failure to remedy the potentially injurious state of affairs: see *Delaware Mansions Ltd v Westminster CC* [2002] 1 AC 321.

[182] *Butler v Standard Telephones and Cables Ltd* [1940] 1 KB 399; *McCombe v Read* [1955] 2 QB 429.

[183] *Midwood & Co Ltd v Manchester Corpn* [1905] 2 KB 597.   [184] [1925] 1 KB 671.

[185] [1967] 1 AC 645.

cases such as this are better seen as involving misfeasance or nonfeasance is by no means easy to decide.[186]

(B) OCCUPIERS

As we noted in the previous section, the occupier of premises will be liable in respect of nuisances that he has himself created. But he may also be liable in other circumstances, too. In the main, these cases turn on the occupier having 'adopted' or 'continued' the nuisance by failing to take reasonable steps to remedy a potential hazard on land that he occupies. Broadly, an occupier adopts a nuisance if he makes use of an 'erection, building, bank or artificial contrivance which constitutes the nuisance', whereas he continues the nuisance if he, with '[actual] knowledge or presumed knowledge of its existence, fails to take any reasonable means to bring it to an end'.[187] In determining what amounts to the reasonable means he might be expected to take, the court, for reasons of justice, *may* have regard to his limited financial and other resources;[188] especially if the defendant has had the state of affairs involuntarily thrust upon him.

So far as the liability of occupiers for nuisance is concerned, there are four main categories of case to consider. But before examining them, it is worth noting that the first three categories would also apparently apply in respect, not just of someone in control of the land, but also of someone in control of the hazard, *but not the land*.[189]

(1) Acts of a trespasser

If the dangerous state of affairs on the defendant's land is created by a trespasser, so long as the occupier knows or ought to know about it, he is liable in nuisance in respect of damage thereby caused to his neighbour. The leading case is *Sedleigh-Denfield v O'Callaghan*.[190] There, a drainage pipe had been laid by a trespasser. Initially, the defendant occupiers had no knowledge of the fact that this had been done. But later, when they discovered it, the defendants used the pipe in order to drain excess water from their own land. Due to misplaced grating, the pipe became blocked. The defendants' servant – who had been responsible for periodically maintaining the drainage system – ought to have noticed the risk of flooding that it posed. But he did not notice it, and the blocked pipe caused water to overflow on to the claimant's premises. In finding the defendant liable, the House of Lords stressed the importance of the defendant's (presumed) knowledge of the risk:

> An occupier is not *prima facie* responsible for a nuisance created without his knowledge and consent. If he is to be liable a further condition is necessary, namely, that he had

---

[186] In the eventuality, the Privy Council treated *Goldman* as a nonfeasance case.
[187] *Sedleigh-Denfield v O'Callaghan* [1940] AC 880, at 894.
[188] But not always, see *Abbahall v Smee* [2003] 1 All ER 465.
[189] *Jones Ltd v Portsmouth CC* [2003] 1 WLR 427.   [190] [1940] AC 880.

knowledge or means of knowledge, that he knew or should have known, of the nuisance in time to correct it.[191]

It is important to distinguish cases such as *Sedleigh-Denfield* from two further kinds of case. First, from those such as *Smith v Littlewoods Organisation Ltd*[192] where the House of Lords held that there was no liability where the trespassers had, *in the absence of actual or presumed knowledge* on the part of the defendants, caused a fire in the defendants' disused cinema which spread to the claimant's property. Second, from those where the third party merely uses the defendant's land as a means of gaining access to the claimant's land rather than, as in *Sedleigh-Denfield*, where the third party's mischievous act or omission actually occurs on the defendant's land. In such cases, the Court of Appeal has held that the defendant will be free of any general liability in respect of the acts of such third parties.[193] A final point that ought to be noted is that, where the defendant's failure to abate a nuisance can be attributed to a pre-existing duty on his part to consult the interested parties before any remedial steps can permissibly be taken, the defendant's inaction will not be taken by the courts to be an unreasonable failure to erase the menacing state of affairs.[194]

(2) Acts of nature

If a dangerous state of affairs arises on the defendant's land due to an act of nature of which the occupier knows or ought to know, he is liable in nuisance if damage occurs to a neighbouring landowner. In *Goldman v Hargrave*, the facts of which we have already noted, the Privy Council extended the rule in *Sedleigh-Denfield v O'Callaghan* – that an occupier must take reasonable steps to remedy a potentially hazardous state of affairs – to cases in which the danger arises by an act of God. However, Lord Wilberforce added the important qualification that the unreasonableness of the defendant's attempts to avert such a danger must be judged in the light of his financial and other resources. He said:

> [T]he law must take account of the fact that the occupier on whom the duty is cast has, *ex hypothesi*, had this hazard thrust upon him through no seeking or fault of his own. His interest and his resources, whether physical or material, may be of very modest character…A rule which required of him in such unsought circumstances in his neighbour's interest a physical effort of which he is not capable, or an excessive expenditure of money, would be unenforceable or unjust.[195]

Although *Goldman* is, strictly, an Australian decision, its underlying rationale was adopted in the English case of *Leakey v National Trust for Places of Historic Interest*

---

[191] Ibid at 904. See also *Lippiatt v South Gloucestershire Council* [1999] 4 All ER 149.
[192] [1987] AC 241.
[193] *P Perl Exporters Ltd v Camden LBC* [1984] QB 342.
[194] *Page Motors Ltd v Epsom and Ewell BC* (1981) 80 LGR 337.
[195] [1967] 1 AC 645, at 663. This might be seen as undermining the supposed strictness of nuisance liability. On the other hand, it might be seen as being a not unreasonable user of the land (and, therefore, a not unreasonable interference).

or *Natural Beauty*.[196] There, the defendants owned land on which there stood a large mound of earth which they knew to be prone to subsidence. When, following a particularly dry summer which caused cracks in the earth to appear, the mound finally gave way causing damage to the claimant's houses, it was held by the Court of Appeal that the defendants were liable in respect of the landslip.[197]Although the defendants had given permission to the claimant to abate the cause of the nuisance, they had themselves done nothing to remove the danger.[198]

(3) Nuisances created by independent contractors

An employer, naturally enough, is vicariously liable for nuisances created by an employee in the course of his employment.[199] But as regards independent contractors, the defendant is only liable in respect of their failure to take precautions if, as Slesser LJ held in *Matania v National Provincial Bank Ltd and Elevenist Syndicate Ltd*,[200] 'the act done is one which in its very nature involves a special danger of nuisance being complained of'. In that case, the occupier of the first floor of a building was held liable to the superjacent occupiers in respect of the dust and noise generated by the alteration works carried out by the independent contractors he had employed.

The nature of an occupier's liability for independent contractors was more widely stated by Cockburn CJ in *Bower v Peate*, when holding a principal liable for his independent contractor's withdrawing support from the buildings of the claimant:

> a man who orders a work to be executed, from which, in the natural course of things, injurious consequences to his neighbour must be expected to arise...is bound to see to the doing of that which is necessary to prevent the mischief, and cannot relieve himself of his responsibility by employing someone else.[201]

(4) Acts of a previous occupier

If the predecessor of the defendant occupier created a hazardous state of affairs and the defendant knows or ought to know of its existence then, according to Scrutton LJ in *St Anne's Well Brewery Co v Roberts*,[202] he is liable in respect of any damage to which it gives rise. Even if the construction created by the occupier's predecessor in title did not pose a threat at the time of its creation, that person may nonetheless be held liable in respect of any hazards it subsequently gives rise to so long as he knew, or ought to have known, that such a threat was posed.[203]

---

[196] [1980] QB 485.

[197] But note that where D's *nonfeasance* is in issue, the court's expectations of him will diminish: *Holbeck Hall Hotel Ltd v Scarborough BC* [2000] 2 All ER 705.

[198] But note that it is doubtful whether liability arises for the presence of animals *ferae naturae* or failure to remove them: *Farrer v Nelson* (1885) 15 QBD 258; *Seligman v Docker* [1949] Ch 53.

[199] *Spicer v Smee* [1946] 1 All ER 489, at 493 (*obiter*). [200] [1936] 2 All ER 633, at 646.

[201] (1876) 1 QBD 321, at 326. Followed in *Spicer v Smee* [1946] 1 All ER 489, at 495.

[202] (1928) 140 LT 1 (part of an ancient wall collapsed damaging C's inn but, on the facts, D was found not liable because of the lack of constructive knowledge that the wall was likely to collapse).

[203] *Bybrook Barn Garden Centre Ltd v Kent CC* [2001] Env LR 30.

(C) LANDLORDS

We have already seen that a landlord who authorises his tenant to commit a nuisance is treated, in law, as the creator of the nuisance, and will himself be liable for that nuisance.[204] But there are three further situations that call for discussion in which the landlord *may* be held liable qua landlord (as opposed to qua creator).

First, if at the date of letting the landlord knows or ought to know of the condition giving rise to the actionable nuisance, he will be liable despite the tenancy if he has not taken a covenant to repair the premises from the tenant.[205] According to Goddard J in *Wilchick v Marks and Silverstone*, a landlord ought to know not only of those defects that are patently obvious but also of those that are capable of being discovered by use of reasonable care.[206] Second, a landlord will also be liable for dangerous conditions that arise from want of repair during the currency of the tenancy if he has covenanted to perform such repairs,[207] reserves the right to enter and repair,[208] or has an implied right to enter and repair.[209] Furthermore, where the landlord's premises are situated on a highway, he will be liable to passers-by or similarly liable to neighbouring landowners regardless of whether the want of repair is attributable to his (that is, the landlord's) want of care.[210] Finally, where a landlord does something to the premises that leads inevitably to a nuisance if the premises are occupied, then he, rather than the tenants, will be liable. In *Toff v McDowell*,[211] for example, the tenants had used the premises in a perfectly normal fashion but, because the landlord had taken up the floor covering, anyone occupying the premises subsequently would sound unbearably loud to the subjacent claimant. The landlord was held liable and directed to replace the flooring.[212]

As regards the liability of a tenant, it is well established that, if he has covenanted to repair the premises, he is liable in nuisance for damage arising from a failure to effect those repairs.[213] On the other hand, the mere fact that the landlord has covenanted to

---

[204] See, eg, *Lippiatt v South Gloucestershire Council* [1999] 4 All ER 149.

[205] *Todd v Flight* (1860) 9 CBNS 377; *Gandy v Jubber* (1864) 5 B & S 78 (reversed (1865) 9 B & S 15); *Bowen v Anderson* [1894] 1 QB 164.   [206] [1934] 2 KB 56, at 67–8.

[207] *Payne v Rogers* (1794) 2 Hy Bl 350. Where there is no such covenant, the landlord will not be liable for adopting or continuing a nuisance if it is attributable to defective construction of the premises: *Jackson v JH Watson Property Investment Ltd* [2008] 11 EG 94.

[208] *Wilchick v Marks and Silverstone* [1934] 2 KB 56; *Heap v Ind Coope and Allsopp Ltd* [1940] 2 KB 476; *Spicer v Smee* [1946] 1 All ER 489.   [209] *Mint v Good* [1951] 1 KB 517.

[210] *Wringe v Cohen* [1940] 1 KB 229 (followed in *Mint v Good* [1951] 1 KB 517). The importance of the rule in *Wringe v Cohen* has since been amplified by the imposition on landlords of onerous obligations to maintain houses, let for fewer than seven years, in a state of good repair (see the Landlord and Tenant Act 1985, ss 11–16). On the other hand, the rule in *Wringe v Cohen* does not apply to premises on a highway, nor does it apply to nuisances arising from acts of trespassers or processes of nature: *Cushing v Peter Walker & Son (Warrington and Burton) Ltd* [1941] 2 All ER 693.

[211] (1993) 25 HLR 650. To similar effect, see *Stannard v Charles Pitcher Ltd* [2002] BLR 441.

[212] Cf *Southwark LBC v Tanner* [2001] 1 AC 1 (D had not done anything to the rented premises so as to render a disturbance to C inevitable: D was not liable).

[213] *Brew Bros Ltd v Snax (Ross) Ltd* [1970] 1 QB 612. But note that the tenant's covenant to repair does not exonerate the landlord from liability for the repair obligations placed upon landlords under the Landlord and Tenant Act 1985, ss 11–16 of which are inescapable.

repair the premises, will not, ipso facto, exonerate the tenant from nuisance liability.[214] As Lawrence LJ explained in *St Anne's Well Brewery Co v Roberts*:[215]

> Any bargain made by the person responsible [ie, the occupier] to his neighbour or to the public that another person should perform that obligation may give rise to rights as between the two contracting parties, but does not, in my judgment, in any way affect any right of third parties, who are not parties or privy to such contract.

SECTION 5   MUST THE INTERFERENCE EMANATE FROM THE DEFENDANT'S LAND?

The land from which the interference has its source will normally be in the ownership or control of the defendant. Indeed, in so far as nuisance law is designed to provide a means of regulating competing land uses, it might even be argued that land ownership on the part of the defendant is as important as the classic requirement that the claimant must have a proprietary interest.[216] Nonetheless, dicta abound to the effect that the defendant need not be the owner of the land from which the nuisance emanates. Thus, in *Sedleigh-Denfield v O'Callaghan* Lord Wright declared 'the ground of responsibility' to be merely 'the possession and control of the land from which the nuisance proceeds'.[217] And in *Halsey v Esso Petroleum Co Ltd*[218] the defendants were even held liable in respect of the noise generated by their lorries driving along a public street late at night.

SECTION 6   DEFENCES

(A) STATUTORY AUTHORITY

The fact that the activity giving rise to the interference complained of is authorised by statute is the single most important defence in the law of private nuisance. Many activities which interfere with the enjoyment of land are carried out by public or private enterprises in pursuance of an Act of Parliament. But if the statute merely confers a permissive power, then, it has been held, the power must be exercised so as not to interfere with private rights.[219] Whether the activity complained of is explicitly authorised by statute, and whether any potential nuisance action is thereby defeated, is a matter of statutory interpretation.

---

[214] *Wilchick v Marks and Silverstone* [1934] 2 KB 56.   [215] (1928) 140 LT 1, at 8.

[216] In *Miller v Jackson* [1977] QB 966, at 980, Lord Denning MR proclaimed that, '[i]t is the very essence of a private nuisance that it is the unreasonable use by a man of *his land* to the detriment of his neighbour' (emphasis added).   [217] [1940] AC 880, at 903.

[218] [1961] 2 All ER 145.   [219] *Metropolitan Asylum District Managers v Hill* (1881) 6 App Cas 193.

In *Allen v Gulf Oil Refining Ltd*[220] D was authorised by statute compulsorily to acquire land near Milford Haven for the purpose of constructing and operating an oil refinery. C complained that the smell, noise, and vibrations made by the refinery constituted a nuisance. D pleaded the defence of statutory authority.

The House of Lords held that the claimants would first have to establish a nuisance, and that the change in the local environment caused by authorising the operation of the refinery was relevant to that issue.[221] If a nuisance could be established, then the company had to prove that it was an inevitable result of carrying on a refinery there.[222]

It follows from this that the defendant must use all due diligence in performing the activity authorised by statute.[223] If he fails so to do, he will be held to have exceeded the level of damage for which he was granted immunity by the statute. So, in *Tate & Lyle Industries Ltd v Greater London Council*,[224] the defendants were held liable in public nuisance where reasonable care in the design and erection of new ferry terminals, which they had been authorised to build by statute, would have at least partially avoided the siltation of the River Thames which damaged the claimants' business.

One further matter that bedevils the law on the defence of statutory authority occurs where the defendant is a public authority. More particularly, the problem surfaces where the public body is invested with a *discretionary* statutory power and it is argued that it ought to have used that power in order to prevent a nuisance. In *Marcic v Thames Water Utilities Ltd*,[225] the Court of Appeal suggested that such powers may well need to be used in this way; but, on appeal, the matter was not considered by the House of Lords.[226] It remains to be seen how influential the approach of the Court of Appeal will be in future cases where the relevant legislation does not, as in *Marcic*, provide an exclusive statutory mechanism for dealing with complaints.

(B) PRESCRIPTION

The right to do something that would otherwise constitute private nuisance may be acquired as an easement by prescription. In order to decide whether this defence avails, one must look to the law of real property to identify whether the right claimed is capable of constituting an easement. The most common way of acquiring an easement is by 20 years' overt and undisturbed user. One may, for example, acquire the right to pour

---

[220] [1981] AC 1001.
[221] This point was endorsed by Buckley J in *Gillingham BC v Medway (Chatham) Dock Co Ltd* [1993] QB 343, at 360 in relation to the (broadly) analogous defence of authorisation by planning permission. But note: an injunction can exceptionally be obtained to restrain D from engaging in a land use authorised by planning permission: *Wheeler v JJ Saunders Ltd* [1995] 2 All ER 697.
[222] In this respect, the House of Lords followed its earlier decision in *Manchester Corpn v Farnworth* [1930] AC 171 (power station established by statute emitted poisonous fumes that damaged C's fields).
[223] *Marcic v Thames Water Utilities Ltd* [2004] 2 AC 42.
[224] [1983] 2 AC 509. See also *Department of Transport v NW Water Authority* [1984] AC 336.
[225] [2002] QB 929.   [226] [2004] 2 AC 42.

effluent into a stream, although not if it is done secretly.[227] Equally, one may acquire the right do such things as discharge surface water,[228] or rainwater from the eaves of one's house,[229] on to a neighbour's land. It is also well established that the user must be continuous. So, where there is perpetual change in the amount of inconvenience caused – as in the case of fumes or noise – it is doubtful whether an easement can be obtained.[230]

One matter beyond doubt is that if the user is prohibited by statute, it cannot be claimed as a prescriptive right.[231] Equally, 'acts which are *neither preventable nor actionable* cannot be relied upon to found an easement'.[232] So, where a confectioner had for more than 20 years made certain noises on his land through the operation of his equipment, which then, for the first time, interfered with the claimant doctor's user of his land, the defendant could not plead a prescriptive right.[233] As there had been no invasion of a legal right before the consulting room was built, there were no steps until then that the claimant could have taken to prevent the interference.

(C) THE CLAIMANT'S CONDUCT

It is no defence that the claimant came to the nuisance by occupying the land adjoining it.[234] Nor is it a defence that the nuisance has only arisen because the claimant has chosen to use a particular part of his land in a way that heightens his sensitivity.[235] In any case, it may be assumed that the claimant has the normal duty in tort to take reasonable steps to mitigate his loss. He should, for instance, take reasonable steps to minimise the damage when his land is flooded in consequence of his neighbour's tortious conduct. The ordinary principles of causation apply in nuisance law and, if the nuisance is caused by the claimant's own acts, he cannot recover.[236] The defences of consent and assumption of risk are also available. *Pwllbach Colliery Co Ltd v Woodman*[237] illustrates the operation of the consent defence.

A lessor allowed his lessee to mine for coal. The issue was whether he could complain when the lessee's non-negligent operations caused coal dust to be deposited on other land owned by the lessor. The House of Lords held that only if the terms of the lease could be construed as authorising a nuisance was there any defence. Their Lordships held that, first, the nuisance was not a necessary consequence of carrying on that trade and, second,

---

[227] *Liverpool Corpn v H Coghill & Son* [1918] 1 Ch 307.   [228] *A-G v Copeland* [1902] 1 KB 690.
[229] *Thomas v Thomas* (1835) 2 Cr M & R 34.
[230] *Hulley v Silversprings Bleaching and Dyeing Co Ltd* [1922] 2 Ch 268. See also the rather bolder, unsupported suggestion that one can never acquire a prescriptive right to produce a noise that would otherwise be a nuisance in the first instance case of *Lawrence v Fen Tigers* [2011] EWHC 360, at [223].
[231] *Liverpool Corpn v H Coghill & Son Ltd* [1918] 1 Ch 307.
[232] *Sturges v Bridgman* (1879) 11 Ch D 852, at 863 (emphasis added).   [233] Ibid.
[234] *Bliss v Hall* (1838) 4 Bing NC 183; *Miller v Jackson* [1977] QB 966 (no defence to a cricket club that the ground first became a nuisance when C built premises close to it).
[235] *Sturges v Bridgman* (1879) 11 Ch D 852.
[236] Cf the case in public nuisance: *Almeroth v Chivers & Sons Ltd* [1948] 1 All ER 53.
[237] [1915] AC 634.

that there had been no express authorisation of the nuisance in the lease. The defence of consent therefore failed.

As regards the assumption of risk, *Kiddle v City Business Properties Ltd*[238] is a case in point. There, the claimant complained of the damage caused to his shop when flooding from the gutter carrying water from a part of the premises retained by the defendant landlord occurred without negligence on the defendant's part. It was held that the tenant took the premises as he found them and must be deemed to have run this risk. Accordingly, his action in nuisance failed.

Contributory negligence on the part of the claimant might also, in principle, be raised as a defence to an action in nuisance; at least where the nuisance arises out of negligent conduct.[239] There is certainly an *obiter dictum* to this effect in the public nuisance case of *Trevett v Lee*.[240]

(D) OTHER DEFENCES

The Fires Prevention (Metropolis) Act 1774 provides that, in an action brought in respect of a fire, it is a defence to prove that the fire began accidentally.[241] But, as Atkinson J held in *Spicer v Smee*,[242] the defence has no application where the fire was caused by the negligence of the defendant, or was intentionally created by him or by those for whom he was responsible. Even when a fire starts accidentally, if the defendant negligently allows it to grow into a raging inferno, the Act will not afford him a defence for the damage it later causes.[243] Accordingly, the defence has no application in nuisance law except, perhaps, where a person would be liable in nuisance even though his conduct was neither intentional nor negligent.

As we saw earlier, an occupier who unreasonably fails to avert a danger to his neighbour arising out of an act of God will be liable in nuisance. Where, however, there is an occurrence alleged by the claimant to be a nuisance, which in truth is an inevitable accident, it is well established that no liability will attach.[244] But it is no defence that the act of the defendant would not have been a nuisance but for the acts of others, provided that the defendant knew what the others were doing.[245]

---

[238] [1942] 1 KB 269.
[239] Query whether the courts would accept this defence where the nuisance was caused by D's deliberate and malicious conduct.
[240] [1955] 1 All ER 406, at 412.
[241] Note that the Act applies generally, not merely to London: *Filliter v Phippard* (1847) 11 QB 347.
[242] [1946] 1 All ER 489.
[243] *Goldman v Hargrave* [1967] 1 AC 645.
[244] *Tennent v Earl of Glasgow* (1864) 2 M 22.
[245] *Thorpe v Brumfitt* (1873) 8 Ch App 650.

SECTION 7   REMEDIES

(A) DAMAGES

The measure of damages in nuisance is similar to that awarded for trespass to land. The claimant is entitled to full reparation for his loss. Where, for instance, a house (or a crop, or something analogous)[246] is destroyed or damaged, then the claimant will recover the difference between the monetary value to him of his interest (whether he is the landlord, tenant, or otherwise) before and after the event.[247] Where business loss is suffered in consequence of the interference, whether by loss of custom[248] or the cost of moving elsewhere,[249] this is also recoverable in nuisance. Where, however, a hotel owner complained of loss of custom caused by nearby building operations, the Court of Appeal reversed an award of damages to the full extent of loss of custom, holding that a certain amount of the interference was reasonable in the circumstances, although likely to lead to some loss of custom. The court therefore assessed what proportion of the business loss was attributable to that excess of noise and dust which alone was actionable.[250] In 1966, in *The Wagon Mound (No 2)*,[251] the Privy Council held that, in public nuisance, it is not enough that the damage is a direct consequence of the wrongful act; it must also be a foreseeable consequence. *Obiter dicta* in the case stated this rule to be applicable also to private nuisance.

The amount to be awarded by way of damages increases the longer the nuisance continues. But, curiously, the law does not treat this as the continuance of the original nuisance complained of, but rather as a new and distinct nuisance. Thus, in one case where a defendant imposed a strain on the claimant's wall by piling earth against it and was sued in nuisance, it was stated that 'a fresh cause of action arises as each brick topples down, and that there is a continuing cause of action until the root of the trouble is eradicated'.[252] Whether the continuance of the interference is characterised as a fresh nuisance or as a prolongation of the original one is largely immaterial so far as the claimant is concerned.[253] He is much more interested in having the nuisance abated and will, in most cases, seek an injunction. However, as we shall see in the

---

[246] See *Marquis of Granby v Bakewell UDC* (1923) 87 JP 105 (destruction of fish).

[247] *Moss v Christchurch RDC* [1925] 2 KB 750. The law does not grant damages based on the cost of restoring the damaged property to its prior state *if* C has no genuine interest in such restoration: *C R Taylor (Wholesale) Ltd v Hepworths Ltd* [1977] 2 All ER 784. See also *Lodge Holes Colliery Co Ltd v Wednesbury Corpn* [1908] AC 323.

[248] *Fritz v Hobson* (1880) 14 Ch D 542.

[249] *Grosvenor Hotel Co v Hamilton* [1894] 2 QB 836, at 840.

[250] *Andrae v Selfridge & Co Ltd* [1938] Ch 1.

[251] [1967] 1 AC 617.

[252] *Maberley v Henry W Peabody & Co of London Ltd* [1946] 2 All ER 192, at 194. See adoption of this approach in *Delaware Mansions Ltd v Westminster CC* [2002] 1 AC 321.

[253] It can, however, be a concern to D who merely continues a nuisance begun by his predecessor. Yet where the nuisance has caused harm of a kind that now requires remedial work, the courts will award dam-

next section, the injunction is a flexible remedy and the court has a statutory power[254] to grant damages in lieu of an injunction (thus enabling it to make an award that takes account of future as well as past harm). The principles governing the exercise of the court's discretion in the exercise of this power were set out by Smith LJ in the leading case of *Shelfer v City of London Electric Lighting Co (No 1)*.[255] There it was stated that the court has jurisdiction to grant damages in lieu where (1) the injury to the claimant is small, (2) it is quantifiable in money terms, (3) it is capable of being adequately compensated in money, and (4) it would be oppressive to the defendant to grant an injunction.[256] The insistence that the harm complained of must be small places an important restriction on the court's ability to grant damages instead of an injunction.[257] In addition, it seems from *Elliott v London Borough of Islington*[258] that a restrictive definition of what amounts to a small degree of harm should be applied. In that case, the pressing of the defendant's tree against the claimant's wall – causing it to move only a few inches – was regarded as 'very considerable harm'. Furthermore, in relation to the fourth limb of the *Shelfer* test, as Bingham MR observed in *Jaggard v Sawyer*, '[i]t is important to bear in mind that the test is one of *oppression*, and the court should not slide into application of a general balance of convenience test'.[259]

(B) INJUNCTION

An injunction is an order from the court directing the defendant to desist from the future commission of any tortious act. It is the remedy most often sought in nuisance cases and is granted on what is often (but inaccurately) described as being a discretionary basis. Thus, even where the claimant can establish an actionable claim, he may nonetheless be refused an injunction. Broadly, there are two factors which influence the courts in deciding whether or not to grant an injunction: the gravity of the interference and the public interest.[260] As regards the first of these, the courts tend to view occasional interferences as insufficiently substantial to warrant the grant of an injunction. Take, for example, *Cooke v Forbes*.[261]

---

ages that reflect the cost of that remedial work regardless of whether some of the harm was occasioned prior to D 'inheriting' the nuisance: *Delaware Mansions Ltd v Westminster CC* [2002] 1 AC 321, at [38].

[254] Senior Courts Act 1981, s 50.

[255] [1895] 1 Ch 287, at 322–3. In this case the court was dealing with the equivalent provision to s 50 of the Senior Courts Act 1981 (Lord Cairns' Act, s 2). The principles enunciated were reiterated in relation to the 1981 Act by Bingham MR in *Jaggard v Sawyer* [1995] 2 All ER 189, at 203.

[256] This means, in effect, that D buys the right to commit the nuisance.

[257] *Wood v Conway Corpn* [1914] 2 Ch 47.

[258] [1991] 1 EGLR 167.

[259] [1995] 2 All ER 189, at 203.

[260] For a fuller account of the principles, see Murphy, *The Law of Nuisance* (2010), ch 6.

[261] (1867) LR 5 Eq 166. Once C has established that a substantial interference has occurred, and is likely to recur, the burden is on D to show special circumstances why an injunction should not be granted: *McKinnon Industries Ltd v Walker* (1951) 3 DLR 577, at 581.

C used a certain bleaching chemical in making cocoa-nut matting. Occasionally, emission of a noxious chemical from D's plant damaged C's manufactures. Without prejudice to a claim in damages, the court refused an injunction because the interference was only occasional.

However, where there is an ongoing interference with the claimant's legal right – eg, his right to light – the courts will presumptively grant an injunction and be prepared to substitute damages for the injunction only in exceptional circumstances.[262]

An example of the role that can be played by the public interest is evident in the judgment of Peter Gibson LJ in *Wheeler v JJ Saunders Ltd*. In that case, the nuisance was caused by the defendant running a pig farm. In relation to the application for an injunction, his Lordship said: 'I can well see that in such a case the public interest must be allowed to prevail and that it would be inappropriate to grant an injunction'.[263]

The fact that the claimant's chief concern is with the future abatement of the nuisance does not mean that he will not also seek damages in respect of the past harm that he has suffered. In consequence, the law of nuisance is complicated by the fact that the claimant may often seek two remedies at once. Of particular note in this context is the Canadian decision that, where both remedies are granted, any damages must not include an element in respect of permanent depreciation in the claimant's land: it is to be presumed that the injunction will be obeyed and that the value of the land will not further depreciate.[264]

SECTION 8   PUBLIC NUISANCE

(A) NATURE OF PUBLIC NUISANCE

Public nuisance is not susceptible to any precise definition. However, in *R v Rimmington; R v Goldstein*,[265] the House of Lords acknowledged that the definition offered in *Archbold* is an acceptable one. There it is stated that:

> A person is guilty of a public nuisance . . . who (a) does an act not by law, or (b) omits to discharge a legal duty, if the effect of the act or omission is to endanger the life, health, property or comfort of the public, or to obstruct the public in the exercise or enjoyment of rights common to all Her Majesty's subjects.[266]

As is obvious from this broad-ranging definition, public nuisance covers a miscellany of acts and omissions. However, three general observations about the nature of public nuisance can be made to help clarify matters. To begin with, it is clear (though this

---

[262] *Regan v Paul Properties Ltd* [2006] 3 WLR 1131.

[263] [1995] 2 All ER 697, at 711. See, too, *Gillingham BC v Medway (Chatham) Docks Co Ltd* [1993] QB 343, at 364. Cf *Kennaway v Thompson* [1981] QB 88.

[264] *Macievich v Anderson* [1952] 4 DLR 507 (Manitoba Court of Appeal).

[265] [2006] 1 AC 456.

[266] Richardson, *Archbold: Criminal Pleading, Evidence and Practice* (2010), 2864.

is not relevant here) that a public nuisance is first and foremost a criminal offence at common law.[267] Second, it is essential that there be a common injury: that is, infringement of a public right. That being so, the accused in *R v Rimmington* (who sent over 500 individual abusive postal packages to different recipients) could not be held guilty of public nuisance.[268] Third, public nuisance may ground a civil action in three ways: by a relator action (brought in the name of the Attorney General on behalf of a private citizen to suppress the criminal activity of the defendant), by a local authority under the Local Government Act 1972, or by an action for damages in tort brought by a private citizen who has suffered 'special damage'.

(1) The relator action

If the defendant is responsible for a nuisance that affects a large number of citizens but fails to occasion any of them special damage, then an individual citizen may seek to persuade the Attorney General to suppress the defendant's activity on his behalf by way of a relator action for an injunction. To do so, the elements of the crime of public nuisance must be established. In practice, this method of obtaining injunctive relief is very seldom used. This is in large part explained by the fact that the Attorney General is unlikely to entertain an application for a relator action where the victim has not experienced special harm; and where special harm has been suffered, the victim is entitled to bring a civil action in his own name.

(2) Local authority applications

Under section 222 of the Local Government Act 1972 a local authority is empowered to bring proceedings in its own name for injunctive relief where it considers it 'expedient to do so for the promotion and protection of the interests of the inhabitants'. This provision extends to injunctive relief to prevent a public nuisance. Thus, in *Nottingham City Council v Zain (a minor)*,[269] it was held that an injunction could be sought to exclude a known drug-dealer from one of the city council's housing estates.

(3) Civil actions for 'special damage'

There are two situations in which a private citizen may mount a civil action for public nuisance. The first arises where the defendant is responsible for an interference which bears the characteristics of a private nuisance *except* that it affects a much greater number of people.[270] And here, just as in private nuisance, it is not a

---

[267] Most established public nuisances are now prohibited by statutes such as the various Public Health Acts, the Food Act 1984, and the Highways Act 1980.

[268] [2006] 1 AC 456, at [6]. Drawing an analogy with abusive phone calls, Lord Rodger said (at [48]): 'no such individual call can become a criminal public nuisance merely by reason of the fact that it is one of a series'. See also *DPP v Fearon* [2010] EWHC 340.

[269] [2002] 1 WLR 607.

[270] The required number of people will vary from case to case; and if the public right at stake is only enjoyed by a relatively small number of people, this will not prevent there being a public nuisance: *Jan de Nul (UK) Ltd v NV Royal Belge* [2002] 1 Lloyd's Rep 583. Examples include driving heavy lorries through

prerequisite that the act itself be unlawful: the nuisance derives from the detrimental effect of the act complained of. The second concerns cases where the interference would not bear the key characteristics of a private nuisance in that it does not affect the claimant's land, or his use or enjoyment of that land. Instead, the nuisance in such cases amounts to an inconvenience occasioned to the public generally, but causes special damage to the claimant (that is, damage beyond that suffered by other members of the public). Such nuisances typically involve obstructing, or creating a danger on, the highway.

Crucial to both kinds of public nuisance is the requirement that the claimant must suffer, or be at risk of, 'special damage'. Special damage – sometimes referred to as 'particular damage' – is a term almost as obscure in its meaning as public nuisance itself. Nonetheless, what is at least clear is that special damage must not be confused with 'special damages', which latter term is used in personal injury actions in negligence to describe pecuniary losses incurred up to the date of the trial which must be specifically pleaded and proved. While it is difficult to supply a precise definition of special damage, it is possible to advert to a number of established categories of such loss. Pecuniary loss stemming from loss of business or custom, where the injury was of a 'substantial character, not fleeting or evanescent' has long been recognised as such a category.[271] But where other members of the public have also suffered economic loss, it is more difficult for the claimant to establish special damage, for he is able only to show the same kind of damage as that suffered by the others[272] and may therefore obtain no remedy.[273] In addition to pecuniary loss, personal injury[274] and property damage[275] have also been held to constitute special damage. So, too, have causing inconvenience or delay, provided that the harm thereby caused to the claimant is substantial and appreciably greater in degree than any suffered by the general public.[276] Thus, in one

---

residential streets: *Gillingham BC v Medway (Chatham) Dock Co Ltd* [1993] QB 343; blasting from a quarry causing vibrations, dust, and noise: *A-G (on the relation of Glamorgan CC and Pontardawe RDC) v PYA Quarries Ltd* [1957] 2 QB 169; holding 'acid-house parties': *R v Shorrock* [1994] QB 279.

[271] *Benjamin v Storr* (1874) LR 9 CP 400, at 407 (C's coffee shop lost custom when D parked horse-drawn vans outside his premises); *Lyons, Sons & Co v Gulliver* [1914] 1 Ch 631; *Blundy Clark & Co Ltd v London and NE Rly Co* [1931] 2 KB 334. See also *Caledonian Rly Co v Walker's Trustees* (1882) 7 App Cas 259 (depreciation in the value of land) and *Tate and Lyle Industries Ltd v Greater London Council* [1983] 2 AC 509 (cost of dredging silted-up river in order to continue use of a ferry). In relation to economic loss, a curious anomaly exists where the loss is caused by negligence on the part of D. Take, eg, a defendant whose lorry breaks down and blocks the highway because he has failed properly to maintain it. If the action is framed in public nuisance it is likely to succeed, but if it is framed in negligence, it will almost certainly fail for want of sufficient proximity to establish a duty of care. For criticism of this anomaly, see the comments in *Ball v Consolidated Rutile* [1991] Qd 524, at 546.

[272] *Martin v LCC* (1899) 80 LT 866.

[273] *Ricket v Directors etc of the Metropolitan Rly Co* (1867) LR 2 HL 175, at 190 and 199. But that this case did not overturn the decision in *Wilkes* is clear from, inter alia, *Blundy Clarke & Co v London and NE Rly Co* [1931] 2 KB 334 and *Colour Quest Ltd v Total Downstream UK plc* [2009] 1 CLC 186.

[274] *Castle v St Augustine's Links Ltd* (1922) 38 TLR 615.

[275] *Halsey v Esso Petroleum Co Ltd* [1961] 2 All ER 145.

[276] *Walsh v Ervin* [1952] VLR 361; *Boyd v Great Northern Rly Co* [1895] 2 IR 555.

case, a claimant could recover in public nuisance both for damage to his vehicle on the highway and for interference with peaceful sleep in his adjoining house.[277]

The majority of public nuisance cases arise where the defendant either creates a danger on, or obstructs,[278] the highway,[279] or the adjacent pavement.[280] As far as rendering the highway unsafe is concerned, there is a long line of cases that establishes liability in public nuisance in respect of walls,[281] fences,[282] windows,[283] etc that fall on to the highway from adjoining premises. But other examples include leaving dangerous articles such as defective cellar flaps or unlighted scaffolding there,[284] or conducting operations off the highway which menace the safety of those upon it.[285] Where all that occurs is a blockage of the highway, it should, on principle, be users of the highway whose right to use the highway has been infringed, rather than shopkeepers who suffer a consequential loss in trade, who can sue. However, the seemingly errant decision in *Wilkes v Hungerford Market Co*[286] points the other way, and it has been rightly criticised by subsequent judges for doing so.[287]

Cases involving a creation of danger on the highway help illustrate the rigid categorisation of the law of torts. If someone falls over a projection on the forecourt (not forming part of the public footpath) leading to a shop, then his rights are merely those owed by an occupier to those who visit his premises – he has no action in public nuisance.[288] Should this happen on the footpath, however, it becomes a case of public nuisance. Equally, if one deviates only slightly from the footpath in order to pass an obstruction, and is injured while thus off the highway, this, too, might be within the area of public nuisance.[289]

As regards the highway, it is well established that temporary and reasonable obstructions of the highway will not attract liability. Consider *Trevett v Lee*.[290]

> Ds, who had no mains connection, laid a hose pipe across the highway in a time of drought in order to obtain a water supply from the other side of the road. C, who tripped over it and

---

[277] *Halsey v Esso Petroleum Co Ltd* [1961] 2 All ER 145. But was Veale J correct in holding that C should recover even though he was unlawfully using the road to park his car when it was damaged?

[278] Whether there is an obstruction is a question of fact: *Harper v G N Haden & Sons* [1933] Ch 298.

[279] The same principles apply to navigable waterways: *Tate & Lyle Industries Ltd v Greater London Council* [1983] 2 AC 509; *Rose v Miles* (1815) 4 M & S 101.

[280] *Ellis v Sheffield Gas Co* (1853) 2 E & B 767.

[281] *Mint v Good* [1951] 1 KB 517.

[282] *Harrold v Watney* [1898] 2 QB 320.

[283] *Leanse v Lord Egerton* [1943] KB 323.

[284] *Penny v Wimbledon UDC and Iles* [1899] 2 QB 72.

[285] *Castle v St Augustine's Links* (1922) 38 TLR 615 (C lost an eye when a golf ball smashed the window of his car). Cf *Stone v Bolton* [1950] 1 KB 201 (a cricket ball escaping the cricket ground was not a public nuisance as it was an isolated event).

[286] (1835) Bing NC 281.

[287] See, eg, *Ricket v Directors etc of the Metropolitan Rly Co* (1867) LR 2 HL 175, at 190 and 199.

[288] *Jacobs v LCC* [1950] AC 36; *Bromley v Mercer* [1922] 2 KB 126.

[289] *Barnes v Ward* (1850) 9 CB 392; *Barker v Herbert* [1911] 2 KB 633.

[290] [1955] 1 All ER 406. Whether it is a defence to say that the obstruction is reasonable because it is for the public benefit is unsettled. In *R v Russell* (1827) 6 B & C 566 (held to be a defence). Cf the doubt in *R v Ward* (1836) 4 Ad & El 384.

suffered injury, failed in an action for public nuisance since Ds' user of the highway was reasonable 'judged both from their own point of view and from the point of view of the other members of the public'.[291]

Although an obstruction of the highway is only partial, it may nonetheless give rise to liability in public nuisance. As Lord Evershed MR explained in *Trevett v Lee*: '[a]n obstruction is something which permanently or temporarily removes the whole *or part of the highway* from public use'.[292] Accordingly, where a vehicle is parked in such a way as to narrow significantly the width of the road, its owner may be held liable in public nuisance.[293] The obstruction need not, of course, be caused by vehicles. A crowd – such as men picketing an employer's premises – may just as easily obstruct the highway and form the basis of an action in public nuisance.[294] But where a demonstration or picket takes place peacefully, the obstruction will prima facie be considered a reasonable (and thus non-actionable) use of the highway.[295]

A final point worth noting in this context is that, where the claimant alleges public nuisance because the matter in question, although regulated by statute is not so regulated so as to confer an action for breach of statutory duty, the courts will be slow to allow the common law to furnish a remedy where Parliament did not see fit to create one.[296]

(B) THE RELATIONSHIP BETWEEN PUBLIC NUISANCE AND PRIVATE NUISANCE

Though many of the decided cases on public nuisance – especially those involving obstructions to, and dangers on, the highway are clearly incapable of founding an action in private nuisance, there has nonetheless been some confusion between the two torts. Certainly some judges (and jurists) seem to suppose a closer relationship than actually exists. For example, since it was recognised that private nuisance protected householders from the nauseous smells generated by their neighbours, it was thought that public nuisance ought logically to be applicable in cases involving the depasturing of pigs in towns and cities,[297] and otherwise impregnating the air on highways with 'noisome and offensive stinks and smells'.[298] However, while such extensions may have been justifiable, there is no basis for the claim that has often been made to the effect that there is a sub-category of public nuisance which 'overlaps with private nuisance and consists of those cases which satisfy the requirements of that tort but affect a much larger number of people than is usual in a private nuisance action'.[299]

---

[291] *Trevett v Lee* [1955] 1 All ER 406, at 412.
[292] Ibid at 409 (emphasis added).
[293] *A-G v Gastonia Coaches Ltd* [1977] RTR 219; *Dymond v Pearce* [1972] 1 QB 496.
[294] *News Group Newspapers Ltd v SOGAT '82 (No 2)* [1987] ICR 181.
[295] *DPP v Jones* [1999] 2 AC 240.
[296] *Ali v Bradford City MDC* [2011] RTR 20; *Wilkinson v York CC* [2011] EWCA Civ 207, at [9].
[297] *R v Wigg* (1705) 2 Ld Raym 1163.   [298] *R v White and Ward* (1757) 1 Burr 333.
[299] Buckley, *The Law of Nuisance* (1996), 67. This is not to say that any given case will not support an action in both private and public nuisance in certain circumstances: see, eg, *Halsey v Esso Petroleum Co Ltd*

The reason the claim is groundless lies in the fact that, while private rights animate the law of private nuisance, a different category of rights – namely, public rights (which are not a mere amalgam of multiple private rights) – underpins the law of public nuisance.[300] There is an important difference. Private rights are personal to each of us whereas public rights are not. So, although Romer LJ once said that 'a normal and legitimate way of proving a public nuisance is to prove a sufficiently large collection of private nuisances',[301] this approach has since been held by the House of Lords to be wrong. Using the example of multiple obscene phone calls, it has been observed that 'each telephone call affects only one individual...[and] no such individual call can become a criminal public nuisance merely by reason of the fact that it is one of a series'.[302] Each and every call lacks the essential element of common injury: that is, the infringement of a *public* right.[303] On top of this, it is safe to assert two further differences between private and public nuisances. First, private nuisance is never a crime while public nuisance can be both a crime and a tort. Second, a more general distinction can be made by reference to the kinds of interests protected by private and public nuisance since these do not overlap at all precisely. For example, while an action for private nuisance will be confined to interests in or over land, and will not accommodate actions in respect of personal injuries,[304] the same is by no means true of public nuisances. Indeed, it was specifically held that personal injuries are compensable in public nuisance in *In re Corby Group Litigation*.[305]

(C) REMEDIES IN PUBLIC NUISANCE

(1) Injunction

As we have already seen, where the victim of a public nuisance cannot establish special damage, a relator action for an injunction may be brought by the Attorney General on his behalf. Alternatively, as we have also seen, an injunction may be sought by a local authority under section 222 of the Local Government Act 1972 to secure 'the promotion and protection of the interests of the inhabitants'. Finally, individual applicants relying on their special damage are similarly able to obtain injunctions in public nuisance.[306]

[1961] 2 All ER 145. Nor are actions for public nuisance and negligence necessarily mutually exclusive: see, eg, *Dymond v Pearce* [1972] 1 QB 496.

[300] In *R v Rimmington; R v Goldstein* [2006] 1 AC 459, at [44].

[301] *A-G v PYA Quarries* [1957] 2 QB 169, at 187. See also at 191.

[302] *R v Rimmington; R v Goldstein* [2006] 1 AC 459, at [48] and [58].

[303] In order to infringe a public right in such a way as to cause a public nuisance, there must be interference with its use to an unreasonable degree: *Westminster CC v Ocean Leisure Ltd* [2004] EWCA Civ 970. In so far as personal injuries are recoverable (on which see *In re Corby Group Litigation* [2008] EWCA Civ 463), it is to be inferred that a *public* right to reasonable safety exists.

[304] *Hunter v Canary Wharf Ltd* [1997] AC 655.   [305] [2008] EWCA Civ 463, at [22]–[24].

[306] *Spencer v London and Birmingham Rly Co* (1836) 8 Sim 193.

(2) Damages

Most commonly, as noted, a claim in public nuisance will be for damages in respect of personal injuries or for pecuniary losses sustained by people using a public highway.[307] In addition, however, occupiers of premises adjoining the highway may also recover in public nuisance when they suffer special damage as a result of a nuisance on a highway. And this is the case even though the damage complained of is not suffered by them qua users of the highway. For example, shopkeepers have succeeded in this tort where access to their premises has been interfered with,[308] or where their customers have been subjected to noxious smells and darkened rooms as a result of the parking of horses and carts outside their premises.[309]

It is clear from the decision of the Privy Council in *The Wagon Mound (No 2)*[310] that damages are available subject to the familiar remoteness of damage principle. That is, the claimant will only recover so far as the defendant ought to have foreseen the type of loss suffered by the claimant. In that case, the claimant's ship was damaged in a fire caused by the defendant carelessly allowing oil to overflow from the defendant's ship into the waters of Sydney Harbour. The defendant was held liable in public nuisance, but only because the fire on the claimant's ship was held to be a foreseeable consequence of the defendant's wrongful act. By contrast, in *Savage v Fairclough*,[311] a pig farmer who had relied on the advice of an expert agronomist was held not liable in respect of the ensuing pollution of the claimant's water since such pollution had not in fact been foreseen, nor had it been reasonably foreseeable.

Two further limitations exist with respect to the quantum of damages. First, as decided in *Gibbons v South West Water Services Ltd* – a case in which the public water supply in Cornwall was seriously polluted – no matter how reprehensible the public nuisance, exemplary damages will never be available. An important element in the court's decision was the following rhetorical question:

> [I]n the case of a public nuisance affecting hundreds or even thousands of [claimants] how can the court assess the sum of exemplary damages to be awarded to any one of them to punish or deter the defendant without knowing at the outset the number of successful [claimants] and the approximate size of the total bill for exemplary damages?[312]

Finally, an award of damages can be reduced or excluded altogether by operation of the defences of contributory negligence or *volenti non fit injuria* respectively.[313]

---

[307] Note, however, that the creation of a mere hazard on the highway may suffice: *Wandsworth LBC v Railtrack plc* [2002] QB 756 (excessive pigeon droppings).

[308] *Fritz v Hobson* (1880) 14 Ch D 542.

[309] *Benjamin v Storr* (1874) LR 9 CP 400.

[310] [1967] 1 AC 617.

[311] [2000] Env LR 183.

[312] [1993] QB 507, at 531.

[313] *Dymond v Pearce* [1972] 1 QB 496.

FURTHER READING

CROSS, 'Does Only the Careless Polluter Pay? A Fresh Examination of the Nature of Private Nuisance' (1995) 111 *Law Quarterly Review* 445

GEARTY, 'The Place of Nuisance in the Modern Law of Torts' [1989] *Cambridge Law Journal* 214

LEE, 'What is Private Nuisance?' (2003) 119 *Law Quarterly Review* 298

LEE, 'Personal Injury, Public Nuisance and Environmental Regulation' (2009) 20 *King's Law Journal* 12

MURPHY, *The Law of Nuisance* (2010)

OGUS AND RICHARDSON, 'Economics and the Environment: A Study in Private Nuisance' [1977] *Cambridge Law Journal* 284

O'SULLIVAN, 'A Poor Reception for Television Nuisance' [1996] *Cambridge Law Journal* 184

SPENCER, 'Public Nuisance – A Critical Examination' [1989] *Cambridge Law Journal* 55

STEELE, 'Private Law and the Environment: Nuisance in Context' (1995) 15 *Legal Studies* 236

TROMANS, 'Nuisance – Prevention or Payment?' [1982] *Cambridge Law Journal* 87

17

THE RULE IN
RYLANDS v FLETCHER

KEY ISSUES

(1) Elements of the rule

The rule in *Rylands v Fletcher* is rather a mouthful: it highlights various elements of the tort, all of which must be present before liability can be imposed. Thus, a claimant must show that (i) the thing causing damage had been kept or collected on land owned by, or under the control of, the defendant, (ii) it is of a kind that will foreseeably cause harm upon its escape, (iii) there has been a non-natural use (which is not the same as a merely unreasonable use) of land; (iv) there has been an escape of the agent.

(2) Comparison with other torts

There is some doubt about the discrete nature of this action. The currently ascendant view in this country is that the rule in *Rylands v Fletcher* is merely a sub-branch of the law of private nuisance. According to this view, the rule in *Rylands v Fletcher* is seen as a spur of nuisance law that deals only with one-off occurrences. There is

also a somewhat less popular view that the rule in *Rylands v Fletcher* ought to be subsumed within the general law of negligence. But this view, too, conflicts with orthodoxy.

(3) Strict liability

A third key issue concerning this tort is whether, despite many a proclamation to this effect, it truly amounts to an instance of strict liability in tort. The greatest doubt as to whether liability is truly strict in this context inheres in what is implied by the test for remoteness of damage in this tort as well as some of the defences that are available.

(4) Interests protected

A fourth key issue concerns the kinds of loss or harm that are actionable under the rule in *Rylands v Fletcher*. If the idea is pressed hard that it is a mere sub-branch of the law of nuisance, then certain forms of harm – in particular physical injury to the person – ought not to be viewed as actionable.

SECTION 1   INTRODUCTION

The rule in *Rylands v Fletcher*[1] is probably the best known example of a strict liability tort in English law and it derives from the nineteenth-century case of that name.

> Ds employed independent contractors to build a reservoir on their land. Through the negligence of the independent contractors, disused shafts upon the site which communicated with C's mine beneath the reservoir were not blocked up. On the filling of the reservoir, the water escaped down the shafts and flooded C's mine.

Although the defendants were neither themselves negligent nor vicariously liable for the negligence of their independent contractors,[2] they were nonetheless held liable both by the Court of Exchequer Chamber and the House of Lords. Blackburn J, delivering the judgment of the Court of Exchequer Chamber, said:

> We think that the true rule of law is that the person who for his own purposes brings on his lands and collects and keeps there anything likely to do mischief if it escapes, must keep it in at his peril, and if he does not do so, is *prima facie* answerable for all the damage which is the natural consequence of its escape.[3]

Lord Cairns in the House of Lords broadly agreed with this judgment, but he restricted the scope of the rule to instances where the defendant had engaged in 'a non-natural use' of the land.[4] Though seemingly innocuous at the time, this addition to Blackburn J's formulation of the rule gave rise to one of the most vexed questions in relation to *Rylands v Fletcher* liability: what is the essence of 'a non-natural use' of land? As we shall see in section 4 of this chapter, there is still no clear answer to this question.

One instructive point, however, is that Blackburn J did not consider himself to be making new law. The following quotation encapsulates his thinking.

> The general rule, as above stated, seems on general principle just. The person whose grass or corn is eaten down by the escaping cattle of his neighbour, or whose mine is flooded by the water from his neighbour's reservoir, or whose cellar is invaded by the filth of his neighbour's privy, or whose habitation is made unhealthy by the fumes and noisome vapours of his neighbour's alkali works, is damnified without any fault of his own; and it seems but reasonable and just that the neighbour, who has brought something on his own property which was not naturally there, harmless to others so long as it is confined to his own property, but which he knows to be mischievous if it gets on his neighbour's, should be obliged to make good the damage which ensues if he does not succeed in confining it to his own property.[5]

---

[1] (1866) LR 1 Exch 265 (affirmed (1868) LR 3 HL 330).
[2] For discussion of vicarious liability and liability in relation to independent contractors, see ch 24.
[3] (1866) LR 1 Exch 265, at 279–80.   [4] Ibid at 338–40.
[5] Ibid at 280.

Yet, close though the analogy with nuisance may ostensibly appear,[6] the fact remains that *Rylands v Fletcher* was the starting point for a form of liability which, as developed by the courts in subsequent decisions, was wider and quite different in kind from any that preceded it.[7] Indeed, this extension of liability gave rise to speculation about whether or not some comprehensive theory of strict liability for harm caused to persons by ultra-hazardous things was being formulated. Such a theory, whatever attraction it may once have had, is certainly no longer tenable after the interpretation put upon *Rylands v Fletcher* by the House of Lords in *Read v J Lyons & Co Ltd.*[8] There, the facts were as follows.

> The appellant, while working in the respondent's factory, was injured by an explosion there. No allegation of negligence was made by her against the respondents, whom she sued in respect of her injuries. The basis of her claim was that the respondents carried on the manufacture of high-explosive shells, knowing that they were dangerous things.

The ground for the decision of the House of Lords in favour of the respondents was that the rule in *Rylands v Fletcher* does not apply unless there has been an escape from a place where the defendant has occupation or control over land to a place outside his control.[9] But the importance of the case does not end there. The decision in *Read v J Lyons & Co Ltd* constituted a denial of a general theory of strict liability for ultra-hazardous activities: there is only liability for non-negligent escapes where the several preconditions for *Rylands v Fletcher* liability (considered in the following sections) are satisfied. Where these preconditions are not met, the claimant's case can only be formulated in terms of the intentional or negligent conduct of the defendant.

Perhaps the most remarkable characteristic of this rule has been its fluidity. Stated in very broad terms by Blackburn J, it was at once modified in the case itself by the House of Lords, who confined it to instances involving a 'non-natural use' of land. But there nonetheless followed its widespread application: *often* cases properly sounding

---

[6] For an early account of the relationship between liability in nuisance and liability under the rule in *Rylands v Fletcher* see Newark (1945) 65 LQR 480. See also *Cambridge Water Co Ltd v Eastern Counties Leather plc* [1994] 2 AC 264, at 298; *Transco v Stockport MBC* [2004] 2 AC 1, at [9]. For trenchant criticism of these understandings, see Murphy (2004) 24 OJLS 643.   [7] See, eg, Nolan (2005) 121 LQR 421.

[8] [1945] KB 216 (affirmed [1947] AC 156). In *Transco v Stockport MBC* [2004] 2 AC 1, there was a good deal of emphasis placed on extraordinary uses of land. Yet such uses do not (despite what some of their Lordships seemed to think in this case) require an ultra-hazardous agent to have been accumulated. It was really only Lord Bingham (at [11]) who took the view that the operation of the rule hinged on an especially dangerous agent. Those agreeing with Lord Bingham also signalled their agreement with Lord Hoffmann's approach to the case, which was markedly different. That being so, it is impossible to identify any unequivocal support for Lord Bingham's view.

[9] There are *obiter dicta* to the effect that the escape of a dangerous thing from D's chattel, located on a highway (*Rigby v CC of Northamptonshire* [1985] 1 WLR 1242, at 1255) or from his vessel, situated on a navigable waterway (*Crown River Cruises Ltd v Kimbolton Fireworks Ltd* [1996] 2 Lloyd's Rep 533) is sufficient to give rise to *Rylands* liability. These dicta are, however, difficult to sustain both in principle, and in the light of existing authority: see *Jones v Festiniog Rly Co* (1868) LR 3 QB 733; *Powell v Fall* (1880) 5 QBD 597; *West v Bristol Tramways Co* [1908] 2 KB 14. Such actions, it is submitted, should sound in negligence, not *Rylands v Fletcher* – which has always been a land-based tort – *unless*, as in the three cases cited, D has a statutory right to occupation of the public thoroughfare.

in nuisance alone were brought within the fold of *Rylands v Fletcher*. Then, the rule was given even greater elasticity by the interpretation of 'non-natural use' by the Privy Council in 1913. They considered it to mean 'some special use bringing with it increased danger to others, and [which] must not merely be the ordinary use of the land or such a use as is proper for the general benefit of the community'.[10] Even after 1913, the rule in *Rylands v Fletcher* continued to be invoked freely; and often it was not sufficiently sharply distinguished from nuisance.[11] Then, in 1947, came something of a *volte-face* in the shape of *Read v J Lyons & Co Ltd*.[12] There, it was made clear that the earlier decisions of the lower courts which had appeared to extend the original rule must henceforth be closely scrutinised before they could be accepted as good authorities.

SECTION 2   'THINGS' WITHIN THE RULE

Blackburn J spoke of 'anything likely to do mischief if it escapes'. These things must not summarily be described as 'dangerous' and then equated (and, in turn, confused) with those things which have been considered 'dangerous' in the context of negligence. Indeed, it would be wise to eschew the word 'dangerous' altogether since it is an inherently protean concept. A simple example of the need for caution in this context can be supplied by reference to the mischievous 'thing' in *Rylands v Fletcher* itself – namely, water. Water is, of course, not 'dangerous' per se. Yet, as Du Parcq LJ observed in the Court of Appeal in *Read v J Lyons & Co Ltd*,[13] what matters is whether the thing is likely to do damage on escaping to other land.[14] Whether or not this involves personal danger is quite irrelevant. Thus, filth and water are both 'things' caught by the rule even though they are not inherently dangerous.

It is equally true that the ultra-hazardous quality of the thing (in the sense that it is intrinsically dangerous) is of no moment. In *Cambridge Water Co Ltd v Eastern Counties Leather plc*[15] – the leading modern *Rylands v Fletcher* authority – it was held by Lord Goff that:

> [T]here is much to be said for the view that the courts should not be proceeding down the path of developing such a theory [of liability for ultra-hazardous activities] ... I incline to the view that, as a general rule, it is more appropriate for strict liability in respect of operations of high risk to be imposed by Parliament, than by the courts.[16]

---

[10] *Rickards v Lothian* [1913] AC 263, at 280.

[11] The most authoritative statement of the continuing affinity between the two torts is set out by Lord Goff in *Cambridge Water Co Ltd v Eastern Counties Leather plc* [1994] 2 AC 264, at 298–9. The remaining four Law Lords in that case concurred.   [12] [1945] KB 216, at 247.

[13] Ibid at 247.   [14] Cf *Read v J Lyons & Co* [1947] AC 156, at 176.   [15] [1994] 1 All ER 53.

[16] Ibid at 76.

In *Read v J Lyons & Co Ltd*, counsel argued that the thing must have the 'capacity for independent movement'[17] as well as being a potential cause of harm. So, for example, glass would be outside the rule. Provided that an extension is made to include a thing likely to give off something such as a gas, which itself has the capacity for independent movement, this contention has much to commend it, and there is some (albeit limited) support for it in the cases.[18]

Things which have been held to be capable of giving rise to *Rylands v Fletcher* liability include electricity,[19] gas likely to pollute water supplies,[20] explosives,[21] fire[22] and things likely to cause fires[23] (including a motor vehicle whether the tank contains,[24] or is empty of,[25] petrol), things likely to give off noxious gases or fumes,[26] water,[27] sewage,[28] and slag heaps.[29] Cases holding planted yew trees[30] and chair-o-planes[31] to be within the rule are also probably sound so long as there is movement of the mischievous thing beyond the boundary of the land under the defendant's control. Whether a decayed and rusty wire fence[32] and a flag-pole[33] have been rightly regarded as being within the rule is, however, doubtful.

A final and interesting illustration of the kind of 'things' that may fall within the rule is supplied by the case of *A-G v Corke*.[34] There it was held that the owner of land who allowed caravan dwellers to live on that land was answerable under the rule for the interferences which they perpetrated on adjoining land.[35]

The last characteristic of those 'things' whose escape may give rise to liability under the rule is that they must have been brought on to the land by the defendant. This final characteristic applies only to 'things artificially brought or kept upon the defendant's land'.[36]

---

[17] [1947] AC 156, at 158.

[18] Eg, *Wilson v Newberry* (1871) LR 7 QB 31, at 33, per Mellor J: 'things which have a tendency to escape and to do mischief'.   [19] *National Telephone Co v Baker* [1893] 2 Ch 186.

[20] *Batchellor v Tunbridge Wells Gas Co* (1901) 84 LT 765.

[21] *Rainham Chemical Works Ltd v Belvedere Fish Guano Co* [1921] 2 AC 465; and CS gas canisters: *Rigby v CC of Northamptonshire* [1985] 1 WLR 1242.

[22] *LMS International Ltd v Styrene Packaging & Insulation Ltd* [2006] TCLR 6.

[23] *Jones v Festiniog Rly Co* (1868) LR 3 QB 733 (sparks from railway engine); *Balfour v Barty-King* [1956] 2 All ER 555 (blowlamp) (affirmed on other grounds [1957] 1 QB 496).

[24] *Musgrove v Pandelis* [1919] 2 KB 43.   [25] *Perry v Kendricks Transport Ltd* [1956] 1 All ER 154.

[26] *West v Bristol Tramways Co* [1908] 2 KB 14; *Halsey v Esso Petroleum Co Ltd* [1961] 2 All ER 145 (acid smuts).

[27] *Rylands v Fletcher* (1868) LR 3 HL 330; *Western Engraving Co v Film Laboratories Ltd* [1936] 1 All ER 106.   [28] *Humphries v Cousins* (1877) 2 CPD 239.

[29] *Kennard v Cory Bros & Co Ltd* [1921] AC 521.

[30] *Crowhurst v Amersham Burial Board* (1878) 4 Ex D 5.

[31] *Hale v Jennings Bros* [1938] 1 All ER 579.   [32] *Firth v Bowling Iron Co* (1878) 3 CPD 254.

[33] *Shiffman v Venerable Order of the Hospital of St John of Jerusalem* [1936] 1 All ER 557.

[34] [1933] Ch 89. In *Smith v Scott* [1973] Ch 314 undesirable tenants were held to be outside the rule, because a landlord has no 'control' over the tenants.

[35] On similar facts, liability has also been imposed under the principles of private nuisance: see *Lippiatt v South Gloucestershire Council* [1999] 4 All ER 149.   [36] *Bartlett v Tottenham* [1932] 1 Ch 114, at 131.

SECTION 3 PARTIES

(A) WHO MAY BE SUED?

Blackburn J said that the rule applies to a 'person who for his own purposes brings on his lands and collects and keeps there' the thing in question. The thing may or may not be something which in its nature is capable of being naturally there: what matters is whether the particular thing has in fact been accumulated there. If, therefore, water flows from A's underground tunnels into B's mines, whether by force of gravitation or by percolation, A is not liable under the rule in *Rylands v Fletcher* for that escape if the water was naturally on A's land and he did nothing to accumulate it there.[37] On the other hand, there was liability in *Rylands v Fletcher* itself because steps had been taken by the defendants to accumulate the water on their land by constructing the reservoir.[38] The cases where flooding of neighbouring land results from pumping or diverting water from the land of the defendant to that of the claimant may be nuisance, or even perhaps trespass. But they cannot be within the rule in *Rylands v Fletcher* if the defendant has not artificially accumulated the water.[39] Similarly, the escape of rocks is outside the rule since there has been no accumulation.[40] If, however, rocks are blasted in quarrying, there may then be liability for accumulating the explosives.[41]

 In the case of vegetation, assuming the other elements of the rule to be satisfied, it will be important to consider whether that vegetation was planted there deliberately, for the planting of it will constitute an accumulation.[42] *Giles v Walker*[43] (assuming the case was decided on the basis of the rule in *Rylands v Fletcher*; and this is not clear), may be a relevant authority in this context. There, in order to redeem some of his forest land, D ploughed it up. Thereafter, thistles grew all over the ploughed land. Thistle-down escaped from D's land to C's land, where it seeded itself. Finding that the thistles were 'the natural growth of the soil', the court held that this was no tort.[44] Yet it seems, from an interjection of Lord Esher MR, during the argument, that the result would have been different had the court found that the defendant had been responsible for the thistles having come on to his land. In other words, had there been a finding of fact that the ploughing up of the land had caused the thistles to come on to, and grow

---

 [37] *Wilson v Waddell* (1876) 2 App Cas 95.
 [38] And in *Broder v Saillard* (1876) 2 Ch D 692, where the water was brought on to the land in connection with the stabling of D's horses.
 [39] Eg, *Palmer v Bowman* [2000] 1 All ER 22; *Baird v Williamson* (1863) 15 CBNS 376. Cf *Hurdman v North Eastern Rly Co* (1878) 3 CPD 168.   [40] *Pontardawe RDC v Moore-Gwyn* [1929] 1 Ch 656.
 [41] *Miles v Forest Rock Granite Co (Leicestershire) Ltd* (1918) 34 TLR 500. If it is not the explosives, but the rocks which have escaped, then presumably there needs to be an analogy drawn with those cases in which D accumulates agent X but X gives off a gas which escapes, in which case there can be liability: see, eg, *Wilson v Newberry* (1871) LR 7 QB 31.   [42] *Crowhurst v Amersham Burial Board* (1878) 4 Ex D 5.
 [43] (1890) 62 LT 933. Cf *Seligman v Docker* [1949] Ch 53.
 [44] But note the limited liability imposed in nuisance for damage resulting from the naturally occurring dangerous condition of land: *Leakey v National Trust* [1980] QB 485.

upon, the defendant's land when they otherwise would not have done, the requirement of artificial accumulation would have been satisfied.[45]

Problems of responsibility for accumulation were also considered by the House of Lords in *Rainham Chemical Works Ltd v Belvedere Fish Guano Co Ltd*.[46]

A and B contracted with the Ministry of Munitions to manufacture explosives on their land. They formed a limited company, C Ltd, and arranged for C Ltd to perform this contract on the land of A and B. C Ltd were thus the licensees of A and B. Neighbouring landowners suffered damage to their land caused by an explosion on the land of A and B while C Ltd were using it, and they sued C Ltd as well as A and B.

It was decided that a licensee who himself accumulates something on the land of another is liable for the consequences of that accumulation.[47] Further, the House of Lords held that those who remain in occupation of land are also liable to landowners injured by the escape of that which their licensee accumulates in discharge of a contractual duty owed by the occupiers to a third party.

Lord Sumner further stated (*obiter*) that if 'they [A and B] ... simply suffered others to manufacture upon the site which they nevertheless continued to occupy' they would be liable for the consequences of an escape.[48] On the other hand, Eve J in *Whitmores (Edenbridge) Ltd v Stanford*[49] held that a landowner, upon whose land some other person had a prescriptive right to accumulate water for his own purposes, would not be liable under the rule. The extent to which an occupier is liable in respect of the accumulations of his licensees cannot be regarded as entirely settled, but it is relevant to observe that in *Rylands v Fletcher* Blackburn J spoke only of a person who 'for his own purposes' brings things on his land.[50] Thus, a local authority which is required by statute to permit the discharge of sewage into its sewers is treated as responsible for the accumulation of that sewage.[51]

A person who authorises another to commit a tort is normally also himself liable for that tort. Thus, a lessor is liable in nuisance if he lets land for a particular purpose in such circumstances that he is necessarily taken to have authorised the interference which the lessee in consequence causes.[52] There were *obiter dicta* in *Rainham Chemical Works Ltd v Belvedere Fish Guano Co Ltd* to the effect that the same rule applies in *Rylands v Fletcher* cases – in short, that a defendant may be liable although he does not occupy the land, if he has authorised another to accumulate something on it, when the thing so accumulated later escapes.[53]

---

[45] (1890) 62 LT 933, at 934. Observations by the CA in *Davey v Harrow Corpn* [1958] 1 QB 60 support the view taken in the text. [46] [1921] 2 AC 465.

[47] Where, however, over 20 years had elapsed since the licensee had acquired the right to enter and accumulate water there, he was held not to be accountable for the escape of water, if he no longer had control of the land: *Westhoughton Coal and Cannel Co Ltd v Wigan Coal Corpn Ltd* [1939] Ch 800.

[48] [1921] 2 AC 465, at 480. [49] [1909] 1 Ch 427. [50] (1866) LR 1 Exch 265, at 279.

[51] *Smeaton v Ilford Corpn* [1954] Ch 450.

[52] See ch 16.

[53] [1921] 2 AC 465, at 476 and 489. Cf *A-G v Cory Bros & Co* (1918) 34 TLR 621, but not considered, at [1921] 1 AC 521. Cf *St Anne's Well Brewery Co v Roberts* (1928) 140 LT 1, at 5 and 7 (*obiter*).

What happens where the accumulation is not on the land owned or occupied by the defendant? In *Rigby v Chief Constable of Northamptonshire* Taylor J, relying on a passage in the then current edition of *Clerk and Lindsell on Torts*, suggested (*obiter*) that there was, so far as he could see, 'no difference in principle between allowing a man-eating tiger to escape from your land onto that of another and allowing it to escape from the back of your wagon parked on the highway'.[54] It is submitted that this view is wrong. How can the requirements that there be an artificial accumulation on, and a non-natural use of, the defendant's land be satisfied if both the accumulation and escape take place elsewhere? The preferable view, it is submitted, is that such cases should be actionable, if at all, as negligent omissions.[55] The rule in *Rylands v Fletcher* is a well-established land-based tort, yet the focus is on land owned by, or under the control of, the defendant.[56]

(B) WHO MAY SUE?

It is clear that this rule permits a landowning claimant, as in *Rylands v Fletcher* itself, to sue in respect of damage to land. Similarly, in relation to damage to chattels, Blackburn J later allowed a claim where sparks from a railway engine set fire to a haystack;[57] and several other cases support the proposition that liability for damage to chattels is recoverable.[58] But what of those who suffer no such property damage, but merely personal injuries? Arguably, the question needs to be addressed in two stages.[59]

First, where the claimant is an occupier of land, *Hale v Jennings Bros* is a binding Court of Appeal authority enabling occupiers to recover in respect of personal injuries.[60] There, a tenant of a stall at a fair suffered personal injuries as the result of an escape of D's chair-o-plane. She was held to have a good cause of action based on the rule in *Rylands v Fletcher*. But, second, what of the claimant who suffers personal injury but has no such proprietary interest? Here, the law is less clear; both in relation to the general question of whether such persons have a right to sue at all,[61] and in relation to

---

[54] [1985] 1 WLR 1242, at 1255.

[55] Negligent omissions are only infrequently actionable, but creating an obvious source of danger that is liable to be 'sparked off' by a third party may give rise to negligence liability: see *Topp v London Country Bus (South West) Ltd* [1993] 1 WLR 976.

[56] See Murphy (2004) 24 OJLS 643. Cf *Read v Lyons* [1947] AC 156, at 173.

[57] *Jones v Festiniog Rly Co* (1868) LR 3 QB 733. Cf *Cattle v Stockton Waterworks Co* (1875) LR 10 QB 453, at 457.

[58] Eg, *Midwood & Co Ltd v Manchester Corpn* [1905] 2 KB 597; *Musgrove v Pandelis* [1919] 2 KB 43; *Collingwood v Home and Colonial Stores Ltd* [1936] 3 All ER 200. Cf *Read v J Lyons & Co* [1947] AC 156, at 169, and *Transco v Stockport MBC* [2004] 2 AC 1 (*obiter*).

[59] The most recent pronouncement on the question exists in the speeches of Lords Bingham and Hoffmann in the *Transco* case. They both stated, *obiter*, that the rule does not permit claims for personal injuries or death. But as the following discussion reveals, this approach is highly suspect.

[60] [1938] 1 All ER 579.

[61] See *McKenna v British Aluminium Ltd* [2002] Env LR 30, at [20]–[28], where Neuberger J questioned, in the context of a striking out action, (a) whether the increasingly close relationship between nuisance and the rule in *Rylands v Fletcher* meant that the proprietary entitlement rule in nuisance applied also to *Rylands*

the narrower question of whether they may sue in respect of personal injuries. In both *Perry v Kendricks Transport Ltd*[62] and *British Celanese Ltd v AH Hunt (Capacitors) Ltd*[63] it was suggested, *obiter*, that even those with no proprietary interests are able to bring an action for personal injuries on the basis of the rule in *Rylands v Fletcher*. Certainly, there was nothing in Blackburn J's judgment in *Rylands* to prohibit such a possibility. Indeed, to the contrary, his Lordship envisaged liability in respect of '*all the damage* which is the natural consequence of the escape'.[64] On this basis, it might be argued that a proprietary interest in land is not (and never has been) a prerequisite to recovery under this tort.[65] On the other hand, the House of Lords have twice stressed (wrongly, it is submitted) the fact that the rule in *Rylands v Fletcher* derives from, and is a sub-species of, private nuisance.[66] That being the case, on the present standing of English law, the rule in *Rylands v Fletcher*, like the law of private nuisance, would seem to be available only to those who possess a proprietary interest in the land affected by the escape.[67]

Recognising the uncertainty surrounding this issue, and recognising, too, that he was likely to fuel further academic debate on the matter, Ward LJ, in *Ribee v Norrie*,[68] steadfastly refused to draw any firm conclusion on the recoverability of personal injuries under the rule in *Rylands v Fletcher*. He contented himself by deciding the case before him on the basis of negligence. More recently, however, three members of the House of Lords have since reasserted, but only *obiter*, the proposition that the rule in *Rylands v Fletcher* only protects interests in land.[69] The truth, then, is that the recovery of personal injuries under the rule is technically an open question.

In the absence of clear authority, it is submitted that the view that anyone suffering personal injury may recover is to be preferred since the closeness between nuisance and *Rylands v Fletcher* is, as we shall see later in this chapter, apt to be overstated. Even so, it should be pointed out that several of their Lordships in *Read v J Lyons & Co Ltd* specifically expressed the view (albeit *obiter*) that personal injuries were irrecoverable

---

v Fletcher and (b) assuming it did, whether it was a sustainable rule in the wake of the enactment of the Human Rights Act 1998.

  [62] [1956] 1 All ER 154.

  [63] [1969] 2 All ER 1252.   [64] (1866) LR 1 Exch 265, at 279.

  [65] Cf *Hunter v Canary Wharf Ltd* [1997] 2 All ER 426.

  [66] First, in *Cambridge Water Co Ltd v Eastern Counties Leather plc* [1994] 2 AC 264 and, second, in *Transco v Stockport MBC* [2004] 2 AC 1, at [9], [52], and [92].

  [67] See *Hunter v Canary Wharf Ltd* [1997] AC 655 (on nuisance) and *Transco v Stockport MBC* [2004] 2 AC 1, at [11], [47], and [68] (on the rule in *Rylands v Fletcher*). In both cases, however, this approach is difficult to reconcile with Art 8 of the European Convention on Human Rights, which affords all citizens an equal right to respect for their private lives. This point was recognised in *McKenna v British Aluminium Ltd* [2002] Env LR 30. In addition, a further weakness in this approach is that it conflates nuisance law with the rule in *Rylands v Fletcher* without any heed to the historical fact that, in nuisance, the emphasis is placed on C having a proprietary interest, whereas under the rule in *Rylands v Fletcher* the emphasis rests upon D's property (or, at least, property under D's control): it is on *D's land* that an accumulation must occur, and from *D's land* that there must be an escape.   [68] [2001] PIQR P8, at [30].

  [69] *Transco v Stockport MBC* [2004] 2 AC 1, at [9], [35], and [52], per Lords Bingham, Hoffmann, and Hobhouse respectively. The first two named even stated in explicit terms their view that claims for personal injury and death were excluded under the rule.

under the rule.[70] To some extent, however, the distinction between personal injuries and property damage is not always easy to sustain since, in the case of personal injury to the occupier or holder of a proprietary interest, injury to the person might be seen to merge into a general injury to the proprietary interest as a whole by way of a diminution in the amenity value of the land.[71]

A final question in this context is whether the claimant who suffers pure economic loss is able to claim for his losses under the rule in *Rylands v Fletcher*. Here, too, the law is somewhat uncertain. It was held in *Weller & Co v Foot and Mouth Disease Research Institute*[72] that the escape of a virus was not actionable by the claimant, a cattle auctioneer, when it caused a loss of profit to his business after making a third party's cattle unsaleable. But, in the case of *Ryeford Homes v Sevenoaks District Council*,[73] the possibility of recovery for pure economic loss was again mooted, as a preliminary issue, and not ruled out. There, Judge Newey QC expressed the view that pure economic loss was, *in principle*, recoverable under the rule in *Rylands v Fletcher* so long as it was 'a sufficiently direct result of an escape of water from sewers'.[74] This view is thought to be correct, and it is entirely consistent with both Blackburn J's judgment in *Rylands v Fletcher* and the decision in *Weller*.[75]

SECTION 4   THE NON-NATURAL USE OF LAND

Blackburn J said that the rule applied only to a thing 'which was not naturally there'.[76] In the House of Lords, Lord Cairns used more ambiguous words[77] which have since been construed as meaning that the defendant is only answerable if, in bringing the thing on to his land,[78] he is making 'a non-natural use' of the land. The expression 'non-natural use' is very flexible and the courts are afforded a great deal of latitude in construing whether the defendant has engaged in a 'non-natural use'. The form in which Lord Moulton, on behalf of the Privy Council, expressed this rule in *Rickards v Lothian* emphasised this flexibility.[79] He said: '[i]t must be some special use bringing with it increased danger to others, and must not merely be the ordinary use of the land

---

[70]   [1947] AC 156, at 173, 178, and 180–1.

[71]   See the analysis of *Hunter v Canary Wharf* in ch 16.

[72]   [1966] 1 QB 569. See also, in similar vein, *Cattle v Stockton Waterworks Co* (1875) LR 10 QB 453 (escape of water which made it more expensive for C to carry out his contract to construct a tunnel; not actionable).

[73]   [1989] 2 EGLR 281.

[74]   On the facts, however, D was able to invoke the defence of statutory authority (see section 7, below).

[75]   The fact that the auctioneer's loss in *Weller* was contingent upon the cattle owners' loss rendered the loss of profit from the would-be auctions an *indirect*, and hence irrecoverable, economic loss.

[76]   Viscount Simon in *Read v Lyons* [1947] AC 156, at 166, described this as 'a parenthetic reference to' the test of Lord Cairns.   [77]   (1868) LR 3 HL 330, at 337–40.

[78]   What matters is whether the accumulation (as distinct from the escape) is a non-natural use: *Read v Lyons* [1947] AC 156, at 186.   [79]   [1913] AC 263, at 280.

or such a use as is proper for the general benefit of the community'.[80] Viscount Simon in *Read v J Lyons & Co Ltd* thought this statement to be 'of the first importance'[81] and Lord Porter said:

> each seems to be a question of fact subject to a ruling of the judge as to whether...the particular use can be non-natural, and in deciding this question I think that all the circumstances of the time and place and practice of mankind must be taken into consideration so that what might be regarded as...non-natural may vary according to those circumstances.[82]

The current tendency is to interpret 'non-natural use' narrowly, and many earlier cases may no longer be followed. For instance, in *Read v J Lyons & Co Ltd*, despite the contrary previous decision of the House of Lords in *Rainham Chemical Works Ltd v Belvedere Fish Guano Co*,[83] it was doubted whether building and running a munitions factory on land in wartime was a non-natural use.[84] Similarly, despite the words of Lord Moulton in *Rickards v Lothian* concerning uses that bring a 'general benefit to the community', Lord Goff emphatically denied the fact that the generation of employment for a local community was sufficient to transform the storage of chemicals used in the tanning industry into a natural use of the land. He said:

> I myself, however, do not feel able to accept that the creation of employment as such, even in a small industrial complex, is sufficient of itself to establish a particular use as constituting a natural or ordinary use of land.[85]

Beyond this, his Lordship offered little to clarify the meaning of the term 'non-natural use'. Instead of taking the opportunity to do so in *Cambridge Water*, he declined to say more than that he did not consider it necessary to redefine the phrase in that context since 'the storage of chemicals on industrial premises should be regarded as *an almost classic case* of non-natural use'.[86]

It thus fell to the House of Lords in the subsequent case of *Transco v Stockport MBC* to clarify this troublesome phrase. There – in holding that the supply of pressurised water to 66 flats constituted a natural use of land so that there could be no liability for the effects of a burst pipe – Lord Bingham offered the following thoughts.

> I think it is clear that ordinary user is a preferable test to natural user, making it clear that the rule in *Rylands v Fletcher* is engaged only where the defendant's use is shown to be extraordinary and unusual. This is not a test to be inflexibly applied: a use may be extraordinary and unusual at one time or in one place but not so at another time or in another place...[T]he question is whether the defendant has done something out of the ordinary in the place and at the time when he does it. In answering that question, I respectfully

---

[80] Ibid. It has since been qualified that this means the 'national community as a whole': *Ellison v Ministry of Defence* (1996) 81 BLR 101, at 119.   [81] [1947] AC 156, at 169.

[82] Ibid at 176.   [83] [1921] 2 AC 465.   [84] [1947] AC 156, at 169–70 and 173.

[85] [1994] 1 All ER 53, at 79.   [86] Ibid (emphasis added).

think that little help is gained (and unnecessary confusion perhaps caused) by considering whether the use is proper for the general benefit of the community.[87]

By contrast, in the very same case, Lord Hoffmann was of the view that a test based
on ordinary user was rather vague and preferred a test based on increased risk.[88] And
confusingly, various other members of the House of Lords agreed with both analyses
of the problem without indicating a preference for either one. That being so, despite
the effort to clear up the meaning of non-natural use, a crepuscular haze continues
to overhang its definition, with the courts nowadays preferring to use the concept of
reasonable user instead.[89]

The following instances can, however, confidently be stated to be natural uses of
land: water-pipe installations in buildings;[90] growing trees, even though planted by
the defendant, so long as they are not poisonous;[91] working mines and minerals on
land;[92] building or pulling down walls;[93] lighting a fire in the fireplace of a house;[94]
using a hot wire-cutter in proximity to flammable material;[95] installing necessary wiring for electric lighting;[96] storing metal foil in a factory;[97] supplying gas to flats in a
tower block.[98] The provision for sewage disposal by a local authority,[99] and the escape
from a ship of generated steam are probably also natural uses.[100] By contrast, it has
been held that storing water, gas, electricity, and the like in abnormal or excessive
quantities,[101] as well as the use of a blowlamp to thaw pipes in a loft[102] and the storage
of ignitable material in a barn[103] constitute non-natural uses of the land. Ultimately,
it is difficult to resist the conclusion that the notion of 'non-natural use' is presently
a narrow one, and that the current interpretation of the term is likely to restrict the
scope of application of the rule in *Rylands v Fletcher*.

---

[87] [2004] 2 AC 1, at [11].   [88] Ibid at [37].
[89] See, eg, *Arscott v Coal Authority* [2005] Env LR 6, at [29].
[90] *Rickards v Lothian* [1913] AC 263; *Tilley v Stevenson* [1939] 4 All ER 207.
[91] *Noble v Harrison* [1926] 2 KB 332.   [92] *Rouse v Gravelworks Ltd* [1940] 1 KB 489.
[93] *Thomas and Evans Ltd v Mid-Rhondda Co-operative Society Ltd* [1941] 1 KB 381; *St Anne's Well
Brewery Co v Roberts* (1928) 140 LT 1.
[94] *Sochaski v Sas* [1947] 1 All ER 344. Ditto holding a torch, at the top of the opening of a grate in order to
test chimney draught: *J Doltis Ltd v Isaac Braithwaite & Sons (Engineers) Ltd* [1957] 1 Lloyd's Rep 522.
[95] *LMS International Ltd v Styrene Packaging & Insulation Ltd* [2005] EWHC 2065.
[96] *Collingwood v Home and Colonial Stores Ltd* [1936] 3 All ER 200.
[97] *British Celanese Ltd v A H Hunt (Capacitors) Ltd* [1969] 2 All ER 1252; *Mason v Levy Auto Parts of
England Ltd* [1967] 2 QB 530.   [98] *British Gas plc v Stockport MBC* [2001] Env LR 44.
[99] *Pride of Derby and Derbyshire Angling Association v British Celanese Ltd* [1953] Ch 149, at 189. Cf
Smeaton v Ilford Corpn [1954] Ch 450, at 470 and *Ryeford Homes Ltd v Sevenoaks DC* [1989] 2 EGLR 281.
[100] *Howard v Furness Houlder Argentine Lines Ltd and A and R Brown Ltd* [1936] 2 All ER 781.
[101] *Northwestern Utilities Ltd v London Guarantee and Accident Co Ltd* [1936] AC 108; *Western Engraving
Co v Film Laboratories Ltd* [1936] 1 All ER 106 (water in unusual quantities brought on to land for manufacturing purposes of D). In *Transco*, the HL expressly distinguished the substantially greater amount of water
stored in *Rylands v Fletcher*.
[102] *Balfour v Barty-King* [1956] 2 All ER 555 (affirmed on other grounds [1957] 1 QB 496).
[103] *E Hobbs (Farms) Ltd v Baxenden Chemical Co Ltd* [1992] 1 Lloyd's Rep 54.

SECTION 5   ESCAPE

According to the orthodox view, an explosion which injures a claimant within the factory where the explosion occurs is outside the rule since there must be an 'escape from a place where the defendant has occupation of, or control over, land to a place which is outside his occupation or control'.[104] Accordingly, a yew tree that poisoned a horse which ate its leaves by reaching its head over on to the land of the defendant was outside the rule since the 'dangerous' leaves never went beyond the boundary of the defendant's land.[105] By contrast, where something escapes from one place of enter-tainment in a fairground to a stall tenanted by another fairground operative (but still within the fairground), there *is*, apparently, a sufficient escape.[106]

   In *Midwood & Co Ltd v Manchester Corpn*,[107] an explosion in a cable belonging to, and laid by, D in the highway caused inflammable gas to escape into C's nearby house and set fire to its contents. There was held to be a sufficient escape to fall within the rule in *Rylands v Fletcher*. Then, in *Charing Cross Electric Supply Co v Hydraulic Power Co*,[108] the Court of Appeal, relying on the *Midwood* case, held that there was a sufficient escape when water from a main, laid by the defendants under the highway, escaped and damaged the claimant's electric cable which was near to it and under the same highway.

   In *Read v J Lyons & Co Ltd*, the House of Lords did not overrule these cases, but sim-ply pointed out that there was, in each of them, an escape on to property over which the defendant had no control, from a container which the defendant had a licence to put in the highway.[109] On the other hand, the proposition that the rule also extends to cases where the defendant has no such licence in respect of a public thoroughfare is thought to be wrong.[110]

   The actual harm wrought by the escape need not be immediately caused by the thing accumulated. So, for example, it was held in *Kennard v Cory Bros & Co* that where parts of a coal slag heap escaped and their pressure on a third party's quarry spoil caused that spoil to damage the claimant's land, the escape requirement of the rule in *Rylands v Fletcher* was satisfied.[111]

---

[104] *Read v J Lyons & Co* [1947] AC 156, at 168.   [105] *Ponting v Noakes* [1894] 2 QB 281.

[106] This point was essential to the decision in *Hale v Jennings Bros* [1938] 1 All ER 579. Similarly, an escape to the lower part of the same building is sufficient: *J Doltis v Isaac Braithwaite & Sons (Engineers) Ltd* [1957] 1 Lloyd's Rep 522. The key to these cases appears to be an escape on to land under another's control, regardless of property ownership on D's part.   [107] [1905] 2 KB 597.

[108] [1914] 3 KB 772.

[109] [1947] AC 156, at 177. Cf ibid at 168 and 183.

[110] See the *obiter* suggestion in *Rigby v CC of Northamptonshire* [1985] 1 WLR 1242, at 1255 to this effect. See also *Crown River Cruises Ltd v Kimbolton Fireworks Ltd* [1996] 2 Lloyd's Rep 533 (escape from a vessel on a navigable waterway).   [111] [1921] AC 521, at 538.

SECTION 6   FORESEEABILITY OF HARM

Since the important decision in the *Cambridge Water* case, it is clear that foreseeability of harm is required if a claimant is to succeed in an action based on the rule in *Rylands v Fletcher*. The facts in that case were as follows.

> Solvents which had been used by Ds in their tannery for many years had a history of being spilt on to the floor of Ds' factory. From there, they seeped into a natural groundwater source drawn upon by C in order to fulfil its statutory duty to supply drinking water to the inhabitants of Cambridge. The seepage caused the water to become contaminated to the extent that it was unwholesome according to European Community standards. No one had supposed that this contamination would take place, mainly because of the volatility of the solvents which it had been thought had simply evaporated from Ds' factory floor.

A unanimous House of Lords held the defendants not liable on the basis of the unforeseeability of the harm caused to the claimant's water supply. Lord Goff, who delivered the only full speech in the case, stated that 'foreseeability of damage of the relevant type should be regarded as a prerequisite of liability in damages under the rule'.[112] What his Lordship failed to make clear, however, is whether damage had to be foreseeable (1) in terms of the *kind* of harm alone or (2) in terms of *both* an escape occurring *and* harm being thereby caused. However, since then it has been made clear that it is the former that is required. As Lord Bingham put it in the *Transco* case:

> It must be shown that the defendant has done something which he recognised, or judged by the standards appropriate at the relevant place and time, he ought reasonably to have recognised, as giving rise to an exceptionally high risk of danger or mischief if there should be an escape, however unlikely an escape may have been thought to be.[113]

SECTION 7   DEFENCES

(A) STATUTORY AUTHORITY

Sometimes, public bodies storing water, gas, electricity, and the like are by statute exempted from liability so long as they have taken reasonable care. It is a question of statutory interpretation whether (and, if so, to what extent) liability under the rule in *Rylands v Fletcher* has been excluded. Only if there is a statutory *duty* (as opposed to a

---

[112] [1994] 1 All ER 53, at 75.
[113] [2004] 2 AC 1, at [10]. This echoes Lord Goff in the *Cambridge Water* case (see [1994] 1 All ER 53, at 71) and *Hamilton v Papakura DC* [2002] UKPC 9, where the Privy Council also emphasised the need to establish the foreseeability of the relevant damage.

mere *permission*) to perform the hazardous activity will there be a defence. *Smeaton v Ilford Corpn*[114] is illustrative.

> Sewage accumulated by Ds in their sewers overflowed on to the land of C in circumstances which were held to constitute neither nuisance nor negligence. According to section 31 of the Public Health Act 1936, under which Ds had acted in receiving the sewage: 'A local authority shall so discharge their functions...as not to create a nuisance'. In interpreting this to mean that Ds were absolved from liability because they were *obliged* to fulfil the duty without creating a nuisance, the court held that Ds had a defence under the statute to an action based on *Rylands v Fletcher*.

Green v Chelsea Waterworks Co[115] provides a further example of the statutory authority defence in operation. In that case, there was no liability when a water main burst because the waterworks company was under *a statutory obligation* to keep the mains charged at high pressure making a damaging escape an inevitable consequence of any non-negligent burst. By contrast, in *Charing Cross Electricity Co v Hydraulic Power Co*,[116] the defendant, upon the true construction of the legislation, had a statutory permission (but no obligation) to keep its water mains charged at high pressure. On this basis, no immunity from liability could be claimed.

A final point in this context is that the defence only operates in respect of *Rylands v Fletcher* liability. So, if the reason for the escape is the defendant's negligence, the presence of a statutory duty to perform the hazardous activity will not afford a defence. This begs a further question: namely, 'Who is to bear the burden of proof, the claimant or the defendant?' There is no English authority on the point but a majority decision of the High Court of Australia once held the onus to lie with the claimant to show negligence.[117] It is submitted that this decision has little to commend it, for '*prima facie*', according to Blackburn J in *Rylands v Fletcher*, a defendant is 'answerable for all the damage which is the natural consequence of [the thing's]...escape'.[118]

(B) CONSENT OF THE CLAIMANT

If the claimant has permitted the defendant to accumulate the thing the escape of which is complained of, then he cannot sue if it escapes.[119] For the purposes of this defence, implied consent will clearly suffice. Thus, a person becoming the tenant of business premises at a time when the condition or construction of adjoining premises is such that an escape is likely to ensue is deemed to have consented to the risk of such an event actually happening. This defence was the crux of *Kiddle v City Business Properties Ltd*[120] where an overflow of rainwater from a blocked gutter at the bottom

---

[114] [1954] Ch 450.
[115] (1894) 70 LT 547.   [116] [1914] 3 KB 772.
[117] *Benning v Wong* (1969) 43 ALJR 467. Since then, Australia has ceased to recognise liability under the rule in *Rylands v Fletcher*: *Burnie Port Authority v General Jones Pty Ltd* (1994) 179 CLR 520.
[118] (1866) LR 1 Exch 265, at 280.   [119] *Kennard v Cory Bros & Co Ltd* [1921] AC 521.
[120] [1942] 1 KB 269.

of a sloping roof in the possession of the landlord, and above the tenant's premises, damaged the stock in the tenant's premises.[121]

If the accumulation benefits both claimant and defendant, this is an important element in deciding whether the claimant is deemed to have consented.[122] Where, therefore, rainwater is collected on the roof for the benefit of the several occupants of a building,[123] or where a water-closet is installed,[124] or water pipes are fitted,[125] the various occupants are presumed to have consented. On the other hand, the defence does not seem to be available as between a commercial supplier of gas (in respect of gas mains under the highway) and a consumer in premises adjoining the highway.[126] In any event, an occupier will not be presumed to have consented to installations being left in a dangerously unsafe state.[127]

(C) CONTRIBUTORY NEGLIGENCE AND RELATED MATTERS

Where the claimants worked a mine under the canal of the defendant, and had good reason to know that they would thereby cause the water from the canal to escape into this mine, it was held that the claimants could not invoke the rule in *Rylands v Fletcher* when the water actually escaped and damaged their mine. Cockburn CJ described the matter thus: 'the plaintiffs saw the danger and may be said to have courted it'.[128] Where the claimant is contributorily negligent, the apportionment provisions of the Law Reform (Contributory Negligence) Act 1945 will now apply. In addition, as was said in *Eastern and Southern African Telegraph Co Ltd v Cape Town Tramways Co Ltd*, 'a man cannot increase the liabilities of his neighbour by applying his own property to special uses, whether for business or pleasure'.[129] In that case, the claimant, who complained that the tramways of the defendant caused electrical interference with the receipt of messages through his submarine cable, failed in his action because no damage to the cable itself was caused. The claimant suffered loss only because he relied on the cable for the transmission of messages.[130]

---

[121] The principle of implied consent does not apply, however, where C and D are not in a tenant–landlord relationship: *Humphries v Cousins* (1877) 2 CPD 239.

[122] *Peters v Prince of Wales Theatre (Birmingham) Ltd* [1943] KB 73. Where C has, by inference, consented to receiving the benefit of D's watercourse, but contends he has not consented to a negligent accumulation of water, C must prove negligence: *Gilson v Kerrier RDC* [1976] 3 All ER 343.

[123] *Carstairs v Taylor* (1871) LR 6 Exch 217.   [124] *Ross v Fedden* (1872) LR 7 QB 661.

[125] *Anderson v Oppenheimer* (1880) 5 QBD 602 (the reasoning is muddled, but this is the most likely basis of the decision).

[126] *Northwestern Utilities Ltd v London Guarantee and Accident Co Ltd* [1936] AC 108, at 120.

[127] *A Prosser & Sons Ltd v Levy* [1955] 3 All ER 577.

[128] *Dunn v Birmingham Canal Navigation Co* (1872) LR 7 QB 244, at 260 (affirmed LR 8 QB 42).

[129] [1902] AC 381, at 393. Cf *Hoare & Co v McAlpine* [1923] 1 Ch 167 which left open the question of whether C, who complains that his buildings have been damaged, could be met by the plea that they were damaged only because they were dilapidated buildings having insecure foundations.

[130] This decision may, however, be better understood in terms of C's loss not being a sufficiently direct consequence of the escape.

(D) ACT OF A THIRD PARTY: THE RULE IN *RYLANDS v FLETCHER* OR NEGLIGENCE?

What must next be considered is whether it is a defence that, although the defendant brought the thing on to his land, it has only escaped through the act of a third party. It is evident from *Rylands v Fletcher* itself that the defendant is liable for an escape attributable to his independent contractors. Further, there is weighty support for the proposition that the defendant is liable for escapes caused by any other third party where the defendant ought reasonably to have foreseen the act of that third party and had enough control of the premises to be able to prevent it. The proprietor of a chair-o-plane was accordingly held liable for the escape of a chair caused by a passenger tampering with it;[131] the owner of a flag-pole was also liable when small children caused the pole to fall and injure the claimant.[132] Similarly, a gas company laying a main in a highway was liable for damage caused by an explosion of gas when the surrounding earth subsided due to a third party's subjacent mines.[133]

On the other hand, in *Rickards v Lothian*, the defendant was not liable where flooding of the claimant's premises was caused by an unknown third party who had maliciously turned on a water tap in the defendant's premises and blocked the waste pipe of the lavatory basin.[134] Nor was there liability in *Box v Jubb* where the defendant's reservoir overflowed when a third party, conducting operations higher up the stream supplying it, discharged downstream an unusually large volume of water without any warning.[135]

There has been a tendency – an example of which is *Perry v Kendricks*[136] – for these two cases to be taken to support the view that once the defendants have proved that the escape was due to the act of a stranger 'they avoid liability, unless the claimant can go on to show that the act which caused the escape was an act of the kind which the owner could reasonably have contemplated and guarded against'.[137] It is the present submission, however, that although the case law itself clearly supports such a proposition, it has nonetheless been somewhat misguided in its approach. Thus, while it is not suggested that the actual decisions in the two cases are wrong, it is nonetheless contended that the legal doctrine according to which they ought to have been decided

---

[131] *Hale v Jennings Bros* [1938] 1 All ER 579.

[132] *Shiffman v Venerable Order of the Hospital of St John of Jerusalem* [1936] 1 All ER 557, at 561 (*obiter* regarding *Rylands v Fletcher*).

[133] *Hanson v Wearmouth Coal Co Ltd and Sunderland Gas Co* [1939] 3 All ER 47.

[134] *Rickards v Lothian* [1913] AC 263.

[135] (1879) 4 Ex D 76. Cf *Black v Christchurch Finance Co Ltd* [1894] AC 48. Analogous cases to those last cited are those suggesting that there is no liability where an unobservable defect of nature causes the escape, or where there is flooding because a rat gnaws through a water cistern: *Carstairs v Taylor* (1871) LR 6 Exch 217.

[136] [1956] 1 All ER 154.

[137] Ibid at 161, per Parker LJ. Likewise, Jenkins LJ held (at 160) that once the act of a stranger is made out, 'one reaches the point where the claim based on *Rylands v Fletcher* merges into the claim in negligence'.

is mistaken: they are, by nature, more in line with negligence, not *Rylands*, principles. The reasoning for this assertion is as follows.

Since the rule in *Rylands v Fletcher* is a strict liability tort, it follows that negligence in the narrow sense (that is, the breach of a duty to take reasonable care) should play no part in determining liability. This much was made abundantly clear by Lord Goff in *Cambridge Water v Eastern Counties Leather plc* when he said: 'the defendant will be liable for harm caused to the claimant by the escape, notwithstanding that he has exercised all reasonable care and skill to prevent the escape from occurring'.[138] Similarly, in *Transco v Stockport MBC*, Lord Hoffmann stressed the immateriality of the fact that the defendant could not reasonably have foreseen an escape.[139] In other words, and contrary to the view in *Perry v Kendricks* just quoted, it should not matter whether the defendant 'could reasonably have contemplated and guarded against' the intervention of a third party. The better approach is to say that such reasoning has nothing to do with the rule in *Rylands v Fletcher*. In essence, these cases do not involve a failure to control (that is, keep in) a dangerous thing (*Rylands*); they centre, instead, upon the question of whether there was a failure to control the unforeseeable harmful acts of third parties (negligence). The distinction between these two classes of negligent omission was staunchly made by the House of Lords in *Smith v Littlewoods Organisation Ltd*.[140]

It is also quite clear that the rule in *Rylands v Fletcher* (which is concerned with escapes) is to be contrasted with deliberate discharges of the dangerous thing on to another's land. Those cases – at least where the discharge is by the person who accumulated the thing – should sound in trespass.[141]

(E) ACT OF GOD

This defence has received a prominence out of all proportion to its practical importance. It arises only where an escape is caused through natural causes and without human intervention, in 'circumstances which no human foresight can provide against, and of which human prudence is not bound to recognise the possibility'.[142] Thus, the defence succeeded in *Nichols v Marsland*[143] where a most violent thunderstorm caused flooding. Yet the defence was put in its proper perspective by the House of Lords in *Greenock Corpn v Caledonian Rly Co*[144] where an extraordinary and unprecedented rainfall was held in similar circumstances not to be an act of God. The explanation of *Nichols v Marsland*, in this case, was that, in *Nichols v Marsland*, the jury found that no

---

[138] [1994] 1 All ER 53, at 71. In Australia, this tort has been abandoned and replaced by a 'non-delegable duty' in negligence: *Burnie Port Authority v General Jones Pty Ltd* (1994) 120 ALR 42.

[139] [2004] 2 AC 1, at [27].

[140] [1987] 1 All ER 710. See also *Topp v London Country Bus (South West) Ltd* [1993] 1 WLR 976.

[141] *Rigby v CC of Northamptonshire* [1985] 1 WLR 1242, at 1255.

[142] A definition of Lord Westbury in *Tennent v Earl of Glasgow* (1864) 2 M 22, at 26–7 (followed in *Greenock Corpn v Caledonian Rly Co* [1917] AC 556).   [143] (1876) 2 Ex D 1.

[144] [1917] AC 556.

reasonable person could have anticipated the storm and the court would not disturb this finding of fact.

The problem with the way in which the defence has been construed by the courts is that they make its incidence referable to reasonable foresight of the cause of an escape. This, on one construction, tends to undermine the strictness of *Rylands* liability because it makes the defendant's liability depend, like the unforeseeable acts of a third party just considered, upon the existence of fault.[145] However, a second (and preferable) construction of the defence is possible. This involves requiring that an act of God be beyond *all*, not just reasonable, human foresight. According to this construction, we are not excusing the defendant because the natural event causing the escape was beyond what could reasonably have been foreseen; instead, we are concerned with identifying the truly unique and freak occurrence (which should be distinguished from the highly unusual – but not unknown – event).[146] On this basis, it might be argued that few phenomena beyond earthquakes and tornadoes are likely to constitute an act of God for the purposes of this defence. Certainly, the paucity of occasions on which the defence has succeeded would tend to vindicate this view.

(F) NECESSITY

If an intentional release of a substance could ground liability under the rule in *Rylands v Fletcher*, then the defence of necessity ought, on principle, to be available in this tort.[147] However, it is probably better to treat such cases as trespass cases in which raising the defence of necessity is well established.[148] Certainly, in one first instance case in which police officers had fired CS gas canisters into the claimant's shop in order to flush out a psychopath, it was suggested that trespass would be the appropriate cause of action.[149]

---

[145] If this construction is accepted, the failure to prevent the escape ought, instead, to sound in negligence.

[146] To allow reasonable foreseeability of the abnormal event to play a part in defining the defence is also, and inescapably, to suggest that foresight of such events is a factor which determines prima facie liability. And while, in the wake of the *Cambridge Water* case, it is clear that foreseeability is a relevant factor in a *Rylands* action, it is important to appreciate that it only operates to characterise the kind of harm, for which D would otherwise be prima facie liable, as too remote. If foreseeability of the 'freak' event were to play a part in defining this defence, however, it would operate at the level of the *definition* (as opposed to *limitation*) of prima facie liability. (For *obiter* judicial support for this view see *Ellison v Ministry of Defence* (1996) 81 BLR 101.)

[147] On the basis of the assumption that the rule in *Rylands v Fletcher* could apply to deliberate releases, this point was conceded in *Rigby v CC of Northamptonshire* [1985] 1 WLR 1242, at 1255. However, the judge was of the view that the rule should not be applied to deliberate releases.

[148] On the defence of necessity, see ch 11.

[149] *Rigby v CC of Northamptonshire* [1985] 1 WLR 1242, at 1255.

SECTION 8   NUISANCE AND THE RULE IN
RYLANDS v FLETCHER

The *Cambridge Water* case suggested that the rule in *Rylands v Fletcher* was properly to be considered a sub-branch of the law of nuisance. But we believe that there are a number of bases on which this understanding can be refuted. To begin with, although they are both land-based torts, the focus in private nuisance is on the land in which the claimant has a proprietary interest.[150] By contrast, under the rule in *Rylands v Fletcher,* the focus is upon the land owned or controlled by the defendant; there is no requirement for the purposes of this tort that the claimant should have a proprietary interest in any land at all.[151] Similarly, while the escape must be from the defendant's land in *Rylands v Fletcher,* there is no requirement in private nuisance that the defendant be an occupier of land.[152]

Second, although the House of Lords made clear in *Hunter v Canary Wharf Ltd*[153] the fact that personal injuries could not be recovered under the tort of private nuisance, there is no such prohibition in operation under the rule in *Rylands v Fletcher,* as cases such as *Hale v Jennings Bros* illustrate. The only judicial suggestions to the contrary that exist were uttered *obiter.*[154]

Third, a use of land may be artificial (and therefore non-natural, so as to fall within the rule in *Rylands v Fletcher*) without being unreasonable (so as to satisfy the unreasonable user test in private nuisance). Thus, while no one would seriously consider the building of a reservoir to be unreasonable (given the importance to society of water storage), nor would anyone consider a reservoir to be anything other than an artificial construction. Furthermore, while the reasonableness of the defendant's user is a relevant *factor* that may be taken into account in assessing nuisance liability, it is not, per se, a *precondition* of liability since it is ultimately only the unreasonableness of the interference that counts.[155] By contrast, the non-natural use of land is absolutely central to *Rylands* liability. The House of Lords specifically insisted on this in their amendment of the rule promulgated by Blackburn J.

Fourth, the occupier of land is readily made liable under the rule in *Rylands v Fletcher* for the accumulations and escapes caused by independent contractors. By contrast, in private nuisance, the liability for independent contractors is markedly less extensive.[156]

---

[150] *Hunter v Canary Wharf Ltd* [1997] 2 All ER 426.

[151] *Hale v Jennings Bros* [1938] 1 All ER 579. But if – as is often dubiously suggested – the rule in *Rylands v Fletcher* derives from nuisance, why not?

[152] *L E Jones (Insurance Brokers) v Portsmouth CC* [2003] 1 WLR 427.   [153] [1997] 2 All ER 426.

[154] See Murphy (2004) 24 OJLS 643.

[155] See, eg, *Sampson v Hodson-Pressinger* [1981] 3 All ER 710, where the ordinary use of premises which, as a result of their being poorly constructed, caused intolerable noise to be perceived in adjoining premises was held to be a nuisance. See also *Toff v McDowell* (1993) 25 HLR 650.

[156] See ch 16.

Beyond these five instances it is difficult to state with certainty further circumstances where the distinction between nuisance and the rule in *Rylands v Fletcher* exists. But this does not mean that such distinctions cannot be suggested. For example, it is generally accepted that *Rylands v Fletcher* cases turn on isolated escapes, whereas in nuisance cases the interference is normally supposed to be an ongoing one.[157] That being so, it becomes difficult to square the 'state of affairs' nuisance cases[158] with nuisance law orthodoxy. And if these cases are truly anomalous, a further distinction – based on persistence *versus* one-off escape – comes into being.

FURTHER READING

HALL, 'An Unsearchable Providence: the Lawyer's Concept of Act of God' (1993) 12 *Oxford Journal of Legal Studies* 227

MURPHY, 'The Merits of *Rylands v Fletcher*' (2004) 24 *Oxford Journal of Legal Studies* 643

NOLAN, 'The Distinctiveness of *Rylands v Fletcher*' (2005) 121 *Law Quarterly Review* 421

OLIPHANT, '*Rylands v Fletcher* and the Emergence of Enterprise Liability in the Common Law' [2004] *European Tort Law* 81

STANTON, 'The Legacy of *Rylands v Fletcher*' in Mullany and Linden (eds), *Torts Tomorrow: A Tribute to John Fleming* (1998)

WILKINSON, '*Cambridge Water Company v Eastern Counties Leather plc*: Diluting Liability for Continuing Escapes' (1994) 57 *Modern Law Review* 799

WILLIAMS, 'Non-Natural Use of Land' [1973] *Cambridge Law Journal* 310

---

[157] Cf Newark (1949) 65 LQR 480, at 488.

[158] See, eg, *Midwood & Co Ltd v Manchester Corpn* [1905] 2 KB 597. But for compelling criticism of this and other such cases, see Nolan (2005) 121 LQR 421.

18

ANIMALS

KEY ISSUES

(1) Five broad categories of liability

Liability in tort for damage caused by animals can be placed into five distinct categories. The first consists of common law liability. The second, third, fourth, and fifth categories are all to be derived from the Animals Act 1971 and they relate, in turn, to liability for dangerous animals, liability for non-dangerous species, liability for straying livestock, and liability for loss of livestock caused by dogs.

(2) Common law liability

Over the years, the courts have held that a range of familiar torts – including negligence, battery, nuisance, and public nuisance – can all be committed through the instrumentality of animals. For these purposes, it does not matter whether the animal is of a kind that is commonly tamed or domesticated.

(3) Liability for dangerous animals under the Animals Act 1971

The 1971 Act creates a somewhat complex rule of strict liability for damage caused by dangerous animals. The Act provides its own definition of what constitutes a dangerous species. And this definition turns upon the pivotal concepts of whether it is a species that is not commonly domesticated in the British

Isles and whether a full-grown animal of that species has either a propensity to cause harm or a propensity to cause severe harm in the event (which need not be independently likely) that it does cause harm.

(4) Liability for other animals under the Animals Act 1971

The 1971 Act also provides a complex liability rule in relation to animals that do not belong to a dangerous species. Critical to such liability is knowledge on the part of the animal's keeper (which term is defined by the Act) that *this particular animal*, though not belonging to a dangerous species, is nonetheless likely to cause harm if unrestrained.

(5) Liability for straying livestock under the Animals Act 1971

The 1971 Act instantiates a third set of rules that apply to straying 'livestock'. The term livestock receives specific definition under the Act.

(6) Liability for injury to livestock caused by dogs under the Animals Act 1971

Within this fourth category of statutory liability, the Act sets specific limits on the circumstances in which liability will be incurred for injury to livestock caused by dogs.

SECTION 1   COMMON LAW LIABILITY

Persons who own or control animals can perfectly well be held liable under established categories of tort law although those categories have nothing specifically to do with animals. Thus, for example, in *Leeman v Montagu*,[1] a poultry farmer was held liable in nuisance in respect of the disturbance caused by his crowing cockerels. And in *Draper v Hodder*[2] the owner of a pack of terriers was found liable in negligence when his dogs bit a neighbour's child; for he had been negligent in failing to control and/or train the pack adequately. An occupier of premises may also be liable under the Occupiers' Liability Acts in respect of injuries inflicted by dogs on his premises,[3] while liability in battery can be imposed where a dog owner or handler sets the dog upon another.[4] Finally, escaping animals may incur liability under the rule in *Rylands v Fletcher*[5] or, most commonly – and as dealt with in depth below – in accordance with the law of trespass.

SECTION 2   STATUTORY LIABILITY FOR DANGEROUS ANIMALS

(A) DANGEROUS SPECIES

Section 2(1) of the Animals Act 1971 imposes strict liability where any damage is caused by an animal that belongs to a dangerous species. A dangerous species, for these purposes, is one that is not commonly domesticated in the British Isles, and whose fully grown animals have such characteristics that (1) they are likely, unless restrained, to cause severe damage, or (2) they are of a kind that any damage they do cause is likely to be severe.[6] 'Damage' for the purposes of the Act embraces harm to either persons or property. The list is thus not confined to animals likely to attack man, such as bears, tigers, etc. An action also lies under the Act even though the damage caused is not of the kind in respect of which the species is known to be dangerous. Furthermore, liability can also arise even though the animal has not escaped from the control of its keeper. So, a keeper would be liable if his elephant slips or stumbles and thereby causes damage. 'Damage' also includes the impairment of any mental condition.[7] So if someone suffered psychiatric illness by virtue of the sudden appearance of a cobra, there would be liability.

---

[1] [1936] 2 All ER 1677.   [2] [1972] 2 QB 556.   [3] *Hill v Lovett* 1992 SLT 994 (OH).
[4] *Roberts v CC Kent* [2008] EWCA Civ 1588.   [5] *Behrens v Bertram Mills Circus Ltd* [1957] 2 QB 1.
[6] Animals Act 1971, s 6(2).
[7] Animals Act 1971, s 11.

(B) NON-DANGEROUS SPECIES

Section 2(2) of the Animals Act 1971 imposes liability in certain (convoluted) circumstances for an animal that does not belong to a dangerous species. It provides:

> Where damage is caused by an animal which does not belong to a dangerous species, a keeper of the animal is liable for the damage if:
>
> (a) the damage is of a kind which the animal, unless restrained, was likely to cause or which, if caused by the animal, was likely to be severe; and
>
> (b) the likelihood of the damage or of its being severe was due to characteristics of the animal which are not normally found in animals of the same species or are not normally so found except at particular times or in particular circumstances; and
>
> (c) those characteristics were known to that keeper or were at any time known to a person who at that time had charge of the animal as that keeper's servant or, where that keeper is the head of a household, were known to another keeper of the animal who is a member of that household and under the age of sixteen.

According to this subsection, three conditions must be met before the keeper may be held liable.[8] First, the damage must be of a kind which the animal, unless restrained, was likely to cause[9] or which, if caused by the animal, was likely to be severe. (There is no need to show that the severity of the potential damage ensues from any abnormal characteristics in the animal.)[10] This formulation would, therefore, cover not only an animal that attacks a person, but also one with a dangerous disease, such as foot and mouth, that spreads the infection to other animals.

The second subparagraph focuses on unusual characteristics in the animal or those that are not normally found in animals of the same species[11] except at particular times or in particular circumstances. This requirement embraces behaviour that is to be expected of a particular species *but only* in special circumstances, such as where the animal is frightened. Thus, in *Mirvahedy v Henly*,[12] a cause of action lay where the claimant was injured by a horse that had been panicked and escaped from its field. A majority of their Lordships took the view that bolting was *not a* normal characteristic of a horse even though in such circumstances it would be typical of the species. It was therefore abnormal behaviour within the meaning of section 2(2)(b). The same applies

---

[8] Note that one keeper may be liable to another keeper: *Flack v Hudson* [2001] QB 698.

[9] In *Smith v Ainger* [1990] CLY 3297 it was held that it is enough to prove merely that the injurious occurrence was one 'such as might happen'. In *Mirvahedy v Henly* [2003] 2 AC 491, however, Lord Scott (at [97]–[98]) disagreed with this test. Instead, he opined (in his dissenting speech) that damage would be 'likely' if it was 'reasonably to be expected'.   [10] *Curtis v Betts* [1990] 1 All ER 769.

[11] Section 11 of the Animals Act 1971 defines 'species' to include subspecies. It seems that different breeds of dogs are treated as subspecies: *Curtis v Betts* [1990] 1 All ER 769.

[12] [2003] 2 AC 491. See also *Cummings v Granger* [1977] QB 397 (C bitten by D's Alsatian dog which was used as a guard dog in his scrap yard. The dog barked and ran around when non-white people, like C, approached. This is not a usual characteristic in Alsatian dogs, except when used as guard dogs. Accordingly, this was held to be a particular circumstance within the Animals Act 1971, s 2(2)(b)).

to the aggression of a bull mastiff dog defending his 'territory'.[13] For the purposes of this subsection, the Court of Appeal have explained that the word 'normally' should be understood in the light of what the species as a whole can be expected to do, rather than in the light of what is normal for the particular creature. Thus, in one case, liability was imposed in respect of a rearing horse that injured the claimant *even though* that particular horse had no record at all of such behaviour.[14]

The third requirement of this subsection is that the animal's unusual characteristics must have been known to the keeper, or to his servant, or to a member of his household under the age of 16. Thus, a cattle owner was held not liable for damage caused by a cow disturbed by the fact that it had been separated from its calf: crucially, there was 'no evidence that cows in general become excessively agitated when they are weaned from their calves'.[15] This part of the subsection further requires that a causal link between the 'abnormal' characteristic and the injury be established.[16]

(C) LIABILITY FOR 'KEEPERS'

Strict liability under the Animals Act 1971 is imposed on the 'keeper' regardless of whether the animal in question belongs to a dangerous or a non-dangerous species. A keeper for these purposes is defined in terms of the person who owns the animal or has it in his possession, or who is head of the household of which a member under the age of 16 owns the animal or has it in his possession.[17] This last provision prevents evasion of liability by making a child in the family the nominal owner. If a person ceases to keep, own, or possess it, he continues to be liable until another person owns or possesses it.[18]

(D) DEFENCES

While liability under the Act is imposed regardless of fault, the defendant is not liable for any damage which is due wholly to the fault of the person suffering it.[19] Damages will certainly be reduced under the Law Reform (Contributory Negligence) Act 1945 where the claimant – through his own fault – contributes to his damage.[20] It is also a defence under the Act that the damage was suffered by a person who has voluntarily accepted the risk.[21] And, according to the Court of Appeal: '[w]hat must be proved

---

[13] *Curtis v Betts* [1990] 1 All ER 769.

[14] *Welsh v Stokes* [2008] 1 WLR 1224. See also *Freeman v Higher Park Farm* [2009] PIQR P6.

[15] *McKenny v Foster* [2008] EWCA Civ 173, at [32].

[16] *Jaundrill v Gillett* (1996) *Times* , 30 January.   [17] Animals Act 1971, s 6(3).

[18] Animals Act 1971. But a person who takes possession only for the purpose of preventing damage or restoring it to its owner is not thereby made liable: s 6(4).

[19] Animals Act 1971, s 5(1). It has been applied where C ignored police warnings to come out and was subsequently bitten by a police dog: *Dhesi v CC of West Midlands* 2000 WL 491455.

[20] Animals Act 1971, s 10.

[21] Animals Act 1971, s 5(2). In *Cummings v Granger* [1977] QB 397, the court found that when C knew of the dog she must be taken to have voluntarily accepted the risk. The court, esp Ormrod LJ (at 408), treated this defence as being wider than the common law defence of *volenti*.

in order to show that somebody has voluntarily accepted the risk is that (1) they fully appreciated the risk, and (2) they exposed themselves to it'.[22] However, an employee who accepts a risk that is necessarily incidental to his employment shall not be treated as accepting it voluntarily.[23]

It is also a defence that the damage occurred on property where the claimant was a trespasser[24] *so long as* it is proved either that the animal was not kept there for the protection of persons or property or, if kept for those purposes, that thus keeping it there was not unreasonable.[25] Presumably it would be difficult to maintain this defence in respect of a dangerous species being kept for protection only, because that might well be unreasonable. Trespassers will never have a remedy when attacked by an animal of a dangerous species not kept for protection.

SECTION 3   LIABILITY FOR STRAYING LIVESTOCK

Section 4 of the Animals Act 1971 imposes liability on a person in possession of livestock which strays on to another's land.[26] Under the Act, 'livestock' means cattle, horses, asses, mules, hinnies, sheep, pigs, goats, poultry, and deer not in the wild state.[27] Liability is for damage done by the livestock to the land or to any property on it.[28] Presumably, 'property' includes other animals as well as goods, but the claimant cannot recover under section 4 for his personal injuries. Either the person in possession, or the owner (even though not in possession), can recover for damage to his land or property.

A claimant may incur expense in keeping livestock while it cannot be restored to its owner, or while it is detained in pursuance of the power conferred by the Animals Act 1971 to detain it.[29] He can recover any such expenses reasonably incurred.[30] Liability is strict under this section, but the defendant is not liable for any damage due wholly

---

[22] *Freeman v Higher Park Farm* [2009] PIQR P6, at P112.

[23] Animals Act 1971, s 6(5); *Canterbury CC v Howletts & Port Lympne Estates Ltd* [1997] ICR 925 (a tiger keeper was killed by one of the zoo's tigers; the zoo especially encouraged 'bonding' between the tigers and their keeper which necessitated entering the cage regularly: the keeper's dependants could recover damages).

[24] Since the creation in the Countryside and Rights of Way Act 2000 of certain rights to roam, there will now be a smaller number of potential trespassers in relation to whom this defence can be raised.

[25] Animals Act 1971, s 5(3); *Cummings v Granger* [1977] QB 397 (it was reasonable to keep an Alsatian dog, known to be ferocious, to protect old cars in a locked yard).

[26] Where an animal strays on to the highway, the ordinary rules of negligence apply: see, eg, *Hole v Ross Skinner* [2003] EWCA Civ 774; *Wilson v Donaldson* [2004] EWCA Civ 972.

[27] Animals Act 1971, s 11.

[28] Cases involving loss (but no damage) would not be covered (eg, if the Ministry of Agriculture makes a foot-and-mouth order restricting movement of cattle, but none of C's cattle are destroyed).

[29] Animals Act 1971, s 7. See *Matthews v Wicks* (1987) *Times*, 25 May; *Morris v Blaenau Gwent DC* (1982) 80 LGR 793.   [30] Animals Act 1971, s 4(1)(b).

to the fault of the claimant.[31] Thus, if the claimant could have prevented the damage by fencing,[32] and the claimant was under a duty (owed to a person having an interest in the land from which the livestock strayed) to fence, the defendant is not liable so long as the straying would not have occurred but for that breach on the part of the claimant.[33]

The Law Reform (Contributory Negligence) Act 1945 again applies in respect of damage in part caused by the claimant's own fault.[34] It is also a defence that the livestock strayed from a highway and its presence there was a lawful use of the highway. This is because the owner of property adjoining a highway is presumed to have accepted risks incidental to such ownership.[35]

SECTION 4 LIABILITY FOR INJURY DONE BY DOGS TO LIVESTOCK

Section 3 of the Animals Act 1971 provides that where a dog kills or injures livestock[36] its keeper is liable for the damage, even though he was not negligent. But a person is not liable if the livestock was killed or injured on land on to which it had strayed and either the dog belonged to the occupier or its presence on the land was authorised by the occupier.[37] It is a defence that the damage was due wholly to the fault of the person suffering it.[38]

FURTHER READING

LAW COMMISSION, *Civil Liability for Animals* (1967)
NORTH, *The Modern Law of Animals* (1972)

---

[31] Animals Act 1971, s 5(1); *Nelmes v CC of Avon and Somerset Constabulary* (9 February 1993) (unreported) (C kicked a police dog, before his arrest, provoking it into biting him).
[32] Fencing includes the construction of any obstacle designed to prevent animals from straying.
[33] Animals Act 1971, s 5(6). In the absence of any such duty to fence, there is no defence under the Act.
[34] Animals Act 1971, ss 10 and 11.
[35] Animals Act 1971, s 5(4), (5).
[36] Livestock for this purpose is a slightly wider category than the one under s 4 in that it includes pheasants, partridges, and grouse while in captivity: Animals Act 1971, s 11.
[37] Animals Act 1971, s 5(4).
[38] Animals Act 1971, s 5(1). If C, by his own fault, has contributed to the damage, the Law Reform (Contributory Negligence) Act 1945 applies to permit a reduction of the damages awarded.

19

BREACH OF STATUTORY DUTY

KEY ISSUES

(1) Deciding when rights of action exist
The simple fact that the defendant is in breach of a statutory duty will not automatically confer a right of action on anyone adversely affected by it. If the statute does not state clearly that an action may be brought, the question is resolved as a matter of statutory interpretation. In order to sue (in the absence of a specifically created right of action) the statute must, on its proper construction, reveal parliamentary intent either to (i) create the obligation either for the benefit of the claimant (or a class to which the claimant belongs) or (ii) create a public right that is actionable by the claimant upon breach of the duty *because* the claimant suffers more severe harm than the public in general.

(2) Breach of statutory duty will not ground an action for negligence
The mere existence of a statutory duty will not support an action for common-law

negligence should the duty in question be performed carelessly. The statutory duty may create a relationship from which a common-law duty will arise; but it is the relationship (not the statutory duty) that is vital in such cases.

(3) The statute must envisage both the claimant and the kind of loss suffered
Any successful action for breach of statutory duty will require the claimant to show *both* that he or she was intended to be protected by the duty *and* that the protection was aimed at preventing the kind of loss actually suffered.

(4) What is needed to establish a breach of duty may vary
Care must be taken to identify the nature of the duty in any given statute. Sometimes liability will be strict (thus exonerating the claimant from proving fault or intention), while on other occasions the duty may require proof of fault.

SECTION 1   INTRODUCTION

Exceptionally, a person suffering damage as a result of a violation of a statute may have an action in tort in respect of that damage, commonly called an action for breach of statutory duty. For the claimant, the great advantage in many cases of such an action is the fact that all he needs to prove is that the defendant failed to fulfil his statutory obligation. There is no requirement to establish that the breach was either intentional or negligent. The early cases on the tort rested on the broad principle that, whenever a violation of a statute caused damage to an individual's interests, a right of action in tort arose.[1] Leading nineteenth-century decisions[2] markedly restricted the scope of the tort, however, and required that anyone claiming for breach of statutory duty must first establish that the legislature intended that a violation of his right or interest should be tortious.

Lord Denning MR attempted (ultimately unsuccessfully) to resurrect the broader principle in *Ex p Island Records Ltd*,[3] arguing, '[if] a private right is being interfered with by a criminal act, thus causing or threatening to cause him special damage over and above the generality of the public, then he can come to the court as a private individual and ask that his private right be protected'.[4] Had this 'Denning principle' taken root, it would have transformed the action for breach of statutory duty and opened up the way for greater protection of individual interests by tort law in two crucial respects. First, in respect of damage to economic and business interests, claimants could have taken advantage of the extensive provision made by statute to regulate the economy in order to obtain compensation for losses falling outside the compass of the economic torts.[5] Second, citizens aggrieved by the failure of public authorities to fulfil obligations designed to protect their welfare could have sought extensive redress from central and local government. The decisions of the House of Lords in *Lonrho Ltd v Shell Petroleum Co Ltd (No 2)*[6] and *X v Bedfordshire County Council*[7] appear, however, to have stifled the further development of the action for breach of statutory duty.

The claimant in *Lonrho* was an oil company which had suffered heavy losses because it had complied with government sanctions orders prohibiting trade with the illegal regime in Rhodesia, while its competitors had flagrantly violated those orders. Relying on *Ex p Island Records*, the claimants sought to sue their competitors for breach of the orders. The House of Lords firmly rejected the 'Denning principle',[8] reasserting that the general rule in a claim for breach of statutory duty is that 'where an Act creates an obligation and enforces performance in a specified manner...that performance cannot be enforced in any other manner'.[9] Where the only manner of enforcing

---

[1] *Couch v Steel* (1854) 3 E & B 402 was the last important case resting on the old broad principle.

[2] *Atkinson v Newcastle and Gateshead Waterworks Co* (1877) 2 Ex D 441; *Groves v Lord Wimborne* [1898] 2 QB 402.

[3] [1978] Ch 122.   [4] Ibid at 139.

[5] According to a majority of the House of Lords in *OBG v Allan* [2008] 1 AC 1, the breach of a regulatory statute shall not be taken to amount to unlawful means for the purposes of the tort of causing economic loss by unlawful means.   [6] [1982] AC 173.

[7] [1995] 2 AC 633.

[8] Technically, the *Lonrho* case involved a claim for damages whereas in *Ex p Island Records* injunctive relief was sought. The CA later clarified that it makes no difference which type of remedy is sought: *RCA Corp v Pollard* [1983] Ch 135.

[9] *Doe d Bishop of Rochester v Bridges* (1831) 1 B & Ad 847, at 859.

performance for which the Act provides is the criminal process, there are only two classes of exception to this general rule. The first is where 'on the true construction of the Act it is apparent that the obligation or prohibition was imposed for the benefit of a particular class of individuals'.[10] The second arises where the statute creates a public right and an individual member of the public suffers damage which is 'particular, direct and substantial damage other and different from that which is common to the rest of the public'.[11] Lonrho's claim fell outside both exceptions. Sanctions orders prohibiting trade with Rhodesia were intended to end all trade and bring down the illegal regime. They were not imposed for the benefit of any class to which Lonrho belonged; nor did they create a public right.

In *X v Bedfordshire County Council* the House of Lords held that no action for breach of statutory duty arose out of *either* legislation imposing duties on local authorities to safeguard the welfare of children in their area and protect them from child abuse, *or* legislation requiring local authorities to meet the educational needs of children in their district. Lord Browne-Wilkinson acknowledged that legislation to protect children at risk and to provide for education was undoubtedly designed to benefit those children, but found that it was not Parliament's intention to allow individual children harmed by a local authority's failure to meet its statutory obligations to recover compensation for that harm from the public purse. His Lordship noted that no case had been cited before the court where statutory provisions creating a general regulatory scheme to promote social welfare had been held to give rise to a private law claim for damages. He went on to say:

> [a]lthough regulatory or welfare legislation affecting a particular area of activity does in fact provide protection to those individuals particularly affected by that activity, the legislation is not to be treated as being passed for the benefit of those individuals *but for the benefit of society in general.*[12]

Subsequent to the House of Lords reaching its decision in the *Bedfordshire* case, the claimants pursued their case in the European Court of Human Rights where it was held that there had been a breach of both Articles 3 and 13 of the European Convention on Human Rights.[13] These Articles provide, respectively, for protection from inhuman or degrading treatment and the right to an adequate remedy under domestic law. However, the Strasbourg court's finding does not affect the action for breach of statutory duty. Instead, its repercussions have been felt in the context of common law negligence actions[14] and, of course, in relation to actions under section 7 of the Human Rights Act 1998, which provides a cause of action where 'a public authority has acted

---

[10] [1982] AC 173, at 186.

[11] Ibid at 186 (citing a test formulated in *Benjamin v Storr* (1874) LR 9 CP 400, at 407).

[12] [1995] 2 AC 633, at 731–2 (emphasis added). See also confirmation of this approach in *Phelps v Hillingdon LBC* [2001 2 AC 619.   [13] *Z v UK* (2001) 34 EHRR 97. See also ch 1.

[14] See, principally, *D v East Berkshire Community NHS Trust* [2005] 2 AC 373. And see also *Barrett v Enfield LBC* [1999] 3 All ER 193 and *Phelps v Hillingdon LBC* [2001] 2 AC 619.

(or proposes to act) in a way which is made unlawful by section 6(1)' (that is, where the public authority fails to act consistently with a citizen's Convention rights).

To succeed, then, in a claim for breach of statutory duty after the decisions in *Lonrho* and *X v Bedfordshire County Council*, the claimant must now satisfy a two-part test. He must establish that, when Parliament enacted the relevant statute,[15] (1) it was intended to protect a class of persons to which he belongs[16] and (2) Parliament envisaged that, in providing that protection of his interests, he should be able to claim compensation for any failure to protect those interests. The matter is entirely, then, one of construction of the statute in question. But as Lord Browne-Wilkinson has observed, while the principles of breach of statutory duty may be clear in theory, 'the application of those principles in any particular case remains difficult'.[17]

SECTION 2   ELUSIVE PARLIAMENTARY INTENT

The success or failure of any attempt to frame an action for breach of statutory duty will turn on parliamentary intention. And as Lord Steyn observed in *Gorringe v Calderdale MBC*, 'the central question is whether from the provisions and structure of the statute an intention can be gathered to create a private law remedy'.[18] Yet in many instances it is probable that the legislature never even considered the issue of whether individuals should be able to claim damages for breach of the obligations embodied in the relevant statute. Only rarely does Parliament expressly declare that any breach of the statute should,[19] or should not,[20] be actionable in tort. On the other hand, since the courts may now refer to Hansard in interpreting statutes, parliamentary intent may sometimes be gleaned from a study of the parliamentary debates.[21] Nonetheless, in the majority of instances, the judges will continue to struggle with principles and policy developed over the years.

It cannot be stressed too forcefully, therefore, that an action for breach of statutory duty will only lie if the court finds that Parliament intended to confer a right to compensation on an individual injured by breach of that duty.[22] It is not enough simply to show that a statute was designed to protect the claimant in some general sense. Loss or injury of a recognised type must be shown, as must the intention of Parliament that victims should be entitled to monetary compensation. Thus, in one case, unauthorised publication of information about the claimant in breach of the Mental Health Tribunal

---

[15]   On the importance of timing, see *Issa v Hackney BC* [1997] 1 All ER 999.

[16]   It does not matter that the class may be very wide and for that reason hard to distinguish from the public in general: *Roe v Sheffield CC* [2004] QB 653 (the class 'road users' was regarded as being sufficiently specific).

[17]   *X v Bedfordshire CC* [1995] 2 AC 633, at 730.   [18]   [2004] 1 WLR 1057.

[19]   For two examples of Parliament expressly creating a civil remedy for breach of statutory duty see the Protection from Harassment Act 1997, s 3 and the Consumer Protection Act 1987, s 41.

[20]   See the Health and Safety at Work Act 1974, s 47(2).

[21]   See *Richardson v Pitt-Stanley* [1995] QB 123.

[22]   *Hague v Deputy Governor of Parkhurst Prison* [1991] 3 All ER 733, at 750.

Rules was held to be insufficient since privacy was not a recognised head of damage.[23] Equally, in *Hague v Deputy Governor of Parkhurst Prison*,[24] where prisoners alleged that they had suffered injury as a result of being held in solitary confinement in breach of Prison Rules, it was held that mere evidence that the Rules were in part designed to protect prisoners was insufficient to show the required parliamentary intention that they should be able to sue. Lord Jauncey put it this way:

> The Prison Act 1952 . . . covers such wide-ranging matters as central administration, prison officers, confinement and treatment of prisoners, release of prisoners on licence. Its objects are far removed from those of legislation such as the Factories and Coal Miners Acts whose prime concern is to protect the health and safety of persons who work therein.[25]

The priority afforded to interests in bodily security by tort law (particularly within an employment context) is reflected in the willingness of the courts to interpret industrial safety legislation so as to confer a right of action on injured workmen. As Lord Jauncey intimated, breaches of statutory rules to fence machinery in the Factories Act[26] and regulations made for miners' safety by the Mines and Quarries Acts[27] represent classic examples of the statutory provisions traditionally supporting tort actions. In such cases, the courts readily find that Parliament envisaged that an injured employee should be able to claim compensation from any employer who failed to provide his workforce with the protection Parliament demanded. Strict liability for injury to employees both offered an overwhelming incentive to employers to ensure that safety rules were complied with, and meant that the cost of any injury which befell a worker fell on the employer, not the hapless individual. Piecemeal legislation on industrial safety was originally intended to be replaced by a new all-embracing statutory regime introduced by the Health and Safety at Work Act 1974. Sections 2–9 of that Act imposed general safety duties on all employers. Breach of those general duties is expressly stated not to be actionable in tort.[28] But section 15 empowered the Secretary of State to make specific health and safety regulations for particular industries.[29] These abound and breaches are actionable unless the regulation in question provides otherwise.[30]

The duties imposed by such regulations vary in form. Some are absolute, thus requiring that employees' safety be guaranteed. Others demand only that the employer do what is reasonably practicable. In the interpretation of these and modern EU Regulations, case law on their predecessors (such as the Factories Acts) may remain

---

[23] *Pickering v Liverpool Daily Post and Echo Newspapers plc* [1991] 1 All ER 622. But given the courts' obligation (under the Human Rights Act 1998) to develop the common law in line with the European Convention on Human Rights, would the same decision be reached today bearing in mind the Art 8 right to respect for private and family life?   [24] [1991] 3 All ER 733.

[25] Ibid at 750–1.   [26] *Groves v Lord Wimborne* [1898] 2 QB 402.

[27] *Black v Fife Coal Co Ltd* [1912] AC 149; *National Coal Board v England* [1954] AC 403.

[28] Health and Safety at Work Act 1974, s 47(1)(a).

[29] Replacing earlier legislation such as the Factories Acts.

[30] Health and Safety at Work Act 1974, s 47(2).

relevant. More importantly, the general principle that employees injured at work should have generous access to compensation for industrial injury remains intact.

There are also precedents for the protection of interests in land and goods against violation of a statute.[31] Economic losses, too, have exceptionally been found recoverable where protection from that kind of loss was within the ambit of the statute. In *Monk v Warbey*,[32] for example, the claimant suffered bodily injuries in a road accident. The driver of the car was uninsured and impecunious. The claimant recovered his consequential financial loss by suing the owner of the car who, in breach of his statutory duty, had allowed his friend to drive uninsured against third party risks.[33] Equally, in *Rickless v United Artists Corpn*,[34] the claimants won a massive award of damages for the defendants' unauthorised use of clips from old Peter Sellers films. The Court of Appeal found that violation of section 2 of the Dramatic and Musical Performers' Protection Act 1958, prohibiting use of such material without the performer's consent, did create a civil right of action. The purpose of the Act was protection of performers' rights and correlative financial interests.

On the other hand, in *Richardson v Pitt-Stanley*[35] a claim against the claimant's employer-company and its directors for failure to comply with provisions of the Employers' Liability (Compulsory Insurance) Act 1969 requiring employers to insure against liability for accidents at work failed. The Court of Appeal held that, in respect of the company, the employee already enjoyed a range of remedies at common law enforceable against company assets. If there were no such assets (and there were not because the company had gone into liquidation), and no insurance policy, no additional claim for breach of statutory duty under the 1969 Act would avail the claimant. The substantial criminal penalties under the Act militated against the existence of a civil claim and some slight indication that Parliament did not intend to create such a private right was to be found in Hansard. Moreover, if no civil action for breach of statutory duty was intended against the company, their Lordships thought it highly unlikely that Parliament intended a claim to lie against individual directors.

In the light of the judiciary's commitment to restricting liability for pure economic loss, very clear evidence that this type of loss was intended to be protected by the statute will be required. In *Richardson v Pitt-Stanley*, Stuart-Smith LJ signalled in the following words that only exceptionally would such losses be recoverable in an action for breach of statutory duty.

> In my opinion, the court will more readily construe a statutory provision so as to provide a civil cause of action where the provision relates to the safety and health of a class of persons rather than where they have thereby suffered economic loss.[36]

---

[31] *Ross v Rugge-Price* (1876) 1 Ex D 269.

[32] [1935] 1 KB 75.

[33] If, however, as in *Bretton v Hancock* [2005] RTR 22, the claim is for *pure* (rather than *consequential*) economic loss, it will fail since the Road Traffic Act 1988 only imposes a duty to insure to cover losses arising out of death and bodily injury.

[34] [1988] QB 40.   [35] [1995] QB 123.   [36] Ibid at 132.

So, in *Wentworth v Wiltshire County Council*,[37] a claimant seeking to recover for damage to his business caused by disrepair of the adjacent highway failed in his claim. The duty to maintain the highway existed to protect users against personal injury not to safeguard the profits of traders. Furthermore, a number of other factors will impact on the courts' readiness to find that Parliament intended that one of the class of persons for whose benefit an Act was passed should have an action for compensation for its breach.

(1) There is a great reluctance to allow a claim for breach of statutory duty against a public authority for failure to provide adequate public services. Claims have failed against health[38] and education ministers[39] for failure to meet their statutory obligations to ensure adequate health care to patients and education for the nation's children respectively. For example, in *X v Bedfordshire County Council*[40] Lord Browne-Wilkinson, addressing claims in respect of the child care protection system, had no doubt that the relevant statutes were intended to protect children from abuse, but that the language and framework of the legislation were not designed to allow individual children or families to sue.[41] Lord Bridge summed up the heart of the case against imposing liability for breach of statutory duty on public bodies when he issued this ringing warning against too great a readiness to do so:

> the shoulders of a public authority are only broad enough to bear the loss because they are financed by the public at large. It is pre-eminently for the legislature to decide whether these policy reasons should be accepted as sufficient for imposing on the public the burden of providing compensation for financial losses. If they do so decide, it is not difficult for them to say so.[42]

> Continuing in this vein, a seven-judge House of Lords ruled out an action based on breaches of the Education Acts 1944 and 1981 in *Phelps v Hillingdon London Borough Council*.[43] Their Lordships have also rejected a claim premised on a local authority's breach of a statutory duty to house homeless persons.[44]

(2) If the alleged breach of duty derives not from a breach of a statute itself, but a breach of a regulation made under a statute, the following tricky question arises. Did the enabling Act, as it must, empower the minister to make regulations conferring private rights of action on individuals?[45] In answering this question, all that is clear is that, where (a) a statute permits a minister to establish rules concerned with the safety of a particular class of persons, and (b) the Act also

---

[37] [1993] QB 654.
[38] *R v Secretary of State for Social Services, ex p Hincks* (1979) 123 Sol Jo 436.
[39] *Watt v Kesteven CC* [1955] 1 QB 408.   [40] [1995] 2 AC 633.
[41] See further Murphy [1993] LS 103.   [42] *Murphy v Brentwood DC* [1990] 2 All ER 908, at 931.
[43] [2001] 2 AC 619.   [44] *O'Rourke v Camden LBC* [1998] AC 188.
[45] *Hague v Deputy Governor of Parkhurst Prison* [1991] 3 All ER 733. Note the rather different answers to the question from Lords Bridge and Jauncey. See also *Olotu v Home Office* [1997] 1 WLR 328, at 339 and *Todd v Adams* [2002] 2 Lloyd's Rep 293.

empowers the minister to exempt certain potential defendants from the rules, the inference will be that there was no legislative intention that those rules would support an action for breach of statutory duty.[46]

(3) The statutory duty itself must be precise in its terms so as to make enforcing it by way of an action in tort fair to the defendant.[47]

(4) Finally it must be shown that, to intend that a private right of action should lie for violation of a statute, Parliament could have envisaged the circumstances in which the claimant came to suffer harm. In *Olotu v Home Office*[48] the claimant was remanded in custody for a period exceeding the 112-day limit set by Regulations. The court found that the Regulations were designed to achieve expedition in the prosecution of crime and to ensure that accused persons did 'not languish in prison for excessive periods awaiting trial'. Protecting accused persons – the class to which the claimant belonged – was clearly an object of the Regulations. However, no claim for breach of statutory duty lay because neither Parliament nor the Secretary of State laying down the Regulations would have foreseen a scenario where loss would arise because (a) the Crown Prosecution Service failed to comply with its duty under the Regulations, *and* (b) the accused failed to apply for immediate bail.

SECTION 3   NATURE OF THE ACTION

Care must be taken to avoid confusion between this tort and negligence, albeit in practice claimants will often make concurrent claims for breach of statutory duty and negligence. Lord Browne-Wilkinson offered instructive analysis in *X v Bedfordshire County Council*.[49] Addressing the extent of the defendant local authority's liabilities in tort generally for failure in child care and educational provision, he distinguished between three possible causes of action in tort, as follows.

(A) BREACH OF STATUTORY DUTY SIMPLICITER

Such a claim – arising from the tort which this chapter centrally addresses – 'depends neither on any breach of the [claimant's] common law rights nor on any allegation of negligence by the defendants'. If a private right of action lies for violation of a statute, the claimant has no need to prove negligence.

---

[46] *Todd v Adams* [2002] 2 Lloyd's Rep 293, at [25].
[47] *Cutler v Wandsworth Stadium Ltd* [1949] AC 398; *X v Bedfordshire CC* [1995] 2 AC 633.
[48] [1997] 1 WLR 328. See also *Issa v Hackney LBC* [1997] 1 All ER 999.
[49] [1995] 2 AC 633, at 731–6. See also *London Passenger Transport Board v Upson* [1949] AC 155, at 168.

(B) THE COMMON LAW DUTY OF CARE

It may be that the existence of a statutory duty creates a relationship from which a common law duty of care in negligence will arise. An example is a relationship created by the statute that is akin, but by no means identical, to that of employer/employee.[50] Importantly, though, it is the relationship created by the statutory duty (as opposed to the statutory duty itself) that forms the basis of the common-law duty.[51] And in any event, a common-law duty will never arise in favour of C2 where it might conflict with the purpose of the statutory duty owed to C1. Thus, in *Jain v Trent Strategic Health Authority*,[52] where a public authority was authorised by statute to protect the residents of a nursing home, the House of Lords held that no common-law duty could arise in favour of the owners of the nursing home in respect of the manner in which that power was exercised. Any such common-law duty could conflict with the purpose, and thus inhibit the exercise, of the statutory power.

(C) CARELESS PERFORMANCE OF A STATUTORY DUTY

If it is not established that Parliament intended to create an action for breach of statutory duty in respect of a particular obligation, and if it cannot be established, either, that the circumstances of the claimant's relationship with the defendant gave rise to a common-law duty of care, no claim in tort lies simply for the careless performance of a statutory duty. On the other hand, if the claim is founded on another tort – say, for example, private nuisance – the fact that the statutory duty has been performed negligently will defeat an otherwise extant defence of statutory authority.[53]

A typical claim for breach of statutory duty requires only that the claimant should prove that the statutory obligation was not fulfilled. This is because liability in this context is frequently strict. In some cases, however, the statute will prescribe that some degree of negligence be proven, while in others it may allow the defendant a defence if he shows that avoiding injury to the claimant was not 'reasonably practicable'.[54] Alternatively, where the duty is cast in terms of reasonable practicability, the courts may instead read into the duty a negligence-like element. For example, in *Baker v Quantum Clothing Group*,[55] the employer's workplace had, so far as reasonably practicable, to be made and kept safe. A 3–2 majority of the Supreme Court held that, whether an employer had discharged this duty was to be judged according to the general knowledge and standards of the time and, thus, by reference to what might

---

[50] *Rice v Secretary of State for Trade and Industry* [2007] ICR 1469.

[51] In *Gorringe v Calderdale MBC* [2004] 1 WLR 1057, Lord Scott said (at [71]): 'the [statutory] duty cannot create a duty of care that would not have been owed at common law'.   [52] [2009] 2 WLR 248.

[53] *X v Bedfordshire CC* [1995] 2 AC 633, at 728–9.

[54] See, eg, the Highways Act 1980, s 41(1A) which provides that a highway authority is only required to keep a highway free from snow or ice so 'so far as is reasonably practicable'.   [55] [2011] 1 WLR 1003.

reasonably have been foreseen by a reasonable employer. But bearing in mind that two members of the court disagreed, citing a range of cases they thought suggested a stricter interpretation, the case illustrates nicely that great care needs to be exercised in assessing the strictness of any given statutory duty.

SECTION 4   WHAT THE CLAIMANT MUST PROVE

(A) AN OBLIGATION ON THE DEFENDANT

A *mandatory* duty must be imposed on the defendant if the action is to lie. The creation of a criminal offence prohibiting members of the public from engaging in certain conduct is insufficient.[56] Similarly, the conferral of a mere power to act is not enough to justify a civil action in respect of a failure to act in that way.

(B) STATUTE MUST IMPOSE A DUTY ON THE DEFENDANT

This issue has been raised most frequently in actions by workers against their employers where they have been injured by some act or omission of fellow workers. In such cases it can be hard to decide whether the duty is imposed on the employer or on those fellow workers. Just such a problem arose in *Harrison v National Coal Board*,[57] where various duties relating to the running of mines were imposed by statute. In that case, the House of Lords held that, when expressed impersonally, the duties were to be understood as binding the mine owner. But where the duties were personal – such as duties relating to shot firing – they were to be treated as binding the shot-firers alone.

Once the statute has been interpreted to impose a duty on the employer, the general principle is clear: the duty will be non-delegable. Thus 'the owner cannot relieve himself of his obligation by saying that he has appointed reasonably competent persons and that the breach is due to negligence on their part'.[58] It would therefore be no defence to an employer of a workman injured by an unfenced machine that the foreman has failed to carry out the instructions to fence which the employer issued to him. The rule is the same where the duty of the employer has been neglected by the independent contractor of the employer.[59] Other problems, however (which will be discussed later), are raised when the defendant has delegated the duty to the claimant himself, and the claimant is injured as a result of his own failure to perform the delegated duty.

---

[56] *Lonrho Ltd v Shell Petroleum Co Ltd (No 2)* [1981] 2 All ER 456.   [57] [1951] AC 639.

[58] *Lochgelly Iron and Coal Co v M'Mullan* [1934] AC 1, at 13.

[59] *Hosking v De Havilland Aircraft Co Ltd* [1949] 1 All ER 540; *Braham v J Lyons & Co Ltd* [1962] 3 All ER 281. Cf *Hole v Sittingbourne and Sheerness Rly Co* (1861) 6 H & N 488.

(C) STATUTE PROTECTS THE CLAIMANT'S INTEREST BY WAY OF A CAUSE OF ACTION IN TORT

The fundamental issue is simply whether the Act was intended to create a right of action in tort.[60] Everything else is subordinate to that. Thus, as Lord Simonds once said: '[t]he only rule which in all circumstances is valid is that the answer must depend on a consideration of the whole Act and the circumstances, including the pre-existing law, in which it was enacted'.[61] The following considerations, then, are no more than guides to the principles which the courts may utilise in identifying (usually unexpressed) legislative intention.

(1) The state of the pre-existing common law

Sometimes, the tort law in force before the passing of the Act[62] is considered to afford adequate compensation to victims in circumstances also covered by the statute.[63] Here, the statute is taken merely to regulate those activities in order to help prevent the occurrence of the kinds of loss which the existing common law would redress.[64] In such circumstances, the statute will not usually confer an additional cause of action. For instance, ordinary negligence law affords adequate protection for the victims of road accidents: yet the need to reduce these accidents is so urgent that there is much legislation regulating road traffic (for example, on seat belt and headlight usage). But persons injured by motorists in breach of such statutory duties cannot rely on the statute to sue, they must pursue their common-law remedy.[65]

If, however, the statute merely affirms an interest of the claimant which the common law already recognises, yet does not purport to be giving that interest statutory protection for some quite different purpose, then the claimant may be free to sue for breach of the statute.[66] Thus, in *Ashby v White*, where the right to vote – a common-law right – had been confirmed by statute, Holt CJ said:

> And this statute…is only an enforcement of the common law; and if the Parliament thought the freedom of elections to be a matter of that consequence, as to give their sanction to it, and to enact that they should be free; it is a violation of that statute, to disturb the [claimant] in this case in giving his vote at an election, and consequently actionable.[67]

---

[60] Eg, *Hague v Deputy Governor of Parkhurst Prison* [1991] 3 All ER 733, at 705; *Atkinson v Newcastle and Gateshead Waterworks Co* (1877) 2 Ex D 441, at 448; *Pasmore v Oswaldtwistle UDC* [1898] AC 387, at 397.

[61] *Cutler v Wandsworth Stadium Ltd* [1949] AC 398, at 407.

[62] So in *Issa v Hackney LBC* [1997] 1 WLR 956, no claim lay in respect of a statutory nuisance because in 1936, when the relevant Act was passed, virtually all victims of such a nuisance would have been able to recover compensation from their landlords.   [63] See *Richardson v Pitt-Stanley* [1995] QB 123.

[64] Sometimes, as in *Square v Model Farm Dairies (Bournemouth) Ltd* [1939] 2 KB 365 (sale of infected milk), the court might decide that no tort was intended to be created because existing contractual remedies were adequate.   [65] See, eg, *Phillips v Britannia Hygienic Laundry Co* [1923] 2 KB 832.

[66] *Wolverhampton New Waterworks Co v Hawkesford* (1859) 6 CBNS 336, at 356. He may then have the choice of the action for breach of statutory duty or the existing common-law remedy: see, eg, *Simon v Islington BC* [1943] 1 KB 188, at 193.

[67] (1703) 2 Ld Raym 938, at 954. Cf the contrary approach in the analogous cases of *Watkins v Secretary of State for the Home Department* [2006] 2 WLR 807 concerning misfeasance in public office.

(2) Alternative remedies provided by statute

It has been suggested that, where a statute fails to provide any alternative means of enforcement in the event of breach of the relevant duty, the claimant's task of establishing that an action in tort was intended by the statute may be eased.[68] But the absence of an alternative remedy is not by any means irrefutable evidence that Parliament intended to grant the claimant redress via an action for breach of statutory duty. Counsel for prisoners claiming damages for breaches of the Prison Rules in *Hague v Deputy Governor of Parkhurst Prison* sought to argue that the absence of any other remedy available to them necessarily meant that an action lay. The House of Lords forcefully rejected that contention.[69] In *every case*, according to their Lordships, evidence must be presented on the central question of parliamentary intent.

Accordingly, even in cases where an alternative remedy is available under the Act, the mere availability of that remedy is not per se determinative of the issue. As Lord Browne-Wilkinson forcefully put it in the *Hague* case, 'the mere existence of some other statutory remedy is not necessarily decisive'.[70] This is an important statement given that provision is often made for some or other bespoke administrative machinery according to which a public authority's compliance with its duties may be sought. For example, it may be provided that representations can be made to the relevant Secretary of State (who can then order a recalcitrant public body to fulfil its responsibilities);[71] or an appeal procedure may be specified.[72] But, importantly, the courts will need to be mindful of the extent to which the relevant administrative 'remedy' will provide the claimant with a means of obtaining financial redress.[73]

Where the 'alternative remedy' is the imposition of a criminal penalty, the onus will be on the claimant to establish that his claim falls within one of the two exceptions to the general rule of non-actionability set out by Lord Diplock in *Lonrho*.[74] In practice, though, this will normally mean that he must show the purpose of the statute was not just to regulate a particular activity in the general public interest, but also to benefit a class of persons to which he belongs.[75] Thus, the existence of criminal penalties in the Factories Acts did not bar concurrent remedies in tort since the duties imposed by those Acts were specifically designed to protect workers.[76] By contrast, however, breach of statutory rules regulating the operation of betting at greyhound tracks

---

[68] *Thornton v Kirklees MBC* [1979] QB 626; but overruled on its facts in *O'Rourke v Camden LBC* [1998] AC 188. And see *Booth & Co (Intl) Ltd v National Enterprise Board* [1978] 3 All ER 624.

[69] [1991] 3 All ER 733.   [70] *X v Bedfordshire CC* [1995] 2 AC 633, at 731.

[71] See, eg, Children Act 1989, s 84(3) in relation to a local authority's duties to children in care.

[72] See, eg, *Neil Martin Ltd v Revenue and Customs Commissioners* [2008] Bus LR 663.

[73] See, eg, *Phelps v Hillingdon LBC* [2001] 2 AC 619.

[74] *Atkinson v Newcastle and Gateshead Waterworks Co* (1877) 2 Ex D 441.

[75] See, eg, *Todd v Adams* [2002] 2 Lloyd's Rep 293.

[76] *Groves v Lord Wimborne* [1898] 2 QB 402. Breach of the duty to stop at a pedestrian crossing is a rare example of a road safety regulation being interpreted so as to create a right of action in tort: *London Passenger Transport Board v Upson* [1949] AC 155.

did not enable an aggrieved bookmaker to sue because the statute was not passed to safeguard or enhance the business of bookmakers.[77]

Special mention should finally be made of cases in which the alternative remedy available to the claimant would be judicial review. This is because the matter received detailed (but ultimately unsatisfactory) consideration by a divided House of Lords in *Cullen v Chief Constable of the Royal Ulster Constabulary*.[78]

> C was detained in custody under terrorism legislation. Contrary to section 15 of the Northern Ireland (Temporary Provisions) Act 1987, C was denied the right to a private consultation with a solicitor. The fact that he was denied this right resulted in no measurable harm to C.

By a bare majority, their Lordships held that the claimant did not have a civil claim for nominal damages based on breach of statutory duty. Material to the decisions of those in the majority was the fact that 'the speedy hearing of an application for judicial review...is a much more effective remedy for a claimant to seek than an action for nominal damages'.[79] Putting to one side the fact that the accuracy of this statement is questionable, the case law leaves us unclear on whether an action based on breach of statutory duty would have been available if the denial of access to a solicitor had resulted in measurable harm.[80]

(3) Public and private rights

Although the case law is not entirely clear on this, one plausible view is that a claimant can rely on breach of statutory duty so long as the breach of duty infringes a *public right* in a way that causes the claimant to suffer to a much greater degree than other members of the public.[81] In support of this there is Lord Diplock's second exception[82] to the general rule against the actionability of criminal law statutes. However, dicta can be found which intimate that this view is no longer tenable. For example, Lord Browne-Wilkinson, in *X v Bedfordshire County Council*, saw actions for breach of statutory duty *simpliciter* as arising only in favour of 'a limited class of the public'.[83] But if the statute creates a public right, which favours all citizens, why object? After all, the law of public nuisance shows that there is nothing in principle wrong with making the infringement of public rights actionable, so long as the claimant suffers to a much greater extent than the generality of the public.

---

[77] *Cutler v Wandsworth Stadium Ltd* [1949] AC 398.   [78] [2003] 1 WLR 1763.

[79] Ibid at [39].

[80] As regards those in the majority, Lord Hutton thought that it would be available (at [41]) while Lord Millett (despite elsewhere signalling his agreement with Lord Hutton) thought it would not (at [69]). Lord Rodger muddied the waters still further by agreeing with both of them, while Lords Bingham and Steyn, dissenting, were of the opinion that such an action would lie (although it is not clear what weight should be given to their dissenting view in the future).

[81] *Phillips v Britannia Hygenic Laundry Co* [1923] 2 KB 832, at 841.

[82] *Lonrho Ltd v Shell Petroleum Co Ltd (No 2)* [1982] AC 173.

[83] [1995] 2 AC 633, at 731. See also *O'Rourke v Camden LBC* [1998] AC 188, at 194.

(D) HARM SUFFERED IS WITHIN THE SCOPE OF THE ACT

The leading case is *Gorris v Scott*.[84]

> A statutory order required that those parts of a ship which were to be occupied by animals should be divided into pens of a specified size. D violated this order on a ship on which he was transporting sheep belonging to C. This violation contributed to C's sheep being washed overboard.

Since the statute was designed to prevent the spread of disease rather than to prevent animals from being drowned, the action for breach of statutory duty failed. In similar vein, the duty imposed on highway authorities to repair the roads in order to protect users from injury was held not to embrace loss of profit to a local trader.[85] And, equally, breach of the requirement that employees be kitted out with steel-toe-capped boots to prevent injury from falling objects does not ground an action based on frostbite.[86]

In the industrial context, too, the House of Lords has held that the statutory duty on an employer to fence every dangerous part of a machine was designed to prevent a workman coming into contact with moving parts of the machine and did not envisage protecting him from injury caused by flying pieces of the machine itself, or the material on which the machine was working.[87] On the other hand, when a bogie was derailed by a stone that had been allowed to fall from the roof of a mine in breach of the defendants' statutory duty, and the claimant was consequently injured, the House of Lords held that 'where the object of the enactment is to promote safety there can be no implication that liability for a breach is limited to one which causes injury in a particular way'.[88] And in *Gerrard v Staffordshire Potteries*[89] the defendant was found liable in respect of a breach of regulations requiring eye protection against any 'reasonably foreseeable risk engaged in the work from particles or fragments thrown off' where a foreign body flew out of a jar the claimant was glazing. The statute was designed to safeguard the worker from any object dangerous to the eye in the course of her work.

(E) CLAIMANT A PERSON PROTECTED BY THE STATUTE

For breach of a statutory duty to give rise to an action in tort, the claimant must be an individual, or member of a class, that the statute aims to protect. *Knapp v Railway Executive*[90] illustrates the point.

> Railway legislation provided for the maintenance of gates at level crossings. C had stopped his car slightly short of a closed gate governed by this Act. Somehow the car moved

---

[84] (1874) LR 9 Exch 125. But see also *Tasci v Pekalp of London Ltd* [2001] ICR 633.

[85] *Wentworth v Wiltshire CC* [1993] 2 All ER 256.

[86] *Fytche v Wincanton Logistics plc* [2004] 4 All ER 221.

[87] *Close v Steel Co of Wales Ltd* [1962] AC 367. Cf *Wearing v Pirelli Ltd* [1977] 1 All ER 339.

[88] *Grant v National Coal Board* [1956] AC 649, at 664.   [89] [1995] ICR 502.

[90] [1949] 2 All ER 508. Cf *Lavender v Diamints Ltd* [1949] 1 KB 585.

forward striking the gate and since the gate had not been properly fenced, it swung into an oncoming train injuring the driver. C was successfully sued by the engine driver so he in turn sought a contribution from D. His claim failed, however, because the Act was only designed to protect road users (not engine drivers). As the engine driver could not have sued D directly for breach of statutory duty, D was not liable to make a contribution to C.

(F) PROOF OF HARM OR LOSS?

As already noted, most statutes that permit a tortious cause of action will only avail a claimant where he or she suffers the particular type of harm or loss envisaged by the Act. There are, however, some rare instances in which a statute may confer a right of action that is actionable per se. For example, in *Ashby v White*,[91] an interference with the statutory right to vote was held actionable per se, while in *Ferguson v Earl Kinnoull*[92] the refusal on the part of the defendant, in the face of a statute, to determine the suitability of the claimant for a living to which he had been presented, was held actionable per se. Oddly, in *Pickering v Liverpool Daily Post and Echo Newspapers plc*, Lord Bridge declared that an action could lie only on proof of 'loss or injury of a kind for which the law awards damages'.[93] This seems an aberration; and, tellingly, neither *Ashby* nor *Ferguson* was cited in that judgment.

(G) NATURE OF THE DEFENDANT'S CONDUCT

Whether a claimant must prove intention or negligence on the part of the defendant depends on the individual statute. Indeed, liability is strict in very many cases. That said, some statutes are more generous in that they only require the defendant to do what is 'reasonably practicable'.[94] There is a mass of case law on the interpretation of statutory provisions laying down particular standards of conduct; but the vital point to be made here is that there is no universal standard of liability for this tort: one must always turn to the particular statute in question to discover whether intention or negligence must be proved.

(H) CAUSATION

As with all torts, the claimant must show that the defendant caused his loss. More particularly, the claimant 'must in all cases prove his case by the ordinary standard of proof in civil actions: he must show that on a balance of probabilities the breach of duty caused or materially contributed to his injury'.[95] Thus, where it was shown that a steel erector would not have worn a safety belt even if it had been provided, the House

---

[91] (1703) 2 Ld Raym 938. Cf *Simmonds v Newport Abercarn Black Vein Steam Coal Co* [1921] 1 KB 616.
[92] (1842) 9 Cl & Fin 251.   [93] [1991] 1 All ER 622, at 632.
[94] See, eg, Provision and Use of Work Equipment Regulations 1998 (SI 1998/2306), reg 11(2)(a).
[95] *Bonnington Castings Ltd v Wardlaw* [1956] AC 613, at 620. Cf *McGhee v National Coal Board* [1972] 3 All ER 1008.

of Lords held that his employers were not liable to him for breach of their statutory duty to provide one.[96] Similarly, where a carpenter fell from a scaffold because the scaffold had been deliberately pushed over by a workmate, it was not the employer's breach of duty that had caused his injury. The employer was required to provide safe equipment and a safe place of work, but the duty incumbent upon him was only one to ensure that employees would be safe from foreseeable risks. The deliberate, wanton act of the workmate did not constitute such a risk:[97] it was a *novus actus interveniens* that broke the chain of causation.

SECTION 5   THE ANALOGOUS 'EUROTORT' ACTION

On the matter of European Union law rights, the English courts have for some time accepted that directly applicable EU law can create obligations the breach of which entitles affected persons to sue for the harm thereby caused.[98] In *Francovich v Italy*,[99] however, the European Court broadened the bases of liability by holding that a failure by a member state to implement an EU Directive designed to create rights on the part of particular individuals would also give rise to a claim in damages on the part of those individuals. Strikingly, in *Francovich*, the EU legislation in question was not directly effective which meant that, in the absence of an action against the state, there would have been no one against whom an action could have been brought. Since then, the European Court has held that the *Francovich* principle applies in even more circumstances: where the legislation *is* of direct effect,[100] where the breach of EU law entails a legislative act (not merely an omission),[101] and in respect of administrative decisions.[102]

The conditions that must be satisfied in order to sue according to this 'Eurotort' principle were set out by Lord Slynn in *R v Secretary of State for Transport, ex p Factortame Ltd*. He said:

Before a member state can be held liable, a national court must find that:

(i) the relevant rule of [EU] law is one which is intended to confer rights on individuals;

(ii) the breach must be sufficiently serious;

(iii) there must be a direct causal link between the breach and the loss complained of.[103]

---

[96] *Cummings (or McWilliams) v Sir William Arrol & Co Ltd* [1962] 1 All ER 623.

[97] *Horton v Taplin Contracts Ltd* [2003] ICR 179.

[98] *Garden Cottage Foods Ltd v Milk Marketing Board* [1984] AC 130.   [99] [1993] 2 CMLR 66.

[100] *Brasserie du Pêcheur SA v Federal Republic of Germany* (Case C–46/93).

[101] *R v Secretary of State for Transport, ex p Factortame Ltd* (Case C–48/93).

[102] *R v Ministry of Agriculture, Fisheries and Food, ex p Hedley Lomas (Ireland)* (Case C–5/94).

[103] [1999] 4 All ER 906, at 916. These conditions derive directly from the decision of the European Court of Justice in *Brasserie du Pêcheur SA v Federal Republic of Germany* (Case C–46/93), at [74].

The similarity between the first requirement and the test adopted in relation to an action for breach of statutory duty is immediately apparent; yet this connection between the two forms of action was arguably furthered in *Three Rivers District Council v Bank of England (No 3)*.[104] There, the House of Lords held that a banking directive concerning the regulation of credit institutions was fundamentally designed to harmonise banking practice, rather than to protect depositors. That being so, a failure to comply with the directive did not avail the depositors: the directive was not primarily intended to confer a right of action upon them.

It has since been explained, in relation to the second limb of *Factortame*, that the pivotal phrase 'sufficiently serious' does not necessarily require negligence or fault (although fault may be a material consideration), and that the seriousness of the breach must be judged in the context of the clarity of the EU rule breached and, where appropriate, the legislative discretion afforded to the member state.[105] Again, the similarities with ordinary breach of statutory duty principles are striking.

SECTION 6   DEFENCES

(A) THE RELATION BETWEEN CRIMINAL AND TORTIOUS LIABILITY

Breach of some statutory duties may give rise to both criminal and tortious proceedings. But it must not be assumed that the defences in each case are identical. For example, the defences open to mine owners under the Coal Mines Act 1911 were held to be wider in criminal law than in actions for breach of statutory duty.[106]

(B) ASSUMPTION OF RISK

Wheeler v New Merton Board Mills Ltd[107] decided that *volenti non fit injuria* is not a defence to an action brought by a workman for breach by an employer of his statutory duty – at least where the statute makes the employer liable whether or not his conduct was intentional or negligent. In *ICI Ltd v Shatwell*,[108] the House of Lords approved the *Wheeler* case in so far as employers' statutory duties are concerned; but it added that the defence of *volenti* 'should be available where the employer was not himself in breach of statutory duty and was not vicariously in breach of any statutory duty through the neglect of some person who was of superior rank to the [claimant] and whose commands the [claimant] was bound to obey'.[109] The grounds for the *Wheeler* decision are not obvious. This makes it all the harder, in the absence of any decision outside the sphere of such duties of employers to workers, to know whether

---

[104] [2000] 2 WLR 1220.

[105] *R v Secretary of State for Transport, ex p Factortame Ltd (No 5)* [1999] 4 All ER 906; *Byrne v Motor Insurers Bureau* [2009] QB 66.   [106] [1933] 2 KB 669.

[107] [1965] AC 656.   [108] Ibid.   [109] Ibid at 687.

the defence is generally inapplicable to actions for breach of statutory duty.[110] It may well be contrary to public policy for anybody (not merely employers) to contract out of a duty imposed by an Act of Parliament. If this is so, assumption of risk may never be a defence to this action.

(C) CONTRIBUTORY NEGLIGENCE

At common law, contributory negligence was once a complete defence.[111] Nowadays, apportionment of damages is possible under the Law Reform (Contributory Negligence) Act 1945.[112] The principles of the defence are the same as those already discussed in a previous chapter, subject to the following points. Legislation and regulations designed to protect health and safety are often expressly designed to protect workers against acts or inattention. Accordingly, a 'risky act due to familiarity with the work or some inattention resulting from noise or strain' will not be contributory negligence,[113] although it might be sufficient negligence to make the employer vicariously liable to a negligently injured third party.[114] Frequently, the employer will have delegated to his employee responsibility for the performance of the statutory duty and that employee will then have been negligent. The House of Lords held in *Boyle v Kodak Ltd*[115] that 'once the [claimant] has established that there was a breach of enactment which made the employer absolutely liable, and that that breach caused the accident, he need do no more'.[116] But, 'if the employer can prove that the only act or default of anyone which caused or contributed to the non-compliance was the act or default of the [claimant] himself, he establishes a good defence'.[117]

In *Boyle v Kodak Ltd* the statutory duty to fix a ladder securely while a storage tank was painted was imposed on both the employers and the employee who was injured through its breach. The Court of Appeal dismissed the action on the ground that the claimant was the sole cause of the accident, but the House of Lords allowed his appeal. The employers had not proved that they had instructed the claimant on how to comply with the regulations. That being so, their breach of statutory duty was a cause of the damage. The significance of the claimant also being in breach of his statutory duty was that it constituted a ground for apportionment of the damages: he was awarded one half. Had the statute imposed the duty on the employers alone, the claimant's damages

---

[110] See *Alford v National Coal Board* [1952] 1 All ER 754, at 757 (*obiter*).

[111] *Caswell v Powell Duffryn Associated Collieries Ltd* [1940] AC 152 (*obiter*).

[112] *Cakebread v Hopping Bros (Whetstone) Ltd* [1947] KB 641.

[113] Where the risk has been consciously accepted by the employee, it will, apparently, be contributory negligence: see, eg, *Sherlock v Chester CC* [2004] EWCA Civ 201, at [32].

[114] *Staveley Iron and Chemical Co Ltd v Jones* [1956] AC 627, at 648 (explaining the similar decision of the House of Lords in *Caswell v Powell Duffryn Associated Collieries Ltd* [1939] 3 All ER 722). On the difficulty of proving contributory negligence in this tort, see *Westwood v Post Office* [1974] AC 1.

[115] [1969] 2 All ER 439. This decision applied *Ross v Associated Portland Cement Manufacturers Ltd* [1964] 2 All ER 452 and *Ginty v Belmont Building Supplies Ltd* [1959] 1 All ER 414.

[116] [1969] 2 All ER 439, at 441.   [117] Ibid at 446.

would not have been reduced, unless the employers proved that the claimant failed to take care for his own safety and was thus contributorily negligent.

(D) ACT OF A THIRD PARTY

This is no defence where the statute is deemed to impose liability so strict that the defendant is responsible for such acts. In other cases it may be a defence; but everything depends on the particular wording and interpretation of the Act.[118]

(E) *EX TURPI CAUSA*

The Court of Appeal has held that the defence of *ex turpi causa non oritur actio* may be invoked in cases where the claimant is relying on a breach of statutory duty.[119]

FURTHER READING

BUCKLEY, 'Liability in Tort for Breach of Statutory Duty' (1984) 100 *Law Quarterly Review* 204
FOSTER, 'The Merits of the Civil Action for Breach of Statutory Duty' (2011) 33 *Sydney Law Review* 67
STANTON, 'New Forms of the Tort of Breach of Statutory Duty' (2004) 120 *Law Quarterly Review* 324

---

[118] *Cooper v Railway Executive (Southern Region)* [1953] 1 All ER 477.
[119] *Hewison v Meridian Shipping Services Pte Ltd* (2003) 147 SJLB 24 (C's fraudulent concealment of his epilepsy led to the defeat of his claim).

PART VI

INTERESTS IN REPUTATION: DEFAMATION

20

DEFAMATION: FOUNDATIONAL PRINCIPLES

KEY ISSUES

(1) Competing interests
The law of defamation is to be found at the point at which interests in free speech and reputation intersect. Liability rules reflect the delicate balance struck by the legislature and the courts between these interests.

(2) Lowering of reputation
Defamation occurs by way of the 'publication' of an explicit or imputed statement that results in injury to the claimant's reputation, in the sense that a substantial and respectable proportion of society thinks less well of him.

(3) Libel and slander
Defamation comes in two forms: libel, which is concerned with statements in 'permanent form' and with respect to which injury to the claimant's reputation is presumed; and slander, which is not in permanent form and with

respect to which damage must be proved by the claimant (subject to certain exceptions).

(4) Defences
Much of the balance between the competing interests of free speech and reputation is struck in the form of the defences available to claims of defamation, which are dealt with in the next chapter.

(5) Reform on the agenda
The Government has indicated its interest in reforming certain aspects of the law of defamation in order to find a better balance between competing interests – and to ensure that the law does not have a chilling effect on worthwhile journalistic, non-government organisation, scientific, and academic endeavour. This chapter includes consideration of provisions from the Draft Defamation Bill 2011.

SECTION 1 INTRODUCTION

There are two types of defamation: libel which, in general, is written; and slander which, in general, is oral.[1] In some respects, different rules are applicable to each.

---

[1] It is inaccurate, however, to say that slander is always oral and that libel is always visual. The use of sign language as between two deaf persons, for example, is probably capable of constituting slander. Equally,

Both, however, protect the interest in the reputation of the claimant. There is, therefore, no tort in either case unless there has been a communication of the defamatory matter to a third party, for it is the opinion held of the person defamed by others that matters.[2] Insults directed to the claimant himself do not in themselves constitute defamation, since the tort is not primarily concerned with the claimant's wounded feelings. Instead, the gist is that the defendant either lowers the claimant in the estimation of reasonable, right-thinking members of society, or causes such citizens to shun or avoid the claimant.

In many ways defamation is unique among torts, and it is best understood in the context of its historical development. Until the sixteenth century, the ecclesiastical courts exercised general jurisdiction over defamation. Thereafter, the common-law courts developed an action on the case for slander where 'temporal' (as distinct from 'spiritual') damage could be established. Much later, the common-law courts acquired jurisdiction over libels, too, and they then forged a distinction between libel and slander on the basis that damage would be presumed in libel, but that the claimant would have to prove 'special damage'[3] for slander.

In the late nineteenth and early twentieth centuries, liability in defamation was extended because of the menace to reputations occasioned by the mass circulation of the new, popular press. The recent history of defamation is marked by continuing conflict between the need to protect the character and privacy of individuals, on the one hand, and the right to freedom of speech, on the other.[4] The intensity of this conflict has naturally been heightened with the enactment of the Human Rights Act 1998, bringing with it formal rights to both privacy and freedom of speech (Articles 8 and 10, respectively, of the European Convention on Human Rights). Of course, the press maintains that the latter is often disregarded at the expense of open and honest criticism of those in authority. And in *Derbyshire County Council v Times Newspapers Ltd*[5] the press scored a notable victory. The House of Lords ruled that public authorities and governmental bodies were not entitled to sue in defamation. As Lord Keith put it:

> It is of the highest public importance that a democratically elected governmental body, or indeed any governmental body, should be open to uninhibited public criticism. The threat of a civil action for defamation must inevitably have an inhibiting effect on freedom of speech.[6]

---

television broadcasts and public theatre performances of a defamatory nature are, by statute, libellous rather than slanderous: see section 3 below.

[2] For a powerful argument that it is not reputation, per se, that matters, but rather the concern that persons ought not wrongly to be judged by false information see Gibbons (1996) 16 OJLS 587.

[3] The phrase 'special damage' is to some extent misleading; 'actual damage' is a more accurate term to capture the sense of what must be proved: see Jolowicz [1960] CLJ 214.

[4] See, eg, Barendt [1993] PL 449.

[5] [1993] AC 534. Note, too, their Lordship's references to (but not reliance on) Art 10 of the European Convention on Human Rights.

[6] [1993] AC 534, at 547. The principle was extended to political parties in the course of an election campaign in *Goldsmith v Bhoyrul* [1997] 4 All ER 268. But what if an individual party member sues qua individual?

Since that case was decided, the fundamentality of the right to freedom of speech conferred by Article 10 has been raised on a number of occasions. In *Tolstoy Miloslavsky v United Kingdom*,[7] for example, the European Court of Human Rights issued a declaration that a libel damages award of £1.5 million granted by an English jury had been excessive and thus a violation of the defendant's freedom of speech. But apart from these decisions of rather limited scope, the English courts have consistently held defamation law to be broadly compatible with Article 10.[8] Furthermore, in *Campbell v MGN*,[9] the House of Lords held that there was no presumption that the Article 10 right to freedom of speech should trump any competing interests, such as the Article 8 right to respect for privacy. It would simply need to be balanced against those interests (in respect of which there was, equally, no presumptive pre-eminence).[10]

On the one hand, a move towards a freestanding right to privacy founded on Article 8 of the Human Rights Convention is becoming increasingly evident. In *Douglas v Hello! Ltd*, Sedley LJ took a bold step towards the general protection of privacy: the thrust of his argument being that, since the courts are public authorities for the purposes of section 6 of the Human Rights Act 1998, they are now bound to develop the common law – including the law of defamation – in accordance with the Article 8 right to respect for privacy.[11] That said, it remains the case that English law has not yet reached the stage of recognising a distinct cause of action based on the wrongful invasion of privacy.[12] But that it will in due course seems probable. Thus, while there are senior judicial figures who believe that it would be inappropriate for the courts (rather than Parliament) to introduce such an innovation,[13] the stated reluctance of Parliament to do so has since prompted the Master of the Rolls to comment that he cannot 'pretend to find it satisfactory to be required to shoehorn within the cause of action of breach of confidence' claims that are fundamentally about privacy.[14]

On the other hand, defamation law is already partly governed by statute; and some of this is ill-considered and badly drafted. The result of this admixture of legislation and common law is a tort characterised by many detailed and complex rules – some substantive, others procedural. Even so, defamation actions remain a popular recourse for wealthy public figures seeking, with the aid of expensive lawyers, to vindicate their reputations publicly in the law courts.[15] Indeed, the tort is to some extent a wealthy

---

[7] (1995) 20 EHRR 442.

[8] See *Reynolds v Times Newspapers Ltd* [2001] 2 AC 127; *McCartan Turkington Breen v Times Newspapers Ltd* [2001] 2 AC 277; *Loutchansky v Times Newspapers Ltd (No 2)* [2002] 2 WLR 640.

[9] [2004] 2 AC 457.

[10] See also *Spiller v Joseph* [2010] UKSC 53, at [74]–[79]; *Clift v Slough BC* [2010] EWCA Civ 1484; *Flood v Times Newspapers Ltd* [2010] EWCA Civ 804, at [21].   [11] [2001] QB 967, at [129].

[12] See *Campbell v MGN Ltd* [2004] 2 AC 457, at [11].

[13] See *Wainwright v Home Office* [2004] 2 AC 406, at [31]–[33].

[14] *Douglas v Hello! (No 3)* [2005] 3 WLR 881, at [53]. See also ch 22.

[15] But note that the scope to litigate was partly curtailed by s 5 of the Defamation Act 1996 which reduced the normal limitation period from three years to one (extendable at the court's discretion – on which, see *Steedman v BBC* [2002] EMLR 17). Equally, the summary procedure under ss 8–10 of the 1996 Act confers considerable powers of disposal on the courts and helps avert protracted litigation, so long as adequate

person's tort since legal aid is not *currently* available either to pursue, or to defend, a defamation action.[16]

Another notable feature of defamation law is the potentially very high level of damages that can be awarded by a jury.[17] To some extent this potential is mitigated by Rules of Court made under section 8 of the Courts and Legal Services Act 1990, which empower the Court of Appeal to substitute for an excessive award 'such sum as appears to the court to be proper'. Just such a substitution occurred in *John v MGN Ltd*.[18] Sir Thomas Bingham MR suggested that, in future, the courts could provide guidance to juries on the level of awards, that jurors might look, by way of comparison, at awards in personal injury cases, and that the judge and the parties' respective counsel could indicate to the jury the award they consider to be appropriate.[19]

'Reputation' is treated as only a transitory interest since no cause of action will survive the defamed person's death.[20] Furthermore, the nature of the available defences in defamation serve to make it also a contingent interest that must sometimes give way to a more pressing public interest. For example, if one informs the police of one's suspicion that a neighbour is abusing a child, one may raise the defence of qualified privilege so long as the (ultimately unfounded) suspicion was honestly held. Similarly, as long as the basic facts are true, the defence of fair comment will protect the press when expressing views on the actions of politicians, public servants, and others in the public eye.

The debate on the correct balance between an individual's interest in his good name and freedom of speech is a vital attribute of a democratic society.[21] That debate continues into the present day. The Government has indicated its interest in reforming certain aspects of the law of defamation in order to find a better balance between competing interests – and to ensure that the law does not have a chilling effect on worthwhile journalistic, non-government organisation, scientific, and academic endeavours. It published a Draft Defamation Bill in March 2011. This has the further

---

compensation can be achieved by an award not exceeding £10,000 (see, eg, *Burnstein v Times Newspapers Ltd* [2001] 1 WLR 579; *Loutchansky v Times Newspapers Ltd* [2001] 3 WLR 404).

[16] This absence of legal aid for Ds facing defamation charges from a powerful corporate entity amounts to a violation of the right to a fair trial under Art 6 of the European Convention on Human Rights: *Steel & Morris v UK* [2005] EMLR 15. It would seem, therefore, that it now falls to the UK Government to make changes in the legal aid entitlements in defamation cases, and in principle not just for Ds.

[17] There is a strong prima facie right to a jury trial in defamation under the Supreme Court Act 1981, s 69(1). Thus, if D seeks to insist upon such a trial, the court will normally treat this prima facie right as being of fundamental importance: see *Safeway Stores v Tate* [2001] QB 1120. Exceptionally, under the Defamation Act 1996, s 8, a judge may determine the level of damages that C is to receive.

[18] [1996] 2 All ER 35. See also *Rantzen v Mirror Group Newspapers (1986) Ltd* [1994] QB 670 and *Jones v Pollard* [1997] EMLR 233. On the other hand, the Court of Appeal will not reduce high (but not excessive) levels of damages: see *Kiam v MGN Ltd* [2002] 2 All ER 219.

[19] *John v MGN Ltd* [1996] 2 All ER 35, at 51–2. As a limit to such guidance, on the other hand, D is not permitted to mention to the jury any of the amounts he may have offered to C in their pre-trial correspondence: *Kiam v Neil* [1995] EMLR 1.

[20] See Law Reform (Miscellaneous Provisions) Act 1934, s 1(1). However, defaming a dead person may still constitute a criminal libel.   [21] See Loveland [2000] EHRLR 476.

aims of simplifying the law, and reducing costs of litigation in this area. More specific reforms would include the following:

(1) A new requirement that a statement must have caused substantial harm in order for it to be defamatory

(2) A new statutory defence of responsible publication on matters of public interest

(3) A statutory defence of truth (replacing the current common law defence of fair/honest comment)

(4) Provisions updating and extending the circumstances in which the defences of absolute and qualified privilege are available

(5) Introduction of a single publication rule to prevent action being brought in relation to publication of the same material by the same publisher after a one year limitation period has passed

(6) Action to address libel tourism by ensuring a court will not accept jurisdiction unless satisfied that England and Wales is clearly the most appropriate place to bring an action...

(7) Removal of the presumption in favour of jury trial, so that the judge would have a discretion to order jury trial where it is in the interests of justice.[22]

The passage of an Act in this form would represent a considerable alteration to the present law. In this book, we highlight provisions in the Draft Bill.

SECTION 2   ELEMENTS OF DEFAMATION

Whether a defamation action is framed in libel or slander, the claimant must always prove that the words, pictures, gestures, etc are defamatory. The claimant must also show that they refer to him and, finally, that they were maliciously published.

(A) THE MEANING OF 'DEFAMATORY'

(1) Injury to reputation

The classic definition of a defamatory statement is one 'which is calculated to injure the reputation of another, by exposing him to hatred, contempt or ridicule'.[23] It is clear that being made a laughing stock is not sufficient. *Blennerhasset v Novelty Sales Services Ltd*[24] provides an example. In that case, a newspaper advertisement was headed 'Beware of Yo Yo' and went on to imply that Mr Blennerhassett, a worthy man, had now been placed under supervision in a quiet place in the country by reason of his fascination

---

[22] Ministry of Justice, *Draft Defamation Bill Consultation Paper* (CP3/11, 2011), 5–6.

[23] *Parmiter v Coupland* (1840) 6 M & W 105, at 108; *Emerson v Grimsby Times and Telegraph Co Ltd* (1926) 42 TLR 238.

[24] (1933) 175 LT Jo 393.

with the defendant's toy, the Yo Yo. Although the claimant, a stockbroker, showed that his arrival at the Stock Exchange on the day after the publication was greeted with 'jeers, ribaldry and laughter', the statement was held not to be defamatory.[25]

The inadequacy of the classic definition is now generally recognised, especially in that it does not embrace injury to trading reputation.[26] Lord Atkin once proposed the alternative test of whether: 'the words tend to lower the claimant in the estimation of right-thinking members of society generally?'[27] But, while this test cures some of the defects of the earlier one, the expression 'right-thinking members of society' is deeply problematic. For example, although it is established that it is defamatory to say that a person is insane,[28] or that she has been raped,[29] do right-thinking people think less well of those unfortunates? On the other hand, that one's associates (being themselves an ordinary cross-section of a respectable part of the community) think less well of one in consequence of a statement does not necessarily make that statement defamatory. Thus, in *Byrne v Deane*[30] it was held that to impute that a member of a golf club had informed the police about an illegal fruit-machine kept in the club was not defamatory even though it lowered him in the esteem of his fellow members. A certain class of society may think badly of police informers, but simply to impute this conduct to someone is nonetheless not defamatory.[31] Similarly, ought it to be regarded as defamatory to say of a worker who stayed at work during a strike that he was a 'scab' or a 'blackleg'?[32] And, do allegations that X is homosexual lower X in the estimation of anyone other than homophobes?[33]

The truth is that English law has not defined 'defamatory' with satisfactory precision.[34] With diffidence it is suggested that the 'right-thinking' person test (which has yet to be subject to an appellate court's close scrutiny) must be understood in one of two ways. First, if most citizens would shun or avoid a person in consequence of the statement, then it will be classed as defamatory. Second, and alternatively, if a

---

[25] On the other hand, so long as it inspires contempt or ridicule, even a caricature has been held to constitute defamation: *Dunlop Rubber Co Ltd v Dunlop* [1921] 1 AC 367. Cf *Dolby v Newnes* (1887) 3 TLR 393.

[26] Eg, *Capital and Counties Bank v George Henty & Sons* (1882) 7 App Cas 741, at 771; *Tournier v National Provincial and Union Bank of England* [1924] 1 KB 461, at 477 and 486–7.

[27] *Sim v Stretch* [1936] 2 All ER 1237, at 1240. In *Rubber Improvement Ltd v Daily Telegraph Ltd* [1964] AC 234, at 285, Lord Devlin said that the test was the effect on the 'ordinary' man, not the 'logical' man. See also *Skuse v Granada Television Ltd* [1996] EMLR 278 and *Berkoff v Burchill* [1996] 4 All ER 1008. Cf *Norman v Future Publishing Ltd* [1999] EMLR 325 (gentle humour short of ridicule is not actionable).

[28] *Morgan v Lingen* (1863) 8 LT 800.

[29] *Youssoupoff v Metro-Goldwyn-Mayer Pictures Ltd* (1934) 50 TLR 581.   [30] [1937] 1 KB 818.

[31] *Sim v Stretch* [1936] 2 All ER 1237. On the other hand, not merely the golfing fraternity, but right-thinking persons will (it has been held) think worse of an amateur golfer who allows his name to be used in the advertising of chocolates: *Tolley v JS Fry & Sons Ltd* [1931] AC 333. Yet, in *Gibbings v O'Dea & Co Ltd* (1948–9) Macgillivray & Le Quesne Copyright Cases 31 it was held not to be libel for D to use the name of C, who was an author, on an advertisement for mattresses in the *Irish Times*.

[32] McCardie J thought not in *Myroft v Sleight* (1921) 90 LJKB 883.

[33] Probably not: see *Quilty v Windsor* 1999 SLT 346. See also *Arab News Network v Al Khazen* [2001] EWCA Civ 118 (a lowering of reputation within a particular racial group is insufficient).

[34] Gibbons' answer would be to change the basis of the action from damage to reputation to awarding a remedy for unsubstantiated allegations that cause C to be falsely judged: (1996) 16 OJLS 587.

substantial and respectable proportion of society would think less well of a person then, again, the statement will be construed as defamatory provided that their reaction is not plainly anti-social or irrational.[35] Both these interpretations accord with *Byrne v Deane* and also support the view that it is defamatory to say that someone is a 'scab' or a member of the National Front.

(a) Words of abuse

To say that abuse is not defamatory is misleading. The cases relied on for this erroneous statement are cases of slander deciding that special damage must ordinarily be proved.[36] The test to be applied to words of abuse is exactly the same as for other allegedly defamatory statements. Thus, it may be defamatory to call a person a villain,[37] a black sheep[38] or a habitual drunkard.[39] What matters is the context and manner in which the words are uttered. Thus, even a word like 'Mafia' can be understood to describe a close-knit group in a metaphorical, but not defamatory, sense.[40]

(b) Words of opinion

A statement may be defamatory, even though the maker states it, not as fact, but as mere opinion.[41] One must take into account circumstances of time and place.[42] Thus, in *Slazengers Ltd v C Gibbs & Co*,[43] it was defamatory to state during the war with Germany that the claimants were a German firm that was likely to be closed down.

(c) Other examples of injured reputation

Several further examples may help to illustrate what is, and what is not, defamatory. It is defamatory to impute to a trader, businessman, or professional person a lack of qualification, knowledge, skill, capacity, judgment, or efficiency in the conduct of his trade or business or professional activity (such as a severe attack on the special anaesthetising technique of a practising dental surgeon).[44] By contrast, it is not per se defamatory merely to criticise a trader's goods: the trader himself must be attacked for a defamation action to lie. If, however, one can read into a criticism of the product

---

[35] If the words would not in themselves convey to the ordinary person the meaning which a special group of experts would give to them, then this interpretation would not apply (unless an innuendo were pleaded: see below) because the basic rule that words must be defamatory in their ordinary meaning would not be satisfied: *Mollo v BBC* (1963) *Times*, 2 February. Nor is it defamatory, without more, for D to say that C is Mr X, even though others have published defamatory articles about Mr X. The libel complained of must be in the statement published by D: *Astaire v Campling* [1965] 3 All ER 666.

[36] Eg, *Thorley v Lord Kerry* (1812) 4 Taunt 355. But in that case, it was explicitly stated (at 365) that, 'for mere general abuse spoken, no action lies'.　　　　　　　　[37] *Bell v Stone* (1798) 1 Bos & P 331.

[38] *M'Gregor v Gregory* (1843) 11 M & W 287.　　　[39] *Alexander v Jenkins* [1892] 1 QB 797, at 804.

[40] *Brooks v Lind* 1997 Rep LR 83 (not defamation to suggest C was associated with a 'Council Mafia').

[41] *Braddock v Bevins* [1948] 1 KB 580.

[42] *Dolby v Newnes* (1887) 3 TLR 393 (a statement at a private dinner party, although not defamatory, may become so if repeated in a magazine).　　　　　　　　　　　　[43] (1916) 33 TLR 35.

[44] *Drummond-Jackson v British Medical Association* [1970] 1 All ER 1094.

a criticism of its manufacturer, then the criticism may be defamatory.[45] Thus, to say that a baker's bread is *always unwholesome* is defamatory.[46] But to say that a product does not answer its purpose is not.[47] To say that a trader is bankrupt or insolvent is defamatory;[48] but to say that he has ceased to be in business is not, for it does not reflect on his reputation.[49] It is also not per se defamatory to say that a trader has been put on a stop-list.[50]

(2) Who may be defamed?

Either a living person or the commercial reputation of a trading company may be defamed under English law,[51] so long as their reputation exists at least partly in this country.[52] Accordingly, it is defamation to claim that X Ltd indulges in black-market activities.[53] Importantly, the fact that commercial enterprises can sue for defamation is seen by the press as a powerful inhibition of vigorous criticism of such entities. The threat to sue for libel has a 'chilling effect' on investigations by the media and may allow corrupt practices to remain hidden from the public. However, the importance of the protection offered to such enterprises by the law of defamation has been affirmed in *Jameel v Wall Street Journal Europe SPRL*, where Lord Bingham remarked that:

> [T]he good name of a company, as that of an individual, is a thing of value. A damaging libel may lower its standing in the eyes of the public and even its own staff, make people less ready to deal with it, less willing or less proud to work for it.[54]

In the same case, Lord Craig observed that other organisations not involved in trading for profit, such as charities and trade unions, may also be harmed by defamatory statements and may have a right of action. In the case of a charity, his Lordship reasoned that 'it is not only its pocket, due to a loss of income, that is liable to be injured. Injury to its reputation in the eyes of those with whom it must deal to achieve its charitable objects may be just as damaging to the purpose for which it exists'.[55]

---

[45] *Evans v Harlow* (1844) 5 QB 624.

[46] *Linotype Co Ltd v British Empire Type-Setting Machine Co Ltd* (1899) 81 LT 331, at 133, (dictum).

[47] *Evans v Harlow* (1844) 5 QB 624.   [48] *Shepheard v Whitaker* (1875) LR 10 CP 502.

[49] *Ratcliffe v Evans* [1892] 2 QB 524. Nor is it defamatory to say that his business is suffering as a result of competition: *Stephenson v Donaldson & Sons* (1981) 262 EG 148. In some circumstances it may constitute the separate tort of injurious falsehood.

[50] *Ware and De Freville Ltd v Motor Trade Association* [1921] 3 KB 40.

[51] In relation to companies, the statement 'must attack the corporation or company in the method of conducting its affairs, must accuse it of fraud or mismanagement, or must attack its financial position': *South Hetton Coal Co v NE News Association* [1894] 1 QB 133, at 141; approved in *Jameel v Wall Street Journal Europe SPRL* [2006] UKHL 44.

[52] In *King v Lewis* [2005] EMLR 4, a boxing promoter who was defamed in an American magazine was able to sue in the English courts on the twin bases that (1) he had a professional reputation in the UK and (2) the article, which had appeared over the internet, had been downloaded in this country. On companies, see *Jameel v Wall Street Journal Europe SPRL* [2006] UKHL 44, at [17].

[53] *D & L Caterers Ltd and Jackson v D'Ajou* [1945] KB 364. Cf *Holdsworth Ltd v Associated Newspapers Ltd* [1937] 3 All ER 872. A company may recover substantial damages even though it suffers no financial loss: *Selby Bridge (Proprietors) v Sunday Telegraph Ltd* (1966) 197 EG 1077.   [54] [2006] UKHL 44, at [26].

[55] Ibid at [96].

By contrast to the position regarding companies, according to *Derbyshire County Council v Times Newspapers Ltd*,[56] public authorities cannot invoke defamation law to protect their 'governing reputation'.

> Ds had published articles questioning the propriety of C's management of pension funds. The House of Lords struck out the claim, holding that democratically elected government bodies and public authorities should be open to uninhibited public criticism. The 'chilling effect' of libel might prevent publication of matters about which the public ought to be informed.

In effect, then, the right of free speech and freedom of the press (enshrined in Article 10 of the European Convention on Human Rights) outweighed the Council's claim to protection of its reputation.[57] On the other hand, the limitation on the authority suing in libel – be it a local council or government ministry – does not apply to any individual working there who can show that he personally has been defamed. To some extent, then, what their Lordships had to say about libel and public authorities in the *Derbyshire* case may be viewed as somewhat specious given that uninhibited criticism may well be appropriate and healthy in respect of many individuals holding important public offices.

(3) The interpretation of defamatory statements

It has so far been assumed that the meaning of the statement complained of is readily ascertainable. But this is not always so; and there are detailed rules of interpretation that must now be considered.

(a) Innuendo

The initial question in any defamation action is whether the words complained of are capable of bearing a defamatory meaning. In the absence of an allegation that those words possess an extended meaning, words must be construed (by a judge)[58] in their ordinary and natural sense.[59] The whole of the statement must be looked at, not merely that part which the claimant alleges to be defamatory (although, of course, it may be relevant to take account of the greater importance of some part of a statement – for example, the headlines of an article in a newspaper).[60] In *Charleston*

---

[56] [1993] 1 All ER 1011 (overruling *Bognor Regis UDC v Campion* [1972] 2 QB 169).

[57] For critique see Loveland [1994] LS 206. Recall, also, that the Convention has all but been incorporated into English law by virtue of the Human Rights Act 1998.

[58] *Turner v Metro-Goldwyn-Mayer Pictures Ltd* [1950] 1 All ER 449, at 465.

[59] *Capital and Counties Bank Ltd v George Henty & Sons* (1882) 7 App Cas 741, at 772; *Skuse v Granada Television Ltd* [1996] EMLR 278: *Gillick v BBC* [1996] EMLR 267. In *Mitchell v Faber and Faber Ltd* [1998] EMLR 807, Hirst LJ stated (at 811) that, '[i]n deciding whether words are capable of conveying a defamatory meaning the court will reject those meanings which can only emerge as the product of some strained or forced or utterly unreasonable interpretation'. Similarly, in *Edwards v Times Newspapers Ltd* (1997) (unreported) it was held that the ordinary meaning of the words used must be construed in the light of the meaning that would be attached to them by 'the ordinary reader'.

[60] *Shipley v Todhunter* (1836) 7 C & P 680.

v News Group Newspapers Ltd,[61] for instance, two soap opera stars sued in respect of material published in the defendants' newspaper which depicted the claimants' faces superimposed upon two near-naked torsos. The article printed beneath the picture castigated the makers of a pornographic computer game which had generated the images in question. It was held that, taken as a whole, the picture and the article were not capable of being defamatory.[62] On the other hand, where an article contains both a defamatory statement *and* a denial of that statement, the court is unlikely to find that the denial necessarily neutralises the defamatory comment. As Simon Brown LJ put it: 'I find it very difficult to conceive of circumstances in which the mere printing of a denial could of itself be said to constitute an antidote sufficient to neutralise the bane'.[63]

There may be circumstances, too, where the context in which the words were uttered must be taken into account. In *Bookbinder v Tebbit*,[64] for example, the alleged slander was made at a political meeting. The court said that the meaning to be attached to the defendant's words could be affected, among other things, by the form of the question to which the words were an answer or the general course of the speech in issue. Similarly, there may be circumstances where the claimant alleges that the statement is defamatory because specific facts known to the reader give to the statement a meaning other than, or additional to, its ordinary meaning. This is known as a 'true' or 'legal' innuendo, and here the claimant must plead and prove such facts[65] because the defendant is entitled to know the meaning of the statement on which the claimant seeks to rely so that he is able to argue either that, even thus construed, the statement is not defamatory or that it is true of the claimant.

There is also a third possibility: that the words may have a meaning beyond their literal meaning which is inherent in them and arises by inference or implication. This is sometimes known as a 'false innuendo' and it is something that the claimant must plead separately. Of course, if there is no obvious, ordinary, or natural meaning to be ascribed to the words complained of, then this obscures the sense in which the words bear a 'false innuendo'. It was for this reason that the court in *Allsop v Church of England Newspaper Ltd*[66] held that the claimant must plead the particular meaning upon which he relies in such cases. A 'false innuendo' differs from a 'true innuendo' in that the pleader of a 'false innuendo' does not generally need to set out any extrinsic facts in support of his plea.

---

[61] [1995] 2 AC 65.

[62] For criticism see *Chakravarti v Advertisers Newspapers* [1998] HCA 37, at [134].

[63] *Mark v Associated Newspapers (No 1)* [2002] EMLR 38.   [64] [1989] 1 WLR 640.

[65] Case law insists that C must prove that those facts were actually known to some people (*Fullam v Newcastle Chronicle and Journal Ltd* [1977] 1 WLR 651) and that those facts were in existence and known to those people at the time of the publication (*Grapelli v Derek Block (Holdings) Ltd* [1981] 2 All ER 272; *Baturina v Times Newspapers Ltd* [2011] EWCA Civ 308).

[66] [1972] 2 QB 161.

(i) True innuendoes

Here are some typical examples of 'true', or 'legal', innuendoes. In one case, the defendant, having engaged the claimant, a well-known singer, to perform at a concert, printed her name third in the order on the programme. The court accepted evidence that in the world of musical performances the best singer is always placed at the head of the programme with those holding only a lesser reputation in the middle. That being so, the programme constituted a defamatory innuendo of the claimant.[67] It has also been held that to include a cartoon of a well-known, amateur golfer in an advertisement for chocolate implied he was being paid for the advert and thus prostituting his amateur status.[68]

In *Hough v London Express Newspaper Ltd*,[69] the question that arose was whether a claimant relying on an innuendo has to prove that there was publication to somebody who interpreted the matter in the defamatory sense alleged.

> D published an account and photograph of the 'curly-headed wife' of a named boxer. C, the boxer's real wife, produced witnesses who gave evidence that they had read the statement to mean that C was not the wife of the boxer. In the event, they were not misled into thinking that she was not his wife, nor was any person that was produced as a witness so misled. Nonetheless, it was held that the appropriate test was an objective one. The court found in C's favour: it was enough to prove that there are people who *might* understand the words in a defamatory sense, but no need for 'evidence that some person did so understand them'.[70]

(ii) False innuendoes

Problems also arise with regard to false innuendoes. In *Rubber Improvement Ltd v Daily Telegraph Ltd*,[71] the defendants published an article which stated that the Fraud Squad of the City of London Police were investigating the affairs of the claimants' company. The article was found to be defamatory in its ordinary meaning because the simple statement that the Fraud Squad was inquiring into his affairs might have damaged his reputation even though such investigation did not, per se, impugn his innocence. However, since what was said was true – the Fraud Squad was conducting the investigations mentioned – no action lay.[72] The claimants also alleged that the words were defamatory in a second way: that is, they carried with them the imputation that there was at least a basis for suspicion about the way in which the business was conducted. The thrust of the plea was that the imputation of reasonable suspicion (while

---

[67] *Russell v Notcutt* (1896) 12 TLR 195.

[68] *Tolley v JS Fry & Sons Ltd* [1931] AC 333.   [69] [1940] 2 KB 507.

[70] Ibid at 515. See also *Theaker v Richardson* [1962] 1 All ER 229.

[71] [1964] AC 234. But see *Hyams v Peterson* [1991] 1 NZLR 711 where the New Zealand Court of Appeal found a statement containing words of suspicion could impute guilt.

[72] There is an important difference between something being defamatory *simpliciter* and something being defamatory and *actionable*. To be defamatory, the statement must merely diminish C's reputation; but to be actionable, the statement must also be untrue. In short, both true and false statements may be defamatory, but only the latter may be actionable

still consistent with the claimants' innocence) was nonetheless capable of diminishing their trading reputation. On the facts, their Lordships held that the words were not defamatory in this second sense; since there was a distinction between, on the one hand, imputing reasonable grounds for suspicion and, on the other (as here), simply reporting the fact of suspicion.

This crucial distinction between a statement and an imputation of suspicion has since been reasserted by the Court of Appeal in *Mapp v News Group Newspapers Ltd.*[73] Nonetheless, the point is that the second plea in *Rubber Improvement Ltd* constituted the allegation of a false innuendo and therefore did not require the claimants to adduce evidence of any extrinsic facts which had to be set out in the pleading (such as details of individual readers who would interpret the words in a particular way). Furthermore, the presumption of falsity – which in fact is irrebuttable in English law (though this does not mean that substantial damage to reputation is also presumed)[74] – has since been confirmed by the European Court of Human Rights not to be incompatible with the Article 10 right to freedom of expression.[75]

When a defendant newspaper described a well-known broadcaster as 'bent', the claimant had to set out the meaning of the word on which he relied.[76] If a statement is capable of many different meanings and the claimant does not specify those on which he relies, the defendant is entitled to justify the statement according to any meaning which it reasonably bears.[77] If, in a long article containing many different meanings in relation to him, the claimant fails to plead the meaning(s) on which he relies, the defendant is entitled to have the claimant's statement of claim struck out as disclosing no reasonable cause of action.[78]

(b) The roles of judge and jury in construing what is defamatory

The judge decides whether a statement is *capable* of bearing a defamatory meaning, whether in its normal meaning or by innuendo.[79] Once that is resolved in the affirmative, the jury then decides whether it *did* bear a defamatory meaning on the occasion complained of.[80] In order to fulfil his task, the judge must construe the particular words used to determine whether they are capable of bearing a defamatory meaning; only once he decides that they may bear such a meaning does the jury then decide whether in fact they were defamatory.[81] The claimant may contend that the statement

---

[73] [1998] QB 520.
[74] *Jameel v Dow Jones* [2005] QB 946, at [30]–[32]. The Court of Appeal also added that, although falsity is presumed, a claim may be struck out as an abuse of process where virtually no damage to reputation has occurred.   [75] *Steel & Morris v UK* [2005] EMLR 15, at [93]–[94].
[76] *Allsop v Church of England Newspaper Ltd* [1972] 2 QB 161.
[77] *London Computer Operators Training Ltd v BBC* [1973] 2 All ER 170.
[78] *DDSA Pharmaceuticals Ltd v Times Newspapers Ltd* [1973] QB 21.
[79] *Adam v Ward* [1917] AC 309, at 329; *Lloyd v David Syme & Co Ltd* [1986] AC 350; *Mapp v News Group Newspapers Ltd* [1998] QB 520. By virtue of s 7 of the Defamation Act 1996, the judge must consider whether the statement is capable (as opposed to being merely 'arguably capable') of bearing a particular meaning.
[80] *Cassidy v Daily Mirror Newspapers Ltd* [1929] 2 KB 331, at 340.
[81] *Jones v Skelton* [1963] 3 All ER 952.

has different defamatory meanings. In such instances, the judge decides which of those the statement is capable of conveying, and the jury then decides which particular meaning within that category the words in fact bear.[82] Take, for example, *Aspro Travel Ltd v Owners Abroad Group plc*.[83]

> The allegations here were that Cs' family company was 'going bust' and the question was whether this was potentially defamatory. Among other things, the court had to consider the alleged false innuendo that it was defamatory in the sense that such allegations would lower the directors of such a company in the estimation of the public by implicitly suggesting that, notwithstanding the company's insolvency, the directors were nonetheless allowing it to continue trading.

Although the determinations of a jury (where empanelled) are taken very seriously in libel cases,[84] it is nonetheless the case that an appellate court may set aside a jury's verdict and enter judgment for the defendant where the jury in the court of first instance found for the claimant after the first instance judge had entrusted the decision to them. Conversely, on the very rare occasions when an appellate court holds that a jury could not reasonably have found that the words were not defamatory, it will set aside the verdict and order a new trial.[85] Where the judge has misdirected the jury on the law, its verdict will also be set aside.[86] The courts seek to ensure that the issues which come to trial are clear-cut in order to eschew the advantage that one party might obtain by clever tactics. It is a fundamental principle in defamation that:

> the trial of the action should concern itself with the essential issues and the evidence relevant thereto and that public policy and the interests of the parties require that the trial should be kept strictly to the issues necessary for a fair determination of the dispute between the parties.[87]

Moreover, what holds for the claimant also holds for the defendant. Thus, defendants pleading the defence of justification must do so in a manner which makes it quite clear what meaning or meanings they seek to justify.[88] Time and again the Court of Appeal has deplored attempts to take advantage of the rules of pleading in order to acquire an unfair advantage at the actual trial.[89]

---

[82] *Slim v Daily Telegraph Ltd* [1968] 2 QB 157.

[83] [1995] 4 All ER 728.

[84] See, eg, *Safeway Stores plc v Tate* [2001] 2 WLR 1377. Cf *Alexander v Arts Council of Wales* [2001] 1 WLR 1840 (a finding of no possible malice justified the judge in withholding the case from a jury).

[85] The jurisdiction to do this exists under the Supreme Court Act 1981, s 69. However a decision to overturn the verdict of a jury can only be taken in exceptional circumstances where the jury's decision cannot be explained on any ground not indicative of perversity: see *Grobbelaar v News Group Newspapers* [2003] EMLR 1.

[86] *Tournier v National Provincial and Union Bank of England* [1924] 1 KB 461. Cf *Dakhyl v Labouchere* [1908] 2 KB 325.   [87] *Polly Peck (Holdings) plc v Trelford* [1986] 2 All ER 84, at 94.

[88] *Lucas-Box v News Group Newspapers Ltd* [1986] 1 All ER 177: *Morrell v International Thomson Publishing Ltd* [1989] 3 All ER 733.

[89] *Morrell v International Thomson Publishing Ltd* [1989] 3 All ER 733, at 733–5.

The Government is proposing to remove the presumption in favour of trial by jury by amending provisions in the Senior Courts Act 1981 and the County Courts Act 1984.[90] Trial by jury would be available by leave of the court only. One of the main reasons for this proposed amendment is that it will supposedly allow for early resolution of various issues in cases that would otherwise have had to await a determination by a jury on the meaning of allegedly defamatory material. However, the true impact of such a provision is likely to be small, given that most defamation cases are, in fact, tried without a jury.[91]

(4) Immateriality of the defendant's knowledge

The general common-law position is that '[a] person charged with libel cannot defend himself by showing that he intended in his breast not to defame'.[92] Nor is it a defence that a person has no actual knowledge that his statement is defamatory. It is usually stated that liability at common law is strict: it matters not whether the defendant could have taken steps to discover that the statement was defamatory. The leading case is *Cassidy v Daily Mirror Newspapers Ltd*.[93]

> With the authority of Mr C, Ds published a photograph, taken at a race meeting, with the following words underneath: 'Mr C, the racehorse owner, and Miss X, whose engagement has been announced'. Ds published the photograph, not knowing that C was already married to the man in question, and having taken no steps whatever to find out whether he was already married. Ds were held liable to C for implying she had been living with him without being married to him.

The case provides clear authority for the proposition that, at common law, one may be liable for a statement which one does not actually know to be defamatory. To this strict general rule, however, there are two exceptions – one statutory; one rooted in the common law. These exceptions can be viewed in two ways: either as 'chinks' in the general rule or as defences to the application of the rule.[94] The second approach is favoured here, and the exceptions are discussed in depth in the next chapter.

(B) REFERENCE TO THE CLAIMANT

'In order to be actionable the defamatory words must be understood to be published of and concerning the [claimant].'[95] The claimant need not be mentioned in the statement, nor need everyone reading it know that he was referred to; it suffices if ordinary sensible people, proved to have special knowledge of the facts, might reasonably

---

[90] Draft Defamation Bill 2011, cl 8.
[91] Ministry of Justice, *Draft Defamation Bill Consultation Paper* (CP3/11, 2011), 36.
[92] *E Hulton & Co v Jones* [1910] AC 20, at 23.   [93] [1929] 2 KB 331.
[94] See also Descheemaeker (2009) 29 OJLS 603 for argument that defamation has been 'infiltrated' by negligence concepts.
[95] *Knupffer v London Express Newspaper Ltd* [1944] AC 116, at 121. Cf *Farrington v Leigh* (1987) *Times*, 10 December.

believe that the statement referred to the claimant.[96] Thus, where the defendant publishes a biography about X, and the biography contains a picture of X together with the claimant *and* a known prostitute, it is defamatory of the claimant to publish that photograph where the claimant's friends would see the picture and identify him even though he is not actually named in the book.[97] On the other hand, in cases such as this, the damages will be lower where only a small proportion of those who read the book would know that it was defamatory of the claimant.

(1) Class libels

Where a statement defamatory of a class of persons is made, the same test is applied to determine whether individuals within the class may sue. If the class is so small that persons would reasonably believe that every member of it is targeted, then each individual member may sue. Thus, where proceedings were pending against 17 persons, it was held that one of them could sue a third party who said of them all that 'these defendants helped to murder HF'.[98] A similar rule applies to directors of a small company,[99] and presumably also to trustees of an institution. But a statement that 'all estate agents are rogues' would not enable any one member of such a large class to sue.

Even where the class is too large to permit every member to sue, an individual within the class may still be able to sue. So, for example, even if the claimant has a very common surname, other facts contained in the statement in question may narrow the class sufficiently for him to be defamed;[100] and, of course, if the claimant can show that the statement was especially referable to him, he may sue. Often this will rest on an innuendo which must be specifically pleaded; and the court will order the claimant to give full particulars of the facts on which the claim rests.[101]

Two cases illustrate the position. First, *Le Fanu v Malcomson*.[102]

> D published an article suggesting that in some of the Irish factories cruelties were practised upon employees. There were circumstances in the article as a whole, including a reference to Waterford, which enabled the jury to identify C's Waterford factory as the one at which the article was aimed. C's action succeeded.

---

[96] *Morgan v Odhams Press Ltd* [1971] 2 All ER 1156. If D publishes a statement defamatory on its face about someone described but not named, and a later publication by D names C so as to identify the subject to readers of the first article, for the first time, the second publication may be relied on to support the allegation that the first one referred to C: *Hayward v Thompson* [1982] QB 47.

[97] *Dwek v Macmillan Publishers Ltd* [2000] EMLR 284.

[98] *Foxcroft v Lacy* (1613) Hob 89. See also *Browne v Thomson & Co* 1912 SC 359.

[99] *Aspro Travel Ltd v Owners Abroad Group plc* [1995] 4 All ER 728. The same may be true in reverse: see *Elite Model Management Corp v BBC* [2001] All ER (D) 334 (ie, defamation of company executives may also be defamatory of the company). Cf *Chomley v Watson* [1907] VLR 502 where the true statement 'Either you or Jones stole the money' was held not to be actionable by the innocent party, Jones.

[100] *Jameel v Dow Jones & Co Inc* [2005] QB 946.   [101] *Bruce v Odhams Press Ltd* [1936] 1 KB 697.

[102] (1848) 1 HL Cas 637.

Second, *Knupffer v London Express Newspaper Ltd*:[103]

> During the war, D's newspaper referred to the Quisling activities of the Young Russian Party. Although the party was international, and had a British branch of 24 members headed by C, the article referred only to the Party's activities in France and the US. But since the total membership was several thousand, each member could not be said to be identified. No facts were proved in evidence that could identify C as being singled out in the article, and therefore his action failed.

(2) Unintentional references to the claimant

The claimant may be defamed although the defendant did not intend it. Where the defamation is intentional, however, a greater level of damages may be awarded.[104] In several cases, newspaper proprietors who did not intend to defame the claimant have been held liable. In *Hulton v Jones*,[105] for example, the defendants published a fictional article about 'Artemus Jones'. The writer of the article did not know of the claimant, of that name, who was a former contributor to the newspaper. But the managing editor, on reading the article in proof, had thought at first that the claimant was intended. The defendants were held liable. Similarly, in *Newstead v London Express Newspaper Ltd*,[106] the defendant published an account of the trial for bigamy of 'Harold Newstead, thirty-year-old Camberwell man'. The reporter had included the address and occupation of the Harold Newstead of whom this was a correct report, but the sub-editor deleted it. This want of particularity caused readers to think that the claimant – another Harold Newstead of Camberwell, of about the same age – was meant. It was held to be no defence that the words were true of, and intended to refer to, another.[107]

Whether cases like these can now withstand the passage of the Human Rights Act 1998, with its requirement that the courts must develop the common law in accordance with the rights enshrined in the European Convention,[108] is highly questionable. There is arguably an infringement of the Article 10 right to freedom of expression in such cases because, for example, the press would effectively be forced to check whether a genuine photograph of person X resembles closely enough any other person so as to amount to a defamation of that other person when a particular story accompanies the photograph. Certainly, the view was taken in *O'Shea v MGN Ltd* that such a requirement would place too onerous a burden on a publisher. As Morland J put it:

> [T]he strict liability principle should not cover the 'look-alike' situation. To allow it to do so would be an unjustifiable interference with the vital right of freedom of expression

---

[103] [1944] AC 116.

[104] *Bridgmont v Associated Newspapers Ltd* [1951] 2 KB 578. [105] [1910] AC 20.

[106] [1940] 1 KB 377. And see *Grappelli v Derek Block (Holdings) Ltd* [1981] 2 All ER 272 and *Hayward v Thompson* [1982] QB 47 (effect of later publications identifying the person defamed).

[107] By contrast, where D publishes details of a person whom he does not actually know (and it is clear that D does not know him), and C shares the same name as the person named by D, and that name is a common name, C seemingly will have to show that a reasonable person known to C would interpret it as a reference to C: *Jameel v Dow Jones* [2005] QB 946, at [45]. [108] See *Douglas v Hello! Ltd* [2001] QB 967, at [129].

disproportionate to the legitimate aim of protecting the reputations of 'look-alikes' and contrary to Article 10.[109]

But whether this first instance decision can be confined to cases involving 'look-alike' photographs, or whether it ought (logically) to be extended to cases where articles alone are printed in newspapers with no accompanying photograph, will be for future courts to decide. Perhaps Morland J simply felt obliged to confine his judgment to cases involving photographs because *Hulton v Jones* and *Newstead v London Express Newspaper Ltd* were decisions of the House of Lords and Court of Appeal respectively. At the very least, it is clear that the courts are increasingly concerned, in general terms, about infringements of Article 10.[110]

(C) 'MALICIOUS' PUBLICATION

Though always referred to as the need for 'malicious publication', the true requirement is for there to have been *mere* publication. The adjective 'malicious' is in practice otiose, save that the presence of malice serves to defeat the defences of honest comment and qualified privilege (both discussed in the next chapter). Publication is 'making known the defamatory matter after it has been written to some person other than the person of whom it is written'.[111] This requirement of publication to a third party merely underlines that the tort protects not an individual's opinion of himself but the estimation in which others hold him. Because of this rule, it is often important to know when the defendant, who perhaps addressed his remarks to the claimant alone, can be held responsible for the fact that third parties have learnt of the defamatory statement. The rule is that, if he intended that it should be published to them, or ought to have foreseen such publication, he is liable, but not otherwise.[112] A defendant is not liable for an 'unsuspected overhearing of the words' spoken by him to the claimant.[113] He is not liable where a father opens his son's letter,[114] or the butler opens even the unsealed letter of his employer.[115] A correspondent should expect that clerks of a businessman-claimant might, in the ordinary course of business, open letters addressed to him at his place of business but not when they are marked 'personal', 'private', etc. He is therefore responsible for the publication to them where the correspondence is not so marked.[116]

---

[109] [2001] EMLR 40, at [47].

[110] See, eg, *Jameel v Dow Jones* [2005] QB 946; *Steel & Morris v UK* [2005] EMLR 15.

[111] *Pullman v Walter Hill & Co* [1891] 1 QB 524, at 527.

[112] *Huth v Huth* [1915] 3 KB 32, at 38; *Slipper v BBC* [1991] 1 All ER 165.

[113] *White v J and F Stone (Lighting and Radio) Ltd* [1939] 2 KB 827.

[114] *Powell v Gelston* [1916] 2 KB 615.

[115] *Huth v Huth* [1915] 3 KB 32. Cf the case if the sender knew that C was blind, and that the butler often opened letters for her.

[116] *Pullman v Walter Hill & Co* [1891] 1 QB 524. But what if one sent a letter marked 'private' to, say, the Prime Minister, or even to any other busy public figure? Might there not be publication to the secretary who opened it?

In general, the original maker of a statement is not liable for its republication by another; yet that other will be responsible even though he expressly states that he is merely reproducing what he has been told from a specified source.[117] So, the writer, newspaper proprietor, and printer of a defamatory article in a newspaper are each liable for its publication.[118] This repetition rule has specifically been held to be compatible with Article 10 of the European Convention on Human Rights,[119] even though it may be seen as forcing journalists to check scrupulously (or distance themselves from) comments made by others. Importantly, however:

> where a man who makes a request to another to publish defamatory matter, of which, for the purpose, he gives him a statement, whether in full or in outline, and the agent publishes the matter, adhering to the sense and substance of it, although the language be to some extent his own, the man making the request is liable to an action as the publisher.[120]

A man who knows that reporters are present when he is making a speech is not thereby responsible for its publication in the press, but he is answerable if he gives the information to them with a view to publication.[121] On the other hand, when a television broadcast foreseeably invites comment in the next day's newspapers, the maker of the original defamatory statement will be liable for its repetition by the press.[122]

The requirement of publication to a third party is satisfied by dictating a letter to one's typist,[123] and probably also when office staff photocopy.[124] A judge at first instance in Northern Ireland has held that a printer does not, by the very act of handing back in a parcel the printed handbills to the customer-author, publish

---

[117] *M'Pherson v Daniels* (1829) 10 B & C 263. The republication principle extends to multiple publications by D: see *Loutchansky v Times Newspapers Ltd (No 2)* [2002] QB 783.

[118] And distributors. In *Goldsmith v Sperrings Ltd* [1977] 2 All ER 566, it was held not to be an abuse of process for C to pursue a claim arising from an article against 37 different distributors with a view to making them settle his claim on the basis of their undertaking to cease distributing the magazine. Note, too, that distributors may require the original publisher to indemnify them against liability. Thus, the original defamer may have to pay out damages several times over.

[119] *Chase v News Group Newspapers Ltd* [2003] EMLR 11. Cf the finding of the European Court of Human Rights in *Thoma v Luxembourg* (2003) 36 EHRR 21 that 'a general requirement for journalists to distance themselves from the content of a quotation' would be irreconcilable with the role of the press and thus an infringement of Art 10.

[120] *Parkes v Prescott* (1869) LR 4 Exch 169, at 179.

[121] *Adams v Kelly* (1824) Ry & M 157; *McWhirter v Manning* (1954) *Times*, 30 October.

[122] *Slipper v BBC* [1991] 1 All ER 165. In effect, this decision is no more than an application of the general law of causation; the foreseeable repetition of the statement by the press is too probable to be regarded as a *novus actus interveniens*.

[123] *Pullman v Walter Hill & Co* [1891] 1 QB 524. The circulation of interdepartmental memoranda within a company is also sufficient publication: *Riddick v Thames Board Mills Ltd* [1977] QB 881.

[124] The official report of *Pullman v Walter Hill & Co* [1891] 1 QB 524 does not expressly state that the press copying in that case was held to be a publication, but Lord Esher MR said in *Boxsius v Goblet Frères* [1894] 1 QB 842, at 849 that the case had so decided, and he was a judge in both cases.

those handbills.[125] The defendant's publication to his own wife is not enough[126] but publication to the wife of the claimant suffices.[127] Against these instances of minimal publication must be weighed a more recent authority, *Jameel v Dow Jones*,[128] in which it was held that a potentially widespread publication that was in fact confined to a very small number of persons should be struck out as an abuse of process. On the facts, only five people saw the libellous material; and of these, three were the claimants' agents while the remaining two had no connection whatsoever with the claimant.There was thus no 'real and substantial tort' and the proceedings were an abuse of process in that there was hardly a genuine attempt to protect the claimant's reputation by way of injunction (since the source of the complaint had been removed from the website by the time of the claim) and any proceedings, if permitted, would have involved needless, substantial costs for all parties concerned. Furthermore, it has since been made clear that a claimant must bear the burden of proving a widespread publication in the case of internet defamation; for there is no legal presumption of substantial publication.[129]

Difficulties of proving publication are eased by certain rebuttable presumptions. If one can prove, for example, that a letter bore the correct address and that it was properly posted, there is a presumption of publication to the addressee.[130] Similarly, postcards and telegrams[131] (though not unsealed letters)[132] are presumed to have been published to Post Office officials. On the other hand, there is no publication for the purposes of defamation law unless the defamatory meaning of the communication would be understood by the third party. Thus, a postcard defamatory of (but not known to be referable to the claimant by persons unaware of the special facts), was held not to be published to Post Office staff.[133]

On occasion, there may be publication by omission. Failure by a defendant who is authorised and able to remove or amend defamatory matter which is the work of another amounts to publication by him. Thus, those in charge of a club will be accountable for defamatory matter placed by another on the notice board of the club if they do not remove it within a reasonable time.[134]

---

[125] *Eglantine Inn Ltd v Isaiah Smith* [1948] NI 29.

[126] *Wennhak v Morgan* (1888) 20 QBD 635.

[127] *Wenman v Ash* (1853) 13 CB 836.

[128] [2005] QB 946.

[129] *Al Amoudi v Brisard* [2006] 3 All ER 294.

[130] *Warren v Warren* (1834) 1 Cr M & R 250.

[131] *Sadgrove v Hole* [1901] 2 KB 1.

[132] *Huth v Huth* [1915] 3 KB 32. It was stated, *obiter*, that had Post Office officials in fact read the letter to check whether it was properly stamped, that would have been publication. Cf *Clutterbuck v Chaffers* (1816) 1 Stark 471 (it was held to be no publication where D handed to X a folded, unsealed letter which X, without reading or showing it to others, handed to C).

[133] *Sadgrove v Hole* [1901] 2 KB 1. The same applies to cipher messages and messages in foreign languages.

[134] *Byrne v Deane* [1937] 1 KB 818. Compare those cases where the matter is carved in stone, or D is not in control of the place where the libel is exhibited. Here the impracticability/impossibility of avoiding the publication negates any prospect of liability.

The Government has proposed amendment to the law relating to publication. In its *Draft Defamation Bill Consultation Paper*, it has drawn attention to the perils for publishers that have arisen from the internet and the development of online archives. 'The effect of the multiple publication rule in relation to online material is that each "hit" on a webpage creates a new publication', which creates the possibility of a new cause of action should the material be defamatory.[135] In the view of the Government, this is not a 'suitable' rule. Thus, the Draft Defamation Bill 2011 includes the following clause:

6. Single publication rule

(1) This section applies if a person –

    (a) publishes a statement to the public ('the first publication'), and

    (b) subsequently publishes (whether or not to the public) that statement or a statement which is substantially the same.

(2) In subsection (1) 'publication to the public' includes publication to a section of the public.

(3) For the purposes of section 4A of the Limitation Act 1980 (time limit for actions for defamation etc) any cause of action against the person for defamation in respect of the subsequent publication is to be treated as having accrued on the date of the first publication.

(4) This section does not apply in relation to the subsequent publication if the manner of that publication is materially different from the manner of the first publication.

...

(6) Where this section applies –

    (a) it does not affect the court's discretion under section 32A of the Limitation Act 1980 (discretionary exclusion of time limits for actions for defamation etc)...

The aim of sub-clause 6(1) is to ensure that the provisions apply with respect to publications having the same or substantially the same content so that the 'essence of the defamatory statement' in a later publication is not very different from that of an earlier publication.[136] With respect to sub-clause 6(4), the following example is provided of a case in which the manner of a second publication will be 'materially different' from the first publication:

> where a story has first appeared relatively obscurely in a section of a website where several clicks need to be gone through to access it, but has subsequently been promoted to a position where it can be directly accessed from the home page of the site, thereby increasing considerably the number of hits it receives.[137]

---

[135] Ministry of Justice, *Draft Defamation Bill Consultation Paper* (CP3/11, 2011), 30.
[136] Explanatory Notes to the Draft Defamation Bill 2011, at [42]
[137] Ibid at [44].

SECTION 3 DISTINGUISHING LIBEL FROM SLANDER

(A) CRITERIA FOR DISTINGUISHING LIBEL FROM SLANDER

Any medium whereby thought and ideas can be expressed or conveyed may constitute the publication of defamation – words, pictures, gestures,[138] music, and statues are all examples.[139] It is, however, the choice of medium which determines whether the defamation is libel or slander; and it is because the rules relating to the two torts differ in some important respects that it is necessary to distinguish between them.

There can be no doubt that anything communicated in the form of a permanent character and visible to the eye is libel, and that anything temporary and merely audible is slander. Thus, defamatory books, newspapers, letters, and even effigies[140] are all libels, while spoken words are slander. What is more difficult, however, is how to characterise things which are in permanent form but only audible, and things which are visible but not in permanent form, such as material posted on the internet.[141] In *Youssoupoff v Metro-Goldwyn-Mayer Pictures Ltd*,[142] the scenes depicted on the screen in a talking film were held to constitute libel. Yet, at most, the case really only supports the view that permanency is an important element in the test for libel. It does not establish that permanency is the sole criterion. Slesser LJ put the *ratio* of the case thus:

> There can be no doubt that, so far as the photographic part of the exhibition is concerned, that is a *permanent matter to be seen by the eye*, and is the proper subject of an action for libel, if defamatory. I regard the speech which is synchronised with the photographic reproduction and forms part of one complex, common exhibition as an ancillary circumstance, part of the surroundings explaining that which is to be seen.[143]

The case, therefore, does not settle authoritatively whether a defamatory anecdote in a film is libel. Nor does it tell us whether defamatory remarks on a CD are slander. Although there are *obiter dicta* in other cases suggesting that permanency alone is a sufficient criterion,[144] the point remains technically undecided. Accordingly, it follows

---

[138] See *Cook v Cox* (1814) 3 M & S 110, at 114.

[139] Even the lighting of a lamp in the daytime in C's garden, thereby inferring that he keeps a brothel, is caught: *Jefferies v Duncombe* (1809) 2 Camp 3; and perhaps so is police shadowing of C's house.

[140] *Monson v Tussauds Ltd* [1894] 1 QB 671.

[141] Defamatory material posted on an internet website has been held to be a libel once downloaded in this country: *King v Lewis* [2005] EMLR 4. Merely being an internet service provider (ISP) is enough to make that provider a publisher at common law; but liability for publication will not automatically follow for there may be a defence depending on whether the provider could and should have prevented further dissemination: *Godfrey v Demon Internet Ltd* [2001] QB 201. See also, to similar effect, the Electronic Commerce (EC Directive) Regulations 2002.

[142] (1934) 50 TLR 581.

[143] (1934) 50 TLR 581, at 587 (emphasis added).

[144] Eg, in *Monson v Tussauds Ltd* [1894] 1 QB 671, at 692, Lopes LJ stated that: 'Libels are generally in writing or printing, but this is not necessary; the defamatory matter may be conveyed in some other permanent form. For instance, a statue, a caricature, an effigy, chalk marks on a wall, signs, or pictures may constitute a libel'.

that it is not possible to say into which category the following fall: tape recordings, talking parrots that have learnt certain phrases from their owners, and sky-writing. On the other hand, dictation of a letter to a typist is only slander,[145] while forwarding of the typed letter is undoubtedly libel, and, moreover, a libel for which the dictator is accountable on the basis that he authorised his agent to forward it. The reading aloud of a letter written by another, where those to whom it was read were aware that the speaker was reading from the document, was held to be libel in *Forrester v Tyrrell*.[146] The short report of this case does not, however, mention whether the point that it may have been slander was argued.[147] In *Osborn v Boulter*,[148] Scrutton and Slesser LJJ thought that the reading aloud of a document was slander, while Greer LJ was inclined to think it libel. It is submitted that the approach in *Forrester v Tyrrell* is preferable since the defamatory material was both visible and in permanent form. The reading of it simply constituted the means of publication.[149]

The uncertainty at common law has prompted statutory intervention to cover mass media communications. Section 166 of the Broadcasting Act 1990 now provides that the publication of any words in the course of any broadcast programme on television or radio shall be treated as publication in a permanent form. It no longer matters whether the broadcast is for general public reception or otherwise. Similarly, the Theatres Act 1968 provides that the publication of words in the course of a performance of a play shall also be treated as publication in a permanent form.[150]

(B) JURIDICAL DIFFERENCES BETWEEN LIBEL AND SLANDER

There are two major juridical differences between libel and slander. First, a libel of sufficient seriousness may be punished as a crime whereas slander is always only tortious.[151] Second, libel is actionable per se[152] whereas slander, subject to the exceptions discussed in the next section, is actionable only upon proof of actual damage.[153] In its Draft Defamation Bill 2011, the Government has signalled its intention to 'remove the

---

[145] But when the typist listens to a dictaphone, a libel is probably being published.

[146] (1893) 57 JP 532. MacDermott J followed this decision with reluctance in *Robinson v Chambers (No 2)* [1946] NI 148 where the audience was aware that D was reading out a letter.

[147] If the secretary simply hands or reads the letter back to the person who dictated it, then there can be no defamation, for there has been no publication.

[148] [1930] 2 KB 226. Slesser LJ left open (at 236) whether 'the circumstance of dictation, and the dictated matter being brought back and considered by the dictator, may constitute in certain cases a libel'.

[149] For additional judicial support for this view, see *Robinson v Chambers (No 2)* [1946] NI 148.

[150] Section 4. But note that performances given 'on a domestic occasion in a private dwelling' are exempted by s 7 of the Act.

[151] Of course, spoken words may constitute a crime where the other elements of that crime are present: eg, blasphemy or sedition. Earlier views that to constitute a crime a libel must be calculated to provoke a breach of the peace were rejected in *Gleaves v Deakin* [1980] AC 477.

[152] It is actionable per se even by a company: *Jameel v Wall Street Journal Europe SPRL* [2006] UKHL 44.

[153] Although the term 'special damage' is used frequently, this is misleading, as noted earlier, since the phrase has other meanings in other contexts. In fact, the use of the term 'special damage' in this context is to be attributed to the *dictum* of Lord Wensleydale in *Lynch v Knight* (1861) 9 HL Cas 577.

scope for trivial and unfounded actions' in defamation.[154] To this end, it is proposed that a new provision create a requirement for 'substantial harm' to be proved in all cases of defamation. Clause 1 provides:

Substantial harm

A statement is not defamatory unless its publication has caused or is likely to cause substantial harm to the reputation of the claimant.

(C) EXCEPTIONAL CASES WHERE SLANDER IS ACTIONABLE PER SE

(1) Imputation of crime

The limits of this exception cannot precisely be defined because it is not settled whether the reason for it is the social ostracism resulting from such a slander, or the putting of the claimant in jeopardy, or even some other matter. At the very least, the following points are incontrovertible. The crime must be one for which the claimant could be imprisoned forthwith. The statement 'I know enough to put you in gaol' is therefore actionable per se.[155] If the perpetrator, having been arrested, can only be punished by a fine for the offence in question (and not by imprisonment), the imputation of the commission of the crime remains outside the exception.[156] And this is the case even though there is a power to commit for non-payment of the fine.[157]

The words used must also be clear and unambiguous. If they convey a mere suspicion – for example, of murder – they do not fall within the exception and the slander is not actionable per se.[158] In addition, in construing the meaning of the words, it is firmly established that they must be looked at in context in order to discover what was imputed. This rule is made clear by *Thompson v Bernard*.[159] The case also illustrates the obvious point that difficult problems of criminal law may need to be resolved in order to determine whether the facts imputed constituted a crime punishable by imprisonment.

If the claimant has to rely on some secondary meaning of the words spoken, he must, according to *Gray v Jones*,[160] prove that they were reasonably capable of being so interpreted. *Gray v Jones* also lends support to the view that the risk of social ostracism is at least one of the reasons for this exception. Having found that the words 'You are a convicted person' might reasonably mean that a crime punishable by imprisonment was imputed, Atkinson J held them to be within the exception because, although

---

[154] Ministry of Justice, *Draft Defamation Bill Consultation Paper* (CP3/11, 2011), 9.
[155] *Webb v Beavan* (1883) 11 QBD 609. This illustration also shows that a general imputation of criminality without reference to a specific offence is sufficient.
[156] *Hellwig v Mitchell* [1910] 1 KB 609; *Ormiston v Great Western Rly Co* [1917] 1 KB 598.
[157] *Michael v Spiers and Pond Ltd* (1909) 101 LT 352.
[158] *Simmons v Mitchell* (1880) 6 App Cas 156.
[159] (1807) 1 Camp 48.
[160] [1939] 1 All ER 798.

they would not place the claimant in jeopardy,[161] they would tend to cause him to be ostracised socially. On the other hand, there have been several cases where something criminal in character, but for technical reasons not punishable in the requisite way, has been held to be outside the rule – presumably because the claimant was not in jeopardy. In *Lemon v Simmons*,[162] for instance, saying that a husband stole from his wife while the couple lived together was held not to impute a crime since husbands were not at the time punishable for such thefts.

(2) Imputation of certain types of disease

To impute that a person has a contagious venereal disease is also to commit a slander actionable per se.[163] Whether the exception has any greater scope is doubtful. There is weak authority that leprosy is within the exception.[164] Yet, even if it *is* defamatory to impute other communicable diseases, such as scarlet fever or tuberculosis, it is submitted that, unless suffering from the particular disease induces moral condemnation or loathing, it is probably not nowadays actionable per se. Even in the case of venereal disease, it is not actionable per se to say that the claimant has suffered from it in the past.[165] This makes good sense, since the rationale for making the imputation of contagious venereal diseases actionable per se was, historically, that it might dissuade people from associating with the victim. Today, with cures easily available for many, if not most, infectious or contagious diseases, it might be questioned whether this exception ought to survive. The last reported case was *Bloodworth v Gray* in 1844.[166] The Government has signalled its intention to abolish this exception.[167]

(3) Slander in respect of office, profession, calling, trade, or business

At common law, a slander in respect of an office, profession, trade, or business was actionable per se if, first, it was calculated to disparage the claimant in his office, and, second, it was spoken in relation to his office. Section 2 of the Defamation Act 1952 now recasts this most important of circumstances in which slander is actionable per se. It provides:

> In an action for slander in respect of words calculated to disparage the [claimant] in any office, profession, calling, trade or business held or carried on by him at the time of the publication, it shall not be necessary to allege or prove special damage, whether or not the words are spoken of the [claimant] in the way of his office, profession, calling, trade or business.

---

[161] On which see *Jackson v Adams* (1835) 2 Bing NC 402.

[162] (1888) 57 LJQB 260.

[163] *Bloodworth v Gray* (1844) 7 Man & G 334. Even if AIDS is not strictly speaking a venereal disease, an imputation that a person is infected with the HIV virus may conceivably be actionable per se.

[164] *Taylor v Perkins* (1607) Cro Jac 144: the words 'Thou art a leprous knave' were held to be actionable per se.

[165] *Taylor v Hall* (1742) 2 Stra 1189.

[166] (1844) 7 Man & G 334.

[167] Ministry of Justice, *Draft Defamation Bill Consultation Paper* (CP3/11, 2011), 9.

The provision thus removes the second common-law requirement: the words are actionable even though they are not said of the claimant in the actual conduct of his profession so long as the imputation they carry is designed to disparage him in his particular calling. Section 2 also nullifies decisions such as *Jones v Jones*,[168] where it was held that an allegation that a headmaster had committed adultery with a school cleaner did not relate to his conduct in his profession. Today, such an allegation would certainly be actionable simply because it had prejudicial effects on his employment.

Words are also actionable per se if they impute some want of integrity or some corrupt or dishonest conduct in the office, whether an office of profit or of honour.[169] But as regards an office of honour, the slander is only actionable per se if it imputes such dishonesty, want of integrity, or incompetence as to justify removal from office.[170]

(4) Imputation of the unchastity of a woman

The loosely worded Slander of Women Act 1891 provides that 'words spoken and published... which impute unchastity or adultery to any woman or girl, shall not require special damage to render them actionable'. Imputation of 'unchastity' has also been held to include the imputation of lesbianism.[171] It is assumed, though the Act does not say so expressly, that it confers upon the woman alone the right to sue (but not her alleged male partner). Slang expressions of unchastity are probably enough, but gestures and other media of communication, not being 'words', fall outside the Act.[172] The Government is of the view that this provision is outdated and has signalled its intention to abolish it.[173]

(D) SPECIAL DAMAGE AND REMOTENESS OF DAMAGE

The question of what 'special damage' must be proved in respect of those forms of slander which are not actionable per se is closely bound up with the problem of remoteness of damage in defamation. Nonetheless, it is at least clear in principle that material loss is required if an allegation of special damage is to be substantiated. Examples include loss of employment,[174] the refusal of persons to enter into contracts with the claimant,[175] and the loss of hospitality from friends proved to have provided food or drink on former occasions.[176] A mere threat of material loss is insufficient,[177] but it is

---

[168] [1916] 2 AC 481.
[169] The distinction between offices of honour and offices of profit is now immaterial. Section 2 applies equally to both: *Maccaba v Lichtenstein* [2004] EWHC 1578.
[170] *Robinson v Ward* (1958) 108 L Jo 491.
[171] *Kerr v Kennedy* [1942] 1 KB 409.
[172] Sign language is a probable exception.
[173] Ministry of Justice, *Draft Defamation Bill Consultation Paper* (CP3/11, 2011), 9.
[174] *Coward v Wellington* (1836) 7 C & P 531.
[175] *Storey v Challands* (1837) 8 C & P 234.
[176] *Davies v Solomon* (1871) LR 7 QB 112. The rationale is that the loss of food and drink represents a loss of material value.
[177] *Michael v Spiers and Pond Ltd* (1909) 101 LT 352.

uncertain whether loss of spousal support, by either a husband or wife, is special damage. Consider *Lynch v Knight*.[178] There, the defendant told the claimant's husband that
the claimant had almost been seduced before their marriage. The husband made her
leave their home, and here her slander action (based on loss of consortium) failed. The
ground of the decision, however, was not that loss of consortium is not special damage,
but rather that the damage was too remote. It is submitted that Lord Campbell was
correct in his assertion that loss of spousal support may constitute special damage.[179]

In *Allsop v Allsop*,[180] the claimant suffered physical illness as a result of the mental
suffering she sustained following the slander. This was held not to be special damage.
Noting that mental distress and bodily harm may be taken into account by way of
aggravation in assessing damages in defamation,[181] *Allsop* must be taken as deciding
that special damage in slander must be damage in respect of a primary interest – that
is, loss of esteem or association – and that the primary purpose of the law of defamation is not to protect against psychiatric harm resulting from the apprehension of the
effects of defamatory matter being published to third persons.

Despite the fact that, historically, the test for remoteness in defamation was one
based on 'the natural and necessary consequences' of the defamation,[182] it now seems
that the test is the same as in most other areas of tort law. Thus, the key question is
whether the kind of damage suffered by the claimant was a reasonably foreseeable
consequence of the defendant's act. Accordingly, if a tabloid newspaper charges a distinguished history professor with sexual harassment and the university suspends him,
he may claim compensation for the whole of that loss.

Particular problems arise in defamation where additional loss results from a repetition of the libel. In *Slipper v BBC*,[183] for example, allegations in an original broadcast
were given even wider publicity in newspaper reviews of the programme. The Court
of Appeal refused to strike out the part of the claim dealing with that damage. While
unauthorised repetition might, on occasion, constitute a *novus actus interveniens*,
there has never been an absolute rule that the original defamer cannot be held liable
for the consequences of such a repetition. Thus, if I write to the Students' Union claiming a colleague is embezzling the Student Law Society's funds, it is very much foreseeable that this allegation will be repeated. If the letter had not been sent, but another
colleague took it from my desk and sent it to the *Sun* newspaper, there would be a break
in the chain of causation, in just the same way as in any other tort.[184]

---

[178]   (1861) 9 HL Cas 577.
[179]   Ibid at 589–9. Approved in *Best v Samuel Fox & Co Ltd* [1952] AC 716, at 732. See also *Wright v Cedzich*
(1930) 43 CLR 493, at 530 and *Lampert v Eastern National Omnibus Co Ltd* [1954] 2 All ER 719.
[180]   (1860) 5 H & N 534.
[181]   Ibid at 539.
[182]   *Ward v Weeks* (1830) 7 Bing 211.
[183]   [1991] 1 QB 283. See also *Sutcliffe v Pressdram Ltd* [1991] 1 QB 153.
[184]   See *Weld-Blundell v Stephens* [1920] AC 956.

FURTHER READING

BARENDT, 'Libel and Freedom of Speech in English Law' [1993] *Public Law* 449

BARENDT, 'What is the Point of Libel Law?'[1999] *Current Legal Problems* 110

DESCHEEMAEKER, 'Protecting Reputation: Defamation and Negligence' (2009) *Oxford Journal of Legal Studies* 603

GIBBONS, 'Defamation Reconsidered' (1996) 16 *Oxford Journal of Legal Studies* 587

KENYON, 'What Conversation? Free Speech and Defamation Law' (2010) 73 *Modern Law Review* 697

MITCHELL, *The Making of the Modern Law of Defamation* (2005)

21

DEFENCES AND REMEDIES IN DEFAMATION

KEY ISSUES

(1) Defences in general
As already noted, the law of defamation attempts to balance the competing interests of freedom of speech and reputation largely through the availability of the defences considered in this chapter.

(2) Consent to publication
It is a defence to defamation that the claimant has consented to the publication of an allegedly defamatory statement concerning him.

(3) Justification
It is a defence to defamation that the statement of the defendant is of a factual nature and that the facts are proved to be true or substantially true. If the statement also includes matters of opinion, these must be proved to be 'accurate' in order to be justified.

(4) Offer of amends
It is a defence under statute where the defendant made a statement that he did not know to be defamatory of the claimant and where he subsequently makes an offer, in writing, correcting and apologising for the statement and where he is willing to publish the correction and pay a sum by way of compensation.

(5) Privilege
Various forms of privilege exist, which protect the defendant from liability in defamation on the occasion on which a statement is made. Privilege is either absolute or qualified in nature. Qualified privilege arises where there is a common interest in publication and it is not made with 'malice'.

(6) Honest comment
It is a defence to defamation that the statement was on a matter of public interest and in the nature of comment upon true or privileged facts, such comment being one that could honestly have been made by a fair-minded person and that was actually made without malice.

(7) Remedies
Remedies to claims of defamation include damages and injunctions.

Most of the defences already discussed in relation to other torts are also available in defamation.[1] But several other defences, peculiar to defamation, warrant separate consideration in this chapter. To a large extent, these defences reflect the fact that defamation law recognises the vital interest in freedom of speech. The defence of absolute privilege, for example, allows comments to be made regardless of whether they are true, and regardless of the defendant's malicious motive.

SECTION 1   CONSENT AND ASSUMPTION OF RISK

Although opinions vary, the better opinion is that consent is an independent defence in defamation.[2] Someone who telephones a newspaper with false information about himself will not be able to sue in defamation when the newspaper publishes it; but he does not consent to the publication in a newspaper of a story about himself that he told at a parish vestry meeting.[3] Importantly, consent may be implied or express, so consent explicitly supplied on a contractual basis will certainly defeat a defamation action.[4] On the other hand, implied consent can sometimes involve a difficult question of fact about whether a claimant has genuinely consented to the repetition of a defamatory statement. If, for instance, the claimant asked the defendant to repeat it, because he did not properly understand on the first occasion, he would not be consenting. Whether express or implied, consent will always be narrowly construed in defamation cases.[5]

The related defence of assumption of risk was applied in *Chapman v Lord Ellesmere*.[6] There the claimant maintained that, even if he had consented to the publication of a report of an inquiry by the Jockey Club, he had not consented to its publication in such a form as to contain an innuendo against him. The Court of Appeal found for the defendant on the ground that the claimant had agreed to run the risk of the particular form that the statement might take.[7]

SECTION 2   JUSTIFICATION

It is no part of the claimant's case to establish that the defendant's statement was untrue: the claimant has merely to prove the publication of a statement defamatory of him. If, however, the defendant can prove that his statement was true, he has a complete defence even if he made the statement maliciously. The rationale is that 'the law will not permit a man to recover damages in respect of an injury to a character which

---

[1] The exceptions are consent and assumption of risk, dealt with in section 1 below.

[2] But see *Russell v Duke of Norfolk* [1949] 1 All ER 109, at 120. This issue may be crucial if, eg, A asks B for a reference and B is actuated by malice in providing one, unless the consent is deemed to be to a non-malicious reference only.   [3] *Cook v Ward* (1830) 6 Bing 409.

[4] *Cookson v Harewood* [1932] 2 KB 478n.   [5] *Howe v Burden* [2004] EWHC 196.

[6] [1932] 2 KB 431.   [7] Ibid at 464.

he does not...possess'.[8] The defendant does not discharge this burden by proving that he honestly believed it to be true. He must prove that it was true.[9] Nor will it help simply to show that he repeated accurately to a third party what he had heard from another, even though he told the third party it was a mere repetition.[10] If the words impute the commission of a specific offence, it is not enough to prove that the claimant was suspected of that offence.[11] In order to invoke the defence of justification in these circumstances, the defendant must be able to identify specific conduct on the part of the claimant which justifies such a suspicion.[12] These restrictions on the defence are clearly necessary to prevent its abuse.

Before deciding whether the defendant can successfully plead justification, one must first discover what the statement complained of has been interpreted to mean.[13] If the statement contains an innuendo, that too must be justified.[14] And even if the defendant justifies the innuendo, he will still fail unless he also justifies the primary meaning of the words used; for they form a separate head of claim.[15] And just as the claimant must specifically plead the meanings he relies on as defamatory, so must the defendant pleading justification 'make it clear to the [claimant] what is the case he is seeking to set up'.[16]

Obviously, then, many problems with justification are merely points of interpretation where the material question is: 'Does that which is proved to be true tally with that which the defendant's statement is interpreted to mean?' In *Jameel v Wall Street Journal Europe (No 3)*,[17] the defendant made reference to 'those with potential terrorist ties'. The claimants argued that the words used meant, at the very least, that they were reasonably suspected of having terrorist links. The defendant counter-argued that the words implied no more than that there were reasonable grounds to undertake an enquiry or investigation of whether there were in fact terrorist links (this meaning being one stage removed from what the claimants alleged). The Court of Appeal accepted that both meanings were feasible and agreed with the claimants, holding that

---

[8] *M'Pherson v Daniels* (1829) 10 B & C 263.

[9] *Peters v Bradlaugh* (1888) 4 TLR 414. In this context it is arguable that the importation of the European Convention on Human Rights into English law might require a relaxation of this rule where the publication relates to matters of public importance: see Art 8(2).

[10] *M'Pherson v Daniels* (1829) 10 B & C 263. On the other hand, repetition of a prevalent rumour may be justified following *Aspro Travel v Owners Abroad Group plc* [1995] 4 All ER 728 where the Court of Appeal refused to strike out Ds' plea of justification on this basis.

[11] *Rubber Improvement Ltd v Daily Telegraph Ltd* [1964] AC 234, at 274–5.

[12] *Shah v Standard Chartered Bank* [1999] QB 241, at 269–70 (it is not enough merely to show that the suspicion emanates from a reliable source). The suggestion that this 'conduct rule' places an unjustifiable restriction on the Art 10 right to freedom of expression has been rejected: *Chase v Newsgroup Newspapers Ltd* [2002] EWCA Civ 1772.   [13] See ch 20.

[14] *Prior v Wilson* (1856) 1 CBNS 95.

[15] *Watkin v Hall* (1868) LR 3 QB 396, at 402; *Rubber Improvement Ltd v Daily Telegraph Ltd* [1964] AC 234.

[16] *Lucas-Box v Associated Newspapers Group* [1986] 1 All ER 177. See also *Morrell v International Thomson Publishing Ltd* [1989] 3 All ER 733.

[17] [2005] QB 904. Reversed on other grounds at [2006] UKHL 44.

the issue should be left for a jury to decide. *Wakley v Cooke* is another case that turned, ultimately, on a point of interpretation.[18] There, the defendant called the claimant a 'libellous journalist'. He proved that a judgment against the claimant for libel had once been obtained; but because the defamatory statement complained of implied that the journalist habitually libelled people, the defendant ultimately failed to justify his remark.

The opposite result prevailed in *Bookbinder v Tebbit*.[19] The defendant had alleged at an electoral meeting that the claimant had squandered public money on a campaign to print 'support Nuclear Free Zones' on council stationery. He sought to justify his claim by advancing evidence of general financial mismanagement on the part of the claimant, who was the leader of the local council. The Court of Appeal struck out those particulars of justification. They did not pertain to the very specific 'sting' of the libel. One cannot justify an express claim of misconduct by generalised evidence of the claimant's behaviour.

The defence will not fail if the statement is substantially true: inaccuracy on minor points of detail are disregarded.[20] Similarly, 'it is unnecessary to repeat every word which might have been the subject of the original comment. As much must be justified as meets the sting of the charge, and if anything be contained in a charge which does not add to the sting of it, that need not be justified'.[21] Consider *Clarke v Taylor*.[22]

> D accused C of taking part in a 'grand swindling concern' at Manchester, and added that '[C] had been at Leeds for one or two days before his arrival in [Manchester] ... and is supposed to have made considerable purchases there. It is hoped, however, that the detection of his plans in Manchester will be learnt in time to prevent any serious losses from taking place'. D justified the statement that C had swindled at Manchester, but not the remainder of the statement. It was held that this was a sufficient plea of justification because the remaining words did not allege any further act of criminality.

Many statements contain both statements of fact and opinion: for example, 'X was drunk again last night; his behaviour was disgusting'. If the defendant relies on a plea of justification in respect of this, he must prove not only that X was drunk but also the accuracy of his claim that X's behaviour was disgusting (in so far as that comment adds to the sting of the libel). If the further statement introduces new matter, or implies the existence of further facts, he must prove those further facts which justify the terms in which he has described the claimant.[23]

---

[18] (1849) 4 Exch 511. On the question of whether it is more defamatory of a woman to allege that she has had an extra-marital affair with one man rather than another see *Khashoggi v IPC Magazines Ltd* [1986] 3 All ER 577. [19] [1989] 1 All ER 1169.

[20] *Alexander v North Eastern Rly Co* (1865) 6 B & S 340. See also *Henry v BBC* [2006] EWHC 386.

[21] *Edwards v Bell* (1824) 1 Bing 403, at 409.

[22] (1836) 2 Bing NC 654.

[23] *Cooper v Lawson* (1838) 8 Ad & El 746. There is sometimes another possible defence: honest comment.

At common law, every material statement had to be justified. Thus, if the defendant could prove the truth of three charges but not a fourth charge, the defence would fail (although proof of three would be relevant in assessing damages). This rule was modified by section 5 of the Defamation Act 1952 which stipulates:

> In an action for libel or slander in respect of words containing two or more distinct charges against the [claimant], a defence of justification shall not fail by reason only that the truth of every charge is not proved if the words not proved to be true do not materially injure the [claimant's] reputation having regard to the truth of the remaining charges.[24]

It is now, therefore, important to know when there are several charges. The section can only apply when the defendant has proved, first, that at least one charge is substantially true, after having been separated from the remaining charges, and, second, that this charge is itself incapable of further severance. At common law, the courts had also to consider when charges were severable, because any severable charge could be separately justified with a view to reducing damages or, perhaps, establishing some other defence in respect of that charge. Presumably, the common-law rules on what is a severable charge also apply under the Act.[25]

The effect of the Act is illustrated by considering its application to the facts of the pre-Act decision in *Goodburne v Bowman*.[26]

> C was alleged by D to have made, in each of his two periods of office as mayor, a small secret profit from the corporation on selling coals to the poor. D justified the statement by pleading that C did this in one of those terms of office only. The plea failed because it did not establish the truth of all the material statements in the libel.

Under the 1952 Act, it is open to the jury, on similar facts, to find that, in view of the truth of one of the two charges, the other did not, separately, materially injure his reputation. The claimant cannot evade the section by basing his cause of action solely on those residual parts of the defendant's statement which are not true if the different parts of an article are not plainly severable. This is so because a defendant may well be able to base a defence of justification on the whole of the article.[27] Accordingly, where several defamatory allegations have a common 'sting', they are not to be regarded as separate and distinct: the defendant must justify the 'sting' and 'it is fortuitous that what is in fact similar fact evidence is found in the publication'.[28] Where separate allegations are made, however, and the claimant relies only on the allegation that cannot

---

[24] If D relies on s 5 he must plead it as a defence: *Moore v News of the World Ltd* [1972] 1 QB 441.

[25] See *Clarkson v Lawson* (1830) 6 Bing 587; *Davis v Billing* (1891) 8 TLR 58; *Fleming v Dollar* (1889) 23 QBD 388.   [26] (1833) 9 Bing 667.

[27] *S and K Holdings v Throgmorton Publications Ltd* [1972] 3 All ER 497 (distinguishing *Plato Films Ltd v Speidel* [1961] AC 1090).

[28] *Polly Peck (Holdings) plc v Trelford* [1986] 2 All ER 84, at 102; *Khashoggi v IPC Magazines Ltd* [1986] 3 All ER 577.

be justified (with no mention of the statement that can be justified) the defendant cannot invoke section 5.[29]

If a defendant persists in a plea of justification and thereby prolongs the period in which the damage from the publication continues to spread, a greater sum by way of aggravated damages may be awarded against him.[30]

Before the enactment of the Human Rights Act 1998, the completeness of the defence of justification required great emphasis. Even if the defendant was inspired by malice, or even if, when he made the statements, he did not believe them to be true, his defence was sound so long as they were true. As we saw in the previous chapter, defamation law offers no protection, per se, against even the grossest invasion of privacy.[31]

A further curb on the freedom of the press to dig up aspects of a person's past is contained in the Rehabilitation of Offenders Act 1974. In relation to 'spent' convictions of 'rehabilitated persons', the Act specifies that after the expiry of certain defined periods – the duration of which differs according to the length of sentence – most convictions become spent, and the convicted person becomes rehabilitated. Section 8(3) of the 1974 Act provides an exception to the general tenor of the legislation according to which convictions become totally spent. It entitles a defendant in a defamation action to adduce evidence of the claimant's conviction; but only so long as the defendant mentions this conviction without malice.[32] The onus of establishing the presence of malice – defined as some spiteful, irrelevant, or improper motive – lies with the claimant.[33]

The Government proposes a statutory defence of 'truth'. Its Draft Defamation Bill 2011 would abolish the common-law defence, and repeal and replace section 5 of the Defamation Act 1952.[34] Provisions of interest are as follows:

3. Truth

(1) It is a defence to an action for defamation for the defendant to show that the imputation conveyed by the statement complained of is substantially true.

(2) Subsection (3) applies in an action for defamation in relation to a statement which conveys two or more distinct imputations.

(3) If one or more of the imputations is not shown to be substantially true, the defence under this section does not fail if, having regard to the imputations which are shown

---

[29] In *Cruise v Express Newspapers plc* [1999] QB 931, at 954, Brooke LJ said: 'It is no defence to a charge that "You called me A" to say "Yes, but I also called you B on the same occasion and that was true"'.

[30] *Cassell & Co Ltd v Broome* [1972] AC 1027, at 1125.

[31] For the extent to which English tort law protects privacy as such, see ch 22.

[32] It is arguable that this qualification of the right to adduce evidence of a spent conviction is antithetical to the right to freedom of speech enshrined in Art 10 of the European Convention on Human Rights. It is therefore possible that an appellate court may, in the future, feel the need to issue a declaration of incompatibility between the 1974 Act and the Convention under s 4 of the Human Rights Act 1998.

[33] *Herbage v Pressdram Ltd* [1984] 2 All ER 769. For an analysis of the provisions, see Descheemaeker [2011] LS 1, esp 16–17.

[34] Ministry of Justice, *Draft Defamation Bill Consultation Paper* (CP3/11, 2011), 14–17.

to be substantially true, the imputations which are not shown to be substantially true do not materially injure the claimant's reputation.

(4) The common law defence of justification is abolished and, accordingly, section 5 of the Defamation Act 1952 (justification) is repealed.

SECTION 3   INNOCENT DISSEMINATORS

There is, technically, still a common-law defence based on innocent dissemination. But this has been largely subsumed within section 1 of the Defamation Act 1996. Furthermore, because the statutory defence is broader in scope, and (normally) no less onerous to invoke, it seems that the common-law defence is all but otiose nowadays. Accordingly, discussion of it is omitted from this book.

Under section 1(1), a person has a defence if he shows that he was not the 'author, editor or publisher'[35] of the matter complained of; that he took reasonable care in relation to its publication, and that he did not know (or have reason to believe) that what he did caused or contributed to the publication of defamatory matter. That being so, the defence is not available where the defendant is an internet service provider (ISP) through whose service an unknown third party posts defamatory material if, after notification of the defamatory nature of the material, the defendant fails to verify its defamatory content and remove it from the Web.[36] At this point, it does not lie in the mouth of the service provider to say that it is not contributing to the publication of the defamatory statement.

The defence is wider than the common-law defence of innocent dissemination in that a much wider class of persons may avail themselves of it.[37] But, again, the defendant has a burden and standard of proof that require him to show his innocence as regards knowledge of the defamatory nature of the statement,[38] and that he took reasonable care in relation to his part in its publication. So far as the reasonable care test is concerned, under section 1(5) of the Act, the court is directed to have regard to three specific factors: (1) the degree of the defendant's responsibility for the content of the statement complained of, or for the decision to publish it; (2) the nature or

---

[35] The notion of publisher, for the purposes of the Act, is confined to that of 'commercial publisher'; ie, 'a person whose business is issuing material to the public': s 1(2).

[36] *Godfrey v Demon Internet Ltd* [2001] QB 201.

[37] Under s 1(3)(a) of the Act, those involved in the production process or printing of books, newspapers, and magazines are also covered. So, too, are those who distribute information by way of electronic media such as internet users (s 1(3)(c)), those, such as chat-show and phone-in hosts, who broadcast information in live programmes (s 1(3)(d)) and those, such as ISPs, who operate communications systems that are used to transmit defamatory statements (s 1(3)(e)).

[38] Strictly, *Vizetelly v Mudie's Select Library Ltd* [1900] 2 QB 170 required ignorance of *a libel* (a narrower concept than that of a defamatory remark). To this extent, the defence is more restrictive than its common law counterpart in that knowledge of a defamatory statement (eg, one known to be defamatory, but believed to be true) will defeat the defence.

circumstances of the publication;[39] (3) the previous conduct or character of the author, editor, or publisher.[40]

SECTION 4   OFFER OF AMENDS

The Defamation Act 1996 creates a defence related to an 'offer to make amends'.[41] The defence is available only to those defendants who did not know, or had no reason to believe, that the statement in question referred to the claimant and was untrue and defamatory of him.[42] 'Having a reason to believe' in this context requires that the defendant must have been reckless as to the matter and not merely that a reasonable person in his position would have realised that the statement was untrue or defamatory. In other words, the test is a subjective, not objective, one.[43]

The defence may only be invoked where the offer to make amends is in writing and states that it is such an offer under the 1996 Act.[44] In addition, the offer must satisfy three further prerequisites: it must contain a correction to, and apology for, the original statement; it must state a willingness to publish that correction and apology; it must make clear that the publisher consents to pay to the aggrieved party such sum as may be agreed between them, or, as may be determined judicially.[45] Where an offer of amends has been made, it will probably serve as significant mitigation.[46]

If the offer of amends is accepted, section 3(2) prohibits the aggrieved party from subsequently bringing or continuing defamation proceedings. An offer which has been accepted creates an agreement between the parties, which will rarely be undone by a court even if new facts come to light. In *Warren v Random House Group Ltd*,[47] the Court of Appeal accepted that it had a discretion to undo an agreement, but insisted that this is of narrow compass. The central issue would be whether any special circumstances supported the avoidance of the agreement 'in the sense of circumstances so different from those contemplated or intended to be governed by the undertaking at the time that it was given that it is appropriate for the undertaker to be released from his promise'.[48]

If the offer of amends is not accepted, the offer may nonetheless be invoked as a defence in any subsequent defamation proceedings brought by the claimant.[49] For this reason, it is suggested that it would normally be unwise for a claimant to reject an offer of amends. Should he instead pursue an action in the courts, in order for the offer not

---

[39] The Act is unclear on what is meant by 'the circumstances of the publication'. Presumably, however, remarks made about infamous or notorious persons would require greater concern than remarks about less-well-known people.

[40] Presumably, here, the standard of care demanded is greater in relation to publishers with a history of producing defamatory material.   [41] Defamation Act 1996, ss 2–4.

[42] Defamation Act 1996, s 4(3).

[43] *Milne v Express Newspapers (No 1)* [2005] 1 WLR 772.   [44] Defamation Act 1996, s 2(3).

[45] Defamation Act 1996, s 2(3), (4).   [46] *Nail v NGN Ltd* [2005] EMLR 12.

[47] [2008] EWCA Civ 834.   [48] Ibid at [26].

[49] Defamation Act 1996, s 4(2).

to constitute a defence, the claimant would have to show, first, that the defendant knew or had reason to believe that the statement referred to the claimant and, second, that it was both false and defamatory.[50]

The offer of amends defence does not require the alleged defamer to prove his innocence.[51] Accordingly, it effects a significant change in the location of the burden of proof. On the other hand, any defendant wishing to use this defence is debarred from resorting to any other defence (such as justification).[52] This means that he is forced to choose between (1) definitely paying moderate damages (either agreed with the claimant, or judicially determined) and (2) risking paying damages in full if another defence – such as justification – should be held not to be available.

SECTION 5   ABSOLUTE PRIVILEGE

Certain occasions are deemed to be so important that those making statements upon them are not liable in defamation despite their statements being untrue and even malicious. These occasions – where the public interest in freedom of communication is paramount – are called cases of absolute privilege.

(A) PARLIAMENTARY PROCEEDINGS

By the law of Parliament, the courts for centuries had no jurisdiction to hear evidence of proceedings in Parliament.[53] This immunity extended beyond all statements made in the course of parliamentary proceedings to all reports, papers, votes, and proceedings published by, or under the authority of, either House.[54] This assertion of 'parliamentary privilege' meant not only that parliamentary proceedings could not found an action in defamation, but also that such proceedings could not be relied on in relation to a claim arising out of a non-parliamentary publication. Thus, in one case, the court would not admit evidence of statements contained in Hansard that the claimant sought to introduce in order to demonstrate malice.[55]

---

[50] C bears the burden of proof by virtue of the Defamation Act 1996, s 4(3) which introduced a statutory presumption of the publisher's innocence, thus giving him the right to invoke his offer of amends as a defence.

[51] This is now presumed under s 4(3). Cf s 4 of the 1952 Act, which it replaces. Another difference between the current provision and s 4 of the 1952 Act is as follows. If the offer is refused, the case will proceed but D may still use the making of the offer as a mitigatory defence (reducing the amount of damages payable) where he (1) knew that the publication was defamatory of C but (2) reasonably believed that what was said was true: s 4(5).   [52] Defamation Act 1996, s 4(4).

[53] Bill of Rights 1688, art 9; *Ex p Wason* (1869) LR 4 QB 573, at 576. See also Government of Wales Act 2006, s 42. Hence, the frequent challenge by the victim to the MP to repeat outside the House his attacks on the victim's reputation. Comments outside Parliament, even if they refer to earlier privileged statements, do not attract absolute privilege: *Jennings v Buchanan* [2005] 1 AC 115.

[54] Parliamentary Papers Act 1840, s 1.

[55] *Church of Scientology of California v Johnson-Smith* [1972] 1 QB 522. See also *Hamilton v Al Fayed* [2001] 1 AC 395. Cf *Rost v Edwards* [1990] 2 QB 460 where Popplewell J did allow evidence drawn from the *Register of Members' Interests* on the basis that this was a public document.

Section 13 of the Defamation Act 1996 introduced a significant change in the law.[56] It permits an MP to waive the prohibition on adducing evidence of parliamentary proceedings enshrined in article 9 of the Bill of Rights 1688.[57] But where an MP waives that privilege in order to enter evidence of the proceedings of a parliamentary committee (or its findings), the waiver will override the privilege of the House as a whole, and thus entitle the defendant to challenge the parliamentary proceedings in question, and even the findings of a prior parliamentary inquiry into the conduct of the MP in question.[58] Section 13 is thus an extremely important (and not uncontroversial) provision. Furthermore, it is clear from section 13(5) that it extends not just to parliamentary proceedings per se, but also to evidence contained in such documents as reports produced by parliamentary committees.[59]

(B) EXECUTIVE MATTERS

In the leading case of *Chatterton v Secretary of State for India*,[60] it was held that a letter from the Secretary of State for India to his Parliamentary Under-Secretary providing material for the answer to a parliamentary question was absolutely privileged. It is impossible to say how high in the hierarchy of civil servants a defendant must be before he enjoys this privilege, but a message from the High Commissioner for Australia to his Prime Minister about a matter of commerce which concerned the Government of Australia was certainly held to be privileged.[61] And complaints made to the European Commission relating to the enforcement of competition proceedings are similarly protected.[62]

It has been doubted whether those below the status of minister may claim the privilege;[63] and if it were not for the cases below relating to military communications, one might confidently suggest that routine communications between persons not in charge of government departments are outside the privilege. Indeed, one might even doubt whether the courts would extend it anywhere beyond the examples contained in the above cases.

---

[56] Cf the common law: *Prebble v Television New Zealand* [1995] 1 AC 321.

[57] Section 13 operates in favour of MPs only. The waiver enables an MP to vindicate his character in a defamation action by adducing evidence of parliamentary proceedings. It does not, by contrast, allow the MP to adduce evidence from a similar source in order to substantiate the main argument.

[58] *Hamilton v Al-Fayed* [2001] 1 AC 395. Note, however, that *the actual words used* by the MP remain privileged: Defamation Act 1996, s 13(4).   [59] See Sharland and Loveland [1997] PL 113.

[60] [1895] 2 QB 189. The Parliamentary Commissioner Act 1967, s 10(5) also gives an absolute privilege to the Parliamentary Commissioner for his reports to Parliament and for certain of his communications to MPs; the Local Commissioners have a similar absolute privilege under the Local Government Act 1974, s 32; so, too, does the Legal Services Ombudsman under s 23 of the Courts and Legal Services Act 1990.

[61] *M Isaacs & Sons Ltd v Cook* [1925] 2 KB 391.

[62] *Hasselblad (GB) Ltd v Orbinson* [1985] QB 475. But should this more properly be regarded as judicial privilege, or even witness immunity: see *Mahon v Rahn* [1998] QB 424.

[63] *Szalatnay-Stacho v Fink* [1946] 1 All ER 303, at 305 (not considered on appeal: [1947] KB 1).

In *Dawkins v Lord Paulet*,[64] it was held that a report on the claimant from his superior officer to his commander-in-chief could not form the basis of an action for libel. The rationale of the case is not clear, however. Cockburn CJ dissented; Lush J based his judgment on the principle that the army was outside the jurisdiction of the courts,[65] yet one of the three grounds of Mellor J's judgment was that such letters were absolutely privileged.[66] It is submitted that this is not strong enough authority for the proposition that communications within the civil service generally, and relating to the character and ability of personnel, are absolutely privileged. Nor does the case decide that civil servants below ministerial rank enjoy this absolute privilege; but their communications, as we shall see, would be adequately protected by the qualified privilege which doubtless attaches to them.

A final point in this context is that absolute privilege must not be confused with the procedural rule that the Crown, whether or not it is a party, cannot be compelled, in any litigation, to produce or disclose the existence of any documents the production or disclosure of which would be contrary to the public interest.[67] In practice, because the Crown can decide at its discretion whether to produce such documents, this rule has prevented claimants from maintaining libel suits, even for communications within the civil service, which were not absolutely privileged.[68]

(C) JUDICIAL PROCEEDINGS

Statements made in proceedings before superior and inferior courts of record and magistrates' courts are privileged. The privilege extends to other tribunals recognised by law,[69] provided they are 'exercising functions equivalent to those of an established court of justice'.[70] In cases of doubt, 'the overriding factor is whether there will emerge from the proceedings a determination the truth and justice of which is a matter of public concern'.[71] Thus, an enquiry before an Inn of Court into the conduct of a barrister was absolutely privileged,[72] even though the body had no power to issue a subpoena, or to take evidence on oath, and sat in private. The disciplinary committee of the Law Society,[73] courts martial,[74] and select committees of the House of Commons[75] are also within the privilege. If the function of the body in question is merely administrative,

---

[64] (1868) LR 5 QB 94.

[65] But see *Dawkins v Lord Rokeby* (1873) LR 8 QB 255 (affirmed (1875) LR 7 HL 744).

[66] In *Merricks v Nott-Bower* [1965] 1 QB 57, the report by one high-ranking police officer to another about a third police officer was held not to be so clearly the subject of absolute privilege that a claim in libel should be struck out. [67] Crown Proceedings Act 1947, s 28. See also *Schneider v Leigh* [1955] 2 QB 195.

[68] *Home v Bentinck* (1820) 2 Brod & Bing 130, *Beatson v Skene* (1860) 5 H & N 838 and *West v West* (1911) 27 TLR 476, are examples of cases where the rule was successfully used for that purpose.

[69] Either under statute or by royal prerogative of justice: *Lincoln v Daniels* [1962] 1 QB 237.

[70] *O'Connor v Waldron* [1935] AC 76, at 81.

[71] *Lincoln v Daniels* [1962] 1 QB 237, at 255–6. [72] *Lincoln v Daniels* [1962] 1 QB 237.

[73] *Addis v Crocker* [1961] 1 QB 11. [74] *Wilson v Westney* [2001] EWCA Civ 839.

[75] In principle, these would seem to have been more properly within the 'legislative privilege', but this is not the basis of *Goffin v Donnelly* (1881) 6 QBD 307. But see now *Rost v Edwards* [1990] 2 QB 460.

and it does not determine the rights, guilt, or innocence of anyone, there is no absolute privilege, even though procedures akin to judicial procedures – such as hearing evidence or summoning witnesses – are used.[76] Thus, justices dealing with applications for liquor licensing,[77] official industrial conciliation processes,[78] and complaints to social security adjudication officers[79] have all been held to be outside the scope of the privilege. Competition proceedings before the European Commission, by contrast, have been held to attract absolute privilege despite the essentially administrative nature of their procedures: the public interest in the Commission's duty to enforce European competition law was held to outweigh the private interests of litigants seeking to vindicate their reputations.[80]

The privilege is enjoyed by judges (even if their statements are malicious or irrelevant),[81] parties, informants,[82] witnesses questioned in relation to a crime,[83] counsel[84] and solicitors,[85] and presumably also jurors. Whether others engaged in the proceedings are privileged is doubtful.[86] They are certainly not protected where the statement is so irrelevant that it is no longer made by a person qua participant in the proceedings.[87] The privilege is probably lost when the court has no jurisdiction.

Finally, it should be noted that the privilege extends to documents initiating[88] or made in the course of the proceedings (for example, pleadings and affidavits).[89] However, documents prepared prior to proceedings that do not have any *necessary* link with those proceedings are not privileged in this way. Accordingly, in one case where a defamatory letter was written by the defendant council to the claimant's solicitor in the course of pre-hearing negotiations, it was held that, since the letter's contents did not have any necessary import for any future legal proceedings, it was inappropriate to allow the defendant to claim a privilege.[90]

---

[76] See, eg, *W v Westminster CC* [2005] 1 FLR 816; *O'Connor v Waldron* [1935] AC 76.

[77] *Attwood v Chapman* [1914] 3 KB 275.   [78] *Tadd v Eastwood* [1985] ICR 132.

[79] *Purdew and Purdew v Seress Smith* [1993] IRLR 77.

[80] *Hasselblad (GB) Ltd v Orbinson* [1985] QB 475.   [81] *Scott v Stansfield* (1868) LR 3 Exch 220.

[82] *Westcott v Westcott* [2008] EWCA Civ 818, although criminal proceedings were never commenced.

[83] *Seaman v Netherclift* (1876) 2 CPD 53. See also *Mahon v Rahn (No 2)* [2000] 4 All ER 41 where a bankers' report sent in response to inquiries to both the Trading Standards Authority and the Serious Fraud Office was covered by absolute privilege.   [84] *Munster v Lamb* (1883) 11 QBD 588.

[85] *Mackay v Ford* (1860) 5 H & N 792. But in non-contentious matters, a qualified privilege may be sufficient: see *Waple v Surrey CC* [1998] 1 WLR 860.

[86] Doubt arises since judicial immunity may derive from the separate defence of judicial act, not that of privilege: *Hamilton v Anderson* (1858) 3 Macq 363. Cf *Law v Llewellyn* [1906] 1 KB 487.

[87] In answer to the question: 'Were you at York on a certain day?' a statement by a witness: 'Yes, and AB picked my pocket there', would not be made qua witness if the proceedings were entirely unconnected with AB: *Seaman v Netherclift* (1876) 2 CPD 53, at 57.

[88] But not if the initiating document is wrongly sent to the Bar Council, instead of to an Inn of Court: *Lincoln v Daniels* [1962] 1 QB 237.

[89] See *Lilley v Roney* (1892) 61 LJQB 727; *Revis v Smith* (1856) 18 CB 126; *Taylor v Director of the Serious Fraud Office* [1999] 2 AC 177. The privilege confers a general defence to all torts, and not merely to defamation: *Marrinan v Vibart* [1963] 1 QB 528.

[90] *Waple v Surrey CC* [1998] 1 All ER 624. See also *Daniels v Griffith* [1998] EMLR 489 (no privilege in respect of a defamatory statement (relating to C) given by D to the police which was later used by a parole

(D) SOLICITOR-CLIENT COMMUNICATIONS

Closely related to the privilege just discussed is the question of how far statements to solicitors by either clients or witnesses before trial are protected. If the purpose of not restricting the prosecution of judicial proceedings is to be attained, it would be unrealistic to deny to a witness privilege in respect of a proof of his evidence made immediately before trial. The House of Lords has therefore held in *Watson v M'Ewan* that a witness making a proof after the issue of a writ, but before trial, is absolutely privileged.[91] This extension by the House of Lords of the privilege surrounding judicial proceedings is restricted to matters outside the proceedings which are necessary for the administration of justice. It does not extend to a complaint to the Bar Council, even though that is a recognised channel for complaints by the public about members of the Bar.[92]

Whether all communications between solicitor and client should be privileged is clearly a different matter. Yet consider *More v Weaver*:[93]

> In a discussion between solicitor and client on whether a loan should be called in, C was defamed. Importantly, the discussion bore no relation to any actual or prospective litigation. The statement was held to be absolutely privileged.

By contrast, in *Minter v Priest*[94] the House of Lords expressly left open the question of whether *More v Weaver* had been rightly decided. It is submitted that *More v Weaver* was wrongly decided. In the cases which it purported to follow,[95] solicitor-client communications were only held to be absolutely privileged because they referred to judicial proceedings actually pending.

(E) REPORTS OF JUDICIAL PROCEEDINGS

A fair and accurate report of judicial proceedings heard in public and published contemporaneously with those proceedings, is absolutely privileged under section 14 of the Defamation Act 1996. For the purposes of this section, 'contemporaneous' publications include those that appear 'as soon as practicable after publication is permitted'.[96] And the 'judicial proceedings' to which the Act refers are specified to mean any proceedings in a UK court, the European Court of Justice or the European Court of Human Rights.[97] Unlike the corresponding provision in the previous legislation – which confined privilege to newspaper, television, and radio reports – section 14 confers absolute privilege on *all* contemporaneous reports regardless of the medium of publication. However, nothing in the legislation changes the common-law rule that

---

board considering C's parole because the parole board was not a court of law). Cf *Mond v Hyde* [1998] 3 All ER 833 (official receiver covered by privilege in respect of statements made in bankruptcy proceedings in so far as those statements were made for the purpose of court proceedings).

[91] [1905] AC 480.

[92] *Lincoln v Daniels* [1962] 1 QB 237.

[93] [1928] 2 KB 520.   [94] [1930] AC 558, at 579.   [95] Eg, *Browne v Dunn* (1893) 6 R 67.

[96] Defamation Act 1996, s 14(2).   [97] Defamation Act 1996, s 14(3).

the jury should decide if the report is a fair and accurate one.[98] And once any absolute privilege is established, it extends to consequential communications in the ordinary course of things to clerks, typists, and the like.[99]

The Government proposes to widen the availability of this privilege. Under clause 5(1) of the Draft Defamation Bill 2011, section 14(3) of the Defamation Act 1996 would be repealed and the following substituted for it:

(3) This section [ie section 14 of the Defamation Act 1996] applies to –

(a) any court in the United Kingdom,

(b) any court established under the law of a country or territory outside the United Kingdom,

(c) any international court or tribunal established by the Security Council of the United Nations or by an international agreement;

and in paragraphs (a) and (b) 'court' includes any tribunal or body exercising the judicial power of the State.

SECTION 6   QUALIFIED PRIVILEGE

In certain circumstances, it is thought desirable that reflections on the reputation of another, although untrue, should not give rise to tortious liability, provided those reflections were not published with 'malice'. These are occasions of qualified privilege. They are characterised by the fact that, in such circumstances, the interest in freedom of speech is more important than the claimant's interest in the protection of her reputation. In practical terms, this is the most widely used defence. It is generally underpinned by the notion that the defendant was under a duty – whether legal, social, or moral – to make the communication complained of.[100] However, since malice – which will defeat this defence – may be evidenced in number of ways, that concept needs to be considered as a preliminary matter.

(A) MALICE

(1) Establishing malice

'Malice', for the purposes of defeating a claim to qualified privilege, means making use of the privileged occasion dishonestly or for some evil or improper purpose, and it may be established in any of the following ways.

---

[98] Although legal precision is not required, a report of a conviction for stealing a car was held not to be a fair report of a conviction for taking it without the owner's consent: *Mitchell v Hirst, Kidd and Rennie Ltd* [1936] 3 All ER 872.

[99] *M Isaacs & Sons Ltd v Cook* [1925] 2 KB 391.

[100] See *Adam v Ward* [1917] AC 309, at 334.

(a) The defendant does not believe in the truth of his statement

By far the most important way of establishing malice (and thereby rebutting the privilege) is to show that the defendant did not believe in the truth of his statement or that he was reckless as to whether the statement was true or false. Thus, '[i]f a man is proved to have stated that which he knew to be false, no one need inquire further'.[101] That being so, a solicitor who writes that his client has admitted his negligence when he knows that he has not admitted it has abused the privilege.[102] Equally, in *Fraser v Mirza*,[103] proof that the defendant had quite blatantly and deliberately lied in parts of the statement complained of was sufficient to establish malice and defeat his claim of privilege. On the other hand, mere proof that the defendant had no reasonable grounds for believing his statement to be true is not enough to rebut the qualified privilege.[104] In *Horrocks v Lowe*,[105] it was held that, if the defendant honestly believed his statement to be true, his privilege would not be lost merely because his conclusion that his statement was true resulted from unreasoning prejudice, or was irrational with regard to the subject matter. Equally, mere carelessness in the choice of one's words is insufficient to establish malice.[106]

There is probably one exception to the rule that a person who does not believe in the truth of a statement forfeits the privilege. Lord Bramwell established this exception thus:

> A person may honestly make on a particular occasion a defamatory statement without believing it to be true; because the statement may be of such a character that on that occasion it may be proper to communicate it to a particular person who ought to be informed of it.[107]

Although authority is lacking, this exception seems sound in principle. There may well be circumstances where the obligation to communicate the defamatory matter is so pressing that the defendant should be free to do so: this is particularly true where such information as the defendant has is properly requested by another, or where an important interest is subjected to a serious risk of harm if the defendant does not publish the information. A good example might be informing a school that the caretaker is a paedophile. Even if the maker of the statement does not believe it of the caretaker, although she heard it from another, she might nonetheless be excused from liability for erring on the side of caution and informing the school authorities.

---

[101] *Clark v Molyneux* (1877) 3 QBD 237, at 247.   [102] *Groom v Crocker* [1939] 1 KB 194.
[103] 1993 SLT 527.
[104] *Clark v Molyneux* (1877) 3 QBD 237. Cf *Pitt v Donovan* (1813) 1 M & S 639. C may, however, be able to circumvent a plea of qualified privilege by suing in negligence: *Spring v Guardian Assurance plc* [1995] 2 AC 296.   [105] [1975] AC 135.
[106] *Oliver v CC of Northumbria Police* [2004] EWHC 790.
[107] *Clark v Molyneux* (1877) 3 QBD 237, at 244. Cf *Botterill v Whytehead* (1879) 41 LT 588, at 590.

(b) Abuse of the purpose of the privilege

If the defendant does not act for the purpose of protecting that interest for which the privilege is given, he loses it.[108] Thus, even if the defendant believes his statement to be true, if the court is satisfied that his dominant motive was an improper purpose, the privilege will be lost.[109] He must use the occasion in accordance with the purpose for which the occasion arose.[110] Thus, it was held that a letter sent to the BBC by a film company about a film critic would be 'malicious' if its purpose was to stifle criticism.[111]

With reference to this class of malice, the courts normally use such expressions as 'wrong motive', 'personal spite', or 'ill-will'.[112] If the defendant is actuated by any such motive, he abuses the privilege. But where he honestly believes in the truth of his statement, the court should be very slow to draw the inference that he is activated by improper motives.[113] The language occasionally used by the courts, and more often by writers, might seem to suggest that whenever, on a privileged occasion, the defendant has exhibited an improper motive, the privilege is rebutted. This is not quite correct: not only must there be an improper motive, that motive must have been a causative factor in the publishing of the defamation. Thus, in *Winstanley v Bampton*, a creditor who wrote a defamatory letter to the commanding officer of the claimant debtor, and believed what he wrote, forfeited his privilege because his indignation and anger had led him to defame the claimant.[114] If, however, the defendant was using the occasion for its proper purpose, but incidentally happened to have feelings of resentment towards the claimant, this would not deprive him of the privilege, which is not lost if the ill-will is not the defendant's primary purpose, but merely one purpose.[115]

In deciding whether there is the requisite ill-will, it is relevant to consider the violence of the language of the communication. That said, the courts will be very reluctant to infer malice from such evidence alone. In *Adam v Ward*, Lord Atkinson said:

> a person making a communication on a privileged occasion is not restricted to the use of such language merely as is reasonably necessary to protect the interest or discharge the duty which is the foundation of his privilege; but that, on the contrary, he will be protected, even though his language should be violent or excessively strong, if, having regard to all the circumstances of the case, he might have honestly and on reasonable grounds believed that what he wrote or said was true.[116]

---

[108] (1877) 3 QBD 237, at 246.   [109] *Horrocks v Lowe* [1975] AC 135, at 149.
[110] *Royal Aquarium and Summer and Winter Garden Society v Parkinson* [1892] 1 QB 431.
[111] *Turner v Metro-Goldwyn-Mayer Pictures Ltd* [1950] 1 All ER 449, at 457–8.
[112] *Wright v Woodgate* (1835) 2 Cr M & R 573, approved in *Adam v Ward* [1917] AC 309, at 349.
[113] *Horrocks v Lowe* [1975] AC 135, at 149–50.
[114] [1943] KB 319.   [115] *Horrocks v Lowe* [1975] AC 135.
[116] [1917] AC 309, at 339. Cf *Spill v Maule* (1869) LR 4 Exch 232 for a good illustration of judicial refusal to deprive D of his privilege on the ground that he used extravagant language.

(c) The inclusion of extraneous matter

The introduction of irrelevant matter in a communication may afford evidence of malice which will defeat the privilege that would otherwise attach to the communication.[117] On the other hand, in circumstances where the material is wholly extraneous to the main statement being made, there will be no privilege in the first place, and the question of whether a qualified privilege is defeated by malice will not arise.[118]

(d) Unreasonable publication to persons outside the scope of the privilege

Malice is present (and rebuts the privilege) if a defendant deliberately slanders another in the presence of persons to whom he has no privilege to communicate the matter (even if he has privilege to inform some of those present), or if he publishes in the press, when he could have protected his interest by a private communication.[119]

(2) Judge and jury and the burden of proof in respect of malice

Lord Finlay summarised the functions of judge and jury in this context thus:

> It is for the judge, and the judge alone, to determine as a matter of law whether the occasion is privileged, unless the circumstances attending it are in dispute, in which case the facts necessary to raise the question of law should be found by the jury. It is further for the judge to decide whether there is any evidence of express malice fit to be left to the jury – that is, whether there is any evidence on which a reasonable man could find malice.[120]

The burden of proving to the jury that the defendant was 'malicious' rests with the claimant. He discharges this burden if he proves the defendant malicious in any of the senses discussed above. In pleas of express malice, as in every other aspect of defamation law, questions may arise of exactly what meaning or meanings the defamatory statement properly bore. In *Fraser v Mirza*,[121] for example, the respondent alleged, in a complaint to the Chief Constable, that the appellant police officer had acted against him on racist motives. He expressly claimed that, when questioned about two television sets, he gave them up without hesitation and that a friend of his in the Pakistani community had been threatened by the officer. The House of Lords held that the whole substance of the complaint was intended to convey that the respondent had been charged with offences relating to the television sets without any evidence. His allegations were shown to be deliberate untruths and constituted sufficient evidence of absence of belief in the overall sting of the libel: namely, that he had been charged on solely racist grounds.

---

[117] *Adam v Ward* [1917] AC 309.
[118] Ibid; *Watts v Times Newspapers Ltd* [1997] QB 650.
[119] *Oddy v Lord Paulet* (1865) 4 F & F 1009.
[120] *Adam v Ward* [1917] AC 309, at 318.
[121] 1993 SLT 527.

(3) Excess of privilege and malice

In *Adam v Ward*, the House of Lords held that there are two separate questions to be answered. The first is whether the privilege has been exceeded. The second is whether there is evidence of malice.[122] The primary importance of the distinction lies in the fact that the judge decides whether the privilege has been exceeded (and therefore lost), but the jury decides whether there is 'malice'. And observations made by judges in directing juries on what is evidence of malice are not necessarily applicable when they have to rule on excess of privilege.[123] There may be such an excess where statements quite unconnected with the main statement are introduced.[124]

An example of excess of privilege is where statements quite unconnected with the main statement are introduced. Take, for example, *Tuson v Evans*.[125]

> In a letter to C's agent setting out the basis of his claim against C for arrears of rent, D added: 'This attempt to defraud me of the produce of land is as mean as it is dishonest'. This 'wholly unnecessary' addition deprived him of his qualified privilege.

The privilege will also be lost by publishing to more persons than is necessary. It was exceeded, for example, when the minutes of a *preliminary* inquiry by a committee of a local authority into alleged petrol thefts by employees were placed in the public library. At that stage, the body of rate-payers did not possess the necessary interest to receive that information.[126] On the other hand, an occasion does not cease to be privileged simply because the defendant publishes to clerks or others in the reasonable and ordinary course of business practice.[127] The fact that persons are present other than those to whom there is a duty to make the statement will not end the privilege if the ordinary 'business of life could not well be carried on' were such restrictions to be imposed.[128] So, for example, a company does not forfeit its protection if, in order to have circulated a copy of the auditor's report, it sends it to printers, for that is reasonable and necessary.[129]

(4) Joint publishers and malice

Some difficult problems relating to the abuse of privilege are raised when there is a publication by joint tortfeasors or the employees of the defendant. An agent through

---

[122] [1917] AC 309, at 318, 320–1, and 327.

[123] Ibid at 321.

[124] If the statement, though not in strict logic relevant to the privileged occasion, is reasonably germane to the subject matter, then it is material only as evidence of malice to take the case out of the privilege: *Horrocks v Lowe* [1975] AC 135, at 151.   [125] (1840) 12 Ad & El 733.

[126] *De Buse v McCarthy* [1942] 1 KB 156.

[127] *Boxsius v Goblet Frères* [1894] 1 QB 842; *Edmondson v Birch & Co Ltd and Horner* [1907] 1 KB 371; *Bryanston Finance Co Ltd v De Vries* [1975] QB 703. The last cited case, following *Toogood v Spyring* (1834) 1 Cr M & R 181, established that where the publication is made only to C, and not to third parties, there is then a qualified privilege for the publication to clerks if it is fairly warranted by any reasonable occasion (but not, as in that case, for a threatening improper letter).

[128] *Toogood v Spyring* (1834) 1 Cr M & R 181, at 194.

[129] *Lawless v Anglo-Egyptian Cotton and Oil Co* (1869) LR 4 QB 262.

whom a person publishes a privileged communication enjoys the same privilege as his principal. Thus, a solicitor has the defence of qualified privilege when he publishes on behalf of his client some matter which his client had a privilege to publish.[130] Correspondingly, if a servant in the course of his employment publishes with malice, the fact that his master was not personally malicious will not exempt the master from vicarious liability since the servant who forfeits the privilege does so in the course of his employment.[131] Where each party responsible for a joint publication has an individual right to publish the statement – for example, trustees or members of a committee – each has an independent privilege which is not affected by the malice of one or more of the other joint publishers.[132] Sometimes, however, one of the persons sued for the publication is a mere ancillary (for example, a printer or typist). Such an ancillary publisher may probably still plead qualified privilege even if all his principals published maliciously. The key question would be whether the ancillary was himself actuated by malice.[133]

(B) INSTANCES OF QUALIFIED PRIVILEGE

(1) General principle

All the instances of qualified privilege discussed in what follows can be captured within the general principle of common interest: that is, they exist where the defendant has an interest or duty (whether legal, social, or moral) to communicate intelligence about the claimant to a third party who has a corresponding interest or duty to receive such information.[134] The underlying rationale has also been summarised thus: it exists for 'the common convenience and welfare of society'.[135] Thus, 'originally and in principle there are not many different kinds of privilege, but rather for all privilege there is the same foundation of the public interest'.[136] The classic statement on the matter is that of Parke B:[137]

> [The defendant is liable for a defamatory statement] unless it is fairly made by a person in the discharge of some public or private duty, whether legal or moral, or in the conduct of his own affairs, in matters where his interest is concerned. If fairly warranted by any reasonable occasion or exigency, and honestly made, such communications are protected for

---

[130] *Baker v Carrick* [1894] 1 QB 838.

[131] *Citizens' Life Assurance Co v Brown* [1904] AC 423; *Riddick v Thames Board Mills Ltd* [1977] QB 881.

[132] *Egger v Viscount Chelmsford* [1965] 1 QB 248.

[133] This was the view of the majority in *Egger v Viscount Chelmsford* [1965] 1 QB 248, who took the bold step of disregarding statements to the contrary in *Adam v Ward* [1917] AC 309 because their Lordships had not heard argument on the point.

[134] *Adam v Ward* [1917] AC 309. This even covers broad-based internet communications to all the members of a particular religious community if they have sufficient interest in receiving the information: *Hewitt v Grunwald* [2004] EWCA Civ 2959.   [135] *Perera v Peiris* [1949] AC 1, at 20.

[136] *Webb v Times Publishing Co Ltd* [1960] 2 QB 535, at 563.

[137] *Toogood v Spyring* (1834) 1 Cr M & R 181, at 193, approved in *Adam v Ward* [1917] AC 309, at 349.

the common convenience and welfare of society; and the law has not restricted the right to make them within any narrow limits.

It is convenient to group the examples of statements afforded qualified privilege – and they are only examples – as follows: privileged reports, statements which protect an interest, and those made in the public interest.

(2) Privileged reports

Fair and accurate reports of proceedings in Parliament or in committees thereof, or a fair summary or sketch of that part of those proceedings which is of special interest,[138] are privileged at common law.[139] These, and other such common-law privileges, are expressly preserved by the Defamation Act 1996,[140] even though section 15 of that Act – read in conjunction with Schedule 1 – endeavours to establish a comprehensive range of reports that attract a statutory qualified privilege. The printing or broadcasting[141] of copies of, or extracts from, reports,[142] papers, votes, or proceedings published by authority of either House of Parliament are also privileged independently of the 1996 Act.[143]

Judicial reports, too, remain privileged at common law, so long as they are both fair and accurate.[144] The question of whether such reports meet the criteria of fairness and accuracy falls to the jury. In view of the different rationale for this privilege, these 'judicial proceedings' (a report of which acquires a qualified privilege) are not the same as those 'judicial proceedings', a report of which attracts an absolute privilege.[145] The former is a much broader class of reports. Yet in *Stern v Piper*,[146] it was held that qualified privilege does not stretch to a report of proceedings that are merely 'pending'. On the other hand, although a tribunal for the purposes of qualified privilege need not perform 'judicial functions' (in the narrow sense of the term), reports of its proceedings may be privileged, provided the public are admitted and the tribunal is not a mere domestic one, such as the Jockey Club.[147] The privilege still applies where

---

[138] *Cook v Alexander* [1974] QB 279.

[139] *Wason v Walter* (1868) LR 4 QB 73. For recent consideration of what constitutes a 'fair and accurate' report, see *Curistan v Times Newspapers Ltd* [2008] EWCA Civ 432, esp at [26]–[36].

[140] Defamation Act 1996, s 15(4)(b).

[141] Defamation Act 1952, s 9(1) extends this privilege to those forms of broadcasting to which the Act applies. [142] Parliamentary Papers Act 1840, s 2.

[143] Including Blue Books and reports of Royal Commissions presented to Parliament: *Mangena v Edward Lloyd Ltd* (1908) 98 LT 640; on appeal (1909) 99 LT 824.

[144] *Furniss v Cambridge Daily News Ltd* (1907) 23 TLR 705, at 706. In *Stern v Piper* [1997] QB 123 it was said that blasphemous or obscene material would not be privileged; nor would pre-trial reporting of allegations in court documents not yet in the public domain.

[145] For the judicial proceedings covered by absolute privilege see s 14(3) of the Defamation Act 1996.

[146] [1997] QB 123.

[147] *Chapman v Lord Ellesmere* [1932] 2 KB 431. Cf *Allbutt v General Council of Medical Education and Registration* (1889) 23 QBD 400, at 410. The privilege applied to foreign courts where the subject matter was of legitimate interest to the English newspaper-reading public (eg, where it was closely connected with the administration of justice in England – as in *Webb v Times Publishing Co Ltd* [1960] 2 QB 535 – but not otherwise).

the tribunal is simply considering the case in order to discover whether it has jurisdiction, even though in fact it has no such jurisdiction.[148]

By far the most comprehensive list of those reports and statements that are afforded a qualified privilege is contained in Schedule 1 to the Defamation Act 1996.[149] Importantly, however, there are limits to this statutory privilege. The Act offers no protection in the instance of a 'publication to the public, of matter which is not of public concern and the publication of which is not for the public benefit'.[150] Nor does it confer a qualified privilege in respect of anything published with malice,[151] or illegally.[152]

So far as it relates to qualified privilege, the protection provided by section 15 of the 1996 Act is broadly similar to its now repealed predecessor, section 7 of the Defamation Act 1952. That, in turn, was little more than a reiteration of section 3 of the Law of Libel Amendment Act 1888 and, importantly, there is authority under that nineteenth-century statute that what has become section 15 requires *both* public concern *and* public benefit to be shown. Furthermore, the burden of proving these things lies with the defendant.[153] Both the questions of what constitutes a matter of public concern, and what constitutes a matter of public benefit, are for the jury to decide.[154]

Reports protected by the Act fall into two distinct groups: (1) those privileged without any explanation or contradiction[155] and (2) those privileged subject to explanation or contradiction.[156] In relation to the former category, protection is conferred, broadly, on a worldwide basis. It lies in respect of reports of judicial, legislative, and international organisation proceedings conducted in public, and reports on official publications. Unlike the absolute privilege that is conferred in relation to reports of judicial proceedings, the protection conferred under section 15 of the 1996 Act applies without requiring the report to be contemporaneous with the judicial proceedings.[157]

In relation to the second class of reports covered by section 15 – those which are privileged subject to explanation or contradiction – no protection will be afforded if the claimant proves that the defendant, despite a request to publish a letter or statement of explanation or contradiction in a suitable manner,[158] has refused or neglected so to

---

[148] *Usill v Hales* (1878) 3 CPD 319. This case is not an authority on absolute privilege for judicial acts done without jurisdiction.   [149] The statutory list is too long to be reproduced here.
[150] Defamation Act 1996, s 15(3). In, eg, *Kelly v O'Malley* (1889) 6 TLR 62, for example, irrelevant, defamatory comments made at a public meeting were afforded no privilege.
[151] Defamation Act 1996, s 15(1).   [152] Defamation Act 1996, s 15(4)(a).
[153] *Kelly v O'Malley* (1889) 6 TLR 62, at 64.
[154] *Kingshott v Associated Kent Newspapers Ltd* [1991] 1 QB 88. But note that sufficient sections of society may well constitute 'the public' for these purposes: see *GKR Karate (UK) Ltd v Yorkshire Post Newspapers Ltd (No 2)* [2000] EMLR 410 and *Al-Fagih v HH Saudi Research and Marketing (UK) Ltd* [2002] EMLR 215.
[155] Defamation Act 1996, Sch 1, Part I.
[156] Defamation Act 1996, Sch 1, Part II. Note that 'Reports' for these purposes will include the summary of a press release that is issued to accompany a press conference: *McCartan Turkington Breen v Times Newspapers Ltd* [2001] 2 AC 277.
[157] *Tsikata v Newspaper Publishing plc* [1997] 1 All ER 655. 'Reports' privileged in this way under s 7 of the 1952 Act continue to be covered under the 1996 Act so the authority of the case remains intact.
[158] That is, in the same manner as the publication complained of, or, alternatively, in a manner that is both reasonable and adequate in the circumstances: Defamation Act 1996, s 15(2).

do.[159] The kinds of reports and statements that fall into this second class include those concerning official parliamentary or judicial notices to the public, meetings of public or quasi-public bodies in the UK, and general meetings of UK public companies.

The essential difference between the first and second class of reports is that those in the latter category tend to be based on notices issued, and meetings held, in the UK or European Union. For this reason it is much more reasonable to expect, say, a newspaper to print a correction or explanation relating to the initial report. By contrast, it is seen as too much of an imposition to expect the newspaper to publish such explanations or corrections when the initial report was on an item of world news.

The Government proposes to widen the availability of this privilege. Under clauses 5(2)–(9) of the Draft Defamation Bill 2011, various extensions would be made to the provisions of the Defamation Act 1996, Schedule 1 concerning the reporting of governmental, public company, and scientific and academic conference proceedings.[160]

(3) Statements to protect an interest

(a) The public interest

(i) Statements by way of help in discovering criminals

Information given to the police[161] in order to detect crime is privileged.[162] Statements made by policemen in the course of their inquiries into suspected crimes are presumably also privileged; and statements made in the course of complaints about police conduct have also been held to be privileged.[163]

(ii) Statements about the misconduct of public officers

When a member of the public brings to the notice of the proper authority any misconduct or neglect of duty on the part of public officers, his doing so is afforded qualified privilege.[164] However, when the defendant, acting in good faith, complains to the wrong official, he is not privileged.[165] Yet a defendant who first addresses his complaint about misconduct to his MP will almost certainly be privileged.[166] One unanswered question, however, is whether the privilege in relation to the misconduct of public officers includes those employed in one of the now privatised public services. By reason of logic, it ought so to apply.

---

[159] Defamation Act 1996, s 15(2).

[160] See Ministry of Justice, *Draft Defamation Bill Consultation Paper* (CP3/11, 2011), 25–8.

[161] But not to the wife of the accused: *Wenman v Ash* (1853) 13 CB 836.

[162] *Padmore v Lawrence* (1840) 11 Ad & El 380.   [163] *Fraser v Mirza* 1993 SLT 527.

[164] Eg, *Harrison v Bush* (1855) 5 E & B 344 (statement to Home Secretary about county magistrate). But see *Blackshaw v Lord* [1984] QB 1: suspicions must be aired to the proper authority and not the public at large unless public safety is at risk.

[165] *Hebditch v MacIlwaine* [1894] 2 QB 54; *Beach v Freeson* [1972] 1 QB 14. Cf *London Association for Protection of Trade v Greenlands Ltd* [1916] 2 AC 15, at 34 (answers to an inquiry in the genuine mistaken belief that the inquirer had a legitimate interest were held to be privileged).

[166] *R v Rule* [1937] 2 KB 375.

(iii) Other statements

The defendant's duty to make a statement about the claimant is sometimes only a moral or social one – for example, to supply a third party with a warning about the claimant.[167] This, however, does not prohibit his statement attracting a qualified privilege. That said, in the absence of a legal or contractual duty to make such a statement, the court may well be wary of granting a privilege unless the defendant can show a strong relationship – for example, one of friendship – between himself and the third party to whom he feels obliged to make the statement.[168] Furthermore, in establishing the existence of such a duty, the defendant is entitled only to rely on matters that were known to him at the time of publication.[169]

The list of moral and social duties is virtually endless. The following is by no means an exhaustive list of the situations under this head. It is merely illustrative, and includes the following: supplying information about credit;[170] protection by a solicitor of his client's interests;[171] answers to confidential inquiries about servants;[172] a member of a woman's family warning her about her fiancé's character (or vice versa).[173] By contrast, the privilege does not cover idle gossip or officious intermeddling by strangers.[174] Consider *Watt v Longsdon*.[175]

> A company director was held to be privileged in passing on to the chairman a report that an employee was associating with another woman and otherwise misconducting himself during his employment overseas, but he was not protected in informing the wife of the employee, although she had an interest in receiving that information.

As regards the social duty on Employer A to provide a reference on behalf of one of his (former) employees to Employer B, it is clear that such a reference would be afforded qualified privilege. On the other hand, in the light of the House of Lords' decision in *Spring v Guardian Assurance plc*,[176] this immunity may be of little use, since it was held in *Spring* that, subject to the usual requirements, the employee would be entitled to sue in negligence rather than defamation for the loss attributable to a carelessly written reference.[177]

It has never been directly decided whether the moral duty to publish an apology, after having published a defamatory statement, attracts a qualified privilege. In *Watts v Times Newspapers Ltd*,[178] the Court of Appeal failed to supply an authoritative answer to this question. In that case, the defendant published a defamatory account

---

[167] See, eg, *Amann v Damm* (1860) 8 CBNS 597; *S v Newham LBC* (1998) 96 LGR 651.

[168] *Todd v Hawkins* (1837) 8 C & P 88.

[169] *Loutchansky v Times Newspapers Ltd* [2002] QB 321; *GKR Karate (UK) Ltd v Yorkshire Post Newspapers Ltd (No 2)* [2000] EMLR 410.

[170] *London Association for Protection of Trade v Greenlands Ltd* [1916] 2 AC 15.

[171] Cf *Baker v Carrick* [1894] 1 QB 838, at 841.   [172] *Kelly v Partington* (1833) 4 B & Ad 700.

[173] *Todd v Hawkins* (1837) 8 C & P 88.   [174] *Coxhead v Richards* (1846) 2 CB 569.

[175] [1930] 1 KB 130.

[176] [1995] 2 AC 296.

[177] But note that the remedy in negligence would be assessed by a judge and might well be lower than that awarded by a jury in a defamation action.   [178] [1997] QB 650.

of the claimant and then subsequently apologised in terms that reiterated the initial libel. Instead of stating generally that such apologies attract qualified privilege, it was merely held that no such claim to privilege could be sustained in the instant case for want of a reciprocal interest in publishing the apology on the part of the defendant.

(b) Reynolds *and the public interest*

There is no general common-law defence of publication of 'fair information on a matter of public interest'. *General* interest in the subject matter of a report made to the public as a whole is, by itself, an insufficient basis upon which to grant the report a qualified privilege.[179] The correlative 'duty and interest' aspects that normally characterise instances of qualified privilege are absent in such cases; for the public at large can but rarely claim a *genuine* interest in the disclosure of information concerning a given individual. However, an item of information may be of genuine public interest and the public may be *entitled* to know of it.[180] Where this is so, and a newspaper or any other person acts responsibly in publishing the item, it may claim a qualified privilege. A somewhat lengthy test for establishing whether a newspaper has acted in this fashion was set out by Lord Nicholls in the House of Lords in *Reynolds v Times Newspapers Ltd*. He said:

> Depending on the circumstances, the matters to be taken into account include the following.
>
> 1 The seriousness of the allegation. The more serious the charge, the more the public is misinformed and the individual harmed, if the allegation is not true.
>
> 2 The nature of the information, and the extent to which the subject matter is a matter of public concern.
>
> 3 The source of the information. Some informants have no direct knowledge of the events. Some have their own axes to grind, or are being paid for their stories.
>
> 4 The steps taken to verify the information.
>
> 5 The status of the information. The allegation may have already been the subject of an investigation which commands respect.
>
> 6 The urgency of the matter. News is often a perishable commodity.
>
> 7 Whether comment was sought from the [claimant]. He may have information others do not possess or have not disclosed. An approach to the [claimant] will not always be necessary.
>
> 8 Whether the article contained the gist of the claimant's side of the story.
>
> 9 The tone of the article. A newspaper can raise queries or call for an investigation. It need not adopt allegations as statements of fact.
>
> 10 The circumstances of the publication, including the timing.

---

[179] The 'public interest' of qualified privilege is narrower and broader in scope than the 'public interest' of honest comment (see below). *Chapman v Lord Ellesmere* [1932] 2 KB 431 illustrates its strictness: in qualified privilege, unlike honest comment, the defence will succeed although the facts are untrue. However, anything submitted to the public for its appraisal can be treated as a matter of 'public interest' in the honest comment defence.   [180] This is the phrase used in *Roberts v Gable* [2007] EWCA Civ 721, at [32].

This list is not exhaustive. The weight to be given to these and any other relevant factors will vary from case to case.[181]

Notwithstanding a general caution regarding the free and easy application of the principle enunciated in *Reynolds*,[182] – after all, matters that are of interest to the public clearly extend beyond those which are strictly speaking in the public interest[183] – Lord Nicholls did envisage that a liberal approach should be taken in relation to defending comments made about political figures. He insisted that any 'court should be slow to conclude that a publication was not in the public interest and, therefore, the public had no right to know, especially when the information is in the field of political discussion'.[184]

Since the decision in *Reynolds*, it has been suggested that the proper benchmark for claiming the privilege may well be 'responsible journalism'.[185] It might be said that a test of responsible journalism alone is too imprecise to constitute the basis for the *Reynolds* privilege because, by itself, it tends to conflate the questions of the existence of a privilege and the presence of malice. That being so, the argument goes, while 'responsible journalism' might attract a privilege, it ought not to be seen as synonymous with a duty to publish,[186] for there must also be a public interest in publication. The argument, however, did not find favour with the House of Lords in its consideration of this issue in *Jameel v Wall Street Journal Europe SPRL*.[187] The House affirmed its disposition towards greater freedom of discussion of matters of public interest.

> The case concerned a newspaper report which, in factual terms, revealed supposed information that the bank accounts of a certain Saudi Arabian company and its managing director were being monitored by the Saudi Arabian Monetary Authority in connection with the funding of terrorist organisations. This was taken to mean, at least, that grounds existed upon which to investigate the involvement of those persons. The report

---

[181] [2001] 2 AC 127, at 205. This test has been said to involve a 'balancing exercise' requiring the use of judgment, but not a 'discretion': *Flood v Times Newspapers Ltd* [2010] EWCA Civ 804, at [46], [49], and [107]. For detailed analysis, see Williams (2000) 63 MLR 748.

[182] See, eg, *Al-Fagih v HH Saudi Research & Marketing (UK) Ltd* [2002] EMLR 215.

[183] For instance, a justification to publish to the public at large matters of speculation and suspicion will arise only in exceptional cases, such as those where public safety is endangered: see, eg, *Camporese v Parton* (1983) 150 DLR (3d) 208. See also *Henry v BBC* [2005] EWHC 2787 (no need for a certain party to be named in a regional television report).

[184] [2001] 2 AC 127, at 205. See, eg *Tsikata v Newspaper Publishing plc* [1997] 1 All ER 655. Cf the USA where all 'political speech' attracts a qualified privilege (*New York Times Co v Sullivan* (1964) 376 US 254) and in New Zealand where political speech concerning existing, former or prospective MPs is thus protected (*Lange v Atkinson* [1998] 3 NZLR 424; *Lange v Atkinson (No 2)* [2000] 3 NZLR 385).

[185] See, eg, *Bonnick v Morris* [2003] 1 AC 300; *Kearns v General Council of the Bar* [2003] 1 WLR 1357. The test of what is responsible journalism is to be judged by reference to whether the steps taken to gather and publish the information were responsible and fair: *Jameel v Wall Street Journal Europe (No 3)* [2006] UKHL 44, at [32], [53], [144], and [149]. But the test seems circular!

[186] *Loutchansky v Times Newspapers Ltd (No 2)* [2002] 1 All ER 652. See also *Al-Fagih v HH Saudi Research and Marketing (UK) Ltd* [2002] EMLR 215 (failure to verify allegations appearing in a newspaper does not necessarily amount to malice).   [187] [2006] UKHL 44.

was defamatory, but was also found to be in the public interest. One question was whether the 'responsible journalism' threshold had been met.

In discussing this, Lord Bingham stressed that the *Reynolds* factors were not to be seen as a 'series of hurdles to be negotiated by a publisher' in order to invoke the privilege. Rather, the factors consisted of 'matters which might be taken into account'.[188] His Lordship, and others, also pointed to the need of the court to place weight upon 'editorial decisions and judgments made at the time, without the knowledge of falsity which is a benefit of hindsight' where considered in nature and not casual or slipshod.[189] In the result, the House held that the *Reynolds* privilege was indeed available to report the matters in question.

In another development, it is now asserted by the Court of Appeal that there is a subspecies of qualified privilege called 'reportage'. This is said to involve cases where statements are merely reported by the press without any adoption of their truth. On the prevailing narrow view, the reportage doctrine applies only to the reporting of allegations made in the course of some political and public interest dispute.[190] According to *Roberts v Gable*,[191] the significance is as follows:

> If upon a proper construction of the thrust of the article the defamatory material is attributed to another and is not being put forward as true, then a responsible journalist would not need to take steps to verify its accuracy. He is absolved from that responsibility because he is simply reporting in a neutral fashion the fact that it has been said without adopting the truth.[192]

It is difficult to see the justification for this rocky outcrop of the *Reynolds* privilege. It appears to miss the point that the seriousness with which, say, an allegation of corruption made by X is treated is all the greater when reported by newspapers Y and Z.[193] It is submitted that all *Reynolds* criteria (which are not inflexible in nature) should remain applicable, otherwise the repetition rule should prevail.[194]

Since the decision in the *Reynolds* case, there has been an exponential increase in 'publication' beyond traditional forms. These publications include much material that is 'self-published' on the internet by way of blogs and the like. In a sign that the courts are clearly aware of the greater accessibility of publication of comment to the 'average person', the Privy Council has stated in *Seaga v Harper*[195] that the *Reynolds* privilege is not to be restricted to newspaper publications. Delivering the judgment of their

---

[188] [2006] UKHL 44, at [33]. See also ibid at [56].

[189] Ibid at [33]. See also ibid at [51] and [108]. For a case where the court rejected the editorial view in favour of publication, see *Flood v Times Newspapers Ltd* [2010] EWCA Civ 804.

[190] This is where the exception began its life: *Al-Fagih v HH Saudi Research and Marketing (UK) Ltd* [2001] EWCA Civ 1634. Contra *Charman v Orion Publishing Group Ltd* [2007] EWCA Civ 972, at [91].

[191] [2007] EWCA Civ 721.

[192] Ibid at [61]. Contra *Galloway v Telegraph Group Ltd* [2006] EWCA Civ 17, at [50]; *Flood v Times Newspapers Ltd* [2010] EWCA Civ 804, at [101].

[193] See, eg, *Truth (NZ) Ltd v Holloway* [1960] 1 WLR 997, at 1003.

[194] For a different, but nevertheless critical, analysis, see Bosland (2011) OJLS 89.

[195] [2008] UKPC 9.

Lordships, Lord Carswell stated that there is 'no valid reason why it should not extend to publications made by any person who publishes material of public interest in any medium', so long as the test of 'responsible journalism' is satisfied.[196]

The Government has noted perceived problems with the *Reynolds* privilege, such as its 'complication' and costliness to run as a defence.[197] In its Draft Defamation Bill 2011, it proposes putting the defence on a statutory footing:

2. Responsible publication on matter of public interest

(1) It is a defence to an action for defamation to show that –

    (a) the statement complained of is, or forms part of, a statement on a matter of public interest; and

    (b) the defendant acted responsibly in publishing the statement complained of.

The intention is that the defence should operate 'regardless of whether the statement complained of is a statement of fact, an inference or an opinion'[198] and that it should be available outside the confines of 'mainstream journalism'.[199] Sub-clause (2) provides a test for determining whether a defendant has acted responsibly by publishing a statement that is very similar in nature to the *Reynolds* factors. These factors are not intended to constitute a 'checklist' and are indicative only.[200] Finally, sub-clause (3) is intended to subsume the reportage doctrine:

(3) A defendant is to be treated as having acted responsibly in publishing a statement if the statement was published as part of an accurate and impartial account of a dispute between the claimant and another person.

As already established by the case law, the Explanatory Notes to the Draft Bill affirm that, where the reportage doctrine applies, the defendant will not need to verify the information reported before publication.[201]

(c) The self-interest of the publisher

Just as self-defence and protection of property are defences in torts against the person and property, so also is a statement made to protect or advance the defendant's interests a matter of qualified privilege in defamation.[202] Thus, a creditor may write to an auctioneer to protect his security.[203] Equally, a man who replied to a letter demanding payment of fees for medical services to his wife (who died from scarlet fever) saying, 'I shall never pay him unless the law compels me, and that I do not fancy it can, as I could more easily indict Dr S for manslaughter', was held to be privileged.[204] Privilege

---

[196] [2008] UKPC 9, at [11].

[197] Ministry of Justice, *Draft Defamation Bill Consultation Paper* (CP3/11, 2011), 10.

[198] Ibid at 12.

[199] Ibid at 11.

[200] Explanatory Notes to the Draft Defamation Bill 2011, at [11].

[201] Ibid at [12].

[202] *Toogood v Spyring* (1834) 1 Cr M & R 181, at 193; *Aspro Travel Ltd v Owners Abroad Group plc* [1995] 4 All ER 728.   [203] *Blackman v Pugh* (1846) 2 CB 611.

[204] *Stevens v Kitchener* (1887) 4 TLR 159.

will also extend to reasonable steps taken by the publisher to collect money owing to him,[205] warnings issued to servants about the bad character of their associates,[206] and replies to attacks on the publisher's reputation.[207]

(d) Common interest

There are cases of privilege based on interest where neither the public nor the publisher *alone* has a sufficiently defensible interest for the case to be brought within any of the preceding subheadings. These cases attract a privilege on the basis that the publisher and the recipient of the communication have a 'common interest' in the subject matter of the communication. A common interest of this kind exists between an employer and his employees. Thus, in one case, the defendants had posted up a circular in such of their premises as would be frequented by their employees, stating (among other things) that the claimant, another former employee, had been dismissed for neglect of duty. The privilege of common interest was held to extend to the defendants.[208]

The range of matters privileged because they are of common interest are manifold and include a bishop replying to an attack on him in the legislature before an assembly of his clergy,[209] communications within a family on matters affecting the welfare of a member of that family,[210] speeches by a company shareholder at a shareholders meeting[211] or by a trustee at a friendly society meeting,[212] a statement made by a creditor to another creditor about their debtor,[213] and communications by the head of the Bar Council to members of the Bar.[214]

In one respect the scope of this privilege has been curtailed by section 10 of the Defamation Act 1952, which provides that publications, even to a qualified voter, by or on behalf of a candidate at a parliamentary or local government election, are not privileged on the ground that they are material to a question in issue in the election.[215]

SECTION 7 HONEST COMMENT

This defence (formerly called 'fair comment') covers comments about the claimant or the claimant's conduct[216] in connection with matters of public interest. Such comments

---

[205] *Winstanley v Bampton* [1943] KB 319.

[206] *Somerville v Hawkins* (1851) 10 CB 583.

[207] *Laughton v Bishop of Sodor and Man* (1872) LR 4 PC 495. But may a representative of the press, theatre, or other section of the community create a privilege by replying to an attack on that section as a whole by C? 'No', held Dixon J in *Penton v Caldwell* (1945) 70 CLR 219 (whose decision was reversed by the High Court of Australia on the ground that D, a newspaper, had itself been attacked by C).

[208] *Hunt v Great Northern Rly Co* [1891] 2 QB 189. See also *Bryanston Finance Ltd v De Vries* [1975] QB 703. [209] *Laughton v Bishop of Sodor and Man* (1872) LR 4 PC 495.

[210] *Todd v Hawkins* (1837) 8 C & P 88. [211] *Parsons v Surgey* (1864) 4 F & F 247.

[212] *Longdon-Griffiths v Smith* [1951] 1 KB 295. [213] *Spill v Maule* (1869) LR 4 Exch 232.

[214] *Kearns v General Council of the Bar* [2003] 1 WLR 1357.

[215] *Braddock v Bevins* [1948] 1 KB 580 must now be read in the light of this section. See also *Plummer v Charman* [1962] 3 All ER 823.

[216] The comment may not be directed towards another matter but incidentally contain an unsubstantiated, defamatory allegation about C: *Baldwin v Rusbridger* [2001] EMLR 1062.

must be in the form of reasonable remarks[217] upon true or privileged statements of fact. They must constitute an honestly held opinion made by a person who did not believe the statements to be untrue and who was not, therefore, actuated by malice.[218]

(A) MATTERS OF PUBLIC INTEREST

The first requirement of this defence is that the statement in question must be made upon a matter of public interest. Here, the defence has been held to cover the public conduct of people in public offices,[219] but not their private conduct (except in so far as it throws light upon whether they possess qualities such as integrity and honesty which are thought to be essential to people in public life).[220] Matters of government and public administration,[221] including local government,[222] are also within its scope. The management of institutions of substantial public concern, such as the media itself,[223] or religious institutions, is also a matter for honest comment.[224]

Anything submitted to the public for its appraisal is of public interest. Books,[225] articles in periodicals and newspapers,[226] plays,[227] and radio broadcasts (themselves being film criticisms),[228] are examples. The work of an architect[229] and the performance of actors in public entertainments[230] are also within the defence. Indeed, any circumstances that may fairly be said to invite comment are within its scope. Traders publishing handbills,[231] or those who issue public advertisements, invite comment on them. On the other hand – and notwithstanding the importance of the question – it remains undecided how far the quality of goods offered for sale to the public is the proper subject of honest comment. Even so, it is submitted that it would be artificially restrictive if the answer were to depend on the extent of the manufacturer's advertising campaign.

(B) COMMENT ON TRUE FACTS

A second part of the defence is that the comment, with one exception,[232] must be made upon true facts (and the rules relating to this part of the defence are unnecessarily

---

[217] The comment must pass an objective test (see below), but beyond this it became difficult to justify the use of the adjective 'fair' in this defence. Hence the renaming of the defence in *Spiller v Joseph* [2010] UKSC 53.   [218] *Reynolds v Times Newspapers Ltd* [2001] 2 AC 127, at 193.

[219] *Seymour v Butterworth* (1862) 3 F & F 372 (Recorder and MP).   [220] (1862) 3 F & F 372, at 382.

[221] Eg, *Henwood v Harrison* (1872) LR 7 CP 606 (the method by which D converted a naval vessel).

[222] *Purcell v Sowler* (1877) 2 CPD 215.

[223] *Telnikoff v Matusevitch* [1992] 2 AC 343 (recruiting policy for the BBC Russian service).

[224] *Kelly v Tinling* (1865) LR 1 QB 699.   [225] *Thomas v Bradbury, Agnew & Co Ltd* [1906] 2 KB 627.

[226] *Kemsley v Foot* [1952] AC 345.   [227] *Merivale v Carson* (1887) 20 QBD 275.

[228] *Turner v Metro-Goldwyn-Mayer Pictures Ltd* [1950] 1 All ER 449.

[229] *Soane v Knight* (1827) Mood & M 74.

[230] *Dibdin v Swan* (1793) 1 Esp 27; *Cooney v Edeveain* (1897) 14 TLR 34; *London Artists Ltd v Littler* [1969] 2 QB 375; *Cornwell v Myskow* [1987] 2 All ER 504.   [231] *Paris v Levy* (1860) 9 CBNS 342.

[232] Comments on statements of fact, not proved to be true, but themselves privileged, also attract the defence.

complicated by many technical rules). The defence requires the facts upon which the comment was made to be stated or identified in or from the comment itself.[233] As was said in *Spiller v Joseph* by Lord Phillips P:

> The comment must…identify at least in general terms what it is that has led the commentator to make the comment, so that the reader can understand what the comment is about and the commentator can, if challenged, explain by giving particulars of the subject matter of his comment why he expressed the views that he did.[234]

At this point it is important to distinguish this defence from that of justification. Honest comment is available only in respect of expressions of opinion; justification is available in respect of both statements of fact and matters of opinion. In honest comment, it is not necessary to prove the truth of the comment, merely that the opinion was honestly held.[235] If justification is pleaded in respect of matters of opinion, the defendant must prove not merely that he honestly held the views expressed, but that they were 'correct' views. Thus, if the statement complained of was: 'X's speech last night was inconsistent with his professions of Socialism', then, on a plea of justification, the defendant would have to prove that it was inconsistent. In honest comment, he would only need to show that he honestly held this opinion on X's speech.

Naturally, in many statements it will be very difficult to unravel fact from comment. Yet the two must be separated in due course by the court as the defence of honest comment only lies in relation to comments upon facts that are proved to be true or, exceptionally, statements that are untrue, but made on a privileged occasion (for example, a witness statement in court).[236] If the statement is not privileged, and the statement is untrue, the defendant will not be able to invoke the honest comment defence simply by proving that his comment is honestly made. Thus, in one case, a defendant who implied that a play was adulterous could not rely on honest comment where the court found as a fact that adultery was not dealt with in the play.[237] The words 'X is a disgrace' led the hearer to believe that they were based on unstated facts. Accordingly, the defendant could not plead honest comment in respect of those words alone. If, however, he had added 'he has deserted his wife and family', the original words might well be regarded as a comment on the stated facts.[238]

The full details of the procedural complexities associated with a plea of honest comment fall beyond the scope of this book. It suffices to say that defendants will attempt,

---

[233] *Spiller v Joseph* [2010] UKSC 53, at [90].

[234] Ibid at [104].

[235] *Reynolds v Times Newspapers Ltd* [2001] 2 AC 127, at 193. But for criticism, see Young (2000) 20 OJLS 89.

[236] *Mangena v Wright* [1909] 2 KB 958; *Grech v Odhams Press Ltd* [1958] 1 QB 310; on appeal [1958] 2 QB 275. It is not necessary for D to justify the facts contained in a privileged statement or report but he must establish that he has given a fair and accurate report of the proceedings in question: *Brent Walker Group plc v Time Out Ltd* [1991] 2 QB 33. The facts must exist at the time of the comment: *Cohen v Daily Telegraph Ltd* [1968] 2 All ER 407.　　　　　　　　　　　　　　[237] *Merivale v Carson* (1887) 20 QBD 275.

[238] See *Cooper v Lawson* (1838) 8 Ad & El 746. For a more modern reassertion of the importance of taking the offending words in context, see *Branson v Bower* [2001] EMLR 800, at [12]–[13].

whenever they can, to cloud the distinction between fact, which they must prove, and comment, which may be permissible if honest. Accordingly, the Court of Appeal has insisted that a plea of honest comment must be made 'with sufficient precision to enable the claimant to know what case he has to meet'.[239] Claimants can require details of the facts that are said to constitute the honest comment,[240] for not always will such facts be apparent. On the other hand, the absence of such facts in the defamatory statement will not necessarily be fatal to an attempt to invoke the defence. Consider *Kemsley v Foot*.[241]

> D attacked a newspaper by publishing an article headed 'Lower than Kemsley'. Kemsley, a newspaper proprietor in no way connected to the newspaper that had been attacked, sued D, arguing that the words amounted to a statement that Kemsley's papers were worthy of contempt in their own right. D's counter-argument was that this was indeed implied in what he had written, but that it was (1) a mere statement of opinion and (2) one that could be justified on the basis of honest comment. Kemsley contended that what D had said was a statement of fact, that no defence of honest comment could be invoked and that D's defence should be struck out. Their Lordships held that the words in question were, on their face, a mere statement of opinion, even though no supporting factual evidence was provided to justify that opinion.

The case also established that, 'where the facts relied on to justify the comment are contained only in the particulars, it is not incumbent on the defendant to prove the truth of every fact so stated in order to establish his plea of [honest] comment, but . . . he must establish sufficient facts to support the comment to the satisfaction of the jury'.[242]

A rather different question arose in *Telnikoff v Matusevitch*.[243] There, the defendant had written an angry and critical letter to the *Daily Telegraph* in response to an article written by the claimant. The key issue was whether, in determining which parts of the letter constituted allegations of fact and which were merely comment, the letter could be read alongside the offending article. The House of Lords held that only the contents of the letter itself could be considered as there were likely to be several readers who saw only the letter and not the article. Lord Keith advised both those writing to newspapers and the editors thereof to take care to use language distinguishing sufficiently clearly between fact and comment.[244]

Difficulties may arise where a defendant can prove some but not all of his factual allegations. It is thus provided in section 6 of the Defamation Act 1952 that:

> a defence of fair comment shall not fail by reason only that the truth of every allegation of fact is not proved if the expression of opinion is fair comment having regard to such of the facts alleged or referred to in the words complained of as are proved.[245]

---

[239] See *Control Risks Ltd v New English Library Ltd* [1989] 3 All ER 577.
[240] *Cunningham-Howie v F W Dimbleby & Sons Ltd* [1951] 1 KB 360.
[241] [1952] AC 345; followed in *Lowe v Associated Newspapers* [2006] EWHC 320.
[242] [1952] AC 345, at 362.   [243] [1991] 4 All ER 817.   [244] Ibid at 823.
[245] Where separate allegations have a common 'sting', it has been suggested that it is permissible in fair comment, as it is in justification, to rely on other un-complained of parts of the relevant statement: *Polly Peck (Holding) plc v Trelford* [1986] 2 All ER 84, at 102.

This provision has been held not to afford a defence where the facts on which the comment is based materially add to the harm to reputation. In such cases, the defendant must also prove those facts since their existence will not be assumed.[246] That said, even if the defence ultimately fails, where some of what the defendant said in relation to the claimant's bad character can be shown to be true, this can be invoked to mitigate the amount of damages payable.[247]

An imputation of corrupt or dishonourable motives will render a comment unfair and the defence not maintainable unless, first, such an imputation is an inference that a fair-minded person might reasonably draw from such facts *and*, second, it also represents the honest opinion of the writer.[248]

(C) COMMENT MUST BE HONESTLY MADE AND NOT ACTUATED BY MALICE

There is only a prima facie case of honest comment if the comment in question is shown to be one that the defendant made honestly.[249] Lord Esher summarised the matter thus:

> Every latitude must be given to opinion and to prejudice, and then an ordinary set of men with ordinary judgement must say whether any fair man[250] would have made such a comment on the work…Mere exaggeration, or even gross exaggeration, would not make the comment unfair. However wrong the opinion expressed may be in point of truth, or however prejudiced the writer, it may still be within the prescribed limit. The question which the jury must consider is this – would any fair man, however prejudiced he may be, however exaggerated or obstinate his views, have said that which this criticism has said of the work which is criticised?[251]

What is clear from this passage – and, in particular, those references to what 'ordinary men' and 'any fair man' might say – is that an objective test is to be applied in order to determine whether the comment in question could have been honestly made.[252] The court's task is to assess whether the comment in question fell within reasonable bounds, given that it is not possible (in most cases) to determine the actual convictions with which a comment was uttered at the time of utterance. Although the test has been

---

[246] *Truth (NZ) Ltd v Avery* [1959] NZLR 274 (in this case there was an identically worded New Zealand statute); approved (*obiter*) in *Broadway Approvals Ltd v Odhams Press Ltd* [1965] 2 All ER 523.

[247] *Turner v News Group Newspapers Ltd* [2006] EWCA Civ 540.

[248] *Campbell v Spottiswoode* (1863) 3 B & S 769 (where Cockburn CJ variously uses the expressions 'well-founded', 'not without cause', and 'not without foundation'); *Peter Walker & Sons Ltd v Hodgson* [1909] 1 KB 239, at 253; approved in *Harris v Lubbock* (1971) *Times*, 21 October.

[249] *Plymouth Mutual Co-operative and Industrial Society Ltd v Traders' Publishing Association Ltd* [1906] 1 KB 403, at 418.

[250] This dictum was approved by Lord Porter in *Turner v Metro-Goldwyn-Mayer Pictures Ltd* [1950] 1 All ER 449 (except for the substitution of 'honest' for 'fair').

[251] *Merivale v Carson* (1887) 20 QBD 275, at 280–1. Note also that a comment may be unfair because a medical fact was omitted from the defamatory statement: *Dowling v Time Inc* (1954) *Times*, 25 June.

[252] For modern support of this objective test, see *Branson v Bower (No 2)* [2001] EMLR 809.

described by the highest of authority as 'elusive', and as one which is rarely in issue (or likely to be in issue),[253] it lives on as a filter of the applicability of the defence.[254] The more important issue, however, will usually be whether the claimant can prove an actual lack of honesty in the making of the comment.

When assessing whether the comment could have been honestly made by a fair-minded person, evidence of the claimant's standing and reputation among his fellows at the time of publication is relevant, but evidence of enhanced reputation by the time of the trial is not. Surprisingly, perhaps, if the comment is proved to be one that could have been honestly made by a fair-minded person, the defendant does not have to prove that he actually believed it to be 'fair'.[255] It is then for the claimant to establish that the relevant criticism was not an opinion honestly held by the defendant; that, in other words, the defendant was actuated by malice. If, for example, a newspaper publishes a defamatory letter from a reader expressing opinions which could reasonably be justified, the publishers and editor are not required to prove they concurred in the comment.[256]

It is not malicious in this context to make a comment one believes to be true, even if one's reason for making that comment is associated with the pursuit of one's own private ends.[257] It is a lack of belief in what was published that goes to the question of malice in connection with this defence.[258] If the purpose of the maker of the honest comment is not to give the public the benefit of his comment but, instead, to injure the claimant, then the defence does not lie.[259] The defendant 'is the person in whose motives the [claimant] in the libel action is concerned, and if he, the person sued, is proved to have allowed his view to be distorted by malice, it is quite immaterial that somebody else might without malice have written an equally damnatory criticism'.[260] 'It is of course, possible for a person to have a spite against another and yet to bring a perfectly dispassionate judgment to bear upon his literary merits, but, given the existence of malice, it must be for the jury to say whether it has warped his judgement.'[261]

If an employee is malicious, so as to lose his defence of honest comment, then in accordance with the ordinary principles of vicarious liability, his employer will also be deprived of the defence. Vicarious liability in defamation may also extend to a principal-agent relationship. Thus, the publisher of a periodical could not establish honest comment when the writer of a book review was malicious: the writer was an agent.[262] On the other hand, the publisher's defence of honest comment is not affected when

---

[253] *Spiller v Joseph* [2010] UKSC 53, at [6].

[254] This is the only way of reading *Spiller v Joseph* [2010] UKSC 53. See, esp, ibid at [83] (outline of elements).   [255] *Telnikoff v Matusevitch* [1991] 1 QB 102; affirmed on this point [1992] 2 AC 343.

[256] For a contrary judgment from Canada see *Cherneskey v Armadale Publishers Ltd* [1979] 1 SCR 1067.

[257] Eg, *Grobbelaar v News Group Newspapers Ltd* [2001] 2 All ER 437 (reversed on other grounds [2003] EMLR 1). On the other hand, if the statement is made as part of a conspiracy, an action may lie in that tort, so long as a damage *beyond* mere damage to reputation can be shown.

[258] *Branson v Bower (No 2)* [2001] EMLR 809.   [259] *Merivale v Carson* (1887) 20 QBD 275, at 281–2.

[260] *Thomas v Bradbury, Agnew & Co Ltd* [1906] 2 KB 627, at 638.   [261] Ibid at 642.

[262] *Gros v Crook* (1969) 113 Sol Jo 408.

the writer of a letter in the correspondence column of his newspaper is malicious.[263] A joint publisher probably does not lose his defence of honest comment because of the malice of another joint publisher unless he is vicariously liable for that other.[264]

(D) BURDEN OF PROOF AND THE FUNCTIONS OF JUDGE AND JURY

The defendant has the onus of proving that the matter is of public concern, that the facts on which the comment is based are true, and that the comment is such as an honest man might make. The claimant must then prove the defendant was actuated by malice. It is for the judge to decide whether the matter is one of public interest.[265] Lord Porter said:

> It is for the jury in a proper case to determine what is comment and what is fact; but a prerequisite to their right is that the words are capable of being a statement of a fact or facts. It is for the judge alone to decide whether they are so capable, and whether his ruling is right or wrong is a matter of law for the decision of an appellate tribunal.[266]

(E) SIMILARITY BETWEEN HONEST COMMENT AND QUALIFIED PRIVILEGE

The honest comment defence resembles that of qualified privilege in that the defendant, in order to raise a prima facie defence, must establish certain facts. Furthermore, both defences fail if the defendant was 'actuated by malice' in publishing the statement.

(F) PROPOSED REFORM

The Government has noted perceived problems with the honest comment defence, such as its 'complexity', technical nature, and the resultant uncertainty that arises in its application.[267] In its Draft Defamation Bill 2011, it proposes putting the defence on a statutory footing and renaming it 'honest opinion'. The relevant provisions are as follows:

4. Honest opinion

(1) It is a defence to an action for defamation for the defendant to show that Conditions 1, 2 and 3 are met.

---

[263] *Lyon and Lyon v Daily Telegraph Ltd* [1943] KB 746.

[264] In *Gros v Crook* (1969) 113 Sol Jo 408 the court held that it would not have found D liable for the writer's malice had he not been vicariously liable. To the same effect, see *Egger v Viscount Chelmsford* [1965] 1 QB 248, at 265

[265] *South Hetton Coal Co v NE News Association* [1894] 1 QB 133, at 141.

[266] *Turner v Metro-Goldwyn-Mayer Pictures Ltd* [1950] 1 All ER 449, at 461.

[267] Ministry of Justice, *Draft Defamation Bill Consultation Paper* (CP3/11, 2011), 18 and 20.

(2) Condition 1 is that the statement complained of is a statement of opinion.[268]

(3) Condition 2 is that the opinion is on a matter of public interest.

(4) Condition 3 is that an honest person could have held the opinion on the basis of [either] –

    (a) a fact which existed at the time the statement complained of was published; [or]

    (b) a privileged statement which was published before the statement complained of.

(5) The defence is defeated if the claimant shows that the defendant did not hold the opinion.

(6) Subsection (5) does not apply in a case where the statement complained of was published by the defendant but made by another person ('the author'); and in such a case the defence is defeated if the claimant shows that the defendant knew or ought to have known that the author did not hold the opinion.

(7) The common law defence of fair comment is abolished and, accordingly, section 6 of the Defamation Act 1952 (fair comment) is repealed.

The intention is that it will be sufficient to prove any relevant fact or facts as the basis of the opinion; 'it will not be necessary for the defendant to prove the truth of every single allegation of fact set out in the statement complained of'.[269] It is also intended that, in condition 3, the law should retain 'the objective element that the opinion must be one which an honest person could have held'.[270]

SECTION 8   APOLOGY

The offer or the making of an apology is not a defence at common law, although it may be given in evidence in mitigation of damages. Under statute, however, it is a defence.

> In an action for a libel contained in any public newspaper or other periodical publication, it shall be competent to the defendant to plead that such libel was inserted in such newspaper or other periodical publication without actual malice, and without gross negligence, and that before the commencement of the action, or at the earliest opportunity afterwards, he inserted in such newspaper or other periodical publication a full apology for the said libel, or, if the newspaper or periodical publication ... should be ordinarily published at intervals exceeding one week, had offered to publish the said apology in any newspaper or periodical publication to be selected by the [claimant] in such action.[271]

This defence is hardly ever used[272] and we need only note two further things in relation to it. First, every such defence must be accompanied by a payment of money into

---

[268] That is, as the ordinary person would understand it: Explanatory Notes to the Draft Defamation Bill 2011, at [23].

[269] Ministry of Justice, *Draft Defamation Bill Consultation Paper* (CP3/11, 2011), 20–1.

[270] Ibid at 21–2.

[271] Libel Act 1843, s 2.   [272] For the reasons as to why this is so, see the 11th edition of this work.

court by way of amends.[273] Second, the issues of malice, gross negligence, and the adequacy of the apology are to be decided separately by the jury.

SECTION 9 REMEDIES

(A) DAMAGES

The main function of the tort of defamation is to compensate the claimant for his loss of reputation: that is, the extent to which he is held in less esteem and respect, and suffers loss of goodwill and association.[274] Damages for this loss of reputation are at large in respect of both libel and slander. The principles ordinarily applicable to damages at large[275] apply here equally. Accordingly, by way of parasitic damages, compensation may be given for insult or injury to feelings.[276] In addition, circumstances of aggravation and mitigation are important. And damages may be aggravated by such matters as the mode, circumstances, and extent of publication as well as the conduct of the defendant from publication to verdict.[277] By contrast, the defendant's belief in the truth of his statements,[278] the fairness of his reports,[279] and his being provoked by the claimant[280] may all serve to mitigate the damages awarded.

Where partial justification is proved, even though the defendant may be unable to prove sufficient facts to establish justification at common law (or bring himself within section 5 of the Defamation Act 1952), he may nonetheless be able to rely on the facts proved to reduce the damages.[281] Indeed, in an exceptional case, he may do so to reduce the damages almost to vanishing point.[282] Persistence in an unsubstantiated plea of justification, however, will lead to a higher award of damages.

Exemplary damages may also be awarded where the defendant calculated that the money to be made out of his wrongdoing would probably exceed the compensation payable for the defamation, and where he defamed the claimant either knowing his conduct to be illegal, or where he was reckless as to its illegality.[283] Where several claimants are libelled, the amount of exemplary damages may properly take into account

---

[273] Libel Act 1845, s 2.

[274] The best judicial survey is in the judgment of Devlin LJ in *Dingle v Associated Newspapers Ltd* [1961] 2 QB 162.   [275] See ch 26.

[276] *Goslin v Corry* (1844) 7 Man & G 342; *Ley v Hamilton* (1935) 153 LT 384, at 386. Are damages recoverable for injuries to C's feelings caused by publishing the libel to him? See *Hayward v Thompson* [1982] QB 47.

[277] *Praed v Graham* (1889) 24 QBD 53.

[278] *Bryce v Rusden* (1886) 2 TLR 435; *Forsdike v Stone* (1868) LR 3 CP 607 (bona fide mistake of identity).

[279] *Smith v Scott* (1847) 2 Car & Kir 580; *East v Chapman* (1827) Mood & M 46.

[280] *Moore v Oastler* (1836) 1 Mood & R 451n.

[281] See, eg, *Burstein v Times Newspapers Ltd* [2001] 1 WLR 579. Note, however, that to introduce such evidence, it must be so clearly relevant to the subject matter of the libel or C's character as to produce an obvious risk of the jury assessing damages on a false basis: *Turner v News Group Newspapers* [2006] EWCA Civ 540.

[282] *Pamplin v Express Newspapers Ltd (No 2)* [1988] 1 All ER 282.

[283] *Cassell & Co Ltd v Broome* [1972] AC 1027.

the fact that the defendant has libelled more than one person; but the total should not exceed that representing a proper sum by way of punishment of the defendant.[284]

At one time, it was feared that damages awards were becoming excessive. The turning point came in *Sutcliffe v Pressdram Ltd*[285] when the Court of Appeal set aside a £600,000 award warning that, in assessing any element of aggravated damages, misconduct by the defendant is relevant only in so far as it increases the injury to the claimant. The jury's own indignation at that conduct was irrelevant in assessing a proper quantum of compensatory damages. Importantly, section 8 of the Courts and Legal Services Act 1990 empowers the Court of Appeal to substitute 'such sum as appears to be proper' for the award of a jury where that award is quashed as excessive.[286] In relation to the meaning of 'excessive', the Court of Appeal has held the test to be whether a reasonable jury would have thought the award proposed was necessary to compensate the claimant and re-establish his reputation.[287] Finally, even beyond section 8 of the 1990 Act, it was held in *John v MGN Ltd*[288] that damages might permissibly be controlled in two further ways. First, by the court drawing the jury's attention to the levels of awards made in personal injuries cases (while recognising that no direct analogy can be drawn because of the different nature of the 'injury' involved) and, second, by allowing the court and counsel to mention to the jury what they consider to be an appropriate award and its appropriate bracket. This last development helps particularly to curtail the huge awards made by juries in the past.

Occasionally the claimant's loss of reputation will cause him a knock-on pecuniary loss – for example, loss of business. That loss is recoverable as special damage and is awarded in addition to general damages so long as the loss can be shown with sufficient precision.[289] On the other hand, evidence of the bad reputation of the claimant will be a ground for mitigating the level of damages, since a reputation already largely lost is necessarily of less value. The rules governing evidence of reputation are complex and, in practice, a trial often becomes little more than a tactical battle over this issue. The governing principle is that general evidence alone is permitted (and then, only after prior notice and particulars have been given). Evidence of specific facts in order to demonstrate the disposition of the claimant is not currently admissible.[290] The court is concerned with the esteem in which the claimant is in fact held – with his established reputation, in other words.[291] It is not concerned with his actual character, or with the reputation that he may deserve. Thus, where, on a privileged occasion, a newspaper published extracts from a parliamentary report, and then embellished this

---

[284] *Riches v News Group Newspapers Ltd* [1986] QB 256.   [285] [1991] 1 QB 153.

[286] In *Rantzen v Mirror Group Newspapers (1986) Ltd* [1993] 4 All ER 975, the Court of Appeal made use of this section and reduced a jury award of £250,000 to one of £110,000. Cf *Kiam v Mirror Group Newspapers* [2002] 2 All ER 219.   [287] *Rantzen v Mirror Group Newspapers Ltd* [1993] 4 All ER 975.

[288] [1997] QB 586.

[289] See, eg, *Collins Stewart Ltd v Financial Times Ltd* [2005] EMLR 5.

[290] *Scott v Sampson* (1882) 8 QBD 491; *Turner v News Group Newspapers Ltd* [2006] EWCA Civ 540.

[291] *Plato Films Ltd v Speidel* [1961] AC 1090 (approving *Scott v Sampson* (1882) 8 QBD 491 and *Hobbs v C T Tinling & Co Ltd* [1929] 2 KB 1).

report with details not found in the report, it could not reduce its damages by asserting that the claimant's reputation was already tarnished by the privileged publication of the parliamentary report.[292] Where the defendant has persisted in a plea of justification, it is the claimant's reputation at the time of the trial which counts in assessing damage to reputation.[293] The ordinary rules of evidence apply. Thus, if the claimant gives evidence, he may be cross-examined as to credit, although evidence to rebut his answers is forbidden. The jury should be directed to disregard this cross-examination when fixing damages.[294]

In the case of slanders not actionable per se, actual damage must be proved. It is doubtful, therefore, whether any other damages than those for actual damage are recoverable for such slanders.[295] If this is correct, the rules in relation to aggravated and exemplary damages do not apply.

(B) INJUNCTIONS

Claimants in defamation actions often seek interlocutory injunctions as soon as they have served the writ so as to prevent further publication. The courts, concerned not to interfere unduly with press freedom, normally do not grant such injunctions when the case is contested and the claimant is unable to show that a defence of justification, honest comment, or privilege is likely to fail at the eventual trial.[296] Section 12(3) of the Human Rights Act is also relevant in this context, for it provides that no injunctive relief may be granted to restrain a publication 'unless the court is satisfied that the applicant is likely to establish [at trial] that publication should not be allowed'. In *Cream Holdings v Banerjee*,[297] the House of Lords arguably watered down a prior Court of Appeal decision in which it had been stressed that section 12(3) had been specifically inserted into the 1998 Act in order to protect freedom of expression.[298] Their Lordships stated that for the purposes of section 12(3), 'likely' meant merely 'more probably than not'.

A somewhat specious case that is worth noting in this context involved the Attorney-General seeking an injunction to prevent further publication of an alleged contempt;

---

[292] *Associated Newspapers Ltd v Dingle* [1964] AC 371.
[293] *Cornwell v Myskow* [1987] 2 All ER 504.   [294] *Hobbs v C T Tinling & Co Ltd* [1929] 2 KB 1.
[295] There is an *obiter dictum* of Williams J in *Brown v Smith* (1853) 13 CB 596 to the effect that no other damages are available. In *Dixon v Smith* (1860) 5 H & N 450, C, a doctor, claimed a guinea, being the loss of a particular patient in consequence of the slander, together with damages for general decline in business, and deterioration of goodwill. After denying, on the grounds of remoteness, such general damages resulting from repetition of the slander, the court held the damages not to be limited to the guinea. Whether the further damages were at large, or for some non-remote business loss besides loss of the patient, is not clear, but an observation by Martin B (at 452), supports the latter interpretation.
[296] *Bonnard v Perryman* [1891] 2 Ch 269. For illustrations see *Crest Homes Ltd v Ascott* [1980] FSR 396; *Harakas v Baltic Mercantile and Shipping Exchange Ltd* [1982] 2 All ER 701.   [297] [2004] 3 WLR 918.
[298] *Greene v Associated Newspapers Ltd* [2005] 3 WLR 281.

it was said that the interest in the protection of justice (as perceived by the Attorney-General) prevailed over the interest in free speech.[299]

Finally, according to the Court of Appeal in *British Data Management plc v Boxer Commercial Removals plc*,[300] if publication of a libel is threatened but has not yet occurred, a *quia timet* injunction may be awarded if the claimant is able to set out with reasonable certainty the gist of the libel.[301] And the courts will also readily grant injunctions to successful claimants if further publication of the offending statement is likely.[302]

FURTHER READING

DESCHEEMAEKER, '"Veritas non est defamatio?" Truth as a defence in the law of defamation' (2011) 31 *Legal Studies* 1

LOVELAND, 'A New Legal Landscape? Libel Law and Freedom of Political Expression in the UK' [2000] *European Human Rights Law Review* 476

SHARLAND AND LOVELAND, 'The Defamation Act 1996 and Political Libels' [1997] *Public Law* 113

WILLIAMS, 'Defaming Politicians: The Not So Common Law' (2000) 63 *Modern Law Review* 748

YOUNG, 'Fact, Opinion and the Human Rights Act 1998' (2000) 20 *Oxford Journal of Legal Studies* 89

---

[299] *A-G v News Group Newspapers Ltd* [1986] 2 All ER 833 (the rule in *Bonnard v Perryman* [1891] 2 Ch 269 does not apply to an action for conspiracy).   [300] [1996] 3 All ER 707.

[301] Note that C need not prove verbatim the wording of the threatened libel.

[302] *Monson v Tussauds Ltd* [1894] 1 QB 671.

PART VII

MISUSE OF PRIVATE INFORMATION

22

MISUSE OF PRIVATE INFORMATION

KEY ISSUES

(1) Origins of the action

The tort of misuse of private information has its origins in the equitable wrong of breach of confidence. Yet the action has developed in several ways in recent years that represent significant departures from those equitable origins. For instance, the person disclosing the information may be liable without ever having been confided in by the victim. Nor is the modern action governed by the traditional maxims of equity. We therefore think that it is best to treat the action as it now stands as a new tort concerned specifically with the wrongful use or disclosure of private information.

(2) Gist and elements of the tort

An action will lie where X unjustifiably discloses to others private information concerning Y. From this description of the tort's gist it will be gathered that its key elements are that (i) the information concerned should be capable of being considered 'private' and (ii) the disclosure of that information should be unjustified. Both the matter of what constitutes private information and the question of what amounts to an unjustifiable disclosure are dealt with in this chapter.

(3) Human rights considerations

An important backdrop to the operation of this tort is the European Convention on Human Rights. Certainly, the case law to date reveals a strong influence being exerted by both the Article 8 right to respect for privacy and the often conflicting Article 10 right to freedom of expression.

(4) Defences

Beyond the role played by public interest in judging whether a disclosure was justified, two defences of potential significance are (i) consent to the disclosure and (ii) the fact that private information (barring photographic information, which is treated differently) is already in the public domain.

SECTION 1   INTRODUCTION

Whereas the wrongful invasion of privacy has for some time been recognised as the basis for an action in tort in the United States[1] and New Zealand,[2] there is as yet no comparable tort under English common law. Indeed, in *Wainwright v Home Office*, Lord Hoffmann saw great danger in the courts attempting to fashion a tort based on the unjustified invasion of privacy. He much preferred the idea that this should be a job for Parliament rather than the courts, not least because of the patent need for any such tort to carry with it a carefully thought-through menu of exceptions and defences.[3]

On the other hand, this does not mean that English common law more generally fails to recognise the interest we all have in our privacy being protected from wrongful invasions. For a start, Article 8 of the European Convention on Human Rights – now imported into English law by virtue of the Human Rights Act 1998 – imposes the obligation on all public authorities (including the police, immigration authorities, etc) to grant positive respect to our private lives. But equally, because the courts are public authorities for these purposes, coupled with the fact that they are required to develop the common law consistently with the rights embodied in the Convention,[4] it seems apparent that the Convention is likely to enjoy a measure of horizontal effect in this context. One basis for this contention is the fact that the European Court of Human Rights has intimated that Article 8 does more than merely impose a negative obligation on the state and public bodies (*not to interfere with* citizens' privacy). It also 'may involve the adoption of [positive] measures designed to secure respect for private life even in the sphere of the relations of individuals between themselves'.[5]

But even beyond the application of the Human Rights Act 1998, there are several extant torts that provide some, albeit specious, protection to our interest in privacy. For example, the law of private nuisance is helpful inasmuch as it confers a cause of action in relation to substantial and unreasonable interferences with the use or enjoyment of land. Equally, the tort of trespass to land offers protection against physical intrusions; while the law of defamation seeks to guard our reputations against the publication of harmful untruths. Most significantly, however – at least in common-law terms – has been the rapid evolution of the protection of privacy out of the longstanding equitable obligation to respect confidences. Indeed, as one judge explained:

> [i]n the great majority of situations where the protection of privacy was justified, an action for breach of confidence would provide the necessary protection... A duty of confidence would arise whenever the party subject to the duty was in a situation where he either knew

---

[1] Second Restatement of Torts at §§ 652A–652I (1977).   [2] *Hosking v Runting* [2004] NZCA 34.

[3] [2003] 3 WLR 1137, at [31]–[33].

[4] Human Rights Act 1998, ss 2 and 6.

[5] *Von Hannover v Germany* (2005) 40 EHRR 1, at [57]. On the other hand, the Convention right could not be construed so as to impose on newspapers a duty to inform people in advance when the newspaper editors propose to publish information which concerns them: *Mosley v UK* (2011) *Times*, May 11.

or ought to know that the other party could reasonably expect his privacy to be protected. The range of situations in which protection can be provided is therefore extensive.[6]

Thus, at the turn of the Millennium, the prevailing view was still that any general protection of privacy was 'grounded... in the *equitable doctrine* of breach of confidence'.[7] Indeed, it took another half a decade before a senior member of the English judiciary was prepared to offer a firm indication that a new *tort* based on the misuse of private information had emerged. In *Campbell v MGN*,[8] cognisant of Commonwealth authority,[9] Lord Nicholls noted that the relevant cause of action had 'shaken off the limiting constraint of the need for an initial confidential relationship' before suggesting that '*the tort* is better encapsulated now as a misuse of private information'.[10] Although his Lordship was the only member of the House of Lords to describe the action in terms of a tort in that case, there are now such profound differences between the action for misuse of private information and the action for breach of confidence that it seems perfectly right that he should have seen the action in this way.[11] We shall take it, then, that a new tort – albeit one falling short of the general protection of privacy – was created in *Campbell v MGN*, the facts of which case were as follows.

> C, a famous model, claimed damages from D, a newspaper group, in respect of an alleged breach of confidence and an infringement of her privacy rights under the Human Rights Act 1998. D had published (1) stories about C attending Narcotics Anonymous, (2) details of her treatment for drug addiction, and (3) a photograph of her at a place where Narcotics Anonymous held meetings. C was prepared to concede that the *Daily Mirror* was entitled to publish the fact that she was a drug addict and that she was in need of treatment, but she alleged that publication of the details of her treatment together with the photograph were a step too far and that this amounted to a wrongful publication by the newspaper of private information.

Recognising fully the need to balance the newspaper group's right to freedom of expression against Ms Campbell's right to respect for privacy, the House of Lords held by a bare majority that publication of Ms Campbell's treatment details along with the photograph suggesting her attendance at a Narcotics Anonymous meeting was a step too far. These details were more than was necessary to put the record straight (bearing in mind that Ms Campbell had previously lied in public, denying her drug addiction). That being so, her claim not to have private information concerning her misused in this way succeeded. However, as has already been observed, the most remarkable feature of the case was the way in which the action was viewed: namely, as an action

---

[6] *A v B plc (a company)* [2002] EMLR 371, at 382.
[7] *Douglas v Hello! Ltd (No 1)* [2001] QB 967, at 1001 (emphasis added).   [8] [2004] 2 AC 457.
[9] *Hosking v Runting* [2004] NZCA 34. In that case, the New Zealand Court of Appeal identified two heads of liability: one, in equity, protecting confidentiality; the other, in tort, protecting wrongful publicity about private lives.   [10] [2004] 2 AC 457, at [14] (emphasis added).
[11] Apart from the absence of any need to impart the information in circumstances attracting confidentiality, another salient difference is the absence of any need to apply the traditional equitable maxims.

based on the misuse of private information. Moreover, several more recent cases seem to have endorsed this understanding of the common law.[12]

SECTION 2   ELEMENTS OF THE TORT

(A) GENERAL OBSERVATIONS

In the immediate wake of *Campbell*, it seemed to have been confirmed that the misuse of private information of a *personal* kind could ground an action for damages. Some three years later, the House of Lords had occasion to consider whether commercially exploitable private information – in the form of photographs taken at a celebrity wedding – would attract the same protection.[13] In that case, their Lordships held that such commercially valuable private information, at least in the hands of a publisher, was to be regarded as falling within the existing law on breach of confidence.[14] That being so, commercially exploitable information must be distinguished from purely private information with no intrinsic commercial value. Lord Hoffmann put it this way: '[t]he information in this case was capable of being protected, not because it concerned the ... private life [of Michael Douglas and Catherine Zeta-Jones], but simply because it was information of commercial value over which the Douglases had sufficient control to enable them to impose an obligation of confidence'.[15]

To some extent, the decision in this case may be seen as a retrograde one in that it stymies the development of the new tort of misuse of private information. It also represents a significant departure from the orthodox approach to the equitable obligation to maintain a confidence in that it involved 'information' acquired by the publisher from a third party, rather than information provided by the Douglases in confidence. Nonetheless, the fact remains that the case was dealt with on the basis of the equitable action, and for this reason it must be seen as running parallel to the new tort where information of intrinsic commercial value is concerned.

(B) PRIVATE INFORMATION AND 'REASONABLE EXPECTATION'

(1) General principles

Not all personal information attracts the protection of the emerging tort. This is because, as the *Campbell* case insists, the claimant must also be able to show that he held a reasonable expectation that the information in question would be kept private.[16] This of course begs the question of what factors will be taken to generate the requisite 'reasonable expectation' of privacy. And while there is currently no clear-cut answer

---

[12] See, eg, *JIH v NGM Ltd* [2011] EMLR 9, at [55]; *Thornton v TMG Ltd* [2010] EWHC 1414, at [36]; *Murray v Express Newspapers* [2008] 3 WLR 1360, at [27].   [13] *Douglas v Hello! Ltd (No 3)* [2008] 1 AC 1.

[14] Ibid at [113]–[119].

[15] Ibid at [124].   [16] *Campbell v MGN* [2004] 2 AC 457, at [21] and [85], and [134].

to this, it is at least apparent that a claimant will not be able to rely upon his peculiar susceptibility to embarrassment to transform an ordinarily innocuous disclosure into an actionable one. As Lord Hope explained in the *Campbell* case, '[t]he law of privacy is not intended for the unduly sensitive'.[17] But this only takes us so far. It does not resolve the way in which the phrase 'reasonable expectation' should be understood. It could, for example, be taken to mean the equivalent of a rational, actual expectation; or it could be taken to connote a legitimate (but not necessarily actual) expectation. So if, for example, certain salacious facts concerning X, a famous pop star, were to come to the attention of a well-known, sensationalist tabloid newspaper, X could hardly be thinking rationally if he genuinely expected that the newspaper would withhold those facts from the public when their publication would undoubtedly generate higher sales. Yet at the same time, he might well have a legitimate expectation that those facts would be kept secret.

According to the various speeches in the *Campbell* case, it would seem that the second interpretation is nearer the mark. What concerned Baroness Hale was that misuse of private information could amount to an infringement of 'the individual's informational autonomy', while Lord Hoffmann stressed the 'protection of human autonomy and dignity'.[18] The lowest common denominator here would seem to be the right to control the dissemination of private information (since this is an aspect of both human autonomy and informational autonomy). But this does not mean that the two categories are coextensive. Indeed, only information that has the capacity to embarrass or cause a decline in one's public standing would seem to fit the thinking of Lord Hoffmann. So, while details of a pop star's drug addiction would fit both tests, publication of his or her mobile telephone number would have no obvious impact on his or her human dignity or social standing. Even so, a publication of the latter kind would almost certainly fall within the category of information the publication of which the pop star would reasonably expect to be able to control.

Since their Lordships were wary of creating a general tort centring on the protection of privacy, it would seem more sensible to adopt the narrower test based on 'human autonomy and dignity' in order to explain the case. Such a test commands broader support from the various speeches in the *Campbell* case which, taken together, in general viewed the action as being centred upon personal information bearing the capacity to cause embarrassment or offence.[19] It also reconciles *Campbell* with the *Douglas* case where the House of Lords sought to maintain the viability of the equitable action for breach of confidence in relation to commercially exploitable information.

---

[17] [2004] 2 AC 457, at 94.

[18] *Campbell v MGN* [2004] 2 AC 457, at [51].

[19] Lord Hope favoured the adoption of a 'substantial offence' test like the one propounded by Gleeson CJ in the High Court of Australia in *Australian Broadcasting Corporation v Lenah Game Meats Pty Ltd* (2001) 208 CLR 199. Cf the doubts of Lord Nicholls in the *Campbell* case about this being 'suggestive of a stricter test of private information than a reasonable expectation of privacy' [2004] 2 AC 457, at [22].

So, to summarise, what appears to lie at the heart of the new tort is private informa-tion about which the claimant can reasonably form the expectation that secrecy ought to be maintained. This reasonable expectation is to be judged objectively (albeit a judg-ment about what the particular claimant might legitimately expect).[20] Thus, recalling the facts of *Campbell*, we can see that while certain disclosures – themselves capable of causing embarrassment – were justified in order to set the record straight, other disclosures, that were not so justified, gave rise to a successful action in tort. Equally, in *Theakston v MGN*,[21] it was thought acceptable to publish general written details of a celebrity's visit to a brothel, but also unnecessary to publish photographic evidence of the event.

For the present, then, it would seem that, on the strength of the present law, a wrongful disclosure of a good deal of private information will not fall within the *Campbell* principle. An individual's private financial information provides a good example. For while there may well be a desire to keep something such as the details of one's earnings or expenditure a secret, it is difficult to see how disclosures about these matters would have any impact on the claimant's autonomy or dignitary interests. On the other hand, a good case could probably be made for extending the new tort in this direction.

(2) Examples of information protected by the tort

As the tort is limited to the misuse of private information, it follows that misuse of public information cannot ground an action.[22] Also, drawing on the existing case law relating to breaches of confidentiality, we might also note that no protection will be afforded to information that is already public knowledge. But in so saying we should also bear in mind the principle according to which something should *not* be construed as being common knowledge just because all the relevant component parts of a par-ticular piece of information are already in the public domain. Thus, just because the public could find something out by putting A and B together in order to get C (when A and B are already common knowledge) does not mean that C cannot be regarded as protected information. If a member of the public has to go through the process of putting A and B together in order to possess the precise information constituting C, then C may well be regarded as private information.[23]

There is no set type (or types) of information in respect of which the claimant can assert a reasonable expectation of privacy. But the following three (non-exhaustive) kinds of information do warrant some discussion.

(a) Compromising and embarrassing photographs

Notwithstanding what has just been said about information already in the pub-lic domain, it is apparent that special rules apply to compromising or embarrassing

---

[20] *Murray v Express Newspapers* [2008] 3 WLR 1360, at [35].   [21] [2002] EMLR 137.
[22] *BBC v Harper Collins Publishers Ltd* [2011] EMLR 6.
[23] *Saltman Engineering Co v Campbell Engineering Co* (1948) 65 RPC 203.

photographs. This is because, as Baroness Hale put it in the *Campbell* case, '[a] picture is "worth a thousand words" because it adds to the impact of what the words convey'.[24] In other words, while it is one thing to report in words that X is a drug addict, it is quite another to publish a photograph of X in all his drug-addicted misery. Thus it was that the Court of Appeal in the *Douglas* case pointed out that '[i]n so far as a photograph does more than convey information and intrudes on privacy by enabling the viewer to focus on intimate personal detail, there will be a fresh intrusion of privacy when each additional viewer sees the photograph'.[25] That being so, although there was an agreement with *OK! Magazine* that various authorised photographs could be published, this did 'not, however, provide a defence to a claim ... [based on] the publication of unauthorised photographs'.[26] Furthermore, the fact that pictures are taken in a public place does not necessarily undermine their intrusiveness if published. If their taking and publication was unauthorised, and particularly if the photographs were taken covertly, an action will lie if 'the person publishing the information knows or ought to know that there is a reasonable expectation that the information in question will be kept confidential'.[27]

(b) Information about health and medical conditions

In just the same way that disclosures of medical information have generally been taken to be capable of grounding an action in equity based on breach of confidentiality, so too – as is apparent from the decision in *Campbell*[28] – may we take it that such information can also form the basis for an action under the new tort of misuse of private information. On the other hand, there would appear to be an important distinction between the two actions in this context. The tort only permits claims by those to whom the information relates personally. By contrast, it would appear possible for, say, a hospital which compiles and holds patients' medical records, to invoke the equitable action since it, too, has a vested interest in their confidentiality being maintained.[29]

(c) Sexual information

Unauthorised disclosure of private details concerning one's sexual relationships (or even sexuality)[30] should also generally ground the tort. However, as a caveat to this point, it might well be the case that such information will not always give rise to a reasonable expectation of privacy. If, for example, the claimant were a public figure whose honesty could be seen to turn on the disclosure of such factual information, then there may be a case for disclosing so much of the otherwise private information

---

[24] [2004] 2 AC 457, at [155].   [25] *Douglas v Hello! Ltd (No 6)* [2006] QB 125, at [105].

[26] Ibid at [107].

[27] *Campbell v MGN* [2004] 2 AC 457, at [134]. See also *Peck v UK* [2003] EMLR 15 where an attempted suicide was captured on CCTV and the European Court of Human Rights held that it was a breach of Art 8 of the European Convention to disclose that footage to newspapers and broadcasters.

[28] See also *Z v Finland* (1997) 25 EHRR 371.

[29] See *Ashworth Security Hospital v MGN* [2001] FSR 559.

[30] See, eg, *Dudgeon v UK* (1981) 4 EHRR 149.

as is necessary in the public interest to confirm or refute the allegations about that person's honesty. So, as Lord Woolf CJ put it in one case: 'where a public figure chooses to make untrue pronouncements about his or her life, the press will normally be entitled to put the record straight'.[31]

If the sexual conduct of the claimant is criminal in nature, this too would apparently justify disclosure.[32]

(C) UNJUSTIFIED DISCLOSURES

An important limit on the availability of this tort made clear by the *Campbell* case is that disclosure, in order to be actionable, must have been unjustified. But so saying merely begs the question of what amounts to an 'unjustified disclosure', and necessarily involves balancing two competing human rights – viz, the right to respect for our private lives and the right to freedom of expression – neither of which is absolute. But before considering the way in which this balancing exercise is to be undertaken, it is necessary to point out the crucial distinction between, on the one hand, misusing private information by *unjustifiably disclosing* it, and, on the other, simply invading our privacy (for example, by observing us through a powerful zoom lens on a camera).[33] Only the former is capable of generating tortious liability on the basis of what Lord Nicholls said in *Campbell*.[34]

As regards the human rights dimension, it has been recognised for some time that there are important limits to both the Article 8 and Article 10 rights. As regards the latter, the then President of the Family Division in *Venables v News Group Newspapers Ltd*[35] held that the right to freedom of expression in Article 10(1) was a strong one that could only be overridden in accordance with the exceptions set out in Article 10(2). Furthermore, her Ladyship insisted that these exceptions – that is, that any restriction on free expression must be in accordance with the law, necessary in a democratic society and, in every case, proportionate to the legitimate aim pursued – were to be construed narrowly and that the burden of showing an Article 10(2) exception lies firmly with the party seeking to restrain publication of potentially injurious information. On the other hand, in *Campbell*, Baroness Hale identified that there were different classes of speech, each of which warranted different levels of protection. Thus, while she clearly saw political free speech as central to a democratic society, she also

---

[31] *A v B* [2003] QB 195, at [43]. This does not mean, however, that public figures have *no* right to privacy. If their honesty is not in question, there is no reason why matters completely unrelated to their public lives should not attract protection: *X v Persons Unknown* [2007] EMLR 10.

[32] *LNS v Persons Unknown* [2010] EWHC 119.

[33] In the case itself, two Law Lords drew a similar distinction between the simple spying through such a lens with the (probably tortious) publication of a photograph taken in such a fashion: see *Campbell v MGN* [2004] 2 AC 457, at [76] and [121]–[123].

[34] But note that if the invasion is deliberately undertaken by a public authority – say, in the form of unjustified state surveillance of an individual – then there can nonetheless be direct liability under s 7 of the Human Rights Act 1998 for breach of Art 8: see, eg, *Halford v UK* (1997) 24 EHRR 523; *Wainwright v Home Office* [2003] 3 WLR 1137.   [35] [2001] 2 WLR 1038.

indicated that mere gossip serving no political, educational, or artistic purpose would be more difficult to justify (even though it may help to sell certain publications) if it were to impact negatively on another's privacy interest.[36] Equally, she envisaged a general freedom to discuss the private lives of 'public figures, especially those in elective office' since this otherwise private information might well be 'relevant to their participation in public life'.[37]

In essence, what her Ladyship was describing was a 'public interest' justification for the disclosure of otherwise private information. (A justification analogous to the long-recognised equivalent in the context of the equitable action for breach of confidence.)[38] Indeed, recent cases amply demonstrate the firm toehold this justification has acquired in the context of the misuse of private information.[39] Thus, we can now say with some confidence that, in order to justify disclosure, the information must of its very nature be of a kind that ought to be disclosed.[40] So, for example, the expression of legitimate doubt about the safety of criminal convictions may well be taken to be a matter of public interest.

> In *Lion Laboratories Ltd v Evans*,[41] Cs sought to prevent publication of internal memoranda leaked by employees to the press. The memoranda cast doubt on the reliability of the intoximeter manufactured by Cs and used by the police to test alcohol levels in drivers. The Court of Appeal refused to grant an injunction. The public interest in the reliability of the product which could, if unreliable, result in unfair prosecutions outweighed any private rights of Cs. Disclosure of this information to the proper authorities was therefore justified.

On the other hand, it has been made clear that the release of private information that satisfies the mere prurient interest of members of the public will not qualify as being in the public interest. Thus, as Eady J has put it: 'it is not for the state or for the media to expose sexual conduct which does not involve any significant breach of the criminal law'.[42] That said, if the defendant truly believed that disclosure of the information was in accordance with a genuine public interest, that might well be enough.[43] And where the conduct about which a revelation is made is criminal in nature, the disclosure will, seemingly, fall within the public interest.[44]

Beyond noting these points, it is difficult to provide any much clearer guidance on what will and will not satisfy the public interest test so as to justify the disclosure of

---

[36] *Campbell v MGN* [2004] 2 AC 457, at [148].

[37] Ibid. Others in respect of whom there is apparently an equivalent public interest include clergymen, headmasters, and senior civil servants (*McKennit v Ash* [2008] QB 73) as well as high-profile bankers at a time of banking crisis (*Goodwin v NGN Ltd* [2011] EWHC 1437).

[38] See, eg, *A-G v Jonathan Cape Ltd* [1976] QB 752 (Crossman diaries) and *A-G v Guardian Newspapers* [1987] 3 All ER 316 (*Spycatcher* affair).

[39] See, eg, *Goodwin v NGN Ltd* [2011] EWHC 1437; *JIH v NGN Ltd* [2011] EMLR 15; *Mosley v NGN Ltd* [2008] EMLR 20.   [40] *Cambridge Nutrition Ltd v BBC* [1990] 3 All ER 523.

[41] [1985] QB 526.   [42] *Mosley v NGN Ltd* [2008] EMLR 20, at [127].

[43] *LNS v Persons Unknown* [2010] EWHC 119, at [96]. See also *Mosley v NGN Ltd* [2008] EMLR 20, at [135].   [44] Ibid.

private information. The degree of public interest that exists, and the extent to which any given person can legitimately claim an expectation of privacy, is likely to vary from one case to another. Thus, in *Murray v Express Newspapers*, a case in which great weight was placed upon the fact that the information concerned a *child* of a famous person, Sir Anthony Clarke MR explained that the question of whether disclosure would be permissible required account to be taken of:

> all the circumstances of the case. They include the attributes of the claimant, the nature of the activity in which the claimant was engaged, the place at which it was happening, the nature and purpose of the intrusion, the absence of consent and whether it was known or could be inferred, the effect on the claimant and the circumstances in which and the purposes for which the information came into the hands of the publisher.

In so saying, his Lordship was clearly echoing the speeches of Lord Hope and Baroness Hale in *Campbell* that the courts ought to adopt a 'relative merits' approach whereby the respective benefits of protecting one right (privacy) rather than the other (freedom of expression) are compared and contrasted (given that one or other right must give way where the two come into conflict).[45]

SECTION 3   DEFENCES AND REMEDIES

It has already been mentioned in passing that a disclosure of private information in the public interest provides a justification for that disclosure. But there are, in terms of defences, several further points worthy of note. First, so far as the tort action is not constrained by the traditional maxims of equity, it seems to us unnecessary for the courts to continue to invoke the oft-quoted dictum that 'there is no equity in the disclosure of an iniquity'[46] in order to show justification for any given disclosure. Second, it will of course be a defence to show that the disclosure was made with the prior consent/authorisation of the claimant. Third, it will also be a defence to show that the information in issue was already in the public domain[47] (although care must be taken in deciding whether something was already in the public domain).[48] That said, as noted above, special rules apply to photographs even if what they convey is merely visual evidence of information already in the public domain.

As regards remedies, both injunctions[49] (prior to disclosure) and compensatory damages (after disclosure) will be available, although exemplary damages appear *not* to be available for this tort.[50] (In principle, however, it is hard to see why such damages

---

[45] *Campbell v MGN* [2004] 2 AC 457, at [105] and [141] respectively.

[46] *Gartside v Outram* (1857) 26 LJ Ch 113.   [47] *BBC v Harper Collins Publishers Ltd* [2011] EMLR 6.

[48] Eg, private information that has already been conveyed to a limited circle of acquaintances has been held *not to be* in the public domain: *HRH Prince of Wales v Associated Newspapers Ltd* [2008] Ch 57.

[49] The availability of a *contra mundum* injunction will be judged according to a balancing of the claimant's Art 8 privacy right and the defendant's Art 10 right to freedom of expression: see, eg, *OPQ v BJM* [2011] EWHC 1059.   [50] *Mosley v NGN Ltd* [2008] EMLR 20.

should not be available where the disclosure of information has made the defendant a profit that exceeds the compensatory sum payable to the claimant.)[51] Also, where X has obtained possession of certain private personal information concerning Y it will be possible to obtain an order for the return of the confidential documents.[52]

FURTHER READING

JONES, 'Restitution of Benefits Obtained in Breach of Another's Confidence' (1970) 80 *Law Quarterly Review* 463

PHILLIPSON, 'Transforming Breach of Confidence? Towards a Common Law Right of Privacy under the Human Rights Act' (2003) 66 *Modern Law Review* 726

---

[51] Such a case would seem to fall neatly within the second category of case for which exemplary damages may be sought according to *Rookes v Barnard* [1964] AC 1129. For details, see ch 26.
[52] See, eg, *Tchenguiz v Immerman* [2011] 2 WLR 592.

PART VIII

MISUSE OF PROCESS AND PUBLIC POWERS

23

MISUSE OF PROCESS AND PUBLIC POWERS

KEY ISSUES

(1) Three main torts
In this chapter, three principal causes of action are considered: malicious prosecution; abuse of process; and misfeasance in a public office. In each case a balance must be struck between the protection of individuals' interests and rights, on the one hand, and the efficient conduct of public administration and the administration of justice, on the other. To help ensure a proper balance is struck, the need to show malicious motives becomes an important touchstone of liability in the first and third causes of action (even though motive is generally an unimportant matter in tort law).

(2) Relative importance of the torts
Both the tort of malicious prosecution and that of misfeasance in a public office had, for a time, slipped into relative desuetude. But, since the latter part of the twentieth century, both seem to have enjoyed considerable resurgence. They are now not infrequently pursued (although they result in success much less often). By contrast, the facility to strike out cases as an abuse of process under the Civil Procedure Rules exerts a stultifying effect over the (now) more contentious action for abuse of process.

(3) Immunities, etc
In the context of malicious prosecution it is necessary to appreciate the limits that exist with respect to witness immunity. In particular it needs to be grasped that the mere fact that someone lies with a view to securing a criminal prosecution of the claimant cannot possibly result in liability for malicious prosecution *unless* an actual prosecution takes place. On the other hand, it may be possible in some circumstances to invoke an alternative basis of liability: namely, abuse of the legal process.

SECTION 1 INTRODUCTION

The motive with which an act is done does not in general make that act tortious. As we shall see in this chapter, there are certain limited exceptions to that general rule. The essence of the wrongful conduct in the following group of torts is the misuse of rights conferred on individuals for the public good. It is the abuse of those rights for private benefit or other improper ends that gives rise to tortious liability. The tort of malicious prosecution is long established and in recent years seems to have revived from the state of torpor which afflicted its development in the middle of the last century. At the same time, the evolution of the tort of misfeasance in a public office continues to expand the role of tort law in controlling the conduct of public officials.

SECTION 2   MALICIOUS PROSECUTION AND MALICIOUS INSTITUTION OF CIVIL PROCEEDINGS

The torts considered in this section are concerned with protecting the interest in freedom from unjustifiable litigation. Their function comes very close to that of defamation. However, the wrongful institution of proceedings may sometimes only cause pecuniary loss or loss of personal liberty without damaging reputation. A second prefatory point that ought to be made concerns the distinction between malicious prosecution and false imprisonment. In false imprisonment, the initial act is wrongful in itself: for example, where an arrest is made without proper adherence to the procedural requirements. By contrast, malicious prosecution presupposes that the proper procedural formalities have been carried out, and is instead concerned with the purposes for which they were used. However, a point of connection between the two torts is that, in both instances, the claimant has a prima facie right to trial by jury.[1]

Nor must the delicate balance of public interests involved in malicious prosecution be underestimated. On the one hand, there is the freedom that everyone should enjoy to engage the legal process in order to prosecute crime. While on the other, there is the need to discourage untruthful accusations made about innocent individuals.[2]

(A) ELEMENTS OF THE TORT

(1) Institution of wrongful proceedings

The rule is that the defendant must have been 'actively instrumental' in instigating the proceedings.[3] In *Martin v Watson*,[4] the House of Lords addressed just what that requirement involved. Their Lordships confirmed the ancient rule that if X merely gives information to a police officer[5] or a magistrate,[6] upon which the police officer or

---

[1] *Cropper v CC of South Yorkshire Police* [1990] 2 All ER 1005.
[2] *Martin v Watson* [1994] 2 All ER 606; *Gregory v Portsmouth CC* [2000] 1 AC 419.
[3] *Danby v Beardsley* (1880) 43 LT 603, at 604. In *Evans v London Hospital Medical College* [1981] 1 All ER 715, it was held that a hospital which provided pathology reports for the police did not institute proceedings.   [4] [1996] AC 74.
[5] *Danby v Beardsley* (1880) 43 LT 603. Nor will supplying information to police which is used to ground an arrest engage liability for false imprisonment: *Davidson v CC of North Wales* [1994] 2 All ER 597.
[6] *Cohen v Morgan* (1825) 6 Dow & Ry KB 8.

magistrate then *independently* decides to launch a prosecution, that does not render X a prosecutor for the purposes of this tort. The decision to prosecute rests with the public officials who determine that legal proceedings against the claimant should go ahead.[7] However, the deliberate provision of false information *may* need to be treated differently where the complainant is the sole person who has knowledge of the facts pertaining to the alleged offence. In *Martin v Watson*[8] the defendant had a history of ill-feeling towards the claimant. She deliberately set out to deceive police officers by making an entirely false allegation that the claimant had exposed himself to her. The House of Lords held her liable for malicious prosecution because the facts relating to the alleged offence were *necessarily* known only to her removing any possibility that the police had exercised any element of independent judgment in bringing the prosecution. It was thus appropriate to treat the defendant as having procured the subsequent prosecution.

Thus, a defendant who complains to the police or magistrates will be regarded as the 'prosecutor' if:

(1) he falsely and maliciously gave information to the police, making it clear that he is prepared to be a witness for the prosecution in circumstances where it can be inferred that he desires and intends that the claimant should be prosecuted;[9] and

(2) the facts of the alleged offence are such that they are exclusively within the defendant's knowledge, so that it is practically impossible for police officers to make any independent judgment about whether or not to proceed with the prosecution.[10]

That there must be an absence of independent judgment is vital. Thus, the point has been made that deliberate, false claims cannot amount to procuring a prosecution unless it can be shown that the information given effectively manipulated the authorities into a course of action that they would not otherwise have undertaken.[11] But what happens if the authorities act upon, and are influenced by, information stemming from a variety of sources, only one of which is the false information knowingly supplied by the defendant? In such a case, it will be much more difficult to sustain the argument that the malicious defendant was a 'prosecutor' in the sense that he or she procured the

---

[7] This is in direct contrast to circumstances where D initiates a private prosecution. However, note that there may be cases where a public prosecution is brought, but on the facts of the case, D has effectively required that the prosecution go ahead, formally accepting responsibility for the initiation of the relevant proceedings: see, eg, *Mohamed Amin v Jogendra Kumar Bannerjee* [1947] AC 322. [8] [1996] AC 74.

[9] Cf *Hunt v AB* [2009] EWCA Civ 1092 (where D had only given evidence under police pressure, thus clearly not intending or desiring that C be prosecuted).

[10] *Martin v Watson* [1995] 3 All ER 559, at 568. As to liability where D continues proceedings after learning of facts which negate the basis of the prosecution, see *Tims v John Lewis & Co Ltd* [1951] 2 KB 459 (reversed on another point [1952] AC 676). A lawyer who does more than advise his client in good faith may be deemed responsible for the prosecution: *Johnson v Emerson and Sparrow* (1871) LR 6 Exch 329.

[11] *Hunt v AB* [2009] EWCA Civ 1092, at [47] and [84].

prosecution.[12] That said, actions against the authorities founded on misfeasance in a public office cannot necessarily be ruled out in such circumstances.[13]

It is one thing to say that the defendant must have instituted wrongful proceedings, but it is less easy to specify which kind of proceedings count for these purposes. Certainly, where the claimant has been subjected to a criminal prosecution as a consequence of which he lost, or risked losing, his liberty and/or his reputation and/or the cost of defending the charge, a remedy in the tort of malicious prosecution will lie.[14] Less clear is whether maliciously instituting civil proceedings may incur liability.[15] In 1698 Holt CJ delivered a judgment in *Savile v Roberts* which suggested the possibility of so doing so long as the proceedings were intended to inflict one of the following:

> 1. ... [D]amage to a man's fame, as if the matter whereof he is accused be scandalous...
> 2. ... such [damages] as are done to the person; as where a man is put in danger to lose his life, or limb, or liberty... 3. Damage to a man's property, as where he is forced to expend his money in necessary charges, to acquit himself of the crime of which he is accused.[16]

Since then the courts have (at least *obiter*) resiled considerably from this judgment.[17] Nonetheless, it does seem that malicious proceedings in bankruptcy and winding up can ground liability in this tort so long as the defendant was the petitioning creditor.[18] The logic here is that the very institution of such civil proceedings may wreck the claimant's business, destroying confidence in his competence and integrity.

By contrast, in *Gregory v Portsmouth City Council*[19] the claimant sued the defendant for maliciously instituting disciplinary proceedings against him. He argued that the disciplinary process was analogous to the criminal process. The charges against him hurt his reputation and put him to expense in defending himself. Yet the House of Lords stated that there were no grounds to extend the scope of a tort of maliciously instituting proceedings beyond criminal prosecutions and exceptional cases such as bankruptcy and winding up.[20] Equally, in *Gizzonio v Chief Constable of Derbyshire*,[21] the Court of Appeal also rejected an attempt to construct a tort of malicious refusal of bail.

---

[12] *Mahon v Rahn (No 2)* [2000] 4 All ER 41 (D, a banker, supplied information about C, but there had also been an investigation by the Serious Fraud Office, therefore D was not liable).

[13] See *L v Reading BC* [2001] 1 WLR 1575.

[14] These three heads of loss were spelt out in *Manley v MPC* [2006] EWCA Civ 879.

[15] It has never been decided formally whether maliciously instituting civil proceedings can incur liability.   [16] (1698) 1 Ld Raym 374.

[17] See esp *Gregory v Portsmouth CC* [2000] 1 AC 419.   [18] *Tibbs v Islington LBC* [2003] BPIR 743.

[19] [2000] 1 AC 419.

[20] Their Lordships' reasoning is highly questionable since even civil proceedings may damage one's reputation, and the immunity granted to those supplying evidence would defeat any action founded on defamation, conspiracy, or malicious falsehood. That being so, C stands to suffer damage in respect of which no cause of action currently lies.

[21] (1998) *Times*, 29 April.

Notwithstanding the position with respect to maliciously instituting civil proceedings, an action will lie for maliciously procuring a warrant of arrest.[22] And, similarly, maliciously procuring a search warrant is an actionable wrong, although actions typically fail[23] because the damage to the claimant ensues not from the warrant being granted, but from its execution (in the form of entry into his premises, or the seizure of property). That said, the issue of a warrant may exceptionally constitute actionable harm.[24]

(2) Termination in favour of the claimant

In order to sue, the proceedings upon which the claim is based must have terminated in the claimant's favour.[25] Even though the claimant has been convicted of a lesser offence,[26] or has had his conviction quashed on appeal,[27] or has been acquitted on a technicality (for example, a defect in the indictment)[28] this requirement is satisfied. The same *may* be true where the claimant has escaped prosecution for offence X but the facts alleged in seeking to secure a prosecution for that offence are later passed on by the police to a local authority in order that it may obtain an anti-social behaviour order against the claimant.[29] If, however, the conviction of the claimant stands, there is no possibility of obtaining a remedy in this tort.[30]

As regards demonstrating a favourable termination of proceedings, the claimant seems to satisfy the test if he proves that the defendant has discontinued the proceedings[31] (but he cannot sue while the proceedings are still pending).[32]

(3) Absence of reasonable and probable cause

Malicious prosecution is treated with some caution by the courts, fearful of discouraging the enforcement of the law against suspected offenders and anxious to protect the interest in bringing litigation to a close.[33] This judicial attitude is reflected in the development of the requirement that there must be an absence of reasonable and probable cause on the part of the prosecutor. Thus, the claimant has the difficult task of proving a negative – a burden which he does not discharge merely by proving malice on the part of the defendant.[34] Furthermore, the court will not order the defendant to give particulars of the grounds on which he prosecuted.[35]

---

[22] *Roy v Prior* [1971] AC 470.

[23] See *Gibbs v Rea* [1998] AC 786, at 797; *Reynolds v MPC* [1985] QB 881.

[24] *Gibbs v Rea* [1998] AC 786.

[25] This requirement is not imposed where, eg, an arrest or search warrant is procured. But it was considered applicable in an action based on an attempt to construct a tort of malicious refusal of bail: *Gizzonio v CC of Derbyshire* (1998) *Times*, 29 April.   [26] *Boaler v Holder* (1887) 51 JP 277.

[27] *Reynolds v Kennedy* (1748) 1 Wils 232.   [28] *Wicks v Fentham* (1791) 4 Term Rep 247.

[29] *Daar v CC of Merseyside* [2005] EWCA Civ 1774.

[30] *Basébé v Matthews* (1867) LR 2 CP 684. Nor can C sue if he is merely bound over to keep the peace: *Everett v Ribbands* [1952] 2 QB 198.   [31] *Gilding v Eyre* (1861) 10 CBNS 592, at 604 (*obiter*).

[32] *Watkins v Lee* (1839) 5 M & W 270.

[33] See, eg, *Martin v Watson* [1994] 2 All ER 606 (reversed [1996] AC 74).

[34] *Johnstone v Sutton* (1786) 1 Term Rep 510.   [35] *Stapley v Annetts* [1969] 3 All ER 1541.

The House of Lords approved the following definition of reasonable and probable cause:

> an honest belief in the guilt of the accused based upon a full conviction, founded upon reasonable grounds, of the existence of a state of circumstances, which, assuming them to be true, would reasonably lead any ordinary prudent and cautious man, placed in the position of the accuser, to the conclusion that the person charged was probably guilty of the crime imputed.[36]

Since then it has further been held that, in order for the claimant to succeed on the issue of reasonable and probable cause, he must prove one or other of the following.[37]

(1) That the defendant did not believe that the claimant was probably guilty of the offence. Evidence should be given by the claimant of some fact or facts which, either inherently or coupled with other matters proved in evidence, would permit the inference that the defendant did not believe in the claimant's guilt.[38] Where there is powerful circumstantial evidence, the defendant's silence in the face of allegations made against him might afford some evidence of absence of reasonable and probable cause.[39] If such evidence is given, the question must be left to the jury whether it has been proved to their satisfaction that the defendant did not believe in the claimant's guilt. But, unless such evidence is given, it is not proper to put a question to the jury as to the defendant's belief.[40] The question put to the jury must be formulated precisely and should not refer to reasonable cause. It should be either: 'Did the defendant honestly believe in the claimant's guilt?' or 'Did the defendant honestly believe in the charges he was preferring?' It must not be: 'Did he honestly believe that there were reasonable grounds for the prosecution?', for that would cause the jury to reflect upon the whole issue of reasonable and probable cause.[41] Merely to prove that the defendant had before him information which might not have led a reasonable man to form an opinion that the claimant was guilty is not evidence that the defendant did not believe him to be guilty.[42] If this ground is relied on, the older cases suggest that the claimant must give some evidence from which an inference may be drawn as to what the defendant's belief actually was: it is not sufficient to give evidence from which a guess may be made as to what it was. Nor is it sufficient merely to supply evidence of reasons for non-belief. (Indeed, according to Canadian judicial thinking, it is perfectly possible for a public prosecutor to have serious personal doubts about the claimant's guilt yet *still* have reasonable and probable

---

[36] *Hicks v Faulkner* (1881) 8 QBD 167, at 171 (affirmed (1882) 46 LT 130); *Herniman v Smith* [1938] AC 305).   [37] *Glinski v McIver* [1962] AC 726; *Reynolds v MPC* [1985] QB 881.

[38] See, eg, *Clifford v CC of Hertfordshire* [2011] EWHC 815 (where an expert had advised the prosecutor in terms creating doubt about the soundness of a prosecution).

[39] *Gibbs v Rea* [1998] AC 786.

[40] *Herniman v Smith* [1938] AC 305, at 317; *Ward v CC of West Midlands Police* (1997) *Times*, 13 December.   [41] *Tempest v Snowden* [1952] 1 KB 130.

[42] See, eg, *Moulton v CC of the West Midlands* [2010] EWCA Civ 524.

cause to institute a charge against him if the evidence is strong but not entirely watertight.)[43] If such evidence is relied on, there must also be evidence that those reasons were in fact operative; but if silence affords some inference of absence of belief in cause, the heavy burden of proof on the claimant may now be somewhat eased.[44]

Or

(2) That a person of ordinary prudence and caution would not conclude, in the light of the facts in which he honestly believed, that the claimant was probably guilty. It is for the judge and not the jury to determine whether a person of ordinary prudence would have so concluded. It is for the judge alone to determine whether there is reasonable and probable cause.[45] The trouble experienced in splitting the functions of judge and jury in consequence of this rule accounts for most of the complexities of this tort. There is the ever-present danger that the questions addressed to the jury will be so general that the ultimate question left to the judge, of reasonable cause, is instead improperly decided by the jury. In conducting the trial the judge has two alternatives: he may direct the jury that, if they find certain facts, or arrive at certain answers to specific questions which he puts to them, there is reasonable and probable cause, leaving it to the jury to find a general verdict on this hypothetical direction; his alternative – and this is the better course – is to direct the jury to settle the facts in dispute, whereupon he decides, upon the whole case, whether there is reasonable and probable cause.[46]

It is impossible to enumerate all the factors which may be relevant in deciding whether there was reasonable and probable cause. However, particularly important points would be that the defendant acted in good faith on the advice of counsel[47] (although this would not be conclusive),[48] or on the advice of the police,[49] where the defendant, however honest his act, had taken reasonable care to inform himself of the facts,[50] and regardless of whether the defendant's mistake was one of fact or law.[51]

(4) Malice: improper purpose

The claimant must also prove malice on the part of the defendant.[52] In this context, this means that he must show 'any motive other than that of simply instituting a

---

[43] *Miazga v Kvello* [2009] 3 SCR 339.   [44] *Gibbs v Rea* [1998] AC 786.

[45] *Lister v Perryman* (1870) LR 4 521.

[46] *Abrath v NE Rly Co* (1883) 11 QBD 440, at 458 (affirmed (1886) 11 App Cas 247).

[47] *Ravenga v Mackintosh* (1824) 2 B & C 693. Cf *Bradshaw v Waterlow & Sons Ltd* [1915] 3 KB 527.

[48] *Abbott v Refuge Assurance Co Ltd* [1962] 1 QB 432.   [49] *Malz v Rosen* [1966] 2 All ER 10.

[50] *Abrath v NE Rly Co* (1833) 11 QBD 440, at 451.

[51] *Philips v Naylor* (1859) 4 H & N 565. In *Riches v DPP* [1973] 2 All ER 935, it was held that allegations of malice and want of reasonable cause in an action against the DPP stood no chance of success when the committing magistrate, the trial judge, and the jury all shared the same view of the evidence held by the DPP.

[52] *Brown v Hawkes* [1891] 2 QB 725. In *Wershof v MPC* [1978] 3 All ER 540, C proved absence of reasonable cause, but failed because he could not prove malice.

prosecution for the purpose of bringing a person to justice'.[53] The judge decides whether there is any prima facie evidence of malice, but it falls ultimately to the jury to decide whether there is in fact any malice in the case.[54] There was, for instance, evidence of malice where a defendant landlord made a charge in order to evict the claimant tenant from his house,[55] and where a defendant accused the claimant of exposing himself to her as part of a long-running vendetta between neighbours.[56] The question is not whether the defendant is angry or inspired by hatred,[57] but whether the defendant has a purpose other than bringing an offender to justice. There is malice, for instance, if the defendant uses the prosecution as a means of blackmail or any other form of coercion. Where the motives of the defendant are mixed, the claimant will fail unless he establishes that the dominant purpose is something other than the vindication of the law.[58] However, it is crucial to note that a claimant who proves malice, but fails to prove want of reasonable and probable cause, still fails.[59] Should a tenant, therefore, establish that his landlord has instituted proceedings against him for stealing the landlord's fixtures, with the object of determining his tenancy, the tenant's action in this tort will not succeed if he fails to prove absence of reasonable cause.[60]

(B) THE CROWN PROSECUTION SERVICE

As will be obvious, the vast majority of precedents establishing this tort predate the Prosecution of Offences Act 1985, although many cases have been decided since its enactment. Under the 1985 Act, the Crown Prosecution Service (CPS), headed by the Director of Public Prosecutions (DPP), took over responsibility for prosecutions initiated by the police. Yet several questions relating to the potential liability of the CPS and the police remain unanswered. Assume the claimant is originally charged and remanded in custody at the instigation of the police. Imagine further that the CPS reviews the evidence and decides to discontinue proceedings. The claimant cannot sue for false imprisonment in respect of the period when he was detained by judicial order. But he may sue under the present tort since discontinuance of the proceedings amounts to a termination of proceedings in his favour.[61] Yet if the CPS continues proceedings, thus endorsing the judgment of the police officers, proving absence of reasonable and probable cause will be a mammoth task.

The CPS and its officers enjoy no general immunity in tort, in particular against claims for malicious prosecution or misfeasance in a public office.[62] However, the CPS

---

[53] *Stevens v Midland Counties Rly Co* (1854) 10 Exch 352. [54] *Brown v Hawkes* [1891] 2 QB 718.
[55] *Turner v Ambler* (1847) 10 QB 252. [56] *Martin v Watson* [1995] 3 All ER 559.
[57] *Brown v Hawkes* [1891] 2 QB 718, at 722. [58] *Abbott v Refuge Assurance Co Ltd* [1962] 1 QB 432.
[59] *Silcott v MPC* (1996) 8 Admin LR 633. [60] *Turner v Ambler* (1847) 10 QB 252.
[61] *Watkins v Lee* (1839) 5 M & W 270.
[62] *Elguzouli-Daf v MPC* [1995] QB 335.

owes no *general*[63] duty of care in relation to the conduct of prosecutions. The Court of Appeal has held that such liability in negligence might have an 'inhibiting effect on the discharge by the CPS of its central function of prosecuting crime'.[64] Furthermore, the courts will be vigilant to ensure that any action in malicious prosecution brought against the CPS is not in reality a disguised claim for negligence. Incompetence is not to be equated with (or taken to be evidence of) malice.[65]

(C) DEFENCES

No questions on defences call for special comment other than that of whether it is a defence to establish that the claimant was guilty of the offence for which he was prosecuted. Obviously, in the rare case where a defendant had no reasonable cause and was malicious, and the proceedings terminated in the claimant's favour, and yet, at the trial for malicious prosecution the defendant is able to establish the guilt of the claimant, the claimant would recover at best a very small sum of damages. There is, indeed, some authority for the view that in such a case the action fails altogether.[66]

SECTION 3 ABUSE OF PROCESS

For the purposes of this tort, the leading case is *Grainger v Hill*.[67]

> D was liable when he had C arrested, ostensibly for non-payment of a debt, but in fact in order illegally to compel him to surrender the register of a vessel, without which C could not put to sea.

The case established that in this tort the claimant need not prove want of reasonable and probable cause; nor need the proceedings have terminated in his favour.[68] The claimant must show simply that the predominant purpose of the other party in using the legal process has been other than that for which it was designed.[69] Thus, a defendant who issued by mistake a plaint note for a debt which had already been paid was

[63] But where prosecutors undertook to provide information to magistrates, a duty of care was owed to C: *Welsh v CC of Merseyside Police* [1993] 1 All ER 692.

[64] *Elguzouli-Daf v MPC* [1995] QB 335.

[65] *Thacker v Crown Prosecution Service* (1997) *Times*, 29 December.

[66] *Heslop v Chapman* (1853) 23 LJQB 49, at 52. Cf *Shrosbery v Osmaston* (1877) 37 LT 792, at 794.

[67] (1838) 4 Bing NC 212; *Gibbs v Pike and Wells* (1842) 9 M & W 351 (maliciously registering a court order); *Speed Seal Products Ltd v Paddington* [1986] 1 All ER 91.

[68] *Speed Seal Products Ltd v Paddington* [1986] 1 All ER 91.

[69] *Metall und Rohstoff AG v Donaldson Lufkin & Jenrette Inc* [1989] 3 All ER 14, at 50; *Clissold v Cratchley* [1910] 2 KB 244.

held not liable.[70] By contrast with malicious prosecution, however, damage to fame, person, or property need not be proved. *Any* special damage suffices.[71]

On the other hand, in *Metall und Rohstoff AG v Donaldson Lufkin & Jenrette Inc,*[72] the Court of Appeal somewhat grudgingly recognised the existence of a tort of abuse of process in *Grainger v Hill*. It did however doubt the existence of a more general tort of maliciously instituting civil proceedings.

SECTION 4   IMMUNITIES

It is a fundamental principle of the common law that no one can be civilly liable for evidence given in court;[73] thus immunity in defamation exists for words uttered as a witness in court.[74] The same is true of false information given to the police which may be used to ground a prosecution.[75] Similarly, no action for conspiracy may be brought against policemen who conspire to defame the claimant at a criminal trial,[76] while a claim in respect of imprisonment caused by the defendant giving false evidence on oath at the claimant's trial is also barred:[77] perjury is a crime, not a tort. Finally, witness immunity extends beyond the actual presentation of evidence to cover also the preparation of evidence that will (or would) be given in court.

On the other hand, a distinction must be drawn between evidence that a witness gives (or has stated he would give) in court, and evidence that has been fabricated (such as a fabricated interview). The House of Lords has made clear that immunity does not extend to the latter.[78] It has also been held that in proceedings for malicious arrest, the claimant can rely on statements made by the defendant in court when seeking the warrant: the wrong is the arrest with malice, of which the statement in court provides evidential support.[79]

---

[70] *Corbett v Burge, Warren and Ridgley Ltd* (1932) 48 TLR 626.

[71] Eg, if a suit in deceit was instituted for the purpose of damaging C's credit. In *Smith v East Elloe RDC* [1956] AC 736, their Lordships held there to be jurisdiction to hear a claim that a clerk to a council knowingly and in bad faith wrongfully procured a compulsory purchase order to be made and confirmed by a minister, even though a statute precluded the courts from challenging the validity of the order itself on grounds of bad faith.

[72] [1989] 3 All ER 14.

[73] *Roy v Prior* [1971] AC 470.   [74] See ch 22.   [75] *Westcott v Westcott* [2009] 2 WLR 838.

[76] *Marrinan v Vibart* [1963] 1 QB 528.

[77] *Hargreaves v Bretherton* [1959] 1 QB 45, approved *obiter* in *Roy v Prior* [1971] AC 470, at 477. In *Evans v London Hospital Medical College* [1981] 1 All ER 715, it was held that this immunity extends to statements made before the issue of a writ or the institution of a prosecution, distinguishing *Saif Ali v Sydney Mitchell & Co* [1980] AC 198. But note *Palmer v Durnford Ford (a firm)* [1992] QB 483 restricting immunities of expert witnesses.   [78] *Darker v CC of West Midlands Police* [2001] 1 AC 435.

[79] *Roy v Prior* [1971] AC 470.

SECTION 5 MISFEASANCE IN A PUBLIC OFFICE[80]

A successful application for judicial review of administrative action which results in an administrative process being quashed as invalid or unlawful does not, of itself, create any liability for loss or damage suffered by the applicant.[81] The tort of misfeasance in a public office may, however, offer a remedy for the gross misuse of administrative powers.[82] Where an individual suffers loss or damage consequent upon egregious, improper administrative action which the relevant officer knows to be unlawful, that loss or damage is recoverable in tort.[83] The underlying rationale is that public power is conferred to be exercised only for the public good, and not for improper purposes.[84] Notwithstanding the fact that the tort allows the courts the opportunity to signal their disapproval of such abuses of public power, it is not actionable per se, and no damages will be available unless special damage is proved. In one case, then, the action failed because the claimant-prisoner failed to show consequential loss resulting from the non-privileged opening of his letters by prison officers.[85] On the other hand, where material damage, such as loss of liberty,[86] is proved the courts may be minded to signal their disapproval in strident terms, and exemplary damages may be awarded.[87]

In *Three Rivers District Council v Bank of England (No 3)*,[88] the House of Lords laid down the test for liability in the tort of misfeasance in a public office. According to their Lordships, liability arises in two situations. The first, malice-based version, is made out where a defendant, in bad faith, abuses his powers (or neglects his duties) as a public officer specifically intending to injure the claimant and the claimant suffers material harm.[89] By contrast, the second form of the tort exists where the defendant, in bad faith, acts knowingly beyond his powers (or inconsistently with his duties) and knows that in so acting he is likely to injure the claimant (or a class of people to which the claimant belongs), and the claimant suffers material harm.

The second version of the tort – to which reckless indifference is an integral part – was later considered in more detail in *Akenzua v Secretary of State for the Home*

---

[80] See Murphy (2011) 31 OJLS (forthcoming).

[81] *Dunlop v Woollahra MC* [1982] AC 158.   [82] *Jones v Swansea CC* [1990] 3 All ER 737.

[83] *David v Abdul Cader* [1963] 3 All ER 579; *Davis v Bromley Corpn* [1908] 1 KB 170.

[84] *Three Rivers DC v Bank of England (No 3)* [2000] 2 WLR 1220; *Jones v Swansea CC* [1990] 1 WLR 54.

[85] *Watkins v Secretary of State for the Home Department* [2006] 2 WLR 807 (misfeasance established, but no harm shown). Cf *Ashby v White* (1703) 2 Ld Raym 938 where there was an analogous wrong without harm – the denial of a right to vote – which was held to be actionable.

[86] See, eg, *Karagozlu v MPC* [2007] 1 WLR 1881.

[87] *Watkins v Secretary of State for the Home Department* [2006] 2 WLR 807; *Kuddus v CC of Leicestershire Constabulary* [2002] 2 AC 122.   [88] [2000] 2 WLR 1220.

[89] Arguably, on this version of the tort, if the public officer believes that his abuse of power is ultimately in the public interest, there is no bad faith present (and thus no liability).

Department.[90] There, the Court of Appeal had to consider whether the class of individuals to which the claimant belonged must be a particular, identifiable class of persons.

> X had been released from custody by the defendant in order to serve as a police informant. X later murdered a woman whose personal representatives subsequently brought an action for misfeasance in a public office based on the fact that a man who had a history of violence and violent proclivities had been recklessly released from custody.

The Court of Appeal – notwithstanding the way in which the test for the tort had been expressed in the *Three Rivers* case – held that there was no need to identify a particular class of persons. As Sedley LJ explained, the reference in *Three Rivers* to knowledge of a class of persons to which the claimant belonged was 'not a freestanding requirement of [this] tort'; instead, it was a requirement 'derived from the antecedent proposition that the intent or recklessness must relate…to the kind of harm suffered'.[91] In other words, demonstrating knowledge of a class was not an end in itself, it was simply *a* means of showing the more fundamental factor: namely, that the manner in which harm occurred was of kind foreseen by the defendant at the time of his act or omission. (The fact that a tort can be committed by *omission* was made clear in the *Three Rivers* case, though their Lordships emphasised that a conscious decision not to act would be required to meet the recklessness requirement.)

In either of its two forms, it is clear that misfeasance in a public office may be used to obtain a remedy where ordinary negligence principles would be of no avail for want of foreseeability and/or proximity for the purposes of establishing a duty of care.[92]

By definition, the tort can only be committed by those in a public office. But this, of course, begs the question of how widely the term 'public office' is to be interpreted. *Roncarelli v Duplessis*[93] provides a good example of the tort being applied to a politician. The *Three Rivers* case clearly shows its applicability to an institution such as the Bank of England. An action for misfeasance in a public office may also lie against a local authority,[94] a government department,[95] or potentially (on the strength of antipodean authority) even a judge.[96]

At one time, in order to relieve an employer of vicarious liability for an employee's tortious conduct, the unlawful conduct had to be beyond the authorised duties of the employee. It was thus extremely difficult to characterise acts of misfeasance in a public office as ones that would support a finding of vicarious liability.[97] Nowadays, however,

　[90]　[2003] 1 WLR 741.
　[91]　Ibid at [19].
　[92]　See further Chamberlain (2010) 88 Can Bar Rev 579.
　[93]　(1959) 16 DLR (2d) 689: C lost his liquor licence after D, the then Premier of Quebec, ordered the Quebec Licensing Commission to revoke the licence. D acted against C as part of his campaign against Jehovah's Witnesses. C recovered damages for this malicious abuse of the licensing process.
　[94]　*Jones v Swansea CC* [1990] 3 All ER 737 (where the action lies against a local council, C must show that the majority of those supporting the relevant resolution did so with intent to harm him).
　[95]　*Racz v Home Office* [1994] 2 WLR 23.
　[96]　*Rawlinson v Rice* [1998] 1 NZLR 454; *Cannon v Tahche* [2002] VR 317.
　[97]　See, eg, *Racz v Home Office* [1994] 2 WLR 23.

the broader-based, 'close connection' test for vicarious liability promulgated in *Lister v Hesley Hall Ltd*[98] is likely to make the imposition of vicarious liability somewhat easier. After all, that test has been used to catch the most flagrant acts of battery and sexual abuse.

Fabrication of evidence by police officers and malicious refusal of bail are further examples of possible misfeasance in a public office. But the usual rules on witness immunity apply to this tort;[99] and misfeasance in a public office cannot be used to circumvent the requirements in malicious prosecution of proof of absence of reasonable and probable cause.

FURTHER READING

MURPHY, 'Misfeasance in a Public Office: A Tort Law Misfit' (2011) 31 *Oxford Journal of Legal Studies* (forthcoming)
WELLS, 'The Abuse of Process' (1985) 102 *Law Quarterly Review* 9

---

[98] [2002] 1 AC 215.
[99] *Silcott v MPC* (1996) 8 Admin LR 633; *Gizzonio v CC of Derbyshire* (1998) *Times*, 29 April.

PART IX

PARTIES AND REMEDIES

24

VICARIOUS LIABILITY

KEY ISSUES

(1) Distinguishing employees and independent contractors

An employer will only be vicariously liable for the torts of his or her employees. No such liability may be imposed in relation to the torts committed by mere independent contractors. That being so, a fundamental issue in this context is whether the person causing loss or harm was an employee or an independent contractor. Various indicia of employment – such as 'control' and 'integration into the employer's organisation' – have been used over the years. But no single test for the existence of an employer-employee relationship is able to be applied universally.

(2) Agents

Vicarious liability can be imposed in some circumstances where the tort in question has been committed not by the principal, but by his agent. These circumstances, along with the special difficulties that can be encountered in relation to agents who commit the tort of deceit, are afforded brief consideration here.

(3) Employers' liability where independent contractors are engaged

Just because vicarious liability cannot be imposed on an employer for those torts committed by his independent contractors does not mean that an employer may never be held liable in tort in such circumstances. So, if the employer has ratified or authorised a contractor's tortious conduct, he may be liable. And if he himself has acted negligently (for example, by engaging incompetent staff), or acted in breach of a non-delegable duty of care, he may nonetheless by liable in tort as a primary wrongdoer.

(4) Non-delegable duties

Special consideration is given to an employer's liability on the basis of a breach of a non-delegable duty of care. Such duties are notably under-theorised, and the guidance provided is largely a survey of the leading cases. There is, however, also an attempt made to offer an account of what seem to be the key characteristics that link these cases.

(5) The course of employment and close connection tests

An employer will only be vicariously liable if the tortious act was *either* (i) authorised conduct on the part of an employee, done in the course of his employment *or* (ii) conduct that was sufficiently closely connected to his contract of employment that it is fair and just that the employer should be held responsible.

SECTION 1   INTRODUCTION

For present purposes, the law divides employed persons into two groups:

(1) Those employed to perform services in connection with the affairs of the employer and who are engaged on a *contract of service*. In tort, we call such persons 'employees'.

(2) Those who do work for another, but who are not controlled by that other in the performance of that work. Normally, such work will be carried out in pursuance of a *contract for services*. In tort law, such persons are referred to as 'independent contractors'.

The distinction between employees and independent contractors is fundamental. If an employee commits a tort in the course of his employment, or in the doing of something that has a sufficiently close connection to his employment, his employer will be vicariously liable for the tort regardless of whether he himself has committed a tort: 'every act which is done by a servant in the course of his duty is regarded as done by his master's orders, and consequently is the same as if it were the master's own act'.[1] Vicarious liability therefore provides one of the clearest examples of strict liability in tort.

Various justifications for the imposition of vicarious liability have been offered over the years. One such justification has been the fact that the employer will normally have much deeper pockets than the primary tortfeasor. For this reason, a claimant will usually be able to target a defendant worth suing (though this cannot be guaranteed).[2] Partly, this will be because the employer will carry insurance for such events and, partly because he will also often be in a position to pass on the cost of such insurance to the public in the form of increased prices for his product.

A second justification is that the prospect of vicarious liability may well encourage employers to maintain high standards of conduct in the running of their businesses, while a third goes like this: because the employer stands to make a profit from his employee working for him, it is only right that he should also bear the risk of potential liability arising from the work done.[3]

If the act complained of is not that of an employee, then the employer is not, without more, liable. If the person who causes injury or loss is not an employee, then the 'employer' cannot be held liable unless he himself has (1) acted in a way so as to be treated as a joint tortfeasor or (2) breached a non-delegable duty owed to the claimant.[4]

---

[1] *Bartonshill Coal Co v McGuire* (1858) 3 Macq 300, at 306.

[2] See, eg, *Merrett v Babb* [2001] 3 WLR 1 (the employer in this case had ceased to trade when the action was brought). Note, too, that where the employer is sued, he may later seek an indemnity from the employee under the Civil Liability (Contribution) Act 1978.

[3] For a decent account of these and other putative justifications for vicarious liability see Neyers (2005) Alberta L Rev 1.   [4] *Bull v Devon Area HA* [1993] 4 Med LR 117.

Put otherwise, an employer is not automatically liable for the torts of his independent contractors.

SECTION 2   EMPLOYEES AND INDEPENDENT CONTRACTORS

(A) CONTROL

The formula traditionally used by the courts to mark the distinction between an employee and an independent contractor is that of 'control'.[5] According to this test, a person is an employee where the employer 'retains the control of the actual performance' of the work.[6] This was a more meaningful test in bygone years when this country was predominantly an agricultural and industrial nation in which work was largely done by labourers or craftsmen under the directions of employers who had the same or even greater technical skill than their workmen. It would ordinarily be enough to say that the employer could tell the worker not merely what task was to be performed, but also how it should be performed. If the employer could do both these things, the person engaged was an employee. Conversely, where a supposed employer lacked the power to direct what the tortfeasor was to do, the absence of any such control would be fatal to the suggestion that person was an employee.[7]

Nowadays, working patterns have changed so much that it is difficult to slot employment relationships into the traditional analytical framework of control. For example, many more employees work at home these days, or possess some technical skill which is often not possessed by their employers. In consequence, the control test does not by itself prove adequate on every occasion.[8] In addition, for policy reasons, the courts may hold someone to be an employee even though aspects of his work suggest more that he is an independent contractor. In *Lane v Shire Roofing Co (Oxford) Ltd*,[9] for example, the Court of Appeal drew attention to the policy reasons that exist within the field of health and safety at work to decide a borderline case in favour of classifying the worker as an employee.

Notwithstanding its limitations, the control test does remain helpful in some instances, and in deciding whether enough 'control' is exercised over another to make him an employee one must take into account several factors, no single one of which is conclusive. The criteria include the extent to which the employer can control the details

---

[5] 'The final test...lies in the nature and degree of detailed control over the person alleged to be a servant': *Performing Right Society Ltd v Mitchell and Booker (Palais de Danse) Ltd* [1924] 1 KB 762, at 767.

[6] *Honeywill and Stein Ltd v Larkin Bros (London's Commercial Photographers) Ltd* [1934] 1 KB 191, at 196.

[7] For recent deployment of this approach, see *Various Claimants v Institute of the Brothers of Christian Schools* [2010] EWCA Civ 1106.

[8] *Short v J & W Henderson Ltd* (1946) 62 TLR 427, at 429. The inadequacy of this test was expressly stated in *Cassidy v Ministry of Health* [1951] 2 KB 343, at 352.   [9] [1995] IRLR 493.

of the work, whether the method of payment is on a time or a job basis,[10] whose tools, equipment, and premises are to be used,[11] the skill called for in the work, the freedom of selection of labour by the employer,[12] and the power to dismiss. All these matters, and possibly more besides, but especially and increasingly the one mentioned in the quotation below from Denning LJ, must be considered in order to decide whether a power to control can be inferred. His Lordship said:

> It is often easy to recognise a contract of service when you see it, but difficult to say wherein the difference [between a contract of service and a contract for services] lies. A ship's master, a chauffeur, and a reporter on the staff of a newspaper are all employed under a contract of service; but a ship's pilot, a taxi-man, and a newspaper contributor are employed under a contract for services. *One feature which seems to run through the instances is that, under a contract of service, a man is employed as part of the business, and his work is done as an integral part of the business; whereas, under a contract for services, his work, although done for the business, is not integrated into it but is only accessory to it.*[13]

Of particular note in relation to the ongoing relevance of the control test is the decision in *Viasystems (Tyneside) Ltd v Thermal Transfer (Northern) Ltd.*[14] In this case, the question facing the Court of Appeal was whether a fitter's mate supplied on a labour-only basis by A to B could trigger the vicarious liability of A or B. It was found that both A and B (through their respective fitters) had sufficient control of the mate to prevent his negligence. That being so, it was held by May LJ that both A and B could be held vicariously liable for the flooding he caused through his negligence.[15] The route to the same conclusion adopted by Rix LJ, however, was rather different. In his view, the critical test to apply is whether the employee 'is so much a part of the work, business or organisation of both employers that it is just to make both employers answer for his negligence'.[16] Importantly, both members of this two-man Court of Appeal recognised that there was never a formal contract of employment between B and the careless mate! They were content to deem him to be the employee of both A and B and impose liability jointly and equally between them.[17] This is a radical step, and, in the wrong hands, it potentially threatens to undermine the principle that one cannot be liable for the torts of an independent contractor, for all one would need to do would be

---

[10] Employees are generally paid by the hour whereas independent contractors are normally paid for the complete job.   [11] *Quarman v Burnett* (1840) 6 M & W 499.
[12] At common law the owner of a ship was not liable for the negligence of a compulsory pilot: *The Halley* (1868) LR 2 PC 193 (see now Pilotage Act 1987; *Oceangas (Gibraltar) Ltd v Port of London Authority* [1993] 2 Lloyd's Rep 292).
[13] *Stevenson, Jordan & Harrison Ltd v MacDonald and Evans* [1952] 1 TLR 101, at 111 (emphasis added). In *Bank Voor Handel en Scheepvaart NV v Slatford* [1953] 1 QB 248, at 295, Denning LJ said: 'It depends on whether the person is part and parcel of the organisation' (reversed on other grounds [1954] AC 584).
[14] [2006] 2 WLR 428.   [15] Ibid at [16].   [16] Ibid at [79].
[17] Since vicarious liability does not require fault to be shown on the part of the employer, it naturally followed that liability would ordinarily be split evenly between the two employers (assuming equal control): ibid at [52] and [85].

to look to the control or degree of integration into the temporary employer's workforce in order to deem the contractor to be an employee of the temporary employer.

It was almost inevitable that *Viasystems* would not supply the final word on dual vicarious liability. Indeed, the ink was barely dry on the judgments in that case when another case, *Hawley v Luminar Leisure*,[18] came before the Court of Appeal. Disappointingly, that case failed to clarify whose was the preferable test since there were echoes of both May LJ's control test and Rix LJ's integration test.[19] Nor has the opportunity been taken since to endorse just one of these tests. In *Colour Quest Ltd v Downstream UK Plc*,[20] Steele J ventured no further than to say that May LJ's control test enabled him to dispose of the case before him, while in *Biffa Waste Services Ltd v Maschinenfabrik Ernst Hese GmbH*,[21] Stanley Brunton LJ applied both tests on behalf of the entire Court of Appeal. It is, then, probably best to conclude for the present that either test will suffice.

(B) PERSONAL INVESTMENT IN THE ENTERPRISE

Another approach to the central issue of who is an employee is to ask: 'Is the worker in business on his own account?'[22] In answering this question the courts will look at who owns the tools used, who paid for the materials, and whether the worker stands to make anything from a profit to a loss on completion of the enterprise. Thus, where a building worker is simply paid, and neither hires his own help nor provides his own equipment and has no say in the control of the site, his position will be that of an employee rather than an independent contractor.[23]

There is, however, another sense in which the phrase 'personal investment in the enterprise' may be used and may also be pertinent to the question in hand. If the person engaged need not personally invest his own endeavour into the enterprise, but has the option of delegating the task to some other person, this is likely to be indicative of a contract for services rather than a contract of service.[24]

(C) INTENTION OF THE PARTIES

The intention of the parties, recorded in the terms of their agreement, can also provide a useful guide as to whether there is a contract of service or a contract for services.[25] On the other hand, their express intentions will not necessarily be conclusive of the matter. Thus, in one case where the parties agreed that the worker should be treated as self-employed for reasons of tax and national insurance payments, the court

---

[18] [2006] EWCA Civ 30.   [19] Ibid at [83] and [85].   [20] [2009] 1 CLC 186, at [220].
[21] [2009] PNLR 12, at [55] (control test) and [58] (integration test).
[22] *Lee Tin Sang v Chung Chi-Keung* [1990] 2 AC 374; *Lane v Shire Roofing Co (Oxford) Ltd* [1995] IRLR 493.   [23] *Montreal v Montreal Locomotive Works* [1947] 1 DLR 161.
[24] *MacFarlane v Glasgow CC* [2001] IRLR 7.
[25] *Johnson v Coventry Churchill International Ltd* [1992] 3 All ER 14.

nonetheless held there to be a contract of employment.[26] The intention of the parties was simply one factor to which the court had regard.

Interestingly, it has been said that the question of the interpretation of documents governing the nature of the parties' relationship is one of law;[27] yet the appellate courts will be loath to reverse the findings of lower courts or tribunals unless there has been a clear misdirection or a conclusion reached that is wholly unsupportable.[28]

(D) SOME PARTICULAR CASES EXAMINED

In the majority of cases, there is no difficulty in determining the status of the worker.[29] Factory hands, office clerical staff, agricultural workers, and the like are clearly employees; whereas garage proprietors, house builders, and dry-cleaners are the independent contractors of the members of the public who employ them. Similarly, a chauffeur is an employee, but a taxi driver is not. However, borderline or hybrid cases will arise from time to time. Sales representatives, for example, might conceivably fall into either category, depending on the circumstances.[30]

(1) Agency workers

Those who work ad hoc on temporary contracts acquired through an employment agency, may, on occasion, be treated as employees of the agency for the purposes of each separate engagement.[31] Whether the general arrangement – that is, the worker being registered on the agency's books – could amount to a contract of employment would appear to turn on the question whether there is a mutuality of obligation between the worker and agency (that is, a duty to provide work on the part of the agency and a duty to accept it on the part of the worker).[32] In turn, this question can be answered not merely by reference to the documentary evidence associated with the engagement[33] but also by reference to what was actually said and done at the time of

[26] *Young & Woods Ltd v West* [1980] IRLR 201. See also *Ferguson v Dawson Partners (Contractors) Ltd* [1976] 1 WLR 1213.   [27] *Davies v Presbyterian Church of Wales* [1986] 1 WLR 323.
[28] See, eg, *Lee Ting Sang v Cheung Chi-Keung* [1990] 2 AC 374; *Kapfunde v Abbey National plc* [1999] ICR 1.
[29] For the special statutory provisions defining when a trade union is vicariously liable for various torts involving industrial action, see the Trade Union and Labour Relations (Consolidation) Act 1992, s 15.
[30] Or the holder of a university research fellowship who is required also to act as a part-time demonstrator.
[31] *McMeechan v Secretary of State for Employment* [1997] IRLR 353. Cf *Montgomery v Johnson Underwood Ltd* [2001] IRLR 269 (the worker here was not an employee because, unlike in *McMeechan*, there was no review or grievance procedure between the agency and the worker that could be taken to be indicative of the formality of their relationship).
[32] In *Carmichael v National Power plc* [1999] 1 WLR 2042 Lord Irvine said (at 2047) that a contract of employment required an 'irreducible minimum of mutual obligations'. See also *Clark v Oxfordshire HA* [1998] IRLR 125; *Dacas v Brook Street Bureau (UK) Ltd* [2004] IRLR 358.
[33] Eg, the fact that the agency only pays the worker according to time sheets supplied by the employer (suggesting that the worker is not an employee of the agency): *Montgomery v Johnson Underwood* [2001] IRLR 269.

the engagement.[34] If the agency has no day-to-day control over the tasks performed by the worker, this will tend to indicate that he or she is not an employee of the agency.[35]

(2) Hospital staff

The courts were once much concerned to decide which members of hospital staff are employees. This issue exposed the problems of the 'control' test. How could lay members of a hospital board be said to 'control' a highly skilled neurosurgeon? After much uncertainty, it is now settled that nurses, radiographers,[36] house surgeons,[37] and assistant medical officers[38] in the full-time service of hospitals are employees.[39] Part-time anaesthetists have also been held to be employees on the basis that they are members of the organisation of the hospital.[40] Surgeons and consultants working under the National Health Service, even though only engaged part-time, will for the same reason be employees. They are all operating as part and parcel of the NHS enterprise. It is only when the surgeon or consultant treats the patient under a private contract between himself and the patient that the hospital is not answerable for his torts.

(3) Borrowed employees

It is often difficult to decide whose employee a person is when he is lent by his employer to another. The leading decision here is *Mersey Docks and Harbour Board v Coggins and Griffiths (Liverpool) Ltd.*[41]

> The Board owned many mobile cranes, each operated by skilled drivers who were engaged and paid by the Board. In the ordinary course of its business, the Board hired out a crane to the respondents, a stevedoring company, for use in unloading a ship. The power to dismiss the driver remained with the board even though the contract provided that he was to be the servant of the hirers. While loading the cargo, the driver was under the immediate control of the hirers in the sense that the hirers could tell him which boxes to load and where to place them, but they could not tell him how to manipulate the controls of the crane. A third party was injured by virtue of negligent handling of the crane by the driver. The House of Lords was called upon to decide whose servant he was at the time of the accident.

---

[34] *Franks v Reuters Ltd* [2003] EWCA 417.

[35] *Dacas v Brook Street Bureau (UK) Ltd* [2004] IRLR 358.   [36] *Gold v Essex CC* [1942] 2 KB 293.

[37] *Collins v Hertfordshire CC* [1947] KB 598; *Cassidy v Ministry of Health* [1951] 2 KB 343.

[38] *Cassidy v Ministry of Health* [1951] 2 KB 343.

[39] Soo, too, are educational psychologists and teachers engaged by a local education authority (*Phelps v Hillingdon LBC* [2001] 2 AC 619), as are education officers performing the statutory functions of such authorities (*Carty v London Borough of Croydon* [2005] EWCA Civ 19).

[40] *Roe v Minister of Health* [1954] 2 QB 66.

[41] [1947] AC 1; *Karuppan Bhoomidas v Port of Singapore Authority* [1978] 1 All ER 956 (although a bye-law stated that those loading and discharging ships shall be under the control of the ship's officers, stevedores remained the employees of the port authority, which was vicariously liable for their torts).

It was held that the Board was solely liable. There is a very strong presumption[42] that someone remains the employee of the general or permanent employer although another employer borrows his services. Where cranes or vehicles are let out on hire with a driver, the owner is responsible for his employee's negligence unless he specifically divested himself of all possession and control.[43] But if the system of work that is used is unsafe, then, according to *Morris v Breaveglen Ltd*,[44] the general employer is liable, for he has a non-delegable duty to ensure the provision and operation of a safe system of work. (On the other hand, it should not be forgotten that where both the general employer and the employer to whom the employee has been loaned have control over the employee, both employers can sometimes be held vicariously liable in respect of the employee's torts.)[45]

(4) Police officers

Under section 88 of the Police Act 1996 the chief officer of police for any police area is vicariously liable for those torts committed by constables exercising or purporting to exercise their functions.[46] And vicarious liability may even be imposed where the tort in question is committed by an off-duty officer who makes it clear that he is a police officer.[47]

SECTION 3　IS THERE A SEPARATE CATEGORY OF AGENTS?

We have seen that a person who does work for another may be either an employee or an independent contractor. But such a person *may* simultaneously be an agent. This is because the category of 'agent' partially overlaps with the categories of both 'employee' and 'independent contractor'. And while agency is primarily of importance within the law of contract, it is not without some significance in this context, too.

An agent may or may not be an employee. A person employed on a weekly wage to sell vacuum cleaners and under orders as to his times and place of employment will be both an agent (in contracting to sell cleaners) and an employee.[48] By contrast, no one would suggest that, if the defendant employed a chartered accountant to settle his

---

[42] For an example where the company 'borrowing' employees did become vicariously liable, even though there was no formal contract of employment between the temporary employer and the employee, see *Hawley v Luminar Leisure* [2006] EWCA Civ 30.

[43] And the original employer will of course be primarily liable if he hires out an incompetent driver: *McConkey v Amec plc* (1990) 27 Con LR 88.

[44] [1993] PIQR P294.

[45] *Viasystems (Tyneside) Ltd v Thermal Transfer (Northern) Ltd* [2006] 2 WLR 428.

[46] See, eg, *Rowlands v CC Merseyside* [2007] 1 WLR 1065.

[47] *Weir v Bettison* [2003] EWCA Civ 111.

[48] Cf a schoolboy distributing milk in his school who will not be the servant of a local education authority, although he may well be an agent: *Watkins v Birmingham CC* (1975) 126 NLJ 442.

liability for income tax on his behalf, the defendant would be liable if the accountant negligently knocked down a pedestrian while driving to the tax office in order to discuss the matter. The accountant would be both an agent and an independent contractor of the defendant.

The tort of deceit provides an important example of where tort law *is* concerned with the existence of an agency arrangement. Where a principal delegates authority to another person to negotiate a contract on his behalf, he may be liable for the fraud of his 'agent'. So, for example, if an estate agent, in the course of negotiating the sale of a house of his principal, knowingly makes untrue statements about that house to a third party who acts on them to his detriment, the principal will be liable in deceit. And yet the estate agent is not the principal's employee. This liability exists only where the principal can be said to have held out the estate agent as someone authorised to make such representations in the course of making the contract.[49] This provides a valuable clue to the key issue here – such misrepresentations, though capable of giving rise to tortious liability, are so intimately associated with, and inseparable from, the contractual relation to which end the agency is directed that they assume the quality of contract, where agency, of course, is important per se.[50]

The concept of agency is also applicable to merely negligent statements made by an estate agent.[51] But it is an essential prerequisite of liability of the principal that the agent acted within the scope of the authority which the principal's acts led the claimant to believe the agent enjoyed. Where the agent is an employee of the principal, the agent cannot act beyond the scope of his authority yet still remain within the general course of his employment.[52]

The other area which demands special attention is the liability of a vehicle owner when the vehicle is driven by someone else. Of course, the owner is liable if his employee drives it negligently in the course of his employment. The courts have not stopped there, however, and the House of Lords in *Morgans v Launchbury*[53] affirmed that if the vehicle is driven by the owner's agent, and he is driving it for the owner's purposes, the owner will again be liable. The facts in *Morgans v Launchbury* were as follows.

> D owned the car. With her permission, her husband took it on a pub-crawl. When he was too drunk to drive, he asked his drinking companion to drive. D was held not liable for the damage caused by the companion's negligent driving.

---

[49] Cf *Uxbridge Permanent Benefit Building Society v Pickard* [1939] 2 KB 248, at 254–5. For further endorsement of the 'holding out' principle, see *Lloyd v Grace, Smith & Co* [1912] AC 716; but for criticism of the way in which this case has subsequently been interpreted by the House of Lords, see Murphy, 'Juridical Foundations of Common Law Non-Delegable Duties' in Neyers et al (eds), *Emerging Issues in Tort Law* (2007), ch 14.

[50] Notably, then, the close-connection test for vicarious liability cannot be used in relation to agents: *M v Hendron* [2007] CSIH 27.

[51] *Kooragang Investments Pty Ltd v Richardson & Wrench Ltd* [1982] AC 462. In that case, therefore, the principal was held not liable for the agent's negligent statement because the agent was not authorised to make the valuations which formed the subject of the negligent statements.

[52] *Armagas Ltd v Mundogas SA, The Ocean Frost* [1986] AC 717.   [53] [1973] AC 127.

The House of Lords held that the driver was not the agent of the owner, and that a car owner is liable only if the driver is his employee acting in the course of his employment or is his authorised agent driving for, and on behalf of, the owner. Lord Wilberforce added that 'agency' in such a context was merely a concept the meaning and purpose of which is that the owner ought to pay.[54] The House rejected the argument that it was so desirable to find someone liable who was covered by compulsory third-party insurance, that it should hold the owner liable for anyone who drove with his permission: only Parliament, not the courts, could make that extension of liability.[55]

SECTION 4   LIABILITY IN RESPECT OF AN INDEPENDENT CONTRACTOR

An 'employer' is not normally liable merely because an independent contractor commits a tort in the course of his employment. Certain exceptions exist in relation to various torts of 'strict liability'. Thus, as noted in earlier chapters, there may be liability imposed on the part of an 'employer' in the context of private nuisance,[56] under the rule in *Rylands v Fletcher*[57] and in respect of a breach of statutory duty.[58] But leaving these examples to one side, it is clear that an employer will generally only be liable in connection with the torts committed by independent contractors in one of three ways.

(A) AUTHORISING, PROCURING, AND RATIFYING TORTS

In many circumstances the law will attribute to a man the conduct of another being, whether human or animal, if he has instigated that conduct. If X sets his dog upon Y it is as much a battery as if X had struck Y with his fist. He who instigates or procures another to commit a tort is deemed to have committed the tort himself.[59] It matters not whether that other was an employee, an independent contractor, or an agent (human or otherwise). In *Ellis v Sheffield Gas Consumers Co*[60] the facts were as follows.

> Having no legal power to do so, Ds' gas undertaking employed an independent contractor to dig up a part of a street. C fell over a heap of earth and stones made by the contractor in the course of digging, and Ds were held liable on the ground that they had authorised this nuisance.

---

[54] [1973] AC 127, at 135.

[55] In *Norwood v Navan* [1981] RTR 457, a husband was held not liable for the negligence of his wife when driving his car for family shopping. Cf *Nelson v Raphael* [1979] RTR 437.

[56] Eg, *Matania v National Provincial Bank Ltd* [1936] 2 All ER 633; *Alcock v Wraith* (1991) 58 BLR 20.

[57] (1868) LR 3 HL 330.   [58] *Hosking v De Havilland Aircraft Co Ltd* [1949] 1 All ER 540.

[59] And even if that other has a defence, the principal may still be liable: *Barker v Braham* (1773) 3 Wils 368 (D authorised a sheriff to arrest C on an illegal warrant; although the sheriff was protected from liability by reason of acting under the warrant, D was still liable in false imprisonment).   [60] (1853) 2 E & B 767.

It is not always easy, however, to decide whether the defendant can be said to have authorised the tortious act. Where a lessee was empowered to erect certain structures, but the lease reserved to the lessor the right to approve the plans for such structures (which right the lessor is not reported to have exercised), this was not enough to make the lessor answerable for the lessee's negligence in the course of building the structure.[61] On the other hand, although a taxi driver is certainly not an employee, if his fare orders him to drive fast or to take other risks, he is jointly responsible for any ensuing tort.[62]

If a person commits a tort while purporting to act on behalf of another, but in fact does so without his authority, and that other later ratifies the act which amounted to a tort, he thereby becomes answerable for the tort in the same way as if he had given authority prior to its commission. However, to be liable on this basis, the principal must know at the time of ratification[63] of the doing of an act which constitutes a tort. But he needn't know that the act was tortious. Thus, if he ratifies the purchase of goods which the vendor had no right to sell, he is still liable in conversion, even though he is unaware that the sale was unlawful.[64]

(B) PERSONAL NEGLIGENCE ON THE PART OF THE EMPLOYER

First, there may be such an element of personal negligence on the part of the employer as to make him liable for the acts of his independent contractor, and this may be so even though the duty of care owed by the employer in a particular case is not so extensive as to make the employer liable merely because his independent contractor has been negligent. For example, the employer is liable where he carelessly appoints an incompetent contractor. Equally, where the risk of harm is foreseeable in the absence of precautions, a failure by the employer to provide in the contract for those precautions, is actionable negligence.[65] *Robinson v Beaconsfield RDC*[66] furnishes another example of personal negligence on the part of the employer.

> Ds employed contractors to clean out cesspools in their district. No arrangements were made for the removal of the deposits of sewage upon their being taken from the cesspools by the contractors. The contractors deposited sewage on C's land. Ds were held liable for their failure to take proper precautions to dispose of the sewage.

It probably follows from the decision in *Robinson* that it would also be negligence to fail to make a proper inspection after a job has been completed. Certainly, in the context of the operation of the Occupiers' Liability Act 1957, proper discharge of the common

---

[61] *Hurlstone v London Electric Rly Co* (1914) 30 TLR 398.
[62] Cf *M'Laughlin v Pryor* (1842) 4 Man & G 48. Mere failure to object or other acquiescence would not be enough. [63] *Freeman v Rosher* (1849) 13 QB 780.
[64] *Hilbery v Hatton* (1864) 2 H & C 822. [65] Cf *Hughes v Percival* (1883) 8 App Cas 443.
[66] [1911] 2 Ch 188.

duty of care where contractors have been engaged involves making such inspections after the work has been completed.[67]

(C) BREACH OF A NON-DELEGABLE DUTY

In some cases, the employer's duty to take care has been so widely drawn that it is not discharged by properly instructing and supervising a competent contractor to perform that duty on the employer's behalf. There is a positive, non-delegable duty to see that care is taken. These non-delegable duties often involve such high standards of care that they appear to (and sometimes do) impose strict liability.[68] In other words, such duties can arise in the context of several torts – some of which involve strict liability, some of which do not. No fail-safe guide to the incidence of such duties is available. The most that can be said by way of certainty is that it is a question of law in any given case whether such a duty is owed, although they commonly arise in the context of work done by independent contractors.[69]

Non-delegable duties also tend to arise where the contractor's activity is particularly hazardous – for example, where open fires on bush land are lit,[70] and where re-roofing takes place on a row of terraced houses where difficulties with the 'joins' between the properties is well known.[71] For example, where employers are carrying out operations on or near a highway, and those operations (performed by independent contractors) may foreseeably harm highway users, those employers will be in the frame for liability for breach of a non-delegable duty of care. Consider *Holliday v National Telephone Co.*[72]

> Ds, in laying telephone wires along a street, employed an independent contractor to solder the tubes in which these wires were carried. In negligently using a benzolene lamp, the contractor injured a passer-by. Ds were held liable.

---

[67] Occupiers' Liability Act 1957, s 2(4)(b).

[68] Note that the law in this area is very confused. One of us thinks that (1) the standard of care involved where the non-delegable duty exists as a subspecies of the law of negligence is often pitched at a very high level because of the degree of risk typically present in such cases, and (2) that where the non-delegable duty exists as a subspecies of nuisance, the duty is necessarily strict (Murphy (2007) 30 University of New South Wales LJ 86). Another of us thinks that the non-delegable duty is an independent tort involving strict liability in every case (Witting (2006) 29 University of New South Wales LJ 38).

[69] In *Farraj v King's Healthcare NHS Trust* [2009] EWCA Civ 1203 Dyson LJ suggested (at [93]) that the question of whether such a duty would be imposed was to be determined on policy grounds according to what is just, fair, and reasonable. For an attempt to theorise the little understood prerequisites for such duties, see Murphy, 'Juridical Foundations of Common Law Non-Delegable Duties' in Neyers et al (eds), *Emerging Issues in Tort Law* (2007), ch 14.

[70] *Black v Christchurch Finance Co* [1894] AC 48. And see *Balfour v Barty-King* [1957] 1 QB 496 (owner liable for a fire when an independent contractor plumber used a blowlamp in a loft to thaw D's frozen pipes).

[71] *Alcock v Wraith* (1991) 58 BLR 20.

[72] [1899] 2 QB 392. In *Pickard v Smith* (1861) 10 CBNS 470, the same principle was applied to hold a railway refreshment room proprietor liable to a passenger who fell down a hole which the employee of D's independent contractor negligently left on the platform.

Another hazardous instance in which a non-delegable duty may be held to arise is where one carries out structural operations that threaten damage to neighbouring premises.[73] Equally, a railway company owes such a duty to passengers to see that bridges along its lines are carefully built by its independent contractors.[74] By contrast, though, removing a hawthorn tree from a garden adjoining a highway is not an inherently dangerous activity, and the garden owner will not be held liable for harm caused by virtue of his contractor removing it negligently.[75]

The categories of non-delegable duties are not closed; and danger is not the only criterion according to which they may be ascribed. It seems equally plausible that an assumption of responsibility on the part of the employer will suffice.[76] Thus, a patient who is accepted for treatment in an NHS hospital will be able to rely upon a non-delegable duty in order to sue the NHS authorities that stand behind those engaged to provide the patient's actual specialist treatment. The rationale here is that hospital authorities have a duty to provide proper treatment at all stages, and this involves a duty that they cannot cast off by simply entrusting it to competent staff. *Lindsey County Council v Marshall*,[77] *Gold v Essex County Council*,[78] and *Collins v Hertfordshire County Council*[79] all suggest that such a non-delegable duty formed the basis of Denning LJ's judgment in *Cassidy v Ministry of Health*[80] where it was held that a hospital authority that ran a casualty department had a duty to provide proper medical and nursing care for all those who presented themselves complaining of illness or injury.[81]

A direct, non-delegable duty to patients may have several consequences in today's health service. Perhaps until about 1980 it did not matter very much whether Denning LJ was right in *Cassidy*.[82] If all the professionals caring for a patient were employees, and it could be proved that someone was negligent, the hospital authority was necessarily vicariously liable for the tort of one of their employees. However, with the increasing use of agency staff, the hospital may now be able to escape vicarious liability by arguing that the patient is unable to prove that a person for whose work the hospital is responsible was at fault. But if the hospital owes its patients a personal, non-delegable duty of care, such an escape route is readily blocked. Even if negligent treatment is provided by an independent contractor, the hospital will be liable.[83]

---

[73] *Hughes v Percival* (1883) 8 App Cas 443 (party wall negligently cut into while contractor was rebuilding part of adjoining premises); *Alcock v Wraith* (1991) 58 BLR 20.

[74] *Grote v Chester and Holyhead Rly Co* (1848) 2 Exch 251.

[75] *Salsbury v Woodland* [1970] 1 QB 324.

[76] Indeed, in some instances it has been said that undertaking an enterprise that carries with it certain severe risks will form the basis for the imputation of such an 'assumption of responsibility' (even though this involves a measure of linguistic inelegance): see Murphy, 'Juridical Foundations of Common Law Non-Delegable Duties' in Neyers et al (eds), *Emerging Issues in Tort Law* (2007), ch 14. That being so, an assumption of responsibility may, more so than the creation of an especial danger, lie at the heart of such non-delegable duties.   [77] [1937] AC 97.

[78] [1942] 2 KB 293, at 301.   [79] [1947] KB 598.   [80] [1951] 2 KB 343, at 362–3.

[81] *Barnett v Chelsea and Kensington Hospital Management Committee* [1969] 1 QB 428.

[82] For a view that he was wrong see *Yepremian v Scarborough General Hospital* (1980) 110 DLR (3d) 513.

[83] See, eg, *M v Calderdale and Kirklees HA* [1998] Lloyd's Rep Med 157.

The Employer's Liability (Defective Equipment) Act 1969 must also be noted at this juncture. It applies when, for the purposes of his business, an employer provides equipment (which includes any plant and machinery, vehicle, aircraft, and clothing) for his employee and the employee suffers personal injury in the course of his employment in consequence of a defect in that equipment. The injury is then deemed also to be attributable to the negligence of the employer if the defect is attributable wholly or partly to the negligence, or other tort, of an independent contractor or other third party. This Act therefore imposes an extensive statutory duty on employers. But it leaves unchanged the common-law duty of the employer to provide and ensure the operation of a safe system of work in respects other than the provision of equipment.[84] And this duty is an especially onerous one as *McDermid v Nash Dredging and Reclamation Co Ltd*[85] illustrates.

> C was employed as a deck hand by Ds. He was instructed to go and work on another tug owned by a different company within the same group as Ds. As a result of the negligence of that tug master, who was not an employee of Ds, C suffered severe injuries. Ds were held liable for failing to provide and ensure the operation of a safe system of work.

It was no excuse that they did not in fact have any control over the operation of the system in question. The breach of the non-delegable duty in respect of the safety of their employee was not discharged by delegating that duty to the master of the tug. The duty was one not just to devise, but also to *ensure the operation of,* a safe system of work.[86] Even so, it must be stressed that that duty remains a duty to take reasonable care, not an absolute duty to guarantee the employee's safety.[87] In *Cook v Square D Ltd,*[88] for example, an employee working in Saudi Arabia was injured falling over an unguarded raised tile. The Court of Appeal held that the employers, who were 8,000 miles away, could not be responsible for every day-to-day event in the workplace.[89] The real question was whether they had done what a reasonable employer should do in order to set up, operate, and monitor a safe system of work.

In one or two instances, the courts have been prepared to extend the categories of non-delegable duty. In *Rogers v Night Riders,*[90] for example, the claimant's mother telephoned the defendants for a taxi to take her daughter to the station and the mother paid for the cab. During the journey, a door flew open and the claimant was injured. The taxi driver was not an employee but an independent contractor for the defendants. Nevertheless the defendants were held to be in breach of their primary duty to the

---

[84] Note the obligation to insure under the Employers' Liability (Compulsory Insurance) Act 1969.

[85] [1987] AC 906. See also *Davie v New Merton Board Mills Ltd* [1959] AC 604, at 646.

[86] For the argument that this case more closely resembles vicarious liability than non-delegable duty, see McKendrick (1990) 53 MLR 770.

[87] That being so, it is possible for the partial defence of contributory negligence to be raised in relation to the employer's non-delegable duty towards his employees: see, eg, *McGarvey v Eve NCI Ltd* [2002] EWCA Civ 374.   [88] [1992] ICR 262.

[89] But note that the incident in *McDermid* also took place abroad. Are the distinctions made between the two cases convincing? See [1992] ICR 262 at 270–1.

[90] [1983] RTR 324.

claimant. As far as she knew, it was the defendants who undertook to convey her safely and carefully to her destination.

What is really required in this area is that the courts set out clearly the bases for such duties. This need arises not simply because such analysis is conspicuous by its absence in the English case law, but also because there has been a tendency for the boundaries between non-delegable duties and vicarious liability to become remarkably confused in recent years, especially in the House of Lords' decision in *Lister v Hesley Hall Ltd*[91] (explored in more detail below).

SECTION 5   CASES WHERE AN EMPLOYER IS NOT LIABLE FOR THE TORT OF AN INDEPENDENT CONTRACTOR

In cases where the employer's duty to the claimant is *not* a non-delegable one – and there are many such cases – the key question will concern the extent of the risk against which the employer has the duty to guard.[92] And here a less stringent standard of care would seem to obtain. *Phillips v Britannia Hygienic Laundry Co*[93] provides a useful example. In that case, the owner of a lorry was held not liable when a third party's vehicle was damaged in consequence of the negligent repair of his lorry by a garage proprietor he contracted with to perform those repairs.

Nor will an employer of an independent contractor be liable for what is commonly termed the 'collateral negligence' of their contractors. *Padbury v Holiday and Greenwood Ltd*[94] both furnishes facts which illustrate the principle, and contains what seems to be the soundest statement of it. In that case, A employed B to fit casement windows into certain premises. B's employee negligently put a tool on the sill of the window on which he was working at the time. The wind blew the casement open and the tool was knocked off the sill on to a passer-by. Holding the employer not liable, Fletcher Moulton LJ said:

> [B]efore a superior employer could be held liable for the negligent act of a servant of a sub-contractor it must be shown that the work which the sub-contractor was employed to do was work the nature of which, and not merely the performance of which, cast on the superior employer the duty of taking precautions.[95]

In short, the employer is liable for those risks of harm created by the work itself which the employer is having done. 'Collateral' means collateral to the risk which marks the

---

[91] [2002] 1 AC 215.

[92] *Dalton v Angus & Co* (1881) 6 App Cas 740, at 831.

[93] [1923] 1 KB 539 (affirmed [1923] 2 KB 832); followed in *Stennett v Hancock and Peters* [1939] 2 All ER 578.   [94] (1912) 28 TLR 494.

[95] Ibid, at 495. Cf *Hardaker v Idle DC* [1896] 1 QB 335, at 342; *Thompson v Anglo-Saxon Petroleum Co Ltd* [1955] 2 Lloyd's Rep 363.

limit of the duty of the employer. If the employer is to be liable, the danger must be inherent in the work; it is not enough that the contractor chooses a negligent way of performing it where the normal manner of performance would create no reasonably foreseeable peril to the claimant.

The negligence must be 'in the employer's department of duty'.[96] A householder who employs a contractor to repair his lamp over the highway is liable if the contractor repairs it in such a way that it falls on to a passer-by, for that is the very risk in respect of which the duty of the householder is imposed on him, but he is not liable if the contractor, while repairing it, allows a hammer to drop on to the passer-by, for that act would be outside the employer's range of duty. If a hospital owes a non-delegable duty to patients in respect of their treatment, it does not follow that the hospital is liable when an agency doctor negligently backs his car into yours when driving from one part of the hospital to another. That act is not within the hospital's non-delegable duty to patients. *Wilson v Hodgson's Kingston Brewery Co*[97] also demonstrates how liability for the acts of independent contractors falls short of vicarious liability for the torts of an employee.

> Ds employed X, an independent contractor, to deliver beer at a public house. X delivered it through a cellar flap on the highway, and he negligently left the flap open, causing C, who was passing along the pavement, to be injured. Pointing out that X could have delivered it through the front door, the court held that the incident was not within the scope of any duty on the part of Ds to take care.

SECTION 6   LIABILITY IN RESPECT OF EMPLOYEES

(A) INTRODUCTION

An employer is liable whenever his employee commits a tort in the course of his employment or in circumstances sufficiently closely connected to his employment. In other words, all the elements of the particular tort[98] must generally occur within, or in close connection with, the employer-employee relationship. Thus, the employer will still be answerable if the tort was committed before the employment relationship ceased to exist, even if the harm occurred after that date.[99]

Where a duty of care imposed on the employer has been broken, but the claimant cannot prove which employee of the employer is responsible for the breach, the employer is nonetheless liable as one might expect.[100] Accordingly, in *Roe v Minister*

---

[96] *Cassidy v Ministry of Health* [1951] 2 KB 343, at 365. This judgment contains a lucid statement of the nature of collateral negligence. For the difficulty in ascertaining exactly D's duty for the purpose of this rule, see *Salsbury v Woodland* [1970] 1 QB 324, at 349.   [97] (1915) 85 LJKB 270.

[98] A procedural bar against suing the servant will not prevent the master from being vicariously liable: *Staveley Iron and Chemicals Co Ltd v Jones* [1956] 1 All ER 403; *Broom v Morgan* [1953] 1 QB 597.

[99] *Briess v Woolley* [1954] AC 333.

[100] *Grant v Australian Knitting Mills Ltd* [1936] AC 85; *Olley v Marlborough Court Ltd* [1949] 1 KB 532 (a guest left the bedroom key at the hotel office; upon the key being taken and the bedroom being burgled, the onus was cast on the hotel to prove that they and their staff had taken reasonable care of the key).

of Health all three judges in the Court of Appeal stated (*obiter*) that, where a claimant established negligence on the part of one or more of several employees of the defendant hospital authority, the defendant authority would be vicariously liable although the claimant could not prove which of those employees committed the negligent act.[101] Further, the *ratio decidendi* of *Cassidy v Ministry of Health* is that, where the claimant has been injured as a result of some operation in the control of one or more employees of a hospital authority (and he cannot identify the particular employee who was in control), and in all other respects the requirements of the res ipsa loquitur rule in respect of the act are satisfied, the hospital authority is vicariously liable unless it ousts the operation of that rule.[102] These two decisions were arrived at on the basis of vicarious liability,[103] *not* on the basis of a breach of a non-delegable duty by the employer.

(B) IN THE COURSE OF THE EMPLOYEE'S EMPLOYMENT

At one time, vicarious liability could only be imposed when the employee did the act complained of 'in the course of his employment'.[104] While a rival test has since emerged, based on acts closely connected to the employee's contract of employment, it is nonetheless still true that any tortious act committed within the course of an employee's employment will suffice to invoke vicarious liability. To hold otherwise would be to negate the rationale behind a vast body of case law that is still regarded as sound. That being so, the *legal* question of when an act falls within a 'course of employment' is by no means redundant (even though it is now of less significance than formerly).[105]

(1) The course of employment: general principles

At one time, it was generally accepted that the crucial distinction to be made lay between an employee's wrongful mode of doing authorised work (for which the employer would be liable), and his performance of some unauthorised act (for which the employer would not be liable).[106] Such a simplistic distinction was never entirely satisfactory,[107] especially from a compensation point of view, for some cases involving deliberate misconduct could at best be viewed as having been 'massaged' in order to fit the somewhat rigid 'unauthorised mode' (as opposed to 'unauthorised act') category.

---

[101] [1954] 2 QB 66.   [102] [1951] 2 KB 343.

[103] Although Denning LJ would have preferred to ground liability on the breach of a non-delegable duty (as noted in section 3 above), he also agreed with Somervell and Singleton LJJ, in respect of the statement in the text.

[104] Even though the act is outside the scope of employment the employer may still be liable for breach of his own duty to provide a safe system of work: see, eg, *Hudson v Ridge Manufacturing Co Ltd* [1957] 2 QB 348.

[105] Just this question was raised in *HSBC Bank Plc v 5th Avenue Partners Ltd* [2009] EWCA Civ 296 (in which case it was said (at [56]) that the question of whether an act was done in the course of employment was a mixed one of fact and law.   [106] *Goh Choon Seng v Lee Kim Soo* [1925] AC 550.

[107] See Cane (2000) 116 LQR 21.

Of course, it is quite properly uncontentious to regard negligence in the performance of a job as a wrongful mode of doing an authorised act; but deliberate, heinous acts by an employee are far more difficult to classify in such terms. That said, the decided cases have on occasion regarded such egregious (even criminal) conduct in terms of wrongful modes of performing authorised acts. Examples will be considered below. But it is useful to begin this section by making the general observation that the possible variations of fact in this context bedevil the exposition of any clear, uncontroversial, and universally applicable formula. Here, as in many areas of tort law, some of the decisions are based more on policy than principle. That said, a few examples do help to illustrate the breadth of the factual variations that may occur. Take, first, *Century Insurance Co Ltd v Northern Ireland Road Transport Board*.[108]

> The driver of a petrol lorry, while transferring petrol from the lorry to an underground tank at a petrol station, struck a match in order to light a cigarette and then threw it, still alight, on the ground. An explosion and a fire ensued.

His employers were held liable for the damage caused: he did the act in the course of carrying out his task of delivering petrol. It was an unauthorised way of doing what he was actually employed to do. Similarly, in *Bayley v Manchester, Sheffield and Lincolnshire Rly Co*,[109] erroneously thinking that the claimant was on the wrong train, a porter of the defendants forcibly removed him. The defendants were held liable. Consider, too, *Harrison v Michelin Tyre Co Ltd*.[110]

> C was injured when an employee of Ds deliberately steered the truck which he was driving a few inches off the designated passageway and knocked C over as he stood at his machine. Ds were held liable. The momentary horseplay engaged in by Ds' servant did not take him outside the course of his employment.

In recent years, however, there has been a rash of cases the Commonwealth over in which the employee committed various crimes of violence and sexual abuse which have forced the courts to abandon their somewhat artificial endeavours to squeeze these cases of deliberate wrongdoing into the traditional 'unauthorised mode' framework.[111] They have preferred to deal with such cases according to the 'close connection test' that will be examined in due course. For now, however, it is useful to provide some general guidance on how the courts determine what does and does not come within the concept of authorised acts.

(2) Authorised conduct within limits of time and space

The conduct of an employee is normally only within the scope of his employment during his authorised period of work. However, he will still be treated as being within the scope of his employment during a period which is not unreasonably disconnected

---

[108] [1942] AC 509.   [109] (1873) LR 8 CP 148.

[110] [1985] 1 All ER 918. See also *Duffy v Thanet DC* (1984) 134 NLJ 680.

[111] See, eg, *Mattis v Pollock* [2003] 1 WLR 2158, *New South Wales v Lepore* [2003] HCA 4, *Bazley v Curry* [1999] 2 SCR 534, and *Jacobi v Griffiths* (1999) 174 DLR (4th) 71; *Lister v Hesley Hall Ltd* [2002] 1 AC 215.

from the authorised period. Thus, someone paid for working until 6 p.m. who stays on for a few extra minutes in order to finish a job will still be within the scope of his employment.[112] But an employee who comes into his employer's premises without permission during his holiday is not within the scope of his job.[113]

By extension from the foregoing, employees travelling to and from their place of work are not ordinarily regarded as being within the course of their employment. However, there are instances where travel is so closely connected with a person's work that the ordinary principle cannot apply. In *Smith v Stages*,[114] for example, an employee had been working away from his home and his usual workplace. He was involved in a road accident driving home in his own car so that he could resume work at his usual place of employment the next day. He was paid for the day he needed to drive back as a normal working day. The House of Lords held that he remained within the course of his employment. His journey from A to B was part and parcel of his job in those circumstances, and his employers, in effect, directed that he make the journey.[115]

There are of course many jobs where travel is itself the essence of the employment. The work of sales representatives is an obvious example. But what if such employees make a detour from their set pattern of work for their own purposes, say, to visit a friend or to do some shopping? The courts have sometimes been called upon to decide whether such detours fall within the scope of employment. The classic ruling is that of Parke B in *Joel v Morison*.

> If he was going out of his way, against his master's implied commands when driving on his master's business, he will make his master liable; but if he was going on a frolic of his own, without being at all on his master's business, the master will not be liable.[116]

Whether the detour by the employee is a 'frolic of his own' is clearly a matter of degree. Here are two cases, one on each side of the line.

> A carter was in charge of a horse and cart during the day. Without permission he drove them home, a ¼-mile out of his way, for his midday meal, and left the horse unattended outside his home. His employer was held liable for damage done by the horse when it ran away.[117]

> A carman, having delivered wine, was to bring back some empties directly to the shop of his employers. On the return journey, before reaching the shop, he deviated from his route in order to pick up a cask at the home of the clerk accompanying him and take it elsewhere for that clerk's private purposes. While on the way to the clerk's home he drove the cart negligently and injured C. His employers were held not liable.[118]

---

[112] See, eg, *Ruddiman & Co v Smith* (1889) 60 LT 708.   [113] *Compton v McClure* [1975] ICR 378.
[114] [1989] AC 928. See also *Vandyke v Fender* [1970] 2 QB 292; *Elleanor v Cavendish Woodhouse Ltd and Comerford* [1973] 1 Lloyd's Rep 313.
[115] In similar vein see *Ministry of Defence v Radclyffe* [2009] EWCA Civ 635.
[116] (1834) 6 C & P 501, at 503.   [117] *Whatman v Pearson* (1868) LR 3 CP 422.
[118] *Storey v Ashton* (1869) LR 4 QB 476.

Consider carefully, in each case, exactly what job the employee was engaged to do. Also, if an employee is found to have gone on a 'frolic of his own', can he be deemed to have re-entered his employer's service at a later stage? An attempt to establish such a resumption failed in *Rayner v Mitchell*.[119]

> X was employed to deliver beer and pick up empties. He took out the cart on an unauthorised trip and on his return picked up some empties. This was held not enough to constitute a resumption of his employment, and his employer was held not liable for his negligent driving while returning to the employer's premises with the empties on board.

(3) Express prohibitions

Often, of course, an employer expressly forbids certain acts. But it does not follow from this that an act done in defiance of the prohibition is thereby placed outside the scope of employment. If it were so, the employer would only have to issue specific orders not to be negligent in order to escape liability for his employee's negligence. The House of Lords has laid down the rule as follows:

> [T]here are prohibitions which limit the sphere of employment, and prohibitions which only deal with conduct within the sphere of employment. A transgression of a prohibition of the latter class leaves the sphere of employment where it was, and consequently will not prevent recovery of compensation. A transgression of the former class carries with it the result that the man has gone outside the sphere.[120]

Again, a few illustrative examples are helpful. In *Canadian Pacific Rly Co v Lockhart*[121] the defendants prohibited their staff from driving uninsured cars on the company's business. In breach of this instruction, S drove an uninsured car negligently, while engaged on the company's business, and injured the claimant. The defendants were held liable, the Judicial Committee holding that:

> it was not the acting as driver that was prohibited, but the non-insurance of the motor car, if used as a means incidental to the execution of the work which he was employed to do. It follows that the prohibition merely limited the way in which, or by means of which, the servant was to execute the work which he was employed to do, and that breach of the prohibition did not exclude the liability of the master to third parties.[122]

Likewise, a garage hand employed to move vehicles in a garage, but forbidden to drive them, was acting in the course of his employment when he drove a van out of the garage on to the highway (in order to make room in the garage for another vehicle), and collided on the highway with the claimant's van.[123] These cases may be contrasted

---

[119] (1877) 2 CPD 357.
[120] *Plumb v Cobden Flour Mills Co Ltd* [1914] AC 62, at 67 (a workmen's compensation case, but the principles are the same).   [121] [1942] AC 591.
[122] Ibid at 601.
[123] *LCC v Cattermoles (Garages) Ltd* [1953] 2 All ER 582. Cf *Limpus v London General Omnibus Co Ltd* (1862) 1 H & C 526 (a bus driver, contrary to instructions, raced a rival bus in order to get custom – a direction to the jury that these instructions defined the scope of employment was held wrong in law). Cf *Iqbal v London Transport Executive* (1973) 16 KIR 329.

with *Rand v Craig*.[124] There, the defendant employed his servants to carry rubbish from X to Y. Instead they deposited some of this rubbish on the claimant's land. The defendant was held not liable for this trespass because the employees were employed, not to carry rubbish generally, but only to carry it from X to Y. The act was therefore of a kind that the defendant was impliedly forbidden to do.

If a driver gives a lift to a third party in breach of his employer's instructions and tortiously injures that passenger through careless driving, the courts approach the question of the employer's liability as follows. The issue does not turn on the fact that the passenger is a trespasser.[125] Instead, the employer will be held not liable if his prohibition has marked the limits of the scope of employment, so that giving the lift was outside that scope. On the other hand, if the prohibition affects only the mode in which the employee is to perform his duties, the employer may be vicariously liable. Two cases show the distinction.[126] In *Twine v Bean's Express Ltd*,[127] the facts were as follows.

> The employer had a contract to employ his vans on Post Office business. Contrary to his express instruction his driver gave a lift to a third party.

It was held that giving the lift was outside the scope of employment. Operating what was in effect a 'free taxi service' was not the job the driver was employed to do. But contrast this case with that of *Rose v Plenty*.[128]

> A milkman employed a 13-year-old boy to deliver and collect milk bottles on his milk round contrary to his employer's order that children were not to be employed by rounds-men in the performance of their duties. The driver negligently injured the boy.

The employer was held vicariously liable because the prohibition affected only the manner in which the roundsman was to perform his duties of delivering milk and did not limit the scope of those duties. He was still delivering milk, and the boy he had wrongly recruited to assist him was part of that enterprise.

(C) CLOSE CONNECTION BETWEEN THE WRONGFUL ACT AND THE EMPLOYEE'S WORK

Frequently, employees do acts which they have no express authority to do, but which are nevertheless calculated to further some proper objective of their employer. Unless the method of accomplishing this objective is so outrageous that no employer could

---

[124] [1919] 1 Ch 1.

[125] *Young v Box & Co* [1951] 1 TLR 798; *Rose v Plenty* [1976] 1 All ER 97.

[126] Though note that the distinction can sometimes appear illusory. In *Gavil v Carroll* [2008] ICIR 122 a specific prohibition against assaulting opposition players did not, apparently, mean a rugby player was act-ing beyond the scope of his employment when he punched an opponent *after the match*.

[127] (1946) 175 LT 131.

[128] [1976] 1 All ER 97. As to the principles applicable when a prohibition is statutory, see *Alford v National Coal Board* [1952] 1 All ER 754.

reasonably be taken to have contemplated such an act as being within the scope of employment, the employer will be liable for torts thus committed, as the following cases show. *Poland v John Parr & Sons* is the leading case.[129]

> H, an employee of Ds, while going home to dinner, reasonably believed that a boy was stealing sugar from a bag on a passing lorry of his employers. He struck the boy, who fell and, in consequence, had to have a leg amputated. Although his act in defence of his employer's property was unreasonable enough to be tortious, it was not sufficiently excessive to be outside the scope of his employment.

Holding that 'a servant has an implied authority upon an emergency to endeavour to protect his employer's property if he sees it in danger or has reasonable ground for thinking that he sees it in danger',[130] the Court of Appeal found the defendants liable. Atkin LJ did, however, point out that:

> where the servant does more than the emergency requires, the excess may be so great as to take the act out of the class. For example, if H had fired a shot at the boy, the act might have been in the interest of his employers, but that is not the test.[131]

Now consider *Warren v Henlys Ltd.*[132]

> A garage attendant employed by Ds accused C, in violent language, of leaving the garage without paying for his petrol. After paying, C called the police and said that he would report the attendant to his employers. The attendant on hearing this assaulted C.

It was held that there was no evidence that 'this assault...was so connected with the acts which the servant was expressly or impliedly authorised to do as to be a mode of doing those acts'.[133]

A very obvious example of conduct unconnected with the employer's work is seen in *Makanjuola v Metropolitan Police Commissioner*.[134] There, a police officer extracted sexual favours from the claimant in return for a promise not to report her to the immigration authorities. It was held that his act was entirely for his own purposes and not an act his employer in any sense authorised. Of course, were the officer's proclivities known to senior officers, it might have been possible to argue that there was a breach of a primary duty of care to the public; but those proclivities were not known. Finally, where the acts of prison officers are broadly in furtherance of the interests of the Home Office, the Home Office remains liable even though the officers' acts amount to misfeasance in a public office.[135]

---

[129] [1927] 1 KB 236.   [130] Ibid at 240.   [131] Ibid at 245.
[132] [1948] 2 All ER 935. In *Keppel Bus Co Ltd v Sa'ad bin Ahmad* [1974] 2 All ER 700, a bus conductor struck a passenger after a quarrel. Although the conductor's duties extended to keeping order, his employer was not vicariously liable because there was no evidence of disorder.   [133] Ibid at 938.
[134] [1992] 3 All ER 617.   [135] *Racz v Home Office* [1994] 2 AC 45.

(1) Criminal assaults, etc

Evidence that the employee's conduct was a criminal or otherwise wilful wrongdoing will not necessarily negate the possibility of imposing vicarious liability.[136] For example, an employer may be liable in respect of acts of harassment[137] or where an over-enthusiastic defence of his interests results in an assault which is in the circumstances a crime as well as a tort.[138] Similarly, in *Vasey v Surrey Free Inns*,[139] an employer was held liable in respect of an assault upon the claimant committed by two doormen in his employ. The doormen's acts were, crucially, in response to the claimant having caused damage to the employer's premises by kicking them. Accordingly, the doormen's actions were construed as being in furtherance of the employer's interests.[140]

There may be cases, however, where the wrongful conduct is in no sense in the employers' interests, but it is so bound up with the employee's job that the employers may be held vicariously liable for that conduct. To put it more bluntly, dishonest or criminal acts are no bar, per se, to the imposition of vicarious liability.[141] The crucial question is whether the act in question either was committed directly in the course of the employee's employment,[142] or was sufficiently connected to it to warrant the imposition of vicarious liability. Thus, the theft of the mink stole in *Morris v C W Martin & Sons Ltd*[143] by the man entrusted with the job of cleaning it has been viewed by the House of Lords in *Lister v Hesley Hall Ltd* as being a case in which the employee used an unlawful mode of doing his job.[144] The theft of the stole by a cook in the canteen at the firm's factory would, however, be an act totally unrelated to his employment. Accordingly, the employer would not in such circumstances be held vicariously liable (which is not to say that he would escape personal liability in negligence for employing persons known to be dishonest, thus placing him in breach of a non-delegable duty to care properly for the fur). The short point is that the employer cannot be held *vicariously liable* simply for supplying an opportunity for the employee to commit the

[136] *Barwick v English Joint Stock Bank* (1867) LR 2 Exch 259; *Lloyd v Grace, Smith & Co* [1912] AC 716.
[137] See, eg, *Iqbal v Dean Manson Solicitors* [2011] EWCA Civ 123, at [63].
[138] *Poland v Parr* [1927] 1 KB 236.   [139] [1996] PIQR P373.
[140] See also *Mattis v Pollock* [2003] 1 WLR 2158 (where a doorman committed an assault some hundreds of metres from the nightclub at which the trouble had started and vicarious liability was still imposed); *Weir v Bettison* [2003] EWCA Civ 111 (a chief constable was held vicariously liable for an assault committed by an off-duty police officer who assaulted a would-be thief after indicating that he was a police officer and that he proposed to take the culprit to a police station).
[141] *Port Swettenham Authority v TW Wu & Co* [1979] AC 580.
[142] *T v North Yorkshire CC* (1998) *Times*, 10 September.   [143] [1966] 1 QB 716.
[144] [2002] 1 AC 215. This interpretation is highly questionable since two members of the Court of Appeal seem to have viewed the case as turning primarily upon the non-delegable duty arising out of the bailment of the fur. It is particularly notable that Lord Nicholls deliberately left this case to one side when considering the close connection test in *Dubai Aluminium Co Ltd v Salaam* [2003] 2 AC 366, at [27]–[28].

crime. Instead, the criminal act must be much more closely connected with the contract of employment. The leading case is *Lister v Hesley Hall Ltd*.[145]

> A warden living in a boarding house attached to a school owned and managed by Ds had systematically sexually abused for about three years Cs, who were boys at the school with emotional and behavioural difficulties. Ds had no knowledge of these facts. Cs claimed damages against Ds for the personal injuries they suffered, arguing, inter alia, that Ds were vicariously liable for the torts committed by the warden. The House of Lords held Ds vicariously liable, emphasising the close contact he had had with the pupils by virtue of his job and the inherent risks his job carried with it.

At the heart of their Lordships' decision was the fact that there was a sufficiently close connection between the work that the warden had been employed to do and the acts of abuse that he had committed for those acts to justify the defendants' vicarious liability.[146] As Lord Steyn put it, in terms reflecting the role of policy in this context:

> The question is whether the warden's torts were so closely connected with his employment that it would be fair and just to hold the employers vicariously liable. On the facts of the case the answer is yes. After all, the sexual abuse was inextricably interwoven with the carrying out by the warden of his duties in [the children's] House.[147]

And for Lord Clyde:

> The opportunity to be at the premises would not in itself constitute a sufficient connection between his wrongful actings and his employment. In addition to the opportunity which access gave him, his position as warden and the close contact with the boys which that work involved created a sufficient connection between the acts of abuse which he committed and the work which he had been employed to do.[148]

What seems to lie at the heart of *Lister*, then, is not that the job provided the mere circumstances in which the tort took place, but rather that the tort in question constituted a particular risk which was inextricably linked to the employer's type of business.[149] As Lord Clyde further explained: '[t]he fact that his employment gave the employee the opportunity to commit the wrong is not enough to make the employer liable. He is liable only if the risk is one which experience shows is inherent in the nature of the business'.[150]

---

[145] [2002] 1 AC 215.

[146] In similar vein, see *Maga v Birmingham Roman Catholic Archdiocese Trustees* [2010] 1 WLR 1441 and *Brink's Global Services v Igrox Ltd* [2010] EWCA Civ 1207.

[147] [2002] 1 AC 215, at [28].   [148] Ibid at [50].

[149] In *Gravil v Carroll* [2008] ICR 1222 the CA preferred to ask whether the occurrence in question was an 'ordinary incident' of a rugby match before holding a rugby club liable for a post-match punch thrown by one of its players at an opposition player. See also *Maga v Birmingham RC Archdiocese Trustees* [2010] 1 WLR 1441.

[150] [2002] 1 AC 215, at [65]. It might be argued that the focus on the nature of the employer's business tends to blur the distinction between the employer's primary and vicarious liability (see *Balfon Trustees Ltd v Peterson* [2001] IRLR 758, at [28]). But the decision in *Lister* is assuredly based on the latter.

In the wake of *Lister*, it is unwise to regard earlier decisions treating wanton, egregious conduct as falling beyond the bounds of a course of employment as cast-iron precedents on vicarious liability. A moment's reflection reveals that child abuse, by whatever means, could never plausibly be viewed as a mere unauthorised mode of performing an authorised act. But the 'close connection test' adopted in *Lister*, which stresses the intimate connection between the employee's tort and the nature of his employment, readily embraces such cases.[151] Of course, while this approach goes a long way towards providing compensation to those who might otherwise go without (if forced to sue, for example, a relatively impecunious warden), it nonetheless gives rise to more problems than it solves. In particular, the language used in *Lister* is more in tune with that deployed in connection with non-delegable duties than with that traditionally associated with vicarious liability.[152] Equally, as Lord Nicholls subsequently pointed out in *Dubai Aluminium Co Ltd v Salaam*, the close connection test 'affords no guidance on the type or degree of connection... [that will be] sufficiently close to prompt the legal conclusion that the risk of the wrongful act occurring, and any loss resulting... should fall on the firm or employer'.[153] In other words, in ensuring that the claimants received a remedy in *Lister*, the House of Lords adopted a very vague test the application of which will prove remarkably popular,[154] but no doubt problematic in the future.

(2) Fraud

Leaving cases of violence and abuse to one side, it is clear that an employee's fraud may also result in vicarious liability. *Lloyd v Grace, Smith & Co*[155] is the leading case.

> In an action to recover title deeds by C (who was a client of D, a firm of solicitors), the material point was whether the firm was liable for the act of its managing clerk, who, when C consulted him about selling her property and realising a mortgage, fraudulently induced her to sign documents transferring those properties to him. The managing clerk was employed, among other things, to carry out conveyancing transactions. Although the firm derived no benefit from these frauds, perpetrated by its employee for his own purposes, it was held liable for his acts.

In such cases, according to *Lloyd*, the usual question that must be posed appears to be whether the employee was acting with either the actual or ostensible authority of the

---

[151] In similar vein, see *Bazley v Curry* (1999) 174 DLR (4th) 45; *Jacobi v Griffiths* (1999) 174 DLR (4th) 71.

[152] *Lister v Hesley Hall Ltd* [2002] 1 AC 215, at [55] and [82]–[83].   [153] [2003] 2 AC 366.

[154] The test has already been adopted on many occasions: see *Dubai Aluminium v Salaam* [2003] 2 AC 366; *JJ Coughlan Ltd v Ruparelia* [2003] EWCA Civ 1057; *Marsh v CC of Lancashire* [2003] EWCA Civ 284; *Mattis v Pollock* [2003] 1 WLR 2158; *A-G v Hartwell* [2004] UKPC 12; *Bernard v A-G of Jamaica* [2004] UKPC 47; *Brown v Robinson* [2004] UKPC 56; *Godden v Kent and Medway Strategic HA* [2004] UKHC 1629; *Frans Maas (UK) Ltd v Samsung Electronics* [2004] 2 Lloyd's Rep 251; *Majrowski v Guy's and St Thomas' NHS Trust* [2006] UKHL 34.   [155] [1912] AC 716.

employer.[156] And, so long as such authority exists, it does not matter that the defrauded party had reasonable grounds for suspicion about what was going on: the court will not require such parties to make enquiries about the legitimacy of a transaction.[157]

Cases of actual authority are unlikely to be very problematic. But cases of ostensible authority do prove tricky. In this respect, it will be important to advert to the fact that the employee appeared to be acting in a manner that would benefit the employer rather than the employee personally. But if the act is only intended to benefit the employee, and the fraud is not intimately bound up with the employee's employment,[158] vicarious liability ought not to be imposed. (This does not mean, however, that the employer could not potentially be held liable in some cases on the alternative basis of breach of a non-delegable duty.)[159]

In *Dubai Aluminium Co Ltd v Salaam*,[160] all the fraudulent acts necessary to make the employee personally liable took place within (or in close connection with) his course of employment, and vicarious liability could be imposed. By contrast, however, in *Crédit Lyonnais Bank Nederland NV v Export Credits Guarantee Department*,[161] part of the fraud was committed by the employee and part of it by a third party. The House of Lords therefore refused to combine the two sets of acts so as to make the employer vicariously liable for the combined acts of the two fraudsters. Crucially, not all the relevant acts occurred within the course of the employee's employment.

SECTION 7   STATUTORY DUTY AND VICARIOUS LIABILITY

For a time it was unclear whether an employer could be held vicariously liable for an employee's breach of a statutory duty imposed directly on the employee but not the employer. Happily, the matter has now been resolved authoritatively in *Majrowski v Guy's and St Thomas' NHS Trust* where it was held that an employer can be so liable. In that case, Lord Nicholls said: '[u]nless the statute expressly or impliedly indicates otherwise, the principle of vicarious liability is applicable where an employee commits a breach of a statutory obligation sounding in damages while acting in the course of his employment'.[162]

---

[156] Ibid at 725. This approach has since been endorsed by the HL in *Stone and Rolls Ltd v Moore Stephens* [2009] 3 WLR 455.

[157] *Quinn v CC Automotive Group Ltd* [2010] EWCA Civ 1106.

[158] In *JJ Coughlan v Ruparelia* [2003] EWCA Civ 1057 the CA stressed the importance of considering whether the transaction in question, 'viewed fairly and properly', was the kind of transaction that forms part of the ordinary business of a solicitor.

[159] Certainly, there were those in the Australian High Court who preferred to see *Lloyd* as a case of non-delegable duty: see *New South Wales v Lepore* [2003] HCA 4, at [110] and [235].

[160] [2003] 1 Lloyd's Rep 65.   [161] [2000] 1 AC 486.

[162] [2006] UKHL 34, at [17]. See also *Iqbal v Dean Manson Solicitors* [2011] EWCA Civ 123 (vicarious liability for acts prohibited by the Protection from Harassment Act 1997).

So far as the Crown is concerned there is specific statutory provision: the rather obscurely worded section 2(3) of the Crown Proceedings Act 1947 has the effect of making the Crown liable for breaches of statutory duty by its employees.

FURTHER READING

CANE, 'Vicarious Liability for Sexual Abuse' (2000) 116 *Law Quarterly Review* 21

FELDTHUSEN, 'Vicarious Liability for Sexual Torts' in Mullany and Linden (eds), *Torts Tomorrow: A Tribute to John Fleming* (1998), 222

MCKENDRICK, 'Vicarious Liability and Independent Contractors – A Re-Examination' (1990) 53 *Modern Law Review* 770

MURPHY, 'Juridical Foundations of Common Law Non-Delegable Duties' in Neyers et al (eds), *Emerging Issues in Tort Law* (2007), ch 14

STEVENS, 'Non-Delegable Duties and Vicarious Liability' in Neyers et al (eds), *Emerging Issues in Tort Law* (2007), ch 13

WEEKES, 'Vicarious Liability for Violent Employees' [2004] *Cambridge Law Journal* 53

WITTING, 'Breach of the Non-delegable Duty: Defending Limited Strict Liability in Tort' (2006) 29 *University of New South Wales Law Journal* 38

25
CAPACITY AND PARTIES

KEY ISSUES

(1) Capacity
A preliminary issue that might arise in a tort action concerns 'capacity'. This refers to the status of legal persons and their ability to sue or be sued in tort.

(2) Capacity examples
Very young children cannot be held responsible in law for the consequences of actions that might otherwise be tortious. However, the law is more accepting of the responsibility of mentally disordered persons, especially where they have some understanding of the nature and quality of their acts.

(3) Concurrent tortfeasors
The claimant's injury might be the result of the torts of more than one person. In such a case, the claimant can sue more than one person. However, the law does not require this; it allows the claimant to sue for the full amount one only of the concurrent tortfeasors whose acts combine to cause the same damage. This reduces the burden upon the claimant in obtaining redress.

(4) Several tortfeasors causing different damage
The claimant's injuries might, alternatively, be the result of the independent acts of more than one person causing separate items of damage. In such a case, the liability of each tortfeasor is several and he is liable only for the damage that he causes.

(5) Contribution
Statute allows any person successfully sued in tort to seek contribution from other joint or concurrent tortfeasors (under (3) above, but not (4)). This might be done in the course of the original action commenced by the claimant, or in separate proceedings between tortfeasors. The law will apportion liability between these parties according to the extent of their responsibility.

SECTION 1   THE CROWN

(A) VICARIOUS LIABILITY

According to section 2(1) of the Crown Proceedings Act 1947, 'the Crown shall be subject to all those liabilities in tort to which, if it were a private person of full age and capacity, it would be subject in respect of torts committed by its servants or agents'. However, notwithstanding this general statement of the Crown's vicarious liability, it is also clear that an employee must *normally* be directly or indirectly appointed by the Crown and paid wholly out of the Consolidated Fund or other specified national funds for this vicarious liability to be triggered.[1] The Crown is not, therefore, vicariously liable for the torts of police officers,[2] or for the torts of borrowed employees.

The Act does not define the term 'Crown', yet it is clear that the Crown Proceedings Act 1947 does not apply to the employees of those bodies that are not deemed to be agents of the Crown. In such cases, the ordinary law affecting public bodies and public officers will apply, and it is clear that many public bodies fall outside the Act.[3] It is thus important to be able to determine which public bodies constitute agents of the Crown. Yet resolving this matter is often difficult. That said, it is certainly the case that the nature of the functions of the body in question, and the extent to which it is under ministerial control, are especially relevant considerations.[4]

(B) NON-VICARIOUS LIABILITY

Section 2(1)(b) and (c) of the Crown Proceedings Act 1947 makes the Crown liable for any breach of those duties owed at common law to employees, agents, or independent contractors by an employer, and for any breach of the duties attaching at common law to the ownership, occupation, possession, or control of property.

Section 2(1) does not seem sufficiently wide to take account of all the cases where an employer is liable otherwise than vicariously. While employers are frequently answerable for the acts of independent contractors – not because the independent contractor has committed a tort in the course of his work, but because the duty is a personal one imposed on the employer – section 2 would not seem wide enough to cover non-delegable duties of this sort.[5] The Crown is liable in tort to the same extent as private persons for breaches of statutory duty that have been imposed on it, provided the duty is also imposed on persons other than the Crown and its officers.[6] If the duty is imposed, not on the Crown, but directly on its employees, and an employee commits a tort while performing or purporting to perform those statutory functions, 'the liabilities of the Crown in respect of the tort shall be such as they would have been if those functions had been conferred or imposed solely by virtue of instructions lawfully given

---

[1] Crown Proceedings Act 1947, s 2(6). The exception, under s 3, is that no such liability can be imposed in respect of the infringement of intellectual property rights except in accordance with s 3.

[2] For the liability of a chief constable to pay damages out of public funds to those harmed by a policeman's torts, see the Police Act 1996, s 88 and *Weir v Bettison* [2003] EWCA Civ 111.

[3] *Tamlin v Hannaford* [1950] 1 KB 18.

[4] *Bank voor Handel en Scheepvaart NV v Administrator of Hungarian Property* [1954] AC 584.

[5] Cf *Egerton v Home Office* [1978] Crim LR 494 (a duty was owed to a sexual offender in prison to keep a protective watch to guard against his being attacked by fellow prisoners).

[6] Crown Proceedings Act 1947, s 2(2). The Occupiers' Liability Act 1957, s 6 provides that that Act shall bind the Crown and that the common duty of care imposed by it shall apply as a statutory duty for the purpose of the Crown Proceedings Act 1947.

by the Crown'.[7] The Crown also has the same liability as other employers under the Employer's Liability (Defective Equipment) Act 1969.

(C) EXCEPTIONS

(1) Judicial errors

Section 2(5) of the Crown Proceedings Act 1947 provides that the Crown shall not be liable 'in respect of anything done or omitted to be done by any person while discharging or purporting to discharge any responsibilities of a judicial nature vested in him, or any responsibilities which he has in connection with the execution of the judicial process'. The first part of the subsection would be otiose if it merely provided that the Crown shall not be liable wherever the judge has the defence of 'judicial act'. It seems, therefore, that whatever doubts there may be about the liability of inferior courts for acts done in excess of jurisdiction which purport to be in discharge of the judicial function, the Crown is exempted from liability.[8] Presumably, also, the first part of the subsection extends not only to that limited class of bodies not being courts, *strictu sensu*, to which the defence of 'judicial acts' applies, but also to other administrative tribunals.

(2) Armed forces

The Crown Proceedings (Armed Forces) Act 1987 repealed section 10 of the 1947 Act, which prevented members of the armed forces suing the Crown in respect of injuries suffered in the course of their duties caused by another member of the armed forces who was on duty. Beyond the statute, it was also established in *Mulcahy v Ministry of Defence*[9] that no alternative liability at common law exists. In that case, the Court of Appeal held that a serviceman did not owe his fellow servicemen a duty of care in warlike conditions for it would not be fair, just, and reasonable to impose such a duty.[10]

(3) Certain statutes imposing liability in tort

It is doubtful whether the Crown is bound by statutes imposing tortious liability unless the particular statute has clearly made the Crown liable. However, most modern Acts making substantial changes in tort law have been made expressly applicable to the Crown.[11]

---

[7] Crown Proceedings Act 1947, s 2(3). Presumably, this rule also applies where the duty in question is not also imposed on persons other than employees of the Crown.

[8] *Welsh v CC of Merseyside Police* [1993] 1 All ER 692. Under s 31(1) of the Courts Act 2003, immunity is granted to a justice of the peace only in respect of acts or omissions 'in the execution of his duty as a justice of the peace', and then only so far as those acts or omissions fall 'within his jurisdiction'.

[9] [1996] QB 732.

[10] Note that this decision must now be read in the light of *Barrett v Enfield LBC* [2001] 2 AC 550 and *Phelps v Hillingdon LBC* [2000] 3 WLR 776.

[11] Eg, Law Reform (Contributory Negligence) Act 1945, the Congenital Disabilities (Civil Liability) Act 1976, the Civil Liability (Contribution) Act 1978, and the Limitation Act 1980. Statutes about which the doubt persists include the Defamation Acts of 1952 and 1996.

SECTION 2 COMPANIES

(A) LIABILITY

A company is a separate legal entity, able to enter into contracts, to own property, and to sue and be sued in its own name. It has a liability that is separate from that of its shareholders. Indeed, the ordinary rule is that the shareholders are not liable for the debts of the company in which they invest, except to the extent of any unpaid amounts on the shares that they hold.[12]

A company will be *vicariously* liable for the acts and omissions of its employees arising in the course of its business, where these cause loss to outsiders. This kind of liability is exactly the same as that which applies with respect to an employer who is a natural person. Vicarious liability is discussed in chapter 24.

The more complex issue to be discussed concerns the *primary* liability of the company, its directors, officers, and employees when a tort is committed. Let us first consider when the company is primarily liable. Directors are said to act *as the company* when they make decisions as the directing mind and will of the company.[13] They act in this way when making decisions at board meetings or on delegation of decision-making power from the board. The range of persons who may qualify as the directing mind and will of the company was extended in various cases, including the decision of the House of Lords in *Director General of Fair Trading v Pioneer Concrete (UK) Ltd & Another (Re Supply of Ready Mixed Concrete (No 2))*,[14] which held that the court could examine the specific individuals who exercised management and control over the activity constituting the wrong. Given the way that decision-making power within the company may be delegated to particular individuals who are not necessarily board members, the directing mind and will might be found in any delegate holding the decision-making power of the board.[15] In these cases, the wrongs of the individual decision makers become the wrongs of the company.[16]

Where recourse to the company would not be viable, outsiders who have suffered a wrong at the hands of an individual director or officer may look to him for redress. The general principle is that individuals are liable for their own torts. 'Whether the principal is a company or a natural person, someone acting on his behalf may incur personal liability in tort as well as imposing vicarious liability or attributed liability upon his principal'.[17] But there must be some act or omission of the director or officer

---

[12] Insolvency Act 1986, s 74(2)(d).

[13] *Lennard's Carrying Co Ltd v Asiatic Petroleum Co Ltd* [1915] AC 705; *Tesco Supermarkets Ltd v Nattrass* [1972] AC 153.

[14] [1995] 1 AC 456. See also *Meridian Global Funds Management Asia Ltd v Securities Commission* [1995] 2 AC 500.   [15] See *Tesco Supermarkets Ltd v Nattrass* [1972] AC 153, at 171 (Lord Reid).

[16] This liability base has been applied in criminal, regulatory, and civil proceedings: CA Png, *Corporate Liability: A Study in the Principles of Attribution* (2001), 19.

[17] *Williams v Natural Life Health Foods Ltd* [1998] 1 WLR 829, at 835. See also *Wah Tat Bank Ltd v Chan Cheng Kum* [1975] AC 507, at 514–15.

that amounts to a tort. A director will be personally liable for his own statements constituting deceit.[18] However, courts are reluctant to impose personal liability upon individual officers of a company for negligent misstatements made while acting for the company. In such cases, the claimant must establish the type of proximity that gives rise to an 'assumption of responsibility'.[19] Further, a claim for conversion rightly made with respect to a company alleged to have been dealing with the claimant's goods in a manner inconsistent with its rights is not, prima facie, good as against one only of its directors, where there are two or more directors.[20]

In some cases, the question arises as to the liability of one company within a group of companies for the acts or omissions of another company in the group – usually the liability of the parent company for its subsidiary's torts. Ordinarily, the courts will respect the separateness of each entity. They will not 'lift the corporate veil' in order to fix liability in a company other than that which interacted with an opposing party.[21] On rare occasions, however, courts have been prepared to disregard the strictness of rules of separate legal personality and even to recognise an extended liability in companies other than the parent. Thus, in *Aventis Pasteur SA v O'Byrne*,[22] the Grand Chamber of the European Court of Justice held that a person injured by a defective product could sue the French producer, or, if out of time, its UK *subsidiary* distribution company, in circumstances where the parent exercised a high degree of control over the subsidiary so as to determine when the product entered into circulation. This is to say that the subsidiary could be *treated as* the manufacturer under the Product Liability Act 1987.

(B) POWER TO SUE

Companies (but not their shareholders)[23] can sue for any tort other than those of which, in the nature of things, they could not be victims – for example, assault. That said, in the context of defamation – for which a company may in principle sue[24] – it is important to identify whether the words in question refer to the company or an individual. Thus, to say of the sole owner of a company that he is a 'bloody crook' is a slur on the individual rather than his company.[25]

---

[18] *Standard Chartered Bank v Pakistan National Shipping Corp (No 2)* [2003] 1 AC 959. See also *Stone & Rolls Ltd v Moore Stephens* [2009] UKHL 39, at [132]–[136].

[19] *Williams v Natural Life Health Foods Ltd* [1998] 1 WLR 829.

[20] *Thunder Air Ltd v Hilmarsson* [2008] EWHC 355 (Ch).

[21] *Adams v Cape Industries plc* [1990] Ch 433.

[22] (2009) 113 BMLR 1. See also subsequent decision of the Supreme Court in *O'Byrne v Aventis Pasteur SA* [2010] UKSC 23, esp at [34]–[35].

[23] Thus if a shareholder suffers a loss in the value of his shareholding due to a tort committed against the company, it is the company, not the shareholder, who can recover: see *Johnson v Gore Wood & Co* [2002] 2 AC 1.

[24] Eg, *Jameel v Wall Street Journal Europe SPRL* [2006] UKHL 44. This case confirmed that there is no need for a company to prove special damage in order to sue. See discussion in ch 20.

[25] *Shendish Manor Ltd v Coleman* [2001] EWCA Civ 913.

We have also seen (in chapter 3) that courts are prepared, no doubt in rare cases only, to 'lift the corporate veil' allowing a parent, controlling, or jointly controlling company to sue for losses affecting, in the first instance, a subsidiary, but leading to the claimant's own financial loss. This was the situation in the relational economic loss case of *Shell UK Ltd v Total UK Ltd*,[26] where the Court of Appeal accepted a claim by the part-owner of certain service companies for economic losses arising after its fuel storage and pipeline facilities were damaged in a fire caused by the negligence of the defendant. The claimant oil company had entered into contractual agreements for the use of these facilities, but had no possession or immediate right to possession. The claimant was held to be the 'beneficial owner' of the damaged property and could recover, at least where the legal owners were joined in the proceedings.

SECTION 3   PARTNERSHIPS AND LIMITED LIABILITY PARTNERSHIPS

The law does not recognise any legal entity known as a 'partnership'. The term 'partnership' simply describes a relationship (based on contract) between a group of persons who carry on a business with a view to a profit.[27] Partners may be jointly and severally liable to any persons not themselves partners[28] for torts committed by any one of them either while acting in the ordinary course of the business of the firm, or with the authority of his fellow partners.[29] The claimant must show that he relied on the individual partner's status *as a partner*.[30] In addition to this 'vicarious' liability, each partner may have a primary duty in tort: for example, the occupier's duty of care to visitors is owed by each partner in a partnership that occupies those premises.[31]

The limited liability partnership (LLP) is a hybrid form of business organisation, incorporating features of both the private company and the partnership. The LLP is a body corporate with legal personality separate from its members,[32] although its capital is not raised through the issuance of shares. The commission of a tort by a partner will render liable both that partner personally, and the limited liability partnership (as principal). The other partners will not be liable personally on the face of the legislation. But one important issue that is unclear from the Limited Liability Partnerships Act 2000 is whether the personal involvement of one partner in linking a client to a second partner can invoke that partner's personal liability. Suppose senior partner X

---

[26] [2010] EWCA Civ 180.

[27] Partnership Act 1890, s 1. See also *Dubai Aluminium Co Ltd v Salaam* [2003] 2 AC 366, at 376.

[28] *Mair v Wood* 1948 SC 83.

[29] Partnership Act 1890, ss 10 and 12; *Dubai Aluminium Co Ltd v Salaam* [2003] 1 All ER 97.

[30] *Nationwide Building Society v Lewis* [1998] Ch 482. Note that the existence of a partnership may be implied from an agreement to carry on a business in common even where the term 'partnership' is not expressly used: *Grant v Langley* [2001] WL 513090.   [31] See *Meekins v Henson* [1964] 1 QB 472.

[32] Limited Liability Partnerships Act 2000, s 1.

recommends to a client, C, that junior partner Y should do C's conveyance. Suppose further that X misrepresents that Y is competent. In such a case, it is clear that Y could be held liable for a negligently performed conveyance, as could the limited liability partnership. But would X remain immune, or would the personal 'assumption of responsibility' principle that causes a director to be personally liable in the case of a limited company[33] be applied in this context, too?

SECTION 4   HUSBAND AND WIFE

The liability of one spouse for the torts of the other is to be decided on the same principles as those applying where the parties are not married. Put simply, there is no presumption that one is responsible for the other.[34] As regards liability, *inter se*, section 1(1) of the Law Reform (Husband and Wife) Act 1962 provides that 'each of the parties to a marriage shall have the like right of action in tort against the other as if they were not married'. This provision is not so peculiar as it may first seem because, of course, the first spouse may well be a mere nominal defendant, the real defendant being an insurance company (for example, where spouse A is injured by spouse B's negligent driving).[35] Notwithstanding section 1(1), Parliament was also anxious to discourage actions founded on petty grievances between spouses. That being so, section 1(2) allows the court to stay the action 'if it appears...that no substantial benefit would accrue to either party from the continuation of the proceedings'.[36]

SECTION 5   MENTALLY DISORDERED PERSONS

The problems here arise mainly from the incomplete analyses often made by the judges of the states of mind required in particular torts. The case most directly in point is *Morriss v Marsden*.[37]

> D violently attacked C, a complete stranger, while he was standing in the entrance hall of a hotel, and D was sued for battery. The defence raised was insanity. The judge found that D was not in a condition of automatism or trance at the time of the attack on C, but that his mind directed the blows which he struck. He also found that at the material time D was a certifiable lunatic who knew the nature and quality of his act but, because of his lunacy, did not know that what he was doing was wrong. He nevertheless held the defence of insanity to be inapplicable.

[33] *Williams v Natural Life Health Foods Ltd* [1998] 1 WLR 830.
[34] Law Reform (Married Women and Tortfeasors) Act 1935, s 3. Husband and wife can be jointly liable in conspiracy: *Midland Bank Trust Co Ltd v Green (No 3)* [1982] Ch 529.
[35] Where another negligent driver is involved, his or her insurers may claim a contribution from the insurers of the negligent spouse in accordance with the principles discussed in section 7 of this chapter.
[36] Note, too, the provision in s 1(2)(b) to allow property disputes to be dealt with under the Married Women's Property Act 1882, s 17.
[37] [1952] 1 All ER 925.

The case is, therefore, authority for the proposition that, if a mentally disordered person has that state of mind which is required for liability in battery, then his insanity is no defence.[38] All that is required in battery is that the defendant must intend to strike the blow at the claimant. The judge in *Morriss* found that the defendant did so intend, and that it therefore followed that he was liable. At a more general level, the case also supports the proposition that, in tort (as distinct from criminal law), a defendant who intentionally invades the claimant's protected interest will not be excused simply because he was unaware that the invasion was a wrongful act. Thus, as Stable J observed in *Morriss v Marsden*:

> if a person in a condition of complete automatism inflicted grievous injury, that would not be actionable. In the same way, if a sleepwalker inadvertently, without intention or without carelessness, broke a valuable vase, that would not be actionable.[39]

The logic of this dictum means that a defence will lie in respect of all torts – including those of 'strict' liability – in which the defendant's conduct was, because of his mental disorder, involuntary. But there will also be a defence even if the conduct was intended, but the tort in question – for example, simple conspiracy – requires an improper purpose or malice.

SECTION 6   CHILDREN

(A) LIABILITY

A person is a child until he attains the age of 18 years.[40] Childhood as such is not a defence: but like all other defendants, a child is not liable for a specific tort if it is shown that he lacked the required capacity for legal responsibility. Should a one-year-old child pick up a letter defamatory of X, written by his father, and throw it through the window, whereupon Y picks it up and reads it, X will have no cause of action for libel against the infant. On the other hand, a 15-year-old youth, who pushes a man into a swimming pool, can be held liable in negligence and trespass.[41]

(1) Where the act of the child is also a breach of contract

With certain exceptions, a child is not liable for breach of contract.[42] Therefore, where the act of the child is merely an improper performance of one of the acts contemplated by such a contract, it will not be open to the person aggrieved to sue him in tort so as

---

[38] This is so even if the defendant's insanity causes him to be under a delusion about the surrounding circumstances. The critical thing is simply that he possessed the state of mind required by the tort in relation to the act done: *Buckley and Toronto Transportation Commission v Smith Transport Ltd* [1946] 4 DLR 721.

[39] [1952] 1 All ER 925, at 927.

[40] Family Law Reform Act 1969, s 1(1).

[41] *Williams v Humphrey* (1975) *Times*, 20 February. Cf *Wilson v Pringle* [1987] QB 237. For comment on some inconsistencies in the law relating to childhood responsibility, see Lyons [2010] LS 257.

[42] See Minors' Contracts Act 1987.

to evade the contractual immunity. But, if the act complained of, though performed upon the occasion of a contract, is independent of it, the claimant may then sue in tort. Of course, this rule is difficult to apply in marginal cases, but its judicial recognition is clear. Thus, a child who had possession of goods under a hire-purchase agreement, and who wrongfully disposed of them to a third party, was liable to the true owner for the independent tort of detinue which he committed by wrongfully disposing of them.[43] The hirer of a mare, hired for riding only, is liable in tort for doing an act of a nature not contemplated by the contract (namely jumping the mare); but if he were merely to ride her too far, this would not be an act of a different nature and no action in tort would lie.[44] The fact that the contract was in both cases void against the child would not, per se, prevent him from being liable in tort.

In this context, the question of suing a child in tort arises most often where he has obtained goods or a loan of money under contract by misrepresenting his real age. In such cases, the courts have held that no action in deceit will lie because that would be tantamount to allowing the enforcement of a void contract.[45]

(2) Liability of the parent

Although a claimant may have no cause of action against the child, he may sometimes be able to recover from the child's parent. The parent is liable only where he is accountable according to some other general principle of tort law. He may be vicariously liable – for example, if the child is acting as her father's chauffeur and drives the car negligently. Similarly, the father will be liable if he instigates the son's commission of a tort, and he will be liable if he himself has been personally negligent.[46] In other words, a father is not necessarily liable merely because his son has thrown a stone through his neighbour's window. Unless the father ordered him to do so, or unless his negligent supervision is proved to have caused the act complained of, he will not be liable.

(B) CAPACITY TO SUE

Except that he must normally sue by his next friend, a child is in the same position as any other claimant when suing in tort. A child may sue either parent, and may wish to do so where the parent has an insurance policy (usually comprehensive household insurance) which covers the particular liability.[47] The Court of Appeal has warned against the danger of too readily imposing liability for the 'rough and tumble of

---

[43] *Ballett v Mingay* [1943] KB 281.

[44] *Burnard v Haggis* (1863) 14 CBNS 45; *Jennings v Rundall* (1799) 8 Term Rep 335. See also *Walley v Holt* (1876) 35 LT 631 and *Fawcett v Smethurst* (1914) 84 LJKB 473.

[45] *R Leslie Ltd v Sheill* [1914] 3 KB 607, at 612.

[46] *Donaldson v McNiven* [1952] 2 All ER 691; *Newton v Edgerley* [1959] 3 All ER 337. The duty of school authorities is also to take the care which a reasonable parent would take: see, eg, *Ricketts v Erith BC* [1943] 2 All ER 629 and *Rich v LCC* [1953] 2 All ER 376.

[47] See, eg, *Ash v Lady Ash* (1696) Comb 357. See also *Young v Rankin* 1934 SC 499.

family life'.[48] And it is certainly well established that a parent (or someone with quasi-parental responsibility) may lawfully exercise reasonable chastisement in respect of the child.[49]

SECTION 7 JOINT TORTS

(A) CATEGORIES

There are three broad categories of circumstance where one person may suffer damage as the result of torts committed by two or more defendants: joint tortfeasors, several concurrent tortfeasors causing the same damage, and several tortfeasors causing different damage.[50]

(1) Joint tortfeasors[51]

In this category there are the following:[52]

(1) An employer and employee in those cases where the employer is vicariously liable for the tort of the employee.[53]

(2) One person together with another whom he prompts to commit a tort. Thus, for example, a landlord who invited his lodger to help him detect an escape of gas on the premises by striking a match was a joint tortfeasor along with the lodger in respect of the damage caused by the ensuing explosion.[54] But a person who merely facilitated (rather than procured) a tort would not be a joint tortfeasor.[55]

(3) Two or more persons who are in breach of a duty imposed on them jointly. Thus, two occupiers of the same premises are joint tortfeasors if they are sued by a visitor for failure to take reasonable care in respect of those premises.

(4) All those persons who take 'concerted action to a common end'[56] where, in the course of executing that joint purpose, any one of them commits a tort. The liability of partners for a tort committed by one of them in connection with the firm's business, the director 'sufficiently bound up in the company's acts',[57] and the liability of joint employers of an employee who commits a tort in the course

---

[48] *Surtees v Kingston-upon-Thames BC* [1991] 2 FLR 559.

[49] See, eg, *R v H* [2001] 2 FLR 431 (allegation of assault by father of his son).

[50] For full discussion, see *Clerk and Lindsell on Torts* (20th edn, 2010), ch 4.

[51] Carty [1999] LS 489.   [52] Cf Scrutton LJ in *The Koursk* [1924] P 140, at 155.   [53] See ch 24.

[54] *Brooke v Bool* [1928] 2 KB 578.   [55] *PLG Research Ltd v Ardon International Ltd* [1993] FSR 197.

[56] *The Koursk* [1924] P 140, at 152. Directors may be joint tortfeasors with a limited company where they directed or procured the tortious act, or informed the company for the express purpose of doing a wrongful act: *Rainham Chemical Works Ltd v Belvedere Fish Guano Co* [1921] 2 AC 465, at 476; or if, after formation, the company adopted a deliberate policy of wrongdoing: *Oertli (T) A-G v E J Bowman (London) Ltd* [1956] RPC 282, at 292.

[57] *Koninklijke Philips Electronics NV v Princo Digital Disc GmbH* [2003] EWHC 2588.

of his employment are three examples. *Brooke v Bool*[58] furnishes another. The landlord and his lodger were looking for an escape of gas, and an explosion occurred as a result of the careless exposure of a naked light to the escaping gas by the lodger. Besides holding that they were joint tortfeasors because the landlord had 'permitted and invited'[59] the lodger to do the act, the court held that they were joint tortfeasors for the further reasons that 'the enterprise in which... [they] were engaged was the joint enterprise of both, and that the act which was the immediate cause of the explosion was their joint act done in pursuance of a concerted purpose'.[60] Similarly, where the first defendant imprisoned the claimant, and the second defendant threatened to strike the claimant if he resisted, they were joint tortfeasors in respect of the claimant's false imprisonment even though the second defendant's act was also an assault.[61]

The Porter Committee summarised the position in defamation as follows:[62]

Where defamatory matter is contained in a book, periodical, or newspaper, there is normally a series of publications each of which constitutes a separate tort. First, there is a publication by the author to the publisher for which the author is solely liable. Second, there is the publication by the author and publisher jointly to the printer, for which the author and publisher are jointly liable. Third, there is the publication of the printed work to the trade and the public, for which the author, publisher, and printer are jointly liable.

(2) Several concurrent tortfeasors causing the same damage

Several, or separate, or independent tortfeasors are of two kinds: either those whose tortious acts combine to produce the same damage, or those whose acts cause different damage, to the same claimant. It is convenient to call the first group several concurrent tortfeasors, and they alone are illustrated in this section, which is concerned with acts that do not fit into any of the four subcategories of joint tortfeasors just listed, but which result in the infliction of the same damage to the claimant. In *Drinkwater v Kimber*,[63] a passenger in a motor car was injured in a collision between

---

[58] [1928] 2 KB 578. Perhaps *Scarsbrook v Mason* [1961] 3 All ER 767 furnishes the most remarkable example. There it was held that where passengers and the driver of a car combine on equal terms for the enterprise of a specific journey by the car of another, each is jointly liable for the driver's negligence.

[59] [1928] 2 KB 578, at 585.   [60] Ibid at 585.

[61] *Boyce v Douglas* (1807) 1 Camp 60. See also the view of Bankes LJ (at 149) in *The Koursk* [1924] P 140, that if X, Y, and Z conspired to attack C, and X and Y carried out the attack, the fact that X and Y were sued in battery, and Z was sued in conspiracy, would not prevent them from being joint tortfeasors; and *White v Whithers LLP* [2009] EWCA Civ 1122, esp at [41], where Ward LJ said that: 'A may commit trespass to goods by removing them from [C's] possession and if he then passes the documents to B who takes possession with the intention of asserting some right or dominion over them..., then B may be guilty of conversion. Assuming for the moment that B is not himself guilty of trespass, he may be liable for A's acts if he is a joint and several trespasser'.

[62] Cmd 7536, at 29. If C must prove malice in order to defeat a plea of qualified privilege, only Ds who are malicious are joint tortfeasors: *Gardiner v Moore* [1969] 1 QB 55.

[63] [1952] 2 QB 281, at 292. See also *Fitzgerald v Lane* [1989] AC 328.

that car and another. Morris LJ said that the two drivers, both of whom were negligent, 'were separate tortfeasors whose concurrent acts caused injury to the female claimant'. *Thompson v LCC*[64] provides a further example.

> C's house was damaged when its foundations subsided due to a combination of two things: first, negligent excavation by D1 and, second, a water company, D2, negligently allowing water to escape from its main.

Finally, the facts in *The Koursk* also illustrate a case in which there was only one unit of damage that was impossible to divide between the various tortfeasors.[65]

> *The Koursk*, while sailing in convoy, negligently changed course so that it bore down on the *Clan Chisholm*, which was careless in failing to reverse its engines in order to avoid a collision. Immediately after the impact, the *Clan Chisholm* collided with the *Itria*. Having recovered damages against the *Clan Chisholm* for an amount less than the loss suffered (because of a special statutory provision), the *Itria* sued *The Koursk*.

The Koursk and *Clan Chisholm* were held not to be joint tortfeasors, but only several tortfeasors causing the same damage.

(3) Several tortfeasors causing different damage

Where two or more persons not acting in concert cause different damage to the same claimant, they are treated differently in law from either joint or several concurrent tortfeasors. In the straightforward kind of case, the two defendants inflict quite separate harm on the claimant. For example, the first defendant gouges out the claimant's eye, and the second defendant fractures his skull, whereupon the first defendant is answerable only for the damage resulting from the loss of the eye and the second defendant solely for the damage attributable to the fracture of the skull. Similarly, suppose that a motorist carelessly knocked down a pedestrian who sustained multiple injuries to his leg, and a surgeon later amputated the wrong leg. Since the motorist would not be answerable for the further damage caused to the pedestrian by the surgeon's negligence, the motorist and the surgeon would be several tortfeasors causing different damage to the same claimant.

While the notional distinction between this category and several concurrent tortfeasors is clear in theory, there are some cases in which it is very difficult to decide whether there was an indivisible unit of damage, or whether the harm was capable of apportionment among the several defendants. The courts appear to have taken a sensible attitude in such cases, avoiding, if possible, saddling any one defendant with responsibility for more harm than he has caused. Accordingly, they display a marked preparedness to declare harm to be divisible.[66] Thus, in the common kinds of case of harm caused by the independent acts of various defendants – for example, pollution

---

[64] [1899] 1 QB 840. Cf *Sadler v Great Western Rly Co* [1896] AC 450.   [65] [1924] P 140.
[66] See, eg, *Royal Brompton Hospital NHS Trust v Hammond (No 3)* [2002] 1 WLR 1397; *Niru Battery Manufacturing Co v Milestone Trading Ltd (No 2)* [2003] 2 All ER (Comm) 365.

of rivers, or nuisance by smell or noise – the courts will not hold each defendant liable for the entire damage. They will endeavour to ascertain the respective contributions to the harm made by each defendant, and, failing that, they will generally apportion the loss equally between them.[67]

Flooding cases, however, can present difficulties. If C's land is flooded for 30 days by the combined flood water of the first defendant and the second defendant, and would have been flooded for 15 days by the flood water of either of them, each is liable for 15 days' loss of farming activity. If, on the other hand, the flooding does not hinder the claimant's work, but actually destroys his crops in circumstances where the flood water of either the first defendant or the second defendant alone would not have destroyed the crops, the first and second defendants will both be liable for the entire loss – the harm being indivisible. When the act of the defendant impinges on existing circumstances – for example, where the first and second defendants are already discharging water into a stream and not causing a flood – and the third defendant, knowing of the first and second defendants' acts, discharges such a further amount as causes the claimant's lands to be flooded, then the third defendant is answerable for the entire flood damage.

Another difficult case concerns a claimant who has contracted mesothelioma in consequence of wrongful exposure to asbestos dust on the part of a number of former employers. In *Barker v Corus UK Ltd*,[68] it was held that, where more than one employer had been in breach of a duty (and may therefore have been responsible for the claimant's mesothelioma), liability should be apportioned among the various former employers according to their respective contributions to the risk of contracting the disease (gauged according to the length and intensity of exposure to asbestos dust).[69] While this indicated a clear desire to treat each employer as a several tortfeasor,[70] it is not at all clear why the different periods of risk were viewed as different damage, or even damage at all (given that risk is not generally treated as actionable loss in negligence law).[71] This difficulty, and others besides,[72] prompted the government to introduce legislation designed to reverse the decision in *Barker*, and to put in its place some form of statutory basis for claims by mesothelioma victims. This occurred in the shape of the Compensation Act 2006 (discussed fully in

---

[67] *Bank View Mills Ltd v Nelson Corpn* [1942] 2 All ER 477, esp at 483 (reversed [1943] KB 337); *Pride of Derby and Derbyshire Angling Association Ltd v British Celanese Ltd* [1953] 1 All ER 179. See also *Dingle v Associated Newspapers Ltd* [1961] 1 All ER 897, at 916. The point was not discussed in the House of Lords: [1964] AC 371. Sometimes the cumulative effect of the actions of D1 and D2 is greater than the sum of their respective contributions – this does not deter the courts from making them liable proportionately for the amount of harm which each would have caused in any event.

[68] [2006] 2 WLR 1027.   [69] Ibid at [48] and [109].

[70] Ibid at [62].

[71] This point was made in the speeches of both Lord Rodger and Baroness Hale.

[72] The most prominent other problem was identified by Lord Rodger: namely, that he could see no 'logical or otherwise compelling connection between the *Fairchild* exception and the introduction of several liability': ibid at [87].

chapter 5). In *Sienkiewicz v Greif (UK) Ltd*, Lord Phillips P explained that the principle to be applied was as follows:

> When a victim contracts mesothelioma each person who has, in breach of duty, been responsible for exposing the victim to a significant quantity of asbestos dust and thus creating a 'material increase in risk' of the victim contracting the disease will be held jointly and severally liable for causing the disease.[73]

But the Act only applies to cases of mesothelioma, creating disparities in the treatment of other forms of physical injury.[74] The resultant liability regime has been the subject of criticism in the Supreme Court. Thus, in *Sienkiewicz*, Lord Phillips P commented that:

> The 2006 Act, coupled with [the test for causation in] *Fairchild* [v *Glenhaven Funeral Services Ltd*],[75] has draconian consequences for an employer who has been responsible for only a small proportion of the overall exposure of a claimant to asbestos dust, or his insurers...[76]

(B) DISTINGUISHING BETWEEN JOINT TORTFEASORS, SEVERAL CONCURRENT TORTFEASORS, AND OTHER TORTFEASORS

There are four points of note that can be made in relation to the distinctions that exist between the various categories of multiple tortfeasors.

(1) Concurrent tortfeasors, whether joint or several, are each answerable in full for the whole damage caused to the claimant. Several non-concurrent tortfeasors are merely answerable for that damage which each has caused. It is therefore often of prime importance to decide whether the defendants were acting in concert. Suppose that A and B are engaged on a hunting expedition and both of them simultaneously fire across a highway at game beyond the highway. If a shot injures a highway user, but it is not known which of A or B fired it, they are joint tortfeasors acting in concert, enabling the claimant to recover full damages from either.[77] If, however, they are several tortfeasors, they have not committed the same damage (for only one has caused damage), and the success of the action depends on proof of the commission of a tort by the one who is sued.[78] Questions of divisible harm do not arise where the defendants are joint tortfeasors because each joint tortfeasor is liable in full for all the harm sustained by the claimant.

(2) Satisfaction[79] by any concurrent tortfeasor discharges the liability of all the others, whereas satisfaction by a several non-concurrent one does not.[80]

---

[73] [2011] UKSC 10, at [1].   [74] Ibid at [176].
[75] [2003] 1 AC 32.   [76] [2011] UKSC 10, at [58].
[77] *Arneil v Paterson* [1931] AC 560.   [78] Cf *Cook v Lewis* [1952] 1 DLR 1.
[79] But note that a mere accord – ie, an agreement by C to accept some consideration in substitution for his strict legal remedy – with a several concurrent tortfeasor does not necessarily have this effect: everything turns on the interpretation of the accord: *Jameson v Central Electricity Generating Board* [2000] 1 AC 455; *Heaton v AXA Equity & Law Life Assurance Society plc* [2002] UKHL 15.
[80] And see *Bryanston Finance Ltd v de Vries* [1975] QB 703. For the effect of C's accepting payment into court by D1 on his right to sue those others jointly liable, see *Townsend v Stone Toms & Partners* [1981] 2 All ER 690.

(3) The courts are less willing to exercise their discretion under the Civil Procedure Rules to allow joinder of the defendants where the defendants concerned are not concurrent tortfeasors.

(4) There is in general a right to contribution in the case of concurrent tortfeasors, but not in respect of other tortfeasors.

(C) JOINT TORTFEASORS AND SEVERAL CONCURRENT TORTFEASORS

The distinction between joint and several concurrent tortfeasors is of much less importance since the enactment of the Law Reform (Married Women and Tortfeasors) Act 1935. Section 6(1) of that Act[81] abolished the rule in *Brinsmead v Harrison*[82] according to which a judgment against one joint tortfeasor barred a separate action, or the continuance of the first action, against the others.[83] The following two rules apply to both joint and several concurrent tortfeasors.

(1) A claimant who has obtained judgment against one wrongdoer for any damage is free to obtain judgment later against anyone else jointly liable for that damage.[84]

(2) The damages in the later actions can exceed the award in the first action. However, the claimant is not entitled to costs in any such later action unless the court is of the opinion that there were reasonable grounds for bringing that action at this later stage.[85]

(D) CONTRIBUTION

(1) Scope

Section 1(1) of the Civil Liability (Contribution) Act 1978 provides that 'any person liable in respect of any damage suffered by another person may recover contribution from any other person liable in respect of the same damage (whether jointly with him or otherwise)'. At one time, the courts gave a wide interpretation to the meaning of the phrase 'same damage'.[86] However, the House of Lords overruled this broad approach in *Royal Brompton Hospital NHS Trust v Hammond (No 3)*.[87]

---

[81] Section 6(1) has been repealed but substantially re-enacted in the Civil Liability (Contribution) Act 1978, s 1.   [82] (1872) LR 7 CP 547.

[83] If C had an unsatisfied judgment against D1 and a retrial is ordered of his action against D2 the judgment against D1 does not prevent C from recovering judgment against D2: *Wah Tat Bank Ltd v Chan Cheng Kum* [1975] AC 507.   [84] Civil Liability (Contribution) Act 1978, s 3.

[85] Civil Liability (Contribution) Act 1978, s 4.

[86] For details, see *Friends' Provident Life Office v Hillier Parker May and Rowden* [1997] QB 85.

[87] [2002] UKHL 14.

A firm of architects had negligently issued extension certificates to contractors in respect of certain construction work commissioned by a developer. The building work was delayed and the developer sued the architects in respect of their negligence. The architects were unable to claim a contribution from the contractors who actually carried out the delayed construction. The contractors were responsible for delayed construction per se, whereas the architects (by issuing the extension certificates) had caused the developer to lose the opportunity to sue the contractors for liquidated damages in respect of that delay. The question was whether the loss of opportunity to sue for liquidated damages was to be regarded as the same damage as the delay, per se.

Their Lordships insisted that the words 'liable in respect of the same damage' were to receive their ordinary and natural meaning and held that the loss of opportunity to sue for liquidated damage was not the same damage as the delayed construction.

(2) Who may claim a contribution?

The Civil Liability (Contribution) Act 1978 reaffirms the general principle that a person who is liable is entitled to claim contribution from anyone else who is also liable.[88] This applies even if an out-of-court settlement is reached. Thus, if a defendant can show that, assuming that the factual basis of the claim against him could be established, he would have been liable, he may claim a contribution from anyone else who would have been liable with him.[89] If the defendant has settled because he was doubtful about his liability in law (even though the facts were established), he can obtain a contribution only if he can prove that he was legally answerable, however bona fide and reasonable his decision to settle the claim. Furthermore, if he were liable at the time he made, was ordered to make, or agreed to make the payment, he is still entitled to recover a contribution, even though he has since ceased to be liable either because of the expiry of a limitation period, or otherwise.[90] And the right to claim a contribution passes on the defendant's death to his personal representatives, whether or not his liability had, before his death, been established or admitted.[91]

(3) Those from whom a contribution may be claimed

Contribution is recoverable from anyone who is liable for the same damage,[92] and on the authority of *K v P*[93] it is clear that the defence of *ex turpi causa* may not be raised in order to defeat a claim for contribution.[94] If one party was originally liable, but

---

[88] Civil Liability (Contribution) Act 1978, s 1(1). A contribution may still be claimed from D2 where D1 made a payment in kind (ie, free remedial work): *Baker & Davies plc v Leslie Wilks* [2005] 3 All ER 603.

[89] Civil Liability (Contribution) Act 1978, s 1(4); *Arab Monetary Fund v Hashim (No 8)* (1993) *Times*, 17 June.

[90] Civil Liability (Contribution) Act 1978, s 1(2).

[91] *Ronex Properties Ltd v John Laing Construction Ltd* [1983] QB 398.

[92] Civil Liability (Contribution) Act 1978, s 1(1). The potential contributory may want to be joined in the original claimant's action as a defendant: see, thus, *Davies v DTI* [2006] EWCA Civ 1360.

[93] [1993] Ch 140.

[94] On the other hand, those factors relevant to raising the defence are also factors of which the court may take note in fixing the level of contribution (which may be 0%).

then ceased to be liable since the time the damage occurred – perhaps because the claimant waived his claim against that person – he would nonetheless remain liable to make a contribution to the other tortfeasor, if that second tortfeasor were to be sued.[95] By contrast, where a settlement is reached with tortfeasor X, but a later action is pursued against tortfeasor Y, the question of whether X (who settled) may later be required to contribute to the damages later paid by Y will turn on the construction of the settlement agreement. *Jameson v Central Electricity Generating Board*[96] is the leading case.

> Jameson was exposed to asbestos at work due to the fault of both his employer, X, and the CEGB where the exposure occurred. Jameson agreed a 'full and final settlement' with X. When Jameson died, his executors made an additional claim for loss of dependency under the Fatal Accidents Act 1976 from CEGB. It was held that this action could not be brought because of the finality of the wording of the settlement between X and Jameson. That being the case, there was no prospect of CEGB paying the additional sum, and then seeking a contribution to this sum from X.

If, on its proper construction, the settlement between X and Jameson had not ruled out a subsequent action brought by his executors against CEGB, then, in principle, X could have been required to contribute.[97] More commonly, the period of limitation for the claimant suing that defendant may have expired (the limitation period being two years after the right to contribution arose).[98] So long as contribution is sought before the expiry of the limitation period, however, the contribution will be payable.[99]

(4) Amount of contribution recoverable

By section 2(1) of the Civil Liability (Contribution) Act 1978:

> in any proceedings for contribution under section 1 above the amount of the contribution recoverable from any person shall be such as may be found by the court to be just and equitable having regard to the extent of that person's responsibility for the damage in question.

---

[95] Civil Liability (Contribution) Act 1978, s 1(3).

[96] [2000] 1 AC 455. For a similar 'constructionist' approach, see *Co-operative Retail Services Ltd v Taylor Young Partnership Ltd* [2002] UKHL 17. But note that a properly interested third party may later invite the court to re-examine the meaning of any such agreement: *AB v British Coal Corp* [2004] EWHC 1372.

[97] See, eg, *Logan v Uttlesford DC and Hammond* [1986] NLJ Rep 541.

[98] The relevant date is the date of judgment or, where the case has been settled out of court, the date of the agreement to pay: Limitation Act 1980, s 10(3), (4). The period may be extended where the person seeking contribution is under a disability or is the victim of fraud, concealment, or mistake Limitation Act 1980, s 10(5).

[99] Civil Liability (Contribution) Act 1978, s 1(3). The subsection has a proviso that he is not liable if, on the expiry of the period of limitation or prescription, the right on which the claim against him was based, was extinguished. But because most tort actions are not extinguished by limitation – conversion is the important exception – this proviso is of very limited importance in tort.

Section 2(2) of the same Act provides that:

> The court shall have power in any such proceedings to exempt any person from liability to make contribution, or to direct that the contribution to be recovered from any person shall amount to a complete indemnity.

Neither causation nor culpability is the sole test to be applied in making the apportionment.[100] Both the moral blameworthiness and the extent to which the act is directly connected to the damage caused are material in making this apportionment.[101] This view that moral blame is not the only criterion is supported by the cases which have authorised apportionment between a defendant liable for negligence at common law and one who was not negligent but who was nonetheless in breach of a strict statutory duty.[102] On the other hand, it has been held that moral blame alone will suffice where there is no causative potency on the part of one of the defendants.[103] This seems odd because it means that one can be liable to pay a contribution even though, if sued directly, one would incur no liability. Less controversially, where two employers are both vicariously liable for the tort of a shared employee, it has been held to follow from the fact that there is no requirement of fault on the part of the employers held vicariously liable, that their liability should be shared equally.[104]

If there is a limit on the amount for which a defendant could be liable to the claimant, by reason of an agreement between the claimant and the defendant, or if the amount would have been reduced by reason of the Law Reform (Contributory Negligence) Act 1945,[105] then the maximum amount of contribution is that amount so limited or reduced.[106]

It will be noted that the statute contemplates tortfeasors being entitled to a complete indemnity in some circumstances. Where, for example, a person who knows that he is not entitled to sell goods authorises an auctioneer to sell them, and he immediately does, the auctioneer, having been held liable in conversion, is entitled to an indemnity from his principal.[107]

---

[100] *Weaver v Commercial Process Co Ltd* (1947) 63 TLR 466.

[101] *Miraflores (Owners) v George Livanos (Owners)* [1967] 1 AC 826, at 845; *Brown v Thompson* [1968] 2 All ER 708, at 709; *Cavanagh v London Passenger Transport Executive* (1956) *Times*, 23 October.

[102] Eg, *Jerred v Roddam Dent & Son Ltd* [1948] 2 All ER 104; *Dooley v Cammell Laird & Co Ltd* [1951] 1 Lloyd's Rep 271.

[103] *Brian Warwicker Partnership plc v HOK International Ltd* [2005] EWCA Civ 962.

[104] *Viasystems (Tyneside) Ltd v Thermal Transfer (Northern) Ltd* [2006] 2 WLR 428.

[105] Suppose that C was injured by defective goods which he bought, but that C was also contributorily negligent. As contributory negligence is not a defence to actions for breach of strict contractual duties (*Barclays Bank plc v Fairclough Building Ltd* [1995] QB 214), the retailer will be liable in full to C, but his claim for contribution against the negligent manufacturer will be reduced to the extent to which a claim by C against the manufacturer would have been scaled down on account of C's contributory negligence.

[106] Civil Liability (Contribution) Act 1978, s 2(3). The reduction to represent the degree of C's contributory negligence must be made before assessing the respective contributions of the tortfeasors: *Fitzgerald v Lane* [1989] AC 328.

[107] *Adamson v Jarvis* (1827) 4 Bing 66. For an illustration of a statutory right of indemnity, see the Civil Aviation Act 1982, s 76(3).

Most important is the relationship between employer and employee. In *Lister v Romford Ice and Cold Storage Co Ltd* the facts were as follows.[108]

> D, employed by C, took his father with him as mate. In reversing his lorry, D injured his father who, in an action against C, recovered damages in respect of D's negligent act. C brought an action against D claiming an indemnity in respect of the amount of the judgment and costs awarded against it.

The House of Lords held that the claimant was entitled to recover from the defendant for breach of the defendant's contractual obligation of care to his employer.[109] It follows that an employer who has been made vicariously liable for the tort of his employee can claim an indemnity from the employee. It was clearly recognised before this decision that when the employer himself was also at fault he would not obtain a complete indemnity but must suffer a reduction in respect of his own fault.[110] But these cases were based on section 6 of the Law Reform (Married Women and Tortfeasors) Act 1935.[111] What remains to be decided is whether, and if so on what principles, a reduction can be made in a claim by the employer based on a breach by the employee of his contract of employment.[112]

FURTHER READING

CARTY, 'Joint Tortfeasance and Assistance Liability' [1999] *Legal Studies* 489
MARTIN-CASALS, *Children in Tort Law Part 1: Children as Tortfeasors* (2006)
OLIPHANT (ed), *Aggregation and Divisibility of Damage* (2009)
WATTS, 'The Company's *Alter Ego* – An Impostor in Private Law' (2000) 116 *Law Quarterly Review* 525

---

[108] [1957] AC 555; distinguished in *Harvey v R G O'Dell Ltd* [1958] 2 QB 78, at 106. And see *Vandyke v Fender* [1970] 2 QB 292, at 303.

[109] The Report of the Inter-Departmental Committee (1959) set up by the Ministry of Labour and National Service concluded that the decision raised no practical problem and that no legislative change was called for at that time. Moreover, in *Morris v Ford Motor Co Ltd* [1973] QB 792, it was held that the agreement in that case, being in an industrial setting so that subrogation against employees was unrealistic, contained an implied term excluding subrogation against them.

[110] Eg, *Jones v Manchester Corpn* [1952] 2 QB 852. Where the master's liability is purely vicarious, involving no personal fault, the master will obtain a 100% contribution from the negligent servant under the Civil Liability (Contribution) Act 1978, as in *Harvey v R G O'Dell Ltd* [1958] 2 QB 78.

[111] *Lister v Romford Ice and Cold Storage Co Ltd* [1957] AC 555 left open the question of whether an indemnity under the Act could also have been given.

[112] How far the Law Reform (Contributory Negligence) Act 1945 applies to a suit in contract is obviously pertinent. But see *Barclays Bank plc v Fairclough Building Ltd* [1995] QB 214 ruling out its applicability in relation to strict contractual duties.

26
REMEDIES: BASIC PRINCIPLES

KEY ISSUES

(1) Types of damages

Although the vast majority of damages awards in English tort law are intended to compensate the claimant for the loss he or she has suffered, occasionally other forms of award are made. These include: (i) nominal damages (where a right has been infringed without the claimant suffering tangible loss), (ii) aggravated damages (where, beyond the mere infringement of a free-standing actionable right – in respect of which ordinary damages will be available – the defendant has also committed an affront to the claimant's human dignity), (iii) exemplary damages (where, exceptionally, tort law recognises the suitability of adding a punitive element to the basic compensatory award) and (iv) contemptuous damages (where the court forms a dim view of the bare legal claim that the claimant advances).

(2) Injunctions

A second form of remedy – often sought in connection with the torts of private nuisance and passing off – is that of the injunction. Various types of injunction can be sought depending on whether harm is ongoing or merely threatened, and on whether the defendant has to take positive steps to do something he is under a duty to do (as opposed to discontinuing the doing of something he is not lawfully entitled to do). In cases where some harm has already been occasioned and more is threatened, an injunction may be sought alongside damages. It is therefore wrong to see injunctions as simply an alternative to damages.

(3) Tort remedies and other areas of law

Sometimes, the commission of a tort that involves the misappropriation of the claimant's property may enable the defendant to make a profit at the claimant's expense. In such cases, the claimant may be in a position to elect between a tort measure of damages and one based on the defendant's unjust enrichment. Equally, there may be occasions when the defendant can be concurrently liable in tort and contract.

(4) Limits to recovery

Both the rules on limitation of actions and the rules on mitigation can serve to exclude or limit the recovery of damages.

SECTION 1   SELF-HELP REMEDIES

The availability of a limited number of extra-judicial, self-help remedies has been touched on earlier.[1] In general, however, the person invoking self-help should remember that he acts at his peril.

SECTION 2   JUDICIAL REMEDIES

(A) DAMAGES

(1) Nominal

Some interests, for example freedom of movement, one's bodily integrity, and the possession of one's property are considered to be so important that any violation of them is a tort. The damages are said to be at large in all such cases. This means that although the interest protected may not have a precise cash value, the court is free, on proof of the commission of the tort, to award substantial damages.[2] By contrast, nominal damages (of typically £5) will be awarded where the court decides in the light of all the facts that no damage has been sustained.[3] The function of nominal damages is simply to mark the vindication of a right that is actionable per se. Damages of this kind can therefore be awarded without the claimant having had to suffer any tangible damage. *Grobbelaar v News Group Newspapers Ltd*[4] provides a good example. There, a professional footballer had been libelled in so far as he had been accused of actually fixing football matches. He had not technically *fixed* the result of the matches, thus the statement was untrue and libellous. He had, however, accepted money in exchange for his attempts to throw the games, and was awarded £1 in nominal damages by the House of Lords. Similarly, in another case in which there was technically a false imprisonment, the appellants would have been detained in any event had the authorities acted in accordance with an existing policy as opposed to the unpublished one they actually followed. Nominal damages were again awarded.[5]

Nominal damages are nowadays given *only* in respect of torts actionable per se[6] and must not be confused with a small sum intended to compensate only limited actual damage. On the other hand, one case runs counter to these principles: *Constantine v Imperial Hotels Ltd.*[7] The claimant, a famous black cricketer, was improperly refused accommodation at the defendants' hotel. This was a tort derived from the former

---

[1] See ch 11.
[2] Eg, £5 damages was awarded to C in *Ashby v White* (1703) 2 Ld Raym 938 (right to vote); £50 in *Nicholls v Ely Beet Sugar Factory Ltd* [1936] Ch 343 (interference with a fishery).
[3] *The Mediana* [1900] AC 113, at 116; *Neville v London Express Newspaper Ltd* [1919] AC 368, at 392.
[4] [2002] 1 WLR 3024.
[5] *R (on the application of WL (Congo)) v Secretary of State for the Home Dept* [2011] 2 WLR 671.
[6] Cf *Embrey v Owen* (1851) 6 Exch 353, at 368.
[7] [1944] KB 693.

action on the case, and actionable per se. Birkett J held that he could not grant substantial damages. The decision seems wrong, however, because damages were at large in accordance with the above principles and he found that the claimant suffered unjustifiable humiliation and distress. He should, therefore, have been awarded damages that reflected the injury to feelings.[8]

(2) Contemptuous damages

These are derisory damages marking the court's low opinion of the claimant's claim, or its disapproval of his conduct.[9] They differ from nominal damages in that they may be awarded in respect of any tort, not merely those actionable per se. Moreover, the award of only contemptuous damages may be material in deciding whether to allow costs to the claimant.

(3) General and special compensatory damages

These expressions have various meanings but the basic principle is this. General damages are those damages that the law presumes to have resulted from the defendant's tort; special damages are awarded for a loss that will not be presumed such as the costs of medical treatment incurred prior to the hearing in a personal injury case.[10] To avoid injustice to the defendant, the claimant must give notice in his pleadings of, and substantiate any claim for, 'special damages'.[11]

(4) Aggravated damages

The general object of an award of damages in tort is normally to compensate the claimant for what he has lost or suffered as a consequence of the tort. Nonetheless, an award of damages may sometimes take into account the motives and conduct of the defendant where they combine to cause the claimant to suffer an affront to his dignity. Such damages are traditionally called 'aggravated damages' and, in sentient adults, they are often available where arrogant or high-handed conduct on the part of the defendant causes outrage or anger in the claimant.[12] However, they should in theory be no less available even to the infantile or mentally incapacitated who are incapable of forming such feelings of outrage or anger. In short, offence to human dignity is not contingent on sentience,[13] but it does mean that we must doubt the correctness of one decision in which aggravated damages were awarded to a (non-human) corporation.[14]

There has been considerable disagreement about the true nature of aggravated damages. Most scholars nowadays consider them a form of compensation (although views

---

[8] There was general confirmation of this in *Cassell & Co Ltd v Broome* [1972] AC 1027.

[9] See, eg, *Reynolds v Times Newspapers Ltd* [1998] 3 WLR 862 (C obtained damages of just 1p).

[10] In *R v Secretary of State for the Home Dept, ex p Greenfield* [2005] 1 WLR 673, at [11]–[12], Lord Bingham equated special damages with pecuniary loss; general damages with non-pecuniary loss.

[11] See, eg, *Domsalla v Barr* [1969] 1 WLR 630.

[12] In *Horsford v Bird* [2006] UKPC 3, at [14], Lord Scott spoke of 'high-handed, insulting or oppressive conduct'. [13] See Murphy [2010] CLJ 353.

[14] *Messenger Newspapers Group Ltd v National Graphical Association* [1984] IRLR 397.

vary on just what it is that they compensate). There is certainly support in the case law for the view that they are compensatory. For example, Sir Thomas Bingham MR once said that the aggravated damages in defamation cases are not an exception to the idea that damages in tort serve a compensatory (as opposed to punitive) function 'since injury to the [claimant's] feelings and self-esteem is an important part of the damage for which compensation is awarded'.[15] But there is also support for the idea that they serve a punitive function (in that the courts will often seem to be attending to the deliberate, arrogant conduct of the defendant).[16] Yet, even in such cases, we believe it is wrong to regard aggravated damages as a form of punishment. It is simply by highlighting conduct of this kind that we can see beyond the tangible injury to the claimant and identify, further, an infringement of his or her dignity. So, for example, even though the level of physical injury may be the same in both cases, there is a very real difference between having one's toes trodden on by mistake, and having them stamped upon deliberately. The affront that accompanies the stamping is what aggravated damages address.

The view of the Law Commission – that aggravated damages are merely a special form of compensation in respect of mental distress – seems to us unsustainable because the existing case law simply does not support such a view. In one study, one of us identified a total of 653 cases in which aggravated damages featured; yet in only 63 of these was there any mention of mental distress.[17] Furthermore, it is possible to identify cases in which the defendant has discriminated against, or harassed, the claimant so as to generate ordinary compensatory damages for the feelings of distress thereby caused but in which an additional sum by way of aggravated damages was also awarded.[18] Such cases clearly support the contention advanced here that there is an important distinction between the infliction of distress and the infringement of human dignity.

The range of torts in relation to which aggravated damages may be awarded is broad. It includes the following: trespass to the person[19] and to land,[20] defamation,[21] other torts based on deliberate falsehoods,[22] and private nuisance.[23] The question of whether such damages should be available in negligence was considered by the Court of Appeal in *AB v South West Water Services Ltd*.[24] The view taken in that case – just as in an earlier case[25] – was that they should not be so available. However, before such damages can be ruled out for this tort, it must be remembered that negligence liability turns ultimately on a failure to meet the standard of care of the reasonable man. There is no absolute requirement that there should be inadvertence on the part of the

---

[15] *AB v SW Water Services Ltd* [1993] QB 507, at 532.
[16] See, eg, *KD v CC of Hampshire* [2005] EWHC 2550. [17] Murphy [2010] CLJ 353.
[18] *Duffy v Eastern Health and Social Services Board* [1992] IRLR 251 (discrimination); *Choudary v Martins* [2008] 1 WLR 617 (harassment). [19] See, eg, *Thompson v MPC* [1998] QB 498.
[20] *Drane v Evangelou* [1978] 1 WLR 455. [21] *Sutcliffe v Pressdram Ltd* [1991] 1 QB 153.
[22] *Khodaparast v Shad* [2000] 1 All ER 545 (malicious falsehood); *Archer v Brown* [1985] QB 401 (deceit). [23] *Thompson v Hill* (1870) LR 5 CP 564.
[24] [1993] 1 All ER 609, at 629. [25] *Kralj v McGrath* [1986] 1 All ER 54.

defendant: deliberate conduct falling short of this standard can perfectly well be relied upon in a negligence action. That being so, it is hard to disagree with Lord Neuberger's comment that: 'I cannot see why such damages should not logically be recoverable in some categories of negligence'.[26]

(5) Exemplary damages

Exemplary damages (which in theory turn upon conduct which outrages the court) may be seen as an anomaly in the law of torts.[27] Their object is to punish and deter. The preponderance of opinion until relatively recently was that exemplary damages should be abolished,[28] for their continued existence, it has been objected, confuses the functions of the civil and criminal law.[29] Furthermore, since the standard of proof is lower in a tort case than in a criminal law case, it has been suggested that a defendant can end up being 'punished' in tort without the safeguard of the higher standard of proof that obtains in criminal proceedings. Finally, such damages have also been opposed on the basis that they bestow upon a claimant an unwarranted windfall. On the other hand, this argument only holds good so long as one accepts that the law of tort is exclusively concerned with securing compensation for harm caused.[30] Yet many do not accept this. Tort, for example, can clearly be shown to possess a deterrent function in certain circumstances. For example, those with managerial control, and thus potentially in the frame for vicarious liability, may feel prompted into taking extra steps to prevent employees behaving in ways that might generate such awards.[31]

But leaving such arguments to one side, it is clear from the decision of the House of Lords in *Kuddus v Chief Constable of Leicestershire*[32] that exemplary damages may nowadays be obtained in connection with virtually any tort.[33] In sweeping away the previous approach – which limited their availability to specific torts that need no longer concern us – the House of Lords rendered the argument about the rights and wrongs of exemplary damages within tort a largely academic one. All that really concerns us in the remainder of this section is an examination of the bases upon which such damages will be awarded. (That said, the section will conclude with a brief consideration of what the future *may* hold for exemplary damages.)

[26] *Ashley v CC Sussex* [2008] 1 AC 962, at [102].
[27] Despite the endorsement of exemplary damages in *Kuddus v CC of Leicestershire* [2002] 2 AC 122, their Lordships nonetheless expressly recognised their anomalous presence in tort.
[28] For examples, see the previous edition of this work.
[29] See, eg, *Cassell & Co Ltd v Broome* [1972] AC 1027, at 1088. But note that this makes an assumption about a *necessary separation* of crime from tort that is difficult to ground when one recalls that many crimes are also torts.
[30] This point was made forcefully by Lord Wilberforce in *Cassell & Co Ltd v Broome* [1972] AC 1027.
[31] See, eg, *Rowlands v CC of Merseyside* [2007] 1 WLR 1065, at [47].   [32] [2002] 2 AC 122.
[33] The only doubt that exists relates to the availability of exemplary damages for breach of statutory duty where the statute in question *does not* specifically authorise such an award: see *Kuddus v CC of Leicestershire* [2002] 2 AC 122, at [45]. Cf *Design Progression Ltd v Thurloe Properties Ltd* [2005] 1 WLR 1 for such an award for breach of s 1(3) of the Landlord and Tenant Act 1998.

The starting point is *Rookes v Barnard*.[34] In that case, Lord Devlin limited exemplary damages awards to three categories of case.

(a) Where the claimant has been the victim of oppressive, arbitrary, or unconstitutional action by servants of government

It has been established that the phrase 'oppressive, arbitrary, or unconstitutional' is to be understood *disjunctively*, so that it is enough if the action was merely oppressive, or arbitrary, or unconstitutional. That being so, if unlawful conduct by a police officer can be proved, it is not necessary to show that it was also arbitrary and oppressive.[35] As regards those who constitute 'servants of government', it has been held that the notion embraces central and local government officers and includes, also, police officers[36] and prison officers guilty of misfeasance in a public office,[37] or false imprisonment.[38] Public utilities, such as the electricity and water companies, fall outside the category, as do other privatised monopoly suppliers; for even though they are endowed with statutory powers and obligations, they are not exercising executive functions.[39]

One question for the future within this category is whether the English courts will follow the lead of the Privy Council in a series of Commonwealth cases involving breaches of constitutional rights and rename such damages 'vindicatory damages'.[40] The English counterpart to such infringements of constitutional rights would, presumably, be the state's infringement of a citizen's Convention rights. But the best guidance so far available suggests that 'if there is any scope for the award of vindicatory damages where exemplary damages are not appropriate, it must be…very limited indeed. Such an award could only be justified where the declaration that a claimant's right has been infringed provides insufficiently emphatic recognition of the seriousness of the defendant's default'.[41]

(b) Where the defendant's conduct has been calculated by him to make a profit for himself which may exceed the compensation payable to the claimant

Within this category fall those such as publishers who, as in *Cassell & Co Ltd v Broome*,[42] calculate that a libel may well sell so many copies of a publication that they will still profit despite having to pay compensatory damages to the victim.[43] The idea is

---

[34] [1964] AC 1129.

[35] *Holden v CC of Lancashire* [1987] QB 380.

[36] *Casssell & Co Ltd v Broome* [1972] AC 1027; *Thompson v MPC* [1998] QB 498.

[37] *Racz v Home Office* [1994] 2 WLR 23.

[38] *Muuse v Secretary of State for the Home Department* [2010] EWCA Civ 453.

[39] *AB v SW Water Services Ltd* [1993] 1 All ER 609.

[40] See, eg, *A-G of Trinidad and Tobago v Ramanoop* [2006] 1 AC 328; *Inniss v A-G for St Christopher and Nevis* [2008] UKPC 38; *Takitota v A-G* [2009] UKPC 11.

[41] *R (on the application of WL (Congo)) v Secretary of State for the Home Dept* [2011] 2 WLR 671, at [256]. Cf *Ashley v CC of Sussex* [2008] AC 962, at [22].

[42] [1972] AC 1027.

[43] Judging whether there is a likely profit is to be construed widely. Potential damages awards are included, as are benefits in kind that may be recovered by C: *Borders (UK) Ltd v MPC* [2005] EWCA Civ 197.

that they should learn that 'tort does not pay'.[44] In this context, it is important to stress that 'carelessness alone, however extreme, is not enough' unless the inference may be drawn 'that the publisher had no honest belief in the truth of what he published'.[45] But the category is not limited to cases of defamation; it can equally well be invoked where conspirators falsely imprison immigrants and force them to work as prostitutes,[46] where trespassers deliberately expropriate part of a neighbour's property,[47] or where landlords commit torts against tenants by driving them out of their property in order to profit by letting it to someone else at a higher rent.[48]

(c) Where authorised by statute

There are very few examples of this final, and least important, category in which the statute expressly permits the claimant to sue for exemplary damages.[49]

(d) Three further considerations

As well as establishing that the tort in question falls into one of the three categories outlined in *Rookes v Barnard*, it also seems that three further requirements must obtain. First, the claimant must be able to show that he himself was the victim of the tort.[50] This requirement is certain, and also means that relatives invested with a cause of action upon the victim's death do not possess the right to sue for exemplary damages.[51] Second, it must also be shown that exemplary damages are necessary to effect proper punishment of the defendant. This requirement is also certain,[52] and means that if the defendant has been prosecuted for the equivalent crime, no award of exemplary damages will normally be made[53] (although the fact that the defendant has been fined will not be absolutely determinative in every case,[54] and confiscation of crime proceeds may not necessarily run the risk of duplication by an award of exemplary damages).[55] Finally, but slightly less certainly, it was established by a bare majority in *A v Bottrill*[56] that when an award of exemplary damages is under consideration, a third fundamental consideration is whether the defendant's behaviour met the criterion of outrageous conduct warranting condemnation. Since *Bottrill* is strictly an authority on New Zealand law, it remains to be confirmed by the English courts. However, it seems very likely that it will be so confirmed given that *Bottrill* was a decision of the Privy Council.

---

[44] Note the limits of this argument in *AB v SW Water Services Ltd* [1993] 1 All ER 609.

[45] *John v MGN Ltd* [1996] 2 All ER 35, at 57.   [46] *AT v Gavril Dulghieru* [2009] EWHC 225.

[47] *Ramzan v Brookwide* [2011] 2 All ER 38.   [48] *Drane v Evangelou* [1978] 2 All ER 437.

[49] See, eg, the Reserve and Auxiliary Forces (Protection of Civil Interests) Act 1951, s 3(2).

[50] *Rookes v Barnard* [1964] AC 1129, at 1227–8.

[51] Specific provision to this effect exists in s 1(2)(a)(i) of the Law Reform (Miscellaneous Provisions) Act 1934.   [52] *Watkins v Secretary of State for the Home Dept* [2006] 2 WLR 807.

[53] See, eg, *Archer v Brown* [1985] QB 401 (no exemplary damages where D imprisoned for offence).

[54] *Devenish Nutrition Ltd v Sanofi-Aventis SA* [2007] EWHC 2394 (appeal on other grounds dismissed: [2009] Ch 390).   [55] *Borders (UK) Ltd v MPC* [2005] EWCA Civ 197.

[56] [2002] 3 WLR 1406.

(e) The future

If the English courts were to adopt the general approach laid down in *Bottrill*, then it might be used to expand both the first and second *Rookes v Barnard* categories. For sure, there is no obvious reason why outrageous conduct on the part of servants of the Crown should be frowned upon more than outrageous conduct on the part of any other citizen. Nor is it logical to confine the availability of exemplary damages to instances of intentional wrongdoing or subjective recklessness where the defendant's conduct is motivated by the prospect of making a profit. Intentional wrongdoing motivated purely by simple spite or malevolence would seem to be perfectly suitable, too. Thus, if the English courts were to adopt the *Bottrill* criterion of outrageous conduct that calls for condemnation, they might well pave the way for a more logical, coherent, and principled law on exemplary damages even if, as their Lordships' most recent statement on the matter makes clear, such damages are not to be encouraged.[57]

A second point that requires final determination is whether a person held vicariously liable for the tort of another can be required to pay exemplary damages. There is Court of Appeal authority suggesting that such a person can be required to pay such damages;[58] but this was later doubted in the House of Lords by one Law Lord, while his brethren declined to reach a settled view on the matter.[59] Then, in *Rowlands v Chief Constable of Merseyside*,[60] the Court of Appeal held the defendant vicariously liable for exemplary damages in respect of a constable's tort. But the case is hardly conclusive since section 88 of the Police Act 1996 specifically makes the chief constable a 'joint tortfeasor for all purposes'.

(6) Mitigation of damage and related principles

This expression covers two separate rules in the law of torts.

(1) There is the situation which is the converse of the circumstances in which aggravated damages may be awarded. That is, evidence may be given of circumstances which justify a lesser award of damages.[61] For example, a defamation award may be reduced where the claimant provoked the defendant.[62]

(2) As noted in the discussion of causation, it is the policy of the law not to allow a claimant to recover to the extent to which he has brought the loss upon himself.[63] Similarly, where a claimant is negligent after the commission of a tort against him, he cannot recover further damages caused by that carelessness. *The Flying Fish*[64] illustrates the point.

---

[57] *Watkins v Secretary of State for the Home Dept* [2006] 2 WLR 807.
[58] *Thompson v MPC* [1998] QB 498.   [59] *Kuddus v CC of Leicestershire* [2002] 2 AC 122.
[60] [2007] 1 WLR 1065.
[61] *Peruvian Guano Co Ltd v Dreyfus Bros & Co* [1892] AC 166, at 174; *Drane v Evangelou* [1978] 2 All ER 437.   [62] *Moore v Oastler* (1836) 1 Mood & R 451n.
[63] See, eg, *Dodd Properties Ltd v Canterbury CC* [1980] 1 All ER 928.   [64] (1865) 2 Moo PCCNS 77.

> C's ship was damaged by the negligence of those in charge of D's vessel. C's captain showed want of nautical skill in that he refused aid after the collision. In consequence of this negligent refusal, the ship was destroyed. C was able to recover the damage caused by the collision but not that additional damage accruing when the ship was destroyed by the negligence of the captain.

In short, contributory negligence is concerned with negligence of the claimant *before* the cause of action has matured by the occurrence of some damage. After damage has occurred and an action in tort is vested in the claimant, he has a duty to take care to mitigate his loss. The burden of showing an unreasonable failure to mitigate lies with the defendant. Thus, where a claimant refuses treatment or surgery that could have lessened the consequences of her injury, the onus is on the defendant to show that the refusal was unreasonable.[65] Even if the claimant shows that the refusal of treatment is presently reasonable, there may still be a discount made if it can be shown that there is a chance both (1) that the claimant will accept the treatment in the longer term *and* (2) that the treatment might succeed.[66]

Where the claimant does take reasonable steps to minimise the consequences of the defendant's tort, he can recover for the harm sustained by him in consequence of his action[67] or expenses thereby incurred,[68] regardless of whether his total loss would have been less had he not acted at all. Thus, in *Rogers v Austin*[69] it was held to be reasonable to hire a replacement car at above the market rate where the basis of the hire agreement was that no hire payment would be required of the claimant until completion of her legal proceedings against the defendant.[70] Equally, if a claimant takes a new job because, by virtue of his injury he can no longer do the old one, and the new job proves to be beyond him, there can be no reduction in the tortfeasor's liability based on the loss of that second job.[71]

Although not strictly mitigation issues, the courts have been required to decide what to do in relation to a claimant whose loss is covered by an insurance policy held by the claimant, or in relation to a claimant who, consequent upon the defendant's tort, happens to benefit from some future windfall. As regards insurance cover, it was held in *Bradburn v Great Western Railway Co*[72] that the amount received under the insurance policy is *not* to be deducted from the claimant's damages. A claimant pays the insurance premiums; and these would be totally wasted if the claimant's tort damages were to be reduced by the amount payable under the policy.

The second issue – namely, that of a windfall payment – arose for consideration in *Needler Financial Services Ltd v Taber*.[73] In that case, the claimant changed to a new pension scheme in line with the defendant's negligent advice. The new scheme (with

---

[65] *Geest plc v Lansiquot* [2002] UKPC 48, at [14].   [66] *Thomas v Bath District HA* [1995] PIQR Q19.

[67] *The Oropesa* [1943] P 32.   [68] *Kirkham v Boughey* [1958] 2 QB 338.   [69] [1997] CLY 1791.

[70] In *Lagden v O'Connor* [2004] 1 AC 1067 it was held that losses flowing from the higher-than-usual expenses incurred by C because of C's impecuniosity are also recoverable

[71] *Morris v Richards* [2003] EWCA Civ 232.   [72] (1874) LR 10 Ex 1.

[73] [2002] 3 All ER 501.

Norwich Union) was less favourable than the claimant's initial scheme, but it did entitle the claimant to a windfall payment when the Norwich Union de-mutualised. It was
held, rather curiously, that this windfall was *not* to be deducted from the loss attributable to the defendant's negligent advice.

(7) Successive actions on the same facts

The guiding rule can be stated shortly. The difficulty lies in defining its terms. If one
and the same act produces two different heads of damage, but it does not give rise to
two separate causes of action, the claimant cannot bring successive actions but must
recover in respect of all his damage in the first proceedings. The policy is to avoid
excessive litigation. The leading case is *Fitter v Veal*.[74]

> C recovered £11 damages from D for assault and battery. Some years later, C discovered
> that his injuries were much more serious than he had at first thought, and he underwent a
> surgical operation for removal of part of his skull. He was held unable to recover any dam-
> ages in a second action for his additional injuries.

(a) Violation of two rights separately protected

If a single act violates two rights which are accorded separate protection by the law
of torts, then there are two separate causes of action, the pursuit of one of which will
not necessarily bar proceedings in respect of the other.[75] *Brunsden v Humphrey*[76] is
illustrative.

> A cab driven by C collided with D's van through the negligent driving of D's servant. In
> county court proceedings, C recovered compensation for the damage to his cab. He then
> brought a second action in the High Court for personal injuries sustained by him in the
> same collision, and the Court of Appeal held that this action was not barred by the earlier
> one.

The interest in bodily security is separate from that in one's goods – hence there were
two separate causes of action. Where a single act caused a shortened expectation of
life and damaged goods, two actions lay.[77] On the other hand, the interest in length
of life and in freedom from pain are deemed to be subsumed under the one interest,
namely that in bodily security. Accordingly, only one action may be brought.[78] The
following interests are distinct for present purposes: interests in land, in reputation,

---

[74] (1701) 12 Mod Rep 542.

[75] But note that it may be regarded as an abuse of process to return to court raising issues that might have
been raised against the same wrongdoer in earlier proceedings: see, eg, *Talbot v Berkshire CC* [1994] QB
290. If it is such an abuse, the second claim will be struck out. But whether it *is* such an abuse is not always a
straightforward question: *Johnson v Gore Wood & Co* [2001] 2 WLR 72.

[76] (1884) 14 QBD 141. See also *O'Sullivan v Williams* [1992] 3 All ER 385.

[77] *The Oropesa* [1943] P 32.

[78] *Derrick v Williams* [1939] 2 All ER 559. Cf *Chant v Read* [1939] 2 KB 346.

in freedom of the person, and freedom from excessive litigation (that is, malicious prosecution).[79]

(b) Consequential damage where two torts protect the same interest

If the primary purpose of two different torts is to protect the same interest, then merely consequential damage that could have been recovered in proceedings for the first tort cannot be claimed in an action on the second tort. *Gibbs v Cruikshank*[80] makes this clear.

> D executed an illegal distress on C's land. In an action of replevin, C recovered the goods and the replevin expenses. This action did not preclude a subsequent suit in trespass to land, but it did preclude a later action in trespass to goods for consequential business loss, since both replevin and trespass to goods primarily protect one's interest in goods and, parasitically, one's business interests.

It would seem that if the chief purpose of the second tort is to protect an interest different from that primarily protected by the first, then damages for the violation of the main interest protected by the second tort can be recovered in proceedings for the second tort even though those damages could have been recovered consequentially in the first action.[81] If, as is supposed, damages for interference with land are recoverable in replevin, *Gibbs v Cruikshank* would be authority for this.[82]

Imagine, also, that X took letters from Z which were in Z's possession and which were defamatory of Z; and then suppose that X gave them to Y. Suppose further that in proceedings in conversion against X, Z recovered damages for his loss of the letters qua goods, but did not claim or recover (as he could by way of consequential damages[83]) damages for loss of reputation. It is submitted that, in such circumstances, he would be able to bring a further action for defamation against X (because defamation primarily protects the interest in one's reputation, quite different in kind from the primary interest covered by conversion).

(c) Successive acts

Successive actions are barred only in respect of one and the same act. If, then, A assaults B today and again tomorrow, two actions lie. Should A, however, in one and the same fight break B's nose and knock out some of his teeth, then B has only one cause of action. In less straightforward cases, one must look to the pleadings of the first action to discover whether the facts there relied on do or do not include those later complained of.[84]

---

[79] *Guest v Warren* (1854) 9 Exch 379.   [80] (1873) LR 8 CP 454.

[81] So if D causes subsidence on C's land, C may not claim for later depreciation in the value of the land *although* he can claim for the cost of remedial work which helps prevent further loss: *Delaware Mansions Ltd v Westminster CC* [2002] 1 AC 321.

[82] See also *Guest v Warren* (1854) 9 Exch 379.   [83] *Thurston v Charles* (1905) 21 TLR 659.

[84] For the principles at play see *Roberts v Gill* [2010] UKSC 22.

(d) One tortious act causing damage on different occasions

Sometimes, a single act may cause the same damage over and over again. If X digs a hole in Y's land, Y's cattle may fall into it and suffer injury both before and after Y has sued X for trespass to land. There is, however, only one act of a tortious nature – digging the hole. It follows, therefore, that only one suit in trespass to land can be brought. If, on the other hand, A throws an object on B's land and B recovers in trespass to land, and thereafter B's cattle stumble over it and are injured, B can bring a second action; for leaving an object on the land of another is an act of trespass in itself, separate from the earlier trespass constituted by throwing the object on to the land.[85]

(B) ACCOUNT OF PROFITS

Sometimes it is more advantageous for the claimant to seek an account of the defendant's profits resulting from the tort rather than to claim damages. Frequently, the victim of passing off will obtain an injunction *and* an account of the defendant's profits, but the remedy is not confined to that tort.

(C) INJUNCTIONS

(1) As a remedy per se, or as an addition to damages

A remedy in damages alone may sometimes be inappropriate or insufficient to vindicate the claimant's rights. Where there is a risk a tort may be repeated, what the claimant wants is an order to prohibit that repetition: an injunction. Injunctions are a critical remedy in many tort claims, but they will be dealt with only briefly here.

There are two broad kinds of injunctions: viz, prohibitory injunctions and mandatory injunctions. A prohibitory injunction may, for example, be issued against someone who has committed a trespass or a nuisance so that he will be restrained from repeating the tort in the future. A mandatory injunction, by contrast, requires the defendant to undertake a positive act to put an end to a state of affairs amounting to an actionable interference with some proprietary interest on the part of the claimant, whether or not that interference is causing actual damage.[86] For example, a mandatory injunction may require him to pull down a wall which interferes with the claimant's right to light.

Where an injunction is granted before the trial of an action, pending fuller investigation into the case that will take place at the trial, and in order to prevent the commission or continuance of an act alleged to be tortious, it is called an interim injunction.[87] Such an injunction is commonly applied for in respect of alleged economic torts where the claimant contends that the state of affairs resulting from the defendant's act is so serious that the defendant ought not to be allowed to continue to create that state of

---

[85] See also *Maberley v Henry W Peabody & Co London Ltd* [1946] 2 All ER 192.
[86] See, eg, *Jones v Llanrwst UDC* [1911] 1 Ch 393.   [87] See Gray [1981] CLJ 307.

affairs pending the hearing. At one level, the granting of an interim injunction might seem to be a prejudgment of the case because it is, of course, a remedy granted to a claimant who has yet to prove that he has had his legal right infringed by the defendant. This begs the question of whether such injunctions should, in justice, ever be granted.[88] So far as the courts are concerned, the matter is clear: there is no offence caused in considering the respective strength of both parties' cases and, if the claimant has a strong prima facie case, in granting such an order.[89] Where, however, an interim injunction would effectively ruin the defendant's livelihood, the courts will be very slow to grant one without a hearing having taken place.[90]

A further restriction on the availability of interim injunctions operates in relation to breach of confidence and is to be found in s 12(3) of the Human Rights Act 1998. There it is provided that no such injunction should be granted if it is likely to restrict freedom of expression *unless* the court is satisfied that the applicant is likely to establish that the publication in question should not be permitted. Of course, everything here turns on what is meant by 'likely'. And the House of Lords, in *Cream Holdings Ltd v Banerjee*,[91] held that the term is susceptible to more or less restrictive interpretations depending on the circumstances of the case, including the severity of the consequences associated with publication. By itself, this is a fairly unhelpful thing to say. But three observations can be made to help clarify matters.

First, it was held by the Court of Appeal in *Greene v Associated Newspapers Ltd*[92] that the common law on defamation has not been changed by section 12(3). Second, and by contrast, it was held in the *Cream Holdings* case that section 12(3) may be especially relevant in cases of breach of confidence; for while one's reputation can be restored for the purposes of defamation law, confidentiality once breached is lost for good. Third, Lord Nicholls did suggest in the *Cream Holdings* case that in a non-exceptional case, the crucial word, 'likely', should be understood to mean 'more likely than not'.

Two highly important forms of interim injunction are the search order and the freezing injunction. A search order is a mandatory injunction (formerly known as an *Anton Piller* order) that requires the defendant to allow the claimant entry to premises to search for property infringing the claimant's rights, or documents relevant to his claim. In actions for breach of intellectual property rights, such orders are crucial to ensure the defendant cannot destroy incriminating documents prior to the trial of the action. By contrast, a freezing injunction prohibits the defendant from moving his assets abroad or from disposing of assets within the jurisdiction.[93] In this way, the claimant ensures that if he obtains judgment against the defendant, there will be property in England against which to enforce that judgment. Both search orders and

---

[88] For the argument that injunctions should be available even before any form of measurable harm has occurred, and even outside an interference with a proprietary interest, see Murphy (2007) 27 OJLS 509.

[89] *Browne v Associated Newspapers Ltd* [2008] QB 103, at [42].

[90] *Series 5 Software Ltd v Clarke* [1996] 1 All ER 853.   [91] [2005] 1 AC 253.

[92] [2005] 1 All ER 30.

[93] *Mareva Cia Naviera SA v International Bulkcarriers SA* [1975] 2 Lloyd's Rep 509.

freezing injunctions are draconian measures[94] and claimants will always be required not only to justify their claim for such orders, but also to give undertakings to return property seized and compensate the defendants should their suit ultimately fail.

A perpetual injunction is a final order issued after the hearing of the action. A *quia timet* injunction may be issued to restrain a tort which has not yet been committed, but commission of which is threatened, so long as substantial damage appears imminent.[95]

The jurisdiction of the High Court[96] to grant injunctions is often said to be discretionary; but this is not strictly a fair description.[97] An interim injunction may be granted even though the claimant has not made out a prima facie case provided there is a 'serious question' to address and the court decides on the balance of convenience that such an order is warranted.[98] The courts exercise sparingly their 'discretion' to grant mandatory injunctions, and will refuse unless very serious damage would otherwise occur.[99] A prohibitory injunction will be granted to a claimant on proof that his proprietary rights are wrongfully being interfered with unless special circumstances exist.[100]

The public interest in not restraining the activity in question will sometimes be a relevant consideration.[101] But even so, it should be noted that the courts will be most reluctant to leave the victim of a serious interference with merely a remedy in damages.[102] The most the courts seem willing to do (almost as a matter of course) in order to mitigate the consequences of their granting injunctions is suspend the coming into force of the injunction for a short period,[103] or impose time restrictions on it.[104]

---

[94] See *Columbia Pictures Industries Inc v Robinson* [1987] Ch 38.

[95] *Lemos v Kennedy Leigh Development Co Ltd* (1961) 105 Sol Jo 178.

[96] Supreme Court Act 1981, s 37(1).

[97] See Waddams, *Dimensions of Private Law – Categories and Concepts in Anglo-American Legal Reasoning* (2003), 180.

[98] *American Cyanamid Co v Ethicon Ltd* [1975] AC 396. See also *Garden Cottage Foods Ltd v Milk Marketing Board* [1982] QB 1114. Public policy considerations certainly also figure: *Department of Social Security v Butler* [1995] 1 WLR 1528.

[99] *Redland Bricks Ltd v Morris* [1970] AC 652 lays down the rules governing the exercise of this 'discretion'.

[100] *Pride of Derby and Derbyshire Angling Association Ltd v British Celanese Ltd* [1953] Ch 149.

[101] See, eg, *Miller v Jackson* [1977] QB 966, at 981 and 988; *Dennis v Ministry of Defence* [2003] EWHC 793.

[102] *Shelfer v City of London Electric Lighting Co* [1895] 1 Ch 287. See also *Kennaway v Thompson* [1981] QB 88 which probably went too far in refusing to consider the public interest and held *Miller v Jackson* not to be binding.

[103] In *Woollerton & Wilson Ltd v Richard Costain Ltd* [1970] 1 All ER 483, Ds (building contractors) operated a crane in Cs' air space. The court suspended the injunction until Ds completed the building because Cs had refused reasonable compensation and the air space had become valuable only because of Ds' activities. Cf *John Trenberth Ltd v National Westminster Bank Ltd* (1979) 253 Estates Gazette 151 (where the court held that *Woollerton* was wrongly decided and refused to follow it).

[104] Eg, *Dunton v Dover DC* (1977) 76 LGR 87.

(2) Injunctions where an action in tort does not lie

The courts have occasionally granted injunctions to protect title to property, even where no tort is established.[105] But this is an exceptional use. The normal rule is that a final injunction will not be granted unless the relevant elements of an extant tort have been shown to be present. The rationale underpinning this general approach, of course, is that it is wrong to restrain another from engaging in some form of lawful conduct in this way, and that it is similarly wrong to compel another to act in a particular way when that other has not transgressed any law. But as regards the title to property exception, *Gee v Pritchard*[106] is instructive. In that case, the claimant obtained an injunction to prevent the defendant from disclosing confidential and private material contained in letters (which had already been returned to the claimant, but of which the defendant had kept copies) written by the claimant to the defendant. Crucially, according to the court, an injunction would serve to protect the claimant's right of property in the letters. English tort law does not (at least as yet) protect privacy as such, but it is interesting that this English case has been the cornerstone of the development in the US of the tort of infringement of privacy.

Until 1982 it seemed that an injunction could be available to protect victims of criminal violations of statutes even though no action for breach of statutory duty lay. However, *RCA Corpn v Pollard*[107] has ruled against the availability of injunctions in such cases.

SECTION 3   LIMITATION OF ACTIONS

(A) INTRODUCTION

At common law there was no time limit restricting the right to sue. Successive statutes from 1623 onwards introduced limitation periods after the expiry of which an action in tort becomes time barred. The victim of an alleged tort must serve his writ within a specified number of years or forfeit his remedy.

The need for limitation periods is self-evident. Potential defendants would otherwise face years of uncertainty not knowing whether or not they will be sued. A fair trial becomes increasingly difficult as witnesses' memories fade and in some cases witnesses even die or leave the country. Accordingly, even if the claimant begins his cause of action within the statutory limitation period, his claim may still be struck out if he pursues it in a dilatory manner on the basis that this will amount to an abuse of process

---

[105] See *Loudon v Ryder (No 2)* [1953] Ch 423; *Springhead Spinning Co v Riley* (1868) LR 6 Eq 551. The possibility of an injunction, even though no tort has been committed, is doubly important when it is noted that s 50 of the Supreme Court Act 1981 enables the court to grant damages in addition to, or in substitution for, an injunction. See *Marcic v Thames Water Utilities Ltd (No 2)* [2001] 4 All ER 326.

[106] (1818) 2 Swan 402.

[107] [1983] Ch 135 and holding that *Ex p Island Records Ltd* [1978] Ch 122 was overruled by *Lonrho Ltd v Shell Petroleum Co Ltd (No 2)* [1982] AC 173.

of the court.[108] But a claim form issued just before the end of the limitation period, yet, through *mere negligence*, served after it expired is not an abuse of process.[109]

Very short and rigid time limits, however, also result in injustice to the claimant. He may not discover for some years that he has been the victim of a tort. Common examples include persons contracting industrial diseases, and the losses suffered by the owners of negligently constructed buildings. Taking first damage to the body from working conditions: this is likely to be stealthy and progressive with definitive symptoms of disease not manifesting themselves until years after the disease was in fact well established.[110] Similarly, when a building is erected on defective foundations, cracks may begin to ruin the fabric of the building years before they become apparent to even the most observant homeowner.[111] It would scarcely be fair to deny the worker suffering from disease or the unfortunate homeowner any remedy at all simply because a rigid limitation period had expired before they could have realised that they might have a right to compensation.

The relevant and complex law on limitation is now mainly contained in the Limitation Act 1980 (as amended by the Latent Damage Act 1986).[112] In the case of actions for personal injury caused by negligence, nuisance, or breach of duty – whether the duty exists by virtue of a contract, a statute,[113] or independently of either a contract or a statute – when the damages claimed by the claimant consist of, or include, damages in respect of personal injuries to the claimant or any other person, the period of limitation is three years.[114] The term 'personal injuries' includes any disease and any impairment of a person's physical or mental condition.[115] It does not, however, involve theft of body products.[116] But what exactly is meant by the broad phrase 'breach of duty'? Does it, in particular, include intentional trespass to the person? English law has flitted to and fro on this question in the past,[117] but the latest pronouncement on the matter by the House of Lords is that it does embrace this kind of intentional wrongdoing.[118]

In cases of actions for negligence, other than for personal injuries or death, the Latent Damage Act 1986[119] introduced a primary limitation period of six years (with

---

[108] *Grovit v Doctor* [1997] 1 WLR 640, at 647.   [109] *Aktas v Adepta* [2011] 2 WLR 945.

[110] See, eg, *Cartledge v E Jopling & Sons Ltd* [1963] AC 758 (pneumoconiosis from inhaling dust); *Thompson v Smiths Shiprepairers (North Shields) Ltd* [1984] QB 405 (industrial deafness).

[111] See, eg, *Murphy v Brentwood DC* [1991] 1 AC 398.

[112] For recommendations in favour of a streamlined, unitary approach to the limitation of actions in this context, see Law Com 270, *Limitation of Actions* (2001).

[113] A breach of a duty embodied in EU law that causes C to suffer the infringement of a right created by EU law will be treated in the same way as the breach of a domestic statutory duty: *R v Secretary of State for Transport, ex p Factortame Ltd (No 7)* [2001] 1 WLR 942.

[114] Limitation Act 1980, s 11(1).

[115] Limitation Act 1980, s 38(1). It also seems capable of embracing the failure to make proper provision for someone suffering from a congenital learning difficulty: *Phelps v Hillingdon LBC* [2000] 3 WLR 776.

[116] *Yearworth v North Bristol NHS Trust* [2010] QB 1.

[117] For details, see earlier editions of this book.   [118] *A v Hoare* [2008] 1 AC 844.

[119] By inserting a new s 14A into the Limitation Act 1980.

provision in special circumstances for a further period of three years to run from the 'starting date' set by that Act). In either case, there is a final 'long-stop' of 15 years from the date of the act or omission constituting the negligence.[120]

An action for libel and slander must ordinarily be brought within one year, but there is a discretion to allow the action to proceed even after the expiry of the one-year period.[121] Where the claimant sues in respect of a defective product under the Consumer Protection Act 1987, he or she must normally bring the action within three years of suffering the relevant damage, or within three years of acquiring the necessary knowledge of the facts to sue if that date be later.[122] No action may be brought under the Consumer Protection Act 1987 more than ten years after the product was first put into circulation.[123] The claimant may still have an action in negligence after that date where, even by then, he has not discovered his injury or damage or other relevant facts pertaining to his right of action in negligence. The limitation period for other tort actions remains six years.[124]

(B) WHEN DOES A CAUSE OF ACTION ACCRUE?

A cause of action accrues, and hence the limitation period begins to run, at that moment in time when a potential claimant is entitled to succeed in an action against a potential defendant. There must then be in existence such a claimant and defendant. If, for example, a tort is committed against the estate of a deceased person, and if his goods are taken away, the cause of action does not accrue until an executor or administrator is appointed.[125] A cause of action against an ambassador does not accrue until his diplomatic immunity ends.[126] On the other hand, a claimant whose car has been stolen by a thief whom he does not know and cannot trace has a cause of action against that thief from the time of the theft.[127] When a cause of action lies without proof of damage, time clearly always runs from the date of the wrongful act. Similarly, in libel, the limitation period runs from the date of publication even if the appropriate defendant cannot be identified at that stage.[128]

By contrast, in negligence, the cause of action accrues only when damage is suffered. In fact, this is the case in all torts where damage is essential to the cause of action. But ascertaining when exactly damage occurs may be difficult; and the crucial date is the date of the damage, not its discoverability.[129] So when a negligently constructed security gate is the reason for a burglary's commission, the time runs from the date of

---

[120] Limitation Act 1980, s 14B.
[121] Limitation Act 1980, s 4A.
[122] Consumer Protection Act 1987, s 5(5) and Sch I.   [123] Ibid.
[124] Limitation Act 1980, s 2.
[125] *Murray v East India Co* (1821) 5 B & Ald 204; *Pratt v Swaine* (1828) 8 B & C 285.
[126] *Musurus Bey v Gadban* [1894] 2 QB 352.   [127] *R B Policies at Lloyd's v Butler* [1950] 1 KB 76.
[128] *Edwards v Golding* [2007] EWCA Civ 416.
[129] *Pirelli General Cable Works Ltd v Oscar Faber & Partners* [1983] 2 AC 1. Cf the Privy Council decision in *Invercargill CC v Hamlin* [1996] 1 All ER 756 (doubting *Pirelli*).

the burglary, not the time of the negligent construction of the gate.[130] Where the relevant negligence consists of negligent advice, the question arises whether the damage founding the cause of action is suffered when the claimant relies on that advice,[131] or when the subsequent financial loss is suffered. The leading case of *Nykredit Mortgage Bank plc v Edwards Erdman Group Ltd (No 2)*[132] supports the latter approach. There, it was held that a purchaser's cause of action accrues at the time of the purchase. For, as Lord Nicholls explained, '[h]e suffers damage by parting with his money and receiving in exchange property worth less than the price he paid'.[133] This, of course, makes sense in that reliance is only relevant to the question of causation; and it is not per se a measurable head of loss.

The injustice to a claimant who would otherwise lose his right to a remedy before he could know of its existence explains why, in the tort of negligence, special provision is now made for all forms of latent damage, with separate rules for personal injuries and other forms of damage.

(C) SPECIAL RULES FOR PERSONAL INJURIES

The impetus for reform of the limitation rules concerning personal injuries came from cases relating to industrial disease. Where, for example, the claimant contracts pneumoconiosis from inhaling dust, his cause of action in negligence arises even though he is unaware of the onset of the disease. In *Cartledge v E Jopling & Sons Ltd*[134] the House of Lords held that, at common law, time started to run as soon as the damage was suffered. In this case, therefore, time ran once material scarring of the lung tissue had occurred, even though an X-ray examination would *not* have revealed it. The Limitation Act 1980[135] seeks to avoid the injustice that would otherwise arise in such circumstances where a cause of action for personal injuries would become time barred before the claimant knew of it. Thus, under the Act, the three-year limitation period begins to run either from the date of the accrual of the cause of action (that is, the date of the damage) or from the date of the claimant's knowledge of that damage, whichever is the later. The limitation period ends only three years after the date of the claimant's knowledge of the cause of action if that date is after three years from the accrual of the cause of action. If the claimant dies before the expiration of the period, the period as regards the cause of action surviving for the benefit of the estate of the deceased, by virtue of section 1 of the Law Reform (Miscellaneous Provisions) Act 1934, is three years from the date of death or the date of knowledge of the personal representative.[136]

---

[130] *Dove v Banhams Patent Locks Ltd* [1983] 2 All ER 833.
[131] *Forster v Outred & Co* [1982] 2 All ER 753.   [132] [1997] 1 WLR 1627.
[133] Ibid.   [134] [1963] AC 758.   [135] Limitation Act 1980, s 11.
[136] Limitation Act 1980, s 11(5), (6). For the corresponding application of these provisions to claims under the Fatal Accidents Act 1976, see ss 12(1) and 33.

Section 14 of the Limitation Act 1980 provides a detailed definition of 'knowledge', the interpretation of which has given rise to complicated case law. When, in a personal injuries case, time runs from the date of a person's knowledge, the date is the date on which he first had knowledge of the following facts:[137]

(1) that the injury in question was significant;[138]

(2) that the injury was attributable in whole or in part to the alleged wrongful act or omission;[139]

(3) the identity of the defendant;[140]

(4) the identity of a third person (and any additional facts supporting the bringing of an action against the defendant) where that third person was guilty of the act or omission on which the claimant's case hangs.

The case law surrounding these factors has been summarised by the Court of Appeal and reduced to the following four rules:

1 The knowledge required to satisfy section 14(1)(b) is a broad knowledge of the essence of the causally relevant act or omission to which the injury is attributable.

2 'Attributable' in this context means 'capable of being attributed to', in the sense of being a real possibility.

3 A [claimant] has the requisite knowledge when she knows enough to make it reasonable for her to begin to investigate whether or not she has a case against the defendant. Another way of putting this is to say that she will have such knowledge if she so firmly believes that her condition is capable of being attributed to an act or omission which she can identify (in broad terms) that she goes to a solicitor to seek advice about making a claim for compensation.[141]

4 On the other hand she will not have the requisite knowledge if she thinks she knows the acts or omissions she should investigate but in fact is barking up the wrong tree; or if her knowledge of what the defendant did or did not do is so vague or general that she cannot fairly be expected to know what she should investigate; or if her state of mind is such that she thinks her condition is capable of being attributed to the act or omission alleged to constitute negligence, but she is not sure about this, and

---

[137] Fatal Accidents Act 1976, s 14(1). Note that there is an important distinction between 'knowledge' and 'belief': see *Nash v Eli Lilly & Co* [1993] 4 All ER 383.

[138] Under the Limitation Act 1980, s 14(2), an injury is deemed significant if the person, the date of whose knowledge is in question, would reasonably have considered it sufficiently serious to justify his instituting proceedings for damages against D who does not dispute liability and is able to satisfy a judgment: see *Albonetti v Wirral MBC* [2008] EWCA Civ 783.

[139] See *Wilkinson v Ancliff (BLT) Ltd* [1986] 3 All ER 427. C need not know the precise details of D's acts or omissions to set time running, only the essence of the act or omission: *Nash v Eli Lilly & Co* [1993] 1 WLR 782.

[140] C may have been knocked down by a hit-and-run driver, or D's firm may be a member of a group of interlocking companies: *Simpson v Norwest Holst Southern Ltd* [1980] 2 All ER 471.

[141] Cf one who merely suspects they have suffered and whose investigation takes the form of seeking medical advice in order to clarify matters: *Sniezek v Bundy (Letchworth) Ltd* [2000] PIQR P213.

would need to check with an expert before she could properly be said to know that it was.[142]

Section 14(1) expressly states that knowledge that any acts or omissions did, or did not, as a matter of law, involve negligence, nuisance, or breach of duty is irrelevant.[143] In effect the claimant is deemed to know the legal significance of facts.[144] Furthermore, as regards knowledge of facts, it is clear that it is not just the claimant's *actual* knowledge that is relevant. Section 14(3) makes the following provision for constructive knowledge of the facts:

> For the purposes of this section, a person's knowledge includes knowledge which he might reasonably have been expected to acquire:
>
> (a) from facts observable or ascertainable by him; or
>
> (b) from facts ascertainable by him with the help of medical or other appropriate expert advice which it is reasonable for him to seek; but a person shall not be fixed under this subsection with knowledge of a fact ascertainable only with the help of expert advice so long as he has taken all reasonable steps to obtain (and, where appropriate, act on) that advice.

The point of section 14(3) is to encourage a claimant to seek expert advice expeditiously.[145] If he fails to do so, and remains ignorant in consequence, the burden lies with the defendant to show that it was unreasonable for the claimant not to seek advice taking account of purely objective criteria, but excluding subjective factors such as the intellect and character of the particular claimant.[146] Once one has ascertained what the claimant actually knew and thereafter added to that such knowledge as can be imputed under section 14(3), the test of whether the claimant ought to have instituted proceedings at an earlier date becomes an objective one.[147]

If the claimant does consult an expert, he is not prejudiced if the expert fails to find, or inform him of, the ascertainable facts.[148] Furthermore, since the subsection only applies to knowledge of a 'fact', it follows that a claimant who delays suing because he has received erroneous legal advice, will find that time runs against him if he has not issued a writ.[149] Similarly, since the subsection is confined to knowledge and what ought to be known, it does not extend to reasonable belief or reasonable suspicion.[150]

---

[142] *Spargo v North Essex District HA* [1997] PIQR P235, at P242.

[143] But where C's action relies on D's omission, 'knowledge' cannot exist until C knows that something else could and should have been done: *Forbes v Wandsworth HA* [1997] QB 402.

[144] See *Brooks v J & P Coates (UK) Ltd* [1984] 1 All ER 702.

[145] See, eg, *B v Ministry of Defence* [2010] EWCA Civ 1317.

[146] *Adams v Bracknell Forest BC* [2005] 1 AC 76.   [147] *A v Hoare* [2008] 1 AC 844, at [34]–[35].

[148] *Marston v British Railways Board* [1976] ICR 124.

[149] *Leadbitter v Hodge Finance Ltd* [1982] 2 All ER 167.

[150] *Nash v Eli Lilly & Co* [1993] 4 All ER 383.

In exceptional cases, the victim of personal injuries who fails to start his action in due time may, with permission of the court, still be able to proceed according to another provision. That is, the claimant who had knowledge of all the relevant facts but was unaware of his legal rights, or the claimant who has received hopeless legal advice, has one last chance to seek a remedy. By section 33(1) of the 1980 Act, the court may still allow an action to proceed notwithstanding the expiry of the limitation periods. The court has a discretion to extend the statutory time limits if it considers it equitable to do so having regard to the degree to which the ordinary limitation rules prejudice the claimant, and the degree to which any exercise of the power would prejudice the defendant. It may have particular significance in cases where the claimant is now an adult but whose claim centres on child abuse suffered many years previously.[151] Whatever the factual basis, the court must have regard to all the circumstances,[152] including the following (listed in section 33(3)):

(a) the length of, and the reasons for, the delay on the part of the claimant;[153]

(b) the effect of the delay on the cogency of the evidence in the case;

(c) the conduct of the defendant after the cause of action arose, including his response to the claimant's request for information;

(d) the duration of any disability of the claimant arising after the cause of action;[154]

(e) the extent to which the claimant acted promptly and reasonably once he knew of the facts which afforded him a cause of action; and

(f) the steps taken by the claimant to obtain medical, legal, or other expert advice and the nature of any such advice received.[155]

A very wide discretion, and one not limited to the six named factors, is given to the court.[156] So, for example, the fact that the defendant is insured is a relevant consideration[157] as, too, is the fact that the case may involve putting the defendant to greater expense in defending the action than the action is actually worth.[158] There is, however, one restriction. Where the claimant has commenced proceedings and then

---

[151] For guidance on the use of the s 33 discretion in such cases, see *AB v Nugent Care Society* [2010] PIQR P3; *XA v YA* [2011] PIQR P1.

[152] Here the court cannot simply consider the effects of not exercising the discretion on just C or D: *KR v Bryn Alyn Community (Holdings) Ltd* [2003] 1 FCR 385. Further, the courts are slow to find the balance of prejudice in favour of C in the absence of cogent medical evidence showing a serious effect on C's health: *Robinson v St Helen's MBC* [2002] EWCA Civ 1099.

[153] Here the delay means the delay after the expiry of the normal time limit: *McDonnell v Walker* [2009] EWCA Civ 1257.

[154] See, eg, *Barrow v Consignia plc* [2003] EWCA Civ 249.

[155] But note that C is not necessarily to be associated with his dilatory (or otherwise negligent) legal advisers *Das v Ganju* [1999] Lloyd's Rep Med 198. Cf *Smith v Hampshire CC* [2007] EWCA Civ 246.

[156] See, eg, *Firman v Ellis* [1978] QB 886; *Steeds v Peverel Management Services Ltd* [2001] EWCA Civ 419.   [157] *Kelly v Bastible* (1996) 36 BMLR 51.

[158] *Nash v Eli Lilly & Co* [1993] 4 All ER 383.

discontinued them, only in the most exceptional case will the discretion be exercised in his favour.[159]

(D) LATENT DAMAGE IN NON-PERSONAL INJURIES CASES

The special provision made by section 11 of the Limitation Act 1980 to assist claimants who lacked the necessary knowledge to start an action was restricted to actions for personal injuries. Yet the problems limitation periods pose for the victim of a latent defect can be just as acute in relation to damage to property. A series of Court of Appeal decisions sought to establish that the cause of action in such cases accrued only when the defect was discoverable.[160] But in *Pirelli General Cable Works Ltd v Oscar Faber & Partners*[161] the House of Lords overruled those decisions as inconsistent with *Cartledge v E Jopling & Sons Ltd*.[162] The facts in *Pirelli* highlight the problems of latent damage.

> In 1969, Cs engaged Ds to advise them in relation to building a new chimney. Ds' design was negligently produced. Cracks occurred in the chimney and it had to be replaced. Cs first discovered the cracks in 1977 but they in fact first occurred in 1970. Cs served their writ in 1978 contending that the (six-year) limitation period did not begin to run until 1977 when they could first reasonably have discovered the defect.

The House of Lords held that the cause of action accrued in 1970 when the damage first occurred so the claim was time-barred. Indeed, it is a general principle in latent damage cases that time begins to run from the date on which damage actually did occur. That said, pinning down the date on which damage *actually* occurred can involve some nice distinctions. So, in one case where A misadvised B so that B entered into a commercially inadvisable insurance arrangement, the critical date was held to be that on which B entered into the arrangement rather than the subsequent date on which an insured party made a claim on the basis of the policy.[163] The financial loss suffered was contingent on entering into a misconceived arrangement, and actually entering into the arrangement was treated as 'the damage which the claimants...suffered'.[164]

Two further acute difficulties for claimants emerged from the decision in *Pirelli*. Lord Fraser, in an *obiter dictum*,[165] suggested that where a defect was so gross that the building was 'doomed from the start',[166] time would begin to run even earlier: from the completion of the building. The result of such a doctrine – that is, that the worse

---

[159] *Walkley v Precision Forgings Ltd* [1979] 2 All ER 548.
[160] See *Sparham-Souter v Town and Country Developments (Essex) Ltd* [1976] QB 858.
[161] [1983] 2 AC 1.   [162] [1963] AC 758.
[163] *Axa Insurance Ltd v Akther & Darby* [2010] 1 WLR 1662.
[164] Ibid at [82]. In similar vein, see *Pegasus Management Holdings SCA v Ernst & Young* [2010] 3 All ER 297. Cf *Law Society v Sephton & Co* [2006] 2 AC 543 (where C's loss was equally contingent, but C was not misled into entering into an inadvisable arrangement).   [165] [1983] 2 AC 1, at 16.
[166] See *Dove v Banhams Patent Locks Ltd* [1983] 2 All ER 833.

the negligence, the more favourable the limitation period would be to the defendant – did not find favour in later decisions.[167]

The second difficulty arising from the case in relation to latent defects affected 'subsequent owners' of buildings. In *Pirelli* it was said that time did not start to run again in favour of the subsequent owner once he acquired the property.[168] But subsequent owners' problems were in fact more acute than simply being entitled only to the tag end of their predecessors' limitation period. Had they any claim at all in respect of damage to property to which, at the time damage occurred, they had no title? The essence of the claim in such a case is a claim for economic loss associated with the diminished value of the property that the subsequent owner has acquired. According to the House of Lords' decision in *Murphy v Brentwood District Council*,[169] such claims will now generally be inadmissible; yet their Lordships also managed to approve *Pirelli* on the basis that it was said to fall within the principle enunciated in *Hedley Byrne v Heller*.[170] As a consequence, there has been continuing confusion.[171]

The Law Reform Committee reported on these several problems concerning latent damage to property in 1984.[172] Their proposals were largely incorporated into the Latent Damage Act 1986 which applies not solely to latent damage to property, but also to all negligence actions other than claims in respect of personal injury or death. The Act took effect by inserting two new sections – sections 14A and 14B – into the Limitation Act 1980. The limitation period in actions to which sections 14A and 14B apply are now either six years from the date on which the cause of action accrued, or three years from the 'starting date' when the claimant had the necessary knowledge of the facts to bring an action.

'Knowledge' in this context is defined in section 14A(6)–(8) in terms virtually identical to those used to define 'knowledge' in the original section 14 for the purpose of extending the three-year period to bring an action in respect of personal injuries.[173] Section 14B of the 1980 Act imposes a 'long-stop' of 15 years from the date of the act or omission constituting the alleged negligence. Once 15 years have elapsed, no action at all may be brought, even though the claimant may not have discovered the relevant damage. This is because section 14B contains no provision similar to section 33 of the 1980 Act, which, as we have already seen, gives a judge the discretion to override this final limitation period.[174]

The Latent Damage Act 1986 represents a worthy attempt at compromise between the rights of claimants and defendants, but it still leaves some key questions unanswered. First, sections 14A and 14B apply to actions for negligence. But are they also

---

[167] See, eg, *Ketteman v Hansel Properties Ltd* [1987] AC 189 (HL adopted a severely restrictive view of 'doomed from the start').   [168] [1983] 2 AC 1, at 18.

[169] [1990] 2 All ER 908.   [170] Ibid at 919.   [171] See McKendrick [1991] LS 326.

[172] Twenty-fourth Report: *Latent Damage* (Cmnd 9390).

[173] See, eg, *Spencer-Ward v Humberts* [1995] 06 EG 148. In assessing C's knowledge, account will be taken of misleading advice that has been provided by 'experts' in the past that now prevents C from knowing that an actionable case exists: *Oakes v Hopcroft* [2000] Lloyd's Rep Med 294.

[174] But see the Latent Damage Act 1986, s 2 regarding fraud, concealment, or mistake.

applicable to actions for nuisance or breach of statutory duty where the essence of the wrong complained of is also often the absence of reasonable care?[175] Second, no clear definition of damage is provided.

One matter – concerning overlapping duties in contract and tort – that was once unclear has now been clarified. The Latent Damage Act 1986 is applicable only to actions in tort.[176] But, notwithstanding its inapplicability to contractual duties of care, some contractual relationships may still be governed by this limitation period where concurrent duties in contract and tort are owed.[177] According to *Henderson v Merrett Syndicates Ltd*,[178] the claimant is entitled to rely on that limitation period which is most advantageous to him; so in such circumstances, a claimant may well have recourse to the extendable limitation periods in tort.

Section 3 of the Latent Damage Act 1986 addresses the rights of successive owners of property. It provides that where a cause of action has accrued to A while he has an interest in that property, 'then provided B acquires the property' after the date on which the original cause of action accrued,

> but before the material facts about the damage have become known to any person who, at the time when he first had knowledge of the facts, has any interest in the property; a fresh cause of action in respect of that negligence shall accrue to that other person on the date on which he acquires his interest in the property.

The limitation period as against the new owner is once again either six years from when his cause of action accrued (that is, his acquisition of the property) or three years from when he acquired knowledge of the relevant facts (subject once again to the 15-year 'long stop' in section 14B of the Limitation Act 1980).

Three further points must be noted about section 3 of the Latent Damage Act 1986. First, and most importantly, how can section 3 be reconciled with *Murphy v Brentwood District Council* which generally denies the existence of any duty of care in such cases?[179] Note that in *Murphy*, section 3 did not even get a passing mention from their Lordships! Second, although drafted with defective buildings in mind, the section applies to all property including goods. Finally, the new cause of action for the subsequent property owner arises only where his predecessor did not have any actual or constructive knowledge of the relevant defect.[180]

---

[175] For a 'yes' answer, see James [1994] NILQ 301.

[176] *Iron Trades Mutual Insurance Co Ltd v JK Buckenham Ltd* [1990] 1 All ER 808.

[177] Note that many professional–client relationships would fall into this bracket.

[178] [1995] 2 AC 145.

[179] *Murphy* does not deny a duty of care where the defective property poses a threat of damage to other property, nor does it do so where the property damage is of the kind often referred to as 'complex structure' damage. These would appear to be the only two exceptions to the seeming redundancy of s 3 in this context.

[180] In what circumstances (if any) could the subsequent owner sue the vendor who failed to disclose his knowledge of the relevant defects?

(E) CONTINUING WRONGS

Where the act of the defendant is a continuing wrong – for example, if he erects a building on the claimant's land and there is a continuing trespass – then, so long as it endures, a cause of action will lie provided it is based on the continuance of that wrong during the six years (or three years in the case of personal injuries) immediately pre-ceding the action.[181] To put it another way, once the wrong ceases, the claimant can claim for all the harm that occurred by virtue of the continuance within the previous six or three years, depending on the kind of harm. An example of a continuing wrong is an ongoing failure to implement an EC Directive as required by statute. The loss associated with failure so to implement is of an ongoing nature and therefore not time barred.[182]

(F) EFFECT OF DISABILITY OF THE CLAIMANT

If, on the date when any right of action accrued, the person to whom it accrued was a minor or a person of unsound mind,[183] the action may be brought at any time before the expiration of six years (or three years in the case of personal injuries) from the date when the person ceased to be under that disability, or died, whichever event first occurred.[184]

Where the cause of action has once vested in a person who is free from disability, and the period has therefore begun to run, should that person (or some other person to whom the cause of action has passed subsequently) become disabled, the period will not on that account be further extended.[185] When a right of action which has accrued to a person under a disability vests, on the death of that person while still under a dis-ability, in another person also under a disability, there, too, there is no further exten-sion of time permitted by reason of the disability of the second person.[186] Where a person, in whom a cause of action has vested, was, at the moment of vesting, under one disability – for example, minority – and, at or before the cessation of that disability, the person becomes insane, time does not begin to run until he has 'ceased to be under a disability',[187] that is until the last of his disabilities has ended.

The fact that disability may persist for a very long time obviously works to the dis-advantage of the defendant. But according to *Headford v Bristol and District Health Authority*[188] it was not an abuse of process to institute proceedings after a 28-year

---

[181] *Hardy v Ryle* (1829) 9 B & C 603; *Earl of Harrington v Derby Corpn* [1905] 1 Ch 205.

[182] *Phonographic Performance Ltd v DTI* [2004] 1 WLR 2893.

[183] By the Limitation Act 1980, s 38(3) 'a person is of unsound mind if he is a person who, by reason of mental disorder within the meaning of the Mental Health Act 1983 is incapable of managing and adminis-tering his property and affairs'.   [184] Limitation Act 1980, ss 28(1) and 28A.

[185] Limitation Act 1980, s 28(2). But in personal injury actions, the court may take account of this factor in deciding whether to exercise its s 33 discretion to extend the limitation period.

[186] Limitation Act 1980, s 28(3).

[187] Limitation Act 1980, s 28(1).   [188] [1995] 6 Med LR 1.

delay, even though the delay was apparently unjustified other than in terms of the Act's provision for an extension of the limitation period.

(G) POSTPONEMENT OF LIMITATION PERIODS IN CASES OF FRAUD OR CONCEALMENT

Where the action is based on the fraud of the defendant or his agent, or of any person through whom he claims (or that person's agent),[189] or where any fact relevant to the right of action is deliberately concealed by any such person, the period shall not begin to run until the claimant has, or with reasonable diligence could have, discovered the fraud or concealment.[190] It is not sufficient if the defendant has merely concealed facts that would strengthen the claimant's claim; they must be central to him framing such a claim in the first place.[191] On the other hand, once a cause of action has arisen, subsequent concealment of facts relevant to the claimant's action will postpone the running of the limitation period.[192]

A tort is 'based upon fraud' only where fraud is a necessary allegation in order to constitute the cause of action.[193] (Presumably, deceit is the only tort based upon fraud in this sense.) Deliberate commission of a breach of duty in circumstances in which it is unlikely to be discovered for some time amounts to deliberate concealment of the facts involved in that breach of duty.[194] The House of Lords – despite the ambiguity of the language used in the provision ('deliberate conduct' does not necessarily imply deliberate harm) – has made it clear that moral wrongdoing on the part of the defendant is an essential ingredient.[195] 'Fraud' in the Act is to be interpreted very widely.[196] It appears, rather than to bear any technical meaning, to signify simply 'conscious wrongdoing'.[197]

SECTION 4   TORT AND CONTRACT

For a time, the Court of Appeal, in a series of decisions,[198] gave support to dicta by Lord Scarman in *Tai Hing Cotton Mills Ltd v Liu Chong Hing Bank Ltd*[199] to the effect that where the relationship between two parties is contractual, no concurrent duty should lie in tort. Yet it has since been authoritatively determined that concurrent

---

[189] In *Eddis v Chichester Constable* [1969] 2 Ch 345, these words included the tenant for life where Cs were the trustees and owners of an heirloom fraudulently sold by the tenant for life.

[190] Limitation Act 1980, s 32(1).   [191] *C v Mirror Group Newspapers Ltd* [1996] 4 All ER 511.

[192] *Sheldon v RHM Outhwaite (Underwriting Agencies) Ltd* [1996] AC 102.

[193] *Beaman v ARTS Ltd* [1949] 1 KB 550 (conversion was held not to be an action based on fraud).

[194] Limitation Act, s 32(2).

[195] *Cave v Robinson Jarvis & Rolf* [2003] 1 AC 384: the moral wrongdoing on the part of D must exist *either* in respect of the act that constitutes the breach of a duty *or* in connection with the concealment of a duty that was breached without any malice.   [196] *Beaman v ARTS* [1949] 1 KB 550.

[197] Ibid at 572.

[198] *National Bank of Greece SA v Pinios Shipping Co* [1990] 1 AC 637; *Johnstone v Bloomsbury Area HA* [1992] QB 333.   [199] [1985] 2 All ER 947, at 957.

duties in contract and tort may in fact lie.[200] Furthermore, the claimant is at complete liberty to choose whichever cause of action he thinks will be most advantageous to him.[201] That choice may be crucial for the following reasons:

(1) Causes of action for liquidated damages may perhaps be assignable if they lie in contract,[202] but not if they lie in tort.

(2) Although the claimant may not freely evade the contractual immunities of minors and mentally disordered persons by suing in tort, in some circumstances he can sue them for torts committed in the course of a contractual relationship.

(3) There are circumstances in which an action in contract will give greater damages than one under the Fatal Accidents Acts.[203] Although the Fatal Accidents Acts may perhaps bind the Crown in tort proceedings, they do not bind the Crown in contract actions (to which they also extend).

(4) The Crown is answerable in tort for the acts of a restricted class of 'servants'.[204] That restricted definition does not apply to actions against the Crown for breaches of contracts made by servants of the Crown.

(5) Trade unions are partially immune from tortious liability but are fully liable for breaches of contract.

(6) Most importantly, the rules relating to limitation of actions differ depending on whether the claimant sues in contract or tort. In contract, time starts to run from the date of the breach of contract; in negligence it runs only from the date damage was suffered, or the date when the claimant had the necessary knowledge of the facts to sue, if that is later. The claimant-friendly provisions of the Latent Damage Act 1986 do not apply to an action for breach of a contractual duty of care.[205] But note that the availability of the defence of contributory negligence no longer depends on which remedy the claimant seeks where the essence of the claim is breach of a duty of care rather than of a strict contractual obligation.[206]

SECTION 5   TORT AND UNJUST ENRICHMENT

(A) ELECTION OF REMEDIES

It has been held that, in appropriate circumstances, a claimant has the choice of suing either in tort or in the law of unjust enrichment.[207] For example, if the defendant

---

[200] *Henderson v Merrett Syndicates Ltd* [1995] 2 AC 145.   [201] Ibid at 194.

[202] *County Hotel and Wine Co Ltd v London and NW Rly Co* [1918] 2 KB 251, at 258 (affirmed on other grounds: [1921] 1 AC 85).   [203] *Sellars v Best* [1954] 2 All ER 389.

[204] Crown Proceedings Act 1947, s 2.

[205] *Iron Trades Mutual Insurance Co Ltd v J K Buckenham Ltd* [1990] 1 All ER 808.

[206] *Forsikringsaktieselskapet Vesta v Butcher* [1989] AC 852.

[207] *A-G v Blake* [2001] 1 AC 268, at 280.

wrongfully takes the claimant's goods and sells them, the claimant is said to have the choice of suing in conversion or bringing an action for restitution based on the price received by the defendant. It is not proposed to examine here the intricacies of the law of unjust enrichment (which would be necessary if every possible circumstance giving rise to both tortious and restitutionary remedies were to be considered).[208] It suffices to note two things: first, that the torts in which such an election is likely to arise are conversion,[209] trespass to goods,[210] trespass to land by removing minerals,[211] and deceit;[212] and second, that it is questionable whether in juridical terms there is a straightforward election between a compensatory remedy (in tort) and a restitutionary remedy (based on the defendant's unjust enrichment). In conversion cases, the loss suffered by the defendant will frequently coincide exactly with the gain made by the defendant. Imagine A steals B's watch and sells it for the market value of £60. If B sues on the basis of A's gain he will receive just the same amount as if he sues on the basis of his own loss. But if B sues on the former basis, this does not *ipso facto* render the damages received restitutionary in nature. In as much as B suffered a loss, and in so far as the damages he receives perform corrective justice, they may perfectly well be viewed as compensatory in nature.[213]

This election by the claimant to sue for 'restitution' has sometimes been erroneously described as a 'waiver' of the tort. The claimant does not 'waive' the tort if he elects to sue for restitution.[214] He is free at any time before he has signed judgment to abandon his restitutionary claim and pursue, instead, a remedy in tort. Equally, his suit in unjust enrichment will not bar proceedings in tort on the same facts against another wrongdoer unless the claimant has not merely obtained judgment, but also had satisfaction of it. It is true that if he signs judgment in unjust enrichment, his claim in tort against that defendant is barred,[215] but that is merely an illustration of the rule that where the claimant has succeeded in one cause of action he has no further cause of action, howsoever framed, in respect of that very same interest for which the first cause of action lay.

These rules are clearly illustrated by the leading case of *United Australia Ltd v Barclays Bank Ltd.*[216]

A cheque payable to Cs was wrongfully sent by their secretary to D1. D1 then presented it to D2 who, in turn, paid over the requisite amount to D1. Initially, Cs tried suing D1 in

---

[208] See Edelman, *Gain-Based Damages: Contract, Tort, Equity and Intellectual Property* (2002).
[209] *Lamine v Dorrell* (1705) 2 Ld Raym 1216; *Thomas v Whip* (1715) cited in 1 Burr 458.
[210] *Oughton v Seppings* (1830) 1 B & Ad 241; *Rodgers v Maw* (1846) 15 M & W 444.
[211] *Powell v Rees* (1837) 7 Ad & El 426.
[212] *Mahesan S/O Thambiah v Malaysian Government Officers' Co-operative Housing Society* [1979] AC 374.
[213] But for complexities concerning damages in conversion see Tettenborn, 'Conversion, Tort and Restitution' in Palmer and McKendrick (eds), *Interests in Goods* (1998).
[214] Hedley (1984) 100 LQR 653. See also *Maheson S/O Thambiah v Malaysian Government Officers' Co-operative Housing Society* [1979] AC 374.
[215] *United Australia Ltd v Barclays Bank Ltd* [1941] AC 1, at 30.
[216] Ibid.

unjust enrichment for money had and received. Cs later discontinued this action without obtaining final judgment and instead began an action in tort against D2 for conversion of the cheque. The House of Lords held that Cs could not be said to have 'waived' their right to sue D2 by having instituted proceedings against D1 – nothing less than satisfaction of a judgment in the first proceedings would have barred this action in tort for the same damage. Cs, therefore, were not precluded from bringing the present action in tort.

(B) RELATIVE ADVANTAGES OF PROCEEDINGS IN TORT AND UNJUST ENRICHMENT

The crucial difference between proceeding on the basis of normal tort principles and suing for the restitutionary remedy lies in the different measure of damages.[217] For example, if A converts B's watch valued at £10, a suit in conversion will allow B to recover £10. But if A sells it to C for £15, B can recover £15 in unjust enrichment as money had and received by A.

Some of the differences between contract and tort mentioned in the previous section are also relevant here: for example, the disabling effect in contract of infancy or insanity[218] and the operation of the Crown Proceedings Act 1947 in relation to tort actions. Finally, if X makes use of Y's land without causing any tangible harm to that land, a restitutionary remedy based on a fair rental value will be available.[219] But such a remedy will not be available if the wrong concerned is a nuisance rather than a trespass.[220] In short, if there is no misappropriation of the claimant's property rights, there can be no restitutionary award.[221]

FURTHER READING

BEEVER, 'The Structure of Aggravated and Exemplary Damages' (2003) 23 *Oxford Journal of Legal Studies* 87

HEDLEY, 'The Myth of Waiver of Tort' (1984) 100 *Law Quarterly Review* 653

JAMES, 'Statutory Liability for Negligence and the Latent Damage Act 1986' [1994] *Northern Ireland Legal Quarterly* 301

LAW COMMISSION, *Limitation of Actions* (2001)

MURPHY, 'Rethinking Injunctions in Tort Law' (2007) 27 *Oxford Journal of Legal Studies* 509

MURPHY, 'The Nature and Domain of Aggravated Damages' [2010] *Cambridge Law Journal* 353

TETTENBORN, 'Conversion, Tort and Restitution' in Palmer and McKendrick (eds), *Interests in Goods* (1998)

---

[217] In *Universe Tankships Inc of Monrovia v International Transport Workers' Federation* [1983] 1 AC 366, the House of Lords held that by bringing an action in unjust enrichment (instead of inducing breach of contract) against a trade union, C evaded the immunity of trade unions under s 13 of the Trade Union and Labour Relations Act 1974.

[218] See *Morriss v Marsden* [1952] 1 All ER 925, at 927.

[219] *A-G v Blake* [2001] 1 AC 268, at 279.

[220] *Forsyth-Grant v Allen* [2008] Env LR 41.

[221] See, eg, *Devenish Nutrition Ltd v Sanofi-Aventis SA* [2009] Ch 390.

27

PRINCIPLES OF COMPENSATION FOR PERSONAL INJURIES AND ASSOCIATED LOSSES

KEY ISSUES

(1) Pre- and post-death awards

One way of classifying the damages available in tort law in respect of personal injuries is according to whether they are made in favour of a living tort victim, or whether they are awarded to someone else after the victim has died.

(2) Personal injury damages available to living claimants

The damages available to living claimants can, themselves, be subdivided into two broad classes. The first of these involves damages for pecuniary losses (such as loss of earnings and the cost of medical and nursing care). The second involves damages for non-pecuniary losses (such as pain and suffering). Often, computing the exact amount of the claimant's pecuniary loss will be impossible (because no one can be sure how long the claimant would have remained fit and well, or how long the claimant would have remained in his current job, had the defendant's tort never been committed). Equally, placing an exact amount on such subjective matters as pain and suffering is, in reality, impossible.

(3) Damages available after the tort victim has died

Damages that are awarded after the tort victim has died break down into two broad types. The first consists of survival actions (as they are known). Such actions are grounded in the Law Reform (Miscellaneous Provisions) Act 1934. With very few exceptions, what the statute allows for here is the victim's estate to pursue a tort claim that vested in the victim prior to his death. The second kind of claim that can be made post-death is one that treats the victim's very death as the basis of the claim. In such cases, the action is brought by the deceased's dependants (for loss of support) under the auspices of the Fatal Accidents Act 1976.

(4) Alternative compensation systems

Though not a part of English tort law, no survey of personal injury awards is really complete without some consideration of various alternative sources of compensation. A brief account of some such sources is therefore supplied at the end of this chapter.

SECTION 1   INTRODUCTION

The function and the anomalies of tort law as a system of loss distribution in society are well illustrated when we consider the overall rules governing the compensation of personal injuries. The victim's financial future may well turn on whether he is success-ful in establishing that his injuries are someone else's 'fault'; essentially, that a tort was committed. Should he succeed, he and his family will receive a level of compensation, which, while its method of assessment may be criticised, will help to meet his mate-rial needs and will far exceed the total of social welfare benefits available to an equally severely injured person unable to prove 'fault'[1] on the part of another.

Consider this rough example. X, Y, and Z, all aged 25, suffer severe brain dam-age rendering them incapable of continuing paid employment. X's accident happens while he is swimming in a cold lake. He gets into difficulties and by the time he is res-cued from drowning and resuscitated, the brain damage inflicted by lack of oxygen is irreversible. Y suffers brain damage in the course of surgery to remove his appendix. Proceedings are started on his behalf but allegations of negligence against the hospital are not substantiated. Z's injuries are inflicted in a road accident for which the driver of the other car accepts liability. All three accident victims, before their misfortunes, were earning £35,000 a year.

Provided X and Y are successful in obtaining the maximum available social secu-rity benefits they will still receive far less than Z, the only victim to benefit from the torts system. This then begs the question of how this discrepancy can be explained or justified. In the case of X, is it that his accident was his own 'fault' and that he took the risk upon himself?[2] What about Y? Anaesthesia is inherently risky. Does Y have to accept the risk to attain the benefit of the surgery? It could even be argued that X and Y should have insured themselves against their respective injuries. But then so could Z. Yet, even if Z had insured himself, he would still receive his insurance monies *in addition to* his award of damages, as we shall see later.

Considerations such as these lead inevitably to evaluations of the operation of the 'fault' system upon which tort law is largely premised.[3] Arguments for and against it draw on notions of corrective justice, the economic analysis of tort law,[4] and the nature of the relationship between tort law and insurance.[5] Some even canvass the idea of replacing tort law (or large chunks of it) with no-fault compensation schemes, such as the one implemented in New Zealand.[6] Yet, while the debate on compensating personal injuries via tort law has raged for over three decades, there seems little to no present prospect of the tort system being overhauled in this country. Even so, for the

---

[1] For critique of the 'fault' principle, see Cane (ed), *Atiyah's Accidents Compensation and the Law* (2006).   [2] See *Tomlinson v Congleton BC* [2004] 1 AC 46.

[3] See esp *Report of the Royal Commission on Civil Liability and Compensation for Personal Injury* (1978) (Cmnd 7054–1) (hereafter *Pearson Report*) paras 1716–17.

[4] See, eg, Calabresi, *The Cost of Accidents* (1970). Cf Schwartz (1994) UCLA L Rev 377.

[5] See, eg, Atiyah, *The Damages Lottery* (1997); Stapleton (1995) 58 MLR 820.

[6] See Harris (1974) 37 MLR 361.

sake of completeness, a short section appears at the end of this chapter which describes briefly various alternative compensation schemes.

SECTION 2   AWARDS OF DAMAGES TO LIVING CLAIMANTS

Damages have historically been granted on a once-and-for-all basis,[7] which inevitably – because of the role played by speculation – leads to imperfections in the compensatory awards made. Indeed, the process of assessing lump-sum damages often consists, in truth, of little more than judicial guesstimates: 'How long will the claimant actually live?', 'Will she develop epilepsy in five years' time?' A claimant whose medical prognosis is judged overly pessimistically will gain a bonus, while the converse is also true. In short, individual corrective justice gets sacrificed in the interests of finality and predictability. Unsurprisingly, such imperfections have attracted much criticism, even from leading members of the judiciary.[8] That being the case, a system of periodic payments that can be adjusted over time to meet the claimant's needs are now generally regarded as a more effective and just compensation mechanism in cases of severe injury.[9] Thus, while lump-sum awards can and will still be made in respect of run-of-the-mill injuries, it is also possible to obtain a periodical payment order in respect of severely injured claimants (which may even be made on a reviewable basis in certain circumstances).[10]

Periodical payments were first made available on a statutory footing in 2005.[11] Yet unlike the voluntary structured settlements that they replaced, these orders can be imposed on the parties even if they are individually or jointly opposed to such an arrangement. (That said, courts will apparently be unlikely to act contrary to the wishes of *both* parties.)[12] Drawing up the necessary initial schedule can be a complex matter (involving such matters as indexing),[13] and it is for this reason that periodical payments orders were made reviewable in certain circumstances so that modifications to the order can be effected in the future in light of, typically, a serious deterioration in

---

[7] One exception is where a provisional award is made enabling C to re-apply for further damages if a risk of further damage (eg, epilepsy) does in fact materialise: see the Supreme Court Act 1981, s 32A.

[8] See, eg, *Wright v British Rlys Board* [1983] 2 AC 773, at 776–8.

[9] But for criticism and doubt, see Lewis, 'Appearance and Reality in Reforming Periodical Payments of Tort Damages in the UK' in Neyers et al (eds), *Emerging Issues in Tort Law* (2007), ch 19.

[10] See the Damages Act 1996, ss 2–2B (as substituted by the Courts Act 2003 and the Damages (Variation of Periodical Payments) Order 2005 (SI 2005/841)).

[11] Damages Act 1996 (as amended by the Courts Act 2003 and the Damages (Variation of Periodical Payments) Order 2005). The impetus for this statute was provided largely by the Law Commission in its review of such settlements: Consultation Paper No 125, *Structured Settlements and Interim and Provisional Damages* (1992); Law Com No 224, *Structured Settlements and Interim Provisional Damages* (1994).

[12] *Thompstone v Tameside and Glossop NHS Trust* [2008] 1 WLR 2207.

[13] See, eg, ibid.

the claimant's condition.[14] On the other hand, it is important to stress that the order needs to be made reviewable at the outset, and that reviewability is by no means the norm.

Whether paid in the form of a lump sum or in the form of periodical payments, compensatory damages in tort can be broken down into two main components:

(1) Pecuniary losses – primarily but not exclusively those resulting from loss of earnings or earning capacity. They also include the costs of medical and hospital expenses.

(2) Non-pecuniary loss – that is, pain and suffering and loss of amenity.[15]

(A) PECUNIARY LOSSES

(1) Loss of earnings

A number of years are likely to elapse between the infliction of the relevant injuries and the trial.[16] Loss of earnings up to the date of trial are part of the claimant's 'special damages' and must be specifically pleaded.[17] In making such pleas it is important to realise that all claims for loss of earnings (including business profits)[18] are computed in a way that is consistent with deductions that would have been made by way of tax.[19] Loss of perquisites will also be taken into account.[20]

One's prospective loss of earnings is also recoverable, though this is sometimes a matter of considerable speculation,[21] since the court is forced to estimate the claimant's future employment prospects,[22] his future incapacity,[23] and the number of working years of which he has been deprived.[24] The traditional judicial method is to arrive at a multiplicand (which represents an estimate of the claimant's net annual loss); and

---

[14] But note that, controversially, no facility for review is made in respect of the escalating costs of health care provision that may well rise at a rate in excess of inflation. See further Lewis, 'Appearance and Reality in Reforming Periodical Payments of Tort Damages in the UK' in Neyers et al (eds), *Emerging Issues in Tort Law* (2007), ch 19.

[15] For a detailed account of the composition of non-pecuniary loss see Law Com No 257, *Damages for Personal Injury: Non-Pecuniary Loss* (1999). See also Ogus (1972) 35 MLR 1.

[16] Matters have improved to some extent in the wake of the changes made to the availability of legal aid and the introduction of the tracking of claims within the civil justice system.

[17] *Ilkiw v Samuels* [1963] 2 All ER 879.   [18] *Kent v British Rlys Board* [1995] PIQR Q42.

[19] *British Transport Commission v Gourley* [1956] AC 185. The case sets out in detail how the notional tax liability is to be calculated.

[20] *Clay v Pooler* [1982] 3 All ER 570. Where a director is able to show that his company suffered a loss of profits through his incapacity, so that his earnings fell, damages for this loss were awarded: *Lee v Sheard* [1956] 1 QB 192.

[21] *Collett v Smith* [2009] EWCA Civ 583 (18-year-old professional footballer with uncertain prospects).

[22] In the tricky case of professional sportspersons, see *Collett Smith* [2009] EWCA Civ 583.

[23] But note that this estimate is now subject to variation if the award takes the form of a reviewable periodic payment: Damages Act 1996, s 2B.

[24] This paragraph is based mainly on the speeches of the House of Lords in *Taylor v O'Connor* [1971] AC 115 and *Cookson v Knowles* [1979] AC 556. For the most modern statement on the correct approach to the computation of loss of earnings in cases of long-term disability, see *Herring v Ministry of Defence* [2003]

then to multiply this by a multiplier (which represents the number of working years lost by the claimant). The starting point for arriving at the multiplier is the number of remaining years in the claimant's working life.[25] This figure is then reduced to take account of contingencies such as future unemployment and sickness and, above all (in the case of a lump sum), the fact that the claimant may receive a capital sum which he is expected to invest in interest-bearing securities. In the important House of Lords decision in *Wells v Wells*,[26] it was held that there is an expectation that the prudent claimant will take advantage of index-linked government securities which yield a low but safe average net return. The relatively low return associated with such securities has to be reflected in a higher initial lump sum than would formerly have been made. The award is calculated on the basis that the claimant will spend the income and part of the capital annually so that the capital will be exhausted at the age the court has assessed to be the appropriate age having regard to all the contingencies. Currently, the courts assume a 2.5% rate of interest which is net after tax.[27] In practice, the experience of the court has resulted in a multiplier which, for example, in the case of a 30-year-old, would ordinarily be about 17, reducing to about 14 in the case of a man of about 40.[28] Practitioners are familiar with current judicial trends and out of court settlements are negotiated on the basis of these current 'going rates'.[29]

Until *Wells v Wells*, actuarial evidence was discouraged by the courts despite the fact that actuaries are accustomed to using statistical tables to work out expectancies and to 'discount' capital awards so as to reflect contingencies and the immediate receipt of the capital sum.[30] The main criticism made against actuarial tables was that, being produced for insurers, they were designed to deal with average expectancies within *groups* rather than with the actual expectancies of particular individuals (with whom the courts had to deal). Put thus, this criticism is somewhat misleading, for it takes no account of the fact that actuarial tables can be drawn up more specifically – for example, on an occupation-specific basis. Furthermore, it fails to indicate why a judicial guesstimate would be any more accurate than such tables. In recognition of this fact, there was support in *Wells v Wells* for counsel generally endeavouring to calculate their clients' claims in accordance with the most well-known set of such

EWCA Civ 528. See also *Clenshaw v Tanner* [2002] EWCA Civ 1848 on the deductions that can be made in order to take account of the likely effects of C's alcohol abuse on his future earning potential.

[25] If there is great uncertainty associated with the calculation, the courts will, instead, grant a lump sum based on the best estimate the court can make as to C's loss: *Chase International Express Ltd v McRae* [2003] EWCA Civ 505.   [26] [1998] 3 All ER 481.

[27] This was set by the Damages (Personal Injury) Order 2001 (SI 2001/2301). However, if any party to the proceedings can show that a different rate is more appropriate in the particular case, the court may use that rate: Damages Act 1996, s 1(2). For details of s 1(2) in operation, see *Clerk and Lindsell on Torts* (2006), 1821.   [28] See *Pritchard v JH Cobden Ltd* [1988] Fam 22.

[29] Relying heavily on publications such as Kemp and Kemp, *The Quantum of Damages* (1975).

[30] *Mitchell v Mulholland (No 2)* [1972] 1 QB 65. The courts seem to take a very different attitude to actuarial evidence when approving those periodical payments formerly known as structured settlements: see Law Com 125, *Structured Settlements and Interim and Provisional Damages* (1992), 53–4.

tables – the *Ogden Tables*.[31] If it ever comes into force, section 10 of the Civil Evidence Act 1995 will afford statutory recognition to the use of these *Ogden Tables*.

The courts will not hear evidence from economists on future inflationary trends.[32] The House of Lords has stated that such evidence is too speculative[33] and has taken the view that, by prudent investment, the claimant can offset the effects of inflation.[34] Only in very exceptional cases will any allowance be made for inflation to offset the effect of higher-rate tax on very large awards.[35]

Although there is no shortage of examples of the courts showing faith in the efficacy of fine-tuning the multiplicand and multiplier in order to provide an award which is just and also meets the claimant's needs,[36] considerable problems have from time to time been encountered. One of these problems centres on the time that may elapse between the date of the accident and the date of the trial. In such a case, the claimant will of course receive his actual loss of earnings up to the trial. Yet the defendants in *Pritchard v J H Cobden Ltd*[37] sought to argue that the multiplier – fixed by reference to the period likely to elapse between the date of the trial and the end of the claimant's working life – should be reduced to allow for the actual loss recovered as special damages and to discourage delay in bringing personal injuries actions to trial. Their contentions were ultimately rejected. The Court of Appeal stressed the need that the claimants had for a certain and predictable sum in lost earnings to defray their immediate post-injury expenses.

A second difficulty that has been encountered concerns fixing a suitable multiplier where the medical evidence suggests that the claimant will die early as a result of his injuries. Should he be able to recover compensation for his 'lost years' when, but for the fatal injury, he would have lived longer? Loss of income in the 'lost years' is now recoverable[38] subject to a deduction for the claimant's living expenses during those 'lost years'.[39] For claimants injured in the middle of their working life when they have families and dependants, such income should clearly be recoverable. It is needed to ensure that even after the claimant's premature death his family does not suffer and that the claimant himself can enjoy some relative peace of mind in what remains of his life. Section 3 of the Damages Act 1996 now provides for this eventuality, allowing dependants to claim for those losses not compensated by the original award of damages.

---

[31] *Actuarial Tables for use in Personal Injury and Fatal Accident Cases* (2004).

[32] *Mitchell v Mulholland (No 2)* [1972] 1 QB 65.

[33] See *Lim Poh Choo v Camden and Islington Area HA* [1980] AC 174, at 193.

[34] *Cookson v Knowles* [1979] AC 556; *Wells v Wells* [1998] 3 All ER 481.

[35] *Hodgson v Trapp* [1989] AC 807, at 835.

[36] For an exception see *Read v Harries* [1995] PIQR Q 25.   [37] [1988] Fam 22.

[38] *Pickett v British Rail Engineering Ltd* [1980] AC 136.

[39] Including a pro rata sum for his consumption of housing, electricity costs, etc: *Harris v Empress Motors Ltd* [1983] 3 All ER 561.

It is now clear that the courts will compensate loss of earning capacity[40] as readily as an actual loss of earnings. So a married woman who at the time of her injuries is engrossed in child rearing will be compensated for any loss of earning capacity running from the time when she would have been likely to return to remunerated work outside the home.[41] Children and young people who have not started earning will receive compensation for the damage to, or destruction of, their employment prospects. The older the child and the more evidence there is of her prospects of remunerated work, the larger the award will be.[42] With a very young child, the highly speculative nature of assessing her loss of earning capacity will not disentitle her from such an award, but it may mean a relatively small amount is received under this head. In *Croke v Wiseman*,[43] for example, a 21-month-old boy was permanently incapacitated in a medical accident. He was 7 at the date of the trial and likely to survive until he was 40. To compensate him for his loss of earnings, a multiplicand of £5,000, and a multiplier of five years, were set by the Court of Appeal. No award was made in respect of loss of earnings in the 'lost years'. This now seems standard for children and young people.[44]

(2) Medical, nursing, and hospital expenses

A claimant is entitled to recover as special damages those medical, nursing, and hospital expenses which he has reasonably incurred up to the date of trial.[45] His predicted future expenses will then be estimated and awarded as general damages.[46] Where the claimant has received private health care or plans to arrange future treatment privately, the possibility that the claimant could have avoided these expenses by using the facilities of the NHS is to be disregarded.[47] Yet, if it is clear that private medical care will not be used, the courts will refuse to entertain any claim that the claimant makes in respect of any such care he *might have elected* to use.[48] In other respects, the expenditure must be reasonable in relation to both the claimant's condition and the amount paid. If he has to live in a special institution or in special accommodation, the additional expense is recoverable.[49] He cannot claim the capital cost of acquiring

---

[40] *Smith v Manchester Corpn* (1974) 17 KIR 1; *Dhaliwal v Personal Representatives of Hunt* [1995] PIQR Q56. But what of C who elects to paint unprofitably rather than do well-paid commercial work? See *Keating v Elvan Reinforced Concrete Co Ltd* [1967] 3 All ER 611.

[41] *Daly v General Steam Navigation Co Ltd, The Dragon* [1980] 3 All ER 696.

[42] See *Housecroft v Burnett* [1986] 1 All ER 332 (£56,000 for loss of earning capacity awarded to an intelligent 16-year-old girl).   [43] [1981] 3 All ER 852.

[44] See *Housecroft v Burnett* [1986] 1 All ER 332. Cf *Harvey v Northumberland CC* [2003] EWCA Civ 338 (C, a young adult, got £9,000 for his thwarted ambition to become a police officer).

[45] Even hospice care is covered: *Drake v Foster Wheeler Ltd* [2011] 1 All ER 63.

[46] The courts will naturally take expert evidence on such matters. But where conflicting medical evidence is presented to the court, the judge will be entitled to form his own view of what care is likely to be needed (bearing in mind what the conflicting medical experts have said): *Huntley v Simmons* [2010] Med LR 83.

[47] Law Reform (Personal Injuries) Act 1948, s 2(4). If C does make use of the NHS he cannot recover what he would have had to pay if he had had private treatment: *Lim Poh Choo v Camden and Islington Area HA* [1980] AC 174.   [48] *Woodrup v Nicol* [1993] PIQR Q 14.

[49] *Shearman v Folland* [1950] 2 KB 43; *George v Pinnock* [1973] 1 All ER 926.

special accommodation since he continues to own that accommodation.[50] But he can claim the additional annual cost over his lifetime of requiring special accommodation and the capital cost of any alterations or conversions needed to meet his disability that do not enhance the value of the property.[51] Any saving to the claimant attributable to his maintenance at public expense in a hospital, nursing home, or other institution is set off against any loss of earnings.[52]

The claimant is able to claim his nursing expenses. If the court finds, however, that at some future time he will be unable to obtain all the private nursing services required, and will have to enter an NHS hospital, an appropriate deduction from future nursing expenses will be made.[53] On the other hand, where the burden of caring for the claimant is largely shouldered by relatives or friends, the claimant's right to compensation to pay for such services is normally unaffected.[54] He is entitled to receive a sum to recompense, for example, his wife, mother, or friend.[55] That the carer has given up gainful employment must be taken into account and generally his or her loss should be made good, although the total cost of care should not exceed current commercial rates for professional nursing care.[56] Recompense is also available even though the relative is simply caring for the claimant voluntarily, out of love.[57] On the other hand, if a spouse provides gratuitous assistance in running her injured husband's business, no award will be made in relation to the value of these essentially commercial services.[58]

There is no need for the injured party to enter into any contractual agreement with his relative or friend. Indeed, any such agreement made for the purpose of increasing the award for care will be treated as a sham.[59] The need for additional help for the family by way of night sleepers to help a paralysed claimant, and substitute help to give family members a holiday, must not be overlooked, however. Nor must the monetary value of gratuitous care formerly provided by the claimant for another member of the family. So, for example, if X is injured by virtue of Y's tort, X may claim the value of the care he used to provide gratuitously for his disabled brother Z.[60]

---

[50] *Cunningham v Harrison* [1973] QB 942.   [51] *Roberts v Johnstone* [1989] QB 878.

[52] Administration of Justice Act 1982, s 5.   [53] *Cunningham v Harrison* [1973] QB 942.

[54] *Hunt v Severs* [1994] 2 AC 350; *Donnelly v Joyce* [1974] QB 454 (mother gave up job to care for 6-year-old C); *Cunningham v Harrison* [1973] QB 942 (a wife gave up her job to nurse her husband); *Roberts v Johnstone* [1989] QB 878 (care provided by adoptive mother). But note the important distinction between caring services and business services: *Hardwick v Hudson* [1999] 1 WLR 1770.

[55] In *Croke v Wiseman* [1981] 3 All ER 852, C had a life expectancy of 33 years, throughout which he would need continuous nursing by professional nurses and his parents. In awarding £119,000 for the future cost of nursing care the court took account of the mother losing her teacher's pension rights, valued at £7,000, on giving up her post.

[56] *Housecroft v Burnett* [1986] 1 All ER 332. Where, however, the carer's net loss of earnings is a lesser amount than the commercial rate for caring, the amount will nonetheless be confined to the carer's net loss: *Fitzgerald v Ford* [1996] PIQR Q72.

[57] But here, it has been suggested that the amount should be equal to 75% of the commercial rate for help: *Fairhurst v St Helens and Knowsley HA* [1995] PIQR Q1.   [58] *Hardwick v Hudson* [1999] PIQR Q202.

[59] *Fairhurst v St Helens and Knowsley HA* [1995] PIQR Q 1.   [60] *Lowe v Guise* [2002] QB 1369.

Exceptionally, nursing care cannot be recouped in the case where the carer was also the tortfeasor who inflicted the injury. In *Hunt v Severs*,[61] for example, a wife had run over her husband in a car but no award was made in relation to the nursing care she later provided, since the House of Lords stated that this head of damage was only to be awarded in circumstances where the claimant had a moral duty to account for those damages to the carer. In other words, the objection was that such damages would have been a perverse award 'compensating the [tortfeasor] carer'.[62]

(3) Additional pecuniary losses and expenses

Loss of earnings or earning capacity, and medical and nursing expenses commonly form the bulk of the pecuniary loss resulting from personal injuries. But other losses and expenses which can be shown to flow from the claimant's injuries will also generally be recoverable. These include obvious additional costs of coping with a life of disability,[63] expenses of removal to a specially adapted dwelling,[64] a specially built invalid car or some other means of giving the claimant mobility,[65] a telephone for emergencies,[66] etc. Similarly, losses resulting from no longer being able to pursue a profitable hobby will also be recoverable. And a married woman whose injuries impaired her capability to do housework received an award for that impairment based on the cost of obtaining household help.[67]

But certain 'losses' resulting from injury are more problematic. Historically, young unmarried women received an award for loss of marriage prospects where they suffered disabling or disfiguring injuries. That award was generally regarded as part of the claimant's recompense for loss of amenity. But young female claimants paid for it in that, in assessing the multiplier for loss of future earnings, account was taken of the likelihood of marriage and motherhood reducing the number of years in which the claimant was likely to be earning.[68] In a break with the past, the judge in *Hughes v McKeown*[69] made no award for loss of marriage prospects and consequently declined to reduce the multiplier used to calculate the award for loss of earnings from that appropriate to a young man of similar age. The Court of Appeal later suggested that either approach is acceptable.[70] But in the modern era, loss of a young woman's marriage prospects coupled with a presumed dependency upon a husband would seem

---

[61] [1994] 2 AC 350.

[62] Ibid at 394. But why should the loss be so seen? Why is it not to be regarded in terms of C's need for such care? For criticism see Matthews and Lunney (1995) 58 MLR 395. Note also the fact that the Australian courts have refused to follow the *Hunt v Severs* approach: *Kars v Kars* (1996) 141 ALR 37.

[63] In *Kroeker v Jansen* (1995) 123 DLR (4th) 652 an award was made to a woman 'disabled from some of her housework beyond the level that her husband ought reasonably to do for her'.

[64] *Moriarty v McCarthy* [1978] 2 All ER 213 (paraplegic moving to a bungalow).

[65] *Housecroft v Burnett* [1986] 1 All ER 332.   [66] *Moriarty v McCarthy* [1978] 2 All ER 213.

[67] The award was made regardless of whether it was actually used to obtain domestic help: *Daly v General Steam Navigation Co Ltd, The Dragon* [1980] 3 All ER 696.

[68] *Moriarty v McCarthy* [1978] 2 All ER 213.   [69] [1985] 3 All ER 284.

[70] *Housecroft v Burnett* [1986] 1 All ER 332; but what of the 20-year-old law student who has a training contract at a London firm? Her prospective earnings may be higher than her speculative 'husband's' and she

to be sexist. If anything, the loss of marriage and parenthood prospects should be reflected in the award for loss of amenity and be available equally to young men.

A second problematic 'loss' occurs where injuries lead to the breakdown of the claimant's marriage. Can he or she recover the additional expenditure involved in running two homes and maintaining a former spouse? The Court of Appeal has held such expenses to be irrecoverable.[71] They are not 'losses' resulting from the injuries but merely a redistribution of assets. In any case, such 'losses' should be excluded as a matter of policy, since the spectre of sham 'divorces' clearly cannot be ignored.

The exclusion of damages on policy grounds has also surfaced in other contexts. In one case, a rapist who had earlier recovered damages for the change of personality he suffered after a traumatic injury, attempted to obtain an indemnity for the damages he was ordered to pay his victims. His attempt failed.[72] In cases in which mothers have attempted to obtain damages for wrongful birth, it is now clear that no award will lie in respect of the ordinary costs associated with raising a healthy child;[73] but damages will be available in respect of the special costs associated with raising a disabled child.[74]

Where a claimant was permanently incapacitated and, in addition to loss of earnings, there was a 'cost of care' claim, the House of Lords sought to avoid any duplication of damages as follows.[75] A full award for loss of earnings was made in the usual way with no deduction for living expenses except in respect of the 'lost years'. In calculating the award for cost of care, however, a deduction was made for the living expenses the claimant would have incurred in any event had she not been injured.

Other miscellaneous losses that would fall into this category include the loss of the opportunity of obtaining affordable health or life insurance,[76] the loss of lodgings which have to be surrendered when the claimant is unable to work any longer because those lodgings had been provided by the employer,[77] and the loss of a company car.[78]

(4) Deduction for benefits received

The pecuniary losses and expenses resulting from injury may on occasion be offset by benefits received whether from social security, insurance provision, or charity. But on what bases should such benefits be set off against the award to be made to the claimant? Social security benefits are now dealt with in the Social Security (Recovery of Benefits) Act 1997. That Act provides protection for damages awards made in respect of pain, suffering, and loss of amenity against the recoupment of

---

may well never give up paid work. And what about the financial loss to a young man deprived of the chance of marrying a high-earning wife?

[71] *Pritchard v J H Cobden Ltd* [1988] Fam 22.

[72] *Meah v McCreamer (No 2)* [1986] 1 All ER 943. See also *Clunis v Camden and Islington HA* [1998] 3 All ER 180.

[73] *McFarlane v Tayside Health Board* [1999] 3 WLR 1301; *AD v East Kent Community NHS Trust* [2002] EWCA Civ 1872.   [74] *Parkinson v St James and Seacroft University Hospital NHS Trust* [2002] QB 266.

[75] *Lim Poh Choo v Camden and Islington AHA* [1980] AC 174.

[76] *A v National Blood Authority* [2001] 3 All ER 289.   [77] *Liffen v Watson* [1940] 1 KB 556.

[78] *Clay v Pooler* [1982] 3 All ER 570.

social security benefits. Taken together, section 8 of, and Schedule 2 to, the Act permit recoupment only as against compensation for loss of earnings, the cost of care, and loss of mobility. The scheme affects the defendant in the following way. As regards those damages that represent the amount payable in respect of pain, suffering, and loss of amenity, the defendant is directly liable to the claimant. As regards the amount now paid to the claimant by way of state benefits in respect of loss of earnings, etc, the defendant is, instead, liable to the Secretary of State. The principle is simple: the state shall not bear the pecuniary cost of the defendant's tort, while the claimant at the same time should not be compensated twice over. But one possible exception to this principle is contained in Part II of Schedule 1 to the Social Security (Recovery of Benefits) Act 1997 which allows for regulations to be made for disregarding small payments.[79]

Social security benefits are not the only collateral benefits which may result from the claimant's injury and consequent disability. Few general principles can be deduced from the authorities about when such benefits should be deducted from the award of damages for loss of earnings and additional expenditure. That being so, any attempt to present a rational picture of the rules is likely to fail. Nonetheless, it does seem clear that the courts will generally make every effort to encourage benevolence so that charitable payments made to the claimant – for example, from a disaster fund – will not be deducted;[80] nor generally will *ex gratia* payments made by employers be deducted.[81] In addition, proceeds of personal insurance policies provided for by the claimant or his family will not be deducted.[82] But where, even despite his sickness or disability, the claimant receives sick pay as part of his contract of employment, he must account for those monies[83] (unless the contract provides that sick pay must be refunded in the event of a successful tort claim).[84]

In *Parry v Cleaver*[85] the House of Lords held that an occupational disability pension was not deductible regardless of whether it was contributory or discretionary. The test, their Lordships held, was twofold: was the money received of the same nature as what was lost; and, if not, was it a benefit still intended to be paid even if the claimant were to be reimbursed from another source? In the light of this test, statutory sick pay payable by the employer under the Social Security and Housing Benefits Act 1982 was held to be deductible.[86] It was seen as essentially the same as a contractual entitlement to sick pay.

---

[79] 'Small payments' are those of £2,500 or less. There is no sign of any such regulations at present.

[80] *Redpath v Belfast and County Down Rly* [1947] NI 167; approved in *Parry v Cleaver* [1970] AC 1.

[81] *Cunningham v Harrison* [1973] QB 942. Cf *Hussain v New Taplow Paper Mills Ltd* [1987] 1 All ER 417 (where D was the employer).

[82] *Bradburn v Great Western Rly Co* (1874) LR 10 Exch 1; approved in *Parry v Cleaver* [1970] AC 1.

[83] *Turner v Ministry of Defence* (1969) 113 Sol Jo 585.   [84] *Browning v War Office* [1963] 1 QB 750.

[85] [1970] AC 1; followed in *Longden v British Coal Corpn* [1998] AC 653.

[86] *Palfrey v Greater London Council* [1985] ICR 437.

In *Hussain v New Taplow Paper Mills Ltd*[87] the injured claimant received long-term sickness benefit provided for by a permanent health insurance scheme arranged by his employers and taken out for their (that is, the employers') benefit. The monies received were held to be indistinguishable from contractual sick pay and were not seen as analogous to a disability pension or private insurance monies. The Court of Appeal suggested that, as between claimant employees and their employers, *ex gratia* benefits ought to be accounted for and that the claimant should generally only recover his net loss. But difficulties arise because two basic principles of compensatory damages conflict. First, as *Hussain* affirmed, the claimant should receive only his actual estimated loss, and should not gain a net benefit from his injuries. Yet, on the other hand, the tortfeasor should not benefit either from the claimant's own prudence in insuring himself, or from the benevolence of others.

'Victory' for the net loss principle in *Hussain* was short-lived. In *Smoker v London Fire and Civil Defence Authority*,[88] the House of Lords affirmed *Parry v Cleaver*. Thus, a contributory disability pension remains non-deductible even if provided and partly paid for by the employer. Similarly, in *McCamley v Cammell Laird Shipbuilders Ltd*[89] the defendant employers took out and paid for personal accident policies on behalf of all their employees. The proceeds of such policies were held to be non-deductible as these were payable whenever an employee suffered a qualifying injury regardless of fault. It was a product of the employers' benevolence not a consequence of the tort which later materialised. *Hussain*, then, is probably best seen as confined it to its own particular facts.[90] That being so, only if part of the claimant's claim is that he has lost the opportunity to accumulate greater pension rights will the pension payable after the normal date of retirement be taken into account.[91]

(B) NON-PECUNIARY LOSSES

(1) Pain and suffering

The claimant is entitled to compensation for the pain and suffering, both actual and prospective, which is caused by the initial injury or subsequent surgical operations.[92] If his expectation of life has been reduced by his injuries, an award of damages for pain and suffering shall take account of any suffering caused or likely to be caused to him by awareness that his expectation of life has been shortened.[93] Neither a permanently unconscious claimant,[94] nor one who experiences anxiety at having developed

---

[87] [1988] AC 514. See also *College v Bass Mitchells & Butlers Ltd* [1988] 1 All ER 536 (redundancy payments).   [88] [1991] 2 AC 502.

[89] [1990] 1 All ER 854.

[90] Tentatively suggested in *McCamley v Cammell Laird Shipbuilders Ltd* [1990] 1 All ER 854, at 860.

[91] *Longden v British Coal Corpn* [1998] AC 653.

[92] *H West & Son Ltd v Shephard* [1964] AC 326; *Cutler v Vauxhall Motors Ltd* [1971] 1 QB 418.

[93] Administration of Justice Act 1982, s 1(1)(b). This Act abolished damages for loss of expectation of life as such, and as a separate head of damage.   [94] *Wise v Kaye* [1962] 1 QB 638.

symptomless (and per se harmless) pleural plaques because of exposure to asbestos,[95] has any claim for pain and suffering. Nor, according to *Kerby v Redbridge HA*,[96] is mere sorrow or upset at the loss of a child actionable.

(2) Loss of amenities

Compensation is also recoverable for loss of faculty. Even though the accident has rendered the claimant a 'human vegetable' so that he is unaware of his injuries, he is still entitled to claim for any loss of bodily function.[97] Damages cannot be refused simply because the claimant will be unable to use the damages in view of the sever- ity of his injuries.[98] This is because the award for loss of amenities must be made on the basis of amenities lost; awareness of deprivation is irrelevant. The court will take into account deprivation of sexual pleasures,[99] loss of a holiday,[100] inability to fish,[101] disfigurement,[102] as well as more obvious losses, such as inability to play games or to walk. In short, damages under this head may take account of a wide range of subjec- tive factors.

(3) Assessing the quantum

Non-pecuniary damages differ from pecuniary damages in that there is not even any suggestion of a scientific method of deciding what sum should be awarded. Damages for loss of amenity and pain and suffering have traditionally been awarded as an aggregate lump sum. This sum represents an amount that society deems fair (fairness being interpreted by the courts in the light of previous decisions); and in this regard there has evolved a set of conventional principles which provide a provisional guide to the comparative severity of different forms of injury. This guide uses a system of brackets of damages into which particular types of injury fall. In other words, loss is generally[103] compensated according to a tariff – for example, a sum between £A and £B for the loss of an arm, between £X and £Y for the loss of an eye, etc. However, the particular circumstances of the claimant, including his age and any unusual depriva- tion which he suffers, are also taken into account.

One particular problem for these guidelines is the continual fall in the value of money. This, of course, necessitates an ongoing reassessment of these awards.[104] What happens in practice, then, is that practitioners' books and periodicals[105] regularly publish judicial awards under all the relevant heads – for example, blindness, loss of

---

[95] *Rothwell v Chemical & Insulating Co Ltd* [2008] AC 281.   [96] [1994] PIQR Q 1.
[97] *H West & Son Ltd v Shephard* [1964] AC 326; *Lim Poh Choo v Camden and Islington AHA* [1980] AC 174.   [98] Ibid.
[99] *Cook v JL Kier & Co Ltd* [1970] 2 All ER 513.   [100] *Ichard v Frangoulis* [1977] 2 All ER 461.
[101] *Moeliker v A Reyrolle & Co Ltd* [1977] 1 All ER 9.   [102] *Oakley v Walker* (1977) 121 Sol Jo 619.
[103] The courts may depart from the standard tariff where the circumstances of a particular case require it. See, eg, *Griffiths v Williams* (1995) *Times*, 24 November (the court took account of the fact that C was a rape victim).   [104] *Birkett v Hayes* [1982] 2 All ER 710.
[105] Especially Kemp and Kemp, *The Quantum of Damages* (1975) and the monthly publication, *Current Law*, under the heading of 'Damages'.

a leg, etc – with brief details of the claimant's circumstances. This enables the claimant's lawyers and the defendant's insurers to agree likely awards, and it also assists the judges in conforming to the (real-value) levels of awards made by their brethren. Nonetheless, the difficulty of awarding a sum given the constant fall in the value of money is well illustrated in *Housecroft v Burnett*.[106]

> The injuries sustained by the 16-year-old claimant resulted in tetraplegia. The life which she could have expected with its pleasures, career prospects, and the hope of a family was replaced by complete dependence on her mother for every aspect of her care. The court recognised the imprecise nature of the task but stressed the need for uniformity where possible. It was held that the bracket of acceptable awards should therefore be set by reference to recent decisions.

When considering the exact amount to award within the appropriate bracket, extreme physical pain, or the impairment of speech or hearing ought to justify an award above the average; whereas a lack of awareness of one's disability might be taken to justify an award at the lower end of the range. The difficulty of comparing levels of injury is well illustrated in *McCamley v Cammell Laird Shipbuilders Ltd*.[107] There, the claimant lost most of an arm and a leg on one side. He continued to suffer great pain and regained very little mobility. The trial judge awarded him £85,000, equivalent to the then going rate for tetraplegia. The Court of Appeal considered the award to be very generous, yet refused to overturn it. The decision thus illustrates the fact that the superior courts are generally reluctant to overturn damages awards unless they are *drastically* out of line with common practice (making the amount awarded, at least in part, a matter of luck). Furthermore, the reluctance of the superior courts to exercise their supervisory function in this context can be quite remarkable on occasion. In *Kiam v MGN Ltd*[108] – admittedly a defamation case – the Court of Appeal refused to disturb an award of £105,000 made by the jury even though the trial judge had suggested a bracket of between £40,000 and £80,000. The amount was not, according to the court, out of all proportion to what might sensibly have been thought appropriate.

(4) Provisional awards

Sometimes, the courts are called upon to award prospective damages where the claimant's medical prognosis is imprecise. For example, the injury may have created a risk of, say, epilepsy developing later in life. The courts used to estimate the percentage chance of such a condition developing and award an equivalent proportion of damages for the results of that condition. Claimants were consequently over-compensated if the risk did not materialise and under-compensated if it did. The Administration of Justice Act 1982 accordingly provided an alternative. Where there is a chance that the claimant at some time in the future will, as a result of the tort, develop some serious disease or suffer some serious deterioration in his physical or mental condition, the court will assess damages on the assumption that the development or deterioration

---

[106] [1986] 1 All ER 332.   [107] [1990] 1 All ER 854.   [108] [2002] 2 All ER 219.

will not occur, but award further damages at a future date if it does so occur, upon an application made by the claimant.[109]

The rules on provisional damages have in the past given rise to problems of application, and it is submitted that the courts will now, where the facility exists, much prefer to make use of reviewable periodical payments (considered above).

(5) Interest

The courts have the power to award interest on all or any part of an award of damages and should do so on awards for personal injuries or death unless there are 'special reasons' not to do so.[110] Detailed exposition of the rules on interest is beyond the scope of this work. It suffices to note simply the general rule that interest on pre-trial pecuniary loss will be payable at half the average rate on short-term investment accounts for that period.[111] No deduction of interest is normally made to take account of social security benefits received by the claimant.[112] Interest payable on non-pecuniary loss will be low – not more than 2% at present.[113]

(C) DAMAGE OR DESTRUCTION OF GOODS

Claimants in personal injury actions often also have a claim for damage to goods such as their cars. Where the car or other goods are destroyed, damages are made up of the cost of buying a replacement, together with compensation for loss of use pending replacement, with a deduction for the salvage value of the destroyed goods.[114] Where there is damage to goods, the damages represent the diminution in value, normally based on the cost of repair.[115] Damages are also given for loss of use, even though the goods were non-profit earning and not replaced during repair.[116] If a substitute has been hired, then the cost can be claimed provided the goods hired and the price paid are reasonable.[117]

SECTION 3   DEATH

Two issues arise when death ensues from a tort. First, the deceased's estate may wish to proceed with the cause of action which the deceased himself would have had if he

---

[109] The 1982 Act merely provided for rules to be made under it that grant this jurisdiction. They have now been made. See Supreme Court Act 1981, s 32A(1) and (2). See also RSC Ord 37, rr 8–10.

[110] Supreme Court Act, s 34A.   [111] *Jefford v Gee* [1970] 2 QB 130.

[112] *Wisely v John Fulton (Plumbers) Ltd* [2000] 2 All ER 545. But where the benefits exceed the damages due to be paid, such a deduction may be made: *Griffiths v British Coal Corpn* [2001] 1 WLR 1493.

[113] *Lawrence v CC of Staffordshire* [2000] PIQR Q349; *Wright v British Rlys Board* [1983] 2 AC 773. The reasons are: (1) damages should take into account inflation up to the time of judgment; and (2) damages for non-pecuniary loss are often difficult to quantify until C's condition has stabilised.

[114] *Moore v DER Ltd* [1971] 3 All ER 517; *Thatcher v Littlejohn* [1978] RTR 369.

[115] *Dodd Properties (Kent) Ltd v Canterbury CC* [1980] 1 All ER 928.

[116] *The Mediana* [1900] AC 113; *HL Motor Works (Willesden) Ltd v Alwahbi* [1977] RTR 276.

[117] *HL Motor Works (Willesden) Ltd v Alwahbi* [1977] RTR 276 (reasonable to hire a Rolls-Royce until C's Rolls-Royce was repaired).

had not died. Second, others – but especially relatives – may claim that they have suffered a loss in consequence of the death. Two statutes need therefore to be examined:
the Law Reform (Miscellaneous Provisions) Act 1934 (dealing with the survival of
actions) and the Fatal Accidents Act 1976 (dealing with death itself giving rise to a
cause of action).

(A) SURVIVAL OF ACTIONS

The Law Reform (Miscellaneous Provisions) Act 1934 provides that, subject to three
significant exceptions, on the death of any person, all causes of action vested in him
survive for the benefit of his estate.[118] The first exception is that actions for defamation
do not survive. Second, the right of a person to claim under section 1A of the Fatal
Accidents Act 1976 for bereavement does not survive for the benefit of his estate.[119]
Third, exemplary damages do not survive in the hands of the deceased's estate.[120]
The reason why these actions die with the initial victim is that they are all regarded
as claims personal to the deceased; although why this should be true of exemplary (as
opposed to aggravated) damages is hard to fathom.

Where the death of the deceased has been caused by an act or omission giving rise to
a cause of action, the 1934 Act enables his estate to bring proceedings in tort against the
defendant.[121] His estate may claim damages according to the usual principles for the
period between when the cause of action arose and the death. Thus, damages may be
awarded for the pain, suffering,[122] and loss of amenity[123] for that period during which
the deceased actually suffered such deprivations. Damages may also be awarded for
lost earnings[124] and medical expenses incurred up to the time of death,[125] including
palliative care in a hospice.[126]

The damages awarded to his estate 'shall be calculated without reference to any loss
or gain to his estate consequent on his death'.[127] Thus, if the deceased loses an annuity to which he was entitled, or if insurance monies become payable upon his death,
these losses and gains are disregarded in computing damages under the 1934 Act. The
rights conferred by the 1934 Act are in addition to any rights conferred by the Fatal

---

[118] Section 1(1).
[119] Administration of Justice Act 1982, s 4(1). It does, however, extend to a registered same-sex civil
partner.   [120] Administration of Justice Act 1982, s 4(2).
[121] For the limitation periods within which these proceedings must be brought, see the Limitation Act
1980, s 11(5)–(7).
[122] *Andrews v Freeborough* [1967] 1 QB 1 (£2,000 awarded to the estate of a child aged eight who remained
unconscious for a year between the accident and death); *Murray v Shuter* [1976] QB 972 (£11,000 awarded
to the estate of a man aged 36 in respect of loss of amenity during the four years he survived the accident in
a coma).   [123] *Rose v Ford* [1937] AC 826 (£2 awarded for loss of leg amputated two days before death).
[124] *Murray v Shuter* [1976] QB 927.   [125] *Rose v Ford* [1937] AC 826.
[126] *Drake v Foster Wheeler Ltd* [2011] 1 All ER 63.
[127] Law Reform (Miscellaneous Provisions) Act 1934, s 1(2). For application see *Harland and Wolff plc v
McIntyre* [2006] EWCA Civ 287.

Accidents Act 1976,[128] and the amount is unaffected by any damages under the later legislation.

No damages may now be awarded to the estate in respect of loss of income in the deceased's 'lost years'.[129] The potential overlap between claims by dependants under the Fatal Accidents Act for loss of dependency and an estate's claims for lost income from the 'lost years' is thus avoided.[130]

Technically, the 1934 Act applies even though death occurs instantaneously upon the commission of the tort (thus removing the possibility that the victim experiences any pain and suffering).[131] But since the Administration of Justice Act 1982 came into force, there is only one circumstance in which a claim may, in reality, be made under the 1934 Act where death is immediate;[132] and even that is of restricted application. However, whether or not the deceased died immediately, a claim for funeral expenses may be made.[133]

Finally, we must consider the situation where a claimant has been awarded provisional damages under section 32A of the Supreme Court Act 1981. If he subsequently dies due to deterioration in his condition, his dependants may now claim those losses that were not compensated by the initial award of damages.[134]

(B) DEATH AS A CAUSE OF ACTION

(1) Introduction

Historically, at common law, no action in tort could be brought by third parties who suffered loss through the killing of another.[135] But fatal accidents became so frequent with the development of railways that in 1846 Parliament had to pass the Fatal Accidents Act of that year which made considerable inroads into the common law rule. The modern principles are now embodied in the Fatal Accidents Act 1976.

The 1976 Act only benefits certain dependants; and even then the class of dependants entitled to sue varies according to whether the claim lies in respect of loss of support, bereavement, or funeral expenses (the three heads of claim permitted under the Act). But for present purposes, the initial point to make is that the Act is rather exceptional in creating an interest for one person in the life of another. No such general principle exists in tort law. Thus, an employee cannot sue a tortfeasor for the resulting

---

[128] Law Reform (Miscellaneous Provisions) Act 1934, s 1(5); *Yelland v Powell Duffryn Associated Collieries Ltd (No 2)* [1941] 1 KB 519.

[129] Law Reform (Miscellaneous Provisions) Act 1934, s 1(2)(a).

[130] See *Gammell v Wilson* [1982] AC 27.

[131] In *Hicks v CC of South Yorkshire Police* [1992] 2 All ER 65 it was held that momentary pain was merely part of the dying process and not an independent period of pain prior to death.

[132] The problem is that, with immediate death, there is no time for the victim to appreciate pain, suffering, etc and for the cause of action to vest. The better view is probably that the cause of action is completed by the injuries, and vests in the deceased at the moment of death.

[133] Law Reform (Miscellaneous Provisions) Act 1934, ss 1(2)(c) and 3(5); *Stanton v Ewart F Youlden Ltd* [1960] 1 All ER 429

[134] Damages Act 1996, s 3.

[135] *Baker v Bolton* (1808) 1 Camp 493; *Admiralty Comrs v SS Amerika* [1917] AC 38.

death of his employer so that the employee loses his job. Nor can an insurance company sue simply because it has to discharge its obligations under a life policy sooner than it otherwise would. In short, interests beyond those of the deceased's family have no recognition when death occurs.

Section 1(1) of the Fatal Accidents Act 1976 provides:

> If death is caused by any wrongful act, neglect or default which is such as would (if death had not ensued) have entitled the person injured to maintain an action and recover damages in respect thereof, the person who would have been liable if death had not ensued shall be liable to an action for damages, notwithstanding the death of the person injured.

(2) Who may sue?

The action is brought in the name of the executor or administrator[136] of the deceased, and lies in respect of loss of support for the benefit of the following relatives:[137] a wife, husband, or former wife or husband;[138] registered same-sex civil partners and former registered same-sex civil partners;[139] children, grandchildren, fathers, mothers, step-parents, grandparents, brothers, sisters, uncles, aunts, and their issue; adopted and illegitimate dependants; stepchildren of the several categories.[140] If there is no executor or administrator, or if he fails to bring the action within six months after the death of the deceased, any dependant may bring the action.[141] The Administration of Justice Act 1982 responded to social changes by including for the first time any person who was living with the deceased in the same household[142] for at least two years before that date, and was living during the whole of that period as the husband or wife of the deceased.[143] The provision now made for same-sex (and former same-sex) partners to claim is a further example of this branch of law responding to social change.

(3) Nature of the act complained of

It must first be proved that the act caused the death.[144] Thereafter, it must be shown that there was a 'wrongful act, neglect or default' by the defendant. These words

---

[136] Fatal Accidents Act 1976, s 2(1).   [137] Fatal Accidents Act 1976, s 1(2)–(5).

[138] By the Fatal Accidents Act 1976, s 1(4), a former spouse includes a person whose marriage has been annulled or declared void as well as a divorced person. This provision still applies even if the surviving former spouse has remarried: *Shepherd v Post Office* (1995) *Times*, 15 June. An equivalent definition is made in respect of a 'former civil partner': s 1(4A).

[139] Fatal Accidents Act 1976, s 1(4)–(5) as amended by s 83 of the Civil Partnership Act 2004.

[140] Fatal Accidents Act 1976, s 1(5)(a): 'any relationship by affinity shall be treated as a relationship by consanguinity, any relationship of the half-blood as a relationship of the whole blood, and the stepchild of any person as his child'. D must be given particulars of the dependants for whom a claim is made and of the nature of this claim: s 2(4).   [141] Fatal Accidents Act 1976, s 2(2).

[142] Note that it is possible for a person to be living in more than one household at any one time: *Pounder v London Underground Ltd* [1995] PIQR P 217.

[143] Fatal Accidents Act 1976, s 1(3)(b). But note that the Act is not so progressive as to recognise same-sex cohabitational relationships unless a registered civil partnership has been entered into. Cf Family Law Act 1996, s 62.

[144] In *Pigney v Pointer's Transport Services Ltd* [1957] 2 All ER 807, the deceased committed suicide while in a depressive state induced by D's negligent act; the death was held to have been caused by that act, so that

presumably embrace any tort.[145] Consequently, if the defendant's act was never actionable because he would have had a defence to any action brought by the deceased in his
lifetime, no action will lie.[146] Where the deceased died partly as the result of his own
fault and partly as the result of the fault of any other person, damages are reduced
to a proportionate extent[147] in the same way that they are under the Law Reform
(Contributory Negligence) Act 1945. If a dependant's contributory negligence is a
cause of the deceased's death, that dependant's damages are reduced but the awards to
other dependants are unaffected.[148]

At the time of his death, the deceased must have been in a position to sue the
defendant had he not died because of the wrongful act. If the limitation period expired
between the injury and his death, the Limitation Act 1980 stipulates that no Fatal
Accidents Act claim can come into existence.[149] This ordinarily[150] means that if more
than three years have elapsed between the injury and death, the claim will be time
barred.[151] The Limitation Act 1980 also provides that if the deceased had settled his
own claim,[152] no action lies under the Fatal Accidents Act,[153] but an action still lies
(and without any limit on the damages) if the claimant had merely agreed beforehand
that no more than, say, £1000 damages should be recoverable in the event of his being
the victim of this tort.[154]

(4) Specific limitations on claims under the 1976 Act

We have already noted the three kinds of action that can be brought under the Act.
But there are certain important limitations on the ability to sue for these. Let us begin
with the action for bereavement.[155] This claim – quite distinct from the action for loss
of support already considered – may be brought only for the benefit of (1) the surviving
'life partner' of the deceased (that is the deceased's wife, husband, or civil partner),[156]
or (2) the relevant parent or parents of any unmarried children.[157] The bereavement
action does not extend to former spouses, former civil partners, or a heterosexual
cohabitant who had been living with the deceased as his or her wife or husband.

There are limits, too, on the ability to sue for loss of support. In particular, any
claim by a dependant lies only upon proof of pecuniary loss (that is, financial support

---

an action under the Fatal Accidents Act 1976 was successful (as was a similar claim in *Watson v Willmott*
[1991] 1 QB 140).

[145] And a negligent breach of contract: *Grein v Imperial Airways Ltd* [1937] 1 KB 50.
[146] *Murphy v Culhane* [1977] QB 94 (if the deceased had failed because of the defence of *ex turpi causa* no
action would lie under the Act).   [147] Fatal Accidents Act 1976, s 5.
[148] *Dodds v Dodds* [1978] QB 543. The negligent dependant may also be required to make a contribution
(under the Civil Liability (Contribution) Act 1978) towards the damages which D has to pay for the benefit
of the dependants.   [149] Limitation Act 1980, s 12(1).
[150] The three-year period can be extended if the deceased did not have 'relevant knowledge' of his cause
of action.   [151] Limitation Act 1980, s 11(1).
[152] *Pickett v British Rail Engineering Ltd* [1980] AC 136, at 146–7 and 152.
[153] Limitation Act 1980, s 12(1).   [154] *Nunan v Southern Rly Co* [1924] 1 KB 223.
[155] Fatal Accidents Act 1976, s 1A(1).   [156] Fatal Accidents Act 1976, s 1A(2)(a).
[157] Both parents may claim if he was legitimate; only the mother if he was illegitimate: s 1A(2)(b).

that he or she would have received).[158] The language ordinarily used by the courts is that there must be a loss of 'prospective pecuniary advantage' and that a 'speculative possibility' of pecuniary gain is not enough.[159] A parent could recover, therefore, when his 16-year-old daughter died, having almost completed her unpaid dressmaking apprenticeship.[160] But the parent of a three-year-old child has been held to have no cause of action.[161] Although it is not essential that the dependant should have a legal right to that aid[162] – the loss of services gratuitously rendered is enough.[163] However, a distinction must be made between a pecuniary benefit to the dependant that would have accrued qua business relationship (as opposed to qua family relationship). If the loss is a business loss, no action is permitted under the Act. Thus, a father could not sue in respect of the loss of business contracts occasioned by the death of his son, who worked for the father's firm.[164]

For public policy reasons, where the pecuniary loss is attributable to an illegal enterprise in which the deceased was engaged, no action will lie under the 1976 Act. Thus, in *Hunter v Butler*[165] it was held that no claim lay where the deceased had been earning wages while fraudulently claiming social security benefits. The court was concerned not to allow monies illegally gained to form the basis of a claim for dependency.

(5) Period of limitation

The action under the 1976 Act must be brought within three years from either the date of the death, or the date on which the claimant had (actual or constructive) knowledge of the death, whichever is the later.[166] Where there are several potential claimants, the limitation period runs separately against each. Where the dependant's limitation period has expired before an action was brought, the court has a further discretionary power to extend the period.[167]

(6) Assessment of damages

The sum to be awarded as damages for bereavement is £18,000.[168] Where both parents claim this sum, it is divided equally between them.[169] Damages other than damages

---

[158] *Duckworth v Johnson* (1859) 4 H & N 653.

[159] *Davies v Taylor* [1974] AC 207: wife deserted husband five weeks before his death; shortly before his death he instructed a solicitor to begin divorce proceedings. The deserting wife had no claim as she failed to show a reasonable expectation of pecuniary benefit. [160] *Taff Vale Rly Co v Jenkins* [1913] AC 1.

[161] *Barnett v Cohen* [1921] 2 KB 461.

[162] *Stimpson v Wood & Son* (1888) 57 LJQB 484 (the mere fact that a wife by her adultery had lost her legal right to maintenance did not bar her claim). [163] *Berry v Humm & Co* [1915] 1 KB 627.

[164] *Sykes v NE Rly Co* (1875) 44 LJCP 191. The decision was followed in *Burgess v Florence Nightingale Hospital* [1955] 1 QB 349 (husband could not recover for loss of services of wife as dancing partner). See also *Behrens v Bertram Mills Circus Ltd* [1957] 2 QB 1 and *Malyon v Plummer* [1964] 1 QB 330.

[165] [1996] RTR 396. See also *Burns v Edman* [1970] 2 QB 541: no claim could be made by a widow who knew that her support came from the proceeds of her husband's crimes.

[166] Limitation Act 1980, s 12(2). [167] Limitation Act 1980, s 33.

[168] Fatal Accidents Act 1976, s 1A(3).

[169] Fatal Accidents Act 1976, s 1A(4). Would this be so where one parent was the tortfeasor who caused the death?

for bereavement are set proportionate to the injury[170] each dependant suffers.[171] Thus, the actual pecuniary loss resulting to each dependant from the death is ascertained separately[172] and the question of division is dealt with later.[173] So, for example, where an award is made to a widow and her children it has been suggested that the proportion awarded to the children should represent their genuine dependency.[174] The court should not simply award the bulk of the money to the widow on the assumption that she will provide for her children.[175] Among other things, the children need protection against the risk of their mother dying and the money passing into the hands of a stepfather.

Lord Wright has explained the traditional method of measuring the damages.

> The starting point is the amount of wages which the deceased was earning, the ascertainment of which to some extent may depend on the regularity of his employment. Then there is an estimate of how much was required or expended for his own personal and living expenses. The balance will give a datum or basic figure which will generally be turned into a lump sum...That sum, however, has to be taxed down by having due regard to uncertainties.[176]

The House of Lords elaborated upon this in *Taylor v O'Connor*.[177] The damages to a widow must make available to her, to spend each year, a sum free of tax equal to the amount of the dependency – an award sufficient to buy an annuity of that amount is not enough because part of the annuity will be taxable. The multiplier must be calculated from the date of the victim's death[178] and should be such that the capital sum awarded, together with the income earned by its investment, will be exhausted by the end of the period intended to be covered. It is supposed that the dependants will spend annually a part of the capital as well as the whole of the income they receive from so much of the capital as remains.[179] The multiplier of the annual loss of dependency is seldom fixed at more than 16 times that annual figure; so if the dependants have lost £8,000 a year from the death, the award will rarely exceed £128,000.

---

[170] 'Injury' includes any disease and any impairment of a person's physical or mental condition: Fatal Accidents Act 1976, s 1(6).

[171] Fatal Accidents Act 1976, s 3(1). For the meaning of this oddly worded provision see *Jameson v Central Electricity Generating Board* [2000] 1 AC 455.

[172] *Davies v Powell Duffryn Associated Collieries Ltd* [1942] AC 601, at 612. A dependant's damages are not reduced because his mother was contributorily negligent: *Dodds v Dodds* [1978] QB 543. Where a husband and wife with either separate incomes or a joint income share their living expenses, the amount by which their joint living expenses are less than twice the expenses of each one living separately is a benefit arising from the relationship, and may be the subject of a claim under the Fatal Accidents Act by the husband in respect of the death of his wife: *Burgess v Florence Nightingale Hospital* [1955] 1 QB 349.

[173] *Dietz v Lennig Chemicals Ltd* [1969] 1 AC 170, at 183. The court is to direct how the award is to be divided: Fatal Accidents Act 1976, s 3(2).   [174] *Benson v Biggs Wall & Co Ltd* [1982] 3 All ER 300.

[175] *Clay v Pooler* [1982] 3 All ER 570 (the children merely received pocket money).

[176] *Davies v Powell Duffryn Associated Collieries Ltd* [1942] AC 601, at 617.   [177] [1971] AC 115.

[178] *Graham v Dodds* [1983] 2 All ER 953.

[179] *Young v Percival* [1974] 3 All ER 677. See also *Taylor v O'Connor* [1971] AC 115.

In assessing future earnings, probable deductions for income tax are to be made.[180] No account may be taken of the fact that the dependant is of independent means, except in so far as it shows what pecuniary aid to that dependant was made by the deceased.[181] So, if a professional woman loses her husband who is also a professional, it is no answer to say that she could well support herself and her children. The question is simply how much of his income the deceased husband spent on his family rather than himself.

In *Cookson v Knowles*,[182] the House of Lords refined further the method of calculation. As a general rule, damages up to the date of trial are to be assessed separately from those after that date. For the first part, the loss of dependency will be multiplied by the actual period between the accident and the trial. Interest on that sum will then be awarded at half the short-term investment rate current during that period. For the second part, the court will arrive at the amount of dependency (the multiplicand) by estimating the probable rate of earnings of the deceased at the date of the trial. It will calculate the multiplier in the usual way. The multiplier will be fixed by reference to the date of the death, and the number of years actually elapsing between the death and the trial will then be deducted.[183] Interest is not awarded on the second sum.[184] Inflation is disregarded except in estimating earnings at the date of trial.

If the dependants have incurred funeral expenses in respect of the deceased, damages may be awarded in respect of those expenses.[185] But in assessing damages payable to a widow in respect of the death of her husband, the court must not take into account the widow's remarriage or her prospects of remarriage.[186]

It will be recalled that subject to certain conditions, persons living together as man and wife, though not married, are treated as 'dependants'.[187] In assessing their damages the court has to take into account the fact that the dependant had no enforceable right to financial support by the deceased as a result of their living together.[188]

To what extent can the courts take account of events occurring between the death and the trial? If such an event enables the courts to fix more precisely that which they are otherwise called upon to estimate, they must have regard to that event.[189] Thus, they have taken into account that, before trial, the defendant died;[190] that war broke

---

[180] *Bishop v Cunard White Star Co Ltd* [1950] P 240, at 250.

[181] *Shiels v Cruikshank* [1953] 1 All ER 874, a Scottish case, but presumably applicable to England.

[182] [1979] AC 556; *Corbett v Barking, Havering and Brentwood HA* [1991] 2 QB 408 (but the multiplier should be adjusted to take account of known facts).   [183] *Graham v Dodds* [1983] 2 All ER 953.

[184] The court's power to award interest in respect of personal injuries is strictly limited: Supreme Court Act 1981, s 35A.   [185] Fatal Accidents Act 1976, s 3(5).

[186] Fatal Accidents Act 1976, s 3(3). Her remarriage prospects might affect awards to her children: *Thompson v Price* [1973] QB 838.

[187] If an unmarried father is killed, even if the mother of his children has no claim, their children recover the loss of all the benefits which their father had provided for them, including such benefits given to the mother for the children's advantage – eg, the cost of her air fares for a family holiday: *K v JMP Co Ltd* [1976] QB 85.   [188] Fatal Accidents Act 1976, s 3(4).

[189] *Corbett v Barking, Havering and Brentwood HA* [1991] 2 QB 408.

[190] *Williamson v John I Thornycroft & Co Ltd* [1940] 4 All ER 61.

out (reducing the deceased's life expectancy);[191] that tax rates had been reduced.[192] Each of these events enables the courts to quantify more precisely a dependant's loss of contribution from the deceased. Hypothetical events which would, but for the deceased's death, have increased the dependant's dependency will not be taken into account. So the claimant widow's greater prospective loss had she, as she would have so desired, given up work to have a family, was rightly disregarded in *Malone v Rowan*.[193] Also to be disregarded under the 1976 Act are benefits which have accrued or will, or may, accrue to any person from his estate, or otherwise, as a result of the death.[194]

The assessment of damages in a Fatal Accidents Act claim can thus be seen to be relatively straightforward where what is in issue is the loss of a family breadwinner. The dependent family seeks to replace the lost income of the deceased parent. In recent years the courts have recognised that the death of a parent gives rise to other pecuniary losses over and above any loss of earned income. A series of cases have considered how damages should be assessed where a mother is tortiously killed. It may be that at the time of her death she was not working outside her home, or was only doing so on a part-time basis. The fundamental principle is that the widower and children are entitled to compensation based on the reasonable cost to them of replacing the mother's services in the home.[195] The starting point for that assessment where the children are under school age[196] will be the national cost of hiring a child-minder/housekeeper.[197] Allowance will be made for the fact that mothers do not work fixed hours and do not limit themselves to cooking, cleaning, and routine tasks. They provide more general care and moral guidance and those wider 'motherly services'[198] should be reflected in the award of damages. Where the father,[199] or other relative,[200] then gives up work to take over these duties, and in the light of the children's needs, that is a reasonable course of action, compensation may be based on his (or their) loss of earnings rather than the cost of a child-minder.

What is said above assumes the existence of a nuclear family where the mother stays at home providing 100% of the child care and the father earns 100% of the family income. That, of course, is seldom the case these days. So there must be a reduction made for loss of 'motherly services' where the mother did not provide full-time care.[201] Interestingly, in *Hayden v Hayden*,[202] it was held that if the father in effect undertook most of the mother's responsibilities after her death, there was no loss to the child in

---

[191] *Hall v Wilson* [1939] 4 All ER 85.   [192] *Daniels v Jones* [1961] 3 All ER 24.
[193] [1984] 3 All ER 402.   [194] Fatal Accidents Act 1976, s 4.
[195] *Hay v Hughes* [1975] QB 790; *Corbett v Barking, Havering and Brentwood HA* [1991] 2 QB 408.
[196] The court in *Spittle v Bunney* [1988] 3 All ER 1031 assumed a diminishing need for 'motherly services' once a child is settled at school.
[197] Based on the net rather than the gross wage payable: *Spittle v Bunney* [1988] 3 All ER 1031.
[198] *Regan v Williamson* [1976] 2 All ER 241.
[199] *Mehmet v Perry* [1977] 2 All ER 529 (note the special needs of these children who suffered from the hereditary disease thalassaemia).
[200] *Cresswell v Eaton* [1991] 1 All ER 484 (aunt gave up job as a traffic warden).
[201] Ibid.   [202] [1992] 4 All ER 681.

this respect. Yet *Hayden v Hayden* must be contrasted with *Stanley v Saddique*[203] where the child's parents were not married. On the death of the mother, the father undertook full responsibility for his son and soon remarried. The evidence suggested that the stepmother was likely to make a much better parent than the deceased mother. The defendants argued that the benefit conferred by the acquisition of a stepmother more than cancelled out the loss of the original mother's services. But the court held that section 4 of the Fatal Accidents Act 1976 prevented any such 'benefit' being taken into account.[204] *Stanley v Saddique* was followed, but with a critical qualification added, in *H v S*.[205] There it was said that the principle enunciated in *Hunt v Severs*[206] should be applied to such cases so that the amount representing the value of the lost gratuitous services should be held on trust for the benefit of the new voluntary carer (in this case, the father who had not previously provided care for the claimant children).

SECTION 4   ALTERNATIVE COMPENSATION SYSTEMS

(A) RESPONSIBILITY AND THE WELFARE STATE

Public responsibility for personal injury victims is recognised in the existence of a safety net of a number of benefits and provisions made for such persons. The complexity of the social welfare system means that a detailed exposition of its workings fall beyond the scope of this book. However, a brief sketch of that system's mechanics can be offered to good effect for anyone trying to assess the comparative merits (or otherwise) of the tort system.

(1) The welfare state provides essential services for accident victims in two main respects. Medical advice and treatment are largely available free of charge within the National Health Service. Where long-term care is required, this may prove to be of significant benefit to the victim. Even beyond hospital care, there is the possibility of various forms of assistance being provided by local authorities to, for example, the aged and the disabled. In practice, however, pressure on local authority budgets often means that only minimal benefits and services are in fact supplied.

(2) A wide range of social security benefits is available to persons incapable of work by reason of accident or disease. The level of payments made is at a subsistence rate, and generally far lower than the loss of earnings suffered by the incapacitated victim. Certain of the non-means-tested benefits are also payable to tort

---

[203] [1992] QB 1.

[204] On the broad meaning of 'benefit' in this context see also *O'Loughlin v Cape Distribution Ltd* [2001] EWCA Civ 178 (business flair of the deceased a benefit for the purposes of s 4).

[205] [2003] QB 965.

[206] But for criticism see Matthews and Lunney (1995) 58 MLR 395. See *Dimond v Lovell* [2002] 1 AC 384.

victims but the social security legislation now provides that the state recovers these payments from the tortfeasor.[207]

One thing is clear in this context: the better off one is to start with, the more one stands to lose and is likely to suffer from an incapacity in respect of which one has no remedy in tort. Thus, the solicitor who succumbs to an inherent risk of surgery stands to lose a great deal more than the single mother already on social security benefits before she is incapacitated. However, if the state has only limited resources to compensate for disability, it can be argued that high earners should have no especial claim for preferential treatment. The solicitor could, after all, have taken out an insurance policy covering her against all forms of personal injury or disease.

(3) Certain groups of the disabled may, in addition, receive extra payments related to their disability. For example, the Vaccine Damage Payments Act 1979 provides for payments to persons suffering 80% disablement consequent on vaccination.

(B) OTHER COMPENSATION SYSTEMS

(1) Criminal Injuries Compensation Scheme

The Criminal Injuries Compensation Authority administers from government funds a statutory scheme for compensating victims of crimes of violence. If they suffer personal injury as a result of violent crime or while apprehending (or seeking to apprehend) a suspect, the Authority may award compensation according to a statutory tariff.

(2) Occupational sick pay

Many members of the workforce are entitled to continued payments from their employer in replacement of loss of earnings (at least in part), for a limited absence from work through sickness or injury.[208] But the number so entitled is on the wane.

(3) Occupational pensions

Many millions of employees are members of pension schemes run by their employers. These entitle the relevant employees to compensation beyond that available under the social security system in the event of personal injury requiring their early retirement.[209]

---

[207] Social Security (Recovery of Benefits) Act 1997, s 6. Note that this provision requires that the 'compensator'– usually D's insurer – must pay the *full amount* of recoverable benefits, which may well exceed the sum that would have been payable as compensation. This means that the state never loses out although, plainly, D might (as might C, depending on future contingencies).

[208] *Pearson Report*, para 137.

[209] For details, see *Pearson Report*, para 145ff.

(4) Industrial injuries scheme

Where injury occurs at work as a result of an industrial accident, a much more generous scheme provides higher levels of disability benefit than that available within the basic social security system.

(5) Insurance

In many cases, the person killed or injured will have taken out an insurance policy providing for benefits in the event of his death or personal injury.[210] There are three main forms of this first-party insurance.[211] The most common is a life policy providing a guaranteed minimum sum on death. Personal accident policies cover death, loss, or disability resulting from accidents for a prescribed period. Permanent health policies provide periodic payments if the insured person becomes unable to pursue his usual occupation because of sickness or accident. Sometimes these forms of insurance are provided by employers for their staff.

The *Pearson Report*[212] estimated that about half the total compensation paid in respect of personal injury and death comes from social security and about a quarter from the tort system. The remaining quarter comes from the other sources listed above. These figures show how limited a view of accident compensation is obtained if one examines only tort, and ignores these other sources of compensation.

(C) THE FUTURE

In 1974 the Royal Commission on Civil Liability and Compensation for Personal Injury was set up under the chairmanship of Lord Pearson. It reported in 1978. Its basic proposal was to retain the mixed system of tort law and social security, with a gradual swing towards social security. It made 188 detailed proposals of which one of the most interesting was a proposal to bring road traffic accidents within social security schemes on the model of industrial injuries. Over 30 years later, it seems that a wholesale change to a social welfare system that abandons 'fault' is highly improbable in this country. In particular categories of accident, there has been some pressure for limited 'no fault' compensation systems. But on what rational grounds should victims of particular types of mishaps – such as medical accidents – be singled out for special treatment? It is equally to be noted that a piecemeal implementation of 'no fault' schemes would be potentially problematic in that it would simply add to the highly complex interweaving of various compensation systems.

---

[210] Much more widespread is insurance against fire or damage to one's buildings, homes, furniture, or car, where the insured has a right of subrogation against tortfeasors.

[211] For greater detail and for arguments in favour of augmenting first-party insurance, see Atiyah, *The Damages Lottery* (1997).

[212] *Pearson Report* (1978).

FURTHER READING

ATIYAH, *The Damages Lottery* (1997)

CANE (ed), *Atiyah's Accidents Compensation and the Law* (2006)

HARRIS, 'Accident Compensation in New Zealand: A Comprehensive Insurance System' (1974) 37 *Modern Law Review* 361

KEMP, 'Discounting Damages for Future Loss' (1997) 113 *Law Quarterly Review* 195

LEWIS, 'Appearance and Reality in Reforming Periodical Payments of Tort Damages in the UK' in Neyers et al (eds), *Emerging Issues in Tort Law* (2007), ch 19

LEWIS, *Deducting Benefits from Damages for Personal Injury* (2000)

MATTHEWS AND LUNNEY, 'A Tortfeasor's Lot is Not a Happy One' (1995) 58 *Modern Law Review* 395

OGUS, 'Damages for Lost Amenities: For a Foot, a Feeling or a Function?' (1972) 35 *Modern Law Review* 1

ROGERS (ed), *Damages for Non-Pecuniary Loss in a Comparative Perspective* (2001)

STAPLETON, 'Tort, Insurance and Ideology' (1995) 58 *Modern Law Review* 820

INDEX

mitigation of loss
   damage on different
      occasions 688
   general principles
      684–686
   successive actions on same
      facts 686–687
   successive acts 686–687
passing off
private nuisance
   character 452
   duration 450–451
   extent 451
   social utility 452–453
recognised harm
   economic loss 93–109
   generally 71–74
   personal injury and
      death 74–76
   property damage 87–90
   psychiatric harm 76–87
   rescuers 75–76
   unborn children 74–75
   unplanned
      pregnancies 90–92
relevance to standard of care
   cost of avoidance 116–118
   likelihood of harm
      113–114
   magnitude of harm 114
res ipsa loquitur 144
slander actionable per se
   imputations of crime
      555–556
   imputations of disease 556
   imputations of
      unchastity 557
   professions, trade, and
      business 556–557
Honest comment
   proof 593
   proposed reform 593–594
   qualified privilege
      compared 593
   scope 587–588
   specific requirements
      honestly made without
      malice 591–593
      public interest 588
      true facts 588–591
Hospital expenses 712–714
Human rights
   breach of statutory duty 514
   false imprisonment 271, 278
   impact on defamation
      534–535

impact on public
      authorities 54, 66
misuse of private
      information
      602–604
protection by tort law 5–9
relationship with
      negligence 72–74
Husband and wife
   capacity 664
   dependency claims 726–728
   private nuisance claims 463

Illegality
   breach of statutory duty 530
   causing loss by unlawful
      means 399–400
   death claims 728
   defence to negligence
      208–210
   effect on damages 213–214
   juridical uncertainty
      344–345
   leading case law 346–347
   reform proposals 214
   types of case
      illegality 213
      joint illegal
         enterprises 210–213
      unilateral illegal acts
         211–212
   unlawful means conspiracy
      harm 407–408
      intention 406
      requirement of
         combination
         405–406
      unlawful means 406–407
   vicarious liability
      assault 653–654
      fraud 653–654
Imprisonment *see* **False**
      imprisonment
Independent contractors
   defective premises 228–230
   employees distinguished
      agency workers
         636–637
      borrowed employees
         637–638
      control 633–635
      hospital staff 637
      importance 632–633
      intention 635–636
      overlap with agents
         638–640

personal investment in
      project 635
   police officers 638
private nuisance 469
vicarious liability for
   authorised torts
      640–641
   collateral negligence
      645–646
   negligence 641–642
   no breach of duty by
      employer 642–645
   strict liability torts 640
Inducement to breach of
      contract
inducing breaches of other
      obligations 397
meaning and scope
   analogous obligations
      397–398
   harm 396
   inducements 392–393
   intention 395–396
   justification 396–397
   knowledge of
      contract 394–395
   meaning and scope
      391–392
   void and voidable
      contracts 393–394
Inevitable accident 327
Injunctions
   breach of confidence 361
   defamation 597–598
   key issues 677
   misuse of private
      information
      394, 610
   no tort established 691
   nuisance distinguished
      442–443
   passing off 381–382
   per se or in addition to
      damages 688–690
   private nuisance 476–477
   public nuisance 482–483
   trespass to land 320–321
Innocent dissemination
   566–567
Innuendos
   false innuendos 544–545
   interpretation 541–542
   role of judge and jury
      544–546
   true innuendos 543
Insanity 348–349